Professional ASP Data Access

Dino Esposito
James De Carli
Jason Hales
Simon Robinson
Richard Anderson
Chuck Fairchild
Aaron Grady
John Granade
Joshua Parkin
Rama Ramachandran
Matthew Reynolds
Ulrich Schwanitz
Julian Skinner
Kent Tegels
Thearon Willis

Wrox Press Ltd. ®

Professional ASP Data Access

Published by Wrox Press Ltd,
Arden House, 1102 Warwick Road, Acocks Green,
Birmingham, B27 6BH, UK
Printed in the United States
ISBN 1-861003-92-7

Trademark Acknowledgements

Wrox has endeavored to provide trademark information about all the companies and products mentioned in this book by the appropriate use of capitals. However, Wrox cannot guarantee the accuracy of this information.

Credits

Authors
Dino Esposito
James De Carli
Jason Hales
Simon Robinson

Contributing Authors
Richard Anderson
Chuck Fairchild
Aaron Grady
John Granade
Joshua Parkin
Rama Ramachandran
Matthew Reynolds
Ulrich Schwanitz
Julian Skinner
Kent Tegels
Thearon Willis

Additional Material
Alastair Ewins
Hope Hatfield
Stephen Mohr

Technical Architect
Julian Skinner

Technical Editors
Gary Evans
Alastair Ewins
Adrian Young

Development Editor
Greg Pearson

Project Administration
Jake Manning

Author Agent
Sophie Edwards

Category Managers
Dominic Lowe
Joanna Mason

Technical Reviewers
Robert Chang
Michael Clarkson
Chuck Fairchild
Damien Foggon
Mark Goedert
Mark Harrison
Jeff Hart
Mark Horner
Stephen Kaufman
Ron Landers
Shawn Murphy
Gerry O'Brien
Matthew Reynolds
Martin Ried
Scott Robertson
David Schultz
Dave Shelley
Marc Simkin
Macer Skeels
Steve Smith
Andrew Watt
Robert Oliver

Production Manager
Laurent Lafon

Production Coordinator
Mark Burdett

Additional Layout
Laurent Lafon
Pip Wonson

Cover Design
Shelley Fraser

Index
Alesandro Ansa
Bill Johncocks

Proofreaders
Lisa Rutter
Diana Skeldon
Keith Westmoreland

About the Authors

Dino Esposito

Dino Esposito is a trainer and consultant who spends most of his time writing (Wrox) books and (MSDN) articles. He also co-founded www.vb2themax.com.

When not traveling to teach ASP(+) and ADO(+) classes Dino lives in the Rome area with his wife Silvia and Francesco - the world's youngest author, 1 book and 10 articles coauthored in his first 2 years of life. You can reach Dino at dinoe@wrox.com.

James R. De Carli

James De Carli's background within the computer industry spans writing,teaching, and applications development. With more than two dozencertification exams under his belt, James has earned several technicalcertifications, including Microsoft Certified Systems Engineer (MCSE),Microsoft Certified Solutions Developer (MCSD), and Microsoft CertifiedDatabase Administrator (MCDBA).

He has made numerous contributions to various technical magazines, and was a contributing author of Wrox's Professional JavaScript. James holds a Masters degree in Computer and Information Sciences and a Bachelors degree in Mathematics and Statistics. He spent many years as an instructor for a Microsoft Authorized Training and Education Center and as a developer for a Microsoft Solution Provider Partner.

Today, he works as Director, Website Architecture and Development with Site Shell Corporation, a Connecticut-based Internet media provider. James is also an Assistant Professor at Fairfield University where he teaches graduate-level Software Engineering courses.

James lives in Connecticut with his lifelong friend and wife Catherine, and their three sons, Kenneth, Robert, and Daniel.

Dedication

To my sons, my parents, and my sisters, who I love and admire. And especially to my wife Cathy, for her tenderness, patience, and understanding.

Jason Hales

Jason Hales BSc is a freelance consultant based in Cambridgeshire, England. He has over 10 years commercial experience in software development focusing primarily on Microsoft development tools in conjunction with SQL Server and Oracle. Prior to VB and ASP, he developed in PowerBuilder, C and Sybase on UNIX.

Jason is president of Digital Tier (www.digitaltier.com) a company formed in January 1995 to promote enterprise-wide scalable Windows and Internet development.

When he's not programming or writing, Jason can be found wind surfing (in the summer months only), studying New Scientist magazine, reading books by Richard Feynman and James Herbert, mountain-biking, or in the company of his family and friends. His main hobbies include general fitness, weight training, listening to music and any form of motor-sports.

Jason has also contributed to *Professional Windows DNA: Building Distributed Web Applications with VB, COM+, MSMQ, SOAP, and ASP*, also from Wrox.

He can be contacted by e-mail at jason.hales@digitaltier.com

Dedication

This work is dedicated, as ever, to my loving wife, Ann, and my two wonderful daughters Emma and Sophie. I'd also like to dedicate this to my mum, Beryl, my nanny, my sisters Jo and Rachel, my brother James, all the nieces and nephews around the world, and John and Sybil Wright for their help.

A big shout also goes out to the "Usual Suspects" from sunny Great Yarmouth: Paul Warnes, Craig Howard, Dan Houghton, Will Bell, Geoff Pryor and Simon Leggett. I'd also like to mention Michael O'Boyle for his never-ending Oracle question and answer sessions.

Simon Robinson

Simon Robinson lives in Lancaster, in the UK, where he shares a house with some students. He first encountered serious programming when he was doing his PhD in physics, modeling all sorts of weird things to do with superconductors and quantum mechanics. The experience of programming was nearly enough to put him off computers for life (though oddly, he seems to have survived all the quantum mechanics), and he tried for a while being a sports massage therapist instead. But he then realized how much money was in computers compared to sports massage, and rapidly got a job as a C++ programmer/researcher instead. Simon is clearly the charitable, deep, spiritual, type, who understands the true meaning of life.

His programming work eventually lead him into writing, and he now makes a living mostly from writing great books for programmers. He is also an honorary research associate at Lancaster University, where he does research in computational fluid dynamics with the environmental science department. You can visit Simon's web site at `http://www.SimonRobinson.com`.

Richard Anderson

Richard Anderson is an established software developer and author who has activity been working with Microsoft technologies for as long as he can remember. Richard works for Business Management Solutions (http://www.bms.uk.com), a leading edge e-commerce company which specializes in next generation hosted payroll systems.

Richard is a co-author of many books, including the recently released *A Preview of Active Server Pages+*, and *Beginning Components for ASP*, both published by Wrox.

Charles Fairchild

Charles K. (Chuck) Fairchild, Ph.D., is an educator teaching course in information technology (Visual Basic, ASP, and database design), business statistics, and economics, and an independent consultant with more than 30 years experience in computer applications development in the public and private sectors. He may be reached at `cfairch@mindspring.com`.

Aaron Grady

Aaron works for Microsoft in Developer Support, supporting Microsoft SNA Server and Host Integration Server 2000. He holds certifications for MCSE+ Internet and MCDBA. In his free time, Aaron enjoys talking with his wife, playing with his kids, listening to The Cure, playing pool, and contemplating the deeper things in life.

Acknowledgements

Aaron gives thanks to Jessica, Eli, Victoria, Gabe, God, and everyone else that he's ever met.

John Granade

John Granade is an Applications Engineering Manager at Data Return Corporation. Data Return Corporation is a leading provider of advanced hosting solutions for customers deploying applications that utilize Microsoft BackOffice products. He works with companies to architect high performance/scalable hosted solutions on the Microsoft platform. He is an MCSE/MCSD living in Atlanta, GA and is a graduate of Auburn University.

John may be reached at jgranade@granadetech.com.

Dedication

I would like to thank my wife for supporting me and loving me (even when it's not easy), my kids for giving me someone to play Nintendo with, my parents for giving me the foundation and the self-confidence needed to succeed, and to Jesus Christ for giving me a new life.

Joshua Parkin

Joshua Parkin currently works with NamSys Inc in Ontario Canada developing currency management and cash handling solutions through imaging and self service. Joshua has also developed with GennexX Software in Ontario Canada to develop a medical software data store using Novell Directory Services and remote interfaces through the web and various hand held devices.

Dedication

A big thanks goes to my wife Melanie for putting up with my time spent in participating in this book as well as Jim Foster for not complaining every time I killed a server. Joshua Parkin can be reached at jparkin@home.com.

Rama Ramachandran

Rama Ramachandran is the Director, Technology with Imperium Solutions, a Microsoft Solution Provider Partner. He is a Microsoft Certified Solution Developer and Site-Builder and designs and develops web and E-commerce applications using ASP, COM, Visual Basic, SQL Server and Windows 2000. He also has extensive experience with building database systems using Visual Basic, Visual InterDev, Access, and FoxPro.

Rama is the contributing author of Professional Visual InterDev 6 Programming (Wrox) as well as the co-author of four books on Visual Basic from Que Publishing. He is also the ASP Pro at Fawcette's www.inquiry.com web site where he answers ASP related questions. He teaches Visual Basic and Web Development at Fairfield University as well as at the University of Connecticut, and lives in Stamford, Conn., with his wife Beena and their sons Ashish and Amit. Reach Rama at rama@imperium.com.

Matthew Reynolds

Matthew Reynolds is an independent e-business consultant and evangelist specializing in building solutions based on the Windows DNA platform. He lives and works in the UK and helps enthusiastic startups realize their goals through his consulting firm, RedPiranha.com.

Ulrich Schwanitz

Ulrich is an architecture specialist with many years of experience in the design and implementation of enterprise NT systems and networks. Meanwhile, he has shifted focus towards Internet technologies. He is currently involved with planning and designing web applications of various kinds.

Ulrich and his family enjoy living in a charming suburb of Antwerpen, Belgium.

Kent Tegels

Kent Tegels, MCSE+I, MCP+SB is a Web Analyst for HDR, Inc. in Omaha, Nebraska. He develops and administers numerous sites on HDR's Intranet, Internet and Extranet. In the few moments of free time he has, Kent tinkers with Perl programming, computer gaming and cooking.

Thearon Willis

Thearon is a senior consultant with 20 years of IT experience. He has over four years of experience building Web applications using Active Server Pages, VB COM components and SQL Server. His Web applications incorporate a combination of DHTML, XML, COM+, MSMQ and ADO.

Thearon is currently working on a B2B application for a dot com company writing COM components that utilize COM+, MSMQ, XML and ADO.

Thearon lives in Charlotte, North Carolina with his wife and daughter.

Table of Contents

Table of Contents

Table of Contents

Section 3: Architecture 259

Table of Contents

Table of Contents

Table of Contents

xii

Table of Contents

Table of Contents

Table of Contents

Table of Contents

Table of Contents

Table of Contents

Introduction

Microsoft's Active Server Pages (ASP) technology has come a long way since its first introduction back in 1997, and it is now very much at the leading edge of internet application development. And at the very core of an effective internet application is *data access*. No matter how an application stores and retrieves information, whether with a traditional relational database, or with some other technique, such as directory services or XML, developing a successful application requires a thorough understanding of your data format, and how to effectively manipulate that data from Active Server Pages.

This book is primarily about just that: how to manipulate data effectively from an ASP application in a wide range of different data stores: SQL Server, Oracle, IBM's DB2, Active Directory, Novell Directory Services, Exchange 2000, and so on. But it is also much more. Amongst other things, we look in detail at the effective design and implementation of multi-tiered applications, the use of XML not only as a means of data *storage*, but also as a medium for data *transfer*, using data mining techniques as a way of extracting useful information from data, and security and performance issues.

Who Is This Book For?

This book is aimed at developers who already have some experience of using ASP, using components, and data access, but who want to develop their understanding of the complexities of data manipulation from an ASP application, and how to access data from a wide range of different types of sources. This book provides a wealth of information which is essential for anyone wanting to develop serious real-world internet applications using ASP, and contains many practical examples which will enable you to effectively deploy the full power of current data access technologies.

Most of the examples in this book are based on VBScript and Visual Basic, and some familiarity with these is assumed. However, there are also some examples which make use of JavaScript and Visual C++, but don't worry if you haven't used these before.

Like all of the Wrox *Professional* series of books, this is designed to give in-depth information that will be useful to the developer. It is *not* a primer in either ASP or data access techniques. If you are not too familiar with using ASP, you might want to try *Beginning Active Server Pages 3.0* or, for those with some experience, *Professional Active Server Pages 3.0*. A good introduction to ASP and data access can be found in *Beginning ASP Databases*, also from Wrox Press.

What Is This Book About?

As its title suggests, this book focuses on manipulating data from Active Server Pages 3.0, as included with Windows 2000. However, there is a broad spectrum of different ways in which data may be stored, and precisely *how* we store our data is going to have important implications for the way we put together our ASP application.

We look at the full range of storing and accessing data from an ASP application: using relational databases, such as SQL Server, Oracle, IBM's DB2 and the open source MySQL; accessing data from directory services such as Novell Directory Services (NDS) and Microsoft's Active Directory; and using legacy data, XML, data mining, and data shaping.

We not only look at data access, but also spend time focusing on more general aspects of ASP application development; development within an *n*-tier architecture, using COM+, and security and performance issues.

Let's take a brief look at what we cover in the individual chapters of this book:

Chapter 1: ASP, Data and Databases

In this chapter we take a general look at data storage techniques, the impact of the internet on application development, and various data access technologies; **ODBC**, **OLE DB** and **ADO**.

Section I: Database Fundamentals

Chapter 2: Database Design Concepts

In this chapter we investigate database design, looking at the distinction between flat file and relational databases, ensuring data integrity, normalization, using indexes, views, and stored procedures, and performance.

Chapter 3: SQL Programming

This chapter gives us an in-depth look at using SQL. This includes looking at how to use SQL for accessing and sorting data, using `JOIN` to access multiple tables, creating and changing tables, and transactional processes.

Chapter 4: Stored Procedures, Triggers and Views

Here we build on Chapter 3 by looking at the construction and use of stored procedures, triggers, and views.

Section II: Data Access Technologies

Chapter 5: Introduction to Data Access

This chapter provides us with an in-depth look at data access technologies; **Open DataBase Connectivity (ODBC)**, **Data Access Objects (DAO)**, **Remote Data Objects (RDO)**, **ODBCDirect**, **ActiveX Data Objects (ADO)**, and **OLE DB**.

Chapter 6: OLE DB

In this chapter we take a more thorough look at using OLE DB providers. In particular, we look at the OLE DB objects and their interfaces, and ways of utilizing OLE DB for data access.

Chapter 7: ActiveX Data Objects

This chapter gives us a thorough look at the **ADO** object model: using ADO to connect to a data store, accessing and using data, and using stored procedures.

Section III: Building ASP Applications

Chapter 8: ASP Application Architecture

In this chapter, we take a different tack, exploring the architecture of an internet application. In particular, we look at the **Windows DNA** architecture, 3-tier application design, **COM+** and component design, and creating components using **Visual Basic**, and **C/C++**, and **ATL**.

Chapter 9: Component Services

Here, we take a more detailed look at the use of components with **MTS** and **COM+**. Amongst other things, we cover transactions, object pooling, and queued components.

Chapter 10: Designing the User Services

In this chapter, we focus on a number of issues that bear on the design on the user services layer of an internet application. In particular, looking at browser compatibility and data display. Here we build the user interface for an application which we develop over the next few chapters.

Chapter 11: Building Data Access Components

This chapter focuses on building components for an ASP application using Visual Basic; how components benefit ASP applications, how to expose a site's functionality as a **COM-based API**, how to build a data access component in Visual Basic, and how a COM-based API simplifies the addition of new functionality.

Chapter 12: Building OLE DB Components

Here we look at developing components for our application using C++; when to use C++ OLE DB components in web applications, how to write ASP components that get data through OLE DB consumers, and issues surrounding the use of ADO with C++.

Chapter 13: Integrating the Application with COM+

This chapter guides us through the deployment of the application that we developed over the previous few chapters. Amongst other things, we look at issues that bear on performance and security such as object lifetime and state, COM+ integration, threading, and how to write a COM+ application through components services.

Section IV: Relational Databases

Chapter 14: SQL Server

This is the first of four chapters in which we investigate the use of relational databases. In this chapter, we look at the use of SQL Server. Amongst other things, we look at creating and using stored procedures, performance issues, creating and scheduling tasks, using triggers, and sending e-mail from SQL Server.

Chapter 15: Oracle8 and Oracle8i

In this chapter, we look at installing and configuring client components for **Oracle**, connecting to an Oracle database using the **OLE DB Provider for Oracle**, **Microsoft's ODBC Driver for Oracle**, and **Oracle Objects for OLE**. We also explore the use of **PL/SQL**, retrieving ADO recordsets from an Oracle stored procedure, and the use of reference cursors, and build an ASP application that manipulates data stored in an Oracle database.

Chapter 16: IBM DB2 Universal Database

Here we look at the use of **IBM's DB2** database. We cover the installation of DB2 client components, using OLE DB and ODBC connection to connect to a DB2 database, and accessing data from ASP pages. We also construct a sample ASP application that utilizes a DB2 database.

Chapter 17: MySQL

In this chapter, we look at the open source **MySQL** database server. We look at the installation and configuration of both the database server and the **MyODBC** data source, connecting to MySQL, user permissions, and MySQL SQL. We also look at some of the limitations of MySQL, before building an 'address book' sample application using ASP pages with MySQL.

Section V: Non-Relational Data

Chapter 18: Directory Services

This chapter is the first in which we look at the use of non-relational data storage. Over the last few years, directory services have gained wide acceptance. This chapter focuses on Microsoft's **Active Directory**. We start by looking at installing Active Directory, before giving an overview of its functionality. We then look in detail at the use of **Active Directory Service Interfaces** (**ADSI**) and the **Lightweight Directory Access Protocol** (**LDAP**), and how to manipulate data in Active Directory from ASP pages.

Chapter 19: NDS and ASP

Here we look at **Novell Directory Services** (**NDS**). After an overview of the product, we look at using the ADSI provider for NDS, LDAP development, and the Novell ActiveX controls for NDS. We also look at creating and manipulating NDS objects from ASP pages, and using NDS as a data store for an ASP application.

Chapter 20: Indexing Service

In this chapter we explore how the Windows 2000 **Indexing Service** can be used as a data store, and see how to construct web searches using it. We look in detail at the atomic units of the Service, such as catalogs, properties, scopes and queries; and two different ways of constructing web searches: through COM objects, or by using the OLE-DB provider for the Indexing Service.

Chapter 21: Semi-Structured Data and Internet Publishing

In this chapter, we look at ways of accessing partially structured data. In particular, we investigate ways of manipulating the contents of a web site from an ASP application. Central to this is the use of **Web Distributed Authoring and Versioning** (**WebDAV**).

Chapter 22: Exchange 2000

Increasingly, large amounts of data are kept on systems such as Microsoft's **Exchange 2000**. In this chapter, we look at how to view, create, modify, search for and delete items in Exchange 2000 from an ASP application, via the Exchange OLE DB provider. We also look at sending and receiving various messages using ASP pages in conjunction with **Collaboration Data Objects** (**CDO**) and Exchange 2000.

Chapter 23: Legacy Data

A great deal of data has been accumulated over the years on systems which, for want of a better term, come under the rubric of 'legacy systems'. In this chapter, we look at different types of legacy data, **Systems Network Architecture** (**SNA**), and ways of using **Microsoft's SNA Server** and **Host Integration Server 2000** to integrate legacy data with some sample ASP applications.

Section VI: XML

Chapter 24: An XML Primer

This is the first of a set of chapters in which we look at the use of XML with ASP. After an overview of XML, we investigate the use of **Document Type Definition** files and **Data Schemas**, look at some practical examples of how to use the Microsoft XML parser, and see how data islands work.

Chapter 25: Rendering and Styling XML

In this chapter we again look at using XML, focusing on the use of stylesheets, XSL tags, developing an application with XML and XSL, and see how to write XML-based server pages. We further develop the XML application from the last chapter.

Chapter 26: Persisting XML

In this chapter, we further develop the XML application developed over the last two chapters. In particular, we look at recordset persistence using XML and ADTG (Advanced Data TableGram), the use of disconnected XML-based recordsets, and see how the ADO 2.5 `Stream` object is used.

Chapter 27: XML and Relational Databases

Here we investigate ways of retrieving data from relational databases in XML format. In particular, we focus on manipulating data stored in Oracle and DB2 using XML as our medium of communication.

Section VII: Advanced Topics

Chapter 28: E-commerce and E-business

In this chapter, we take a general look at developing an e-commerce site using ASP and SQL Server. We concentrate on developing an e-commerce site which implements some simple personalization and membership functionality, and on general e-commerce issues such as security.

Chapter 29: Data Shaping

In this chapter, we examine the use of data which is stored in a relational format, but which we need to *access* in a hierarchical format. Microsoft's data shaping provider, MSDataShape, provides us with a way of *transforming* the structure of the data as we extract it from the database.

Chapter 30: Multi-Dimensional Data

Here we focus on using **On Line Analytical Processing** (**OLAP**), in particular, Microsoft's **Analysis Services**, as a means of extracting useful information from data stored in a relational database. We look at generating an OLAP database, using **MDX** (**Multi-dimensional Extensions**), and building an ASP application that will access and display information from an OLAP database.

Chapter 31: Data Mining

In this chapter, we look at data warehousing and data mining techniques, and run through some practical examples using Microsoft's **SQL Server 2000 Analysis Services**. We also see how to integrate use of Analysis Services with an ASP application.

Chapter 32: Remote Data Services

We here look at the use of **Remote Data Services** (**RDS**). This provides the means to instantiate a COM component on a client from a remote server. We focus in particular on a detailed look at the RDS 2.6 object model, data binding, using RDS with custom objects, and constructing a sample application using RDS.

Chapter 33: Advanced Query Interfaces

In this chapter, we take a look at more sophisticated ways of accessing data from a relational database. We focus in particular on executing heterogeneous queries with SQL Server, **XPath**, using natural language queries through **MSEQ** (**Microsoft English Query**), and creating an advanced ASP based data access interface.

Section VIII: Performance and Security

Chapter 34: Scalability and Performance

In this chapter, we are given a detailed look at ASP application design issues that bear on performance and scalability. Amongst other things, we look at numerous techniques for ensuring the optimum performance of an application, software and hardware issues, and clustering and load balancing.

Chapter 35: Security

And in this final chapter, we look at a wide range of security issues, including security within Windows 2000, IIS authentication, cookie-based authentication, certificate-based authentication, Web Server authentication, and ways of preventing hacking.

Section IX: Case Studies

Case Study 1: Web-Based Reports

In this first of two case studies, we integrate many of the technologies and concepts we encountered in earlier chapters (such as ASP pages, HTML, client-side and server-side scripting, Visual Basic COM components, Component Manager, stored procedures, views, table indexes, and security) to produce a 3-tier application that will summarize activity on a web site.

Case Study 2: Dynamic Elements

In this case study, we look at how to dynamically create HTML elements in a form in a web page. In particular, we look at creating table relationships, creating dynamic HTML elements on a client, the server-side processing of dynamic elements, and presenting these using ASP pages.

What You'll Need to Use This Book

To get the most from this book, you should be running Windows 2000 or Windows NT 4.0. Ideally, you should also have access to the following:

- ❑ An enterprise relational database, such as SQL Server
- ❑ Visual Studio
- ❑ Ideally ASP 3.0, shipped with IIS 5.0 and Windows 2000
- ❑ ADO 2.5 or 2.6

Most of the examples assume that you are running the IIS 5.0 web server (which ships with Windows 2000), but most of the examples will work with IIS 4.0 (shipped with Windows NT4) and PWS (supplied with Windows 95/98).

Some of the chapters require the use of specific software, such as Oracle, NDS or Exchange 2000. In some cases, evaluation or developer editions of this software can be downloaded from the Internet, and in these cases we indicate in the relevant chapters where specific applications can be downloaded.

Conventions Used

You are going to encounter different styles as you are reading through this book. This has been done to help you easily identify different types of information and to help you avoid missing any key points. These styles are:

> **Important information, key points, and additional explanations are displayed like this to make them stand out. Be sure to pay attention to these when you find them.**

General notes, background information, and brief asides look like this.

- ❑ Keys that you press on the keyboard, like *Ctrl* and *Delete*, are displayed in italics.
- ❑ If you see something in a fixed-width font like `BackupDB`, you'll know that it is a filename, object name or function name.
- ❑ The first time you encounter an **important word**, it is displayed in bold text.
- ❑ Words that appear on the screen, such as menu options, are in a similar font to the one used on screen, for example, the File menu.

This is how code samples look the first time they are introduced:

```
Private Sub Command_Click
    MsgBox "Don't touch me"
End Sub
```

Whereas code that you've already seen, or that doesn't relate directly to the point being made, looks like this:

```
Private Sub Command_Click
    MsgBox "Don't touch me"
End Sub
```

Customer Support

We want to know what you think about this book: what you liked, what you didn't like, and what you think we could do better next time. You can send your comments, either by returning the reply card in the back of the book, or by e-mail (to feedback@wrox.com). Please be sure to mention the book title in your message.

Source Code

Full source code for all the examples in this book can be downloaded from the Wrox web site at: http://www.wrox.com.

Errata

We've made every effort to make sure that there are no errors in the text or the code. However, to err is human, and as such we recognize the need to keep you informed of any mistakes as they're spotted and corrected. Errata sheets are available for all our books at www.wrox.com. If you find an error that hasn't already been reported, please let us know.

P2P.WROX.COM

For author and peer support join the ASP mailing lists. Our unique system provides **Programmer to Programmer™ support** on mailing lists, forums and newsgroups, all *in addition* to our one-to-one e-mail system. Be confident that your query is not just being examined by a support professional, but by the many Wrox authors and other industry experts present on our mailing lists. At p2p.wrox.com you'll find support, not only while you read this book, but also as you start to develop your own applications.

To enroll for support just follow this four-step system:

1. Go to p2p.wrox.com.

2. Click on the ASP button.

3. Click on the type of mailing list you wish to join.

4. Fill in your e-mail address and password (of at least 4 digits) and e-mail it to us.

Why this System Offers the Best Support

You can choose to join the mailing lists or you can receive them as a weekly digest. If you don't have the time, or facility, to receive the mailing list, then you can search our online archives. Junk and spam mails are deleted, and your own e-mail address is protected by the unique Lyris system. Any queries about joining or leaving lists, or any other queries about the lists, should be sent to `listsupport@p2p.wrox.com`.

1

ASP, Data, and Databases

As developers, we create applications that work with data. It is our hope that our applications organize, process, and present this data, in ways in which the data can be seen as more than just a collection of facts. Since our applications model the real world, and apply business rules, data is transformed into *information*.

In today's marketplace, this data can come from a wide variety of sources. Although databases are still the most frequently used source of data, other providers of data, such as libraries of documents, electronic mail, streaming media, and security credentials are becoming commonplace. To meet the requirements of integrating such a wide range of data sources, developers today need flexible technologies and standards for accessing and retrieving data from these sources and technologies.

Many of the approaches to designing and deploying applications often fail when used to create web applications. What worked when there was only a single machine running a program and a limited number of users won't meet the needs for today's marketplace. Web applications need to be designed to support many users over a wide variety of hardware, use a mix of technologies, and need to be *fast!* Because data will come in many forms, we need an infrastructure that can support a variety of data sources. In addition, we need to be able to acquire and process these disparate forms of data in a fast and efficient manner.

Active Server Pages, together with **ActiveX Data Objects** (**ADO**) and **OLE DB**, can bring about this access to a myriad of data stores. Existing data access technologies have concentrated on relational databases, but ADO now brings the benefits of semi-structured data. So not only can we provide fast access to existing stores of data, but we can also access data in a variety of structures, such as mail messages, web pages, XML, and so on.

The primary goal of this book is to help you, the developer, build applications that stitch together these sources of data by using proven technologies and methods. To meet this goal, we'll take a look at the obstacles facing developers today, the technologies available to us, and how these technologies may be utilized. In addition, we'll discuss the nature of the data that can be accessed and approaches used to organize and process this data.

It is our hope that this book will assist you in the design and production of applications that meet the needs demanded of today's Internet.

Data vs. Information

As developers, we try to create applications that model "the real world". A model is really just a set of rules that we apply to data to produce some result. The rules that are applied in the model represent some business practices, such as "all merchandise will be priced 10% lower during the month of August" and "no credit shall be made available for accounts with unpaid balances older than 30 days." The data in the model might include today's date or some company's account number.

Data is essentially just facts, and facts have little meaning unless they are given in some *context*. For example, let's assume that you are with 11 people. It is a fact that you are part of a group of a dozen individuals. But what else can you say about this group? Do 12 individuals constitute a big group of people? That depends on the context. If these 11 individuals were with you in your bathroom, we would probably consider them to be a large group. If, on the other hand, these 11 were the only spectators in a football stadium, then you may consider this number small.

When we develop a model for an application, we add context to the data processed and thereby transform this data into more meaningful *information*. In the most general sense, information is a collection of facts that is both qualitative and quantitative. In our prior example, it is important to know that we have twelve people (a quantitative assessment) and that number is considered small (a qualitative assessment). With information, decisions can be made, businesses can operate, and economies can function. It is information that is at the core of the global economy.

The importance of information can't be overstated. Unfortunately, information is the most difficult thing for software to deliver. Often software supplies lots of data and we require the user to glean information from this data. Internet search engines are a good example of supplying lots of data, but not necessarily lots of information.

Part of the reason why some software doesn't deliver enough information is that our models are often too simplistic. Simple models are often used because they are easier to implement, they don't require as many resources to execute, and therefore can execute at acceptably fast speed. If we design and implement our applications more efficiently, then we can allow for more sophisticated models that can provide more meaningful information.

Acquiring and Storing Data

How our applications acquire data has changed over the years and is still changing. Forty years ago, an application would typically have got its data from a punch card reader. Twenty years ago, the data would have come from a keyboard or magnetic tape. Subsequently, we have accessed data stored on disk drives and bar code readers, and more recently still, data access over the Internet has become commonplace. Today, we have sources such as wireless phones, email servers, and directory services. In the next few years, we could well see even more sources as Cable TV, PC, and cellular services converge into one giant, global, broadband network.

Traditionally, most business data was collected and stored in databases for applications to use. Databases are still the single most-used data storage tool. But increasingly, what we are asked to store is a complex collection of related data items that require different methods of storage. Often we can't store the entire collection of data together, so we store data that is of different types in their own format or with different services. And when we want to access this data, we need some strategy for retrieving each of the various related items from these different sources.

It is commonplace today to mix media types to produce hybrids of data. One example of this is an e-mail message that is composed of a web page that contains a form for the user to submit to a database. What the user reads is a mixture of HTML and JavaScript code that has been delivered via some e-mail message. This "mail merge" may construct the e-mail messages by cross-referencing peoples' names and e-mail addresses in a database with some generic text, and is processed by some mail server.

The applications we develop today will frequently need to integrate the services from multiple sources using a mixture of technologies. One of the challenges that we as developers face today is to make these technologies work together in an efficient, fast, and reliable manner. With our goal of using software to transform data into information, we can recognize that at the heart of these technologies is *data access*.

A Brief History of Data Access

It is often said, that in order to see where we're going, it is important to know where we've been. Where we are today in application development is a direct result of what was done in the past. To more fully appreciate the options available to us today for accessing data, and how these options may be used, let's review how applications have been developed in recent years. By illustrating the obstacles that each new design strategy addressed and the technologies they used, we can get a better appreciation for what we can use today to develop modern applications.

When we talk about application development prior to the Internet, we need to consider the environment programs ran in at that time. Years ago, the processing power of computers was very limited. Most $5 calculators today have more processing power than the computer onboard the *Eagle* lunar module that Neil Armstrong used to land on the moon in 1969. Because of such meager processing power, early computing was quite limited. Even though processing power increased dramatically in the years that followed our trips to the Moon, applications built in the 1970s and 1980s were humble by today's standards. Every technology is evolutionary in nature and digital computing is no exception.

Early Computing Environments

With early mainframes, the vast majority of processing power came from a single powerful machine. Data and program code were often provided from simple tape devices or punch card readers. Programs could rely upon having exclusive access to data; and that data was stored on devices that were directly connected to the mainframe. The workstations that accessed the mainframe were simple dumb terminals that did little more than render text-based forms for input. The amount of code required to run on the terminal was minimal. In today's computer jargon, we would call these "thin clients."

Communications between the mainframe and its peripheral devices were relatively simple, since they basically entailed commands to start programs, read or write data against some local data source, and transmit the results to a printer or text-based terminal. Early personal computer applications had a surprisingly similar environment. Each PC was a stand-alone machine that communicated only with a local monitor or printer and accessed data found on local disk drives. The PC operating systems used were capable of running only one program at a time, so there wasn't competition for resources among different programs.

Isolation of Data

When a program needed to read or write data, it was accessed using routines built specifically for that program using proprietary technologies and custom file formats. Custom file formats had to be used because of the lack of widespread standards. Eventually, as computers became more ubiquitous, standards did develop, and so did databases.

Databases were the single most influential type of application in the history of computing. Most early applications dealt with the storage, processing, and retrieval of data. Database systems provided developers with a set of tools to store and retrieve data, so they could then focus their attention on how the data needed to be processed.

Several types of databases were developed. But one type, the **relational database**, eventually became dominant. Relational databases are based upon a branch of mathematics that deals with the mapping of data sets and the breakdown of data into small, non-duplicating items of information. Relational databases, such as DB2 and Oracle, were introduced, but accessing the data stored in these products often meant dealing with proprietary data access interfaces. This meant that databases were usually costly to construct and maintain.

In the early to mid 1980s, databases designed to be run on the PC were introduced. Microcomputers were inexpensive compared to mainframes and products like Ashton Tate's dBase II became wildly popular. Soon there were many competing database products for PCs, such as Foxpro, DataEase, and FileMaker. Most of these products used vendor specific file formats and therefore did not encourage the sharing of data amongst systems.

This difficulty in sharing data wasn't simply a matter of different data storage formats; it was also due to the fact that programs didn't work together. If we wanted to produce a graphical chart of a company's sales figures, we would have had to use one program, such as a database or accounting application, to produce a paper report with the numbers to graph. These values then had to be manually keyed into a second application, such as Harvard Graphics or Lotus 1-2-3, to produce the chart.

If you were knowledgeable with the software, you might be able to speed up this process somewhat by exporting the data to text file and then importing that file into the charting program. Still, this was a time consuming and error-prone process. Data was duplicated and transferred, but not really shared. If the data was changed on the source application, the entire export /import process needed to be repeated.

The Beginnings of Interoperability

In the early to mid 1980s, IBM and Apple introduced operating systems for desktop computers. These operating systems were multitasking, so more than one application was able to execute concurrently. Just as important as multitasking was that these operating systems provided a system-wide clipboard feature. By using the clipboard, users were able to share data between applications through "cut and paste". One understated feature of this clipboard was that data saved to it could be stored in different formats. This allowed the source application, using one format, to post the data to the clipboard. Another application, which may have used a different data format, was able to read this data, thus allowing the application into which the data was pasted to select from the most appropriate format. This went a long way to help resolving issues with isolated data.

Over time, the interoperability between applications became more and more robust. Windows included a feature called **Object Linking and Embedding** (OLE) that greatly extended the use of technology that made the clipboard possible. Applications could actually display their data and functionality without human intervention. OLE allowed us to do things such as change values in an Excel spreadsheet and have those changes reflected in a chart contained in a Word document.

OLE also evolved to provide not just data sharing, but automation. **OLE Automation** made it possible for one application to be in full communication and control of another application. Programs controlled with OLE could be considered components of an application. The result was that hybrid solutions could be developed utilizing several specialized applications. For example, a macro in Microsoft Word could cause Microsoft Excel to load and perform a calculation that would be too complex for the word processor to perform.

Advances in interoperability weren't limited to the desktop computer. Mainframes and minicomputers were also evolving and becoming increasingly important. Large-scale databases couldn't properly be supported by PCs, so the heavy iron computers were still in great demand. Databases such as Oracle and DB2 ruled.

And as PCs became more common in the workplace, people realized the advantages of importing data from some back-end database and performing additional processing at the desktop. Remote access utilities and emulation programs started to be released. Vendors started to offer interfaces that could be programmed to access the data. This approach started the client-server revolution. Unfortunately, the complexity of creating, maintaining, and programming the proliferation of data access interfaces and file formats slowed the wide-scale acceptance of client-server computing. To address this need, an industry standard called **Open Database Connectivity** (**ODBC**) was developed.

Client/Server Development with ODBC, DAO, and RDO

ODBC offered the ability to easily connect PCs with powerful back-end databases. It became one of the most widely used data access technologies and is still in wide use today. ODBC works as a layered system, thereby offering a flexible architecture.

When the application makes the call to use a database, it references a **Data Source Name** (**DSN**), which contains settings on which type of database to access, and how that database should be accessed, as well as login credentials. The DSN is used by an ODBC manager, which redirects the call to the appropriate ODBC driver. It is this driver that actually does the appropriate data access translations required to communicate with the back-end **Relational Database Management Systems** (RDBMS). If the back-end database lacks certain features typically found in a database, the driver is normally capable of simulating the missing feature to provide the correct data to the client.

By only having to reference a DSN in our code, ODBC makes it very simple to change which database is used. All we need to do is update the DSN definition, and little or no code needs to change in the application. This makes it very easy to move from a development environment to a testing environment, and then into production.

ODBC has a number of other features that make it extremely attractive:

- ❑ It makes use of SQL, a database access language, which has become the standard database access language.
- ❑ It uses a simple layered approach with "plug-in" database drivers to simplify implementation.
- ❑ Its call-level interface supports a broad range of tools.

But despite its advantages, ODBC has a number of shortcomings. It was originally designed as a Windows-based API with many of its features requiring low-level programming to implement. Microsoft recognized this and released **Data Access Objects** (DAO), in part, to make ODBC access easier. DAO was released with Microsoft's PC relational database product, Access, as well as Visual Basic 3.0.

DAO went a long way in simplifying the use of ODBC, but DAO proved to be too resource intensive in some cases. It relied upon a file-based database engine called JET engine that had some performance issues. These issues caused a performance hit with applications using ODBC because when an application acquired its data from some back-end database such as Oracle, the Jet engine still had to process the data. In these situations there was little need for the JET database engines to process the data if the back-end database was already doing so.

To address this, Microsoft came out with **Remote Data Objects** (RDO). This provided objects that acted as wrappers around the ODBC API and bypassed the JET engine entirely. It was made to resemble DAO so it would be familiar to programmers. RDO proved to be very robust and is still highly regarded as a preferred access technology for WANs and LANs.

The Impact of the Internet

Today, most companies are developing applications that are geared up for use on the Internet. Because of this, we have to tailor our applications to take advantage of the way in which the Internet works. Interoperability has also become more significant for web applications, as have security and reliability.

What we know today as the Internet began as a joint venture between the U.S. military and a number of academic institutions back in the late 1950s and early 1960s. The original military goals for the network, which eventually became known as ARPANET, still govern how the Internet works today. The United States was convinced that a centralized computer network couldn't survive a sustained missile attack, so a network of decentralized servers was designed. The idea was that if any single server went off-line (that is to say it was blown up), the rest of the system would continue to function.

In order for this to happen, when two computers needed to communicate, they would not use a fixed, predetermined route. Rather, the data would move throughout the network by "hopping" from one server to the next, and at each server determine which next available server would bring it closer to its intended destination. The result was a system that could meet their military objectives, but at the cost of maintaining persistent connections between machines.

When this network was opened for use by the general public when the Supercomputer Network Study Act went into effect in the late 1980s, its use was limited. But, as is well known, its popularity grew very quickly. In time, this network became known as the Internet, and it started to become widely used for commercial purposes. As the Internet was used more, two major trends started to become apparent. These two trends, which are still evolving, were the rise of the Internet as a database applications platform and the rise in importance of non-relational data; data which does not directly fit the database model encapsulated by ODBC.

Due to the fundamental design of the Internet and the trends of users on the Internet, we have to consider a number of issues in the design and use of applications built today.

Security, Scalability, Performance, and Reliability

An Internet application might typically have to support a much larger number of users than a LAN-based application. And because users can access such an application from virtually anywhere, security issues have become more important. As the Internet is accessible from all time zones, twenty-four hours a day, reliability has also become increasingly important.

In an application built for use in a corporate environment, you probably have lots of knowledge about the users: their names, job responsibilities, where they are accessing the application from, when they are most likely going to be using the application, etc. Most corporate users simply want the application to help them with their jobs. They have a vested interest in seeing the application perform well.

With an Internet application, you don't have the same level of confidence about your knowledge of the users. You don't know much, if anything, about the users. Having relative anonymity, some Internet users may be hostile and attempt to hack into your site. Although a great deal may be done at the operating system level to deter such attacks, it is advisable to add a certain level of security to your applications as well. Security is important, not just against keeping hackers at bay, but also for confidentiality and for public relations. A customer is less likely to use your site if they feel that their personal information is going to be accessible to others.

Another issue important to Internet applications is that of **scalability**. Scalability refers to the ability of an application to perform satisfactorily no matter how many users are accessing it. What may work in an application that supports only 10 users may not be able to handle hundreds or thousands of simultaneous users. Since any Internet web page may be accessible to anyone with an Internet connection, every Internet application has the potential of getting huge volumes of users. Most Internet applications need to be designed with an eye towards an ever-increasing user base.

Where we have a large number of interconnected computers, network performance issues need to be considered. In a corporate environment, a slow running LAN application is tolerated because employees are a captive audience – they have to use the application for their jobs. On the Internet, a slow running application will only encourage the user to move onto a different site. This illustrates an important change in application development; from developing applications that users *had* to use to developing applications that users *choose* to use. If an Internet application is not fast enough to satisfy the typical user, it is doomed to fail.

Consider the recent on-line retailers that have crashed and burned. One common contributing factor to these failures was that their sites were too slow for the average user. The most frequently stated reason people shop on-line is for convenience. If a user has to wait too long for a page to load or the connection times out, then the site will not seem convenient and users will move on.

But just how fast is the average user's connection? At the time of printing, less than 10% of the Internet subscribers in the U.S. have a broadband connection, such as through a cable modem, DSL, or a T1/T3 line. This percentage is significantly less in Europe. Currently, most Internet access is through a 56K modem, and in many places 24K modems is the maximum rate supported. If pages don't process and load in a reasonable time frame at this speed, we have need for some improvements.

Client/Server Architecture and the Internet

Traditional client/server applications execute on machines that exist in an isolated LAN/WAN with a known configuration. We know in advance the hardware we are going to use for both the client and the server. We also know that the client machines will be able to connect to the server and maintain that connection as long as they need it.

By its very nature, the Internet is a distributed medium, with many potential points of failure and network performance issues. Due to the network protocols used by the Internet, persistent connections cannot be guaranteed. Client and server computers are now virtually independent. Client computers need to be able to accomplish more with less support from the server and, at times, without a server connection.

Without persistent connections, technologies such as RDO fail. Even if we could establish a persistent connection, the sheer volume of users on the Internet would cause so many concurrent connections to the servers that the system would quickly become overloaded.

Client/Server applications generally use a 2-tiered approach; the client communicating directly with the server. The client-side tier pulls raw or semi-processed data from the server for processing on the desktop. These applications are typically written in 3rd generation languages such as Delphi, Visual C++, or Visual Basic. Such applications possess quite a bit of processing power through a significant amount of code. These types of applications are often called "fat clients", as opposed to the "thin clients" of the early mainframe era that required little processing on the desktop. Although we could use robust languages to produce powerful fat client desktop applications, the distribution and installation of these applications is not realistic over the Internet. One reason for this is the amount of time required to download the setup files. Another reason why these fat client applications are difficult to deploy over the Internet is that we typically wouldn't know what operating system would be used by the client.

If we cannot rely upon having fat client applications, we have to perform the bulk of the processing on the server. This too presents a number of challenges because as the number of users on the Internet increases, more and more will be demanded of the server. A single server may not have the resources to provide such high-volume service.

Use of Non-Relational Data

The Internet brought with it another interesting challenge, namely, the use of non-relational data, such as streaming media and electronic mail. The Internet, while using existing data and databases in new ways, is also composed of massive amounts of text, images, and other media. Organizations will need to manage these new data types effectively if they are to utilize them as a valuable source of information.

Relational data – data that can be broken down into small items of non-duplicated information such as a person's name or address – is almost always stored in a database. Relational Database Management Systems (RDBMS) have matured over the past 20 years or so and have become fast, efficient, and relatively inexpensive. Unfortunately, RDBMS' don't handle large, complex objects such as video very well. Also, some kinds of non-relational data, such as directory services for an operating system or e-mail, can't be incorporated easily into a RDBMS. If we are going to produce fast, efficient Internet applications that work well with a variety of large and complex objects, we will need to consider more than RDBMS' for storing our data.

Interoperability between Web Sites

The Internet enables information and operations to be shared. Early web sites that were static in nature and functioned only as on-line brochures didn't have a great need to share information. As long as a user could navigate to the site, the site was able to fulfill its purpose. But as e-commerce has developed, the need to share information between sites has increased.

Although any given web site may provide numerous resources and information, most do not share that information well with other sites. Take, for example, a financial web site that wants to obtain real-time stock market data from another web site, or a merchant site that wants to display the manufacturer's current catalog of products. Although these kinds of information sharing can be done, they are usually limited to simple requests.

One simple technique used to share data between pages of a given site as well as between different web sites today is through the use of **query strings**. These are the strings of characters often seen in the browser's address line when you navigate to different pages using a hyperlink. For example, the following text is used on the Wrox site to display a description of a book. In order to know what book to display information about, this text includes a query string that identifies an ISBN number of the book: "`http://www.wrox.com/Consumer/Store/Details.asp?ISBN=1861003927`". Hit counters and banner ads often rely upon such query strings.

Another common method is to utilize frames, where the source for a content frame is provided from another site's web server. This approach works well if all we want to do is display a page from another site, but there is no real data sharing involved. Also, there can be legal, content, and design problems with this method.

More sophisticated resource sharing uses alternative strategies that require some sort of low-level understanding between the participating sites as to the format and processing of the information. Unless there are standards to follow, this would quickly become unmanageable if more than a handful of sites participated.

Interoperability becomes even more important if we start to consider web sites that do not have a traditional user interface. Such sites provide data services to other sites. For example, some web based e-mail services allow us to programmatically access their POP3 mail servers, or a package tracking site may offer two ways of viewing tracking information. In addition to a set of web pages allowing users to enter their order number and view the shipping status, the site may allow this information to be obtained entirely through code. For such a site to be successful, a simple, standardized way of accessing their services must be available.

Challenges Facing Developers

As we have discussed, the very nature of the Internet and the habits of those who use it, bring new challenges to developers. The Internet presents new data access challenges on many levels, including the following:

- ❏ The sheer number of users and machines increased the importance of performance, reliability and security.
- ❏ The amount and type of data available on the Internet, as well as the synthesis of different data types, demands new data management approaches.
- ❏ With data and applications distributed across many machines, a new emphasis has been placed on the integration of systems and services. Often this means that a significant amount of processing was no longer done on the client machine – "thin clients" like those of the earlier mainframes had again become desirable.

Building Solutions Today

Although the challenges facing enterprise and Internet applications development are considerable, there are numerous ways in which they may be addressed. **Microsoft Windows Distributed interNet Applications Architecture** (Windows DNA) provides one such way. According to Microsoft, Windows DNA is a comprehensive, integrated platform for building and operating distributed Web applications and services.

What does this mean to developers? If we cut through the hype, we will find that Windows DNA isn't a single technology or product such as ODBC or Visual C++, but rather a collection of products and technologies along with an architecture for constructing applications. Windows DNA includes:

- ❏ Services from Windows 2000, which includes web page serving and scripting, messaging support, XML parsing, and security.
- ❏ Microsoft Commerce Server 2000 (which went into beta in July 2000) to provide e-commerce building blocks.
- ❏ Microsoft BizTalk Server for information exchange and workflow management using XML.
- ❏ Integration with third-party data sources and systems with Microsoft Integration Server (codenamed Babylon).

❑ A number of clustering and load balancing services found in Windows 2000 and Microsoft Application Center 2000 for distributing the workloads of components, servers, and the network.

❑ Data management and warehousing with Microsoft SQL Server 2000.

❑ Development tools such as Visual Studio.

At the time of printing, some of these products hadn't been released, and are still in beta, but we can still use our existing software with Windows DNA. This is because Windows DNA isn't just a collection of products, it is also an architectural model. The software that we use today – whether it is from Microsoft or not – can benefit from this model.

It should also be pointed out that there are many other technologies that exist for building robust web applications, such as Java; also, Microsoft has already announced a successor to Windows DNA called Microsoft.NET, but that is for the foreseeable future. DNA is still *the* framework for ASP development.

The Windows DNA 2000 Architecture

In the Windows DNA architecture, "tiers" or "layers" of technology are used to separate vital functions such as data access, business logic, and presentation logic. These tiers are useful, amongst other reasons, for performance and maintenance issues. As we saw earlier, the traditional 2-tiered approach taken by client/server applications often fails with Internet applications. 2-tiered applications don't scale well, are not easily distributed across multiple servers, don't easily encapsulate business logic, and often the code is not easily reusable.

The Windows DNA architecture uses 3 (or more) tiers or "application services". These include a **Data Layer**, a **Business Logic Layer**, and a **User Layer**. Each layer encapsulates a specific type of functionality depending upon the nature of the service it will provide to the rest of the application; and each layer is implemented independently, usually on different machines, to provide the highest level of scalability and performance, as well as to provide flexibility for continued development and maintenance.

The following diagram illustrates this tiered architecture. As we can see, the Presentation Layer may reside on any number of devices, such as a high-powered desktop machine or some low-end laptop or handheld device. The Data Layer may contain a variety of data sources that could include databases, other applications, or non-relational data providers; and the Business Logic Layer sits between the Presentation and Data Layers to provide the intelligence required to move requests from the Presentation Layer to the Data Layer, and data from the Data Layer to the Presentation Layer.

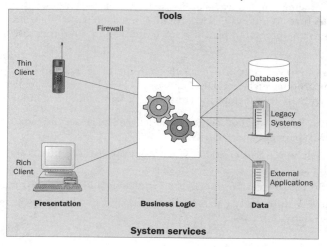

Data Layer

This layer includes any application or data storage program that provides data for the application. It could include database management systems, non-relational data providers, (such as mail servers and directory services) and may also include connections to other legacy systems. A significant amount of this book will deal with the topic of how to design and implement the data layer using various products.

Business Logic Layer

This layer provides the business rules used to model the real-world business process that the application is designed to automate. In an e-commerce application, the business rules applied in this layer could dictate the code required to validate credit card numbers, manage inventory levels, or track customer profiles.

This is the layer that interacts the most with the other application services. It is responsible for accepting requests from the Presentation Layer and providing that layer with data. The Business Logic Layer gets its data from interactions with the data layer. This is the Business Logic Layer that is most often used to transform data into meaningful information.

The layer is created as one or more dynamic link libraries using a standard called the **Component Object Model** (COM). By using the COM standard, the various layers of the application can interact with the DLLs created even though the DLL and the other layers may have been created using different languages. We'll discuss COM in detail in Chapter 8.

When another layer of the application needs to enact some business function, such as add a new employee or determine the status of an order, an object is instantiated from the DLL. The properties and methods of the object will be used by the calling layer to process the business operations. For example, the DLL may expose an object called "Employee", that contains methods to hire, retire, and promotes employees. If the method requires data from the database, it may instantiate additional data access objects that interact directly with the database. For example, we could have a method on this help object called ExecuteSQL that accepts as an argument a string that is sent to the database and is executed as a command.

The DLL can be written in any number of 3rd generation languages, such as Visual Basic or C++. Rather than using RDO or DAO, the data access technology generally used within DNA is ActiveX Data Objects (ADO).

ADO was created to be fast and lightweight, and was specifically optimized for use over the Internet. It is language neutral, meaning that it is not tied to any one particular language. It can be used in a range of languages, such as C/C++ (and soon C#), Java, Visual Basic, and VBScript. ADO uses OLE DB, an access technology that allows ADO to work with traditional data sources, such as databases, as well as non-relational data sources such as directory services; Active Directory Service Interfaces (ADSI) and NetWare Directory Services (NDS). We'll discuss ADO in detail in Chapter 7.

XML is becoming the de facto standard for exchanging data in the Business-to-Business (B2B) marketplace. XML is not a single, predefined markup language like HTML. XML is a *metalanguage*; a language for describing other languages. With XML, we can define customized classes of documents describing and exchanging data. XML is discussed in chapters 24 through 27.

Presentation Layer

The Presentation layer, also called the User Layer, represents the layer at which all interaction with the user takes place. This is the "client-side" of an n-tier application. This layer consists of all of the HTML, controls, graphics, and other content that is presented to the user. This content is usually in a browser, but other containers, such as Microsoft Office applications or some other stand-alone application, may be used. For the purposes of our discussion, we will only talk about using the most common container; the web browser.

The content contained in the browser may include executable code, such as JavaScript scripts, Dynamic HTML, Java applets, and ActiveX controls. Client-side code is useful for such things as data entry validation and for caching frequently used data so as to help reduce accessing the other application layers.

Layer Interactions

To understand how each of these layers interacts with one another, let's describe a simple Windows DNA application. This application allows customers to purchase a product on-line. The application is first invoked when the customer uses their browser to navigate to the web site hosting the application.

When the customer submits the URL in their browser, a request is sent to the web server. We want the customer to view a page that displays the name, description, and current price of the product, and an HTML form that will be submitted to place the order. In order for the customer to see this content, we will use an ASP document to construct the page.

We can assume that the name and description of the product won't change often, so information could be hard coded in the VBScript; but the current price is something that we need to look up. In order to get the current price for the product, we need to access our Microsoft SQL Server 2000 database.

To do this, the VBScript code in the ASP document creates an instance of the Business Logic Layer object. The code then uses the `GetPrice` method on the object, passing it the appropriate `ProductID`. The code in the `GetPrice` method uses ADO to establish a connection to the database, issues the appropriate command to get the current price, and then disconnects from the database. The value of the current price is then returned to the ASP script and is used to assemble the HTML that is sent to the customer's browser.

As the customer fills out the HTML form, client-side JavaScript code checks to make sure that the customer enters valid data, such as an order quantity greater than zero and the correct number of digits for the credit card. The advantage of using client-side scripting here is that, in many circumstances, this validation may be done without having to make a call to the data layer, thus providing better performance and scalability.

After the customer fills out the HTML form and submits it, ASP code processes the purchase request. This code may be in the same document that originally assembled the page or it could be a different document. The ASP code again creates an instance of the Business Logic Layer object and calls the method that validates the customer's credit card number. This method establishes a connection to a third party credit card service and returns a value indicating if the credit card has been accepted. Next, the ASP code calls the `CustomerPurchase` method on the Business Logic Layer object. Like `GetPrice`, used earlier, this method uses ADO to establish a connection to the database and invoke the necessary commands to record this customer's purchase and update the inventory records.

The Advantages over 2-Tiered Applications

From this relatively simple example, we can see this approach has a number of advantages over the traditional 2-tier client/server approach.

- ❑ First, the database is accessed for only a brief period of time, so the number of concurrent server connections is kept to a minimum. This becomes more important as the number of users increases.

- ❑ Second, because we are using ADO, we can access the database server regardless of whether it is in the same LAN or connected through the Internet.

- ❑ Third, by using ASP, we can acquire the data needed to assemble the page before sending that page to the customer's browser, thus minimizing download time. The customer's computer did not access the COM objects directly, so there is no need for software to be installed on that machine.

- ❑ A fourth advantage comes from the fact that the data layer may only be accessed from our COM objects, and therefore we have better security on our system.

- ❑ A fifth advantage concerns our ability to maintain and enhance only certain parts of the application without having to re-deploy the entire application. If there is some change that is required to the business rules, we can update the Business Logic Layer without having to update the other layers.

- ❑ Finally, this multi-tier model also makes it much easier to break apart an application for development by different developers or teams of developers.

Windows DNA Data Access

At the core of the Windows DNA data access technologies is OLE DB. OLE DB, along with other technologies, is part of Microsoft's **Universal Data Access** (UDA) strategy. This strategy is designed to provide access to information wherever that information happens to be.

UDA is delivered in a collection of technologies called **Microsoft Data Access Components** (MDAC) that includes:

- ❑ ActiveX Data Objects (ADO).
- ❑ OLE DB.
- ❑ Open Database Connectivity (ODBC).
- ❑ Installation and distribution utilities.

ODBC

As we saw earlier, ODBC became a dominant technology for accessing relational databases and is still widely used. It is based on the non-proprietary specifications for database APIs and uses Structured Query Language (SQL) – the de facto standard language for accessing relational databases.

OLE DB

OLE DB, a set of interfaces for data access, is Microsoft's component database architecture that provides universal data integration regardless of the data type. Although ODBC continues to be used, it is limited to accessing relational data. OLE DB can be used to access and manipulate all types of data, not just relational information.

It is the fundamental Component Object Model (COM) building block for storing and retrieving records and unifies Microsoft's strategy for database connectivity.

ADO

Most developers would not directly code the object interfaces exposed by OLE DB. Rather, they would construct their applications using ADO. ADO is actually a collection of objects, organized in an object model, that provides easy access to the features of OLE DB. The object model was purposely made to resemble other data access objects, such as DAO and RDO, to help ease the learning curve for experienced developers.

Because ADO is based upon OLE DB, it provides easy access to any data source, including relational and non-relational databases, e-mail, file and directory systems, graphics and multimedia, custom business objects, and more. ADO was designed to be lightweight and high performance to help meet the needs of many Internet development scenarios. By having a small memory footprint, a relatively flat object model to reduce access layers, and requiring minimal network traffic, ADO avoids many of the issues that have plagued other data access technologies.

ADO is also language independent and may be used in any language that supports COM. This independence allows us to develop data access components in virtually any modern Windows programming language.

Orchestrating Data Access with Windows DNA

The multiple tier architecture encouraged by Windows DNA guides us on how we can break our application down into a series of interacting services. By having separate services, we can split our application across more than one machine to help increase scalability, performance, and availability. Much of the data access in a Windows DNA application will come from the Business Layer, but it is also possible that different data providers will need to communicate with each other. Regardless of which players are involved, there are technologies and products that we can use to help coordinate and manage these interactions.

Component Management

At the Business Layer, Active Server Pages is ideal for managing data flow. By using server-side scripting, we can apply logic to acquire the needed data and package it before sending it to the Presentation Layer. Because of COM, ASP scripts can also create instances of objects provided by DLLs created in some other compiled language. In most circumstances, using COM objects in ASP is faster than simple scripting, so the ability of ASP to access these components can provide performance enhancements.

To better manage the resources of these DLLs, they can be installed as packages in Windows 2000 Component Services. Microsoft Transaction Server (MTS) under Windows NT provided a similar service. MTS is now incorporated into Windows 2000 Component Services and works with the next generation of COM, called COM+. Internet Information Server and Component Services work together to form a basic architecture for building web applications. IIS uses the functionality provided by Component Services to:

❑ Isolate applications into distinct processes.

❑ Manage communication between COM components (including the ASP built-in objects).

❑ Coordinate transaction processing for transactional ASP applications.

❑ Provide sharing of resources, such as objects, for greater efficiencies in managing resources.

Queuing

When a component or script on one server needs to communicate with a different server, it is possible that a connection to that server can't be established immediately. Rather than imposing long delays waiting for the connection to be established or requiring that the operation be retried at some future time, message queuing can be used to provide asynchronous communications.

Microsoft Message Queuing, which is built into Windows 2000, is a message queuing communications technology that works something like a voice mail system. If someone calls you and you are not there, they can leave a message. When you get back, you can listen to the message and respond to it. MSMQ enables applications on different systems to communicate with each other, even if systems and networks occasionally fail.

Replication

Data on one server frequently needs to be copied and/or merged with data on different servers. This activity is called **replication**. We usually think of replication as something that is done between database servers, and although database replication is quite common, replication of files and directories is also possible.

Microsoft SQL Server 2000 has many replication features that can be controlled using SQL Server's Enterprise Manager utility. We may also control replication using a set of replication objects provided in SQL Server. A Replication Distributor Interface allows us to programmatically implement and manage replication; and Microsoft ActiveX controls provide much of the functionality that would normally require using Enterprise Manger.

The replication features of the Active Directory services of Windows 2000 allow us to keep shared resources current on multiple machines. Rather than copying records from one database to another, we can copy objects such as files and folders between machines. Directory replication can provide load balancing by maintaining identical folder content across multiple machines. A rich object interface from the Active Directory services is available to construct custom data solutions.

Summary

The applications that we create, work with a combination of data and business rules to model real-world business processes. Although databases are still the most frequently used source for data, other non-traditional sources of data are becoming commonplace. Relational and non-relational data is being combined to produce new forms of hybrid data. In order for us to properly handle such hybrids, our applications need to integrate the services from multiple servers using a mixture of technologies.

By reviewing approaches to data access in recent years, we have identified issues and obstacles facing developers today. With the advent of the Internet, we find that there are problems with using traditional software development approaches. Issues concerning scalability, performance, and efficient usage of resources and data lead us to use the n-tiered approach as encapsulated in Windows DNA. At the heart of this approach is Active Server Pages. Together with Microsoft's Universal Data Access technologies; ADO, with its simple object model, OLE DB, providing access to many different types of data, and COM, which holds it all together, development is made considerably easier.

By leveraging the technologies and architecture of Windows DNA, we can build fast, efficient, and robust applications that can meet the demands of today's business climate. These first few pages give only a brief overview of what can be done. In the chapters that follow, we'll take a much closer look at how we can organize and access our data using these technologies.

Section 1

Databases

Database Design Concepts

2

Web site designers think in terms of seconds when describing slow-loading pages. There are many reasons why a web site may be slow: too many heavy graphics, multimedia streams, a lousy design. Add to all of this that a database-enabled site must also request and acquire data from a database, which is probably on a different server, adding even more to the load time of the web page. A poorly designed database can stretch the load time of a page from a few seconds into several minutes and can even cause the web page to fail. When data is requested for a web page, the response needs to be nearly immediate. If your database isn't fast enough to work within such a timeframe, then your web site is doomed to failure.

If this sounds a bit alarmist, just consider the number of recent online retailers that have crashed and burned. One common contributing factor to these failures was that their sites were too slow for the average user. The most frequently stated reason people shop online is for convenience. If a user has to wait too long for a page to load or the connection times out, then the site will not seem convenient and users will move on. But just how fast is the average user's connection? Less than 10 per cent of the 50 million or so internet subscribers in the US have broadband, cable modems, or Digital Subscriber Line (DSL) and this percentage is substantially lower in Europe. The most common Internet access is through a 56K modem. If your pages don't process and load in a "reasonable timeframe" at this speed, you have to make some improvements.

Unfortunately, many of us now working with Active Server Pages did not start out as database programmers. Some of us started as HTML programmers and picked up databases as we went along. Others of us started as Visual Basic programmers and migrated over to ASP. And others started out as mainframe report writers. Regardless of how you came to be working with ASP, the fact is that most of us don't have as strong a database background as we should have if we are to develop browser-based database applications.

It is very likely that when you develop a web-based database application, you will do more than just access the information from the database. You will probably be designing the database as well, so a quick review of design concepts is in order. We will all have worked with databases at some point and each of us has a pretty good idea of how databases are used, so we can readily construct our own database. Actually, with the wide range of available tools in the marketplace today, creating a database is really easy. Even Microsoft Access provides a number of wizards that step you through the database creation process allowing you to produce a database in a matter of a few minutes. Although Microsoft Access is a fine product, most wizard-generated applications are sufficient only for low volume and relatively simple data access. For many professional applications, especially for high-volume internet access, we need a database that is efficient, flexible, and fast enough to handle many simultaneous users. To create such a database, a human touch is usually required. The main focus of this chapter is to discuss what makes for a good database design and the concepts constructing a database so that it meets internet performance expectations.

A Brief History of Database Systems

Today's most widely used database system is the relational database. These databases use a collection of related tables to store information. The design of the tables and how they relate to one another is based on a process called **normalization**. This process was initially developed by Dr Edgar F Codd, and is based upon a branch of mathematics that deals with the mapping of data sets and the use of relational calculus. Although Codd's publication of this subject, "*A Relational Model of Data for Large Shared Data Banks*", came out in 1970, its proposed data model was so radically different that it wasn't until around 1980 that it started to become widely used.

Today's Relational Database Management Systems (RDBMS) are not "purely relational" in the sense that they do not conform exactly as Dr Codd had envisaged. Instead, they have added to the capabilities of the relational database model by including features found in other types of database systems that have been developed. For the sake of completeness, a few comments concerning the various types of database systems that influenced today's RDBMS developers are warranted.

Hierarchical Databases

Hierarchical databases, which were first developed by IBM for its IMS mainframe database product line, organized data in tree-like structures where each level in the tree contains data items that are different from other levels. This type of database was attractive to use as it easily models real-world processes. Perhaps the most intuitive way to visualize this type of relationship is by imagining an upside down tree of data. In this tree, a single table acts as the "root" of the database from which other tables "branch" out. This approach to organizing data is very similar to the way files and folders are organized when viewed in Windows Explorer.

The relationship between the data items is thought of in terms of parents and children: a child may only have one parent but a parent can have multiple children. Parents and children are tied together by links called "pointers". A parent will have a list of pointers to each of their children. The following illustration demonstrates a hierarchical relationship of courses, students, and grades.

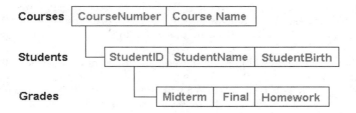

However, there were some serious data access issues that plagued these databases. In the data structure on the previous page, if you wanted to find out the value of a given field, such as the `Final` grade, you needed to traverse the tree starting from the top. This approach to navigation was often slow with large databases. Also, you could not add a record to a child table until it had already been incorporated into the parent table. This might be troublesome if, using our example, you wanted to add a student who had not yet signed up for any courses. Worse yet, the hierarchical database model required much repetition of data within the database. For example, if a student was enrolled on more than one course, then the `StudentName` and `StudentBirth` fields would need to be repeated for each course.

Hierarchical database have been widely used but slowly have been replaced with relational systems. Even though the use of hierarchical databases has been in decline in recent years, data access to hierarchical systems has more recently been making a comeback. This is most notable in the form of directory services such as Microsoft's Active Directory, and through support of irregularly shaped records in ADO.

Network Databases

The first standardized and widely accepted database model for mainframe computers was the network database model, which was developed by the Committee for Data Systems Languages (CODASYL). This is the same organization that produced the COBOL language, partially with the goal of accessing data in these network databases.

In many ways, the network model was designed to solve some of the more serious problems with the hierarchical database model. Specifically, the network model solves the problem of data redundancy (that is repetition) by representing relationships in terms of sets rather than a hierarchy. It was developed as a more flexible version of the hierarchical model. However, instead of using a single-parent tree hierarchy, the network model allowed child tables to have more than one parent.

Nevertheless, though it was a dramatic improvement, the network model was far from perfect. Most profoundly, the model was difficult to implement and maintain. Most implementations of the network database model were used by computer programmers rather than real users. What was needed was a simple model that could be used by real end-users to solve real problems.

From the mid 1970s through the early 1990s, this database type was widely used. Although network databases still have a significant presence, they are increasingly being replaced by relational databases.

Object-Oriented Databases

Like object-oriented programming languages such as C++, object database management systems (ODBMSs) are object-oriented systems. These databases were introduced in the early 1980s but because of performance issues (and the rise of relational databases) they never became widely used. With the increasing demand to store and access non-traditional data, such as digital images, sound files, etc., the benefits of using objects has become increasingly important. With today's faster and less expensive machines, many of the major database vendors have been including support for objects in their relational databases so that complex data may be managed.

The Importance of Good Design

As a developer, you will most likely need to come up with the data model yourself or in partnership with a database administrator. A well-designed structure for your database can make the crucial difference between creating a "successful" database application and one that is, shall we say, "less than successful". The data stored in the database needs to be organized such that the data is easily retrieved, and may be stored and processed in a fast, efficient manner. A well-designed data model will accurately represent the real world and allow business rules to be applied, thus transforming the data from mere bits and bytes into meaningful information.

A poor design will inflict performance problems, integrity problems, and functionality limitations, and the best SQL statements and program code in the world won't help much. A solid design will go a long way in avoiding these problems and make it much, much easier to code the application that uses the database. The importance of database design cannot be stressed highly enough.

Database design is not rocket science and if one follows some basic rules and guidelines, it is not difficult to produce a good quality design. Of course, the final design will depend on a great many factors, including the type of database with which you are working and the information that you are trying to organize. There are several types of databases, including hierarchical, relational, network, and object. Since each database type uses a different model to organize its data, the database design for each will be slightly different. Today, relational database management systems are by far the most commonly used database type and it is these that we will discuss in detail. Bear in mind, though, that much of what follows is applicable to all database types.

Business Before Architecture: The Logical Design

With all applications, the ultimate goal is to effectively and efficiently build and implement a solution that meets your business needs. This means that you must understand the business needs before you develop a business application! The starting point for an effective database design is always the same, regardless of the database type, that is, you have to know what your business goals are when developing the application and what information and processes are needed to meet these goals. A considerable amount of research on the business needs must be conducted before you can begin designing the architecture of the system.

Understanding the business is sometimes the most difficult task in this stage of development, especially since most business operations have a certain degree of complexity to them. Although there are many specific reasons that make understanding the business difficult, such as logistics, industry specializations, and legal issues just to name a few, these reasons can be generalized as complexity. An inability to deal successfully with complexity is often a cause of failure in software development. Complexity leads to incomplete understanding, which in turn leads to a poor design. The key to dealing with complexity is to come up with a representation of the system that has been organized into manageable chunks and which simplifies things by eliminating unnecessary details. This is often called **decomposing** the project. By breaking the project into its constituent parts it is easier to understand the processes required.

To gain a good understanding of the various business components for the project, enlist the aid of the stakeholders – the key employees of the business who have a vested interest in the project. These stakeholders will be able to provide the resources for you to understand the business. Do whatever you can to get the business resources involved early in the design process. Hold focus sessions and interviews with the business people. Find out such things as criteria for performance, detailed objectives, data retention requirements (such as how much history is needed and how long to keep it), and other expectations. It is during this research phase that you should start asking how the success of the project will be measured. By knowing this factor, you can start developing your quality assurance plans. Also, knowing this will give you a better idea of what is important in the application. As you start to develop your model for the business, let the business people review and evaluate your work and then use their input to refine the model and help in establishing priorities.

To illustrate some of these ideas, consider the fictitious bookstore, Books For You. In their initial meetings with you, the developer, they present their business objectives. As seen by the company, these objectives are fairly simple and are listed in order of importance to the company:

1. Establish a presence on the Internet

2. Allow on-line purchases

3. Provide an attractive and user-friendly interface

4. Begin gathering customer profiles

5. Begin tracking customer purchase histories

Some of these objectives are easy, like the first one to establish a presence on the Internet. Any static web page will do that. The other objectives are a bit more involved. There is quite a lot to the operation of such a site that may not be obvious. With the help of the people who will operate the bookstore, you can figure out what the site needs to do to meet these objectives. First look at what a typical visitor to the site would need to do in order to buy a book:

- ❏ The shopper navigates the site looking for the book that he or she is interested in.
- ❏ When the shopper finds the book, it is added to a shopping cart.
- ❏ The shopper may continue to look for another book and may add more books to the shopping cart.
- ❏ Once all books have been selected, the shopper proceeds to a checkout area and provides the information needed to pay for the books and have them delivered.

For the shopper to perform these activities, the bookstore will need a catalog of books to sell and some mechanism to display them to the shopper. The store may also provide a search feature that allows quicker access to the books of interest to the shopper. There must be a way to store the contents of the shopping cart for each shopper and make sure each shopping cart is kept separate from the others. When the shopper wishes to check out, the billing, and credit card information will need to be gathered and stored. If the shopper is a returning customer, there may be a need to provide some personalization, like automatically filling in address details such as city, state and ZIP into the order form. Also, some interaction with a third party for credit card verification is required as well as receipt generation via e-mail.

Rather than trying to come up with a design for all of this at once, evaluate each part of the application independently. Attacking the problem one step at a time makes the task of designing the application and the database itself much easier. With the primary activities identified, we look more closely at each of them. Some of the questions asked might be:

- ❏ What basic information do we need to store about the customer's shopping cart?
- ❏ What basic information is needed for the catalog of books?
- ❏ What is the minimal information that is required by the third party for credit card verification?

Don't try to determine every last detail about the data at this stage. That will come later. If you try to collect every minute detail now, you risk getting bogged down in the details. At this point we need to determine the most significant pieces of information required for the business. Eventually, the information stored for each one of the previous questions will become a table (or tables) in the database, but at this stage in the design phase, these collections of related data items are referred to as **entities**.

Once you have a rough idea of what entities are required, you need to consider how they will coexist. How does a shopping cart interact with the catalog of books? The interaction between entities may require that you include additional information that you didn't think of at first. After you have roughed out the major components to the application, go over it again, but this time, pay a bit more attention to details. Again, don't try to get too detailed; just put in enough detail to be confident in the design. Later on in the process, you review these entities and their interactions and refine them.

One common technique for identifying the entities and their relationships is to extract short English phrases from a narrative that describes the data being modeled. For example, consider the following fictitious conversation between a developer (Dev) and the client, "Books For You" (BFY):

Dev: "How does your store get the books that it sells?"

BFY: "Our store orders its books from any number of distributors. We just call them on the phone, give them our account number and place an order."

Dev: "When you order a book, what information about that book do you need for that order?"

BFY: "Typically, all we need to tell them is the ISBN number of the book and the number of copies required. ISBN numbers are unique, so just having that one bit of information, we can find the book we want. If we have the ISBN number, the distributor can usually find out any other information needed. If we don't have an ISBN number, we can usually order a book if we have its title, its author or authors. Also, it often useful to know the name of the publisher, or the publication date."

Dev: "What are your options if the distributor doesn't have the book?"

BFY: "Well, we can always check with other distributors."

From this brief exchange we can determine quite a bit. We can identify several entities and traits of these entities:

Entity	Traits
Stores	Account Number
Books	ISBN Number, Publisher's Name, Publication Date, Title, Author's Name
Distributors	Phone Number
Authors	Author Name

We can also determine relationships between entities. Note that some relationships may be described differently depending upon which entity you begin with:

Entity 1	Entity 2	Relationship
Stores	Books	Stores Order Books
Distributors	Books	Distributors Supply Books
Authors	Books	Authors Write Books

One convenient way of documenting this information is to use a diagram. Below is an example of such a diagram:

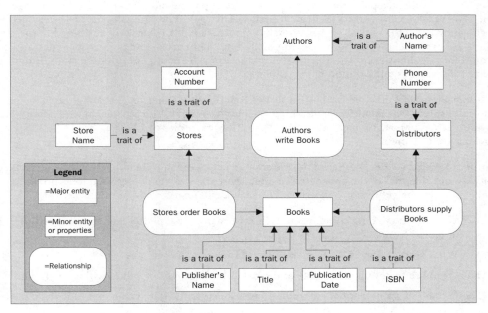

The diagram above illustrates an early draft of a portion of our data store. As we investigate the business and more clearly understand the data we are modeling, we will add more entities and relationships and will probably make changes. For example, we may very well determine that since the Account Number of the Store is assigned differently by each Distributor, we may not wish to the Store entity to contain this data, but rather in the Distributor entity.

One great practice when designing a database (or any other type of application for that matter) is to discuss problems and ideas with other developers. Hold a meeting with them and explain the objectives of the application, the major obstacles, the known business process, and your proposed design. Having your data model represented in easy-to-view diagrams like the one above will make it easy for your associates to understand and comment on your work. Let them look things over, evaluate what has been done, and provide you with feedback. This peer-review process will almost always save you time and effort since any given application will have similarities with other applications. By enlisting others, you can understand how they approached their designs and learn from their efforts. Take the ideas and suggestions offered in the reviews and evaluations to refine your model and add greater detail.

Keep cycling through these activities – researching the business, identifying the components, identifying relationships, business review, peer review, and refining the model – until a clear and understandable model of the system is developed.

The goal of this exercise is to come up with a meaningful representation of the system, with the various entities identified and an understanding of what services those entities will provide. The result of this effort is called a **conceptual design**. The conceptual design will not describe *how things are done*, but rather *what needs to be done*.

Developing a Logical Design

Once you have a conceptual design you can then start paying more attention to how things will be done. The result of this will be the **logical design**. The logical design will provide a very detailed specification of all the entities. It has to include more than just what was considered in the conceptual design. It has to include all the processing, including the housekeeping, and the audit trails. It has to account for peculiarities in database query optimization. It should consider the skills of the team, the build strategy, and configuration management.

Most logical designs take the form of an **Entity Relationship Diagram** (**ER Diagrams**), which are pictorial displays that identify details about the entities required for various business functions and how the entities may reference each other. We'll see a few examples of ER Diagrams below as we discuss the concepts used by them.

In order to construct ER Diagrams, details about each element of data needs to be determined for each entity. In our diagram of the conceptual model, these data elements, referred to as **attributes**, are often displayed as minor entities or properties. For each attribute ask such questions as:

- ❑   Where will the data come from? Will it be manually typed in, generated somehow, or obtained from another source?
- ❑   What kind of data is it? Numeric? Text? Date?
- ❑   What are the limits to the size of the data? What ranges of values will it need to hold?
- ❑   Is the data value dependent upon other values? Is the data value derived? If so, how?
- ❑   What are valid values? How do we test for valid values?
- ❑   What format should the data be displayed in?

In many ways, the logical design is usually much simpler to come up with than developing the conceptual design, although the process is much more detailed. Starting with a good conceptual design, much of the information needed to be stored in the database will be obvious. All you need to do now is organize it in a way that fits the technology to the business rules.

As with the conceptual design, keep the people on the business side of things involved in this process. Historically, one of the major risks to a project's success is lack of end-user involvement. By keeping business people involved and by having them frequently review the designs, the more likely it is that the final product will be a success. With each review, you are managing user expectations and fine-tuning the feature set of the product. Although the business people can help in many ways, it is your responsibility to make the design work. You will have to ensure that the database schema will model the business appropriately and that the data stored in it is efficiently maintained.

Ensuring Data Integrity

One of the purposes of the logical design is to organize the information in ways so that the business rules are followed and to make sure that every process useing this information does not corrupt the data. A poor design can cause data anomalies such as invalid values, missing information, or information that is not changed consistently throughout the database.

Data integrity falls into four categories:

- ❑   Entity integrity – which ensures that every row of data can be properly identified.

- ❑   Domain integrity – which validates the information stored in a particular field.

- ❑   Referential integrity – which ensures that values are consistent between entities.

- ❑   User-defined integrity – which allows you to specify business rules that do not fall into one of the other integrity categories.

As we continue our discussion of developing a logical design, we shall see how data integrity can be ensured through the careful implementation of several key concepts, including normalizing data, providing referential integrity, and applying validation rules to the data.

Relational versus Flat File Databases

After we have defined the entities for our design, our next step is to organize their attributes so that each piece of data is stored once and that it is stored in the correct place. Without a well-organized set of entities, our information will be susceptible to data anomalies and data integrity will be lost. In order to explain and illustrate the organizational process, we will begin with a poorly organized database, such as those created with spreadsheet or word-processing programs.

It is quite common for people not to use a database system like Oracle, SQL Server or even Microsoft Access as their first database. This is often because, when developing their first database, most people don't actually think of their work as being a database. Phone lists stored in a word-processing document, clients listed in some contact management software, and a check register kept in a spreadsheet are all such examples. Typically these are simple lists that have a few pieces of information for each entry. When the information is displayed or printed, it looks like one big table. These examples are called **flat file databases**. The term 'flat' comes from the fact that these tables are two-dimensional – they are usually wide and tend to be very long. Flat files are often wide because of the great many items of information people store in them. They tend to be long because each new record in the file adds to its overall length.

Many successful applications are based on flat-file databases, but they are almost always small applications limited to a single user. When such a database has to store and retrieve large volumes of data, it is often too inefficient and prone to development errors. To illustrate some of the issues with flat-file databases, we will consider the fictitious mail order company named **ACME Aquarium Products**.

ACME takes orders from customers on the phone and stores each order in a spreadsheet:

Date	Invoice Number	Customer Name	Customer Address	Ship To Address	1st Item Product	Price	Qty	2nd Item Product	Price	Qty	Total
13-Dec-99	5106	Jason Trickey	27 Federal Road Westport, CT 06880	27 Federal Road Westport, CT 06880	PA422	$ 19.99	1	AF812	$ 14.99	3	$ 64.96
13-Dec-99	5107	Catherine Crean	62 Fern Street Naugatuck, CT 06720	821 Main Street Waterbury CT 06914	PA422	$ 19.99	1				$ 19.99
14-Dec-99	5108	Jason Tricky	27 Federal Road Westport, CT 06880	27 Federal Road Westport, CT 06880	PA422	$ 19.99	2	AS101	$ 15.99	2	$ 71.96
14-Dec-99	5109	Elizabeth Remes	3 Fawn Hill Road Huntington, CT 06484	3 Fawn Hill Road Huntington, CT 06484	FF545	$ 12.99	6	AF812	$ 14.99	6	$167.88
14-Dec-99	5110	Margaret Barry	39 Hemmingway Drive Oxford, CT 06462	PO Box 266 Monroel, CT 06268	AS101	$ 15.99	2	FF545	$ 12.99	2	$ 57.96

There are a few serious problems with this approach. One such problem is that the data is limited – this system does not allow for more than two items to be ordered on a single invoice. Another problem concerns redundancy of data between records – the data-entry clerk will need to type in the customer's name with each item purchased regardless whether they are purchasing more than one item at a time or are a returning customer. Not only is this tedious for the data-entry clerk, but also encourages typographical errors. Notice that the name of the customer "Jason Trickey" is spelled differently in invoice 5106 and invoice number 5108. When storing data, a consideration should be made for how much disk space you are willing to provide for the application. Although hard disk space is relatively inexpensive, storing lots of redundant data can often be costly.

One way we could address some of these issues is by creating a "lookup table" for the customers. Each customer would be assigned a customer number on their first purchase and that number would be used to identify the customer each time they placed an order. This approach offers a number of improvements. First, the chances of typographical errors decrease since fewer characters are entered for a customer number than are with a full name. Second, each customer's full name is recorded only once so the overall amount of space required to store all customer's names should be reduced. You can further reduce space by placing information specific to each customer, like the customer address, in the customer lookup table.

It is said that the customer lookup table is *related* to the invoice table. The key to this relationship is the customer number. As long as you know the customer number from an entry in the invoices table, you can search through the customer table to find the appropriate customer entry and therefore find out every detail stored about that customer. A widely used database model, called the **relational database**, uses these cross-table lookups to provide an easy and efficient means to organize and retrieve data.

The single most important design attribute of a relational database is how the tables are set up. The tables should be organized so that they are properly related and store the data efficiently. One widely used process of organizing the data is called **normalization**.

The term normalization comes from the mathematical term "normal" which means "to be at right angles". (The term was also a play on the political jargon "normal relations".) If we were to imagine the database tables laid out like a crossword puzzle, with each data item representing a letter in a word of the puzzle, our example may look like the following:

Invoices Table

We will take a detailed look at the process of normalization, as it is quite complex.

The Normalization Process

Normalization is the process of applying successive rules to a database design to improve its structure and reduces data integrity issues. This process identifies and decreases data redundancy and produces a simple structure for the data that clearly indicates the relationships between data items. It also eliminates data anomalies thereby ensuring consistency within and between tables.

When certain rules of normalization are applied to a table, it is said to be in **first normal form**, or 1NF for short. If a table is already 1NF and additional rules are applied to it, it is said to be in **second normal form** (**2NF**). As more and more rules are applied, tables may reach higher forms, such as **third normal form** (**3NF**), the **Boyce-Codd normal form** (BCNF), **fourth normal form** (**4NF**), and **fifth normal form** (**5NF**).

When normalization is applied to the tables of a database, not all tables necessarily will achieve the same "level" of normalcy. Some tables may be in 3NF while others are in 4NF and yet others in 2NF. This is fine, since our ultimate goal is to have a fast, efficient, and meaningful design. Normalization helps in achieving these goals, but normalization can be overdone in some cases. With each increasing form of normalcy there are trade-offs between efficiencies in storage and performance, so we should strive to have an "appropriate" amount of normalization based upon the particular needs of the application. For most commercial applications, tables will be in either 3NF or 4NF.

In the broadest sense, there are three basic steps in normalization:

- ❑ Elimination of repeating groups
- ❑ Removal of derived data
- ❑ Making certain that each table represents only one single business entity. (Related entities are placed in other tables and cross-referenced using keys.)

To better understand how the normalization process works and its benefits, let's examine each normal form.

First Normal Form

For a table to be in first normal form each row must be **identified**, all columns in the table should be **atomic**, and each field must be **unique**. What do we mean by identified, atomic, and unique? To understand how these terms are used in database theory, consider the following:

Identification

In a relational database, we never record information about something we cannot identify. To distinguish each row in the table, we define a **primary key** (PK). Think of the primary key as being the row's name. When we need to refer to any given row, we do so by its primary key. Since database systems spend much of their time searching for data, the primary key is used to uniquely identify each row so that searching is efficient.

The primary key may be selected from one or more of the columns in the table, or we may create a new column for this purpose. If there are columns already in the table whose values are guaranteed to be unique, then they should be used rather than taking up additional space for a new column. If a new column is to be created, then the values in this column will typically be in some sequence, such as an order number or employee ID, which increments by a value of one with each new row.

If you have a choice of which column(s) to use for the primary key, it is generally best to choose the most concise column(s) – meaning, those with the smallest usable data type. Since most database systems process numbers more efficiently than character strings, consider using numbers for this column, preferably an integer value. Integer values are often very efficiently stored in most RDBMSs. Also, the column (or columns) used for the primary key should be one that is static or changes very infrequently. The best type of primary key is a single column that contains integer values that never change.

> *It should be noted that, since the purpose of a primary key is to uniquely identify every row of a table, missing values (called **null** values) should not be allowed in any of the columns comprising the primary key. If fact, RDBMSs will not allow you to include a "nullable column" as part of the primary key. This "no nulls" rule applies only to primary keys. Columns that contain nulls and are therefore not used as part of the primary key may be used to assist searches by including these columns as part of an **index**. It should also be noted that it is possible to uniquely identify each row of the table by using two different columns (or sets of columns). Although each would be considered a **candidate key**, only one can be selected for use as the primary key. We'll cover indexes and candidate keys later on in this chapter.*

In our invoice example, when we think of any given order, we identify that order by its invoice number. This column can be used because every order will have a unique invoice number. The business will assign a new invoice number to each order in sequence. We couldn't use any other column since their values may be repeated from invoice to invoice: 'Jason Trickey' placed more than one order, so using the customer name column would not uniquely identify a single row. With some tables, there may not be a single unique column. In these cases, we define the primary key to be some combination of two or more columns that together will be unique.

A common example of this is to use both a person's social security number and their last name. Although it is not widely known, social security numbers in the United States are not unique and are re-issued every so many years. Obviously, a person's last name is not unique. Although neither piece of information is unique, if we use a combination of the two, the probability of two people having the same social security number and last name is minute, so together they are "sufficiently unique".

Atomic Values

For a column to be atomic, it should only contain one piece of information. It should not be an array or a list or anything with its own structure.

To illustrate the requirement of being atomic, consider the `Ship To Address` column in the preceding `Invoices` example. This column contained four items of data in one field: a street address, a city, a state and a ZIP code. Having compound data items makes operations such as selecting and sorting very arduous. So, if you wanted to sort the data by ZIP code, you would need to know at which character in that column the ZIP code started. This will rarely be the same from entry to entry:

```
        1         2         3         4
1234567890123456789012345678901234567890
3 Fawn Hill Road, Huntington, CT 06484
61 Fern Street, Naugatuck, CT 06720
```

As you can see, the ZIP code in the first entry is in the seventh word and starts at the 34th character, whereas the second entry has its ZIP code as the sixth word, which starts at the 31st character. If the data is grouped together like this in a single column, we would have to parse the individual data items, which would take time and consume resources.

To resolve this problem, the first normal form rules require that each of these items of data must be in their own column: a column for street address, a column for city, a column for state, and a column for ZIP.

Unique Columns

Having unique columns means that every column in a table is different from every other column in the same table. In other words, the table should contain no repeating groups, that is, columns or groups of columns with the same name. This requirement should not be confused with having unique values within a column, as is required for primary keys.

To illustrate the uniqueness requirement for each column, think of a home mortgage loan. Let's say that the loan is for 30 years to be paid off in monthly installments. You could create a table that contains one column for every scheduled payment, and since interest is usually accrued on a daily basis at least, you will also need to have a column for the date each payment is made:

```
LoanNumber
Payment1
DateOfPayment1
Payment2
DateOfPayment2
Payment3
DateOfPayment3
    :
Payment360
DateOfPayment360
```

This approach has a number of problems associated with it. First, it uses storage space inefficiently. At the beginning of the loan, nearly every column is empty but the space required to store the values of each column must be reserved when the table is created. Only when the loan has been fully paid off will all the columns actually be used. A second problem with this table concerns how calculations must be made. In order to compute something as essential as the current balance, you will need to construct a fairly complex formula that checks each of the more than 700 columns!

If you think about it, there really isn't any difference between `Payment1` and `Payment2` columns – each holds a value of how much you paid on a given month. These columns aren't unique, and therefore the unique columns requirement is violated. A much better solution is to use multiple rows rather than multiple columns. The table should only have columns for `LoanNumber`, `Payment`, and `DateOfPayment`. Each time a payment is made, a new row is inserted into the table. If no payments have been made for a given loan, no rows will be stored, so no space is wasted.

For another illustration, again consider our invoice example. This system allows for only two items to be purchased with one invoice. The information for the first product is saved in the `Product`, `Price`, and `Qty` fields under the group "1st Item". The information for the second product is saved in columns with the same name but under the group "2nd Item". Clearly, these two sets of columns are redundant and this approach wastes space when only one item is ordered.

To resolve this problem, we eliminate one set of the columns and add a new row for the second item. By having one row for each line item, we use only the space we need and we are able to add any number of line items to the invoice. Since we can now have more than one row for each invoice, we need some way of grouping all of the line items to a single invoice. We get around this by using two tables, one for the invoice itself and another table for the line items. Let's call the first table "`Invoices`" and the second table "`InvoiceLineItems`." The line items table will hold the product, price and quantity data whereas the invoice table will hold the invoice number, invoice date, customer number, and the address.

To make sure that we can match each row in the `Invoices` table with the correct (that is, related) rows in the `InvoiceLineItems` table, we need store some common information in each table. Each invoice will have a unique invoice number. We also include the invoice number for each row in the line items table. We can then match the rows from both tables that share the same invoice number values.

Invoices

InvoiceNumber	CustomerID	...	...	SalesTaxRate
2140	101	...	...	0.08
2141	184	...	...	0.08
2142	101	...	...	0.06

InvoiceLineItems

LineNumber	InvoiceNumber	ProductID	...	...	Discount
1	2140	PA422	...	...	12.95
2	2140	MR002	...	...	34.19
1	2141	PA100	...	...	19.67
1	**2142**	MR100	...	...	23.88
2	**2142**	MR202	...	...	18.44

This table-to-table relationship goes two ways:

❑ You can take any row in the first table and find all of the related rows in the second table.

❑ You can take any row in the second table and find all of the related rows in the first table.

So the third row in the top table (with an ID of 2142) will match the fourth, fifth and sixth rows in the bottom table.

In most circumstances, the primary key from one table is used to match against some column in a second, related table. The column in the second, related table that is used in the relationship is called a **foreign key**. We'll cover more about how tables are related in a later section.

Second Normal Form

Part of the goal of normalization is to eliminate redundant data. Storing duplicate data unnecessarily will take up disk space, slow down performance and may cause problems when it comes to changing or deleting data. The second normal form is applied to help ensure that redundant data does not exist. For a table to be in Second Normal Form (2NF), it must pass two tests. The first test is that it must already be in First Normal Form. The second test is that all fields that are not part of the key are dependent upon all of the columns that make up the key. In more mathematical terms, the table has no partial key dependencies.

To illustrate this, consider the following movie schedule:

Theater	Movie	ShowingTime	Telephone
Empire Theater	Toy Story 2	5:30 PM	(203) 555-1111
Empire Theater	Toy Story 2	7:30 PM	(203) 555-1111
Empire Theater	Being John Malkovich	7:45 PM	(203) 555-1111
Royal Heights	Being John Malkovich	9:00 PM	(860) 221-9876
Empire Theater	The Blair Witch Project	9:15 PM	(203) 555-1111

This table describes which movies are played at what times at certain theaters. In this table, the primary key is composed of the `Theater` and the `Movie` fields. Since the same movie can be shown at different times and at different theaters, we need to know both the theater and the movie before we can determine the show time. It said that there is a **functional dependency** between the `ShowingTime` field and the two fields of the primary key. This is usually denoted as "`(Theater, Movie) ? (ShowingTime)`" while can be read as "`Theater` and `Movie` determine `ShowingTime`". The `Telephone` field violates the 2NF rule since it is not functionally dependent upon all of the fields in the primary key. Telephone is an attribute of the theater and it is independent of the movie being played.

To resolve this, remove the `Telephone` field from this table and place it in a new table that describes each theater:

ShowingTimes

Theater	Movie	ShowingTime
Empire Theater	Toy Story 2	3:15 PM
Empire Theater	Toy Story 2	5:30 PM
Empire Theater	Being John Malkovich	7:45 PM
Royal Heights	Being John Malkovich	7:45 PM
Empire Theater	The Blair Witch Project	10:00 PM

Theaters

Theater	Telephone
Empire Theater	(203) 555-1111
Royal Heights	(860) 221-9876

Let's take another look at our Invoices example and determine if our tables are all in 2NF. Currently, our tables should be defined as follows:

Invoices

Invoices	InvoiceLineItems	Customers
InvoiceNumber (PK)	InvoiceNumber (PK)	CustomerID (PK)
InvoiceDate	LineNumber (PK)	CustomerName
CustomerID	ProductCode	Address
ShipToAddress	ProductDescription	City
ShipToCity	Price	State
ShipToState	Qty	ZIP
ShipToZIP	Discount	Phone
SalesTaxRate		

For each table, we need to determine if each field is dependent upon the primary key. The primary key is used to identify each record in the table, so each field in a given table must be dependent upon that key, or in other words, each field must describe the entity that the primary key represents.

One technique for determining if a field is dependent upon the primary key is to ask the question "Does *field* describe *PK*?" for each field in the table. For example "Does InvoiceDate describe the InvoiceNumber?" Since the primary key identifies each invoice, it is easier to answer the question if we restate the question as "Does InvoiceDate describe the Invoice." The answer is, of course, yes. The InvoiceDate describes when the invoice was created. "Does CustomerID describe the Invoice?" Yes, the CustomerID describes what customer placed the invoice. If we continue through the Invoices table, we find that we can answer yes for every field, so the Invoices table is in 2NF.

With the `InvoiceLineItems` table, we have a compound primary key that is composed of both `InvoiceNumber` and `LineNumber`. This is needed since more than one product may be ordered in a single invoice. The `LineNumber` field will contain a value of 1 for the first item order for a given invoice. It will have a value of 2 for the second item, and so on. Therefore, the primary key identifies the *nth* item order in the invoice. When we ask our questions, we state them such as "Does `ProductCode` describe the 1st item ordered in the invoice?" When we answer these questions we find that this table is also in 2NF. Similarly, we find that the `Customers` table is also in 2NF.

Third Normal Form

The requirements for Third Normal Form (3NF) are similar to those for Second Normal Form in that it considers functional dependencies. Where the rules for 2NF required that each column is dependent upon the primary key, the rules for the 3NF require that each field be dependent *only* on the primary key and no other columns. A table is considered to be in Third Normal Form if it is already in Second Normal Form and all columns that are not part of the primary key are dependent entirely on the primary key. In other words, every column in the table must be dependent upon the key, the whole key and nothing but the key. If a column describes some non-key column, it should be removed and placed into a different table.

Let us again take a look at our `Invoices` example and apply the rules for 3NF. Starting with the `InvoiceLineItems`, let's make sure that each column in the table that isn't part of the primary key directly describes the key, `InvoiceNumber`, and `LineNumber` (that is, the "line item"). `ProductCode` identifies the product that is being order for the line item, so that column looks good. The next column is `ProductDescription`. Although you can think of this column as identifying the product that is being ordered, in actuality, `ProductDescription` describes the product, which we identify by its `ProductCode` value. If the product were changed for this line item (which we identify with the `ProductCode`), then `ProductDescription` column would change accordingly. Therefore, `ProductDescription` is dependent upon `ProductCode`, not the primary key, so this violates the rule for 3NF.

To remedy this violation, we do not include `ProductDescription` in the `InvoiceLineItems` table, but rather, store this column in a different table, one that describes each product that is sold. This new table, `Products`, can use the `ProductCode` column as a primary key. Since the `InvoiceLineItems` table will still contain the `ProductCode` column, we can relate the two tables.

After applying 3NF rules to our schema, the resulting tables would be:

Invoices	InvoiceLineItems	Products	Customers
InvoiceNumber (PK)	InvoiceNumber (PK)	ProductCode (PK)	CustomerID (PK)
InvoiceDate	LineNumber (PK)	ProductDescription	CustomerName
CustomerID	ProductCode	Price	Address
ShipToAddress	Qty		City
ShipToCity	Discount		State
ShipToState			ZIP
ShipToZIP			Phone
SalesTaxRate			

Boyce-Codd Normal Form

When E F Codd initially developed the normal forms, he envisaged five of them. As we know, he numbered these forms 1 through 5. Later on, it was discovered that there was a problem with some tables in 3NF and a stricter version of 3NF was developed. Since there was already a form called 4th Normal form, it was decided to name this form after the people who developed it, hence the name Boyce-Codd Normal Form (BCNF).

It should be noted that tables that are in BCNF are also in 3NF. Only in special circumstances, which we will describe, will a table in 3NF not be in BCNF.

Although the earlier normal forms address dependencies of columns with the primary key, the Boyce-Codd Normal form (BCNF) deals with dependencies within keys. The BCNF is concerned with which fields may be selected to make up the primary key of a 3NF table. To understand this form, we first need to define a couple of terms. If each row in a table can be uniquely described by more than one set of fields, you have to choose which set of fields will comprise the primary key. Each set of fields that you may choose from is called a **candidate key**. If a key contains more than one field, it is said to be a **composite key**. If each of the candidate keys shares some of the same fields, it is said that they are both "composite and overlapping".

A table is said to be in BCNF if it is already in 3NF and there are no dependencies within the fields that comprise the candidate keys. Thus BCNF differs from the 3NF *only* when there is more than one candidate key and these keys are composite and overlapping.

To illustrate the need for the BCNF, consider a financial application where you need to keep track of loans across and number of banks for a variety of people. A `Borrower` table could be constructed that contains the columns: `BankNumber`, `LoanNumber`, `CustomerID`, and `Amount`. This table could have its primary key selected from any of the following functional dependencies:

> `BankNumber, LoanNumber, CustomerID -> Amount`
>
> `BankNumber, LoanNumber -> CustomerID and Amount`
>
> `CustomerID, LoanNumber -> BankNumber and Amount`

Since each of these candidate keys contains more than one column, they are all composite keys. Also, each key uses the `LoanNumber` column, so they are also overlapping. Although this table is in 3NF, there is a redundancy problem, in that for each customer associated with a loan, we must repeat the bank name and amount of the loan. We can eliminate this redundancy by decomposing the table into two tables that are each in BCNF. One table that describes the loans themselves and a second table describing which customers are associated with each loan:

> `BankLoan` table: `LoanNumber, BankNumber and Amount`
>
> `CustomerLoan` table: `LoanNumber and CustomerID`

This works because no single bank will issue two loans with the same loan number, and no single customer will get the same loan number from two different banks.

If we look at our `Invoices` example, we can confirm that each table is in BCNF since there are no other fields or combinations of fields that are candidate keys.

Fourth Normal Form

Our rules of normalization have so far resolved redundancies among columns in a table, but these rules did not address all types of redundancies. Tables in 4NF resolve problems that arise from tables having composite primary keys but still possess redundant data between rows.

In order to describe a table in 4NF, consider the following scenario that illustrates the problems that 4NF tables resolve. Suppose we are asked to add to a university database a table that contains, for each course, a list of all teachers who are qualified to teach the course and a list of all the textbooks required for the course. In this scenario, the required text for a course is dictated by the course, not the teacher.

CourseNumber	TeacherID	RequiredText
SW460	101	Instant JavaScript
SW460	101	Professional JavaScript
SW460	177	Instant JavaScript
SW460	177	Professional JavaScript
SW481	96	Visual Basic Oracle 8 Programmer's Reference
SW523	177	ADO 2.1 Programmer's Reference
SW523	177	Professional Active Server Pages 3.0
SW523	177	Professional SQL Server 7 Programming

The primary key for this table is a composite of each of the three fields. There are no non-key columns. The table is in at least BCNF.

There is a redundancy between rows worth noting: every `CourseNumber` of "SW460" uses "Instant JavaScript" or "Professional JavaScript" as the `RequiredTexts`. There can be problems when updating a table that allows such redundancies. For example, the addition of one new textbook requires the insertion of a new row for each teacher who teaches the course, and the addition of a new qualified teacher requires the insertion of a new row for each textbook on the list. These problems are due to the fact that, although neither `TeacherID` nor `RequiredText` are functionally dependent on `CourseNumber`, the *list* of `TeacherID`s and the *list* of `RequiredText`s are dependent on `CourseNumber`. In other words, the lists of qualified teachers and texts both depend on `CourseNumber` but have nothing to do with each other.

The solution for this problem is to decompose this table into two new tables. One table will define which teachers are qualified for which course and the second table will define which texts are required for each course. These new tables will be in Fourth Normal Form.

Teachers

CourseNumber	TeacherID
SW460	101
SW460	77
SW481	101
SW524	77

Texts

CourseNumber	RequiredText
SW460	Instant JavaScript
SW460	Professional JavaScript
SW481	Visual Basic Oracle 8 Programmer's Reference
SW524	Professional Active Server Pages 3.0

Fifth Normal Form

The aim of the fifth normal form is to have tables that cannot be decomposed further. In other words, a table in 5NF cannot be constructed from several smaller tables.

Consider the following situation:

AuctionSite	Seller	Buyer
CyberAuction	Richards	Russell
CyberAuction	Davis	Ryan
HighBid	Richards	Ryan
CyberAuction	Richards	Ryan

Let us see what happens when we decompose this 4NF table into two tables using (AuctionSite, Seller) and (AuctionSite, Buyer). For simplicity, let us call the first table AS and the second table AB.

Table AS

AuctionSite	Seller
CyberAuction	Richards]
CyberAuction	Davis
HighBid	Richards

Table AB

AuctionSite	Buyer
CyberAuction	Russell
CyberAuction	Ryan
HighBid	Ryan

Now let us see what happens when we join these tables. For this join, let us relate the two tables using AuctionSite. The first record from AS is that of Richards using CyberAuction. This record matches up with two records from AB, those for Russell and Ryan, to produce:

AuctionSite	Seller	Buyer
CyberAuction	Richards	Russell
CyberAuction	Richards	Ryan

So far, so good. These records match exactly with our original table. Now let us consider the second record of AS, which produces:

AuctionSite	Seller	Buyer
CyberAuction	Davis	Russell
CyberAuction	Davis	Ryan

There is a problem here: Davis never sold anything to Russell using CyberAuction! Therefore, we can conclude that tables AS and AB are not in 5NF. The solution is to decompose our original table into three tables: (AuctionSite, Seller), (AuctionSite, Buyer), and (Seller, Buyer) as follows:

Table AS

AuctionSite	Seller
CyberAuction	Richards
CyberAuction	Davis
HighBid	Richards

Table AB

AuctionSite	Buyer
CyberAuction	Russell
CyberAuction	Ryan
HighBid	Ryan

Table SB

Seller	Buyer
Richards	Russell
Davis	Ryan
Richards	Ryan

The last table shows the result when we join these tables two at a time. The result of any two tables being joined will produce some false rows, but when this result is joined with the third table, these data anomalies will disappear:

Table ASB: AS Joined With AB

AuctionSite	Seller	Buyer
CyberAuction	Richards	Russell
CyberAuction	Richards	Ryan
CyberAuction	Davis	Russell
CyberAuction	Davis	Ryan
HighBids	Richards	Ryan

Now let us walk through the joining of table ASB with table SB. We will match records from both tables that share the same (Seller, Buyer) values. The first record of ASB, Richards selling to Russell using CyberAuction has a match in SB, so the following record is produced:

AuctionSite	Seller	Buyer
CyberAuction	Richards	Russell

Similarly for the second record in ASB, so our resulting table becomes:

AuctionSite	Seller	Buyer
CyberAuction	Richards	Russell
CyberAuction	Richards	Ryan

When we come to the third record of ASB, we find no corresponding record in SB. Therefore our resulting table is left unchanged.

We continue with the fourth record of Davis selling to Ryan using CyberAuction and find matching values in SB to produce:

AuctionSite	Seller	Buyer
CyberAuction	Richards	Russell
CyberAuction	Richards	Ryan
CyberAuction	Davis	Ryan

Finally, we match the record in ASB of Richards selling to Ryan using HighBid to a record in SB to produce a table containing the same records as our original 4NF table!

AuctionSite	Seller	Buyer
CyberAuction	Richards	Russell
CyberAuction	Richards	Ryan
CyberAuction	Davis	Ryan
HighBid	Richards	Ryan

Although the order of the records may not be the same between our 4NF table and our result, such differences are not considered in relational theory. As long as the two tables contain the same records, regardless of the order, we can consider them to be the same. Therefore, tables AS, AB, and SB are all considered to be in 5NF.

How Far to Normalize

When you normalize tables, you are able to better organize the data and reduce the amount of storage required. Although these benefits are very important, there are situations where the benefits of normalized tables are compromised by the reduction in performance. Whenever more than one table needs to be joined, additional processing power must be expended. If the number of tables being joined is small or the tables themselves hold few rows, this performance hit is negligible, but when many tables are involved with a large number of rows, the execution time can increase significantly. What is needed is the "optimal amount" of normalization.

But what is the optimal amount of normalization? You really can't know for sure until you get some test data in the database and you start running some stress tests and get some empirical performance measurements. As a general rule though, it is better to over-normalize than not to normalize enough. When coming up with the initial logical design, it is generally good practice to normalize each table to at least the fourth normal form. At this level, the design is sound and will work well for applications that use it. If you find that there is sufficient justification not to use 4NF or 5NF tables, you can always "flatten" the tables easily.

It is common for people designing databases to stop at 3NF because of some idea that it is actually more efficient when coding to not use 4NF or 5NF. In fact, a large number of databases in business today rarely go beyond 3NF. The argument for stopping at 3NF usually stems from the practice of using simplified queries, which include fewer joins. While this may be true is some cases, you will risk introducing data anomalies if you stop at 3NF. We either have to live with these anomalies or we have to write additional code to deal with them whenever they occur. Sometime the errors introduced by these anomalies are inconsequential; sometimes they are not. Bear in mind that any additional code written will need to be duplicated in every application that uses the database. This increases the likelihood of human error and increases complexity. You need to carefully consider the impact of how far you normalize. Many would argue that a slightly slower application that is 100 per cent accurate is preferable to a slightly faster application that is 97% accurate. I'd prefer to be safe and go with the more accurate approach.

Another common violation of the normalization rules is the use of **summary tables**. These are tables that contain aggregations or calculations from other tables. Examples of summary tables are:

❏ Calculating last year's sales statistics from individual stores of a national retailer on a region-by-region basis and storing these statistics in a new table for use in enterprise reporting queries.

❏ Copying the daily records for a single department from one table into another.

The use of summary tables should be discouraged in most circumstances, though a strong case can be made in favor of the first type of summary table, as the data contained in the table would be created just once and would never need updating. However, the second example of a summary table, which is more commonly found, can be avoided. A simple view can be defined on the database that would accomplish the same result without the extra processing and disk space that would be required for a new table to be generated each day.

The use of summary tables would be acceptable if all of the following conditions were met:

1. The processing required in order to compute the statistics is exceptionally time-consuming if carried out regularly.

2. There is little or no chance that the statistics would ever change, such as with historical values, or the effort required to recalculate the statistics is trivial.

3. Storage space for the additional tables will always be available.

It should be stressed that this recommendation not to use summary tables does not apply in every circumstance. There are some very good reasons for the duplication of data in summary tables, but these are almost always due to technology – such as when data is being transferred between databases for purposes of replication or data warehousing, or when conforming to some business rule. For example, telephone companies are prohibited by law from retaining certain information about telephone traffic, except in an aggregate.

Relationships, Cardinality, and ER Diagrams

In relational databases, being able to match related records between two tables is essential. Given any row in one table, in order to find its related row or rows in the second table, we use keys.

When we join two tables, the RDBMS takes the value of one field of the first table and searches for records that have the same value in some specified field in the second table. The field from the first table used in this search is called the **foreign key**. Usually, the field that is searched in the second table is the **primary key** of that table. As we have seen, primary keys are used to distinguish one record in a table from all other records in that table. Primary keys will always be unique within any given table. If they were not unique then they couldn't be very useful in distinguishing individual records! It is this pairing of fields that will be used for referencing the two tables which is called the **relationship**. A common way of diagramming the relationship of two tables (referred to as **entities** in database theory) is through **Entity-Relationship Diagrams** (ER Diagrams). Here is an example of an ER Diagram:

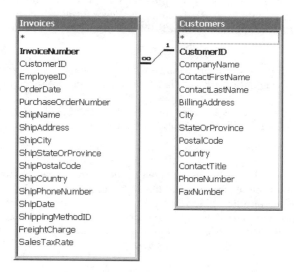

The primary key of the `Customers` table is `CustomerID`, which is matched with the `CustomerID` field from the `Invoices` table. In this case, we say that the `CustomerID` field of the `Invoices` table is the foreign key to the `Customers` table.

Since it is possible for any one customer to place more than one order, any number of rows in the `Invoices` table will exist for a customer. When a single row in one table can be related to more than one row in a second table, the relationship between the tables is called a **one-to-many** relationship. This relationship is denoted in the above ER Diagram by the line connecting the two tables with the "1" and infinity "∞" symbols. The counting of the number of rows that may be matched between tables is referred to the cardinality of the relationship. The cardinality value of the `Customers` table in this relationship is "one" while the value of the cardinality of the `Invoices` table in this relationship is "many."

Although there may be a relationship between tables, it is possible that some rows in one table will not match any rows in the related table. This would happen if a customer had not yet placed any orders (therefore having no rows in the `Invoices` table), but was still listed in the `Customers` table. Since it is possible for zero rows to match, a cardinality of zero is possible. In some circumstances, only a single row in one table will be matched with one and only one row in the related table.

One-to-One Relationships

One-to-one (1:1) relationships require that one and only one row in a table can be matched with a single row in its related table. This type of cardinality is not common in many relational databases, but will happen occasionally depending upon business rules. For example, suppose the business rules for your application state that a sales representative will service one and only one corporate client. In this case, the sales representative's row in a `SalesReps` table will be matched with only one particular customer in a `Clients` table. Similarly, each company listed in the `Clients` table will be matched with one and only one sales representative in the `SalesReps` table.

In many ER Diagramming tools, 1:1 relationships are simply denoted with a single line connecting the two entities, while other tools add a "1" next to the line as a notation. In the following example, we are displaying a 1:1 relationship that joins patients to beds in a hospital.

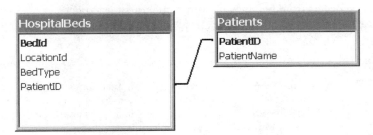

It is possible that a patient is found in the `Patients` table but a corresponding bed assignment has not been entered. This would be the case for ambulatory patients that do not need to be admitted overnight or when the information on the patient was first being entered into the database. In these situations, we have a "1: 0 or 1" relationship or a "cardinality of zero or one." Although some diagramming tools explicitly denote these relationships, many diagramming tools assume that 1:1 and 1: 0 or 1 relationships are the same.

One-to-Many Relationships

One-to-many (1:M) relationships allow one row in a table to be related to one or more rows in the related table. For an example of a one-to-many relationship, look back at the first illustration of this section that shows the relationship between `Customers` and `Invoices`. Any one customer found in a `Customers` table may be matched with one or more invoices in an `Invoices` table. This relationship could also be described as "one or more invoices can be matched with only one customer". Many-to-one relationships are the same as one-to-many relationships, except for a matter of perspective.

Many-to-Many Relationships

Many-to-many (M:M) relationships are also provided for in ER Diagrams. With these types of relationships, multiple rows in one table match multiple rows in the related table. As with one-to-one relationships, these are not as common as one-to-many relationships in most business applications. When they are needed, they are often difficult to work with and are inefficient.

Whenever a situation arises when a many-to-many relationship is needed, often a new intermediary table is used to link the two tables. This new table is often called a junction table. The idea behind a junction table is to record every combination of records that match in the tables with the M:M relationship. This junction table is designed to hold the primary keys of other tables. Both of the original tables then are linked to the junction table in a many-to-one relationship.

Referential Integrity

When we have two related tables, we must define a relationship that describes how rows are matched between the tables. This definition is important so that information in related tables is kept complete and consistent. **Referential Integrity** (RI) preserves the defined relationships between tables when rows are entered or deleted. RI helps ensure that key values are consistent across tables so that there are no references to nonexistent values. It is a simple rule: "If B references A, then A must exist".

Some examples of how RI can ensure data integrity include:

❑   Preventing orders from being taken from nonexistent customers.

❑   Preventing the deletion of an employee record if there exists a corresponding entry in, say, an `EmployeeSchedule` table.

❑   Automatically changing the records in related tables when the primary table is updated.

Under most RDBMSs, you can set referential integrity only when certain conditions are met. Since we are comparing values between two tables when the tables are related, the fields that are being referenced must be of the same or "compatible" data types and size. Compatible data types are those that contain the same values although the precision of the data may differ. For example, it is possible to join an integer field with a real number field, or a character field whose maximum width is 20 with another character field whose maximum width is 25 characters. Another condition that is required for referential integrity is that the matching column from the primary table be uniquely identifiable, by either its primary key or candidate key. The last condition is that both tables in the reference belong to the same database.

One significant advantage of defining RI rules on the database is that once the rules are established, the burden of enforcing these rules is removed from your application's code. Your application's code does not have to explicitly check for conditions that violate referential integrity. Instead, the RDBMS will raise an error to inform you when an attempt that violates the rules has been made. Your application will still need to check for and respond to the error, but the majority of the work is done by the database where such errors are more efficiently processed.

By having these rules as part of the database and not in the application, more than one application may be written for the same database and still use the same rules. If the logic for RI was only contained in the application and some business rule changed, then updates would be required to all applications that use that database.

To illustrate this, consider the scenario where a company uses Visual Basic to develop an order entry system for use by their sales department. The database requires that orders may be placed only products in their inventory. The developers decided to put code in the Visual Basic application to ensure that this rule is followed. Some time later, the company develops a web site that allows customers to place orders directly, and the same business rule concerning what products may be ordered was to be used. Because the code for this business rule is not in the database, the company would have to duplicate this logic for the web site. By having the logic in two places, you need to maintain two sets of code and risk having inconsistencies between the two versions. If the business rules logic is located on the database, where both applications can access it, then the business rules are more easily maintained and are guaranteed to be consistent.

Enforcing Business Rules

Table columns have properties other than just data type and size. The other properties form an important part of the support for ensuring the integrity of data in a database. These additional properties include **integrity constraints**, and **triggers**. By using these, the database system can help enforce referential integrity, apply business rules, and validate the data being stored in the columns.

Enforcing Business Rules with Integrity Constraints

Integrity constraints (or constraints for short) define rules regarding the values allowed in columns and they are the preferred mechanism for enforcing integrity. Because constraints may be used to validate data for a given column, they are said to help maintain **domain integrity**, where the term "domain" refers to the values of a column. Constraints may also be used by the database system to process queries quickly and more efficiently. These are simple to use because they are declared when the table is defined.

There are many different classes of constraints. The following are the most commonly supported types in the major RDBMS systems today:

1. **Nullability** – specifies that the column does or does not accept `Null` values.

2. **Uniqueness** – specifies that the value entered is not currently found in the column, although `Null` values may be allowed in multiple rows.

3. **Primary Key** – identifies the column(s) whose values uniquely identify a row in a table. Although similar to the uniqueness constraint, primary key constraints do not allow any `Null` values.

4. **Foreign Key** – identifies the relationships between tables by identifying a column (or columns) in the table that is to be used with another table when enforcing referential integrity. A foreign key constraint does not have to be linked to a primary key constraint in another table; it can also be defined to reference the columns of a uniqueness constraint in another table.

5. **Check** – provides a validation rule that is applied to the data before it can be stored in the column, such as limiting the values to positive numbers or a set of possible values.

To illustrate the creation of these constraints, let's see how this is done in Microsoft SQL Server 2000's Enterprise Manager. As you can see in the illustration below, Microsoft SQL Server 2000 allows you specify the nullability for each field when defining the table:

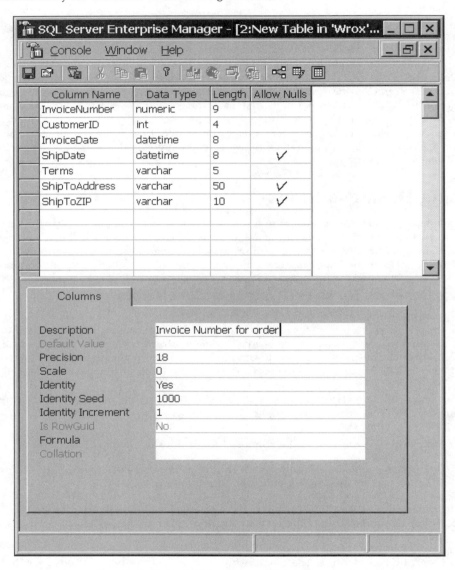

To specify a primary key, select the field (or fields) to be used by clicking on the gray button to the left of the field. If you wish to use more than one column, hold the *Ctrl* key down when selecting the second column.

After the column (or columns) has been selected, click on the button in the toolbar that resembles a key:

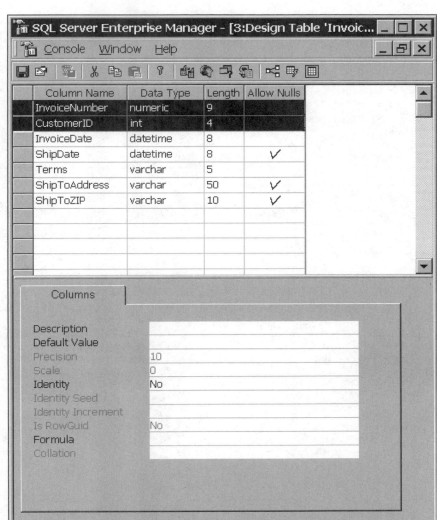

Alternatively, you can set the primary key using the Properties dialog for the table. To display this dialog, select the "Index and Properties tool" on the toolbar or press *Alt-F10*. When the Properties dialog is displayed, select the Indexes/Keys tab to display the definition of the primary key. By default, Microsoft SQL Server 2000 names the primary key using "PK_" followed by the table name.

Alternatively, if you wish to change the primary key, simply use the drop-down lists under **Column Name**:

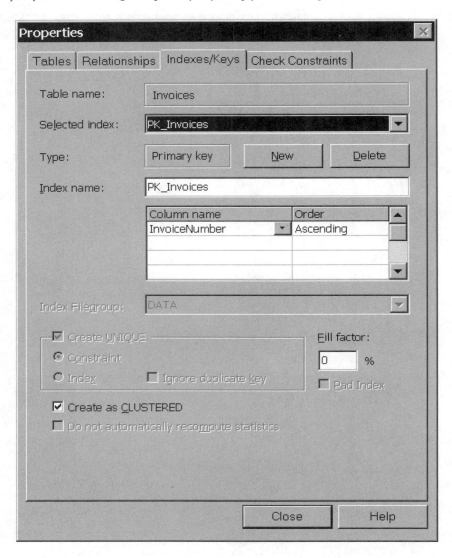

With Enterprise Manager, the procedure for specifying that a column is to be unique is through defining a unique index. This is similar to defining a primary key and also using the **Indexes/Keys** tab.

Select the New button, give the index a name and then pick the column to use:

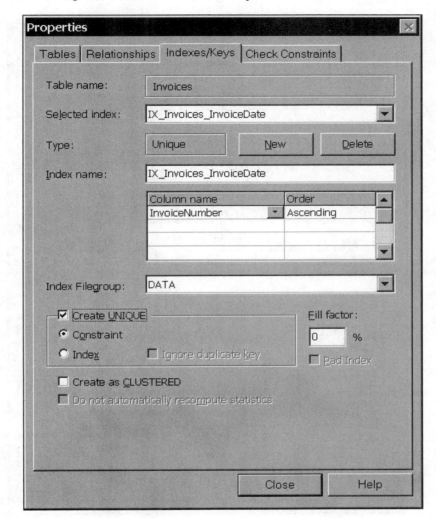

To make this index force only unique values in the column, select the Create UNIQUE checkbox and then select the Constraint option button.

As you might expect from its name, the Relationships tab is used to define foreign key relationships:

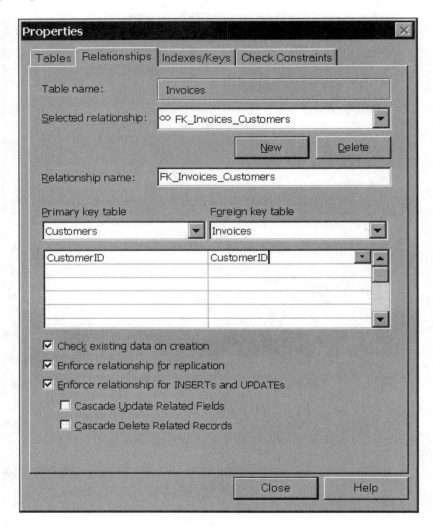

To create a new relationship, first select the New button and provide a name for the relationship. Next, by using the Primary key table and Foreign Key table drop-down controls, we specify which two tables we are establishing a relationship for. Finally, we need to identify which field or fields from the first table will match with which field or fields in the second table.

Check constraints are defined on the **Check Constraints** tab. In the following illustration, we define a validation rule that is applied to the `Terms` column. This rule forces the `Terms` column to accept only three possible values: "Net90", "Net60", and "Net30". To define a new constraint, select the **New** button, supply a name for the constraint, and then enter a formula **Constraints Expression** text box. SQL Server uses brackets to identify the names of fields and automatically wraps the entire expression in parentheses.

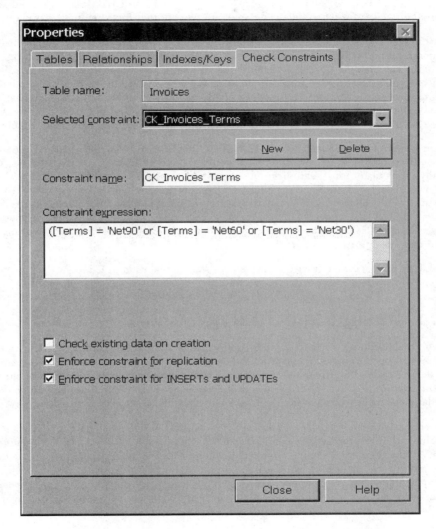

Once you have finished with this dialog, close it and then save the table definition using the **Save** button on the toolbar.

It should be noted that the SQL language defines statements that will accomplish the same results as what was just illustrated. We'll see more about the SQL language in the next chapter.

Enforcing Business Rules with Triggers

In many cases, integrity constraints will be able to enforce most data integrity rules in a database, but there may be certain business rules that are too complex for simple constraints. Triggers are compiled procedures stored in the database that are associated with a table and are executed (fired) when some condition is met. Most RDBMSs will allow a trigger to be executed when data is added, deleted or changed in a table. You can specify a trigger (or triggers, in some RDBMSs) to be fired for when data is added, another trigger for when data is deleted, and yet another for when data is updated.

Consider the scenario of an online auction site where bidders and sellers can change their `UserID` no more than once a month. In order for this business rule to apply, the current data must be compared with the date of the last time the `UserID` was modified. We would be unable to enforce this rule with simple constraints. To do so, we need a procedure to execute that will check if the required amount of time has elapsed and to update a `LastModifiedDate` field if the user is allowed to make the change. Another scenario is when a student graduates from a university. The business rule states that when a student leaves the university, their student row is moved from the `Students` table into the `Alumni` table.

Triggers are useful in a number of ways. First of all, they provide logic inside the database to relieve an application from having to execute a series of commands to perform a single operation. This approach is generally much faster for the application since it will reduce the number of calls to the database and therefore reduce network traffic. Second, the statements that fire within a trigger are treated as a single transaction. If a severe error is detected, the entire transaction automatically rolls back. A third benefit comes from the fact that triggers can be defined to fire before and after attempts are made to modify a table. Triggers can disallow or roll back changes that violate referential integrity, thereby canceling the attempted data modification.

We'll be taking a closer look at triggers and how they may be used in Chapter 4.

Physical Design and Tuning

When you finish building the logical model and it has been reviewed and accepted by all the interested parties, you will need to actually construct the database. The construction of the database will require that you decide upon all of the details for column datatypes and constraints, physical storage assignments, and other physical properties of the database. This detailed design, which defines exactly how the database will be implemented on your target database system, is called the **physical design**.

The physical design requires that you get very, very specific. You will need to decide whether to use an integer value or a real number for a column, or if the column should contain variable-length data or fixed length data. Other decisions, such as what will be the physical ordering of the rows in the table, if any, and what mechanisms will be used to assist searches in the table. By implementing these details, you turn your columns into "fields" and the rows into "records". The actual implementation requires that you invoke the commands required to construct the database your design describes. This can be done by manually entering the specifications for each object that is defined, or by using some CASE tool.

If you are using an ER Diagramming program such as Visio (www.visio.com) or PLATINUM ER*win* (www.platinum.com), you can choose the Generate Database option to produce a definition of the database's physical structure and, optionally, execute that definition in the RDBMS to generate the database itself. Most of the better-known ER Diagramming tools can generate a design for servers (Oracle, SQL Server), desktop databases (Paradox, Access, FoxPro), the Visual Basic Access Engine, or a generic SQL database. They recognize product-specific features such as cascading referential integrity in Access or T-SQL triggers (SQL Server) and exploit those features when it generates the physical design.

As clever as these products may be, don't expect that everything will generate properly or in the optimal manner. For example, both Oracle and Microsoft SQL Server provide mechanisms for how and where the files for the database should be stored. You should check with the product documentation for details on Data Clusters for Oracle and File Groups for Microsoft SQL Server.

Once the database is generated in the RDBMS, you can then start refining the design. First, you will need to load into the database test data that will reasonably represent production data. After this is done, you can then consider such things as index creating and (possibly) de-normalization of tables. Theorectically, some of this work should have been done during the logical design phase, but in reality, much of this work needs to be done after some empirical testing.

Using Indexes

An **index** is used in a database to speed up the referencing of data. In many ways, an index does exactly what an index of a book does – it provides you with a fast way to locate a particular topic. In a book, all of the important words should be listed, along with the page numbers that deal with each of those topics. The index is in alphabetical order, for easy look-up. In databases, an index specifies the order of each record in a table if you wanted to reference it by some column (or columns). If you often need to search through a table of employees in order of length of service to the company, to speed up those searches you could create an index that is based upon the HireDate field.

Indexes are critical to the operation of most databases. A well-placed index will improve the performance of searches and joins in a database significantly, often by several orders of magnitude. It is highly recommended that every table have at least one index. This "one index minimum" is generally a trivial requirement since normalized databases will assign a primary key to virtually every table, and primary keys are actually indexes themselves. The issues with indexes concern how many additional indexes should be applied and how they should be constructed.

There are two basic types of index. The first type forces the table to physically sequence the records. This way, when you issue a query against the table, the records returned will be presented in this physical order. Obviously, if this type of index causes the records in the table to be placed on disk in some physical order, you can have only one index of this type for any single table. When the index orders the records in the most commonly used sort order, then significant performance gains may be achieved. This type of index is often called a **clustered index**. The second type of index, often called a **non-clustered index**, works by keeping track of the order of the records as if the table was sorted by a particular column or columns. When the database engine processes a query against a table with an index, that index can be used, often increasing the performance of the query several fold.

While indexes can greatly improve performance of applications, they are not appropriate for every column. Creating too many indexes can actually hurt performance. This is because with every index created, there is some overhead required for storage and maintenance. You need an *appropriate* number of indexes – not too many to degrade performance, but enough that they are available when needed.

So how many indexes should a table have? There really is no correct answer since different tables will have differing numbers of columns and differing contents. A better question to ask is "Which columns should be indexed?" To answer this, we need to consider each table one-by-one as well as how the tables reference each other. First, consider which columns *not* to index. Most RDBMSs will create an index for every primary key and for every field with a uniqueness constraint, so these columns should not require indexes. One of the main benefits of an index is to quickly find the desired rows without having to perform lots of disk I/O, which has a considerable impact on performance. If the table contains only a small number of rows, the RDBMS will be able to store the entire table in memory, so having an index will not reduce the amount of disk I/O. Also, avoid placing an index on a column whose values do not vary much. For example, a Gender field that stores only "M" or "F" would not be a good candidate for an index. A similar case can be made against columns that contain a significant number of Null values.

Once you have eliminated from consideration all of the columns that are not good candidates for an index, we then should consider which of the remaining columns would offer the most benefit if indexed. The fields that are used by query statements to join tables make excellent candidates for indexing. In most cases, joins are made between the first table's primary key and the second table's foreign key. Since primary keys are already indexed, all you need to do is index the foreign key field(s). Other excellent candidates are those fields that are often used as part of the selection criteria of queries or those fields that are often used to sort the results of a query.

There are a few other considerations when choosing fields for indexes. Fields that are updated less frequently typically make better index candidates than fields that have their values changed often. Also, when given a choice of two equally qualified fields, it is often better to use the numeric values over string values and shorter data types over longer ones.

You may also create indexes that include more than one field. These **composite indexes** can be useful when you don't have a wide variation of values in any of the candidate fields. Composite indexes can also improve performance when a query retrieves only the fields contained in the index. However, keep in mind that there are usually limits to the number of fields that may be included in a composite index as well as limits on the total length of the data contained in a composite query.

There are products available that you can use that will help identify which fields would provide a benefit if indexed. For example, Microsoft SQL Server 7 and 2000 included SQL Server Profiler and Index Tuning Wizard which may be used to help analyze queries and determine which indexes to create.

Once the indexes have been created, you should regularly administer them. For a variety of reasons, indexes can become corrupt, inaccurate, or inefficiently organized over time. If a table is subject to a great deal of updating and deleting, the indexes may become "scattered" or "uncondensed". When this happens, the gains from using indexes decrease. To correct these problems, the indexes will need to be rebuilt. Most RDBMSs offer commands that will reconstruct an index. You can also reconstruct an index by dropping it and then creating it again. You may wish to consider establishing a regular schedule of rebuilding the indexes in your database.

Using Views and Stored Procedures

As sophisticated as constraints and triggers are, there are often many places in the database that require additional programming logic. Centralizing this logic in the database is almost always preferable to expecting the applications that use the database to implement the logic. Today's modern RDBMSs offer a range of commands that you would find in any high-level language for developing this logic, such as conditional statements and looping and constructs. **Views** and **stored procedures** provide means of executing this logic.

A view is one of several ways to store SQL statements. Once a view is created, you can use it as if it were a table itself, since the SQL statements that define the view select and return rows. There are many advantages to using views. They can help simplify queries, isolate application logic, add additional security, and since they can include logic in their definitions, views can provide ways to incorporate business rules.

Stored procedures are functions that, like views, contain a mixture of SQL commands and programming logic. Unlike views, stored procedures can accept and return parameters. Stored procedures are also compiled on the server for faster execution.

Views

To see how views may be of use, imagine that you had an `Employees` table that contained records of all employees, including those no longer with the firm. Assume that the table contains a field named `Active`, which distinguishes current employees from past employees specifying some selection criteria. Naturally, most of the interaction with this table will be for current employees only, so we will need to explicitly specify the active employees every time we query the database. To simplify things, we can create a view that is designed to always select active employees. Once we have the view defined, we can reference it as if it were a table itself.

Although this example is fairly trivial, we can see how using a view can shield end users from having to know certain details about the table we draw information from. You may also use views to prevent users from accessing sensitive information. If we did not want users to be able to access all fields from the `Employees` table, such as the `Salary` field, we can use the view to return only particular columns. We could also use view to perform calculations, translations of data, or acquire data from multiple sources.

If you code your applications to use only views, you are providing the ability to change the names of tables or to use different tables in the future. By implementing views, if you needed to change the name of a table, you can hide the renaming of the table by updating only the views that your application uses. If you didn't use views and a table name changed, you would be forced to modify your application's source code, recompile it and then redistribute the application.

Views are discussed in more detail in Chapter 4.

Stored Procedures

Like views, stored procedures will contain statements and may return a set of records from the database. Views, at the most basic level, act as filters for existing information that must be accessed as part of a query statement. Stored procedures are much more dynamic and offer a number of performance advantages. Unlike views, stored procedures can accept arguments when they are invoked and may return a set of records, a return code, or an output argument that may be used outside the stored procedure to access data.

One of the most important advantages of stored procedures is that they are compiled when they are created and stored within the database ready to be executed. For most RDBMSs, executing pre-compiled routines is several times faster than executing similar commands sent as raw SQL statements. When a SQL statement is received by a RDBMS, the statement is parsed, analyzed, and then the database engine evaluates the most efficient approach for executing the statement. All of this takes time. By using a stored procedure, most of this work is done at compilation time. Using stored procedures can also reduce network traffic since only the call to the stored procedure and parameter values needs to be transmitted.

For example, consider the processing required for placing an order for a product. A check needs to be made to see if the quantity ordered of the product is available. If it is not, then the quantity that is required needs to be placed on back order and the order updated accordingly. If these actions were taken on the client side, then several queries would be required, causing many round trips to the server. If this logic was all part of a single order request stored procedure, network traffic would be reduced and the operation would be significantly faster.

Like views, stored procedures can shield users from knowing the details of the tables in the database. This may be done for security reasons or to make using business functions easier. Also, the internal logic of a stored procedure may be updated without affecting the code of the applications that use them, thus making maintenance easier.

Stored procedures are discussed in more detail in Chapter 4.

Performance Tuning

Much of the work done up to this point has been theoretical: we analyze entities relations, evaluate columns for indexes, and determine data types. Even if we are very careful and have thought of every possible option, we are bound to miss something. Usually, what we missed becomes apparent when the application goes live. The trick is to make sure we have tested the application sufficiently that whatever we miss is relatively harmless and minor. It is also very likely that, in spite of our best efforts with the logical design, some of the decisions made do not provide the performance that we expected. The best way to shake out performance problems before going live with the database is to do some empirical testing.

After testing and analyzing the database and the server itself, you should be able to resolve most issues through one or more of the following actions:

❑ Further normalization of tables to eliminate duplicate data.

❑ The de-normalization of some tables to reduce the time required for joins.

❑ The creation, modification, or removal of indexes.

❑ Redistributing various database objects across physical devices.

❑ Adding additional hardware, especially memory and fast-access disk drives.

Stress Testing

One effective way to test the application is to stress-test it. Stress testing will often make design flaws obvious. The first requirement of stress testing is data, lots of data. Many of the ER Diagramming tools available will be able to generate sample test data if you cannot obtain a sufficient amount of real world data to test against. It's also possible to write cross-join queries that will produce large amounts of data from a relatively small amount of test data. With a large enough data set to work with you will be able to use performance analysis tools to optimize your stored procedures, views, and queries substantially. Many of these tools will not only time the execution of your routines, but breakdown this time statement-by-statement to help identify bottlenecks.

Performance monitoring tools tend to fall into certain categories: analysis; system monitoring; and error trapping. Each has a different focus, and they often are most useful when used together. All of the major RDBMS vendors provide such tools with their products, so you should check the accompanying documentation to see what utilities are included. It is also worth browsing through the RDBMS installation CDs, since some tools might not be automatically installed when you install the database server software.

Microsoft Windows NT and Windows 2000 also provide the Performance Monitor utility that may be used to track a variety of variables on the server that can be useful in getting a better understanding of how the database is responding. By using Performance Monitor, you can track real time statistics such as CPU utilization, disk I/O, and network throughput. There are literally hundreds of items of information that can be tracked, although, to start with, the most important deal with memory usage, user connections, disk I/O, processor usage and locking. Once you have tracked these items over a period of time, you will be able to establish patterns of behavior. Only after you have a good baseline of operations will you be able to best judge the impact of changes that you implement.

There are also many good third-party products available for stress testing. The product from Benchmark Factory (www.benchmarkfactory.com) can be used to simulate thousands of simultaneously connected users over several hours when carrying out rigorous load testing. Mercury Interactive (www.merc-int.com) offers a number of highly regarded products such as LoadRunner, TestDirector, and TestSuite which may be of tremendous use in testing large-scale applications. Active Measurement and eMeasure from Bluecurve Software (www.bluecurve.com) are also worth looking at, as is Rational Suite PerformanceStudio from Rational Software (www.rational.com).

Query and Procedure Optimization

An important aspect to a database application's performance is the efficiency of the code using it. The various SQL statements and stored procedures used by the RDBMS can be analyzed and bottlenecks may be found. Examples of such tools include Oracle's SQL Trace and Microsoft's Query Analyzer. In addition, most RDBMSs support a Show Plan or Explain Plan SQL command that gives details on what the database query engine is doing when it executes a SQL statement. The usefulness of tools like these cannot be overstated. Analyzing the queries and code won't make them faster, but the analysis will give you insight on what needs to be adjusted to make execution faster. With the right tool, some experimentation, and some patience, the performance of SQL statements and stored procedures can be drastically improved – sometimes the code can run several times faster.

The following illustration comes from Microsoft SQL Server Query Analyzer. It shows the execution plan for running a stored procedure. The execution plan displays details of the relative costs required for each portion of the SQL statement executed within the stored procedure. It shows the SQL statement being executed at the top, which in this case is contained in a stored procedure. In the lower half of the screen, a step-by-step breakdown of the actions taken by the database query engine in order to process the stored procedure. At each step, a cost (usually based on time) is calculated and the type of operation is identified. Additional information on each step can be obtained when the mouse pointer is moved onto each step's icon. Right-clicking the icon displays a context menu allowing you to manage performance-related items such as indexes.

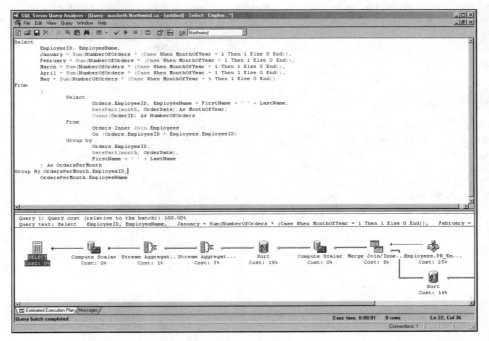

Creating and Maintaining Statistics

Most modern RDBMSs use what is called a cost-based query optimizer to determine how best to execute a query. The optimizer analyzes the various alternative methods that may be used to execute the query and determines which one is the "optimal". It is this optimal execution plan that is used and saved for later reference.

This begs the question: "How does the optimizer compare the various ways a query may be executed and determine which one is optimal?" The exact process will vary from RDBMS to RDBMS, but each follows the same general approach. The optimizer parses the statements into discrete steps that require a particular type of action: sorting records, searching through tables, matching records between tables, etc. At each step, the optimizer determines if there is more than one way to execute the action. For example, should a table been scanned using an index, and if so, which index. As each step is examined, the various alternative approaches are evaluated based upon an estimate of CPU and I/O usage and other factors such as the physical layout of the tables. The greater the usage, the higher the "cost". The optimizer chooses the least expensive execution path to process the query.

The next question that arises from this explanation is: "How does the optimizer estimate the cost at each step?" Again, this varies with each RDBMS, but they all base these estimates on a set of statistics stored for the database. These statistics include such things as the number of rows in the table, a measure of uniqueness of the values in an index, and the distribution of data stored on disk.

Statistics are usually generated and updated automatically, but over time you may find that the statistics are less representative of the data they describe. This is due to the fact that some of the statistics are based upon a sampling of the data and not all of the data. Also, certain database operations, such as bulk inserts, deletes, and updates that effect large numbers of records may make these statistics less accurate. When the statistics are inaccurate, the query optimizer will base its decisions on faulty information and the most optimal plan may not be used. To alleviate this problem, you should periodically regenerate the statistics used. This is especially true after loading test data into the system. Most RDBMSs provide an `Update Statistics` command that regenerates the statistics. If your RDBMS doesn't have such a command, or you are not able to find it, try dropping and rebuilding the various indexes in the database to force at least some of the statistics to be regenerated.

Summary

There are many reasons why applications suffer from poor performance. A poorly designed database should not be one of them. To construct a fast efficient database, a good design is essential. All good designs start with an understanding of the business process that we are modeling. By enlisting the aid of key stakeholders and making use of the knowledge of co-workers, you start constructing a conceptual design. The conceptual design identifies the major entities used in the database and the relationships between these entities to describe what needs to be modeled.

After you are confident enough in the conceptual design, begin working on the logical design. The logical design describes how things are done and provides details on the mechanics of the database by specifying such things as data types, keys, calculations, and data integrity rules. One major aspect of the logical design is the organization of the data into tables. Using the rules for normalization, we can efficiently store and access the information without risking data loss. After the tables have been structured, we then apply data integrity rules and enforce business practices through the use of constraints and triggers.

With a detailed logical design in hand, we generate the statements that define our objects and execute these statements to physically generate the database. Security and application access is also applied as well as various tools to stress-test the server. After loading the database with meaningful test data, we double-check our work through stress testing. We also begin to tune the database, by adding additional indexes and by generating statistics.

The end result will be a fast, flexible, and efficient database that will be able to keep up with the demands of today's web-based industries.

3

SQL Programming

When accessing relational databases, a standardized version of **Structured Query Language** (**SQL**) is usually used. Indeed, SQL is so frequently used that it is considered the *de facto* standard data access language for database systems. All of the major RDBMS, such as those from Sybase, IBM, Oracle, and Microsoft, support SQL. The chances are that when you are developing a database-enhanced web site, you will use SQL.

In database-enabled web sites, we need to be able to get at data and manipulate it. Often, this data needs to be obtained from more than one source table and combined, and if we are accessing this data from a web site, the need for speed becomes important. With these requirements in mind, in this chapter we will take a look at how to use SQL to acquire, modify and delete information, including how to specify which records are to be acted upon from individual tables, as well as from multiple tables. We shall also see how SQL may be used to create and destroy tables in a database, consolidate information, and to insure that we can combine many related actions that are applied together as a single transaction. Towards the end of the chapter, we'll see how we can use these approaches to solve complicated problems in ways that are fast and efficient. In later chapters, we will cover in detail how you can use SQL with ASP.

What is SQL?

Originally, SQL was designed and implemented at IBM Research for a relational database system called SYSTEM R. This soon became very popular and many commercial vendors were developing their own variations of this language. Due to this widespread use, there have been efforts made to standardize the language. To date, there have been four major versions of SQL approved by the American National Standards Institute (ANSI). The International Standards Organization (ISO) has approved the first three versions and is expected to approve the fourth in 2000:

❑ **SQL-86** was defined in 1986 as a "bare bones" standard and defined the union or common features of the most important DBMS products at the time.

❑ **SQL-89** is a superset of SQL-86 and added a small number of new features .

❑ **SQL-92** or **SQL-2** or **International Standard Database Language SQL** was completed in 1992 and includes extra data types, additional ways to relate different tables together, catalog specifications, and other features.

❑ **SQL-99** or **SQL-3** was approved by ANSI on December 8th 1999, and formalized many features that had been available on many database systems through proprietary implementations. This version included support for flow control statements, international character sets, new data types, and binary objects.

You can purchase downloadable copies of the five document SQL-3 standard, ISO/IEC 9075-1:1999 through ISO/IEC 9075-5:1999, at https://webstore.ansi.org.

As suggested by the number of years between the releases of the major versions, these standards don't happen overnight. Between each major version, a series of minor additions and amendments are made. Currently, enhancements are being made concerning area such as object language bindings, on-line analytical processing, management of external data, and time-based operations. The next major release is expected around 2003.

Virtually all RDBMS' fully support SQL-2, and the major vendors support much of what is defined in SQL-3. Although SQL-3 was only recently approved by ANSI, it was first developed back in 1995, and most of the major vendors have been adding support for the new version based upon the draft proposal. Unfortunately, without an official standard, each vendor implemented many of the proposed changes differently. You should see a greater adherence to the SQL-3 standard in the next major releases from the major RDBMS vendors. Although each vendor may have some minor differences in how they implement SQL-3 features, SQL is almost universally supported. The similarities between versions are so strong that if you learn any one vendor's version, you will be able to work with the other major vendors' versions with little difficulty.

What is in SQL?

Historically, SQL has been a non-procedural language, unlike languages such as C, C++, Visual Basic, and Java. In these procedural languages, your code provides statements on *how* to process information. In the SQL language, statements describe *what* information gets processed and you allow the database engine to determine the best method for getting that information. This doesn't imply that SQL is void of commands that allow you to govern the order of the processing and other logic. It does contain most of the typical constructs that we would find in most modern languages, like While loops, If and Case statements, and the like. But even with these procedural features, the basis of the language is telling the RDBMS what needs to be done and the RDBMS figures out the best way to do it.

The SQL commands may be issued directly to the database using a query tool such as Microsoft SQL Server's oSQL (which is included with SQL Server 7 and 2000), Microsoft Query, or Oracle's SQL Worksheet. These commands may also be executed via a programming language such as VBScript, VBA (Visual Basic for Applications) or C++. When you construct your ASP documents, you will be using SQL to access and manipulate your database.

Language Components of SQL

As the name suggests, SQL includes syntax for executing queries. We can ask questions of the database and have the results returned in tabular form. In addition to extracting data from a database, we can insert new records, delete records, and update existing records. The query and update commands together form the **Data Manipulation Language** (DML) component of SQL. There are only four basic statements in the DML component: SELECT, UPDATE, DELETE and INSERT. We'll see how these commands work in the next section.

There is also a **Data Definition Language** (DDL) component of SQL that is used to create new tables and other objects. As we discussed in the previous chapter, Database Design Concepts, the characteristics of a table are defined by specifying column names and types, as well as possibly defining keys and restrictions on the data (called constraints), and relationships between tables. The main DDL statements in SQL are CREATE TABLE, ALTER TABLE and DROP TABLE. These commands are discussed later in this chapter.

Data Types

Data types in SQL are analogous to data types in other languages. A data type, regardless of the language, is a set of representable values. Every representable value belongs to at least one data type though some belong to several data types. All items in SQL that can be referenced by name, such as fields and variables, must have a declared type.

SQL-3 supports three sorts of data types: **predefined data types**, **user-defined types** and **constructed types**. Predefined data types are sometimes called the "built-in data types", or "intrinsic data types" and include integers, floating point numbers, and character strings. User-defined data types can be created by an application in the RDBMS and are based upon predefined data types. For example, you can declare a data type called "PostalCode" that defines a fixed length character string. A constructed type is specified using one of SQL's data type constructors, ARRAY, REF, and ROW, to create data types such as arrays and collections.

SQL defines distinct data types as named by the following: CHARACTER, CHARACTER VARYING, CHARACTER LARGE OBJECT, BINARY LARGE OBJECT, BIT, BIT VARYING, NUMERIC, DECIMAL, INTEGER, SMALLINT, FLOAT, REAL, DOUBLE PRECISION, BOOLEAN, DATE, TIME, TIMESTAMP, and INTERVAL. These data types may be summarized as follows:

Character String Types	The data types CHARACTER, CHARACTER VARYING, and CHARACTER LARGE OBJECT are collectively referred to as character string types. A character string is a sequence of characters. A character string has a length, which is the number of characters in the sequence. The length is zero (for a null or empty string) or a positive integer.
Binary String Types	The data type BINARY LARGE OBJECT is referred to as the binary string type and the values of binary string types are referred to as binary strings or BLOBs.
Bit String Types	The data types BIT and BIT VARYING are collectively referred to as bit string types. A bit string is a sequence of bits, each having the value of zero or one. A bit string has a length, which is the number of bits in the string. The length is zero or a positive integer.

Boolean Types	The data type BOOLEAN comprises the distinct values, true and false. Unless prohibited by a NOT NULL constraint, the BOOLEAN data type also supports the situation where a definite true or false is unknown or undetermined, which evaluates to NULL.
Numeric Types	The data types NUMERIC, DECIMAL, INTEGER and SMALLINT are collectively referred to as exact numeric types. The data types FLOAT, REAL, and DOUBLE PRECISION are collectively referred to as approximate numeric types. Exact numeric types and approximate numeric types are collectively referred to as numeric types. Values of numeric types are referred to as numbers.
Temporal Types	The data types TIME, TIMESTAMP, and DATE are collectively referred to as date-time types. The data type INTERVAL is referred to as an interval type. Values of these types may include the following information:

YEAR	Year (0001-9999)
MONTH	Month within year (0-11)
DAY	Day within month (0-31)
HOUR	Hour within day (0-23)
MINUTE	Minute within hour (0-59)
SECOND	Second within minute and possibly fraction of a second within minute (0-59.999...)

Nulls	SQL-3 also defines a NULL value, which is used to indicate the absence of any data value. When an object (variable, field, etc) is declared, its data type is specified, as well as if the object will allow NULL values to be stored, regardless of data type.

You will find that different RDBMS' will name these data types differently from the SQL-3 standard. For example, Microsoft SQL Server 2000 uses varchar rather than CHARACTER VARYING to specify variable length character strings. If you specify CHARACTER VARYING with Microsoft SQL Server 2000, the data type will be mapped to a varchar.

Below are listed some of the most common data types as implemented by Microsoft SQL Server, Oracle and DB2, as well as data type mappings for Visual Basic and C:

SQL-3 Data Type	MS SQL Server	Oracle	DB2	Visual Basic	C	Description
BOOLEAN	bit	number	Decimal	Boolean	short	True and false
BIT	bit	number	Decimal	Boolean	char	Values of 0 or 1
INTEGER	integer	integer	Integer	Long	long	Integer values
DECIMAL	decimal	number	Decimal	Single		Fixed single precision real values

QL-3 Data Type	MS SQL Server	Oracle	DB2	Visual Basic	C	Description
FLOAT	float, real	float	Float	Single		Floating precision real values
DOUBLE PRECISION	float, real	number	Float	Double	double	Fixed double precision real values
DATE	datetime	date	Date	Date		Date and time data
CHAR	char	char	Character	String	char	Fixed-length non-Unicode character data
VARCHAR	varchar	varchar, varchar2	Varchar	String	char	Variable-length non-Unicode character data

The different RDBMS' will also support data types that are not defined by the formal SQL standard. This was expected and has been included in the SQL-3 standard:

> *"Each host language has its own data types, which are separate and distinct from SQL data types, even though similar names may be used to describe the data types... Not every SQL data type has a corresponding data type in every host language."*

Some of these "non-standard" data types were developed to provide additional functionality and features. Others were developed as specific implementations of SQL data types, such as Microsoft SQL Server's MONEY data type, which is a special case of a REAL. Others are simply different from the SQL standards, such as SQL Server's use of the datetime type rather than DATE.

> *In the late 1990s, a tremendous effort was made to correct various "Y2K issues". Many of these issues were due to the use of data types that were capable of holding a very limited range of numbers. These data types were usually used in order to save memory and disk space. Today, most RDBMS' still support such "small footprint" data types. For example, Microsoft SQL Server 2000 supports both an Integer and a TinyInt. The Integer type can hold values from -2,147,483,648 through 2,147,483,647, where as the TinyInt can hold values from only 0 through 255. Another similar data type is the smalldatetime, which may hold date values from January 1, 1900, through June 6, 2079. If you use the smalldatetime data type with your database applications, then your application will fail if it uses a date past June 6, 2079. This isn't something to be ignored. Some financial calculations, such as those issuing 100 year leases or bonds, use end dates far beyond the year 2079.*

Accessing Data Using SELECT

In the English language, when you ask a question, the basic structure of the sentence is always the same: "What is the birthday of each of our clients?" "Which restaurants offer Sunday Brunch?" "How many snow boards were sold on January 15, 2000?" In each case, you are requesting information by name. The first question specifically asked for a list of dates. The second question asked for the names of restaurants that meet a particular requirement. The third question asked for a statistic about a quantity of a given product for a specific date. When phrasing a question in SQL, we need to be very specific about which columns of data are to be returned, as well as under what conditions the data should be pulled from.

The Basic Structure of the SELECT Statement

Since SQL is not nearly as flexible as the English language, the format of a question in SQL must be phrased in some exact format. To ask a question in SQL, we use the SELECT statement, which takes the following general form:

```
SELECT column1, column2, ..., columnN
    FROM table
    WHERE condition
    ORDER BY columnA, columnB, ..., columnX ;
```

The SELECT clause of the statement identifies the fields (or calculations) that are to be returned. The statement uses the FROM clause to identify the table (or tables) from where the data will be obtained. The WHERE clause allows you to specify restrictions limiting which rows of the table will be select, and the ORDER BY clause is used to sort the resulting records.

Although the SQL-3 standard does not require the use of a terminating semicolon, in some implementations of SQL, a semicolon must be placed at the end of the statement. This is one example of the differences between the versions of SQL that are implemented by different vendors. Some other differences may be less apparent. You should check the documentation that accompanies your RDBMS to see if it contains a section comparing their version of SQL with the ANSI standard for further details.

In its simplest form, the SELECT statement is used to return all columns from all records in a given table. Rather than specifying which columns to return in the SELECT clause, we can use an asterisk character (*) to select all columns in the table. Let us assume that we have a table called Clients that describes customers of a company. To list all of the information we have in our Clients table, we could issue the following command:

```
SELECT * FROM Clients
```

The results of this query will look similar to the following:

ID	Fname	Lname	Phone	Email	DateOfBirth	Zipcode
1	Walter	Remes	860-914-9921	wremes@net.net	10/22/1954	06891
2	Diane	Asmus	203-922-9212	cybergirl@ola.net	09/06/1966	06614
3	Jason	Trickey	212-870-1211	jct@nyzap.net	05/03/1965	10012
4	Suzanne	Crean	203-722-2281	suz@crean.com	06/13/1963	06720
5	Pamela	Trickey	212-870-1211	pt@nyzap.net	06/06/1966	10012

The preceding example of a SQL statement used the "*" to select all columns from a table. The order the columns appear in the output is determined by the database. To specify the order of the columns, you could explicitly list each field, separated by commas after the keyword SELECT. When the columns are listed explicitly, you are not required to list every field. If we specify particular columns rather than the asterisk, only those columns will be returned. For example, if we are interested in only the birthday of each client, we could use the statement:

```
SELECT Fname, Lname, DateOfBirth FROM Clients
```

Since we want to find out the birthdays of all of our clients, there are no restrictions to the query, so the WHERE clause is not used. This statement will return all the value of the Fname, Lname and DateOfBirth fields for every record in the table named Clients. The results that are returned are in a column layout:

Fname	Lname	DateOfBirth
Walter	Remes	10/22/1954
Diane	Asmus	09/06/1966
Jason	Trickey	05/03/1965
Suzanne	Crean	06/13/1963
Pam	Trickey	06/06/1966

*Although using SELECT * is convenient, it does come with a performance hit when used from ADO. ADO makes two queries to the database. Before it fills your recordset, ADO must query the system tables to determine the name and data types of all your fields. It is much faster to specify your fields' names in the SQL query, as the system table lookup no longer happens. Note that this behavior doesn't exist when you issue this command from within a stored procedure since ADO is not used.*

Selecting Unique Records

Now consider the following statement that requests the values of the Zipcode field found in our table:

```
SELECT Zipcode FROM Clients
```

This statement would produce the following results:

Zipcode
06891
06614
10012
06720
10012

Notice that in each SQL statement executed, five were returned – one for each record. The statement `SELECT Zipcode FROM Clients` is interpreted as "Select the value of the `Zipcode` field for every record in the `Clients` table". However, what if we wanted to ask the question "What are the unique `Zipcode` values found in the `Clients` table?" To eliminate duplicates from the resulting set of records, we add the `DISTINCT` keyword:

```
SELECT DISTINCT Zipcode FROM Clients
```

Which produces:

Zipcode
06891
06614
10012
06720

A Note on Formatting

The SQL language allows for a great deal of flexibility when adding whitespace in commands. SQL requires that the keywords must be separated by at least one space character or carriage return. Any additional space characters and carriage returns will be ignored. Therefore, the following two statements are considered identical:

```
Select LName, FName, Email From Clients
```

```
Select
    LName,
    FName,
    Email
From
    Clients
```

Having the option of placing extra spaces and carriage returns allows us to format the text of the commands for easier reading. So when you have a fairly long SQL statement, feel free to break it apart on several lines to make it more readable.

Also, most RDBMS' allow you to use either upper or lower case with the keywords. For readability, you should be consistent in using case.

Computing Statistics and Other Calculations

When using the `SELECT` statement, we can have the database compute formulas and calculations based on our data. By using basic mathematical operators such as +, -, *, and /, we can construct most of the formulas we may need. The SQL-3 standard defines a limited number of functions as well (although most RDBMS' include many additional functions) to allow you to create robust and sophisticated calculations.

To create a calculation, simply enter a formula rather than a column name in the SELECT statement. If the calculation is to operate on certain fields, you may include those fields as if they were variables in the formula. When the query is executed, the formula will be computed for each row selected from the database, and a table of results will be returned.

For example, if we wanted to find out the earliest birth date of our clients we could use:

```
SELECT Min(DateOfBirth)
FROM Clients
```

Which would return:

10/22/1954

Specifying Column Names

Notice that the column returned in the previous example is unnamed. Some database systems will supply a default name of column1 or generate a name such as MinOfDateOfBirth, but most systems will simply not name the column. If you wish to provide a name to any column in the resulting set of records, you may do so by using the AS keyword followed by the desired name. For example, if we wanted to name the resulting column EarliestDOB we would write the query as:

```
SELECT Min(DateOfBirth) AS EarliestDOB
FROM Clients
```

Now the results of this query would have the resulting column named appropriately:

EarliestDOB
10/22/1954

Of course, you can't assign column names that are reserved words in SQL, but most common sense names will be accepted. Most RDBMS' have some restrictions on column names, but if you stick with letters and numbers, you will not have any problems. You can include some other characters such as a dollar sign ($) or tilde (~), but it is generally not recommended. Often, programmers will use an underscore (_) in column names, but in light of the way the Internet passes arguments, even this character should be avoided. Recent usability research suggests that the easiest for the eye to read is all lower case names with the first letter of each word capitalized. You should also try to use names that will not be likely to become reserved words in future versions of SQL; take care to avoid identifiers beginning with CURRENT_, SESSION_, SYSTEM_, or TIMEZONE_, or ending in _LENGTH.

We can also obtain more than one statistic in a single query by listing each statistical function separated by commas:

```
SELECT
    In(DateOfBirth) AS EarliestDOB,
    Max(DateOfBirth) AS LatestDOB,
    Count(DateOfBirth) AS NumberOfDOB
FROM Clients
```

Which returns:

EarliestDOB	LatestDOB	NumberOfDOB
10/22/1954	09/6/1966	5

It should be pointed out that this result does not correspond to any given record in the database. Although the values returned are derived from data found in the database tables, this result is an entirely new row.

The COUNT function may also be used to count the number of records in a table. Rather than specifying some particular field when using the COUNT function, use an asterisk:

```
SELECT COUNT(*) AS NumberOfClients
FROM Clients
```

Which returns:

NumberOfClients
5

This COUNT(*) query is particularly useful in many situations. It is often advantageous to determine if a table has any records of interest before attempting to process those records. Most RDBMS' have optimized their query engines to process the COUNT(*) query as quickly as possible and will most likely be the fastest single query you will find against any single table. You should do some testing to see if, in your particular application and RDBMS, the time taken by making two queries will increase performance, since there are many factors influencing access speed such as volume of data and the availability of indexes.

If we needed to compute some specific, non-statistical formula, we can construct it using the standard mathematical operators. Here is a chart of these operators, in order of decreasing precedence:

Operator Symbol	Name	Type	Meaning
( )	Parentheses	Infix	Used to force the order of calculations. For example, under normal precedence 8 − 4 / 2 would equal 6. If we wanted to force subtraction of the 4 from the 8 before dividing by 2, we would use parentheses in the calculation, (8 − 4) /2, which would yield the value of 2.
+	Positive	Prefix	Unary Addition
−	Negative	Prefix	Unary Subtraction
*	Multiply	Infix	Multiplication
/	Divide	Infix	Division.
+	Add	Infix	Addition.
−	Subtract	Infix	Subtraction.
|	Concatenate	Infix	Concatenation

Individual RDBMS will offer operators beyond those explicitly defined in the SQL standard. Commonly offered operators include:

Operator Symbol	Name	Type	Meaning
%	Modulo	Infix	Returns the integer remainder of a division. For example, 11 % 5 = 1 because the remainder of 11 divided by 5 is 1. This function is useful when calculating intervals.
^	Exponentiation	Infix	Raises a number to a power. For example, 2^3 yields 8.

As with aggregate functions, the formula is entered to define a new column in the SELECT clause of a query. For example, if we needed to calculate the total cost for items ordered, the query might look like:

```
SELECT
    InvoiceNumber,
    StockNumber,
    QtyOrdered,
    UnitPrice,
    (QtyOrdered * UnitPrice) * (1 + SalesTax)
        AS TotalCost
FROM
    Invoices
```

Commonly Found Functions

When constructing formulas in SQL, most RDBMS provide a widerange of functions that may be included. Although the SQL standard did not explicitly define these functions, they have become widespread amongst the major database vendors. In most cases, these functions are to be used with an individual value and not with records. As always, consult your RDBMS documentation for specifics.

Mathematical Functions	
ABS(X)	Returns the absolute value of X.
CEIL(X)	Returns the smallest integer greater than or equal to the given numeric expression.
FLOOR(X)	Returns the largest integer less than or equal to the given numeric expression.
MOD(X,Y)	Returns the remainder of X / Y.
POWER(X,Y)	Returns X to the power of Y.
ROUND(X,Y)	Rounds X to Y decimal places. If Y is omitted, X is rounded to the nearest integer.
SIGN(X)	Returns –1 when X is negative, a 0 when X is zero, or +1 when X is positive.
SQRT(X)	Returns the square root of X.

Character Functions	
LEFT(string, X)	Returns the leftmost X characters of the string.
RIGHT(string, X)	Returns the rightmost X characters of the string.
UPPER(string)	Converts the string to all uppercase letters.
LOWER(string)	Converts the string to all lowercase letters.
LENGTH(string)	Returns the number of characters in the string.
string || string string + string	Combines the two strings of text into one, concatenated string, where the first string is immediately followed by the second.
SUBSTR(string, X, Y)	Extracts Y letters from the string beginning at position X.
NVL(expression, value) ISNULL(expression, value)	If the expression passed is a Null, then value is returned, otherwise the value of the expression is returned.

Date Functions	
DateAdd(unitsoftime, X, date)	Adds X number of unitsoftime to date. The unitsoftime may be year, month, week, day, hour, minute or second.
Year(date) DatePart(year, date)	Returns the year of the given date.
Month(date) DatePart(month, date)	Returns the month of the year (1 - 12) of the given date.
Day(date) DatePart(day, date)	Returns the day of the month (1 -31) of the given date.
Weekday(date) DatePart(weekday, date)	Returns the day of the week (1-7) of the given date.
Sysdate Getdate() Current_Date	Returns today's date.

Data Types And Calculations

Obviously, you can't construct a formula using incompatible data types and get a meaningful result, such as dividing a text value by a number. When you do attempt to use a formula like this, the query engine will return an error such as:

```
Syntax error converting the nvarchar value 'Smith' to a column of data type int.
```

However, some data types are considered compatible, that is, they are easily converted to the same data type. For instance, you can add the value 2.1 (a real number) to 3 (an integer number). The query engine examines the two data types used and converts one value into the data type of the other. In this example, the value 3 is converted into the real number value of 3.0 and the result of the expression is a real number. In general, this conversion is performed on the least precise data type, in this case, integer. So, if you wish to explicitly convert a value to a particular data type, you can use a conversion function. The most commonly used conversion function is named CAST. This function takes the form:

```
CAST (expression AS datatype)
```

For example, to convert the integer value of a field called NumberOfVisits into a variable length character string you may use either:

```
CAST(NumberOfVisits AS varchar(5))
```

❑   Microsoft SQL Server supports the CAST function as well as an equivalent function named CONVERT, which takes the form:

```
CONVERT (datatype [(length)], expression)
```
where length describes the precision of the data type that you are converting to.

Sometimes, it is not obvious when you would need to explicitly perform a conversion. Consider the following OrderDetails table and SELECT statement:

OrderID	ProductID	UnitPrice	Quantity
10248	11	14.0000	11
10248	42	9.8000	10
10248	72	34.8000	5
10249	14	18.6000	9
10249	51	42.4000	40

```
SELECT Quantity / 2 AS HalfOfQty FROM OrderDetail
```

You would expect that the results of this SELECT statement would return values such as 5.5, 5, 2.5, 4.5, and 20. Surprisingly, the values returned are 5, 5, 2, 4, and 20. The reason for this is because the Quantity field contains integer values and 2 is an integer. When the query engine determines the data type of the resulting column, it too will be an integer. Since integers can't hold any digits to the right of the decimal point, they are discarded.

To alleviate this problem, you must make sure that, value you are dividing by is a real number. To do this, we may use the CAST function:

```
SELECT Quantity / CAST(2 AS FLOAT) AS HalfOfQty FROM OrderDetail
```

Although this statement does produce the correct results, there is a simpler and more efficient way to get the same result. All we need to do is make sure that the denominator is written explicitly as a real number:

```
SELECT Quantity / 2.0 AS HalfOfQty FROM OrderDetail
```

Sorting Data Using a SELECT Statement

Unless we specify otherwise, the records returned from a SELECT statement will be displayed in "natural order." This means that the records are displayed in the order in which the RDBMS found them. If the table uses an index that forces the records to be saved in a particular sequence, then the returned records will also be presented in the indexed order. Otherwise, the order of the records will be in an order determined by the RDBMS and this order may even vary between SELECT statements.

If we wish to have the resulting records from a SELECT statement presented in some specific order, we can add the ORDER BY clause to the SELECT statement. This clause allows you to specify a field or fields and/or a calculation that will be used to sort the results. Using our example above to select the birthday of each client, we can add an ORDER BY clause to sort the results by age:

```
SELECT Fname, Lname, DateOfBirth
FROM Clients
ORDER BY DateOfBirth
```

The records returned would be presented as:

Fname	Lname	DateOfBirth
Walter	Remes	10/22/1954
Suzanne	Crean	06/13/1963
Jason	Trickey	05/03/1965
Pamela	Trickey	06/06/1966
Diane	Asmus	09/06/1966

As you can see, the data is presented in ascending order. If we wished to sort the results with the youngest client first, we add the DESCENDING (or DESC) modifier:

```
SELECT Fname, Lname, DateOfBirth
FROM Clients
ORDER BY DateOfBirth DESCENDING
```

You may explicitly state that sequencing is to be in ascending order by using either ASCENDING or ASC. Since ascending order is the default, there is little reason to include this modifier.

If two records possess the same value in the field used to sort by, you may include additional fields for sub-sorting, provided that each field is separated by a comma. Therefore, to get a listing of our clients' names and birth dates, sorted by last name, and then by first name, we could use:

```
SELECT Fname, Lname, DateOfBirth
FROM Clients
ORDER BY Lname, Fname
```

Fname	Lname	DateOfBirth
Diane	Asmus	09/06/1966
Suzanne	Crean	06/13/1963
Walter	Remes	10/22/1954
Jason	Trickey	05/03/1965
Pamela	Trickey	06/06/1966

Obviously, the query engine will have to perform extra work to sort the results. This extra work may well cause significant reductions in performance if the result set is large, so do not idly use the ORDER BY clause unless there is a good reason for returning the records in a particular order. When this clause is used, the query engine will attempt to utilize an appropriate index to sort the records faster, if an index is available. If you know that certain columns will be used frequently for sorting, you may consider creating indexes on those columns. However, even adding an index may not help in the end. Since indexes must be maintained when data is added, deleted or changed, they incur a certain amount of overhead. By adding too many indexes, you may speed up your queries but slow down other activities in the database.

Obtaining Only the First Records

We can extend the idea of sorting our results to find out which of our clients is the oldest or youngest to asking queries such as "Who are the three oldest clients?" Rather than having the query engine return all results, we can have only superlative records returned. This is done by adding a modifier to the SELECT clause called a **predicate**. The TOP n predicate may be added immediately after the keyword SELECT to restrict the result to the first n records. For example,

```
SELECT TOP 3 Fname, Lname, DateOfBirth
FROM Clients
ORDER BY Lname, Fname
```

Would return only:

Fname	Lname	DateOfBirth
Diane	Asmus	09/06/1966
Suzanne	Crean	06/13/1963
Walter	Remes	10/22/1954

These particular records are chosen because this result set was ordered using ORDER BY Lname, Fname. If different sort columns were used in the ORDER BY clause, then the first records presented in that other sequence would be returned. You can use the TOP predicate without an ORDER BY, but the records presented will not be in any particular order (unless the records are stored in a particular sequence).

If you add a percent symbol (%) immediately after the number in the TOP predicate, you will limit the results to the first *n%* of the records processed. By using the version of the TOP predicate, you can construct queries that ask questions such as "Which students are in the top 10% of their class?" and "Which products account for the top 15% of sales?"

Applying Conditions to a SELECT Statement

With most database applications, we often are more concerned with certain subsets of the data rather than every record in a table. To restrict the data selection to particular records, we add the WHERE clause to the SELECT statement which sets the criteria to be used to acquire records. The WHERE clause must immediately follow the FROM clause in the statement. For example, if we want to know which clients live in the city of Hartford, we could phrase the select statement as:

```
SELECT Lname, Fname
FROM Clients
WHERE City = 'Hartford'
```

The database would scan through all records in the `Clients` table to find those that had a value of `Hartford` in the `City` column. From these records, only the values of each record's `Lname` and `Fname` fields will be returned.

Please note that we use an apostrophe character to delineate text. Some RDBMS also support the use of the double-quote character, but you will hardly ever go wrong by using the apostrophe. However, if the data you are searching for includes an apostrophe, such as in the name "D'Angelo", you should use a pair of apostrophe characters to indicate a literal apostrophe in the string, for example

```
SELECT * FROM Clients WHERE Lname ='D''Angelo'
```

If we wish to construct a condition that references a numeric field, no delimiters are needed. If, for instance, we are asking "Which restaurants offer Sunday Brunch?" and we know that the value 1 will be assigned to the `SundayBrunch` column for any row in the `Restaurant` table that offers Sunday brunch, we could write the SQL statement as:

```
SELECT RestName
FROM Restaurants
WHERE SundayBrunch = 1
```

When specifying the search criteria, SQL provides operators that are common to most other languages:

Operator	Meaning/Use
=	Equal to.
>	Greater than.
<	Less than.
>=	Greater than or equal to.
<=	Less than or equal to.
<>	Not equal to.
Not	Boolean Negation.
And	Boolean And.
Or	Boolean Or.

In addition, many database systems will provide alternate notation for those operators that are not strictly the SQL standard. It is worth noting some of them, since translating between the various dialects of SQL is often commonplace:

Operator	Meaning
!	Not.
!=	Not equal to.
!<	Not less than.
!>	Not greater than.

It is also possible to use more than one condition in our SELECT statements. To construct the question "How many snowboards were sold on January 15, 2000?", we need to specify more than one condition in the WHERE clause. The first condition is that the sale must be on January 15th. The question specifically asks for the sum of a specific product type, so we need to add to the WHERE clause a second restriction to count only snowboards. SQL specifies the logical AND and OR operators in order to allow multiple conditions. So, in order to have the database return the total number of snowboards sold, we need to specify this is the SELECT and place the multiple conditions in the WHERE clause. SQL supports the aggregate functions of SUM, COUNT, AVERAGE, MIN, and MAX. Therefore, the SQL statement might be phrased as follows:

```
SELECT Sum(QtySold) AS SalesQuantity
FROM Sales
WHERE ProductCategory = 'Snowboard'
    AND DateOfSale = '01/15/2000'
```

The result would contain a single column with a single value since we are asking for a single statistic:

SalesQuantity
76

We can change the query to ask for the sales of two particular snowboards. To do so, we would specify the stock numbers of the two snowboards using an OR operator:

```
SELECT Sum(QtySold) As SalesQuantity
FROM Sales
WHERE (StockNumber ='SB4022'
    OR StockNumber = 'SB6510')
    AND DateOfSale = '01/15/2000'
```

The SQL language also provides a NOT operator so that we can exclude certain records. If we wanted to determine the quantity sold of all products except for the two snowboards, we could add a slight modification to our query:

```
SELECT Sum(QtySold) As SalesQuantity
FROM Sales
WHERE NOT (StockNumber ='SB4022'OR StockNumber = 'SB6510')
    AND DateOfSale = '01/15/2000'
```

It is sometimes easier (and perhaps faster) to use Boolean algebra to rewrite statements that use ANDs, ORs, and NOTs. When we need to construct a condition in the form:

NOT ConditionA AND NOT ConditionB

*we can use **DeMorgan's Theorem** from the rules of sentential logic to rewrite the condition a:*

NOT (ConditionA OR ConditionB).

Similarly, if we have a condition in the form:

NOT ConditionA OR NOT ConditionB

it can be rewritten as

NOT (ConditionA AND ConditionB)

If we were asking for the sales of many different products, we could use an abbreviated notation when specifying the stock numbers. This is done using the IN operator. When using this operator, each value must be separated with a comma, and the entire set of acceptable values enclosed in parentheses:

```
SELECT Sum(QtySold) AS SalesQuantity
FROM Sales
WHERE StockNumber IN ('SB4022','SB6510','SB6512','SB7666')
    AND DateOfSale = '01/15/2000'
```

Most database systems will internally convert a WHERE clause that uses the IN operator into a WHERE clause that uses a series of OR operators. The time required for this conversion is not great, but extra time is required. Therefore, to increase performance, consider using the OR operator rather than the IN operator when you know in advance what values you are searching for.

If we want to ask a similar question as before, but include all sales in January 2000, we could use the following statement that utilizes inequality operators to limit the range of dates to days in January:

```
SELECT SUM(QtySold) AS SalesQuantity
FROM Sales
WHERE StockNumber IN ('SB4022','SB6510','SB6512','SB7666')
    AND DateOfSale >= '01/01/2000'
    AND DateOfSale <= '01/31/2000'
```

As an alternative to specifying an upper and lower bound for the DateOfSale field using inequality operators, SQL provides the BETWEEN statement. This statement still requires that upper and lower bounds be specified. For example, we could rewrite the above query as follows:

```
SELECT SUM(QtySold) AS SalesQuantity
FROM Sales
WHERE ProductCategory = 'SnowBoard'
    AND DateOfSale
    BETWEEN '01/01/2000' AND '01/31/2000'
```

As with using the IN operator, when processing the query, most database systems will convert bounds specified by the BETWEEN keyword into a pair of conditions using inequality operators and an AND operator; so functionally they are equivalent but the BETWEEN operator takes a small amount of additional effort. If query processing speed is crucial, avoid using the BETWEEN operator if possible.

We may also use the NOT operator together with the IN operator. By using the two operators together, you can select all records except those records contained in a defined set. For example, consider the following statement that returns the sum of the quantities sold in January 2000 for all products except those with the specified stock numbers:

```
SELECT SUM(QtySold) AS SalesQuantity
FROM Sales
WHERE StockNumber NOT IN ('SB4022','SB6510','SB6512','SB7666')
    AND DateOfSale >= '01/01/2000'
    AND DateOfSale <= '01/31/2000'
```

There is another interesting operator that may be used to select multiple records. It is the LIKE operator. This operator allows you to use wild card characters for pattern matching of strings. Using these wildcard characters makes the LIKE operator more flexible than using the = and <> comparison operators. Let us say you wanted to see the total quantities sold for all products whose product category description started with the word "snow":

```
SELECT SUM(QtySold) AS SalesQuantity
FROM Sales
WHERE ProductCategory LIKE 'Snow%'
```

The percent sign (%) is used to represent any possible character (number, letter, or punctuation) or set of characters that might appear after the characters "snow". To restrict the selection to products that have product categories ending with the word "board", use "%board". For categories including the word, "board", try using "%board%".

Other characters may be used with the LIKE command for other pattern matching. The following table describes the characters that are common in most implementations of SQL:

Character(s)	Purpose	WHERE clause example
%	Any string of zero or more characters.	WHERE City LIKE '%new%' finds all city names with the word 'new' anywhere in the name. New Haven, Newtown, Old Newcastle, Agnew, etc.
_ (underscore)	Any single character.	WHERE State LIKE 'C_' finds all two letter state abbreviations that start with a 'C'. CA, CO, CT.
[ ]	Any single character within the specified range ([a-f]) or set ([abcdef]).	WHERE Fname LIKE '[a-h]ean' finds the first name of Dean but not Jean. WHERE Lname LIKE 'Sm[iy]th' finds both Smith and Smyth.
[^]	Any single character not within the specified range ([^a-f]) or set ([^abcdef]).	WHERE StockCode LIKE '[^k-m]%' finds all product codes that do not begin with a k, l, or m.

There are some important performance considerations when using pattern matching. If the column you're scanning is indexed, the query engine of most RDBMS' will use the index with LIKE operation such as LIKE Lname='smith' or LIKE Lname='smith%'. However, if you look for LIKE Lname='%smith' or LIKE Lname='%smith%' the index will not be used and therefore performance will suffer.

Special Considerations for Null Values

Most RDBMS' will record a Null value when the data is unknown or unavailable. Null values should not be confused with a zero (which is a legitimate number), a zero-length string (a string data type with no characters), or the space character. Null values are usually ignored when using aggregate functions such as MIN, MAX or AVG as well as when including a WHERE clause that searches for specific values. For instance, consider if we were to issue the following SQL statements together in a single query window using Microsoft SQL Server:

```
SET ANSI_NULLS OFF
SELECT title, price FROM titles WHERE price = NULL
```

These statements disable support for the ANSI standard behavior for using null values and then issue a `SELECT` statement. As we see in the results, there are two records that have null values for the price column.

Title	Price
The Psychology of Computer Cooking	NULL
Net Etiquette	NULL

Now let's execute the same statements again, but enabling the default behavior for `Nulls` under the ANSI standard:

```
SET ANSI_NULLS ON
SELECT title, price FROM titles WHERE price = NULL
```

These statements return the following records – none!

Title	Price

The reason behind this behavior is that, under the ANSI standard, if certain records have a column that contains a null value, then that column cannot be evaluated in a conditional statement, not even the null value itself can be evaluated.

Using Groupings With Statistical Functions

As we have seen, SQL provides a number of aggregate functions that are used to calculate statistics on the data. Although we can use a `WHERE` clause in the `SELECT` statement to limit the rows used to compute the statistics, it is more common that we compute these statistics on collections of our data. If we needed to find the total sales for each of five stores, we could approach this by issuing five separate queries, limiting each to a particular store. A more efficient approach is to issue a single query which groups the records based upon the different stores and then calculates the required statistics on each group. To cause the `SELECT` statement to group similar records, use the `GROUP BY` clause along with instructions on how the database query should organize the selected records.

To see how this works, let us assume that we have the following `Sales` table:

OrderDate	CustomerID	StoreNumber	StockNumber	QtyOrdered	UnitPrice
02/14/2000	212	1	PA422	2	19.95
02/14/2000	387	2	RS200	100	2.45
02/15/2000	166	2	TS4552	1	67.88
02/15/2000	201	1	PA400	4	23.99

OrderDate	CustomerID	StoreNumber	StockNumber	QtyOrdered	UnitPrice
02/16/2000	143	5	SD332A	50	4.87
02/16/2000	387	2	TS3111	10	98.10
02/16/2000	076	3	DR65	1	210.00
02/16/2000	412	4	TS4552	1	67.88
02/17/2000	287	3	PA422	20	19.95

To find out the total number of products ordered from each store, try:

```
SELECT StoreNumber, Sum(QtyOrdered) AS TotalQuantity
FROM Sales
GROUP BY StoreNumber
ORDER BY StoreNumber
```

This query produces:

StoreNumber	TotalQuantity
1	6
2	111
3	21
4	1
5	50

As we saw earlier, we can request multiple statistics in a single query. To compute the total and average sales per day for all stores, we could use:

```
SELECT OrderDate, SUM(QtyOrdered * UnitPrice) AS TotalQuantity,
               AVG(QtyOrdered * UnitPrice) AS AverageSales
FROM Sales
GROUP BY OrderDate
ORDER BY OrderDate
```

which returns:

OrderDate	TotalQuantity	AverageSales
02/14/2000	284.9	142.45
02/15/2000	163.84	81.92
02/16/2000	1502.38	375.595
02/17/2000	399.0	399.0

If the ORDER BY clause is not specified, groups returned using the GROUP BY clause are not in any particular order. Because of this, you will usually use the ORDER BY clause to specify a particular ordering of the data when the GROUP BY clause is used. As was mentioned above, the query engine has to perform extra work to sort the results. This will cause a performance hit. Therefore, do not idly use the ORDER BY clause unless there is a good reason for returning the records in a particular order.

Some Notes on Using GROUP BY

There are a few important comments to mention when using the GROUP BY clause. First, any field listed in the SELECT clause that is not used in an aggregate function must be listed in the GROUP BY clause. Therefore, the first of the following statements is legal, while the second is not:

```
SELECT DateOfSale, SalesPersonID, SUM(QtyOrdered) AS TotalQuantity
FROM Sales
GROUP BY
     SalesPersonID
     DateOfSale,
ORDER BY
     SalesPersonID,
     DateOfSale
```

```
SELECT DateOfSale, SalesPersonID, SUM(QtyOrdered) AS TotalQuantity
FROM Sales
GROUP BY
     DateOfSale
ORDER BY
     SalesPersonID
     DateOfSale
```

This second statement would produce an error message from the database such as:

```
Dynamic SQL Error
-SQL error code = -104
-invalid column reference
```

or

```
Server: Msg 8118, Level 16, State 1, Line 1
Column 'SalesPersonID' is invalid in the select list because it is not contained in
either an aggregate function or the GROUP BY clause.
```

You may include a search condition for a group by adding the HAVING clause to the select statement. The HAVING clause acts like a WHERE clause, but for the grouped records rather than individual records. The elimination of records from using HAVING will occur after the WHERE clause has executed and the HAVING clause will set conditions based upon the value of the field being grouped. To illustrate the use of the HAVING clause, let's step through what happens to produce the result set for the following query:

```
SELECT CategoryName, SUM(UnitsInStock) AS TotalOnHand
FROM Products
WHERE CategoryName LIKE 'S%'
GROUP BY CategoryName
HAVING
    SUM(UnitsInStock) < 50
```

To understand how HAVING works, let us first look at what the query would produce without using either the WHERE or HAVING clauses:

```
SELECT CategoryName, SUM(UnitsInStock) AS TotalOnHand
FROM Products
GROUP BY CategoryName
```

produces:

ProductCategory	TotalOnHand
Skis	43
Snowboards	50
Apparel	386
Boots	39
Safety & First Aid	28

If the WHERE clause is included, this resultset would be reduced to only those product categories that began with the letter S:

ProductCategory	TotalOnHand
Skis	43
Snowboards	50
Safety & First Aid	28

When the HAVING clause is used, it would examine each row of the current resultset and eliminate any row that has a total on hand of 50 or more:

ProductCategory	TotalOnHand
Skis	43
Safety & First Aid	28

Queries Using Multiple Tables

Although the tables in a database are carefully organized so that they efficiently store and maintain data, when we request information from the database we will more than likely need to draw that information from more than one table. When we specify more than one table in a SELECT statement, it is said that the tables are being **joined**.

Typically, in order for two tables to be joined, they need to share some common information. For instance, the Clients table may include such fields as Name, Address, and Zipcode and a Zipcodes table may contain the fields Zipcode, City, and State. Each table holds a Zipcode field that may be used to relate the two tables. In this case, the Zipcode field in the Clients table is a foreign key that references the primary key of the Zipcodes table, which is the Zipcode field. When you query against two tables, the database's query engine may not know implicitly which columns should be used for the join, and when it comes to constructing the query, you must explicitly state which tables are being used and which fields hold the common information.

In the following Select statement, the Clients table is joined with the Zipcodes table:

```
SELECT
    ContactFirstName,
    ContactLastName, BillingAddress,
    City,
    State,
    Zipcodes.Zipcode
FROM
    Clients JOIN Zipcodes
        ON (Clients.Zipcode = Zipcodes.Zipcode)
```

Notice that the FROM clause now lists the names of the two tables being joined along with the keyword JOIN and an ON (...) operator that specifies the columns from each table used for referencing. Both tables have a field named Zipcode, so in the SELECT clause of the statement, we need to explicitly state from which table the Zipcode value would be drawn. The other fields listed in the statement have names that are unique between the two tables, so there is no need to specify which tables their values are drawn from.

Alternative Syntax for Joins

It should be noted that this syntax of using the JOIN keyword and the ON operator was introduced with SQL-92. Some RDBMS' that have been around for longer may still have code that uses the pre-SQL-92 syntax. In addition, some of us will still need to work with these older RDBMS', so knowing how this older syntax is used is worthwhile. This older syntax simply lists each table to be referenced in the FROM clause, separated by a comma, and the join condition is presented in the WHERE clause:

```
SELECT
    ContactFirstName, ContactLastName, BillingAddress, City, State,
    Zipcodes.Zipcode
FROM
    Clients, Zipcodes
WHERE
    Clients.Zipcode = Zipcodes.Zipcode
```

If your RDBMS supports both versions of the syntax, you should test each version to see which provides the best performance. There is often a significant difference in speed between the two versions, and usually the newer JOIN...ON syntax is substantially faster.

When performing the joins described above, only those records that have a Zipcode value that is found in both tables will be presented in the results. This is the default behavior and this type of join is called an **inner join**, and you would usually use the INNER JOIN construct in the FROM clause to specify this. To better understand how inner joins work, consider the following sample tables and a SELECT statement that queries both of them:

TableA	
ColumnA1	**ColumnA2**
1	A
2	A
3	C
4	D
5	A
6	H
7	A
8	Null

TableB	
ColumnB1	**ColumnB2**
A	Blue
B	Green
C	Yellow
D	Black
F	Orange
G	White
I	Red

```
SELECT * From TableA JOIN TableB ON (TableA.ColumnA2 = TableB.ColumnB1)
```

As the query engine processess the query it starts with the first table listed in the statement, in this case it is `TableA`. The first record of `TableA` is referenced and the value of its `ColumnA2` field is sought in `ColumnB1` field of `TableB`. Since the value "A" is found in both of the joining columns, the first record of the result set is determined:

ColumnA1	ColumnA2	ColumnB1	ColumnB2
1	A	A	Blue

Now, the second record in `TableA` is referenced and the value of its `ColumnA2` field is looked for in `TableB`. Again, a match is found and a new record for the resultset is generated:

ColumnA1	ColumnA2	ColumnB1	ColumnB2
1	A	A	Blue
2	A	A	Blue

This process continues with the third, fourth, and fifth records of `TableA` to produce:

ColumnA1	ColumnA2	ColumnB1	ColumnB2
1	A	A	Blue
2	A	A	Blue
3	C	C	Yellow
4	D	D	Black
5	A	A	Blue

When the sixth record of `TableA` is referenced, a corresponding record is not found in `TableB` since no record in `TableB` has a value of "`H`" in `ColumnB1`. With the lack of a matching record in `TableB`, the query engine skips this sixth record in `TableA` and the result set is not added to.

The process continues with the seventh record in `TableA`, matching it to a record in `TableB` and adding a new record into the result set. When the eighth record of `TableA` is processed, we again cannot find a match in `TableB`, so this record is also discarded. The result displayed will be the following:

ColumnA1	ColumnA2	ColumnB1	ColumnB2
1	A	A	Blue
2	A	A	Blue
3	C	C	Yellow
4	D	D	Black
5	A	A	Blue
7	A	A	Blue

Notice that not just the records from `TableA` were discarded. Four records in `TableB` were also ignored. This is again due to the behavior of inner joins to select only the records that are common between the two tables.

Outer Joins

There will be occasions when you need to obtain *all* records from one table and the matching records from the second table, if available. Such a `JOIN` is called an **outer join**. There are three types of outer joins: **right outer join**, **left outer join**, and the **full outer join**.

Left joins work very much like inner joins except that all records in the first (left) table that meet the `WHERE` clause condition are returned, regardless of if a matching record is found in the second (right) table. For example, if we were to reissue the last SQL statement as a `LEFT JOIN`, the resultset would be displayed as:

```
SELECT * FROM TableA LEFT JOIN TableB ON (TableA.ColumnA2 = TableB.ColumnB1)
```

ColumnA1	ColumnA2	ColumnB1	ColumnB2
1	A	A	Blue
2	A	A	Blue
3	C	C	Yellow
4	D	D	Black
5	A	A	Blue
6	H	*Null*	*Null*
7	A	A	Blue
8	*Null*	*Null*	*Null*

Notice that when a matching record was not found in the right-side table, `Null` values are assigned.

Right outer joins work exactly as left outer joins except that all records from the right-side table are returned and values from the left table are provided if a matching record is found.

```
SELECT * FROM TableA RIGHT JOIN TableB ON (TableA.ColumnA2 = TableB.ColumnB1)
```

ColumnA1	ColumnA2	ColumnB1	ColumnB2
1	A	A	Blue
2	A	A	Blue
7	A	A	Blue
Null	Null	B	Green
3	C	C	Yellow
4	D	D	Black
Null	Null	F	Orange
Null	Null	G	White
Null	Null	I	Red

Full outer joins act like a double-ended left and right join. All records from both tables are returned (assuming they meet the `WHERE` clause requirement) and `Null` values are used for columns where a matching record was not found.

```
SELECT *
FROM TableA FULL OUTER JOIN TableB ON (TableA.ColumnA2 = TableB.ColumnB1)
```

ColumnA1	ColumnA2	ColumnB1	ColumnB2
1	A	A	Blue
2	A	A	Blue
3	C	C	Yellow
4	D	D	Black
5	A	A	Blue
6	H	Null	Null
7	A	A	Blue
8	Null	Null	Null
Null	Null	B	Green
Null	Null	F	Orange
Null	Null	G	White
Null	Null	I	Red

Alternative Syntax for Outer Joins

As with inner joins, you may use an alternate syntax for outer joins. Like the older syntax for inner joins, the old syntax for outer joins lists each table to be referenced in the FROM clause, and the JOIN condition is presented in the WHERE clause. What differs with the outer join syntax is that rather than using an equal sign as the comparison operator in the WHERE clause, use *= for left outer joins and =* for right outer joins. The following are examples of outer joins using the pre-SQL2 syntax:

Left Outer Join Using pre-SQL2 Syntax

```
SELECT
    ContactFirstName,
    ContactLastName,
    BillingAddress,
    City, State, Zipcodes.Zipcode
FROM
    Clients, Zipcodes
WHERE
    Clients.Zipcode *= Zipcodes.Zipcode
```

Right Outer Join Using pre-SQL2 Syntax with Aliases

```
SELECT
    Orders.EmployeeID,
    Orders.OrderID,
    AvgUnitPrice = Avg(OD.UnitPrice)
FROM
    OrderDetails AS OD INNER JOIN Orders ON (OD.OrderID =* Orders.OrderID)
GROUP BY
    Orders.EmployeeID, Orders.OrderID
ORDER BY
    Orders.EmployeeID, Orders.OrderID
```

Creating And Changing Tables Using SQL

All tables within a database must be created at some point. As the application is used, there may be call to add or change these tables. Most modern RDBMS' have easy-to-use utilities with nice graphical interfaces that make table creation and maintenance convenient. These utilities may be easy to use, but there are many times when you need to create or alter tables with SQL, especially within stored procedures.

This section will cover how you can generate tables and columns and update the database using SQL. As always, there are variations in notation and data types between RDBMS', so you will need to check with your database vendor's documentation to confirm some of the specific syntax used here.

Creating Tables

The SQL Data Definition Language (DDL) provides the CREATE TABLE command for generating empty tables. Here is the most basic syntax:

```
CREATE TABLE tablename (
columnname datatype {identity | null | not null}
[, ...]
)
```

For example, you could create a seven-column table called `Orders` using this statement that works in both Sybase and Microsoft SQL Server:

```
CREATE TABLE Orders
(
    InvoiceNumber DECIMAL(5,0)
        IDENTITY(1000,1) NOT NULL,
    CustomerID DECIMAL(5,0) NOT NULL,
    OrderDate DATETIME NOT NULL,
    ShipDate DATETIME,
    Terms CHAR(5),
    ShipToAddress VARCHAR(100) NOT NULL,
    ShipToZip CHAR(5)
)
```

In the above statement, the data type `decimal(5,0)` defines a numerical format that stores five digits to the left of the decimal point and zero digits to the right of the decimal point. The `char(5)` data types define a five character wide fixed-length string, while `varchar(100)` defines a variable-length string of up to 100 characters. The keyword `IDENTITY` specifies that the column contain a sequence of values that will be used to identify each row uniquely. The `IDENTITY` keyword requires a "seed" value and an increment value. In this case the first record inserted into this table will have a value of 1000 in this field, the second will have 1001, and so on. Finally, the `NOT NULL` modifier prohibits null values in the column.

The ANSI-2 standard defined a limited number of data types. Since then, additional data types have been widely adopted, although the names used for them differ slightly from RDBMS to RDBMS. The most common data types found are:

❑   `Char(x)` – A fixed-length string of characters, where x is a number designating the number of characters. If the data to be saved has fewer characters than x, the data will be padded with spaces.

❑   `VarChar(x)` or `VarChar2(x)` – A variable-length string of characters, where x is a number designating the maximum number of characters allowed (maximum length) in the column.

❑   `Integer` – Integer values. These may be positive, negative, or zero.

❑   `Decimal(x, y)` or `Numeric(x, y)` – Real numbers, where x is the maximum length in digits of the decimal numbers in the column, and y is the maximum number of digits allowed after the decimal point. The maximum `(4,2)` number would be `99.99`.

❑   `Date` or `DateTime` – A date column in a RDBMS-specific format.

❑   `Boolean` – A column that can hold only two values: `TRUE` or `FALSE`.

When specifying character data types for columns, you should consider if the data that is to be stored would use a particular character set. With the Internet having no national boundaries, it is likely that text will be sent to your database, containing characters that are not part of the default character set for your system. There are typically two ways of storing such characters correctly; the first is to install your RDBMS to store its character data in a Unicode format. The second way is to use the Unicode equivalents of fixed-length and variable-length character data. In most of the major RDBMS', these data types are `nchar` and `nvarchar`.

When creating a table, the names that you employ should follow some general guidelines. The name of the table should be less than 64 characters long, start with a letter and should not contain spaces or most of the symbol characters. Some RDBMS' allow longer names or different symbols to be included, so you should consult your vendor's documentation for specifics. If you keep your table names less than 64 characters long and include only alphanumeric characters, your names will be acceptable to most RDBMS'.

When defining a table, in addition to declaring column names and data types, you may also declare other properties that specify data integrity restrictions. These additional properties include such things as check constraints, primary keys, foreign keys, and default values. Refer back to Chapter 2 for descriptions and uses of these integrity properties.

The following example illustrates how these data integrity properties may be defined. The example uses Oracle data types:

```
CREATE TABLE Orders
(
    InvoiceNumber NUMBER(5, 0) PRIMARY KEY,
    CustomerID NUMBER(5,0) NOT NULL,
    OrderDate DATE NOT NULL,
    ShipDate DATE,
    Terms CHAR(5)DEFAULT 'Net60',
        CHECK
            (Terms IN ('Net30', 'Net60', 'Net90')),
    ShipToAddress VARCHAR(100) NOT NULL,
    ShipToZip CHAR(5),
    FOREIGN KEY (ShipToZip) REFERENCES ZipCodes,
    FOREIGN KEY (CustomerID) REFERENCES Customers
)
```

Using SELECT to Create Tables

When working with databases, we must be aware that any actions that we take may effect the operation of the other activities in the database. If you are issuing a series of SQL statements against a subset of records from a table (or tables), each statement has the potential of delaying the execution of activity elsewhere. It is often advantageous to first extract the subset of records that you need into a new table and then perform subsequent statements on the new table.

One convenient way of creating a table is to use the SELECT statement. After the select clause of the statement, add the INTO clause:

```
SELECT *
INTO
    DecemberOrders
FROM
    OrderDetails
WHERE
    OrderID BETWEEN (1000 AND 2000)
```

Some databases, such as Oracle, provide an alternative method for creating tables by using a SELECT statement within the CREATE TABLE statement:

```
CREATE TABLE DecemberOrders
AS
    SELECT *
    FROM
        OrderDetails
    WHERE
        OrderID BETWEEN (1000 AND 2000)
```

Other RDBMS' may allow you to use yet another syntax:

```
INSERT DecemberOrders
    SELECT *
    FROM
        OrderDetails
    WHERE
        OrderID BETWEEN (1000 AND 2000)
```

Regardless of the method that you try, it is possible that you will not be allowed to use the command. You need to have the appropriate permission to create tables in the database. In addition, some databases will, by default, explicitly prohibit these commands, because these types of "bulk inserts" are very costly to perform and can cause inaccuracies with the database statistics. In Microsoft SQL Server and Sybase SQL Server, use the db_options command to set the ability to use bulk inserts. Check your RDBMS's documentation for details.

Deleting Tables

It is important that, after you no longer need the new table, it is removed from the database. To do so, use the DROP TABLE command. This command takes a single argument, the name of the table to be removed:

```
DROP TABLE DecemberOrders
```

Altering Tables Using SQL

Sometimes, in designing a database we might overlook some item of data that needs to be stored, or, after some time, we might find that our business requirements have changed. In these situations, you will need to change a table, either by adding or removing column, or by changing some of the properties of the table. To make changes to table using SQL, we may use the ALTER TABLE command.

This command is very similar to CREATE TABLE, and follows a very similar syntax. To add a new column to an existing table use the syntax:

```
ALTER TABLE table
    ADD newcolumnname <column_definition>
```

For example, if we wanted to add the columns "StartDate" and "VestingDate" to the Employees table, we would use:

```
ALTER TABLE Employees
    ADD
        StartDate DATE NOT NULL,
        VestingDate DATE NULL
```

101

Similarly, we can remove columns from a table:

```
ALTER TABLE table
    DROP columnname
```

```
ALTER TABLE Employees
    DROP StartDate, VestingDate
```

There are similar approaches to changing the data type for a column and to add, remove or alter constraints on columns, but such actions are more typically performed using one of the graphical tools provided by the RDBMS.

Adding, Deleting, and Changing Data

A database management system has three major purposes. The first of these is to provide a structured way of storing data. The second purpose is to provide a mechanism for searching the data stored in the database. The third and final purpose of a DBMS is to get the data into the database and manipulate it.

Adding Data to Tables

The `INSERT` statement is used to add rows of data to a table. The command requires that you specify the destination of the new records (either a table, or in some cases a view) as well as the data. If you are not providing data to every field in the table, you will also be required to specify which fields are to be populated with the data.

The `INSERT` statement takes the following general form:

```
INSERT tablename (column1, column2, ..., columnX)
    VALUES (value1, value2, ..., valueX)
```

To insert a new record in all fields of the `Employee` table, we could use the following:

```
INSERT Employee
    VALUES (298, 'Conover', 'Susan', '040-70-1887', '3 Fawn Hill Road', '06484')
```

This statement adds data to the `EmployeeID`, `LastName`, `FirstName`, `SocialSecurity`, `Address`, and `Zipcode` fields. If the identifier of the table, in this case the `EmployeeID` field, was generated automatically, we would not want to specify its value, in this case `298`. We would thus exclude the `EmployeeID` value, but we would also have to explicitly specify what other fields are being populated:

```
INSERT Employee (LastName, FirstName, SocialSecurity, Address, Zipcode)
    VALUES ('Conover', 'Susan', '040-70-1887', '3 Fawn Hill Road', '06484')
```

There is another advantage to using this second syntax, namely, we can list the fields to be populated in any order. Therefore, the following statement is equivalent to the above:

```
INSERT Employee (SocialSecurity, FirstName, LastName, Address, Zipcode)
    VALUES ('040-70-1887', 'Susan', 'Conover', '3 Fawn Hill Road', '06484')
```

The INSERT statement may be used in conjunction with the SELECT statement. The syntax is virtually the same, except that the VALUES clause is substituted for the SELECT statement. You would use these two statements together to copy data from one table to another. The following statement adds employees with more than five years of service to the PensionPlan table.

```
INSERT PensionPlan (EmployeeID, SocialSecurity)
    SELECT EmployeeID, SocialSecurity
    FROM Employees
    WHERE StartDate <= DateDiff(year,-5,GetDate())
```

Deleting Data From Tables

In order to remove records from a table using SQL, the DELETE statement may be used. This statement takes the general form:

```
DELETE
FROM tablename
WHERE conditions
```

To remove all records in the Orders table that are older than five years, we could use:

```
DELETE
FROM Orders
WHERE OrderDate <= DateDiff(year,-5,GetDate())
```

The WHERE clause of this statement uses the same syntax as in the SELECT statement. As with the SELECT statement, if the WHERE clause is omitted, the query engine will select all records in the table. Therefore, if you wish to purge an entire table of records simply use the statement:

```
DELETE FROM tablename
```

Sybase SQL Server and Microsoft SQL Server offer another method, called the TRUNCATE TABLE statement, for purging all rows from a table. It operates like a DELETE statement without WHERE clause, and therefore can be used only to remove all records from a table. This statement offers some advantages over the DELETE statement, but it also has some drawbacks. The DELETE statement removes records one at a time and the action is recorded in transaction logs by the server. Since each record's deletion is recorded record by record, it is possible to undo the deletion. When the TRUNCATE TABLE statement is used, the records are removed and the action is not recorded in the logs. The advantage of not recording the deletion of individual records is that TRUNCATE TABLE is extremely fast and does not cause the transaction logs to grow. The disadvantage of using TRUNCATE TABLE is that if you issue this command by mistake, you can't undo the action. You'd have to hope that you have a good backup on tape!

Updating Data in Tables

To change the values of columns in a table, we use the UPDATE statement. The general format of this statement is:

```
UPDATE targettablename
SET field1 = newvalue1, field2 = newvalue2
FROM sourcetablename
WHERE conditions
```

The following statement changes the `UnitPrice` field of all snowboards to 90% of the original `Unitprice`:

```
UPDATE
SET Unitprice = Unitprice * 0.9
FROM Products
WHERE CategoryName = 'snowboards'
```

Since this statement is updating fields based upon their current values, there is no need to specify a target table. When a target table is not included, the query engine assumes that source and target tables are the same. In the following statement, only those products that have sold more than 10 units at a time during the month of January will have a unit price discount:

```
UPDATE Products
SET UnitPrice = P.UnitPrice * 0.9
FROM
    Products AS P Inner Join Sales AS S
    ON (P.ProductID = S.ProductID)
WHERE
    S.OrderDate
    BETWEEN '01/01/2000' AND '01/31/2000 23:59'
    AND OrderQuantity > 10
```

To determine the target records in the `Products` table, we need to refer to the `Sales` table. With more than one table being used in this statement, it is required that we explicitly specify which table is being updated and explicitly state which fields will be used in the calculation of the new `UnitPrice`.

Transactional Processing

In many commercial applications, we need to perform a series of operations. If any single operation fails, then the entire series of operations cannot be used. Take, for instance, a transfer of funds from a savings account to a checking account. For this to happen, a withdrawal needs to be made from one account and a deposit to the other. If, for any reason, we are unable to perform either of these actions, we need to cancel the other.

SQL provides a mechanism to group such operations into what are called **transactions**. All database systems that support transactions must have a way to explicitly tell the system that a transaction is beginning (although the syntax used may vary for each RDBMS). There is also a statement that will identify the end of the transaction, specifying if the entire transaction was a success or a failure. If successful, all of the actions taken between the command that started the transaction and the command that ended it will be saved to the database. If the transaction was not successful, then the state of the records prior to the start of the transaction will be reinstated.

A transaction must exhibit four properties, called the ACID (Atomicity, Consistency, Isolation, and Durability) properties. Together these properties ensure that a transaction does not corrupt your data if some problem occurs while it is being processed:

❑   **Atomicity** – this means that a transaction is an indivisible unit of work: all of its actions succeed or they all fail. If any single action in the transaction fails, then the entire transaction fails and any changes to the system are reversed.

❑ **Consistency** – a transaction never leaves the database in an inconsistent state. All data integrity rules will be applied and any other required changes to the data. If a change is made, it can be undone if the transaction fails at a later point.

❑ **Isolation** – a transaction behaves as if it were in complete isolation from other concurrent transactions in the system. A transaction either sees data in the state it was in before another concurrent transaction modified it, or it sees the data after the other transaction has completed. It will never see the data changes currently being made by another transaction. This allows us to reload the starting data and replay a series of transactions to end up with the data in the same state it was in after the original transactions were performed.

❑ **Durability** – this means that even in the event of some catastrophic failure, for example, an operating system failure, the results of committed transactions will not be lost and the partial results of uncommitted transactions will be rolled back.

The syntax in Oracle for marking the start of a transaction is:

```
SET TRANSACTION
```

For Sybase SQL Server and Microsoft SQL Server, the syntax is:

```
BEGIN TRANSACTION
```

Following the command that starts the transaction, all the subsequent SQL statements perform the required operations within the transaction. If all these statements execute without incident, then we can save the results of the operations with the COMMIT statement for Oracle, or the COMMIT TRANSACTION statement for the Microsoft and Sybase products. If an error is raised before the COMMIT command is invoked, all of the changes made will be reversed or **rolled back**. You can explicitly cause the transaction to roll back by issuing the ROLLBACK command in Oracle, or ROLLBACK TRANSACTION in Microsoft and Sybase SQL Servers.

Therefore, if we issue the following block of SQL statements, by wrapping them in a transaction, we can insure that they all are executed or none are executed.

```
BEGIN TRANSACTION
    INSERT INTO Alumni
        SELECT *
        FROM Students
        WHERE GraduationDate < GetDate()
    DELETE FROM Students
        WHERE GraduationDate < GetDate()
COMMIT TRANSACTION
```

The code transfers the details of already graduated students into the Alumni table, before deleting them from the Students table.

Transactions are possible because the RDBMS keeps track of every change that takes place in the database: when a record is inserted into a table, a record is deleted, or a value is updated in a column. This record is kept in a **transaction log**. If the transaction fails, the database is able to reconstruct the values of the database before the transaction by reading this log. It is this transaction log that is used to undo the changes to the database if the transaction is rolled back.

105

However, transactions have the potential to affect performance. Typically, when data is modified in a table, the database engine will prevent other operations from accessing or changing that data, in a process called **locking**. When a particular row in a table is locked and another operation requests that data, the second operation is delayed until the lock is released. To minimize the impact on other operations, locks are generally applied to the smallest subset of data in the table, the record. If your transactions issue a large number of operations, then you may be locking out other processes from using the data. Therefore, if it is possible, you should design your code to minimize the time required to process the transaction.

Alternatively, if there are many statements that lock various parts of the same table, the time and resources needed to lock and unlock all of the records one at a time can be considerable. When transactions are used, the database engine can lock the entire table (or larger portions of a single table) at the start of the transaction and release this lock when the transaction is completed.

> *Some RDBMS', like Microsoft SQL Server 2000, incorporate "lock escalation", which automatically provide this ability for individual SQL statements that are not explicitly defined in a transaction.*

Query Tricks

As we become more familiar with SQL, we come to realize that some of the syntax present may be written in creative ways to make the query engine do things that we might not originally expect. Often, this alternative syntax provides much faster access or it radically simplifies complex operations. In addition, we can use functions and special operators in our queries to combine them in ways that will allow us to process commands sequentially or in groups. This section will present some different ways of constructing SQL statements, which under certain circumstances can provide elegant solutions to difficult problems. The exact implementation of the code discussed will vary somewhat with each dialect of SQL, so you may need to experiment with your particular database server. But then again, experimenting is half the fun.

Combining Sequences of Queries

There are situations where we would want to return a single set of records that are the result of more than one query. These situations may arise because the data we are interested in require vastly different selection criteria, or the data is located on different tables that cannot be joined. Consider a query that asks for the top 5 and the bottom 5 sales items, or the query that acquires names, addresses, and, phone numbers from the Clients, Vendors, and Employees tables.

To combine the results of two or more SELECT statements into a single resultset, we can use the UNION operator. To use this operator, simply add the keyword UNION between each of the SELECT statements:

```
SELECT TOP 15 SUM(Quantity) AS QtySold, ProductID
FROM OrderDetails
GROUP BY ProductID
ORDER BY SUM(Quantity) DESC

UNION

SELECT TOP 15 SUM(Quantity) AS QtySold, ProductID
FROM OrderDetails
GROUP BY ProductID
ORDER BY Sum(Quantity) ASC
```

Some conditions must be met in order to use UNION. First, each of the queries being combined must produce resultsets with the same number columns. Secondly, these resulting columns must have the same or compatible data types. Finally, the fields must be listed in the same order, if a resulting column is to be populated by values from different fields. For instance, you would not be able to combine SELECT OrderDate, Quantity FROM Orders with SELECT LastName, FirstName FROM Clients since the two SELECT statements return different data types in their columns.

When the query executes, the resultset will be based upon the properties of the first SELECT statement presented. It will be this first SELECT statement that defines the names and data types of the columns. In addition, when the final records are selected, duplicate values will be eliminated. To illustrate this, let's consider the following UNION query:

```
SELECT FirstName, LastName, Address, City, State, Zip FROM Employees

UNION

SELECT C.Fname, C.Lname, C.Address, Z.City, Z.State, Z.Zipcode
FROM Clients AS C LEFT JOIN Zipcodes AS Z ON (C.Zipcode = Z.Zipcode)

UNION

SELECT FirstName, LastName, Address, City, StateOrProv, PostalCode
FROM Vendors
```

Let us assume that when each of the SELECT statements is issued without the UNION operator, it returns the following resultsets:

FirstName	LastName	Address	City	State	Zip
Vishu	Honnaya	71 Apple Tree Drive	Monroe	CT	06268
Raj	Honnaya	71 Apple Tree Drive	Monroe	CT	06268
Desire	Williams	226 Elm Street	Southbury	CT	06488

Fname	Lname	Address	City	State	Zipcode
James	Conrad	166 Jeremy Drive	Trumbull	CT	06261
Mike	Russell	4 Hemmingway Drive	Oxford	CT	06486
Robert	Conover	3 Fawn Hill Rd	Shelton	CT	06484

FirstName	LastName	Address	City	StateOrProv	PostalCode
Robert	Conover	3 Fawn Hill Rd	Shelton	CT	06484
Gloriann	Pudimat	720 Spring Hill Rd	Oxford	CT	06486

The results of the UNION query will combine these records, using the field names from the first SELECT statement and eliminate any duplicates:

FirstName	LastName	Address	City	State	Zip
Vishu	Honnaya	71 Apple Tree Drive	Monroe	CT	06268
Raj	Honnaya	71 Apple Tree Drive	Monroe	CT	06268
Desire	Williams	226 Elm Street	Southbury	CT	06488
James	Conrad	166 Jeremy Drive	Trumbull	CT	06261
Mike	Russell	4 Hemmingway Drive	Oxford	CT	06486
Robert	Conover	3 Fawn Hill Rd	Shelton	CT	06484
Gloriann	Pudimat	720 Spring Hill Rd	Oxford	CT	06486

Therefore, the record for "Robert Conover" found in the Vendor table will be eliminated since this record was first found in the Clients table. If you wish to prevent the elimination of duplicate records, add the ALL predicate to the UNION operator in the following way:

```
SELECT FirstName, LastName, Address, City, State, Zip FROM Employees

UNION ALL

SELECT C.Fname, C.Lname, C.Address, Z.City, Z.State, Z.Zipcode
FROM Clients AS C Left Join Zipcodes AS Z ON (C.Zipcode = Z.Zipcode)

UNION ALL

SELECT FirstName, LastName, Address, City, StateOrProv, PostalCode FROM Vendors
```

*The SQL-3 specification (ISO/IEC 9075:Annex D - Deprecated features) identifies UNIONs as being **deprecated**, meaning that it is intended that the feature will be removed from a revised version of the SQL standard at a later date. Although UNION joins may be removed from the official specification for SQL, it is very likely that most RDBMS' will continue to support it for backward compatibility.*

Creating Cross Tabulation Queries

Have you ever wanted to produce a "cross tabulation" or "pivot table" report? These reports summarize data row-by-row in groups, but present the group totals in columns. Let us assume that you have the following sales table;

OrderID	EmployeeID	OrderDate	CustomerID
10248	2	Oct 28 1999	1005
10249	2	Oct 29 1999	1004
10250	3	Nov 1 1999	1000
10251	3	Nov 1 1999	1006
10252	1	Nov 2 1999	1008
10253	3	Nov 3 1999	1000
10254	1	Nov 4 1999	1003
10255	2	Nov 5 1999	1001
10256	3	Nov 8 1999	1000
10257	2	Nov 9 1999	1005
10258	1	Nov 10 1999	1008
:	:	:	:

You would like to run a single query that produces an output similar to this:

EmployeeID	October	November	December
1	12	11	16
2	11	4	13
3	17	15	15
4	14	20	16
5	4	6	5
6	5	6	9
7	7	7	6
8	12	10	16
9	11	9	17
10	14	12	17
11	13	14	12
12	26	20	18

If you think about it for a while (and with a little reading up on date functions), you will see that it is pretty easy to produce any one of these month counts by using the COUNT function:

```
SELECT
    EmployeeID,
    DatePart(month,OrderDate) As MonthOfYear,
    COUNT(OrderID) AS NumberOfOrders
FROM
    Orders
GROUP BY
    EmployeeID, DATEPART(month,OrderDate)
```

Although the results of this query give you the information you are looking for, it is not in a very good arrangement for an easy to read report:

EmployeeID	MonthOfYear	NumberOfOrders
2	10	11
1	11	11
3	10	17
1	12	16
2	12	13
1	10	12
3	12	15
3	11	15
2	11	4

What we need to do is to take the results of this query and present each month as a different column for any given employee. Since we can perform sums and counts very easily in SQL, we could create a formula that adds up the number of orders per month for each employee, assigning a value of zero for any data that is not associated with a particular month. In SQL, the IF keyword cannot be used as part of a formula, the CASE keyword can. The basic usage of a CASE statement is:

```
CASE
    WHEN ConditionA THEN ValueUsedWhenConditionAIsTrue
    WHEN ConditionB THEN ValueUsedWhenConditionBIsTrue
    ELSE Value_Used_When_All_Of_The_Above_Conditions_Fail
END
```

Therefore, we can construct the definition for any given month in a similar way to the following:

```
October = SUM(NumberOfOrders * (CASE WHEN MonthOfYear = 10 THEN 1 ELSE 0 END) )
```

This formula multiplies each quantity of orders by either a zero or a one depending upon the month. For this formula to work, we still need to use the resultset that lists each employee's month-by-month counts, so we will use a sub-query to produce this table.

```
SELECT
    EmployeeID,
    October = SUM(NumberOfOrders
        * (CASE
                WHEN MonthOfYear = 10 THEN 1
                ELSE 0 END)),
    November = SUM(NumberOfOrders
        * (CASE
                WHEN MonthOfYear = 11 THEN 1
                ELSE 0 END)),
    December = SUM(NumberOfOrders
        * (CASE
                WHEN MonthOfYear = 12 THEN 1
                ELSE 0 End)),
FROM
    (
        SELECT
            EmployeeID, DATEPART(month, OrderDate) AS MonthOfYear,
            COUNT(OrderID) AS NumberOfOrders
        FROM
            Orders
        GROUP BY
            EmployeeID, DATEPART(month, OrderDate)
    ) AS OrdersPerMonth
GROUP BY EmployeeID
```

An alternative formula is derived from a solution presented by David Rozenshtein, Ph.D, Anatoly Abramovich, Ph.D, and Eugene Birger. Their version is significantly faster since the relatively slow CASE construct is replaced with a mathematical formula. On a sample test database, their solution was about twice as fast as the solution presented above.

Their formula uses the Sign function which returns a value of 1 if its parameter is positive, -1 if it is negative, and zero when the parameter is zero. If the result of subtracting 1 from the MonthOfYear column is zero, then you know that the month is for January. Similarly, by subtracting 2 from the MonthOfYear column, you can test for February, and so on. The ABS function takes the absolute value of this result, so the term ABS(Sign(MonthOfYear - 1)) can only have a value of zero (if the month is January) or one (if it is another month). The (1 - ABS(Sign(MonthOfYear - 1))) portion of the formula converts the result to 1 if the month is January and zero otherwise:

```
SELECT
    EmployeeID,
    January = Sum((1 - ABS(Sign(MonthOfYear - 1)))
        * NumberOfOrders),
    February = Sum((1 - ABS(Sign(MonthOfYear - 2)))
        * NumberOfOrders),
    March = Sum((1 - ABS(Sign(MonthOfYear - 3)))
        * NumberOfOrders),
    April = Sum((1 - ABS(Sign(MonthOfYear - 4)))
        * NumberOfOrders),
    May = Sum((1 - ABS(Sign(MonthOfYear - 5)))
        * NumberOfOrders),
    June = Sum((1 - ABS(Sign(MonthOfYear - 6)))
        * NumberOfOrders),
```

```
        July = Sum((1 - ABS(Sign(MonthOfYear - 7)))
            * NumberOfOrders),
        August = Sum((1 - ABS(Sign(MonthOfYear - 8)))
            * NumberOfOrders),
        September = Sum((1 - ABS(Sign(MonthOfYear - 9)))
            * NumberOfOrders),
        October = Sum((1 - ABS(Sign(MonthOfYear - 10)))
            * NumberOfOrders),
        November = Sum((1 - ABS(Sign(MonthOfYear - 11)))
            * NumberOfOrders),
        December = Sum((1 - ABS(Sign(MonthOfYear - 12)))
            * NumberOfOrders)
FROM
    (
        SELECT
            EmployeeID, DATEPART(month, OrderDate)
            AS MonthOfYear,
            Count(OrderID) As NumberOfOrders
        FROM
            Orders
        GROUP BY
            EmployeeID, DATEPART(month, OrderDate)
    ) AS OrdersPerMonth
ORDER BY EmployeeID
```

One lesson to be learned from this comparison is that a purely mathematical solution will usually be faster than a procedural one.

Using Dynamic Tables

When we use the FROM clause of a SELECT statement, what we are doing is identifying the source of the records for the query. We generally think of these sources as being tables, but they need not be. Views may be used in many queries. Views are objects that are defined using SQL statements to acquire data for us on the fly. If we can use dynamically acquired data from a view, why can't we use it from other sources that produce sets of records?

There are many situations where the information that you need to use is not found in any particular table, such as when you need to query against the results of a previous query. You can take the approach of issuing one query and saving the results in a table, then issuing a second query and saving those results as well, and then performing a third query that joins the first two tables. Not only is this inefficient (especially if done from the client-side), there are timing issues as well. How accurate will your data be? What if someone makes changes to the data in between the time the first query and the second are executed? It is possible to **lock** these tables so that they can't be altered while you are issuing the series of queries. However, if you do this, you risk affecting other operations in the database.

One way to solve this problem is to use queries rather than tables in the FROM clause of the SELECT statement. SQL statements like these comprise a **nested query** (or **sub-query**) and the results produced by these nested queries are sometimes referred to as **dynamic tables**.

Consider the following SQL code that calculates the fraction of time a user spent on-line during one week compared to the amount of time spent on-line during a month:

```
SELECT
    A.UserID,
    A.MinutesOnlineForWeek/B.MinutesOnlineForMonth
FROM
    (
        SELECT UserID, SUM(SessionDuration)
            AS MinutesOnlineForWeek
        FROM
            Sessions
        WHERE
            Login BETWEEN '1999-12-12' AND '1999-12-17'
        GROUP BY UserID
    ) AS A
    INNER JOIN
    (
        SELECT UserID, SUM(SessionDuration)
            AS MinutesOnlineForMonth
        FROM
            Sessions
        WHERE
            Login BETWEEN '1999-12-01' AND '1999-12-31'
        GROUP BY UserID
    ) AS B
    ON (A.UserID = B.UserID)
ORDER BY A.UserID
```

This query calculates the sum total of the time spent on-line for each user during the week of December 12, 1999 and uses the results of the query as the "left" table of the join. Similarly, the second query calculates the sum total of time for each user spent on-line during the entire month and its results are used as the "right" table of the join.

Sub-Queries and JOINS

Generally speaking, a sub-query is any SELECT query that is nested inside another SQL statement to provide a set of records. In some cases, a sub-query performs a similar function to a join since it is providing data. Often a sub-query can be rewritten as a query that uses joins. For example, consider a query that requests the average price of items sold per order for each Employee. This query could be written using a join:

```
SELECT
    Orders.EmployeeID,
    Orders.OrderID,
    AvgUnitPrice = Avg(OD.UnitPrice)
FROM
    OrderDetails AS OD INNER JOIN Orders
    ON (OD.OrderID = Orders.OrderID)
GROUP BY Orders.EmployeeID, Orders.OrderID
ORDER BY Orders.EmployeeID, Orders.OrderID
```

Using a sub-query, the same results can be obtained with:

```
SELECT
    EmployeeID, OrderID,
    AvgUnitPrice = (
        SELECT AVG(OD.UnitPrice)
        FROM OrderDetails AS OD
        WHERE OD.OrderID = Orders.OrderID)
FROM
    Orders
```

The interesting features of the sub-query solution is that for every `OrderID` found in the `Orders` table, a `SELECT` statement is issued that calculates the average unit price for all line items for all line item records that have the same `OrderID` value. Therefore, if the `Orders` table contains 1000 `OrderIDs`, then there will be 1000 average values computed. Because 1000 averages are being calculated one after the other, you would expect that the sub-query would be significantly slower that the `JOIN` query, but timing tests we carried out showed the opposite to be true: the `JOIN` took 378 milliseconds whereas the corresponding sub-query took 285 milliseconds! How could this be? There is no simple explanation, but factors such as the size of the data, the indexes used, and the performance of the physical disk drives may have had an affect on these results. Under different conditions, the `JOIN` query may have performed better.

In general, sub-queries like these do tend to be slower than `JOIN`s, since these sub-queries typically incur more physical I/O operations than joins. One important conclusion to draw from this experiment is that you should time different versions of your queries to determine which is the fastest for your system and your data.

Producing Combinations of Records

Consider a situation where you need to associate every record in one table with every record in a second table. For example, a clothing retailer may need to associate each item with all available sizes or colors. If the retailer has a table of item numbers (often called **SKUs**, for **S**tock **K**eeping **U**nits), and a table of colors, you can produce a result set that shows every combination of SKUs and colors. This type of query is called a **cross join** or **Cartesian join.** To use a cross join, we identify the two tables to join but do not provide any join condition. Without a join condition specifying how the records in the two tables are to be matched, any record from the first table may be matched with any record in the second table:

```
SELECT
    Inventory.SKU, Attributes.Color
FROM
    Inventory, Attributes
```

Since each record from the first table is matched with every record in the second table, the number of records in the result set will be equal to the number of records in the first table multiplied by the number of records from the second table. Therefore, in our above example, if there are 100 SKUs and 5 colors, the result set would contain 500 records.

Cross joins are particularly useful for generating sequences and intervals, which have many uses in databases. Look at the following query. It assumes that we start with two tables, `HoursOfOperation` and `DaysOfOperation`. The `HoursOfOperation` table contains an `HourOfDay` field that holds the values of 0 through 23. The `DaysOfOperation` table contains a `DateOfDay` field that holds date values from December 1, 1999 through December 31, 1999. This query adds each hour to every day to produce 744 record hour by hour lists of times within the month of December.

```
SELECT
    DateAdd(hour,HourOfDay,DateOfDay)
        AS PeriodBeginning
FROM
    HoursOfOperation, DaysOfOperation
ORDER BY DateAdd(hour,HourOfDay,DateOfDay)
```

PeriodBeginning
1999-12-01 00:00:00.000
1999-12-01 01:00:00.000
1999-12-01 02:00:00.000
1999-12-01 03:00:00.000
1999-12-01 04:00:00.000
1999-12-01 05:00:00.000
1999-12-01 06:00:00.000
1999-12-01 07:00:00.000
...

PeriodBeginning
1999-12-31 15:00:00.000
1999-12-31 16:00:00.000
1999-12-31 17:00:00.000
1999-12-31 18:00:00.000
1999-12-31 19:00:00.000
1999-12-31 20:00:00.000
1999-12-31 21:00:00.000
1999-12-31 22:00:00.000
1999-12-31 23:00:00.000

Using Comparison Conditions with Joins

As we have seen, when specifying a query that uses more than one table, we can use the JOIN...ON keywords to specify which fields are referenced when the tables are joined. We did this by specifying that a field in one table would be equal to some other field found in a different table:

```
FROM Clients INNER JOIN ZipCodes
    ON (Clients.Zipcode = Zipcodes.Zipcode)
```

The condition specified in the ON portion of this clause is a direct comparison of two fields and because this condition used an equals sign as the comparison operator, the two fields must be exactly the same for the join to occur for any given record. Who ever said that you *have to* use the equal sign? This condition is a Boolean operation and as long as you place a valid expression which can be resolved into either True or False, you can use that expression in the FROM clause.

Let's consider the scenario where you need to report the number of users on the system. When users sign onto the application, the time that they log in is recorded, as well as the time when they log out. Let's further assume that these times are recorded in a table called Sessions:

Login	Logout	UserID
1999-12-19 12:45:12.000	1999-12-19 14:30:23.000	2
1999-12-19 12:46:43.000	1999-12-19 13:25:20.000	1
1999-12-19 13:10:30.000	1999-12-19 16:35:45.000	3
1999-12-19 15:25:40.000	1999-12-19 17:33:29.000	2
1999-12-19 15:34:32.000	1999-12-19 15:45:56.000	1
1999-12-19 19:02:54.000	1999-12-19 23:23:23.000	4

Our report needs to count how many users were connected to the application during each hour of a given day, for example December 19, 1999. If we try to determine these counts on the client using a procedural language like VBScript, we could loop through each hour of the day and issue a query to count how many users had log in times during each hour. This would tell us how many users logged on and logged off during each hour but what about those users logged on one hour and logged off in another hour? You can get creative and write an algorithm that will solve this puzzle, but SQL offers a much more elegant solution.

To simplify things, let's assume that we have a table named `HoursToProcess` that contains the hour that we wish to report. It contains a single field named `PeriodBeginning` that contains date values from midnight on December 19th 1999 through 11:00pm on the same day:

PeriodBeginning
1999-12-19 00:00:00
1999-12-19 01:00:00
1999-12-19 02:00:00
:
1999-12-19 21:00:00
1999-12-19 22:00:00
1999-12-19 23:00:00

Before we construct the SQL statement, let's take a look at what we have available to work with:

❑   We know that SQL provides a COUNT aggregate function, and since we want to count the users for each hour, it seems like a likely candidate to use in our solution.

❑   Aggregate functions typically require a GROUP BY clause, and since we want to get counts by each hour, it makes sense to group by the `PeriodBeginning` field.

❑   If we want to list all hours, regardless of how many users were logged on, we should use a LEFT JOIN, with the `HoursToProcess` table playing the role of the "left" table.

❑   The report should probably list the midnight hour first, then 1am, then 2am, and so on, so an ORDER BY PeriodBeginning clause will be required.

❑   If a user logs onto the system, logs off and then logs on again all within the same hour, they should only be counted once, so we should use a SELECT DISTINCT, to eliminate counting the same data twice.

We will count a user as being logged on during any given hour if the log on time was on or after the beginning of the hour and the log off time was also on or after the beginning of the hour. Therefore, if a user logged on at 12:46pm, and logged off at 1:25pm, this user would be counted in both the 12:00pm and 1:00pm data. When the tables are joined, we will need to compare the start of each hour with the log in and log out times. The problem is, how do we specify the join condition? If we look at some sample data closely, we should be able to discover a pattern:

Login	Logout	Hours Of Day Online
1:01am	1:59am	1
1:01am	2:01am	1, 2
1:59am	2:01am	1, 2
1:59am	3:01am	1, 2, 3

If we subtract one hour from each of the log in times, then we determine if a record meets our join condition by checking if the `PeriodBeginning` field (which holds the start of each hour) falls between the log in and log out times. In Microsoft SQL Server, we can use the `DateAdd` function to subtract one hour from the log in time.

Pulling all of this together, we will select each hour from `PeriodBeginning` and count the number of distinct users by grouping on `PeriodBeginning`. We will perform a left join using a comparison of the log in and log out times to the `PeriodBeginning` date, where `PeriodBeginning` must be greater than one hour before the log in time and one hour before the log out time. The results will be sorted by `PeriodBeginning`:

```
SELECT DISTINCT
    H.PeriodBeginning, Count(S.UserID) As CountOfUsers
FROM HoursToProcess AS H LEFT JOIN Sessions AS S
    ON (H.PeriodBeginning BETWEEN DateAdd(hour,-1,S.Login) AND S.Logout)
GROUP BY H.PeriodBeginning
ORDER BY H.PeriodBeginning
```

This query produces the following result set under SQL Server:

PeriodBeginning	CountOfUsers	PeriodBeginning	CountOfUsers
1999-12-19 00:00:00.000	0	1999-12-19 12:00:00.000	2
1999-12-19 01:00:00.000	0	1999-12-19 13:00:00.000	3
1999-12-19 02:00:00.000	0	1999-12-19 14:00:00.000	2
1999-12-19 03:00:00.000	0	1999-12-19 15:00:00.000	3
1999-12-19 04:00:00.000	0	1999-12-19 16:00:00.000	2
1999-12-19 05:00:00.000	0	1999-12-19 17:00:00.000	1
1999-12-19 06:00:00.000	0	1999-12-19 18:00:00.000	0
1999-12-19 07:00:00.000	0	1999-12-19 19:00:00.000	1
1999-12-19 08:00:00.000	0	1999-12-19 20:00:00.000	1
1999-12-19 09:00:00.000	0	1999-12-19 21:00:00.000	1
1999-12-19 10:00:00.000	0	1999-12-19 22:00:00.000	1
1999-12-19 11:00:00.000	0	1999-12-19 23:00:00.000	1

If we want to make this query more generic so that it can be used with any date, we can replace the reference to the `HoursToProcess` table with a dynamically generated table. We will still need a table that holds integer values from 0 to 23, which represent the hours of the day, and we will still need to supply a date. Let's assume that a table named `HoursOfOperation` exists and it contains an `HourOfDay` field that holds the values of 0 through 23. To add a certain number of hours to a date, we can use the `DateAdd` function. This function may be used to add different units of time, so one of its required arguments specifies the unit of time being added. This function takes two other arguments, the number of time units being added, and the date.

Pulling all of this together, we construct the following SQL statement:

```
SELECT DISTINCT
    H.PeriodBeginning, Count(S.UserID) AS CountOfUsers
FROM (Select DateAdd(hour,HourOfDay,'Dec 19 1999') AS PeriodBeginning
    From HoursOfOperation) AS H
    LEFT JOIN Sessions AS S
    ON (H.PeriodBeginning Between DateAdd(hour,-1,S.Login) And S.Logout)
GROUP BY H.PeriodBeginning
ORDER BY H.PeriodBeginning
```

To make this query work with other dates, all we need to do is edit the reference to December 19th 1999 so that it contains the date in which we are interested.

Summary

SQL is the *de facto* standard query language for data access. When you construct your ASP application, you will most likely use SQL to access data sources. In this chapter, we looked at the non-procedural nature of SQL statements to acquire, modify and delete information. In these statements, we need to specify what records are to be acted upon. We covered accessing data from single tables using simple `SELECT` statements, and from multiple tables using join conditions in the `WHERE` clause of `SELECT` statements. By using `INNER`, `LEFT`, `RIGHT`, and `CROSS JOIN`s we have a great deal of control over what data is selected and how information from different tables can be combined.

Acquiring, deleting, and changing data are not the only actions we need to perform when working with databases. Having the ability to create tables on the fly provides us with mechanisms to consolidate data for faster, and more efficient, operations. By using transactions, we can combine many related actions into batches of statements that we can guarantee to be applied together as a group, or not at all. The ability to commit command sequences or roll them back as needed is vital to the operation of today's e-commerce applications.

Finally, we took a survey of some creative ways of using queries to solve complicated problems that, if done in a procedural language like Visual Basic or C++, would probably require substantially more time and resources.

With the information covered in this chapter, we should now be able to develop efficient SQL commands that can be used in ASP applications that are sufficiently robust to meet the needs of today's database-driven Internet applications.

4

Stored Procedures, Triggers and Views

There are many places in an application where programming logic is required. If our application uses a database, there are some compelling reasons to place some of this logic in the database itself. One of the reasons for doing this is that when we architect our application, we should segregate the various portions of the application into layers, where each layer encapsulates some specific type of functionality. We do this for maintenance, scalability, and performance purposes. If the application uses a database, the centralizing application logic on the database itself, can offer many advantages over requiring code outside the database to implement the logic. By placing certain strategic application logic inside the database, you can reduce redundancy of code, provide faster overall execution, and maintain state information of your users.

When we want to add programming logic into a database, there are three main ways of achieving this: views, stored procedures, and triggers. We also have the ability to place data validation and restrictions at the table and column level for further control, but such features can only use relatively simple logic.

A **view** is one of several ways to store SQL SELECT statements on the database. Once a view is created, we can use it almost as if it were a table itself, since the SQL statements that define the view select and return records. There are many advantages to using views. They can help simplify queries, isolate application logic, add additional security, and since they can include logic in their definitions, views can provide ways to incorporate business logic.

Stored procedures are functions that, like views, contain a mixture of SQL commands and programming logic. Like views, stored procedures may be used to return a set of records, but unlike views, stored procedures can use parameters and provide return codes. Stored procedures are also compiled on the server for faster execution.

A **trigger** is a special kind of stored procedure that is executed when data is inserted, deleted, or changed in a specified table. Triggers can help to maintain the referential integrity of your data by maintaining consistency among logically related data in different tables. Like stored procedures, triggers are compiled, so they have the potential to improve performance. The main advantage of triggers is that they are automatically executed regardless of who or what caused the data modification.

Used separately or in combination, views, stored procedures, and triggers provide a rich programmable environment for processing and managing your data.

In this chapter, our discussions will include:

- ❑ General overviews of using views, stored procedures, and triggers.
- ❑ The advantages and disadvantages of using each of these database objects.
- ❑ How these database objects are created.
- ❑ How to retrieve and update data through views and stored procedures.
- ❑ How to use triggers to enforce business rules.

Views

A **view** is an alternative way of organizing and presenting data from one or more tables. You can think of a view as a filter through which you can work with the data you are interested in. Unlike tables, views don't store data in the database. Instead, a view stores a SQL SELECT statement. When a view is referenced, the RDBMS uses the SQL defined in the view to query the database and access a resultset. This allows us to use views as data sources, just as we do tables. This is why views are described often as "virtual tables". When the view is used in a SELECT statement, the rows and columns referenced in the view are returned. When used with INSERT or UPDATE statements, the rows and columns mapped by the view are modified. Similarly, views may be used to delete data.

Creating and Using Views for Data Selection

To illustrate how views are used to select data, imagine that you had an employee table that contained records of all employees, including those no longer with the firm. Assume that the table contains a Boolean field named `Active`, which has the value `True` for current employees and `False` for former employees. Naturally, most of the interaction with this table will be for current employees only. When we query this table, we can restrict the results to current employees by using a WHERE clause, as follows:

```
SELECT * FROM Employees WHERE Active = True
```

If we were to use this same query as the definition of a view, we would be able to use the view to filter out former employees. For example, if the view was called `ActiveEmployees`, then we could use the following to return the same results as above:

```
SELECT * FROM ActiveEmployees
```

In order to create a view for this SQL statement, we use the CREATE VIEW command. To illustrate the use of this command, consider the following code that may be used with Microsoft SQL Server, Oracle or DB2:

```
CREATE VIEW ActiveEmployees
AS
SELECT * FROM Employees WHERE Active = True;
```

Only after this CREATE VIEW command has been executed (for instance, in a query utility such as Microsoft Query Analyzer, SQL*Plus or the DB2 Command Center), will the view object exist in the database.

The SQL-3 specification for the CREATE VIEW command is as follows:

```
CREATE VIEW view_name [(column [ ,...n ])]
AS
query_expression
[WITH CHECK OPTION]
```

The optional column attribute in this syntax allows us to give new names for each column that is returned by the view. This works just like declaring aliases in a SELECT statement – if we omit naming each column, then the view columns acquire the same names as the columns returned in the SELECT statement. Naming columns is only required when two or more columns may otherwise have the same name or when a column is derived from a calculation.

WITH CHECK OPTION is only used when the view will be further used to modify or insert data. We will discuss this attribute when we discuss using views for data modification below.

The SQL-3 standard specifies a few restrictions on the SELECT statement that defines the contents of a view. For instance, views cannot include the ORDER BY clause or use the INTO keyword in the SELECT statement. Vendor-specific implementations of SQL may differ somewhat in these restrictions, so you should check your RDBMS documentation. One such example, is that under Microsoft SQL Server 2000, an ORDER BY clause may be used in the view definition if there is also a TOP predicate in the select list of the SELECT statement.

It is interesting to note that we can reference existing views when we use the CREATE VIEW command to create a new view. This makes a lot of sense, since we can use the name of a view in a SELECT statement and a view is defined by a SELECT statement. Therefore, we can create a new view from our existing ActiveEmployees view:

```
CREATE VIEW ActiveMaleEmployees
AS
SELECT * FROM ActiveEmployees WHERE Gender<>'F'
```

Views and Permissions

By using a view, you can provide access to one or more tables, or parts of tables, without giving the user direct access to the table. For example, consider an Employee table that contains confidential information. You may want to deny direct access to this table for all company staff except for people in the Payroll department. Other users may be allowed access to the nonconfidential data in this table, such as FirstName, LastName, and Telephone, by referencing a view that selects only those columns. Furthermore, these users may be given limited access permissions for the table, such as the ability to read records from the table but not the ability to add to or change records.

Views, like all objects in a database, have permissions associated with them that allow or deny use by individual users or groups of users. By using the GRANT and REVOKE commands in SQL, permissions must be assigned on an object-by-object basis. Users may access only those views where they have the appropriate permissions. Also, any operations that are allowed on the view are determined by what permissions have been granted to the user. Permissions that may be granted for a view are the same as those for a table: SELECT, INSERT, UPDATE, and DELETE (and Declarative Referential Integrity in Microsoft SQL Server).

Typically, a view is created by the database administrator or developer who has the appropriate permissions to access the tables that the view uses. After the view has been created, permissions are assigned to individual users or groups of users so that they can use the view. Permissions to the view are assigned using the GRANT statement, which uses the following general syntax:

```
GRANT operations ON viewname
TO users
```

Such as:

```
GRANT INSERT, UPDATE, DELETE ON ActiveMaleEmployees
TO PayrollDept, JohnM
```

> Note: A user must have the correct permissions for a table before he can use its data in a view. That applies to reading data using SELECT as well as manipulation data using INSERT, UPDATE and DELETE.

Changing and Deleting Views

As with other objects in a database, you may need to change or delete a view. How you can delete or change views is fairly straightforward, but a few points are worth mentioning.

Deleting a View

To delete a view, use the DROP VIEW statement:

```
DROP VIEW ActiveMaleEmployees
```

Unless you are the owner of the view, have system administrator permissions, or have been granted explicit permission to do so, you will not be allowed to delete the view.

Redefining a View

In ANSI SQL, there is no command for changing the definition of a view. If you need to change the view's definition, you will need to drop the view and then recreate it. Just bear in mind that when you delete an object, all permissions associated with that object for all users will be lost and you will need to regrant these permissions as needed.

Although the ANSI SQL specification doesn't allow for the changing of view definitions, most major RDBMSs provide this functionality. If you are using Microsoft SQL Server, Sybase SQL Server, or Oracle, you may use the ALTER VIEW statement. The major benefit of using ALTER VIEW is that view is changed while retaining its permissions.

```
ALTER VIEW ActiveMaleEmployees
AS
SELECT * FROM ActiveEmployees WHERE Gender='M'
```

Oracle offers the REPLACE option in the CREATE VIEW command which functions just like the ALTER VIEW command.

```
CREATE OR REPLACE VIEW ActiveMaleEmployees
AS
SELECT * FROM ActiveEmployees WHERE Gender='M'
```

Renaming a View

The SQL standard does not provide a command for changing the name of a view. The workaround to this is to drop the view and then recreate it using the new name. Unfortunately, when you drop the view, all permissions associated with the object are lost. You will need to reapply all permissions associated with that object for all of your users after recreating the view under the new name.

To help avoid this inconvenience, most of the major RDBMSs provide their own means to rename views. For example, in Microsoft SQL Server 2000, you may rename a view using the Enterprise Manger utility. To do so, first right-click on the name of the view, select rename from the pop-up menu and type the new name. Next, double-click on the view's name to display its properties and then edit the definition of the view so that it uses the new name.

You may also rename the view with the system procedure sp_rename. Here is the syntax:

```
EXEC sp_rename oldname, newname
```

For example, to rename ActiveMaleEmployees to EmployeesActiveMale:

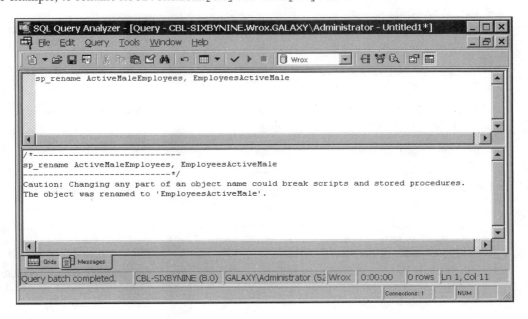

As with using the rename menu item to rename a view, you will still need to edit the definition of the view so that it uses the new name. Of course, if you change the name of a view, you will need to update any other view or code that refers to it to use the new name.

Using Views for Data Modification

Views may be used to insert, delete, or update data. To illustrate this use of views, consider the following SQL statement that uses the `ActiveEmployees` view created above:

```
DELETE *
FROM ActiveEmployees
WHERE EmployeeID = 1868
```

This statement would be functionally equivalent to using:

```
DELETE *
FROM Employees
WHERE Active = True AND EmployeeID = 1868
```

As with using views for selecting data, all we have to do is reference the name of the view in the SQL statement, and the operation is mapped into the view's result set. Unlike using views for selecting data, there are a number of restrictions on using views for deletes:

- ❑ The view can only reference a single table in its FROM clause. In other words, you can't use views to delete records if the view includes a join.

- ❑ The query expression in the view cannot use aggregate functions in the select list, such as SUM, COUNT, or MAX. Aggregate functions can be used in a subquery in the FROM clause as long as the values returned by the functions are not modified.

- ❑ The query expression in the view doesn't use TOP, GROUP BY, or DISTINCT.

- ❑ The FROM clause in the query expression references at least one table. For example, the following view cannot be used for deletes. This view uses only the ANSI reserved word Current_Date to return the system date:

  ```
  CREATE VIEW ThisMoment AS
  SELECT RightNow = Current_Date
  ```

  In contrast, this next view can be used for deletes, since it returns system date along with a value referenced from an existing table:

  ```
  CREATE VIEW CurrentEmployeeCount AS
  SELECT COUNT(*), AsOf = Current_Date FROM Employees
  ```

These restrictions are nearly the same for using views to insert or update records. There are two exceptions:

- ❑ Data inserts and updates can be made on views that include joins, but the UPDATE or INSERT statement has to be written so that it modifies data in only one of the base tables referenced in the FROM clause of the view.

- ❑ All columns being modified must adhere to all restrictions for the data modification statement as if they were executed directly against the base table. This applies to column nullability, constraints, identity columns, and columns with rules and/or default values.

Data Modification Issues with Views

When using views, we need to be aware of some wider database issues when adding, modifying, and deleting data. Specifically, we need to be aware of data integrity (as with inserting data directly into a table), and we need to be aware of the possibility of inserting data into a table through a view which cannot be accessed through that view.

Data Integrity Constraints and Views

As we know from our earlier chapter on database design, data integrity provides for consistency between related tables within a database and helps ensure that the business model is being followed. For example, let us assume that a bank has a list of customers in the Customers table and a list of customer accounts in the Accounts table. It wouldn't make sense to allow a new account to be added to the Accounts table unless an associated customer exists in the Customers table. Integrity rules on the Accounts table will force a new customer record to be created before a new account can be added.

These integrity rules must be followed regardless of whether the table is modified directly or indirectly because of a view. In other words, you can't get around these integrity rules by using a view. If you attempt an action that violates these rules, an error will be thrown and the operation will be rolled back.

Disappearing Data

Unfortunately, there are some situations where it may become confusing when you use a view for data modification. This may happen when you insert or update records using a view containing a WHERE clause, and you add or change records such that they can no longer be selected by the view. To illustrate this, consider the view defined as follows:

```
CREATE VIEW MISGroup AS
SELECT * FROM Employees WHERE DeptName = 'MIS'
```

This view works with only a single table, so we may use it for selecting as well as inserting and updating records. Let us assume that when we issue the statement:

```
SELECT * FROM MISGroup WHERE LastName = 'Remes'
```

We get back the following records:

EmpID	LastName	FirstName	DeptName	Gender
1762	Remes	Brian	MIS	M
2387	Remes	Brenden	MIS	M

We could then use this view to add a new record to the Employees table. However, we can add a record using this view as follows:

```
INSERT INTO MISGroup (EmpID, LastName, FirstName, DeptName, Gender)
VALUES (3401, 'Remes', 'Elizabeth', 'Sales', 'F')
```

The row can be inserted into the table through the view but it cannot be retrieved and subsequently displayed through the same view. The row effectively disappears when retrieved through the view, but it can nevertheless be accessed through the table upon which the view is based.

127

To avoid potential confusion that may occur in such a situation, we can add the WITH CHECK OPTION clause to our view definition. This clause will prevent insert and update operations from SQL statements that do not satisfy the requirements of the WHERE clause provided.

```
CREATE VIEW MISGroup AS
SELECT * FROM Employees WHERE DeptName = 'MIS'
WITH CHECK OPTION
```

If an attempt was made to insert or update records for employees not in the MIS group using this view, the operation would fail and an error would be raised. With Microsoft SQL Server, the error information returned includes the following:

```
Server: Msg 550, Level 16, State 1, Line 1
The attempted insert or update failed because the target view either specifies
WITH CHECK OPTION or spans a view that specifies WITH CHECK OPTION and one or more
rows resulting from the operation did not qualify under the CHECK OPTION
constraint.
The statement has been terminated.
```

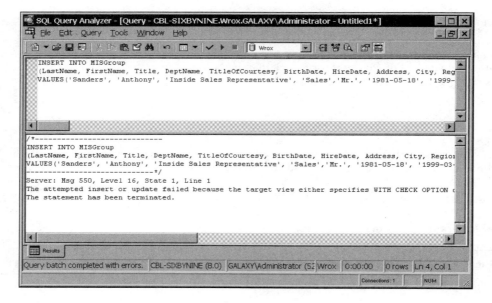

The Advantages of Views

There are a number of advantages to using views, which range from the simplification of SQL statements, to being able to customize how the data is presented, to development efficiencies and enhanced security.

Simplification of SQL Statements

Views make our queries simpler because they can, in many cases, substitute for lengthy SQL statements.

If we have a view defined that performs a complex join, we can use the view instead of the complex join. For example, if we have a view called AuthorPayments that is defined to invoke the following SQL statement:

```
CREATE VIEW AuthorPayments
(AuthID, BookID, Amount, ActivityDate)
AS
SELECT
    t.AuthID,
    t.ISBN,
    Amount = (t.price * r.royalty) * s.total_sales
FROM
    titles AS t INNER JOIN royalties AS r
    ON t.ISBN = r.ISBN
    LEFT JOIN sales AS s
    ON t.ISBN = s.ISBN
```

If we wanted to determine the amount of royalties paid to each author, we could use the relatively simple SQL statement that refers to the view:

```
SELECT AuthID, SUM(Amount) FROM AuthorPayments GROUP BY AuthID
```

Because the user doesn't have to specify all the conditions and qualifications every time operations are performed on the data, the SQL statements are easier to understand and construct. If a view is not used, the same results would require a much more complicated nested query, such as:

```
SELECT AuthID, SUM(Amount)
FROM
    (
    SELECT
        t.AuthID,
        t.ISBN,
        Amount = (t.price * r.royalty) * s.total_sales
    FROM
        titles AS t INNER JOIN royalties AS r
        ON t.ISBN = r.ISBN
        LEFT JOIN sales AS s
        ON t.ISBN = s.ISBN
    ) AS A
GROUP BY AuthID
```

Easier Maintenance

If you code your applications to use views, you are providing the ability to change the names of tables or to use different tables in the future. By using views, if you need to change the name of a table, you can hide the renaming of the table by updating only the views that you use and not the code that calls the view. If you don't use views and a table name is changed, you would be forced to modify your application's source code, recompile it and then redistribute the application.

Most applications will undergo modification from time to time. However, by using views in your applications, you will find that maintenance will be much easier. Views help to shield applications from changes in the structure of the tables if such changes become necessary. For example, say the database is restructured so that a table is replaced by two new tables and the original table is dropped. If you were not using a view to access this data, you would be forced to recode all references to the table to include a join. If you were using a view, you would only have to make a single code change: alter the definition of the view to include the join. Although using a view doesn't shield your application for every change made to a table, it can make these changes much easier to manage.

129

Access to Data Can be Customized

As we have seen, views can be constructed to provide access to parts of one or more tables. The records that are returned may be restricted with a WHERE clause to provide "horizontal partitioning" of the data. The columns that are returned by a view may be specific fields from the table(s) providing "vertical partitioning". In addition, the columns returned may include calculations based upon the fields or system information. Such capabilities allow us to construct very customized presentations of data. Having such abilities is particularly important when users that share the same database have different interests, skill levels, and security settings. Here are a few examples to illustrate how views may be used to customize access to data:

❑ One view of a sales table may show month end sales figures by region that may be of interest to upper management. A district manager may want to see sales per salesperson for each office, so he may access the sales data using one view, while the shipping and receiving department may use a different view to show sales for each product.

❑ Power users that have access to the database may query data using views in their SELECT statements without having to specify details of how the various tables are related.

❑ Views may be used to limit access to sensitive data for various applications or for users with different levels of authority. For instance, we might not want nonmanagers to be able to access all fields from the Employees table, such as the Salary field, so we can use a view to return only particular columns and grant all users access to this view. To prevent nonmanagers accessing the whole table, we can make sure that they do not have the permissions to access the Employees table directly. Alternatively, we can create a second view for accessing the entire table and give only manager permission to use the view.

❑ We can also use views to perform calculations, translations of data, or to acquire data from multiple sources. The following view definition performs a UNION query that returns rows from two different tables. The first table contains all active full-time employees and the second table returns temporary employees. Together, the rows returned represent all staff currently employed:

```
CREATE VIEW ActiveEmployees AS
BEGIN
    SELECT
        FirstName + ' ' + LastName AS EmployeeName,
        Department,
        Phone,
        Email,
        Category =
            CASE
                WHEN EmpCode = 1 THEN 'Exempt'
                ELSE 'Hourly'
            END
        FROM Employees
        WHERE Active = True
    UNION
    SELECT
        FirstName + ' ' + LastName AS EmployeeName,
        Department,
        Phone,
        Email,
        Category = 'Hourly'
    FROM TemporaryStaff;
END
```

Stored Procedures

If your application is to get the most from your database server, the use of stored procedures is essential. Stored procedures are code modules that are precompiled, optimized, and saved on the server. They contain functionality that, like views, use SQL commands. Although views may be able to contain simple logic, such as a CASE statement in a calculation, stored procedures can contain robust program logic and flow control. A single stored procedure can consist of one or more SQL statements; they can use views and call other stored procedures.

Because stored procedures can contain multiple SQL statements as well as programming logic, we can perform a series of related operations by executing a single stored procedure. These could even be transactional operations, such as posting a credit for one account along with a debit for a different account. Such operations could produce output for a series of analyses, for example:

```
Summary of Sales by Month
Month Ending Monthly Sales
------------ ---------------
Jan          202,143.71
Feb          177,749.26
Mar          213,051.30
Apr          250,187.45
May          75,567.75
Jun          78,198.10
Jul          141,295.99
Aug          133,301.03
Sep          82,964.00

Year to Date Sales
Statistic    Value
------------ ---------------
Sum          1,354,458.59
Max          250,187.45
Min          75,567.75
Average      150,495.39

The largest single sale was: 23,076.10
The most active salesperson was: Mike Russell
```

Advantages of Using Stored Procedures

Using stored procedures has many advantages, many of which make use of the rich functionality of the RDBMS itself, including improved design, better database performance, greater efficiency in the execution of tasks, and improved security.

Faster Execution

One of the most important advantages of stored procedures is that they are compiled. In most modern RDBMSs, there is a tremendous difference in performance between executing precompiled routines and the equivalent commands sent to the database engine as SQL statements.

To understand why stored procedures are fast, we need to discuss what happens when a SQL statement is executed. The first thing that happens is that the text of the SQL statement is transmitted over the network to the server. Once the server receives this information, the SQL statement itself is parsed to determine just what is being requested. During this parsing process, the statements may be reordered or rewritten for better efficiency. For instance, the IN operator used in a SELECT statement might be rewritten as a series of OR conditions. Now that the server knows what information needs to be processed, it starts to figure out the best strategy for performing the requested operations. As the optimizer steps through the commands, it determines if there is more than one way to process each statement, and if so, each way is recorded and analyzed. The end result is something that resembles a decision tree, which is called a **query plan**.

In order to determine which sequence of commands in the query plan produces the best performance, some information is needed about the data that is being processed by the query. Information about the database is then checked, such as how many rows are in each table, how much storage is needed to hold these rows, and what indexes are available. Such information is referred to as **database statistics**. The RDBMS navigates the query plan's decision tree and by using these statistics, tries to estimate the cost (that is the time required to execute) for each of these alternatives. The query engine then selects the path in the query plan that is the most efficient. The result is called an **execution plan**.

With stored procedures, most of this work is done when the procedure is saved. The query optimizer is able to parse the statements and generate the query plan. When the stored procedure is called, all the optimizer has to do is determine which of the execution plans, stored in the query plan, to employ. Once an execution plan has been selected, it is cached in memory and reused if the stored procedure is called again. The amount of time saved by having the query plan available right at the start can be significant.

Multiple Statements Executed With a Single Call

Since a stored procedure may contain more than one SQL statement, a *single request* to run a stored procedure can invoke *multiple* SQL statements. This has several advantages. To illustrate these advantages, imagine that a stored procedure contains ten SQL statements. By having these statements in a single stored procedure, we have the benefit of determining the query plan in advance. Another benefit comes when remote applications are used to call the stored procedure. Without a stored procedure, the remote application will need to make ten round trips to the server, thus causing delays and increasing network traffic.

Easier Maintenance

Like views, stored procedures allow for easier maintenance for both your database and your applications. If the database changes, you may need only update the stored procedure without having to touch any of the applications that use the database. Also, if more than one application uses the same database, a set of common stored procedures could quite possibly be used to reduce the amount of code that needs to be maintained.

Better Code Organization

One advantage of using stored procedures is that it helps centralize your code. Centralizing code on a database is better than requiring data access applications to implement the same logic. Having redundant code like this would increase the time and cost required to maintain the applications and would greatly increase the likelihood of errors and discrepancies among the applications. Stored procedures assist in achieving a consistent implementation of logic across applications. The SQL statements and logic needed to perform a commonly performed task can be designed, coded, and tested once in stored procedures, and then any application needing to perform these tasks can simply execute these stored procedures. Coding business logic into a small set of stored procedures also offers a single point of control for ensuring that business rules are correctly enforced.

It should be pointed out that, although placing logic in a database has advantages, it is usually not appropriate to place *all* of your application's logic there. In the n-tier application model, some of the business rules may be better located in a COM component used to access the database. By distributing the logic between the various tiers of your application, you can avoid overworking any given server. You must strike a balance between placing your logic in the database or within the components.

Customization of Data and Operations

Like views, stored procedures can be used to customize the presentation of data and simplify data access. It is common to allow power user access to portions of the data in the database. Rather than requiring these users to know SQL well enough to construct queries, power users can execute stored procedure to acquire and analyze data. Not only will this save time for the user, it will help avoid data errors from poorly constructed queries. By providing stored procedures for these users to work with, you can avoid such disasters as a user deleting the entire contents of a table by mistake or performing a join that takes an hour to run and locks out other users in the process.

Better Security

Stored procedures, like all other objects in the database, will have permissions associated with them that allow or deny user access. By prohibiting direct access to the tables and forcing access through the stored procedure, you have greater control over security, since you can dictate what data is accessed and how it is accessed.

For example, you may want users of your web site to log in before they can access personal or confidential information. You would not want to allow users to select rows from the table that contains the usernames and passwords for the site, so you would revoke all access to this table except through the stored procedure and grant access only to the administrator. The web site log in page would collect the credentials from the user, and post the details to the database, invoking a log in stored procedure and passing the details as parameters. This stored procedure would check the validity of these credentials and a success or failure value would be returned to the page that called it. With this information, the web page could then respond accordingly.

Using Stored Procedures and Views

Although stored procedures and views may be used to produce the same results in many situations, the use of each has advantages. Used together, views and stored procedures provide a better, more secure, and flexible environment.

Stored procedures also have the ability to accept and return parameters where views cannot. Views, at the most basic level, act as filters for existing information that can only be accessed as part of a SQL statement. On the other hand, stored procedures are more dynamic since they can contain multiple SQL statements as well as procedural language commands to create algorithms. Both may be used to return records, though stored procedures cannot be used in the FROM clause of a SELECT statement whereas a view can.

Ideally, applications will use views to access data from stored procedures, which means that these two object types complement each other: stored procedures allow access from the users to the RDBMS, while views allow access to the data from the stored procedures. This delegation of function between the two objects can provide better security than would be possible if they were used independently. It can also make the calling application less sensitive to changes to the database structure. With control flow language constructs, such as looping and condition statements, the stored procedure can determine which view is appropriate for use under specific conditions.

Running a Stored Procedure

Stored procedures may be run using the SQL command EXECUTE from a query utility, such as Microsoft SQL Server's Query Analyzer, or a call to the database from a data access technology such as ADO. The syntax for the EXECUTE command is pretty simple:

```
EXECUTE procedure_name
```

Many RDBMSs allow you to abbreviate the command EXECUTE to EXEC. Some, like Microsoft SQL Server, even allow you to skip the EXEC keyword altogether by supplying just the name of the stored procedure; this is only allowed if executing the stored procedure is the first command submitted.

If the stored procedure has any parameters, their values are placed after the name of the stored procedure in a comma-separated list, for example:

```
EXECUTE spGetpendingAccounts 'January 23 2000'
```

When a stored procedure executes, the SQL statements defined in the procedure will execute sequentially. If the stored procedure selects records, these records are returned to the application that called the stored procedure. For example, the following illustration shows the results that are returned when a stored procedure is invoked in Microsoft's Query Analyzer:

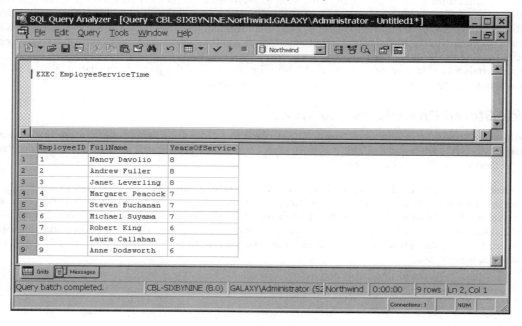

We will look at calling stored procedures from an ASP application via ADO in Chapter 7.

Creating Stored Procedures

The process required to create a stored procedure is not very different from what is required to create a view. The SQL command to do this is CREATE PROCEDURE:

```
CREATE PROCEDURE proc_name (parameters)
AS
BEGIN
   sql_statements
END
```

This command, like any SQL command, needs to be executed on the RDBMS to create the stored procedure. You can run this command in a query utility, such as Microsoft's Query Analyzer, Oracle's SQL*Plus or DB2's Command Center. Each of these major RDBMSs provide editors and tools to help build your stored procedures. Many developers find that it is more convenient to construct the code in a query tool, and carry out preliminary testing there, before creating a stored procedure with the CREATE PROCEDURE command.

To change the contents of a stored procedure, you may use the ALTER PROCEDURE command. Apart from the difference in the name of the command, ALTER PROCEDURE has exactly the same syntax as CREATE PROCEDURE. Like ALTER VIEW, the primary benefit of using this command, rather than deleting and then recreating the stored procedure, is that you will retain whatever permissions were granted to users for the object. This is a *very important* feature whose value should not be underestimated.

Creating Stored Procedures in Microsoft SQL Server

As an alternative to typing the CREATE PROCEDURE and ALTER PROCEDURE commands in a query tool, let's take a look at how we can use Microsoft SQL Server's Enterprise Manager. This example assumes that you already have a Microsoft SQL Server database. To start a new stored procedure, select the Stored Procedures group under your database. Next, right-click and choose New Stored Procedure...

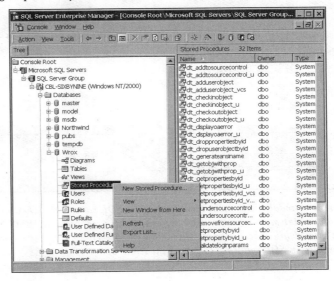

The Stored Procedure Properties editor will then be displayed:

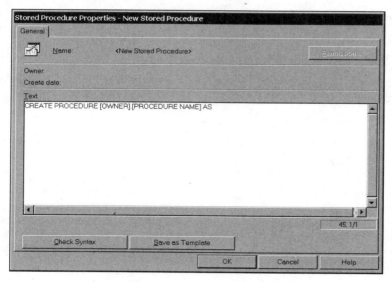

In this simple editor, you will enter the SQL commands for your routine. The editor opens with the command used to create the routine already supplied – the CREATE PROCEDURE statement. The first thing needed is to name this routine. The [OWNER] portion of the name identifies an owner if you wish to create the stored procedure for someone else. If you omit this, it is assumed that the owner is the current logged on user. Microsoft SQL Server allows for spaces in the names of its objects, so the bracket characters are used as delimiters for the names. Although including spaces may make the procedure name easier to read, it is best not to use them.

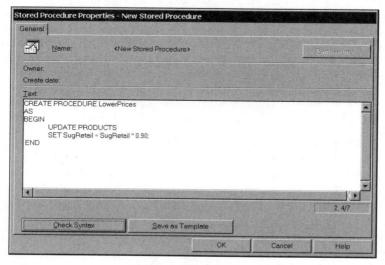

*The above example introduces **statement terminators** for SQL statements. These are used to indicate the end of a statement when multiple statements are used. Some RDBMS products, such as Oracle, require them, while others, such as Microsoft SQL Server, do not. The mostwidely used statement terminator in SQL implementations is the semicolon.*

After keying in your commands, select the OK button to cause Microsoft SQL Server to check the code, compile the statements, and save the stored procedure.

Creating Stored Procedures in Oracle

We can of course use the SQL*Plus utility to create a stored procedure in Oracle, specifying the appropriate SQL command:

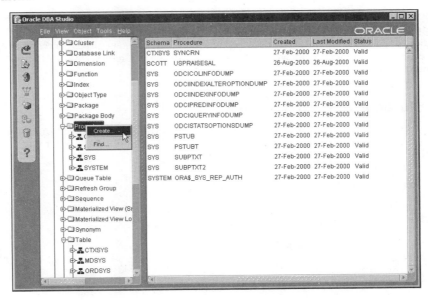

Note that the forward slash (/) character is used to indicate the end of procedure.

However, we can also create stored procedures using DBA Studio. In the tree view in the left-hand pane, right-click on the Procedure node in the Schema group, and select Create... from the context menu:

This opens the **Create Procedure** dialog, which allows us to specify the name of the procedure and the SQL statements which it will contain:

All the SQL for the procedure, except for the CREATE PROCEDURE keywords themselves, must be included, so parameters must be listed in parentheses with their data types before the initial AS keyword. When we've finished writing the procedure, we simply click on the **Create** button.

> Note that Oracle stored procedures may not contain SELECT statements which return datasets. This means that we cannot retrieve OLE DB rowsets or ADO recordsets directly from an Oracle stored procedure. We will see in Chapter 15 how to get around this problem.

Creating Stored Procedures in DB2

DB2 allows us to create stored procedures using the standard CREATE PROCEDURE SQL command. For example, to create a stored procedure that returns all columns in the EMPLOYEE table of the SAMPLE database:

```
CREATE PROCEDURE DB2ADMIN.uspSelectEmp()
RESULT SETS 1
LANGUAGE SQL
P1:BEGIN
    DECLARE cursor1 CURSOR WITH RETURN FOR
    SELECT * FROM ADMINISTRATOR.EMPLOYEE;
    OPEN cursor1;
END P1
```

Note that we need to specify the number of resultsets that will be returned from the procedure, and the language in which the procedure is written. We must also declare, and open, a cursor if we want our stored procedure to return a resultset; we will discuss cursors later on in this chapter.

DB2 allows us a number of ways of executing SQL commands against a database. For example, we could use the **Command Center**, the **Script Center**, or the **Command Window** (passing the SQL statements as a parameter to the db2 command):

Note that we must first connect to the database, and that the entire CREATE PROCEDURE statement (up to END P1) must be entered as a single line, if we use either of these utilities.

However, DB2 also provides a GUI for creating stored procedures, either in SQL or in Java, called the **Stored Procedure Builder**. This provides a wizard which automatically generates much of the SQL for us – for example, in declaring and opening the cursor – as well as handling the parameters.

Note that we can't create stored procedures in DB2 using the Control Center.

To create a stored procedure using this wizard, open the Stored Procedure Builder and create a new project. Expand the tree, right-click on the Stored Procedures node, and select Insert | SQL Stored Procedure Using Wizard... from the context menu:

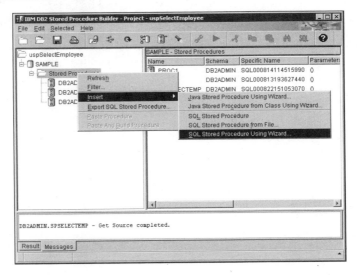

The first screen of this wizard requires us simply to specify a name for the procedure. This name is in the form *Schema_name*. *Procedure_name*, for example, DB2ADMIN.uspSelectEmployee. If the schema isn't specified, the procedure will be assigned to the default schema for the currently logged on user.

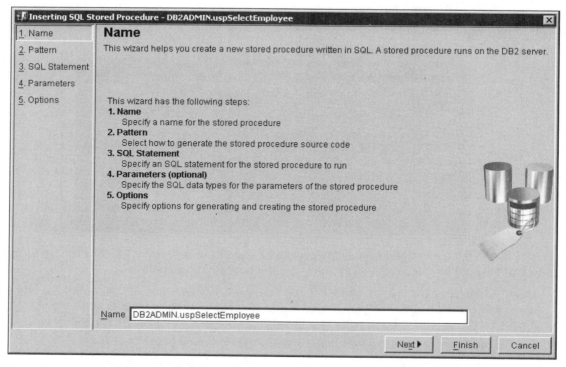

The next step is to specify the general characteristics of the procedure. First, we must decide whether the stored procedure will consist of a single SQL statement, or whether the procedure will choose one SQL statement from several, or whether no SQL statement will be generated. If the stored procedure contains multiple SQL statements, a parameter will be passed to the procedure to determine which statement will be executed. Secondly, we can also indicate whether the procedure will return a resultset (that is, if it contains SELECT statements that aren't assigned to a variable within the procedure), and we can specify how errors will be handled. If an error occurs when the procedure is run, we can either cause an exception to be thrown, or assign a SQL error code to an output argument:

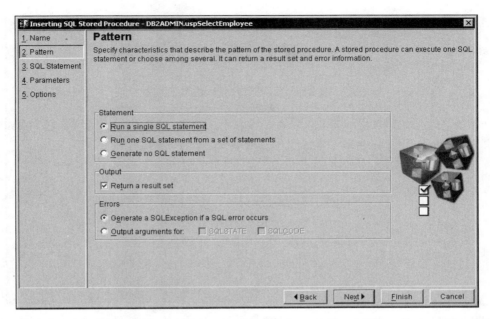

The wizard then allows us to enter the SQL statement for the stored procedure. Parameters used within the procedure should be prefixed by a colon (:), so that the wizard can automatically generate the parameter declarations for the procedure:

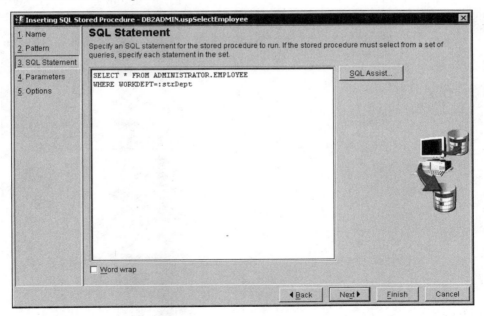

The next screen allows us to enter new parameters for the stored procedures, and to check the ones created by the wizard. We can specify the mode (whether this is an input or output parameter), the data type and the name for the parameter:

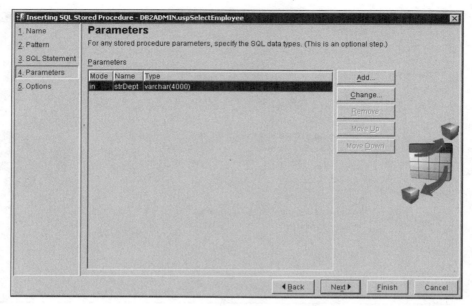

Finally, there are a couple of options we can specify for the procedure. First, we can assign a specific name (of no more than eight characters), which is used to identify the stored procedure uniquely from other database objects. If we don't assign a specific name, DB2 will generate one for us. Secondly, we can specify whether to compile the stored procedure immediately, or only generate the SQL code which builds the procedure. Lastly, we can choose whether to enable debugging for the procedure:

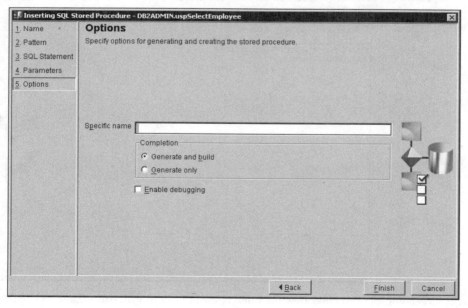

Clicking on the Finish button will now cause the wizard to generate the SQL for the stored procedure, and build the procedure, if this option was chosen.

Deleting a Stored Procedure

To delete a stored procedure from the database, use the DROP PROCEDURE command:

```
DROP PROCEDURE procedure_name
```

As with any other database object, if a stored procedure is dropped, and then recreated, all permissions that were assigned to the original object will need to be regranted.

Deleting a Stored Procedure from Microsoft SQL Server

In addition to using the DROP PROCEDURE statement, we can delete a stored procedure from within Enterprise Manager. To do so, simply right-click on the procedure name from the Stored Procedures folder, and then select Delete from the context menu:

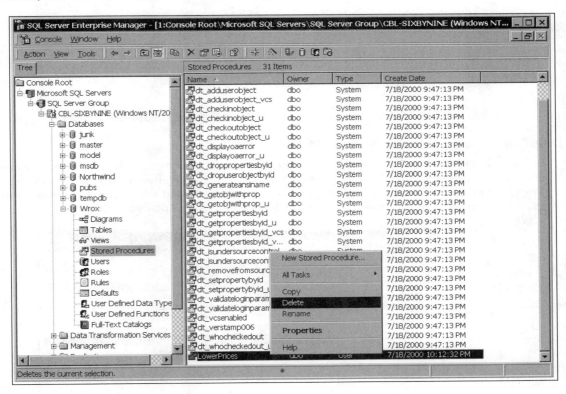

Deleting a Stored Procedure from Oracle

This is equally easy: we simply right-click on the name of the stored procedure we wish to remove in DBA Studio and select Remove from the context menu:

Deleting a Stored Procedure from DB2

In DB2, as well as deleting a stored procedure through a DROP PROCEDURE SQL command, we can use either the Control Center or the Stored Procedure Builder to remove procedures. In either case, we simply right-click on the name of the procedure we want to delete, and select Drop. In Control Center, stored procedures are found in the Stored Procedures group under Application Objects:

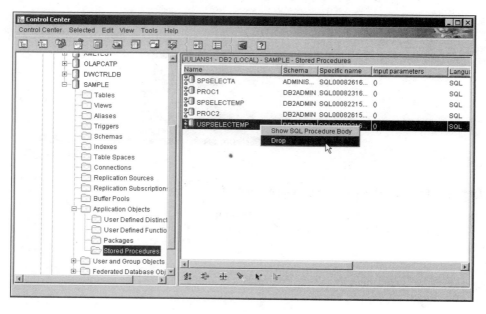

Recompiling a Stored Procedure

When a stored procedure is saved, a query plan is determined. This query plan will be used to determine an execution plan when the stored procedure is first executed. This execution plan will be reused with later calls to the stored procedure. Normally, having a predetermined execution plan makes the execution of a stored procedure much faster, since it doesn't need to be created every time.

The problem with this is that the execution plan may not work as expected. Recall that the execution plan is based upon the database statistics at the time when the plan was created. If the database changes considerably – and databases are constantly changing – then this plan may no longer be the best one to use. Actions such as adding indexes, changing data in indexed columns, and changing table definitions can change the database enough to make your stored procedures run sluggishly or not at all. Therefore, it is often advantageous to periodically recompute the execution plan so that we get the best performance possible. To cause a new execution plan to be created we need to *recompile* the stored procedure.

In general, you should consider recompiling your stored procedures under any of the following circumstances:

- ❑ The initial roll out of the application after test data has been purged.
- ❑ After large bulk processes, like importing many new records or mass deletions.
- ❑ When columns have been added, removed, or changed from one or more tables used by the stored procedure.
- ❑ When indexes have been added, removed, or changed from one or more tables used by the stored procedure.
- ❑ After restoring a backup.

There are a few ways to recompile a stored procedure. The first is to edit and resave the stored procedure, for example, by using ALTER PROCEDURE. In fact, this is the only use for ALTER PROCEDURE in Oracle's PL/SQL. The act of resaving the stored procedure will cause the RDBMS to rebuild the execution plan. Another way to recompile a stored procedure is using a WITH RECOMPILE clause in the CREATE PROCEDURE statement. This clause forces a new execution plan to be computed with each execution of the stored procedure, rather than caching the plan in memory:

```
CREATE PROCEDURE procedure_name
WITH RECOMPILE
AS
BEGIN
    sql_statements
END
```

It is important to stress that when creating the procedure using the WITH COMPILE option, the RDBMS will recompile the procedure before *every* requested execution. This can cause serious performance problems since we give up the advantage of having a precompiled execution plan. This should only be done when the cost of computing the plan with each execution is outweighed by the increased efficiency gained with an up-to-date execution plan. The WITH RECOMPILE option is usually used when frequent mass changes are made to the data or if the database structure itself changes frequently.

Different RDBMSs will provide other mechanisms for forcing a stored procedure to recompile. Microsoft SQL Server and Sybase SQL Server provide a system stored procedure, sp_recompile, that forces a new execution plan to be determined for a stored procedure the next time that procedure is executed. The WITH RECOMPILE option should be used with care.

Coding for Stored Procedures

By using the CREATE PROCEDURE command, the actual creation of a stored procedure is easy – the hard part deals with the code to use inside the stored procedure. A stored procedure contains one or more SQL statements. These statements may include commands from the SQL Data Manipulation Language (SELECT, UPDATE, DELETE, and INSERT), and the SQL Data Definition Language (CREATE TABLE, ALTER VIEW, etc), and flow control commands (branching and looping). As with any other high-level programming language, you will need to be concerned with such things as variables, passing parameters, specifying return values, and error handling.

Let's take a look at how these are implemented in a stored procedure. Since many of these topics behave like many of the high-level programming languages, we will focus on how these commands and constructs are implemented in the major RDBMSs.

> *Bear in mind that, with each vendor's product, there will be differences in syntax for the code within a stored procedure as well as additional proprietary features, so make sure that you check with the vendor's documentation.*

To illustrate this, the following small stored procedure adds a new employee to the Employees table. After looking through this example to get a feel for the coding of stored procedures, we'll take a closer look at the various commands and constructs. This example uses Microsoft SQL Server syntax.

```
CREATE PROCEDURE spAddEmployee
(
    @LastName varchar(50),
    @FirstName varchar(30),
    @SocialSecurityNumber char(9)
)
/* This routine adds a new employee to the Employees table. */
AS
BEGIN
    DECLARE @dtCurrent datetime
    SELECT @dtCurrent = GetDate()
    INSERT INTO Employees (FirstName, LastName, SocialSecurity, StartDate)
        VALUES (@FirstName, @LastName, @SocialSecurityNumber, @dtCurrent)
    RETURN @@Error          -- Send 0 upon success or the error number otherwise
END
```

Now let's examine the code in detail to explain a few important items about stored procedure coding.

This routine accepts three arguments, each of which is declared starting with an @ symbol. The argument list must be enclosed in a set of parentheses immediately after the procedure's name. If the procedure does not accept any arguments, then the parentheses should not be included.

> *In Microsoft SQL Server and Sybase SQL Server, the @ symbol is used to identify all arguments and variables in SQL. DB2 SQL and Oracle's PL/SQL do not require this symbol when naming variables.*

Following the argument list is a comment line. Comments can be made in two ways. The first is by using two successive hyphens. This method causes the compiler to ignore all text to the right of the hyphens on the current line. The second method, as shown above, allows us to create single or multiple-line blocks of comments using C-style syntax. The block of comment lines starts with /* and ends with */.

You will also see the keywords BEGIN and END, which are used to identify blocks of code. Strictly speaking, these are not needed in our simple example, although it is good practice to use them. These keywords are used to identify a **batch** of SQL statements.

> Microsoft SQL Server creates a separate execution plan for each batch, so the statements found in a batch are always executed in a group. Because the BEGIN...END blocks define an execution plan, you *must* have at least one statement contained within the block – empty blocks are not permitted.

After the BEGIN keyword is a declaration of the local variable @dtCurrent as a variable with a data type of datetime. Following this declaration is the assignment of the current system date to this variable using the SELECT statement. All variable assignments in Microsoft SQL Server are made by using SELECT or SET. If you did not include the keyword SELECT or SET and simply used @dtCurrent = GetDate(), the query engine would interpret this as a Boolean comparison, which in this case would cause an error. DB2 also uses SET, but Oracle's PL/SQL does not require either the SET or SELECT command to be used when assigning values to variables. Instead, PL/SQL requires that you use the := operator for assignments:

```
DECLARE dtCurrent date;
dtCurrent := SYSDATE;
```

The next statement in the procedure is the INSERT statement itself. The values assigned to the new record are provided by the values of the argument variables and @dtCurrent. Following the INSERT statement is the Return @@Error statement. The RETURN keyword is used to assign a return value for the procedure, which, in this case, is equal to the value of the @@Error system variable. In Microsoft SQL Server, all variables that are accessible to the entire system are identified by having @@ at the start of their name. The @@Error variable is set after SQL Server completes the execution of any SQL statement. If @@Error is zero, then the statement executed successfully, otherwise it is assigned an error code value. Because @@Error is reassigned after each statement is executed, it should be checked immediately after the statement is executed.

> *Error handling is done quite differently in Oracle. Rather than requiring an explicit check to determine if an error occurred, **exception handlers** are used. Errors and exception handling in Oracle and DB2 are discussed below.*

Once you have typed in all of the code for the stored procedure, select the Check Syntax button. This will cause the compiler to scan your code for obvious syntactical mistakes. If an error is detected, a dialog will be displayed giving you some indication of what the problem is, and in which line in the procedure it was first detected.

Once you have found and resolved all of the syntax issues, select the OK button to save and compile the stored procedure. This will also close the edit window and return you to Enterprise Manager. If you don't see your new procedure listed, try right clicking on the Stored Procedures folder in the left pane and select Refresh or press the F5 key to update the display.

Variable Naming Conventions

Notice that the data types used for the variable are the same data types that are used when defining a field in a table. Indeed, variables in SQL Server are fundamentally no different to fields. As with fields, you should consider using a naming convention. Whether using fields or variables, having a standardized naming convention will save you, and any developers that will later support this application, a great deal of time and frustration, and ultimately it will reduce the overall cost of ownership of the application.

When naming objects, bear in mind that there are rules specific for each RDBMS. Most modern databases allow you to use names that are dozens of characters in length, so there is little need for abbreviations. Abbreviated names can be easily misunderstood and therefore should be avoided. There are few limitations with naming objects, whether they be stored procedures, variables, tables or some other objects, so be descriptive and clear when naming your objects. Just don't use reserved words, and special characters, or start names with a number. Some RDBMSs, like Microsoft SQL Server, allow spaces and underscore character within names, but it is generally good practice to avoid these. This is especially true with databases that are used for Internet applications since these characters make debugging query strings a nightmare.

One common naming convention for variables is to start the name with an abbreviation for the data type. Some of the more commonly used data types for variables are listed below along with their abbreviation, usage, and a sample name:

Data Type	Description	Abbrev.	Example Name
integer	Integer values	i or n	iUserCount
decimal	Fixed precision real values	d	dCommission
float	Floating precision real values	f	fMarketValue
datetime date	Date and time data	dt	dtStart
char	Fixed length non Unicode character data	c	cSocSecNumber
varchar varchar2	Variable length non Unicode character data	vc	vcLastName

Using Output Parameters and Default Values

As we have already discussed, stored procedures can be defined with a list of parameters or arguments. These arguments may be used to supply information to the stored procedure that will be manipulated or to control the flow of execution within the procedure. When we define what arguments are to be included in the stored procedure, we can specify default values for each argument. Also, we can decide if each argument will provide the stored procedure with information or send results from the stored procedure back to the calling program, or both.

Default Values

If a stored procedure is defined to accept an argument and the call to the stored procedure does not include that argument, SQL provides a mechanism so that the missing argument will be assumed. This is done by specifying a **default value**.

Default values are specified as part of the CREATE PROCEDURE command. If we expand the general syntax that was listed above for this command, we find that default values are specified following the declaration of the parameter's data type:

```
CREATE PROCEDURE procedure_name (parameter_name data_type [= default])
WITH RECOMPILE
AS
BEGIN
    sql_statements
END
```

To illustrate this, let's consider the following CREATE PROCEDURE command:

```
CREATE PROCEDURE uspOrdersForDay (@dtDay datetime)
AS
BEGIN
    DECLARE @dtTarget datetime
    IF @dtDay IS NULL
        SELECT @dtTarget = GetDate()
    ELSE
        SELECT @dtTarget = @dtDay
    SELECT * FROM Orders WHERE DateDiff(dd,OrderDate,@dtTarget) < 1.0
END
```

In this example, the procedure expects a single argument to be passed. If we attempt to run the stored procedure without passing it a date value, an error will occur:

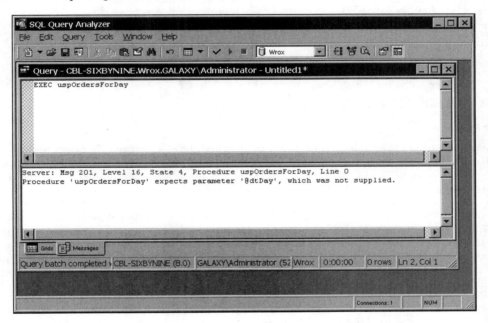

Now let's edit the stored procedure so that a value of NULL will be assumed if the @dtDay argument is not provided:

```
CREATE PROCEDURE uspOrdersForDay (@dtDay datetime = NULL)
AS
BEGIN
    DECLARE @dtTarget datetime
    IF @dtDay IS NULL
        SELECT @dtTarget = GetDate()
    ELSE
        SELECT @dtTarget = @dtDay
    SELECT * FROM Orders
        WHERE DateDiff(dd,OrderDate,@dtTarget) < 1.0
END
```

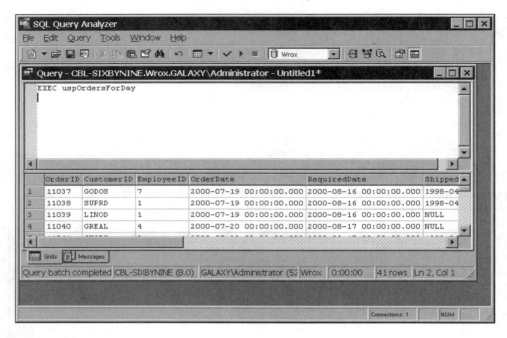

Output Parameters

When we construct subroutines or functions in most high-level languages, we can define these routines with arguments. Typically, these arguments are used to pass values into the routine so these values may be acted upon. In these situations, these arguments are considered **input parameters**. In SQL, arguments are considered to be input arguments by default.

However, a stored procedure parameter can also be declared as an **output parameter**. Output parameters allow the external procedure or program that called the stored procedure to retrieve a value set during the procedure's execution. Output parameters act similarly to arguments that are passed by reference in Visual Basic, meaning that when an output parameter is used, the RDBMS will modify the variable passed. After the stored procedure has been called, the new value of the variable will become available to the calling routine.

To use output parameters, two things must be done. First, the keyword OUTPUT (in SQL Server) or OUT (in DB2 and Oracle) must follow the data type of the parameter in the declaration of the argument list. The second requirement is that when the procedure is called, the variable passed to the procedure must be followed with the same keyword, OUTPUT. If you don't place this keyword after the variable name when executing the stored procedure, the stored procedure will still run, but the modified value of the variable will not be sent back to the calling routine.

The code below provides a simple demonstration of using output parameters in Microsoft SQL Server. The first group of statements creates a stored procedure that declares an output parameter. The second group invokes this procedure and then displays the value of the variable that was modified.

```
CREATE PROCEDURE spDemoOutputParameter
    @InArg int,
    @OutArg int OUTPUT
AS
    SELECT @OutArg = @InArg * 2
```

```
DECLARE @SomeVal int, @SomeReturnVal int
SELECT @SomeVal = 4
SELECT @SomeReturnVal = -1                    -- initialize with a known value
EXECUTE spDemoOutputParameter @SomeVal, @SomeReturnVal OUTPUT
SELECT @SomeReturnVal AS SomeReturnVal
```

Running this code in a query window produces the following result:

```
SomeReturnVal
-------------
8
```

If you do not supply the keyword OUTPUT in the call to the stored procedure, @SomeReturnVal will not be modified and the result will be:

```
SomeReturnVal
-------------
-1
```

When a parameter is identified as an output parameter, the value of the variable passed will be available to the stored procedure. Therefore, output parameters are actually bidirectional. However, you should not use any parameter for both input and output; modifying input values is generally considered to be an unsafe programming technique. Having separate parameters for input and output produces cleaner and more robust code.

Assigning Database Values to Variables

A common task in stored procedures is to save the value of a field or calculation from the database in a variable. How we get the value of a field into a variable differs slightly with each major RDBMSs. In Microsoft SQL Server and Sybase SQL Server, a variable assignment uses either the SET or SELECT command, which uses the general syntax:

```
SELECT variablename = expression FROM tablename
SET variablename = expression FROM tablename
```

The expression could be the name of the field or can be a calculation based upon a field or some other variable. For example:

```
DECLARE @vcLastName varchar(30)
DECLARE @iEmployeeCount int
DECLARE @NewEmployeeID int
SET @vcLastName = LastName FROM Employees WHERE EmployeeID = 3
SET @iEmployeeCount = COUNT(*) FROM Employees
SET @NewEmployeeID = @ iEmployeeCount + 1
```

Oracle's PL/SQL uses a slightly different syntax for assigning variables. If the value being assigned is from a field from a record, the SELECT...INTO syntax is used:

```
DECLARE iCustomerID integer;
SELECT CustID INTO iCustomerID FROM Customers WHERE ID = 433;
```

The SQL standard also defines **cursors** as another way to populate variables with the values from a field. Cursors are essentially a reference to the results of a multirow query, much like a Recordset object in ADO. Due to the multirow nature of cursors, they are almost always used in conjunction with loops. We'll come back to cursors later on in this chapter.

Specifying Return Values

As we have already seen, a stored procedure can return data to the calling code by using output parameters and by sending back a resultset for each SELECT statement contained in the stored procedure. SQL provides yet another way of sending back data to the caller of the stored procedure – **return values**.

To see return values in action, let's look at another stored procedure. This routine inserts a new account in a Customer table. This table has an automatically incrementing CustomerID field. After we insert the new record into the table, we will cause the stored procedure to set the output parameter @CustomerID to the CustomerID value of the newly created Customer record and return a success value. In this example, using Microsoft SQL Server, the @@Error system variable will be zero upon success and nonzero otherwise. This variable identifies the type of error.

```
CREATE PROCEDURE CreateCustomer
(
    @CustName varchar(20),
    @CustomerID int OUTPUT
)
AS
BEGIN
   DECLARE @iRetValue int
   INSERT INTO Customer(FullName)
      VALUES (@CustName)
   SELECT @CustomerID = Max(CustomerID)+ 1 FROM Customer
   RETURN @@Error
END
```

> *It should be noted that many RDBMSs offer a feature to automatically determine the value of identity column of a newly inserted row, such as the @@IDENTITY system variable in Microsoft SQL Server. The design for this example works on a broader range of products because it does not rely upon product specific features such as @@IDENTITY.*

Flow Control

Although most people would not consider SQL to be a procedural language, it does contain procedural commands that allow us to develop simple algorithms for our stored procedures. These commands were formally introduced in SQL-3 only recently, so you may find some slight differences in implementation in RDBMSs.

The flow control constructs in SQL-3 behave very much like those that are found in high-level languages such as Ada, VBScript, Pascal, and C. You will probably find that most of what is presented in this section is already familiar to you. Most developers need only to see how SQL implements these commands, so let's take a brief look at what procedural commands SQL has to offer.

Conditional Statements Using IF

The IF statement allows different commands to be executed depending upon a Boolean condition. Depending upon the RDBMS you are using, the IF statement follows one of two general forms:

Form 1

```
IF condition1
    sqlstatement1
ELSE
    sqlstatement2
```

Form 2

```
IF condition1 THEN
    sqlstatement1
ELSEIF condition2 THEN
    sqlstatement2
...
ELSEIF conditionN THEN
    sqlstatementN
ELSE
    sqlstatementX
END IF
```

Oracle and DB2 use the second form, while Sybase and Microsoft's products use the first. Notice that the IF statement in the first form does not support an ELSEIF clause. You can achieve the same functionality of an IF...ELSEIF structure by using the CASE statement, (which is discussed below), or by nesting a series of IF statements.

As with most other languages, the ELSE clause is optional. When we wish to execute more than one statement, we enclose the statements within a BEGIN...END block. Here is an example using Microsoft SQL Server that demonstrates using blocks with IF statements:

```
CREATE PROCEDURE spPostUserGroup
(
    @ActionType int,    -- 1: Add user to existing group;
                        -- 2: Drop user from existing group;
                        -- 3: Create new group.
    @UserID int,
    @GroupID integer,
    @GroupName varchar (50) = NULL
) AS

IF @ActionType < 3
    BEGIN
        -- We are editing the membership of an existing group.
        IF @ActionType = 1
            EXEC spAddUserToGroup @GroupID, @UserID
        ELSE
            EXEC spDropUserFromGroup @GroupID, @UserID
    END
ELSE
    BEGIN
        -- We are creating a new group.
        EXEC spCreateUserGroup @GroupID, @GroupName
    END
RETURN @@ERROR
```

Conditional Computations Using CASE

When used with ELSEIF, the IF statementexecutes different statements based upon whether on of several conditions are met. Rather than determine what statements are executed, the CASE statement is used to determine how a single statement is executed.

The CASE statement has two formats. The first format compares an expression to a set of possible values. The expression is evaluated against the first value in the set. If the expression equals the value, then the corresponding result is used. If the expression doesn't equals the first value, then the second value is evaluated. If the second value doesn't match, then the third value is evaluated, and so on. This continues until a matching value is found or all of the values have been exhausted, when the ELSE portion of the expression is used. Since this format keeps comparing values until a match is found, this format is often called the "search format".

153

The syntax of the "search" format of the CASE statement is:

```
CASE input_expression
    WHEN value1 THEN result_expression1
    WHEN value2 THEN result_expression2
    ...
    WHEN valueN THEN result_expressionN
    ELSE else_result_expression
END
```

And an example of a CASE statement in this format is:

```
SELECT
    EmployeeID,
    LastName,
    FirstName,
    Status =
        CASE StatusCode
            WHEN 1 THEN 'Full time, Non-exempt'
            WHEN 2 THEN 'Part-time, Non-exempt'
            WHEN 3 THEN 'Contractor'
            ELSE 'Full time, Exempt'
        END
    FROM Employees
```

The second format operates similar to the IF...THEN...ELSEIF block found in many languages. In this format, different expressions may be evaluated. The result that is used is based upon the first expression that evaluates to True.

The "If" format of the CASE statement has the syntax:

```
CASE
    WHEN Boolean_expression1 THEN result_expression1
    WHEN Boolean_expression2 THEN result_expression2
    ...
    WHEN Boolean_expressionN THEN result_expressionN
    ELSE else_result_expression
END
```

For example:

```
SELECT
    EmployeeID,
    AverageSales =
        CASE
            WHEN Count(OrderID) > 0 THEN Avg(OrderTotals)
            ELSE Null
        END
    FROM OrderDetails
    GROUP BY EmployeeID
```

Although not part of the procedural language components, the SQL standard contains NULLIF, which is an extremely useful function that may be used for conditional testing. NULLIF returns a Null value when a Boolean expression is true.

Microsoft SQL Server and other RDBMSs also define the function ISNULL that may be used to replace Null values with some other value. Take a look at these functions in the product documentation to give you some ideas on how they may be used.

Redirecting Execution Flow with GOTO

Although many developers have been taught that using a GOTO statement is not good practice, there will be situations where a properly placed GOTO statement will be appropriate. GOTO statements in SQL operate just as they do in most other high-level languages, by redirecting execution to a line in the routine identified by a label. In most dialects of SQL, such as that of Microsoft SQL Server and DB2, labels are defined by placing a valid object name on a separate line of code followed by the colon character.

GOTO statements and labels can be used anywhere within a procedure or statement block: and GOTO statements may even be nested. The only condition imposed upon the use of the GOTO statement is that it can only refer to labels within the current routine.

The following example demonstrates the use of the GOTO statement. This code snippet also demonstrates the use of SQL Server's WAITFOR statement, which suspends execution for a period of time. This statement is similar to the Windows Sleep API function. Unlike Sleep, which only allows the process to be delayed for a certain duration, the WAITFOR statement can be used to pause execution for a period of time or until a specific time of the day.

```
DECLARE @i int

SELECT @i = 1
TopOfLoop:
SELECT @i = Count(*) FROM UsersInQueue
IF @i > 0 THEN
    BEGIN
        -- pause for 5 seconds for queue to empty.
        WAITFOR Delay '00:00:05'
        GOTO TopOfLoop
    END
ELSE
    EXEC spCleanupQueueResources
END
```

Repeating Statements Using the While Statement

The WHILE statement is used to repeat a statement or block of statements as long as a specified condition remains true. The WHILE statement in SQL Server also includes a BREAK statement that exits the loop, and a CONTINUE statement that is used to restart the loop. The syntax is very similar to other languages:

```
WHILE BooleanExpression
BEGIN
    SqlStatements
END
```

Here's an example of using the WHILE construct that processes a week's worth of records:

```
DECLARE @dtDayToProcess datetime
SELECT @dtDayToProcess = GetDate()

WHILE @dtDayToProcess > DateAdd(day, -7, GetDate())
    BEGIN
        EXEC spDailyStatusReport @dtDayToProcess
        SELECT @dtDayToProcess = DateAdd(day,-1, @dtDayToProcess)
    END
```

Iterative Control: The LOOP Statement

The SQL-3 standard defines the LOOP construct which allows us to repeatedly execute a sequence of statements. The LOOP statement encloses a sequence of statements between the keywords LOOP and END LOOP that will continue to execute until the LEAVE command is reached.

The general format of a construct using LOOP is as follows:

```
LOOP
     sequence_of_statements;
     IF condition THEN LEAVE;
END LOOP
```

The actual implementation of LEAVE varies between the major RDBMSs:

❑ In DB2, the LEAVE command expects the name of a label to be supplied before the loop. When execution of the loop stops, this label will identify which loop will be terminated, and execution will continue on the line after the END LOOP statement for that loop.

❑ In Oracle, the LEAVE command is named EXIT, and does not require the use of a label. Instead, when the EXIT command is reached, execution redirects to the first statement following the END LOOP statement.

> Note that Microsoft SQL Server does not support the LOOP...END LOOP construct. Instead, Microsoft SQL Server relies upon the WHILE construct.

The following is a trivial example to illustrate this construct under DB2. It simply keeps incrementing the value of the variable iCount until it reaches 23, and then continues execution after the loop which is prefixed by the label1 label.

```
SET iCount = 0
label1:
LOOP
    SET iCount = iCount + 1;
    IF iCount => 23 THEN
        LEAVE label1;
    END IF;
END LOOP;
```

Defining and Using Cursors

SQL is designed to work with sets of data. For example, when we issue an UPDATE statement, every record that meets the criteria of the WHERE clause is affected. There are situations where we need to process records not as a set, but one at a time in a sequence. On the client-side, this process regularly occurs. We execute a query and get back a resultset, and store this resultset in an object. Then we use the methods of that object, such as MoveNext, to walk through the records and process them one at a time. The ability to traverse these records is a feature of the object model used (ADO, DAO, RDO, etc.). SQL provides a similar mechanism that runs on the RDBMS called **cursors**.

Cursors with Microsoft SQL Server

The procedure to set up and use a cursor has similarities to using a data access object model such as the ADO recordset. With ADO, you declare a variable of data type `"ADODB.Recordset"`, open it, navigate through the records, close the recordset, before finally destroying the object. In SQL Server, we first declare a variable to be of a cursor type. When we declare this variable, we specify a `SELECT` statement that will be used to populate the results. Next, we open the cursor. We navigate through the results by issuing the `FETCH` command, which retrieves a row from the cursor. When we have finished using the cursor, we close it, and then destroy the cursor object with a `DEALLOCATE` statement.

ADO is discussed in detail in Chapter 7.

Let's take a look at the details of how to use a cursor by examining the following code. It is a simple inventory allocation process. A certain number of cases arrive at a warehouse and we must allocate these cases to the stores with the greatest need. By using a cursor, we can allocate the cases based upon determining which of the stores has the lowest inventory:

```
DECLARE @iQtyOfCases int
DECLARE @iUnitsPerCase int
DECLARE @iStoreID int

SELECT @iQtyOfCases = 6
SELECT @iUnitsPerCase = 8

DECLARE curStores CURSOR FOR
SELECT Top 3 StoreID
    FROM Inventories
    WHERE ProductID = 1
    ORDER BY QtyInStock
WHILE @iQtyOfCases > 0
    BEGIN
        SELECT StoreID, QtyInStock
            FROM Inventories ORDER BY QtyInStock
        OPEN curStores
        FETCH FROM curStores INTO @iStoreID
        WHILE (@@Fetch_Status = 0 AND @iQtyOfCases > 0)
            BEGIN
                UPDATE Inventories
                    SET QtyInStock = QtyInStock + @iUnitsPerCase
                    FROM Inventories
                    WHERE StoreID = @iStoreID
                SELECT @iQtyOfCases = @iQtyOfCases -1
                FETCH NEXT FROM curStores INTO @iStoreID
            END
        CLOSE curStores
    END
DEALLOCATE curStores
SELECT StoreID, QtyInStock FROM Inventories ORDER BY QtyInStock
```

At the start of the routine, we identify how many cases will be distributed and how many units there are in each case. Then, the cursor is declared and named (curStores), specifying that when it is opened, it should retrieve the StoreIDs of the stores with the three lowest inventory levels. The outer WHILE loop is used to loop through the allocation process for as long as we have cases to distribute. To better illustrate the allocation process, a SELECT statement is issued to show the initial and final inventory levels. The initial values are:

```
StoreID     QtyInStock
-----------  -----------
2            0
5            2
6            12
1            15
3            18
7            20
4            22
```

We use the FETCH statement to retrieve the first row and assign the value of this record's field to @iStoreID. If the cursor was defined to select more than one column; we would list additional variables after @iStoreID to have the cursor populate the variables in the order listed in the SELECT statement.

The global variable @@Fetch_Status is similar to the EOF property of ADO recordsets. It is used to detect if the fetch was successful. If it was successful, @@Fetch_Status will hold a value of zero. When the bottom of the cursor is reached, this variable will have a value of −1, so we can use this variable as one of the conditions for our allocation loop.

Now that we have the StoreID of the store with the lowest inventory, we can use this value in an UPDATE statement that adds one case worth of units to that store. We decrement the number of cases now available and then use the FETCH NEXT statement to retrieve the next record in the cursor. After the first round of allocation, our inventory levels become:

```
StoreID     QtyInStock
-----------  -----------
2            8
5            10
1            15
3            18
6            20
7            20
4            22
```

If you compare these values with the ones above, you'll see that Stores 2, 5, and 6 went from 0, 2, and 12 to 8, 10, and 20, respectively. After we allocate the first three cases, we close the cursor and restart the outer WHILE loop. The cursor is reopened, causing it to select those stored that currently have the lowest inventories. In this case, the stores are 2, 5, and 1. We continue this process of computing (twice in total), determining which the three most under stocked stores are, and then allocating cases to them, until we run out of cases to distribute.

Once we have finished using the cursor, we need to issue the DEALLOCATE statement. Just like setting an object to Nothing in Visual Basic, the DEALLOCATE statement destroys the cursor and releases all resources that were used by it.

> The DEALLOCATE statement completely frees all resources allocated to the cursor, including the cursor name. Therefore, after a cursor is deallocated, you must issue another DECLARE statement if you wish to rebuild the cursor.

The following shows the output generated when the entire code block is executed:

```
StoreID      QtyInStock
-----------  -----------
2            0
5            2
6            12
1            15
3            18
7            20
4            22

StoreID      QtyInStock
-----------  -----------
2            8
5            10
1            15
3            18
6            20
7            20
4            22

StoreID      QtyInStock
-----------  -----------
2            16
3            18
5            18
6            20
7            20
4            22
1            23
```

Cursors do not scale and are usually only used in special circumstances. In addition, if you are using cursors more than once then you should probably use variables.

Cursors with Oracle

You might wonder, if Oracle stored procdures can't contain SELECT statements which return recordsets, why we'd need cursors in Oracle procedures. In fact, as we'll see in Chapter 15, cursors play a vital role in the workaround which allows us to retrieve an ADO Recordset from an Oracle stored procedure. But cursors do also have a use even within Oracle procedures, since they are used in conjunction with the SELECT INTO statement.

If a cursor is not declared explicitly, Oracle will implicitly create one whenever we execute a SELECT INTO statement. For example, the following stored procedure returns the name and job title of an employee based on their ID number:

```
CREATE OR REPLACE PROCEDURE spSelectEmp
   (i_empno  IN number,
    o_name   OUT varchar2,
    o_job    OUT varchar2)
AS
BEGIN
   SELECT ename, job
   INTO o_name, o_job
   FROM EMP
   WHERE EMPNO=i_empno;
END;
```

Behind the scenes, Oracle creates a cursor to contain the row returned by the SELECT statement. We can rewrite the same procedure, explicitly declaring our cursor, opening it, retrieving the values, and closing the cursor again:

```
CREATE OR REPLACE PROCEDURE spSelectEmp
    (i_empno IN number,
     o_name   OUT varchar2,
     o_job    OUT varchar2)
AS
    CURSOR cursor1
    IS
        SELECT ename, job
            FROM EMP
            WHERE EMPNO=i_empno;
BEGIN
    OPEN cursor1;
    FETCH cursor1 INTO o_name, o_job;
    CLOSE cursor1;
END;
```

This involves several more lines of code, so why would we do this? Explicitly declared cursors are slightly more efficient, but there's also another advantage. Implicit cursors can only contain one row, so if we want to iterate through several rows within our procedure, we'll need to declare a cursor explicitly. Since an explicitly declared cursor can contain several rows, we need to be able to iterate through them one row at a time. PL/SQL provides a construct called a **cursor for loop** which allows us to do this. The following stored procedure uses a cursor for loop to iterate through each record in the EMP table, and decreases the salary of every manager by a hundred dollars, while increasing everyone else's by a hundred (OK, not a likely scenario, unfortunately, but it illustrates the technique):

```
CREATE OR REPLACE PROCEDURE spCursorLoop
AS
    CURSOR cursor1
    IS
    SELECT * FROM EMP;
BEGIN
    FOR record IN cursor1
    LOOP
        IF record.JOB = 'MANAGER' THEN
            UPDATE EMP SET SAL = SAL - 100 WHERE EMPNO=record.EMPNO;
        ELSE
            UPDATE EMP SET SAL = SAL + 100 WHERE EMPNO=record.EMPNO;
        END IF;
    END LOOP;
END;
```

We declare the cursor as usual, but we don't need to open it explicitly with a cursor for loop. The actual loop is a little like a Visual Basic For Each loop. It has the syntax:

```
FOR record_name IN cursor_name
LOOP
    -- SQL statements
END LOOP;
```

The `record_name` is used to identify the current record within the loop. We prefix this to the name of the specific column we want to reference for the record, in much the same way as we use the `table.column` syntax to identify a specific column in a table. So, to return the value of the `JOB` column for the current record in the loop, we use `record.JOB`, where `record` is the name we used in the `FOR` statement to identify the current record. For each record, we check this value to see if it equals `'MANAGER'`, and if so, we update the `EMP` table, decreasing the value of the `SAL` column for the current record where `EMPNO` is equal to the value of the current record's `EMPNO`. Unfortunately, we can't just say `record.SAL = record.SAL - 100` otherwise, we increase the salary by a hundred.

Cursors with DB2

Cursors play a vital role in DB2 stored procedures, since they are required if we are to return a set of records back from the procedure. In order to return a data set from a DB2 stored procedure, we must declare a cursor for the `SELECT` statement which will return our recordset. The syntax for declaring a cursor in DB2 SQL is:

```
DECLARE cursor_name CURSOR
    [WITH HOLD]
    [WITH RETURN [TO CALLER | TO CLIENT]]
    FOR select_statement
```

The optional `WITH HOLD` clause indicates that the cursor can be maintained over multiple transactions or units of work. If a cursor is declared `WITH HOLD`, it will be kept open after the call to `COMMIT` the transaction; otherwise it will be closed when the transaction ends, regardless of whether it is committed or rolled back. If the transaction is aborted, any open cursors will be closed, even if they are declared `WITH HOLD`.

The `WITH RETURN` clause (also optional) specifies that the cursor may return a set of data. If the cursor is declared `WITH RETURN TO CALLER`, the stored procedure can return a resultset to either a client application or a calling function such as another stored procedure. However, if it is declared `WITH RETURN TO CLIENT`, the dataset will be returned directly to the client application, and will be invisible to any intermediate stored procedures through which the current procedure was called.

Finally, we specify the `SELECT` statement which will be used to populate the cursor, preceded by the `FOR` keyword. Note that cursors must be opened before they can be used, using the `OPEN` statement. They must also be left open if the data is to be available to our client application. So a simple procedure which returns a dataset from a `SELECT` statement might look like this:

```
CREATE PROCEDURE db2admin.spSelectSales()
RESULT SETS 1     -- Return one resultset
LANGUAGE SQL
P1: BEGIN
-- Declare our cursor, specifying we want to
-- return a dataset
DECLARE cursor1 CURSOR WITH RETURN FOR
    SELECT * FROM Administrator.Employee
       WHERE JOB='SALES';

    -- Open the cursor. Must remain open at the end of the SP.
    OPEN cursor1;
END P1
```

You might be wondering what's stopping us having more than one cursor, and returning multiple recordsets? And the answer is – nothing! If we want our stored procedure to return several distinct datasets, we simply declare and open multiple cursors with different SELECT statements. We can indicate in the RESULT SETS clause of the CREATE PROCEDURE statement how many recordsets our procedure will return:

```
CREATE PROCEDURE db2admin.spSelectMgr()
RESULT SETS 2   -- Two resultsets this time!
LANGUAGE SQL
P1: BEGIN
DECLARE cursor1 CURSOR WITH RETURN FOR
    SELECT * FROM Administrator.Employee
        WHERE JOB='MANAGER';

DECLARE cursor2 CURSOR WITH RETURN FOR
    SELECT * FROM Administrator.Staff
        WHERE JOB='Mgr';

    OPEN cursor1;
    OPEN cursor2;
END P1
```

Running this procedure gives these results:

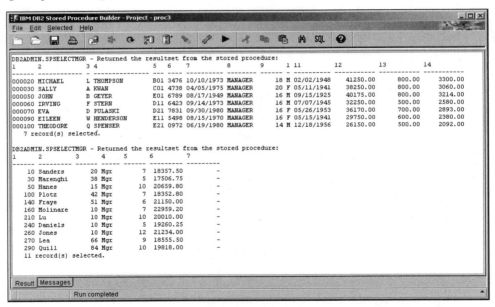

Error Handling

Error conditions are inevitable in just about every application that is coded. To account for unexpected (or expected) errors, we need to plan our routines so they react properly. The SQL language standard doesn't explicitly specify how errors should be handled, so this varies between various RDBMSs. The major RDBMSs implement error handling in one of two general ways, using **exception handlers** or using an error status indicator. Oracle uses the former and Microsoft SQL Server, the latter, while DB2 uses a combination of these two approaches.

The exception handler approach defines code in each procedure that is automatically executed when the system determines that an error has occurred. This is very much like the approach taken in C++, Java, and the new version of Visual Basic, which use `try...catch` blocks to run code identified by the `catch` keyword if an error occurs anywhere in a block of code identified by the `try` keyword.

The error status indicator approach uses a system variable that maintains a code to indicate the success or failure of the last command executed. The code must explicitly check the value of this variable to determine if an error occurred. This is analogous to using `On Error Resume Next` in Visual Basic and then having to check the `Number` property of the `Err` object for a nonzero value to see if an error had been thrown.

Error Handling in Microsoft SQL Server

Microsoft SQL Server uses the error status indicator approach to error handling. The `@@ERROR` system function returns zero if the last T-SQL statement executed successfully; if the statement generates an error at any point, `@@ERROR` returns the error number. The value of `@@ERROR` changes on the completion of each T-SQL statement. You will be required to explicitly refer to the `@@ERROR` variable to determine if error processing is required.

> *You can find a list of error messages, along with related information, in the Microsoft SQL Server 2000 Books Online under the "Error Messages" section of "Troubleshooting".*

The following is a stored procedure that refers to the `@@ERROR` variable after attempting to post a new record. If the insert failed, an error condition will have been generated that can be detected in the `@@ERROR` variable. The value of the `@@ERROR` variable is also cached in a local variable and sent back as a return value to indicate success or failure. By responding to the value of this variable, the procedure can set the appropriate status message describing the success or failure of the process.

```
CREATE PROCEDURE CreateNewAccount
(
    @UserName varchar(20),
    @Password varchar(20),
    @Status varchar(40) OUTPUT
)
AS
BEGIN
    DECLARE @iRetValue int
    IF Len(@Password) < 6
        BEGIN
            SELECT @Status = 'Account not created: invalid password'
            RETURN -1
        END
    ELSE
        BEGIN
            INSERT INTO Customer(LastName)
                VALUES (@UserName)
            SELECT @iRetValue = @@ERROR
            IF @iRetVal = 0
                SELECT @Status = 'Account was created.'
            ELSE
                SELECT @Status = 'An error occurred creating the account.'
            RETURN @iRetValue
        END
END
```

Error Handling in Oracle

As we mentioned earlier, error handling is implemented in Oracle using exception handlers which we can compare to a `try...catch` construct in C, JavaScript, etc. Each batch of SQL statements marked by the `BEGIN...END` keywords may contain an exception handler (indicated by the keyword `EXCEPTION`), which should be placed at the end of the batch. Should an exception occur during the execution of the SQL statements in the batch, control will pass to this exception handler.

Within the handler, we can specify SQL statements to execute depending on the nature of the error which occurred. If the error isn't handled by any of the statements in the exception handler, control will pass to the exception handler in an outer block, if there is one.

The syntax used to handle exceptions is:

```
WHEN condition THEN sql_statements;
```

Where `condition` can be one of:

- `no_data_found`: Raised when a `WHERE` clause matches no records in the database.
- `too_many_rows`: Raised when more than one row is fetched into an implicit cursor.
- `dup_val_on_index`: Raised when a value is assigned to an indexed field which already exists in that field.
- `value_error`: Raised when a value is assigned to a field which is longer than the maximum length of the field.
- `others`: Handles any exceptions not covered by other handlers.

The following stored procedure illustrates this technique. We attempt to insert a new record into the `EMP` table of the `scott` database. If an exception is raised, control will pass to the exception handler marked by the keyword `EXCEPTION`. We handle each type of error (although, in fact, `too_many_rows` won't occur in this procedure). For each error, we simply set an output parameter, `o_status`, to a descriptive string:

```
CREATE OR REPLACE PROCEDURE spInsertEmp
    (i_empno IN number,
     i_name IN varchar2,
     i_job IN varchar2,
     i_mgr IN varchar2,
     i_hiredate IN date,
     i_sal IN number,
     i_comm IN number,
     i_dept IN number,
     o_status OUT varchar2)
AS
BEGIN
    INSERT INTO EMP
        VALUES (i_empno, i_name, i_job, i_mgr,
                i_hiredate, i_sal, i_comm, i_dept);

EXCEPTION
    WHEN no_data_found THEN o_status := 'No data found';
    WHEN value_error THEN o_status := 'Value too long for field';
    WHEN too_many_rows THEN o_status := 'Implicit cursors may
                                        only retrieve one row';
    WHEN dup_val_on_index THEN o_status := 'Row contains a duplicate value
                                        in an indexed field';
    WHEN others THEN o_status := 'Unknown error occurred';
END;
```

Oracle also lets us define and raise our own errors to the client application. We simply declare a variable of type EXCEPTION, RAISE it when necessary, and in our exception handler call RAISE_APPLICATION_ERROR with a code and description for the error. For example, if we want to raise an application error when someone attempts to insert a new employee with the JOB column set to 'PRESIDENT':

```
CREATE OR REPLACE PROCEDURE spInsertEmp
    (i_empno IN number,
     i_name IN varchar2,
     i_job IN varchar2,
     i_mgr IN varchar2,
     i_hiredate IN date,
     i_sal IN number,
     i_comm IN number,
     i_dept IN number)
AS
president_error EXCEPTION;
BEGIN
    IF i_job = 'PRESIDENT' THEN
        RAISE president_error;
    ELSE
        INSERT INTO EMP
            VALUES (i_empno, i_name, i_job, i_mgr,
                    i_hiredate, i_sal, i_comm, i_dept);
    END IF;
EXCEPTION
    WHEN president_error THEN RAISE_APPLICATION_ERROR(-20000,
        'Cannot insert a new president');
END;
```

If we call this stored procedure via ADO from ASP, this error will be passed back from Oracle through the OLE DB provider to our ASP page:

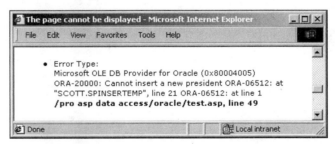

Error Handling in DB2

Error handling in DB2 stored procedures is implemented by a combination of these two methods. DB2 makes available to us two variables, SQLCODE and SQLSTATE, which inform us of any errors which have occurred. SQLCODE is an integer which returns the code for any error which occurred (or zero if no error occurred), while SQLSTATE is a five character string and holds the standard SQL state code for the previous operation. Any attempt to access either of these values will cause both to be reset. To use these variables in our procedure, they first need to be declared. They are usually assigned default values indicating that no error has occurred:

```
DECLARE SQLCODE INTEGER DEFAULT 0;
DECLARE SQLSTATE CHAR(5) DEFAULT '00000';
```

By default, DB2 will halt execution of a stored procedure if any error occurs, so we need a way of allowing the procedure to continue execution if anything does go wrong. To do this, DB2 allows us to specify an exception handler, which indicates what action to take when an exception or warning is raised. The format for the handler declaration is:

```
DECLARE handler_type HANDLER FOR error_type
BEGIN
    -- SQL statements
END;
```

The BEGIN and END keywords can be omitted if the handler only contains a single SQL statement.

The handler_type indicates what action DB2 should take should this handler be invoked. This can be one of the following:

❑ CONTINUE. After the SQL statements in the handler have been executed, the stored procedure will continue execution at the line after the one which caused the error.

❑ EXIT. The stored procedure will stop execution once the handler has finished.

❑ UNDO. This can only be used within transactions; it will roll-back any changes made in the current transaction, and continue execution at the end of the transaction.

The error_type specifies the type of error or warning for which the handler will be invoked. This can be one of:

❑ SQLEXCEPTION. The handler will be invoked whenever a SQL exception is raised.

❑ SQLWARNING. The handler will be invoked when a SQL warning is raised.

❑ NOT FOUND. Raised when a WHERE clause matches no records in the database.

The following stored procedure illustrates how these two features work together. The procedure inserts a new row into the DEPARTMENT table of the SAMPLE database. We declare handlers in case any error or warning is raised, and in each of these handlers, we store the current value of SQLCODE in a variable named iRetVal. Finally, we return this value to our client application:

```
CREATE PROCEDURE DB2ADMIN.spNewDept ( IN sDeptNo varchar(4000),
                                      IN sDeptName varchar(4000),
                                      IN sMgrNo varchar(4000),
                                      IN sAdmrDept varchar(4000),
                                      IN sLocation varchar(4000) )

    LANGUAGE SQL
    MODIFIES SQL DATA

P1: BEGIN
    DECLARE SQLCODE INTEGER DEFAULT 0;
    DECLARE iRetVal INTEGER DEFAULT 0;

    DECLARE CONTINUE HANDLER FOR SQLEXCEPTION SET iRetVal = SQLCODE;
    DECLARE CONTINUE HANDLER FOR SQLWARNING SET iRetVal = SQLCODE;
    DECLARE CONTINUE HANDLER FOR NOT FOUND SET iRetVal = SQLCODE;

    INSERT INTO ADMINISTRATOR.DEPARTMENT
        VALUES (sDeptNo, sDeptName, sMgrNo, sAdmrDept, sLocation);

    RETURN iRetVal;
END P1
```

We can't retrieve the values of both the SQLCODE *and* SQLSTATE, *because accessing one will cause both of them to be reset.*

As in Oracle, we can also raise our own exceptions within an Oracle stored procedure. To do this, we raise a specific SQLSTATE. Note that raising an invalid SQLSTATE will generate an error, so it is generally advisable to raise a SQLSTATE which is reserved for application specific errors (that is, which begin with the characters '7' to '9' or 'T' to 'Z'). To raise a SQLSTATE, we use the SIGNAL SQLSTATE statement. This may optionally contain a SET MESSAGE_TEXT clause, which specifies the text description of the error which will be returned to the calling application.

As an example of the SIGNAL SQLSTATE statement, let's rewrite the stored procedure above to prevent any users entering a new department number beginning with the character 'A':

```
CREATE PROCEDURE DB2ADMIN.spNewDept ( IN sDeptNo varchar(4000),
                                      IN sDeptName varchar(4000),
                                      IN sMgrNo varchar(4000),
                                      IN sAdmrDept varchar(4000),
                                      IN sLocation varchar(4000) )

    LANGUAGE SQL
    MODIFIES SQL DATA

P1: BEGIN
    IF sDeptNo LIKE 'A%' THEN
        SIGNAL SQLSTATE '75000'
            SET MESSAGE_TEXT = 'New departments cannot have an A... code';
    ELSE
        INSERT INTO ADMINISTRATOR.DEPARTMENT
            VALUES (sDeptNo, sDeptName, sMgrNo, sAdmrDept, sLocation);
    END IF;
END P1
```

Triggers

Triggers are stored procedures that run automatically whenever a change occurs in a record on the database. A trigger is specific to one or more of the data modification operations; UPDATE, INSERT, or DELETE. In some RDBMSs, triggers are executed before the operation is committed, while others allow triggers to run before or after the operation is committed. For example, in Microsoft SQL Server 2000, triggers are only executed before the change is made to the database, while DB2 and Oracle allow for triggers to be executed either before or after the data modification operations.

Triggers that run before the database is altered, may change any incoming data values and may also abort the posting altogether and cause a transactional roll-back. Due to this control over what changes are posted, triggers are very useful for enforcing business rules, keeping running totals or summaries, and many other purposes. Some situations where triggers are useful include:

❑ Situations when changes need to "cascade" into related tables to maintain referential integrity.

For example, if we delete an employee from an Employees table, we may also want to delete any records for that employee in a related EmployeeTrainingSchedule table.

❑ Performing simple "what if" analyses.

For example, a trigger can compare the state of a table before and after a data modification, and take actions based on that comparison.

❏ Rolling back changes that would violate a business rule, thereby canceling the attempted data modification transaction.

For example, suppose a company's policy is that an employee cannot enroll in a company's medical benefits program until that employee has worked in the company for a minimum of 30 days. In this situation, an insert trigger in the `Benefits` table would check to see if the employee number in the record being inserted was in fact a valid employee (their `EmployeeID` existed in the `Employees` table), and that the employee's start date was at least 30 days ago.

❏ Automatically invoking a related program or routine to provide additional processing.

For example, when a new customer registers with your web site, an insert trigger could call a stored procedure that causes a confirmation e-mail message to be composed and sent to the customer.

Creating Triggers

To create a trigger, we use the CREATE TRIGGER command. As part of this command, we will need to identify which data modification commands will cause the trigger to execute, and if applicable, when the trigger will execute – either before or after posting.

Here is a simple example for Microsoft SQL Server. This trigger invokes a stored procedure that will send an e-mail message whenever anyone tries to add or change data in an `articles` table:

```
CREATE TRIGGER t1
ON articles
FOR INSERT, UPDATE
AS
EXEC spSendChangeNotificationEmail      -- send using xp_sendmail
```

Triggers in Microsoft SQL Server

For the most part, triggers are simply, stored procedures that execute when a data modification command is attempted on a table. In Microsoft SQL Server 2000, triggers are executed in response to any change of data to a table. This implies that a trigger will fire if the query acted directly against the table or against a view that is based upon the table.

Any one trigger may be defined so that it executes in response to an insert, update, or delete. In other words, we can have a different trigger fire for each modification event (DELETE, INSERT, or UPDATE), or we can have the same trigger execute some or all of these events. Microsoft SQL Server also allows us to define more than one trigger for the same event. For example, we can have TriggerA and TriggerB both fire when an INSERT event occurs.

The general syntax for the CREATE TRIGGER command is as follows:

```
CREATE TRIGGER trigger_name
ON table
    FOR [DELETE[,]] [INSERT[,]] [UPDATE]
AS
    sql_statements
```

Under this syntax, we use the FOR clause to identify what events the trigger will respond to. Although Microsoft SQL Server will execute a trigger for most data modification commands, there are a couple of notable exceptions to what triggers will respond to. Microsoft SQL Server 2000 fires a trigger for a table when it detects a data modification command in the transaction log. This means that non-logged activities, such as TRUNCATE TABLE, will not cause a trigger to execute. Also, if a trigger from one table attempts a data modification command on a second table, and that second table has a trigger, this additional trigger is executed. This second trigger could possibly cause a third trigger to run, and it, a fourth trigger, and so on, to a maximum of 32 triggers.

> *You can disable this "nesting" of triggers by setting the* nested triggers *option to 0 by using the* sp_configure *system stored procedure.*

When the code in the trigger is executing, you can examine the contents of the record being inserted or modified. A single record table named Inserted will contain the values of the fields for the record being inserted or updated. Please note that even when an update is occurring, this table will still be named Inserted. The Deleted table stores copies of the affected rows during DELETE and UPDATE statements. During the execution of a DELETE or UPDATE statement, rows are deleted from the table with the trigger and transferred to the Deleted table. The Deleted table and the table with the trigger will have no rows in common.

The following example creates a trigger named tiuSales1 on the table Sales that will fire whenever a record is changed or inserted. The trigger insures that the selling price is greater than zero. If it is not, the trigger forces a roll-back:

```
CREATE TRIGGER tiuSales1
ON Sales
FOR INSERT, UPDATE
AS
BEGIN
    IF Inserted.Price < 0
        ROLLBACK TRANSACTION
END
```

Here is another example. Here we see how a trigger may be used to update the contents of a field in the table:

```
CREATE TRIGGER tuSetUpdateTime
ON Customer
FOR UPDATE
AS
UPDATE Customer
    SET LastUpdate = GetDate()
WHERE RecordID = (SELECT RecordID FROM Inserted)
```

This next example demonstrates how a trigger may be used to perform a "cascading delete", that is, a deletion in a different table:

```
CREATE TRIGGER tdDelete_Related_Transactions
ON Inventory
FOR DELETE
AS
    DELETE FROM ReorderLevels
    WHERE ProductID IN (SELECT ProductID FROM Deleted)
```

There are clauses in the command that can determine if a particular field in the table is being modified. The IF UPDATE(`column_name`) clause evaluates to TRUE whenever the column is assigned a value:

```
CREATE TRIGGER tuSales2
ON Sales
FOR UPDATE
AS
BEGIN
    IF UPDATE(Price) AND Inserted.Price < 0
        ROLLBACK TRANSACTION
END
```

Alternatively, the IF COLUMNS_UPDATED() clause can be used to check which columns in a table were updated by an INSERT or UPDATE statement. This clause returns a varbinary data value that indicates the columns that have changed. To determine exactly which columns have been changed, we need to perform a bitwise comparison of the value returned by COLUMNS_UPDATED and a bitmask of the column(s) we are interested in.

So, how do bitwise comparisons work? To understand how, consider the binary number 00001100. Each digit in this number represents a single on/off indicator of whether a particular column was changed. The digits are to be read from right to left, where the right-most digit indicates the first column of the table, the digit to the left of that indicates the second column, and so on. So, the number 00001100 (decimal 12) tells us that the third and fourth columns have been changed. Similarly, if columns 1, 3, and 5 had been updated, the value returned by COLUMNS_UPDATED would be 00010101 in binary, or decimal 21. Therefore, if we use:

```
IF COLUMNS_UPDATED = 21
```

We can determine if columns 1, 3, and 5 were the only columns to be changed.

But how do we check if columns 1, 3, and 5 were updated, regardless of whether any other columns were changed? To do this, we use the bitwise AND operator, which in Microsoft SQL Server is represented by the pipe symbol (&). For example:

```
IF COLUMNS_UPDATED & 21 = 21
```

To see why this works, let us assume that we have two values, tblA and tblB, where tblA holds the value of COLUMNS_UPDATED and tblB is our mask containing the value 21. If tblA has the value 00011101, then columns 1, 3, 4, and 5 have been updated. If we want to see if 1, 3, and 5 were updated, we use the mask 00010101 and compare digits. If both have the value 1, then the result is 1, otherwise it is 0:

```
(tblA & tblB):
tblA   00011101
tblB   00010101
       --------
       00010101
```

Therefore, if the columns we are checking for all have values of 1 for their corresponding bits, the result of the bitwise AND will be identical to the mask. To illustrate this further, consider the results of using this same mask with a COLUMNS_UPDATED that indicates that only columns 3 and 4 were updated:

```
tblA    00001100
tblB    00010101
        --------
        00000100
```

Here the result does not equal the value of the mask, so we know that columns 1, 3, and 5 were not all updated.

Triggers in Oracle

Unlike SQL Server, Oracle allows us to specify whether triggers are to be executed before or after the event which produced them is performed, and to also indicate an action we should take *instead of* the requested insert, delete or update. The syntax for creating a trigger in PL/SQL is:

```
CREATE [OR REPLACE] TRIGGER trigger_name
   BEFORE | AFTER | INSTEAD OF
   DELETE | INSERT | UPDATE [OF column [, ...]]
   ON table
   [REFERENCING
      OLD [AS] oldtable | NEW [AS] newtable]
   [FOR EACH ROW]
   [WHEN (condition)]
   -- SQL statements
```

There are a couple of points where this syntax differs from that used in creating SQL Server triggers. Firstly, we need to state explicitly if we wish to refer to the tables containing the values of altered rows before and after any changes take place. We do this using the REFERENCING clause, specifying the OLD or NEW keyword to indicate which table we wish to access, and giving the table an alias by which we can refer to it within the trigger. The optional FOR EACH ROW clause specifies that the trigger is to fire for each row that is modified, rather than once for the entire statement. Finally, we can also include a WHEN clause which we can use to restrict the trigger to fire only under a given condition.

For example, the following trigger is fired before an insert on the EMP table if the new hire date is greater than the current date. We check this by looking in the NEW table, to which we give the alias newEmpTbl. If the trigger is fired, we raise an exception to prevent the invalid row being entered:

```
CREATE OR REPLACE TRIGGER tbiEmp
BEFORE INSERT ON EMP
REFERENCING NEW AS newEmpTbl
FOR EACH ROW
WHEN (newEmpTbl.HIREDATE > SYSDATE)
BEGIN
    RAISE invalid_date_error;

EXCEPTION
    WHEN invalid_date_error THEN RAISE_APPLICATION_ERROR (-20000,
        'Cannot have a hire date in the future.');
END;
```

If we want our trigger to fire for more than one action (say, for updating and inserting), we join the actions with the OR keyword. We can also cause the trigger to fire only if particular columns have been updated using the UPDATE OF ... syntax. For example, we can modify the trigger above so that it will also ensure that our hire date field isn't updated with a value later than the current date:

```
CREATE OR REPLACE TRIGGER tbiEmp
BEFORE INSERT OR UPDATE OF HIREDATE
ON EMP
REFERENCING NEW AS newEmpTbl
FOR EACH ROW
WHEN (newEmpTbl.HIREDATE > SYSDATE)
DECLARE invalid_date_error EXCEPTION;
BEGIN
    RAISE invalid_date_error;

EXCEPTION
    WHEN invalid_date_error THEN RAISE_APPLICATION_ERROR (-20000,
        'Cannot have a hire date in the future.');
END;
```

Triggers in DB2

The syntax for creating triggers in DB2 is very similar to that for Oracle:

```
CREATE TRIGGER trigger_name
    NO CASCADE BEFORE | AFTER
    DELETE | INSERT | UPDATE [OF column [, ...]]
    [REFERENCING
        [OLD [AS] oldrow][,]
        [NEW [AS] newrow][,]
        [OLD_TABLE [AS] oldtable][,]
        [NEW_TABLE [AS] newtable]]
    FOR EACH ROW | FOR EACH STATEMENT
    MODE DB2SQL
    [WHEN (condition)]
    BEGIN ATOMIC
        -- SQL statements
    END;
```

The chief differences here, are that a trigger in DB2 can only apply to one action, such as updates or deletes (we will need to write multiple triggers if we want to react to different actions on the table); and that our REFERENCING clause can have up to four parts:

❑   OLD: The row prior to being updated.

❑   NEW: The row as it will be after any changes have been made.

❑   OLD_TABLE: The entire set of rows prior to being updated.

❑   NEW_TABLE: The entire set of updated or inserted rows after the changes have been made.

To illustrate this syntax, let's rewrite the Oracle trigger that we saw earlier for the DB2 SAMPLE database. Again, we'll fire a trigger before a new row is inserted into the EMPLOYEE table, if the new value for the HIREDATE is later than the current date:

```
CREATE TRIGGER ADMINISTRATOR.tiEmployee
    NO CASCADE BEFORE
    INSERT
    ON ADMINISTRATOR.EMPLOYEE
    REFERENCING NEW AS newrow
    FOR EACH ROW
    MODE DB2SQL
    WHEN (newrow.HIREDATE > CURRENT DATE)
    BEGIN ATOMIC
        SIGNAL SQLSTATE '70001' ('Hire date cannot be in the future');
    END;
```

The SIGNAL SQLSTATE statement we use in triggers has a slightly different form to the one we saw earlier. In this case, we include the descriptive text in parentheses after the SQLSTATE code, rather than specifying it in a SET MESSAGE_TEXT clause.

Summary

When coding an application that uses a database, there are several objects that we can use to develop our algorithms and apply business rules. This chapter introduced the primary objects used in database programming: views, triggers, and stored procedures.

By using views; we can simplify queries, isolate application logic, and add additional levels of security. Views allow us to create a layer of abstraction between the raw data and the consumer of that data. Not only does this extra layer provide customized sets of data for the user, it also helps to ease maintenance issues when changes are made to the tables.

Stored procedures, with a combination of SQL statements, flow control logic, and error handling, provide us with a rich environment to develop our algorithms and business rules. By placing data manipulation routines within the database itself, we can achieve better organization of our code and with it better performance. These performance gains come from the fact that stored procedures are compiled so that a single call to a stored procedure can invoke multiple SQL operations. Like views, we can grant permissions on a user basis for added security.

By using triggers, we can associate routines that are fired when data modification events occur. This provides us with an efficient and convenient way to apply business rules and enforce data integrity within tables and between tables.

Section 2

Data Access

Introduction to Data Access

In order to understand the current technologies available for data access, let us begin by looking at what we mean by **data access**. The expression is formed from two words that symbolize a source of data with its own format, internal rules, and schemas (the *data* part) and a public interface to allow external clients to read and write it (the *access* part). Being able to access data, wherever it is located and in whatever format, has been a goal of many developers since the beginning of the modern programming era.

For a long time, the originator of the data lived with the certainty that the data represented a valuable asset to defend, protect, and keep hidden from any prying eyes, with both good and bad intentions. Of course, protecting data is a necessity, and data always represents a significant part of enterprise assets. However, making it accessible to external users in a standard way is not necessarily a bad thing.

Six or seven years ago, I struggled to build a desktop application that maintained a small database of descriptions. We needed to keep the data away from unauthorized people, but, at the same time, enable authorized users to merge their own data with ours. Having chosen a certain desktop database engine, we soon realized that a degree of interoperability between our application and other databases would have been required for the product to be successful. Understanding different database formats was the key problem we faced, and a possible solution that was considered was the creation of general purpose libraries containing these formats. However, such a solution was not achievable in practice due to the limited extensibility of the various databases. Those were the bad old days when establishing interoperability between databases required a great deal of effort.

The modern era of database programming began when software developers proposed **Open Database Connectivity** to provide a means of allowing any application to access any database format through a common set of API functions. ODBC was Microsoft's implementation of this open data access proposal, whereas the equivalent technology in the Java world was Java Database Connectivity or JDBC. Below this common layer of code, a database-specific tool, the **driver**, did all the hard work of mediating between the client and the database itself, getting the data and returning it back to the client. Because the API calls were the same, all the user had to do was change the driver and the data source without having to change any code. This quickly became the preferred method of general data access and formed the basis of what followed – first the standardization of driver architectures, leading to the object-oriented data access methodologies of today.

In this chapter, we'll take a whistle-stop tour of the various technologies available for data access. I'll introduce each one in some kind of chronological order, while providing just enough details on each of them to allow you to understand the evolution of data access over the past five years. We'll touch on:

❑   ODBC

❑   DAO and RDO

❑   OLE DB

❑   ADO

Finally, I will mention the latest addition to the family – ADO+.

Open Database Connectivity

Open Database Connectivity (ODBC) is an architecture that Microsoft presented back in 1991. It was aimed at giving developers the ability to access a number of different types of data sources through the same API. Before then, developers were limited to database-specific APIs, such as DBLib, which provided great performance when accessing their native databases, but could not be used for any other databases.

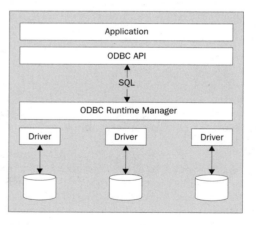

In the overall ODBC architecture, two components play a central role and do most of the tasks – they are the ODBC Driver Manager and the driver, which basically took the database connectivity problems and solved them with the same technology used to solve hardware driver problems. ODBC provides a set of drivers with common interfaces which know how to deal with the database in order to get the desired data.

The Runtime Driver Manager

As I said before, the ODBC API defines a set of protocols that allow a client application to access data directly. By 'protocol', I mean a sequence of well-defined steps, or a set of functions that are called in a certain order. So, if you issue one set of commands, you get a recordset copied into the local memory cache or, if a difference set of commands are used, any changes you made are entered into the underlying database. Once the application knows about this API and these high-level protocols, it can work with any data source for which an ODBC-compliant driver module exists. While making the call to the database, the application specifies the driver through which it wants the command to execute.

The ODBC Driver Manager is the module responsible for locating the correct driver. It starts and sustains communication with the driver and makes sure a command is executed properly. The application never calls the driver manager directly – the API functions invoked by the client do this under the hood.

The use of drivers solves the problem of accessing multiple database management systems (DBMS); however, the code needed to accomplish this can be rather complex. Applications that need to work with more than one driver cannot be statically linked to any of them. Otherwise they would need recompiling to support a new driver or if a new version of an existing driver were released. So, applications must load drivers at runtime and indirectly call the functions in them.

> *For C++ Programmers: ODBC drivers are Dynamic Link Libraries (DLLs) and as such they may have a static-link import library. If you link to a driver at compile time then the compiler and the linker will be able to resolve any function name. If you plan to use any possible driver, you will need to load it dynamically at runtime. In this case, you cannot use function names in your code and must resort to function pointers. The ODBC Driver Manager solves the recompilation and relinking problem.*

How the Manager Works

The Driver Manager implements all the ODBC functions. Generally speaking, these functions are pass-through calls to similar functionality implemented in the drivers themselves. The Driver Manager library is usually statically linked to the application. However, nothing prevents applications from loading the library at run time. Since the Driver Manager is a proxy module, any change in any of the available drivers will not affect it. Thus, the application can call ODBC functions by name in the Driver Manager and have it do the dirty job of mapping them to the corresponding functions in the specific driver.

From the application's point of view, a particular driver is identified by a string. The picture alongside shows some of the ODBC drivers installed on a typical machine:

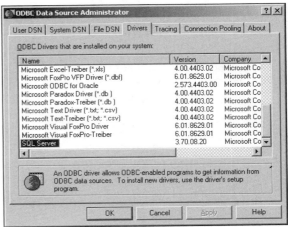

The string that identifies the driver is any of those listed under the **Name** column. You can get that dialog box by opening the Control Panel and selecting the **ODBC Data Sources** applet. Notice that under Windows 2000 this applet is contained in the **Start** menu item called **Data Sources (ODBC)** under the **Administrative Tools** menu.

Invoked by an API call that contains the driver's name, the Driver Manager locates and loads the driver and stores the address of each function it exports. This table of functions is often referred to as a **connection handle**:

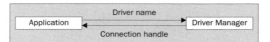

To call a function, the application makes a call to it in the Driver Manager and passes the connection handle for the driver, and information on the function that is to be called. The Driver Manager then calls the function by using the address stored earlier:

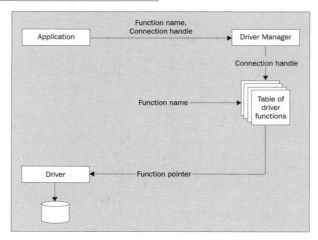

A different driver is required for each data source that supports ODBC. The driver implements the functions in the ODBC API. To use a different driver, the application just needs to load the new driver and call the functions in it, and there is no requirement for recompilation. To access multiple data sources simultaneously, the application loads multiple drivers, and there would then be multiple connection handles.

ODBC Drivers

The ODBC specification was originally proposed by Microsoft but rapidly gained a broad acceptance and has become a standard for all platforms. How drivers are implemented is specific to the operating system. For example, on the Windows platform drivers are dynamic link libraries (DLLs).

The ODBC specification provides a number of features implemented by all the common database systems, though ODBC functionality allows for more specific database features to be accessible from the client. However, implementing every last feature or obscure functionality of a rich database system such as Oracle or SQL Server would mean that the driver would become more complex and less efficient. So a balance has to be struck in deciding which advanced features to implement and which not to. Having implemented the chosen set of ODBC functionality in the driver, there are two more criteria that the ODBC API takes care of:

❑   How to determine whether a certain driver supports a given feature

❑   Establish a number of conformance levels for drivers

Two functions provide the necessary information for the first criterion: `SQLGetInfo` returns general information about the driver and its RDBMS capabilities, and `SQLGetFunctions` returns the list of functions the driver supports. For the second criterion, note that there are three ODBC interface conformance levels: Core, Level 1, and Level 2. For more details, please refer to the ODBC Programmer's Reference (see http://msdn.microsoft.com/library/psdk/dasdk/odin8w4s.htm).

Bear in mind that ODBC defines a common interface for all of the features it exposes. Consequently, applications can reason in terms of cross-database features rather than RDBMS-specific features. Thus, applications don't need to be updated when a new version of an RDBMS is released, nor when a driver is updated.

Connecting to ODBC Data Sources

ODBC applications talk to a **data source**, which is simply the repository of the data. It can be a file or a particular database defined within an RDBMS. Typical examples of data sources are SQL Server, Oracle and DB2 databases, a collection of XBase files in a server directory, and an Access file.

A data source gathers into a single place all of the information needed to access the data, including the driver name and the physical location – all of these details are hidden from the user. The user will simply refer to the data using high-level names such as `Inventory` or `Orders` without knowing where the data resides or how the application gets to it. There are two types of data sources: machine data sources and file data sources. Both contain similar information but differ in the way it is stored.

Machine Data Sources

Machine data sources are stored on the machine with a user-defined name. On machines running Windows 95 or higher, this information is stored in the system registry. Depending on the registry key that the information is stored under, the data source is known as a **user data source** or a **system data source**. A user data source is visible only to the user that created it and only on the current machine. Conversely, a system data source is visible to all users that can access the machine, including NT services.

The data source contains all of the information the Driver Manager and driver need to connect to the indicated data source – the name of the driver, the name of the database, and other network information. For example, for an Oracle database, a machine data source contains the name of the Oracle driver, the server where the Oracle RDBMS resides, the SQL*Net connection string that identifies the SQL*Net driver to use, and the system ID of the database on the server. A SQL Server database contains the name of the server, user ID and password, authentication method, the database name, and optional settings such as the locale ID and the log file.

Registry Settings

A user data source is stored under the `HKEY_CURRENT_USER` registry hive. The exact path is:

```
HKEY_CURRENT_USER
  \Software
    \ODBC
      \ODBC.INI
```

A system data source is stored under the same path below the `HKEY_LOCAL_MACHINE` hive:

```
HKEY_LOCAL_MACHINE
  \Software
    \ODBC
      \ODBC.INI
```

Under this path the ODBCINST.INI sub-tree contains references to all drivers installed. In versions of Windows prior to Windows 95, these settings were kept in system INI files called odbc.ini and odbcinst.ini using sections to distinguish between machine and user-specific data sources.

File Data Sources

File data sources are stored in a .dsn file in this location:

```
C:\Program Files\Common Files\ODBC\Data Sources
```

The Driver Manager reads the content of the file before making the connection to the data source. A file data source has no data source name, and the data is referred to by DRIVER, SERVER and DATABASE attributes. This is the typical content of a .dsn file:

```
[ODBC]
DRIVER=SQL Server
UID=sa
DATABASE=pubs
APP=Microsoft(R) Windows NT(TM) Operating System
SERVER=(local)
Description=MTS Samples
```

A .dsn file allows connection information to be used repeatedly by a single user or shared among several users.

The Role of SQL

In addition to a standard programming interface, ODBC defines a standard query language based on the X/Open SQL CAE specification (see http://msdn.microsoft.com/library/psdk/dasdk/odch32ax.htm). This language is nearly identical to the SQL language that is supported by most of the common RDBMSs. Applications can submit statements using either ODBC - or RDBMS-specific SQL grammar. If a statement uses ODBC grammar that is different from that used by the RDBMS, the driver converts it before sending it to the data source. However, such conversions are rare because most RDBMSs already use standard SQL grammar.

ODBC applications perform almost all their data access operations through SQL statements. These statements can be constructed in one of three ways: hard-coded during development, constructed at runtime, or entered directly by the user. This depends upon the specific needs and goals of the application.

Beyond ODBC

Architecturally speaking, ODBC is based on SQL. This provides an advantage to the user as long as relational data is being targeted. In this respect, ODBC is good at its job and has served the database programming community well. However, nowadays it has several crucial shortcomings:

❑   It depends too much on the relational model and the SQL language.

❑   It exposes a function-based API that is difficult to use from a VB/ASP perspective.

Also, what if your data is not contained in a RDBMS system or a file-based database engine? What if your data has to be collected by several different drivers? What if your data cannot be easily expressed as homogeneous rows and columns, such as spreadsheet data? The simple answer to this is that in these situations, you have data that cannot be accessed through ODBC. But is that really a valid answer? In other words, do we really have two different categories of data – relational and non-relational? Or is data just data – regardless of the format, the storage medium and the internal representation?

A complete solution to these issues came only recently with the launching of Microsoft's **Universal Data Access** (UDA). However, before then, they had been working on resolving the difficulty of accessing the ODBC API from a script-based environment. The shift from a call-based to an object-based data access model was addressed several years ago with the release of DAO and the Jet Database Engine. I'll cover UDA later on in this chapter. In the meantime, let's resume the historical review of data access evolution and consider what has been developed since ODBC.

Towards Data Object Models

A client that wants to obtain data programmatically from an ODBC data source needs to call a number of API functions and handle pointers and memory buffers. This can be done by dedicated C++ programmers with a lot of time, but it is not exactly easy for Visual Basic developers or ASP script authors. Using object-oriented programming models is easy to use and is much less error-prone. In this section, I shall review three such technologies:

- ❑   DAO – Data Access Objects
- ❑   RDO – Remote Data Objects
- ❑   ODBCDirect

DAO – Data Access Objects

The very first example of object-oriented database programming was **Data Access Objects** or **DAO**, a high-level programming interface built on top of the Jet Database Engine, which is the native database engine behind Microsoft Access. For early Visual Basic users, DAO was the best way of accessing data on local Access databases. It was not the only tool of its kind at the time, and probably was not the most efficient, but it was highly popular.

DAO offers a hierarchy of objects that allow users to get both records and data definitions from Access sources. Indeed, the DAO objects map to the various objects of a database that applications need to access, such as tables, views, queries, and indexes. In effect, the DAO object model was designed to be a reproduction of the Access database objects, and in terms of efficiency, elegance, and productivity, DAO is tailor-made for Access. The latest version of Jet (4.0), which shipped with Access 2000, supports Unicode and ANSI-compliant SQL syntax as well as row-level locking, improved replication and the ability to track logged on users. As you would expect, DAO exposes all of this new functionality to the developer. Jet 4.0 is also completely compatible with SQL Server 7 and later, which makes the task of migrating from Access to SQL Server easier than ever.

The DAO object model is summarized in the figure below:

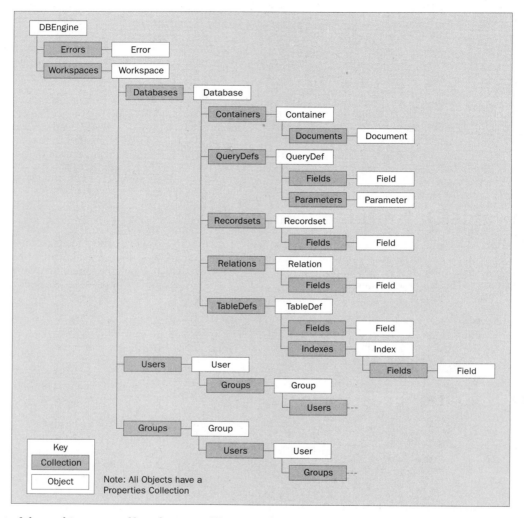

Most of these objects are self-explanatory. However, the `Workspace` object contains information on the current user session and transaction scope, whereas the `Database` object represents the database with a single open connection. It follows that if you have more than one database open, you have to have more than one `Database` object. The `TableDef` object contains the table definitions whereas the `QueryDef` object is where the SQL statements are stored. The `Container` object represents the objects on the database where you can assign access permissions for a secure workgroup. The `Relation` object specifies a relationship between fields in tables and queries. You can use this object to create, delete, or change the type of relationship.

Many of the DAO objects have very limited functionality when used with non-Access databases. For all databases other than Access, the Jet engine is required to translate the data access commands before they are sent on. Thus, if you wanted to use DAO to access an Oracle or a SQL Server database (via ODBC), or an ISAM database such as FoxPro, this translation process compromises performance.

DAO also leaves a lot to be desired when accessing remote data sources over the Web. Connecting via ODBC to a client/server database such as Microsoft SQL Server is handled in a very clumsy manner. In client/server data access, data retrieved from the database is parsed on the *server*, and then the client only receives the data that was originally requested. However, when DAO retrieves data from an ODBC database, Jet pulls *all* of the data and then parses it on the client machine, which is a terrible use of network bandwidth and client resources. Thus, DAO is not at all optimized for use in a Web environment. For these reasons, and with the rise of ADO, the future of DAO is uncertain, though it would still fill a niche when it comes to programming Access from Visual Basic or C++.

RDO – Remote Data Objects

The next step in the evolution of object-oriented data access was **Remote Data Objects** or **RDO** – which allows programmers to access relational database servers without having to go through the Jet engine. RDO is a set of objects that encapsulates the ODBC API, thereby enabling a much more direct access to ODBC data sources than can be achieved through Jet. Since Jet is not used, the calls to data sources do not require this extra level of translation, which results in faster data access and retrieval.

So RDO provided the speed of making direct calls to the ODBC API while presenting the programmer with a COM-based architecture that was simple to use. However, RDO was restricted to using ODBC, and therefore accessing Jet and ISAM data sources was very inefficient. This proved to be a limitation of RDO, in that it was not able to access the wealth of data contained in mainframe archives and other non-relational formats, such as spreadsheets, mail messages, and text files.

> **ISAM stands for** Indexed Sequential Access Method, **which provides a way of accessing data where almost all the data handling takes place on the client, with the server used merely to store records. ISAM data sources include Microsoft Access, Microsoft FoxPro, dBase and Paradox.**

RDO offers a simpler object model than DAO as shown in this figure:

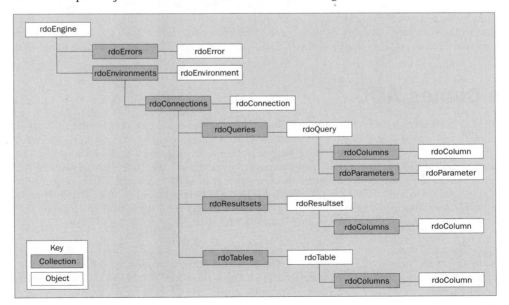

The main objects of note are the `rdoEnvironment` object, which defines a set of connections and a transaction scope for a user and sets a security context for database operations; the `rdoQuery` object, which contains SQL statements; the `rdoResultset` object, which contains the returned recordset; and the `rdoTable` object, which represents the table or view definition.

RDO inherits all the good and bad of ODBC; that is, support for relational data and a significant loss of efficiency when requested to deal with non-ODBC data sources. RDO certainly earned its place in the history of data access, but it was not developed with the Web in mind, being a pre-Web technology, and hence does not work well in this environment. For these reasons, it has now largely been superseded by ADO.

ODBCDirect

ODBCDirect, introduced with Visual Basic 5, provides another means to access data. Based on RDO, it enables DAO applications to bypass Jet to access ODBC data sources directly. In this way, you can use the same DAO code to access data sources that would otherwise be costly in terms of performance if Jet were used. Programmatically enabling your application to use ODBCDirect is very simple. All you have to do is add the following line to the beginning of your application before any DAO objects are referenced:

```
DBEngine.DefaultType = dbUseODBC
```

In order to access a data source, ODBCDirect-enabled applications must create a workspace object, which defines the connection in terms of standard data access criteria such as a user session, user name, password, and database type. The connection is made by supplying a standard semicolon-delimited connection string to the data source.

Although it is easy to upgrade a DAO application to an ODBCDirect application, there are several key differences in the way they are programmed. For instance, ODBCDirect applications must be handled at the workspace level rather than the database level and a separate workspace object is required for each recordset returned from the data source. Also, you cannot use ODBCDirect to carry out any changes to the database structure or assign access permissions, neither can you perform heterogeneous joins. However you are able to access any ODBC-enabled source, and can perform batch updates.

Here Comes ADO

When Microsoft introduced **ADO, ActiveX Data Objects**, it seemed like they wanted to just scramble things once again and come up with yet another TLA to amaze people. What's ADO anyway? Is it just a permutation of DAO? Despite the programming community's initial diffidence towards ADO, it was destined to play an important role in any database programmer's life. The first versions of ADO provided just an alternative way of doing the same things as DAO and RDO. In terms of functionality, ADO was inferior to both RDO and DAO, and it had a different object model. The only advantage in using ADO was the introduction of Remote Data Services (RDS), a set of objects to carry out client-to-server data access across the HTTP protocol and the Internet.

The real change of perspective for ADO arrived with ADO 2.0 and its support for the then relatively new data access technology: OLE DB. OLE DB is the unifying approach for data access without any distinction between local and remote, relational and non-relational. OLE DB is at the very heart of Microsoft's Universal Data Access to which we now turn.

Universal Data Access

Universal Data Access (UDA) is Microsoft's strategy that aims to provide high-performance access to potentially any data sources. UDA introduces a common programming interface for both relational and non-relational data that can be used with almost all of today's programming languages and development tools. It is not tied to a single vendor but, like ODBC, is open to the contribution of third parties, who supply the tools and products that make the integration of data storage formats possible at low cost. Integration and low cost of ownership are two fundamental principles of UDA. These form the basis of other important design goals for UDA applications, such as ease of deployment and upgrading.

UDA was originally designed to provide the strategy for all data services built into Windows distributed applications and utilizes COM as the means of putting together the various pieces of its puzzle. But if it is a philosophy inspiring the data access services on the Windows DNA platform, what functionality do we need to implement UDA applications?

Here Comes OLE DB

OLE DB is the layer of code that actually turns the UDA vision into practice. OLE DB can be seen as the equivalent to ODBC but with potentially unlimited scope regarding the format of the data that is to be accessed. After all, OLE DB and ODBC share the same goal, by providing a common API to allow data access. The main differences between OLE DB and ODBC are summarized like this:

- ❏ OLE DB follows a COM-based approach while ODBC is a function-based technology managed by a separate Driver Manager.

- ❏ OLE DB boasts a general architecture that encompasses both relational and non-relational data. With OLE DB 2.5, the same unifying approach extends also to hierarchical and semi-structured data. ODBC is only designed to act on relational data.

- ❏ OLE DB utilizes COM components (providers) instead of a library of functions (implemented in ODBC drivers) to facilitate data access.

- ❏ OLE DB can support any query language that the specific provider understands. ODBC is restricted to a generic brand of SQL.

- ❏ Because it is COM-based, OLE DB doesn't need the equivalent of the ODBC Driver Manager.

- ❏ OLE DB exposes the data through COM interfaces and avoids copying the rowsets directly into the application's memory.

Two OLE DB compliant applications work according to a sort of client-server system where the client is called **consumer** and the server is the **provider**. Both are instances of COM objects.

UDA vs Universal Data Storage

An alternative strategy to Universal Data Access is **Universal Data Storage**. UDA depends on defining and implementing a layer of code capable of shielding users and programmers from the diversity of the underlying data sources. By contrast, Universal Data Storage integrates different data formats by importing all the different data formats into a unique environment. One example of such a system is a powerful RDBMS capable of supporting many different types of data. Such a system is Oracle 8i, which allows you to import and display as native tables any sort of document, including Word documents and e-mails.

Another product was Informix Universal Server, which introduced the revolutionary concept of **data-blade**. This gave us a chance to write callback modules capable of analyzing proprietary data and exposing it in a standard way. Despite having very different low-level architectures, data-blades and OLE DB providers have certain features in common. The only significant difference at the higher level of abstraction is that data-blades import new data sources into the Informix's RDBMS, while OLE DB allows you to import new data sources into an existing enterprise or user information system.

Without Further ADO

Directly programming OLE DB interfaces is largely the domain of C/C++ developers. For performance reasons, OLE DB code was written using C++ and raw COM fundamentals, and is a hard beast for other developers to comprehend, let alone use. The vast majority of VB and ASP programmers would barely be able to take advantage of the technology. For this reason, Microsoft reinvented its preferred data access object model, ADO, to make it fully OLE DB compliant.

*Actually, ADO only does half the task of enabling VB and ASP developers to use OLE DB. ADO enables the writing of OLE DB consumer code but doesn't enable the writing of OLE DB providers. For this purpose, Microsoft released another framework, called the **OLE DB Simple Provider** (OSP) Toolkit that we will discuss in more detail in the next chapter.*

ADO 2.0

ADO 2.0 certainly represents a major upgrade in the story of ADO. With this version, ADO becomes functionally equivalent to RDO and DAO, with a few additional capabilities and facilities. The most important feature, however, is the support for OLE DB. All the ADO data access goes through OLE DB, even when it explicitly declares to use ODBC. In this case, ADO utilizes the OLE DB provider for ODBC drivers.

The ADO object model is characterized by a hierarchy of objects. In other words, to create a recordset you can just create and fill it without creating any other object, say, a connection. On the fringes of the object model, you also find interesting features such as disconnected recordsets, data-shaping and persistence. ADO 2.0 is part of the Microsoft Data Access Components toolkit (MDAC), which also includes some OLE DB providers (for Oracle, JET, Active Directory, Index Server, and SQL Server) and Remote Data Services version 2.0.

ADO 2.1

Microsoft released this minor upgrade a few months after shipping the MDAC 2.0 as a patch for several bugs and misbehaviors. The basic ADO programming model didn't change in this release, though a very important new feature was included: support for XML. In fact, since ADO 2.1 you can save a recordset to an XML document that follows a pre-defined schema.

ADO 2.5

This version of ADO, which shipped with Windows 2000, is characterized by a couple of new objects – Record and Stream – that enhance the way in which you are able to work with the content of the single field. Being based on the OLE DB 2.5 interfaces, ADO 2.5 is also capable of taking advantage of things like **direct URL binding** and providers that return hierarchical recordsets. By the time you read this, a minor update of ADO, ADO 2.6, which includes more functionality for SQL Server 2000 integration, will have been released.

ADO+

ADO+ is the latest evolutionary improvement to ADO, which is designed to improve platform interoperability and is an integral part of the forthcoming .Net platform. It is characterized by an extensive use of strongly typed programming in which business objects figure prominently. A concept crucial to ADO+ is the **dataset**, which is an in-memory copy of the database data. A dataset is able to exist in memory without any active connection to the database containing the exposed tables and views. Because of this and because of the strongly typed programming model, applications using ADO+ datasets will operate with faster execution times than their ADO contemporaries, because they will not need to walk through ADO collections every time they need to get some database-specific information.

The dataset is passed from the database through a middle-tier business object to the user interface, and ADO+ employs XML to ensure data persistence and transmission. In other words, the whole dataset is converted into an XML format before being exchanged between the different components. Because of the platform neutrality of XML, any application on any platform has the potential to read and manipulate ADO+ datasets.

Summary

The average database client application of today probably uses ADO as its preferred method of accessing data. This happens for a number of good reasons: ease of use, inherent simplicity, a powerful object model. In terms of performance, ADO is not exactly the fastest way of getting records but is highly optimized for the things it is supposed to do. The continued evolution of the framework is an indirect guarantee that it is much better than commonly believed.

If anyone is about to write a client module for an existing system, then ADO will probably be his or her first choice of data access technology. The earlier object-oriented data access technologies – RDO, DAO and ODBCDirect – have been superseded by ADO and OLE DB, though they might still be employed for specific uses. If you still have to maintain RDO or ODBC-based systems, be assured – Microsoft will continue supporting and providing ODBC resources and won't be dropping RDO. However, you should plan to migrate to ADO as soon as possible. Doing this from RDO won't be too difficult. If, however, you're planning to choose a data access technology for a brand new system, you should adopt the latest ADO version available. ADO was designed to facilitate use of OLE DB functionality, and inherits all the advantages that this COM-based API has to offer.

In this chapter, in fact, we've quickly reviewed the data access technologies that crossed the Windows world in the past decade:

- ❑ Open Database Connectivity
- ❑ The DAO object model for Jet
- ❑ RDO as a COM-based ODBC
- ❑ OLE DB as the practical implementation of the UDA strategy
- ❑ ADO in all of its flavors

In the chapters that follow, we'll look at the last two technologies in more detail, starting with OLE DB.

6

OLE DB

Many people welcome the idea of being able to access data from different stores, regardless of the internal structure of the data and the method used to store it. For a typical company, its data store does not just consist of tables, indexes, stored procedures, and triggers contained within a commercial DBMS system (usually a relational DBMS), but also includes Word documents containing details of the company's employment and security policies. For example, faxes, spreadsheets, e-mail messages, pictures, web pages – anything that can be expressed in a digital format.

Data access applications have to be designed so that they can access data wherever it resides and whatever its format, which is much better and much more practical than having the company's entire data store migrate to a new, fully integrated data system. A real-world corporate data store is always a highly heterogeneous one, and, as a developer, you might be asked to create an application that combines the contents of a table of customers with e-mail messages and faxes received from each of these customers. Actually, this would be relatively easy to do, if all the data was integrated in the same environment, but this is rarely, if ever, the case. Microsoft's answer to the demand for tools to manage heterogeneous data is contained in the UDA strategy that we covered in the previous chapter.

UDA is aimed to provide a layer of code that is capable of accessing all possible data sources with the same API. It defines a very flexible interface. To write a UDA compliant module you're required to implement a minimum core functionality, though you can exceed this minimum standard should your application need it. The technology at the very center of the UDA vision is OLE DB, namely a COM-based specification to define both the way data is exposed and the way a client can access it. OLE DB is the low-level layer that acts as middleware between client applications and data sources wrapped by data providers.

In this chapter, we'll cover the basics of OLE DB as follows:

❏ The OLE DB architecture.

❏ The role of OLE DB services.

❏ The fundamental COM interfaces.

❏ Newest changes to the OLE DB model.

❏ Accessing data through OLE DB.

OLE DB is based on COM and extensively utilizes interfaces. Working with interfaces is a relatively difficult programming task which can only be carried out by advanced C++ users. However, many applications are written with either Visual Basic or ASP, which cannot implement the OLE DB interfaces directly. For this reason, Microsoft introduced ADO, a set of objects that sits on top of OLE DB. The ADO objects map directly onto the COM interfaces that OLE DB providers expose. Using ADO and its web counterpart, Remote Data Service (RDS), is relatively easy from within ASP pages or Visual Basic applications. However, if speed and optimized performance is your aim, an application using the raw OLE DB API gives an edge over an ADO based application.

The Rationale Behind OLE DB

The big picture of data access according to Microsoft's technologies is shown here:

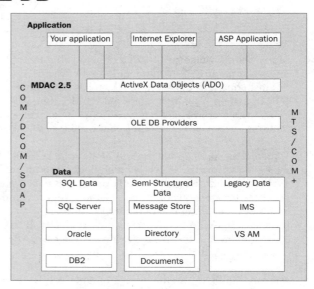

Win32 and Web-based applications can either take advantage of OLE DB directly or use ADO. This depends upon the specific development tools used to build the application. The diagram above illustrates a typical Windows DNA three-tier system, where the client can be any Win32 application or a web application. The middle tier consists of the business objects that use ADO or OLE DB to fetch data from data providers. COM, **Distributed COM** (DCOM) and, more recently, SOAP (**Simple Object Access Protocol**) provide the plumbing that ties up together all the pieces of a DNA 2000 system that uses OLE DB to manipulate data. The middle-tier layer is powered by MTS/COM+ services to improve the overall scalability and transaction support. All client applications can rely on a common API to access any sort of data regardless of the storage medium and the format: relational, nonrelational, proprietary formats, semistructured, hierarchical, ISAM, and so on.

OLE DB is an evolving technology and has been enhanced to include support for OLAP and multidimensional data (as of version 2.1 of the specification) as well as semi-structured, non-tabular data (as of version 2.5). Providers exist for all common RDBMS, and many nonrelational formats – such as legacy archives on mainframes, though if you have data in an unsupported data format (such as Excel worksheets) then you may have to pay your software developers to create a provider for you! For example, exposing a single Excel worksheet through OLE DB is possible. The cells of a single worksheet model a table of records. However, an Excel file may consist of multiple worksheets that need to be rendered in some way. The fact that Excel files can consist of one or more than one worksheet means that they are at best semistructured data sources that the OLE DB version 2.1 cannot work with. Word documents provide even more of a problem – they cannot be logically expressed as a single table. However, it is possible to break a Word document down into a collection of tables (paragraphs, comments, bookmarks, styles), or render it as a tree. Whatever you do, you end up working with semistructured data.

It's only with OLE DB 2.5 that Microsoft addresses the problem of rendering semistructured and hierarchical data. Defining a standard interface, though, doesn't mean that all the providers implement it. At this time, the only OLE DB providers fully compliant with OLE DB 2.5 are those for SQL Server 2000 and Exchange 2000.

The Limitations of OLE DB 2.1

There are a few characteristics of the earlier version of OLE DB that needed to be improved in order to make it able to access all types of data. First, OLE DB 2.1 **rowsets** (they are called recordsets in ADO jargon, but are basically the same thing) can only be tabular, that is they have to present the same number and type of columns for all rows. It is not possible to have rows with varying numbers of columns. Difficulty arises when attempting to model hierarchical data. While you can append a field to an existing table to hold a child rowset, this has to be repeated for each row in the rowset. As a result, you can contain a hierarchical structure in a tabular rowset, but not a real tree or a collection of nodes. Also, a consumer application has to know the details about the provider it wants to connect to, such as its name (ProgID) or its CLSID, as well as about the syntax of the supported query language.

These caveats have been fixed with OLE DB version 2.5, as we will demonstrate later in this chapter. However, as mentioned a moment ago, only a few providers to date expose features specific to OLE DB 2.5.

The OLE DB Architecture

Let's put aside for a moment the differences between the various versions of the OLE DB specification and focus on the main architectural issues. This figure shows the structure of OLE DB:

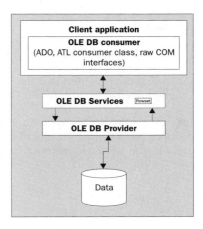

You see that there are three categories of OLE DB modules: consumers, providers and services. A client application uses consumer interfaces to invoke an OLE DB provider, which embeds the data source and is responsible for updating the data and for returning the selected subset of records. Between consumers and providers, OLE DB services play an interesting role; they wrap the standard data access process into a handful of new interfaces and software services. OLE DB services can interact with the data passing through to the caller, to filter it and make it available through more powerful services.

OLE DB Consumers

An OLE DB consumer is the application that acts as the client in a purely OLE DB environment. A consumer application invokes an OLE DB provider (with or without the intervention of an intermediate service), issues its query in a language that the provider can understand, and obtains a rowset.

Writing OLE DB Consumers

An OLE DB consumer can be written in two ways. First, it can be written as a raw C++ application that includes the proper header files, instantiates the right COM components and goes on and on querying them for the needed interfaces. A more elegant approach is to use the Active Template Library (ATL). As we're going to show you later on, you write ATL consumer applications by inserting a consumer object into your ATL project which inherits from a few basic ATL classes. These classes, in turn, inherit from OLE DB interfaces.

Outside the C++ world, ADO is by far the easiest way to access an OLE DB data source. From Visual Basic programs as well as from ASP pages or client-side script, you ask the ADO objects to open a connection with the data source and issue a command. The result of this process is the data, contained in an ADO `Recordset` object, which you can then manipulate on the client.

OLE DB Providers

An OLE DB provider is a component that exposes a standard set of OLE DB interfaces to the consumer. Behind the scenes, the provider is responsible for translating the commands received from the consumer to a format that is recognizable by the data store. OLE DB interfaces are expected to return records of data, but the provider does not necessarily own the data it returns. In some cases, the OLE DB provider is simply a wrapper module for another component that takes care of retrieving and formatting the data. In other cases, the OLE DB interfaces are directly exposed by the data store (that is, the database server).

As a COM component, an OLE DB provider is identified by a program identifier (ProgID) and a CLSID. The consumer refers to it through the ProgID. The COM Service Control Manager (SCM) identifies the providers that the consumer wants to talk to and there's no need for a special proxy module such as that used with ODBC.

An OLE provider is required to support a certain number of mandatory interfaces, though it can further implement a handful of optional ones. A special property based mechanism allows consumers to know in advance whether that certain provider supports that given feature.

OLE DB providers are registered as regular COM objects but require a couple of extra registry entries; the OLE DB Provider branch, and the OLEDB_SERVICES node:

- ❑   OLE DB Provider
- ❑   OLEDB_SERVICES

Those entries have to be created under the CLSID node of the component. For example, suppose the CLSID of your provider is {...} these nodes are under

```
HKEY_CLASSES_ROOT
  \CLSID
    \{...}
```

The first node contains the provider's name and is purpose is simply for identification. All the CLSIDs with that node are the CLSIDs of an OLE DB provider. The OLEDB_SERVICES node, instead, enables or disables the OLE DB services. The value is a DWORD – a 32-bit integer – and works as a bitmask. The default value is 0xFFFFFFFF which means insert everything that is available.

Existing Providers

Once you install MDAC 2.5, your system should contain at least the following OLE DB providers:

Provider	ProgID	Description
MSDASQL	MSDASQL	Provides access to data through an ODBC data source.
Index Server	MSIDXS	Provides read-only access to file system and Web data indexed by Microsoft Indexing Service.
SQL Server	SQLOLEDB	Provides access to SQL Server databases
Active Directory	ADSDSOObject	Connects to heterogeneous directory services through ADSI.
Oracle	MSDAORA	Provides access to Oracle databases
OLAP	MSOLAP	Provides access to multidimensional data that conform with the Microsoft OLE DB for OLAP specification.
Internet Publishing	MSDAIPP.DSO	Provides access to resources served by FrontPage or Internet Information Server, including HTML files or Windows 2000 Web folders.
JET 4.0	Microsoft.Jet.OLEDB.4.0	Provides access to Access databases.
DB2	DB2OLEDB	Provides access to IBM DB2 databases.
AS/400 and VSAM	SNAOLEDB	Provides access to AS/400 and VSAM tables on a host machine.

New and improved providers (such as a provider for accessing Sybase databases) are expected to ship with Microsoft Host Integration Server, which will be discussed in Chapter 23.

Not all of these providers implement exactly the same features, or in the same way. Later on in this chapter, we'll present the minimum set of characteristics an OLE DB provider must have.

> *When connecting to OLE DB data sources through raw C++ code, you usually create instances of the COM component representing the provider. You can also use mnemonic constants to refer to the component's CLSID. For example, CLSID_SQLOLEDB is the constant for the OLE DB provider for SQL Server.*

Writing OLE DB Providers

C++ is the only language that can be used to develop OLE DB providers. As we said earlier, an OLE DB provider is a COM object that implements a set of COM interfaces. However, there are a couple of aspects that differentiate an OLE DB provider from other COM objects – for one thing, the registry settings that we mentioned above. Secondly, an OLE DB provider is required to conform to a specific object model. (More on this later in the section about OLE DB interfaces and objects.)

You could write a provider using raw C++, or you could exploit some ready-to-use ATL classes. If you are not familiar with C++, there is a way of writing data providers that can even be used with Visual Basic.

The OLE DB Simple Provider Toolkit

If you want to write a data provider with Visual Basic, the first problem is that you have to implement special interfaces, which can be done with the help of type libraries. The second problem is that you have to manipulate pointers and memory buffers, which has never been easy in Visual Basic. The third problem is that certain COM data types used in OLE DB provider interfaces are not supported in Visual Basic. To be able to write data providers with VB, you need a wrapper that shields your code from these unsupported features, and exposes the supported interfaces to external callers (ADO and C++ consumers). It is also necessary to implement the most important of their methods through handlers provided by a VB COM object. The wrapper is written once and can be considered as a binary part of the MDAC. Through special registry settings, you can link it to a certain VB COM object and have a two-part data provider: the run-time wrapper plus the VB object. The former provides the plumbing, while the latter injects the particular code that retrieves and updates the recordsets. This wrapper is the **OLE DB Simple Provider** toolkit (OSP).

OSP originally shipped with Internet Explorer 4.0 and comprises a DLL (`msdaosp.dll`), some type libraries, and a number of examples written in different languages, including C++, Visual Basic and Java. Basically, it provides you with a generic layer of precompiled code (that is, `msdaosp.dll`) to enable communication with any OLE DB consumer. It exposes three interfaces that evaluate to the minimum implementation requirement for OLE DB interfaces: `DataSource`, `Session` and `Rowset`. Behind these interfaces there are lots of methods to code. The OSP toolkit does most of this work for you. The only thing you must do is write a VB COM object that looks like a VB data source class. Such an object is said to be an **OSP Data Object**.

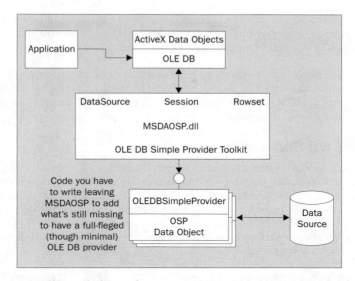

An OSP Data Object actually implements the OLEDBSimpleProvider interface that has 14 functions that span from data retrieval to updating, and from row counting to searching. OSP maps the functions of OLEDBSimpleProvider to various functions within the three objects it exposes. The sum of the methods of all the interfaces for the DataSource, Session and Rowset objects will always be higher than 14 – the excess functionality coming from the msdaosp.dll.

An OLE DB simple provider is a legitimate provider whose registered server is always msdaosp.dll. How is the link between this and your specific OSP Data Object established? Through the registry, of course. While registering the data object, the Default entry of the following registry key should be set to the ProgID of your OSP component. This ensures that msdaosp.dll is able to get in touch with it:

```
HKEY_CLASSES_ROOT
  \CLSID
   \{CLSID of your OSP data object}
    \OSP Data Object
```

Differences with non-Simple Providers

There's good and bad with OSP. On the plus side, it lets you easily write small providers with a significant number of features such as updating and searching. Its fairly simplified programming interface also makes it possible to write OLE DB providers with languages like Visual Basic or Java. However, the providers created using the OSP toolkit are not extensible since all of their exported functionality is defined by the OLEDBSimpleProvider interface. Also, the OSP providers do not support commands, which means that they are useful when the data to render is simple and doesn't require the use of complex queries.

OLE DB Service Providers

One of the reasons that make OLE DB a better architecture than ODBC is the lack of a run-time layer that maps the client calls to the entry points of the ODBC driver module. The presence of a COM programming interface allows the consumer to connect directly to the provider's functionality without any layer in the middle.

However, for ASP and Visual basic programmers, the ADO objects sit in between the consumer and the provider providing an intermediate run-time layer. ADO magically transforms calls to its methods and objects into calls directed to the provider's v-tables of functions.

There's another example of intermediate modules that allow you to customize the way in which the consumer/provider interaction takes place. These special modules are called **OLE DB Services**. The closest analogy for OLE DB services (or service providers) are MTS service components, namely interceptors that get dynamically loaded at run-time and are activated through a declarative syntax.

Settings for OLE DB Services

OLE DB provides a standard set of services to enrich the native functionality of OLE DB providers. These services include resource pooling, automatic transaction enlistment, and the client cursor engine. There are several ways to instantiate an OLE DB provider, but not all of them automatically enable services. In particular, when a consumer connects to a provider through CoCreateInstance, passing the CLSID, then OLE DB services are not enabled. If you're using ATL, use the XXX::OpenWithServices method instead of the more common XXX::Open that the ATL wizard silently inserts in the code it generates.

The following table shows all the valid values for the OLEDB_SERVICES registry node:

Value	Description
-1	All services (default).
-4	All except resource pooling and automatic transaction enlistment.
-5	All except Client Cursor Engine.
-8	All except resource pooling, automatic transaction enlistment, and the Client Cursor Engine.
3	Resource pooling and automatic transaction enlistment only, session level aggregation only.
0	No services.

If the registry entry does not exist for the provider, no service will be enabled, even if explicitly requested by the consumer programmatically.

The OLE DB Objects

An OLE DB data provider's COM interfaces are logically grouped to form an object hierarchy. This object model dictates the step-by-step procedure through which a consumer gains access to the real data supplied by a provider.

The OLE DB object model revolves around four main objects: Datasource, Session, Command and Rowset. The OLE DB 2.5 added a couple of new objects to this list: Row and Stream. We can see their relationships in the following diagram:

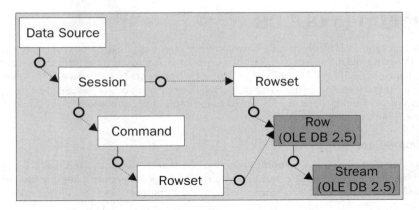

The Datasource is the logical link with the location where the data is kept and contains all the information needed to access it safely and successfully - network address, log on parameters, database name. Through a Datasource object, an application specifies the connection parameters.

A Session object represents a stand-alone transaction between the application and the data source. It can be seen as a physical channel to exchange data. A data source can manage multiple sessions at the same time.

According to the OLE DB specification, a Command object is not a required object and represents an operation done on the data source within the session. It can be a stored procedure, a SQL query or a string in any language that the provider can understand.

The Rowset is the object that renders a table of data with rows and columns of homogeneous data. There are two ways to get a rowset: through a command and through the session object. In either case, you'll be using different interfaces.

The Row and the Stream objects are for allowing semistructured data management. The Row object represents the content of a single row of data. The most important aspect of OLE DB 2.5's support for semistructured data is that the rows of a rowset don't need to be homogeneous. The Stream object serves the purpose of allowing a better manipulation of binary and streambased data within a row field.

Behind either of these objects there's a group of COM interfaces that you need to implement. Thus, summarizing:

- ❑ An OLE DB provider must implement at least the Datasource, Session and Rowset objects.
- ❑ Each object includes a number of COM interfaces with their own set of methods.
- ❑ For each of these interfaces you need to implement all the methods marked as mandatory.
- ❑ Accessing OLE DB data means getting a Rowset object.
- ❑ To get a rowset you need to work with an instance of both the Datasource and the Session objects.

Mapping ADO to OLE DB

ADO is an automation library that sits between your client application and the data provider. Your application uses the ADO objects, which then correlates any invocation with the OLE DB provider interfaces. Consequently, ADO is a kind of proxy that presents to users an easy to use programming interface. The main ADO objects are: `Connection`, `Command`, `Recordset`, `Record` and `Stream`. For some of them, the OLE DB mapping is straightforward. For others, it needs just a little more explanation.

The Connection Object

The ADO `Connection` object combines together the features of both the OLE DB's `Datasource` and `Session` objects. The various attributes let you define the connection string for the data source and the `Open` method creates the `Datasource` object and obtains a `Session` object instance from it. The `Execute` method needs an underlying `Command` or `Recordset` object.

The Command Object

The ADO `Command` object is nearly identical to the OLE DB's `Command` object.

The Recordset Object

The ADO `Recordset` object is the ADO counterpart of the OLE DB `Rowset` object.

The Record Object

The `Record` object evaluates to the OLE DB's `Row` object.

The Stream Object

Evaluates to the OLE DB `Stream` object. In ADO 2.5 the `Stream` object can be seen as a powerful replacement for the `GetChunk` and `AppendChunk` methods.

> **The remainder of this chapter discusses the fine details of OLE DB, which require a detailed knowledge of C++ and COM. If you don't program in C++ or COM then move onto the next chapter.**

OLE DB Interfaces

Let's discover more about the specific OLE DB interfaces for each object. The starting point for an OLE DB conversation is the `Datasource` object. You create it using either of two interfaces:

❑ `IDataInitialize`

❑ `IDBPromptInitialize`

The data source object is created programmatically using a connection string. You can also retrieve a connection string from an existing data source object. The `IDBPromptInitialize` interface allows the display of the data link dialog boxes programmatically. Using the data link user interface, users can build a connection string dynamically or select an existing data link file. Data link files have a `.udl` extension. Once you get the connection string, you can then use `IDataInitialize` to get a data source object based on that.

The Data Link File

A data link file is a plain text file with .udl extension and contains all the information needed to access a data source. When the user double-clicks on a UDL file in Explorer, the Data Link Properties dialog (shown below) is displayed and the user can select the provider and connection details. This is useful if the user doesn't know in advance which provider to use or which database servers are available.

The Data Link File can be used to open a data source as follows:

```
objConn.Open "File Name=c:\Temp\Data.udl"
```

Here's the typical content for a UDL file:

```
[oledb]
; Everything after this line is an OLE DB initstring
Provider=SQLOLEDB;User ID=sa;Initial Catalog=pubs;Data Source=EXPOWARE
```

A data link file is OLE DB's equivalent to the ODBC file DSN. When using the IDBPromptInitialize interface to create a connection through the above UDL, the dialog box that appears looks like this:

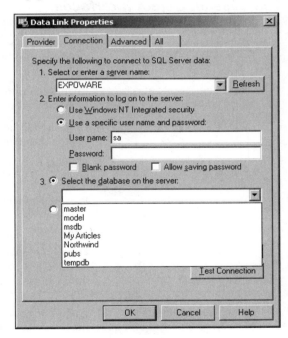

The settings for the provider (SQL Server in this case) can be set using the Provider tab.

The Datasource Object Interfaces

Interface	Description
IDBCreateSession	Returns the requested interface on the newly created session object. (**Mandatory.**)
IDBDataSourceAdmin	Represents a unique place to create, destroy and modify data source objects.

Table continued on following page

Interface	Description
IDBInfo	Provides information about keywords and literals that a provider supports.
IDBInitialize	Initializes and uninitializes a data source object. (**Mandatory**.)
IDBProperties	Gets and sets the values of the properties available for the data source object. (**Mandatory**.)

The mandatory interfaces are fully supported by the ATL provider template classes.

> *A data source object is the consumer's view of the physical data store. Destroying a data source simply releases the connection between the consumer's space and the data store.*

The Session Object Interfaces

Interface	Description
IDBCreateCommand	Creates a command object for those providers that support commands.
IDBSchemaRowset	Enables consumers to get information about a data store without knowing its structure in advance.
IGetDataSource	Gets an interface pointer on the data source object that created the session. (**Mandatory**.)
IOpenRowset	Enables consumers to work directly with individual tables or indexes in a data store. (**Mandatory**.)
ISessionProperties	Provides information about the properties the session supports. It also lets you know the current settings of those properties. (**Mandatory**.)
ITransactionJoin	Enlists the session in a coordinated transaction. This interface is exposed only by those providers that support distributed transactions.

The mandatory interfaces are fully supported by the ATL provider template classes, as are the optional IDBCreateCommand and IDBSchemaRowset interfaces.

The Command Interfaces

Interface	Description
IAccessor	Allows a consumer to manipulate accessors. (**Mandatory**.)
IColumnsInfo	Provides information about the columns returned by a rowset or a command. (**Mandatory**.)
IColumnsRowset	Provides information about the columns returned by a rowset or a command.

Interface	Description
ICommand	Governs the command execution. (**Mandatory**.)
ICommandPrepare	Validates and optimizes the command execution and results in an execution plan.
ICommandProperties	Allows the user to set the properties that the returned rowsets must support. (**Mandatory**.)
ICommandText	Gets and sets the text for the command. (**Mandatory**.)
ICommandWithParameters	Gets and sets the list of the command's parameters, their names, and their types.
IConvertType	Provides information about the supported type conversions on the command. (**Mandatory**.)

The mandatory interfaces are supported by the ATL template classes.

*An **accessor** is a data structure, created by the consumer, that describes how row or parameter data from the data store must be mapped and stored in the consumer's data buffer. For each column in a row, the accessor contains a structure that holds information about the column's ordinal value, data type, and position in the consumer's buffer.*

The Rowset Interfaces

Interface	Description
IAccessor	Allows a consumer to manipulate accessors. (**Mandatory**.)
IColumnsInfo	Provides information about the columns returned by a rowset or a command. (**Mandatory**.)
IConvertType	Provides information about the supported type conversions on the command. (**Mandatory**.)
IRowset	Provides methods for fetching rows sequentially and reading the content of the various columns. (**Mandatory**.)
IRowsetChange	Enables updatability in an OLE DB provider.
IRowsetIdentity	Enables the comparison of two row handles to see whether they refer to the same underlying row. While this interface is optional, general consumers expect the Rowset object to implement this interface, either natively or via OLE DB Services.
IRowsetInfo	Gives more detailed information on the rowset's capabilities. (**Mandatory**.)
IRowsetLocate	Allows a consumer to fetch nonsequential rows.

The mandatory interfaces are supported by the ATL template classes plus the optional IRowsetIdentity interface.

The Row Interfaces

Interface	Description
IColumnsInfo	Provides information about the columns returned by a row. (**Mandatory**.)
IConvertType	Provides information about the supported type conversions on the command. (**Mandatory**.)
IGetSession	Returns an interface pointer on the session object within whose context the row object has been created. (**Mandatory**.)
IRow	Allows a consumer to read column data from a row object. (**Mandatory**.)
IRowChange	Enables a consumer to update the content of a row's columns.
IRowSchemaChange	Allows a consumer to modify the structure of the row by adding or deleting columns.
IScopedOperations	Supports recursive insert/update operations on a tree based data source. The scope of the row object is determined by the tree or subtree whose root node is bound to the row object.

The Row object makes rows available as objects that can exist independently from rowsets. Using the Row object's interfaces, any consumer can reach the requested row within a rowset and access its columns more directly without an intermediate accessor. A consumer can get a Row object, either by opening a rowset on a Session object or by executing a SQL SELECT statement, and requesting the IRow interface.

There is no current support for the Row object in ATL 3.0

The Stream Interfaces

Interface	Description
ISequentialStream	Provides simple sequential access to a stream object. It is a subset of the IStream interface and has to offer forward only reading and writing capabilities. (**Mandatory**.)
IStream	This is the standard interface for compound files and contains a richer set of functionality than the mandatory ISequentialStream interface.
IGetSourceRow	Returns an interface pointer to the row object within whose context a stream object was created.

There is no current support for the Stream object in ATL 3.0

New Features of OLE DB 2.5

The new features in OLE DB 2.5 can be summarized as follows:

❑   Support for semistructured data.

❑   Direct URL binding.

OLE DB 2.5 lets you manage data in both tabular and non-tabular format and provides a URL-based alternative to connection strings and command texts. Such a feature, known as **direct binding**, brings you an immediate advantage – you don't need to know any details about the provider. Just use a URL-based description of the data source you want to access and a new OLE DB service will do the rest, as we will see later on. Also, the new features will not require you to rewrite existing consumers or providers – they will still work.

Support for Semistructured Data

Semistructured data is data expressed in a nonrectangular, heterogeneous way. Typical examples are directories and files in a file system, or folders and messages in an e-mail system, or data that can be rendered through trees or hierarchical storages. XML documents are another great example of semistructured data. The document can be seen as a set of rows (tags), but each tag can have its own set of attributes resulting in an irregularly shaped rowset, where only a few groups of records have the same number of columns. The Row object has been introduced to help users to efficiently manage this.

A Row object can represent a row in a rowset, the result of a single SQL query, or a node in a tree-structured namespace. With this object, the granularity of the OLE DB object model becomes finer. With OLE DB 2.1 you were restricted to Rowsets, now you can go down one more level with Rows.

Rows can exist independently from rowsets. A row can be either a row in a rowset or an object including a rowset as one of its column values. It can also come from a single SELECT statement (SELECT INTO) that is a SELECT command where you retrieve a single row of data and copy the contents of its fields to variables. In this case, you can have a row with as many columns as the number of retrieved variables.

Rowsets were designed for high-volume access and use accessors to bind the provider's columns to the consumer's provided return buffer. Since the rows within a rowset are supposed to be of the same format, the accessor caches information, resulting in better performance. Row objects have been designed to model three types of data: hierarchies, rows of a rowset, and single objects containing a 'traditional' rowset. They are fast and efficient. They are also extensible in schema, that is, you can add and delete columns.

Direct URL Binding

The idea behind direct URL binding, is to get rid of all the intermediate objects that a consumer needs to create in order to access a resource like a rowset or a row. However, these steps don't actually disappear but are simply hidden by the direct binding service that maps a URL to a resource. As a result, the consumer doesn't have to know any details about the provider, such as its ProgID and address. All an application has to do is connect to a URL and retrieve a rowset: all the usual OLE DB procedures required to produce that rowset, including the name of the actual provider, take place behind the scenes.

To support direct URL binding, a provider must implement the `IBindResource` interface and must define the URL schema of the data in such a way that the OLE DB infrastructure can locate the correct provider. In between the consumer and the provider there's a new OLE DB service, called the Root Binder that acts as a proxy and dispatches the URL based calls from the consumer to the provider. The picture below illustrates the architecture of direct URL binding:

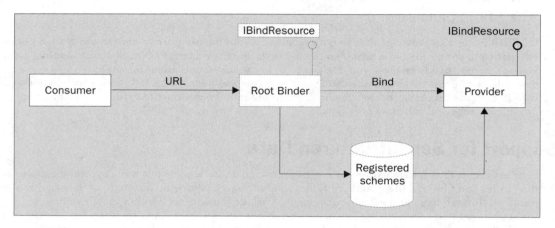

The consumer requests the Root Binder's `IBindResource` interface and calls the `Bind` method passing a URL based string and specifying the type of the object required (`Row`, `Rowset`, `Command`, `Session`, `Stream` or `Datasource`) and the particular interface it wants.

The root binder matches the URL with the content of the registry node where the registered URL is mapped. If successful, it loads the provider and queries its `IBindResource` interface. Then it silently calls the same `Bind` method on the provider using the same arguments it received.

As well as implementing `IBindResource`, any provider that supports direct URL binding must devise its owned data in a web-compliant way. It defines a URL schema according to the logical structure of the namespace of the data it represents. For example, an OLE DB provider that scans the file system for documents written by a certain author might use URLs like these:

```
http://filesys/diskC/author='Joe Users'&format='.doc'
http://filesys/AllDisks/author='Joe Users'&format='all'
```

In the first example, the provider is supposed to return a recordset with all the file system's information (modification date, name, size, attributes) available for the `.doc` files whose author is Joe Users and which is located on disk C. In the second example, the provider retrieves all the documents from all the disks for a certain user. Interpreting the URL-specific syntax is up to the provider, analyzing its components and then doing whatever task is required. All this takes place from within the provider's `Bind` method.

URL Registration

`IRegisterProvider` is the root binder interface responsible for URL schemas registration and unregistration. This is an interface that providers call during the set up to register their URL schemas for the direct URL facility. The `SetURLMapping` method allows providers to store their URLs and declare their ability to process them. When calling this method, the provider just passes in the URL schema and its CLSID.

The advantages of direct binding are quicker, more direct access to the resources, and a simplified hierarchy navigation. You can also identify a row with a URL or you can embed commands in the URL. Remember, deciding the schema of your own provider is completely up to you.

A provider that exposes direct URL binding capabilities is also said to contain a **binder object**, which is actually the COM class exposing those extra interfaces. ICreateRow is a mandatory interface for the OLE DB Root Binder object and for all direct URL enabled providers. A consumer uses ICreateRow, and in particular the CreateRow method, to create a new URL named object and ask for data.

> *Only the root binder implements the* IRegisterProvider *interface. There's no need for providers to expose it.*

Accessing a Data Source through OLE DB

Let's take you through the step-by-step procedure that takes place between a consumer and a provider. Then, we'll turn this into source code using Visual C++, and also using Visual Basic plus ADO.

Connecting to a data source means the following:

- ❑ Creating an instance of the Datasource object.
- ❑ Setting the data source properties such as address, database name, and log on information.
- ❑ Initializing the Datasource object.
- ❑ Creating a Session object.

At this point, you can create a Command object and run it. Through the Command object you can obtain a rowset depending upon the command text used. A command like the SQL SELECT returns a rowset, whereas a command like INSERT or UPDATE simply modifies the existing database without returning a rowset. A rowset object can also be obtained directly from the Session object. To obtain a rowset, there's one extra step to carry out: the definition of an accessor structure. An accessor sructure determines the way in which the consumer expects to receive the data. It is given by an array of structures each describing a column of data. The consumer calls the provider's IAccessor interface and passes that information through the CreateAccessor method. Let's now see all these steps in more detail. Next, we'll wrap up a demo application using both Visual C++ and ADO/ASP.

Initializing the Datasource Object

The first step that an OLE DB consumer accomplishes is getting an instance of IDBInitialize. You call CoCreateInstance and specify the CLSID of the provider. If the provider is SQL Server, the code will look like this:

```
IDBInitialize *pInit = NULL;
hr = CoCreateInstance(CLSID_SQLOLEDB, NULL, CLSCTX_ALL,
                      IID_IDBInitialize, (LPVOID*) &pInit);
```

To make sure that all the definitions are regularly available remember to add:

```
#include <oledb.h>
#include <sqloledb.h>
```

Of course, the latter is needed as long as you're using SQL Server as the data provider. A fundamental prerequisite for this to work is that you initialize the COM run-time environment through a call to `CoInitialize`.

The `Datasource` object is using memory but is not yet ready to work. You need to specify the actual data source you want to connect to and then explicitly initialize the object.

Setting Properties

Every object in OLE DB can be customized through properties that vary quite a bit from object to object. Properties are grouped in structures called **property sets**. A property set contains an array of structures and is identified via a GUID. Let's see how to set up a `Datasource` object to work on the Northwind SQL Server database, impersonating the system administrator.

```
const ULONG cProperties = 3;
DBPROP rgProperties[cProperties];

// sets the userID
rgProperties[0].dwPropertyID = DBPROP_AUTH_USERID;
rgProperties[0].vValue.vt = VT_BSTR;
rgProperties[0].vValue.bstrVal = T2OLE("sa");

// sets the password
rgProperties[1].dwPropertyID = DBPROP_AUTH_PASSWORD;
rgProperties[1].vValue.vt = VT_BSTR;
rgProperties[1].vValue.bstrVal = T2OLE("");

// sets the initial catalog
rgProperties[2].dwPropertyID = DBPROP_INIT_CATALOG;
rgProperties[2].vValue.vt = VT_BSTR;
rgProperties[2].vValue.bstrVal = T2OLE("northwind");
```

This is the array of properties that must be inserted in a property set structure:

```
DBPROPSET rgPropSets[1];
rgPropSets[0].rgProperties    = rgProperties;
rgPropSets[0].cProperties     = cProperties;
rgPropSets[0].guidPropertySet = DBPROPSET_DBINIT;
```

There are several predefined groups of properties. `DBPROPSET_DBINIT` is the most important one that must be always supported by a provider. To set the initialization properties we query the interface for a pointer to the properties object, and then call a method in the property object:

```
IDBProperties *pProp = NULL;
pInit->QueryInterface(IID_IDBProperties, (LPVOID*)&pProp);
pProp->SetProperties(1, rgPropSets);
```

Once you've fixed up the properties, it's time to initialize the `Datasource` object:

```
pInit->Initialize();
```

Creating the Session

Creating the session from the data source is a relatively quick matter:

```
IDBCreateSession *pSession = NULL;
IOpenRowset *pOpenRowset = NULL;
pInit->QueryInterface(IID_IDBCreateSession, (LPVOID*)&pSession);
pSession->CreateSession(NULL, IID_IOpenRowset, (IUnknown**) &pOpenRowset);
```

Obtain the IDBCreateSession interface by querying the IDBInitialize pointer you hold and invoking CreateSession. Then you can implement the required interface, such as IOpenRowset. If all goes well, you hold a pointer to open a Rowset object. However, this doesn't mean that you already own the actual data.

You need to open the Rowset object through the OpenRowset method to get an IRowset interface. One of the parameters for this method is just the name of the table to open, in this case the pwszTableName variable:

```
DBID dbcolid;
dbcolid.eKind        = DBKIND_NAME;
dbcolid.uName.pwszName = pwszTableName;

IRowset *pRowset = NULL;
pOpenRowset->OpenRowset(NULL, &dbcolid, NULL, IID_IRowset, 0, NULL,
                        (IUnknown**) &pRowset );
```

The DBID structure encapsulates various ways of identifying a database object. In this case, it specifies the table name on the data source object. It's only at this point that the most interesting part of the story begins: it's about time to pull data from the rowset.

Creating an Accessor

A consumer pulls the data from a Rowset object by first getting some meta data for the Rowset's columns. Then it uses the meta data to create column bindings. A column binding is a mapping between the rowset columns and the actual buffer of memory where the consumer expects to receive the records. The binding is represented by a structure called DBBINDING. The meta data is returned by the IColumnsInfo interface:

```
IColumnsInfo *pColInfo = NULL;
pRowset->QueryInterface(IID_IColumnsInfo, (LPVOID*) &pColInfo);

LONG nCol;
WCHAR *pwszColNames;
DBCOLUMNINFO* pdbColInfo;
pColInfo->GetColumnInfo(&nCol, &pdbColInfo, &pwszColNames);
```

The content of the array of DBCOLUMNINFO structures is used to set up bindings, filling DBBINDING structures. Finally, the array of DBBINDING structures constitutes the necessary input for creating an accessor.

```
// rgBind is the array of DBBINDINGs and nBindings is the size
IAccessor* pAccessor = NULL;
pRowset->QueryInterface(IID_IAccessor, (LPVOID*)&pAccessor);
HACCESSOR hAccessor;
pAccessor->CreateAccessor(DBACCESSOR_ROWDATA, nBindings, rgBind,
                          0, &hAccessor, NULL);
```

The accessor is the key to getting the actual rowset data through the `IRowset`'s methods `GetNextRows` and `GetData`.

A C++ Test Application

The application you see below has been built using the Microsoft Foundation Classes (MFC) AppWizard in Visual C++ 6.0. It is a dialog based application that imports an ATL data consumer object.

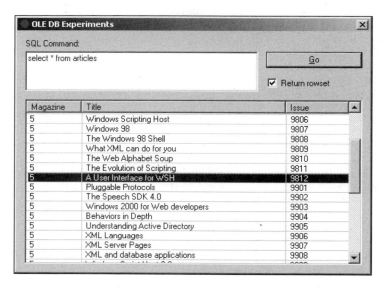

When you attempt to insert a data consumer ATL object, the following dialog box appears:

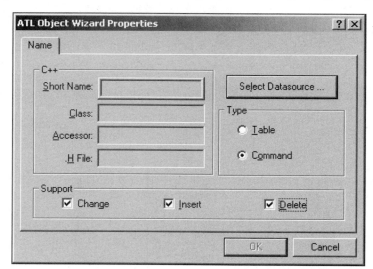

Set the type of support we'll need in addition to query (update, insertion, deletion) and select the data source (both the provider and table). The wizard generates a header file for you with the name of the chosen table. In that header file, there are the definitions for the accessor and the rowset class. In this demo, we'll link up to an Access database (`articles.mdb`) containing articles information (magazine code, title, abstract, issue, URL, publisher). The header `articles.h` is generated automatically. You can download the code from the Wrox web site at www.wrox.com if you want to look at `articles.h`.

The `CArticlesAccessor` class, which is present in the code, represents the intermediate buffer, the consumer and the provider will use to exchange data. The `CArticles` class, instead, is what you'll be using in your code.

About the Accessor

The wizard functionality is somewhat limited. In particular, it codes both the accessor structure and the command. It fixes the structure of the accessor assuming that command is what is specified by the `DEFINE_COMMAND` macro. By slightly changing the source code of `articles.h` you can make it run any SQL command and not just the one defined. However, it'll work as long as the returned rowset is compatible with the accessor. In other words, you cannot use this code to run SQL commands that return a rowset with extra fields or even a narrowed set.

If you need to use consumer code that needs to use dynamically defined accessors then you should resort to other ATL accessor classes such as `CDynamicAccessor`. This class will dynamically create an accessor at run-time based on the column information of the rowset. Use this class when you retrieve data from a data source with unknown structure.

Querying for Data

We want the sample application to be able to query the database as well as enter updates or insert or delete records. Its typical usage would be; enter a SQL command in the edit box and click **Go**. The list view below shows the results.

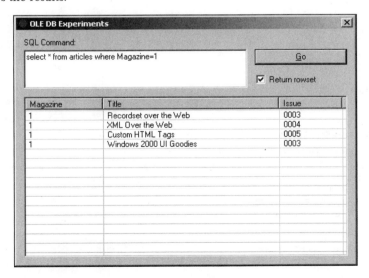

The source code that handles the click on the **Go** button is:

```
#include "articles.h"

void CQueryOLEDBDlg::OnOK()
{
    CArticles arts;
    arts.Open();

    // Loops through the records and refreshes the listview (m_pLV)
    int    i=0;
    m_pLV->DeleteAllItems();
    while(arts.MoveNext() == S_OK)
    {
        TCHAR szMagCode[20];
        wsprintf(szMagCode, _T("%d"), arts.m_Magazine);

        // The listview header has been set in OnInitDialog
        m_pLV->InsertItem(i, szMagCode);
        m_pLV->SetItemText(i, 1, arts.m_Title);
        m_pLV->SetItemText(i, 2, arts.m_Issue);
        i++;
    }
}
```

In this way, though, you cannot specify any run-time command. To be able to pass arts.Open() the SQL command we need to manually change articles.h is as follows:

```
class CArticles : public CCommand<CAccessor<CArticlesAccessor> >
{
public:
    HRESULT Open(LPCTSTR szCommand)
    {
        HRESULT hr;

        hr = OpenDataSource();
        if (FAILED(hr))
            return hr;

        return OpenRowset(szCommand);
    }

    HRESULT OpenDataSource()
    {

    //Code unchanged

    }

    HRESULT OpenRowset(LPCTSTR szCommand)
    {
        // Set properties for open
        CDBPropSet     propset(DBPROPSET_ROWSET);
        propset.AddProperty(DBPROP_IRowsetChange, true);
        propset.AddProperty(DBPROP_UPDATABILITY,
            DBPROPVAL_UP_CHANGE |
            DBPROPVAL_UP_INSERT |
            DBPROPVAL_UP_DELETE);

        return CCommand<CAccessor<CArticlesAccessor> >::Open(
            m_session, szCommand, &propset);
    }

    CSession     m_session;
};
```

At this point, we're taking text from the text box and passing it to the Open method of the CArticles object, as in the following code:

```
CArticles arts;
CString buf;
m_pEdit->GetWindowText(buf);
arts.Open((LPCTSTR) buf);
```

Modifying the Table

You receive a run-time error if you try to enter a command like this:

```
update articles set issue='march 2000' where issue='0003'
```

One of the assertions throughout the ATL base code gets violated at a certain point. The problem is that UPDATE (as well as INSERT or DELETE) has nothing to do with rowsets and accessors. If we want the same application (or the same business component) to manipulate both read and write commands we need to fork the code and follow different policies when it comes to accessors.

The user interface of the program has a check box that, when checked, tells the program you want to generate a rowset. The source code of articles.h changes again:

```
class CArticles : public CCommand<CAccessor<CArticlesAccessor> >
{
public:
    HRESULT Open(LPCTSTR szCommand, BOOL bRowsetWanted)
    {
        HRESULT hr;

        hr = OpenDataSource();
        if (FAILED(hr))
            return hr;

        if (bRowsetWanted)
            return OpenRowset(szCommand);
        else
            return ExecuteCommand(szCommand);
    }

    HRESULT OpenDataSource()
    {

    // Code unchanged

    }

    HRESULT OpenRowset(LPCTSTR szCommand)
    {

    // Code unchanged

    }

    HRESULT ExecuteCommand(LPCTSTR szCommand)
    {
        // Set properties for open
        CDBPropSet     propset(DBPROPSET_ROWSET);
        propset.AddProperty(DBPROP_IRowsetChange, true);
        propset.AddProperty(DBPROP_UPDATABILITY,
            DBPROPVAL_UP_CHANGE |
            DBPROPVAL_UP_INSERT |
            DBPROPVAL_UP_DELETE);
```

```
        CCommand<CNoAccessor, CNoRowset> cmd;
        return cmd.Open(m_session, szCommand, &propset);
    }

    CSession     m_session;
};

#endif // __ARTICLES_H_
```

The rowset class' Open method now takes a second argument; the value of the check box. If you want to generate a rowset (that is, you're running a SELECT command) then it works as it has so far. Otherwise, it goes through the new ExecuteCommand method that requires no accessors and creates no rowsets.

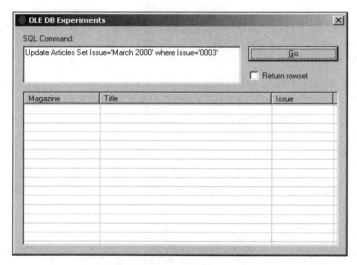

The "update articles..." command shown above doesn't produce any errors:

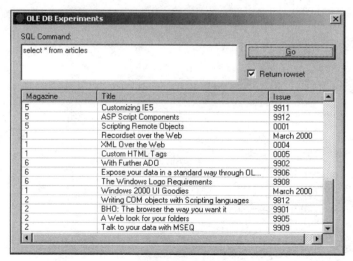

The use of ATL classes greatly simplifies the development of OLE DB consumer modules. Yet you need to learn the whole and underlying model of OLE DB to be able to intervene in the right place to optimize or enhance the basic wizard generated code.

You might wonder why in an ASP book like this, we're spending so many pages covering OLE DB from a C++ perspective. The reason is simple: ADO is great but also adds overhead. Looking at C++, you gain performance in two respects. First, you get to see what's going on under the hood and therefore you are able to get the most out of the ADO object model. Second, ATL and OLE DB make it possible to write more efficient C++ business objects once you become experienced in C++ and the OLE DB object model.

The use of ADO from Visual Basic is discussed in the next chapter.

Enumerating OLE DB Providers

As explained earlier, an OLE DB provider requires special registry settings. In more detail, they require that a key called `OLE DB Provider`, is placed below the CLSID node:

```
HKEY_CLASSES_ROOT
  \CLSID
    \{...}
```

There is no other place in the Windows system where registration information about OLE DB providers is kept. So if you need to enumerate all the providers installed on your system, all you have to do is loop through all the registered CLSIDs and check for a child `OLE DB Provider` node. Writing such a component is not that hard. You just need to be familiar with the Win32 registry API functions.

However, this is a sort of under-the-hood approach that doesn't save you, should Microsoft change the way in which OLE DB providers are registered. There's a probably better, but not necessarily easier, way to enumerate providers. This method relies on a system provided service called the OLE DB **Root Enumerator**. It's a COM component whose CLSID is hard-coded in the `CLSID_OLEDB_ENUMERATOR` constant. Once you've instantiated it, query for the `ISourcesRowset` interface and call the `GetSourcesRowset` method. You are returned a rowset object that defines two columns; the name and the CLSID of all the providers installed in the system.

A COM Object to Enumerate using the OLE DB Root Enumerator

Getting details of all the installed providers is quite difficult in C++, but it is impossible in Visual Basic. To make this functionality available for a broad range of clients, let's wrap it up as a COM automation server. To make it even easier, let's expose the list of provider names, via a collection, so that VBScript's `For Each` construct or JScript's `Enumerator` object can use it.

After creating an empty ATL COM object, let's insert a "simple object" and add to it the `_NewEnum` property. The library in the example is called `MyOleDb` and the object is `EnumProviders`. You can directly edit the IDL code to add both `_NewEnum` and `Count`:

```
import "oaidl.idl";
import "ocidl.idl";
[
    object,
```

```
        uuid(364A1CDF-74BA-4CA5-BEF8-06214669909F),
        dual,
        helpstring("IEnumProviders Interface"),
        pointer_default(unique)
    ]
    interface IEnumProviders : IDispatch
    {
        [propget, id(DISPID_NEWENUM)]
            HRESULT _NewEnum([out, retval] LPUNKNOWN *ppEnum);
        [propget, id(1), helpstring("property Count")]
            HRESULT Count([out, retval] long *pVal);
    };


    [
        uuid(BCAC14D5-E521-4CAF-942E-7DD5654299A1),
        version(1.0),
        helpstring("MyOleDb 1.0 Type Library")
    ]
    library MYOLEDBLib
    {
        importlib("stdole32.tlb");
        importlib("stdole2.tlb");

        [
            uuid(BF3018DD-1743-4F91-A021-D0E69BCBF517),
            helpstring("EnumProviders Class")
        ]
        coclass EnumProviders
        {
            [default] interface IEnumProviders;
        };
    };
```

A property called _NewEnum with an ID of DISPID_NEWENUM has a special meaning. It enables enumeration using For Each or similar constructs. The Count property, however, has a straightforward meaning – it returns the number of installed providers.

The source code is in the enumproviders.cpp file. The implementation needs a number of preliminary declarations and #includes:

```
// EnumProviders.cpp : Implementation of CEnumProviders
#include "stdafx.h"
#include "MyOleDb.h"
#include "EnumProviders.h"
#include <oledb.h>
#include <msdaguid.h>

#define NUMELEM(p1) (sizeof(p1) / sizeof(p1[0]))
#define COLUMN_ALIGNVAL 8
#define ROUND_UP(Size, Amount)  \
    (((DWORD)(Size) + ((Amount) - 1)) & ~((Amount) - 1))

const ULONG    SOURCES_MAXLEN = 64;
const ULONG    MAX_NUM_PROVIDERS = 32;
```

```
enum enumSOURCES_COLUMNS
{
    eid_SOURCES_NAME = 1,
    eid_SOURCES_PARSENAME,
    eid_SOURCES_DESCRIPTION,
    eid_SOURCES_TYPE,
    eid_SOURCES_ISPARENT,
    eid_SOURCES_CLSID,
};

struct SOURCES
{
    ULONG      iOrdinal;
    DBTYPE     wType;
    ULONG      cbMaxLen;
};

struct COLUMNDATA
{
    DBSTATUS    wStatus;        // status of column
    DWORD       dwLength;       // length of data (not space allocated)
    BYTE        bData[1];       // data here and beyond
};
```

_NewEnum is a read-only property that corresponds to a get__NewEnum method like this:

```
STDMETHODIMP CEnumProviders::get__NewEnum(LPUNKNOWN *ppNewEnum)
{
    USES_CONVERSION;

    // *****************************************
    //    DECLARATIONs
    // *****************************************
    BYTE *pData = NULL;
    ULONG cRows=0;
    HROW rghRows[MAX_NUM_PROVIDERS];
    HROW *pRows = &rghRows[0];
    HRESULT hr = S_OK;
    ULONG ul = 0;
    DWORD dwOffset = 0;
    IAccessor *pIAccessor = NULL;
    IRowset *pIRowset = NULL;
    SOURCES s_rgSources[] =
    {
    eid_SOURCES_NAME, DBTYPE_STR, SOURCES_MAXLEN,
    eid_SOURCES_PARSENAME, DBTYPE_WSTR, SOURCES_MAXLEN * sizeof(WCHAR),
    eid_SOURCES_TYPE, DBTYPE_UI4, sizeof(ULONG),
    };

    // Param check
    if (ppNewEnum == NULL)
        return E_POINTER;
    *ppNewEnum = NULL;
```

```
    // Declare the enumerator object
    typedef CComEnum<IEnumVARIANT, &IID_IEnumVARIANT, VARIANT,
        _Copy<VARIANT> > EnumObj;
    CComObject<EnumObj>* pE = NULL;

    // Declare the array to store the providers names
    CSimpleArray<CComVariant> m_Array;
    m_Count = 0;
```

At this point we've declared both the IEnumVARIANT object that powers the _NewEnum property and the internal structure (a CSimpleArray class) that will hold the providers' names. Now we're ready to run the actual OLE DB code that enumerates the installed providers.

```
    // Create the enumerator object
    ISourcesRowset *pISrcRowset = NULL;
    hr = CoCreateInstance(CLSID_OLEDB_ENUMERATOR, NULL,
        CLSCTX_INPROC_SERVER, IID_ISourcesRowset,
        (LPVOID*)&pISrcRowset);
    if (FAILED(hr)) goto EXIT;

    // Retrieve the rowset
    hr = pISrcRowset->GetSourcesRowset(NULL, IID_IRowset, 0, NULL,
        (LPUNKNOWN *)&pIRowset);
    if (FAILED(hr)) goto EXIT;

    // Set up the DBBINDING array
    DBBINDING rgBind[3];
    memset(rgBind, 0, sizeof(rgBind));

    // Get the accessor interface
    hr = pIRowset->QueryInterface(IID_IAccessor, (LPVOID*)&pIAccessor);
    if (FAILED(hr)) goto EXIT;
```

To pull data from the rowset we need to define an accessor:

```
    for (ul=0; ul< NUMELEM(s_rgSources); ul++)
    {
        rgBind[ul].dwPart = DBPART_VALUE | DBPART_LENGTH | DBPART_STATUS;
        rgBind[ul].eParamIO      = DBPARAMIO_NOTPARAM;
        rgBind[ul].iOrdinal      = s_rgSources[ul].iOrdinal;
        rgBind[ul].wType        = s_rgSources[ul].wType;
        rgBind[ul].obValue      = dwOffset + offsetof(COLUMNDATA,bData);
        rgBind[ul].obLength      = dwOffset + offsetof(COLUMNDATA,dwLength);
        rgBind[ul].obStatus      = dwOffset + offsetof(COLUMNDATA,wStatus);
        rgBind[ul].cbMaxLen      = s_rgSources[ul].cbMaxLen;
        rgBind[ul].dwMemOwner    = DBMEMOWNER_CLIENTOWNED;

        dwOffset += rgBind[ul].cbMaxLen + offsetof( COLUMNDATA, bData );
        dwOffset = ROUND_UP(dwOffset, COLUMN_ALIGNVAL);
    }
```

You create the accessor like this:

```
// Create the accessor
HACCESSOR hAccessor;
hr = pIAccessor->CreateAccessor(DBACCESSOR_ROWDATA,
    NUMELEM(s_rgSources), rgBind, dwOffset, &hAccessor, NULL);
if (FAILED(hr)) goto EXIT;
```

Initiate the procedure to get the data from the rowset:

```
// Retrieve the row data info
hr = pIRowset->GetNextRows(NULL, 0, MAX_NUM_PROVIDERS, &cRows, &pRows);
if (SUCCEEDED(hr))
{
    // Local buffer for the data
    pData = new BYTE[dwOffset];
    if (pData == NULL)      goto EXIT;

    // Scans rows of data, collecting providers but not enumerators..
    for (ul=0; (ul<cRows) && (ul<MAX_NUM_PROVIDERS); ul++)
    {
        memset(pData, 0, dwOffset);

        hr = pIRowset->GetData(rghRows[ul], hAccessor, pData);
        if (SUCCEEDED(hr))
        {
            if (*((ULONG*)(pData + rgBind[2].obValue)) ==
                DBSOURCETYPE_DATASOURCE)
            {
                TCHAR temp[SOURCES_MAXLEN*2+1];
                wsprintf(temp, _T("%s,%s"),
                    (TCHAR *)(pData + rgBind[0].obValue),
                    OLE2T((WCHAR*)(pData + rgBind[1].obValue)));

                CComBSTR buf(temp);
                m_Array.Add((CComVariant)temp);
                m_Count++;
            }
        }
    }
}
else
    goto EXIT;
```

I've chosen to store a single comma-separated string in the array obtained by concatenating the provider's name and CLSID. When the enumeration ends, we're ready to create an object the clients can scroll at their leisure. This object is the ATL Enumerator object initialized with an array of contiguous data:

```
// Create the enumerator object
hr = CComObject<EnumObj>::CreateInstance(&pE);
if (FAILED(hr))
    return hr;

// Initialize the enumerator
if (pE)
{
    CComVariant *pVA = m_Array.m_aT;
    pE->Init((VARIANT*)&pVA[0], (VARIANT*)&pVA[m_Count],
        NULL, AtlFlagCopy);
    return pE->QueryInterface(IID_IUnknown,
        reinterpret_cast<void**>(ppNewEnum));
}
}
```

Finally, the source code for the Count property:

```
STDMETHODIMP CEnumProviders::get_Count(long *pVal)
{
    *pVal = m_Count;
    return S_OK;
}
```

Enumerating from ASP

Let's see how to use this component from within an ASP page:

```
<%
    Response.Write "<h2>Installed Providers</h2>"
    Response.Write "<table style='font-family:verdana;font-size:10'>"
    Response.Write "<thead><td><b>Name</b></td>"
    Response.Write "<td><b>CLSID</b></td></thead>"

    set ep = Server.CreateObject("MyOleDb.EnumProviders")

    for each provider in ep
        a = split(provider, ",")
        Response.Write "<tr>"
        Response.Write "<td>" & a(0) & "</td>"
        Response.Write "<td>" & a(1) & "</td>"
        Response.Write "</tr>"
    next

    Response.Write "</table>"
%>
```

The key instruction is the creation of a
MyOleDb.EnumProviders object. Then you just
scan the collection of providers and split the string
returned for each of them.

Summary

In this chapter, we delved deep into the OLE DB object model and architecture. OLE DB is the set of components that transforms the universal data access strategy into reality, and establishes an access method based on the data source connection and rowset extraction. The best way of interacting directly with the interfaces is by programming in C++. However, ADO is an excellent object model that sits on the top of OLE DB and facilitates data access in other programming environments such as Visual Basic and ASP. Here you learned about:

❑ The OLE DB architecture.

❑ Which interfaces are mandatory in every OLE DB object.

❑ How ADO relates to OLE DB.

❑ How to use ATL consumer classes to read and write a data source.

❑ How to enumerate the installed providers.

Further Reading

We've touched on a number of related topics in this chapter. An overview of OLE DB can be found in *OLE DB for ODBC Programmers* available in Technical Articles section of MSDN. Some interesting reflections about OLE DB are also in the Don Box's *House of COM* column on MSJ, July 1999. To know more about the new features in OLE DB 2.5 check out the following resources:

❑ Using OLE DB and ADO 2.5 to represent Nonlinear, Nonrelational Types of Data – Bob Beauchemin, MSJ November 1999

❑ New Features in OLE DB 2.5 – Dino Esposito, MIND, October 1999

❑ Professional ADO 2.5 – Dave Sussman et al., Wrox Press

Finally, two code-intensive articles that demonstrate how to write OLE DB providers are my July 2000 Cutting Edge column on MSDN Magazine and *Exposing Custom Data in a Standardized Way through OLE DB and ADO*, that appeared in MSJ June 99. While the latter provides an overview of ATL provider classes, the former piece shows how a provider can implement a custom language and variable length rowsets.

7

ActiveX Data Objects

In earlier chapters, we discussed how ASP applications are constructed and how databases may be constructed and programmed. This chapter covers the use of **ActiveX Data Access Objects** (**ADO**), a mechanism that may be used by the client to access the information provided in a database. We'll see how ADO may be used from client-side scripting as well as from other languages, such as Visual Basic. By having the ability to use ADO to query information from the server and integrate that information into the pages we send to the client, we can build dynamic web applications, rather than just simple static web sites.

ADO contains a set of low memory footprint objects that provide an easy to use interface to OLE DB, and are optimized for use over the Internet. Because ADO is a COM-based OLE DB consumer, we can use ADO to access not just databases, but a variety of data stored on different types of servers. Consider an e-commerce site. The inventory may be saved in an Oracle database. The customer data may be saved in Site Server's LDAP membership directory. Technical support information may be stored in Microsoft Exchange Server public folders. Finally, the site needs to interact with its inventory suppliers using some specific EDI documents. By having OLE DB in use, developers don't have to know the internal workings of all of these sources of data. As long as the developer knows how to use and manipulate ADO, the OLE DB technology will do the rest.

In order for us to know how to use and manipulate ADO, we need to be familiar with the objects found in ADO; how we may use them to establish a connection with the server and retrieve data, as well as how to process that data. With these objectives in mind, in this chapter we will discuss:

- ❑ Connecting and Disconnecting from a Data Store.
- ❑ Retrieving Data.
- ❑ Editing Data and Record Locking.
- ❑ Viewing and Manipulating Data after Dropping a Connection.
- ❑ Using Stored Procedures.
- ❑ Performance Considerations.

An Overview of the ADO Object Model

To developers that have used either DAO or RDO, the object model of ADO will look very familiar. Let's take a quick look at the object model, and then we'll discuss each of the major objects in more detail.

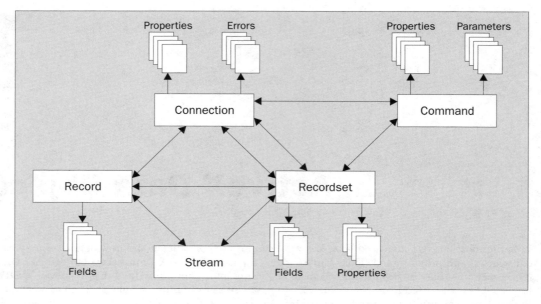

The Record and Stream objects were introduced in ADO 2.5, and are used principally for accessing semistructured data. We will look at these in more detail in Chapter 21.

As we can see, the object model isn't as hierarchical as either DAO or RDO; rather, the ADO object consists of separate independent objects. The model is organized in this way to provide the developer with greater flexibility. For example, a Command object, which holds instructions on how to invoke a SQL statement, may be configured to perform some maintenance operation, and we may then reuse the object with many different databases.

In general, the interaction between the process that requests the data (the client) and the data store (the server) works as follows. Keep in mind that the client here may be script code running on a browser, or some application written in a language such as Visual Basic or Visual C++, or some COM object:

1. On the client, a Connection object is created to establish a "pipeline" from the client to the server.

2. A Command object is created on the client and it is configured to invoke some SQL statement.

3. The Command object is sent to the server through the pipeline established by the Connection object.

4. The server processes the SQL statement specified by the Command object and produces a set of records that are contained in a Recordset object.

5. The Recordset object is sent down to the client using the established connection.

6. The client receives the recordset (or pointers to the records in the recordset) and navigates through the records it contains, referencing the fields that comprise the records.

7. Additional SQL statements may be sent to the server. Again, these statements are defined using the Command object and sent to the server using the Connection object. Any returned recordsets are processed.

8. The connection to the server is released.

Connecting to a Data Store

The Connection object provides all of the functionality needed to establish, maintain, and release a session with a database or some other provider of data (called a **data store**). In order for the Connection object to do its job, we need to set properties of the Connection object with the information needed to locate and use with the data store. These values used for these properties roughly correspond to the information found in an ODBC **Data Source Name** (**DSN**). Although the exact values may vary depending upon the data store, they typically include connection string information (such as User ID and password), the name of the server, the default database, as well as time out settings and the type of data store. We'll see some specific examples below.

In order to use a Connection object, we must first create an instance of the object. From within Visual Basic Script this is done with the CreateObject method of the Server object:

```
<%@ Language="VBScript" %>
<%
  dim cnPubs

  Set cnPubs = Server.CreateObject("ADODB.Connection")
  :
%>
```

How to Connect to a Data Store

When we create a Connection object, a connection to the data store will not be established immediately. To do this, we use the Connection object in one of two ways:

❑ We assign values to properties of the object with information on how and where the connection should be made. Once the Object's properties have been set, we can use its Open method to establish the connection.

❑ We pass the connection information as arguments of the Open method.

There isn't a great deal of difference in performance between these two approaches, but each has a few minor advantages (and disadvantages). By using properties, we can avoid specifying the same information if we reuse the Connection object, whereas using arguments reduces the number of times that object needs to be accessed. Any difference in performance will most likely be dwarfed by other factors, such as logic inefficiencies and network congestion, so we should use the approach that is most convenient for our application.

The ConnectionString Property

Once we have created the object, a number of its properties need to be set with information on how to establish the connection to the data store. The first such property is ConnectionString, which stores the information used to establish a connection to a data store.

The value of this property contains semi-colon separated values, similar to the connection strings found in ODBC DSNs. Like DSNs, which identify such things as the ODBC driver to be used and the name of the server, the Connection String can identify the OLE DB Provider to be used, the server name, or some other resource that will supply the data.

ADO supports five arguments for the ConnectionString property; any other arguments pass directly to the provider without any processing by ADO. The arguments ADO supports are as follows.

Argument	Description
Provider= or File Name=	This specifies the name of the provider to use for the connection. This is required only if the Provider *property* is not used. This specifies the name of a provider specific file (such as a persisted data source object) which contains connection information, such as a File DSN or Data Link File. Note that File Name and Provider are mutually exclusive.
Remote Provider=	This specifies the name of a provider to use when opening a client-side connection. This would only be used for Remote Data Services.
Remote Server=	This specifies the path name of the server to use when opening a client-side connection. Again, this would be used only for Remote Data Service.
URL=	This specifies the connection string as an absolute URL which uniquely identifies a particular file directory. This argument was first introduced with ADO 2.5.

The first argument, Provider, identifies the *OLE DB Provider* to be used, which in turn identifies the type of data store that will be accessed. OLE DB Providers are similar to ODBC drivers, in that they are used to provide native access to a vendor's data store system. But unlike ODBC drivers, which only allow access to databases, and certain kinds of files, such as text files and Excel worksheets, OLE DB Providers can provide access to any number of sources of data.

> For details on specific OLE DB Providers, refer back to Chapter 6. For a list of available OLE DB products, including third party providers, see
> http://www.microsoft.com/data/partners/products.htm.

If you have Microsoft Office 2000 installed, you can find out which OLE DB providers are installed on your system by using the Microsoft System Information utility. This tool, MSINFO32.EXE, is located in the Program Files\Common Files\Microsoft Shared\MSInfo folder. It may also be launched from any Microsoft Office product by selecting the System Info... button found in the About dialog:

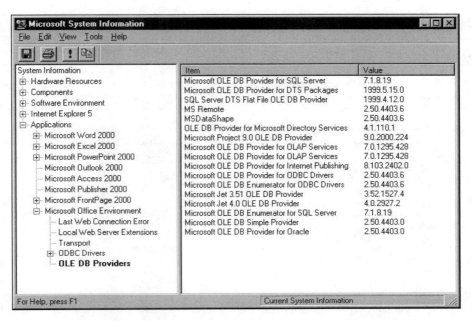

In most situations, only the `Provider` argument is used, with additional information specific to the OLE DB Provider. For example, the following uses the `Provider` argument, but the rest of the string is sent directly to the server to specify the database and security information;

```
<%@ Language="VBScript" %>
<%
  Option Explicit
  Dim cnPubs

  Set cnPubs = Server.CreateObject("ADODB.Connection")
  cnPubs.ConnectionString = _
    "PROVIDER=SQLOLEDB;DATA SOURCE=MyServer;" _
    & "USER ID=pwilliams;PASSWORD=Babylon5At10pm"
  :
%>
```

Note that the `ConnectionString` property is read/write when the connection is closed, and read-only when the connection is open.

The following table lists OLE DB connection strings for several common data sources:

Data Source	Connection String
Microsoft Access 2000	`Provider=Microsoft.Jet.OLEDB.4.0;Data Source=`*physical path to .mdb file*`;Password=`*password*`;User ID=`*userid*`;`
Microsoft Access 97	`Provider=Microsoft.Jet.OLEDB.3.5;Data Source=`*physical path to .mdb file*`;Password=`*password*`;User ID=`*userid*`;`
Microsoft SQL Server	`Provider=SQLOLEDB.1;Data Source=`*server*`;Password=`*password*`;User ID=`*userid*`;Initial Catalog=` *databasename*`;`

Table continued on following page

227

Data Source	Connection String
Oracle	`Provider=MSDAORA.1;Data Source=server;Password=password;` `User ID=userid;Initial Catalog= databasename;`
Microsoft Indexing Service	`Provider=MSIDXS.1;Data Source=server; Password=password;` `User ID=userid;Initial Catalog=databasename;`

Note that when using this syntax, we must make sure that we do not use a space character on either side of the equal sign following the `Provider` keyword and do not break these connection strings across lines of code.

We would create a connection for Microsoft Access in the following way:

```
<%@ Language="VBScript" %>
<%
  Option Explicit
  Set cnSales = Server.CreateObject("ADODB.Connection")
  cnSales.ConnectionString = "Provider=Microsoft.Jet.OLEDB.4.0;" _
    & "Data Source=C:\Data\ProjectedSales.mdb"
  cnSales.Open
%>
```

and would create a connection for Microsoft SQL Server like this:

```
<%@ Language="VBScript" %>
<%
  Option Explicit
  Set cnSales = Server.CreateObject("ADODB.Connection")
  cnSales.ConnectionString = "Provider=SQLOLEDB.1;Password=!jX6k0qYYb3;" _
    & "User ID=WebUser;Initial Catalog=marketing;" _
    & "Data Source=192.151.222.214"
  cnSales.Open
%>
```

Currently, the most common technology used to access databases is ODBC. Microsoft distributes an OLE DB provider that utilizes existing ODBC drivers. This provider, the OLE DB Provider for ODBC Drivers, is the default provider for ADO. If we do not explicitly define a provider, ADO will expect to find an ODBC Data Source Name that we specify in the ConnectionString.

Unfortunately, because the OLE DB Provider for ODBC Drivers relies upon existing ODBC Drivers, performance can suffer. This is not strictly because of ODBC, but rather, this performance hit comes from having two layers of data access technologies. For the fastest performance, use a "native OLE DB Provider" – one built for use with a specific data store. These providers, such as those for Oracle and Microsoft SQL Server, are substantially faster than using ODBC since they can access the RDBMS directly without having to be processed through ODBC.

The Open and Close Methods

Once we have set the appropriate properties of the connection object, we initiate the session with the data store by invoking the `Open` method of the connection object. After this method successfully completes, the connection is live, and we can issue commands against it and process the results. When we have finished performing our operations over an open connection, we use the `Close` method to terminate the session and to free any associated system resources. Closing an object does not remove it from memory; we can change its property settings and use the `Open` method to open it again later. To completely eliminate an object from memory, we set the object variable to `Nothing`.

The Open method is flexible enough so that if we do not specify values for the ConnectionString or Provider properties, we may do so as arguments to the Open method. The syntax for using the Open method with arguments is:

```
Connection.Open ConnectionString, UserID, Password, Options
```

The ConnectionString is specified as described above. The UserID, and Password provide the credentials needed to access the data stores, although these are not needed if they are included in the ConnectionString, or if we use a File DSN or Data Link File. We'll take a look at File DSNs and Data Link Files next. The Options argument will vary from provider to provider, so we have to make sure that we check our provider's documentation for the exact details.

Here is an example of using the Open method using the ConnectionString parameter:

```
<%@ Language="VBScript" %>
<%
   Option Explicit
   Dim cnPubs

   Set cnPubs = Server.CreateObject("ADODB.Connection")
   cnPubs.Open ConnectionString = "Provider=SQLOLEDB.1;Password=!jX6k0qYYb3;" _
     & "User ID=WebUser;Initial Catalog=marketing;" _
     & "Data Source=192.151.222.214"
   :
   cnPubs.Close
   Set cnPubs = Nothing
%>
```

Some OLE DB Providers are smart enough to display a dialog box for logging on when connection information is missing. Microsoft's SQL Server provider is one of these 'smart providers.' It is often more secure to leave out UserID and Password information from the ConnectionString and force the user to enter these credentials manually.

It is worth taking account of the following points when creating connections:

❑ If we specify a ConnectionString as an argument to the Open method, the ConnectionString property will automatically be assigned the value of this argument, overwritting any prior value.

❑ If we pass user and password information both in the ConnectionString argument and in the optional UserID and Password arguments, the UserID and Password arguments will be used and the values specified in ConnectionString will be overwritten.

❑ The connection can be closed and we can later call the Open method to reestablish the connection to the same, or another, data source. While the Connection object is closed, calling any methods that require an open connection to the data source generates an error.

Using A Data Link File to Connect to a Data Store

Data link files are very similar to File DSNs in that they are text files which contain all of the information normally specified to control how a connection is made to the data store. If we open up a Data Link File, its contents would contain the information normally found in a connection string:

Note that Data Link Files have an extension of .udl, for **Universal Data Link**, and, by default, are located in the C:\Program Files\Common File\System\OLE DB\Data Links folder.

To use a Data Link File with the Open method of the Connection object, we will need to instruct ADO to read the file for the connection information. This is done by specifying the fully qualified file name of the Data Link File as the value to the File Name argument:

```
<%@ Language="VBScript" %>
<%
    Option Explicit
    dim cnPubs

    '-- Create the connection and start a session.
    Set cnPubs = Server.CreateObject("ADODB.Connection")
    cnPubs.Open "File Name=D:\Webs\808_Pubs\pubs.UDL"


    :
    cnPubs.Close
    Set cnPubs = Nothing
%>
```

To create a new UDL file, we right-click on the file listing pane in Windows Explorer and choose **Text Document** from the **New** menu. We name this file with an extension of .udl. When we change the file extension, Windows will warn us that the file may become unusable. We simply confirm that we wish to use the UDL extension by selecting 'Yes'. Next, we right-click on this file and open its **Properties** window. Since Windows associates the UDL extension with Data Link Files, a multitabbed properties dialog for the UDL will be displayed:

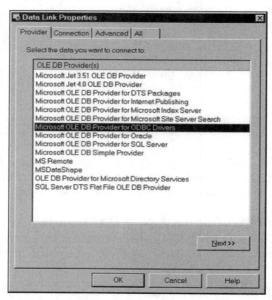

Note that on Windows 9x and Windows NT 4 systems, where Data Access components are installed, when we right-click on the file listing pane in Windows Explorer, and choose the **New** menu, 'A Microsoft Data Link' is included as one of the possible document types to create. Microsoft has removed this document type from the default **New...** menu in Windows 2000.

Using the first tab, we specify the OLE DB Provider that will be used when connecting. Next we click on the **Connection** tab to specify which database should be accessed, as well as which username and password will be used. Depending upon the type of provider specified, different options would be enabled and disabled. For example, when using the OLE DB Provider for SQL Server, we will have options to specify the server, but when using the OLE DB Provider for ODBC Drivers, the server is specified as part of the connection string.

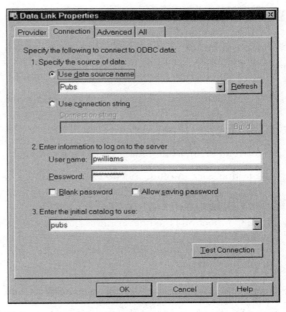

After specifying the connection information on this tab, we should validate the parameters by using the **Test Connection** button. Of course, the server we are connecting to should be running, or we will be unable to test the connection. If the server is not running, we will receive a connection timeout error.

If a connection can be established, we will receive a message box saying that the test was successful.

The **Advanced** tab can then be used to specify a Windows NT User account to be used as the log in ID when establishing the connection. This tab also provides options for specifying a connection time-out value as well as what read/write access this connection will be granted.

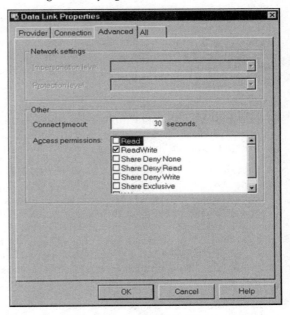

Although UDL files are typically stored in the `C:\Program Files\Common File\System\OLE DB\Data Links` folder, they may be placed anywhere on a computer or network. By using NTFS security, we can set access permissions for those who can access this file.

The DefaultDatabase Property

Another property of the `Connection` object is the `DefaultDatabase` Property. The value of this property indicates the default database for a connection object. This property is not required, since it can usually be included as part of the `ConnectionString`, specified as part of the SQL statements that are executed, or set automatically by the RDBMS.

By having a default database, our SQL commands may be simpler since we will not need to specify which database to use. But we should be careful when using this property since some providers allow only one database per connection, in which case, we cannot change the `DefaultDatabase` property. Also, different providers that don't support this property may respond to its use differently - some may return an error while others ignore the setting.

Note that we can often specify the name of the target database as part of the connection string.

The ConnectionTimeout Property

The ConnectionTimeout property indicates how many seconds to wait while attempting to establish a connection before terminating the attempt and generating an error. The default value is 15 seconds, but we may wish to adjust this value if we expect a lot of network traffic or heavy server usage. If the time from the `ConnectionTimeout` property setting elapses prior to the opening of the connection, an error occurs and ADO cancels the attempt. If we set the property to zero, ADO will wait indefinitely until the connection is opened. For most web applications, it is not advisable to set this property to zero.

❏ The ConnectionTimeout property is read/write when the connection is closed and read-only when it is open.

Connection Pooling

One of the biggest hits to performance when using data stores concerns establishing the connection. Ideally, our application would maintain a persistent connection to the backend for all of our data access, but the nature of the Internet makes such persistent connections unrealistic. With each page of our application, when the user requests information from the data store, connections are created, used, and then dropped. The resources and time required for creating a new connection with each request may be significant.

To help alleviate this burden, a scheme for reusing connections, called **pooling** has been developed. Pooling enables an application to use a connection from a pool of connections that do not need to be reestablished for each use. Once a connection has been created and placed in a pool, an application can reuse that connection without performing the complete connection process.

OLE DB resource pooling, also known as **OLE DB Session Pooling**, is handled by the OLE DB core components. When ADO is used with an OLE DB data source object, the OLE DB services query the data provider for pooling supported capabilities and uses them if available. When we issue the `Close` method to disconnect from the data store, OLE DB informs our application that the connection has been closed, but in reality, the connection is still maintained for a short period of time. OLE DB marks these now idle connections as being available for reuse. If a new connection is attempted by the same user, OLE DB first checks to see if that user's connection still exists in its cache of idle connections. If such an idle connection exists, it is used rather than expending the time and effort to create a new `Connection` object, set its properties, and establish a new connection to the server.

Although this pooling scheme has the potential of increasing performance, it does have a downside when a server has a limited number of connections. Let's assume that our server can support ten simultaneous connections and ten different users have just hit the database and then disconnected. These ten connections are then placed into the pool of idle connections.

By default, idle connections are held for a period of 60 seconds before they are abandoned. If an eleventh user attempts to use the database before one of the idle connections is released, that user will have to wait. This is because these connections are configured for the particular ten users who have just logged off. Of course, such a situation would occur only where connections are specific to individual users. In many ASP applications, this might not be an issue.

Starting in MDAC version 2.5, which is the bundled set of data access technologies that include ADO, we can control pooling for our application on a provider-by-provider basis. This may be done in the following ways:

❑ We can set the **Retry Wait** registry value to control the length of time, in seconds, to wait between connection attempts. It is entered as a DWORD value under HKEY_LOCAL_MACHINE/SOFTWARE/Microsoft/DataAccess/Session Pooling.

❑ We can set the length of time, in seconds, that unused connections are held in the pool for an individual provider through the registry. We set the SPTimeout value as a DWORD value under a provider's CLSID entry, found under HKEY_CLASSES_ROOT/CLSID/ClassID, where ClassID is the CLSID of the OLE DB provider.

❑ We can disable pooling for an individual provider through the registry. This is done by setting a DWORD value of 0xfffffffe for the OLEDB_Services registry entry under the provider's CLSID. This is found under HKEY_CLASSES_ROOT/CLSID. Use the value 0xffffffff to enable all services, including pooling.

❑ We can control pooling through the properties we set when connecting to the database by writing directly to the OLE DB API. See http://msdn.microsoft.com/library/techart/pooling2.htm for more information concerning this option.

Retrieving and Using Data

When using ADO to retrieve data from a data store, we can use three objects: a Connection, a Command, and a Recordset object. As we saw above, the Connection object establishes the session with the server. We use the Command object to specify what actions are to be taken with the data store, such as selecting a series of records, as well as to specify the properties of the Recordset object that will hold these records.

The process required to obtain data from a data store is fairly straight forward. First we create a Command object using the CreateObject method of the Server object. Then set its CommandText property with the SQL statement to be invoked. Next, we need to tell the Command object where to find the data, so we set its ActiveConnection property to the Connection object to be used. We then use the Server.CreateObject method to create a Recordset object to hold the results of the command. Finally, we invoke the Command object's Execute method to run the SQL statement and assign the results of the command to a Recordset object:

```
<%@ Language="VBScript" %>
<%
    Option Explicit
    Dim cnPubs, cmdAuthors, rsAuthors

    Set cnPubs = Server.CreateObject("ADODB.Connection")
    cnPubs.ConnectionString = "Provider=SQLOLEDB; Data Source=Pubs"
    cnPubs.Open
```

```
Set cmdAuthors = Server.CreateObject("ADODB.Command")
Set rsAuthors = Server.CreateObject("ADODB.Recordset")
cmdAuthors.CommandText "Select au_fname, au_lname From Authors"
cmdAuthors.ActiveConnection = cnPubs    ' use the connection to pubs.
Set rsAuthors = cmdAuthors.Execute      ' open the recordset.
    :
%>
```

When possible, we should create our ADO objects as late as possible and release them as soon as we're done with them. This frees up the database and other resources that may be expensive to hold for an extended period.

Once the Recordset has been populated with data, we can use its methods to navigate through the records and examine the contents of the fields comprising the records. If we are familiar with using DAO or RDO, we will find moving about through a recordset is nearly identical in ADO. Navigation is performed by using the Move, MoveFirst, MovePrevious, MoveNext, MoveLast, and AbsolutePosition members of the Recordset object:

Method	Usage
Move	Moves the position of the current record position by a specified number of records.
MoveFirst	Moves the current record position to the first record in the Recordset.
MovePrevious	Moves the current record position one record backward (toward the top of the Recordset).
MoveNext	Moves the current record position one record forward (toward the bottom of the Recordset).
MoveLast	Moves the current record position to the last record in the Recordset.
AbsolutePosition	Moves to a record based on its ordinal position in the Recordset object, or to determine the ordinal position of the current record.

As with RDO and DAO, there are two properties that may be used to determine when we have navigated to the top or bottom of the recordset: BOF and EOF. BOF will have the value of True when we are at the first record of the recordset. Similarly, EOF will be True when the last record of the recordset is reached. If both BOF and EOF are True, then the recordset contains no records.

Using the Field Object

Just as records in a database table are comprised of fields, a Recordset object is comprised of Field objects. Field objects may be referenced through the recordset by the name of the field or ordinal position of the Field object in the Recordset. The Value property of the Field object will hold the contents of the field that was returned.

For example, if a Command object was executed with the CommandText:

```
Select FirstName, LastName, Phone From Clients
```

and the result was stored in a `Recordset` object named `rsClientPhones`, we would be able to use the following references to the `LastName` field:

```
rsClientPhones.Fields("LastName").Value
rsClientPhones.Fields(1).Value
rsClientPhones("LastName").Value
rsClientPhones(1).Value
rsClientPhones("LastName")
rsClientPhones(1)
```

The first reference explicitly refers to the `Value` property of the `Field` that is named `LastName`. The second reference uses the fact that in this `Recordset`, the ordinal position of the `LastName` field is 1. (Ordinal values has the base 0, so the second field has the index of 1.) The next two references work because the default property of the `Recordset` object is the `Fields` property. The last two references take advantage of the fact that `Value` is the default property of the `Field` object.

Referencing a `Field` object by its ordinal position is faster than referencing it by the field name. But of all these ways to reference the value of a field, the last one is the fastest because it uses the ordinal position and it uses the default property, which is always faster than explicitly naming a property.

> In general, the fewer periods used in a reference, the better it will perform because the period notion implies that a nondefault member of the object's interface is being used.

When we have finished working with the Recordset, we release the memory and resources used by it by invoking the `Close` method. If more actions need to be taken in the database, we can use additional `Command` objects (or modify existing ones) with the same `Connection` object. Finally, when we are done working with the database, we shut down the connection using the `Close` method of the `Connection` object. Of course, we finish by setting all of our objects to `Nothing` to force the release of all resources they used.

Here's an example of issuing a query and processing the resulting records:

```
<%@ Language="VBScript" %>
<%
    Option Explicit
    Dim cnPubs, cmdAuthors, rsAuthors, strOutput

    '-- Create the connection and start a session.
    Set cnPubs = Server.CreateObject("ADODB.Connection")
    cnPubs.ConnectionTimeout = 60
    cnPubs.Open "File Name=D:\Webs\808_Pubs\data\pubs.UDL"

    '-- Create a Command object and set it up to query the database.
    Set cmdAuthors = Server.CreateObject("ADODB.Command")
    Set rsAuthors = Server.CreateObject("ADODB.Recordset")
    cmdAuthors.CommandText = "Select au_fname, au_lname From Authors"
    cmdAuthors.ActiveConnection = cnPubs    ' use the connection to pubs.
    Set rsAuthors = cmdAuthors.Execute       ' open the recordset.

    '-- Display the author information.
    StrOutput = ""
    Do While Not rsAuthors.EOF
```

```
      strOutput = strOutput & rsAuthors(0) & " "  & rsAuthors(1) & "<BR>"
      rsAuthors.MoveNext
   Loop
   Response.Write strOutput

   rsAuthors.Close
   cnPubs.Close

   Set rsAuthors = Nothing
   Set cmdAuthors = Nothing
   Set cnPubs = Nothing
%>
```

There is yet another way to refer to a field. That is to bind a field to a field object. In order to bind a field in a Recordset to a field object, we need to declare a variable to reference the field object and then use the Set command to assign the field to the variable. For example:

```
Dim fldFirstName, fldLastName
Set fldFirstName = rsAuthors(0)
```

As we navigate through the Recordset, the variable fldFirstName will point directly to the value of that field for the current record. This approach minimizes the often slow internal referencing required when working with objects. The result is better performance, especially with large recordsets. Here is the same code as above, but using bound fields:

```
<%@ Language="VBScript" %>
<%
   Option Explicit
   Dim cnPubs, cmdAuthors, rsAuthors, strOutput, fldFirstname, fldLastName

   '-- Create the connection and start a session.
   Set cnPubs = Server.CreateObject("ADODB.Connection")
   cnPubs.ConnectionTimeout = 60
   cnPubs.Open "File Name=D:\Webs\808_Pubs\data\pubs.UDL"

   '-- Create a Command object and set it up to query the database.
   Set cmdAuthors = Server.CreateObject("ADODB.Command")
   Set rsAuthors = Server.CreateObject("ADODB.Recordset")
   cmdAuthors.CommandText = "Select au_fname, au_lname From Authors"
   cmdAuthors.ActiveConnection = cnPubs    ' use the connection to pubs.
   Set rsAuthors = cmdAuthors.Execute    ' open the recordset:

   '--  Display the author information.
   StrOutput = ""
   Set fldFirstName = rsAuthors(0)
   Set fldLastname = rsAuthors(1)
   Do While Not rsAuthors.EOF
      strOutput = strOutput & fldFirstName & _
                  " " & fldLastname & Chr(13) & Chr(10)
      rsAuthors.MoveNext
   Loop
   Response.Write strOutput

   rsAuthors.Close
   cnPubs.Close

   Set rsAuthors = Nothing
   Set cmdAuthors = Nothing
   Set cnPubs = Nothing
%>
```

Opening Recordsets With Different Behaviors

We have seen how to open a Recordset by using the Execute method of the Command object. When we do so, the Recordset that is created uses the default properties for the provider. Although each provider's defaults may vary, the most common defaults specify a forward only, server-side cursor with Read-only access. If we wish to use values other than the defaults, we will need to explicitly create a Recordset object and then set its values before the records are obtained.

To populate a customized Recordset object with data, we may take one of two approaches. The first is to use the Recordset's Open method with parameters that will dictate the characteristics of the recordset. The second approach is to specify these characteristics by setting various properties of the Recordset object before issuing the Open method. Since a method is being used, the Recordset object must exist before Open can be issued. Therefore, the Recordset object is not being generated implicitly by some Command object.

Without a Command object to use, we will need to supply the Recordset object with the information normally found in the Command object. The properties we may use for this are Source, ActiveConnection, CursorType, LockType, and Options. These properties may also be passed as parameters to the Open method of the Recordset object:

The syntax for the Open method is as follows:

```
recordset.Open Source, ActiveConnection, CursorType, LockType, Options
```

The Source parameter may be the name of an existing Command object, an SQL statement, a table name, a stored procedure call, a URL, or the name of some file (a Stream object) that will identify what data is to be accessed. The ActiveConnection parameter may be an existing Connection object or a ConnectionString. The CursorType and LockType parameters are explained below. The Option parameter is used to indicate how the Recordset should be processed. Some of the more common values for the Options parameter are:

Constant	Description
adCmdText	Evaluates CommandText as a textual definition of a command or stored procedure call, such as a SELECT statement or call to a stored procedure.
adCmdTable	Evaluates CommandText as a table name whose columns are all returned by an internally generated SQL query.
adCmdStoredProc	Evaluates CommandText as a call to a stored procedure.
adCmdUnknown	The default. Indicates that the type of command in the CommandText property is not known. When this option is used, ADO will make a second round-trip to the server – the first to determine if the CommandText is calling an existing stored procedure or table, and then a second to execute the call. Although this option will work with any valid SQL command, for performance reasons, this option should be avoided if at all possible.
adCmdFile	Evaluates CommandText as the file name of a persistently stored Recordset.

Table continued on following page

Constant	Description
adCmdTableDirect	Evaluates CommandText as a table name whose columns are all returned.
adAsyncExecute	Indicates that the command should execute asynchronously.
adAsyncFetch	Indicates that the remaining rows after the initial quantity specified in the CacheSize property should be retrieved asynchronously.
adAsyncFetchNonBlocking	Indicates that the main thread never blocks while retrieving. If the requested row has not been retrieved, the current row automatically moves to the end of the file.
adExecuteNoRecords	Indicates that the command text is a command or stored procedure that does not return rows (for example, a command that only inserts data). If any rows are retrieved, they are discarded and not returned.
adOptionUnspecified	Indicates that the command is unspecified.

The command options in this list (such as adCmdText and adCmdStoredProc) are also options available on the Command object.

The values of these constants and others defined in the ADO Type Library are not normally available in ASP code. To obtain these constants, we need to reference the ADO Type Library by using the following meta data tag:

```
<!-- METADATA TYPE="typelib"
FILE="C:\Program Files\Common Files\System\ado\msado15.dll" -->
```

As an alternative, IIS 5.0 introduces the ability to bind to a component's type library using the following:

```
<!-- METADATA NAME="Microsoft ActiveX Data Objects 2.5 Library"
       TYPE="TypeLib" UUID="{00000205-0000-0010-8000-00AA006D2EA4}" -->
```

Each of these parameters is optional, but their order is not. If we wish to use an optional parameter which is preceded by some parameter that we don't want to use, we will need to include commas to identify each parameter. For example, the following specifies the Source and Options parameters only:

```
.Open "spSomeProcedure",,,, adCmdStoredProc
```

If the parameter we want to exclude is at the end of the statement, then the commas are not needed. For example:

```
.Open "Select * From Orders",cnBooks
```

Let's look at a detailed example of how some of the properties of the Recordset object may be used. This example creates a recordset from a SELECT statement using a Connection object, and then writes the results of the query to the page.

```
<%@ Language="VBScript" %>
<!--METADATA TYPE="typelib"
    FILE="C:\Program Files\Common Files\System\ADO\MSADO15.dll" -->
<%
    Option Explicit
    Dim cnPubs, rsAuthors, strCmdText, strOutput, fldFirstname, fldLastName

    '-- Create the connection and start a session.
    Set cnPubs = Server.CreateObject("ADODB.Connection")
    cnPubs.ConnectionTimeout = 60
    cnPubs.Open "File Name=D:\Webs\808_Pubs\data\pubs.UDL"

    Set rsAuthors = Server.CreateObject("ADODB.Recordset")
      With rsAuthors
          ' Populate the recordset
        ' args: Source, ActiveConnection, CursorType, LockType, Options
           .Open "Select au_fname, au_lname From Authors", cnPubs,,,adCmdText
      End With

    '-- Display the author information on the page.
    StrOutput = ""
    Set fldFirstName = rsAuthors(0)
    Set fldLastname = rsAuthors(1)
    Do While Not rsAuthors.EOF
        strOutput = strOutput & fldFirstName _
        & " " & fldLastname & Chr(13) & Chr(10)
        rsAuthors.MoveNext
    Loop
    Response.Write strOutput

    rsAuthors.Close
    cnPubs.Close

    Set rsAuthors = Nothing
    Set cnPubs = Nothing
%>
```

Cursor Locations

One consideration when using cursors is where the resources for managing them come from. Depending upon the cursor type and the capabilities of the provider, the cursor may be located on the server or on the client. Some data providers, such as Microsoft FoxPro and Microsoft Access do not have the facility to manage cursors, so OLE DB Cursor Service is required to manage the cursor on the client. Other providers, such as Microsoft SQL Server have the ability to manage the cursor or allow ADO to do so on the client.

It is worth pointing out, that in an n-tier ASP situation, the "client" is the machine running IIS/ASP and the "server" is the machine running the database. The choice of cursor location may have performance implications due to the resources required to maintain and service the cursor. With a high volume of connections, these resource requirements can be significant. We should do some performance testing to determine the most appropriate location for our cursors.

The location of the cursor is specified by the `CursorLocation` property of the `Recordset` object. The values that this property may have are:

Constant	Use
adUseServer	To have the server manage the cursor (default).
adUseClient	To have the cursor managed on the client by the OLE DB Client Cursor Engine. This is an OLE DB service provider which provides facilities for client-side data manipulation such as sorting, filtering and searching recordsets.

Note that this property setting affects connections established only after the property has been set. Changing the `CursorLocation` property has no effect on existing connections.

Note also that only a setting of `adOpenStatic` is supported if the `CursorLocation` property is set to `adUseClient`. If an unsupported value is set, then no error will result; the closest supported `CursorType` will be used instead. Cursor Types are described below.

If a provider does not support the requested cursor type, it may automatically substitute a different cursor type. We can determine the cursor type returned by examining the `CursorType` property once the recordset object is open. To verify specific functionality of the returned cursor, we use the `Supports` method. After we close the `Recordset`, the `CursorType` property reverts to its original setting.

Cursor Types

One significant difference between ADO and the earlier data access technologies is that the methods that are available in the ADO objects will vary depending upon the recordset being used. Recordsets are categorized by the type of **cursor** they use.

When a `Recordset` object is opened, it is constructed using an administrative element called a cursor. There are several types of cursors, each providing a specific range of functionality. Some cursors will enable us to change the data in recordsets and have the change seen by others accessing the database, while other cursor types prevent other users from seeing our changes. Some cursors allow us to move through the recordset in any direction, whilst others allow movement only from the start of the recordset to the end. Cursors are also an indicator, called the **Current Record Pointer**, which identifies which record is currently being accessed.

There are four types of cursors available in ADO: **Forward-only**, **Static**, **Keyset**, and **Dynamic**. The cursor type is specified when the `Recordset` is opened by the value of the `CursorType` argument of the recordset's `Open` argument. We'll see an example of using this method after we discuss the details of using cursors.

Forward Only

This cursor restricts navigation of the records in the recordset in such a way that we cannot move backwards.
Only forward movement (from the start of the recordset to the bottom of the recordset) is allowed. In fact, if we attempt to navigate backwards by using a method such as `MovePrevious`, we will get an error. By restricting movement in this way, there is no need for ADO to keep track of records that have already been accessed. This results in faster movement within the recordset and fewer resource requirements.

The data stored by a Forward-only cursor is a *copy* of the information found in the data store at the time when the recordset was opened – a "snapshot" of the data at some moment in time. This snapshot will not be affected by any changes made to the original records in the data store. Therefore, it is quite possible that, over time, the values found in our recordset will begin to diverge from the values of those records found on the server.

We may even edit the values found in the recordset and posted back to the database. We should be careful, though; because the recordset isn't notified of any changes made to the source records, we may end up overwriting someone else's updates. We'll discuss editing strategies in a few paragraphs when **LockTypes** are introduced.

Forward-only cursors are usually a good choice for populating dropdown lists, for reporting purposes, and for most web oriented tasks. Forward-only cursors are the default cursor type. The constant used when defining a Forward-only `Recordset` is `adOpenForwardOnly`.

> *If the `Recordset` is forward only and we want to support both forward and backward scrolling, we can use the `CacheSize` property to create a record cache that will support backward cursor movement through the `Move` method. Because cached records are loaded into memory, we should avoid caching more records than is necessary.*

Static

Like Forward-only cursors, static cursors also duplicate the data from the data store, so any changes that are made in the recordset will not affect the data in the data store unless we explicitly post those changes. Unlike Forward-only cursors, Static cursors allow for both forward and backward movement within the Recordset.

This cursor type is useful when we need to see a "snapshot" of the data at a particular point in time or we need to process information after being disconnected from the data store. (We'll look at Disconnected Recordsets a little later.)

The constant used when defining a Static cursor Recordset is `adOpenStatic`.

Keyset

Keyset cursors are like static cursors in that a fixed set of records are selected when the recordset is opened. When opened, the records that meet the requirements of the query are determined and their identifiers (called **keys**) are saved in the recordset. By having the keys for the selected records stored in the recordset, ADO is able to fetch the current values of the records from the database as we move up and down the recordset. There is one important limitation though, if the new records are added to the database, or if records are changed so that they meet the query requirements, keyset cursors will not detect them.

Keyset recordsets are fairly lightweight and are quick to open, since only the key values of the recordset need to be determined; although they do generate more network traffic and require more resources since each record's current value needs to be transmitted as we navigate the recordset. This type of cursor is good when our data doesn't change rapidly (or changes are unimportant) or we need to edit the data.

Unfortunately, Keyset records require that the connection to the server needs to be maintained. While this is acceptable in traditional client/server applications such as those written in Visual Basic, it really doesn't apply to Internet applications. This is because there is no way to continuously update the data in the browser without having the client refresh his screen or use some browser-specific tricks.

The constant used when defining a Keyset cursor `Recordset` is `adOpenKeyset`.

Dynamic

Dynamic cursors work very much like Keyset cursors by allowing navigation both forwards and backwards through the recordset. They differ from Keyset cursors in that the set of records that the `Recordset` will hold is not fixed when the `Recordset` is first opened. Any changes made to the data in a recordset or in a database will be seen by ourselves and by others.

If new records are added or existing records deleted or updated, our recordset will reflect these changes. Like Keyset cursors, a connection to the server must be maintained, and for the same reasons as stated above, Dynamic cursors are not very useful with most Internet applications.

The constant used when defining a Dynamic cursor `Recordset` is `adOpenDynamic`.

> *The JET database engine in Microsoft Access doesn't support this cursor type. With ADO 2 and later, any attempt to use a Dymanic cursor will degrade gracefully to a Keyset cursor. ADO versions prior to 2.0 degraded to ForwardOnly cursors.*

Lock Types

The last major topic concerning the set up of Recordset objects is locking. Locking deals with preventing more than one person from changing a record's data at the same time. By specifying a **lock type,** we can determine how and when records will be updated in a multi user application. ADO supports four types of locks: **Read Only**, **Pessimistic**, **Optimistic**, and **Batch Optimistic**.

Read Only

This type of lock prevents any changes from being made to the Recordset. This is the default lock type and uses the fewest resources of all the lock types, since ADO and the server will not need to track or post any changes. The ADO constant for this lock type is `adLockReadOnly`.

Pessimistic

This type of lock prevents any other person from changing a record from the moment that we begin to edit it. The record remains locked until we post the changes with an `Update` method or abandon the edit. Although this lock type insures that no two people will attempt to change the same record at the same time, it often causes many other operations in the data store to wait until we are done with our editing. The ADO constant for this lock type is `adLockPessimistic`.

Optimistic

This type of lock assumes that no one will attempt updating a record that we are editing. Only at the last possible moment will other users be prevented from updating the record. Just before the record's new values are posted (when the `Update` method is called), the server will protect the record from being changed (locking it), insert the changed values, and then release the lock.

This type of lock is useful because it minimizes the interference our actions will have on others using the data store. Unfortunately, it is possible that two people will begin to edit the same record at the same time. When this happens, the changes made by the last person to post their data will survive. The ADO constant for this lock type is `adLockOptimistic`.

Batch Optimistic

This lock type is similar to Optimistic Locks in that a record being changed will not be locked until just before the data is posted. This lock type differs from the other lock types because they allow only one record at a time to be edited, whereas the Batch Optimistic lock type allows multiple records to be updated simultaneously. When using Batch Optimistic locking, the `UpdateBatch` method is used to post the changes, not `Update`.

When the `UpdateBatch` method is invoked, the server locks all records that have been modified, posts the changes, and then releases the locks. As with Optimistic locking, there is a chance that one user will overwrite the changes posted by another, but this lock type is typically faster than Optimistic locks and also allows for editing of Disconnected Recordsets. The ADO constant for this lock type is `adLockBatchOptimistic`.

Using Recordsets With Different Behaviors

Let's look at an example of how some of the properties of the `Recordset` object may be used. This example creates a server-side, read-only cursor, and writes the results of the query to the page:

```
<%@ Language="VBScript" %>
<!--METADATA TYPE="typelib"
   FILE="C:\Program Files\Common Files\System\ADO\MSADO15.dll" -->
<%
   Option Explicit
   Dim cnPubs, rsAuthors, strOutput, fldFirstname, fldLastName

   '-- Create the connection and start a session.
   Set cnPubs = Server.CreateObject("ADODB.Connection")
   cnPubs.ConnectionTimeout = 60
   cnPubs.Open "File Name=D:\Webs\808_Pubs\data\pubs.UDL"

   Set rsAuthors = Server.CreateObject("ADODB.Recordset")
     With rsAuthors
       ' Specify we should use the connection to pubs.
       .ActiveConnection = cnPubs
          ' Specify the cursor's location
          .CursorLocation = adUseServer
          ' Specify the cursor's lock type
          .LockType = adLockReadOnly
          ' Populate the recordset
          .Open "Select au_fname, au_lname From Authors"
     End With

   '-- Display the author information on the page.
   StrOutput = ""
   Set fldFirstName = rsAuthors(0)
   Set fldLastname = rsAuthors(1)
   Do While Not rsAuthors.EOF
      strOutput = strOutput & fldFirstName _
      & " " & fldLastname & Chr(13) & Chr(10)
      rsAuthors.MoveNext
   Loop
   Response.Write strOutput

   rsAuthors.Close
   cnPubs.Close

   Set rsAuthors = Nothing
   Set cnPubs = Nothing
%>
```

Disconnected Recordsets

We have stated before that, as a general rule of thumb, we should connect to the data store as late as possible and release our connection as early as possible. This approach minimizes the amount of time the data store's server has to maintain our objects and frees up resources for other requests. The main advantage of this approach is that it frees the server's resources for other users, thus providing additional concurrency and scalability.

There are many situations where we need to obtain some data from the server and then perform some lengthy operation on that data on the client. In many cases, these operations do not require a connection to be held while the data is being processed. When possible, we should *disconnect* the recordset from the databases after it has been populated. This does not mean that we should close the Connection object. If we do, we will lose the recordsets associated with that connection. Rather, we set the ActiveConnection property to Nothing, or the Recordset or Command, depending upon which object is used.

In order to have a disconnected recordset, it must use a client-side cursor. This makes a lot of sense since we will be disassociating the recordset from any connection to the database.

```
<%@ LANGUAGE="VBSCRIPT" %>
<!--METADATA TYPE="typelib"
  FILE="C:\Program Files\Common Files\System\ADO\MSADO15.dll" -->
<%
  Option Explicit
  Dim cmdSP, cnStore, rsProducts, StrOutput
  Dim fldProductID, fldProductPrice, fldProductName, fldProductDescription

  '-- Create the connection and start a session.
  Set cnStore = Server.CreateObject("ADODB.Connection")
  With cnStore
      .ConnectionTimeout = 60
      .Open "File Name=C:\Inetpub\wwwroot\3927_Ch07\link.udl"
  End With
  Set cmdSP = Server.CreateObject("ADODB.Command")
  With cmdSP
      .CommandText = "SELECT * FROM dbo.Titles"
      .ActiveConnection = cnStore
  End With
  Set rsProducts = Server.CreateObject("ADODB.Recordset")
  With rsProducts
      'Specify the cursor's location
      .CursorLocation = adUseClient
      .LockType = adLockReadOnly
  End With
  Set rsProducts = cmdSP.Execute
  Set cmdSP. ActiveConnection = Nothing

  if rsProducts.EOF then
  %>
  No items found
  <%
  else
  %>
<TABLE>
<!-- BEGIN column header row for Table-->
<TR>
  <TH>Title_ID</TH>
  <TH>Title</TH>
  <TH>Type</TH>
  <TH>Pub_ID</TH>
  <TH>Price</TH>
</TR>
<%
```

```
'--  Display the product information in the table.
   do until rsProducts.EOF
   %>
   <TR>
      <TD><%=rsProducts(0) %></TD>
      <TD><%=rsProducts(1) %></TD>
      <TD><%=rsProducts(2) %></TD>
      <TD><%=rsProducts(3) %></TD>
      <TD>$ <%=rsProducts(4) %></TD>
   </TR>
   <%
      rsProducts.MoveNext
   Loop
   %>
</TABLE>
<%
   rsProducts.close
   cnStore.Close
   Set rsProducts = Nothing
   Set cmdSP = Nothing
   Set cnStore = Nothing
end if
%>
```

Using Saved Recordsets

ADO has the ability to save the contents of a Recordset object to a file. These files are often refered to as **saved recordsets** or **persisted recordsets**. Once saved to a file, a saved recordset can be closed and reopened without an active connection.

Consider, for example, a sales application used by a salesperson on the road, where he doesn't always have an Internet connection to access the database. When the salesperson is at the home office and can access the network, the application acquires data from a database and saves it as a saved recordset. By saving the information as a recordset, the laptop application may later access that data without being connected to the network.

To create a saved recordset, we simply use the Save method of the Recordset object when the Recordset is open. The syntax for the Save method is:

```
recordset.Save filespec, PersistFormat
```

The filespec argument is a string that specifies the file to be created. The PersistFormat argument specifies the file format to be used when the recordset is saved. Currently, there are only two file formats that are supported: XML or ADTG. ADTG is the default format and indicates that the file should be saved in the Microsoft Advanced Data TableGram format. The constants available for this argument are:

Constant	Value	Description
adPersistADTG	0	Indicates **Microsoft Advanced Data TableGram** (**ADTG**) format.
adPersistXML	1	Indicates **Extensible Markup Language** (**XML**) format.

For example, to create a saved recordset on a floppy disk with the name Account.dat using the XML format, we could use:

```
rsAccount.Save "A:\Accounts.dat", adPersistXML
```

It should be pointed out that if we want to persist the recordset on a client machine, we should create our recordset object so that it uses a static, client-side cursor.

Here is a more detailed example, written in Visual Basic. This routine establishes a connection to the database and executes an SQL statement that selects all records from an inventory table. The results of this query are then saved to a file using the default ADTG format.

```
Public Sub GetInventory()

    ' -- Create objects as needed.
    Set mconnInv = CreateObject("ADODB.Connection")
    Set mcmdGetInv = CreateObject("ADODB.Command")
    Set mrsResults = CreateObject("ADODB.Recordset")

    ' -- Attempt the connection.
    mconnInv.Open "File Name=C:\SalesData\Inventory\Inventory.UDL"

    ' -- Configure the command.
    Set mcmdGetInv.ActiveConnection = mconnInv
    mcmdGetInv.CommandText = "Select * From Inventory"

    ' -- Configure the recordset to be saved.
    mrsResults.CursorType = adOpenStatic
    mrsResults.CursorLocation = adUseClient
    Set mrsResults.Source = mcmdGetInv

    ' -- Get the recordset.
    mrsResults.Open
    mrsSource.Save "C:\SalesData\Inventory\Inventory.dat" '-- save the recordset.
    mrsResults.Close

End Sub
```

Recordset Property Values and Performance

ADO defaults to using a "firehose cursor" – a server-side, forward-only cursor that is read-only to provide the best possible performance for using a forward-only scan through the records. If we don't need additional functionality, we shouldn't set up the recordsets to provide more than the defaults. If we do need movement back and forth within a Recordset, then we should use a client-side cursor, since, in most situations, we will be much better off. The exception here is for very large recordsets where a server-side cursor may offer better performance.

Another property of the Recordset object that may effect performance is CacheSize. ADO uses this property to determine the number of rows to obtain (fetched) at one time. Once the Recordset gets these rows, they are cached in memory. When we navigate through the Recordset, ADO will check to see if the record we are moving to is in the cache.

If it is, then the values found in the cache are provided. If the record is not in the cache, ADO discards what is currently in the cache and fetches another set of records. If the size of the cache is too small, we will not benefit from having the cache. If it is too big, then we may be wasting valuable resources. There is no specific formula for determining how big the cache should be. It is necessary to experiment with different cache sizes to determine the best value for the particular Recordset.

Using a small CacheSize value significantly improves performance for fetching data from an Oracle data store.

Using Stored Procedures

Whenever possible, stored procedures should be used to extract the fastest possible performance. We can use stored procedures for queries that insert, modify, and delete data; as well as use them to return a recordset. To use a stored procedure, we specify the `adCmdStoredProc` value for the `CommandType` property.

```
<%@ LANGUAGE="VBSCRIPT" %>
<!--METADATA TYPE="typelib"
    FILE="C:\Program Files\Common Files\System\ADO\MSADO15.dll" -->
<%
Option Explicit
dim cnPubs, cmdPubs

'-- Create the connection and start a session.
Set cnPubs = Server.CreateObject("ADODB.Connection")
cnPubs.ConnectionTimeout = 60
cnPubs.Open "File Name=D:\Webs\808_Pubs\data\pubs.UDL"

Set cmdPubs = Server.CreateObject("ADODB.Command")
With cmdPubs
    .ActiveConnection = cnPubs
    .CommandText = "spGenerateDailyEmail"
    .CommandType = adCmdStoredProc
    .Execute
End With

cnPubs.Close

Set cnPubs = Nothing
Set cmdPubs = Nothing
%>
```

Passing Parameters

Most stored procedures operate by providing having one or more arguments passed to them. And we will need to supply these arguments before the stored procedure is invoked. We may do this in two ways.

- ❑ Add them to the `CommandText` property
- ❑ Create parameter objects

To add the arguments to the `CommandText` property, we simply include these arguments as part of the text assigned to the property:

```
cmdpubs.CommandText = "spGenerateEmailForDay 'Jan 28 2000', 110"
```

More commonly, the argument to be passed to the stored procedure will have been passed to the page as part of the query string. In this case, we simply concatenate the value as so:

```
<%@ LANGUAGE="VBSCRIPT" %>
<!--METADATA TYPE="typelib"
    FILE="C:\Program Files\Common Files\System\ADO\MSADO15.dll" -->
<%
Option Explicit
dim cnPubs, cmdPubs, dtDateToProcess
```

```
dtDateToProcess = Request.QueryString("d")

'-- Create the connection and start a session.
Set cnPubs = Server.CreateObject("ADODB.Connection")
Set cnPubs.ConnectionTimeout = 60
cnPubs.Open "File Name=D:\Webs\808_Pubs\data\pubs.UDL"

Set cmdPubs = Server.CreateObject("ADODB.Command")
With cmdPubs
   .CommandText = "spGenerateEmailForDay '" & dtDateToProcess & "'"
   .CommandType = adCmdStoredProc
   .Execute
End With

cnPubs.Close

Set cnPubs = Nothing
Set cmdPubs = Nothing
%>
```

The preferred way to pass arguments to a stored procedure is to use the Parameter objects. By explicitly creating the parameters, the query engine will not have to parse the command line sent, and it will know the data types of each argument sent.

Each Command object has a Parameters collection, which, by default, has no members. We will need to create a new Parameter object for each argument to be passed the stored procedure and then append the Parameter object to the collection. Unlike other ADO objects that use the Server.CreateObject method to produce the object, to generate a new Parameter object we use the CreateParameter method of the Command object. To append the Parameter we use the Append method of the collection.

When we generate the parameter using the CreateParameter method, we may explicitly describe the argument being passed. This method accepts a name for the argument, the data type and size, whether the argument is for input or output, as well as the value for the parameter. The syntax of this method is:

```
Set parameter = command.CreateParameter (Name, Type, Direction, Size, Value)
```

Take note of the following points:

❑ The Name argument of this method must match exactly the name of the argument as defined in the stored procedure.

❑ The Type argument to this method is any data type supported by ADO. The more commonly used data type constants are listed opposite.

❑ Direction specifies if the argument's value will be supplied by the client for the stored procedure to use, or if that argument will have its value populated by the stored procedure.

   ❑ If the argument is to be supplied to the stored procedure, we use the adParamInput constant.

   ❑ If its value is determined by the stored procedure, use the adParamOutput constant.

   ❑ There is also a constant, adParamInputOutput, which may be used to specify a parameter that will act as both an input and an output parameter.

❑ Size specifies how much memory is required for the argument, in bytes.

❑ The Value argument is used for input parameters only, and assigns the value to be sent to the stored procedure.

The following table lists the more commonly used data types:

Constant	Description
adBinary	Indicates a binary value.
adBoolean	Indicates a boolean value.
adChar	Indicates a fixed length string value.
adCurrency	Indicates a currency value.
adDate	Indicates a date value.
adDecimal	Indicates an exact numeric value with a fixed precision and scale.
adDouble	Indicates a double precision floating-point value.
adEmpty	Specifies no value.
adInteger	Indicates a four byte signed integer.
adLongVarBinary	Indicates a long binary.
adLongVarChar	Indicates a long string value.
adLongVarWChar	Indicates a long null-terminated string value.
adNumeric	Indicates an exact numeric value with a fixed precision and scale.
adSingle	Indicates a single-precision floating-point value.
adSmallInt	Indicates a two byte signed integer.
adTinyInt	Indicates a one byte signed integer.
adUnsignedInt	Indicates a four byte unsigned integer.
adUnsignedSmallInt	Indicates a two byte unsigned integer.
adUnsignedTinyInt	Indicates a one byte unsigned integer.
adVarBinary	Indicates a binary value.
adVarChar	Indicates a variable-length string value.
adVarWChar	Indicates a variable-length null-terminated Unicode character string.
adWChar	Indicates a null-terminated Unicode character string.

As an example, let us assume that we have a Command object named cmdSP, and we want to add a Parameter object to this Command. This parameter will be used for the @password argument of a stored procedure, and the parameter will pass to the stored procedure a variable length string up to 32 characters long. First, we need to create an instance of a parameter object:

```
Dim param
Set param = cmdSP.CreateParameter("@vcPassword", adVarChar, adParamInput, 32)
```

In order for this `Parameter` object to be associated with the `Command` object, we need to append it to the `Parameters` collection:

```
cmdSP.Append param
```

We can combine these two actions, thus eliminating the need for a separate parameter object:

```
cmdSP.Append  cmdSP.CreateParameter("@vcPassword", adVarChar, adParamInput, 32)
```

To make this code just a bit faster, we can enclose this line within a `With` block:

```
With cmdSP
    .Parameters.Append .CreateParameter("@vcPassword", adVarChar, adParamInput, 32)
End With
```

We need to take care to make sure that there is a space character following the `Append` method or a run-time error will occur.

Below is code that illustrates the use of parameters with a stored procedure. The stored procedure uses two input parameters, `@vcUsername` and `@vcPassword`, which it uses as credentials. If the username and password are valid, then the user's customer id is returned in a third parameter. If the username or password is invalid, the third parameter will contain a value of -1. This routine assumes that the values for the input parameters have been sent to the page as part of form fields.

```
<HTML><HEAD>
<TITLE>authenticate.asp</TITLE>
</HEAD><body bgcolor="#FFFFFF">
<%@ LANGUAGE="VBSCRIPT" %>
<!--METADATA TYPE="typelib"
    FILE="C:\Program Files\Common Files\System\ADO\MSADO15.dll" -->
<%
    Option Explicit
    Dim strUsername, strPassword
    Dim cmdSP, cnAuthenticate, p
    dim intCustomerID, strMsg

    '-- Get credentials from user.
    strUsername =request.form("username")
    strPassword =request.form("password")

    '-- Create the connection and start a session.
    Set cnAuthenticate = Server.CreateObject("ADODB.Connection")
    With cnAuthenticate
        .ConnectionTimeout = 60
        .Open "File Name=D:\Webs\808_Pubs\data\pubs.UDL"
    End With

    Set cmdSP = Server.CreateObject("ADODB.Command")
    With cmdSP
        .CommandText = "spValidatePassword"
        .CommandType = adCmdStoredProc

    '  -- Add the following input parameters to the collection:
    '  @vcUsername of type Character with a size of 64 bytes
    '  @vcPassword of type Character with a size of 32 bytes
```

```
        ' Add the output parameter to the collection:
        ' @iCustomerID of type Integer with a size of 4 bytes

        set p =.Parameters
        p.Append  .CreateParameter("@vcUsername", adVarChar, _
                                         adParamInput, 64)
        p.Append  .CreateParameter("@vcPassword", adVarChar, _
                                         adParamInput, 32)
        p.Append  .CreateParameter("@iCustomerID", adInteger, _
                                         adParamOutput,4)

        ' -- Assigning values to the input parameters.
        cmdSP("@vcUsername ") = strUsername
        cmdSP("@vcPassword") = strPassword

        Set .ActiveConnection = cnAuthenticate
        .Execute
    End With

    intCustomerID= p("@iCustomerID")

    cnAuthenticate.close
    Set cnAuthenticate = Nothing
    Set cmdSP = Nothing

    '-- React to success or failure.
    If intCustomerID = -1 Then
        StrMsg = "Invalid Username or password<BR>"
           & "<A REF=' authenticate.asp'>Try again</a>
    Else
        session("username")= strUsername
        '-- Redirect to secured area of site.
    End If
%>
</BODY></HTML>
```

Output Parameters vs. Recordsets

The use of output parameters is extremely efficient and should be used whenever possible. Consider, for example, a situation in which we know that the stored procedure will return a single row of values. Why should we require the generation, maintenance, and closing of a `Recordset` object? Output parameters will provide the same functionality, but with much less overhead. Also, when we use a `Recordset`, the query results include data and meta data. When the recordset is small, as is the case with a single record returned, the meta data may very well be much larger than the data itself. By using output parameters we can avoid the transmission of this extra, unneeded information.

Getting Return Values From Stored Procedures

Stored Procedures have the ability to provide a return value. The return values for stored procedures are handled differently than most functions found in Visual Basic Script. In VBScript, a variable may be assigned the return value of a function:

```
intA = MyFunction(intX,intY)
```

Perhaps the VBScript function returns a `True` upon success and a `False` upon failure, so that we may use the function as part of a conditional statement:

```
If Not Login(strUserName, strPassword) Then Exit Sub
```

With stored procedures, what is normally returned is a set of records, so such simple assignments are not possible. Although stored procedures may assign a return value, we must acquire it through the use of a paramater created as a `adParamReturnValue` type.

Consider a stored procedure `spDoSomething` that assigns a value of 0 upon success, and a non zero value upon failure. To retrieve this return value we could do something like the following:

```
<%@ LANGUAGE="VBSCRIPT" %>
<!--METADATA TYPE="typelib"
    FILE="C:\Program Files\Common Files\System\ADO\MSADO15.dll" -->
<%
    Option Explicit
    Dim cmdSP, cnDB, p, intRetval

    '-- Create the connection and start a session.
    Set cnDB = Server.CreateObject("ADODB.Connection")
    With cnDB
        .ConnectionTimeout = 60
        .Open "File Name=D:\Webs\808_Pubs\data\pubs.UDL"
    End With

    Set cmdSP = Server.CreateObject("ADODB.Command")
    With cmdSP
        .CommandText = "spDoSomething "
        .CommandType = adCmdStoredProc
        ' Add the output parameter to capture the return value:
        set p =.Parameters
        p.Append .CreateParameter("returnStatus",adInteger,adParamReturnValue)
        .ActiveConnection = cnDB
        .Execute
    End With
    intRetval = p("returnStatus")

    cnDB.close

    Set cnDB = Nothing
    Set cmdSP = Nothing

    '—The code to react to the success or failure goes here.
%>
```

Let's look at another example of using a return value that shows how identity values may be used.

In most RDBMSs we may define one field in a table to be an "ID" field that will hold a unique identifier, such as an `OrderNumber` or `EmployeeID`. It is a very common to insert a new record into a table and then need to know the ID of that newly inserted record.

For this demonstration, let us assume that we have a table in Microsoft SQL Server named `Employees`. This table defines an "auto-number" field named `EmployeeID` that will assign a value of 1 to the first record inserted, a value of 2 to the second, 3 for the third, and so on. Here is the SQL code to generate this table. The number of fields used in this table have been kept to a minimum so we can keep this demonstration simple.

```
CREATE TABLE [Employees] (
    [EmployeeID] [int] IDENTITY (1, 1) NOT NULL ,
    [LastName] [varchar] (32) NULL
    [FirstName] [varchar] (32) NULL
)
```

When we wish to insert a new record, we will use a stored procedure that accepts the first and last name of the employee, inserts these values into the table, and then returns the value of the EmployeeID that was generated:

```
CREATE procedure usp_AddNewEmployee
(
    @vcLName varchar(32),
    @vcFName varchar(32)
)
```

```
    as
        set nocount on
        insert Employees (LastName, FirstName) VALUES (@vcLName, @vcFName)
        return @@identity
```

Next comes the ASP code that uses ADO objects to invoke the stored procedure. It is worth noting that when we create the parameter for the return value, we can use any name we wish. When we create the other parameters used for input into the stored procedure, the parameter names must match exactly the names of the arguments defined in the stored procedure itself.

```
<%@ LANGUAGE="VBSCRIPT" %>
<%
Option Explicit
%>
<!--METADATA TYPE="typelib"
    FILE="C:\Program Files\Common Files\System\ADO\MSADO15.dll" -->
<%
Dim cmdSP, cnDB, p, intRetval

'-- Create the connection and start a session.
Set cnDB = Server.CreateObject("ADODB.Connection")
With cnDB
    .ConnectionTimeout = 60
    .Open "File Name=C:\Webs\DreamJOBS\objects\SQL01.udl"
End With

Set cmdSP = Server.CreateObject("ADODB.Command")
With cmdSP
    .CommandText = "usp_addjunk "
    .CommandType = adCmdStoredProc
    ' Add the output parameter to capture the return value:
    set p =.Parameters
    p.Append .CreateParameter("ReturnStatus",adInteger,adParamReturnValue)
    p.Append .CreateParameter("@vcLName", adVarChar, adParamInput, 32)
    p.Append .CreateParameter("@vcFName", adVarChar, adParamInput, 32)
    cmdSP("@vcLName") = "Ryan"    '-- value hard coded for testing only.
    cmdSP("@vcFName") = "Matt"    '-- value hard coded for testing only.
    .ActiveConnection = cnDB
    .Execute
End With
intRetval = p(0)        ' ReturnStatus is the first (0th) parameter

cnDB.close
Set cnDB = Nothing
Set cmdSP = Nothing

Response.Write "The new EmployeeID is: " & intRetval
%>
```

Describing Parameters

ADO provides a mechanism for us to ask the database to set all of the parameters of a stored procedure, rather than having us explicitly create each parameter. This is done by issuing the Refresh method of the Parameters collection. Refresh will cause ADO to contact the database and determine how many parameters there are, what their data types are, their size, and whether they are input or output parameters. Once the parameters have been obtained, all we need to do is supply the values to be passed:

```
<%@ LANGUAGE="VBSCRIPT" %>
<!--METADATA TYPE="typelib"
    FILE="C:\Program Files\Common Files\System\ADO\MSADO15.dll" -->
<%
```

```
        Option Explicit
        Dim cmdSP, cnDB, p

        '-- Create the connection and start a session.
        Set cnDB = Server.CreateObject("ADODB.Connection")
        With cnDB
            .ConnectionTimeout = 60
            .Open "File Name=D:\Webs\808_Pubs\data\pubs.UDL"
        End With

        Set cmdSP = Server.CreateObject("ADODB.Command")
        With cmdSP
            .ActiveConnection = cnDB
            .CommandText = "spCreditRequest"
            .CommandType = adCmdStoredProc
            .Parameters.Refresh
            .Parameters(1).Value = 500
            .Execute
  End With
  :

  %>
```

But, as convenient as this trick may be, it comes at a cost. In many data stores, obtaining parameter information is often as expensive as executing the command itself. So when possible, we should describe the command parameters ourselves.

XML Support

Widely accepted standards are crucial to building web based applications. HTML is one such standard. It enables us to create a page once, and have it displayed at different times by many browsers. While HTML provides rich facilities for display, it does not provide any standards based way to manage data. Just as HTML has helped to standardize the presentation of our pages, we need a standard for representing data itself, so software can better search, move, and manipulate information. This data standard is called **Extensible Markup Language** (**XML**).

In the most general terms, we may use XML to define our data in much the same way as the definition of a table in a database. However, XML may be used to describe much more complicated structures than a database table. We'll see how XML may be used in detail in Chapters 24-27, but it is worth mentioning here that ADO supports XML.

A Brief Background on XML

Like HTML, XML is a markup language. If fact, XML is a subset of the same language that HTML was created from, **SGML** (**Standard Generalized Markup Language**). XML defines tags that are used to describe data and how it is structured. An XML source is made up of XML elements, each of which consists of a start tag (`<title>`), an end tag (`</title>`), and the information between the two tags (referred to as the content).

Unlike HTML, which describes how the content should be displayed, XML tags describe what the content *means*. This is somewhat analogous to defining fields in a table. For example, an XML element might be tagged as a unit price, an invoice number, or a customer name. It is up to each document's author to determine what kind of data to use and which tag names fit best. To illustrate this, consider the following XML document:

```
<weather-report>
   <date>August 15, 2000</date>
   <time>11:00</time>
   <location>
      <city>Shelton</city>
      <state>CT</state>
   </location>
   <measurements>
      <skies>mostly sunny</skies>
      <temperature>86</temperature>
      <wind>
         <direction>NW</direction>
         <windspeed>8</windspeed>
      </wind>
      <humidity>75</humidity>
      <visibility>10</visibility>
   </measurements>
</weather-report>
```

Rather than describing how the data should be displayed, these XML tags identify what each data item means. As long as they know what the tags mean, anyone reading this file may use this data as they see fit.

XML and ADO

Starting with version 2.1, ADO has supported XML, allowing us to read XML documents as if they were ADO recordsets. In version 2.5 of ADO, this support was expanded to allow us to save ADO recordsets as XML files.

In order to read an XML file, we need to use the `Open` method of the `Recordset` object with the `adCmdFile` option.

```
rs.Open "orders.xml",,,,adCmdFile
```

To save the contents of a `Recordset` object, we use the `Save` method with the `adPersistXML` argument:

```
rs.Save "orders.xml", adPersistXML
```

We cannot hoped to have even scratched the surface of XML here. However, we look at it in far more depth in Chapters 24-27.

Using ADO Efficiently

The following are a few suggestions, in no particular order, on how we can maximize performance when using various ADO objects.

Always Use Option Explicit

Although this will be familiar to many of us, it can do no harm to reiterate the old maxim that the `Option Explicit` directive should always be used in every `.asp` file. This directive, placed at the top of the `.asp` file, forces the developer to declare all variables that will be used. If we try executing code using this directive, and a variable is found that was not explicitly declared, then an error will be thrown.

This directive requires only a small amount of additional code to type, but the time saved debugging may be substantial. Many programmers consider using this directive very helpful in debugging applications, as it avoids the chance of mistyping a variable name and inadvertently creating new variables (for example, `rsOrdesr=...` instead of `rsOrders=...`).

There is another advantage to explicitly declaring variables: declared variables are faster to process than undeclared variables. Under the covers, the scripting run time engine references undeclared variables by name every time they are used. Declared variables, on the other hand, are assigned an ordinal, either at compile time or run time, and this ordinal value is always used for referencing the variable. Referencing a variable by ordinal value is significantly faster than referencing them by name.

Opening a Recordset Without an Explicit Connection

Since ADO has a "flat" object model, we do not need to explicitly create a `Connection` to use a `Command` object, nor do we need to explicitly create a `Command` object to use a `Recordset` object. Normally, when we use the `Close` method to close a `Connection` object it also closes any active `Recordset` objects associated with the connection. A `Command` object associated with the `Connection` object we are closing will persist, but it will no longer be associated with a `Connection` object. That is, its `ActiveConnection` property will be set to `Nothing`. Since both the `Command` and `Recordset` objects can exist without a `Connection` object, we can create and use them without ever having a `Connection` object explicitly defined.

When we issue the `Execute` method of a `Command` object without an existing `Connection` object specified in the `ActiveConnection` property, ADO will automatically create a `Connection` object for us. In order for the new connection to be established, we will need to provide connection information in the `ActiveConnection` property:

```
<%@ Language="VBScript" %>
<%
   dim cmdAuthors, rsAuthors

   Set cmdAuthors = Server.CreateObject("ADODB.Command")
   Set rsAuthors = Server.CreateObject("ADODB.Recordset")

   cmdAuthors.CommandText = "Select au_fname, au_lname From Authors"
   cmdAuthors.ActiveConnection = _
      "PROVIDER=SQLOLEDB;DATA SOURCE=MyServer;" _
      & "USER ID=pwilliams;PASSWORD=Babylon5At10pm"

   Set rsAuthors = cmdAuthors.Execute    ' open the recordset.

%>
```

Use a Connection Object for Single Execution

ADO has some optimizations for one-time command executions when done through `Connection` object. This is a common user scenario, where the code typically opens a connection, executes a statement, processes the results, and closes the connection. For such scenarios, we can use the `Execute` method of the `Connection` object rather than explicitly creating and using `Command` and `Recordset` objects. By using this method, ADO doesn't preserve any command state information and therefore performs better.

Executing Commands that Do Not Return Records

When we issue a command against the database, ADO will assume that records are to be returned. In order to send the records back to the client, a `Recordset` object is produced. This takes time and resources and is not necessary when we are executing some SQL statement or stored procedure that we know will not return any records.

We can prevent ADO from going through the process of instantiating a recordset by using the `adExecuteNoRecords` option. Whenever possible, we should use this option:

```
<%@ LANGUAGE="VBSCRIPT" %>
<!--METADATA TYPE="typelib"
    FILE="C:\Program Files\Common Files\System\ADO\MSADO15.dll" -->
<%
    Option Explicit
    Dim cnStore, strSQL, strFN, strLN

    strFN = Request.form("f")
    strLN = Request.form("l")
    strSQL = " Insert Into Employees (LastName, FirstName) " _
        & "Values ('" & strLN & "','" & strFN & "')"

    '-- Create the connection and start a session.
    Set cnStore = Server.CreateObject("ADODB.Connection")
    With cnStore
        .ConnectionTimeout = 60
        .Open "File Name=D:\Webs\808_Pubs\data\Store.UDL"
        .Execute strSQL, , adExecuteNoRecords
    End With
    CnStore.Close

    Set cnStore = Nothing
%>
```

Summary

This chapter introduced us to the ADO object model. This allows us to obtain information from the data store and integrate it with scripting code on our client. By having the ability to use ADO to query information from the server, and then use ASP code to integrate that information into the HTML and client script that is sent to the client, we can build dynamic applications rather than just simple static web sites.

We discussed each of the major objects used in ADO and the procedures available to specify how we should connect to the data store. One way was through the use of such properties of the `Connection` object as `ConnectionString`, `DefaultDatabase` and `ConnectionTimeout`. Another way was using a Data Link File.

Once we had defined how we should connect, we saw how the `Open` method established the connection. We then used this open connection to invoke SQL commands via the `Command` and `Recordset` objects. By taking advantage of ADO's flexible object model, we were able to construct recordsets that use a variety of cursor types and locking schemes.

Since one of our mandates in developing internet applications is high performance, we also discussed a number of performance related topics, such as the use of stored procedures, connection pooling, and disconnected recordsets.

Section 3

Architecture

ASP Application Architecture

Whether we're building a commercial web application supporting thousands if not millions of users, or a private extranet/intranet application supporting fewer users that more typically contains more commercially sensitive information, modern day web applications tend to have similar high-level requirements:

- ❑ They should run all the time: 24 hours a day, 7 days a week, 365 days a year. There should be little or no apparent downtime to the users of the system.

- ❑ They should be able to scale to support growth trends. The Web provides a unique problem in that there are millions of people connected to the Internet, and potentially tens of thousands connected to intranets (think Oracle and MS). So a web application should be able to deal with this potentially huge user base and demand.

- ❑ They should be easily maintainable, extensible and designed with change *and* longevity in mind. Web applications should not need to be rewritten every six months due to bad design, and they should allow for frequent changes in the user interface.

- ❑ They need to be secure, protecting data from unauthorized individuals>

- ❑ Most importantly, they should be delivered on time and meet the original business requirements to keep the customers happy.

All of these points are critical to the success of a web application (Internet or intranet), but achieving them can be extremely difficult if we allow ourselves to fall into some common traps:

- ❑ We don't spend enough time planning and developing an understanding of the web application and its overall architecture. Web applications are different from traditional client-server applications, so we need to spend time understanding important new concepts such as stateless components, and understand the importance of techniques like resource pooling.

❑ We try to apply traditional application design principles and methodologies to web development, without understanding the implications of doing so. Web development introduces a new set of problems to solve, which typically require a different solution to the one we'd use for client-server applications.

❑ We don't make full use of the services provided by our development platform, so our developers spent too much time writing and maintaining plumbing code, rather than writing core business functionality. The Windows 2000 operating systems provide a rich plumbing infrastructure for web applications that is stable and efficient, so we should ensure that we make good use of it.

❑ We don't make use of cheap ready-built software. For example, Site Server from Microsoft provides many pre-built component, for user management functions, personalization and much more. Such products are cheap when compared to developer resources, and are also well tested and stable.

Any of these points can lead to the failure of a web application. In most cases, projects that fall into these traps are delivered late, over budget, and often tend to use the wrong technologies. In the worst cases, such applications are just unable to scale and cope with user demand, and can even be out of date by time they do finally work.

The aim of this chapter is not to scare you into thinking web application architecture is very difficult or complex. It isn't really that hard, it just needs a lot of care given to it throughout the design and development cycle of a project, as it is easy to get things wrong. We need to understand that the web introduces a new set of problems to solve, and that there are lots of helpful blueprints for web development like Windows DNA, and online guides like MSDN to help solve design problems with proven approaches.

In this chapter, we'll be looking at:

❑ Using Microsoft DNA as a blueprint when designing our application architecture.

❑ General design considerations when writing ASP applications, such as component and interface design.

❑ Using Microsoft COM and other services of the Windows operating system to provide the core plumbing of a web application.

Windows DNA

Windows DNA (Distributed interNet Architecture) is the umbrella term used by Microsoft to describe their web application development and deployment platform. It has evolved from the original Windows DNA released in 1997, back when web development was first starting to explode in popularity, and Microsoft was busy trying to communicate its web vision to the world. Windows DNA is Microsoft's platform for building and deploying interoperable web solutions.

> **Microsoft Windows DNA is a platform for building and deploying highly scaleable enterprise web applications.**

Windows DNA originally focused on providing a guiding architectural blue print for client-server application developers, migrating their two-tier applications to three-tier web applications. The client would typically be a web browser communicating, via HTTP, with a web server, provided by IIS, using ASP for page generation and MTS for transaction management. DNA also catered for standard WIN32 applications built using a three-tier model making use of MTS and DCOM.

The key challenges facing developers around the time DNA was originally release included:

❑ Understanding the architecture differences between client-server and multi-tiered web applications.

❑ Coping with a potentially huge user base and its associated scalability requirements.

❑ Securely exposing and manipulating internal enterprise data stored in multiple databases via a web interface.

Each of these points is critical to the success of a web-based application, and similar to the point discussed earlier.

The first two points really go hand-in-hand. Most client-server applications have fat clients, so called because they are functionally rich, typically written as Win32 applications, and make use of client machine resources. A common trait of this type of application is that they tend to hold onto resources such as database connections throughout the lifetime of the application, allocating them when they are first started, and releasing them at the end.

This isn't a problem with a small group of users accessing the same server, but with the Web we potentially face having to accommodate thousands of concurrent users. Whilst back end applications like SQL Server and Oracle are powerful, ask them to deal with 1000+ connections and we'll soon see them spend most of their time managing connections rather than doing work, resulting in terrible performance. For this reason, web applications and products like IIS carefully manage concurrency and technologies like MTS allow us to pool precious resources.

Scalability

The way to ensure **resource scalability** in applications with huge numbers of users is, in theory at least, rather simple: don't hold on to resources, grab them as late as possible, use them, and release them as soon as possible. This approach is best described as **just in time resource acquisition** and **as soon as possible resource release**. With this technique, the number of resources used is not equal to the number of clients, but equal to the number of requests being processed at any given point in time. For example, web servers like IIS limit the number of concurrent web requests (the IIS5 configurable default is 25 per processor – see `AspProcessorThreadMax` metabase setting), so we know that the maximum per-resource usage peak is equal to the product of the maximum number of concurrent requests and the maximum resources used per request.

The limit of concurrent users enforced by IIS for web application is configurable, but it is not typically suggested that we change it. If IIS just keeps creating threads and processing more concurrent requests, more and more server resources would be used, increasing machine load and reducing overall throughput. We can, of course, adjust the number for more powerful machines, but if the average web request can be optimised down to a sub-second time, the actual throughput of requests can easily be sufficient to support thousands of user requests a second. If we need to scale beyond this, the best approach is to introduce additional web servers and create a web farm, balancing load across the each machine in the farm.

> The term 'scale out' is used when describing the process of adding additional machines to cope with user demand. The term 'scale up' is used to describe increasing the power of a single machine.

Creating resources such as database connections can be a time-consuming and expensive process requiring several network round trips for authentication if the database is located on another machine. For just in time resource acquisition to work, we need to pool resources so this expensive initialisation time doesn't kill the throughput of our application. To achieve this, rather than destroying a resource when we have finished with it, we place it into a resource pool so another web request being processed can take it out of the pool and use it, with little or no initialisation overhead. Providing other requests check the pool for resources before creating them, we have an effective resource recycling mechanism, and avoid the unnecessary overhead required to continuously create resources. Enter MTS and COM+.

The plumbing required for resource scalability is provided by MTS under NT4, and COM+ under Windows 2000. We'll discuss the finer points of MTS and COM+ in more detail in the next chapter, but for now, we can just picture it as an execution environment that is there to help us solve our plumbing and resource usage problems.

> In Windows 2000 MTS is part of COM+, referred to as Transaction Services.

Security

Once an application is connected to the Internet in any way, we face the threat of external hackers, who might decide one day to attack our site. They may then attempt to steal information, or worse still, corrupt data. We also face an arguably more common risk of bored or unhappy company personnel attempting to break into an application. To help reduce these risks, Windows DNA makes use of Windows security services to **authenticate** users, allowing our application to differentiate the good guys and the bad guys, and **authorize** users, determining who can do what.

Windows Integrated Security (NTLM and Kerberos)

For intranet/extranet applications we'd typically use Windows Integrated security, such as NT Lan Manager (NTLM) for NT4, and/or Kerberos for Windows 2000, which are both supported by the IE range of browsers. IIS using COM+ services enables us to determine who is calling into our ASP pages and components (i.e. what user account) when using Windows Integrated security, enabling us to perform various security checks.

An abstraction called **roles** is used by COM+ to encapsulate domain-specific group and user information from application business logic (assuming we are using Windows integrated security). Rather than checking if a specific user is invoking our business component, we can check if the user is part of a role. For example, to successfully delete an employee from a database, the business object invoked to perform the delete can ensure the caller is in the role called `managers`, thus indicating that the user is authorized to perform a destructive action. COM+ can also perform this check for us, if we use declarative security.

COM+ provides an administrative UI called component services (an MMC snap-in) that allows roles to be defined for an application, for users to be assigned to roles, and for security to be defined in a declarative fashion. The net gain of using roles is that our security checks can be logically defined using problem domain terminology, and our code isn't tied to our security domain.

NTLM security is supported by most browsers, natively in IE4 and above, and via plugins for Netscape and earlier versions of IE. IE 5 and above also support Kerberos.

Windows DNA 2000

Windows DNA has evolved to provide a much richer web development and deployment platform based around Windows 2000 and other Microsoft back office products like SQL Server. The current incarnation extends the original Windows DNA in three core ways:

❑ Our application will use one of the Windows 2000 operating systems, and therefore have the stability and application services which that platform provides (i.e. COM+, XML, IIS).

❑ Our application is *likely* to make use of peripheral Microsoft products such as SQL Server to provide database access, MSMQ for queuing (shipped as a Windows 2000 service), Visual Studio for Development, BizTalk Server for e-Commerce exchanges, AppCenter for replications and farm management, and Host Integration Server 2000 for backend system integration.

❑ Our application is more likely to have much greater interoperability and be programmable thanks to XML and SOAP (Simple Object Access Protocol). SOAP is a protocol that defines how we can expose programmatic functions over the web. The idea is quite simple: rather than just exposing interactive pages, a web site can have its content consumed programmatically, and data can be uploaded programmatically. More information on SOAP can be found at `http://www.develop.com/soap`.

Now we've discussed some of the important development issues facing a web developer, and briefly discussed Windows DNA, lets look at how web applications are built in Windows DNA using n-tier architecture.

N-Tier Architecture

Since the days networked PCs became popular in large companies as cheaper alternatives to mainframes, many languages such as VB and tools like Access have provided development environments that make it easy to create data bound GUI interfaces. These applications are typically structured as in the diagram opposite:

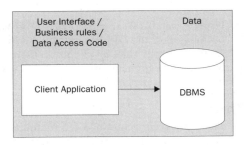

In this type of architecture, the client application contains the GUI code, business logic, security code (sometimes performed by the backend database too), data access logic, and just about anything else not provided by third party database engines. Although suitable for deployment to a small group of users, this type of **2-tier** application structure soon breaks down when used by larger groups. Two of the core problems are:

❑ Deployment – Each time a change is made to a component or the database structure, every client machine has to be updated. This is an administrative nightmare in large companies. For instance, rumour has it that new applications and components in certain well-known banks have been known to take 12 months to deploy to all client machines.

❑ Maintenance – With so many user desktops to go wrong, you can be sure of a very busy helpdesk.

❑ Scalability – All clients are hitting the same back-end data sources and services, competing for resources. As we saw earlier, most applications like this tend to hold on to expensive server resources for too long, and the server chokes on managing resources, rather than doing useful data access work.

If we examine a web application, it must typically perform a number of tasks:

❑ Render HTML to the user, accepting input via forms, and sending back responses.

❑ Check that information received from the user is valid, and doesn't break any defined business rules.

❑ Store the client information, where applicable, in a back-end data source, probably using data stored in the server to process the request.

These functions in a web application built by following the Windows DNA guidelines are divided into three distinct logical tiers:

❑ **User Services** – Responsible for rendering user interfaces and dealing with any user interactions. This tier is also commonly referred to as the presentation services or presentation tier.

❑ **Business Services** – Contains application functionality for carrying out the application core processing, abiding by any business rules and accessing enterprise data. This tier is also commonly referred to as the middle tier or business tier.

❑ **Data Services** – Contains the data for an application, residing in one or more *data sources* (not just relational databases) such as SQL Server, Oracle, Excel Spreadsheets, MailStores, Directories, ERP systems such as SAP and other back-end (and sometimes legacy) systems hosted on mainframes, AS400s etc. This tier is also commonly referred to as the data tier.

Factoring an application using these tiers results in a much more robust, scalable and maintainable application structure. Logical tiers can be deployed on one or more machines. Later in this section we will discuss **physical tiers**.

Using a web browser and HTML/DHTML interfaces effectively solves the client deployment problem, because all of the UI is downloaded dynamically from a central server. Any change made on the server is automatically seen by clients on their next visit. To resolve the scalability issue, the Business Services tier of a web application uses COM+, which provides resource pooling, and other techniques that improve overall scalability.

Three-Tiers

The basic architecture of a DNA application is quite cleanly divided up into three tiers. Each tier provides a layer of indirection that affords us security, encapsulation, flexibility and scalability. The following diagram shows our client-server application from earlier restructure into a 3-tier architecture:

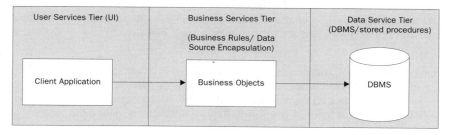

Although not shown in this diagram, some DNA applications also use data access components. Rather than having the same ADO/OLE DB code duplicated in one or more business objects, we can move it into data access components and reuse it. Data access components also provide potential flexibility with regard to changes in the back-end data source, assuming the interface between the business and data component does not change.

So, by developing n-tier applications we gain more flexibility in our application, because the client application has less knowledge about how data is stored, validated and manipulated, so it can focus on doing what it is at good at: UI. We can also now run these objects as part of a COM+ application.

> **A COM+ application is a collection of components (business objects) defined using the component services MMC snap-in, which execute in a managed runtime execution environment and can make use of COM+ services such as transaction management and resource pooling. If you are used to programming for NT4, a COM+ application is the equivalent of an MTS package.**

In this 3-tier approach, changes in business objects do not necessarily affect the UI, unless the programming interface used by the UI and exposed by the business object changes. This approach also means that more intelligence can be built into the components, allowing them to connect to different back-end data sources on different machines, without requiring any UI changes.

DNA is about web applications more than anything else, so most 3-tier applications are written to make use of Windows DNA technologies and products.

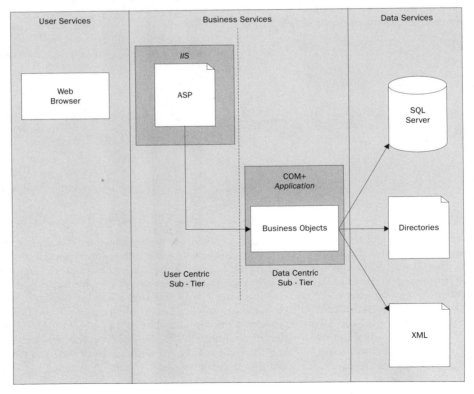

The basic 3-tier architecture is the same here, except the client is now a web browser, and our business objects are now accessed by ASP pages. This layered approach also means the same business objects could also potentially be used to deliver content to other channels such as WAP phones/PDAs, interactive TV etc.

Let's examine each of the three tiers in a little more detail.

User Services (Presentation Tier)

Windows DNA defines four types of application that can exist on the user services or presentation tier:

- **Browser-neutral** – Works on the widest possible range of browsers by ensuring that only HTML 3.2 is emitted by ASP pages, or sticking to a thin subset of DHTML supported by 4.x browsers. These interfaces are functional, but most UI actions such as changing a selection typically require round trip back to serve.

- **Browser-enhanced** – DHTML based, typically requiring a modern day browser such as Internet Explorer 5.x or Netscape 6.x. This type of interface can be very sophisticated, and reduce server round trips by using the DHTML object model, Java Script and XML.

- **Internet-enhanced** – A traditional Win32 application such as Microsoft Money that can be used with or without the Internet, but exhibits additional features and functionality such as online banking when internet enabled. Services of Windows 2000 like COM+ can be used.

- **Internet-reliant** – A traditional Win32 application that needs a internet connection to function.

As we see in the next diagram, starting from the top of the diagram and moving down, the client application becomes fatter, and thus functionally more complex providing a richer UI, at the expense of requiring more deployment on client machines:

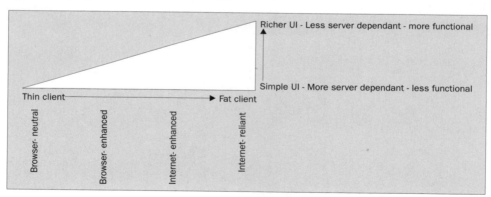

Most web sites support *a browser neutral* interface as it enables the widest possible range of users to visit and make use of the site. The only problem with this type of UI is that we still spend a lot of time ensuring that UI works as expected across browsers, because there are behavioral differences in the way different browsers process HTML 3.2. As we move up to browser-enhanced we basically have to start maintaining browser-specific code bases, or force our clients to adopt a specific browser (common for intranets or extranet applications). ASP doesn't help solve these problems, so we should be prepared for a lot of hard work keeping our UI working across browsers, and be extra careful of not using non-HTML 3.2 tags. The only good news is that in the future ASP+ does address this problem by providing declarative controls that automatically emit the right HTML for different browsers, and which automatically make use of extended capabilities if available.

> **More information about ASP+ can be found in the Wrox book - *A Preview of Active Server Pages+, ISBN 1861004753***

Sites like Microsoft.com that can predict what browsers their viewers are likely to use, or basically have lots more time and money to invest, tend to make use of browser-enhanced UI to give their users a much richer experience. The great feature about these UIs is that they tend to require far fewer roundtrips back to the server, so the user experience is quicker and usually more exciting with popup menus, tree controls and other dynamic elements made possible by DHTML. Although these UIs can be very sophisticated, be prepared to sacrifice features for cross-browser compatibility, or be prepared to spend extra time writing code that a browser sniffs: detects the browser type (user agent) and dynamically adapts the content.

Most intranet and extranet application are browser-enhanced, as the user base tends to be more controlled, and often the browser used can be dictated. These applications tend to have fewer users, but the numbers can still be in the thousands or tens of thousands, so the deployment gain of having a thin client that just consists of a web browser is very attractive.

The last two options are really aimed at high-end, high-cost deployment applications that don't tend to change too often. These types of applications can benefit from using the Web, but really need more traditional Win32/OS functionality to run, and have their own UI requirements (complex GUIS, multiple windows etc).

Business Services (Middle Tier)

The business services tier is all about providing nuggets of functionality to the presentation tier (our ASP pages and Win32 applications), without exposing too much implementation detail. One of the key reasons for having an independent business services tier is that the business rules can all be located in one place; the business component. This means that if an application needs to enforce a particular business rule in many circumstances, a single business object can be used in to enforce the rule in all the different circumstances. Should the rule change, all locations instantly reflect the new rule. If we'd duplicated that rule through 20 ASP pages, we'd have to change 20 pages.

Resource Management

We've briefly touched upon the point that the biggest problem faced when trying to achieve scalability is resource management: Making sure that precious resources are shared, and ensuring that too many clients and too much concurrent processing doesn't occur can lead to more time being spent managing work to be done, than actually doing it. We have also discussed that MTS and COM+ are provided by Microsoft to help us solve this problem.

To recap, to address resource management issues in web application and to support transaction across objects and across machine boundaries, Microsoft created Microsoft Transaction Server (MTS), which is now an integral part of Windows 2000 referred to as Transaction Services. MTS works on the principle that many concurrent clients can be active, and that these activities consist of business objects being created and called by the presentation tier. This unit of work being performed is termed an **activity**. MTS dynamically injects itself into work being performed within an activity, and does some very clever things, which are discussed in detail in the next chapter. However, we'll cover some of the basic details now.

Processes and Threads

To understand how MTS works, we need a quick primer on process and threads.

When we start an application in Windows, the operation system will create a process in which the code for the application will execute. A process is a fairly heavyweight system resource, and has its own address space (up to 4GB of addressable memory) that is isolated from all other processes. If the process crashes for any reason, no other processes are directly affected. IIS runs in its own process, inetinfo.exe, as can COM+ applications (dllhost.exe) depending how they are configured.

To actually run code loaded into a process, the operating system creates a main thread for each process. Threads are the basic units to which the operating system schedules CPU time. A thread doesn't own its own system resources like memory, but it provides an execution path from the code within a process, and accesses the resources of a process. Applications such as IIS create a number of threads (a thread pool) to process ASP requests. Threads are fairly lightweight, and so use fewer machine resources than would be used if we were to create multiple processes to handle multiple concurrent ASP requests.

A process can contain one or more threads, and many processes can be active at the same time. Each thread within every process is allocated a percentage of CPU time depending upon its scheduling priority. If a machine has multiple CPUs, threads can run concurrently.

MTS and COM+ provide the plumbing services to manage processes and threads efficiently on our behalf. IIS makes use of these services when handling ASP requests. IIS5 by default will limit the number of created threads to 25 threads per CPU.

Data Services (Data Tier)

This is where the most important and valuable aspects of most applications live; the back-end data sources and data.

When writing n-tier applications, we'd typically use a back end database like SQL server or Oracle, and use ADO to access it from VB and/or ASP, and ADO and/or OLE DB from C/C++. OLE DB gives a slight performance advantage over ADO (ADO is a thin wrapper on top of OLE DB), but is slightly more complex, and for many web application there really isn't that much benefit in using OLE DB. It takes much longer to develop OLE DB code, and the performance gain it gives us really isn't usually worth the effort.

The data services tier typically contains the following elements:

❑   Back-end data sources – typically SQL Server or Oracle, but as we have discussed XML, MailStores, and Directories also fall into this category.

❑   Stored procedures within the database product.

❑   Data access component to encapsulate data access and provide an additional layer of security.

Stored Procedures

One of the best ways of improving the performance and security of an n-tier application is to use stored procedures. With products like SQL Server and Oracle, using stored procedures results in good performance because the code manipulating the data source is being hosted within the database, therefore the database engine can compile the SQL statements. The stored procedure can also perform multiple tasks (for eample several selects and then an update), so code doesn't have to go through numerous layers of indirection for each operation, unlike ADO or OLE DB.

From a security perspective stored procedures allow you to control access to your database. It is possible to turn off direct table access with products like SQL server, so the only access possible is done via stored procedures. If coded correctly, stored procedures can therefore act as a solid guard around important data.

The biggest performance win with stored procedures comes when performing multiple operations against the database, especially if you're processing in a loop, maybe moving over a recordset containing many rows. Looping through a connected recordset is a fairly expensive operation, especially when done remotely. Where possible, try and move such code into stored procedures, and just perform one local/remote function call to invoke the procedure.

Whatever development we do and no matter what database engine we use, stored procedures should always be used for data access if possible. They shield developers from the actual structure of our database, and give us increased performance. However, we should not create stored procedures that are hundreds of lines long, and that contain too much business logic. This may be tempting to do – especially if you have a good database administrator (DBA) – , but it can result in business logic being spread in too many places throughout your application. Instead, considering wrapping the business logic into a middle-tier component, so it can be re-used in several places.

Data Access Layers

Stored procedures provide performance, but not all database engines are equal, and some stored procedures can have sufficiently complex parameters to merit encapsulation within data access components within the data access layer. This layer simply consists of a number of components that perform one or more tasks:

❑ Shield the programmer from directly accessing stored procedures. This way the stored procedure could in theory change or even be replaced by straight ADO/OLE DB code, and existing code would work.

❑ Provide an additional layer of business logic. If certain data oriented rules must be applied to all of our data, placing them into the data access layer prevents duplication throughout the business objects.

❑ Providing additional security checks or possibly creating audit trail.

As Many Tiers As We Want

DNA applications can consist of more than just three tiers. We can add additional tiers, maybe sub-dividing tiers into several sub-tiers. For example, the business services tier could be sub-divided into three tiers: one that contains ASP pages, one that contains COM components that generate HTML output, and one that contains our business logic. There are no strict rules on how we sub-divide the tiers of an application, so use a common sense approach that suits your team's requirements.

> Each tier in an n-tier web application provides a layer of functionality that affords us flexibility and scalability at the potential cost of some performance.

Physical Tiers of an Application

Conceptually, *logical* tiers are very important, but an application is deployed across **physical tiers**. A physical tier is a machine on which the elements defined in one or more logical tier reside and execute. Each logical tier can be deployed on one or more physical tiers, or they can co-exist on the same machine. Below is a diagram showing our application from earlier being deployed across two physical tiers.

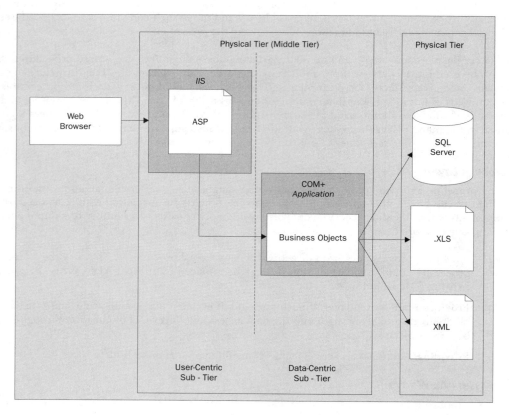

Please note that I've left off firewalls from this diagram. Most secure systems would have a firewall between the end user and the web servers, and a firewall between the business objects and the back-end database. The second firewall is typically there to slow down access to the back-end database, with the hope that alarm bells would already be ringing by the time the first firewall is hacked.

The diagram below shows IIS and COM+ running on one machine, with the back-end database sources such as SQL running on another machine. This is probably the most common way of deploying applications. As an application grows, it is relatively simply to horizontally scale the middle tier across multiple machines using load-balancing software, such as Windows Network Load Balancing (NLB) provided in Windows 2000 Advanced Server. This also has the added benefit of adding fault tolerance to our applications, as a single machine (or several) can fail, and NLB will dynamically adjust its loading balancing to route the work to machines that are still running:

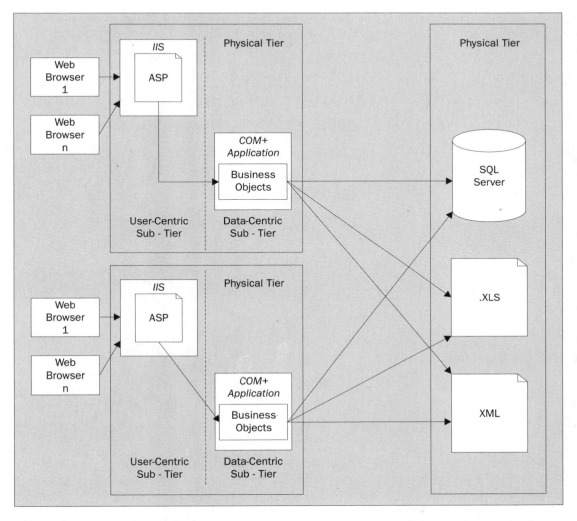

This horizontal scalability can be achieved with no code changes if we make use of the new Application Center 2000 (referred to here as AppCenter) product from Microsoft. This product, due to be released September 2000, effectively manages the replication of an application across a number of machines in a web farm, and it automatically manages any server affinity for an individual user session may have. Server affinity is important, especially if an ASP application makes use of session state. We'll discuss session state later in the chapter, when we look at stateless components. For stateless application we can achieve horizontal scalability without using products like AppCenter, but we then have to take on responsibility for managing machine replication and configuration of NLB and Component Load Balancing (CLB is discussed shortly). This can be a somewhat tedious and error prone task.

Should the machine providing data access become the hot spot in our application, we can easily partition distinct types of data across multiple machines:

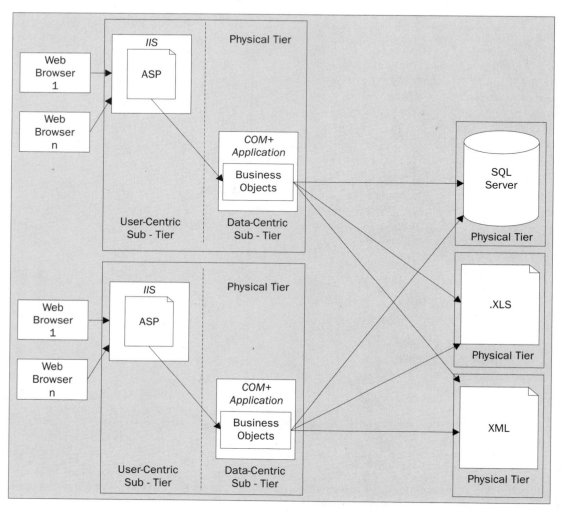

Because each business object encapsulates the location of the data from our ASP pages, they can easily be modified to access different servers this way. Whether we'd use a machine for different types of files, as shown here, is questionable, but it certainly it is very common to use multiple instances or SQL server to share data access load. Of course, having multiple SQL servers does mean we need to be able to partition our database. This isn't a trivial task, and possibly we'd want to look at clustering the data tier before partitioning, or investing in more advanced RAID disk controllers. We look at clustering and the use of RAID devices in Chapter 35.

Component Tier

Another popular physical tier architecture is to split the middle tier across two machines, introducing a component tier:

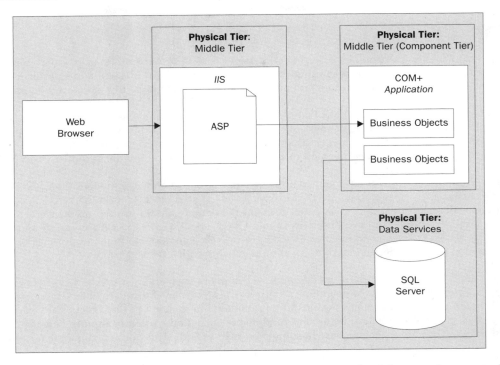

In this architecture, the web server is only responsible for receiving and validating web requests, before forwarding the request to a remote machine for processing by the component tier. This physical architecture can easily be set up using AppCenter 2000 that supports Component Load Balancing (CLB). With this we can define one or more machines as component servers, and requests will be dynamically routed to servers depending on their current load. All component servers are identical, so they all have the same components installed.

We might suspect that using this architecture would result in a single web request being processed more slowly, due to the machine hop, and we'd probably be right most of the time, unless our web servers are under excessive load and just don't have much spare CPU time to do anything except handle HTTP requests. If a component tier is used to perform expensive operations that consume a lot of machine resources, this approach may be preferable. It also shields our web server from potentially fragile components (we all write bad code at some time or other) that could effect our application uptime or responsiveness.

To recap, AppCenter effectively takes over management of Network Load Balancing (NLB) and Component Load Balancing (CLB) that is installed as part of Windows 2000 Advanced Server and Windows 2000 Data Center. It performs all the necessary configuration and makes web farm development simple. AppCenter can also be configured to support external load balancers like Cisco systems Local Director.

Now we have spent time looking at how the architecture of our web application can be divided into a number of logical and physical tiers, lets take a closer look at glue used to empower Windows DNA: COM – the Component Object Model.

COM / COM+

Microsoft COM is a technology built into all versions of Win32 that enables us to build applications in a highly structured and flexibly way using components. A component is essentially a package of code that can be dynamically located, created and pragmatically used at runtime through a well-defined **interface**.

An interface describes the methods that can be called on a component at runtime, but it does not describe how the component has implemented those methods. This black box system is important because any number of components can implement the same interface, allowing us to switch components from different companies, or to simply re-use common interfaces in many components.

The consumer of a component requires no knowledge about where a component is located. Whether it is located locally or remotely, the COM runtime acts as an **Object Request Broker** (**ORB**) and automatically loads the DLL or EXE that contains the component if it resides on the same machine. Or, if configured to do so, it will use Distributed COM (DCOM) to establish a connection to a remote machine. Wherever the component is located, we can use a component in the same way. This ability to use the component independent of its location is called **location transparency**.

COM defines a binary standard, specifying how compilers must emit code to be COM compatible. For the most part, this is an implementation detail we really don't need to worry about. What we do need to understand is that a component must expose funtionality in such a way that functionality written in one language, such as C/C++, can be used at runtime by a program written in another language, such as VB, or via a scripting language based technology, such as ASP. This doesn't happen magically, it is the COM binary standard that enables this interoperability.

COM provides the core server-side plumbing for Windows DNA applications. ASP is a COM based technology, and exposes its intrinsic objects for use in ASP pages as COM objects. For example, when we access the Response object, we are using a COM object.

```
<%
    Response.Write "COM is Cool!"
%>
```

As we can see from screen shotopposite, the Write method used, is just one of the methods that make up the IResponse interface. The ASP Response object has implemented this interface, and we can call any of the methods shown:

ASP makes use of COM as its extensibility mechanism. By this, I mean that ASP exposes its functionality to us as COM objects. The ASP object model is a set of COM objects. We access data sources using ADO and ADSI (among others) which again are both COM object models. We can also create and access our own components, as shown here:

```
<%

    dim objAccount
    set objAccount = CreateObject("ProASPData.Account")

    objAccount.CreateAccount "Wrox1", "Jon Doe"

%>
```

In this code, the first line declares a variable to hold the created object. The second line creates a COM object by calling CreateObject, passing the **programmatic identifier** (**ProgID**) for the component to create (the component created here is discussed later). And the third lines call a function of the COM object.

The ProgID is a mechanism used by COM to associate a string identifier with a specific component. When we create a class module in VB, it generates a ProgID for us using the following format:

[ProjectName].[ClassModuleName]

The following screenshot shows the ProgID of our component:

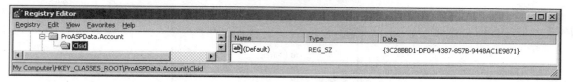

The naming convention is similar in C/C++, but, as with most things, C/C++ gives us more flexibility, so we can specify any string identifier we want.

> *Under the hood, COM maps the Prog ID to a class identifier (CLSID) using the registry. As with most COM information, this mapping is held in the registry under the HKEY_CLASSES_ROOT key.*

Interfaces

As we saw earlier, interfaces are, in effect, small contracts that define groups of functions a component will expose. Each COM component exposes at least one interface called IUnknown, but typically a component supports multiple interfaces. For example, a simple account component may support three interfaces: IUnknown, IDispatch and IAccount. IUnknown and IDispatch are known as **standard interfaces**. They are defined by Microsoft and have a specific role which we'll discuss shortly. IAccount is a **custom interface** that is defined by us for our custom requirements.

We won't cover standard interfaces in much detail in this chapter, but as every component must implement IUnknown, we will now briefly review its role.

IUnknown

The IUnknown interface plays a pivotal role in COM and has two main purposes – **reference counting** and **dynamic discovery** of interfaces.

Because COM is object oriented, an instance of a component (an object) must not be destroyed until every object using it has finished with it (released all of the interfaces they obtained from it). To track these references, the methods AddRef and Release of the IUnknown interface are called by consumers of a component to inform it that its services are either being used or not, enabling the component to maintain a **reference count**.

AddRef increases the reference count and Release decrements the reference count. When the reference count reaches zero the object knows to destroy itself.

Whilst being very simple, reference counts are very powerful. However, they can become difficult to deal with in languages such as C++, as the programmer has to remember to balance them by manually calling AddRef and Release. In VB, programmers are very lucky because this is done for us when a component is used; the same applies to ASP.

The second role of IUnknown is to provide interface navigation at runtime. A component can support multiple interfaces, so IUnknown allows you to request these individual interfaces. This is beyond the scope of this chapter, but for more information on this subject, see Beginning Components for ASP, ISBN 1-861002-88-2.

VB Creation of Interfaces

When we write a class module in VB, a **default interface** is automatically created for us. Each of the public methods and properties that we define in a class module are added to this interface. As the VB language has no programming construct to represent interfaces (although this will be available in Visual Basic 7), we define interfaces by simply defining classes.

The default interface of a class module can be implemented by another class module using the VB `implements` keyword. This is the way VB supports the creation of components that support multiple interfaces. Under the covers, VB is creating component and interface definitions using the **Interface Definition Language** (**IDL**). This is a language-neutral syntax used for defining COM coclasses, interfaces, enumerations etc. Here is a basic example of IDL that VB created for the account component that we saw briefly in the ASP page earlier. We will build this later in this chapter:

```
[
    uuid(56DEE5A3-90A1-429C-B3B1-E5A9A881E1AD),
    version(1.0),
    hidden,
    dual,
    nonextensible,
    oleautomation
]
interface _Account : IDispatch {
    [id(0x60030000)]
    HRESULT CreateAccount(
                    [in] BSTR AccountCode,
                    [in] BSTR AccountHolder,
                    [in, out] VARIANT* ErrorText,
                    [out, retval] VARIANT_BOOL* );
    [id(0x60030001)]
    HRESULT DeleteAccount(
                    [in] BSTR AccountCode,
                    [in, out] VARIANT* ErrorText,
                    [out, retval] VARIANT_BOOL* );
};
```

So that we can compare this to the VB class, let's take a look at the function prototypes for the Account class:

```
Function CreateAccount(ByVal AccountCode As String, _
                    ByVal AccountHolder As String, _
                    ByRef ErrorText As Variant) As Boolean

' code deleted...

End Function

' Delete a bank account

Function DeleteAccount(ByVal AccountCode As String, _
                    ByRef ErrorText As Variant) As Boolean

' code deleted...
End Function
```

The IDL definitions and VB class prototypes are similar. Here are a few interesting points to note:

❑ There are no VB or C/C++ specifics anywhere in the IDL; it's language neutral (although some IDL features are not supported by VB, so C/C++ developers must be aware of this and be careful when targeting VB markets).

❑ The default interface for our VB class module has the same logical name as our class name prefixed with an underscore. In C/C++, interfaces are typically prefixed with an I to denote interface. In IDL the `default` attribute is used to indicate what interface is the default interface.

❑ The IDL interface created for us derives from the interface IDispatch. This enables the functionality of the interface to be accessed by late-bound clients like ASP. We'll discuss the IDispatch interface shortly.

❑ The interface is assigned a physical name (IID/GUID). This is different to the physical name (CLSID) assigned to the class module (CLSID/GUID).

❑ Each method is assigned a unique ID that is used by late-bound clients to identify it.

❑ Each method has a return type of HRESULT. This enables errors to be reported in a consistent way. HRESULT was briefly covered in Chapter 6.

❑ Parameters have attributes to describe in generic form if they are ByRef (in,out) or ByVal (in). IDL has to specify these hints so the COM runtime knows how to invoke functions and pass/return parameters.

By automatically creating interfaces for our class modules, VB is saving the amount of COM we have to understand to get applications written. However, it conceals a few details that we should be aware of.

When creating components in C/C++ and ATL we actually work with IDL. This is a bit scary at first, but various wizards do help create the IDL for us. We only have to manipulate the IDL by hand if we need to modify existing function prototypes, which you'll doubtless do unless you define a perfect interface first time.

Now we have covered the basic principles of interfaces, let's review the IDispatch interface. This is what ASP pages use to access all COM components.

The IDispatch Interface – Late Binding

IDispatch is an interface that allows methods of a component to be discovered and invoked by a client application runtime. Invocation of components' functionality by this interface is termed **late binding**. Before the method can be invoked, the component has to be asked if it supports the function at runtime. The opposite of late binding is **early binding**. This is only applicable to compiled languages, where knowledge about how to invoke a method can be hard wired into the code at compile time.

> **ASP only supports late binding using** IDispatch.

Late binding has two key drawbacks:

❑ It's slower than early binding, because a component has to be asked if it supports a method before it can be invoked.

❑ As the functionality is being queried for at runtime, it's possible that an error will occur because a method is not supported. For instance, if we were to misspell a method name, a call will fail at runtime.

The advantage of late binding is that a component can be extended, and ASP code will not break unless the methods the ASP is dependant upon are changed. In contrast, early bound code can, and usually does, break if an interface is changed once it is published.

Generally speaking we should always use early binding where possible, which in VB requires that you have a type library. All interfaces generated in VB can support both early and late-bound clients, because every interface created by VB derives from IDispatch, the same rule applies for most C/C++ COM classes written using ATL, although you can opt not to support IDispatch. You might decide not to support IDispatch if you know late binding is never a requirement.

ASP Uses IDispatch

ASP is built using Active Scripting Engines that are not capable of accessing anything but the default interface for a component using the `IDispatch` interface. This will only be a problem if you develop components with multiple interfaces that you want to use from ASP, or if you want to use such components from ASP. You just won't be able to access all the functionality of the component, unless you write your own component that exposes the functionality via its own interface, or uses the functionality itself as part of an ASP request.

Components and interfaces are modeled using lollypop diagrams as shown here:

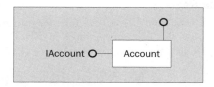

These lollypop diagrams show the interfaces supported by a component extruding from the left side of the box, with the box itself containing the name of the component (coclass). The single line on the top of the box represents the interface called `IUnknown` that every component must implement.

> The good news is that ASP+ allows us to access any interface of a COM component so we don't have to use late binding.

Runtime Identification of Components, Interfaces etc. – GUIDs

When we compile a class module in VB and create a COM component, VB assigns a **Globally Unique IDentifier** called a GUID to the component. A GUID is a 128bit number that is generated based upon the system clock and the MAC address found in the computer's network card, and is guaranteed to be unique. If there is not a network card on the machine, a GUID will still be unique, but will only be *guaranteed* unique on that particular machine. C/C++ also uses GUID but you can either assign GUIDS automatically or by hand.

When a GUID is used to identify a class module it is called a **Class Identifier** (**CLSID**). GUIDs are used in COM to identity lots of things, so there are various other names given to GUIDs when used in a specific context, as we will discuss shortly. These contexts include **interface identifiers** (**IID**), **application identifiers** (**APPID**), and many more.

So why do we need a 128bit number to identify a component? Isn't the name we assign to our class module enough? The answer is no. Analysts and programmers all around the world are assigning names to their class modules every minute of the day, so there are bound to be numerous cases where the same names will be used by two people, especially when people are designing applications for the same program domain. To solve this problem a third party could assign names, but wouldn't that be a pain?

Because 128bit numbers are pretty meaningless to the human eye, they are represented by a string notation in the registry and other places where we have to deal with them. Here is the `CLSID` used to identify a component for the Microsoft RDO Connection component:

```
{E791964C-208A-11CF-8146-00AA00A40C25}
```

If two companies use identical component names, the only real issue is that Programmatic Identifiers can conflict. The chance of this happening is reduced because:

> *COM provides the API* `CoCreateGUID` *for generating GUIDs, but for the most part VB will always generate them on our behalf. If we really want to create our own GUIDs, we can use* `GUIDGEN.EXE` *or* `UUIDGEN.EXE`, *located in the Visual Studio* `common/tools` *directory.*

The Registry

COM uses the registry to store information about all components registered on a machine. You can view this by running the REGEDIT.EXE application. The screen below shows where the various identifiers and information are contained in the registry:

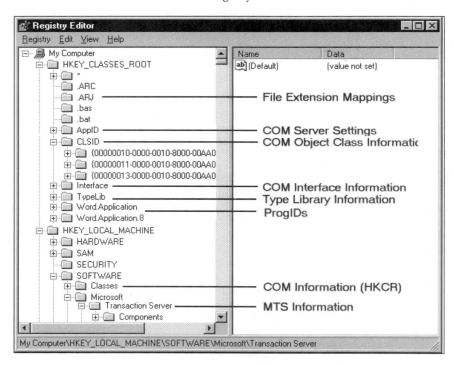

Typically you shouldn't edit these keys as they are installed by applications and components. However, it can be an interesting exercise to explore the registry.

Apartments

Languages like VB shield programmers from the concepts of threads. When you write code, you do not have to worry about two or more threads accessing your code. VB ensures that only one thread (always the same thread) will create and access a specific instance of class module, or in COM-speak a COM object. This guarantee is made because VB does not provide synchronous primitives required to write code that can be safely accessed by two or more threads. Because languages like VB have this restriction, and because COM has to ensure that languages like C/C++ that do support multiple thread will not break these concurrency rules, COM defines the concepts of **threading models**.

Each and every COM component has a threading model. By default, VB6 components have a threading model of **apartment**. An apartment-threaded COM component can be created by any thread, but only the thread that creates an instance of a COM component can access it. This complies with the 'rules' for VB, but doesn't expose the concepts of VB to the user of the component. It just states that the component is thread phobic. An alternative threading model is **single**, which is similar to the apartment-threading model, except that it ensures that only a single thread in a process is used to create ALL single threaded COM components.

For components written in languages like C/C++ that do provide synchronization primitives, COM defines the **free**-threading model. A free-threaded component can be created on one thread, and accessed by any other thread. A component marked as free threaded guarantees it can cope with such access, and will protect its data. For components that don't care about thread affinity (whether they are accessed by a specific thread), and are happy to be accessed by one, two, or more threads, there is the threading model of **both**. This implies that the semantics are of both apartment and free threading.

When an instance of a COM component is created, it is created in and associated with an apartment. An apartment ensures the threading model requirements for a component are adhered to. Without going into much detail, each thread within a process can register its apartment type. This can either be: apartment threaded (referred to as single-threaded apartment – STA) or free threaded (referred to as a Multi-Threaded Apartment or MTA). There can be multiple STAs within a process, but there is only one MTA.

Component Design

Designing components is an art form, and is in many ways reminiscent of object oriented analysis, design and programming. Give three programmers the same problem statement, and they'll all probably come up with different component architectures. Of course, the individual designs of three good programmers would also have similarities. It is these common aspects of good design that we'll take a look at in this section.

Component Granularity

We should try to logically group functionality within components, not making them too fine grained so our system is composed of thousands of components, and not too coursed grained such that our system is only composed of one or two components.

A fine-grained component simply performs a number of small, related tasks and can be re-used. An example of a fine-grained component would be one which performs ISBN validation.

Course-grained components that perform several tasks to perform specific processing tasks are less likely to be easily reusable; an example of this would be a component that validates an ISBN number and enters some details into a database. Such a component is less re-usable due to the database access. This is one reason why we should endeavor to make use of fine-grained component functionality.

Component Families

When designing components we should try to build up component families, and logically divide them up, deciding which tier of our application they belong to, and how the various families interact. For example, we may have one generic component family for data access, within which we have sub-families for such things as relational database access and file access. These would probably all reside within the data access tier.

Use Components instead of complex ASP pages

Where possible, we should ensure all business logic is placed in components. We should avoid creating large ASP pages with lots of code. The code will execute more quickly when compiled as part of a component, as it is early bound and compiled, and it is less likely that we would end up duplicating business logic in components.

Design for the Environment and Distance

Environment dependant components are restricted to how they can be deployed, and have certain run-time requirements. For example, if we write a component that requires access to the ASP intrinsics, this component will not be overly successful at running effectively in the data tier on a different machine. We should architect components to run as closely as possible to their environment dependency, and we should also try to factor such environment dependencies into a separate layer. This would enable us, if we wished, to use our components outside of ASP one day.

Designing for Enterprise Scalability

To cater for enterprise level scalability, applications should try to avoid using session level state. All session state should be stored either within client-side hidden fields, and/or within a back-end database. The reason for doing this is simply so that any server in a web farm can process a web request. If we use session state, a request must always be routed back to the same server using sticky sessions.

Sticky Sessions is a term used to describe ASP user sessions that must always be redirected to the same front-end web server in a web farm. Generally, sticky sessions are required in applications that depend upon state stored in the session object. This is typically a bad design decision because if the machine hosting the sticky session falls over, all session state is lost and the user has to start an entirely new session.

Using a database to store session state (such as a shopping cart) does add a degree of overhead to an application, but it makes it more resilient in the case of failures. If a web server fails during a user's request, another server can handle it and no information will be lost. If we'd used a session-based shopping cart, our customers would lose everything created during their session if the machine hosting that session failed.

On some sites, such as payroll systems, all data must be protected by Secure Sockets Layer security (SSL). In this scenario it is OK to use the session object for some state storage, as SSL requires sticky sessions. The secure negotiation that occurs during session negotiation is too expensive to re-establish on each HTTP request. We should still use session level state wisely, as a machine can still fall over, and all transient state not in the database will be lost.

Instrumentation - Understanding What's Going On Under the Hood at Runtime

When designing web applications, we should make sure we implement a good tracing/logging framework. It is necessary to bear in mind that cross machines calls will be occurring, and sessions will be executing concurrently on different threads. We should consider using performance counters to track what is going on inside an application. They enable system administrators to monitor the state of a deployed application using the Windows performance monitor application, and provide invaluable live feed information about the performance and overall well-being of an application.

Don't Forget Commercial Components

There are plenty of commercial components around for doing generic things like compression and file uploading. Be sure to check out companies like Component Source (http://www.componentsource.com) for such functionality, as this can save time and money in the long run. It might be interesting as a programmer to write code to implement an RFC for file uploading, but there is no way we'd match the functionality of commercial components or their stability. (Of course, there are also some bad commercial components, so evaluate free downloads where possible.)

Design for a Dead Line and Expect Changes

The most important design consideration is of course designing a component architecture that will allow us to implement it within our deadlines. This should probably be the most important point on our list, and as much as we'd like to have complex component architecture, successful systems often start with fairly course-grained component architecture, and evolve over time to a more elegant fine-grained system. Web applications tend to change and evolve a lot, and a very fine-grained architecture is sometimes more difficult to change during the development process. Of course, there are exceptions to this rule, and it really does depend on how good a development team is. But it is a good rule of thumb to keep things as simple as possible at the outset.

Interface Design

When building COM components, we should try to create well-factored interfaces. Here is a list of some good design rules when creating components:

- ❏ We should ensure that components can be used in environments in which they are intended to be deployed. For the most part, this isn't really a problem for VB/ASP, but in C/C++ we can create interfaces that ASP cannot use. In C/C++ we should always expose the IDispatch interface for components that are to be used in ASP pages, and always stick to using automation types.

- ❏ When designing components to be used by ASP pages, in/out parameters (byref parameters in VB) should by of the type Variant. This requirement stems from a limitation in the Active Scripting engines used by ASP. Return parameters do not need to be of the type Variant.

- ❏ We should make our interface names and method names descriptive. That is, not calling an interface ISomething or a method DoIt, but giving them clear, non-ambiguous names. For example, if we have a component that renders some common HTML, we could have an interface called IScreenPainter and methods called DrawPageHeader, DrawPageBody and DrawPageFooter.

- ❏ We should factor interfaces well. That is, trying to group functionality logically in multiple interfaces. For example, in ASP we have interfaces like IRequest and IResponse that group functionality based upon whether it is used to access an HTTP request, to build an HTTP response. In our interfaces, we should try to define similar factoring.

- ❏ We should try to stick to strong types, but consider flexibility. VB programmers often use the VARIANT data type. This has some advantages in that it can give some flexibility (passing different value types or representing nothing), but it can make an interface less intuitive.

There is one caveat that must be mentioned regarding the use of ASP with components. ASP is built using the Microsoft Active Scripting technology. This limits the way in which it can be used with COM, in that it can only access the default interface of a component. When designing components that are only going to be used in ASP pages, we normally shouldn't implement multiple interfaces. To keep well-factored interfaces, and to work around the limitations of ASP only being able to access the default interface of a component, we have a few choices:

- ❏ Have a one-to-one mapping between components and interfaces.

- ❏ Implement multiple interfaces per component, and then write wrapper components that re-expose the functionality of multiple interfaces to scripting clients like ASP as one consolidated interface.

- ❏ Use helper classes to expose non-default interfaces to ASP. These are beyond the scope of this chapter, but more details and an examination of such an implementation can be found at http://www.sellsbrothers.com/tools/multidisp/index.htm.

COM+

COM+ extends COM by adding the notion of services. These are discussed more fully in later chapters. For now, we can think of a service as functionality that is dynamically added to our components after they have been compiled, based upon declarative attributes defined in the MTS/COM+ catalog. The MTS/COM+ catalog is like the registry in that it contains details about components, but it is actually a set of files located within the Windows directory. With MTS/COM+ (more precisely, the MMC component services snap-in) we can specify that the work of a component must occur within a transaction:

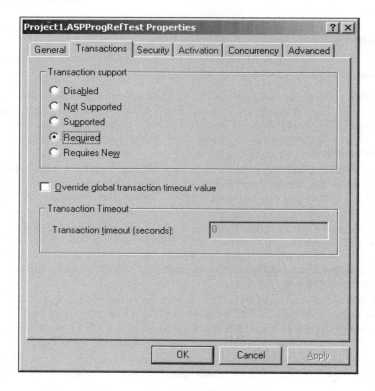

This screen can be reached by viewing the properties of a component from within either the MTS explorer or component services.

As component developers, we don't need to create the transaction; COM+ will automatically create it for us at runtime and enlist our component into the transaction. Any work our component does (or any work any child component it uses does) that involves the use of a database or other traditional data source such as MSMQ, will be performed under the transaction, and have ACID properties. This means that is, it will have Atomicity, Consistency, Isolation, and Durability; more details can be found on Microsoft Developer Network at http://msdn.microsoft.com/library/partbook/asp20/acidproperties.htm.

Now we have discussed various aspects of web development at a high level, let's get our hands dirty and create a simple VB component that is used in an ASP page. The component won't be functionally rich, and is designed simply to show an example of component development in VB.

Creating a Component Using VB

VB is a high-level language that shields developers from most of the low-level implementation details of COM. It lets us create many types of COM servers, but initially, we are going to focus on ActiveX DLLs.

Creating a Simple COM Component

Open up VB, and create a project of the type ActiveX DLL. Change the project name to ProASPData, and the class name to Account:

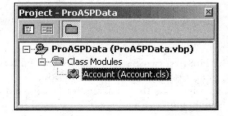

In the code window for the class, enter the following code (this can be downloaded, if required, from the www.wrox.com):

```
' Create a bank account

Function CreateAccount(ByVal AccountCode As String, _
                       ByVal AccountHolder As String, _
                       ByRef ErrorText As Variant) As Boolean

CreateAccount = False

If Len(AccountCode) < 4 Or Len(AccountCode) > 8 Then
   ErrorText = "Account code must be 4 to 8 characters long"
   Exit Function
End If

If Len(AccountHolder) < 4 Or Len(AccountHolder) > 16 Then
   ErrorText = "Account Holder must be 4 to 16 characters long"
   Exit Function
End If

CreateAccount = True

End Function


' Delete a bank account

Function DeleteAccount(ByVal AccountCode As String, _
                       ByRef ErrorText As Variant) As Boolean

DeleteAccount = False

If Len(AccountCode) < 4 Or Len(AccountCode) > 8 Then
   ErrorText = "Account code must be 4 to 8 characters long"
   Exit Function
End If

DeleteAccount = True

End Function
```

This code declares two functions called `CreateAccount` and `DeleteAccount`. Both functions don't actually do that much except validate the input values to ensure length constraints are followed. I've not included the ADO code here, because this is covered later in the book, and at this point we are really just interested in calling functions in COM, rather than the writing code.

If we look at the function prototype for `CreateAccount` we can see that three parameters are passed into the function:

```
Function CreateAccount(ByVal AccountCode As String, _
                       ByVal AccountHolder As String, _
                       ByRef ErrorText As Variant) As Boolean
```

The first two parameters are passed **by value**, which in COM terms means they are **in parameters**: they can be accessed by the function, but any changes made to the parameters will not be returned to the caller. The third parameter is a passed **by reference**, which in COM terms mean it is an **in/out parameter**: a value can be passed in, and any changes to the variable are returned to the caller.

The `DeleteAccount` function has a similar prototype to `CreateAccount`, except that the `AccountHolder` parameter is not included. All other parameters are the same.

To use our component, I've created a simple UI that allows accounts to be created and deleted:

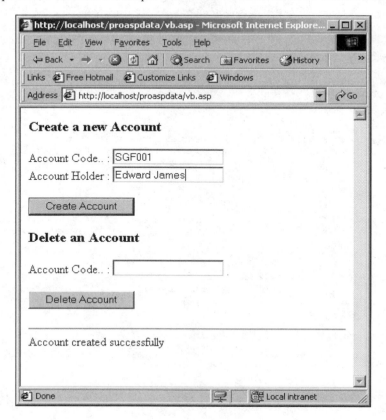

The code to generate this page is as follows:

```
<%

dim sStatus
dim objAccount
dim bReturnCode
dim sErrorText

sStatus = ""

' Are we creating an account

if Request.Form("Action") = "CreateAccount" then

   set objAccount = CreateObject("ProASPData.Account")

   bReturnCode = objAccount.CreateAccount( Request.Form("AccountCode"), _
                                           Request.Form("AccountHolder"), _
                                           sErrorText )

   if bReturnCode = true then
      sStatus = "Account created successfully"
   else
      sStatus = sErrorText
   end if

end if

' Are we deleting an account

if Request.Form("Action") = "DeleteAccount" then

   set objAccount = CreateObject("ProASPData.Account")

   bReturnCode = objAccount.DeleteAccount( Request.Form("AccountCode"), sErrorText )

   if bReturnCode = true then
      sStatus = "Account deleted successfully"
   else
      sStatus = sErrorText
   end if

end if

%>

<form action="vb.asp" method="post">

<H3>Create a new Account</H3>
Account Code   : <input type="text" name="AccountCode" />
<BR />
Account Holder : <input type="text" name="AccountHolder" />
<BR />
<BR />
<input type="submit" value="Create Account" />
<BR />
<input type="hidden" name="Action" value="CreateAccount" />
```

```
</form>

<form action="vb.asp" method="post">

<H3>Delete an Account</H3>
Account Code.. : <input type="text" name="AccountCode" />
<BR />
<BR />
<input type="submit" value="Delete Account" />
<BR />
<input type="hidden" name="Action" value="DeleteAccount" />

</form>
```

```
<HR />

<%
if sStatus <> "" then

    response.write sStatus
end if
%>
```

Let's take a brief look at some of the more important aspects of this code.

CreateObject

When creating a VB COM object in ASP we use the `CreateObject` function, and pass in a string value which is basically of the form `Project Name.Class Name`:

```
set objAccount = CreateObject("ProASPData.Account")
```

As we saw earlier, this string is called a programmatic identifier, or ProgID for short. VB automatically creates ProgIDs for us, which are stored in the registry under the HKEY_CLASSES_ROOT key. We are repeating the screen shown that was shown here, using the RegEdit utility to show the ProgID:

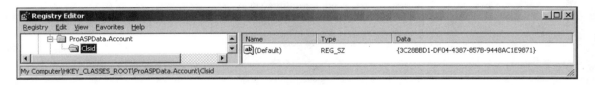

These register keys are used by the `CreateObject` API to access the class identifier for the component.

In Out Parameters

Both of the component functions return `False` if an error is raised, and the `ErrorText` parameter is set to a descriptive string that describe the error:

Because the error text is passed out using a variable that was passed in a `ByRef` parameter, the parameter type is defined as a `Variant`. All variables defined in ASP script are variants, and if we specify any other variable type for `ByRef` parameters ASP, we'll raise a type mismatch error.

Creating a Component Using C/C++ and ATL

Creating COM components in VB is fairly painless, as VB hides the majority of COM details from us. We just create VB class modules, and if we want them to be COM components we just create those classes as part of an ActiveX project and mark the classes as public. With C/C++ there is no such shielding. We have to understand the mechanics of COM, creating IDL, understand how to map C/C++ types to COM types etc.

Creating COM components in plain C/C++ isn't difficult, but it requires us to write a lot of code. A substantial amount of this code is the same for every component. Recognizing this, the guys in Redmond created the Microsoft Active Template Library (ATL). ATL is a set of C/C++ templates that implement boilerplate COM functionality for us. This doesn't shield us completely from COM details, but it does mean we can focus on business logic and writing more interesting code.

To introduce you to creating COM components using ATL we are going to quickly recreate the VB account component from earlier using ATL. To do this we'll use the built-in wizard support, and briefly review the code and IDL it spits out. We won't discuss the dialog options in detail, more information can be found on the MSDN.

New Project

First off, we fire up VS and create a new project (file | new project) and select the ATL COM application wizard:

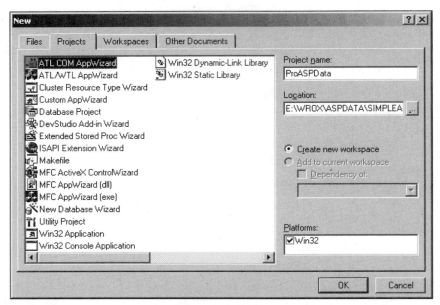

We click OK, and then select the defaults on the next page to create a DLL based COM server:

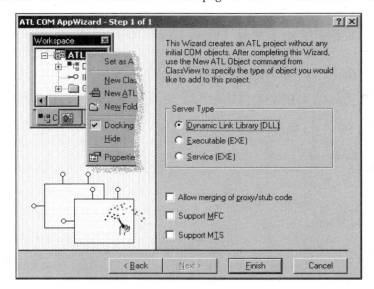

Once the finished button is clicked, the wizard will create a new project with the basic files that are needed to compile a DLL that can expose COM components.

To create a COM component, we use the insert | new class menu, specifying a class type of ATL Class, and specify a name of Account:

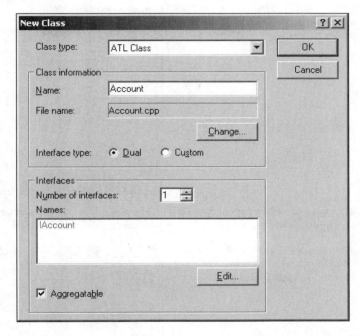

Click OK, and we can then see that the class workspace windows class tab shows the following:

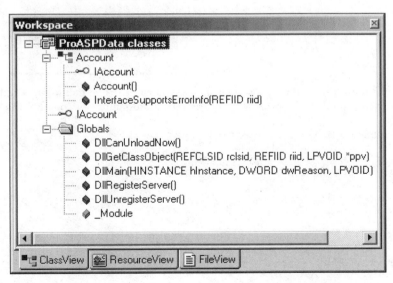

The wizard has created a C/C++ Project called **Account**, and a COM interface called **IAccount**. If we switch to the file view, we can see a number of files have been created, including the IDL file for the project:

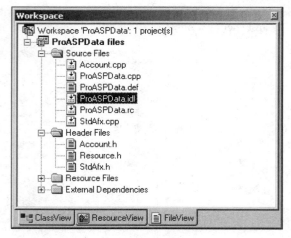

Unlike VB, in C/C++ we are fully exposed to IDL all the time. Various wizard options can help us create the IDL (adding methods etc.), but we have ultimate control and do need to understand it.

If we go back to the class view and right-click on the entry **IAccount item**, we can select the menu item **Add Method** to define a new method:

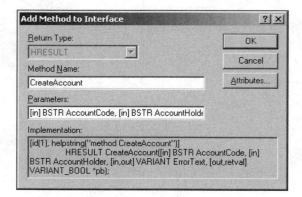

As the implementation section of this screen shows, you can see I've had to type in the full IDL signature for this method. When we click **OK**, the IDL is automatically added to the IDL file:

```
// ProASPData.idl : IDL source for ProASPData.dll

// This file will be processed by the MIDL tool to
// produce the type library (ProASPData.tlb) and marshalling code.

import "oaidl.idl";
import "ocidl.idl";

    [
        object,
        uuid(D42931A5-6836-4297-AC1D-187B34A6E6DA),
        dual,
        helpstring("IAccount Interface"),
        pointer_default(unique)
    ]
```

```
    interface IAccount : IDispatch
    {
        [id(1), helpstring("method CreateAccount")]
        HRESULT CreateAccount([in] BSTR AccountCode,
                              [in] BSTR AccountHolder,
                              [in,out] VARIANT ErrorText,
                              [out,retval] VARIANT_BOOL *pb);
    };

[
    uuid(A4BA2BEE-874E-4A55-8111-982CFC64FBF7),
    version(1.0),
    helpstring("ProASPData 1.0 Type Library")
]
library PROASPDATALib
{
    importlib("stdole32.tlb");
    importlib("stdole2.tlb");


    [
        uuid(5C2032B6-A1AC-46E9-AA88-DACD12C6B514),
        helpstring("Account Class")
    ]
    coclass Account
    {
        [default] interface IAccount;
    };
};
```

The function prototype and shell implementation is also added to any class that implements the COM interface, such as the `InterfaceSupportsErrorInfo(REFIID riid)` class:

```
STDMETHODIMP Account::CreateAccount(BSTR AccountCode, BSTR AccountHolder, VARIANT
ErrorText, VARIANT_BOOL *pb)
{
    // TODO: Add your implementation code here

    return S_OK;
}
```

I'm not going to implement the code for this component in this chapter, but assuming we added the `DeleteAccount` method using the add method dialog too, our ASP page from earlier would work against this C/C++ ATL component without any change.

Summary

In this chapter we've looked at how to approach your web application design and architecture correctly from day one. We looked at the how Windows DNA provides the foundations from which we should architect our web applications, and we have seen how COM provides the plumbing to create and deploy applications, based upon this model.

In the next chapter, we'll take a much more detailed look at COM+ and at implementing and deploying our COM components.

9

Component Services

In Chapter 8, we looked at Microsoft's Component Object Model (COM) and how it has evolved to become a very robust, binary standard for developing modular applications. Applications that are built on the foundation of COM are termed COM-compatible, and if these applications expose their methods and properties via COM interfaces to other applications, they are called COM components. We looked at simple examples of developing COM components in Visual Basic and Visual C++; however, you can develop COM components in a multitude of languages.

In this chapter, we'll look at deploying these components using the component services available on the Windows platform. Under Windows 2000, a variety of component services have been melded together as **COM+**. Much of the core functionality of COM+ was first introduced as Microsoft Transaction Server, or MTS. MTS was introduced in 1996 and version 2 was released with Windows NT 4.0. We'll also look at using MSMQ (Microsoft Message Queue Server) to implement asynchronous communication between components and applications.

Under Windows 2000, MTS and MSMQ have been merged together with COM and DCOM to form Component Services (COM+). There are also many extra features which are either currently available under COM+, or are scheduled for release in the near future. We will look first at the functionality available to us with MTS, and then go on to see what COM+ brings to the party. Then we will look in detail at message queuing using MSMQ, and see how we can implement queued components using COM+. Finally, we'll have a quick look at some of the enhancements which are expected to be released in the next version of COM+ (currently called COM+ 1.x).

Microsoft Transaction Server

Imagine a simple ASP application consisting of an ASP page and a COM component. The ASP page calls the component, which processes data in a recordset and neatly formats it as an HTML table. It then sends the formatted data back to the calling program (the ASP page) via a string variable. The ASP page, in turn, simply does a `Response.Write` to dump this information on to the `Response` object's stream. The browser fetches this response stream and displays the results on the client machine.

Instead of doing all that, wouldn't it be efficient to have our COM component directly access the `Response` object and be able to do a `Response.Write` statement instead of having to pass data via a string variable? Yes it would. But there is one problem. A web site can be hit simultaneously by a number of users, and at the same instant a given ASP page could be executing under the context of each of those users. For each user, a separate instance of the ASP page is run, and within it, a separate instance of the COM component is instantiated. If we need to get a handle to the `Response` object, we need to make sure that we are obtaining the `Response` object that is linked to the user who requested our page, and not to other users. It would be nice if there were a way to manage these COM component instantiations, so that we could have better control on them. And there is a way.

When developing web applications, there is another issue, especially when it comes to the scalability of your applications. Consider a web page that is accessing a database. If there are 1000 users hitting your web site at the same time, there will be 1,000 instances of the web page in action. If this web page accesses a database directly (which may be what you have been doing with ASP pages), there will be 1000 simultaneous connections to your database. On the other hand, if you had a means for the 1000 users to access, say, 20 server applications, which in turn accessed the database, you would only need 20 unique identities and consequently, only 20 connections. Intelligent management of database connections is only one of the requirements for a scalable internet solution. You wish there was a way for you to write components that would also handle connections intelligently. And there is a way.

What you need is a mechanism that manages COM components for you. What you need is a COM component manager.

Microsoft ships a COM component manager along with Internet Information Server (IIS) that has the ability to manage the registering and instantiating of COM components from within your web pages. Don't try to look for it under that name however. It has been terribly misnamed as Microsoft Transaction Server (MTS). In reality, it is a COM component manager. However, as we write more sophisticated COM components, about 80% of the time we will be using database transactions within our COM components. So managing COM components will essentially be equal to managing transactions taking place within those COM components, hence the name Microsoft Transaction Server.

What is MTS?

Although it can be used in a non-web environment, MTS is probably most frequently used with Active Server Pages on one side and Internet Information Server on the other. Think of it as a piece of "middleware" software. Sitting in the middle, it enables VB or VC developers to build scalable, distributed web applications. It performs a task very similar to Transaction Processing (TP) monitoring software used in traditional mainframe applications. TP monitoring software enables an application to scale and support a large number of concurrent users. It does this by efficiently managing system resources such as processes and threads, and enabling the sharing of these threads among thousands of concurrent users for a system. A good example is the software running ATM machines, which may be accessed at the same time by thousands of users spread across the nation. MTS provides a similar service to COM components, thereby freeing the COM programmer from having to worry about network resources, distributed transactions, and memory management. The COM programmer can therefore focus on the business logic within the COM component, instead of having to worry about multi-user programming issues such as thread creation and termination, connection pooling, etc.

Microsoft Windows NT Server is the recommended platform for deploying MTS. However, Microsoft Transaction Server version 2.0 will run on both Microsoft Windows NT Workstation and Microsoft Windows 95/98. In Windows 2000, MTS is, of course, incorporated into COM+.

Physically, Microsoft Transaction Server ships in the form of an MTS run-time environment and an MTS administration program (MTS Explorer). The MTS Explorer is a Microsoft Management Console (MMC) snap-in that allows us to create and manage MTS COM components.

In addition, MTS exposes a set of methods and properties via an Application Programming Interface that we can use within our COM components. This allows us to interact programmatically with MTS within our COM components.

The MTS run-time environment is a set of services that provide distributed transactions, automatic management of processes and threads, and object instance management.

Why Use MTS?

MTS allows us to build COM objects that are simple, yet powerful and scalable. MTS provides a range of services to our applications, including thread management, efficient object activation, and support for transactions. MTS instantiates our component within its own process space, separate from our web server, so that if the component crashes, it does not bring down the web server. By providing all these things automatically, MTS shoulders much of the burden in developing powerful, scalable COM components. Not only that, MTS functionality is part of standard Windows NT, and (in the guise of COM+) of Windows 2000, and is going to stay that way for the foreseeable future – so it is best to take advantage of it.

MTS offers four ways to create scalable web applications:

❑ Thread Management – Automatic thread pooling of components ensures the creation, allocation, and termination of system threads, so that developers do not have to program thread management into their solution.

❑ Object Instance Management – Object instance management and Just-In-Time (JIT) activation – deactivating and reactivating an object while a client holds a reference to it – enables MTS applications to scale more efficiently. From the client's point of view, only a single instance of the object exists from the time the client creates it to the time it is finally released. In actuality, the object may be deactivated and reactivated many times.

❑ Resource Dispensers – One of the main goals of the Microsoft Transaction Server is to manage resources in an effective way to provide scalability. MTS includes several resource dispensers that share system resources across multiple, concurrent application components. For example, the ODBC Resource Dispenser specifically provides pooling for connections to ODBC data sources. These Resource Dispensers provide a significant performance improvement in a multi-user environment.

❑ State Management – MTS objects should not maintain state for any length of time, because maintaining state prevents objects from being reused. Therefore, the state of an application should be maintained in the Presentation Layer. In an ASP application, this can be done in several ways, including the use of cookies for storing permanent or long-term information, and passing data from one page to another through an HTML form (for example, in a hidden element).

Let's have a more detailed look at a couple of these features.

Object Instance Management

Traditionally there have been two ways to create and use objects:

❑ A client can create, use, and then destroy an object. The next time you need the object, you create it again. This is a great technique because it conserves server resources. You use the object and get rid of it quickly. The drawback, however, is that as your web application scales up (so that you are getting more and more hits on your application at the same time), you are creating and destroying more and more objects. Object creation is very expensive in terms of resources and this will affect performance. So your web application will not scale well. In addition, if your object is created on a remote computer, each time it is created, there must be a network round trip which also affects performance.

❑ A client can create, use, and then hold on to the object until the client no longer needs it. This is the technique most Visual Basic programmers are familiar with. For example, in a VB program, you hold on to a persistent connection to a database till you no longer need it. However, a web application using the HTTP protocol is by definition, stateless. The only way to hold on to an object is to place it in a `Session` variable or in the `Application` object. This approach is faster than the first one; however, it will cause a lot of problems when you try to scale your web applications. As the number of users accessing our page at any one time builds up, so does the number of concurrent database connections – with the inevitable impact on the performance of the application.

In both the above cases, scalability of the web application is the problem. MTS comes to the rescue by providing object instance management by providing Just-In-Time (JIT) activation that uses the best of both techniques. When your ASP page creates an MTS COM component, it receives an object that it can use just like a normal COM object – as far as your ASP application is concerned, there is no difference. However, your COM component can signal to MTS that its job is done by using the `ObjectContext.SetComplete` MTS API function. When this function is called, MTS goes to work behind the scenes and releases the object, freeing up the server resources, including any database connections. However, the client application is fooled into thinking that the object is still available for use. Later on, when the client application calls a method on the (now deactivated) object, a new object is automatically created and used instead of the old one. The client has the impression that there was a single object available to the client all along, when in fact, many objects were created and destroyed for it.

Context Management

When we create a standard in-process COM component (that is an ActiveX DLL), which is developed without regard to MTS, it is instantiated within the process of the client application that invokes it. The COM component does not have a handle to the context of the client application.

> An object's context is a set of properties which represent the object's execution requirements, such as whether the object needs to be part of a transaction. We'll look at contexts in more detail in the section on COM+.

In the case of an ASP/COM environment, this means that within our ASP page, we can write the following code to output content to the web browser:

```
Response.Write "Hello"
```

However, we will get an error if we use the same code from within our COM component. Instead, we need to write our COM component so that it returns the content back to the ASP page, which in turn writes it out to the browser. This is because, without MTS, our COM component cannot handle context management – it has no way of knowing which client to perform the `Response.Write` on.

When we create an MTS COM component (a COM component that runs within the MTS runtime environment), it is hosted within the MTS Executive. The MTS Executive is a DLL that provides runtime services for MTS COM components, such as thread and context management services. Using the API for the MTS Executive, our COM component can access the context of the ASP page that calls it and can write content directly to the browser.

Resource Dispensers

If our COM component accesses a database, then each time a method is called, it creates, uses and then releases a database connection. A database connection is a very valuable resource. The most efficient model for resource usage in scalable applications is to use resources sparingly, acquire them only when we really need them, and release them as soon as possible.

MTS implements connection pooling to conserve valuable database connections. MTS provides an architecture for resource sharing through its Resource Dispenser Manager and resource dispensers. A resource dispenser is a service that provides synchronization and management of resources within a process, such as the ODBC Driver Manager. The Resource Dispenser Manager works with specific resource dispensers to pool and recycle resources automatically.

When we use any COM component that does not use any MTS-specific API function calls under MTS, MTS uses the ODBC resource dispenser. This is true even if the component does not use ODBC directly, but uses the OLE DB Provider for ODBC Drivers. Whenever any component running in the MTS run-time environment uses ODBC directly or indirectly, the component automatically uses the ODBC resource dispenser.

When our component releases the database connection, the connection is returned to a pool. When the COM component later requires a connection again, it requests a connection with the same details. Instead of creating a new connection, the ODBC resource dispenser recycles the pooled connection, which saves time and server resources. However, connections can only be recycled if they use exactly the same connection details.

COM+

Under Windows 2000, MTS has morphed into a new set of services, now (more appropriately) called Microsoft Component Services, or COM+. COM+ is the next step in the evolution of COM and MTS. COM+ handles many of the resource management tasks that MTS handled before, including thread allocation, security, and JIT activation. COM+ also protects the integrity of our data by providing transaction support, even if a transaction spans multiple databases over a network or multiple components. First of all, let's take an overview of the services provided by COM+:

❑　Context Management. As we saw above, contexts are essentially a set of properties associated with an object which define the environment in which the object runs. In Windows 2000, every COM object has an associated context, although this is ignored if the component does not run under COM+. COM+ uses the context when providing runtime services for our component.

❏ Transaction Processing. Transactions allow us to group together individual operations, so that any changes made as a result of these operations will only be committed if all of the operations are successful. If one or more operation fails, any changes made within the transaction will be undone, and our data will be in exactly the same state as at the start of the transaction. COM+ components can make use of MTS transactions, which can be distributed across components, and even systems.

❏ Concurrency. If our application provides services to multiple users, it may be called simultaneously by several clients. COM+ shields developers from the issues which might arise from this, such as thread management, and allows us to write multi-user applications as though they only needed to support a single user. COM+ achieves this through **activities**. Activities represent a group of objects executing on behalf of a single client, and thus isolate these objects and their contexts from other objects.

❏ Role-based Security. COM+ allows us to construct a security policy for an application. Individual user and group accounts are abstracted into roles, and COM+ allows us to specify what permissions particular roles are to be granted on the object. These roles are then mapped to NT user accounts. As well as defining these permissions administratively, we can verify programmatically that the application which called our component is running in a certain role, and act accordingly.

❏ Object Pooling. COM+ object pooling allows us to reuse existing instances of our components, instead of creating new ones. We will look at object pooling in more detail a little later in this chapter.

❏ JIT Activation. For the sake of performance, we often want our COM object to be created once, used for the entire life of the client application and then destroyed, rather than follow the create-use-destroy cycle each time we want to use the COM component. However, if we are trying to create a large-scale web application, the create-use-hold approach is detrimental to scalability, since large volumes will force large number of object instances to be created. This will increase the burden on our server, causing it to fail at high volumes. When a component is configured as being JIT activated, COM+ will at times deactivate an instance of it while a client still holds an active reference to the object. The next time the client calls a method on the object, which it still believes to be active, COM+ will reactivate the object transparently to the client, *just in time*. The advantage of doing this is that we enable clients to hold references to objects for as long as they need them, without necessarily tying up server resources – such as memory – to do so.

❏ Queued Components. Queued components are a result of the integration of MSMQ into COM+. They allow us to communicate asynchronously with COM+ components via MSMQ messages, without the need for writing MSMQ code ourselves. We will look at queued components towards the end of this chapter.

❏ COM+ Events. COM+ also introduces a new asynchronous event system. Prior to COM+, COM events required a client to poll the server periodically to see if a specified change had occurred. COM+ events reverse this process: the server (or 'publisher') publishes an event. Clients (or 'subscribers') can opt to subscribe to this event, and the publishers will broadcast changes to all subscribers. The type of event is known as a "loosely-coupled event", and is designed for distributed environments.

One of the other new benefits is the introduction of 'asynchronous COM'. In our ASP page, when we instantiate a COM component and then invoke a method on it, the code in the ASP page does not continue to execute unless the COM component method call either returns back with a success or results in an error. If the method call takes a long time to process, our ASP page will also have to wait for this period. This wait is of course passed on to the end user, and can eventually result in the page timing out. Programmers have sometimes worked around this by setting the `Server.ScriptTimeOut` property to a very large value. However, it still means that the end user cannot continue using the web application till the ASP page completes processing. And the ASP page cannot complete processing till our COM component finishes its processing. COM+ introduces the concept of asynchronous COM, whereby a method call on a COM component can execute asynchronously. This new service includes synchronization, object pooling, and the concept of queued components. Although we can achieve this under Windows NT using MSMQ to communicate with our component, COM+ allows us to implement asynchronous communication without any changes to our code.

COM+ Applications

If you're familiar with MTS programming, COM+ applications are the COM+ equivalent of MTS packages. A COM+ application is the primary unit of administration and security for Component Services. Within a COM+ application, we can have one or more components, all of which should provide some logical, related functions. Each COM component within the COM+ application exposes its methods and properties via the mechanism of COM interfaces. By grouping them together as one "package", a COM+ application allows us to control, administer, and secure the entire COM+ application programmatically:

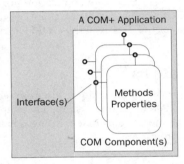

There are distinct benefits to grouping COM components within a COM+ application. These include:

- ❑ Making it easier to deploy COM components as a group.
- ❑ Administration and configuration of scope, boundary and security for the group of COM components is easier.
- ❑ Enabling COM+ to provide additional services (including synchronization and transaction support) to the entire group as a whole.
- ❑ Component DLLs can get loaded into the host process as required.
- ❑ Enabling COM+ to effectively manage threads used by the components.
- ❑ Allowing the COM Components easier access to resource dispensers for shared resources (including database connections).

There are four types of COM+ applications, and we can define our COM components to belong to any of these types of COM+ applications :

- ❑ Server Application
- ❑ Library Application
- ❑ Application proxies
- ❑ COM+ preinstalled applications

Server Applications

These are COM+ applications that run in their own processes. They can support all COM+ services and are similar to server packages under MTS. Server applications give us greater control over the security and role configurations for a COM+ application than library applications. They can use role-based security, and support remote access and queued components.

Library Applications

A library application runs in the process space of the client application that called it. COM components within a library application are always loaded into the process of the calling client application. Library applications are similar to MTS library packages. They cannot support remote access or queued components.

Application Proxies

If we write a server application and want it to be accessed and executed remotely, we can create an application proxy. The application proxy runs on a client computer and enables the client computer to access and use a server application remotely. The application proxy contains a set of files containing registration information; when the proxy is run on the client, it writes this information on the client computer. This information includes the details of the COM+ server application – including Class IDs, Prog IDs, Remote Server Name, and marshalling options.

COM+ Preinstalled Applications

COM+ preinstalled applications make up the runtime environment and other COM+ services that are available as part of the Windows 2000 operating system. These applications handle the internal functions of COM+ and cannot be modified or deleted. These include COM+ system applications, COM+ utilities and IIS System applications.

How COM+ works

COM+ is part of the Component Services that ship with Windows 2000. COM+ includes preinstalled applications that provide a number of services for your COM components.

Contexts, Apartments and Processes

A COM object, when invoked, runs in a process. COM+ divides a process into segments called "apartments". A process can contain one or more apartments. Each apartment contains one or more contexts. A context is the smallest execution context of a component. It is a set of runtime properties maintained for a specific instance of an object. Each COM component object is associated with exactly one context:

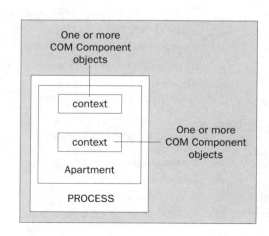

When a business-tier COM component is instantiated from an ASP page, the instance runs within a context, which in turn resides within an apartment within a process. If the business-tier COM component further instantiates a data-access-tier COM component (to access the database back end), then the data access COM component exists in its own context. The two contexts share the same apartment within the same process, but have different run-time properties. Each context has a unique COM object called the `ObjectContext` object. The `ObjectContext` provides the programmer with access to our component's context, allowing us, for example, to commit or abort the MTS transaction to which it belongs, or to check whether the caller is in a specific role.

MTS used to provide wrappers around the context of a COM object. This allowed us to pass the reference to an object to another object. With COM+, we no longer need context wrappers. Every COM object is created with an associated context by default. As we saw above, a context is a set of runtime properties maintained for one or more objects. These runtime properties maintain state information. Every COM object is associated with one context between the time it is activated to the time it is deactivated. Each context resides in a COM apartment. A context can contain multiple objects – so a context can be shared between objects. One or more contexts can reside in the same COM apartment. You can access the context associated with each object by using the `IObjectContext` interface of the `ObjectContext` object. As in the case of MTS COM objects, once you get a reference to the `IObjectContext` interface, you can invoke its `SetComplete` and `SetAbort` methods to signal success or failure within your component code.

Object Pooling

As you are probably aware, the creation and initialization of an object is probably the most expensive operation when it comes to instantiating and using a COM object. If an object already exists in memory, then it is far more efficient to use that than to create one from scratch. COM+ can provide automatic object pooling for our COM components. This enables us to configure a component to have instances of it kept active in a pool, ready to be used by any client that requests the component. We can configure and monitor the pool maintained for a given component, specifying characteristics such as pool size and creation request timeout values. Once the application is running, COM+ manages the pool for us, handling the details of object activation and reuse, according to the criteria we have specified. This can dramatically speed up COM component usage for specific types of COM components – for example, database access COM components used by our business layer. However, in order to take advantage of object pooling, our COM component has to follow certain "poolable" guidelines. For example, the COM component cannot hold client-specific state information since poolable components can be used by one or more client applications. In addition, poolable COM objects cannot be marked as apartment-threaded, since that would bind the object to a particular thread in a process. If an object needs to be used within a pool, it cannot be associated with a single thread alone. Because of this restriction, we cannot use Visual Basic to create poolable COM objects, since VB can only create apartment-threaded objects – for now. However, we can create poolable COM objects in Visual C++.

Developing COM+ Components

Let's take the Visual Basic COM component (`ProASPData.Account`) which we developed in the previous chapter, and modify it to run under COM+. However, before we do that, let's give it some real functionality, rather than just performing a little basic validation. Firstly, we'll create a database, and whenever an account is created or deleted, we'll add or delete a row in a database accordingly. We'll also provide functionality for transferring money from one account to another. Of course, in a live component, you wouldn't modify the interface (although adding methods or properties is more acceptable than removing them), but it's useful for this example to use the same component.

We'll use SQL Server for this example, but any other database could be used, just by changing the ADO connection string. The database, which we will call `Bank`, consists of a single table named `Accounts`. This table has two `varchar` columns named `AccountCode` (the primary key) and `AccountHolder`, and a money `column` called `Balance`:

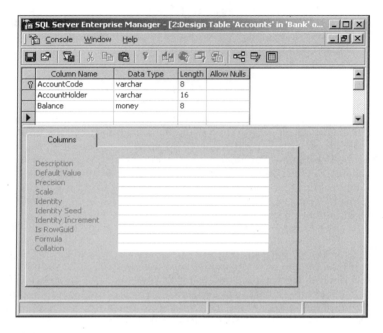

Creating a Transactional Component

Now let's modify our component's code so that it actually updates this database, and so that it takes advantage of COM+. When we've loaded up the project we created in the previous chapter into VB, our first task is to specify that our class will run under MTS/COM+. To do this, we set the class' `MTSTransactionMode` property:

This property indicates not only whether the object will run under MTS/COM+, but also its level of support for MTS transactions. The `MTSTransactionMode` specifies whether the object will form part of any transaction to which the calling application belongs. If it does, then any errors which occur in our object will cause this transaction to fail. We can also specify that the object should force the creation of a new transaction of its own. The possible values are:

- ❏ **0 - NotAnMTSObject** (the default). The object doesn't run under MTS/COM+, and can't take advantage of any COM+ services.

- ❏ **1 - NoTransactions.** The object can run under MTS/COM+, but doesn't support MTS transactions.

- ❏ **2 - RequiresTransaction.** The object runs under MTS/COM+, and must form part of a transaction. If the calling application is not transactional, COM+ will create a new transaction for this object, but otherwise an existing transaction will be used.

- ❏ **3 - UsesTransaction.** The object supports MTS transactions, but COM+ won't create a new transaction if the calling application is not transactional.

- ❏ **4 - RequiresNewTransaction.** COM+ will always create a new transaction for this object, even if the calling application is in a transaction.

In this case, we will require our object to be transactional, but we will allow it to be part of the caller's transaction, so set the `MTSTransactionMode` to **2 - RequiresTransaction**.

Next, we need to add a reference to the COM+ Services type library to gain access to the `ObjectContext` object. Because we're actually going to access the database now, we'll also need to add a reference to ADO:

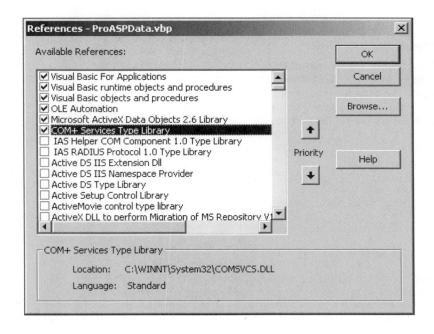

The ObjectControl Interface

Before we update our methods, there are a couple of lines we'll have to add to the General Declarations section of our class. Firstly, we'll implement the ObjectControl interface. This is optional, but it allows us to perform context-specific initialization and clean-up operations for our class. If we implement ObjectControl, COM+ will call its Activate and Deactivate methods whenever our object is instantiated or released. We can use ObjectControl_Activate to create an instance of the ObjectContext object which will be available to all our methods for as long as our component is instantiated, and we can release this object when our component is deactivated:

```
Option Explicit
Implements ObjectControl
Private objContext As ObjectContext
```

```
Private Sub ObjectControl_Activate()
    Set objContext = GetObjectContext
End Sub
```

```
Private Sub ObjectControl_Deactivate()
    Set objContext = Nothing
End Sub
```

There is one more method exposed by the ObjectControl interface: CanBePooled. As we noted above, VB6 doesn't allow us to implement object pooling for our own objects, but we are obliged to expose all the methods of any interface we implement, so we just return False from this method:

```
Private Function ObjectControl_CanBePooled() As Boolean
    ObjectControl_CanBePooled = False
End Sub
```

Using the ObjectContext Object

Now let's go on and extend our existing methods. First, let's modify the CreateAccount method. We'll do a few things here: we'll add some basic error handling, add the ADO code to update the database, and of course the code for managing our MTS transactions. However, first of all we want to check that the context has really been created for this object, by checking that the ObjectContext object is not Nothing. If it isn't, we set the ErrorText and exit the function:

```
Function CreateAccount(ByVal AccountCode As String, _
                       ByVal AccountHolder As String, _
                       ByRef ErrorText As Variant) As Boolean
```

```
Dim objConn As ADODB.Connection
```

```
On Error GoTo CreateAccError
```

```
CreateAccount = False
```

```
If objContext Is Nothing Then
    ErrorText = "Object context does not exist"
    Exit Function
End If
```

The `ObjectContext` object allows us to commit or roll back MTS transactions, by calling its `SetComplete` or `SetAbort` methods. Calling either of these methods will cause the component to be released as soon as the current method has finished execution, under COM+ As Soon As Possible Deactivation. However, we can also call `EnableCommit` or `DisableCommit`. The first of these tells COM+ that the current transaction can be committed, but that the object shouldn't be deactivated. In contrast, `DisableCommit` tells COM+ that the transaction can't yet be committed, but that the object shouldn't be released. After `DisableCommit` has been called, COM+ cannot commit any parent transaction until `SetComplete` or `EnableCommit` is called for this transaction.

So, if all goes well, we will call `SetComplete` at the end of the method. However, if our validation fails, and either the account code or the name of the account holder is not within the permitted length range, we call `SetAbort` to abort the transaction, and then exit the function:

```
If Len(AccountCode) < 4 Or Len(AccountCode) > 8 Then
    ErrorText = "Account code must be 4 to 8 characters long"
    objContext.SetAbort
    Exit Function
End If

If Len(AccountHolder) < 4 Or Len(AccountHolder) > 16 Then
    ErrorText = "Account Holder must be 4 to 16 characters long"
    objContext.SetAbort
    Exit Function
End If
```

If we've got this far, we can go ahead and update the database, so we open up an ADO connection, execute a SQL `INSERT` statement, and close and release the `Connection` object:

```
Set objConn = CreateObject("ADODB.Connection")
objConn.Open "Provider=SQLOLEDB;Data Source=JULIANS1;" & _
            "Initial Catalog=Bank;User ID=sa;Password="

objConn.Execute "INSERT INTO Accounts VALUES ('" & AccountCode & "', '" & _
            AccountHolder & "', 0)"

objConn.Close
Set objConn = Nothing
```

If the database updated without an error, we can commit the transaction, and exit the function, returning `True` to indicate the operation was successful:

```
objContext.SetComplete
CreateAccount = True
Exit Function
```

However, if an error did occur, execution will pass to our error handler. In this case, we set the `ErrorText By Val` parameter to the `Description` of the `Err` object, abort the transaction, and return `False` from the function:

```
CreateAccError:
CreateAccount = False
ErrorText = Err.Description
objContext.SetAbort

End Function
```

The updated `DeleteAccount` and `TransferMoney` methods are very similar, except that we first check that the accounts actually exist, before attempting to delete them or transfer money between them. The code for `DeleteAccount` is:

```
Function DeleteAccount(ByVal AccountCode As String, _
                       ByRef ErrorText As Variant) As Boolean

Dim objConn As ADODB.Connection
Dim objRS As ADODB.Recordset

On Error GoTo DeleteAccError

DeleteAccount = False

If objContext Is Nothing Then
   ErrorText = "Object context does not exist"
   Exit Function
End If

If Len(AccountCode) < 4 Or Len(AccountCode) > 8 Then
   ErrorText = "Account code must be 4 to 8 characters long"
   objContext.SetAbort
   Exit Function
End If

Set objConn = CreateObject("ADODB.Connection")
objConn.Open "Provider=SQLOLEDB;Data Source=JULIANS1;" & _
             "Initial Catalog=Bank;User ID=sa;Password="

' Check that account actually exists
Set objRS = objConn.Execute("SELECT AccountCode FROM Accounts WHERE " & _
                            "AccountCode='" & AccountCode & "'")

' If the recordset is at EOF, it must be empty,
' so the account can't exist
If objRS.EOF Then
   ErrorText = "Account code is not valid"
   objContext.SetAbort
   objRS.Close
   Set objRS = Nothing
   objConn.Close
   Set objConn = Nothing
   Exit Function
End If

objConn.Execute "DELETE FROM Accounts WHERE AccountCode='" & AccountCode & "'"

objConn.Close
Set objConn = Nothing

objContext.SetComplete
DeleteAccount = True
Exit Function

DeleteAccError:
DeleteAccount = False
ErrorText = Err.Description
objContext.SetAbort

End Function
```

And for `TransferMoney`:

```
Function TransferMoney(ByVal FromAccount As String, _
                       ByVal IntoAccount As String, _
                       ByVal Amount As Currency, _
                       ByRef ErrorText As Variant) As Boolean

Dim objConn As ADODB.Connection
Dim objRS As ADODB.Recordset

On Error GoTo TransferError

TransferMoney = False

If objContext Is Nothing Then
    ErrorText = "Object context does not exist"
    Exit Function
End If

If Len(FromAccount) < 4 Or Len(FromAccount) > 8 Or _
    Len(IntoAccount) < 4 Or Len(IntoAccount) > 8 Then
    ErrorText = "Account codes must be 4 to 8 characters long"
    objContext.SetAbort
    Exit Function
End If

If FromAccount = IntoAccount Then
    ErrorText = "Account codes must be different"
    objContext.SetAbort
    Exit Function
End If

Set objConn = CreateObject("ADODB.Connection")
objConn.Open "Provider=SQLOLEDB;Data Source=JULIANS1;" & _
             "Initial Catalog=Bank;User ID=sa;Password="

' Check that the 'from' account actually exists
Set objRS = objConn.Execute("SELECT AccountCode FROM Accounts WHERE " & _
                            "AccountCode='" & FromAccount & "'")

If objRS.EOF Then
    ErrorText = "Account code is not valid"
    objContext.SetAbort
    objRS.Close
    Set objRS = Nothing
    objConn.Close
    Set objConn = Nothing
    Exit Function
End If

' Check that the 'into' account actually exists
Set objRS = objConn.Execute("SELECT AccountCode FROM Accounts WHERE " & _
                            "AccountCode='" & IntoAccount & "'")

If objRS.EOF Then
    ErrorText = "Account code is not valid"
    objContext.SetAbort
    objRS.Close
    Set objRS = Nothing
    objConn.Close
    Set objConn = Nothing
    Exit Function
End If
```

```
' If both accounts exist, we can update the database.
' If either of these statements fails, the transaction will be aborted.
objConn.Execute "UPDATE Accounts SET Balance = Balance - " & Amount & _
                " WHERE AccountCode = '" & FromAccount & "'"

objConn.Execute "UPDATE Accounts SET Balance = Balance + " & Amount & _
                " WHERE AccountCode = '" & IntoAccount & "'"

objConn.Close
Set objConn = Nothing

objContext.SetComplete
TransferMoney = True
Exit Function

TransferError:
TransferMoney = False
ErrorText = Err.Description
objContext.SetAbort

End Function
```

We've also added a method for retrieving the account codes from the database, but since this doesn't write to the database, we don't need to make it transactional. Here, we simply retrieve a disconnected recordset from the database containing the account codes:

```
Function GetAccounts() As ADODB.Recordset

Dim objConn As ADODB.Connection
Dim objRS As ADODB.Recordset

Set objConn = CreateObject("ADODB.Connection")
objConn.Open "Provider=SQLOLEDB;Data Source=JULIANS1;" & _
             "Initial Catalog=Bank;User ID=sa;Password="

Set objRS = CreateObject("ADODB.Recordset")
objRS.CursorLocation = adUseClient
objRS.Open "SELECT AccountCode FROM Accounts", objConn, _
           adOpenStatic, adLockBatchOptimistic

Set objRS.ActiveConnection = Nothing
Set GetAccounts = objRS
Set objRS = Nothing

objConn.Close
Set objConn = Nothing

End Function
```

Finally, we just need to update our ASP page to reflect the new interface. We will add an extra form where we will allow the user to transfer money between two accounts. The account codes can be selected from a listbox, which is populated using our GetAccounts method:

```asp
<%

dim sStatus
dim objAccount
dim bReturnCode
dim sErrorText
dim objRS

sStatus = ""

' Are we creating an account

if Request.Form("Action") = "CreateAccount" then

    set objAccount = CreateObject("ProASPData.Account")

    bReturnCode = objAccount.CreateAccount( Request.Form("AccountCode"), _
                                            Request.Form("AccountHolder"), _
                                            sErrorText )

    if  bReturnCode = true then
       sStatus = "Account created successfully"
    else
       sStatus = sErrorText
    end if

end if

' Are we deleting an account

if Request.Form("Action") = "DeleteAccount" then

    set objAccount = CreateObject("ProASPData.Account")

    bReturnCode = objAccount.DeleteAccount( Request.Form("AccountCode"), sErrorText )

    if  bReturnCode = true then
       sStatus = "Account deleted successfully"
    else
       sStatus = sErrorText
    end if

end if

' If we're transferring money, call TransferMoney method
if Request.Form("Action") = "TransferMoney" then

    set objAccount = CreateObject("ProASPData.Account")

    bReturnCode = objAccount.TransferMoney(Request.Form("FromAccount"), _
                                           Request.Form("IntoAccount"), _
                                           Request.Form("Amount"), sErrorText)

    if  bReturnCode = true then
       sStatus = "Money transferred successfully"
    else
       sStatus = sErrorText
    end if

end if
```

```
%>

<form action="vb.asp" method="post">

<H3>Create a new Account</H3>
Account Code    : <input type="text" name="AccountCode" />
<BR />
Account Holder : <input type="text" name="AccountHolder" />
<BR />
<BR />
<input type="submit" value="Create Account" />
<BR />
<input type="hidden" name="Action" value="CreateAccount" />

</form>

<form action="vb.asp" method="post">

<H3>Delete an Account</H3>
Account Code.. : <input type="text" name="AccountCode" />
<BR />
<BR />
<input type="submit" value="Delete Account" />
<BR />
<input type="hidden" name="Action" value="DeleteAccount" />

</form>

<form action="vb.asp" method="post">
```

```
<!-- The extra form for transferring a sum between two accounts -->
<H3>Transfer Money</H3>
<!-- Get the account codes from the database
     and put them in a select box -->
Account to Transfer From.. : <select name="FromAccount">
<%
   Set objAccount = Server.CreateObject("ProASPData.Account")
   Set objRS = objAccount.GetAccounts
   objRS.MoveFirst
   While Not objRS.EOF
      Response.Write "<option>" & objRS("AccountCode") & "</option>"
      objRS.MoveNext
   Wend
%>
</select>
Account to Transfer Into.. : <select name="IntoAccount">
<%
   objRS.MoveFirst
   While Not objRS.EOF
      Response.Write "<option>" & objRS("AccountCode") & "</option>"
      objRS.MoveNext
   Wend
   Set objRS = Nothing
   Set objAccount = Nothing
%>
</select>
<BR />
Amount to Transfer.. : <input type="text" name="Amount" />
<BR />
<BR />
<input type="submit" value="Transfer Money" />
```

```
<BR />
<input type="hidden" name="Action" value="TransferMoney" />

</form>

<HR />

<%
if sStatus <> "" then
    response.write sStatus
end if
%>
```

The new page looks like this in the browser:

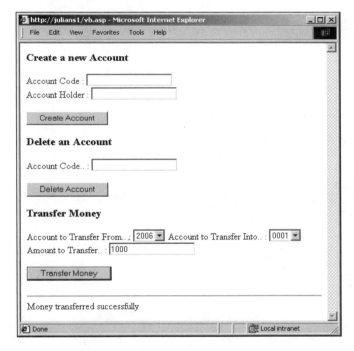

Installing COM+ Applications

The next step, before we can install our component into a COM+ application, is to compile the component into a DLL. Select File | Make ProASPData.dll from VB's menu, and Visual Basic will compile and register the component.

> If you have already loaded the component into memory to be called from ASP, the system will lock the file and deny access if you try to recompile. You can sometimes get round this by setting the **Application Protection** to High (Isolated) on the **Virtual Directory** tab of the ASP application's Properties page. If this fails, you can unload the component by right-clicking on the COM+ application from Component Services Explorer and selecting **Shut down**. If this still doesn't work, try stopping and restarting the web server. Finally, if all else fails, reboot the computer.

Creating a COM+ Application

Before registering our component with COM+, we need to create a new application to contain it. To do this, select Programs | Administrative Tools | Component Services from the Start menu to load the Component Services Explorer:

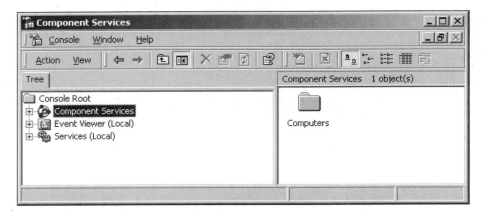

To create a new COM+ application on the current computer, open up the Component Services node in the tree view on the left, then open Computers and My Computer under that. Right-click on the COM+ Applications node under My Computer and select New | Application:

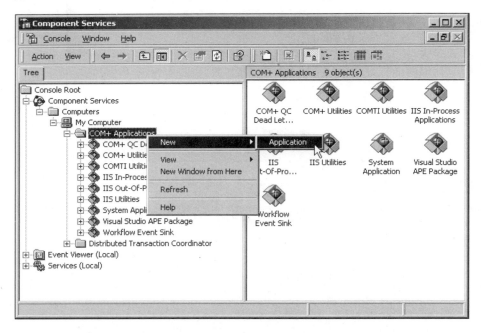

This starts the COM Application Install Wizard. After a splash screen, we can select whether to install an existing application which has been exported from another computer, or create a new application:

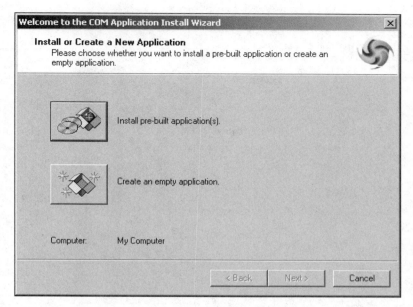

Since we are creating a new application, select the second option (Create an empty application). This moves us on to the next screen, where we can choose a name for our application, and select the application type – library or server application:

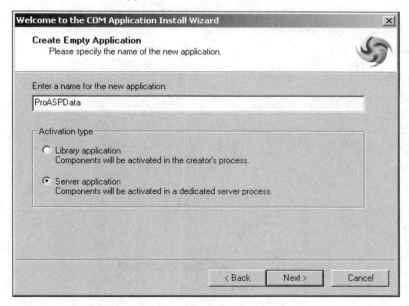

As we saw earlier, server applications provide greater safety (although there can be a performance cost), so we have gone for that option.

The next step allows us to specify the user account under which the COM+ application will run. The default is for the application to run as the user who is currently logged on, but we can also specify that a particular account should be used:

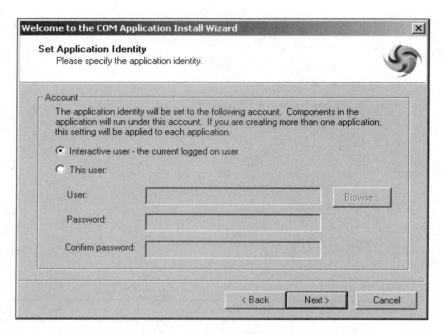

Clicking Next causes the application to be created, and it should now appear under the COM+ Applications node in Component Services Explorer.

Registering a Component with COM+

Our next task is to install our `ProASPData.Account` component into this newly created application. Expand the node representing our new COM+ application, right-click on the Components nodes directly underneath this, and select New | Component:

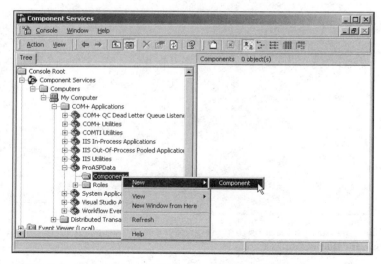

This launches the COM Component Install Wizard. Again, there is a splash screen, after which we are invited to choose whether to install a new component, import a registered component, or install a new event class:

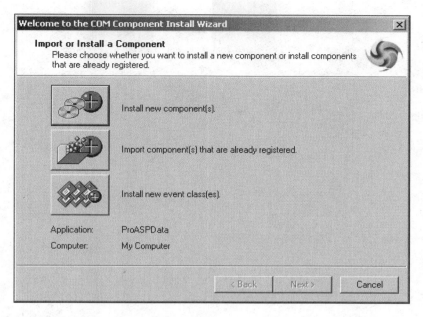

Visual Basic has already registered our component for us, so select the second of these options. The next screen presents us with a list of all the registered components on the machine. Our component should be there, listed as `ProASPData.Account`:

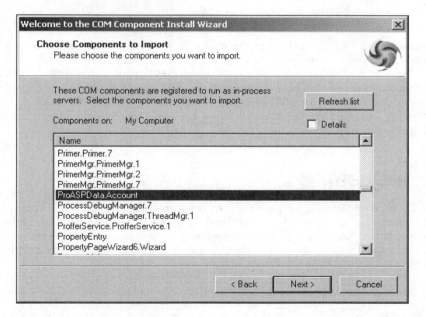

Select this and press Next. This will complete the wizard, and our component should be added to our COM+ application. However, before we're finished with the Component Services Explorer, there's just one more change we need to make. Right-click on our newly added component, and select Properties. This will bring up the property pages for our components. In this dialog, select the Transactions tab:

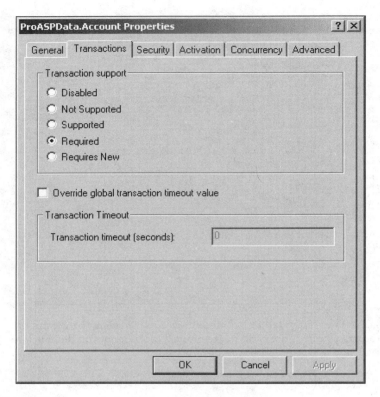

When we created our COM+-enabled component in VB, we set its `MTSTransactionMode` property to 2 - RequiresTransaction, so we need to set the component's Transaction support level to the equivalent value here (Required). The Transaction support levels correspond to the `MTSTransactionMode` values, except that here we also have a Disabled option. This specifies that COM+ will completely ignore the component's transactional requirements. If possible, COM+ will create the component in the creator's context, but otherwise it will create a new context. Therefore, the object may or may not belong to the creator's transaction.

Message Queuing

The second component service we'll look at is **message queuing**. In Windows NT, this is provided by Microsoft Message Queue Server, or MSMQ, and MSMQ is still supported in Windows 2000. Although, as we shall see later in the chapter, COM+ allows us to create queued components without writing any MSMQ code manually, there are limitations to this approach, and a knowledge of MSMQ is still vital for developing asynchronous components.

So, what is message queuing? Normally, our client application calls a method on a server component, waits for a response, and then continues to go about its business. This means that if the server is busy, or if the method takes a long time to execute, the client will be locked until the server has finished executing the method. And worse, if the server is temporarily unavailable, the request won't be processed at all.

The answer to this problem is message queuing. Message queuing is a way of enabling asynchronous communication between components – the client simply sends a message to the server, and continues executing straight away. The messages are left in a queue (hence the name), and the server retrieves messages from the queue when it's able to. Message queuing is sometimes compared to a telephone answering machine – when we phone someone and get an answering machine, we don't know when they will actually listen to their messages, but we do know that the message is waiting there for them. If they didn't have an answering machine, we wouldn't be able to deliver the message at all if they were out, or if the phone were engaged – we would just have to try again later. Message queuing is similar; the message is dropped in a specific queue of messages, and the client has no way of knowing when the server will retrieve the message. But it does allow us to store a message even if the network is down, or if the server is unavailable.

Messages

Another common analogy for message queuing is "email for applications". A sending application sends a message to a receiving application. There is a difference, though – MSMQ messages can be read by any application which has access to the queue to which the message is sent, not just a single application. In this sense, messages are perhaps more closely equivalent to a post to a public folder.

MSMQ messages have three main parts:

❑ The **label**. This is comparable to the subject of an e-mail. It can be used to identify the message, or to group messages together, so the receiving application can tell what the message contains.

❑ The **body**. Similar to the body of an e-mail message, but it doesn't necessarily contain a string; it could contain anything from a string to an array to a COM object. MSMQ itself doesn't examine the contents of the message, so the only restriction is that the receiving application will need to know the format of the body.

❑ The **destination queue**. This is the queue – which can be either on the same machine as the application sending the message, or on another machine – to which the message is sent, and from which it can be retrieved by the receiving application.

Message Queues

The message queue can be compared to the public folder where an e-mail can be posted. Typically, messages are sent to queues on the machine where the receiving application resides, but it is also possible to retrieve messages from queues on remote servers. There are four types of queues available in MSMQ 2.0 (the version shipped with Windows 2000):

❑ **Outgoing queues**. This is where messages are kept until they can be sent to a destination queue on a remote MSMQ server which is unavailable. It is comparable to an e-mail Outbox.

❑ **System queues**. These are used internally by MSMQ itself, and are not available to custom applications.

❑ **Public queues**. This is the most commonly used type of queue. Public queues are available to our custom applications. Because public queues are stored in the Active Directory, they are visible throughout the enterprise.

❑ **Private queues**. These are similar to public queues, but are not stored in Active Directory, so are only visible on the local computer.

Creating Queues

We can administer MSMQ through the Computer Management MMC snap-in. Load this up by selecting Programs | Administrative Tools | Computer Management from the Start menu. Opening up the Services and Applications node reveals a Message Queuing node, where we can add, remove, and configure queues. The Message Queuing folder contains four subfolders, one for each of the available types of queue.

> If Active Directory isn't installed on the machine, we cannot create public queues on that machine. However, the node will still appear.

To create a new public queue, right-click on the Public Queues node and select New | Public Queue. We need to specify just two things to create the queue: the name for the queue, and whether or not the queue supports transactions:

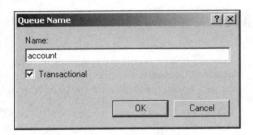

Setting Security Permissions

However, before we use the queue, we need to specify the user accounts which have permissions to read from, write to, and administer the queue. To do this, open up the Public Queues node in the MMC tree view, and our newly created queue should appear in this folder. Right-click on this, select Properties and then select the Security tab:

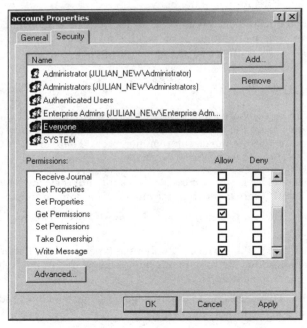

Here we can select user accounts from the Active Directory, and grant them permissions on the queue. Note that, by default, Everyone has write access to the queue but not read access, so all users can send messages to the queue, but only specific users can retrieve these messages.

MSMQ Object Model

In order to create and read messages programmatically, we can use MSMQ's COM API. The full object model is quite large:

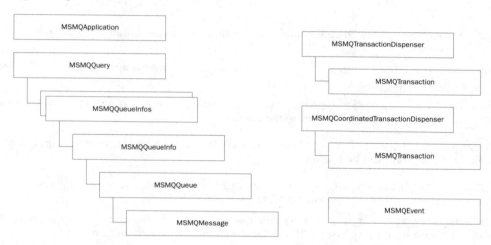

However, only four of these are frequently used in conjunction with ASP applications:

❑ The MSMQQueueInfo object. Used to open, create, and delete message queues.

❑ The MSMQQueue object. Represents a specific message queue.

❑ The MSMQMessage object. Represents an individual message in the queue.

❑ The MSMQEvent object. We use this object in a client application to receive event notification when a message arrives in the queue.

Opening a Message Queue

The starting point for interacting with message queues via the MSMQ API is usually the MSMQQueueInfo object. We can create this using the VB/VBScript CreateObject function, or the ASP Server.CreateObject method:

```
Set objQueueInfo = CreateObject("MSMQ.MSMQQueueInfo")
```

Once we have this object, we can point it at a specific queue by specifying its PathName property. The path name of a queue takes the form "*server_name**queue_name*", where *server_name* is the machine name of the server where the queue resides, and *queue_name* is the name of the queue itself. For example:

```
objQueueInfo.PathName = "myserver\myqueue"
```

If the server is the local machine, we can replace the server name with a period (.), for example, ".\myqueue".

We can now call the Open method to open the queue. The syntax for this method is:

```
Set objQueue = objQueueInfo.Open(Access, ShareMode)
```

The Access parameter indicates whether we want to open the queue for reading or sending messages and can be one of:

- ❑ MQ_PEEK_ACCESS. Open the queue for reading – messages cannot be sent to or removed from the queue.

- ❑ MQ_SEND_ACCESS. Open the queue for sending only – we cannot read messages or remove them from the queue.

- ❑ MQ_RECEIVE_ACCESS: Open the queue for reading or receiving messages. If messages are received, they are removed from the queue.

If Access is set to MQ_RECEIVE_ACCESS, we can use the ShareMode parameter to specify that we want to lock the queue. This can be one of:

- ❑ MQ_DENY_NONE (the default). The queue will not be locked. This is the only option if Access is set to MQ_PEEK_ACCESS or MQ_SEND_ACCESS.

- ❑ MQ_DENY_RECEIVE_SHARE. Locks the queue so that only the current process can retrieve messages from it. An error will occur if the queue has already been opened with MQ_RECEIVE_ACCESS by another process.

For example, to open a queue for sending messages, we would use:

```
Set objQueue = objQueueInfo.Open(MQ_SEND_ACCESS, MQ_DENY_NONE)
```

Or to open a queue for retrieving messages, locking the queue so that no other application can retrieve messages until we've finished:

```
Set objQueue = objQueueInfo.Open(MQ_RECEIVE_ACCESS, MQ_DENY_RECEIVE_SHARE)
```

Reading Messages

Once we've opened our queue with receive access, we can read messages from it. MSMQ provides two ways to do this. We can 'peek' at the message, in which case the message will remain in the queue, or alternatively, we can retrieve the message from the queue, removing it from the queue altogether. To do this, we can use the MSMQQueue object's Receive method:

```
Set objMessage = objQueue.Receive([Transaction], [WantDestinationQueue], _
                                  [WantBody], [ReceiveTimeOut])
```

Where:

Name	Data Type	Description
Transaction	Variant	This can either be an MSMQTransaction object representing the transaction to which the operation belongs, or one of the constants:
		MQ_NO_TRANSACTION (the operation does not form part of a transaction);
		MQ_MTS_TRANSACTION (the default; the operation forms part of an MTS transaction);
		MQ_XA_TRANSACTION (the operation forms part of an external XA-compliant transaction).
WantDestinationQueue	Variant	Indicates whether the MSMQQueueInfo object representing the message's destination will be updated when the message is received. The default is False.
WantBody	Variant	Indicates whether the body of the message needs to be retrieved. If it doesn't we can increase the speed of the operation by not retrieving the body. The default is True.
ReceiveTimeOut	Variant	Specifies the timeout period (in milliseconds) which MSMQ will wait for a message to be available.

You might notice there's no way here of specifying *which* message we want to open, if there's more than one in the queue. The Receive method actually opens the first message in the queue. So what if we want to open a different message? When the queue is opened, MSMQ creates a cursor which we can use to scroll through the messages. To retrieve the message at the current position in the cursor, we can use the ReceiveCurrent method. This has the same parameters as the Receive method.

To move to the next message in the queue (without removing it from the queue), we can use the PeekNext method:

```
Set objMessage = objQueue.PeekNext([WantDestinationQueue], _
                                   [WantBody], [ReceiveTimeOut])
```

Again, the parameters are the same as those for the Receive method, except that we cannot specify the transaction type. This makes sense, since we're only looking at the message – we're not performing any operation on it. There are also Peek and PeekCurrent methods (with the same parameters as PeekNext), which allow us to look at the contents of the first message in the queue or the current message respectively, without removing it from the queue.

Once we've got a reference to the message, we can examine its contents using the `MSMQMessage` object's `Body` property. Because the body of a message could be of almost any data type, this is a variant. Once we've finished with the queue, we should close it, especially if it was opened in `MQ_DENY_RECEIVE_SHARE` mode. For example:

```
Set objQueueInfo = CreateObject("MSMQ.MSMQQueueInfo")
objQueueInfo.PathName = "myserver\myqueue"
Set objQueue = objQueueInfo.Open(MQ_RECEIVE_ACCESS, MQ_DENY_RECEIVE_SHARE)
Set objMessage = objQueue.Receive
strBody = objMessage.Body
objQueue.Close
```

Sending Messages

Sending messages is a bit easier. We simply open the queue with send access, create an `MSMQMessage` object, set its body and/or any other properties, and call the `Send` method. The syntax for this is:

> *objMessage*.Send *objQueue*, *[Transaction]*

Where *Transaction* can again be an `MSMQTransaction` object or one of the constants `MQ_NO_TRANSACTION`, `MQ_MTS_TRANSACTION` (the default), or `MQ_XA_TRANSACTION`. The first parameter is the `MSMQQueue` object representing the queue to which we want to send the message. This queue must, of course, have previously been opened with send access. For example:

```
Set objQueueInfo = CreateObject("MSMQ.MSMQQueueInfo")
objQueueInfo.PathName = "myserver\myqueue"
Set objQueue = objQueueInfo.Open(MQ_SEND_ACCESS, MQ_DENY_NONE)
Set objMessage = CreateObject("MSMQ.MSMQMessage")
objMessage.Body = "This is the body"
objMessage.Send objQueue
objQueue.Close
```

Implementing Message Queuing

Now that we've seen the basics of message queuing, let's put this in to practice by modifying our component to make use of message queues. First of all, we need to create a public queue which our application will use. For simplicity's sake, we can use our existing component for the actual database update. Let's call the queue `account`, and make it transactional:

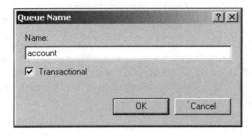

Next, we have to modify our `ProASPData.Account` component so that, instead of updating the database directly, it will send a message to this queue. Firstly, we'll need to add a reference in the VB project to the MSMQ object model:

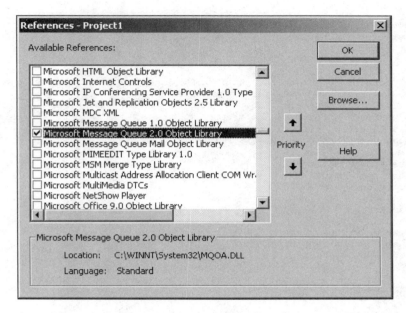

We're going to need MSMQQueue, MSMQQueueInfo, and MSMQMessage objects, so let's declare a couple of additional variables:

```
Option Explicit
Implements ObjectControl
Private objConn As ADODB.Connection
Private objContext As ObjectContext
Private objQueueInfo As MSMQ.MSMQQueueInfo
Private objQueue As MSMQ.MSMQQueue
Private objMessage As MSMQ.MSMQMessage
```

Now we can modify the body of our function to send a message to our account queue, instead of updating the database directly. We'll leave out the validation checks here, because you've probably seen enough of them by now!

We create an MSMQQueueInfo object, and set its PathName property to the path of our queue. We can then use this object to open and retrieve a reference to our queue. Next, we create an MSMQMessage object and set its Body property to our message string. In this case, we'll use a semicolon-delimited string consisting of the action we want the client to take when it receives the message (here "create", to indicate we want to create an account), and the parameters for the eventual method call on our original component. We can now send this message to our queue by calling the Send method. We pass in the MQ_MTS_TRANSACTION constant as the second parameter to indicate that the message forms part of an MTS transaction:

```
Function CreateAccount(ByVal AccountCode As String, _
                       ByVal AccountHolder As String, _
                       ByRef ErrorText As Variant) As Boolean

On Error GoTo CreateAccError

CreateAccount = False
```

```
If objContext Is Nothing Then
    ErrorText = "Object context does not exist"
    Exit Function
End If

Set objQueueInfo = CreateObject("MSMQ.MSMQQueueInfo")
objQueueInfo.PathName = "myserver\account"
Set objQueue = objQueueInfo.Open(MQ_SEND_ACCESS, MQ_DENY_NONE)
Set objMessage = CreateObject("MSMQ.MSMQMessage")
objMessage.Body = "create;" & AccountCode & ";" & AccountHolder
objMessage.Send objQueue, MQ_MTS_TRANSACTION

objContext.SetComplete
CreateAccount = True
Exit Function

CreateAccError:
CreateAccount = False
ErrorText = Err.Description
If Not objContext Is Nothing Then
    objContext.SetAbort
End If

End Function
```

The code for the `DeleteAccount` method is almost identical; the only real difference is in the body of the message we send:

```
Function DeleteAccount(ByVal AccountCode As String, _
                       ByRef ErrorText As Variant) As Boolean

On Error GoTo DeleteAccError

DeleteAccount = False

If objContext Is Nothing Then
    ErrorText = "Object context does not exist"
    Exit Function
End If

Set objQueueInfo = CreateObject("MSMQ.MSMQQueueInfo")
objQueueInfo.PathName = "myserver\account"
Set objQueue = objQueueInfo.Open(MQ_SEND_ACCESS, MQ_DENY_NONE)
Set objMessage = CreateObject("MSMQ.MSMQMessage")
objMessage.Body = "delete;" & AccountCode
objMessage.Send objQueue, MQ_MTS_TRANSACTION

objContext.SetComplete
DeleteAccount = True
Exit Function

DeleteAccError:
DeleteAccount = False
ErrorText = Err.Description
If Not objContext Is Nothing Then
    objContext.SetAbort
End If

End Function
```

Finally, we must update the code for the `TransferMoney` method. Again, this only really differs from the `CreateAccount` and `DeleteAccount` methods in the body of the message that we send:

```
Function TransferMoney(ByVal FromAccount As String, _
                       ByVal IntoAccount As String, _
                       ByVal Amount As Currency, _
                       ByRef ErrorText As Variant) As Boolean

On Error GoTo TransferError

TransferMoney = False

If objContext Is Nothing Then
    ErrorText = "Object context does not exist"
    Exit Function
End If

Set objQueueInfo = CreateObject("MSMQ.MSMQQueueInfo")
objQueueInfo.PathName = "myserver\account"
Set objQueue = objQueueInfo.Open(MQ_SEND_ACCESS, MQ_DENY_NONE)
Set objMessage = CreateObject("MSMQ.MSMQMessage")
objMessage.Body = "transfer;" & FromAccount & ";" & IntoAccount & ";" & Amount
objMessage.Send objQueue, MQ_MTS_TRANSACTION

objContext.SetComplete
TransferMoney = True
Exit Function

TransferError:
TransferMoney = False
ErrorText = Err.Description
If Not objContext Is Nothing Then
    objContext.SetAbort
End If

End Function
```

Building an MSMQ Client

However, it's no good sending messages if they are never picked up, so we also need a client application to deal with the messages we send. For this example, let's use Visual Basic, so create a new **Standard .EXE** project in VB, and add references to the MSMQ object model and to our original `ProASPData.Account` component, which we'll use to perform the actual database access. Just so we can see something happening on this client, we'll add a listbox to the form and add an item to this whenever a message arrives.

Next, in the **General Declarations** section of the form, we need to add a couple of variable declarations. All the time the client is listening to the queue, we will need to have an `MSMQEvent` and an `MSMQQueue` object instantiated, so these will have to be declared at the class level. The `MSMQEvent` object's `Arrived` event will fire when a message arrives in our queue, so we need to declare this variable `WithEvents`:

```
Option Explicit
Dim WithEvents objMSMQEvent As MSMQ.MSMQEvent
Dim objQueue As MSMQ.MSMQQueue
```

When the form loads, we need to start listening to the queue. To do this we create a new `MSMQQueue` object, as we did in our component, and also an `MSMQEvent` object. To start listening, we call the `EnableNotification` method of the `MSMQQueue` object. This method takes one parameter – the `MSMQEvent` object for which the `Arrived` event will fire when a message arrives in the queue:

```
Private Sub Form_Load()
    Dim objQueueInfo As MSMQ.MSMQQueueInfo

    Set objQueueInfo = CreateObject("MSMQ.MSMQQueueInfo")
    objQueueInfo.PathName = "myserver\account"
    Set objQueue = objQueueInfo.Open(MQ_RECEIVE_ACCESS, MQ_DENY_NONE)
    Set objMSMQEvent = CreateObject("MSMQ.MSMQEvent")
    objQueue.EnableNotification objMSMQEvent

    Set objQueueInfo = Nothing
End Sub
```

Now that we've called `EnableNotification`, when a message arrives in our queue, the `Arrived` event of the `MSMQEvent` object will be fired. The handler for this event has two parameters. The first is a `Queue` object representing the queue for which the event has fired. The second is a long integer that indicates whether the event is fired when a message is at the first position in the queue (the default), at the current position in the queue, or at the new position in the queue when the current position changes:

```
Private Sub objMSMQEvent_Arrived(ByVal Queue As Object, ByVal Cursor As Long)
    Dim objMessage As MSMQ.MSMQMessage
    Dim objBank As ProASPData.Account
    Dim strBody As String
    Dim arrBody() As String
    Dim strCode As String
    Dim strHolder As String
    Dim strFrom As String
    Dim strInto As String
    Dim strAmount As String
    Dim strError As String
    Dim blnSuccess As Boolean

On Error GoTo ErrorHandler
```

Our first task is to retrieve the body of the message. We can retrieve the message from the queue by calling the `MSMQQueue` object's `ReceiveCurrent` method. Notice that, as well as retrieving a reference to the `MSMQMessage` object, this also removes the message from the queue:

```
Set objMessage = Queue.ReceiveCurrent
strBody = objMessage.Body
```

Next, we'll add an item to the listbox to show that a message has arrived. We'll write the date and time, and the body of the message. We're going to use the earlier version of our `ProASPData.Account` component to perform the database updates, so we'll create an instance of this before we look at the contents of our message. We formed the message body as a semicolon-delimited string, so we'll use the VB `Split` function to retrieve an array of its constituent parts:

```
List1.AddItem Now & ": " & strBody
Set objBank = CreateObject("ProASPData.Account")
arrBody = Split(strBody, ";")
```

We stored the action to be performed as the first item in the message string, so we'll use a `Select Case` construction to check the first element of this array, and call the appropriate method of our business object, extracting the parameters from the other elements in the array:

```
Select Case arrBody(0)
   Case "create"
      strCode = arrBody(1)
      strHolder = arrBody(2)
      blnSuccess = objBank.CreateAccount(strCode, strHolder, strError)
   Case "delete"
      strCode = arrBody(1)
      blnSuccess = objBank.DeleteAccount(strCode, strError)
   Case "transfer"
      strFrom = arrBody(1)
      strInto = arrBody(2)
      strAmount = arrBody(3)
      blnSuccess = objBank.TransferMoney(strFrom, strInto, _
                      strAmount, strError)
End Select
```

Finally, before we exit the sub, we have to call `EnableNotification` again. The `Arrived` event will only fire once for each call to `EnableNotification`:

```
ExitHandler:
   objQueue.EnableNotification objMSMQEvent
   Exit Sub

ErrorHandler:
   Resume ExitHandler
End Sub
```

To test this, make sure both components are installed, and run the client application we've just created. Now load up our ASP test page in the browser, and try creating, deleting, and transferring money between accounts. The database should be updated, and the messages should be displayed in the listbox:

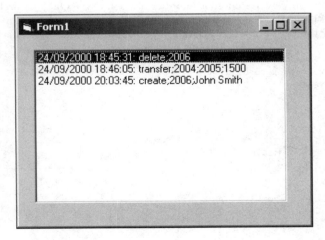

COM+ Queued Components

COM+ **queued components** allow us to take advantage of message queuing to reach an equivalent level of reliability when issuing COM method calls, either locally or across an unreliable network. Before Windows 2000 and COM+, we had to handle the second situation manually using MSMQ, as we did above. Our client application creates a message and hands it to a special outbox within the local installation of MSMQ Server. This ensures that the message is delivered as soon as the network connection is available. COM+ queued components hide the creation of the message and the intervention of MSMQ in a system service, so we don't have to write the MSMQ code ourselves.

Queued components provide an easy way to execute components asynchronously. A client communicates with a queued COM object through MSMQ services. The beauty of COM+ services is that all this happens without any change either to the COM object or the client source code. COM+ interceptors play a significant role in this architecture.

Where the client had to use the MSMQ object model directly to implement messaging, now a COM+ interceptor hooks onto the client's activity, figures out what it is about to do, and replaces the method call with a MSMQ message that silently slips in the MSMQ outbox. The client never actually sees MSMQ in action. It is still there, playing a significant role, but behind the COM+ queued components.

How COM+ Queuing Works

We can transform a COM+ component into a queued component, without any change in the code in either the component or on the client. How is this possible? The client calls a method on an object; when the object is marked as queued, any call directed to it is intercepted and filtered by a Recorder application. The Recorder is one of the system elements that comprise the COM+ queuing services architecture. Such an application stores all the information that a client is about to send to the server in a MSMQ message: method name, parameters, context, and security roles. The MSMQ message is then placed in the outbox folder.

However, a message queue server like MSMQ only ensures that the original request is placed in the server's inbox. But, just as with e-mails, we never know if we're ever going to get a reply! We always need a server-side module that periodically checks the inbox, and extracts and processes any incoming message. The system component that is responsible for polling the MSMQ server inbox is called the Listener, which calls the Player – another member of the COM+ Queuing architecture – to reproduce the client-side conditions when the method was invoked. It goes almost without saying that unchecking the queued flag for the COM object deactivates the Recorder and the Listener, as well as the Player:

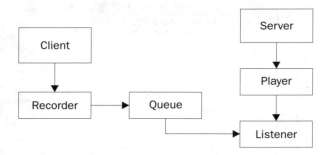

The same mechanism and the same system elements are used when the component needs to send messages back to the client.

Programming Issues With Queued Components

When using queued components, there are certain programming restrictions. For instance, they require that all application methods contain only input parameters – neither return values nor output arguments are admitted. It goes without saying that we must have MSMQ already installed in order to use them. MSMQ must be selected during the operating system set up, or by using Add/Remove programs. Note that MSMQ is not installed by default in Windows 2000.

Implementing Queued Components

To convert a COM+ component into a queued component, all we have to do is change its properties in Component Services Explorer. Right-click on the COM+ application to which the component belongs, select Properties, and then turn to the Queuing page in the dialog box:

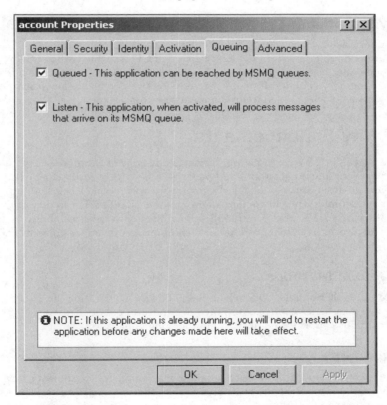

We need to check both the Queued and the Listen boxes here. Checking the Queued box will convert the component to a queued component and cause COM+ to create a public queue for this application. However, we also need to select Listen to ensure that the component listens for the arrival of messages in this queue and can process them.

Next Generation of Component Services

The next generation of Component Services (COM+ 1.x) will be released with the next version of Windows 2000 (currently code named 'Whistler'), and will build on top of existing technologies including COM and COM+ (officially version 1.0). The enhancements fall into three categories: scalability, manageability and availability.

Scalability Enhancements

In terms of scalability, an interesting feature is a configurable isolation level for COM+ applications. In COM+ 1.0 the isolation level was the highest possible to ensure robustness. Also, a COM+ 1.0 application cannot currently run as an NT service. Through the forthcoming COM+ Admin SDK, we will be able to set both the isolation level, and configure an application to run as a service. That is, it will operate independently from the logon/logoff procedures.

Low-Memory Situations

Sometimes, under low-memory situations, we end up having enough memory to create a component instance, but not enough to use it. In the next version of COM+, this particularly troublesome situation will finally come under control. The Service Component Manager will check in advance whether 90% of all the virtual memory is in use. If memory usage is above this level, then it will return an E_OUTOFMEMORY error, when asked to instantiate a new component.

Manageability Enhancements

In terms of manageability, we can now programmatically control component activation, or, in other words, we can prevent future activations and pause an object without affecting existing instances. When we attempt to create an instance of a paused component, we'll get an E_APPPAUSED error. The IComAdminCatalog interface will contain a new method called Pause to do just this. Notice that this feature will only work for COM+ server applications. We'll also have the ability to disable components, a feature that will also be available for in-process components. It simply prevents callers from using that library.

Private and Public Methods

Up until COM+ 1.0, all methods were considered public. Now, by using the public and private keywords, we will gain better control over function exposure; public methods will be externally callable, while private methods can be called only within the same application.

Aliased Components

COM+ 1.x will provide support for aliased components, which are components that share the same native code, but can be compiled and registered under different CLSIDs to satisfy different configuration requirements. Without aliases, we should write different components by duplicating the source code, thereby making the maintenance of the application that little bit more difficult.

Availability Enhancements

In terms of availability, application partitions are the most important enhancements. At the moment, only a single configuration is allowed on a single machine for both applications and components. The goal is to allow multiple configurations of the same application/component on the same machine. The concept of partitions is central to realize this objective.

A partition is a logical machine within a single physical machine. In COM+ 1.x, applications will be able to be installed onto one or more partitions. The **base partition** is the whole machine and anyone with the right privileges can access it. Partitions can be grouped in partition sets subject to security restrictions and make available only to authorized users or organizations.

Summary

In this chapter, we've looked in more detail at some of the services Windows provides for us for managing our components. These include MTS and COM+, which manage transaction processing and the context of our components; and MSMQ which allows us to create asynchronous components. We looked at the changes we need to make in the code of our simple component to support these services, and we saw how to deploy components under COM+.

This chapter and the previous one are intended as a crash course in using components with ASP pages. Don't worry if you haven't taken it all in straight away. In the next four chapters, we will look in more detail at creating COM components and COM+ applications in practice, building a complete ASP application using some of the technologies we've met in the last two chapters.

10

Designing the User Services

The **web browser** has been an integral component in the explosive development of the Web over the last decade. Indeed, browser software has radically changed the lives of programmers, along to a similar extent to object-oriented programming and components. The web browser is the quintessence of web applications. Although we will often use it as the entry-point of a modern distributed system, I believe we're much closer to really thinking of the web browser as the perfect user terminal for web-based systems.

In some years' time, companies that do not make effective use of the Internet will cease to exist as viable players in the world economy. Considering this in terms of software development, it seems that in the not so distant future, an application will have to be a web-based application if it is to have any real commercial or business use.

Many predictions regarding the future of software have been shown to be totally inaccurate in only a short period of time. One of my favorite such predictions was the claim, commonly made a few years ago, that Java would kill off C++ within five years! There is no evidence today to suggest that this is coming true, unless we want to see a Java flavor in the forthcoming C#.

The current prediction is that web-based systems will be the way of doing Internet business within five years. Thus, we are rapidly approaching an historic moment in which a significant share of worldwide distributed systems will be web systems. Microsoft's recent announcement of the **.Net** platform is a response to the way in which the Internet will evolve; it's a platform which is tailored to utilizing the Web as a source of **service providers**. In this scenario, the browser is simply the client-side terminal of such a system: a universal key to access any kind of functionality. Behind the browser, we have the uppermost layer of the distributed architecture, commonly called the **presentation** layer. It's a fundamental, but often neglected, building block of any web application. Indeed, the user interface is where we start to design our system, and also where we finish our coding.

In this chapter, we'll look at a number of aspects of the design of user services from both a theoretical and a practical perspective. Over the next few chapters, we'll present a complete overview of a web-based system for data access. In this chapter, however, we'll begin with the presentation layer.

Specifically, we'll cover:

❑ Principles of good UI and ASP code design

❑ How to use HTML to serve as many browsers as possible

❑ How to simulate simple Dynamic HTML effects

❑ Preparing per-browser pages

❑ Exposing content through XML

This book is about data access, but no matter how efficiently we retrieve data, it is of little use if we have no means of effectively displaying it to the user. Moreover, we also need a means for users to specify what data they're looking for. This is why it is essential to develop a well-designed user interface.

Within the chapter we'll develop a sample web site (The Article Bazaar) through which I'll illustrate some principles for a well-designed user interface and some tricks to write better ASP code. In the next chapters, we'll complete the site by adding middle-tier objects.

The Browser Compatibility Problem

Until a couple of years ago, we could visit a client, demonstrate the effectiveness of an application, and then conclude a presentation with an encouraging: "*It's only HTML, so you only need a web browser to use it.*" Since those happy days, though, the browser has evolved from being a simple and relatively unobtrusive presentation tool to become the preferred user interface for distributed applications.

This change has been driven by the increased power of the HTML language. So rapidly did HTML develop, that the W3C couldn't keep up. However, for a few years the differences between the various browsers, although perceptible, weren't as evident as they are today. The big split in the functionality of the browsers occurred when Dynamic HTML (DHTML) was introduced. With the implementation of DHTML features in Microsoft's Internet Explorer, this has evolved from being a simple browser to being the preferred UI terminal of a web-based platform.

Internet Explorer 5.5 now looks more like a new edition of the Win32 GUI SDK than a plain old HTML browser. Features like page runtime updatability, a rich page object model, behaviors, scriptlets, XML and XSL, cascading stylesheets, support for all scripting languages, multimedia enhancements and, above all, COM support, have made it, at least over the past few years, functionally richer than any other browser.

Most of the success that ASP has gained is due to its inherent ability to send code that can be rendered by any browser. Though a native part of Microsoft's IIS, ASP is also available on other platforms thanks to special third-party products such as Chili!Soft ASP. As long as our ASP pages don't assume special browser capabilities, ASP provides an effective solution for the development of any kind of web application.

ASP can continue working with unchanged effectiveness whether the browser supports DHTML, behaviors, or just plain HTML 3.2. On one hand, customers want pages that can be viewed with all the different kinds of browsers. On the other hand, developers would like to arrange really powerful applications which need to make use of powerful, feature-rich UI terminals. This is undoubtedly a highly debatable point. The more we exploit advanced features of a browser, the more we restrict the potential users for our web application. Alternatively, the more we make it open and browser independent, the more we have to pay in terms of development effort, time, maintenance and performance, or else it will have to contain fewer features and less functionality.

Whether we like it or not, especially when writing a web site that does a bit more than simply presenting data, we should figure out a way to make two apparently contrasting points fit together:

❑ Our web pages should work through any browser, even if the appearance of the data changes.

❑ Our web site should serve a page that is specifically targeted at the requesting browser.

Netscape Communicator and Internet Explorer may have different characteristics, but they are both designed to be used on standard operating systems; Windows, UNIX, Apple Macintosh, etc. However, the time has arrived when we need to consider a whole new generation of browser devices such as WAP phones, palm-top devices, and interactive TV, not to mention other problems such as internationalization and localization of content. Any effort to find a common denominator, even at the price of reduced functionality, is now doomed to failure. This means that ASP pages need to be designed in a more modular way; cut into independent pieces, and we need to provide the means of fitting these pieces together in different ways for different types of clients.

> A detailed look at browser compatibilities may be found in *Alex Homer's Techniques for Webmasters, ISBN 1861001797*, also from Wrox Press.

Principles of Good Design

For large-scale applications, the use of special editors and development tools is crucial. However, using such tools can lead us to rely too much on their functionality and project view. Can drag-and-drop really be a substitute for good partitioning of functions? Personally, I don't think so. We should always have a clear idea of how our ASP pages should look *in code* before we start writing and testing them through a tool.

Unlike static HTML pages, ASP pages are software components, and a web site completely based on ASP technology is a software application. A web application moves from page to page, whereas any other application moves from state (or window) to state. An ASP page, therefore, can be seen to represent a state of a web application. And we wouldn't want to project a complex Win32 application through wizards and drag-and-drop.

Well, this is probably just what happens with many Visual Basic applications. However, the extremely high interest in component design, and the extremely high fees that companies usually pay to top consultants, prove that developing viable applications through wizards and drag-and-drop is neither code-effective nor cost-effective.

Design of the ASP Code

Any ASP page can be divided up into at least three modules:

❑ Initialization

❑ Graphical layout

❑ Content

The initialization should accomplish any task that will be needed to set the page up to work, such as detecting the browser's capabilities. The graphical layout should provide the necessary graphical infrastructure that is common to all, or at least most, of the pages – this normally includes the headings, the logos, the menus and whatever else we want. In most cases, such a page is commissioned to designers and exposes links where we insert the content for specific pages. While the graphical layout is common to most, if not all, pages on a site, the content, of course, is specific to each one.

Almost all of the ASP pages running on the Internet follow these principles. However, it's possible to suspect that a large proportion of them conform to these principles by accident rather than by design. Suppose we start writing the home page and give it a certain layout. If each time we need a new page, we cut and paste code from an existing one, we are recognizing and accepting the modular structure of the pages.

However, this is not an efficient way of achieving structure in our pages – copying lines and lines of identical code across many pages is not the best coding practice. However, once we're aware of the inherent modularity of an ASP page, we can decide which is the best way to implement it.

There are a number of ways in which we can modularize ASP pages, thereby cutting down on code repetition:

- ❑ Server-Side Includes (SSI)
- ❑ Windows Script Components (WSC)
- ❑ COM components
- ❑ Embedded ASP pages

Let's discuss these in a bit more detail.

Server-side Includes

The SSI #include directive gives us a way to insert the content of another file into an ASP page before the web server processes it. We can indicate the file through a file system path or a virtual directory:

```
<!-- #include file ="scripts\consts.inc" -->
<!-- #include virtual ="scripts/consts.inc" -->
```

An included file can, in turn, include other files, provided that the #include directives do not cause a loop. ASP includes the files before executing any script commands. This means that we cannot use a script command to build the name of an included file, we have to insert code that is available in the memory context where the page is being processed. We can obtain the same effect through a scriptless <script> tag, where we just make the src attribute point to the desired file. An SSI include also affects the way in which the page is generated. It doesn't inject portions of the final page.

Windows Script Components

WSCs (Windows Script Components) are COM objects written in scripting languages. We use them in exactly the same way we do with standard COM objects. The advantage is that they require much less time to build and don't require that we stop the web server to refresh or recompile – they are interpreted at runtime. They are a great way to restructure the script that we have in our ASP pages.

With respect to SSI, WSCs are more powerful and flexible as they are processed when we invoke them. On the other hand, though, they use the COM infrastructure which incurs a performance overhead. In my opinion, WSCs are preferable so long as we don't need to squeeze out every little bit of performance from the server.

To write a WSC, all we need is knowledge of a scripting language, such as VBScript or JScript. However, if we want to use some other language, we can also include the parser for that language on the web server. Syntactically speaking, a WSC is an XML file that embeds script code, and exposes it through a well-known programming interface.

COM Components

COM components act like WSCs, though they have a much more complex implementation procedure and offer a much richer functionality. They're harder to code than WSCs since they require knowledge of a language such as Visual Basic, Visual C++/ATL, Java or Cobol, to name but a few. However, the edit-compile-test cycle of a COM object under IIS does require frequent restarting of the web server. This weakness is more than balanced by the fact that COM components are compiled modules that give much better performance when compared to script components. Use of COM components also allows the same business logic to be utilized by both a web application and a win32 client.

Embedded ASP Pages

This is my favorite solution, yet the most recently introduced. Thanks to the new features of the `Server` object in IIS 5.0, we can execute an external ASP page, and inject its output in exactly the same place where we called it. For example:

```
<HR>
<%
    ' Must be a relative URL
    Server.Execute "external.asp"
%>
<HR>
```

The output of `external.asp` goes between the two `<hr>` tags. This is just like calling a script function, without the burden of including the script file and utilizing a string-based interface to return the text to `Response`. On IIS 4.0, we can obtain the same effect with the following code:

```
<!-- #include file ="scripts\external.vbs" -->
<HR>
<%
    buf = External()      ' a function in external.vbs that produces
                          ' the same output as external.asp
    Response.Write buf
%>
<HR>
```

Another advantage of using an embedded ASP page through `Server.Execute` is that we just have to write another ASP page. This is normally much more straightforward than writing a function that returns HTML code.

Sometimes code repetition cannot be avoided. The `Server.Execute` method is only available with ASP 3.0 under IIS 5.0 and Windows 2000. If you're running a different version of the web server, you must resort to the workaround.

Database-driven Pages

If we delegate the graphical layout of a group of ASP pages to a helper page, this doesn't mean that we don't need to change some details here and there (such as titles, descriptions, image, or links). Thus, it's a good idea to make sure that these helper pages are also customizable. The `Server.Execute` method, though, cannot accept query string arguments such as:

```
<HR>
<%
    ' Must be a relative URL
    Server.Execute "external.asp?Name=Dino&LastName=Esposito"
%>
<HR>
```

The method only takes relative URLs without `GET` arguments. The line above will produce an error like the one below:

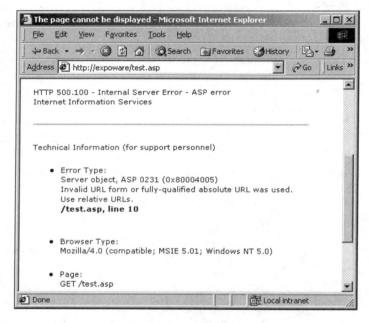

To make the helper page customizable, either we can use the `Session` object, or we can store this information in a database. Deciding which of these methods to employ may depend on the specific features of the application.

A database-driven set of pages has an undoubted advantage: it greatly simplifies site maintenance. However, does it really make sense to have dozens of structurally identical pages that only differ in their content? ASP script code usually provides the content – so why not make it generate the surrounding graphics too?

Optimizing a site for maintenance is important, especially when the site delivers data, and when this data is produced by a separate editorial team. In such cases, we would normally have another factor to consider – making the web site easily localizable. This is not a problem where, say, English is the common language, but within companies where English is not the native language, this is a common request.

Design of the Page

Ideally, a web site should be such that it can be used by the largest possible audience. We have already said that, ideally, its data should be readable using any browser. However, the lowest common denominator (LCD) approach to browser compatibility exposes us to the risk of deploying a site that comes nowhere near to exploiting the functionality and features of the richer client UI. Today, the gap between Internet Explorer 5.5 and Netscape Navigator 3.0 is too wide to make the LCD approach a reasonable option.

Alternatively, developing a page that makes the most of the maximum features of each browser is not recommended either. It would add complexity and risk making site maintenance very difficult. How many different versions of each page should we preserve? The ideal solution lies somewhere in the middle of these two extremes. One possibility is to create just two versions of an application: one for IE 4.0+, and one for all the other browsers.

There are three major versions of IE in use (3.x, 4.x and 5.x), each with significantly different features and functionality. Which is the minimum version of IE that we should target? In most cases, version 4.0, which provides full support for DHTML, data binding, CSS and scriptlets. If we really need to implement behaviors, which allow us to customize HTML tags, we will need the support of IE 5.01+. This is recommended when we need either or both of these two features:

❑ Client-side script code

❑ Highly interactive application with a complex, yet maintainable, UI

Designing IE 5.5-specific pages for an Internet application makes sense only when we need the very special multimedia and graphical features it supports such as HTML + TIME, in-place editing, windowless frames, and UI effects.

Having decided on the version of IE to support, the other output from our site must be HTML 3.2.

> *This is also the direction where ASP+ is taking us. It allows us to write server-side code to address a specific client platform. The lowest level entry is just HTML 3.2.*

User Interface Guidelines

Without pretending to be the ultimate and all-encompassing guide to web page UI design, this section will list a few recommendations for good practice, gleaned from years of real-world experience:

❑ Make all functions a few clicks away

❑ Control the page length and minimize the need for scrolling

❑ Do your utmost to make the rendering of pages faster

❑ Don't make the page script-dependent

❑ Minimize the use of applets and ActiveX controls

❑ Minimize the need for page refreshing

Some of these suggestions obviously conflict. How can we minimize both the scrolling and refreshing? How can we take as much script as possible out of the page while avoiding the use of controls and applets? In general, we should prioritize constraints for a particular project, and apply them uniformly to the design of a web site. Wherever two constraints are in conflict, go for the most prioritized one.

Before going any further with the demo, let's look a little more at the use and the abuse of client-side script code.

Using Client-side Script Code

There are occasions when we would use client-side script code and when we would not. Having script on the client raises some security issues, since that code will expose aspects of the business logic.

In some browsers, support for client-side scripting can be disabled. In these circumstances, we should be prepared to degrade gracefully and, in case the denied functionality is absolutely necessary, we should inform the user that their browser is unable to support the application. We could use, for instance, the <NOSCRIPT> tag:

```
<NOSCRIPT>
Sorry, but this browser does Not currently support scripting
</NOSCRIPT>
```

Alternatively, the server can detect whether the calling browser supports scripting or not. We would only need to check for JavaScript support, since IE is the only browser that supports other languages, such as VBScript. We could use the following to do this:

```
<%
    Set oBC = Server.CreateObject("MSWC.BrowserType")
    If oBC.javascript Then
        Response.Write "<script>...</script>"
    Else
        ' disable those controls (i.e. buttons) that rely on script
    End If
%>
```

The script uses the features of the MSWC.BrowserType server-side object that reads its information from a system file called browsecap.ini. If we detect that client-side scripting is not supported, we might then take the opportunity to disable some script-dependent components.

So, why would we have JavaScript code on our client-side pages? Because script enables the page to be much more interactive and responsive and, in conjunction with other technologies such as **Remote Scripting**, can minimize the need for full page refreshes and save a few round-trips to the server to accomplish some validation tests.

Designing a Web Site: The Article Bazaar

The Article Bazaar is a relatively simple web site that works like a repository for article-related information. It allows us to do basically two things:

- ❏ Search for articles matching a certain pattern
- ❏ Insert information about a new article

It consists of a home page and two additional pages for search and insertion. The screenshot opposite shows how it looks when viewed through Netscape Communicator 4.5:

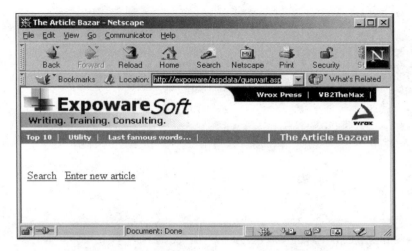

I've deliberately used an old version of the Netscape browser to show that our ASP-based solution will provide a browser-neutral UI.

The web site is powered by a SQL Server 7.0 database called My Articles whose tables contain information about the articles (abstract, URL, title, author, magazine and issue) and magazines (name, publisher).

> *The data for this can be downloaded from* www.wrox.com *as an Access database, and then imported into SQL Server.*

The user interface mimics the look-and-feel of some Microsoft web sites. Once again, I've chosen this one because it effectively combines a number of important features:

❑ Attractive user interface

❑ Simplicity

❑ Reasonable mix of images and text

❑ Limited script code

This page looks like a big tab with a rounded corner. However, it is only with IE 5.x and its support for Vector Markup Language (VML), that we can obtain these effects without resorting to the use of images. We can obtain a similar result using a very complex hierarchy of nested tabs, but that would obtain only a similar effect with the extra burden of a larger volume of HTML code for the browser to render. To keep things simple, we don't use VML or nested tabs in this example.

The two flat menus that can be seen in the screenshot above have not been produced by DHTML code, but are simple hyperlinks placed horizontally without any text decoration. The UI is based only on the capabilities of the <table> tag, and for this reason it's rendered in the same way by both IE and Netscape.

Structuring the ASP Code

I've designed the few pages of this site following the modular pattern mentioned earlier. Let's take a look at the source code for the default.asp page:

```
<HTML>

<!-- INITIALIZATION -->

<HEAD><TITLE>The Article Bazaar</TITLE></HEAD>
<BODY leftMargin=0 topMargin=0 marginheight=0 marginwidth=0>


<!-- PAGE LAYOUT -->

<%
   Server.Execute "layout.asp"
%>

<!-- BODY OF THE PAGE -->

  
<A href="queryart.asp">Search</A>
  
<A href="newart.asp">Enter new article</A>

</BODY>
</HTML>
```

It's rather simple and moves all the complexity of the user interface to the `layout.asp` page. The topmost part of the page deals with any initialization code that's needed for the body of the page. This could be script code as well as a link to a cascading stylesheet. The body of the page renders the actual content that is specific to the page.

The Page's Layout

What follows is a static way of providing the page layout as shown in the figure above:

```
<TABLE bgColor=#ffffff border=0 cellPadding=0 cellSpacing=0 width=100%>
<TR>
   <TD height=60 rowspan=2 vAlign=top width=250>
      <IMG height=60 src=images/expoware.gif></TD>

   <TD align=right height=20 vAlign=top>
      <IMG border=0 src=images/curve.gif width=18 height=20></TD>
   <TD align=right bgColor=#000000 height=20 noWrap vAlign=center>
      <FONT color=#ffffff face=Verdana,Arial size=1>
         <B>  
            <A style="color:#ffffff; text-decoration:none"
               href="http://www.wrox.com">Wrox Press</A>  
            <FONT color=#ffffff>|</FONT>  
            <A style="color: #ffffff; text-decoration: none"
               href="http://www.vb2themax.com">VB2TheMax</A>  
         </B>
      </FONT>
   </TD>
</TR>
<TR>
   <TD align=right colSpan=3 height=40 noWrap vAlign=top>
      <IMG align=right src=images/wroxlogo.gif height=40 width=40></TD>
```

```
</TR>
</TABLE>

<TABLE width=100% border=0 cellspacing=0>
<TR>
   <TD bgColor=#ff6600 colSpan=4 height=20 vAlign=center>
      <FONT color=#ffffff face=Verdana,Arial size=1>
         <B>  
            <A style="color:#ffffff; text-decoration:none"
               href=top10.asp>Top 10</A>  
            <FONT color=#ffffff>|</FONT>  
            <A style="color:#ffffff; text-decoration: none"
               href="utils.asp">Utility</A>  
            <FONT color=#ffffff>|</FONT>  
            <A style="color:#ffffff; text-decoration: none"
               href="words.asp">Last famous words...</A>  
         </B>
      </FONT>
</TD>
   <TD bgColor=#ff6600 height=20 vAlign=center align=right>
      <FONT color=#ffffff face=Verdana,Arial size=2>
         <B>|  The Article Bazaar  </B>
      </FONT>
   </TD>
</TR>
</TABLE>
<BR><BR>
```

There's nothing wrong with the above, except one thing. Should we need to modify an image, a string, or a menu item for any page on the site, we would need to modify the code itself. However, it's reasonable to suppose that we would want to maintain the same layout for all pages, but just change the odd detail here and there. Thus, the page should contain the minimum possible hard-coded layout details. These details should be supplied as parameters.

Adding script code to the calling page to check for these details is one solution. Much better is making the page data-driven. That is, we could create a simple table and use the name of the calling page as the key. The various fields will give the page-specific information we need to complete the processing.

The table we will use has a column called PageName as the primary key. Other data fields are TopLogo, BottomLogo, Content, TopLinks, BottomLinks, and Content:

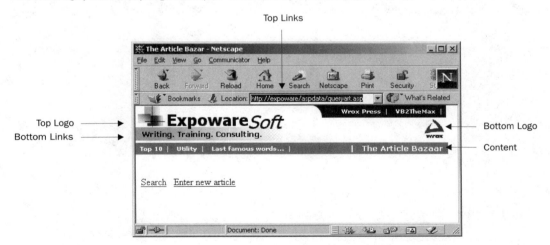

The menus (TopLinks and BottomLinks) are coded in the database through strings separated by a semicolon character. Each string identifies an item. Since each represents, in turn, a hyperlink, it is given by a comma-separated string where the former part is the description and the final part is the URL. For example:

```
Wrox Press,http://www.wrox.com;VB2TheMax,http://www.vb2themax.com
```

Now the layout code looks like this:

```
<%
    ' Grab the name of the calling page
    scriptName = Request.ServerVariables("SCRIPT_NAME")
    n = InstrRev(scriptName, "/")
    curPage = Right(scriptName,Len(scriptName)-n)

    Set rs = Server.CreateObject("ADODB.Recordset")
    sql = "SELECT * From PageLayout "
    sql = sql & "where PageName='" & Trim(curPage) & "'"
    rs.open sql, "provider=SQLOLEDB;uid=sa;Initial Catalog=My Articles"
%>
<TABLE bgColor=#ffffff border=0 cellPadding=0 cellSpacing=0 width=100%>
    <TR>
        <TD height=60 rowSpan=2 vAlign=top width=250>
<%
    Response.Write "<IMG src=" & Trim(rs("TopLogo")) & ">"
%>
        <TD align=right height=20 vAlign=top>
            <IMG src=images/curve.gif width=18 height=20></TD>
        <TD align=right bgColor=#000000 height=20 noWrap vAlign=center>
<%
    a_TopLinks = split(rs("TopLinks"),";")
    For each item in a_TopLinks
                If Len(Trim(item)) then
                a = split(Trim(item), ",")
            Response.Write "<FONT color=#ffffff " & _
                "face=Verdana,Arial size=1><B>  "
            Response.Write "<A style='color:#ffffff; text-decoration:none'"
            Response.Write "href=" & a(1) & ">" & a(0) & "</A>  "
            Response.Write "<FONT color=#ffffff>|</FONT>  "
        End If
    Next
    Response.Write "</B></FONT></TD>"
%>
    </TR>
    <TR>
        <TD align=right colSpan=3 height=40 noWrap vAlign=top>
<%
    Response.Write "<IMG width=40 height=40 align=right src=" & _
                        Trim(rs("BottomLogo")) & ">"
%>
        </TD>
    </TR>
</TABLE>

<TABLE width=100% border=0 cellspacing=0>
<TR >
```

```
<TD bgColor=#ff6600 colSpan=4 height=20 vAlign=center>
<%
   a_BottomLinks = split(rs("BottomLinks"),";")
   For each item in a_BottomLinks
      If Len(Trim(item)) then
         a = split(Trim(item), ",")
         Response.Write "<FONT color=#ffffff " & _
                            "face=Verdana,Arial size=1><B>  "
         Response.Write "<A style='color:#ffffff; text-decoration:none'"
         Response.Write "href=" & a(1) & ">" & a(0) & "</A>  "
         Response.Write "<FONT color=#ffffff>|</FONT>  "
      End If
   Next
   Response.Write "</B></FONT></TD>"
%>
<TD bgColor=#ff6600 colSpan=3 height=20 vAlign=center align=right>
   <FONT color=#ffffff face=Verdana,Arial size=2>
   <B>|  
   <%= rs("Content") %>
     </B>
</TD>
</TR>
</TABLE>
<BR><BR>
<% rs.close %>
```

The `layout.asp` page needs to know about the caller page to get the key for the database. This is information that can easily be obtained through the `Request` object:

```
scriptName = Request.ServerVariables("SCRIPT_NAME")
n = InstrRev(scriptName, "/")
curPage = Right(scriptName,Len(scriptName)-n)
```

The `SCRIPT_NAME` server variable contains the relative to the page from the web server, so we might have to strip off the virtual folder name.

The source code for the `search.asp` page has an identical structure, but produces a slightly different layout:

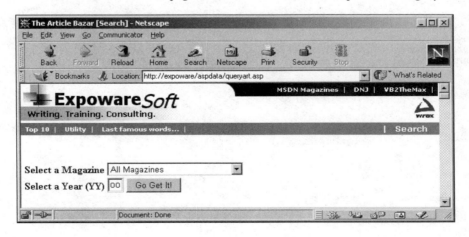

Notice, in particular, the different group of top links. Using a database, we avoid the task of going through a complex of nested `select...case` statements.

Coding the Web Site

The Search Page

By defining a common layout page, we concern ourselves only with the content of the remaining pages on the site. The `Search` page contains a few form elements to gather the information we need to run the query. The form posts to the same page to preserve the user interface.

```
<form name="Main" action="QueryArt.asp" method="post">
```

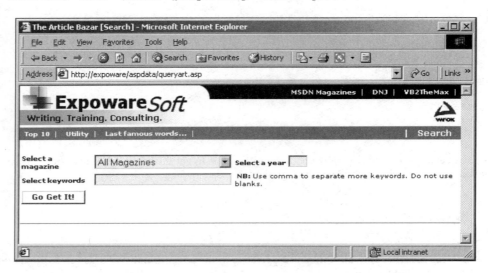

The code for this the page currently looks like this:

```
<HTML>
<HEAD><TITLE>The Article Bazaar [Search]</TITLE></HEAD>

<!-- INITIALIZATION -->
<LINK rel=stylesheet href=tablestyles.css>
<BODY leftmargin=0 marginwidth=0 marginheight=0 topmargin=0>

<%
    ' If GET, this is the first time
    bFirstTime = (Request.ServerVariables("REQUEST_METHOD")="GET")

    strConn = "Provider=SQLOLEDB;uid=sa;Initial Catalog=My Articles"
    Set oRS = CreateObject("ADODB.Recordset")
%>

<!-- PAGE LAYOUT -->
<%
    Server.Execute "layout.asp"
%>
```

Since the form posts to itself, the default values for the query (all years, all magazines, and no keywords) will be used when we access the page for the first time. Thus, the page issues a full query to the database as soon as it is selected. However, we don't want this to occur every time we want this page displayed. We want the code to distinguish between situations where the page is accessed for the first time and when it is accessed subsequently. This is achieved in the previous code by using a GET request for the first access, and a POST request subsequently.

```
strYear   = Request.Form("txtYear")
strKey    = Request.Form("txtKey")
strMagID  = Request.Form("cboMagz")
```

The Request object lets us grab from the Form collection the content of the form's elements:

```
<form name="Main" action="QueryArt.asp" method="post">
<TABLE cellspacing=2><TR>
<TD><font face=verdana size=1><B>Select a magazine</TD>
<TD><font face=verdana size=1>
<SELECT style="background-color:beige;width:200px" name="cboMagz">
   <option value="0">All Magazines</option>

<!-- FILL THE COMBOBOX -->

<%
   Set oRS = Server.CreateObject("ADODB.Recordset")
   oRS.Open "SELECT MagID, Name from Magazines", strConn
   Set oRS.ActiveConnection = Nothing

   While Not oRS.EOF
      s = ""
      If Trim(oRS("MagID")) = strMagID then
         s = " selected "
         strMagz = Trim(oRS("name"))
      End If

      Response.Write "<option " & s & _
                  "value=" &    Trim(oRS("MagID")) & ">" & _
                         Trim(oRS("Name")) & "</option>"
      oRS.MoveNext
   Wend
   oRS.Close
%>
</SELECT>
</TD>

<TD><font face=verdana size=1><B>Select a year</B>
   <input class=MyTextbox name=txtYear value="<%= strYear %>"
         size=2 maxlength=2></input>
</TD>
</TR>

<TR>
<TD><font face=verdana size=1><B>Select keywords</B></TD>
<TD><font face=verdana size=1>
   <input class=MyTextbox name="txtKey" value="<%= strKey %>"
         style=width:200px></input></TD>
```

```
<TD><font face=verdana size=1>
   <B>NB: </B>Use comma to separate more keywords. Do Not use blanks.</TD>
</TR>

<TR>
<TD><font face=verdana size=1>
   <input type=SUBMIT class=MyButton value="Go Get It!"></input></TD>
</TR>
</TABLE>
</form>
```

Since the page is reinterpreted each time we make a query, the combo-box will be created each time. To include a default item in the combo-box, we just need to add the name of the item within the <option> tag. If we initialize the text boxes and the combo-box using the same ASP variables from the beginning of the page, we can maintain the same page state between two successive queries.

At this point, the form has been drawn. If we don't want to start the query the first time we enter the page, we just close the session.

```
If bFirstTime then Response.End
```

Otherwise, we can retrieve the recordset. The fields to select are:

```
SELECT Magazines.Name, Articles.Issue, Articles.Title, Articles.Abstract
FROM Magazines
INNER JOIN Articles
ON Magazines.MagID = Articles.Magazine
```

Each article refers to the magazine through an ID that is the primary key for the magazine table. The above code retrieves all the available records. Based on the content of the form, we should include a WHERE clause to narrow down the records returned:

```
strWhereYear = ""
If strYear <> "" then strWhereYear = "Issue Like '" & strYear & "%'"
strWhereMagz = ""
If strMagID <> 0 then strWhereMagz = "Magazine=" & strMagID

strWhere = ""
If strWhereYear <> "" And strWhereMagz <> "" then
   strWhere = " where " & strWhereYear & " and " & strWhereMagz
Else
   If strWhereYear <> "" Or strWhereMagz <> "" then
      If strWhereYear <> "" then strWhere = " where " & strWhereYear
      If strWhereMagz <> "" then strWhere = " where " & strWhereMagz
   End If
End If

sqlFld = ""
sqlFld = sqlFld & "Magazines.Name, Articles.Issue, Articles.Author,"
sqlFld = sqlFld & "Articles.Title, Articles.Abstract"
If strKey <> "" then sqlFld = sqlFld & ", Articles.Keyword"
sqlCmd = "SELECT Magazines.Name, Articles.Issue, Articles.Author, " & _
            "Articles.Title, Articles.Abstract" & _
```

```
            "FROM Magazines INNER JOIN Articles " & _
            "ON Magazines.MagID = Articles.Magazine"

oRS.Open sqlCmd & strWhere, strConn
Set oRS.ActiveConnection = Nothing
```

If we select 2000 as the year, and MSDN Magazine (ID of 1) as the magazine, the resulting SQL statement is:

```
SELECT Magazines.Name, Articles.Issue, Articles.Author, Articles.Title,
      Articles.Abstract FROM Magazines
INNER JOIN Articles
WHERE Issue LIKE '00%' AND Magazine=1
```

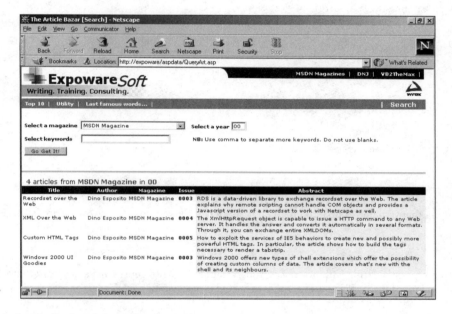

The recordset is displayed through a `<table>` tag:

```
<TABLE cellspacing=0 cellpadding=2 border=0 width=100%>

<TR align=center bgcolor=0>
<TD><font face=verdana size=1 color=#ffffff
   style=font-weight:bold>Title</font></TD>
<TD><font face=verdana size=1 color=#ffffff
   style=font-weight:bold>Author</font></TD>
<TD><font face=verdana size=1 color=#ffffff
   style=font-weight:bold>Magazine</font></TD>
<TD><font face=verdana size=1 color=#ffffff
   style=font-weight:bold>Issue</font></TD>
<TD><font face=verdana size=1 color=#ffffff
   style=font-weight:bold>Abstract</font></TD>
</TR>

<%
```

```
      While Not oRS.EOF
          Response.Write "<TR valign=top>"
          sFont = "<font face=verdana size=1>"
          Response.Write "<TD>" & sFont
          Response.Write oRS("title")
          Response.Write "</TD>"
          sFont = "<font face=verdana size=1 color=blue>"
          Response.Write "<TD>" & sFont
          Response.Write oRS("author")
          Response.Write "</TD>"
          sFont = "<font face=verdana size=1 color=blue>"
          Response.Write "<TD align=center>" & sFont
          Response.Write oRS("name")
          Response.Write "</TD>"
          sFont = "<font face=verdana size=1 style=font-weight:bold>"
          Response.Write "<TD>" & sFont
          Response.Write oRS("issue")
          Response.Write "</TD>"
          sFont = "<font face=verdana size=1>"
          Response.Write "<TD bgcolor=lightcyan>" & sFont
          Response.Write oRS("abstract")
          Response.Write "</TD>"
          Response.Write "</TR>"

          oRS.MoveNext
      Wend
%>
</TABLE>
```

The only thing that remains to be implemented is support for keywords. A keyword string looks like this:

```
Web,DHTML,Win32
```

It is a comma-separated string with no spaces in between. Each word represents a keyword that is checked against the content of the corresponding `Keyword` field in the database.

Full-Text Indexing

Checking for a keyword is not that simple, since we have to check whether at least one of a certain number of substrings is contained within a given string. However, the T-SQL syntax includes a powerful clause called `CONTAINS`. We just add it to the `WHERE` part of the `SELECT` statement and we're done. The complete SQL command is:

```
SELECT Magazines.Name, Articles.Issue, Articles.Author, Articles.Title,
        Articles.Abstract FROM Magazines
INNER JOIN Articles
WHERE Issue LIKE '00%'
        AND Magazine=1
        AND CONTAINS (Keyword, "'Web' or 'DHTML' or 'Win32'")
```

Here's the source code that generates the `CONTAINS` clause from a comma-separated string:

```
buf = ""
a_Keywords = split(strKey, ",")
```

```
For each k in a_Keywords
   If buf <> ""
      buf = buf & " or " & '" & k & "'"
   Else
      buf = buf & '" & k & "'"
   End If
Next
strWhereKey = "CONTAINS(Keyword," & Chr(34) & buf & Chr(34) & ")"
```

For the CONTAINS clause to work, the database needs to be full-text indexed, otherwise we cannot use a CONTAINS predicate on the table. Full-text indexing a database is as easy as selecting the right menu item from the SQL Server Enterprise Manager.

If for any reason we don't want to use this solution, we can do the same thing by scanning all the records and checking manually whether they match the keywords. We can do this from ASP code, a COM object, or directly on the database server through a stored procedure.

The Insert Page

The procedure to add a new article to the repository is no more difficult than adding a new record to the database. In this next section, we will not look at the code which will actually add a new article to the database; we will look at that in the next chapter, but we will prepare our ASP pages for that code here.

The page newart.asp has a general structure like this:

```
<HTML>
<HEAD><TITLE>The Article Bazaar [New]</TITLE></HEAD>

<!-- INITIALIZATION -->

<LINK rel="stylesheet" href="tablestyles.css">
<BODY leftmargin=0 marginwidth=0 marginheight=0 topmargin=0>

<!-- PAGE LAYOUT -->
<%
   Server.Execute "layout.asp"
%>

<!-- BODY OF THE PAGE -->
<FORM name="Main" action="NewArtConfirm.asp" method="post">
<%
   Server.Execute "newartdlg.asp"
%>
</FORM>

</BODY>
</HTML>
```

The content of the form has been placed in a separate ASP page: newartdlg.asp. There is a specific reason for this, as we'll see later in the chapter.

```
<%
   strConn = "Provider=SQLOLEDB;uid=sa;Initial Catalog=My Articles"
   Set oRS = Server.CreateObject("ADODB.Recordset")
```

```
%>
<HR>

<TABLE cellspacing=2><TR>
<TD><font face=verdana size=1><B>Select the magazine</TD>
<TD><font face=verdana size=1>
<SELECT style="background-color:beige;width:200px" name="cboMagz">
<%
    oRS.Open "SELECT MagID, Name from Magazines", strConn
    Set oRS.ActiveConnection = Nothing

    While Not oRS.EOF
        Response.Write "<option " & "value=" & _
            Trim(oRS("MagID")) & ">" & Trim(oRS("Name")) & "</option>"
        oRS.MoveNext
    Wend
    oRS.Close
%>
</SELECT>
</TD>
<TD><font face=verdana size=1><B>Issue (YYMM)</B>
<input class=MyTextbox name=txtYear value="<%= strYear %>"
    size=4 maxlength=4></input>
</TD>
</TR>


<TR>
<TD><font face=verdana size=1><B>Specify keywords</B></TD>
<TD><font face=verdana size=1>
<input class=MyTextbox name="txtKey" value="<%= strKey %>"
style=width:200px></input></TD>
<TD><font face=verdana size=1>
<B>NB: </B>Use comma to separate more keywords. Do Not use blanks.</TD>
</TR>


<TR>
<TD><font face=verdana size=1>
<input type=SUBMIT class=MyButton value="Save it!"></input></TD>
</TR>
</TABLE>

<HR>

<TABLE cellspacing=2><TR>
<TR>
<TD><font face=verdana size=1><B>Title</B></TD>
<TD><font face=verdana size=1>
<input class=MyTextbox name="artTitle" style=width:200px></input>
</TD>

<TD><font face=verdana size=1><B>Author</B></TD>
<TD><font face=verdana size=1>
<input class=MyTextbox name="artAuthor" style=width:200px></input>
</TD>
</TR>
```

```
<TR>
<TD><font face=verdana size=1><B>URL</B></TD>
<TD><font face=verdana size=1>
<input class=MyTextbox name="artURL" style=width:300px></input>
</TD>
<TD> </TD><TD> </TD>
</TR>

<TR valign=top>
<TD><font face=verdana size=1><B>Abstract</B></TD>
<TD><font face=verdana size=1>
<textarea class=MyTextbox name="artAbstract" rows=6 cols=40></textarea>
</TD>
</TR>

</TABLE>
```

The output will look like this:

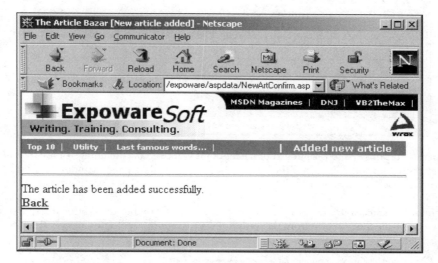

By clicking on the Save it! button, the form is posted to another page: newartconfirm.asp, which confirms whether the operation is successful or not:

```
<HTML>

<!-- INITIALIZATION -->
<HEAD><TITLE>The Article Bazaar [New article added]</TITLE></HEAD>
<BODY leftMargin=0 topMargin=0 marginheight=0 marginwidth=0>

<!-- PAGE LAYOUT -->
<%
   Server.Execute "layout.asp"
%>

<!-- BODY OF THE PAGE -->
```

```
<%
    ' insert the new record
%>

<HR>
The article has been added successfully.<BR>
<A href="newart.asp"><B>Back</B></A>

</BODY>
</HTML>
```

Using a separate response page is standard practice, but if you can take advantage of the tools that allow you to get to the server, run some code and then return back to the calling page (without a refresh), then by all means use alternative approaches.

The problem of these accessory technologies is that they place a number of additional requirements on the browser. The only one that, at least from this point of view, is more accommodating is Remote Scripting.

Tips for Cross-Browser Programming

Writing ASP pages that have a similar appearance in different browsers has never been an easy task. Specifically, two particular issues make this task difficult:

❑ Different page object models

❑ Different support for cascading stylesheets

However, the second point is arguably tougher to solve than the first. While Netscape browsers and Internet Explorer have two very different page object models, we can do a number of basic tasks in roughly the same way. The main difficulties here arise from the fact that IE and Netscape support DHTML in different ways.

In general, Netscape is much less forgiving than Internet Explorer when it comes to HTML source code. For example, Netscape requires us to embed `<input>` tags inside `<form>` tags, and doesn't allow us to use spaces in URLs; it assumes we have escaped them first. Not being aware of these features can lead to unpleasant surprises when we try to run code through other browsers. By contrast, IE understands what we're trying to do and automatically escapes the spaces in our URLs.

My favorite approach to developing cross-browser web pages is this: develop the core set of functionality using Netscape, and then enhance them using IE.

What You Can Do With IE Only

There are a number of things that we can only achieve using IE. These include support for components through scriptlets and COM. However, Netscape does allow us to create instances of COM components, but through a plug-in module.

What You Can Do With Netscape and IE

Remote Scripting is a client-side scripting technology that allows us to run a method on a remote ASP page without leaving the current page. It also enables us to invoke remote methods asynchronously. Being based on ECMAScript code and Java applets, it works on almost any browser platform. We can take advantage of it on Win32 with both Netscape Navigator 3.0+ and IE 3.02+, as well as on Solaris HotJava and Netscape for Linux. However, it doesn't work on Win16 and the Apple Macintosh OS because of limitations within the Java virtual machine on those platforms.

We can customize fonts and colors for HTML tags within Netscape by wrapping the tag body with a `<font>` tag. If we want to do more ambitious things, then we should use the `style` property. The `class` attribute is a sort of shortcut for the `style` property.

Browser-Specific Pages

Armed with much patience and being able to make use of CSS styles and HTML constructs, we can build a user interface that works almost identically on a number of different browsers. However, because of the number of different features on different browsers, exploiting the functionality of a particular browser to the full will prevent us from developing browser-neutral web applications.

Instead of having a different page for each family of browser, we can use a single page containing the necessary programming logic to distinguish between IE (DHTML) and all the other browsers (HTML 3.2). The NewArt.asp page, as we will shortly see, shows an example of this.

A DHTML Drop-down Window

The following code is an amended version of `default.asp`:

```
<HTML>
<!-- INITIALIZATION -->
<HEAD><TITLE>The Article Bazaar</TITLE></HEAD>
<%
    browser = Request.ServerVariables("HTTP_USER_AGENT")
    bMSIE = (Instr(browser, "MSIE") >0)
%>
<SCRIPT language=VBScript>
    Function EnterNew()
        Set oStyle = EnterNewPanel.style
        If oStyle.display = "none" then
```

```
              EnterNewButton.innerHTML = "[Close New Article...]"
              oStyle.display = ""
              ContentTitle.innerText = "New Article"
         Else
              EnterNewButton.innerHTML = "Enter New Article..."
              oStyle.display = "none"
              ContentTitle.innerText = "The Article Bazaar"
         End If
    End Function
</SCRIPT>
<BODY leftMargin=0 topMargin=0 marginheight=0 marginwidth=0>
<!-- PAGE LAYOUT -->
<%
    Server.Execute "layout.asp"
%>
<!-- BODY OF THE PAGE -->
<B>
  
<A href="queryart.asp">Search...</A>
  
<%
    If Not bMSIE then
         Response.Write "<A href=newart.asp>Enter new article...</A>"
    Else
         Response.Write "<A id=EnterNewButton " & _
              "href=vbscript:EnterNew>Enter new article...</A>"
         Response.Write "</B>"
         Response.Write "<DIV id=EnterNewPanel style=display:none>"
         Response.Write "<FORM name='Main
                            action='NewArtConfirm.asp' method='post'>"
         Server.Execute "newartdlg.asp"
         Response.Write "</FORM></DIV>"
    End If
%>
</BODY>
</HTML>
```

The page reads the content of the HTTP_USER_AGENT server variable and determines whether or not the browser is IE. (Admittedly, this code is not very precise in determining the version of the browser; it just makes sure it is IE). Using the HTTP_USER_AGENT variable is a simple but effective way of getting this information. Using the MSWC.BrowserType component gives us much more information about the browser capabilities.

If the user agent string contains the string "MSIE" then the page takes a different branch. It still adds a hyperlink to insert a new article, but this time the link doesn't point to a new page.

```
<A id=EnterNewButton href=vbscript:EnterNew>Enter new article...</A>
```

Instead, it points to a VBScript procedure that runs each time we click on it:

```
Function EnterNew()
    Set oStyle = EnterNewPanel.style
    If oStyle.display = "none" then
```

```
            EnterNewButton.innerHTML = "[Close New Article...]"
            oStyle.display = ""
            ContentTitle.innerText = "New Article"
        Else
            EnterNewButton.innerHTML = "Enter New Article..."
            oStyle.display = "none"
            ContentTitle.innerText = "The Article Bazaar"
        End If
    End Function
```

Other than changing a few of the captions, the function does something quite important: it causes the otherwise hidden <DIV> element to be made visible. This element contains the output of the newartdlg.asp page, and this is the reason why we isolated the form elements from the rest of the newart.asp page.

```
    Response.Write "<DIV id=EnterNewPanel style=display:none>"
    Server.Execute "newartdlg.asp"
    Response.Write "</DIV>"
```

The final effect is shown below:

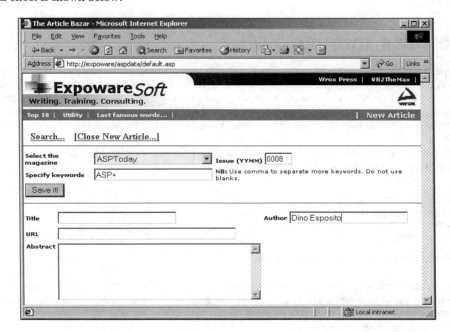

Of course, this requires IE 4.0 or higher to work. If we access the page through Netscape or Opera browsers, we will go through a different route, accessing the same dialog box through newart.asp.

The Special Case of WAP

In most cases, when we decide to serve browser-specific pages, we do this to make the application much more attractive to the user and exploit the special effects that DHTML and IE 4.0 and higher guarantee. As long as we supply code that produces two different types of HTML output – as we did here, then the approach we took above, based on the user agent, works just fine.

However, if we want to extend our pages so that they are viewable by an even wider range of browsers, then we should start thinking in terms of complete separation between the data we're exposing and the views we provide of them.

The rise of WAP (Wireless Application Protocol) devices should encourage us to take this view. WAP devices are generally cell phones with a very limited display, limited navigation facilities, and no easy-to-use keyboard. A WAP device can access any web site that exposes its data as WML (Wireless Markup Language). This is an offshoot of XML. The question is: how do we write WML pages that fit into the device's screen? Can we simply convert HTML into WML via ASP? The simple answer to this is that it depends on how complex our HTML is.

A realistic approach to this situation is to extract the essence of our pages and be ready to deliver it according to the capabilities of the device. But how do we extract the essence of an existing web site? Can XML help us out? Well, yes it can.

> A detailed look at WAP can be found in *Professional WAP, ISBN 1861004044* also from Wrox Press.

Expose Data through XML

The ASP pages that form a web site that delivers data are accomplishing a very simple task. They get the information from a data source and shape it up into a viewable format such as HTML before dispatching it to the browser. What the user receives is a representation of some data. Such a representation may include graphics to make it more attractive and easier to interpret. HTML, on the other hand, is only for defining the page layout; it is not a data description language. With HTML we use data, but we do not define it.

Interfacing with the increasing number of non-PC clients shows that we should make our data available to more than just PC web browsers. Such clients include:

❑   WAP devices

❑   PDA (Personal Digital Assistant) devices

❑   Interactive TV

❑   Web applications through web services

As we saw earlier, the future of web development points in the direction of web services – applications that expose their functionality through HTTP, and send and receive data using XML. The recently announced .Net architecture will define the details of the web services interface, but we will be in a good position to embrace .Net if we expose data via XML.

Our first step will be adding a few extra ASP pages to a site, which simply read in command line arguments, access data, and return the information as an XML string. These pages allow other applications to contact our web site and get what they need: raw information. It'll then be up to them to use the information to populate their own user interface.

The following listing shows the structure of such a page for our Article Bazaar web site. We will look at this page in more detail at the beginning of the next chapter.

```
<%
  ' <--- Collect the arguments --->
  magazine = Request.QueryString("Magazine")
  yearofissue = Request.QueryString("Yearofissue")

  ' Set the MIME type
  Response.ContentType = "text/xml"

  ' Call the necessary components to get the data
  ' Convert them to XML If necessary
  ' Response.Write <the XML data>

  Response.End
%>
```

We would call it in the following way:

```
xmlquery.asp?magazine=9&year=00
```

The caller application will receive XML data as if it were calling a local API function. In the next chapter, which covers middle-tier components, we'll look in more detail at this.

Another way of exposing data via XML is through using XSL. We will look at this approach in Chapters 24 and 25.

Summary

In this chapter, we've looked at the basic principles of designing and creating a good user interface for web applications, and seen how to build a very simple web site that takes advantage of ASP. In particular, we've looked at:

❑ How to effectively structure ASP code

❑ Writing browser-specific ASP code

❑ Tips for cross-browser HTML code

❑ The basic principles of exposing content through XML

In the next chapter, we'll look at developing middle-tier components.

Building Data Access Components

In the previous chapter, we developed an ASP web site that presents a graphical user interface which allows the user to search for articles from a database and display them, as well as add new articles to the database. The web site works perfectly well as it is. However, is this enough?

The application from the previous chapter does have several drawbacks, such as excessive client side processing, which could seriously affect the performance and maintenance of the site. In order for a well-designed user services layer to be effective, it must be integrated well with the technologies that effectively drive the web site; they are located on the server and effectively hidden from the user.

In this chapter, we'll continue to focus on the design of an application, although we will pay more attention to what happens on the server back-end. We'll see how components are used to provide a more effective set of pages and also deliver a common API (Application Programming Interface) exposing the site's functionality. This API will enable us to carry out operations such as exposing data through XML.

Also, we will look at how to build a data access component that accesses a SQL Server database and provides data for the ASP-based web site we built in the previous chapter. While practical data access and manipulation remain the main aims, a short mention of background topics such as middle-tier data validation and business rule implementation cannot be left out. Here we'll look at:

❑   How components benefit ASP applications

❑   How to expose the site's functionality as a COM-based API

❑   How to build a data access component in Visual Basic

❑   How a COM-based API simplifies the addition of new functionality

In this chapter, we'll use Visual Basic and ADO as the main development tools. In the next chapter, the same features will be implemented using C++, the Active Template Library (ATL), and OLE DB consumers.

The Benefits of Components

As mentioned earlier, the application we built in the previous chapter has two significant drawbacks in its data access strategy. All the pages, in fact, utilize direct calls to the ADO objects to get what they need. This means that:

❏ The whole data access process is handled through scripting.

❏ Nearly identical code is used each time we connect to the data source.

The former point affects the overall performance. The latter makes the maintenance harder and adds unnecessary complexity when it comes to extending the site with newer functionality. As we're going to see in this chapter, the use of components can resolve these problems and give us a leaner yet more functional application.

What Components Can Do

This is an ASP book and, accordingly, for us components mean COM automation components, as we saw in Chapter 8. However, 'component' is a much more general and generic term that identifies anything that:

❏ Is a self-contained *piece* of software

❏ Is *somewhat* controllable by external callers

❏ Provides *functionality* through a fixed interface

❏ Completely hides its implementation details (is *encapsulated*)

These are general characteristics that apply to COM, CORBA or even ECMAScript components that can be written using a variety of tools and platforms: from Java to JavaScript and from C++ to Visual Basic and Visual FoxPro. The component is a black box that exposes an immutable programming interface, which is the only way it can communicate with the external world. It takes commands and returns results – the actual implementation details are hidden from the end user.

In our situation, the self-contained piece of software is a COM component that relies on system services and exposes dual interfaces. In other words, it must be callable through COM both from within ASP or Visual Basic applications, and C++ code, among other things. ASP and VB applications would use the IDispatch automation interface. C++ applications would more efficiently bind to the native interfaces, although they could also use Idispatch, so long as they are prepared to take a performance hit.

The available functionality will be expressed in terms of properties and methods, and callers would set these properties and call these methods to get the output from the component. However, using properties also affects the **state** of the component – more on that later on.

The ASP Back-End

Components have many benefits, but they are essentially only wrappers for the functionality they contain – unlike a classic API, their methods and properties are not available directly. As such, they do add overhead to an application, although the benefits of using components far outweigh the performance drawbacks.

To be effective and really interoperable, components must exist in a binary, compiled form, and be highly specialized. Components that are specialized can be highly responsive and simple to use, and also allow us to keep the internal code as clean as possible, thus avoiding any redundancy and minimizing overhead.

Writing components that carry out a few highly specialized tasks will make our whole application more scalable, in that the same component can be used regardless of the size and scope of an application. When designing our application, it is crucial to understand where to employ such specialized components. Depending on the complexity of the site's back-end, we may need to call them either from within ASP code or from the body of additional middle-tier components acting as specific processors for user requests. The diagram below shows a possible, though rather complex, component architecture:

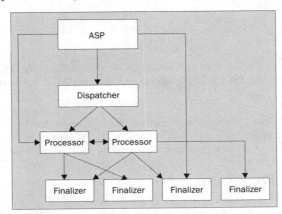

The ASP front-end talks to a tree of components, generically called dispatchers, processors, and finalizers. The back-end hierarchy breaks up the user request, cuts it into pieces of information, and processes these separately and as concurrently as possible. This processing occurs as a series of steps until it reaches the final level of the component hierarchy where, in this case, the finalizer object generates a data access request. If we have a situation where there are few middle-tier components, the finalizer object can be called, if required, directly from the ASP page; this is what happens with our Article Bazaar site.

In any case, using a component is nearly always preferable to inserting raw ADO code into an ASP page.

What About Performance?

It's widely known that ASP is relatively straightforward to use, and owes its simplicity to its script-based nature. However, this strength also turns out to be ASP's most significant weakness – running script has an effect on the performance of the application. The golden rule for any ASP application is that if we want it to serve more pages to more users, we have to take as much of the script out of the pages as we can.

Ideally, we should have a scriptless server-side application – such as an ISAPI DLL running under Internet Information Services (IIS). However, ISAPI applications can only be written in C++ and as such, many programmers find them difficult to program. ASP is still useful, but if we want to improve our server's responsiveness, then we should reduce the amount of script code in our pages using VBScript merely to link together what the components return.

In today's programming world, a common solution is to use a combination of script code and calls to component functionality. The balance of script and component code will vary according to the skills of the development team or the customer's needs.

> *Visual Studio .Net will contain a tool that provides a compromise between ease of use and power. The ATL Server will enable us to write template-based pages (like ASP pages) that contain entry-points where COM objects can insert their output. These pages will look like ASP, but without script engines running in the background.*

Types of Components

Component specialization is the key to good performance and effectiveness. Basically, there are three categories of components:

- ❏ Data Validation
- ❏ Business Object
- ❏ Data Access

Such a classification doesn't affect the way in which we write any of them. Technically speaking, a data validation object is no different from a business object or a data access component. The difference is in the functionality they provide.

In order to create a well-designed object architecture, we should determine in which category our required functionality fits. Then we can design our hierarchy of objects, taking into account the order in which any requests are processed: data input validation, application of business rules, and finally data access.

Data Validation Component

A data validation component can either be called by the originating ASP page, from another business object, or from a Win32 application. The main goal of validation is to verify that the data entered is compatible with the current context and to ensure that it can be used for further operations. On some occasions, carrying out data validation on the client is the preferred option, because it saves at least one round trip to the server. However, this cannot be done all the time. For example, if we need to verify a value against a database entry, we need to do this on the server. An appropriately designed object can simplify the task considerably.

> By using Remote Scripting, we can now control some server-side data validation from the client. If we invoke a remote method asynchronously, we can continue working on the same page and get the response as soon as possible. A detailed look at Remote Scripting and Asynchronous calls may be found at http://www.asptoday.com/articles/19990930.htm.

Business Objects

Business objects are the components that contain all the logic necessary to implement the core functionality of the distributed application. They take input, usually validated beforehand, and process and transform it as required. A business object usually ends up calling the objects that finalize the user request by reading or writing from the data source.

Data Access Component

A data access component has just one task: getting data from a data source or writing data to it, and all the remaining functionality in the component serves to fulfill this role. The typical structure is given by some parameters that fill up the query command to execute. The output depends on the infrastructure we're using; if we use ADO objects, they can either return a disconnected recordset or an XML string.

Building Components

Let's see now how to build a data access component – the element that finalizes the back-end of a web application. The design guidelines are:

❑ Keep the object's programming interface as simple as possible

❑ Minimize the number of arguments

❑ Minimize the number of things it has to do

❑ Try not to rely too much on properties to set up the context where the object must work

The latter point becomes important in the context of stateless component programming – more on this later. First, we will look at actually constructing a component.

Visual Basic ActiveX DLLs

An ActiveX DLL component is an in-process component that runs in the same address space of the caller, in our case IIS, and is invoked through ASP pages. In this next section, we will look at the construction of a data access component for our Article Bazaar.

In Visual Basic, a data access component is actually an ActiveX DLL that we create as shown in the figure below:

We name the project `ArticleBazaar`, to which we add a class which we call `query`. The program identifier (**ProgID**) for this is thus `ArticleBazaar.Query`. All we now have to do is define the public programming interface. Now, however, we can accept all the default settings for an ActiveX DLL:

The object is set, by default, to be non-persistent, to allow the creation of instances outside a Visual Basic project, and to not take advantage of the MTS/COM+ infrastructure.

COM APIs

When writing COM objects that will be called from within ASP pages we can take one of two programmatic approaches. Either they can be designed to work as general-purpose objects, or they can be tied up to the ASP paradigm and programmed as ASP components.

In the first case, the object is just a software component that provides a service. It takes arguments and returns results in the form that the author specifies. Such an object can work in a variety of environments including ASP, generic COM applications, or from client-side script. An ASP component, on the other hand, is totally dependent on its surrounding ASP environment, and can only be used within IIS (although there are ways of constructing components so that they do not have such a dependency). However, the component knows that it is used only from within IIS/ASP, and as such is able to link to the ASP type library, and its code can issue calls to the ASP intrinsic objects.

How we proceed depends on our development needs. An ASP component will be optimized to produce as many pages as possible in the shortest time, whereas a general purpose data access component simply encapsulates the code needed to access a data source to get or set some records. An ASP component typically writes to the output console, and sends HTML code back to the browser, whereas a general data access component will generally not be involved with presentation, thereby concentrating on the data.

We will be using the more flexible solution of a general purpose data access object for the Article Bazaar web site.

The purpose of the component is to develop a set of COM functions which the front-end ASP pages will use. HTML is the favorite language for output. However, we will also be able to convert the data into XML with ease and simplicity. Including XML support will prepare us for future integration with BizTalk applications and general B2B scenarios.

The ArticleBazaar.Query Component

The Article Bazaar web site is relatively simple. Apart from the ASP UI pages already discussed, it has just two components. The first one connects to the SQL Server database, runs a query and returns a recordset, the second inserts a new record into the table. If we want to extend this, we could add other components to deal with deletions and updates.

For a Visual Basic data access component, we must reference the ADO 2.5 object model. Although we could reference other data access objects, ADO 2.5 is currently the best in the context of ASP development:

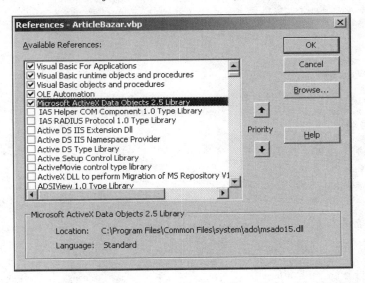

In the figure above, we're making an **early bind** to the ADO 2.5 library. If our application is still taking advantage of Windows NT 4.0 Server and IIS 4.0, or if we haven't installed version 2.5 of the Microsoft Data Access Components (MDAC) toolkit, we can link to the ADO 2.1 library. The code in this project does not use the newer features of ADO 2.5.

> ADO 2.5 can be downloaded from `www.microsoft.com/downloads`. If you are using Access 2000, you will need ADO 2.1 or higher.

Setting Up the Query

The method `GetArticles` has two parameters: the magazine ID, and a string representing the year of publication. After processing, it returns a disconnected recordset with all the articles matching the supplied parameters:

```
'    ***********************************************************
'       GetArticles
'    -----------------------------------------------------------
'       Prepares and runs a query against My Articles.
'       Returns all the articles that match the magazine ID
```

```
'    and the year of publication
' ***********************************************************

Public Function GetArticles(ByVal nMagID As Integer, _
                            ByVal strYear As String) As ADODB.Recordset
    Dim strWhereYear As String      ' builds the WHERE clause
    Dim strWhereMagz As String      ' builds the WHERE clause
    Dim strWhere As String          ' the WHERE clause
    Dim strSQL As String            ' the SQL statement
    Dim strConn As String           ' the connection string
    Dim oRS As New ADODB.Recordset  ' the ADO Recordset

    ' *** if year has been specified...
    strWhereYear = ""
    If strYear <> "" Then
        strWhereYear = "Issue Like '" & strYear & "%'"
    End If


    ' *** if the magazine ID has been specified...
    strWhereMagz = ""
    If nMagID <> 0 Then
        strWhereMagz = "Magazine=" & nMagID
    End If


    ' *** prepares the WHERE clause...
    strWhere = ""
    If strWhereYear <> "" And strWhereMagz <> "" Then
        strWhere = " where " & strWhereYear & " and " & strWhereMagz
    Else
        If strWhereYear <> "" Or strWhereMagz <> "" Then
            If strWhereYear <> "" Then strWhere = " where " & strWhereYear
            If strWhereMagz <> "" Then strWhere = " where " & strWhereMagz
        End If
    End If


    ' *** prepares the full SQL statement...
    strSQL = "SELECT Magazines.Name,Articles.Issue," & _
             "Articles.Author,Articles.Title," & _
             "Articles.Abstract " & _
             "FROM Magazines " & _
             "INNER JOIN Articles ON " & _
             "Magazines.MagID=Articles.Magazine"

    strSQL = strSQL & strWhere

    ' *** prepares the connection string...
    strConn = "Provider=SQLOLEDB;uid=sa;Initial Catalog=My Articles"

    ' *** runs the query...
    With oRS
        .CursorLocation = adUseClient
        .Open strSQL, strConn
    End With
    Set GetArticles = oRS
```

```
        ' *** disconnects the recordset
        Set oRS.ActiveConnection = Nothing
  End Function
```

Much of this code has been taken from the `queryart.asp` page from the previous chapter.

The part of the ASP page which produces the list of the articles, is altered in the following ways:

```
<%
  If bFirstTime Then
    Response.End
  End If
  Set o = Server.CreateObject("ArticleBazaar.Query")
  Set oRS = o.GetArticles(strMagID, strYear)
  Response.Write "  "
  Response.Write "<font face=verdana size=2>"
  Response.Write "<span style='color:red;font-weight:bold'>" & _
      oRS.Recordcount & " </span>"
  Response.Write "articles from "
  Response.Write "<span style='color:red;font-weight:bold'>" & _
      strMagz & "</span>"
  If strYear <> "" Then
    Response.Write " in "
    Response.Write "<span style='color:red;font-weight:bold'>" & _
      strYear & "</span>"
  End If
  Response.Write "</font>"
%>
```

The data access code is now hidden from the ASP page, which neatly separates the database details from the ASP programmer, and as long as the recordset interface remains unchanged, we need not worry about how the recordset is obtained. More importantly, however, we now have a general-purpose tool that can be used from any COM environment to get this information. Thus, we have created some reusable code, and because the ASP page is much slimmer, site maintenance has become that little bit easier.

Writing Slimmer Code

In our `queryart.asp` page, there is another point where farming code out to a component helps us to obtain both slimmer and more functional code. The dropdown list that allows the user to select a magazine is built by querying the database for all the available magazine titles. In the old version of the page, this was achieved through raw ADO calls. Why not use a new method wrapped in a component to do this? Doing this means that our site's COM functionality gets richer. `GetMagazines` gets a list of the magazines from the database:

```
'   *********************************************************
'      GetMagazines
'   ---------------------------------------------------------
'      Prepares and runs a query against My Articles.
'      Looks up and returns all the magazines available
'      in the database
'   *********************************************************
```

```
Public Function GetMagazines() As ADODB.Recordset
    Dim strSQL As String            ' the SQL statement
    Dim strConn As String           ' the connection string
    Dim oRS As New ADODB.Recordset  ' the ADO Recordset

    ' *** prepares the connection string...
    strConn = "Provider=SQLOLEDB;uid=sa;Initial Catalog=My Articles"

    ' *** prepares the full SQL statement...
    strSQL = "SELECT MagID, Name FROM Magazines"

    ' *** runs the query...
    With oRS
        .CursorLocation = adUseClient
        .Open strSQL, strConn
        Set GetMagazines = oRS
    End With

    ' *** disconnects the recordset
    Set oRS.ActiveConnection = Nothing
End Function
```

The caller receives a recordset containing the list and can use it how he or she wants. While it is good to obtain this information, it requires lots of code to make the contents visible in the browser. We can do two things to deal with this: either write an ASP components that gets the recordset and sends it out through the Response object, or modify the method to make it return an HTML string. The GetMagazinesAsHTML method does the latter:

```
' ***********************************************************
'     GetMagazinesAsHTML
' ----------------------------------------------------------
'     Looks up and returns all the magazines available
'     in the database. The magazines names are packed
'     as a list of <OPTION> HTML tags
' ***********************************************************

Public Function GetMagazinesAsHTML(ByVal bIsQuery As Boolean, _
         Optional ByVal nSelected As Integer) As String
    Dim oRS As ADODB.Recordset       ' the worker recordset
    Dim strBuf As String             ' the internal buffer
    Dim temp As String

    ' *** get the magazines
    Set oRS = GetMagazines()

    ' *** starts preparing the HTML string...
    strBuf = ""
    If bIsQuery Then strBuf = "<option value=0>All Magazines</option>"
    If IsMissing(nSelected) Then nSelected = 0

    ' *** prepares the HTML string...
    While Not oRS.EOF
        If oRS("MagID") = nSelected Then
            temp = " selected "
```

```
        Else
            temp = ""
        End If

        strBuf = strBuf & "<option " & temp & _
                          "value=" & oRS("MagID") & _
                          ">" & Trim(oRS("Name")) & _
                          "</option>"
        oRS.MoveNext
    Wend
    GetMagazinesAsHTML = strBuf

    ' *** close and release the object...
    oRS.Close
    Set oRS = Nothing
End Function
```

This code has also been copied from the `queryart.asp` page. The combo-box could have an extra item, **All Magazines**, which is required only when the combo-box is filled by the search page. The Boolean parameter, `bIsQuery`, serves just the purpose of letting us know whether such an extra item is needed or not.

When the form is submitted, the `queryart.asp` page is refreshed to reflect the results of the query. In this case, it would be useful to automatically select the magazine item containing the chosen articles. The optional argument `nSelected` does just this. While enumerating the recordset, if the magazine ID matches the specified index, the `selected` attribute is added to the `<option>` tag.

Since we may need to set some styles for the dropdown list (such as the background color, and the list width), the method returns only the list of the `<option>` tags. The resulting ASP code (found in `queryart.asp`) looks like this:

```
<select style="background-color:beige;width:200px"
  onchange="chg()" name="cboMagz">
<%
  set o = Server.CreateObject("ArticleBazaar.Query")
  Response.Write o.GetMagazinesAsHTML(True, strMagID)
  set o = Nothing
%>
</select>
```

Note the slight change in the `<select>` tag. A bit of client-side script code executes when the selection changes:

```
onchange = "chg()"
```

In the previous chapter, the `strMagz` variable was used to keep track of the name of the magazine being selected. This variable was set while filling the dropdown list:

```
While Not oRS.EOF
  If Trim(oRS("MagID")) = strMagID then
    s = " selected "
    strMagz = Trim(oRS("name"))
  Else
    s = ""
```

```
    End If

    Response.Write "<option " & s & "value=" & _
        Trim(oRS("MagID")) & ">" & Trim(oRS("Name")) & _
        "</option>"
    oRS.MoveNext
Wend
```

Moving this code into the GetMagazinesAsHTML method raises the problem of how to set this variable. Of course, this variable is local to the ASP page while the method is contained in the component. It is not good programming practice to couple two logically separated sections of an ASP application, such as collecting the input parameters and filling up a combo-box. But we would probably never notice this, until we came to adapting code for components – writing components always forces us to write well-designed code.

To work around this problem, we have to define a new hidden control:

```
<input type=hidden name=txtMagName></input>
```

We supply it with the name of the selected magazine each time the selection changes:

```
<script language=javascript>
function chg()
{
  f = document.forms["Main"];
  s = f["cboMagz"];
  f["txtMagName"].value = s.options[s.selectedIndex].text;
}
</script>
```

The value of the input box can be retrieved in the usual way through the Request.Form collection:

```
<%
  strYear  = Request.Form("txtYear")
  strKey   = Request.Form("txtKey")
  strMagID = Request.Form("cboMagz")
  strMagz  = Request.Form("txtMagName")
%>
```

Inserting a New Article

The code that inserts a new article into the database is found in the body of the newartconfirm.asp page. As we saw in the previous chapter, this page is invoked by an HTML form either from newart.asp (for non-IE browsers) or default.asp (for IE):

```
<HTML>
<!-- INITIALIZATION -->
<HEAD><TITLE>The Article Bazaar [New article added]</TITLE></HEAD>
<BODY leftMargin=0 topMargin=0 marginheight=0 marginwidth=0>

<!-- PAGE LAYOUT -->
```

```
<%
  Server.Execute "layout.asp"
%>

<!-- BODY OF THE PAGE -->
<%
  strMagID  = Request.Form("cboMagz")
  strYear   = Request.Form("txtYear")
  strKey    = Request.Form("txtKey")
  strURL    = Request.Form("artURL")
  strTitle  = Request.Form("artTitle")
  strAuthor = Request.Form("artAuthor")
  strAbstr  = Request.Form("artAbstract")

  ' adds the record
  Set o = Server.CreateObject("ArticleBazaar.Insert")
  bResult = o.InsertArticle(strMagID, strYear, strAuthor, strTitle, _
                            strAbstr, strURL, strKey)
  Set o = nothing
%>

<hr> 

<%
If bResult = True then
  Response.Write "The article has been added successfully."
Else
  Response.Write "An error occurred while adding the article."
End If
%>

<hr>
  
<A href="newart.asp"><B>Back</B></A>

</BODY>
</HTML>
```

The `ArticleBazaar.Insert` object has a single method called `InsertArticle` that takes one string argument for each database field:

```
' **********************************************************
'     InsertArticle
' ---------------------------------------------------------
'     Executes a command to insert a new record in
'     "My Articles"
' **********************************************************

Public Function InsertArticle(ByVal strMagID As String, _
        ByVal strYear As String, ByVal strAuthor As String, _
        ByVal strTitle As String, ByVal strAbstr As String, _
        ByVal strURL As String, ByVal strKey As String _
    ) As Boolean

    Dim strSQL As String              ' the SQL statement
```

```
    Dim oCN As New ADODB.Connection ' the ADO Connection object
    Dim oCM As New ADODB.Command    ' the ADO Command object

    ' *** prepares the SQL statement...
    strSQL = "INSERT INTO Articles " & _
            "(Magazine,Author,Issue,Title,Abstract,URL,Keyword) " & _
            "VALUES (" & _
            strMagID & ",'" & strAuthor & "','" & strYear & "','" & _
            strTitle & "','" & strAbstr & "','" & strURL & "','" & _
            strKey & _
            "')"

    ' *** creates the connection...
    oCN.ConnectionString = DATASOURCE
    oCN.Open

    ' *** runs the command...
    oCN.Errors.Clear
    With oCM
        Set .ActiveConnection = oCN
        .CommandText = strSQL
        .CommandType = adCmdText
        .Execute
    End With

    ' *** errors?
    If oCN.Errors.Count > 0 Then
        InsertArticle = False
        oCN.Errors.Clear
    Else
        InsertArticle = True
    End If

    ' closes and returns
    Set oCN = Nothing
    Set oCM = Nothing
End Function
```

The method returns a Boolean value denoting the success or the failure of the operation. Note the use of an ADO Command object and the explicit creation of a Connection object. The Command object provides a more direct and efficient way to work. Alternatively, we could have selected a recordset, added a new record to it, and then updated the table. With only a small change to the code structure, we could use a parameterized stored procedure in case we decide to refine the server-side SQL code.

The Connection object provides the means to manage possible errors. ADO 2.x provides the Errors collection that informs us about the most recent errors that occurred throughout the operation. To be able to catch errors during the insertion, we need to create an explicit connection. (Alternatively, we could have set the Command's ActiveConnection property to the connection string.) In this case, ADO creates and destroys the connection behind the scenes, but we are not given any chance to manage the Errors collection.

Towards Stateless Components

Back in 1996, Microsoft introduced something code-named Viper that came to life in early 1997 as **Microsoft Transaction Server** (MTS), now an integral part of COM+. This defined a programming model for developing distributed, component-based transactional applications. It also provided a run-time infrastructure that acted like an object broker, and a user interface for deploying and managing such applications.

MTS is tightly integrated with IIS (since version 4.0) and provides support for transactional ASP pages. In other words, MTS allows ASP script code blocks to execute within an MTS-managed transaction. Thus, we can shape up our ASP scripts to take into account the outcome of a transaction. This extends the benefits of MTS transaction protection to an entire web application.

An MTS application, called a **package**, contains a group of logically related components that follow a certain programming model. IIS applications execute within their own MTS package, providing process isolation and crash protection for web applications.

The MTS Programming Model

Years of real-world experience prove that when developing distributed systems, we spend much of our time supplying code that has nothing to do with the business objects we are developing. Thread pooling, security and permissions, the pooling of database connections, memory management, etc., are all non-trivial activities required by virtually every real-world distributed system. The idea behind MTS is both simple and attractive: leave the system to deal with all of this and concentrate our efforts on developing our custom objects to implement our business applications.

MTS is like an interceptor that hooks on all calls that any client makes to the objects it controls. Any method invocation on any of these objects is governed by MTS. It takes care of transaction enlistment, pooling, and security, and establishes a concurrency between object instances that can speed up the application performance. The key to this is what is called the MTS programming model.

Components that need to operate under MTS must comply with a few behavior rules. Respecting these rules ensures that MTS can do its own work successfully, which benefits the overall system. The rules can be summarized as:

- ❑ Let the MTS runtime know when it can feel free to manage objects at its (and our) best convenience

- ❑ Get critical resources later and release them earlier

- ❑ Get references to MTS components as soon as possible in our application

We soon come to realize that an object that complies with these rules is a component with a special notion of **state**. MTS owes its strength to its ability to manage the object's lifetime better than the average programmer, and as such requires total control of the component.

In situations where many clients are repeatedly calling the same page and the same object, MTS is designed to use any instances of any objects as efficiently as possible. If an instance of an object is unused, MTS will reassign it to another client session that is waiting to use it. And when the first session wants to reuse the object instance that it lost, then MTS can find another unused instance for it.

How can a single object instance serve two different applications? What about the state? This can happen only when an instance of an object explicitly declares that it has no state to maintain. Objects that comply with MTS rules are said to be **stateless** objects. It doesn't mean they don't have any notion of state; they periodically get rid of it either because they don't need it or because it has been stored into a persistent storage medium such as a database table.

The Object Context

MTS implicitly maintains a **context** for each object it controls. This contains information about the object's execution environment such as the identity of the object's creator and, optionally, the transaction where the object is enlisted. In other words, it is responsible for maintaining state that is implicitly associated with an object hosted inside MTS. In conjunction with the MTS Executive, the **Context Object** enables such features as Just In Time Activation, As Soon As Possible Deactivation and transaction monitoring.

We saw at the beginning of this chapter how COM provides a Context Wrapper Object for each of our objects hosted in MTS. The following diagram illustrates the relationship between the Context Wrapper Object, the Context Object, and our object that we're hosting in MTS:

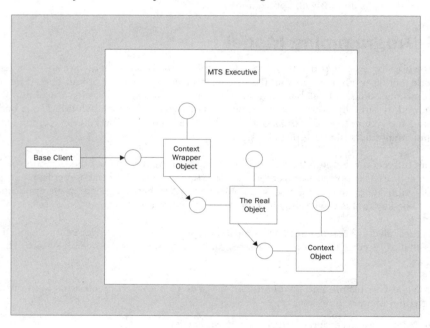

The context object is accessible programmatically through the `IObjectContext` interface. This exposes two important methods that we'll be using soon to make our `ArticleBazaar` component MTS-compliant:

❑   `SetComplete`
❑   `SetAbort`

These two methods indicate when the object doesn't need to hold its state any longer. In particular, `SetComplete` declares that the transaction that the object executes can be committed. Furthermore, the object can be deactivated or re-used after the method returns. `SetAbort` indicates that the transaction must be aborted. We will see how to use these a little later.

From MTS to COM+

COM+ combines both COM and MTS. COM+ appropriates the MTS notion of state and significantly extends COM functionality with new services such as synchronization, object pooling, Queued Components (formerly Microsoft Message Queue). Furthermore, COM+ offers a new distributed application administration and packaging service. In a nutshell, MTS packages become **COM+ applications** and have a new set of extra services to exploit.

> *There's much more to say and know about MTS and COM+. However, this is not the book to cover design and coding issues for COM+ applications in detail. Detailed information about COM+ can be found in* Professional ASP 3.0, *ISBN 1861002610, and information about MTS may be found in* Visual Basic MTS, *ISBN 1861002440, both from Wrox Press.*

A COM+ Compatible ArticleBazaar

Let's see how to modify our `ArticleBazaar` component to make it run as a COM+ application. The new project is called `ArticleBazaarPlus` and references an additional type library: **COM+ Services**, available under Windows 2000:

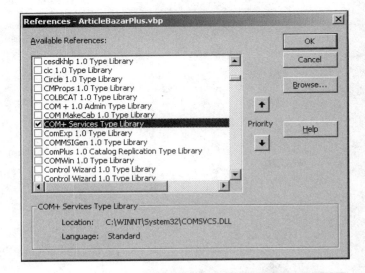

Let's start with the `Insert` object. Actually, there's not much to do that we haven't already done before. We need to reference ADO 2.5. In addition, we need to make sure to set the `MTSTransactionMode` property in the object's property box to `1 - No Transactions`:

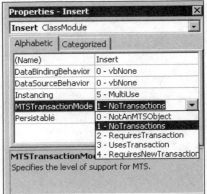

The default value for this is 0 - **NotAnMTSObject**, which means that it will not be associated with a context at runtime. Other than 0 and 1, the remaining values make sense only if the object participates in a transaction, which does not apply in our case.

Having referenced the COM+ Services library, we can now call the `GetObjectContext` function which returns an `ObjectContext` object. Our earlier code will still work fine, but, without appropriate changes, it will not be able to take full advantage of the COM+ runtime.

Here's how the `Insert.cls` file changes now that we're supporting COM+:

```
'   *********************************************************
'     InsertArticle
'   ---------------------------------------------------------
'     Executes a command to insert a new record in
'     "My Articles"
'   *********************************************************
Public Function InsertArticle(ByVal strMagID As String, _
        ByVal strYear As String, ByVal strAuthor As String, _
        ByVal strTitle As String, ByVal strAbstr As String, _
        ByVal strURL As String, ByVal strKey As String _
        ) As Boolean

    Dim strSQL As String            ' the SQL statement
    Dim oCN As New ADODB.Connection ' the ADO Connection object
    Dim oCM As New ADODB.Command    ' the ADO Command object

    ' *** prepares the SQL statement...
    strSQL = "INSERT INTO Articles " & _
            "(Magazine,Author,Issue,Title,Abstract,URL,Keyword) " & _
            "VALUES (" & _
              strMagID & ",'" & strAuthor & "','" & strYear & "','" & _
              strTitle & "','" & strAbstr & "','" & strURL & "','" & _
              strKey & _
            "')"

    ' *** creates the connection...
    oCN.ConnectionString = DataSource
    oCN.Open

    ' *** runs the command...
    oCN.Errors.Clear
    With oCM
        Set .ActiveConnection = oCN
        .CommandText = strSQL
        .CommandType = adCmdText
        .Execute
    End With

    ' *** errors?
    If oCN.Errors.Count > 0 Then
        GetObjectContext.SetAbort
        InsertArticle = False
        oCN.Errors.Clear
    Else
        InsertArticle = False
```

```
        GetObjectContext.SetComplete
    End If

    ' closes and returns
    Set oCN = Nothing
    Set oCM = Nothing
End Function
```

In this case, the code grabs a reference to the `ObjectContext` object through the `GetObjectContext` function. In methods that need a tighter interaction with the COM+ object context, storing the context reference in a variable is a more efficient solution since we query for the object's interface only once. We would do this in the following way:

```
Dim objCtxt As COMSVCS.ObjectContext
Set objCtxt = GetObjectContext()
```

At this point we have a COM+ enabled object but not a COM+ application. We'll further develop this application in Chapter 13. But first, we will look a little more at data access components that use XML and C++ OLE DB consumers.

Advantages of a COM-based API

We've mentioned the importance of having a COM-based API, whose functionality ASP pages can easily call. It's now time to put this into practice.

In the previous chapter, we mentioned that extra ASP pages could be used to make data available to a client rather than HTML pages containing data and graphics. Our Article Bazaar web site contains information that can be shared with any sort of application, not just traditional web browsers. If we have the need to broaden the scope of potential users to our site, then we'll soon come to realize that HTML is not our best friend. The reason is that HTML is a mixture of both data and graphics. While this is good for clients accessing the site using a web browser, this doesn't provide a good service to those applications that only require raw data in order to operate. XML provides the ideal means of returning only data.

Components are the easiest way to power all kinds of ASP pages; those that write HTML code and those that do not. An ASP page that does not output HTML can be considered to be a predecessor of a new type of web application, the **web service**.

An XML-Based Web Service

In this section, we're going to briefly look at using XML to populate our web page. Let's add a new page to the web site and call it `xmlquery.asp`. The skeleton of the page looks like this:

```
<%
  ' <--- Collect the arguments --->
  magazine = Request.QueryString("Magazine")
  yearofissue = Request.QueryString("Year")

  ' Set the MIME type
  Response.ContentType = "text/xml"
```

```
' Call the necessary components to get the data
' Convert them to XML if necessary
' Response.Write <the XML data>

Response.End
%>
```

The page supports two parameters: the magazine ID and the year of publication. This is only for the sake of simplicity; we could add more arguments if we so wished. The purpose of the page is to return an XML string to the caller through HTTP, which is why the MIME type is set to text/xml.

An important design issue is the XML schema that will be used. The XML schema, namely the structure of the XML stream being returned, and the name and query syntax of the page will have to be fully documented if external callers are able to connect to our site and use our data. We look at schemas in more detail in Chapter 24.

For our purposes, let's use the following XML schema:

```
<articles>
  <article title="…" author="…" magazine="…"
    issue="…" URL="…" keyword="…" >
    abstract
  </article>
...
</articles>
```

Our ASP page will now look like this:

```
<%
  function Quote(s)
    Quote = Chr(34) & Trim(s) & Chr(34)
  end function
%>
<%
  ' <--- Collect the arguments --->
  magazine = Request.QueryString("Magazine")
  yearofissue = Request.QueryString("Year")

  ' Set the MIME type
  Response.ContentType = "text/xml"

  ' Call the necessary components to get the data
  set o = Server.CreateObject("ArticleBazaar.Query")
  set oRS = o.GetArticles(magazine, yearofissue)

  ' Convert them to XML if necessary
  outBuf = "<articles>"
  while Not oRS.EOF
    outBuf = outBuf & "<article "

    outBuf = outBuf & "title=" & Quote(oRS("title")) & " "
    outBuf = outBuf & "author=" & Quote(oRS("author")) & " "
    outBuf = outBuf & "magazine=" & Quote(oRS("name")) & " "
    outBuf = outBuf & "issue=" & Quote(oRS("issue")) & " "
```

```
    outBuf = outBuf & "URL=" & Quote(oRS("URL")) & " "
    outBuf = outBuf & "Keyword=" & Quote(oRS("keyword")) & " "

    outBuf = outBuf & ">"
    outBuf = outBuf & oRS("abstract")
    outBuf = outBuf & "</article>"
    oRs.MoveNext
  wend
  outBuf = outBuf & "</articles>"

  ' Return the XML data
  Response.Write outBuf
  Response.End
%>
```

This ASP page and `queryart.asp` are using the same data access component. This ensures consistency across the application and simplifies maintenance. Suppose our web server is `http://expoware`, and the ASP pages are in the `aspdata` folder, we can call this page in any of the following three ways:

```
http://expoware/aspdata/xmlquery.asp?magazine=2&year=99
http://expoware/aspdata/xmlquery.asp?magazine=2
http://expoware/aspdata/xmlquery.asp?year=99
```

In the first case, we're asking for all the articles published in 1999 on the magazine with an ID of 2. The second URL returns all the articles from that same magazine for any year. Finally, the third URL is for all the articles published in 1999 for any magazine. Here's how Internet Explorer 5.0 displays the data:

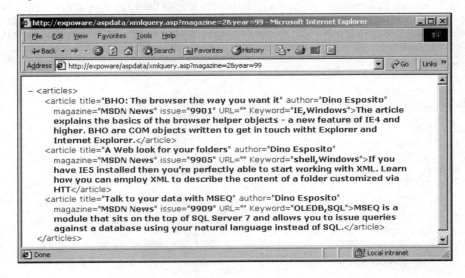

The XmlHttpRequest Object

One of the components that forms part of IE 5.x's object model is `XmlHttpRequest`, which issues an HTTP command wrapped up in a COM object. Any COM-aware application, from VBScript scripts to C++ or Visual Basic programs, can use this object to connect to a URL and get the required information via XML. Here's a first VBScript demo:

```
set xmlhttp = CreateObject("Microsoft.XmlHttp")
xmlhttp.open "POST", _
    "http://localhost/xmlquery.asp?magazine=2&year=99", 0
xmlhttp.send ""
msgbox xmlhttp.responseText
```

*More information about the syntax of this object can be found at
http://msdn.microsoft.com/library/psdk/xmlsdk/xmld8bp0.htm*

And this the output, inserted into a standard message box:

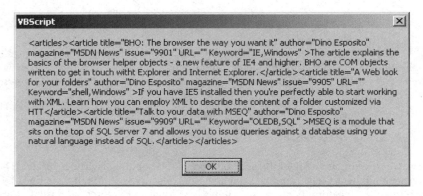

The Visual Basic code shown below gives us a more precise idea of how a desktop application takes advantage of the data we expose through XML. Instead of dumping the raw XML to the message box, the VB application uses the MSXML DOM (Document Object Model) and runs two queries against the Article Bazaar web site: one to get all the magazines, and one to get the selected articles. We'll look at the MSXML DOM in Chapter 25.

```
Private g_xmlHttp As New MSXML.XMLHTTPRequest
Const MYURL = "http://localhost/xmlquery2.asp?"

Private Sub Form_Load()
    Dim nIndex As Integer
    Dim xmldom As MSXML.DOMDocument
    Dim url As String
    Dim xmlItem As MSXML.IXMLDOMNode

    url = MYURL & "magazine=all"
    g_xmlHttp.open "POST", url, 0
    g_xmlHttp.send ""

    Set xmldom = g_xmlHttp.responseXML

    nIndex = 0
    For Each xmlItem In xmldom.documentElement.childNodes
        cboMags.AddItem xmlItem.Attributes(1).Text
        cboMags.ItemData(nIndex) = xmlItem.Attributes(0).Text
        nIndex = nIndex + 1
    Next
```

```
        cboMags.ListIndex = 1
    End Sub

    Private Sub cmdGo_Click()
        Dim xmldom As MSXML.DOMDocument
        Dim url As String

        url = MYURL
        url = url & "magazine=" & cboMags.ItemData(cboMags.ListIndex)
        url = url & "&year=" & txtYear.Text

        g_xmlHttp.open "POST", url, 0
        g_xmlHttp.send ""

        Set xmldom = g_xmlHttp.responseXML

        ' process XML
        nIndex = 0
        For Each xmlItem In xmldom.documentElement.childNodes
            List1.AddItem xmlItem.Attributes(0).Text & ",  " & _
                    xmlItem.Attributes(1).Text
            nIndex = nIndex + 1
        Next
    End Sub
```

We also need to expose the list of all the available magazines. The schema for magazines will be of the following form:

```
<magazines>
  <magazine magID="..." name="...">
  </magazine>
...
</magazines>
```

To actually expose a list of all the available magazines, we would use the following command:

```
http://expoware/xmlquery.asp2?magazine=all
```

The xmlquery.asp page is modified as follows:

```
<%
  function Quote(s)
    Quote = Chr(34) & Trim(s) & Chr(34)
  end function

  ' <--- Collect the arguments --->
  magazine = Request.QueryString("Magazine")
  yearofissue = Request.QueryString("Year")

  ' Set the MIME type
  Response.ContentType = "text/xml"

  ' Call the necessary components to get the data and convert it to XML
  set o = Server.CreateObject("ArticleBazaar.Query")
```

```
    if magazine = "all" then
      set oRS = o.GetMagazines()
      outBuf = AllMagazines(oRS)
    else
      set oRS = o.GetArticles(magazine, yearofissue)
      outBuf = SelectedArticles(oRS)
    end if
  ' Return the XML data
  Response.Write outBuf
  Response.End


Function SelectedArticles(oRS)
  outBuf = "<articles>"
  while Not oRS.EOF
    outBuf = outBuf & "<article "

    outBuf = outBuf & "title=" & Quote(oRS("title")) & " "
    outBuf = outBuf & "author=" & Quote(oRS("author")) & " "
    outBuf = outBuf & "magazine=" & Quote(oRS("name")) & " "
    outBuf = outBuf & "issue=" & Quote(oRS("issue")) & " "
    outBuf = outBuf & "URL=" & Quote(oRS("URL")) & " "
    outBuf = outBuf & "Keyword=" & Quote(oRS("keyword")) & " "

    outBuf = outBuf & ">"
    outBuf = outBuf & oRS("abstract")
    outBuf = outBuf & "</article>"
    oRS.MoveNext
  wend
  outBuf = outBuf & "</articles>"
  SelectedArticles = outBuf
End Function

Function AllMagazines(oRS)
  outBuf = "<magazines>"
  while Not oRS.EOF
    outBuf = outBuf & "<magazine "

    outBuf = outBuf & "id=" & Quote(oRS("magID")) & " "
    outBuf = outBuf & "name=" & Quote(oRS("name")) & " "

    outBuf = outBuf & ">"
    outBuf = outBuf & "</magazine>"
    oRS.MoveNext
  wend
  outBuf = outBuf & "</magazines>"
  AllMagazines = outBuf
End Function
%>
```

Here's what the final Visual Basic form looks like:

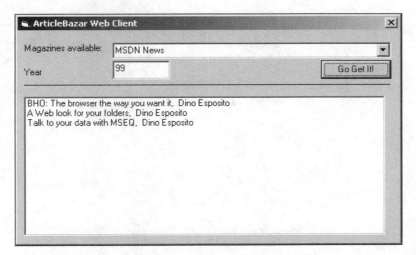

This application is completely responsible for drawing the user interface, yet it takes its XML-formatted data from the web site. Both the web site and the application make use of the same data access components.

Summary

In this chapter, we created some data access components, and improved the Article Bazaar web site by delegating all our data access code to components written with VB and using ADO objects. In developing our application, we discussed what stateless objects are and how they might be used and also showed how to expose the site content to desktop applications through XML.

In the next chapter, we'll revisit most of these topics as show we how to create a custom OLE DB consumer using C++ and ATL.

12

Building OLE DB Components

In the previous chapter we developed some COM-based functionality for our Article Bazaar web application, and we put in a link to the COM+ runtime environment, which enabled the application to scale up and give better performance – more on this in the next chapter. However, when we develop any web solution using ASP and Visual Basic components, we have to come to a compromise between two contrasting programming criteria. On one hand, we want to develop easy, less error-prone solutions. On the other hand, we also want to maximize performance, although we know that the system itself and the network latency can have *the* critical effect on the overall performance of an application – there is little advantage of developing very fast, efficient code if our network cannot cope with it. Most of today's real-world systems sacrifice speed and efficiency in favor of ease of development and simple project management, thereby minimizing the risk of nasty bugs arising from memory leaks or invalid pointer assignment. This means that a "managed" runtime environment like that of Visual Basic's, combined with the intuitiveness of ASP and the inherent simplicity of VBA, is perceived as an attractive solution, especially for those consulting companies that get their bread and butter from building distributed DNA systems.

However, if there is a need for raw programming power, and we are prepared for longer development time, then we can write and deploy C++ components. However, spending days to test and tune a complex C++ component is difficult for two reasons. First, it might now be quite difficult to find C++ experts that are both available and relatively cheap. Secondly, although inherently less scalable, elegant, and perhaps even ethically dubious, employing faster hardware has the same effect as using more efficient components, and more often than not, this also turns out to be the most cost-effective solution.

In this chapter, we'll look at the benefits of employing C++ components in the context of a DNA system, and we'll briefly recap the main reasons for adopting Visual C++, ATL and custom OLE DB consumers (rather than ADO) to optimize a web application. Of course, if any in your development team feels comfortable with C++, there is really nothing to stop you from using ISAPI DLLs in place of ASP, and ATL components instead of ADO. Such applications might be harder to debug and inherently more error-prone, but if we know what we're doing, then we can create some very useful applications.

By the end of this chapter, we will have looked at:

❑ When to use C++ OLE DB components in web applications.

❑ How to write ASP components that get data through OLE DB consumers.

❑ The trials and tribulations of using ADO with C++.

❑ Why stored procedures always provide the best way of optimizing an application.

By way of illustration, we'll start off by implementing the same components as in the previous chapter, but this time using Visual C++ and ATL.

C++ Components Aren't Second Class Components

I don't know why, but it seems that when it comes to writing distributed, Web based systems using Microsoft technologies, the preferred tools are undoubtedly ASP and Visual Basic. Even though the advantages of using C++ are clearly evident, many project managers prefer to push their top-notch experts towards Visual Basic development instead of putting them to work on C++ and ATL. If more speed is required, then the solution that is often imposed on us involves purchasing faster hardware rather than producing faster code.

ASP and Visual Basic are a good compromise between usability, ease of development and performance. Yet this is very much a historical compromise; ASP is powered by interpreting scripting engines, while VB still retains the virtual machine model behind the compiled code. Only C++ can deliver truly compiled, fast and compact code.

The ideal replacement for ASP would be an ISAPI DLL. However, we shouldn't forget that ASP came after ISAPI DLLs, and was introduced to make up for the scarcely practical solution represented by ISAPI extensions. ASP allows us to "see" the page while we're writing it, and we can intersperse raw HTML tags and code blocks without writing our own parser for our own page template, as was the case during the glorious age of CGI.

Considering ASP an essential component in a modern Web based architecture, to improve server-side performance and try to serve more pages in the same timeframe, we must consider using C++ components instead of VB ones. C++ components are definitely not a second-class choice when designing and building a distributed system. However, there is a degree of psychological risk when choosing to adopt C++. We might be expert developers, but if we think that writing error handling and debugging code consists of just using "On Error" constructs, we are in for a shock.

So the question is, under which circumstances would we consider using C++ components?

❑ To implement particularly complex business rules.

❑ To access data via raw OLE DB providers.

❑ When we absolutely need to squeeze out every little bit of performance.

Normally, developing business rules requires us to code complex algorithms, and these require the use of fast code if they are to run efficiently. Business objects that provide the logic of the application must function as quickly as possible – so the faster the code, the better.

Microsoft created OLE DB with performance in mind – it is supposed to be the fastest way to get and set data. Not every application we would want to write would need this level of optimization, but OLE DB's speed and power is there if required. However, what is OLE DB reputed to be faster than? It is faster than any other general-purpose API at accessing data. It is certainly faster than ADO, but is not necessarily and automatically faster than ODBC.

C++ components run generally faster than Visual Basic components, even though the overall performance of a web application is determined by the network bandwidth, latency and the amount of data to be transferred. Normally, using C++ components only really ensures that the components themselves are faster, they do not automatically ensure that our users are given better performance. This somewhat obvious consideration is what ultimately causes developers to adopt the ASP/VB model. On the other hand, companies don't normally invest resources into producing elegant and perfect projects – an imperfect and rather patched up system that works on time and on budget is often seen as better than a system that meets all the criteria of a perfect world, but is not ready to work on demand.

Towards C++ Active Server Pages

The beauty of the ASP model is that it brings the effectiveness of C++ templatized code to a new type of application model, the product tentatively called **ATL Server**.

ATL (**Active Template Library**) is a library of class templates that support COM components. It enables us to create classes that form the basis for ActiveX components, but without the large overhead associated with using **MFC** (the **Microsoft Foundation Class** library). In other words, it enables us to produce very efficient, lightweight components; just what we want if we want to optimize performance.

ATL Server will form part of Visual C++ .Net, an integral part of the Visual Studio .Net environment. It provides a set of classes that interact natively with IIS through ISAPI. As developers, most of the complexities of ATL will be hidden from us to a much greater degree than in ATL 3.0.

With ATL Server, we should be able to design dynamic ASP-like pages using C++ code to insert dynamic blocks of text. Any code block will evaluate to a method of the C++ template class that sends HTML text through the I/O standard console. The result is a new template file (using a `.srf` extension instead of `.asp`), which contains a mix of HTML tags and calls to C++ functions with a predefined signature and running compiled code. The overall model is just like ASP, but without the burden of the scripting engines.

OLE DB, ODBC and ADO

Microsoft pushes OLE DB as the preferred technology for data-driven applications deployed over the Web. Architecturally speaking, OLE DB is superior to ODBC only because it was designed to be. As we saw in Chapter 6, OLE DB is heavily based on COM and this eliminates the need for a runtime layer that locates the ODBC driver and maps calls to the actual driver entry-points. It is also true that OLE DB is much more flexible when it comes to accessing data. Through services and data providers we can grab just about any data – no matter what the storage media involved and their physical location.

In our imperfect world, though, flexibility always comes at a price. The more flexible we are, the more layers of code we need to traverse in order to get the expected results. So questions do arise: is OLE DB really faster than ODBC? And what about ADO?

ODBC is generally faster if we want to fetch sequential rows, and in particular when we do bulk fetching. The reason is that ODBC takes only one call to retrieve all the needed rows.

OLE DB is generally faster when we want to fetch individual rows from a database. OLE DB takes two calls to retrieve data. In the first step, we call the `IRowset::GetNextRows()` to get a handle to the row (`HROW`). Next, we invoke `IRowset::GetData()` to obtain the data for a given row. `GetData` takes the previously retrieved `HROW` to identify the specific record.

OLE DB doesn't implement bulk fetching in quite the same way as ODBC. We can fetch multiple row handles in OLE DB, but we can only get data for one row at a time. The SQL Server 7.0 provider constitutes a pleasant exception, since it implements a specific `IRowsetFastLoad` interface to enable a consumer application to obtain a true bulk fetch capability. Once we hold a connection to the data source, we set the provider-specific property `SSPROP_ENABLEFASTLOAD` to `True`, and create the session:

```
IDBProperties *pIProps;
DBPROP rgps[1];
DBPROPSET PropSet;
rgps[0].dwPropertyID = SSPROP_ENABLEFASTLOAD;
rgps[0].vValue.boolVal = VARIANT_TRUE;
PropSet.rgProperties = rgps;
pIDBInit->QueryInterface(IID_IDBProperties, &pIProps);
pIProps->SetProperties(1, &PropSet);
```

For general applications that access traditional databases, if we use ODBC or OLE DB, we will not detect any great difference in performance. The introduction of OLE DB was meant to facilitate access to both relational and non relational data through the same functionality. As we said earlier in this book, ODBC can only access relational data.

When choosing between OLE DB and ODBC, we have to consider what functionality we want the provider or driver to provide. I remember a client who enthusiastically embraced OLE DB when it shipped with Visual Studio 6.0 more than two years ago. He had to maintain an Oracle database and planned to use the Oracle OLE DB provider. However, we found out to our cost that at that time MDAC 2.0, the OLE DB provider for Oracle, lacked several key classes of useful functionality, so we turned back to ODBC.

Is ADO Faster or Easier?

Whereas OLE DB and ODBC are two comparable data access technologies, ADO is different from both. In fact, ADO provides a means of utilizing either OLE DB or ODBC to get data, though in reality, it only has direct access to OLE DB functionality. Unless we specify an OLE DB provider, ADO defaults to the OLE DB provider for ODBC drivers, which makes it *seem* like we are using ODBC.

Although highly optimized, ADO is not as fast as raw OLE DB, and should not be expected to be. ADO constitutes an extra layer of components that our ASP script or VB code has to use. ADO exposes an object model which normalizes all types to `Variant` – a process which itself incurs a large performance hit. It also performs validation tasks, checks the values we assign to properties, and the overall context in which any method call takes place. For example, ADO automatically converts the cursor location to the right value according to the cursor type, and vice versa. As we can imagine, this process involves repeated database checks that will slow down the application.

So ADO is never faster than OLE DB, and in my experience – somewhat confirmed by non-scientific opinions of colleagues and friends – OLE DB has been shown to work twice as fast as ADO. ADO might be easy to use, and suffices for most applications, but if we really need that extra kick, we should consider writing custom OLE DB consumers in C++ instead of going with the mainstream and choosing ADO and VB.

When ADO is Easier

ADO was developed specifically for VB/ASP programmers, being geared specifically to the VB programming environment. Using ADO with C++ is possible, but is rather troublesome.

- ❏ Setting properties in C++ is not as easy as with VB or VBScript.

- ❏ If we avoid or limit the use of properties, we end up working with methods with rather long parameter lists without having the facility of optional parameters.

- ❏ We see pointers everywhere.

When C++ Is Not Enough

Raw OLE DB calls can improve the overall speed of the component, but what about components that spend much of their time waiting for a response from a database server? In this case, the advantage of optimized code is often negligible, since the overall performance is determined by the database. C++ enhances the performance of a component if it has to preprocess or postprocess data it gets from the database. Unless C++ is our favorite programming language, or the language of choice for the project, doing a simple `select * from authors` and returning is overkill.

Data Access in C++

Now that we've explained some of the guidelines for using C++ to build data access components, let's see how to do it in practice. We'll start by looking again at the `ArticleBazaar.Query` object from the previous chapter. However, this time we will be using ATL and Visual C++ 6.0 to create it.

To start, we create an ATL project using the ATL Object Wizard. We insert a new ATL object from the Data Access category. The type of object we're interested in is the Consumer.

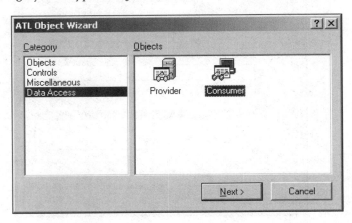

The next step requires us to select the data source and set a few options to support deletes and inserts, as well as to use a table or a command base class for the consumer. The values in the C++ box are filled out by the Wizard after we have selected the table. We can change these if we so wish.

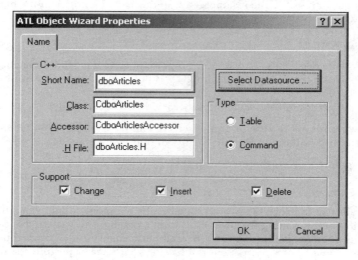

By clicking on Select Datasource, we can set the OLE DB provider and its connection string arguments.

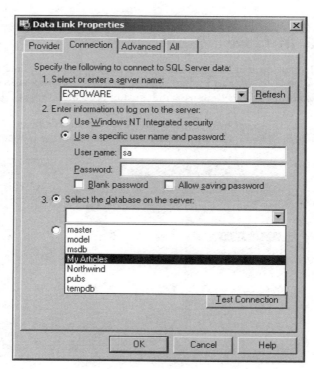

We select the database and then the specific table we want – in this case, `dbo.Articles`.

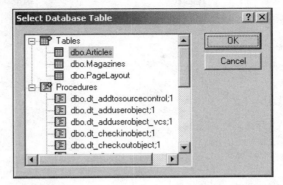

The wizard adds a new header file to our Visual C++ project. In this case, the file is `dboArticles.h`. The wizard generates the following code. So far there's really nothing different from what we saw back in Chapter 6 when we were discussing the OLE DB basics:

```cpp
// dboArticles.H : Declaration of the CdboArticles class

#ifndef __DBOARTICLES_H_
#define __DBOARTICLES_H_

class CdboArticlesAccessor
{
public:
    SHORT m_Magazine;
    TCHAR m_Author[51];
    TCHAR m_Issue[51];
    TCHAR m_Title[51];
    TCHAR m_Abstract[1024];
    TCHAR m_URL[51];
    SHORT m_ArticleID;
    TCHAR m_Keyword[51];

BEGIN_COLUMN_MAP(CdboArticlesAccessor)
    COLUMN_ENTRY(1, m_Magazine)
    COLUMN_ENTRY(2, m_Author)
    COLUMN_ENTRY(3, m_Issue)
    COLUMN_ENTRY(4, m_Title)
    COLUMN_ENTRY(5, m_Abstract)
    COLUMN_ENTRY(6, m_URL)
    COLUMN_ENTRY(7, m_ArticleID)
    COLUMN_ENTRY(8, m_Keyword)
END_COLUMN_MAP()

DEFINE_COMMAND(CdboArticlesAccessor, _T(" \
    SELECT \
        Magazine, \
        Author, \
        Issue, \
        Title, \
        Abstract, \
        URL, \
        ArticleID, \
        Keyword \
        FROM dbo.Articles"))
```

397

```
        void ClearRecord()
        {
            memset(this, 0, sizeof(*this));
        }
};

class CdboArticles : public CCommand<CAccessor<CdboArticlesAccessor> >
{
public:
    HRESULT Open()
    {
        HRESULT hr;

        hr = OpenDataSource();
        if (FAILED(hr))
            return hr;

        return OpenRowset();
    }
    HRESULT OpenDataSource()
    {
        HRESULT hr;
        CDataSource db;
        CDBPropSet     dbinit(DBPROPSET_DBINIT);

        dbinit.AddProperty(DBPROP_AUTH_USERID, OLESTR("sa"));
        dbinit.AddProperty(DBPROP_INIT_CATALOG, OLESTR("My Articles"));
        dbinit.AddProperty(DBPROP_INIT_DATASOURCE, OLESTR("EXPOWARE"));
        dbinit.AddProperty(DBPROP_INIT_LCID, (long)1033);
        dbinit.AddProperty(DBPROP_INIT_PROMPT, (short)4);
        hr = db.Open(_T("SQLOLEDB.1"), &dbinit);
        if (FAILED(hr))
            return hr;

        return m_session.Open(db);
    }
    HRESULT OpenRowset()
    {
        // Set properties for open
        CDBPropSet     propset(DBPROPSET_ROWSET);
        propset.AddProperty(DBPROP_IRowsetChange, true);
        propset.AddProperty(DBPROP_UPDATABILITY,
            DBPROPVAL_UP_CHANGE |
            DBPROPVAL_UP_INSERT |
            DBPROPVAL_UP_DELETE);

        return CCommand<CAccessor<CdboArticlesAccessor> >
                ::Open(m_session, NULL, &propset);
    }

    CSession m_session;
};

#endif // __DBOARTICLES_H_
```

The file describes the consumer class CdboArticles. Through its methods, we open a session with the hard-coded data source (see the OpenDataSource method) and run a full table SELECT command. As we saw in Chapter 6, by slightly modifying this code we can make it work for SELECT as well as INSERT, UPDATE or DELETE commands.

The listing contains what the wizard generated from our input. This needs some refinement in order to work as the C++ equivalent of the `ArticleBazaar.Query` component. This is what we will do:

❑ Obtain a data consumer class that can either run a query, or insert, or new record in the ArticleBazaar database.

❑ Define a wrapper automation component that uses the consumer class.

❑ Determine a way to make the results externally available to the caller page.

Defining the Consumer Class

The wizard-generated code makes a number of assumptions that might not be appropriate for us. First, it assumes that we have a static default command to execute – this is what the `DEFINE_COMMAND` macro does. It expands to a class member function called `GetDefaultCommand()` that is in turn called by the `CCommand::Open()` method to figure out what to do. See `atldbcli.h` for more details.

In our case, we have a parameterized command that is given by a `SELECT` command plus a dynamically determined `WHERE` clause. The `WHERE` clause depends on the magazine ID and the particular issue we want to get data for. The SQL command will now look like this:

```
SELECT   Magazines.Name,
         Articles.Author,
         Articles.Issue,
         Articles.Title,
         Articles.Abstract,
         Articles.URL,
         Articles.Keyword
FROM Magazines
INNER JOIN Articles ON
         Magazines.MagID=Articles.Magazine
```

To this string, we will need to add a proper `WHERE` clause. As a result, we will not need to use `DEFINE_COMMAND`, and so we can get rid of it.

A second modification is the addition of a method to prepare the SQL string from the magazine ID and the issue string – `GetFinalCommandText`.

Finally, the signature of the consumer's `Open` method needs to be altered. The wizard assigns no arguments to it and in Chapter 6 we showed how to modify it to accommodate a command string and make the whole consumer class more dynamic. Here, we could move all the command preparation phase into the `Open`'s body and make it accept only the magazine ID and the issue. The following listing presents the final version of the `CdboArticles` consumer class:

```
// dboArticles.H : Declaration of the CdboArticles class

#ifndef __DBOARTICLES_H_
#define __DBOARTICLES_H_

// ***********************************************************
//    Constants
// ***********************************************************
const TCHAR *QUERYCMD_BASETEXT = _T(" \
    SELECT \
        Magazines.Name, \
```

```
          Articles.Author, \
          Articles.Issue, \
          Articles.Title, \
          Articles.Abstract, \
          Articles.URL, \
          Articles.Keyword \
     FROM Magazines \
     INNER JOIN Articles ON \
          Magazines.MagID=Articles.Magazine ");

// *****************************************************************
//    The Accessor class
// *****************************************************************
class CdboArticlesAccessor
{
public:
    TCHAR m_Name[51];
    TCHAR m_Issue[51];
    TCHAR m_Author[51];
    TCHAR m_Title[51];
    TCHAR m_Abstract[1024];
    TCHAR m_URL[51];
    TCHAR m_Keyword[51];

BEGIN_COLUMN_MAP(CdboArticlesAccessor)
    COLUMN_ENTRY(1, m_Name)
    COLUMN_ENTRY(2, m_Issue)
    COLUMN_ENTRY(3, m_Author)
    COLUMN_ENTRY(4, m_Title)
    COLUMN_ENTRY(5, m_Abstract)
    COLUMN_ENTRY(6, m_URL)
    COLUMN_ENTRY(7, m_Keyword)
END_COLUMN_MAP()

    void ClearRecord()
    {
        memset(this, 0, sizeof(*this));
    }
};

// *****************************************************************
//    The data consumer class
// *****************************************************************
class CdboArticles : public CCommand<CAccessor<CdboArticlesAccessor> >
{
public:
// -------------------------------------------------------------
// Prepares the parameterized command text for execution
// -------------------------------------------------------------
HRESULT GetFinalCommandText(long nMagID, LPCTSTR szYear, LPTSTR szCommand)
{
    if (szCommand == NULL)
        return E_POINTER;

// *** if year has been specified...
    TCHAR szWhereYear[50];
    lstrcpy(szWhereYear, _T(""));
    if (lstrlen(szYear))
        wsprintf(szWhereYear, _T(" Issue Like'%s%%'"), szYear);
```

```
        // *** if the magazine ID has been specified...
        TCHAR szWhereMagz[50];
        lstrcpy(szWhereMagz, _T(""));
        if (nMagID >0)
            wsprintf(szWhereMagz, _T("Magazine=%d"), nMagID);

        // *** prepares the WHERE clause...
        TCHAR szWhere[100];
        lstrcpy(szWhere, _T(""));
        if (lstrlen(szWhereYear) && lstrlen(szWhereMagz))
            wsprintf(szWhere, _T(" WHERE %s AND %s"), szWhereYear, szWhereMagz);
        else
        if (lstrlen(szWhereYear) || lstrlen(szWhereMagz))
        {
            if (lstrlen(szWhereYear))
                wsprintf(szWhere, _T(" WHERE %s"), szWhereYear);
            if (lstrlen(szWhereMagz))
                wsprintf(szWhere, _T(" WHERE %s"), szWhereMagz);
        }

        // completes the base command attaching the WHERE clause...
        wsprintf(szCommand, _T("%s%s"), QUERYCMD_BASETEXT, szWhere);
        return S_OK;
}

// ------------------------------------------------------------
// Runs the command and returns a rowset if any
// ------------------------------------------------------------
HRESULT Open(long nMagID, LPCTSTR szYear)
{
    HRESULT hr;
    // prepare the query command text
    TCHAR szCommand[1024];
    hr = GetFinalCommandText(nMagID, szYear, szCommand);
    if (FAILED(hr))
        return hr;

    // open the data source and go...
    hr = OpenDataSource();
    if (FAILED(hr))
        return hr;
    return OpenRowset(szCommand);
}


// ------------------------------------------------------------
// Open the data source
// ------------------------------------------------------------
HRESULT OpenDataSource()
{
    HRESULT hr;
    CDataSource db;
    CDBPropSet    dbinit(DBPROPSET_DBINIT);

    dbinit.AddProperty(DBPROP_AUTH_USERID, OLESTR("sa"));
    dbinit.AddProperty(DBPROP_INIT_CATALOG, OLESTR("My Articles"));
    dbinit.AddProperty(DBPROP_INIT_DATASOURCE, OLESTR("EXPOWARE"));
    dbinit.AddProperty(DBPROP_INIT_LCID, (long)1033);
    dbinit.AddProperty(DBPROP_INIT_PROMPT, (short)4);
    hr = db.Open(_T("SQLOLEDB.1"), &dbinit);
    if (FAILED(hr))
        return hr;
```

```
        return m_session.Open(db);
    }

    // ----------------------------------------------------------
    // Return the rowset in case of SELECT command
    // ----------------------------------------------------------
    HRESULT OpenRowset(LPCTSTR szCommand)
    {
        // Set properties for open
        CDBPropSet      propset(DBPROPSET_ROWSET);
        propset.AddProperty(DBPROP_IRowsetChange, true);
        propset.AddProperty(DBPROP_UPDATABILITY,
            DBPROPVAL_UP_CHANGE |
            DBPROPVAL_UP_INSERT |
            DBPROPVAL_UP_DELETE);

        return CCommand<CAccessor<CdboArticlesAccessor> >
            ::Open(m_session, szCommand, &propset);
    }

    CSession m_session;
};

#endif // __DBOARTICLES_H_
```

A client module would start the conversation by calling the CdboArticles::Open() method and specifying the magazine ID and the year of publication. This allows the consumer to prepare the SQL command and get the articles rowset, using GetFinalCommandText and OpenRowset. But who will be using the CdboArticles consumer class? We need the component to implement the IDispatch interface that would make it callable from within ASP pages.

Defining a Wrapper Component

Let's add a new object that provides methods to obtain all the records that match the specified criteria, again using the ATL Object Wizard. What we're doing here is adding methods that provide equivalent functionality to the VB component that we built earlier.

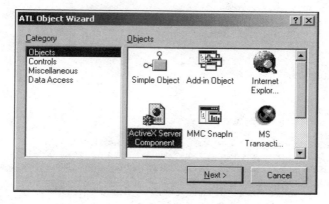

Let's pick up an ActiveX Server Component item from the objects category. The reasons for this will become clear later on. Such a component will be an ASP component in the sense that it can capture and pass a reference to ASP built-in objects to the OLE DB consumer.

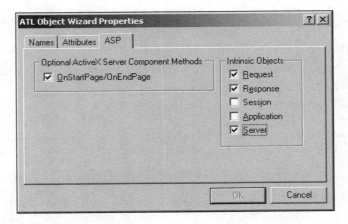

The extra **ASP** tabbed page allows us to customize the way in which the component works. The component will handle both an `OnStartPage` and an `OnEndPage` event and will make all the ASP intrinsic objects available except`Session` and `Application`. Here's the source code for this new `CArticleQuery` component class that is the coclass of the new `IArticleQuery` interface:

```cpp
// ArticleQuery.h : Declaration of the CArticleQuery

#ifndef __ARTICLEQUERY_H_
#define __ARTICLEQUERY_H_

#include "resource.h"       // main symbols
#include <asptlb.h>         // Active Server Pages Definitions

/////////////////////////////////////////////////////////////////////////////
// CArticleQuery
class ATL_NO_VTABLE CArticleQuery :
    public CComObjectRootEx<CComSingleThreadModel>,
    public CComCoClass<CArticleQuery, &CLSID_ArticleQuery>,
    public IDispatchImpl<IArticleQuery, &IID_IArticleQuery,
        &LIBID_ARTICLEBAZAARCPPLib>
{
public:
    CArticleQuery()
    { m_bOnStartPageCalled = FALSE; }

public:

DECLARE_REGISTRY_RESOURCEID(IDR_ARTICLEQUERY)
DECLARE_PROTECT_FINAL_CONSTRUCT()

BEGIN_COM_MAP(CArticleQuery)
    COM_INTERFACE_ENTRY(IArticleQuery)
    COM_INTERFACE_ENTRY(IDispatch)
END_COM_MAP()

// IArticleQuery
public:
    //Active Server Pages Methods
    STDMETHOD(OnStartPage)(IUnknown* pUnk);
    STDMETHOD(OnEndPage)();
```

```
private:
    CComPtr<IRequest> m_piRequest;        // Request Object
    CComPtr<IResponse> m_piResponse;       // Response Object
    CComPtr<IServer> m_piServer;          // Server Object
    BOOL m_bOnStartPageCalled;            // OnStartPage successful?
};

#endif //__ARTICLEQUERY_H_
```

To complete the object, let's add a new method called `GetArticles` that mimics the analogous method in the VB object. To do this, right-click on the `IarticleQuery` interface icon and select **New Method**.

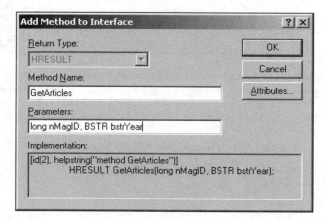

The method takes two arguments: a `long` being the ID of the magazine, and a `BSTR` denoting the year of publication. (Remember, the year of publication is a `yymm` string.) What follows is an excerpt of the component's IDL which describes the methods of the `IArticleQuery` interface. This is in the `ArticleBazaarCpp.idl` file.

```
interface IArticleQuery : IDispatch
{
    //Standard Server Side Component Methods
    HRESULT OnStartPage([in] IUnknown* piUnk);
    HRESULT OnEndPage();
    [id(1), helpstring("method GetArticles")]
        HRESULT GetArticles(long nMagID, BSTR bstrYear);
};
```

The declaration of the `CArticleQuery` class changes like this:

```
// IArticleQuery
public:
    STDMETHOD(GetArticles)(long nMagID, BSTR bstrYear);

    //Active Server Pages Methods
    STDMETHOD(OnStartPage)(IUnknown* IUnk);
    STDMETHOD(OnEndPage)();
...
```

An ASP page can contact the component through the standard automation interface and call into the `GetArticles` method.

`GetArticles` utilizes the `CdboArticles` class to do its data access:

```
#include "dboarticles.h"

...

STDMETHODIMP CArticleQuery::GetArticles(long nMagID, BSTR bstrYear)
{
    USES_CONVERSION;
    CdboArticles arts;

    arts.Open(nMagID, OLE2T(bstrYear));
    while(arts.MoveNext() == S_OK)
    {
        // do something with the rowset
    }

    return S_OK;
}
```

At this point, we come to a new problem. We need to enable the calling ASP page to display information taken from a recordset. The VB component returns a pointer to an ADO recordset object – which is immediately usable from within ASP. The C++ component manipulates a rowset object which is not directly usable from either VB or ASP. If we want our `GetArticles` method to return information about the records it selected, we have to do one of the following:

❑ Put ADO in our component and utilize it for the data access.

❑ Transform the rowset into a string – possibly, an XML string.

❑ Call the ASP objects from the C++ code, thereby minimizing the information transported from the component to the page.

Let's analyze the pros and the cons of each solution.

Why an ASP Component?

To make an ADO `Recordset` object available from a C++ component, we must include the ADO type library in our project before we can accomplish any data access tasks through ADO objects. Alternatively, we can dynamically create a recordset from an XML string, or instantiate it as an empty object and fill it up one record at a time.

To import ADO, we can do the following:

```
#import "c:\program files\…\msado15.dll"
    no_namespace rename("EOF", "EndOfFile")
```

The #import directive makes all the required ADO definitions and declarations available in the current scope.

The following code shows how we would run a query through ADO.

```
void RunQueryThruADO(LPCTSTR szSql)
{
    HRESULT          hr = NOERROR;
    _RecordsetPtr    pRS = NULL;
    FieldPtr         *rgflds = NULL;
    _variant_t       vValue;
    long             lNumFields;

    // open the recordset
    pRS.CreateInstance(__uuidof(Recordset));
    pRS->CursorLocation = adUseClient;
    pRS->Open(szSql, g_pszConnection, adOpenForwardOnly,
        adLockReadOnly, adCmdUnspecified);

    // disconnection
    _variant_t vNull;
    VariantInit(&vNull);
    pRS->put_ActiveConnection(vNull);

    // number of fields
    lNumFields = pRS->Fields->Count;

    // zero memory for fields
    rgflds = new FieldPtr[lNumFields];
    if (!rgflds)
        return;
    ZeroMemory(rgflds, lNumFields * sizeof(FieldPtr));

    // fill the array of fields
    for (long i=0; i<lNumFields; i++)
        rgflds[i] = pRS->Fields->GetItem(i);

    // process the records
    while (VARIANT_FALSE == pRS->EndOfFile)
    {
        long lFieldIndex = 1;
        vValue = rgflds[lFieldIndex]->Value;
        // do something with the field value
        pRS->MoveNext();
    }

    pRS->Close();
    delete [] rgflds;
    pRS = NULL;
    return;
}
```

Using ADO in a consumer module written in C++ doesn't make much sense, since ADO has been developed and documented with Visual Basic in mind. This doesn't strictly impact the code but makes all the code to write more expensive and somewhat repetitious. A second reason is that C++ is the tool of choice if we need optimal performance, which ADO cannot achieve. On the other hand, by using ADO, we can return recordsets back to the caller without having to do any extra processing. If getting recordsets is all that is required, then by all means go for ADO in C++.

XML As a Universal Glue

If returning recordset objects is a problem, we can force the component's method to return a string. In other words, the rowset can be transformed into a string or an array. In both cases, we need to write custom client-side code to process the data. From this point of view, a much better solution is to use XML. The advantages of doing this are:

❑   It is platform-independent.

❑   It allows for data to be described.

The rowset content could be marshaled through XML using a customized schema. The ASP page would then be responsible for postprocessing the XML stream and building a valid object that can work properly in its context.For example, we might use the XML data as the input data to create a recordset based on that information.

Direct Use of ASP Intrinsic Methods

Earlier in the chapter, we identified the practical limitation of ASP in that it is based on interpreted scripts. Then, the solution was to take as much script code out of the page as possible. On the other hand, to swing over to the opposite extreme – putting all the code into a component – we will probably encounter serious development problems with testing, debugging, and maintenance.

The choice of using an ActiveX Server component – an ASP component –saves us from this potential problem. In fact, it is just this type of component that enables us to call the ASP intrinsic objects from within C++ code. Therefore, we can write to the standard output console and bring a portion of the ASP page into the compiled component. In this way, we solve the problem of returning information back to the client and also reduce overhead, although performance takes a hit.

The ATL wizard can prepare the code infrastructure for accessing Response and Request objects. The ASP property page we saw above allows us to choose which ASP object we want to manipulate. In our example, the CArticleQuery class stores three pointers to Response, Request and Server:

```
private:
    CComPtr<IRequest> m_piRequest;        // Request Object
    CComPtr<IResponse> m_piResponse;      // Response Object
    CComPtr<IServer> m_piServer;          // Server Object
    BOOL m_bOnStartPageCalled;            // OnStartPage successful?
```

These variables are initialized during the initialization of the page that refers the object. From the object's point of view, this means that the OnStartPage method is invoked and passed a pointer to the IUnknown interface of the ASP runtime. This interface can then be queried for IScriptingContext and then for IResponse, IRequest and Iserver:

```
STDMETHODIMP CArticleQuery::OnStartPage (IUnknown* pUnk)
{
    if(!pUnk)
        return E_POINTER;
```

```
        CComPtr<IScriptingContext> spContext;
        HRESULT hr;

        // Get the IScriptingContext Interface
        hr = pUnk->QueryInterface(IID_IScriptingContext, (void **)&spContext);
        if(FAILED(hr))
            return hr;

        // Get Request Object Pointer
        hr = spContext->get_Request(&m_piRequest);
        if(FAILED(hr))
        {
            spContext.Release();
            return hr;
        }

        // Get Response Object Pointer
        hr = spContext->get_Response(&m_piResponse);
        if(FAILED(hr))
        {
            m_piRequest.Release();
            return hr;
        }

        // Get Server Object Pointer
        hr = spContext->get_Server(&m_piServer);
        if(FAILED(hr))
        {
            m_piRequest.Release();
            m_piResponse.Release();
            return hr;
        }

        m_bOnStartPageCalled = TRUE;
        return S_OK;
}
```

From now on, we use m_piResponse each time we need to send HTML code back to the browser.

The Creation of the Query Page

The ProgID of the ATL-based component is ArticleBazaarCpp.ArticleQuery. As usual, the first part of the name is the name of the project (as well as the name of the resulting DLL) while the second part is the name of the class implementing the functionality. The class has a GetArticles method that returns a COM error code (HRESULT) and sends HTML code directly through Response. In this way, the overall structure of the page gets simplified. Before delving into the code for GetArticles, let's see what the main part of the queryart.asp page looks like now:

```
<%
    if bFirstTime then
        Response.end
    end if

    set o = Server.CreateObject("ArticleBazaarCpp.ArticleQuery")
    o.GetArticles strMagID, strYear
%>
```

We no longer need to code the HTML table, or scan the recordset and fill the various rows. All this takes place in the `GetArticles` method of the C++ component:

```cpp
STDMETHODIMP CArticleQuery::GetArticles(long nMagID, BSTR bstrYear)
{
    USES_CONVERSION;
    const MAXBUFSIZE = 1024;

    CdboArticles arts;
    TCHAR buf[MAXBUFSIZE], temp[MAXBUFSIZE];
    LPTSTR pszYear = OLE2T(bstrYear);
    HINSTANCE hInst = _Module.m_hInst;

    // open the data source and get the rowset
    arts.Open(nMagID, pszYear);

    // count the records
    int nRecs = 0;
    while(arts.MoveNext() == S_OK)
    { nRecs++; }

    // create the result string "N articles from XXX in YYYY"
    LoadString(hInst, IDS_RESULTS1, temp, MAXBUFSIZE);
    wsprintf(buf, temp, nRecs, arts.m_Name);
    m_piResponse->Write(CComVariant(buf));

    if (lstrlen(pszYear)) {
        LoadString(hInst, IDS_RESULTS2, temp, MAXBUFSIZE);
        wsprintf(buf, temp, pszYear);
        m_piResponse->Write(CComVariant(buf));
    }

    // no record found
    if (nRecs==0)
        return S_OK;

    // write the table header
    LoadString(hInst, IDS_TABLEHEADING, buf, MAXBUFSIZE);
    m_piResponse->Write(CComVariant(buf));

    // fill the table
    arts.MoveFirst();
    while (TRUE)
    {
        // column: Title
        LoadString(hInst, IDS_COLUMNTITLE, temp, MAXBUFSIZE);
        wsprintf(buf, temp, arts.m_Title);
        m_piResponse->Write(CComVariant(buf));

        // column: Author
        LoadString(hInst, IDS_COLUMNAUTHOR, temp, MAXBUFSIZE);
        wsprintf(buf, temp, arts.m_Author);
        m_piResponse->Write(CComVariant(buf));

        // column: Name
        LoadString(hInst, IDS_COLUMNNAME, temp, MAXBUFSIZE);
        wsprintf(buf, temp, arts.m_Name);
        m_piResponse->Write(CComVariant(buf));

        // column: Issue
        LoadString(hInst, IDS_COLUMNISSUE, temp, MAXBUFSIZE);
        wsprintf(buf, temp, arts.m_Issue);
```

```
            m_piResponse->Write(CComVariant(buf));

            // column: Abstract
            LoadString(hInst, IDS_COLUMNABSTRACT, temp, MAXBUFSIZE);
            wsprintf(buf, temp,arts.m_Abstract);
            m_piResponse->Write (CComVariant(buf));

            // jump to the next row
            HRESULT hr = arts.MoveNext();
            if (hr != S_OK)
                break;
    }

    // write the table footer
    LoadString(hInst, IDS_TABLEFOOTER, buf, MAXBUFSIZE);
    m_piResponse->Write (CComVariant(buf));

    return S_OK;
}
```

The query page has two main elements: the row with the results (the number of articles found), and the table with the selected records. The equivalent VB `GetArticle` and `GetArticleXML` methods return a disconnected ADO recordset that gives the total number of records as well as the content. Here, we just scroll the list of records and fill in the table.

However, in C++ we manipulate rowsets, which are wrapped by ADO `Recordset` objects. However, rowsets and recordsets are quite different. For instance, a rowset doesn't allow us to know easily how many rows have been selected, whereas we can easily find out how many records a recordset contains. Knowing how many rows there are in a rowset is the first practical problem we have to solve in order to use the component from the `queryart.asp` page. The second problem is how to handle all the calls to `Response.Write` that are necessary to complete the page. Let's take a look at how we can overcome these problems.

Determining the Length of a Rowset

A simple solution to the first problem is scanning the rowset until the end and putting the count into a variable.

```
arts.Open(nMagID, pszYear);
int nRecs = 0;
while(arts.MoveNext() == S_OK)
{ nRecs++; }
```

If we need to scroll back and forth through a rowset, we need to pay attention to the real first row fetch position of the rowset. When we create a new rowset, the internal pointer that indicates which is the next row to fetch is set to a position *before* the first record, rather than to the first record itself. When this pointer is moved using `MoveNext` or `MoveFirst`, this initial predefined state is lost. In other words, the two following code snippets return different values. The following code:

```
' Rowset pointer set to a position before the first record
arts.Open(nMagID, pszYear);
int nRecs = 0;
while(arts.MoveNext() == S_OK)
{ nRecs++; }
```

returns a different value to this:

```
' Rowset pointer set to first record
arts.MoveFirst();
int nRecs = 0;
while(arts.MoveNext() == S_OK)
{ nRecs++; }
```

The second loop skips the first record.

This happens because in the first code section, when the rowset is opened, it is in its initial state – that is, the state it holds immediately after being created. Calling `MoveFirst` doesn't restore this initial state but simply moves the pointer to the first record. The loop governed by the `while` statement, though, begins with a `MoveNext`. This means that if the rowset is in the BOF state, the first iteration will move the pointer to the first record. But, if the rowset pointer is already on the first record, it will be skipped. This can be explained by looking at the ATL consumer classes source code. Open `atldbcli.h` and search for `MoveFirst`. The code looks like this:

```
// Move to the first record
HRESULT MoveFirst()
{
    HRESULT hr;

    // Check the data was opened successfully and the accessor
    // has been set.
    ATLASSERT(m_spRowset != NULL);
    ATLASSERT(m_pAccessor != NULL);

    // Release a row if one is already around
    ReleaseRows();

    hr = m_spRowset->RestartPosition(NULL);
    if (FAILED(hr))
        return hr;

    // Get the data
    return MoveNext();
}
```

We can programmatically set the initial state using `IRowset::RestartPosition`. In the code of `MoveFirst`, though, it is followed by a call to `MoveNext` that cancels the effect. The `RestartPosition` method is exposed by `IRowset` but is not replicated by the ATL's `CRowset` class. In other words, we cannot call `RestartPosition` (or any other `IRowset` method for that matter) through the consumer class.

The simplest solution is to modify the structure of the second loop so that it goes through the records and fills in the table. So, instead of using this code:

```
while (arts.MoveNext() == S_OK)
{ nRecs++; }
```

we can use this:

```
while (true)
{
    nRecs++;

    // next record
    if(arts.MoveNext() != S_OK)
        break;
}
```

Making Use of the Resources

To fill up the ASP page we need the C++ component to output lots of HTML code. This means a lot of calls to Response.Write from C++. This would not be a big issue if it was not for the fact that calls to Response.Write will probably use concatenated strings. In C++, string manipulation is not as easy to do as in Visual Basic. ATL's CComBSTR data type helps considerably, but the real problem lies elsewhere. Too many hard-coded strings in compiled code is not good programming practice. An alternative solution is to use the application's resources, contained in the project's .rc file. We can store HTML strings there in the form of patterns like this:

```
<td>%s</td>
```

If we keep the strings separated from the rest of the code, this produces more readable code. This is the code to fill a table column:

```
LoadString(hInst, IDS_COLUMNNAME, temp, MAXBUFSIZE);
wsprintf(buf, temp, arts.m_Name);
m_piResponse->Write(CComVariant(buf));
```

The corresponding HTML code is:

```
<td align=center><font face=verdana size=1 color=blue>%s</td>
```

As a final note, remember that Response, as well as any other ASP object, utilizes only the Variant type for its parameters. This is why we use the CcomVariant(<var>) method when outputting to the response object.

> If we write ASP components in Visual C++, we have to use the ASP intrinsic objects if we don't want to link to ADO or return a text string to the caller page.

Creating ASP Instances of Objects

When we use an ASP component, that is, a COM object with the ability to access the ASP intrinsic objects, we must always use Server.CreateObject to create an instance of the object instead of language-specific calls such as JScript's ActiveXObject or VBScript's CreateObject. The reason is that, during initialization, the OnStartPage method has to be invoked to bring the pointers to the five ASP objects into use. This is exactly what Server.CreateObject does and the VBScript's CreateObject does not.

Using Stored Procedures

Queries are relatively straightforward to use as they never change the status of the data source. On the other hand, there are operations (INSERT and DELETE in particular) that can have side-effects that we have to handle programmatically. The risk is that we might end up having to access the database repeatedly to sort out a single operation. This is where **stored procedures** fit in.

A stored procedure is a program written in a custom SQL-based language that the database server executes. All the commands within a stored procedure take place from a single call to the database, thereby reducing the stress on the network and ultimately making data access that much quicker. In general, a real-world system will use stored procedures as much as possible to optimize the performance of the system. So, to implement the functionality to insert a new article into the database, we will use C++ to create a component that will call a stored procedure to do the insert.

Designing the Stored Procedure

In the previous chapter, we designed a component for insertion that simply took an array of values and assigned each to the corresponding fields in the database table. We could only do this with new articles. The functionality could not allow us to add a new magazine through the web interface. However, we now want to allow users to add a new article from any magazine, and if the magazine itself doesn't exist, it is added to the Magazines table on the fly.

As we can see, two different operations are requested: one to check for the magazine and one to insert the article. This will be done using a single stored procedure, which means only one call to SQL Server. A SQL Server 7.0 stored procedure is written in Transact-SQL. We have covered stored procedures in more detail in Chapter 4.

```
CREATE PROCEDURE sp_InsertArticle
    @nMagID int,
    @sMagName varchar(50),
    @sTitle varchar(50),
    @sAuthor varchar(50),
    @sIssue varchar(50),
    @sURL varchar(50),
    @sAbstract varchar(50),
    @sKeyword varchar(50)
AS

DECLARE @temp int
SET @temp = 0

/* new magazine */
IF (@nMagID = -1)
BEGIN
    INSERT Magazines ([Name])  VALUES (@sMagName)
    SELECT @temp = MagID FROM Magazines WHERE [Name]=@sMagName
END
ELSE
    @temp = @nMagID

/* only new article */
INSERT Articles (Magazine,Title,Author,Issue,URL,Abstract,Keyword)
    VALUES (@temp, @sTitle, @sAuthor, @sIssue,@sURL, @sAbstract,
        @sKeyword)

/* return the magazine ID if new, 0 otherwise */
RETURN @temp
```

The user gets the name of the magazine from a combo-box that contains the existing magazines, and in doing so, invokes the stored procedure, the @nMagID argument set to a positive integer value. If, however, the user chooses to add an article from a new magazine, then the value of @nMagID is –1.

The sp_InsertArticle procedure checks the magazine ID and adds a new magazine if it is set to –1.

```
INSERT Magazines ([Name])  VALUES (@sMagName)
```

From the code above, we can see that in the record for the inserted magazine, only the Name field contains a non-null value. If we want to add more information than this, we could modify the syntax of sp_InsertArticle to accommodate details on the magazine, or make it return a new magazine ID and fill the rest of the record with a second procedure. Here's what this new procedure might look like:

```
CREATE PROCEDURE sp_FillMagazine
    @nMagID int,
    @sName varchar(50)
AS

UPDATE Magazines
SET
    Name=@sName

WHERE MagID=@nMagID
```

We can invoke the two procedures like this:

```
DECLARE nMagID int

EXEC @nMagID = sp_InsertArticle <arguments>

/* @nMagID is nonzero if a new magazine has been added */
IF @nMagID = -1
    sp_FillMagazine @nMagID, <magazine_name>
```

where <arguments> is a comma separated list of field values to be added to the table, and <magazine_name> is the name of the new magazine. Note that the code does not assign a value of magID to the new magazine – you have to do this yourself.

The sp_InsertArticle procedure sets the ID of the new magazine into a temporary variable that defaults to 0:

```
DECLARE @temp int
SET @temp = 0
:
SELECT @temp = MagID FROM Magazines WHERE [Name]=@sMagName
```

This value is then returned to the caller:

```
/* return the magazine ID if new, 0 otherwise */
return @temp
```

Now that we have set up our sp_FillMagazine stored procedures, we need call to it from an OLE DB consumer component.

Calling a Stored Procedure from C++

Starting a stored procedure is simply a matter of running a T-SQL command from a consumer module. The syntax looks like this:

```
execute sp_InsertArticle <arguments>
```

where, as before, <arguments> refers to a comma separated list of field values.

In Chapter 6, we showed how to write a C++ query processor that takes a T-SQL command and executes it using ATL template classes. To make it work, we only needed to make a few changes in the wizard-generated code to take into account that INSERTs, DELETEs and stored procedures should be handled without accessors because these may or may not return rowsets.

Instead of using the wizard generated Open() method, we can write a brand new method whose job it is to execute a stored procedure. In dboArticles.h, the following code should be added to the body of the CdboArticles class:

```
// Runs the sp_InsertArticle stored procedure
HRESULT OpenStoredProcedure (long nMagID, LPTSTR szMagName,
                    LPTSTR szTitle, LPTSTR szAuthor, LPTSTR szIssue,
                    LPTSTR szURL, LPTSTR szAbstract, LPTSTR szKeyword)
{
    HRESULT hr;
    hr = OpenDataSource();
    if (FAILED(hr))
        return hr;

    // Prepares the SP command line
    TCHAR szCommand[4096];
    wsprintf(szCommand,
        _T("execute %s %d,'%s','%s','%s','%s','%s','%s','%s'"),
        _T("sp_InsertArticle"),
        nMagID, szMagName, szTitle, szAuthor, szIssue,
        szURL, szAbstract, szKeyword);

    return ExecuteCommand(szCommand);
}

// Executes the specified command without using accessors or
// returning rowsets
HRESULT ExecuteCommand(LPCTSTR szCommand)
{
... // Code already in file
}
```

To make this consumer class available to the ASP page, we need another automation object that calls OpenStoredProcedure.

We've called this new object InsertArticle, and it is an ATL **Simple Object** driven by an interface named IInsertArticle. The object has a single method called Insert. Here's the IDL that describes the object:

```
interface IInsertArticle : IDispatch
{
    [id(1), helpstring("method Insert")]
    HRESULT Insert(long nMagID, BSTR bstrMagName,
        BSTR bstrTitle, BSTR bstrAuthor, BSTR bstrIssue,
        BSTR bstrURL, BSTR bstrAbstract, BSTR bstrKeyword,
        [out, retval] BOOL *pbResult);
};
```

415

The method mimics the signature of sp_InsertArticle and returns a Boolean value to indicate the success or failure of the operation.

```cpp
#include "dboArticles.h"

STDMETHODIMP CInsertArticle::Insert(long nMagID,
    BSTR bstrMagName, BSTR bstrTitle, BSTR bstrAuthor, BSTR bstrIssue,
    BSTR bstrURL, BSTR bstrAbstract, BSTR bstrKeyword,
    BOOL *pbResult)
{
    USES_CONVERSION;

    // SP consumer class
    CdboArticles sp;

    // Call sp_InsertArticle
    HRESULT hr = sp.OpenStoredProcedure(nMagID,
        OLE2T(bstrMagName),
        OLE2T(bstrTitle),
        OLE2T(bstrAuthor),
        OLE2T(bstrIssue),
        OLE2T(bstrURL),
        OLE2T(bstrAbstract),
        OLE2T(bstrKeyword)
    );

    // Sets the return value
    *pbResult = SUCCEEDED(hr);

    return S_OK;
}
```

The ASP page responsible for the insertion (newartconfirm.asp) only requires a couple of lines to be changed:

```asp
<%
    ' adds the record
    set o = Server.CreateObject("ArticleBazaarCpp.InsertArticle")
    bResult = o.Insert(strMagID, "", strTitle, strAuthor, strYear, _
        strURL, strAbstr, strKey)
    set o = nothing

    Response.Write "<br>" & strSQL
%>
```

Each time we need to do complex data manipulation, stored procedures can be very helpful and save us time on two accounts. First, we only need call the database once for all of our operations, and because they are compiled, they execute quickly. Second, once we have encapsulated them in a COM component with a defined signature, they allow us to change the SQL without recompiling the component or restarting IIS. In addition, SQL Server compiles stored procedures dynamically, so they run even faster from the second call onwards.

Summary

Building on what we learned in Chapter 6 and Chapter 11, we have used C++ and ATL to create an OLE DB consumer using equivalent functionality to that of the VB component – that is, to select and insert articles into the database. In doing so, we've covered a number of issues including:

- ❑ The most effective way of building C++ components for ASP pages.

- ❑ Why ADO and C++ is not always a great combination.

- ❑ How tp use the ASP intrinsic objects from C++ code.

- ❑ How to modify the OLE DB consumer wizard generated code to comply with update commands.

- ❑ Calling stored procedures from the component

So far we haven't integrated our applications with MTS/COM+. In the next chapter, we'll see how to deploy the components we developed over the last two chapters as a COM+ application.

13

Integrating the Application with COM+

Now that we've completed our ASP-based application, and created our middle-tier components to facilitate data access, we can discuss how to improve and enhance the application. Having coded all our business logic and UI, all we need to do now is set up the ASP application, and link it to the COM+ runtime. Thus, this chapter is separated into two parts:

❑ Things to be aware of when deploying the ASP application

❑ How to write a COM+ Application through Component Services

Let's start with minimal security and deployment issues.

Deploying the ASP Application

The core of an ASP application consists of `.asp` files, usually a `global.asa` file, and COM components that implement business rules. In addition, we may have images, script files and static HTML pages. All this must be available on the web server machine or be easily reachable from it. Deploying web applications is really quite straightforward, but before we jump for joy, remember that there is more to web site deployment than putting files into folders and setting IIS running. Many other important factors, such as web site access logging, are the responsibility, not of the web site developer, but the system administrator.

For example, we should be aware that any web application is vulnerable to attack, so any deployment feature that can help to improve security is welcome. In particular, these factors should be considered when deploying a web site:

❑   Rename our administrator account

❑   Set up the web logs

❑   Install the web files in separate folders according to category (images, scripts etc.)

❑   Use partitioned disks

❑   Configure all the IIS settings for our application

❑   Decide the proper application protection level

Do not consider these suggestions as mandatory; they are only meant to help in setting up a web site that is relatively safe and well positioned for more ambitious security settings. To implement most of these settings, we need to interact with the Internet Services Manager – one of the Control Panel applets available, within Windows 2000, under the Administrative Tools folder.

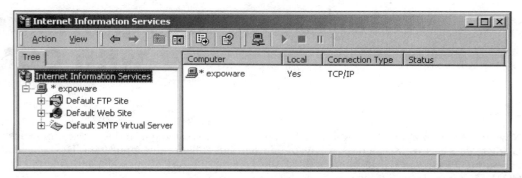

Hiding the Administrator Account

What's the most commonly used and powerful account on a system? The admin account, of course. With the security of our web site in mind, we can create another account with administrator privileges, and reduce the standard administrator account to the rank of an ordinary user.

The Web Logs

Logging is a key aspect of web-site administration, and it is carried out for at least two reasons – security and traffic monitoring. By properly setting up the log parameters, we have a precise record of what is going on in and around our server. We can, for example, monitor this activity for security reasons, or learn more about our users' preferences.

A detailed look at the use of log files can be found in Alex Homer's Pro ASP 3.0 Web Techniques, ISBN 1861003218, also from Wrox Press.

IIS provides a dialog box to let us configure logging activities, including the ability to disable it. The log format choosing can be one of three types:

- ❏ NCSA Common Log Format
- ❏ Microsoft IIS Log Format
- ❏ W3C Extended Log File Format

This screenshot shows the property dialog box we get by right-clicking on the web server name in the IIS window:

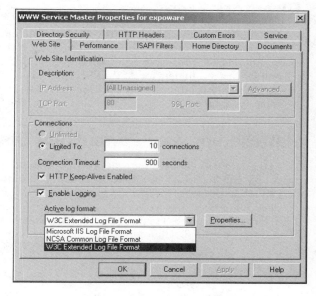

The NCSA Common Log Format stores a fixed set of information, not too detailed for today's requirements. The alternative Microsoft IIS Log Format returns a larger, but still fixed, number of fields which include the IP address of the client, the user name, date and time, processing time, the request, and the number of bytes sent and received.

Both formats save their data as a text file. The default format is the W3C Extended Log File Format. It also saves its data as a text file, but has two advantages over the previous formats – it lets the administrator decide which information is to be logged and it supports many more fields as shown in this screenshot:

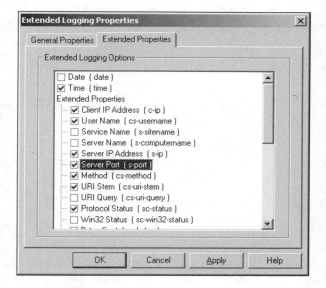

However, note that the more fields we choose for logging, the bigger the log file becomes. One option for keeping the size of the log file to a minimum is to copy the log tables into a database table for later analysis. For an increased level of security, make sure that only trusted users have access to it.

Directory Tree

For security reasons and also ease of administration, we should create a directory structure for our web site based on the type of file. Once we've created the virtual folders for our application, store the files in subfolders according to type. Thus, we would have a folder for server-side includes, one for scripts, one for images, folders for ASP and HTML pages related to specific parts of a site, and so on. This structure allows administrators to apply permissions for groups of files rather than having to do so for each file in turn.

Partitioning and Formatting Disks

Make sure that the partition where both the application and the web server are running is formatted as NTFS. Having a FAT or a FAT32 formatted disk doesn't affect how the application works, but it cannot make use of NTFS 2000 security features. For example, NTFS 2000 supports encryption and decryption at the file system level. It also defines **Access Control Lists** (ACLs) for directories and files. We could also choose to partition our hard disk and install the application on a secondary partition. In this way, our application's files are safer and a bit further removed from attacks by hackers.

Application Configuration

Once our application has been installed in an IIS virtual folder, we can configure our web site. The Configuration dialog box looked like this:

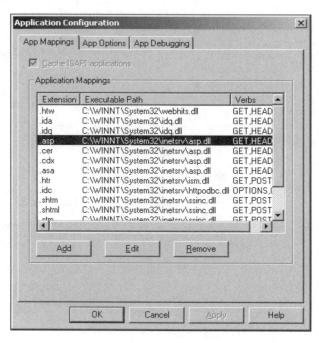

The **App Mappings** tab lists all the file extensions that IIS will recognize as web files on our site. Of course, if we don't want to support any of these extensions, we can highlight it and press **Remove**. Likewise, if we want to manipulate custom extensions, we do the opposite, clicking **Add**.

We can also set up the session timeout as well as define the maximum time for an ASP script to execute:

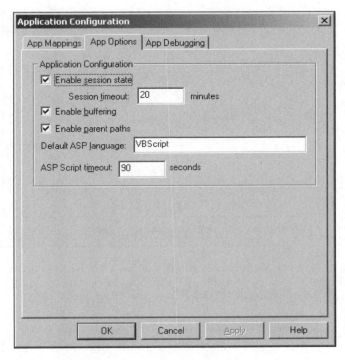

In IIS 5.0 the buffering is enabled by default, which is a change from IIS version 4.0. If we decide that our application works better without buffering, we just uncheck the **Enable buffering** box. What the enable buffering option does is tell ASP to send the page back to the client only after it has finished processing, or if `Response.Flush` is called. This operation speeds up the processing of the page, though this might not be perceived as such by the user. However, we can enable or disable buffering at the page level by using the `Response.Buffer` property.

Another checkbox that we might want to uncheck is **Enable parent paths**. If enabled, it allows the client to use the double-dot operator (..) to point to the parent folder, which might present a problem if we have restricted areas on our site. Indeed, jumping to the parent path might mean that a user is placed into an area of the site that is forbidden to him.

> **IMPORTANT NOTE. When we deploy the application, we should make sure that the server-side debugging feature is turned off.**

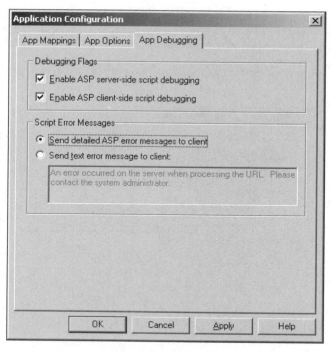

If our application, or the network, produces an error at run-time, we should ensure that the users get the most detailed error information possible. We can define a customized HTML page for each and every HTTP error. We do this via the IISHelp Properties dialog box:

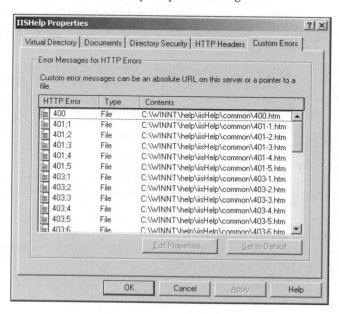

Application Protection

We install a web application by creating a virtual folder under IIS, which means establishing an association between a name and a physical path. For example, the name "ArticleBazaar" might be used to map to the d:/inetpub/wwwroot/aspdata folder. The next step is to set the access permissions for the folder. Normally, for an ASP application, we don't need more than the rights to read and run script code. However, we can enable users to browse the content of the folder, upload and run executables such as CGI scripts or ISAPI extensions. As a general guideline, consider enabling only the features that we really want the user to be able to do on our site:

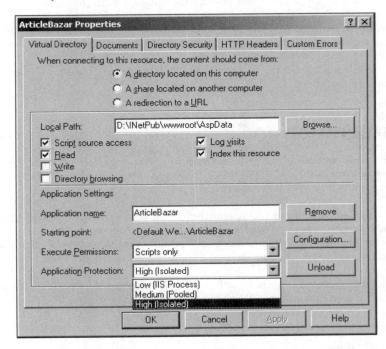

We must also decide on the setting for the protection level for our application: low, medium (the default) or high.

An application with a low level of protection runs in the same process as IIS. While this provides the highest speed of execution and the shortest response time, it does not help the overall stability of the system. Indeed, any blocking error in a component may bring down the entire web server. This option should only be used for highly trusted applications and for situations where the site has to be run with maximum performance.

The highest level of protection is obtained when there is a neat separation between the application and IIS. By choosing the High (Isolated) option, we specify that the application has to run in the context of an isolated process. Any possible crash, in this case, affects only this host application (contained in dllhost.exe) and leaves IIS intact. An isolated component is also easier to debug since we don't have to touch IIS when we need to recompile the component. The drawback to this option is that the application is a completely separate entity with respect to IIS and requires more time to respond. Any application with this setting is automatically started in a separate instance of dllhost.exe.

With IIS 5.0, Microsoft introduced a third possibility: running in a pool of applications. The advantage of running the application in the same context as IIS is that any communication between them comes at a very convenient price in terms of time taken to exchange information. However, this improved performance does not always justify the risk of the web server breaking down should an application trip. The default "medium" level of protection, new to IIS 5.0, lies between the two extreme positions represented by low and high. All the web applications marked as pooled will share the same instance of dllhost.exe. This arrangement minimizes the number of running processes, yet protects IIS from breaking down. The risk incurred by pooling objects is that a blocking failure in any of the applications will bring down all the others with it. So, in practice, it is wise to assign a high protection level for mission-critical applications and pool all the others (within reason!).

With these measures, the ASP application should run without much trouble. So, if we have followed all the steps in this section, we will have created and successfully deployed the web site.

However, this is only half the story. The next stage in deploying a modern web site is to link it to the COM+ run-time environment.

COM+ Integration

The application we have built in the previous three chapters does not make that much use of COM+ services. All we did was write a MTS/COM+ component using Visual Basic. Now it's time to make the objects COM+-enabled.

COM+ is aptly named, in that it is COM plus something else. The plus of COM+ basically stands for a handful of new services added to the COM run-time – like transaction management (formerly known as MTS), message queuing (MSMQ), and resource pooling. These services work not just at the level of the application but involve all the applications and the object in a distributed system.

COM+ brings a rich feature list for both web and component developers. Transforming an otherwise dispersed set of components into a COM+ application can lead to:

- ❑ Simplified deployment of the application
- ❑ Extremely flexible and declarative configuration for context-related properties such as transaction handling and security
- ❑ The ability to run any single component both in-process and out-of-process.

In addition, COM+ takes care of all the threading issues and manages the lifetime of the object much better than we can.

The Development of COM+

Initially, COM provided the mechanism for externally calling component functionality with the sole intervention of the Service Control Manager (SCM). With NT Option Pack 4, COM came with MTS. This came between our objects and our clients. MTS had a very precise and ambitious mission: making our code run faster while taking on tasks like thread pooling, resource pooling, transaction handling, object instantiation, and so on.

Because MTS took away from developers the burden of doing this essential housekeeping, MTS forced them to adopt a slightly modified programming model (often referred to as **stateless**) where objects were to maintain state only when necessary. Along with MTS came **Microsoft Message Queue (MSMQ)**, which was a tool specifically designed to implement a store-and-forward mechanism through messaging. Ideal for connectionless scenarios, MSMQ became the loyal companion to MTS in many distributed systems.

With Windows 2000, Microsoft brought us COM+. Here, COM, MTS and other services such as MSMQ now run under the same infrastructure. However, what COM+ has changed is the way in which a COM call now takes place. The client can ask an object to execute a method either in the traditional COM way, or with a little help from the available run-time services. In enabling this second method of invoking function calls, the COM programming model has broadened out to embrace what was the MTS programming model.

What are the practical benefits of COM+ for a client application? For a start, it can run in a managed environment – that is, as a COM+ application. A COM+ application is just a named container that we fill with object references and security roles. These settings form an environment that influences the way in which the objects will work. All the objects contained within a COM+ application will be managed according to these settings and are given the ability to exploit any of the available services. Of course, those services will not be available for those objects that are not found in the COM+ environment.

By placing our components in COM+, our web application will have the following features:

❑   A run-time that manages the object's lifetime and state

❑   A context that we do not need to explicitly invoke for each object

❑   Automatic thread pooling and neutral-threaded apartments

> *Notice also that being a COM+ application is not just privilege of a new application. Pre-built applications can be transformed in COM+ applications, simply by using the COM+ services wizard.*

Lifetime and State

One key feature of MTS was its ability to manage an object's lifetime in a far more efficient way than the client, despite the fact that it is the client that is apparently creating and destroying it. Even though the client creates an instance of an object, when MTS is involved the object gets created (or acquired) only when the client is about to use it. This feature is known as **Just-In-Time Activation**.

Also, a co-operative object (the Context Object) allows MTS/COM+ to release the object's instance as soon as possible after its task is completed. The point when an object is released depends on internal state, which is where the idea of co-operation fits in. A co-operative object manages state and lets COM+ know when there is no longer any reason to maintain it. The object does this through the `SetComplete` or `SetAbort` we examined in chapter 11.

When an object has no more state to maintain, it can be re-used to serve another request for the same service, that is, the object is pooled, or it can be destroyed. As we can imagine, this is one key factor that makes COM+ inherently scalable. COM+ takes complete responsibility for creating, pooling and destroying of the objects under its control and not the client. COM+ knows how to process objects according to service demand and the state of any pooled objects.

The Object Context

The **context** is the memory structure that COM+ utilizes to keep track of the run-time settings and the services required by an object from a certain application. A context would typically hold information such as whether the object will be pooled, or whether it uses transactions, and it also supports a fixed number of **security roles**. The context is entirely managed by COM+ and the object will actually be unaware of its existence. The information needed to create a context for a given object (or obtain one from the existing pool) is taken from the **COM+ Catalog**.

The COM+ Catalog is a system data store that contains configuration information for COM+ applications for a given server machine.

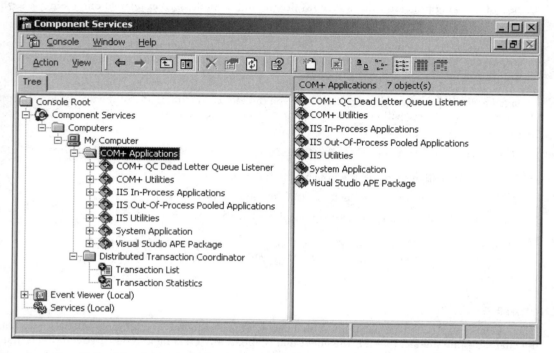

For example, all the settings entered through the Component Services administration tool are written to the COM+ catalog.

COM+ Threading

A problem that we have with COM components is how they react if the same method – or the same internal resource – is called by two concurrent threads. When writing a COM component we can choose between a Single-Threaded Apartment (STA) and a Multi-Threaded Apartment (MTA), where the term **apartment** refers to a logical repository for the threads that manipulate objects.

An STA object is always called by the same thread for its entire lifetime; this is called thread affinity. Furthermore, COM ensures that an STA object will receive calls sequentially via the specified thread.

On the other hand, an MTA object can receive calls from any of the threads in the apartment. However, the object is itself responsible for the necessary synchronization.

With COM+ another model has been added – the **Neutral-Threaded Apartment** (NTA). An NTA object works like an STA object, but accepts calls from any thread, not just one. In other words, NTA is STA but without thread affinity. NTA has one main advantage: it doesn't require cross-thread marshaling. In fact, STA thread affinity forces the COM+ runtime to marshal the data involved with the call from the calling thread to the only one authorized to talk to the service.

NTA is the preferred threading model for COM+ servers as an NTA object doesn't require a specific thread to reply to callers. When a thread instantiates an NTA object, it receives a lightweight wrapper for the object. Access is then as direct as possible, and doesn't require either thread switching or cross-thread data transportation. A process can have only one neutral apartment.

Writing Thread-Neutral Components

NTA components cannot be created with Visual Basic 6.0. This is due to inherent limitations in the current VB6 runtime engine that uses STA thread-affinity. The new Visual Basic .Net is expected to remove this limitation.

To select a neutral apartment for a C++ component, we need to set the `ThreadingModel` attribute to Neutral in the following registry node:

```
HKEY_CLASSES_ROOT
  \CLSID
    \{clsid}
      \InProcServer32
```

Neutral apartment threading is the preferred model for components that do not use a UI. However, Microsoft recommends that components that use a UI use the Single Threading Apartment model.

Preparing COM+ Applications

As we've already seen, a COM+ application is a group of logically related components that the COM+ run-time manages as a complete unit, and we can set declarative properties for them. We can interact with COM+ applications through the **Component Services Explorer** – the MMC snap-in seen a moment ago.

To create a new COM+ application, we select a machine from the CSE, right-click and choose New | Application. The wizard that runs looks like this:

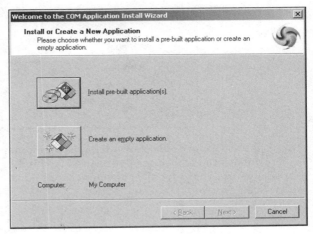

We can choose either to install an existing application or create a new one. If we choose the first option, then we will be asked to select an `.msi` or `.pak` file. MSI files are ready-to-ship packages assembled by Microsoft Installer Service, whereas PAK files are old-style MTS packages. This option is useful if we develop the application on one machine and want to install it on another. Otherwise, we would create a new application.

The Activation Type

The second step requires us to specify a name for the application and choose between two different activation types: server (the default) and library. A server application enables all its components to run from within a single process (`dllhost.exe`) and access the whole range of COM+ services. Furthermore, this activation type makes the entire application more stable since any crash will not affect IIS. The alternative library application type runs in the context of the caller. These in-process components tend to run faster but will not be able to access all the COM+ services, that is, they cannot be queued or load-balanced.

Server applications are also easier to test because we will not have to stop and restart IIS to unload components from memory, but can rely on a more comfortable and quicker context menu.

Application Identity

Next, the wizard asks us to set the account for the application components to run under. The default choice is for the currently logged on user:

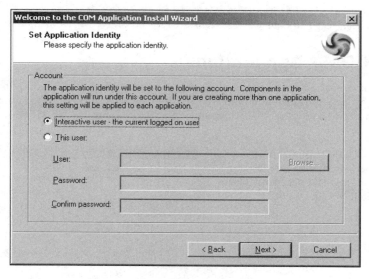

This is the usual choice for most ASP-based applications. The interactive user means anonymous access through the IUSR_computername account. It is a standard user account that IIS creates during installation and allows for all anonymous access – that is, when the web browser doesn't provide a user name and a password when connecting.

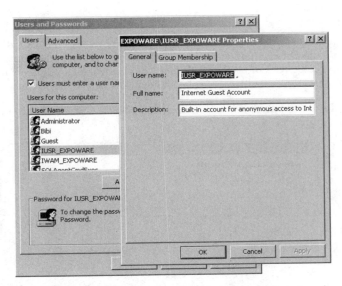

If we choose a particular user identity, then each application that needs to invoke any of our components will impersonate this identity:

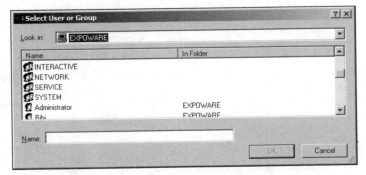

The next step completes the wizard, and the CSE now displays a new, yet empty, element:

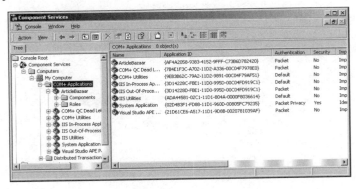

Adding Components

Under each node in the COM+ Applications subtree, we find two folders called Components and Roles. The first contains information about the components that form the application's package. The second describes the categories of users (roles) that can access the components in the application and their security permissions. We will look at roles in detail in just a short while.

Right-clicking on the Components folder, and selecting New   Application, we can add and configure a new component through another wizard:

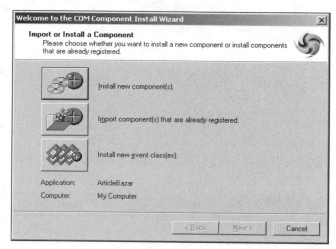

The first option lets us add a new component to the application. If we developed or compiled the component on the server machine, then there will be no need to register it since this is something that Visual Basic and Visual C++ carry out after the linking process. The second option allows us to simply import already registered components into the COM+ application.

Selecting Components

We pick up the components we need from the list of the available COM components:

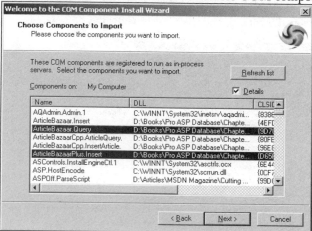

For each component, we can set a number of properties, such as transaction support, the timeout, just-in-time activation, security roles, and the queuing exception class. To edit, just-right click on the component name:

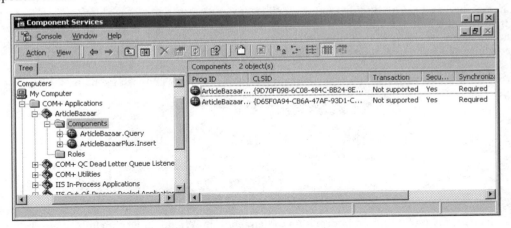

Importing/Exporting the Application

The application's context menu contains an Export... menu which allows us to create an MSI package for deployment on other machines. The wizard lets us set the name of the MSI package and decide, for a server application, whether it is to be for a full installation or an application proxy. The latter is a lightweight installation that simply copies on the host machine what is needed to invoke the components on the primary machine:

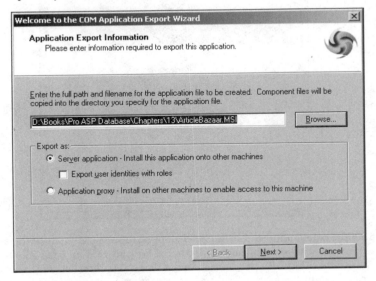

Click Next > and our MSI file is ready to ship in a matter of seconds.

Things aren't that much different when it comes to importing a COM+ application – just copy the MSI files and open the COM+ explorer. Choose to install a new application, but make sure, this time, to select the pre-built applications option.

Role-Based Security

As mentioned earlier, roles define access permissions for an application's components and functionality, and are used to determine whether or not a particular user is able to access a component. An application that uses role-based security needs to know the details of the caller's role membership but can easily be configured to show different groups of functions per user based on this. The programmer will be required to check the membership before each call.

From the administrative point of view, creating a role is as easy as choosing a name for it:

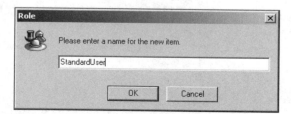

The name is the only required information to define a role. We might also include a description through the role's Properties page:

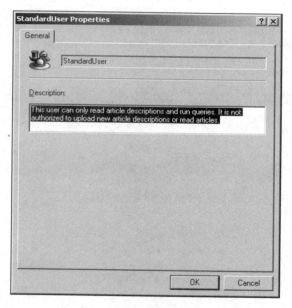

However, defining the roles supported by a COM+ application is only part of the story. Roles make sense only if they are associated with users and groups. For this reason, each role has a Users subfolder that we should fill in with the user accounts that fall under that role. This is the essence of declarative security. Within the CSE, there is nothing that associates users with available functions or resources – this is jealously hidden in the component's code. The following code snippet shows how to programmatically check for a role and apply different settings accordingly:

```
Dim oCtxt As IObjectContext
Set oCtxt = GetObjectContext()
If oCtxt.IsCallerInRole("AdminUser") Then
    ' enable article upload
Else
    ' disable article upload
End If
```

Role-based security is another COM+ service. It has several advantages:

- ❑ We configure the security administratively.
- ❑ No need to write modules to define and apply security rules, unless we really need a stronger security mechanism.
- ❑ Any check is done at resource level, that is, before actually calling the method.
- ❑ Easier interaction between developers and administrators – the application security policies are clearly defined, and administrators have just to populate roles with user groups.

Role-based security presupposes that we trust our clients and think they are exactly who they claim to be. Verifying the client identity is under the charge of the authentication service.

COM+ Enabling C++ Components

In Chapter 11 we saw how to write a COM+ enabled component with Visual Basic. Let's see briefly how to proceed with C++ components.

> **If you did not work through the C++ component examples from Chapter 12, then you can skip this section and go straight to the section entitled Queuing Services.**

The key point is linking in the necessary library files. We need to link to three libraries to successfully compile a COM+ enabled component: `mtx.lib`, `mtxguid.lib` and `delayimp.lib`. If we selected the **Support MTS** checkbox on the front-end page, the ATL AppWizard will add them to the project. Alternatively, they silently slipstream into the project settings when we choose to add an MTS object.

> **Note that the ATL 3.0 Wizards became available before the term "COM+" became widely known, so they still refer to MTS and require linking to the MTS libraries.**

The `mtx.lib` library contains the declaration for `GetObjectContext`, the COM+ entry point:

```
HRESULT hr = GetObjectContext(&m_spObjectContext);
```

Delayed Loading of MTS Library

This `delayimp.lib` system library allows executables to implement the **delayed loading** feature when compiled with Visual C++ 6.0 or higher. This feature enables us to link to a specified DLL only when strictly necessary, but not a second before. Delayed loading combines the best of two apparently contrasting features: dynamic library loading and static linking. First, we statically link to a library and use the function names as-is throughout the code. Second, with a linker option like this specified:

```
/delayload:mtxex.dll
```

we tell the linker not to implicitly link to the specified function names for that library. Instead, it connects those entry-points to a standard function in `delayimp.lib`. This function, when needed at runtime, loads this library through `LoadLibrary` and calls the functions through `GetProcAddress`.

MTS/COM+ Objects

Once we link the three MTS libraries, any COM object we create can call `GetObjectContext`, obtain a reference to `IObjectContext` and call `SetComplete` and `SetAbort` whenever it needs to. If we insert an MTS/COM+ object into our ATL project, we also have the option of making it poolable. Notice, though, that only COM+ supports poolable objects:

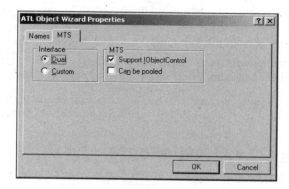

The key point to note here is that we have to implement the `IObjectControl` interface. The header file looks like this:

```
// Foo.h : Declaration of the CFoo

#ifndef __FOO_H_
#define __FOO_H_

#include "resource.h"       // main symbols
#include <mtx.h>

/////////////////////////////////////////////////////////////////////////////
// CFoo
class ATL_NO_VTABLE CFoo :
    public CComObjectRootEx<CComSingleThreadModel>,
    public CComCoClass<CFoo, &CLSID_Foo>,
    public IObjectControl,
    public IDispatchImpl<IFoo, &IID_IFoo, &LIBID_TESTLib>
{
public:
    CFoo () {}

DECLARE_REGISTRY_RESOURCEID(IDR_FOO)
DECLARE_PROTECT_FINAL_CONSTRUCT()

BEGIN_COM_MAP(CFoo)
    COM_INTERFACE_ENTRY(IFoo)
    COM_INTERFACE_ENTRY(IObjectControl)
    COM_INTERFACE_ENTRY(IDispatch)
END_COM_MAP()
```

```
    // IObjectControl
public:
    STDMETHOD(Activate)();
    STDMETHOD_(BOOL, CanBePooled)();
    STDMETHOD_(void, Deactivate)();

    CComPtr<IObjectContext> m_spObjectContext;

    // IFoo
public:
};

#endif //__FOO_H_
```

`IObjectControl`'s methods, `Activate` and `Deactivate`, get called when the object is activated and released:

```
HRESULT CFoo::Activate()
{
    HRESULT hr = GetObjectContext(&m_spObjectContext);
    if (SUCCEEDED(hr))
        return S_OK;
    return hr;
}

BOOL CFoo::CanBePooled()
{
    return FALSE;
}

void CFoo::Deactivate()
{
    m_spObjectContext.Release();
}
```

An object is poolable if it returns TRUE from the `CanBePooled` method, which means that when the object goes out of scope, or when a client requests to destroy it, it is not physically unloaded from memory, but put into a deactivate state ready for re-use by another client. Implementing the `IObjectControl` interface is optional and we should do it only when we need specific initialization and cleanup procedures and object recycling.

> If `CanBePooled` returns TRUE there's no guarantee at all that the object will be recycled – this is the responsibility of the COM+ run-time environment. On the other hand, if the method returns FALSE, then there's absolute certainty that instances of that component will not be recycled.

Summary

The aim of this chapter has been to illustrate the various services and technologies that we don't strictly need to set up a web application, but which can help considerably when refining and enhancing it. In particular, we focused on component settings with and without COM+ and analyzed the benefits of COM+ enabling a web application. In summary, this chapter covered:

❑ Issues related to ASP application deployment

❑ Benefits of MTS and COM+

❑ How to write and configure COM+ applications

Section 4

Relational Databases

14

Microsoft SQL Server

Applications developed with Active Server Pages have the ability to access virtually any database. As with most products in general, Microsoft SQL Server offers features and functionality that differ somewhat from its competitors. This chapter does not try to cover everything that you can possibly do with the product. There are many other fine books available that cover Microsoft SQL Server in a much broader scope, most notably, Rob Vieira's *Professional SQL Server 7 Programming* from Wrox Press. Rather, we shall take a look at a few of the many Microsoft SQL Server features and implementations that are important to the ASP developer. In this chapter we will be concentrating on Version 7.0 of Microsoft SQL Server.

So what are the topics that are important to an ASP developer using Microsoft SQL Server? First of all, we will look at how to build code modules in the database to perform various business and maintenance operations. By centralizing such services available in the database itself, different client applications can behave consistently, performance can be improved, and the amount of redundant code across platforms can be reduced. We'll discuss a number of topics concerning stored procedures, such as how to create and optimize them, and the procedural language features found in SQL Server. We'll take a look at how SQL Server differs from standard SQL, which can have an effect on how the stored procedures run, and how environmental variables can be set to control this.

Another item on our list of topics concerns automation. It is often very helpful to be able to execute procedures at regular intervals or on some schedule, so we'll take a look at SQL Server's task scheduling features. As in languages such as C++ and VBScript that use an event-driven programming model, we can create events within SQL Server and have our stored procedures invoked when these events are raised. How about automated e-mail? Later in this chapter, we will go over an example of executing a query in SQL Server and have the results sent via e-mail.

Our last major topic concerns some of the Web-related features found in Microsoft SQL Server, such as the **Web Assistant Wizard** which was released with version 7.0 to generate HTML documents from SQL Server data. The Web Assistant Wizard generates HTML files by using TSQL queries, stored procedures, and extended stored procedures. You can use the wizard to generate an HTML file one time, generate an HTML file as a regularly scheduled SQL Server task, or you can update an HTML file using a trigger.

Connecting to a SQL Server Database from ASP

In this section we will cover the basic concepts of how to connect to a SQL Server Database using ASP. We will cover SQL Server Security and how to use ASP code to connect to a SQL Server Database using various security methods – SQL Server 7.0 has two different methods.

SQL Server Security–Integrated vs Standard

Starting with SQL Server 7.0, there are two ways to set up security:

❑ Windows 2000 integrated security – the user logs into Windows 2000, not SQL Server.

❑ Standard Security – the user logs into SQL Server using a Login and Password.

With Integrated Security, authentication is carried out by Windows 2000 using trusted connections. There is no need to log into SQL Server separately, therefore there is no SQL Server username and password needed. With Standard Security, authentication is done by SQL Server. The user is required to enter a login and password to get into SQL Server. You would use Standard Security when some or all of your users are not using Windows 2000 (or Windows NT). You would use Integrated Security when all of your users and your database server are using Windows 2000.

How to Connect to a SQL Server Database using ASP Code

There are two common ways to connect to a SQL Server database using ASP code. One is to use a DSN and the other is to use a DSN-less Connection. Both methods use the Connection object to connect to SQL Server. If you use a DSN connection, there is less coding required but you must maintain a DSN connection to SQL Server. If you use a DSN-less connection, there is more coding but you don't have to maintain a DSN on the user's machines. DSN connections are also slower, since they use both OLE DB and ODBC, and so add an extra layer to the architecture. Native OLE DB DSN-less connections should be used if at all possible. Below are four examples: 1) using a DSN connection with integrated security, 2) using a DSN connection with standard security, 3) using a DSN-less connection with integrated security, and 4) using a DSN-less connection with standard security.

ASP Code Using a DSN Connection with Integrated Security

The following example assumes that you have a DSN named Northwind set up on your computer which points to the Northwind sample database on your SQL Server. It also assumes that you are using integrated security so that you don't have to pass a login (username) and password to SQL Server. The first line Dims the variable name (oConn), the second line instantiates the Connection object, and the third line creates the connection to the database:

```
Dim oConn
Set oConn=Server.CreateObject("Adodb.Connection")
OConn.open = "DSN=Northwind"
```

ASP Code Using a DSN Connection with Standard Security

The following example assumes that you have a DSN named Northwind set up on your computer which points to the Northwind sample database on you SQL Server. It also assumes that you are using standard security which requires you to pass a login and password to connect to SQL Server. The login in this example is 'SA' and the password is 'admin'. The first line Dims the variable name (oConn), the second line instantiates the Connection object, and the third line creates the connection to the database.

```
Dim oConn
Set oConn=Server.CreateObject("Adodb.Connection")
OConn.open = "DSN=Northwind;UserID=SA;pwd=admin"
```

ASP Code Using a DSN-less Connection with Integrated Security

The following example assumes that you are using a DSN-less connection to the Northwind sample database on a SQL Server named Wrox. It also assumes that you are using integrated security so that you don't have to pass a login (username) and password to SQL Server. The first line Dims the variable name (oConn), the second line instantiates the Connection object, the third line specifies the OLE DB provider (sqloledb for SQL Server), and the last line creates the connection to the database passing the server name (Wrox), and the database name (Northwind), and specifying that we are using integrated security (Trusted_Connection='Yes'):

```
Dim oConn
'Create an Ado connection
Set oConn=Server.CreateObject("Adodb.Connection")
'Specify the OLE  DB provider
oConn.Provider="sqloledb"
'open the connection
oConn.Open "Data Source=Wrox;Initial Catalog=Northwind;Trusted_Connection=yes;"
```

ASP Code Using a DSN-less Connection with Standard Security

The following example assumes that you are using a DSN-less connection to the Northwind sample database on a SQL Server named Wrox. It also assumes that you are using standard security so that you have to pass a login (username) and password to SQL Server. The first line Dims the variable name (oConn), the second line instantiates the Connection object, the third line specifies the OLE DB provider (sqloledb for SQL Server), and the last line creates the connection to the database passing the server name (Wrox), the database name (Northwind), the login (SA), and the password (admin):

```
Dim oConn
'Create an Ado connection
Set oConn=Server.CreateObject("Adodb.Connection")
'Specify the OLE  DB provider
oConn.Provider="sqloledb"
'open the connection
oConn.Open " Data Source=Wrox; Initial Catalog=Northwind;User ID=SA;Password=Admin;"
```

Extended Stored Procedures

Extended stored procedures allow you to create your own external routines in a programming language such as C. As with Windows API calls, extended stored procedures need to be declared inside the database, but the code that is executed is found in dynamic link libraries or executables on disk. The declarations are found in the master database and usually start with xp_. The extended stored procedures only exist in the master database, which has the following impacts:

❑   You will need to fully qualify the extended stored procedures (for example, master..xp_sendmail) if the Master database is not current.

❑   Rights to execute the extended stored procedures are granted in the Master database.

❑   You will need to rebuild the extended stored procedures on the new server if you move your application's database.

An example of an extended stored procedure that you might use routinely is the xp_cmdshell. The syntax looks like this:

```
xp_cmdshell <'command_string'> [,no_output]
```

The command_string holds the command, exactly as you would have typed it into the command line. The no_output parameter stops the return of any results. For example, if you wanted to list the contents of the c:\mssql7 folder on your hard drive you could use the following code in the query analyzer:

```
Exec Master..xp_cmdshell 'Dir c:\mssql7'
```

Now that we have examined security, and extended stored procedures, we will look at SQL Server specifics: SQL Server has some unique features which can have a considerable impact on how our stored procedures operate. We will now look at a few of the more important of these features.

Setting the Environment in Microsoft SQL Server

Although Microsoft's implementation of SQL, called T-SQL, is fully compatible with ANSI SQL-92 and generally compatible in the SQL-3 (which was released while Microsoft SQL Server 2000 was in beta), Microsoft SQL Server provides optional enhancements not found in the ANSI standard. How closely T-SQL behaves like the SQL standard is controlled by a series of configuration settings at the server level. Many of these settings can be altered for execution on a temporary basis within a stored procedure or query. Since it is often risky to make assumptions about the server's configuration, it is good practice to set the appropriate configuration options for a stored procedure within the procedure itself.

Most configuration settings may be changed within a stored procedure or query by using the SET command. The general format of this command is:

```
SET ConfigurationSettingName value
```

For example, SET LANGUAGE us_english changes the default language used to United States English.

These configuration settings may also be set from within Query Analyzer, by selecting the Connection Properties tab of the Options dialog. You can get to the Current Connections Options dialog by selecting Tools | Options:

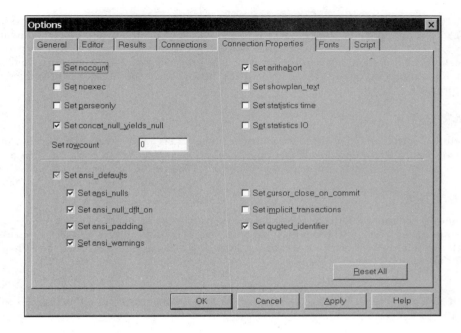

NOCOUNT

When you issue a SQL statement in SQL Query Analyzer, Microsoft SQL Server executes the statement, and then displays the results. These results will usually include a result set and a message indicating how many rows were affected:

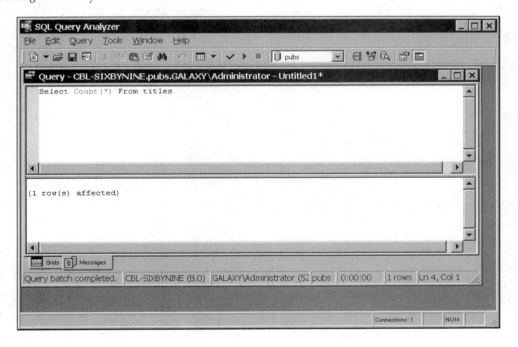

The NOCOUNT setting is used to prevent SQL Server from displaying the "number of rows affected" message. Now you might be thinking why is this setting important? The reason is that if you are using versions of ADO later than 2.0, this message will still get passed back to your client as part of your results. This can cause a number of problems such as preventing you from obtaining your data. For this reason, it is strongly recommended that you place the SET NOCOUNT ON statement at the start of your stored procedures.

ARITHABORT

This setting controls whether or not the query or procedure is aborted when an overflow or divide-by-zero error occurs. The values for this setting are either ON or OFF. When set to ON, the standard ANSI behavior will be used which terminates the procedure. When set to OFF, the procedure is not terminated.

ARITHIGNORE

This controls whether or not error messages are returned from an overflow or divide-by-zero error during a query or within a stored procedure. The values for this setting are either ON or OFF. When set to ON, the standard ANSI behavior will be used that will generate the error message. When set to OFF, no error message is generated.

> If both ARITHABORT and ARITHIGNORE are set to ON, ARITHABORT will take precedence.

CONCAT_NULL_YIELDS_NULL

This setting controls whether or not the concatenation of a text string with a NULL is treated as a null. The values for this setting are either ON or OFF. When set to ON, the concatenation of a null value with a string will produce a null value. When set to OFF, such concatenations will return the string itself.

To demonstrate the effects of this setting, take a look at the following two queries and their results:

```
SET CONCAT_NULL_YIELDS_NULL ON
SELECT 'XYZ' + NULL AS ResultWithOn
```

```
ResultWithOn
------------
NULL

(1 row(s) affected)
```

```
SET CONCAT_NULL_YIELDS_NULL OFF
SELECT 'XYZ' + NULL AS ResultWithOff
```

```
ResultWithOff
-------------
XYZ

(1 row(s) affected)
```

ANSI_WARNINGS

This configuration setting is used to specify how error conditions are responded to. The values for this setting are either `ON` or `OFF`. When set to `ON`, the standard ANSI actions will be carried out:

- If `Null` values appear in aggregate functions (such as `SUM`, `AVG`, `MAX`, `MIN`, or `COUNT`), a warning message is generated.
- Divide-by-zero and arithmetic overflow errors will cause an error message to be thrown and force a roll-back of any current transaction.
- If an `INSERT` or `UPDATE` attempts to add a value to a string or binary field, and the length of the new value exceeds the maximum character length of the field, the action is cancelled and an error is thrown.

When `ANSI_WARNINGS` is set to `OFF`, the following behavior will be used:

- If `Null` values appear in aggregate functions, a warning message will not be generated.
- Divide-by-zero and arithmetic overflow errors will not cause an error; instead a `Null` value is returned.

If an `INSERT` or `UPDATE` attempts to add a value to a string or binary field, and the length of the new value exceeds the maximum character length of the field, the data is truncated to fit the field and no error is thrown.

Performance Considerations with Stored Procedures

As we discussed earlier, there are three major influences affecting the performance of stored procedures: the database statistics, the execution plan, and optimizing the procedures. Let's take a look at each of these and discuss what can be done to maximize the performance of your stored procedures.

Database Statistics

From SQL Server 7 onwards, statistics are maintained automatically. Whenever an index is created, statistics are computed on that index. SQL Server also monitors the statistics and if they are considered to be out of date, a background process is initiated to recalculate them. Having SQL Server provide such services reduces the need for manual intervention and provides an overall better performing database.

The statistics that are kept on tables differ from those that are kept on indexes. The statistics kept on tables include the:

- Number of rows in the table
- Number of blocks of disk space, called pages, that are used by the table
- Number of modifications made to the keys of the table since the last update to the statistics

For indexes, the statistical information stored includes:

- A histogram on the first column of the index, which provides an indication of how the records are grouped
- A measure of uniqueness, called density, on all columns used in the index
- Average amount of storage required to store a key in the index, called the *key length*

To keep this statistical information as current as possible, without generating unnecessary overhead, SQL Server 7.0 introduced **AutoStat**. This agent monitors the number of modifications that are made to a table and causes its statistics to be recomputed when a certain threshold of change has been reached.

> *SQL Server 7.0 also introduced an automatic statistics creation feature, which causes the server to automatically generate all statistics required for the accurate optimization of a specific query.*

To determine if this 'change threshold' has been reached, a system table named sysindexes contains a record describing each index in the database. In this table is a field named rowmodctr, which stores a running total of the number of modifications made to the table that the index describes. This field is incremented by one each time a row is inserted or deleted or an update is made to an indexed column. If the number of rows in the table is less than six, then the statistics are recomputed after every six modifications to the table. If the table has more than six rows, but less than 500 rows, statistics are recomputed every 500 modifications. If the table has more than 500 rows, then the statistics are recomputed after 20 percent of the table has been modified after the 500th change. For example, if the table contains 10,000 records, then the statistics will be updated when 500 + 10,000 * 20% = 2500 modifications have been made to the table.

> *When computing statistics, if the table is small (less than 8 MB), the entire table is read. If the table is large, then SQL Server uses statistical sampling techniques rather than reading the entire set of values.*

After new statistics are generated and a stored procedure is invoked, a check is made to see if its execution plan is sensitive to statistics, and if so, the plan for the stored procedure will be recompiled. The advantage to this approach is that, on average, your stored procedures will execute using a fairly accurate set of statistics. But with that said, there are a number of issues that arise from this approach. The first is on large tables, say those with more than 10,000 records, it may be unacceptable to have to wait until more than 20% of the table has been changed before the statistics are recomputed. The second issue arises when AutoStat starts computing statistics during heavy production periods.

To view the current statistics for an index of a table, use the **Database Consistency Checker** (DBCC) utility from a query window. The following is the syntax for the DBCC Show_Statistics command: The table is the name of the table for which to display statistics information and the target is the object (index name or collection) for which to display statistics information:

```
DBCC SHOW_STATISTICS (table, target)
```

To show the statistics for the PK_Customers index on the Customers table you would run the following command in the Query Analyser (with the **Northwind** database selected):

```
DBCC Show_Statistics (Customers, PK_Customers)
```

The results in the grid window would look similar to this:

	Updated	Rows	Rows Sampled	Steps	Density	Average key length	
1	Sep 22 2000 2:33PM	91	91	91	1.0989011E-2	9.9999952	

	All density	Columns	
1	1.0989011E-2	CustomerID	

Steps	

To examine the status of an index in the `sysindexes` table, try using a query similar to the following. We are using the primary key index (`PK_Customers`) for the `Customer` table of the Northwind database:

```
SELECT id, rows, rowmodctr, name
FROM sysindexes
WHERE name = 'PK_Customers'
```

The grid window would display something similar to the following

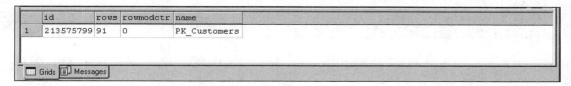

You can turn AutoStat on and off at will and you can monitor the values of the statistics and the values of the `rowmodctr` in the `sysindexes` table to evaluate if it would be appropriate to manually update statistics. During heavy production periods or other heavy usage periods it would be appropriate to manually update statistics. If you wish to disable AutoStat, you may use the system stored procedure `sp_autostats`. This procedure may be used to enable, disable, or view the current automatic statistics settings for a table. The general form used to call this procedure is:

```
sp_autostats table_name, stats_flag, index_name
```

where `stats_flag` is either `'ON'` or `'OFF'`.

Let's look at some examples of using `sp_autostats`. The first example is used to view the AutoStat settings for the `titles` table in the `pubs` database. The `UPKCL_titleidind` index is a clustered index for the `title_id` field and the `titleind` is a nonclustered index for the `title` field:

```
EXEC sp_autostats titles
```

The messages window would display something similar to the following:

```
Global statistics settings for [pubs]:
  Automatic update statistics: ON
  Automatic create statistics: ON

Settings for table [titles]
|

(2 row(s) affected)
```

The grid tab would display something similar to the following:

	Index Name	AUTOSTATS	Last Updated
1	[UPKCL_titleidind]	ON	1998-11-13 03:11:07.360
2	[titleind]	ON	1998-11-13 03:11:07.373

Grids Messages

449

This next example enables automatic statistics for all indexes of the titles table:

```
EXEC sp_autostats titles, 'ON'
```

This statement returns a confirmation message:

```
(2 row(s) affected)

Automatic statistics maintenance turned ON for 2 indices.
```

Grids Messages

This last example disables the automatic statistics setting for the `titleind` index of the titles table:

```
EXEC sp_autostats titles, 'OFF', titleind
```

This statement also returns a confirmation message:

```
(1 row(s) affected)

Automatic statistics maintenance turned OFF for 1 indices.
```

Grids Messages

Recomputing Statistics

Now that we know how to check the status of our statistics, we can manually recalculate the statistics. With Microsoft SQL Server, we use the UPDATE STATISTICS command to force this recompilation. This command may be used to update a single statistic or all statistics on a given table.

The three most common forms of this command are:

❑   Update all statistics for a single table

```
UPDATE STATISTICS tablename
```

Example:

```
UPDATE STATISTICS titles
```

When the command is finished you will get the following message: 'The command(s) completed successfully'.

❑   Update only the statistics for a single index

```
UPDATE STATISTICS tablename indexname
```

An example of this would be:

```
UPDATE STATISTICS titles _titleind
```

❑   Update all statistics for a single table by sampling a specific percentage of the table's values:

```
UPDATE STATISTICS tablename WITH SAMPLE n PERCENT
```

An example of this would be:

```
UPDATE STATISTICS titles WITH SAMPLE 68 PERCENT
```

> *68 percent is a significant number in statistical analysis, since it represents one standard deviation of normally distributed values.*

There are other options that are available when using the UPDATE STATISTICS command, such as:

❑   Forcing the statistics to be computed by reading every row in the table

❑   Turning off AutoStat on the index after the new statistics are computed

❑   Calculating the statistics based upon a fixed number of rows

It is important to realize that manually forcing the update of statistics is not critical with small tables, or for tables that are changed infrequently. Databases that hold a very large volume of data, like millions of rows of data, will usually have a Database Administrator (DBA) monitoring and maintaining the system. It will be this professional's responsibility to monitor and analyze the system and take the appropriate actions as needed.

If you are building an application that will not have a dedicated DBA to monitor it, you should place enough maintenance features into your code so that the database will be self-sufficient. History is replete with tales of applications that worked very well when delivered, but over time became slow and unresponsive because basic maintenance activities were not followed.

Execution Plans

This section will discuss the impact of the execution plan on your procedures.

It is often beneficial to regenerate the execution plan from time to time. The execution plan can be regenerated in four different ways. The first way is when SQL Server has determined that the database statistics used in the plan have been updated and the execution plan is automatically recompiled. Unfortunately, stored procedures are not re-optimized when indexes are added, so in this case SQL Server won't rebuild the execution plan for you.

The second way is to include the WITH RECOMPILE statement in the stored procedure itself. This statement must follow the argument list, if any, and before the AS keyword. For example, you would use the following code to change the byroyalty stored procedure in the pubs database to include the WITH RECOMPILE option :

```
ALTER PROCEDURE byroyalty @percentage int
with recompile
AS
select au_id from titleauthor
where titleauthor.royaltyper = @percentage
GO
```

This statement causes the execution plan to be regenerated each time the stored procedure is called. This approach should be used only when the increase in performance gained by a new execution plan will greatly outweigh the extra cost involved in recalculating the execution plan every time the procedure is used. If your database is relatively small or doesn't change often, the WITH RECOMPILE clause may not gain you much.

The third way to regenerate the execution plan is to drop and rebuild the procedure. To do this, first right-click on the stored procedure's name in Enterprise Manager and choose All Tasks | Generate SQL Scripts... to create a file containing the SQL commands required to build the procedure. The script generated will add code to drop the existing stored procedure before re-creating it. Next, use Query Analyzer (using the File | Open option to load the script you created) or some other query tool to run the script that was just created.

The fourth way to regenerate the execution plan is to use the sp_recompile system stored procedure. Using sp_recompile will not immediately recreate the execution plan. Rather, it will cause SQL Server to recompile the stored procedure the next time it is invoked. The syntax for using this command is:

```
Execute sp_recompile storedprocedurename
```

Although this command can recompile only one stored procedure at a time, you can create a helper routine that will query SQL Server's system tables for all of your stored procedures and then issue the sp_recompile command on each of them:

```
-- Initialize Environment.
SET NOCOUNT ON
DECLARE @vcProcedureName varchar(255)

-- Create a cursor to "walk" the result set.
DECLARE curAdmin CURSOR FOR
    SELECT  ProcedureName = name
    FROM    sysobjects
    WHERE   type = 'P'

-- Activate the cursor and retrieve the first record in it.
OPEN curAdmin
FETCH FROM curAdmin INTO @vcProcedureName

/* As long as the cursor has rows, recompile the stored procedure named in the
current cursor row. */
WHILE @@FETCH_STATUS = 0
BEGIN
    SELECT 'Recompiling Procedure: ' + @vcProcedureName
    EXEC ('sp_recompile ' + @vcProcedureName) -- Execute the recompile statement
    FETCH NEXT FROM curAdmin INTO @vcProcedureName
END
CLOSE curAdmin
DEALLOCATE curAdmin

-- Clean up.
SET NOCOUNT OFF
```

Optimizing a Stored Procedure's Content

When talking about how best to optimize the content of a stored procedure, the discussion is effectively the same as talking abouthow to optimize queries in general. Since a stored procedure is simply a collection of SQL statements with flow control statements, there are only two things that can be done to improve performance: improving the speed of the queries and developing more efficient algorithms. This section of the chapter will offer a few comments about what can be done in general to improve both of these aspects.

Using SQL Query Analyzer

There are no quick and easy ways to make a query faster. In most cases, you will need to adjust more than one thing in a given query to earn greater performance. The best single recommendation that can be given to improve the performance of a query is to analyze it by using tools such as SQL Query Analyzer to understand how it is being processed and where the bottlenecks are. Once you know where your inefficiencies are, you are in a better position to adjust the query accordingly.

To use SQL Query Analyzer, start the tool by selecting SQL Query Analyzer from the Tools menu in Enterprise Manager. With the tool open, select Show Execution Plan from the Query menu. This will cause a second tab to be displayed in the lower pane when a query is executed:

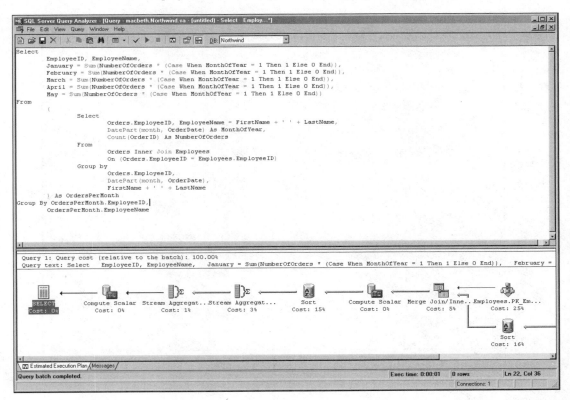

If you hover your mouse pointer over any of the "node icons" in the Execution Plan tab, a tooltip (see example below) window will be displayed showing detailed information about what took place to process that portion of the query:

Compute Scalar

Computing new values from existing values in a row.

Physical operation:	Compute Scalar
Logical operation:	Compute Scalar
Row count:	9
Estimated row size:	50
I/O cost:	0.000000
CPU cost:	0.00178
Number of executes:	1
Subtree cost:	0.143
Estimated row count:	62

Argument:
DEFINE:([Expr1007]=If ([Expr1008]=0) then NULL
else [Expr1009])

If requested, SQL Query Analyzer will provide you with statistics on disk I/O and execution times. To request this data, check the Set statistics time and Set statistics I/O from the Current Connections Options dialog, which we saw earlier:

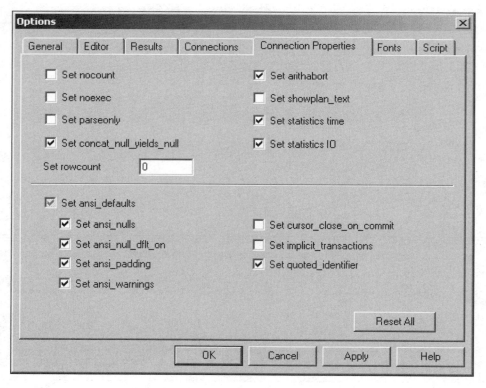

With these options set as ON, when a query is executed, the statistics on disk I/O and execution times will be presented along with the results of the query. The message box output is shown, then the grid box output:

```
SQL Server Execution Times:
   CPU time = 0 ms,   elapsed time = 21 ms.

SQL Server Execution Times:
   CPU time = 0 ms,   elapsed time = 0 ms.
SQL Server parse and compile time:
   CPU time = 10 ms, elapsed time = 14 ms.

(9 row(s) affected)

Table 'Orders'. Scan count 1, logical reads 22, physical reads 0, read-ahead reads 0.
Table 'Employees'. Scan count 1, logical reads 2, physical reads 0, read-ahead reads 0.

SQL Server Execution Times:
   CPU time = 20 ms,   elapsed time = 19 ms.
SQL Server parse and compile time:
   CPU time = 0 ms, elapsed time = 0 ms.
```

Grids Messages

	EmployeeID	EmployeeName	January	February	march	april	may
1	2	Andrew Fuller	11	11	11	11	11
2	9	Anne Dodsworth	6	6	6	6	6
3	3	Janet Leverling	17	17	17	17	17
4	8	Laura Callahan	12	12	12	12	12
5	4	Margaret Peacock	14	14	14	14	14
6	6	Michael Suyama	5	5	5	5	5
7	1	Nancy Davolio	12	12	12	12	12
8	7	Robert King	7	7	7	7	7
9	5	Steven Buchanan	4	4	4	4	4

Grids Messages

The results show the total execution times, cpu times, number of scans per table, number of logical reads per table, physical reads per table, etc. If a query takes too long to process, you can restructure it for better performance. You can change your queries, rerun them and compare the new timing information with the old to determine if you have made your queries more efficient. With this timing information, you can better judge how changes to your queries will affect performance.

Guidelines for Better Queries

Although empirical testing will help you isolate inefficiencies in your queries, there are some general guidelines that should be considered when deciding how best to alter your code. Below is a list of recommendations that may prove useful in constructing and modifying queries:

❑ The Inner Join, Left Join, Right Join syntax is generally much faster than using the older SQL syntax of joining tables by using the WHERE clause.

❑ Avoid using the NOT operator in WHERE clauses when possible.

❑ The = (equals) sign is best if a unique index is available. Closed ranges are next (col1>5 AND col1<10); open intervals are next (c1>5). IN lists are treated as multiple OR clauses. BETWEEN is treated as a closed interval. LIKE with a trailing and/or leading wild card is treated as a closed interval.

❑ Higher priority will be given to indexes that "cover" the query (include all of the columns in the select list) because it is then no longer necessary to access the actual data pages.

455

❏ Do not use expressions or data conversions in index and join-selection WHERE clauses or the optimizer may not recognize that the expression evaluates to a constant.

❏ Local variables in WHERE clauses are considered to be "unknown" and are not considered by the optimizer, except for the input parameters of stored procedures.

❏ If possible, avoid creating temporary tables; instead, use queries against the source tables directly. There are exceptions to this recommendation, especially if the same temporary table could be used repeatedly in subsequent joins.

❏ Don't use the ORDER BY clause in subqueries if the outer query will also sort the results.

❏ If a table has a clustered index which sorts its records in the order desired by the query, there is no need for an ORDER BY clause.

Automation

Queries, views, and stored procedures are objects that may be used to process information, and are invoked either by the client application or when certain events occur. Triggers are an example of event-based execution of these objects and they can be scheduled to fire when a table is updated, or when a record is inserted or deleted. Triggers are discussed in detail in Chapter 4. But how can these database objects be invoked if the use of a trigger is not appropriate? Maybe you don't want some code to run every time a table is updated, but want a procedure to run at a preset time or when a certain condition is met. Perhaps you want to perform a backup on a nightly basis, or notify the DBA when the transaction log is nearly full. Historically, mainframe systems would employ computer operators to perform many of these functions manually. However, using people to do these jobs is not always ideal.

Microsoft SQL Server addresses many of these problems with a wide range of features that perform operations on your behalf without any manual intervention. You can use a scheduler within SQL Server to perform operations on a regular basis or at set times. You can even define your own events that are executed when specific conditions in the database are met. Like event handling routines in languages such as Visual C++ or Visual Basic, you can specify what actions should be performed when these events are raised. Since SQL Server can be integrated with your e-mail systems, you can use these events to provide interaction with users and customers.

Creating and Scheduling Tasks

You can create and schedule tasks easily by using the **SQL Server Agent** (previously known as the SQL Executive in previous releases of Microsoft SQL Server). To start, right-click on the Jobs option from the **SQL Server Agent** node in Enterprise Manager and select New Job from the popup menu, as shown here:

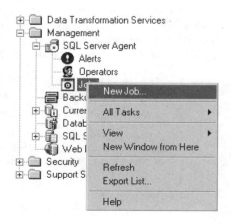

This will bring up the New Job Properties dialog which has 4 tabs: General, Steps, Schedules, and Notifications. On the General tab, you set the name of the job, its category, which provides a means of grouping together jobs, and here is where you specify the owner of the job and the target – in this case the administrator (sa) and the local machine respectively:

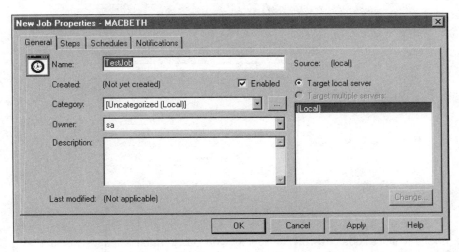

On the Steps tab, you create the tasks that are part of the job and set the options for the tasks, such as what to do if the action is successful or if the action fails. In the Command box, you enter the name of the stored procedure you want to run, or some SQL code:

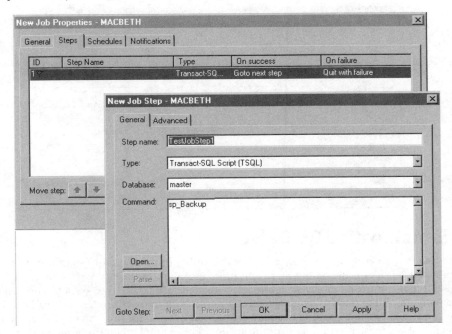

On the Schedules tab, you manage when and how often the job is to run. For example, you can set the job to run every Monday night at 9:00 PM. as follows:

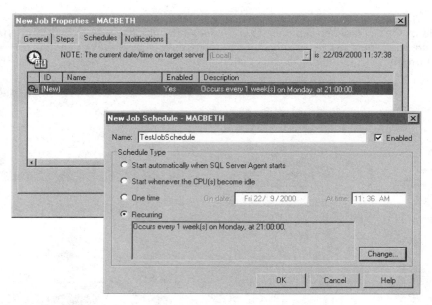

Finally, on the Notifications tab, you can specify who gets notified when a scheduled event occurs, when the notification takes place and what form the notification takes. For example, you can send an e-mail message and a page message to a user when a job fails, or as the screen shot shows, just record any failure in the system log:

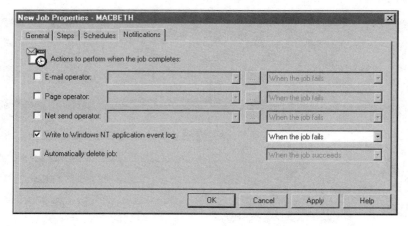

Using E-Mail with SQL Server

With the rise in popularity of e-commerce sites, the ability of database applications to work with electronic mail services is becoming more and more essential. In today's market place, it is virtually a requirement that some kind of e-mail support is provided. Think about it – would you feel confident about making an online purchase on a site that required you to place a telephone call during normal business hours just to ask a simple question? E-mail can be used for more than just product support or marketing, it also can be used for site administration. For example, you can e-mail nightly status reports or alert the DBA when available disk space is reduced to a critical level.

Microsoft SQL Server lets you send, receive, and process mail using two different services. The first service is **MSSQLServer**, which processes mail by connecting to an existing mail server. The second service is the **SQL Server Agent**, which processes mail by establishing an extended MAPI connection.

When MSSQLServer processes mail, the work is done using a series of mail-related stored procedures and a component called **SQL Mail**. This component uses a Simple MAPI (Messaging API) connection with a mail server, such as Microsoft Exchange, Microsoft Windows NT Mail, or another POP3 server. By using Simple MAPI, this service will almost certainly work with most modern mail systems. Outgoing messages may be sent from either a trigger or a stored procedure, allowing you to do such things as send a confirming e-mail to a customer when a new order is processed and recorded in your database tables. The SQL Mail stored procedures can also accept incoming mail and invoke the appropriate queries or stored procedures for processing.

> *The Messaging Application Programming Interface (MAPI) is an extensive set of functions that developers can use to create mail-enabled applications. The full function library is known as Extended MAPI and a limited subset of the library is known as Simple MAPI. Simple MAPI provides basic messaging functionality, such as logging onto the mail system, composing new messages, adding and resolving recipients, and reading messages from the inbox. Extended MAPI allows complete control over the messaging system on the client computer, such as the creation and management of messages, management of the client mailbox, service providers, and so forth.*

The SQL Server Agent doesn't use SQL Mail, but has its own mail system, referred to as **SQLAgentMail**, which is configured separately from SQL Mail and can use either Simple or Extended MAPI. SQLAgentMail is an event-based application, meaning that it is run when an alert is generated, or when a scheduled task either succeeds or fails. Since many wireless devices (phones, pagers, etc.) now support an e-mail address, it's possible to have the SQLAgentMail automatically notify the database administrator of any problems whenever they occur. This differs from SQL Mail, which uses the SQL Mail extended stored procedures to send messages from either a trigger or a stored procedure.

Configuring SQL Mail

Configuring SQL Mail is fairly straightforward. All that needs to be done is to specify the accounts and servers that will be used to send and receive mail. SQL Mail can be configured to use either Exchange or a simple POP3/SMTP server.

Setting Up SQL Mail for Use with Exchange

When setting up SQL Mail for Exchange, you will reference a mailbox on the Exchange server by specifying an Exchange User profile. Exchange mailboxes are set up for specific network logins and so the local system account cannot be used for the profile. Instead you must use a named Windows NT account, so it is recommended that you create an account specifically for SQL Server's use. This can be done using the User Manager utility found in the Administrative Tools (Common) folder (Windows NT) or the Local Users and Groups system tool under Computer Management (Windows 2000). This account must also have administrator privileges on the SQL Server machine, so it should also be added to the local administrator group. Just make sure that you explicitly revoke all accesses to other machine or network resources for this account.

The following are the steps required to set up SQL Mail for using Exchange. It is assumed that your Exchange Administrator has already created a new mailbox to be used by SQL Mail:

1. Log on to Windows NT/2000 using the Windows NT account that has been set up in advance for SQL Server.

2. Change the NT account for the SQL Server service to match your SQL Server Windows NT account by using the Services applet found in Control Panel (or Administration Tools).

3. Restart SQL Server.

4. Install Outlook, Win 2000, or an Exchange client (also known as Windows Messaging) and then reboot the machine.

5. On the SQL Server machine, create a new mail profile for the Exchange service, which can be done by using the Mail applet in Control Panel. This profile needs to be set up using the Connect to my Local Area Network (LAN) option. Also, this exchange profile should not have a Personal Message Store (*.pst) file associated with it, which can also be checked by using the Mail applet in Control Panel. The only services associated with this profile should be Microsoft Exchange Server and, if you want it, the Outlook Address Book.

6. Verify that the mail client just installed can connect to the Exchange Server and that you can pass mail back and forth.

7. From Enterprise Manager, right click on the SQL Mail icon and select Properties. Select the profile name that you just created.

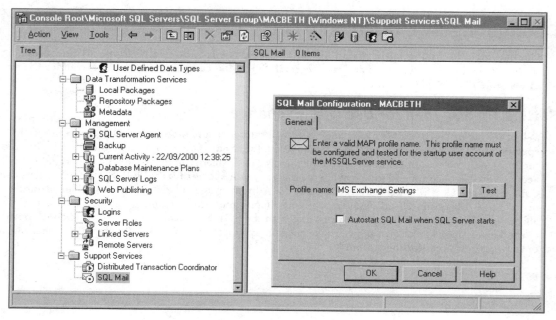

Note that, if you have configured your accounts correctly, the name of the profile should appear in the drop-down list.

8. Start SQL Mail by right-clicking the SQL Mail icon and selecting Start. You can also start SQL Mail programmatically by running the xp_startmail procedure.

9. From Query Analyzer, execute xp_sendmail to send a test message to the mailbox you created for the SQL Mail account:

```
EXEC xp_sendmail 'SQLMailAccount', 'Test message.'
```

10. If you start up your mail client, you should see the test message appear in the inbox.

11. Use the Services applet from Control Panel (or Administration Tools) to cause the SQL Agent to start automatically.

12. Update the system registry to enable SQL Mail service to start when the SQL Server Agent starts by setting the value of the following entry to 1:

```
HKEY_LOCAL_MACHINE\SOFTWARE\Microsoft\MSSQLServer\SQLServerAgent
Name: MailAutoStart
Type: REG_DWORD
Data: 1
```

Setting Up SQL Mail for Use with a POP3/SMTP Server

To use SQL Mail for use with a POP3/SMTP server, you will need to install Windows Messaging, obtain a POP or SMTP mail account and you will also need to install a mail client, such as Outlook or Outlook Express. As in the set up of SQL Mail for Exchange, you will need to use a named SQL Server account. This account should have the same set of requirements and restrictions:

1. Log on to Windows NT/2000 using the Windows NT account that has been set up in advance for SQL Server.

2. Install Windows Messaging.

3. Create the new mail profile by right-clicking the Inbox and selecting Properties. This profile should use only Internet Mail as an option and connecting through the network. Specify the name of the mail server and an automatic transfer method, the e-mail address, and something appropriate in the Full Name box. In the mailbox name box, enter the login name for the mail server. Use the default address book and folder settings.

4. After finishing the creation of this profile, select the profile name that will be used when Windows messaging starts up.

5. Stop the SQL Server and SQL Executive services and change the NT account for these services to match your SQL Server Windows NT account by using the Services applet found in Control Panel (or Administration Tools). Then restart these services.

6. Start the mail client that was just installed and create a new connection for your mail server. This connection needs to be set up to use a LAN.

7. Verify that the mail client just installed can connect to your mail server and that you can pass mail back and forth.

8. From Enterprise Manager, expand the Support Services folder and then right-click on the SQL Mail icon. Enter the profile name that you just created. Once again, if you have configured your accounts correctly, the name of the profile should be in the drop-down list.

9. Start SQL Mail by right-clicking the SQL Mail icon and selecting Start.

10. From Query Analyzer, execute `xp_sendmail` to send a message to the mailbox you created for the SQL Mail account:

```
EXEC xp_sendmail 'SQLMailAccount', 'Test message.'
```

If you start up your mail client, you should see the test message appear in the inbox.

Examples of How to Send E-Mail with SQL Server

Assuming that you have SQL Mail or SQLAgentMail installed, it is very easy to send and receive mail messages. For example, if you wanted to send an e-mail to the webmaster at ACME Aquarium Products, you might use:

```
EXECUTE master.dbo.xp_sendmail 'webmaster@acmeaquarium.com', 'Your site is great!'
```

Note: Since the `xp_sendmail` extended stored procedure is defined in the master database, you will usually need to include the `master.dbo.` prefix to identify that the stored procedure is to be found in the master database rather than the current database.

The `xp_sendmail` extended stored procedure is the only one you need for sending outgoing mail once the service has been started using `xp_startmail`. This stored procedure accepts over 15 different arguments for you to specify such things as a subject line, copy recipients (CCs), blind carbon copy recipients (BCCs), as well as the text of the message and any attachments. Like many other stored procedures, you don't need to include every argument when you invoke the routine; you only need to list the things that you want to be passed. If you don't explicitly name the arguments, SQL Server will assume that you are providing the arguments in a predefined order, according to the syntax described in the help file:

```
xp_sendmail {[@recipients =] 'recipients [;...n]'}
[, [@message =] 'message']
[, [@query =] 'query']
[, [@attachments =] attachments]
[, [@copy_recipients =] 'copy_recipients [;...n]'
[, [@blind_copy_recipients =] 'blind_copy_recipients [;...n]'
[, [@subject =] 'subject']
[, [@type =] 'type']
[, [@attach_results =] 'attach_value']
[, [@no_output =] 'output_value']
[, [@no_header =] 'header_value']
[, [@width =] width]
[, [@separator =] 'separator']
[, [@echo_error =] 'echo_value']
[, [@set_user =] 'user']
[, [@dbuse =] 'database']
```

The only parameters that are required are the recipients and the message. For example, if we want to send an e-mail that includes a subject line and is copied to another recipient, the call to the stored procedure will look like the following:

```
EXEC master.dbo.xp_sendmail
    'webmaster@acmeaquarium.com',
    @copy_recipients = 'jsmith@xyz.com'
    @message ='Your site is great!.',
```

Since the @recipients argument is listed first, as the syntax specifies, its argument name is not needed. The other two arguments are not listed in the syntax order (message then query), so they must be explicitly named.

Unlike traditional e-mail, mail with SQL Server can automatically include the results of queries. This is done by specifying a valid SQL statement as a text string for the @query argument. If you include a message argument as well, the message text will be displayed first, followed by the results of the query. Let's try this out with the following:

```
master.dbo.xp_sendmail
    'jsmith@acmeaquarium.com',
    @message = 'Here is the list of current employees that you asked for.',
    @query = 'Select emp_id, fname, lname from pubs.dbo.employee',
    @subject = 'Current Employees'
```

When the recipient jsmith@acmeaquarium.com receives the mail message, it will look like this:

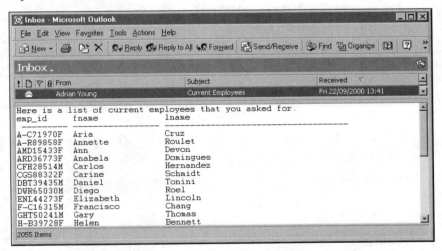

This next example sends a message, executes a stored procedure (sp_configure) rather than a query, and includes the results as an attachment. The @width parameter is used to prevent line breaks in the output lines:

```
master.dbo.xp_sendmail
    'jsmith@acmeaquarium.com',
    @message = 'Attached is the current configuration of the TERRA server.',
    @query = 'sp_configure',
    @attach_results = 'TRUE',
    @width = 250,
    @subject = 'Current configuration of the TERRA server '
```

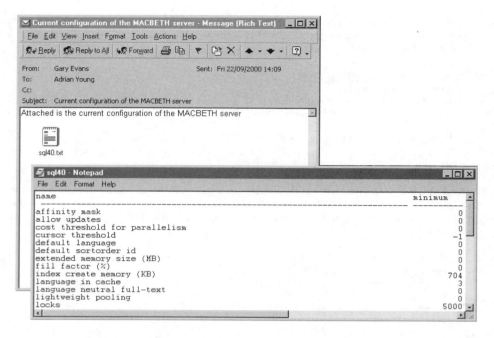

Using Alerts with SQLAgentMail

Alerts are another feature of Microsoft SQL Server that allows for event-driven programming. As with object-oriented languages, you can specify the conditions that will cause an alert to be triggered, whereupon it may send an e-mail message, call a pager, send a message over the LAN, or invoke a stored procedure to address the problem.

SQL Server is installed with a number of sample alerts. You can view these alerts in Enterprise Manager by selecting the Alerts icon under the SQL Server Agent:

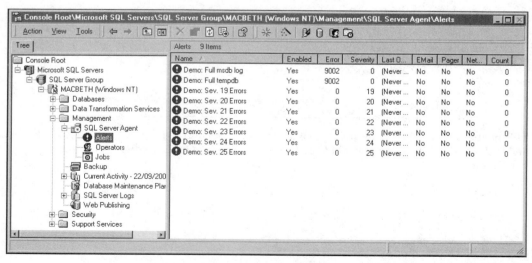

Let's take a look at one of these alerts to see how they are constructed. Right-click on the alert named Demo: Full tempdb and select Properties...:

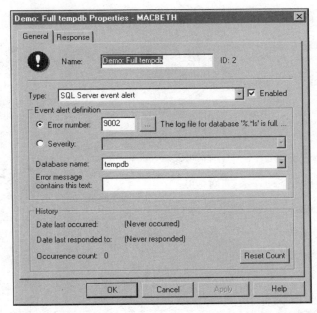

As you can see, this alert is configured when error number 9002 is raised by SQL Server, which indicates that a database is full. The Database name dropdown list specifies which database this alert applies to. In this case, only the tempdb database will be listened to.

If we select the Response tab, we can see what will happen in response if this error is raised:

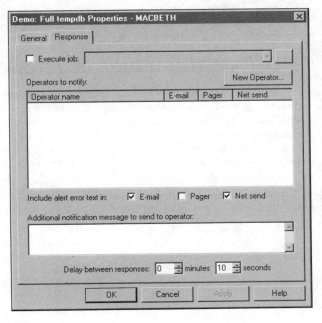

This demonstration alert is not currently set up to respond in any way. If we select the New Operator... button, we can tell SQL Server who to e-mail when this alert is raised.

The New Operator Properties dialog is displayed as follows:

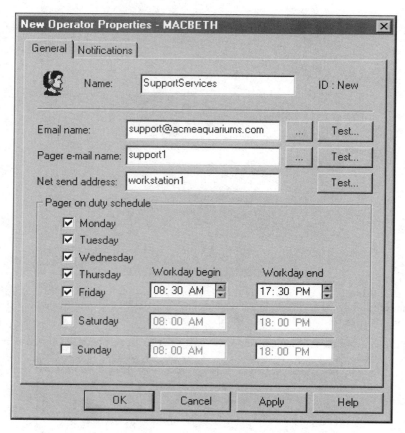

When this particular alert is raised, we want to notify the appropriate support personnel, so let's name this operator "SupportServices". Let's also enter in the e-mail and pager addresses, and if we know the name of the computer, that can be entered into the Net send address box to cause a message dialog box to appear on that computer's monitor. Test buttons are provided to help you verify that you have entered the correct information. After filling in what hours Support Services will be available for paging, select the OK button to save this new operator and return to the Alert properties dialog.

> *If you wish to have more than one person receive the e-mail message, you can always define more than one operator, but a better way is to create a distribution list in your mail system.*

All that remains is to check the boxes that tell SQL Server to send messages to Support Services by e-mail, pager, or straight to the workstation over the Internet:

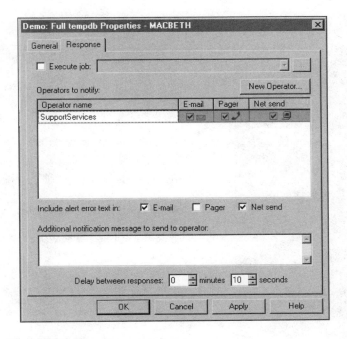

Using the Web Assistant Wizard

You can use the Web Assistant Wizard to generate standard HTML files using SQL Server data by using TSQL queries, stored procedures, and extended stored procedures. You can use the wizard to generate an HTML file once, as a regularly scheduled SQL Server task, or update an HTML file using a trigger. The Web Assistant Wizard runs from the Web Publishing option in SQL Server Enterprise Manager:

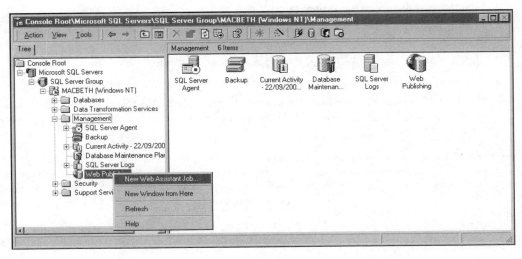

This generates the opening screen of the wizard:

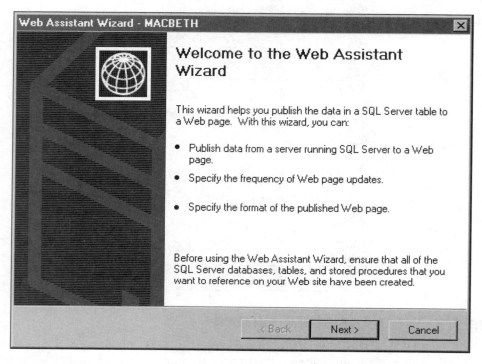

The Web Assistant Wizard consists of eleven screens where you can do the following:

❑ Schedule a task to update a web page automatically.

❑ Publish and distribute management reports.

❑ Publish server reports with information about who is accessing the server currently, which locks are being held, and by which users.

❑ Publish information outside SQL Server using extended stored procedures.

❑ Publish server jump lists using a table of favorite web sites.

❑ Use the sp_makewebtask stored procedure to generate an HTML file. This system stored procedure can be called by any TSQL program. You can also call system stored procedures to run or drop the task.

The Wizard first invites you to select a database from the list on your server – for this example we shall use pubs. Then you supply a name for the job and specify how the data is to be retrieved, either by a stored procedure, by a T-SQL statement, or manually by specifying tables and columns – which is what we will do. The next screen gives you the opportunity to select the table and columns for your web report:

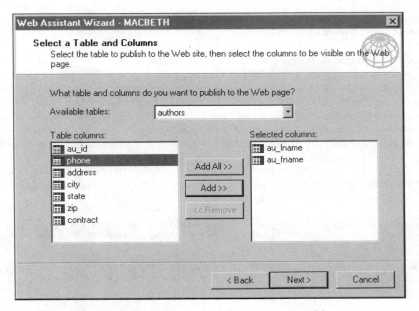

Our report will consist of the first and last names from the `authors` table.

Next you select which rows are to be included in the output. The default setting is for all rows to be returned, though you can specify some restrictions on the output using Boolean comparisons by supplying a T-SQL statement.

Next we specify how the updating of the Web data is scheduled. The options are shown in this screenshot:

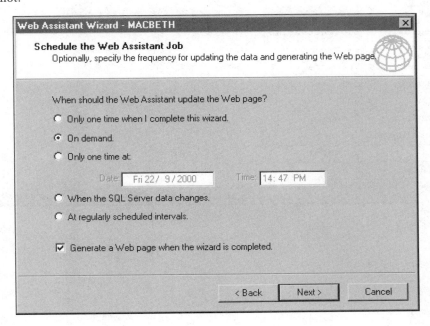

You can see that there is quite a range of options from a single occurrence (either immediately or at a preset time) through to updating on demand.

The next screen deal is with the output HTML page. First you supply a name and path for the file, and then you specify whether SQL Server handles the formatting or whether you supply your own template. The former option is the default. If you let SQL Server determine the formatting, you will be asked to supply a name for the table, and formatting details, and whether or not you want live hyperlinks in your page. Finally, you are asked how many rows you want in your output and whether or not they should be placed on one page or spread across pages. The default scenario is for all rows to be written to a single web page, which would not be ideal if you have a vast number of rows. For large data you can specify now many rows you want per page.

This is what your output should look like, using the author's first and last names from pubs and accepting the default HTML formatting options:

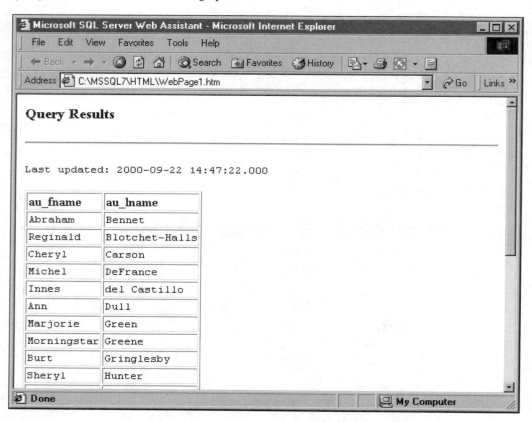

Summary

In this chapter we have looked at many aspects of using SQL Server, specifically:

❏ How security settings need to be taken into account when accessing SQL Server from ASP.

❏ How the environment in which stored procedures are run can be changed.

❏ An in-depth look at stored procedures, and how they can be monitored and the performance improved.

❏ How important tasks can be scheduled to run at certain times or triggered in response to certain events occurring on the database.

❏ How SQL Server can be used to send e-mail messages.

❏ How to configure SQL Server to produce data output as HTML files.

15

Oracle8 and Oracle8i

Wouldn't life be a lot easier if everyone used the same operating system, the same Internet browser software and the same relational database? Unfortunately things aren't that simple, so we need to be as flexible as possible. This book introduces all the main databases and data sources that you, as an ASP developer, may come across. Here, we will cover one of the most important relational databases – Oracle.

In this chapter we will cover the basics of configuring a web server to connect to a remote Oracle8 or Oracle8i database, although many of the techniques apply equally well to previous versions of Oracle 7.x. We'll show you how to use the common **ODBC Drivers** and **OLE DB Providers** in conjunction with ActiveX Data Objects (ADO) to manipulate data stored within an Oracle database from within an ASP application.

We'll build upon each area by creating a collection of ASP scripts that will use the sample `scott` database schema showing how to retrieve and update data in a flexible and more importantly, scalable manner. We will finally cover the (unfortunately), *advanced* concept of retrieving **recordsets** from an Oracle **stored procedure**. Don't worry though, it's relatively easy to use scalar `INPUT` and `OUTPUT` parameters to return individual parameters from an Oracle stored procedure – which we'll also be covering in this chapter.

> All of the SQL and ASP code for this sample application can be downloaded from the Wrox web site at `http://www.wrox.com`.

A Brief History of Oracle

Way back in June 1970, Dr E F Codd published a paper *entitled A Relational Model of Data for Large Shared Data Banks*. This relational model, sponsored by IBM, then came to be accepted as the definitive model for relational database management systems – RDBMS. The language developed by IBM to manipulate the data stored within Codd's model was originally called Structured English Query Language, or SEQUEL, with the word 'English' later being dropped in favor Structured Query Language – SQL.

In 1979 a company called Relational Software, Inc. released the first commercially available implementation of SQL. Relational Software later came to be known as Oracle Corporation.

Oracle Version 8

You'll find versions of Oracle8 available for many of today's popular computing environments, in particular Windows, UNIX and Linux. This is one of the reasons why it's so popular, and luckily for us as developers, doesn't make that much of a difference which platform it is running on.

The original version of Oracle8 was designed to support applications in the up-and-coming network-computing era, ranging from a small departmental application right up to a high-volume enterprise-wide system. In order to provide this level of flexibility, Oracle8 comes in two different editions:

❑ Oracle8

❑ Oracle8 Enterprise Edition

Both editions actually share the same code base, but the difference is that the standard edition (referred to simply as Oracle8) is aimed at smaller applications, whereas its big brother, the Enterprise Edition, comes with a number of high-end features that allows it to support the thousands of users of larger enterprise-wide applications. The Enterprise Edition provides greater support for very large databases containing hundreds of terabytes of data, whilst the number of columns per table and maximum database size, for both editions, has been increased compared to previous versions of Oracle.

In order to support large numbers of users, both the Oracle8 and Oracle8 Enterprise Edition servers provide a method of connection pooling that temporarily drops and then re-uses a physical connection for those users that are idle, in conjunction with its networking software **Net8**. With this type of technology there is no reason why an Oracle server cannot support many thousands of concurrent users.

With that said, it's worth remembering that our ASP-based applications, if designed correctly, should connect and disconnect from the Oracle database as soon as they have completed a certain task, rather than hold onto a database connection for the life of the user's session. Don't forget that Microsoft Transaction Server and OLE DB also offer connection-pooling techniques to save the valuable time taken to initialize database connections.

> *Traditional client/server applications that maintain a user's connection, until the application has closed, will more than likely utilize Oracle's own connection pooling rather than that of OLE DB which pools connections based on the same username and password combination.*

The actual edition of Oracle8 that we connect to again makes little practical difference to the front-end applications that we develop, as we use the same query language and networking software to manipulate the data.

Both editions of Oracle8 provide support for the emerging SQL-3 standard for object-type definition. SQL-3 allows us to create object types that, for example, define a person's address that we could then use directly in our database, and access through our programs.

> *For a full investigation into Oracle's object support, check out the Oracle TechNet at* `http://technet.oracle.com`.

Oracle Version 8i

Oracle8i is the latest incarnation of the Oracle8 data server. If you hadn't already guessed it, the 'i' in Oracle8i refers to the **Internet**. Oracle Corporation bills Oracle8i as "the database for Internet computing".

All of the above Oracle8 features apply just the same to the new Oracle8i, with the Oracle8i data server also being available in two editions – the standard edition, Oracle8i, and the high-end version, Oracle8i Enterprise Edition.

The major change to the Oracle8i Enterprise Edition is the inclusion of support for the **Java Virtual Machine** allowing developers to execute Java code directly from within the database engine. Whereas previously, the only way to procedurally manipulate Oracle data was through its PL/SQL language, you can now use Java to do exactly the same job.

> *So are they doing away with PL/SQL? This does seem to be the general trend if you consider that the next version of SQL Server (the one after version 2000) will allow stored procedures written in any .Net language and that DB2 already provides support for Java stored procedures. SQL is here for the foreseeable future, but maybe for the benefit of ODBC and OLE DB access.*

Oracle8i includes the Internet File System, **iFS**, a Java application that brings the combination of an integrated file system and database into one server to provide text searches and querying of files and data stored within iFS.

Another new technology in Oracle8i is **Oracle WebDB** that allows dynamic web sites to be built and deployed from within the Oracle database. WebDB provides an HTML interface so that non-programmers can develop their own web-based database applications. It includes a lightweight HTTP listener that can act as a web server and a PL/SQL interface to the database. As web developers, we might want to discourage non-programmers from developing their own web sites; this is not just because of our own job security, but also due to the fact that small in-house projects have a tendency to grow into large projects that may not have been designed with scalability in mind through poor programming techniques.

Oracle8i's new **interMedia** feature provides additional support for multimedia content such as image, video, text, and audio. interMedia allows users to query data held within common document formats such as HTML, Adobe Acrobat (PDF) and the Microsoft Office applications such as Word documents and Excel spreadsheets, and provides support for the delivery of *streaming* media in conjunction with common streaming servers such as Oracle Video Server and RealVideo.

> *Release 2 of Oracle8i (version 8.1.6) also brings native support for XML.*

If you've used Oracle8 prior to Oracle8i, then you'll notice that the developer's tools such as the Schema Manager, Oracle Installer and Net8 Assistant have had a radical interface makeover. I personally find them slightly slower to use than their previous counterparts owing to the fact that most are now written in Java, but they do appear more user friendly.

Installing Oracle Client Components

In this section we will be installing the Oracle client components on an IIS-based web server to enable our ASP scripts to communicate with an Oracle database server. Once the client programs have been installed we will be using Oracle's configuration utilities to configure our web server to connect to Oracle.

> *With the exception of cosmetics, there are very few differences between the Oracle8 and Oracle8i installation programs, so we will be showing screen shots from the Oracle8i installation.*

In order to access an Oracle database, a number of software components need to be installed on a client computer. Oracle8 uses its networking component **Net8** to provide client-server and server-server connectivity for many common protocols and platforms.

In versions prior to Oracle8, the forerunner to Net8 was **SQL*Net** version 2 – you'll find lots of documentation that still refers to SQL*Net. Net8 is backwardly compatible with SQL*Net version 2, allowing Net8 to access both Oracle7 and Oracle8 databases. It is possible, however, to connect to an Oracle8 database using SQL*Net but some of the new network features will not be available.

Once you've installed the Oracle client components, the **Net8 Easy Config** and **Net8 Assistant** applications can be used to configure your Net8 settings. Both applications use a number of .ora configuration files that you can, if you know what you're doing, edit yourself in Notepad. We'll go through the installation of the client components before we go into the details of the applications.

> **The Oracle client components are supported on all 32-bit Windows platforms:**
> **Windows 95, Windows 98, Windows NT 3.5 and NT 4 Server and Workstation, and**
> **Windows 2000.**

By running the familiar setup.exe file you will be presented with a screen welcoming you to the **Oracle Universal Installer**, or **Oracle Installer** as Oracle8 calls it. After clicking Next your first choice is to tell the Installer where to put the physical files that it installs. This location is known as the **Oracle Home** setting:

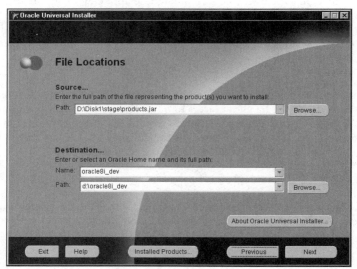

This allows you to install multiple versions of the Oracle products onto the same machine without an installation conflicting with any other installation. Oracle Home essentially defines the location of a folder into which the software is installed. If you only plan to have one set of Oracle products installed on the machine, which is very often the case, then choose DEFAULT_HOME for the Name. In my case, I have a number of Oracle products installed, so I have given it a name of oracle8i_dev with the files being located in the d:\oracle8i_dev folder.

Clicking the Next button takes you to the Available Products screen:

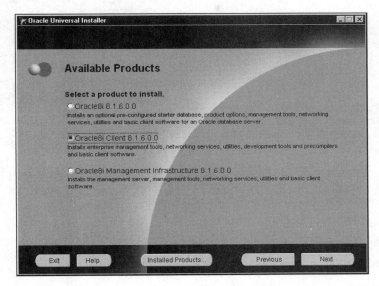

Here you must choose the actual product to install: the database server, client software, or management infrastructure software. In many cases you will be connecting to an Oracle database running on a different server to that of your web server, so you should select the second option, Oracle8i Client. If your web server also happens to be your database server then you will need to select the first option to install the actual database sever and, optionally, a starter database accessed via the scott account. The Management Infrastructure option installs the client components along with directory services components.

In my case, I am installing the Oracle client on a web server that will connect to Oracle on a remote server, so I selected Oracle8i Client.

Once you've clicked Next, you will be asked about the Installation Type (the Oracle8 installation calls this the Primary Function). The list of options shown is dependent upon the item selected from the previous screen. If you had chosen to install the Oracle server then you will see a list of options, such as whether to include the pre-configured starter scott database.

In the case of the Oracle Client installation you can specify the type of installation required for the client components depending upon the features that the client machine needs:

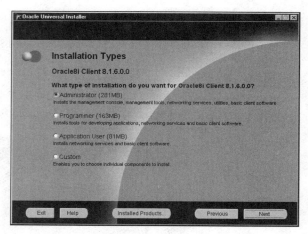

If you need to perform DBA tasks such as creating and backing-up databases, and stopping the server then choose the Administrator option. This will install all of the utilities required to administer an Oracle server.

If the machine is used as your development server then it's a good idea to choose the Programmer option to install a subset of the Administrator tools. However, you won't get utilities such as the **Enterprise Manager Console** used to administer an Oracle server.

The Application User option should be selected if the machine is used as your web server. This will only install the basic networking and client components and none of the admin or programming tools.

The last option, Custom, allows you to specify exactly which components should be installed.

> *You can decide which items should be installed on your machine, but some organizations do not allow developers to perform traditional DBA functions such as stopping servers - for very good reasons. You can always add or remove components using the Installer at a later date. Personally I'd want everything that's available so I'd choose Administrator anytime!*

After you've clicked Next (for the last time) the Installer will show a summary page confirming the options that you have selected:

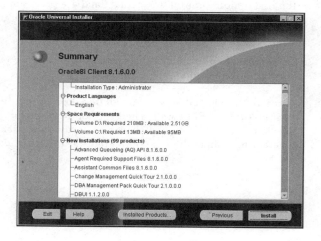

Now it's just a case of pressing the Install button to install all of the required programs. Once the installation has been completed you can move onto configuring Net8, the client software, to connect to your Oracle server.

Configuring Net8

As mentioned earlier, we need to install a layer of network software on our web server that allows us to communicate with Oracle. By selecting the **Client** installation, the Oracle Installer will have installed Net8, which we now have to configure.

Net8 supports standard network protocols, such as TCP/IP, to connect to Oracle8 servers through the use of user-friendly aliases called **service names**. A service name is simply a name used to refer to an Oracle server much as we use URLs in preference for hard-to-remember IP addresses.

You have a number of ways in which to store these lists of service names:

❑   Domain Name System (DNS)

❑   Local client configuration files

❑   Oracle Name Server

❑   Non-Oracle name server

Net8 uses **Oracle Protocol Adaptors** to map the following industry-standard network protocols into a standard that it can recognize internally:

TCP/IP	Widely-used Internet network protocol
SPX	Another commonly used network protocol
Named Pipes	Microsoft's networking protocol specific to PC-based LANs
Bequeath	Used for local Windows 95 and 98 Personal Oracle8 installations
Logical Unit Type	Part of IBM's peer-to-peer SNA network

Oracle8 comes with two utilities to configure Net8: **Net8 Easy Config**, to edit our list of service names, and **Net8 Assistant**, an advanced utility that allows us to configure service names, network listeners, Oracle Names Servers and local configuration files. Configuration using Net8 Assistant is primarily a DBA role so we won't cover it here. We will be using the Net8 Easy Config application to configure our client.

There are a number of ways to store the list of service names with the two most commonly used methods being:

❑   **Host Naming** – Uses existing DNS-based or a centrally maintained HOSTS file for name resolution. By simply using the host's network name, no client configuration is required.

❑   **Local Naming** – Uses a local configuration file, TNSNAMES.ORA, to resolve names.

Host Naming does not require any client configuration so we will take a look at Local Naming using the Net8 Easy Config program. Net8 Easy Config edits a file called TNSNAMES.ORA in the *installation_folder*\Net80\Admin folder, which can be edited manually using Notepad. In many Oracle sites it is a common practice to simply copy the TNSNAMES.ORA file from the Oracle server machine onto the client.

*TNS stands for **Transparent Network Substrate** (TNS). This is a non- proprietary low-level interface that manages the opening and closing of sessions and the sending or receiving of requests.*

The screens that make up the Oracle8 and Oracle8i Net8 Easy Config (Net8 Configuration Assistant in Oracle8i) applications do differ somewhat so we'll work through both versions to configure connecting to an Oracle8 and Oracle8i server.

If you are configuring an Oracle8 client then start the Oracle Net8 Easy Config and select **Add New Service**. Our DBA has called the Oracle8 server `Oracle8_Dev`, so we'll type that name in – you'll have to use the name of your own Oracle8 server. You may find that this is the name of the actual server, provided that it is only running one instance of Oracle.

You may see a dialog box warning you that Net8 Easy Config has found a number of comments in the configuration file `TNSNAMES.ORA`. It is generally safe to ignore this warning message.

In the case of our Oracle8i database, we have a server called `Oracle8i_Dev` so we'll use that for the name. Before you can enter the Oracle8i service name, choose the **Local Net Service Name configuration** option, click **Next** and then choose the **Add** item to add a new service name before pressing **Next** again. Finally you must tell the Oracle8i Configuration Assistant that you want to access an Oracle8i database. Clicking **Next** will take you to the Service Name screen:

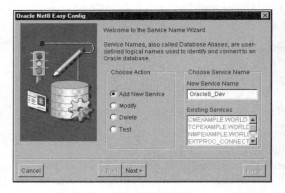

The next step is to choose the type of network protocol used to communicate with the server. Typically this will most likely be TCP/IP:

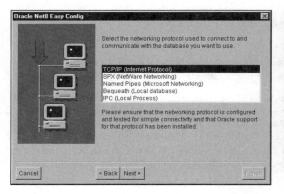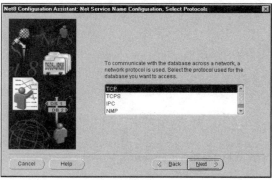

The host name is the resolved name used to refer to the server, which in our case is the same name given to this service name – for ease. It is possible to install the Oracle server software to listen on a different TCP/IP port number. By default, port number **1521** is used for Oracle installations, in much the same way that port number 80 is used for HTTP requests. Unless your DBA has used a different port number for additional security, select the default option:

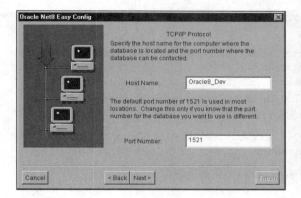 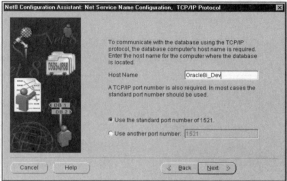

There is one additional step to complete before testing an Oracle8 connection: you have to type in the name of the database System Identifier, or **SID** to connect to. It is possible to run more than one **instance** of Oracle on the same server by giving each instance a unique SID by which it can be identified. If there is only one instance installed, then the Oracle server installation will default to calling it ORCL, which your DBA can confirm:

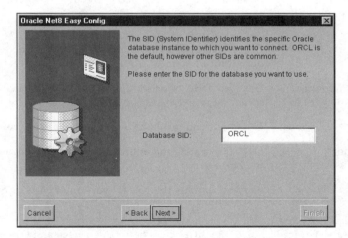

If you do have a number of SIDs per server then it might be a good idea to use the SID as the name for each service.

To test the new service name, you must enter a valid user name and password when using Oracle8. Typically you can enter the `scott/tiger` username/password combination provided that the pre-configured `scott` database has been installed. The Oracle8i version actually defaults to using `scott/tiger` for you.

If you've entered the correct host name and username/password then you should receive a message saying that the connection test was successful. If you receive the error message ORA-12545: connect failed because target host or object does not exist, you need to recheck the values of your host name, port number and SID. You should also confirm that Oracle is actually running on the host specified.

The message ORA-01017: invalid username/password; logon denied is a lot more encouraging; it means that you successfully communicated with the Oracle server, but you entered the wrong username or password.

ORA-12545 and ORA-01017 are the common error messages that you are likely to come across, but you may receive any of the following messages as well:

ORA-12154: "TNS:could not resolve service name"	Net8 could not find the service name specified in your TNSNAMES.ORA file. Make sure that the TNSNAMES.ORA file actually exists and that you do not have multiple copies of the TNSNAMES.ORA file. Make sure that you do not have duplicate copies of the SQLNET.ORA file. When using domain names ensure that your SQLNET.ORA file contains a NAMES.DEFAULT_DOMAIN value.
ORA-12198: "TNS:could not find path to destination" and ORA-12203: "TNS:unable to connect to destination"	The client could not find the required database. Is the service name spelled correctly? Is TNSNAMES.ORA file in the correct folder? Check that the service name ADDRESS parameter in the connect descriptor of your TNSNAMES.ORA file is correct. Get your DBA to check that the Oracle Listener on the remote server has started and is running.
ORA-12224: "TNS:no listener"	Could not connect because the listener is not running. Does the destination address match one of the addresses used by the listener. Are you running the correct version of Net8 or SQL*Net?

> Now that we've covered some of the differences between Oracle8 and Oracle8i, from now on we'll refer to them both collectively as Oracle8. When we come across a distinction between the two, we'll highlight it.

Much like SQL Server's **user spaces**, Oracle groups database objects, such as tables, indexes and procedures, into what is called a **schema**. A schema maps to an actual login name. So, in the case of the scott login name you will find a whole host of database objects under the scott account. scott is the sample database schema created by the Oracle Installer when you first install the Oracle server. Typically, a new default Oracle installation will have the following logins created:

Username	Password	Password
scott	tiger	Sample login.
sys	change_on_ install	Database administrator. Can perform all operations such as stopping and starting the database.
system	manager	Operations user that can perform operational tasks such as database backups.

We've gone through the process of installing Oracle's client networking software, Net8, then added and tested a new Net8 service name to connect to an Oracle8 server called Oracle8_dev and an Oracle8i server called Oracle8i_dev. Now it's time to look at how we connect to an Oracle database through ASP.

Connecting to an Oracle Database

There are a number of ways in which we can connect to an Oracle database in order to manipulate its data from within our ASP scripts. Which one you use rather depends what you are trying to achieve and whether your organization prefers access through stored procedures, as the features supported by one method may not be supported in another.

As well as Oracle Corporation, there are many third-party vendors such as Microsoft and Intersolv that provide a number of products to communicate with Oracle. The following list represents the more commonly used tools:

- ❑ Microsoft OLE DB Provider for Oracle
- ❑ Microsoft OLE DB Provider for ODBC
- ❑ Microsoft ODBC Driver for Oracle
- ❑ Oracle ODBC Driver
- ❑ Intersolv's Merant range of OLE DB providers and ODBC drivers
- ❑ Oracle Objects for OLE by Oracle
- ❑ Oracle Provider for OLE DB by Oracle

Microsoft's Universal Data Access (UDA) initiative contains a set of tools that we can use to communicate with an Oracle database. With the integrated Microsoft Data Access Components (MDAC) suite we can use **ActiveX Data Objects** (ADO) in conjunction with the **Microsoft OLE DB Provider For Oracle** (MSDAORA.DLL) or the **Microsoft ODBC Driver for Oracle** (MSORCL32.DLL) to communicate effectively with Oracle in a way that is reliable, scalable and offers high performance when using ADO.

Microsoft also offers the universal **OLE DB Provider for ODBC Drivers** (MSDASQL.DLL) that allows any ODBC data source to make use of the improvements in OLE DB. This, the default provider used by ADO, was developed so that any existing ODBC-based data could fit into the UDA environment efficiently and without losing an organization's ODBC investment.

As if this didn't give us enough flexibility, we also have the universal **Merant** range of OLE DB providers and ODBC drivers from Intersolv (**www.merant.com/products/datadirect/oledb /Connect/factsheet.asp**), and **Oracle Objects for OLE** (OO4O).

We've discussed how Oracle8's Net8 networking component is used to communicate with an Oracle8 database, but we haven't mentioned the **Oracle Call Interface** (OCI) library. We won't go into much detail except to say that this low-level layer exposes certain procedures that the OLE DB providers and ODBC drivers call in order to communicate with the database, in much the same way as DBLib for SQL Server databases.

After that brief overview, it is now time to show you how to connect to an Oracle8 database using the more popular technologies so that you can see the relative pros and cons of each in terms of feature support, performance, and ease.

> There are bound to be times when you need the ability to fetch recordsets from an Oracle stored procedure with ADO. At the time of writing you have no choice but to use the ODBC driver for Oracle or Oracle's Oracle Provider for OLE DB, both of which will be covered later.

OLE DB Provider for Oracle

The OLE DB Provider for Oracle supports most of the Oracle8 data types:

Data Type	Supported	Data Type	Supported
BFILE		LONG RAW	Yes
BLOB		NCHAR	
CHAR	Yes	NCLOB	
CLOB		NUMBER	Yes
DATE	Yes	NVARCHAR2	
FLOAT	Yes	RAW	Yes
INTEGER	Yes	VARCHAR2	Yes
LONG	Yes	MLSLABEL	

This table shows that many of the standard data types are supported but those such as the LOB (Large Object) and object-based extensions are not supported.

The provider is a *native* provider, in that it accesses the Oracle's API directly rather than through ODBC. This provides us with *generally* the best performance when compared to other methods of connecting to Oracle, but does mean that some functionality is not available.

In order to use the provider, you must set its name in the ConnectionString property of the ADO Connection object or as the ConnectionString argument to the Open method. As with any provider for ADO, unpredictable results can occur if you specify the name of the provider in more than one place.

Let's start by connecting to the Oracle database using the `scott` username to execute two simple built-in Oracle functions to retrieve the system date, `sysdate`, and current username, `user`:

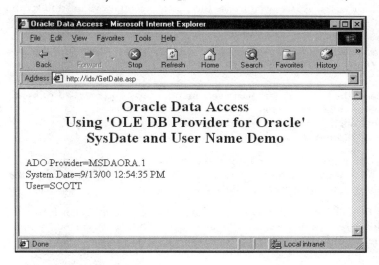

Create a new ASP script called `GetDate.asp`:

```
<% Option Explicit %>
<HTML>
<HEAD><TITLE>Oracle Data Access</TITLE></HEAD>
<BODY>
<CENTER>
   <H2>
      Oracle Data Access<BR>
      Using 'OLE DB Provider for Oracle'<BR>
      SysDate and User Name Demo<BR>
   </H2>
</CENTER>
<%
Dim objConnection
Dim objRecordset

Set objConnection = Server.CreateObject("ADODB.Connection")
With objConnection
   .ConnectionString = "Provider=MSDAORA;Data Source=Oracle8_dev;" & _
                       "User ID=scott; Password=tiger;"
   .Open
   Response.Write "ADO Provider=" & .Provider & "<BR>"

   Set objRecordset = .Execute("SELECT sysdate, user FROM dual")
End With
```

We use the `Connection` object's `ConnectionString` property to tell ADO how to connect to our Oracle database before calling the `Open` command to attempt to connect to the database. Don't forget that the `Data Source` property, `Oracle8_dev`, is the **service name** that we created earlier, rather than the actual machine name – but in my case, both are actually the same value.

The `Provider` section tells ADO to use the OLE DB Provider for Oracle. We can use either the class name of the provider, in this case `MSDAORA`, or the full provider name: `'OLE DB Provider for Oracle'`. As we want to use the `scott` account, we need to set the `User ID` and `Password` accordingly.

> *Our Oracle8 server is located on a server called* `Oracle8_dev`. *You'll have to change this to reflect your own Oracle database server.*

If you've not used the `With...End With` statement, it serves as a way to call multiple methods on a single object without having to refer to the name explicitly every time. It makes your code easier to read and actually runs slightly faster as the ASP processor doesn't have to do extra processing to establish the address of the `objConnection` object.

By calling the `Open` method, we should get a connection to the Oracle database. By way of a confirmation, we write out the name of the `Provider` property. This shows us the name as defined in the Registry along with any version number if there are multiple versions installed on the server.

The `Execute` method returns back a `Recordset` representing the records that were fetched from the database, in this case a single record with a column containing the current system date and the current user name. The argument passed to `Execute` is the command that we want Oracle to run for us.

> *Notice the word* `dual` *in our SELECT statement? Oracle does not allow you to execute a SELECT statement without an accompanying FROM clause;* `dual` *is a logical pseudo-table, available to all accounts, provided for that purpose. It is not a physical table that you can alter.*

```
Response.Write "System Date=" & objRecordset.Fields("sysdate") & "<BR>" & _
               "User="        & objRecordset("user")

Set objConnection = Nothing
Set objRecordset = Nothing
%>
</BODY>
</HTML>
```

We finish off by reading the `Fields` collection of our `objRecordset` object to get the value for the `sysdate` and `user` functions. In the case of the `user` field we've left out the `.Fields` statement as this is the `Recordset` object's default property, though you can make your code run faster if you use it.

There's no need to navigate through the `objRecordset`, as there will only be one record returned. With any objects that we create in our scripts, it's always a good idea to shut them down explicitly as soon as possible using the `Set ... = Nothing` statement in order to free up server resources.

> As we mentioned earlier, if you received the Oracle error message **ORA-12545: connect failed because target host or object does not exist** then you need to recheck the values of your host name, port number and SID that were entered when your created the new service name using Net8 Easy Config.

That was a relatively easy example, so let's have a look at a more complex statement in which we return a number of records. The `scott` schema comes with four sample tables that you can look at yourself. The tables opposite represent an employee's bonus and salary tracking system:

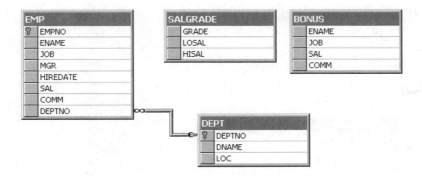

This isn't the best schema that Oracle could have used as their pre-configured sample database. The SALGRADE and BONUS tables are not referenced by any other tables and contain no primary keys.

Table Name	Purpose
DEPT	Stores a list of department names
SALGRADE	Stores a list of salary grades
EMP	Stores a list of employees
BONUS	Stores a list of employee bonuses

Our example ASP script will be using the DEPT and EMP tables to show a list of all employees sorted by their name (later on we'll be using them in our sample application):

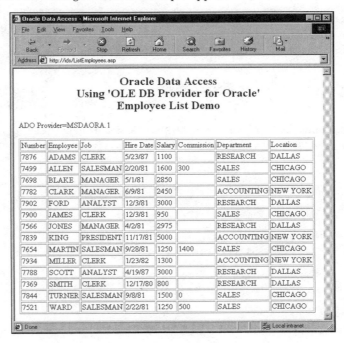

The code used to produce the previous screenshot looks like this:

```
<% Option Explicit %>
<HTML>
<HEAD><TITLE>Oracle Data Access</TITLE></HEAD>
<BODY>
<CENTER>
    <H2>
        Oracle Data Access<BR>
        Using 'OLE DB Provider for Oracle'<BR>
        Employee List Demo<BR>
    </H2>
</CENTER>
<%
Dim objConnection
Dim objRecordset
Dim varSQL

Set objConnection = Server.CreateObject("ADODB.Connection")
With objConnection
    .ConnectionString = "Provider=MSDAORA; Data Source=Oracle8_dev; " & _
                        "User ID=scott; Password=tiger;"
    .Open
    Response.Write "ADO Provider=" & .Provider & "<P>"
```

We start off as before by defining two variables for our Connection and Recordset objects and then connect to the database using the scott/tiger combination. We've added a new variable, varSQL, to hold a nicely formatted SQL statement:

```
    varSQL = "SELECT emp.empno, emp.ename, emp.job, emp.hiredate," & _
             "        emp.sal, emp.comm, dept.dname, dept.loc" & _
             " FROM emp, dept" & _
             " WHERE emp.deptno = dept.deptno" & _
             " ORDER BY emp.ename"

    Set objRecordset = .Execute(varSQL)
End With
```

The SQL statement joins the employee table, EMP, to the department, DEPT, to return a list of employees and their departments. Again we use the Execute command to return back a Recordset of data:

```
Response.Write "<TABLE BORDER=1><TR>" & _
               "   <TD>Number</TD>" & _
               "   <TD>Employee</TD>" & _
               "   <TD>Job</TD>" & _
               "   <TD>Hire Date</TD>" & _
               "   <TD>Salary</TD>" & _
               "   <TD>Commission</TD>" & _
               "   <TD>Department</TD>" & _
               "   <TD>Location</TD>" & _
               "</TR>"
```

We use `Response.Write` to write out the start of our table of results:

```
Do While Not objRecordset.EOF

    Response.Write "<TR>" & _
                   "    <TD>" & objRecordset("empno")    & "</TD>" & _
                   "    <TD>" & objRecordset("ename")    & "</TD>" & _
                   "    <TD>" & objRecordset("job")      & "</TD>" & _
                   "    <TD>" & objRecordset("hiredate") & "</TD>" & _
                   "    <TD>" & objRecordset("sal")      & "</TD>" & _
                   "    <TD>" & objRecordset("comm")     & " </TD>" & _
                   "    <TD>" & objRecordset("dname")    & "</TD>" & _
                   "    <TD>" & objRecordset("loc")      & "</TD>" & _
                   "</TR>"

    objRecordset.MoveNext
Loop
Response.Write "</TABLE>"
```

Now it's just a case of writing out each record by retrieving the value for each column from the `Fields` collection of our `Recordset` object `objRecordset` and moving to the next record using the `MoveNext` method. We loop through using a `Do While...Loop` that will stop as soon as it gets to the end of the `Recordset`.

Some of the records in the `comm` column contain a null value, so we add the HTML non-breaking space tag (` `) to ensure that the browser draws the cell border correctly.

```
Set objConnection = Nothing
Set objRecordset = Nothing
%>
</BODY>
</HTML>
```

As with our previous example, it's a good idea to explicitly close our `objConnection` and `objRecordset` objects as soon as we've finished with them.

We've now managed to connect to an Oracle8 database using the OLE DB Provider for Oracle to retrieve a single record of the current system date and username and a full list of employees in the `scott` database's `emp` table. It is suggested that the OLE DB Provider for Oracle be used for the majority of Oracle data access as it executes faster and supports Microsoft's new direction in data access – OLE DB.

Microsoft ODBC Driver for Oracle

The Microsoft ODBC Driver for Oracle supports the same set of Oracle8 data types as the OLE DB Provider for Oracle. When using this driver with ADO, we are actually using the **OLE DB Provider for ODBC Drivers** (MSDASQL), which in turn uses the Microsoft ODBC for Oracle Driver.

Microsoft released the OLE DB Provider for ODBC (MSDASQL) so that all existing ODBC-based applications could use the new features found in OLE DB through ADO. When connecting to any data source using ADO, this is the default provider that is used.

ODBC connection strings use the older `DRIVER=`, `DSN=`, `UID=`, `PWD=` and `SERVER=` (optionally in the place of DSN=) parameters to connect to a data source. Don't forget that there must be a valid Data Source Name, DSN, registered through the ODBC Data Source Administrator in the Administration Tools (or Control Panel) if you are going to use the `DSN` parameter.

Each time you connect to a database using a DSN, ODBC must look through the Windows Registry in order to retrieve connection details for your DSN. There may be some performance improvements in your application if you use DSN-less connections, as the Windows Registry is notoriously slow to access. If you do need to use DSNs, then remember to use System DSNs rather than File DSNs as anonymous users, which your server is more than likely to use, have access to them.

We are going to create a simple ASP script that uses some of the principles we used with the OLE DB Provider for Oracle to show a list of departments from the `scott` database's `dept` table.

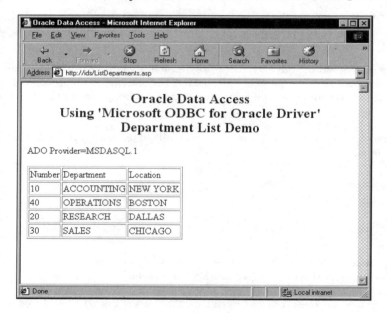

The only real difference to this code is the connection string used, so we'll just show that line of code:

```
.ConnectionString = "Provider=MSDASQL;" & _
                    "DRIVER={Microsoft ODBC for Oracle}; " & _
                    "SERVER=Oracle8_dev; UID=scott; PWD=tiger;"
```

We make use of the `DRIVER` property to tell MSDASQL to use the Microsoft ODBC Driver for Oracle, `SERVER` points to our database server, `Oracle8_dev`, and we use `UID` and `PWD` rather than the `User ID` and `Password` combination.

Notice that we didn't specify a DSN so we don't have to create one, and although it's not actually necessary in this case, we've specified the name of the `Provider` to use.

Oracle Objects for OLE (OO4O)

Oracle provides us with its own native client software that sits above the Oracle Call Interface, as mentioned earlier, allowing us to communicate with an Oracle database using a COM/OLE component.

Oracle Objects for OLE, or OO4O as it is usually abbreviated to, allows us to execute SQL and PL/SQL statements in a native "pass-through" format. This means we can make use of all Oracle data types as well as additional features, such as **bind variables**.

Bind variables are an efficient way to execute the same SQL statement with differing parameters without Oracle having to re-parse the statement each time. Unfortunately, it won't make that much of a performance difference to our web page, as we will only execute the statement twice and then close our database connection. However, this feature is ideal for client/server applications that maintain the database connection until the application is closed. We will be discussing bind variables in the following examples.

Unfortunately, by using OO4O we'll have to forfeit the usual methods found in ADO. However, OO4O does implement the same, or very similar methods, so the learning curve is not that steep.

Version 2.3 of OO4O,which shipped with Oracle8, has the following object model:

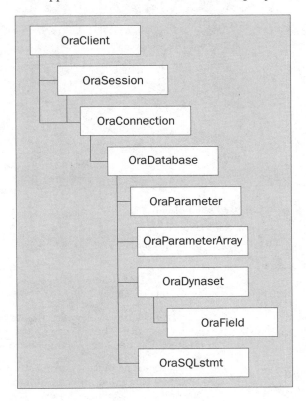

You'll find that the later version, 8.1, as shipped with Oracle8i, has a similar model with a number of extra objects:

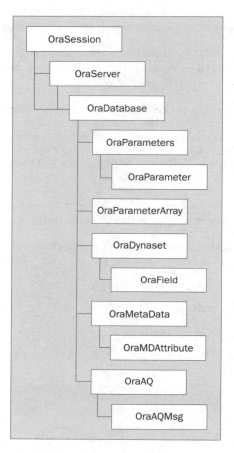

The table gives a brief description of each object:

Name	OO4O Version	Description
OraSession	2.3 8.1	This is the first top-level object needed before we connect to an Oracle database.
OraServer	8.1	Represents a physical connection to an Oracle database server instance. The OpenDatabase function can be used to create client sessions by returning an OraDatabase object.
OraConnection	2.3	Returns various pieces of user information about the current OraSession object. It can be shared by many OraDatabase objects, but each OraDatabase must exist in the same OraSession object.

Name	OO4O Version	Description
OraDatabase	2.3 8.1	Represents a single login to an Oracle database. Similar to the ADO `Connection` object. `OraDatabase` objects are returned by the `OraSession.OpenDatabase` function.
OraDynaset	2.3 8.1	Similar to an ADO `Recordset` object. Represents the results retrieved by a call to the `OraDatabase.CreateDynaset` function.
OraField	2.3 8.1	Represents a column of data within an `OraDynaset` object. Similar to the ADO `Field` object of an ADO `Recordset`.
OraClient	2.3	Automatically created by OO4O as needed. Maintains a list of all active `OraSession` objects currently running on the workstation.
OraParameter	2.3 8.1	Represents a bind variable for a SQL statement or PL/SQL block to be executed using the `OraDynaset` object. Similar to the `Parameter` object in an ADO `Command` object.
OraParamArray	2.3 8.1	Allows **arrays** of parameters to be set for the `OraDatabase.Parameters` function.
OraSQLStmt	2.3 8.1	Represents a single SQL statement. Typically used with SQL statements that include bind variables to improve performance as Oracle does not have to parse the statement each time it is executed. Can be thought of as conceptually similar to the ADO `Command` object.
OraMetaData	8.1	Returns meta data to describe a particular schema such as column names. Similar to the SQL Server DMO object library. See the meta data example below.
OraAQ	8.1	The `CreateAQ` method of the `OraDatabase` returns an `OraAQ` object. This provides access to Oracle's Advanced Queuing message system that allows messages to be passed between applications, much like MSMQ.

We are going to create a sample ASP script that executes a SQL statement to return a list of employees for a specific department number using bind variables. This example, which is compatible with both the 2.3 and 8.1 versions of OO4O, will use `OraSession`, `OraDatabase`, `OraDynaset` and `OraFields` objects, as they are the most commonly used objects in OO4O.

Using Bind Variables

Our script contains simple VBScript function, `CreateEmployeeTable`, declared at the bottom of the script, to handle the refreshing of the `Parameters` collection and writing out of the HTML results table each time.

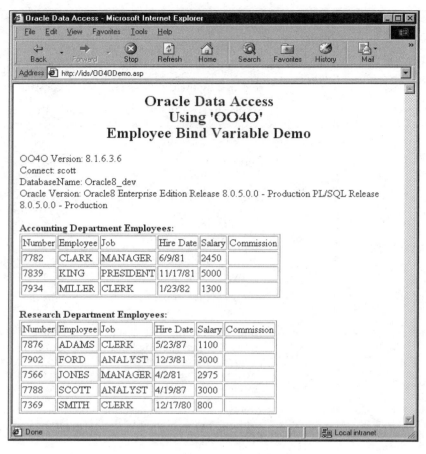

```
<% Option Explicit %>
<HTML>
<HEAD><TITLE>Oracle Data Access</TITLE>
<BODY>
<CENTER>
    <H2>
       Oracle Data Access<BR>
       Using 'OO4O'<BR>
       Employee Bind Variable Demo<BR>
    </H2>
</CENTER>
<%
Const cAccountingDeptCode = 10
Const cResearchDeptCode = 20

Dim varOraSession
Dim varOraDatabase
Dim varOraDynaset
Dim varSQL
```

We've made use of two constants to store the department code for the Accounting and Research departments. These are passed into our `objDatabase.Parameters` object for each department.

Each of the remaining variables defined stores a reference to the `OraSession`, `OraDatabase`, and `OraDynaset` objects respectively. Again we use a variable called `varSQL` to store our nicely formatted SQL statement:

```
Set varOraSession = Server.CreateObject("OracleInProcServer.XOraSession")
Set varOraDatabase = varOraSession.OpenDatabase("Oracle8_dev", _
                                                "scott/tiger", 0)
```

The only object that we have to create ourselves explicitly is the `OraSession` object as all other objects are created from other existing objects. We use the familiar `Server.CreateObject` to create an instance of the OO4O component whose internal `ProgID` is `OracleInProcServer.XOraSession`.

The `OpenDatabase` function returns an `OraDatabase` object, which in our case is the `scott` account on the `Oracle8_dev` service. `OpenDatabase` is called in the following way:

```
Set oraDatabase=oraSession.OpenDatabase(db_name, connectstring, options)
```

Where *db_name* is the **service name** to connect to, *connectstring* is the standard Oracle connection format of "*username/password*", and *options* is a collection of bit flags to indicate the mode in which the database should be opened. In our case we are passing in 0 to indicate that we want the database to be opened in the default mode, which means that any fields that we do not explicitly set a value for using the `AddNew` or `Edit` methods will be set to `Null` (this will incidentally override any server column default values!), rows will be locked as soon as the `Edit` method is called, and that non-blocking SQL functionality will **not** be used. A non-blocking call provides the same concept as an asynchronous ADO call in which the calling application does not have to wait until the server completes a request before continuing.

> **Some client installations may cause the Oracle error "Credential Retrieval Failed" whenever you try to connect. If this is the case then your client installation is trying to use a different form of client authentication to that of the server. Client authentication should be set to none, rather than native (NTS), so edit your `sqlnet.ora` file, located in the same folder as `tnsnames.ora`, and replace the line**
>
> `SQLNET.AUTHENTICATION_SERVICES=(NTS)`
>
> **with**
>
> `SQLNET.AUTHENTICATION_SERVICES=(NONE).`

```
Response.Write "OO4O Version:" & varOraSession.OIPVersionNumber & "<BR>" &_
               "Connect: " & varOraDatabase.connect & "<BR>" & _
               "DatabaseName: " & varOraDatabase.DatabaseName & "<BR>" & _
               "Oracle Version: " & varOraDatabase.RDBMSVersion & "<P>"
```

Just for our benefit we write out some information about the version of OO4O and the Oracle server that we are connecting to:

```
varSQL = "SELECT empno, ename, job, hiredate," & _
         "          sal, comm" & _
         " FROM emp" & _
         " WHERE deptno = :deptnoparam" & _
         " ORDER BY ename"
```

varSQL stores the SQL statement to execute using an Oracle bind variable, :deptnoparam. As we hinted at above, using bind variables can improve the performance of data access when you have the same SQL statement to execute, but need to alter a parameter. Each time Oracle executes a statement it has to go through the statement to understand how it should be executed. By using the bind variable, we can get Oracle to parse it only once. Remember, though, that this only exists for the life of your OraDatabase object – which should only be kept around for the life of the script and not in an ASP Session variable.

```
varOraDatabase.Parameters.Add "deptnoparam", 0, 1
```

Before we can tell Oracle about the bind variable we need to add it to the OraDatabase object's Parameters collection using the Add command, which is called in this way:

```
OraParameters.Add Name, Value, IOType
```

The Name argument is a string that represents the name of the parameter to add, and it must match that of the bind variable defined in the SQL statement, Value is a variant, IOType indicates the direction of this parameter:

Enumerator	Value	Description
ORAPARM_INPUT	1	Use as an input variable only
ORAPARM_OUTPUT	2	Use as output variable only
ORAPARM_BOTH	3	For variables that are both input and output

IOType is much like the adDirection enumerator used in the ADO Command object's Parameters collection to set the direction of SQL parameters.

In our example we passed in a value of 0 as a default because we don't actually have a value to use and a 1 to indicate that is for input use only.

```
Set varOraDynaset = varOraDatabase.CreateDynaset(varSQL, &H4)
```

Now it's just a case of calling the OraDatabase.CreateDynaset to retrieve an OraDynaset object. CreateDynaset is called in this way:

```
Set oradynaset = oradatabase.CreateDynaset(sql_statement, options)
```

Where sql_statement is the SQL to execute and options contains a bit flag of settings to define how the OraDynaset object behaves, such as whether it is updateable, or to cache data on the client. In our case we're passing in the hex value &H4 to indicate that it should be opened in read-only mode as we only want to display some data.

Behind the scenes, Oracle parses the statement ready for execution. It doesn't actually fetch any data until we set the `deptnoparam` parameter's `Value` property in `OraDatabase.Parameters` collection and ask OO4O to refresh the dynaset using `OraDynaset.Refresh`:

```
Response.Write "<B>Accounting Department Employees:</B><BR>"
CreateEmployeeTable cAccountingDeptCode

Response.Write "<BR><B>Research Department Employees:</B><BR>"
CreateEmployeeTable cResearchDeptCode
```

Here we can see our VBScript procedure `CreateEmployeeTable` being called to set the value for each of the department number parameters to create a nicely formatted table, as defined below:

```
Set varOraDatabase = Nothing
Set varOraDynaset = Nothing
Set varOraSession = Nothing
```

As always, we close down all of our objects as soon as possible in order to save server resources. Now to the `CreateEmployeeTable` function:

```
Sub CreateEmployeeTable(ByVal varDeptCode)

    varOraDatabase.Parameters("deptnoparam").Value = varDeptCode
    varOraDynaset.Refresh
```

`CreateEmployeeTable` is passed the required department code, which it binds to the original SQL statement's bind variable `deptnoparam`. Each time you specify a new value for a bind variable, you must call the `Refresh` method to fetch the new data.

Calling `Refresh` cancels all record edit operations that may have been pending through the `Edit` and `AddNew` methods, executes the SQL statement, and then moves to the first row of the resulting dynaset.

```
Response.Write "<TABLE BORDER=1><TR>" & _
               " <TD>Number</TD>" & _
               " <TD>Employee</TD>" & _
               " <TD>Job</TD>" & _
               " <TD>Hire Date</TD>" & _
               " <TD>Salary</TD>" & _
               " <TD>Commission</TD>" & _
               "</TR>"

Do While Not varOraDynaset.EOF
```

So now we create the `TABLE` tag and loop through the records until we come to the end of file, `EOF`, exactly as we would with the ADO `Recordset.EOF` property.

```
Response.Write "<TR>" & _
               "    <TD>" & varOraDynaset.Fields("empno").Value & _
               "</TD>" & _
               "    <TD>" & varOraDynaset.Fields("ename").Value & _
               "</TD>" & _
```

```
      "     <TD>" & varOraDynaset.Fields("job").Value & _
      "</TD>" & _
      "     <TD>" & varOraDynaset.Fields("hiredate").Value & _
      "</TD>" & _
      "     <TD>" & varOraDynaset.Fields("sal").Value & _
      "</TD>" & _
      "     <TD>" & varOraDynaset.Fields("comm").Value & _
      " </TD>" & _
      "</TR>"
```

The `Fields` collection returns a named list of columns for the current record, which we use to create a new table row for each record. We haven't shown it, but as with an ADO `Recordset` object, the `Fields` property is the default value, and for a `Field` object, the `Value` is the default so `varOraDynaset.Fields("sal").Value` is equal to `varOraDynaset("sal")`. For better performance you should use the latter.

```
        varOraDynaset.MoveNext
    Loop
    Response.Write "</TABLE>"
End Sub
%>
</BODY>
</HTML>
```

As with ADO, the `MoveNext` method moves to the next record.

Getting Meta Data

For our final look at OO4O we will use the `OraMetaData` object found in version 8.1 to retrieve a list of attributes for the `emp` table within the `scott` schema. As we said earlier, `OraMetaData` can retrieve all sorts of information about a schema, by calling the `OraDatabase` object's `Describe("schema_name")` function to return an `OraMetaData` object. The `OraMetaData` object returns a collection of `OraMDAttribute` objects that actually describe the data found and contains the following methods and properties:

Name	Description
Count	Returns the number of `OraMDAttribute` objects contained in the collection.
Type	The type of object described, for example `ORAMD_TABLE` which enumerates to the value 1 for an Oracle table.
Attribute(pos)	Returns an `OraMDAttribute` object at the specified position. This can be the 0 based index or a string name, such as "ColumnList".

To make things slightly complicated the `OraMDAttribute` object has a property called `IsMDObject` that returns `True` if the `Value` property contains yet another `OraMetaData` object. This allows you to recursively search through a hierarchy of `OraMetaData` objects. If it returns `False` then `Value` contains a string representation of the item.

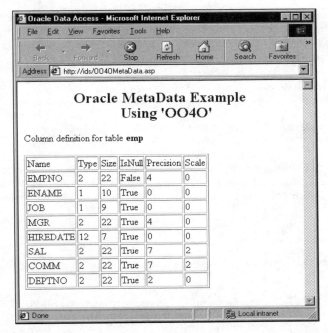

The following code produces the screenshot shown above. We start off with the usual header:

```
<%Option Explicit%>
<HTML>
<HEAD><TITLE>Oracle Data Access</TITLE>
</HEAD>
<BODY>
<CENTER>
    <H2>
        Oracle MetaData Example<BR>
        Using 'OO4O'<BR>
    </H2>
</CENTER>
```

The cTableName constant contains the name of the table that we want to describe. As usual we are using the OraSession object to hold a reference to OO4O and OraDatabase to connect to our Oracle8i server:

```
<%
Const cTableName = "emp"

Dim objOraSession
Dim objOraDatabase
Dim objOraMetaData
Dim objOraMDAttribute
Dim objColumnList
Dim objiColCount
Dim objColumnDetails
```

objOraMetaData is used to store our top-level OraMetaData object returned by the Describe function and objOraMDAttribute stores the item name "ColumnList" from the objOraMetaData object, which represents the list of columns in the emp table. The actual Value for objOraMDAttribute is stored in objColumnList.

```
Set objOraSession = CreateObject("OracleInProcServer.XOraSession")
Set objOraDatabase = objOraSession.OpenDatabase("Oracle8i_dev", _
                                                "scott/tiger", 0)
Set objOraMetaData = objOraDatabase.Describe(cTableName)
Set objOraMDAttribute = objOraMetaData("ColumnList")
```

We connect to the Oracle8i_dev service and call the OraDatabase object's Describe function to return our first OraMetaData object to objOraMetaData for the emp table. objOraMetaData will contain a collection of OraMDAttribute items, so we pass in ColumnList to retrieve the list of column names.

```
If objOraMDAttribute.IsMDObject Then

    Response.Write "Column definition for table <B>" & cTableName & _
            "</B><P>" & _
            "<TABLE BORDER=1><TR>" & _
            "<TD>Name</TD><TD>Type</TD><TD>Size</TD>" & _
            "<TD>IsNull</TD><TD>Precision</TD>" & _
            "<TD>Scale</TD>" & _
            "</TR>"

    Set objColumnList = objOraMDAttribute.Value
```

Even though it's not strictly necessary with this example, we check the IsMDObject property to see if the Value property contains another objMetaData object. In our case, it will always be True, since we asked for the list of column names, which is another objMetaData object.

> IsMDObject **is a property so if you try to call it as a function by adding** () **to the end you'll get runtime error 'Object doesn't support this property or method'.**

To make the code easier to read and run quicker we transfer the Value property into a new variable objColumnList:

```
    For iColCount = 0 To objColumnList.Count - 1
        Set objColumnDetails = objColumnList(iColCount).Value
        Response.Write  "<TR>" & _
            "<TD>" & objColumnDetails("Name")      & "</TD>" & _
            "<TD>" & objColumnDetails("DataType")  & "</TD>" & _
            "<TD>" & objColumnDetails("DataSize")  & "</TD>" & _
            "<TD>" & objColumnDetails("IsNull")    & "</TD>" & _
            "<TD>" & objColumnDetails("Precision") & "</TD>" & _
            "<TD>" & objColumnDetails("Scale")     & "</TD>" & _
        "</TR>"
    Next
    Response.Write "</TABLE>"
End If
```

Now it's just a case of moving through the zero-based collection of column details and writing out the value for each item. We finish off by shutting down our objects:

```
Set objColumnDetails = Nothing
Set objColumnList = Nothing
Set objOraMDAttribute = Nothing
Set objOraMetaData = Nothing
Set objOraDatabase = Nothing
Set objOraSession = Nothing
%>
</BODY>
</HTML>
```

That covers our introduction into the common objects you'll come across in OO4O. OO4O offers a rather flexible approach to connecting to an Oracle database and also provides us with additional PL/SQL functionality not available through ADO, such as the use of input arrays for stored procedures.

So, which one should you use in your ASP applications? Unfortunately, there is no simple answer. Each method claims to be faster than the next whilst providing support for additional functionality. It really does pay to try each of the methods in your own environment before committing to any particular one.

An Overview of PL/SQL

We've shown you a number of techniques available to connect to an Oracle database. Now we shall provide a quick overview of Oracle's own procedural extensions to SQL.

> *This section doesn't aim to be a PL/SQL bible. Instead, we'll cover some of the main differences between PL/SQL and standard ANSI SQL.*

The "PL" in PL/SQL is short for **Procedural Language**. It is an extension to SQL that allows you to create PL/SQL *programs* that contain standard programming features such as error handling, flow-of-control structures, and variables, all allowing you to manipulate Oracle data. By itself, SQL does not support these concepts.

Block Structure

A PL/SQL program consists of any number of *blocks* or sections of code. In our ASP scripts we can create any number of chunks of code to execute on the server using the <%...%> tags. This is similar to PL/SQL, where a set of statements can be grouped logically together as part of a larger set of instructions:

```
DECLARE TotalSal NUMBER(5);
BEGIN
   SELECT SUM(Sal) INTO TotalSal
     FROM emp
    WHERE ename LIKE 'S%';

   dbms_output.put_line('totalSalary=' || TotalSal );
   IF TotalSal < 10000 THEN
      UPDATE emp SET
         Sal = Sal * 1.1
      WHERE ename LIKE 'S%';
   END IF;
```

```
    COMMIT;

  EXCEPTION
    WHEN NO_DATA_FOUND THEN
      dbms_output.put_line('No records found.');
    WHEN OTHERS THEN
      dbms_output.put_line(SQLERRM);
  END;
```

A PL/SQL block has three distinct sections:

- ❏ Declarations
- ❏ Statements
- ❏ Handlers

They are defined in the following way:

```
[DECLARE declarations]
BEGIN
    statements
    [EXCEPTION handlers]
END;
```

The declarations section contains any variables or constants that are going to be used within the statements section. You can have any number of statements to execute, but if an error occurs in any of them, processing will stop and execution will move to the exception section for trapping, if any are defined.

In above example we declare TotalSal as a variable in the declarations section:

```
DECLARE TotalSal NUMBER(5);
```

All of the remaining code up to the EXCEPTION line forms the statements section, followed by two exception handlers: NO_DATA_FOUND and OTHERS.

When you declare an exception handler you must tell Oracle which one of the in-built exceptions you want to trap, such as ZERO_DIVIDE. In our case we've trapped NO_DATA_FOUND, which is raised when an empty result set is retrieved, and OTHERS, which is a catch-all handler that will trap any other exceptions that you have not explicitly named. You can have any number of exception handlers and you can also set up your own exception types, but that is beyond the scope of this chapter.

Once an exception has been trapped you cannot issue the equivalent to a VBScript RESUME NEXT as the PL/SQL program will exit at the last line in the exception handler. This is somewhat different to the operation of SQL Server's T-SQL in which you can check the value of @@Error after any statement, provided that the error was of a trappable nature.

The dbms_output.put_line('No records found.'); statement allows us to briefly mention PL/SQL debugging. dbms_output is a built-in Oracle Package (a package is a way to group together collections of stored procedures) that can be used to send messages to the console. In order to actually see these messages you must execute the SET SERVEROUTPUT ON; statement from within the SQL*Plus SQL editor. Each call to dbms_output.put_line will write out the string message passed to it.

> Oracle uses the / character to mark the end of a block of SQL to execute within SQL*Plus.

Variable Declaration

At the start of a PL/SQL block you must define any variables that are to be used, after the DECLARE statement. You can use any of the standard Oracle data-types such as NUMBER, VARCHAR2 or any PL/SQL data-type, such as BOOLEAN. It is just a case of defining the variable name followed by the data-type and using a semi-colon between multiple declarations:

```
DECLARE TotalBonus  NUMBER(6);
        BonusPaid   BOOLEAN;
```

For a full list of Oracle data-types check out
http://technet.us.oracle.com/doc/server.804/a58227/ch6.htm#649

Assigning Values to Variables

In ASP we use the = statement to assign a value to one of our variables. In PL/SQL it is slightly different, in that we must use :=.

```
SalePrice := (ProductPrice / 100)  * SalesTax;
```

If we are returning a value from a database table or system function, then we use the INTO statement:

```
SELECT SUM(Quantity) INTO ItemsOrdered FROM OrderBasket;
```

Conditional Flow of Control

We use the If...Then...Else construct to control the execution flow of our ASP scripts. PL/SQL also supports this construct in a similar format:

```
IF SaleCount > 10 AND SaleCount < 20 THEN
   UPDATE emp SET sal = sal * 0.3;
ELSIF SaleCount = 5 THEN
   UPDATE emp SET sal = sal * 0.2;
ELSE
   UPDATE emp SET sal = sal * 0.1;
END IF;
```

Surprisingly, PL/SQL doesn't yet provide support for the CASE statement.

Looping Flow Control

To loop through a section of code, PL/SQL supports a number of LOOP statements. The first is similar to the VBScript For...Next statement:

```
FOR countervar IN start..end LOOP
   statements to execute
END LOOP;
```

Where `countervar` is the counter variable, `start` is the initial starting value and `end` is the final value. For example:

```
FOR intCounter IN 1..5 LOOP
    INSERT INTO OrderLine(ID)
        VALUES(OrderLineID.NEXTVAL);
END LOOP;
```

The equivalent loop in VBScript would be:

```
FOR intCounter = 1 To 5
    Response.Write "Value=" & intCounter
NEXT
```

The `WHILE...LOOP` allows us to execute a section of code until a certain condition is true, just as we do with the `Do...Loop` structure in ASP:

```
WHILE TotalBonus < 10000 LOOP
    SELECT Bonus, EmpID INTO EmpBonus, MyEmpID
        FROM emp
        WHERE EmpID <> MyEmpID;
    Totalbonus := TotalBonus + Bonus;
    RecordCount := RecordCount + 1;
END LOOP;
```

Of course, there's a lot more to PL/SQL than that. PL/SQL is like any programming language with many constructs, statements and functions, but these are the typical building blocks that you will come across in any PL/SQL program.

Oracle Packages

We covered stored procedures a few chapters ago, so now we'll take a quick look at **Oracle Packages**. An Oracle package serves as a way to group procedures and functions into common groups typically based upon their functionality. A package has two sections: the **specification** that contains a definition of any objects that can be referenced outside of the package, and a **body** that contains the implementation of the objects. The specification section must be declared first:

```
PACKAGE package_name
IS
    {variable and type declarations }
    {cursor declarations}
    [module specifications]
END {package_name};
```

For example:

```
CREATE OR REPLACE PACKAGE Employee_pkg
AS

    PROCEDURE GetEmployeeName(i_empno    IN    NUMBER,
                              o_ename    OUT   VARCHAR2);
END Employee_Pkg;
```

This defines a package called `Employee_pkg` that contains a single stored procedure called `GetEmployeeAge`.

The package body contains the actual implementation of the procedures within the package. This effectively allows us to hide procedures inside the package by not declaring them in the package specification:

```
PACKAGE BODY package_name
IS
   {variable and type declarations}
   {cursor specifications - SELECT statements}
   [module specifications]
BEGIN
   [procedure bodies]
END {package_name};
```

The specification for our `Employee_pkg` could look like this:

```
CREATE OR REPLACE PACKAGE BODY Employee_pkg
AS

   PROCEDURE GetEmployeeName(i_empno    IN    NUMBER,
                             o_ename    OUT   VARCHAR2)
   IS
   BEGIN
      SELECT ename
         INTO o_ename
         FROM emp
      WHERE empno = i_empno;
   END GetEmployeeName;

END Employee_pkg;
```

To call the `GetEmployeeName` procedure within `Employee_pkg` from ASP we use must prefix the stored procedure name with the package name. We'll be covering the execution of stored procedures in much more detail in the next section:

```
With objCommand
   .CommandText = "{call Employee_pkg.GetEmployeeName(?, ?)}"
   .CommandType = adCmdText
   .Parameters(0).Direction = adParamInput
   .Parameters(0).Value = varEmpNo
   .Parameters(1).Direction = adParamOutput
   .Execute
   Response.Write "Name=" & .Parameters(1).Value
End With
```

Now that we've had a brief look at Oracle packages we can use some of their features in the final section in this chapter, when we come to retrieving ADO resultsets from an Oracle stored procedure. Before we do that, let's create a sample application that uses a number of stored procedures to perform common data-entry actions.

A Sample Oracle ASP Application

We are going to bring together all of the concepts discussed so far into a small ASP application based around the scott database schema. This application will show a list of employees from the emp table and allow the user to perform the usual data-entry procedures:

- Create a new employee
- Edit an existing employee
- Delete an employee

To implement this application we will be using four ASP script files, an include file, and the `global.asa` file. The include file is an ADO helper file that we have created ourselves called `ADOFunctions_inc.asp` used to create our database connections as needed.

> *It is often a good idea to rename your included ASP files from `.inc` to `.asp` to prevent unauthorized people from simply opening them in a browser. We've done this with `ADOFunctions_inc.asp` as it contains a username and password which we don't want people to have access to. I've kept the _inc suffix so that I know it's an include file.*

We will be retrieving lists of data using simple `SELECT` statements whereas the add, edit, update and delete functionality will be provided by four Oracle stored procedures. This will let us examine how we go about calling Oracle stored procedure using `INPUT` and `OUTPUT` parameters with the aid of the Microsoft OLE DB Provider for Oracle.

> *It is notoriously difficult to retrieve an ADO `Recordset` from an Oracle stored procedure. Oracle simply does not allow us to execute a `SELECT` statement from within stored procedure without assigning the returned values to a PL/SQL variable using the `INTO` keyword. There is a way to achieve this functionality with ADO using **PL/SQL tables** or by using **reference cursors**. In the next section, we will be covering the retrieval of an ADO `Recordset` from Oracle stored procedures using PL/SQL tables and then we'll look at doing the same thing using reference cursors and a PL/SQL package.*

One word of warning though, in order to concentrate on the Oracle fundamentals, we won't be using any DHTML features, so the screens do look rather bland!

global.asa

We won't use `global.asa` to handle application and session events, but we will use it to add a reference to the ADO type library to all of our ASP scripts. This will allow us to use the constants such as `adCmdText` for our ADO `Command` object. Enter the following line into `global.asa`:

```
<!-- METADATA TYPE="TypeLib"
     FILE="C:\Program Files\Common Files\System\ado\msado15.dll" -->
```

This uses the `METADATA` tag to include a `TYPELIB` file from the location specified. This is the default location into which the ADO library is located, but you should update it to reflect your own installation if it is different. By adding this line we can make use of all of the standard ADO constants and enumerators.

> *Traditionally, ASP developers would include the Microsoft ADO include file, `ADOVBS.inc`, in order to refer to the ADO constants. This would have to be done on every ASP script and is potentially difficult to support. By using the `METADATA` tag you only have to declare it once which is faster for your web server.*

ADOFunctions_inc.asp

This include file is used in all of our ASP scripts that need to connect to the database. It is much better to put commonly used code into a single include file and reference that in each of our pages, as there would be only one place in which we need to change the username and password if we ever needed to.

So create a new folder called `includes` and add a new file called `ADOFunctions_inc.asp` containing the following code:

```
<%
Function GetDBConnection()
   Dim objConnection

   Set objConnection = Server.CreateObject("ADODB.Connection")
   With objConnection
      .ConnectionString = "Provider=MSDAORA; " & _
                          "Data Source=Oracle8_dev; " & _
                          "User ID=scott; Password=tiger;"

      .Open
   End With

   Set GetDBConnection = objConnection
End Function
%>
```

The `GetDBConnection` function simply returns an `ADODB.Connection` object which points to our Oracle database using the `scott` account.

Default.asp

Our home page, `Default.asp`, displays a list of all employees from the `emp` table using a `SELECT` statement ordered by name. This page allows the user to create a new employee record by clicking the **create employee** link, delete an employee by pressing the **Delete** link, or edit an employee by clicking the employee's name. Both the edit and add employee link go to the `EditEmp.asp` page.

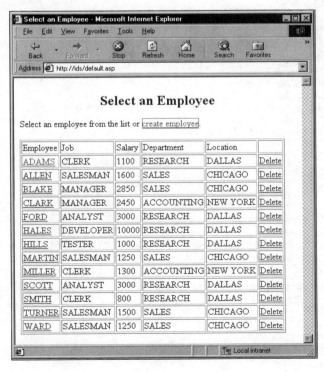

So let's have a look at the ASP code behind this page:

```
<% Option Explicit
   Response.Expires = 0 %>
<!-- #include file="includes/ADOFunctions_inc.asp" -->
<HTML>
<HEAD>
   <META HTTP-EQUIV="Pragma" CONTENT="no-cache">
   <TITLE>Select an Employee</TITLE>
</HEAD>
<BODY>
   <CENTER><H2>Select an Employee</H2></CENTER>
      Select an employee from the list or
      <A HREF="EditEmp.asp">create employee</A>.<P>
```

As usual we start off with the `Option Explicit` statement so that we must declare all variables and constants used in our code. We don't want this page to be cached by the browser so that any amended records are displayed each time the page is shown. We achieve this using `Response.Expires = 0` to tell the browser that this page expires immediately. If your site is going to be accessed by users in different time zones then it's a good idea to actually set this to a large negative number.

The line `<META>` tag is used to tell any proxy servers that they should not cache this page for the same reason.

You'll notice this is the first time that we include our `ADOFunctions.inc` using the `#include` directive.

```
<%
Dim objRecordset
Dim varSQL
Dim varEmpNo

varSQL = "SELECT emp.empno, emp.ename, emp.job, " & _
        "         emp.sal, dept.dname, dept.loc" & _
        "  FROM emp, dept" & _
        "  WHERE emp.deptno = dept.deptno" & _
        "  ORDER BY UPPER(emp.ename)"
Set objRecordset = GetDBConnection().Execute(varSQL)

Response.Write "<TABLE BORDER=1><TR>" & _
            "   <TD>Employee</TD>" & _
            "   <TD>Job</TD>" & _
            "   <TD>Salary</TD>" & _
            "   <TD>Department</TD>" & _
            "   <TD>Location</TD>" & _
            "   <TD> </TD>" & _
            "</TR>"
```

The `objRecordset` variable stores the result of our `SELECT` statement executed by calling the `GetDBConnection` function to return an ADO `Connection`.

As with SQL Server, Oracle also supports table name aliases that can be used for long or duplicated tables, such as:

```
SELECT EmpHol.Name
FROM EmployeesOnHoliday EmpHol
WHERE EmpHol.Department=1
```

Now we fill out the table with the data:

```
Do While Not objRecordset.EOF

    varEmpNo = objRecordset.Fields("empno")

    Response.Write "<TR>" & _
                   "   <TD><A HREF=EditEmp.ASP?EmpNo=" & varEmpNo & ">" & _
                                    objRecordset("ename") & "</A></TD>" & _
                   "   <TD>" & objRecordset("job") & "</TD>" & _
                   "   <TD>" & objRecordset("sal") & "</TD>" & _
                   "   <TD>" & objRecordset("dname") & "</TD>" & _
                   "   <TD>" & objRecordset("loc") & "</TD>" & _
                   "   <TD><A HREF=javascript:deleteEmployee(" & _
                   varEmpNo & ");>Delete</A></TD>" & _
                   "</TR>"

    objRecordset.MoveNext
Loop
Response.Write "</TABLE>"
```

We navigate through the records contained in the Recordset object, creating a table row for each employee. We cache the employee number as it is used as part of the URL for the hyperlink to EditEmp.asp.

```
Set objRecordset = Nothing
%>

<SCRIPT>
function deleteEmployee(EmpNo) {
    if (window.confirm("Are you sure you want to delete employee?") == true)
    {
        window.location = "DeleteEmp.ASP?EmpNo=" + EmpNo;
    }
}
</SCRIPT>
</BODY>
</HTML>
```

We finish by closing off the ASP script and defining the local JavaScript function deleteEmployee. This function uses the window.confirm function to confirm whether the record should be deleted. If Yes, then the employee delete script, DeleteEmp.asp is called.

DeleteEmp.asp

This page simply calls an Oracle stored procedure, emp_Delete, passing in the employee number so that it can be deleted from the emp table.

We've covered stored procedures earlier in this book, so we'll just explain the important parts of this new procedure. This stored procedure doesn't come as part of the default database, so we are going to create it ourselves. Using SQL*Plus, or your preferred Oracle editor, you will need to connect to the scott account and execute the following SQL to create the new procedure:

```
CREATE OR REPLACE PROCEDURE emp_Delete
    (i_empno IN NUMBER)
AS
BEGIN
    DELETE
        FROM emp
        WHERE empno = i_empno;
END;
```

As you can see, it is a very simple procedure that takes one input parameter, i_empno, and deletes the record with the corresponding employee number from the emp table. We use the IN statement to tell Oracle that this parameter is for input only. You must tell Oracle if you want the value of parameters to be updated as the procedure exits, using the OUT statement, in exactly the same way that you should use the ByVal and ByRef statements in your own ASP procedures. I tend to prefix the name of each parameter with an i_ or o_ to denote the direction. You can also specify a parameter as being both IN and OUT but that's not a recommended practice.

So jumping back to DeleteEmp.asp, we have the following code:

```
<% Option Explicit
   Response.Buffer = True
%>
<!-- #include file="includes/ADOFunctions_inc.asp " -->
<HTML>
<%
Dim objCommand
Dim varEmpNo

varEmpNo = Request.QueryString("EmpNo")

Set objCommand = Server.CreateObject("ADODB.Command")
Set objCommand.ActiveConnection = GetDBConnection()
```

This time we are using the ADO Command object to execute our stored procedure because we need to get at the parameters that make up this stored procedure. This is more important when you want to retrieve the value of output parameters, as they are only accessible from the Command object's Parameters collection rather than a Recordset.

```
With objCommand
    .CommandText = "{call emp_Delete(?)}"
    .CommandType = adCmdText
    .Parameters(0).Value = varEmpNo
    .Execute()
End With

Set objCommand = Nothing
Response.Redirect "default.asp"
%>
</HTML>
```

We use the CommandText property to tell the Command object the SQL statement to execute using the {call procname} syntax. Each ? refers to a parameter to this stored procedure and can be referenced in the Command object's Parameters collection – starting from 0. We simply set the first and only parameter to that of the employee number passed in through the URL and then run the procedure using the Execute function.

Finally, we redirect the user back to our home page, default.asp.

Another approach could have been to open a new pop-up window to confirm the delete, which would have then refreshed default.asp using the JavaScript window.opener property, if the delete was successful. If the delete operation failed, for any reason, the pop-up window could have stayed open displaying the error message that was returned.

EditEmp.asp

This page allows existing employee's records to be updated or new ones to be added. If this is an existing employee record, we will be passed the employee number as part of the URL. If there is no employee number, then the page assumes that the user wants to add a new employee record.

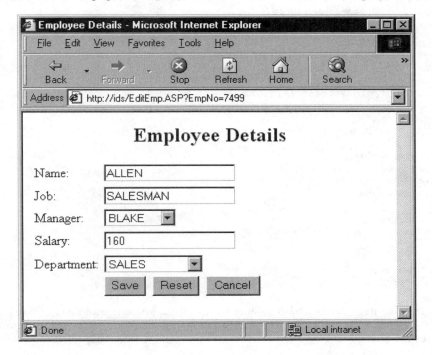

This page uses a stored procedure, emp_GetData, to return the fields for this employee through a number of output parameters, so you'll need to create the following stored procedure:

Remember that with Oracle, we cannot simply execute a SELECT statement inside a stored procedure to return some records as we can with SQL Server!

```
CREATE OR REPLACE PROCEDURE emp_GetData
  (i_empno    IN    NUMBER,
   o_ename    OUT   VARCHAR2,
   o_job      OUT   VARCHAR2,
   o_mgr      OUT   NUMBER,
   o_sal      OUT   NUMBER,
   o_deptno   OUT   NUMBER)
AS
BEGIN
  SELECT ename, job, mgr,
         sal, deptno
    INTO o_ename, o_job, o_mgr,
         o_sal, o_deptno
    FROM emp
   WHERE empno = i_empno;
END;
```

This time we have only one input parameter and five output parameters that are used to store the employee details using the SELECT...INTO statement to transfer the values.

The ASP script has to do quite bit of work to display this page. It populates the list of departments and managers using a custom VBScript procedure that writes out a list of OPTION statements based on a Recordset of data, as we'll see shortly.

```
<% Option Explicit %>
<!-- #include file="includes/ADOFunctions_inc.asp " -->
<HTML>
<HEAD>
    <TITLE>Employee Details</TITLE>
</HEAD>
<BODY>
    <CENTER><H2>Employee Details</H2></CENTER>
<%
Dim objConnection
Dim objCommand
Dim objRSDepartments
Dim objRSManagers

Dim varEmpNo
Dim varEName
Dim varJob
Dim varMgr
Dim varSalary
Dim varDeptNo
```

We use a separate Recordset object to store the list of departments and managers so that we can populate the SELECT list in the correct place. I always find it easier to transfer the record values to local variables in one place.

```
On Error Goto Next
Set objConnection = GetDBConnection()

If Request.QueryString("EmpNo") = "" Then
   varEmpNo = 0
```

We create a database connection using GetDBConnection, and if there is no employee number passed in the URL, we set the employee number to zero. If the user clicked on an employee's name, we would have been passed the correct employee number.

For new employees, we use an Oracle Sequence to generate the new employee number, which we'll cover shortly.

```
Else
    varEmpNo = Request.QueryString("EmpNo")
    Set objCommand = Server.CreateObject("ADODB.Command")
    Set objCommand.ActiveConnection = objConnection
    With objCommand
        .CommandText = "{call emp_GetData(?, ?, ?, ?, ?, ?)}"
        .CommandType = adCmdText
        .Parameters(0).Value = varEmpNo
        .Execute()
```

If we have an employee number then we need to create a `Command` object and specify the `emp_GetData` stored procedure. This time we have six parameters with the first one being the input parameter, the employee number, and the remaining five output parameters storing the employee's details.

```
        varEName    = .Parameters(1)
        varJob      = .Parameters(2)
        varMgr      = .Parameters(3)
        varSalary   = .Parameters(4)
        varDeptNo   = .Parameters(5)
    End With

End If
```

Once we've called the `Execute` function, each of the `Parameters` items will contain our employee's fields so it's just a case of transferring them to our local variables.

```
Set objRSDepartments = objConnection.Execute( _
                    "SELECT deptno, dname FROM dept ORDER BY dname")
Set objRSManagers = objConnection.Execute( _
                "SELECT empno, ename FROM emp ORDER BY ename")

Set objCommand = Nothing
Set objConnection = Nothing
```

We use our connection object, `objConnection`, to retrieve a list of departments and managers for our `SELECT` lists and then shut down the `Command` and `Connection` objects as soon as we've finished with them.

```
Sub PopulateSelectOptions(ByVal objRecordset, ByVal varCurrentID)

    Dim varHTML
    Dim varSelected

    objRecordSet.MoveFirst

    Do While Not objRecordset.EOF
        If CLng(varCurrentID) = Clng(objRecordset.Fields(0)) Then
            varSelected = " SELECTED"
        Else
            varSelected = ""
        End If

        varHTML = varHTML & "<OPTION VALUE=" & objRecordset.Fields(0) & _
                varSelected & ">" & objRecordset.Fields(1) & "</OPTION>"
        objRecordset.MoveNext
    Loop
    Response.Write varHTML
End Sub
%>
```

`PopulateSelectOptions` is a general-purpose procedure that is passed a `Recordset` of data and the ID of the default item to select. Its purpose is to navigate through each record and create a collection of HTML `OPTION` tags using the field at position 0 as the ID and field 1 as the text to display. If this was a full-blown application we'd probably put this function in an include file so that other pages could use its functionality, but as this is an example, we'll leave it in the ASP.

```
<FORM ACTION="EditEmp_HND.ASP?EmpNo=<%=varEmpNo%>" METHOD="POST">
   <TABLE>
      <TR>
         <TD>Name:</TD>
         <TD><INPUT NAME="varEName" VALUE="<%=varEName%>"></TD>
      </TR>
      <TR>
         <TD>Job:</TD>
         <TD><INPUT NAME="varJob" VALUE="<%=varJob%>"></TD>
      </TR>
```

Now we can define the FORM that allows the user to enter the employee details. Notice that we append the employee number, which can be zero for new employee records, to the query string for the form action handler, EditEmp_HND.asp.

```
      <TR>
         <TD>Manager:</TD>
         <TD><SELECT NAME="varMgr" SIZE="1">
           <%
               Call PopulateSelectOptions(objRSManagers, varMgr)
               Set objRSManagers = Nothing
           %>                  </SELECT></TD>
      </TR>
```

This is the first time that we call PopulateSelectOptions to create our list of OPTION tags. We already have the <SELECT> tag so PopulateSelectOptions will generate the corresponding list of <OPTION> tags for each record in objRSManagers.

```
      <TR>
         <TD>Salary:</TD>
         <TD><INPUT NAME="varSalary"
                     VALUE="<%= varSalary %>"></TD>
      </TR>
      <TR>
         <TD>Department:</TD>
         <TD><SELECT NAME="varDeptNo" SIZE="1">
           <%
               Call PopulateSelectOptions(objRSDepartments, varDeptNo)
               Set objRSDepartments = Nothing
           %>
           </SELECT></TD>
      </TR>
      <TR>
         <TD></TD>
         <TD>
            <INPUT TYPE="SUBMIT" VALUE="Save">  
            <INPUT TYPE="RESET" VALUE="Reset"> 
            <INPUT TYPE="BUTTON" VALUE="Cancel"
                   onclick="document.location.href='/';">
         </TD>
      </TR>

   </TABLE>
   </FORM>
</BODY>
</HTML>
```

We finish off by completing the input form, again using `PopulateSelectOptions` to show a list of departments, and adding a Submit to submit the form, a Reset button to clear any edits and a Cancel button to take the user back to the home page.

EditEmp_HND.asp

This page is the form handler that is called when the user submits the data-entry form. It calls the parameterized stored procedure `emp_Update` to update an existing record or add a new one using `emp_Add`.

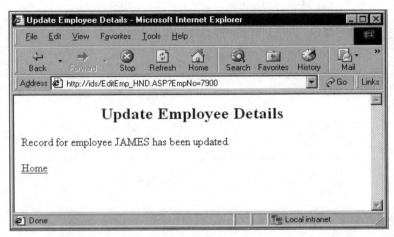

Again, we are going to create these new stored procedures, so jump back to your SQL editor and execute the following lines:

```
CREATE OR REPLACE PROCEDURE emp_Update
   (i_empno    IN  NUMBER,
    i_ename    IN  VARCHAR2,
    i_job      IN  VARCHAR2,
    i_mgr      IN  NUMBER,
    i_sal      IN  NUMBER,
    i_deptno   IN  NUMBER)
AS
BEGIN
   UPDATE emp SET
      ename = i_ename, job = i_job,
      mgr = i_mgr, sal = i_sal,
    deptno = i_deptno
   WHERE empno = i_empno;
END;
```

Now that we've created the stored procedure for updates, we need to create an Oracle `Sequence` object before we create the `emp_Add` procedure. A sequence is an object that generates sequential numbers that we can use as primary keys for our employee number column. Oracle does not support the `IDENTITY` column that you would use in SQL Server so we must create a `Sequence` object to generate the numbers for us. Sequences are created separately from the table that they are created for, so if a table happens to be deleted (that is *dropped*) the sequence object will still exist. Each time you request the next number in the sequence using the `NEXTVAL` property, the sequence will automatically update itself irrespective of the table to column that it was originally created for.

So from your SQL editor execute the following statement to create the sequence:

```
CREATE SEQUENCE empno_seq START WITH 9000;
```

The sequence is called `empno_seq` and starts at 9000. The reason why I've decided to start at 9000 is because the `emp` table already contains some records and, in my case, the largest employee number was 7934, so I want to start at a number greater than 7934. A sequence has a number of properties that you can call, but `NEXTVAL` is the one we need to get the next number in the sequence.

Now that's done we can create the add stored procedure by running the following SQL:

```
CREATE OR REPLACE PROCEDURE emp_Add
    (i_ename    IN   VARCHAR2,
     i_job      IN   VARCHAR2,
     i_mgr      IN   NUMBER,
     i_sal      IN   NUMBER,
     i_deptno   IN   NUMBER)
AS
BEGIN
    INSERT INTO emp(empno,
                    ename, job, mgr,
                    sal, deptno)
            VALUES(empno_seq.NEXTVAL,
                   i_ename, i_job, i_mgr,
                   i_sal, i_deptno);
END;
```

The ASP script is relatively simple:

```
<% Option Explicit %>
<!-- #include file="includes/ADOFunctions_inc.asp " -->
<HTML>
<HEAD>
    <TITLE>Update Employee Details</TITLE>
</HEAD>
<BODY>
    <CENTER><H2>Update Employee Details</H2></CENTER>
<%
Dim objCommand

Dim varEmpNo
Dim varEName
Dim varJob
Dim varMgr
Dim varSalary
Dim varDeptNo
```

We will be using a `Command` object in order to set the stored procedure's parameters and local variables to store the value from the submitted form.

```
With Request

    varEmpNo = .QueryString("EmpNo")
    varEName  = .Form("varEName")
    varJob    = .Form("varJob")
    varMgr    = .Form("varMgr")
    varSalary = .Form("varSalary")
    varDeptNo = .Form("varDeptNo")

End With
```

We transfer the form fields into local variables.

```
Set objCommand = Server.CreateObject("ADODB.Command")
Set objCommand.ActiveConnection = GetDBConnection()

If varEmpNo <> 0 Then

    With objCommand
        .CommandText = "{call emp_Update(?, ?, ?, ?, ?, ?)}"
        .CommandType = adCmdText
        .Parameters(0).Value = varEmpNo
        .Parameters(1).Value = varEName
        .Parameters(2).Value = varJob
        .Parameters(3).Value = varMgr
        .Parameters(4).Value = CInt(varSalary)
        .Parameters(5).Value = varDeptNo
        .Execute()

        Response.Write "Record for employee " & varEName & _
                        " has been updated."
    End With
```

If we have employee number then it's just a case of calling the `emp_Update` stored procedure and pass in each of the values.

```
    Else
        With objCommand
            .CommandText = "{call emp_Add(?, ?, ?, ?, ?)}"
            .CommandType = adCmdText
            .Parameters(0).Value = varEName
            .Parameters(1).Value = varJob
            .Parameters(2).Value = varMgr
            .Parameters(3).Value = CInt(varSalary)
            .Parameters(4).Value = varDeptNo
            .Execute()

            Response.Write "Record for employee " & varEName & " has been added."
        End With
    End If

    Set objCommand = Nothing
%>
    <P>
    <A HREF="default.asp">Home</A>
</BODY>
</HTML>
```

In the case of a new record, we call the `emp_add` stored procedure and pass in the new employee's details.

That concludes our brief ASP sample application based on the `scott` employee data. We've seen how it is possible to call stored procedures using the `{call procname?}` syntax to retrieve data for a single record and to manipulate records using the `Command.Parameters` collection. We made use of a standard include file to create our database connection and a useful function to output a list of `OPTION` tags based on a `Recordset` of data.

Retrieving ADO Recordsets from an Oracle Stored Procedure

We'll finish off with something of a holy grail. Unlike SQL Server, PL/SQL does not allow us to execute a SELECT statement within a stored procedure without a corresponding INTO statement. This means we cannot easily return a recordset back to the calling client whether it is an ASP script or another PL/SQL program.

Consider the following SQL Server stored procedure:

```
CREATE PROCEDURE sp_GetAuthors
AS
BEGIN
    SELECT au_lname, au_fname
    FROM authors
    ORDER BY au_lname, au_fname
END
```

Try creating the following very similar stored procedure in Oracle:

```
CREATE PROCEDURE sp_GetAuthors
AS
BEGIN
    SELECT ename
    FROM emp
    ORDER BY ename;
END;
```

You'll receive the following error messages:

```
Errors for PROCEDURE SP_GETAUTHORS:

LINE/COL ERROR
-------- -------------------------------------------------------------
4/3      PLS-00428: an INTO clause is expected in this SELECT statement
4/3      PL/SQL: SQL Statement ignored
```

Once upon a time, I searched Oracle's own PL/SQL documentation for an answer to this, and I got the impression that this will never be implemented. I believe the reason was, that they feel a calling program, X, should pass parameters into another program, Y, allowing Y to populate the results so that X can then deal with them. This approach doesn't really help us from an ADO point of view.

However, it can actually be achieved by using **PL/SQL tables** and the **Microsoft ODBC for Oracle**, or **reference cursors** with Oracle's **Oracle Provider for OLE DB**. We'll start off with PL/SQL tables and cover reference cursors in the next section.

PL/SQL Tables are somewhat of a misnomer as it might be easier if they were called *PL/SQL Arrays*. The following diagram shows three records from the emp table and how they would be represented in three PL/SQL Table variables:

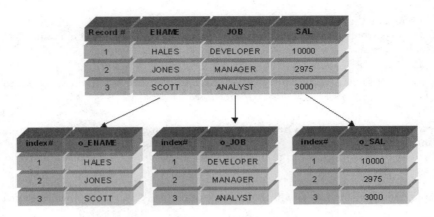

We have three columns, ENAME, JOB and SAL in our source result set. For each column of data we have a corresponding PL/SQL table variable, o_ENAME, o_JOB and o_SAL, each mapping to a value of each column. The PL/SQL table variables are distinct entities in their own right. In order to populate the PL/SQL tables we need to scroll through the records in the source resultset, and add an entry for each column to the corresponding element in each PL/SQL table.

PL/SQL tables have the following characteristics:

❑ **One-Dimensional**: each PL/SQL table can contain only one column of data.

❑ **Integer-Indexed**: Each element of the array is indexed by a single integer much like a VBScript array.

❑ **Unbounded Dimensions**: There is no limit to the size of a PL/SQL table, as the structure will alter in size to accommodate new elements.

❑ **Uniform Data Type**: Only a single uniform data type can be stored in a particular PL/SQL table. So, if you start off with a NUMBER data-type, then all other elements must also be a NUMBER.

PL/SQL table types are defined using the TYPE statement, for example:

```
TYPE tblFirstName IS TABLE OF VARCHAR2(30) INDEX BY BINARY_INTEGER;
```

This would declare a PL/SQL table type called tblFirstName that could be used by a variable to store an array of strings up to 30 characters in length. A variable of this type could be declared as the parameter to a stored procedure, thus:

```
PROCEDURE GetEmployeeList(o_FirstName OUT tblFirstName)
```

Each PL/SQL table type that you want to use must be defined within the **specification** section of an Oracle **Package**.

In the case of a stored procedure that returns a list of employee names and numbers, we must create an individual parameter for both the employee name and the employee number values, both being declared using the PL/SQL table type as defined in our package specification.

In order to populate the employee number and employee name PL/SQL tables with data, we can use a **cursor** that loops through a selection of records and transfers each item of data into the corresponding PL/SQL table element.

> *A cursor allows you to programmatically step through a result set of data, performing operations based on the current row until the end of the result set is reached.*

The easiest way to implement an Oracle cursor is by declaring it outside of a program block and then opening it using a cursor FOR...LOOP. The cursor FOR...LOOP opens the cursor for you, repeatedly fetches rows of values from the result set into fields and then closes the cursor once all rows have been processed.

For example, the following cursor will calculate the total salary for all employees in the emp table:

```
DECLARE CURSOR emp_cur IS SELECT sal FROM emp;
            TotalSalary NUMBER;
BEGIN
   FOR emp_rec IN emp_cur LOOP
      TotalSalary := TotalSalary  + emp_rec.sal;
   END LOOP;
END;
```

We'll start our example off by creating a simple package that contains one stored procedure called EmployeeSearch. This will allow us to retrieve a list of employees from the emp table within the scott schema, based on their name.

Jump to your SQL editor and add the following package specification to the scott schema:

```
CREATE OR REPLACE PACKAGE Employee_Pkg
AS
TYPE tblEmpNo    IS TABLE OF NUMBER(4)      INDEX BY BINARY_INTEGER;
TYPE tblEName    IS TABLE OF VARCHAR2(10)   INDEX BY BINARY_INTEGER;
TYPE tblJob      IS TABLE OF VARCHAR2(9)    INDEX BY BINARY_INTEGER;

PROCEDURE EmployeeSearch
   (i_EName    IN     VARCHAR2,
    o_EmpNo    OUT    tblEmpNo,
    o_EName    OUT    tblEName,
    o_Job      OUT    tblJob);
END Employee_Pkg;
```

Our package is called Employee_Pkg, which we will need to use when referencing the EmployeeSearch procedure. We will be returning three columns in our Recordset: employee number, name and job, so we have created a separate PL/SQL table type for each column.

Note that EmployeeSearch doesn't actually include any code – that's the job of the package body. If you try to define the implementation here you'll get an error from Oracle.

We've defined one input parameter, the name to search for, and a separate output parameter for each of the columns to return. Now we can create the package body – the bit that does the actual work, so execute the following SQL script:

```
CREATE OR REPLACE PACKAGE BODY Employee_Pkg
AS
PROCEDURE EmployeeSearch
    (i_EName    IN      VARCHAR2,
     o_EmpNo    OUT     tblEmpNo,
     o_EName    OUT     tblEName,
     o_Job      OUT     tblJob)
IS
```

We start off by adding the word BODY before the package name, dropping the PL/SQL table definitions, and adding the word IS to start the implementation.

```
CURSOR cur_employee (curName VARCHAR2) IS
    SELECT empno,
           ename,
           job
    FROM emp
    WHERE UPPER(ename) LIKE '%' || UPPER(curName) || '%'
    ORDER BY ename;

    RecordCount NUMBER DEFAULT 0;
```

If you recall from our overview of PL/SQL blocks, we need to declare any variables or cursors that are going to be used by our procedure. We define a cursor called cur_employee that has its own input parameter called curName and a number variable called RecordCount to store a count of the records processed.

Our cursor isn't that sophisticated: it uses || to add the wildcard character '%' to the beginning and the end of the required search name. In SQL Server, we would have used the + string concatenation operator. This enables the LIKE statement to find any employee's names that contain the specified characters. As we populate each of the PL/SQL table parameters we need to keep a track of the current element being set, so we use RecordCount. PL/SQL tables are 1-based so we must increment the RecordCount first as it starts from 0 initially.

```
    BEGIN
        FOR curRecEmployee IN cur_employee(i_EName) LOOP

            RecordCount:= RecordCount + 1;
            o_EmpNo(RecordCount):= curRecEmployee.empno;
            o_EName(RecordCount):= curRecEmployee.ename;
            o_Job(RecordCount):=   curRecEmployee.job;
        END LOOP;
    END EmployeeSearch;
END Employee_Pkg;
```

Here we have defined the actual implementation of the EmployeeSearch procedure. We simply open the cursor and ask it to transfer each record into a cursor variable called curRecEmployee. Notice that we didn't actually define the variable curRecEmployee, as this is simply a reference name to the record structure for the cursor. We can still refer to it within our cursor FOR...LOOP as though it was declared.

Then it's just a case of moving through each record, incrementing the record count, and transferring each individual field into each output parameter in the identical element position using RecordCount.

Now we need to call the procedure from an ASP script to populate the data. This is where you're likely to have the most problems when writing your own procedures. The following rules *must* be remembered, otherwise it simply won't work and you could spend days and days trying to work out why – as I did!

❑ Use the Microsoft ODBC Driver for Oracle.

If you try to use the OLE DB Provider for Oracle you'll get an error message saying "Catastrophic Error"! You should also try to ensure that you're using at least version **2.573.4202.00** of the driver.

❑ Argument Naming and Positioning.

When setting the `Command` object's `CommandText`, you must ensure that you use *exactly* the same name and same position for each parameter as you did when you declared each parameter in your stored procedure. If not, you'll get the rather misleading ODBC error message "Resultset column must be a formal argument".

❑ Maximum Records Returned.

You must use the `resultset` qualifier as part of your `CommandText` string to tell the driver which parameters are recordsets, such as:

```
"{call Employee_Pkg.EmployeeSearch("?, {resultset 100, o_EmpNo, o_EName,
o_Job})}"
```

The number after `resultset` indicates the maximum number of records to be returned in this call. The driver actually allocates a memory cache to store this amount of data. (There appears to be no documentation that confirms what happens when the number of records is a lot less than this number.) If you exceed this number, by even one record, then you will receive Oracle error ORA-06512. It is suggested that you limit the number of records within your cursor population by passing the required value as an additional parameter to your stored procedure and limiting the cursor `FOR...LOOP`. We didn't do this in our example but it might be a nice exercise to try.

So we can now create a simple ASP script to call our procedure. I'm going to use a single ASP script that contains a form that submits to itself and writes out the search results.

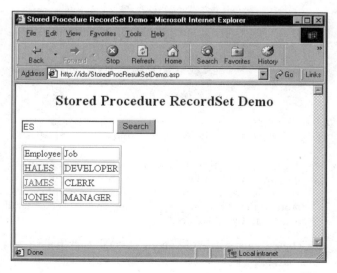

```
<% Option Explicit
    Response.Expires = 0%>
<HTML>
<HEAD>
    <TITLE>Stored Procedure Recordset Demo</TITLE>
</HEAD>
<BODY>
    <CENTER><H2>Stored Procedure Recordset Demo</H2></CENTER>
<%
Dim strSearchName
Dim objConnection
Dim objCommand
Dim objRecordset
Dim varEmpNo

strSearchName = Request.Form("txtSearchName")
If strSearchName = "" Then strSearchName = "%"
```

We transfer the `txtSearchName` input field from the form into a variable. If it was empty, which it will be the first time, we set it to % so that we get all matching names.

```
Set objConnection = Server.CreateObject("ADODB.Connection")
With objConnection
    .ConnectionString = "driver={Microsoft ODBC for Oracle};" & _
                        "server=Oracle8_dev;UID=scott;PWD=tiger;"
    .CursorLocation = adUseClient
    .Open
End With
```

Here we connect to the database using the **Microsoft ODBC Driver for Oracle**.

Now for the fun part:

```
Set objCommand = Server.CreateObject("ADODB.Command")
With objCommand
    Set .ActiveConnection = objConnection

    .CommandText = "{call Employee_Pkg.EmployeeSearch(" & _
                "?, {resultset 100, o_EmpNo, o_EName, o_Job})}"
    .CommandType = adCmdText

    .Parameters(0).Value = strSearchName
    Set objRecordset = .Execute()
End With
%>
```

We are using the standard {call...} and ? syntax to define the first input parameter. Notice that we have included the {resultset 100....} string, as mentioned above, to define those parameters that are to be returned in the Recordset object and that we only want 100 records returned. We have simply pasted in the names of the parameters exactly as we declared them. The only parameter that we actually set is the first input parameter, the search name. Finally, we call the Execute statement to get our data.

What you do is navigate through the records in the `Recordset` and creating a nicely formatted HTML table.

```
<FORM ACTION="StoredProcResultSetDemo.asp" METHOD="POST">
<INPUT NAME="txtSearchName" VALUE="<%=strSearchName%>">
<INPUT TYPE="SUBMIT" VALUE="Search">
<P>
<TABLE BORDER=1>
  <TR><TD>Employee</TD><TD>Job</TD></TR>
<%
Do While Not objRecordset.EOF
    varEmpNo = objRecordset.Fields("o_EmpNo")
    Response.Write "<TR>" & _
                "    <TD><A HREF=EditEmp.ASP?EmpNo=" & varEmpNo & ">" & _
                        objRecordset.Fields("o_EName") & "</A></TD>" & _
                "    <TD>" & objRecordset.Fields("o_Job") & "</TD>" & _
                "</TR>"

    objRecordset.MoveNext
Loop

Set objRecordset = Nothing
Set objCommand = Nothing
Set objConnection = Nothing
%>
</TABLE>
</FORM>
</BODY>
</HTML>
```

Retrieving ADO Recordsets using Reference Cursors

Oracle has released version 8.1.6 of its own provider, **Oracle Provider for OLE DB**. This provider has a class name of **OraOLEDB.Oracle** that is used when defining your ADO connection string. It supports the same set of Oracle data types as Microsoft's OLE DB Provider for Oracle with the additional support for the binary object types BLOB, CLOB, NCLOB, and BFILE, but as with Microsoft's provider, it also does not provide support for the Oracle8i object data types.

This provider gives us pretty much the same level of functionality as Microsoft's, except that it supports the use of Oracle reference cursors so that we can return back an ADO `Recordset` object from a stored procedure. A **reference cursor** is a pointer to a memory location that can be passed between different PL/SQL clients, thus allowing query result sets to be passed back and forth between clients.

A reference cursor is a variable type defined using the PL/SQL `TYPE` statement within an Oracle package, much like a PL/SQL table:

```
TYPE ref_type_name IS REF CURSOR RETURN return_type;
```

Here, `ref_type_name` is the name given to the type and `return_type` represents a record in the database. You do not have to specify the return type as this could be used as a general catch-all reference cursor. Such *non-restrictive* types are known as *weak*, whereas specifying the return type is *restrictive*, or *strong*. The following example uses `%ROWTYPE` to define a strong return type that represents the record structure of the `emp` table:

```
DECLARE TYPE EmpCurType IS REF CURSOR RETURN emp%ROWTYPE;
```

So let's jump straight to an example. We'll create a new Oracle package that contains a single procedure, `EmployeeSearch`, which returns a list of matching employee names. From your SQL editor, execute the following code to create the package specification:

```
CREATE OR REPLACE PACKAGE Employee_RefCur_pkg
AS

    TYPE empcur IS REF CURSOR;
    PROCEDURE EmployeeSearch(i_EName      IN   VARCHAR2,
                             o_EmpCursor OUT empcur);
END Employee_RefCur_pkg;
```

We've created a new type called `empcur` that returns a weak reference cursor that we use as an output parameter to the `EmployeeSearch` procedure. Now we need the package body:

```
CREATE OR REPLACE PACKAGE BODY Employee_RefCur_pkg
AS
    PROCEDURE EmployeeSearch(i_EName      IN   VARCHAR2,
                             o_EmpCursor OUT empcur)

    IS
    BEGIN

        OPEN o_EmpCursor FOR
            SELECT emp.empno, emp.ename, emp.job,
                emp.sal, dept.dname, dept.loc
            FROM emp, dept
            WHERE ename LIKE '%' || i_EName || '%'
                AND emp.deptno = dept.deptno
            ORDER BY UPPER(emp.ename);
    END EmployeeSearch;
END Employee_RefCur_pkg;
```

This code is very similar to our previous stored procedure, except that we don't need to transfer each column in distinct PL/SQL tables, as the reference cursor, `o_EmpCursor`, is returned back to the client. The Oracle Provider for OLE DB converts any parameters that reference cursors into an ADO `Recordset` for us – but only if we add `PLSQLRSet=1` to our connection string, which we'll cover next.

Let's have a look at the results page that calls this stored procedure:

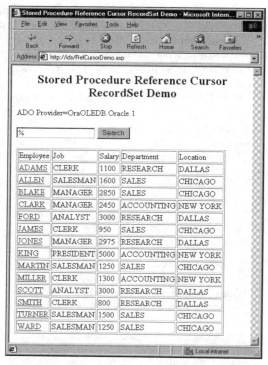

The actual ASP is very similar to our previous example so we'll just concentrate on the sections that are different:

```
<%
Dim strSearchName
Dim objConnection
Dim objCommand
Dim objRecordSet
Dim objNameParam
Dim varEmpNo

strSearchName = Request.Form("txtSearchName")
If strSearchName = "" Then strSearchName = "%"

Set objConnection = Server.CreateObject("ADODB.Connection")
```

So far it's just the same, except that we define a new variable, objNameParam, that we'll use as an ADO Parameter object to pass in the search name entered.

```
With objConnection
   .ConnectionString = "Provider=OraOLEDB.Oracle;" & _
                       "Data Source=Oracle8i_dev;" & _
                       "User ID=scott;" & _
                       "Password=tiger;" & _
                       "PLSQLRSet=1;"
   .Open
   Response.Write "ADO Provider=" & .Provider & "<P>"
End With
```

Here we tell ADO to use the Oracle Provider for OLE DB, `OraOLEDB.Oracle`, and we set the `PLSQLRSet` attribute to tell the provider that it should parse the PL/SQL stored procedures to determine if any parameters return a record set. `OraOLEDB` can only return one recordset per stored procedure. If you call a stored procedure that returns more than one recordset then `OraOLEDB` will only return the first argument of a ref cursor type.

If you omit the `PLSQLRSet` attribute, or you set it to 0, then you'll receive the following Oracle error:

```
ORA-06550: line 1, column 7: PLS-00306: wrong number or types of arguments in call
to 'EMPLOYEESEARCH' ORA-06550: line 1, column 7: PL/SQL: Statement ignored
```

The rest of the code goes as follows:

```
Set objCommand = Server.CreateObject("ADODB.Command")
With objCommand
    Set .ActiveConnection = objConnection

    .CommandText = "{call Employee_RefCur_pkg.EmployeeSearch(?)}"
    Set objNameParam = .CreateParameter("SearchName", adBSTR, _
                                        adParamInput, , strSearchName)

    .Parameters.Append objNameParam

    Set objRecordSet = .Execute()
End With
```

Although our stored procedure has two parameters, the search name and the reference cursor that is returned, you must *not* bind the reference cursor as a parameter using the ? attribute when using `OraOLEDB`, so we've included only one ? character to represent the `Name` input parameter.

The ADO `Parameter` object, `objNameParam`, is created using the `Command` object's `CreateParameter` function. `CreateParameter` is called in the following way:

```
Set parameter = command.CreateParameter(Name, Type, Direction, Size, Value)
```

`objNameParam` is declared as an `adBSTR` type because this maps to Oracle's `VARCHAR2` data type. Once we've created the `Parameter` we need to add it to the `Command` object's `Parameters` collection using the `Append` method.

Finally we call the `Execute` function to return a `Recordset` object that represents the result set from the `o_EmpCursor` reference cursor parameter. That's all there is to it. We can then navigate through the `Recordset` object as usual.

It's worth remembering that if you try to call the stored procedure using the `Parameters` collection directly:

```
.CommandText = "{call Employee_RefCur_pkg.EmployeeSearch(?)}"
.Parameters(0).Type = adBSTR
.Parameters(0).Direction = adParamInput
.Parameters(0).Value = strSearchName
```

527

you'll get the following runtime error:

```
The provider cannot derive parameter info and SetParameterInfo has not been called
```

Therefore you must use the CreateParameter function.

That wraps up our look at retrieving ADO Recordset objects from Oracle stored procedures. As you've seen, we have two choices: PL/SQL tables with the Microsoft ODBC for Oracle Driver or reference cursors with Oracle's Oracle Provider for OLE DB. On the face of it, the use of PL/SQL tables does appear rather convoluted in comparison to the ease of reference cursors. Both are relatively inefficient in terms of server performance and the Oracle Provider for OLE DB has been regarded as rather buggy. Again, it's your choice; it's difficult to define what each can and can't do. As ever, you should investigate how both methods perform in your own environment, looking at response times along with CPU and memory usage.

Summary

That just about brings us to the end of this guide to connecting to an Oracle database from an ASP application. We covered quite lot of ground here:

- ❑ Installation and configuration of the Oracle8 client software, Net8
- ❑ Using the Microsoft OLE DB Provider for Oracle
- ❑ Using the Microsoft OLE DB Provider for ODBC
- ❑ Using Oracle Objects for OLE (OO4O)
- ❑ PL/SQL fundamentals
- ❑ Creating a sample ASP application based on the scott account
- ❑ Showing that it is possible to retrieve an ADO Recordset from an Oracle stored procedure, using both PL/SQL tables and reference cursors

Before we finish this chapter, take look at the chart below comparing each of the common methods of data access for Oracle. I added an additional 7000 records to the emp table and then used each of the methods to retrieve these records and display them using an ASP script. Each method was executed three times and after each test I rebooted the server machine so that there would be very little chance of data being cached by either Oracle or the web server (for this test the web server also doubled as the Oracle database server to cut the time taken to shutdown and restart).

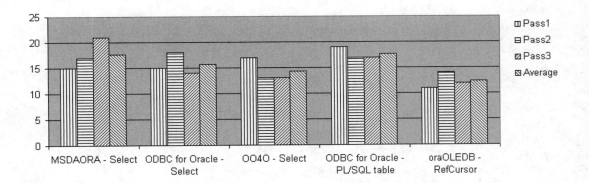

In these tests, MSDAORA was used with a standard SQL SELECT statement, as was the ODBC Driver for Oracle and OO4O, and finally I used the ODBC Driver for Oracle in conjunction with PL/SQL tables, and Oracle's Oracle Provider for OLE DB with a reference cursors as just described. The Y-axis shows the amount of time taken to complete each test in seconds. I also monitored the CPU and memory usage and they were all very similar for each test.

You can see that there is not that much difference between each method. When choosing which method to use, the underlying factor will always be good database design and coding practices.

Don't forget that you can download all of the SQL and ASP scripts for this chapter from the Wrox web site at http://www.wrox.com.

16

IBM DB2 Universal Database

DB2 Universal Database Version 7.1 is IBM's latest release of its cross-platform database system. With this release, IBM has added new features that extend the universality of DB2, integrated support for related technologies, and improved the user interfaces. In this chapter, we will discuss the features of DB2 using the V7.1 Developer's Edition. We will look at some installation issues, before going on to explore how we might use DB2 for web-based database access using Active Server Pages and ODBC.

IBM refers to DB2 as a *Universal Database*, and while we may be justified in suspecting that this is little more than a marketing expression, it is a very powerful application that could be effectively used in almost any situation where we want to store and access large amounts of data efficiently. Enterprise database management systems such as DB2, Oracle, and SQL Server differ from desktop database systems in important ways. The most important differences are that, on enterprise systems, SQL commands are executed on the remote server, not on the desktop, SQL programs can be compiled and optimized as callable stored procedures; and *triggers* or procedural programs can be implemented to respond to database updates. Of course, another critical difference is that enterprise systems can process and store far more information far quicker than a lowly desktop database system.

DB2 7.1 also includes support for, amongst other things, Online Analytical Processing (OLAP), data warehousing, distributed query processing across OLE DB data sources and Oracle databases, XML handling, including parsing XML documents into DB2, Java standards (including JDBC and embedding SQL in Java code), compilation of stored procedures in either Java or C.

DB2 is a cross-platform relational database management system (RDBMS) with roots in mainframe and minicomputer hardware. In its latest releases, DB2 runs on Windows-based systems (workstation versions 95, 98, NT4, and 2000 and server versions of NT4 and 2000), Unix-based systems (AIX, HP-UX, Linux, and Solaris), OS/2; and mini/mainframe OSs (OS/390, AS/400, VSE, and VM). We have also been promised versions for Windows CE and hand-held computers. DB2 capabilities are not identical on all platforms, but the functionality of the product is comparable over all platforms.

> *DB2 Universal Database Version 7.1 may be downloaded, free of charge, from* `http://www6.software.ibm.com/dl/db2udbv7/db2udbv7-p` *for WinNT/2000, AIX, Linux and Solaris.*

With DB2, stored procedures may be compiled from SQL code. However, they may also be compiled from C++ and Java code. The appropriate C++ or Java compilers must be installed when DB2 is installed. DB2 supports Microsoft Visual C++ 5 and 6 compilers, as well as IBM's Visual Age. If the Visual C++ compiler is to be used, then it must be installed with the option to register environment variables switched *on*. This can be done on the last screen of the installation screens:

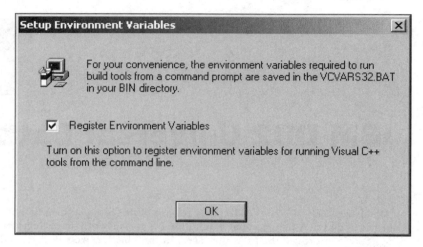

However, in this chapter we will not be looking at building stored procedures with C++ or Java, concentrating instead on using SQL with ASP.

Without further ado, let's take a look at the installation of DB2 components. As we will work on the assumption that a DB2 database is already installed, we will focus on installing the DB2 client components on a web server.

Installation of Client Components

If we were running a large DB2 database, we would want to run our web services on another machine. However, in order to access data from our database, we would have to install the appropriate client components on our web server machine.

We might also want to install appropriate components onto another machine for development purposes. This would enable us to develop our application without having to interfere with the database server machine or the web server.

On running the DB2 installation program, we are given a choice of what products we would like to install. For our web server, as we are only interested in installing client components, we could select **DB2 Administration Client**. For our development machine, we should select **DB2 Application Development Client**.

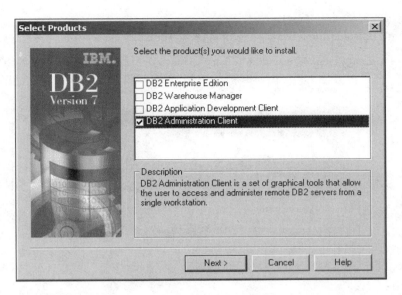

However, we would not necessarily want to install all the components that would typically be installed. So, on the next screen, we should select **Custom**. This will allow us to specify exactly which components we want to install. This would apply for both our web server machine and our development machine.

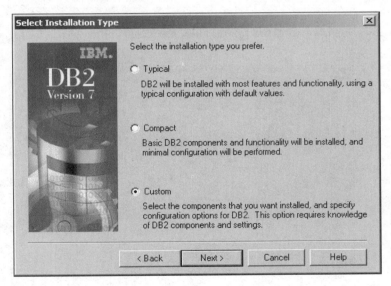

On our web server machine, it would be most important to ensure that we install **Base DB2 Client Support**. The components installed on this selection would provide us with the basic functionality needed to connect to the database.

It might also be beneficial to select the **Communication Protocols**. On clicking on the **Subcomponents** button, we are able to specify the types of protocol components we want installed. For instance, we could install APPC, IPX/SPX, Named Pipes, Net BIOS, or TCP/IP components. The defaults are TCP/IP and Named Pipes.

If we envisage accessing a data warehouse from our web pages, we might also want to install the Data Warehousing Tools and the Data Warehousing ISV Toolkit.

For the development machine, it would be very useful to have the Stored Procedure Builder installed. This is an application with a graphical interface with which we can develop, build and test stored procedures. We might also want to install the Sample Applications.

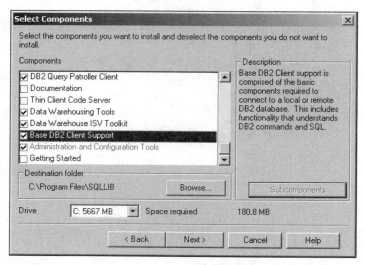

On the following screen, we are asked to provide a user name and password for logging onto the database:

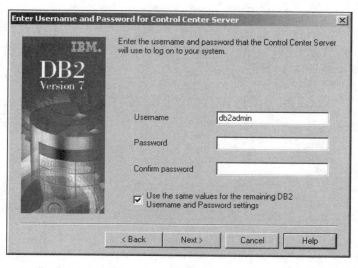

The default username is db2Admin. If this username already exists on your system, then you must use the same password for it. Otherwise, it will be created on the system.

After being presented with a screen that gives us a summary of our installation configuration, DB2 will install the components we specified.

Further Steps

In this chapter, we will be using the Sample database, which comes with DB2. You will need to make sure that this exists on your DB2 database. If it doesn't, then it can be set up from the First Steps option from the DB2 menu. If *this* hasn't been installed, then it will be necessary to install it from the DB2 disks.

The DB2 object hierarchy, as in SQL Server, follows the syntax <SCHEMA>.<TABLE> to use tables in a database.

If the schema name is different to the current network User ID, then the <SCHEMA>.<TABLE> syntax is mandatory. Since the schema name on web servers will *always* be different to the anonymous or blank network User ID, we should plan ahead to write code that will work and to use schema names that do not compromise server security, even if they are discovered by a user (or an intruder).

The Control Center

DB2's **Control Center** is the central user tool for viewing and managing databases.

The Control Center lists all DB2 servers connected to the user's computer. Drilling down the object hierarchy, one finds the SAMPLE database and its objects. The figure below shows the list of tables. The first column in the Tables list is the table name and the second is the schema name. As shown in this example, the samples were installed under a specific User ID, not a generic ID as suggested in the previous note. **The schema name cannot be changed**. If you choose (or allow DB2 to choose) an inappropriate schema name, you must create a new database and import the data into it. (With the DB2 samples, you could drop the database, log on as the appropriate user, and re-install the samples.)

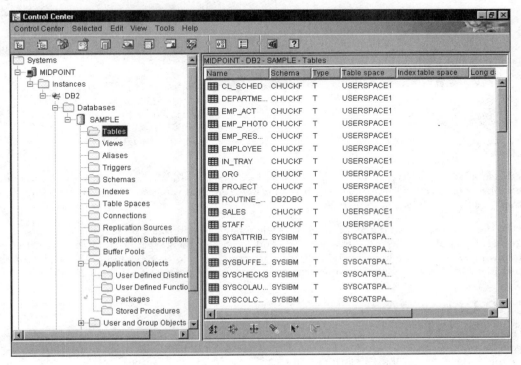

The Control Center gives access to all of the objects in DB2. The figure shows the list of tables, including both those in the USERSPACE, or user data tables, and those in the SYSCATSPACE, or system tables. The primary emphasis of this chapter is upon working with USERSPACE tables created under a specific schema.

The Control Center can manage databases across several servers or systems. In this illustration, the MIDPOINT server is shown, while other servers are out of view on the tree. Multiple instances, or RDBMS systems, comprising a distributed database can be managed from one location. And obviously, multiple databases can be managed within DB2.

Within each DB2 database, many objects can be created, viewed, or modified from the Control Center, including tables, views, aliases, schemas, indexes, table spaces, connections, replication sources and subscriptions, buffer pools, application objects (especially stored procedures), and users and user groups.

We can view the partial contents of any table by right-clicking the table name and selecting Sample Contents:

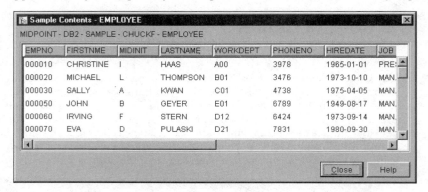

In the Control Center, double-clicking any table name initiates an Alter Table tool for that table, shown in the figure below. The Alter Table tool can be used to view and change the table definition, but not table contents.

> *Of potential interest to those of us who need to develop SQL using Data Definition Language (DDL) commands, the Alter Table tool generates SQL code that can be executed to make changes. That SQL code can be viewed, altered, copied, and stored using the Show SQL command button.*

OLE DB

DB2 supplies its own native OLE DB Provider: IBMDADB2.1. Ideally we would want to use this to establish a connection to the database. It is a far more efficient way than using ODBC because it bypasses the ODBC layer altogether.

However, we encountered unexpected errors when navigating through a recordset using the Connection object's OpenSchema method. And, as we will be navigating through a recordset in the following examples, we have used the ODBC Driver in the following examples. But do bear in mind that it would always be better, in other circumstances, to use the native OLE DB Provider.

ODBC Connections

Open Database Connectivity (ODBC) Drivers enable client programs to access database management systems through drivers provided by the RDBMS vendor. ODBC connections to DB2 databases can be established using the IBM DB2 ODBC DRIVER.

To establish a connection to an existing DB2 database, we can use the ODBC Data Source Administrator. We simply click on the System DSN tab, and click Add. We then select the IBM DB2 ODBC DRIVER and reference the SAMPLE database.

After this has been installed, we can configure the connection by clicking Configure. We can then, if we wish, specify a new User ID and Password for accessing the database via this connection. It is a good idea to make the ODBC User ID and Password different from any valid server logon in order to increase the security of the server. We can also, if we wish, also specify an alias for the database:

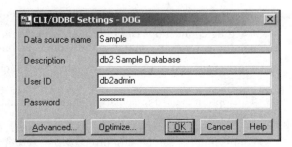

ODBC Advanced Configuration

During the process of creating the connection, or at any time thereafter, we may accept default settings or change them in advanced configuration options.

The advanced options are available under eight tabs, as shown in the following screenshot: Transactions, Data Type, Enterprise, Optimization, Compatibility, Environment, Service, Static SQL.

Using these options, DB2 can be configured and tuned for each server and application.

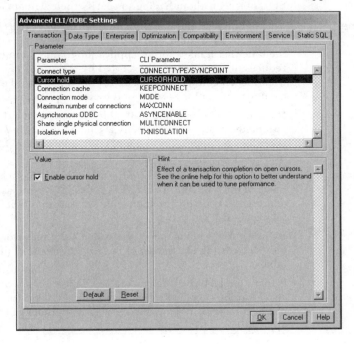

The following may be of particular interest here, but this is by no means an exhaustive list. Under the Transaction tab, we find the following:

Cursor Hold	This is used to control how cursors are dealt with when a transaction completes: 1 = cursors are maintained (this is the default). 0 = cursors are destroyed when a transaction completes.
Connection Cache	This indicates the number of database connections that are cached. Caching connections can improve the performance of applications that need to constantly connect and disconnect from the same database.
Connection Mode	This sets the CONNECT mode to either SHARE or EXCLUSIVE. The default is SHARE.
Maximum number of connections	This option is used to specify the maximum number of connections permitted for each CLI/ODBC application. A value of 0 may be used to represent no limit. This would allow an application to open up as many connections as can be supported by the system resources.
Asynchronous ODBC	This option enables us to specify whether queries may be executed asynchronously. Of course, this is only useful with applications that have been specifically written to take advantage of asynchronous queries.

And under the Enterprise tab:

MVS Current SQLID	If this option is set, a SET CURRENT SQLID statement is sent to the DBMS on connection, which specifies a schema name. This allows us to name SQL objects without having to specify their schema name.
MVS DB Name Filter	This option is useful if a large number of tables exist in the DB2 for a MVS/ESA subsystem. A database name can be specified, and this reduces the time that it takes for an application to query table information, and reduces the number of tables listed by the application. This option is only useful when connecting to DB2 for MVS/ESA, and only if (base) table catalog information is requested by the application.
Schema List	If there are a large number of tables defined in the database, this parameter enables us to specify a schema list. This will reduce the time it takes for an application to query table information, and reduce the number of tables listed by the application.
System Schema	This option can be used to indicate an alternative schema to be searched in place of the SYSIBM (or SYSTEM, QSYS2) schemas when the DB2 CLI and ODBC Catalog Function calls are issued to obtain system catalog information. By using this schema name, the system administrator can define a set of views consisting of a subset of the rows for most of the system catalog tables:
Table Types	If there are a large number of tables defined in the database, a tabletype string can be specified to reduce the time it takes for the application to query table information, and reduce the number of tables listed by an application.

A couple of the **Optimization** parameters are:

Optimization Level	This specifies the query optimization level at which the optimizer should operate the SQL queries. It can be set from 0 to 9.
Parallelism Level	This specifies the degree of parallelism for the execution of SQL statements. If we specify ANY, then the database manager will determine the degree of parallelism allowed.
	Clearly, this is only applicable when connecting to a cluster database system.

And under the **Compatibility** tab we find:

Multithreading (Common)	The CLI/ODBC driver is capable of supporting multiple concurrent threads.
	This option is used to enable or disable multi-thread support.
	A setting of 0 enables multithreading. This is the default. A setting of 1 disables multithreading.
Early Cursor Close	This option specifies whether or not the temporary cursor on the server may be automatically closed, without closing the cursor on the client, when the last record is sent to the client.
	A setting of 0 indicates that the temporary cursor is not to be closed early. While a setting of 1 indicates that the temporary cursor on the server is to be closed early. This latter is the default.
	Having this option set to 1 will speed up applications that access many small result sets.

Understanding and carefully configuring the ODBC parameters is essential in establishing an efficient and effective connection.

Accessing DB2 from ASP

We use a single ASP application file to connect to the database and display the results.

We will call this file `Default.asp`. Initially, we want to specify a file to include, declare some general variables, and introduce some formatting:

```
<% @language=vbscript %>
<!-- #include file="adovbs.inc" -->
<%
'Declarations, Functions, and Subs
' cn and rs are declared to make them available to all procedures
    dim cn   ' connection
    dim rs   ' recordset
    thisPage = "Default.asp"


' Main code follows here
%>
<html>
<head>
```

```
</head>
<body bgcolor = #FFF8DC>
<font face='Arial' size='1'>
<center>
<A HREF=<% = thisPage %> >Home</a>
<font face='Arial'>
<h1>DB2 Database Sample</h1>
<FORM ACTION=<% = thisPage %> METHOD="Post" TARGET="_self">
<%
' Code to process user input goes here

%>
</form>
</body>
</html>
```

The include file `adovbs.inc` defines the ADO constants used in VBScripts to allow mnemonics to be used where a constant is needed. This code assumes the file is in the current folder, although in practice, we would normally have to give the full path name. The variables `cn` and `rs` are dimensioned at the beginning, to make them available to all procedures, and the variable `thisPage` is used to facilitate testing.

Let's take a look at the code required to connect to our DB2 database.

Recordsets

The ASP code needed to connect to the server database as installed is simply:

```
<%
sub MakeCN
    strProvider = "DSN=Sample;UID=db2Admin;PWD=password;Database=Sample;"
    set cn = Server.CreateObject("ADODB.Connection")
    cn.Open strProvider
end sub
%>
```

In this example, the connection code is contained in the `MakeCN` procedure, which is called from the main procedure. Separating the connection code from the data access code simplifies code development and maintenance, and allows user logins to be completely separated from database access:

```
<%
    Call MakeCN

    ' Do something here

    'Close the connection

    cn.Close
    set cn = nothing
%>
```

Opening a recordset is similarly straightforward:

```
strQuery = "SELECT * FROM Administrator.Employee;"
Set rs = Server.CreateObject("ADODB.Recordset")
rs.Open strQuery, cn, adOpenForwardOnly
```

The DB2 SQL syntax for selecting records (and indeed for any other procedure) conforms to ANSI standards. An important detail is that the schema name (in this case Administrator) is here specified as part of the table name in the SQL statement. This is necessary unless the MVS current SQLID parameter is set under the Enterprise tab of the Advanced CLI/ODBC Settings screen (which we looked at earlier). This usage is allowed but is not required by SQL Server if the table name is unique, and is not relevant for Microsoft Access, where the database name identifies the schema uniquely.

The CursorTypeEnum in the recordset open command (adOpenForwardOnly in this case) must be chosen to correspond to the use intended for the recordset. If we have the adovbs.inc file included from the code, this can be specified as a mnemonic.

The choices of cursor types are:

```
'---- CursorTypeEnum Values ----
Const adOpenForwardOnly = 0
Const adOpenKeyset = 1
Const adOpenDynamic = 2
Const adOpenStatic = 3
```

Similarly, a LockType Enum can be specified as needed for the recordset instance. By default it is left unspecified for recordsets that are read-only.

```
'---- LockTypeEnum Values ----
Const adLockReadOnly = 1
Const adLockPessimistic = 2
Const adLockOptimistic = 3
Const adLockBatchOptimistic = 4
```

Data Display

Given that these are ordinary ADO recordsets, there is no limit on how the data can be displayed. In the sample mini-app at the end of the chapter, the data is displayed in a table that can be sorted by clicking a column header. Employee records in that application can be edited by clicking the employee identifier.

Accessing the Database Schema

Developers may need to obtain information from the database schema itself for any number of purposes. For example, new views or tables may be added to the database, it may be necessary to verify privileges before actions are taken, and the like. The more complex the database, the more likely it is that the developer will need to use this information. The key is found in the ADO OpenSchema method. OpenSchema allows the developer to retrieve information about any part of the database schema.

The following procedure displays just the table names associated with the `Administrator` schema name:

```
Sub ShowAdminTables(cn)
    Set rsSchema = cn.OpenSchema(adSchemaTables)
    Response.Write "<H2>Tables in Sample Database</H2>"
    Response.Write "<TABLE>"
    With rsSchema
        Do While Not .eof
            If .Fields("TABLE_SCHEMA") = "ADMINIST" Then
                Response.Write "<TR BGCOLOR='beige'>"
                Response.Write "<TD><FONT SIZE='1'>" & _
                               .Fields("TABLE_NAME").Value & "</TD>"
                Response.Write "</TR>"
            End If
            .MoveNext
        Loop
    End With
    Response.Write "</TABLE>"
End Sub
```

We will call this just after we establish the connection with the following call:

```
call ShowAdminTables(cn)
```

The output from this code is shown in the screen shot opposite.

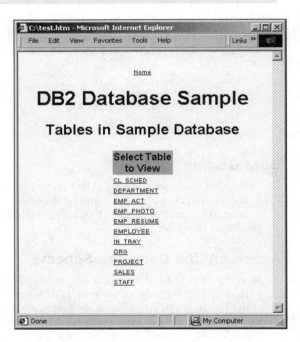

In the Mini-Application presented at the end of this chapter, the table names become live links that are used to generate SQL queries that retrieve the contents of the tables and display them on the web page.

Stored Procedures

DB2 can act as an OLE DB consumer to utilize data from any OLE DB Provider. Once the interface between DB2 and the provider is established, DB2 can manipulate the data as if it were part of the DB2 database.

The key to making this work is to create and register in DB2 a user-defined function (UDF) that refers to the OLE DB Provider and the relevant rowset. In other words, the UDF must specify the database and the table, query, or stored procedure from which the data will be retrieved. The DB2 installation supplies sample code for Microsoft Access, ODBC, SQL Server, Index Server, as well as for Oracle, Lotus Notes, and Intersolv. These samples include both the UDF syntax and SQL code or stored procedures needed to use the UDFs to access data.

To illustrate how to use this capability, we will develop a UDF to retrieve data from the Microsoft Access Northwind database. Specifically, we will retrieve data from the Employees table, and perform a union with the DB2 SAMPLE database Employee table.

The UDF must specify the individual fields and their attributes, the language (OLEDB), and the external name, including connection string. The UDF is inserted into the DB2 database using a command line script. The specific script for this function is:

```
-- First drop the function, in case this is a revision

DROP FUNCTION jet.employees();

CREATE FUNCTION jet.employees ()
   RETURNS TABLE (EmployeeID INTEGER,
       Lastname VARCHAR(20),
       FirstName VARCHAR(12),
       Extension CHAR(4),
       Title VARCHAR(30),
       Birthdate DATE,
       DATASOURCE CHAR(5)
       )
   LANGUAGE OLEDB
   EXTERNAL NAME '!EMPLOYEES!Provider=Microsoft.Jet.OLEDB.3.51;' & _
               'Data Source=c:\files\nwind.mdb;';

-- Test the function (should print a count of 9 to CLP window)

SELECT COUNT (EmployeeID) FROM TABLE (jet.employees ()) AS t;
```

Of course, you must specify the path to nwind.mdb on your server.

We save the script as JetEmp.db2.

The function can now be used to retrieve a rowset of employees from the Employees table of the Northwind database. This is done using:

```
SELECT * FROM TABLE (jet.employees()) as t
```

This can now be used to perform a UNION between the jet.employees table with the DB2 employee table using a stored procedure.

The complete stored procedure (Which we will save as PROC2) would be as follows:

```
CREATE PROCEDURE ADMINISTRATOR.Proc2 (  )
    LANGUAGE SQL
------------------------------------------------------------------------
-- SQL Stored Procedure
------------------------------------------------------------------------
P1: BEGIN
  -- Declare cursor
  DECLARE c1 CURSOR WITH RETURN TO CLIENT FOR
    SELECT EMPNO, LASTNAME, FIRSTNME, PHONENO, JOB, BIRTHDATE, 'DB2' AS DATASOURCE
      FROM ADMINISTRATOR.EMPLOYEE
  UNION
  SELECT CHAR(EmployeeID) AS EMPNO,
    LASTNAME,
    FirstName AS FIRSTNME,
    Extension AS PHONENO,
    Title AS JOB,
    BIRTHDATE,
    'NWIND' AS DATASOURCE
  FROM TABLE (jet.employees ()) AS t
    ORDER BY LastName, FirstNME;
  OPEN c1;
END P1
```

We here select the appropriate fields from the DB2 EMPLOYEE table and assign DB2 as the data source. We then convert the Northwind EmployeeID from integer to character, substitute field names as needed to match the EMPLOYEE table, and assign NWIND as the data source. We then perform the UNION and sort the records by last name and first name.

The stored procedure declares the cursor with return to client, and the last step is to open the cursor and leave it open. This action returns the rowset to the client.

A straightforward way of storing the procedure in DB2 is to use DB2's Stored Procedure Builder, which performs syntax checking and allows us to run the query. We can here see the results of running this stored procedure:

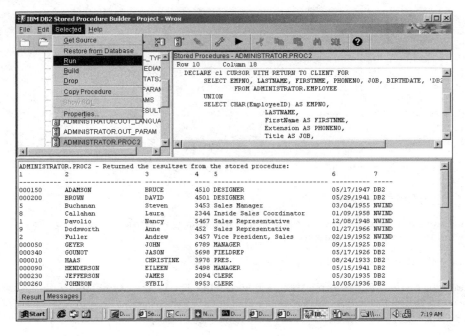

One important point to note in using DB2 stored procedures is that the rowset returned does not contain field names, only field numbers. This also holds true when used in an ADO recordset. Therefore, any field customization for output must not rely on field names in the recordset.

The stored procedure is accessed from the client program using the ADO command in the following way:

```
sub SendProcRequest()
    Set cm = Server.CreateObject("ADODB.Command")
    set cm.ActiveConnection = cn
    cm.CommandText = "Administrator.Proc2"
    cm.CommandType = adCmdStoredProc
    Set rs = Server.CreateObject("ADODB.recordset")
    rs.Open cm.CommandText, cn, adOpenForwardOnly
    call ShowUnion(rs, "Stored Procedure")
end sub
```

If a stored procedure requires parameters, then these must be appended to the command text prior to executing rs.open. The ShowUnion procedure called in the last line of this sub writes the recordset to the browser, as we will see in more detail a little later.

A Mini Application

The following mini-application suggests some of the ways Active Server Pages can connect to and use a DB2 database. This mini-application consists of the following parts:

- ❑ Internet Information Services

- ❑ ADO 2.5 (although only ADO 2.0 services are used)

- ❑ The DB2 sample database, installed to the Adminstrator schema on the web server and accessed through the ODBC connection name Sample2 with the User ID db2Admin and the password Password

- ❑ The DB2 user-defined function (UDF) jet.employees and the stored procedure administrator.proc2 that uses the UDF

- ❑ The Default.asp, which will contain all the code for the application

- ❑ Adovbs.inc, the Microsoft ADO verbs and constants supplied with ADO

- ❑ Startup.txt, a simple file displayed as part of the main menu

The goal of this mini-application is to illustrate key techniques that allow data tables from DB2 to be displayed and edited without the use of session variables or cookies. While cookies pose no security risk, users are becoming more sensitive to possible intrusions, and we should avoid the appearance of intrusion. No effort has been made to optimize the application either for speed or for conservation of server resources.

The opening screen displays the list of available tables and a brief message about the application:

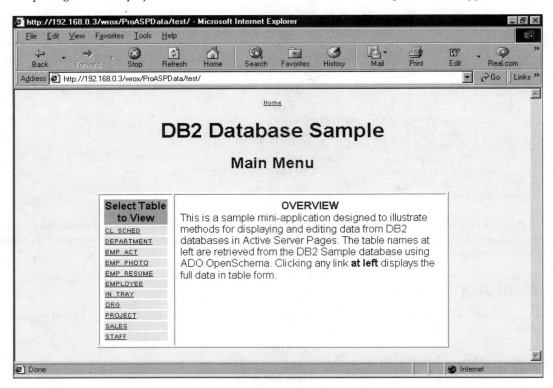

This screen is generated by the ShowMenu sub, which in turns calls ShowAdminTables. The code is as follows:

```
Sub ShowMenu
    Response.Write "<CENTER><B><H2>Main Menu</H2></B><BR>"
    Response.Write "<TABLE BORDER CELLPADDING='5'>"
    Response.Write "<TR BGCOLOR='white' VALIGN=TOP><TD>"
  Call ShowAdminTables

    Response.Write "</TD><TD>"
    Response.Write "<TABLE WIDTH=400>"
    Response.Write "<TR BGCOLOR='white'><TD><FONT FACE='Arial'>"
%>
<!-- #include file='startup.txt' -->
<%
    Response.Write "</TD></TR>"
    Response.Write "</TABLE>"
    Response.Write "</TD></TR>"
    Response.Write "</TABLE>"

    Response.Write "<INPUT TYPE='Hidden' NAME='Message' VALUE='Menu'>"
End Sub
```

```
sub ShowAdminTables
    ' Shows the menu of tables in the Administrator schema
    Set rsSchema = cn.OpenSchema(adSchemaTables)
    response.write "<table width=100>"
    response.write "<tr bgcolor='tan'><td align=center><b>Select Table to
View</b></td></tr>"
    with rsSchema
    do while not .eof
        if .fields("TABLE_SCHEMA") = "ADMINIST" THEN
            response.write "<tr bgcolor='beige'>"
            response.write "<td><font size='1'>"
            response.write "<a
href='default.asp?MenuBtn=Table&Message=Table&TableName=" &
rsSchema.Fields("TABLE_NAME").Value & "'>"
            response.write rsSchema.Fields("TABLE_NAME").Value & "</a>"
            response.write "</td>"
        response.write "</tr>"
    end if
    .movenext
    loop
    end with
    response.write "</table>"
end sub
```

The tables available for display are limited to those included in the Administrator schema. Clicking any table link causes a call to ShowTable, which displays the contents of the entire table. The main code that receives user input is as follows:

```
' Connect to the database
call MakeCN

If Request("EditBtn") <> "" then
    call ShowEditForm(Request("EditBtn"))
elseif trim(Request("EditAction")) = "Save" then
    call SaveEditForm(request("EMPNO"))
elseif trim(Request("MenuBtn")) <> "" then
    select case trim(Request("MenuBtn"))
        Case "Table"
            ' --- Show the table
            call SendSQL(Request("Message"),request("TableName"))
        Case "SQLRequest"
            ' --- Call the Function with SQL
            Call SendSQLRequest()
        Case "Procedure"
            ' --- Call the Proc2 stored procedure
            Call SendProcRequest()
        Case Else
            ' --- The default is show the Employee table
            call SendSQL(Request("Message"),"Employee")

    end select
elseif trim(Request("SortBtn")) <> "" then
    call SendSQL("Table",Request("TableName"))
else
    call ShowMenu
end if
' Close the connection
on error resume next
cn.Close
set cn = nothing
```

If the user has not clicked any button or link, the default action is Call ShowMenu. Each possible user action is tested in order using the syntax request(<anything>) to process parameters from the calling page. This handles form and link requests the same way and allows flexibility when pages are redesigned to get rid of those unsightly Submit buttons.

When the user selects a table, the table name is sent to sub SendSQL, which generates an appropriate SQL command and opens a recordset with the returned data from DB2:

```
sub SendSQL(strMsg,strTable)
    Select Case strMsg
        case "Table"
            strQuery = "SELECT * FROM Administrator." & strTable
            if Request("SortBtn") <> "" then
                strQuery = strQuery & "  ORDER BY " & Request("SortBtn")
            end if
            strQuery = strQuery & ";"
        case else
            strQuery = "SELECT * FROM Administrator.Employee;"
    end Select
    Set rs = Server.CreateObject("ADODB.recordset")
    rs.Open strQuery, cn, adOpenForwardOnly
    call ShowTable(rs)
end sub
```

ShowTable processes the recordset in the following way:

1. It calls MakeHeadingButton to create column headings of submit buttons using the field names.

2. It creates a submit button for the EMPNO in the EMPLOYEE table to allow records to be selected for editing.

3. It formats several fields using standard functions and the custom Proper function to convert DB2 upper to initial caps.

The ShowTable function is defined as follows:

```
sub ShowTable(rs)
    response.write("<h2>" & strTable & " Table</h2>")
    response.write "<font size=2>Click column heading to sort.<br>"
    ' --- set an outside border for the table
    response.write "<table border><tr><td>"
    response.write "<table>"
    response.write "<tr BGCOLOR='tan'>"

    for i = 0 to rs.fields.count - 1
        MakeHeadingButton(rs.fields(i).name)
    next
    response.write "</tr>"
    do while not rs.eof
    response.write "<tr BGCOLOR='beige'>"
```

```
    for i = 0 to rs.fields.count - 1
        select case rs.fields(i).name
            Case "EMPNO"
                response.write "<td><font face = 'Arial' size=1>"
                response.write "<INPUT TYPE='Submit' NAME='EditBtn' VALUE='" &
rs.fields(i).value & "'>"
            case "FIRSTNME", "LASTNAME", "JOB"
                response.write "<td><font face = 'Arial' size=1>"
                response.write Proper(rs.fields(i).value)
            case "SALARY", "BONUS", "COMM"
                response.write "<TD ALIGN='right'><font face = 'Arial' size=1>"
                response.write FormatCurrency(rs.fields(i).value,0)
            case "HIREDATE", "BIRTHDATE"
                response.write "<TD ALIGN='right'><font face = 'Arial' size=1>"
                response.write rs.fields(i).value
            case "PICTURE"
                ' --- this field is present in the EMP_PHOTO table
                response.write "<TD ALIGN='right'><font face = 'Arial' size=1>"
                response.write "Pictures not viewable."
            case else
                response.write "<td><font face = 'Arial' size=1>"
                response.write (rs.fields(i).value)
        end select
        response.write "</td>"
    next
    response.write "</tr>"
    rs.movenext
    loop
    response.write "</table>"
    rs.Close
    set rs = nothing
    ' --- close the outside table
    response.write "</td></tr></table>"
    %><INPUT TYPE="Hidden" NAME="TableName" VALUE="<%= request("TableName") %>"><%

end sub
```

A small function for correcting the case of the returned fields is defined by:

```
Function Proper(str)
    Proper = UCase(left(str, 1)) & LCase(mid(str, 2, len(str) - 1))
end function
```

A function for displaying the title of a particular table is:

```
Function MakeHeading(str)
    response.write "<td><font face = 'Arial' size=2><b>"
    response.write Proper(str) & "</b></td>"
end function
```

And a function for creating the buttons corresponding to the columns and rows of a table is given by:

```
Function MakeHeadingButton(str)
    response.write "<td><font face = 'Arial' size=1><b>"
    response.write "<INPUT TYPE='Submit' NAME='SortBtn' VALUE='" & Proper(str) &
"'>"
    response.write "</b></td>"
end function
```

549

The figure below shows part of the `Employee` table query. The column headings can be clicked for sorting, and `Empno` can be clicked to edit a record. In a complete application, codes such as Workdept A00 would be replaced by the text equivalent from the Department table.

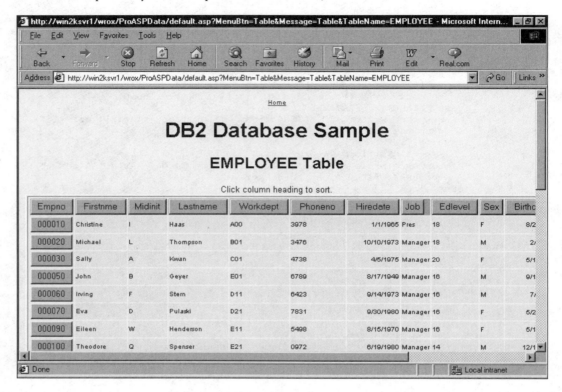

Clicking any column heading in any table causes the table to be sorted by that column. The operative code is as follows:

```
strQuery = "SELECT * FROM Administrator." & strTable
if Request("SortBtn") <> "" then
    strQuery = strQuery & "  ORDER BY " & Request("SortBtn")
end if
strQuery = strQuery & ";"
```

We build the query string the same way as in the initial display. If a field name (sort button) was clicked, we append the ORDER BY clause to the SQL statement. For DB2 it is essential to terminate the string with a semicolon.

For the EMPLOYEE table only, a record can be edited by clicking on the Empno field command button. A complete application would, of course, allow all tables to be edited, but preservation of data integrity would require additional programming (via triggers or stored procedures in the database or application code in the ASP program).

The simple edit form is:

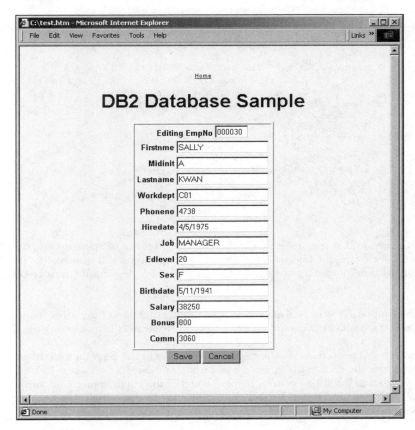

The edit form contained in this mini-application is quite simple and could be used to display data from any of the tables except the binary large objects (BLOB) fields, which we will look at below. The code for the EditForm sub is:

```
Sub ShowEditForm(strID)
    strQuery = "SELECT * FROM Administrator.Employee WHERE EMPNO='" & _
            strID & "'"
    Set rs = Server.CreateObject("ADODB.Recordset")
    rs.Open strQuery, cn, adOpenKeyset, adLockOptimistic
    i = 0
    Response.Write "<TABLE BORDER><TR><TD><FONT FACE='Arial' SIZE=2>"
    Response.Write "<B><CENTER>Editing EmpNo " & _
            "<INPUT TYPE='Text' SIZE='6' NAME='" & _
            rs.Fields(i).Name & "' VALUE='" & rs.Fields(i).Value & _
            "'>" & "</B><BR>"
    Response.Write "<TABLE>"
    For i = 1 to rs.Fields.Count - 1
        Response.Write "<TR BGCOLOR='beige'>"
        Response.Write "<TD ALIGN='right'><FONT FACE='Arial' SIZE=2><B>" & _
                Proper (rs.Fields(i).Name) & "</B></TD>"
```

```
            If Instr(rs.Fields(i).Value,"'") = 0 Then
                ' no apostrophes present
                Response.Write "<td><INPUT TYPE='Text' NAME='" & _
                               rs.Fields(i).Name & "' VALUE='" & _
                               rs.Fields(i).Value & "'></TD>"
            Else
                Response.Write "<TD><TEXTAREA ROWS='1' NAME='" & _
                               rs.Fields(i).Name & "'>" & rs.Fields(i).Value & _
                               "</TEXTAREA></TD>"
            End If
        Response.Write "</TR>"
    Next
    Response.Write "</TABLE>"
    Response.Write "</TD></TR></TABLE>"
%>
    <INPUT TYPE="Submit" NAME="EditAction" VALUE=" Save ">
    <INPUT TYPE="Submit" NAME="EditAction" VALUE="Cancel">
    <INPUT TYPE="Hidden" NAME="Message" VALUE="EditForm">
<%
End Sub
```

It is vitally important that text fields be checked for the presence of apostrophes (as in the case of the name O'Neil, for example), because an ordinary text input type will truncate the text when an apostrophe is written (producing the name "O", for example). A text area must be used to display such fields.

Note that the Empno ID field is displayed in a text field at the top of the form. This was done to avoid passing a session variable, but should be avoided to prevent users from altering the field.

The SaveEditForm procedure is called when the user clicks the Save button. It compares the data from the form with the data in the recordset and updates the recordset where fields have changed. Additional validation should, of course, be performed in the client application, through ActiveX DLLs installed on the server, and through triggers stored in the database itself. If any changes are detected, the recordset update method is called.

```
sub SaveEditForm(strID)
    strQuery = "SELECT * FROM Administrator.Employee WHERE EMPNO='" & strID & "';"
    Set rs = Server.CreateObject("ADODB.recordset")
    rs.Open strQuery, cn, adOpenKeyset, adLockOptimistic

    blnChanged = false
    for i = 1 to rs.fields.count - 1
        if trim(request(rs.fields(i).name)) <> trim(rs.fields(i).value) then
            blnChanged = true
            ' --- A complete application would have data validation here
            rs.fields(i).value = trim(request(rs.fields(i).name))
        end if
    next
    if blnChanged then
        rs.Update
        response.write "Record Updated<br>"
    else
        response.write "No changes found for this record.<br>"

    end if
    call ShowEditForm(rs.fields(0).value)
end sub
```

Two of the tables (EMP_PHOTO and RESUME) contain binary large objects (BLOB) fields that are not displayable on the web page. In EMP_PHOTO the Picture field is suppressed. In RESUME, the Resume field displays binary garbage. To display these binary fields, we would either have to devise our own methods, or write this binary data to a file and load this in an <IMG> tag. This latter approach isn't very elegant, (and we should do it in a component, rather than ASP) but is perhaps the only reliable solution to date.

Finally, we add the code to display the links to the jet.employees OLE DB function linking NWIND to the DB2 Sample. We add one line to ShowMenu and activate the LinkSTP procedure. LinkSTP displays some descriptive text and two links, one for the SQL and one for the stored procedure. Both are shown because, as discussed previously, the SQL returns file names, but the stored procedure does not.

```
%><!-- #include file='startup.txt' --><%
response.write "</td></tr>"
call LinkSTP
response.write "</table>"
```

```
sub LinkSTP
    ' Stored procedure call menu link
    Response.write "<tr><td><hr><font size='2'>"
    Response.Write "<CENTER><b>Call OLE DB Function and Stored
Procedure</b></CENTER>"
    Response.Write "The OLE DB User Defined Function (UDF) connects the NWIND.MDB
Employees table to the DB2 Sample database. The union of the DB2 Employee table
and the NWIND Employees table can be displayed using SQL or a stored
procedure.<br>"
    Response.Write "<a
href='default.asp?MenuBtn=SQLRequest&Message=Proc2&TableName='>SQL Code</a><br>"
    Response.Write "<a href='default.asp?MenuBtn=Procedure&Message=" & _
                "Proc2&TableName='>Stored Procedure</a>"
    Response.Write "</td></tr>"
end sub
```

The revised menu form with the added selections is shown in the figure below:

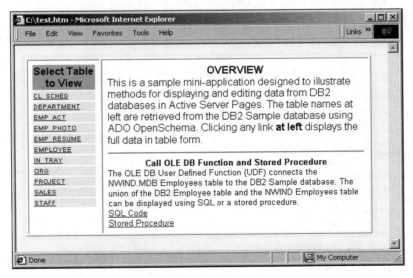

The SQL Code link triggers that send the SQL to DB2 performs the union of the two `employee` `rowsets`, while the Stored Procedure link triggers `Proc2`, as described above:

```
sub SendSQLRequest()
    ' Sends SQL to DB2 to request union of DB2 'employees' with the NWIND
'employees'
    ' using the OLE DB function defined in UDF 'jet.employees'
    Set rs = Server.CreateObject("ADODB.recordset")
    strQuery = "SELECT EMPNO, LASTNAME, FIRSTNME, PHONENO, JOB, BIRTHDATE, 'DB2' AS
DATASOURCE "
    strQuery = strQuery & "FROM ADMINISTRATOR.EMPLOYEE "
    strQuery = strQuery & "UNION "
    strQuery = strQuery & "SELECT CHAR(EmployeeID) AS EMPNO, LASTNAME, FirstName "
& _
                          "AS FIRSTNME, Extension AS PHONENO, Title AS JOB, " & _
                          "BIRTHDATE, 'NWIND' AS DATASOURCE FROM TABLE " & _
                          "(jet.employees ()) AS t ORDER BY LASTNAME, FIRSTNME;"
    rs.Open strQuery, cn, adOpenForwardOnly
    call ShowUnion(rs, "SQL Request")
end sub


sub SendProcRequest()
    Set cm = Server.CreateObject("ADODB.Command")
    set cm.ActiveConnection = cn
    cm.CommandText = "Administrator.Proc2"
    cm.CommandType = adCmdStoredProc
    Set rs = Server.CreateObject("ADODB.recordset")
    rs.Open cm.CommandText, cn, adOpenForwardOnly
    call ShowUnion(rs, "Stored Procedure")
end sub
```

Both procedures send their recordsets to `ShowUnion` for display. `ShowUnion` performs essentially the same steps as `ShowTables` discussed previously, with two changes.

1. The field names are output as ordinary text, not submit buttons (using `MakeHeader`), because the stored procedure was not designed to allow sorting.

2. The `Empno` is output as ordinary text, because the recordset cannot be edited.

Both of these limitations would be relatively straightforward to address:

```
sub ShowUnion(rs, strSrc)
    response.write("<h2>OLE DB Example: " & strSrc & " Recordset</h2>")
    ' --- set an outside border for the table
    response.write "<table border><tr><td>"
    response.write "<table>"
    response.write "<tr BGCOLOR='tan'>"

    for i = 0 to rs.fields.count - 1
        MakeHeading(rs.fields(i).name)
    next
    response.write "</tr>"
    do while not rs.eof
    response.write "<tr BGCOLOR='beige'>"
    for i = 0 to rs.fields.count - 1
        Select case rs.fields(i).name
```

```
     'Case "EMPNO"
     '    response.write "<td><font face = 'Arial' size=1>"
     '    response.write "<INPUT TYPE='Submit' NAME='EditBtn' VALUE='" &
                         rs.fields(i).value & "'>"
     case "FIRSTNME", "LASTNAME", "JOB"
        response.write "<td><font face = 'Arial' size=1>"
        response.write Proper(rs.fields(i).value)
     case "SALARY", "BONUS", "COMM"
        response.write "<TD ALIGN='right'><font face = 'Arial' size=1>"
        response.write FormatCurrency(rs.fields(i).value,0)
     case "HIREDATE", "BIRTHDATE"
        response.write "<TD ALIGN='right'><font face = 'Arial' size=1>"
        response.write rs.fields(i).value
     case "PICTURE"
        ' --- this field is present in the EMP_PHOTO table
        response.write "<TD ALIGN='right'><font face = 'Arial' size=1>"
        response.write "Pictures not viewable."
     case else
        response.write "<td><font face = 'Arial' size=1>"
        response.write (rs.fields(i).value)
     End select
     response.write "</td>"
  next
  response.write "</tr>"
  rs.movenext
  loop
  response.write "</table>"
  rs.Close
  set rs = nothing
  ' --- close the outside table
  response.write "</td></tr></table>"
%><INPUT TYPE="Hidden" NAME="TableName" VALUE="<%= request("TableName") %>"><%
end sub
```

Summary

This chapter has provided an overview of DB2 v 7.1, with an emphasis on using DB2 data in active server pages.

DB2 is a powerful but complex enterprise database system. This chapter has concentrated on the simplest examples of how to access and manipulate data from a DB2 database from Active Server Pages. The sample database provided with DB2 illustrates both simple methods for accessing the database and important design issues that should be addressed in production databases. In particular, we have looked at:

❑   Installation of client components

❑   OLE DB and ODBC connections

❑   Accessing DB2 from ASP

❑   Using stored procedures and user defined functions

In the next chapter, we will be looking at a very different type of database; MySQL.

17

MySQL

We've looked at some of the popular database systems available today, and now we're going to take a look at a database management system that is available from a somewhat different source – **MySQL**. MySQL is growing in popularity, because of its cross-platform support and favorable licensing agreements, combined with very good performance and stability.

In this chapter, we are going to look at the basics of connecting to a MySQL database on a remote server using the ODBC driver – **MyODBC**. We'll look at:

❑ How MySQL manages user permissions

❑ The fundamentals of MySQL's SQL language

❑ What we can and cannot do with MySQL

❑ Building an ASP application that connects to a MySQL database

In order to concentrate on the key concepts that will interest us as ASP developers, we will not be covering the typically DBA-based activities such as installing the MySQL database server, database backups or replication. We will, however, look at the basics of using MySQL, and how to install the MyODBC Driver.

Introduction to MySQL

MySQL is classified as **Open Source Software**. However, what does Open Source actually mean? Essentially it means that we can download the MySQL source code and change it to fit our own requirements. MySQL uses a GNU General Public License to define what we can and cannot do with the software. For example, if an Internet Service Provider hosts our MySQL database server, then we don't need a license to use it. However, if we are selling MySQL as an integral part of a commercial application, then a license is required.

Further information about the GNU General Public License can be found at http://www.gnu.org.

In terms of performance, MySQL compares quite favorably many of the other commercially available database management systems such as Oracle, Sybase and SQL Server. The MySQL web site, http://www.mysql.com, provides many standard performance benchmarks to show how fast MySQL actually performs on various platforms.

One last introductory point: 'MySQL' is officially pronounced *My Ess-Que-Ell*, and not *My-Sequel*.

Supported Environments

MySQL is available on many of today's popular operating systems, such as:

❑   AIX

❑   BSDI

❑   DEC Unix, HP Unix, SCO UnixWare, Tru64 Unix

❑   FreeBSD, NetBSD, OpenBSD

❑   Linux

❑   MacOS X Server

❑   OS/2 Warp

❑   SGI Irix

❑   Solaris

❑   Windows 95, 98, NT, and 2000

As the source code is Open Source, this list is ever expanding. However, in this chapter, we will only be looking at MySQL in the Windows environment.

What does MySQL Offer?

MySQL offers very fast and reliable access to relational data, particularly that of web-based applications that perform a large number of data retrieval queries. The server software is multi-threaded, so it can support multiple users without major degradation in response times.

MySQL supports all of the standard ANSI-SQL92 column data-types, so it is as flexible as any other database system:

Numeric Data Types			
TINYINT	SMALLINT	MEDIUMINT	INT/INTEGER
BIGINT	FLOAT	DOUBLE/REAL	DECIMAL/NUMERIC

Date and Time Data Types			
DATE	DATETIME	TIMESTAMP	TIME
YEAR			

Text and BLOB Data Types			
CHAR	VARCHAR	TINYBLOB	TINYTEXT
BLOB	TEXT	MEDIUMBLOB	MEDIUMTEXT
LONGBLOB	LONGTEXT		

Other Data Types	
ENUM	A single string value from a list of enumerated possible values.
SET	A string of zero of more values from a list of possible values.

As we might expect, MySQL allows us to join to other tables using the ANSI-SQL or ODBC syntax, such as:

```
SELECT *
   FROM table1,table2
   WHERE table1.id=table2.id;
```

or:

```
SELECT *
   FROM table1 LEFT JOIN table2
                   ON table1.id = table2.id;
```

It also supports up to 16 indexes per table for speed, and has been tested with tables containing 50 million records.

> *The figure of 50 million records in a table may not seem that great to you, but it does serve to prove a point that MySQL can handle relatively large database tables.*

At present, MySQL does not provide any extensions to SQL to support stored procedures (including triggers). However, considering the rate at which MySQL is being developed, support for these features may not be that far away. The same was formerly true of database transaction support, which has recently been added and is, at the time of writing, in beta test.

The standard function and operator commands can be used in SELECT and WHERE clauses, such as:

```
SELECT ProductName, MONTH(OrderDate) FROM orders WHERE price * 1.175 > 50;
```

MySQL also supports the GROUP BY and ORDER BY clauses and the associated grouping functions such as COUNT, AVG, SUM, MAX and MIN.

It's also worth remembering that MySQL's string searches are case insensitive by default.

Installing MyODBC

MyODBC is the name of the 32-bit public domain ODBC Driver, created by TCX Datakonsult AB, which allows us to connect to a MySQL database from ASP scripts.

559

However, at the time of writing, there is no native OLEDB Provider for MySQL.

> **The MySQL product does not actually come bundled with MyODBC. It has to be downloaded separately from** `http://www.mysql.com/Downloads/MyODBC`.

Once we've downloaded and unzipped the setup files, we can run the installation program, `SETUP.EXE`.

The *full* installation program includes some rather old versions of Microsoft's ODBC setup utilities. Don't worry though – the version stamping embedded in the ODBC setup files will ensure that you don't end up with any DLLs dating back to 1996! If the ODBC setup program does find that you have newer versions of DLLs installed on your machine, then it will confirm with you before attempting to overwrite them with old DLLs.

We will be asked to select which ODBC Driver we want installed. As the only choice is MySQL, select MySQL and click OK. The Advanced button allows you to specify whether the selected drivers should be installed using version checking (which **is** selected by default) and whether the additional Driver Manager (the software that controls access to the ODBC Drivers) and Translators (these perform the task of converting character data between the data source and other applications) should be installed. Again, these settings are selected by default and you will not need to alter them:

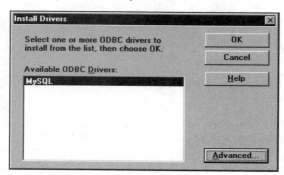

After the driver has been successfully installed, you will be shown a list of existing ODBC Data Sources. It's probably a good idea to select the Close button and configure the ODBC settings using Control Panel's ODBC Data Sources applet.

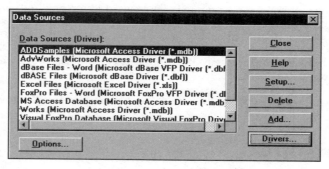

That's all there is to installing the ODBC Driver. Now it's just a case of adding a new data source name pointing to the MySQL server using the Control Panel, or alternatively, using a DSN-less connection from ADO whereby the SERVER property of our connection string points to the relevant MySQL server.

As with Oracle, Sybase and SQL Server, MySQL uses the industry-standard **TCP/IP** protocol to communicate with other MySQL servers. Your machine should have the latest WinSock2 library installed in order to communicate with remote MySQL servers. If your machine is running an older release of Windows 95 then you may actually be running an old version of WinSock, which needs to be upgraded to WinSock2 from the Microsoft FTP site ftp://ftp.microsoft.com/bussys/winsock/winsock2. In the majority of cases, you shouldn't need to perform any further configuration, if your PC is configured to use DNS to resolve server names.

Configuring the MyODBC Data Source

If you prefer to use ODBC data source names (DSNs) to define the location of our MySQL server, then you can add a new MyODBC DSN with the Control Panel's ODBC Data Sources applet.

> *Each time we connect to a database using a DSN, ODBC must look through the Windows Registry in order to retrieve connection details for our DSN. There may be some performance improvements in an application if we don't use the DSN parameter, as the Windows Registry is notoriously slow to access.*

On the System DSN tab of the ODBC Data Source Administrator, it is necessary to press the Add button and scroll through the list of drivers until you find an entry for MySQL.

Next, we are presented with a screen displaying connection options. In my case, the remote MySQL database runs on a Windows NT server called MySQL_dev, which I have entered into both the Window DSN name and MySQL host fields. The key piece of information is actually the host field, which I have also chosen as the name of the DSN to make it easier to identify.

As with other databases, MySQL allows us to have a number of databases running on the same server. By default, it does not actually log us straight into a specific database unless we set the MySQL database name property accordingly. In our case, we want to look at the standard MySQL database.

> *The MySQL database is a system database that stores details about users, database and access permissions.*

Notice that we have left the Port and SQL Command on connect fields blank. MySQL can be configured to listen for requests on specific port numbers, the default being 3306. However, if your database is situated behind a firewall and port 3306 has not been opened for access, you might need to change this.

The SQL Command on connect field allows a SQL statement to be executed as soon as the connection is made. This option might be used to log access to a database by issuing an INSERT statement into an audit table.

We can now set any of the 18 different options that affect the behavior of MyODBC. Typically, we will not need to alter any of these settings, but if we experience difficulties connecting to the MySQL database, it would be worthwhile setting the Trace MyODBC and Safety options to provide additional logging information.

Connecting to MySQL

ODBC allows us to connect to any ODBC data source using either a DSN defined in the ODBC Data Source application or through a DSN-less connection in which we explicitly set the SERVER and DATABASE properties ourselves. (The DATABASE property is not strictly required but it is nice to jump to the required database rather than having to issue a USE *database* command.)

Both connection approaches give the same result. However, you may find DSN-less connections slightly faster, though code changes might be required as an application moves from development into production where the server name or even the database name is different.

There are always going to be times when we need to connect to a MySQL using the command line utilities rather than an ASP script. The MySQL Monitor program, MySQL.exe, allows us to connect to a MySQL database and execute SQL commands. By specifying a **host** we can connect to a remote MySQL database.

> *If you are attempting to connect to a remote MySQL database, then it is worth checking with your DBA that your hostname (computer name) and login name have been registered with the remote MySQL database. MySQL uses a non-standard approach when validating users; not only does it validate login names and passwords, but it also checks the name of the host machine that you are connecting from, as we will see in the MySQL User Permissions section.*

When we need to directly manipulate records, the MyODBC Driver can also be very useful when connecting to an application such as Microsoft Access using its ability to attach to 'linked tables'. Access will display a formatted data-entry grid allowing us to edit any number of records without worrying about the underlying SQL commands that are being executed on our behalf.

Connecting Through the MySQL Monitor Command Line Client

By default MySQL is installed in the `C:\MySQL` folder when running under Windows. A whole host of useful command line and GUI applications can be found in the `Bin` folder.

Open up a Command Prompt window, and move to the `C:\MySQL\Bin` folder. `MySQL.exe` accepts a number of command line arguments that allow us to specify our host name, user name and password:

```
mysql [-h hostname] [-u username] [-ppassword]
```

Notice that `MySQL.exe` allows the host name and user name arguments to include a space before the actual value, whereas the password cannot.

```
C:\>cd mysql\bin

C:\mysql\bin>mysql -u root
Welcome to the MySQL monitor.  Commands end with ; or \g.
Your MySQL connection id is 9 to server version: 3.23.22-beta

Type 'help' for help.

mysql>
```

Now we can execute SQL scripts directly on the server. MySQL uses the semicolon or `\g` as command terminators so that we can enter long SQL commands over a number of lines. MySQL will not attempt to execute them until it comes across a semicolon or `\g`. To close the MySQL monitor program, type `quit` or `exit` and press *Return*.

If we need to enter more than a few SQL commands, it is simpler to type them out and edit them in a separate editor. MySQL enables us to execute commands directly from a file by using the `source` command. To execute the commands contained in a file called `sqlscript.sql`, we would simply enter the following:

```
source sqlscript.sql
```

Of course, if necessary the, path of the file should also be entered.

Connecting Through a DSN Connection

Earlier we created a new ODBC Data Source that made use of the MyODBC Driver, so we can now attempt to connect to that DSN through ADO using an ASP script.

Our simple ASP script will connect to the MySQL server, `MySQL_dev`, to retrieve a list of users and their global permissions from the `user` table in the `MySQL` database. For each record found, we will create a formatted table row. We will connect as the `root` user, so we will have full access to all tables and databases on the server.

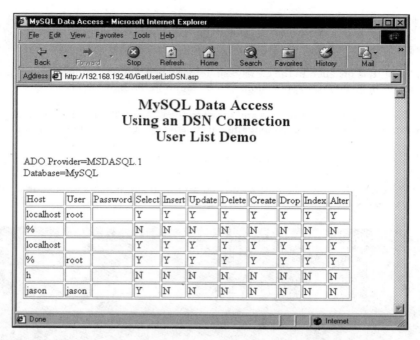

Create a new ASP file called `GetUserListDSN.asp`. This script will use the `MySQL_dev` DSN to retrieve a list of MySQL users and their default permissions from the `user` table within the `MySQL` database using the default `root` user to connect to the server.

```
<%Option Explicit

Const cConnection = "DSN=MySQL_dev;UID=root;PWD=;"

Dim objConnection
Dim objRecordSet

Set objConnection = Server.CreateObject("ADODB.Connection")
```

The constant, `cConnection`, is used to store the connection string. The `DSN` property points to our `MySQL_dev` DSN. When we originally created the DSN, we didn't specify the user ID or password so we must specify them now.

`objConnection` stores a reference to the ADO `Connection` object, created using `Server.CreateObject`. The results of our `SELECT` statement are stored in the `objRecordSet` variable.

```
With objConnection
  .ConnectionString = cConnection
  .Open
  Response.Write "ADO Provider=" & .Provider & "<BR>" & _
              "Database=" & .DefaultDatabase & "<P>"

  Set objRecordSet = .Execute("SELECT * from user")
End With
```

Now it's just a case of setting the `Connection` object's `ConnectionString` property and calling the `Open` method to connect to our MySQL database. Once we've connected, we write out the name of the ADO `Provider` used, in this case the OLE DB Provider for ODBC, MSDASQL, and the default database that we have connected to.

MSDASQL.DLL is the default OLE DB Provider that ADO uses when connecting to an ODBC-based data source. Microsoft developed MSDASQL so that any application that uses ODBC can make use of ADO functionality without the need to rewrite the original application.

The results of our `SELECT` statement are transferred into the `objRecordSet` variable by calling the `Connection` object's `Execute` function, passing in the SQL that we wish to execute.

```
Response.Write "<TABLE BORDER=1><TR>" & _
            "   <TD>Host</TD>" & _
            "   <TD>User</TD>" & _
            "   <TD>Password</TD>" & _
            "   <TD>Select</TD>" & _
            "   <TD>Insert</TD>" & _
            "   <TD>Update</TD>" & _
            "   <TD>Delete</TD>" & _
            "   <TD>Create</TD>" & _
            "   <TD>Drop</TD>" & _
            "   <TD>Index</TD>" & _
            "   <TD>Alter</TD>" & _
            "</TR>"
```

Use `Response.Write` to output a nicely formatted table containing the list of fields that we are showing.

```
Do While Not objRecordSet.EOF

  Response.Write "<TR>" & _
        "   <TD>" & objRecordSet.Fields("host")          & " </TD>" & _
        "   <TD>" & objRecordSet.Fields("user")          & " </TD>" & _
        "   <TD>" & objRecordSet.Fields("password")      & " </TD>" & _
        "   <TD>" & objRecordSet.Fields("Select_Priv")   & " </TD>" & _
        "   <TD>" & objRecordSet.Fields("Insert_Priv")   & " </TD>" & _
        "   <TD>" & objRecordSet.Fields("Update_Priv")   & " </TD>" & _
        "   <TD>" & objRecordSet.Fields("Delete_Priv")   & " </TD>" & _
        "   <TD>" & objRecordSet.Fields("Create_Priv")   & " </TD>" & _
        "   <TD>" & objRecordSet.Fields("Drop_Priv")     & " </TD>" & _
        "   <TD>" & objRecordSet.Fields("Index_Priv")    & " </TD>" & _
        "   <TD>" & objRecordSet.Fields("Alter_Priv")    & " </TD>" & _
        "</TR>"

      objRecordSet.MoveNext
Loop
Response.Write "</TABLE>"

objRecordSet.Close
Set objRecordSet = Nothing

objConnection.Close
Set objConnection = Nothing
%>

</BODY>
</HTML>
```

We navigate through each of the records in the `Recordset` object, writing out a list of the selected fields for each column. Finally we set the `objConnection` and `objRecordSet` objects to nothing as soon as we have finished with them.

> *The `user` table stores a list of users that have access to the MySQL server. We'll cover this table in more depth when we look at MySQL user permissions later.*

Connecting Through a DSN-less Connection

We've seen how easy it is to connect to a MySQL database using a DSN connection to retrieve a list of users so now we'll repeat the same exercise except that we'll be using a DSN-less connection to retrieve the list of users. A DSN-less connection allows us to connect to a MySQL server in a similar fashion, but allows us to specify more of the connection string properties, such as `SERVER` and `DRIVER`.

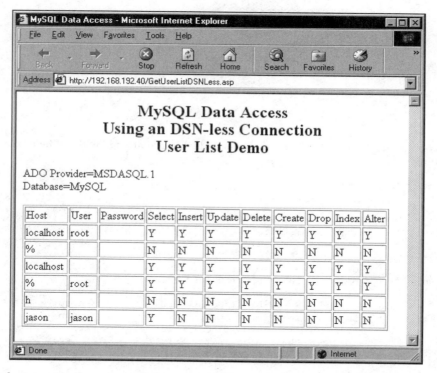

The ASP code is exactly the same as the previous DSN sample except that we have a different connection string:

```
Const cConnection = _
        "DRIVER={MySQL};SERVER=MySQL_dev;UID=root;PWD=;DATABASE=MySQL"
```

This time we tell ADO to use the `MySQL` driver to connect to a server called `MySQL_dev` using the `root` account with no password. The `DATABASE` property tells ADO to move to the `MySQL` database.

Now that we've successfully connected to a remote MySQL database running on the `MySQL_dev` server and retrieved a list of users, we can now take a look at user permissions within MySQL.

MySQL User Permissions

We mentioned earlier that MySQL uses a non-standard approach to authenticate users. As well as the usual username and password combination, it also includes an additional verification parameter, the **host name**. The host name is the name or IP address of the client machine that is attempting to connect to MySQL.

There are two stages involved in MySQL authentication:

❑ Connection Verification – Verifies that the user can actually connect to the server.

❑ Request Verification – Verifies that the user has sufficient privileges to perform the required operation.

Each of these stages is executed by examining a collection of **grant** tables in the MySQL database:

The User Table

The user table determines which users and hosts have access to the MySQL server. The privilege columns are known as **superuser** permissions and they apply to **all** databases within the server regardless of how you set individual permissions within the lower-level db table, which will be discussed shortly.

For example, if we give a host/user the delete privilege at the user table level then we are effectively giving that privilege for all databases. It is best to set the privileges to N for standard users and define their own level of privileges at database level using the db table. So, if we created a user called jason, say, with the superuser delete permission we would add a record to the user table. Now if we add his name to the db table and revoke his delete permission for a specific database, he would still be able to delete from that database, since the user table defines his overall level of permissions. On the other hand, if we set his superuser delete permission to N, we could still allow him to delete from a specific database by granting him the delete permission for that database.

Name	Type	Description
Host	CHAR(60)	The name of a host that can connect to the server. In the case of an ASP implementation this would be the name of the IIS machine. Supports the use of the wild card characters % or _ so that you can specify parts of a host name. This value can also be left blank to declare that you are not interested in which host this user is connecting from. Examples: "localhost" – the local machine. "%" – any host machine. "192.1.34.216" – a host with this IP address. "digitaltier%" – any host that starts with the name digitaltier.

Table continued on following page

Name	Type	Description
User	CHAR(16)	The user name. Cannot contain wild cards but can be left blank for different combinations of hosts. By leaving this field blank you are effectively saying that this set of permissions applies to **any** user from a specific host. Examples: "jason" "reportsystem" "iis_app"
Password	CHAR(16)	An encrypted user password. We can alter this column manually, but must do so in conjunction with the PASSWORD function: For example: UPDATE user SET Password = PASSWORD('my_password') WHERE user='root';
Select_priv	ENUM('N','Y')	Can select from any database table.
Insert_priv	ENUM('N','Y')	Can insert into any database table.
Update_priv	ENUM('N','Y')	Can update any database table.
Delete_priv	ENUM('N','Y')	Can delete from any database table.
Index_priv	ENUM('N','Y')	Can create an index on any database table.
Alter_priv	ENUM('N','Y')	Can alter any database table.
Create_priv	ENUM('N','Y')	Can create a database table.
Drop_priv	ENUM('N','Y')	Can drop any database table.
Grant_priv	ENUM('N','Y')	Can pass on any set database permissions to another user.
References_priv	ENUM('N','Y')	Can create references to any database table.
Reload_priv	ENUM('N','Y')	Can tell MySQL to reload the grant tables.
Shutdown_priv	ENUM('N','Y')	Can shutdown the server.
Process_priv	ENUM('N','Y')	Can see and kill other processes.
File_priv	ENUM('N','Y')	Can read and write files into and from the operating system.

As we can see, the host/user combination is very flexible. The table below shows some typical combinations and how they apply:

Host	User	Valid Connections
'mysqldev.digital tier.com'	'jason'	The user 'jason' connecting from mysqldev.digitaltier.com.
'mysqldev.digital tier.com'	' '	Any user from mysqldev.digitaltier.com.

Host	User	Valid Connections
'%'	'jason'	Any user called 'jason' from any host. For example, 'jason' could connect through one web site such as billing.customers.com and from another called, say, accounts.customers.com. A situation like this might occur if a number of sub-domains connect to the same database.
' '	' '	Any user from any host – very insecure!

The db Table

The db table determines which users and hosts have permissions to access specific MySQL databases. An entry in this table is needed for each database that a user requires access to.

Name	Type	Description
Host	CHAR(60)	The name of a host that this set of privileges applies to. Can be blank and can also contain wildcards. **If the this field is left blank then MySQL will consult the host table for further privilege information**.
DB	CHAR(64)	The name of the database that this set of privileges applies to. Can be blank and can also contain wildcards.
User	CHAR(16)	The user name that this set of privileges applies to. Can be blank but cannot contain wildcards.
Select_priv	ENUM('N','Y')	Can select from any table in the database.
Insert_priv	ENUM('N','Y')	Can insert into any table in the database.
Update_priv	ENUM('N','Y')	Can update any table.
Delete_priv	ENUM('N','Y')	Can delete from any table.
Index_priv	ENUM('N','Y')	Can create an index on any table.
Alter_priv	ENUM('N','Y')	Can alter any table.
Create_priv	ENUM('N','Y')	Can create a table.
Drop_priv	ENUM('N','Y')	Can drop any table.
Grant_priv	ENUM('N','Y')	Can pass permissions on to another user.

The host Table

The host table provides an extension to the db table so that a set of database permissions can be assigned to several hosts. If the host field in the db table is left blank, MySQL will search through this table to find any other permissions for collections of hosts. In some MySQL installations the host table can be used to store a list of servers that are "secure", such as those machines found within a local network.

Name	Type	Description
Host	CHAR(60)	The name of a host that this set of privileges applies to. Can be blank and can contain wildcards.
DB	CHAR(64)	The name of the database that this set of privileges applies to. Can be blank and can contain wildcards.
Select_priv	ENUM('N','Y')	Can select from any table in the database.
Insert_priv	ENUM('N','Y')	Can insert into any table in the database.
Update_priv	ENUM('N','Y')	Can update any table.
Delete_priv	ENUM('N','Y')	Can delete from any table.
Index_priv	ENUM('N','Y')	Can create an index on any table.
Alter_priv	ENUM('N','Y')	Can alter any table.
Create_priv	ENUM('N','Y')	Can create a table.
Drop_priv	ENUM('N','Y')	Can drop any table.
Grant_priv	ENUM('N','Y')	Can pass permissions on to another user.

MySQL also provides a finer-grained level of security that determines which permissions are allowed at table and column level through the tables_priv and columns_priv tables. These are similar to the db table.

The tables_priv Table

This table determines permissions for specific tables within a database.

Name	Type	Description
Host	CHAR(60)	The name of a host that this set of privileges applies to. Can be blank and can contain wildcards.
DB	CHAR(64)	The name of the database that this set of privileges applies to. Can be blank and can contain wildcards.
User	CHAR(16)	The name of the user that this set of privileges applies to. Can be blank but cannot contain wildcards.
Table_name	CHAR(64)	The table name that this set of privileges applies to. Can be blank and can contain wildcards.
Grantor	CHAR(77)	The user that granted this permission.
Timestamp	DATETIME	Timestamp of record.
Table_priv	CHAR(68)	Indicates the permissions to apply from the SET list of Select, Insert, Update, Delete, Create, Copy, Drop, Grant, References, Index, Alter.
Column_priv	CHAR(60)	Indicates the permissions to apply from the SET list of Select, Insert, Update, References.

The columns_priv Table

This table determines permissions for specific columns on tables within a database.

Name	Type	Description
Host	CHAR(60)	The name of a host that this set of privileges applies to. Can be blank and can contain wildcards.
DB	CHAR(64)	The name of the database that this set of privileges applies to. Can be blank and can contain wildcards.
User	CHAR(16)	The name of the user that this set of privileges applies to. Can be blank but cannot contain wildcards.
Table_name	CHAR(64)	The table name that this set of privileges applies to. Can be blank and can contain wildcards.
Column_name	CHAR(64)	The column name that this permission applies to.
Timestamp	DATETIME	Timestamp of record.
Column_priv	CHAR(60)	Indicates the permissions to apply from the SET list of Select, Insert, Update, References.

So how do we go about setting these privileges? Well you can directly manipulate any of the tables using the SELECT, INSERT, UPDATE or DELETE SQL commands. Don't forget that the password field is encrypted, so we must use the PASSWORD function when setting its value.

> *Along with the selection of GUI and DOS based applications that are included with MySQL, you might find NetAdmin and MyAccess2000 very useful utilities for administering your MySQL databases, see:*
>
> *http://www.mysql.com/Downloads/Contrib/netadmin.zip*
> *http://www.mysql.com/Downloads/Win32/MyAccess2000_Ver_1_01.zip*

To create a new user account called 'paul' from any host with the password 'maestro' with **all** of the superuser privileges, we would execute the following statement using the MySQL.exe command line utility:

```
INSERT INTO user VALUES('%','paul',PASSWORD('maestro'),
        'Y','Y','Y','Y','Y','Y','Y','Y','Y','Y','Y','Y','Y','Y');
```

Alternatively, we can add new users by using the preferred GRANT statements. These are easier to read and safer to use.

```
GRANT ALL PRIVILEGES ON *.* TO paul@"%" IDENTIFIED BY 'maestro' WITH GRANT OPTION;
```

Again, this gives the user all permissions in all databases and all tables.

The following statement allows the local iis_user to perform SELECT, INSERT or DELETE operations on all tables within the personnel database.

```
GRANT SELECT,INSERT,DELETE ON personnel.* TO iis_user@localhost;
```

In this section, we learned how MySQL provides us with a very flexible model for defining top-level and fine-grained security to users connecting from different hosts. We have also learned that MySQL allows us to use wildcards to define host names and that we can edit the security tables directly or use the SQL GRANT statements.

In the next section we will take a brief look at the fundamental aspects of MySQL's SQL language.

Introduction to MySQL SQL

MySQL's SQL provides most of the ANSI-SQL commands that are available in other database systems. However, at the time of writing, it doesn't provide the functionality to support stored procedures, packages or user functions, though that is likely to change very soon.

In this section we shall not be covering the standard SQL statements, such as SELECT or DELETE. Instead, we will be looking at the distinctive aspects of MySQL SQL.

> *The MySQL web address www.mysql.com/documentation/ contains an excellent set of files that details the SQL language in great depth.*

Case Sensitivity

MySQL uses operating system files to store databases and tables, so if the operating system that your MySQL database is running on is case sensitive then your database and table names will also be case sensitive. Thus, in the case of Windows, they will *not* be case sensitive. However, note that the actual column names defined in a table are case insensitive by default, as are string comparisons.

MySQL allows non-ASCII characters, such as those with an accent, to be stored in one of many common character sets such as ISO-8859-1, Big5 and UJIS. However, the character set value for the server must be configured correctly so that it indexes non-standard characters accordingly.

Date Validation

MySQL does not provide strict date validation. The people at MySQL believe that it is the responsibility of the application to verify dates. It only checks that the month element is in the range 1-12 and the day is in the range 1-31. Dates are quoted by wrapping them in single or double quotes and must be specified in the year-month-day format.

Supported Functions

MySQL supports a wide variety of standard SQL functions that can be used in both the SELECT and WHERE clauses.

> *MySQL does not permit any white-space between the function name and the parenthesis, but they can be used between arguments, for example the following statement.*

```
SELECT MAX (Salary) FROM employee
```

will not work, though he following statement will:

```
SELECT MAX(Salary) FROM employee
```

Conditional Functions

The conditional functions can be used to return values in accordance with particular rules.

`IFNULL(expr1, expr2)`	If `expr1` is not `NULL` then `expr1` is returned, otherwise `expr2` is returned, for example: `SELECT IFNULL('jason', 'ann');` returns `'jason'`

`NULLIF(expr1, expr2)`	Returns `NULL` if `expr1` is equal to `expr2`, otherwise `expr1` is returned, for example:
	
	`SELECT NULLIF('jason', 'ann');`
	
	returns `NULL` and:
	
	`SELECT NULLIF(100, 100);`
	
	returns `100`.

`IF(expr1, expr2, expr3)`	Returns `expr2` if `expr1` is true, otherwise returns `expr3`, for example: `SELECT IF(Age>100, "Yes", "No");` returns `Yes` if the age is above 100.

`CASE value WHEN comparison THEN result [WHEN comparison THEN result] [ELSE result] END`	Returns `result` when `value` is equal to `comparison`, for example:
	
	`SELECT CASE MyDay`
	   `WHEN 'Saturday' THEN 'Clean Car'`
	   `WHEN 'Sunday' THEN 'Clear Garage'`
	   `ELSE 'Clean House'`
	`END;`

Mathematical Functions

We have access to many of the standard mathematical functions such as `ABS`, `MOD`, `FLOOR`, `PI`, `SIN`, and `TAN`. In addition, MySQL provides the following functions:

`RAND(X)`	Returns a random number in the range 0 to 1.0 with `X` being the seed value.
`LEAST(A, B, C)`	Returns the smallest argument from the list of values. This is not the same as the aggregate `MIN` function that returns the lowest (minimum) value from a group of records. Example: `SELECT LEAST(1, 55, 20);` returns 1.
`GREATEST(A, B, C)`	Returns the largest argument from the list of values. This is not the same as the aggregate `MAX` function that returns the largest (maximum) value from a group of records. Example: `SELECT GREATEST(1, 55, 20);` returns 55.

String Functions

In addition to the standard string-based functions such as ASCII, CHAR, LEFT, RIGHT, and SOUNDEX we have some particularly useful string manipulation functions:

REPEAT(str, count)	Returns a string containing the value of str repeated count number of times, for example: SELECT REPEAT('OVERAND ', 2); returns 'OVERAND OVERAND '
INSERT(str, pos, len, newstr)	Returns the value of str with the substring beginning at position pos and len characters in length, replaced by the value of newstr.
ELT(N, str1, str2, ...)	Returns the string argument at position N, for example: SELECT ELT(2, 'jason', 'ann', 'sophie') will return 'ann'.
LOAD_FILE(filename)	Loads in the operating system file specified in filename and returns the contents as a string. This function could be very useful when you have an operating system file that is created by an external application on a regular basis of which you have no specific control over, such as with some kind of automated data-feed.

Date and Time Functions

There are dozens of useful date and time functions provided by MySQL. Some of the more obscure or useful functions are:

DAYNAME(date)	Returns the name of a weekday, such as 'Friday', so SELECT DAYNAME('2000-04-01'); returns 'Saturday' whereas, SELECT DAYNAME('2000-03-32'); returns NULL because March does not have a 32st day.
MONTHNAME(date)	Returns the name of a month, such as 'April'.
DATE_ADD(date, INTERVAL value type)	Adds value to the date using the type to indicate the interval. The interval type can be one of any of these values: SECOND, MINUTE, HOUR, DAY, MONTH, or YEAR, for example: SELECT DATE_ADD('2000-12-31', INTERVAL 1 DAY); returns '2001-01-1', i.e. the 31st December 2000 with a single day added to it.
CURDATE(), CURRENT_DATE()	Both return the current date.

`CURTIME(),` `CURRENT_TIME()`	Both return the current time.

`NOW(),`
`SYSDATE(),`
`CURRENT_TIMESTAMP()`
	Both return the current date and time.

Miscellaneous Functions

Like all good database servers, MySQL contains a collection of useful system functions:

`DATABASE()`	Returns the current database name.

`USER(),`
`SYSTEM_USER(),`
`SESSION_USER()`
	All return the current user name.

`PASSWORD(str)`	Returns an encrypted string representing the value of `str` for use with the `Password` column in the user table.

`ENCODE(str, keycode)`	Encrypts `str` using the keycode, for example:
	
	`SELECT DECODE('wrox', 'mypassword');`
	
	returns `'ad•ê'`
	
	`If you plan to use the result from this function`
	`in a table then its type is a BLOB.`

`DECODE(str, keycode)`	Decrypts the encrypted string using the keycode. This is the opposite function to `ENCODE`, for example: `SELECT ENCODE('ad•ê', 'mypassword');` returns `'wrox'`

`LAST_INSERT_ID(expr)`	Returns the last value automatically generated into an `AUTO_INCREMENT` column. To create this type of incrementing column you need to add the `AUTO_INCREMENT` modifier when creating a table, for example:
	
	`CREATE TABLE ContactType`
	`   (TypeID   INT(4) NOT NULL AUTO_INCREMENT,`
	`    TypeName VARCHAR(20) NOT NULL);`

`FORMAT(X, D)`	Formats the number `X` to include commas rounded to `D` decimal places, for example:
	
	`SELECT FORMAT(1234.56, 1);`
	
	returns `1,234.6` and:
	
	`SELECT FORMAT(1234.56, 4);`
	
	returns `1,234.5600`

`VERSION()`	Returns the current version of MySQL.
`CONNECTION_ID()`	Returns the current connection ID.

Group By Functions

MySQL supports the standard GROUP BY functions such as MAX, MIN, COUNT, and SUM. However, it also extends them so that we do not have to include columns or calculations from the SELECT statement that also appears in the GROUP BY clause, unlike many other database servers. This can improve performance by not having to group by or sort unnecessary items. This feature, however, is not supported whilst running in ANSI mode.

For example, the following ANSI-compliant statement will return a count of the number of orders grouped by the customer name:

```
SELECT customer.name, COUNT(order.OrderID)
  FROM customer, order
  WHERE customer.CustID = order.OrderID
  GROUP BY customer.custID, customer.name
```

With MySQL we can omit the customer.name from the Group By clause as it unnecessary.

```
SELECT customer.name, COUNT(order.OrderID)
  FROM customer, order
  WHERE customer.CustID = order.OrderID
  GROUP BY customer.custID
```

In the next section we are going to discuss some of the limitations that we should be aware of when developing applications using MySQL.

Limitations of MySQL

We've seen that MySQL is a very flexible and effective database server providing many of the standard ANSI-SQL features found in other database servers. It also provides additional extensions, which make our code less portable should we need to move to another SQL server in the future, such as the PASSWORD, ENCODE, DECODE and LOAD_FILE functions.

However, there are a number of limitations to MySQL. These limitations are not absolute showstoppers, as we'd probably find a work-around that can be used to achieve the same result. As this book went to press the latest version, 3.23, contained the following limitations that may affect the way that we work with MySQL, but will quite likely be addressed in future versions.

User Spaces

MySQL allows us to access tables within other MySQL databases on the same server using the standard database_name.table_name syntax. It does not, however, provide support for **user spaces**. (A user space allows us to create objects that belong to a specific user within a database, thus allowing access to tables with the same name but owned by different users, such as SELECT * FROM jason.invoice_table and SELECT * FROM emma.invoice_table.)

We can, however, specify the name of the database in which a table exists. Thus, SELECT * FROM MySQL.user will return all records from the user table within the MySQL database, whereas SELECT * FROM MySQLXXX.user will result in the following error, if a database called mysqlxxx does not contain a table called user:

```
ERROR 1146: Table 'mysqlxxx.user' doesn't exist
```

Sub-Queries

MySQL does not yet support sub-queries. In a sub-query, an *inner* statement is executed within an *outer* statement in such a way that the outer statement can refer to the results of the inner SELECT statement. A typical sub-query could look like this:

```
SELECT employee.*
   FROM employee
   WHERE employee.employee_id IN (SELECT employee_id
                                    FROM employee_bonus)
```

In some cases, these types of statements can be rewritten without a sub-query by using the LEFT JOIN statement to join the employee and employee_bonus tables:

```
SELECT employee.*
   FROM employee
        LEFT JOIN employee_bonus
        ON employee.employee_id  = employee_bonus .employee_id
   WHERE employee_bonus.employee_id IN NULL
```

To overcome more complex types of sub-query we would need to use a client-based language to interactively process the required records.

Transactional Support

MySQL was recently updated to provide support for transactions. For performance reasons, MySQL will, by default, create new tables that are of a type called MyISAM. However, these default tables are *not* transaction safe.

We must explicitly tell MySQL which tables we would like to be transaction safe by declaring them as BDB tables using the statement TYPE=BDB when we create or alter a table. BDB, or Berkeley DB, tables were implemented in version 3.23.15 of MySQL and use the familiar BEGIN TRANSACTION/COMMIT TRANSACTION/ROLLBACK TRANSACTION syntax to wrap groups of statements into a transaction.

Stored Procedures

Stored procedures are groups of SQL statements that are compiled together and stored on the database. They offer good performance improvements compared to having a client send large chunks of SQL across the network that then need to be parsed each time they're used. MySQL does not currently support stored procedures, but the documentation suggests that this is something MySQL will implement in the future.

Triggers

A trigger is a stored procedure that can be called automatically whenever a record is updated, deleted or inserted. Typically, they are used to update or verify records in other tables based on the current record activity. MySQL does not support triggers as they tend to slowdown the server, and MySQL has been developed with performance in mind. It's not apparent from the documentation whether MySQL will support triggers in the near future.

Foreign Keys

We use foreign keys as a constraint to prevent master-detail records from becoming orphaned by altering a primary key on a referenced table. MySQL does not yet support the use of foreign keys but it may do so in the future. It does allow the FOREIGN KEY syntax, but simply ignores it.

Views

Views provide a way in which we can group tables together using a SELECT statement, and then saved in that format. They can then be worked upon in a manner similar to standard tables. Support for views may be provided in the near future.

Date Validation

We mentioned earlier that MySQL does not actually validate the values that are entered for date fields. It only checks to ensure that the month field is in the range of 1 to 12 and the day is from 1 to 31. It is our responsibility to ensure that any dates entered into our application are valid before storing them in a MySQL table. If you attempt to insert an invalid date such as 31st February into a date field, MySQL will accept it without raising an error. When it comes to searching or ordering this field using MySQL's date based functions you'll find that this value will return a NULL in most cases.

> For ASP developers, the IsDate() function can be used to check the validity of date fields before passing them over to MySQL.

UNION Operator

The UNION operator allows the results from a number of different SELECT statements to be grouped into one recordset as long as the output fields are the same. As with foreign keys and views this is a fundamental operator that is currently missing from MySQL.

For our final section we will bring together the areas that we have covered so far in order to create a sample ASP application that uses a MySQL database to provide a simple electronic address book.

MySQL Address Book Sample Application

We've gone through the main features of MySQL and how we connect to a MySQL database using ADO and the MyODBC driver. Now we'll take a look at creating a simple ASP application that uses a new database and tables to manage an electronic address book.

We will be using the CREATE DATABASE and CREATE TABLE statements to create a new database and associated tables for our application. We'll then be using ADO to connect to and manipulate the address book data in each of these tables.

> **All of the ASP and SQL scripts that make up this sample application can be downloaded from the Wrox web site at http://www.wrox.com.**

Creating the AddressBook Database

By using the MySQL monitor program, `mysql.exe`, we can execute any number of SQL statements on the server machine. We are going to create a new database called `AddressBook` with a number of contact tables.

To create a new database we start the MySQL monitor, connect using the `root` user and execute the following statement:

```
CREATE DATABASE AddressBook;
```

There's not much to say about this statement except that it creates a new MySQL database called `AddressBook`.

> *Behind the scenes, MySQL, will have created a new folder called `AddressBook` in the data folder within your server's MySQL installation directory. At this stage this folder will be empty. It is not until you actually create tables that MySQL will itself create any files there.*

Next we need to jump into the `AddressBook` database with the `USE` statement and create a new table called `ContactType` to store a list of possible contact types, such as 'Friend' and 'Colleague':

```
USE AddressBook;
CREATE TABLE ContactType
  (
  ContactTypeID   INT(4)       NOT NULL AUTO_INCREMENT,
  ContactTypeName VARCHAR(20) NOT NULL,
  PRIMARY KEY(ContactTypeID)
  );
```

The `ContactTypeID` is a primary key to identify each record uniquely. We use `AUTO_INCREMENT` to automatically generate sequential numbers for this field starting from 1. You can specify a starting value for your `AUTO_INCREMENT` column by adding `AUTO_INCREMENT=x` to the end of your table creation statement, where x is the value to start from:

```
CREATE TABLE Status
  (ID TINYINT NOT NULL AUTO_INCREMENT PRIMARY KEY,
  Name VARCHAR(10))
  AUTO_INCREMENT=5;
```

However, you cannot specify the amount that the value in the field is incremented by; this is always 1.

Next, we can use a number of `INSERT` statements to add some standard contact types:

```
INSERT INTO ContactType(ContactTypeName)
  VALUES ('Friend');
INSERT INTO ContactType(ContactTypeName)
  VALUES ('Colleague');
INSERT INTO ContactType(ContactTypeName)
  VALUES ('Family');
```

Notice that we only specify the `ContactTypeName` as the `ContactTypeID` column is generated automatically for us.

Our `Contact` table will be used to store a list of contact details such as the person's name, contact type, e-mail address, date of birth and telephone number. So execute the following SQL statement to create the `Contact` table:

```
CREATE TABLE Contact
(
ContactID        INT(4)       NOT NULL AUTO_INCREMENT,
ContactTypeID    INT(4)       NOT NULL,
FirstName        VARCHAR(20),
LastName         VARCHAR(20) NOT NULL,
DateOfBirth      DATE,
EMailAddress     VARCHAR(50),
Telephone        VARCHAR(20),
PRIMARY KEY(ContactID),
KEY ContactName_IDX(LastName),
KEY ContactTypeID_IDX(ContactTypeID)
);
```

As we said earlier, this SQL code can be written to a text file and run from the command line using the `source` command.

We are using the `AUTO_INCREMENT` option again to generate a unique primary key on the `ContactID` column. For performance reasons we have also created two indexes using the `KEY` option, the first on the `LastName` column. The second index, on the `ContactTypeID` column, allows us to search for specific contact types faster.

The `ContactType` table has a foreign key relationship with the `Contact` table, in that the `ContactTypeID` column is populated using a list of `ContactTypeIDs` from the `ContactType` table. Unfortunately, at present, MySQL does not support the use of foreign keys so it will not check that a record exists in the `ContactType` table for the ID specified.

That's all we need to do to create our MySQL database objects. Now we can move straight to our ASP application scripts.

The AddressBook ASP Application

Our AddressBook application consists of four ASP files and one `include` file. The `include` file, added to each ASP file using the `#include` directive, allows us to put commonly used routines into one file. Our application allows the user to search for contacts and to edit or create contact details.

Within IIS we've created a new virtual directory called `MySQLAddressBook` that will contain the four ASP files and a folder called `Includes`.

DBFunctions.inc

This ASP file, stored in the `Includes` folder, is a general purpose include script containing two functions. The first, `GetDBConnection`, returns a valid ADO `Connection` object this has been opened and which points to our MySQL database. The second function, `FixQuotes`, makes sure that any strings passed to MySQL do not cause it to return an SQL error.

This is `GetDBConnection`:

```asp
<%
Function GetDBConnection()

  Const cConnection = _
    "DRIVER={MySQL};SERVER=MySQL_dev;UID=root;PWD=;DATABASE=AddressBook"

  Dim objConnection

  Set objConnection = Server.CreateObject("ADODB.Connection")
  With objConnection
    .ConnectionString = cConnection
    .Open
  End With

  Set GetDBConnection = objConnection
End Function
```

Rather than have every ASP file create its own database connection, we use this function to create the connection for us. This allows us to store the connection details in one place should we need to amend them.

We use the now familiar ODBC Driver, `MySQL`, to connect to our `MySQL_dev` server using the `root` user ID with no password. (I haven't included any error handling, but in practice it is a good idea to add such code when communicating with a database, rather than show raw SQL errors to your end user.)

MySQL allows us to use the single or double quote characters around a string literal. We've used the single quote character, as it's more readable from ASP. The only problem when using this character is that when a user enters a name that includes a single quote such as O'Boyle, MySQL does not know where the end of the string is, so as a result it will raise an error. A standard technique to prevent this from happening is to replace every single quote with two single quotes, and this is the purpose of `FixQuote`, which is used in a number of ASP scripts that `INSERT` or `UPDATE` contact details.

```asp
Function FixQuote(ByVal varString)
  FixQuote = Replace(varString, "'", "''")
End Function
%>
```

Default.asp

As with all address books we need some way to search for the names that we've stored. We have an ASP page called `default.asp` which allows the user to enter search criteria to use against the `contact` table.

> Most web servers have a default page name that they will show if a URL does not include the name of a file to serve to the client browser. In the case of IIS this file is called `default.htm` or `default.asp`.

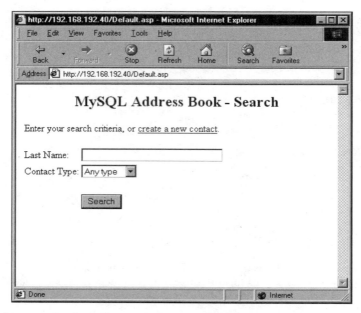

The code behind this page is relatively simple. We start off by creating a title for the page and link in our `DBFunctions.inc` include file using the `#include` statement:

```
<HTML>
<HEAD>
  <!-- #include file="includes/DBFunctions.inc"-->
</HEAD>
<BODY>
  <CENTER>
    <H2>MySQL Address Book - Search</H2>
  </CENTER>
```

Next we create an ASP procedure, `GetContactTypes`, which will write out a list of contact types enclosed with the standard HTML `OPTION` tags:

```
<%
Sub GetContactTypes()

  Dim objRecordSet
  Dim varHTMLResult

  Set objRecordSet = Server.CreateObject("ADODB.Recordset")

  With objRecordSet
    Set .ActiveConnection = GetDBConnection()
    .Open("SELECT * from ContactType ORDER BY ContactTypeName")
  End With

  Do While Not objRecordSet.EOF
    varHTMLResult = varHTMLResult & _
      "<OPTION VALUE=""" & objRecordSet.Fields("ContactTypeID") & """>" & _
      objRecordSet.Fields("ContactTypeName") & "</OPTION>"
```

```
      objRecordSet.MoveNext
   Loop

   Set objRecordSet = Nothing

   Response.Write varHTMLResult

End Sub
%>
```

We next define the data-entry form and call the `GetContactTypes` procedure to give us the options for the contact types `SELECT` list:

```
<FORM ACTION="SearchResults.asp" METHOD="POST">
  <TABLE>
    <TR>
      <TD COLSPAN=2>
        Enter your search critieria, or <A HREF="ContactDetails.asp">
        create a new contact</A>.
        <BR> 
      </TD>
    </TR>
    <TR>
      <TD>Last Name:</TD>
      <TD><INPUT TYPE="TEXT" NAME="txtLastName" SIZE="30"></TD>
    </TR>
    <TR>
      <TD>Contact Type:</TD>
      <TD><SELECT NAME="1stContactTypeID">
            <OPTION VALUE=0 SELECTED>Any type</OPTION>
            <%Call GetContactTypes()%>
          </SELECT>
      </TD>
    </TR>
    <TR>
      <TD> </TD>
    </TR>
    <TR>
      <TD> </TD><TD><INPUT TYPE="SUBMIT" VALUE="Search"></TD>
    </TR>
  </TABLE>
</FORM>
</BODY>
</HTML>
```

You may have noticed that we've added a link to the `ContactDetails.asp` page, thereby enabling the user to create a new contact record. Note that this is the same page that lists the details of contacts, which will be discussed shortly.

When submitted, the user is transferred to the `SearchResults.asp` script to fetch a list of matching contacts. Notice that we create the `SELECT` control and then call `GetContactTypes` to retrieve the list of contact types from the database.

SearchResults.asp

When the user clicks the Search button in `default.asp`, they are transferred to this form handler page. This script takes the search criteria and builds an SQL string in order to retrieve a list of matching contacts from the `Contact` table. We make use of MySQL's `LIKE` and `SOUNDEX` statements to provide additional search flexibility.

For each matching contact found, we create a table row and add a hyperlink to the name allowing the user to edit or view the details using the `ContactDetails.asp` file.

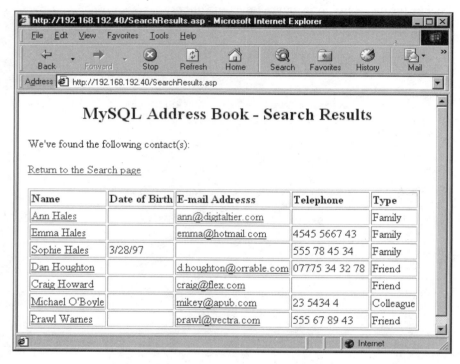

We use the `varSQLCriteria` variable to store a SQL `SELECT` string, which is created on the fly based on the user's search criteria. `objRecordSet` is an ADO `Recordset` object that will hold the results of the user's search. For performance purposes, `varFrmLastName` and `varFrmContactTypeID` are used to cache the contents of the `Request.Form` variables, as they are referred to a number of times.

```
<%Option Explicit

Dim varSQLCriteria
Dim objRecordSet
Dim varFrmLastName
Dim varFrmContactTypeID
```

For each record found, we transfer the contents of the `Recordset` object into a number of local variables. We could have simply written out the value for the field as each record is processed but by transferring the fields into variables we can do some extra formatting if required.

```
Dim varContactID
Dim varFirstName
Dim varLastName
Dim varContactTypeName
Dim varDateOfBirth
Dim varEMailAddress
Dim varTelephone
```

Our standard SELECT statement returns the contact details along with the ContactTypeName from the ContactType table:

```
varSQLCriteria ="SELECT Contact.ContactID, Contact.FirstName," & _
                "     Contact.LastName, " & _
                "     Contact.DateOfBirth, Contact.EMailAddress, " & _
                "     Contact.Telephone, " & _
                "     ContactType.ContactTypeName " & _
                " FROM Contact, ContactType " & _
                " WHERE Contact.ContactTypeID = ContactType.ContactTypeID"
```

If the user has specified a name to search against then we need to add it to our search criteria string. SOUNDEX is a commonly used SQL function that returns a number based on an input string. It uses standard rules such as removing vowels and numbers and allows searches such as "HAILES" to match "HALES". For additional functionality we've used the wildcard character % in conjunction with the LIKE statement to find the search name at any position within the last name column.

In order to retrieve the name of contact type from the foreign key table, ContactType, we use the WHERE clause to join to the ContactTypeID.

```
varFrmLastName = Trim(Request.Form("txtLastName"))
If varFrmLastName <> "" Then
  varSQLCriteria = varSQLCriteria & _
               "    AND (SOUNDEX(Contact.LastName) = " & _
               "        SOUNDEX('" & FixQuote(varFrmLastName) & "') " & _
               "    OR Contact.LastName LIKE '%" & _
                   FixQuote(varFrmLastName) & "%')"
End If
```

If the user has specified the type of contact to search for then we shall add that on to the search criteria and finish off by ordering the results using the last name and then the first name.

```
varFrmContactTypeID = CLng(Request.Form("lstContactTypeID"))
If varFrmContactTypeID <> 0 Then
  varSQLCriteria = varSQLCriteria & _
               "    AND Contact.ContactTypeID = " & varFrmContactTypeID
End If

varSQLCriteria = varSQLCriteria & _
               "    ORDER BY Contact.LastName, Contact.FirstName"
```

Now it's just a case of opening up a database connection and executing the SQL.

```
Set objRecordSet = Server.CreateObject("ADODB.Recordset")
With objRecordSet
  Set .ActiveConnection = GetDBConnection()
  .Open(varSQLCriteria)
End With
%>
```

We create a title for the page and a title row for the search results table:

```
<HTML>
<HEAD>
  <!-- #include file="includes/DBFunctions.inc"-->
</HEAD>
<BODY>
  <CENTER>
    <H2>MySQL Address Book - Search Results</H2>
  </CENTER>
<TABLE>
  <TR><TD>We've found the following contact(s):<BR> <BR>
        <A HREF="Default.asp">Return to the Search page</A><BR> <BR>
        <TABLE BORDER=1>
          <TR>
            <TD><B>Name</B></TD>
            <TD><B>Date of Birth</B></TD>
            <TD><B>E-mail Addresss</B></TD>
            <TD><B>Telephone</B></TD>
            <TD><B>Type</B></TD>
          </TR>
```

For every matching record in the Recordset we transfer each column into a local variable. Notice that we prefix those columns that could be NULL with an empty space to coerce any possible NULL values into empty strings. If you attempt to concatenate a NULL field and string you will end up with a NULL value:

```
<%
Do While Not objRecordSet.EOF
  varContactID       = objRecordSet("ContactID")
  varFirstName       = "" & objRecordSet("FirstName")
  varLastName        = "" & objRecordSet("LastName")
  varContactTypeName = "" & objRecordSet("ContactTypeName")
  varDateOfBirth     = "" & objRecordSet("DateOfBirth")
  varEMailAddress    = "" & objRecordSet("EMailAddress")
  varTelephone       = "" & objRecordSet("Telephone")
%>
```

We create a hyperlink around the contact's first and last name that points to the ContactDetails.asp script so that the user can edit the details for this contact. The person's ContactID is appended to the URL so that ContactDetails.asp gets the correct person's details.

```
<TR>
  <TD NOWRAP>
    <A HREF="ContactDetails.asp?ContactID=<%=varContactID%>">
      <%=varFirstName & " " & varLastName%>
    </A>
  </TD>
```

If there is a date of birth then we format it, otherwise we just enter a non-breaking space character ( ) so that the table cell's border is drawn correctly:

```
<TD><%
    If varDateOfBirth <> "" Then
      Response.Write _
            FormatDateTime(objRecordSet("DateOfBirth"), _
                           vbGeneralDate)
    Else
      Response.Write " "
    End If
    %>
</TD>
```

If this person has an e-mail address we write it out with a `mailto` hyperlink, again using ` ` to make sure that the cell borders are drawn correctly if there is no value for the e-mail address.

```
<TD><%
    If varEMailAddress <> "" Then
      Response.Write "<A HREF=""mailto:" & _
              objRecordSet("EMailAddress") & """>" & _
              objRecordSet("EMailAddress") & "</A>"
    Else
      Response.Write " "
    End If
    %>
</TD>
```

We finish off the person's contact details by displaying the telephone number and contact type before moving to the next record. Once we have got to the end of the `Recordset`, we destroy the `Recordset` object by setting it to `Nothing`.

```
        <TD><%=varTelephone%> </TD>
        <TD><%=varContactTypeName%></TD>
      </TR>
    <%
      objRecordSet.MoveNext
    Loop
    Set objRecordSet = Nothing
    %>
      </TD>
    </TR>
  </TABLE>
</BODY>
```

ContactDetails.asp

When passed a `ContactID` as part of the URL, this script allows the user to edit an existing person's contact details. If a `ContactID` is not passed, as is the case if the create new contact link on the home page is clicked, the script is used to create a new contact record.

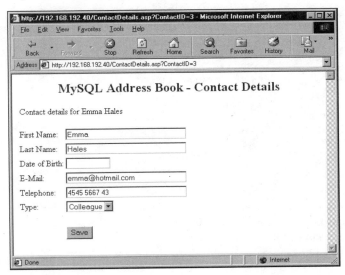

As with our search results page, we transfer the values for each of the columns to local variables so that we can transform them into a friendly display format:

```
<%Option Explicit%>
<HTML>
<HEAD>
  <!-- #include file="includes/DBFunctions.inc"-->
</HEAD>
<BODY>
  <CENTER>
    <H2>MySQL Address Book - Contact Details</H2>
  </CENTER>
<%
Dim objRecordSet

Dim varContactID
Dim varFirstName
Dim varLastName
Dim varContactTypeID
Dim varDateOfBirth
Dim varEMailAddress
Dim varTelephone
```

The `varHTMLSelected` variable is used when we create the list of contact types. We will be using `objRecordSet` to retrieve the person's details and also to store a list of valid contact types:

```
Dim varHTMLSelected

Set objRecordSet = Server.CreateObject("ADODB.Recordset")
Set objRecordSet.ActiveConnection = GetDBConnection()
```

If a `ContactID` has been passed to the script, we fetch the current values from the `Contact` table and transfer them to our local variables. We explicitly call the `Recordset Close` method, as we will be using the `Recordset` again to retrieve a list of contact types:

```
If Request.QueryString("ContactID") <> "" Then
  varContactID = Request.QueryString("ContactID")
  objRecordSet.Open("SELECT * from Contact WHERE ContactID = " & _
                   varContactID)
  varFirstName     = "" & objRecordSet("FirstName")
  varLastName      = "" & objRecordSet("LastName")
  varContactTypeID = "" & objRecordSet("ContactTypeID")
  varDateOfBirth   = "" & objRecordSet("DateOfBirth")
  varEMailAddress  = "" & objRecordSet("EMailAddress")
  varTelephone     = "" & objRecordSet("Telephone")
  objRecordSet.Close
End If
%>
```

The data-entry form is created to call its handler script, `ContactDetails_HND.asp`, when the user clicks the Save button. A short message string states that this is either a new contact record or that the details of the chosen contact are being displayed:

```
<FORM ACTION="ContactDetails_HND.asp?ContactID=<%=varContactID%>"
    METHOD="POST">
  <TABLE>
    <TR>
      <TD COLSPAN=2>
        <%
        If varContactID = 0 Then
          Response.Write "New contact details"
        Else
          Response.Write "Contact details for " & varFirstName & " " & _
                                            varLastName

        End If
        %>
        <BR> 
      </TD>
    </TR>
```

For each of the data-entry fields we create a TEXT input field and write out the current value, if it exists:

```
    <TR>
      <TD>First Name:</TD>
      <TD><INPUT SIZE="30" TYPE="TEXT" NAME="txtFirstName"
          VALUE="<%=varFirstName%>"></TD>
    </TR>
    <TR>
      <TD>Last Name:</TD>
      <TD><INPUT SIZE="30" TYPE="TEXT" NAME="txtLastName"
          VALUE="<%=varLastName%>"></TD>
    </TR>
    <TR>
      <TD>Date of Birth:</TD>
      <TD><INPUT SIZE="10" TYPE="TEXT"  NAME="txtDateOfBirth"
          VALUE="<%=varDateOfBirth%>"></TD>
    </TR>
    <TR>
      <TD>E-Mail:</TD>
      <TD><INPUT SIZE="30" TYPE="TEXT" NAME="txtEMailAddress"
          VALUE="<%=varEMailAddress%>"></TD>
    </TR>
    <TR>
      <TD>Telephone:</TD>
      <TD><INPUT SIZE="30" TYPE="TEXT" NAME="txtTelephone"
          VALUE="<%=varTelephone%>"></TD>
    </TR>
```

Now we can create a SELECT list of contact types and populate it with a valid list from the ContactType table:

```
  <TR>
      <TD>Type:</TD>
      <TD>
        <SELECT NAME="lstContactTypeID" SIZE=1>
          <%
  objRecordSet.Open("SELECT * FROM ContactType ORDER BY ContactTypeName")
```

In this next section of code, `varHTMLSelected` is set to the value `SELECTED` if the current record's `ContactTypeID` matches that of our contact's current `ContactTypeID` so that the correct type is selected:

```
            If Not objRecordSet Is Nothing Then
              Do While Not objRecordSet.EOF
                If CLng(objRecordSet("ContactTypeID")) = _
                                                varContactTypeID Then
                  varHTMLSelected = "SELECTED"
                Else
                  varHTMLSelected = ""
                End If
        %>
```

For each record we write out an `OPTION` tag with the correct value and display text. We've used the `Is Nothing` statement to check that our `Recordset` object contains an initialized object. It is also possible to use the `IsObject()` function to achieve the same result:

```
        <OPTION <%=varHTMLSelected%>
          VALUE="<%=objRecordSet("ContactTypeID")%>" >
          <%=objRecordSet("ContactTypeName")%>
        </OPTION>
```

Once we get to the end we can shutdown the `Recordset` object and close the `SELECT` tag:

```
        <%
               objRecordSet.MoveNext
          Loop
          objRecordSet.close
        End If
        Set objRecordSet = Nothing
        %>
      </SELECT>
```

Finally, we add the **Save** button to submit the form. To be ultra user-friendly we could have also added a **Clear** button to clear the current values:

```
      </TD>
    </TR>
    <TR>
      <TD> </TD>
    </TR>
    <TR>
      <TD> </TD><TD><INPUT TYPE="SUBMIT" VALUE="Save"></TD>
    </TR>
  </TABLE>
</FORM>
</BODY>
</HTML>
```

ContactDetails_HND.asp

This is a form submission handler, hence the HND suffix in its name. When the user clicks the **Save** button on our ContactDetails.asp script they are transferred to this script so that the record can be updated or inserted accordingly. We haven't included any validation ourselves, but this would be the best place to make sure any required fields have been entered before we attempt to update the Contact table:

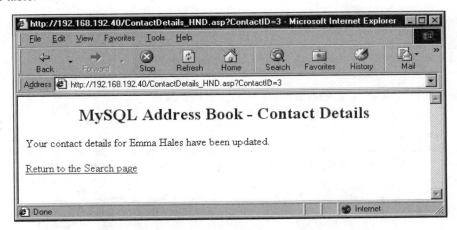

In the case of a new contact record being added, we alter the wording slightly:

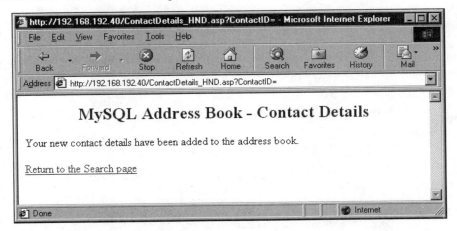

Initially, we transfer the data-entry fields into local variable in preparation for our SQL command:

```
<%Option Explicit%>
<HTML>
<HEAD>
  <!-- #include file="includes/DBFunctions.inc"-->
</HEAD>
<BODY>
  <CENTER>
    <H2>MySQL Address Book - Contact Details</H2>
  </CENTER>
<%
```

```
Dim objConnection
Dim varSQL
Dim varContactID
Dim varFirstName
Dim varLastName
Dim varContactTypeID
Dim varDateOfBirth
Dim varEMailAddress
Dim varTelephone

varFirstName      = Request.Form("txtFirstName")
varLastName       = Request.Form("txtLastName")
varContactTypeID  = Request.Form("lstContactTypeID")
varDateOfBirth    = Request.Form("txtDateOfBirth")
varEMailAddress   = Request.Form("txtEMailAddress")
varTelephone      = Request.Form("txtTelephone")
```

If we weren't passed a `ContactID`, then this is a new record, so we need to execute an `INSERT` statement. Once again, we have used the `FixQuote` function from our `DBFunctions.inc` file to ensure that MySQL accepts any single quote characters contained in the user's string:

```
If Request.QueryString("ContactID") = "" Then
  varContactID = 0
  varSQL = "INSERT INTO Contact(FirstName, LastName, ContactTypeID, " & _
           "                     DateOfBirth, EMailAddress, Telephone)" & _
           "   VALUES(" & _
           "      '" & FixQuote(varFirstName) & "'," & _
           "      '" & FixQuote(varLastName) & "', " & _
         varContactTypeID & ", "
```

We add the remaining fields to the `INSERT` statement, ensuring that the date of birth is in the format year-month-day, as required by MySQL:

```
If varDateOfBirth = "" Then
  varSQL = varSQL & "NULL, "
Else
  varSQL = varSQL & _
         "      '" & Year(varDateOfBirth) & "-" & _
                  Month(varDateOfBirth) & "-" & _
                  Day(varDateOfBirth) & "', "
End If

varSQL = varSQL & _
       "      '" & FixQuote(varEMailAddress) & "', " & _
       "      '" & varTelephone & "')"
```

If the contact already exists, we will use the `UPDATE` statement and add the `ContactID` to the `WHERE` clause. We use exactly the same date formatting options to set the `dateofbirth` field.

```
Else
  varContactID = Request.QueryString("ContactID")
  varSQL = "UPDATE Contact SET " & _
         "  FirstName = '" & FixQuote(varFirstName) & "', " & _
         "  LastName = '" & FixQuote(varLastName) & "', "
```

```
    If varDateOfBirth <> "" Then
      varSQL = varSQL & _
            "  DateOfBirth = '" & _
                Year(varDateOfBirth) & "-" & _
                Month(varDateOfBirth) & "-" & _
                Day(varDateOfBirth) & "', "
    End If

    varSQL = varSQL & _
            "  EMailAddress = '" & FixQuote(varEMailAddress) & "', " & _
            "  Telephone = '" & varTelephone & "', " & _
            "  ContactTypeID = " & varContactTypeID & _
            "  WHERE ContactID = " & varContactID

End If
```

We call `GetDSBConnection` to return an ADO `Connection` object pointing at the MySQL database and attempt the UPDATE or INSERT:

```
Set objConnection = GetDBConnection()
Call objConnection.Execute(varSQL)
```

Finally a message declares whether the data was updated or whether a new contact was entered. Again we haven't added any error handling but you should in case there is a problem with the data.

```
If varContactID = 0 Then
   Response.Write "Your new contact details have been added to the " & _
                   "address book."
Else
   Response.Write "Your contact details for " & varFirstName & " " & _
                   varLastName & " have been updated."
End If
%>
<P>
<A HREF="Default.asp">Return to the Search page</A><BR> <BR>
</BODY>
</HTML>
```

That concludes our sample application for accessing a MySQL database. We saw typical data-entry operations such as searching for records using a SELECT statement created on the fly and making use of MySQL's SOUNDEX and LIKE statements to provide additional search functionality.

We also provided the user with the ability to edit and save any existing contact details, while using the same data-entry form to create new contacts. You can see that with the inability to use stored procedures in MySQL, some of our SQL statements did become rather long.

Summary

This section also wraps up our discussion of MySQL. In this chapter we covered a number of the important aspects of MySQL, and looked at how to utilize it in conjunction with ASP. In particular, we have looked at:

❑   The environments supported by MySQL.

❑   MySQL's features.

❑   Installing and using the ODBC Driver, MyODBC.

❑   MySQL's security model.

❑   An overview of MySQL's SQL implementation.

❑   Outlines the limitations of MySQL.

❑   Constructing a sample MySQL/ASP application.

MySQL can be summarized as a fast, stable and effective database server. It is ideal for web-based applications where large numbers of records needs to be read from. Its SQL language provides a rich set of SQL commands and functions that are close to those offered by other commercially available database servers.

Section 5

Non-Relational Data

18

Directory Services

So far, we've looked almost exclusively at how to use ASP to access relational data – that is to say, data that is stored in databases such as SQL Server, DB2, and Oracle, and which is usually accessed using some form of SQL. However, not all data is suited to this format. In these days of the Web, we are growing increasingly accustomed to storing such data as lists of e-mail addresses, resources and various pictures and audio-visual files. Over the next few chapters we're going to look at some of the different ways that some of this data can be stored and what tools and APIs are available to make it easy for us to get at this data from our ASP pages.

In this chapter, we're going to look at **directory services** –which, roughly speaking, means information that is stored hierarchically for frequent look-ups. The information might, for example, be a directory of employees of an organization, or a directory of user accounts on a local domain, though in principle there's no restriction on the kind of information that can be stored in a directory.

On the Windows 2000 platform, the term 'directory services' is becoming synonymous with **Active Directory**, the directory of all network resources and security information that is used by Windows 2000 domain controllers to manage Windows domains. Active Directory isn't the only directory around by any means, but it is an important one that is frequently encountered. For this reason, we're going to start off this chapter with a closer look at Active Directory and the facilities it offers. We're going to use it to illustrate some of the principles of directories in general, so we can then move on to explore in more detail what a directory actually is, what sorts of information we'd store in it, and the different types of directories that are commonly available.

We'll also take a look at the **Lightweight Directory Access Protocol**, version 3 (**LDAP**). This is an industry standard that defines how to communicate with directories. Most common directories these days are compliant with LDAP, so it's worth knowing a bit about the protocol. Once we've got this background, we can go on to look at the API that we'll use to get at and modify the information in directories: the **Active Directory Service Interfaces**, or **ADSI**.

Up to this point, we've been using ADO as our route to get at information from data sources, but there are various reasons why ADO isn't the best choice for directory information. In this chapter we'll see why this is so, and show how ADSI makes it easy to use information stored in directories. However, having said that, we will find ADO creeping back in when we look specifically at how to search for information in directories.

Active Directory

It's hard to read much about Windows 2000 without seeing some reference to Active Directory pretty quickly. In many ways it's *the* flagship technology that distinguishes Windows 2000 from its predecessor, Windows NT4. The point is that any organization needs some means to organize its computers – to determine user accounts, and to indicate which users have access to which facilities on the network. And at the same time we need to protect the organization's network and files from being accessed by people not authorized to view or modify them. The way that Windows achieves this has traditionally been through the Windows **domain** (not to be confused with an Internet domain – which is a different concept altogether). In Windows 2000, the domain is managed by one or more **domain controllers** – that is, machines that are running either Windows 2000 Server, Advanced Server, or DataCenter Server, and to which all requests for authentication or authorization of domain resources are made. To perform this task, these machines must have access to some kind of data store with all the required security information in it. And in Windows 2000 that data store is Active Directory.

> *With previous versions of NT, there was also a data store that contained the security information. However, in NT4, this data store was more restricted in its abilities, and could be accessed only through a Windows-specific API. Active Directory is more powerful and is open, in the sense of complying with the industry LDAP standard for directories.*

Before looking at how we actually utilize Active Directory, we will take a quick look at how to install it.

Installing Active Directory

Active Directory is quite easy to install. If you are running any version of Windows 2000 Server then you do so using the Configure Your Server wizard. This wizard can be found in the Start Menu under Programs | Administrative Tools. To make things even easier, when we install Windows 2000 Server, this wizard is set by default to run automatically when we start Windows, though we can change this setting.

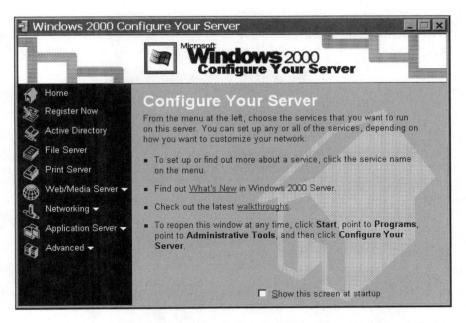

To install Active Directory, we simply select the Active Directory tab on the left and the wizard will then guide us through the process of installing it. Note that installing Active Directory amounts to exactly the same thing as promoting the machine to being a domain controller – since in Windows 2000 a machine is a domain controller if and only if it has Active Directory installed. For this reason, we cannot install Active Directory on Windows 2000 Professional.

Exploring Active Directory

We're going to start off with a very hands-on approach in this chapter. At this point we could go into some of the theory of what makes a directory a directory and why Microsoft didn't just use a relational database for hands-on approach in this chapter. At this point we could go into some of the theory of what makes their security information, but instead we're going to illustrate the concepts directly, by exploring Active Directory.

The tool we're going to use for this is an executable file called adsvw.exe. This is a user interface tool that uses ADSI to allow us to browse around any of the directories installed on a network that are accessible through ADSI.

The adsvw.exe utility is available as part of the ADSI SDK, which can be downloaded from http://www.microsoft.com/ntserver/nts/downloads/previews/ADSI25/default.asp. In order to run it, it will be necessary to have ADSI itself installed as well as the SDK. If you are running a Windows 2000 machine, you will have ADSI as part of the operating system, though if you are running NT4 or Windows 9x, you will need to download ADSI separately (from the same URL as the ADSI SDK).

> Note that adsvw.exe, being a UI tool, is not something we'd be able to use directly in our ASP pages. We're introducing it here both because it is an excellent tool for illustrating how directories work, and because it is also very useful when debugging ASP pages. When our pages seem to be failing or returning incorrect data from directories, it's very simple to use adsvw.exe to check what the data in the directories actually is or whether the data we think we've written to them in our pages has been stored correctly.

When we start `adsvw.exe`, we get presented with a dialog box asking if we want a new ObjectViewer or Query. In other words, do we want to just explore the directories, or are we looking for some specific data (**searching**)? We just want to look around at the structure of the directories, so we'll pick ObjectViewer here:

Another dialog will appear asking us from what point we want to browse:

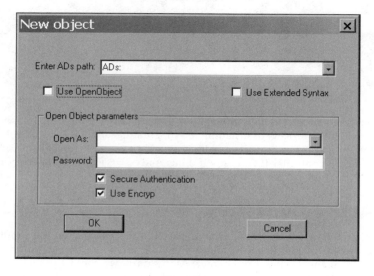

Type in ADs: in the combo box marked Enter ADs path (this is the path that means we want to be able to look at anything that's accessible through ADSI). You should also enter authentication credentials if necessary. If you are logged in with domain administrator privileges, you can leave out the user name and password and make sure the Use OpenObject checkbox is unchecked. (Unchecking this box means user credentials will be taken from the account you're logged into Windows as.) Otherwise you should check this box and enter a User Name (in the Open As combo box) and a password that will give you the necessary privileges.

We then get presented with a 2-pane view, with the left hand pane showing a tree structure of objects in Windows-Explorer style, while the right-hand pane shows various information about the object that's selected in the tree view. It also has various controls allowing the data to be modified. For some objects, as shown in the next screenshot, some data is unavailable, and is therefore indicated by question marks.

This screenshot shows this view with the tree expanded just a little bit:

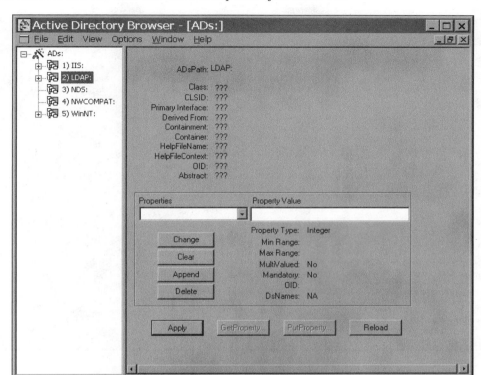

What we see in the left pane is the node called **ADs:** that we specified earlier. This represents an object called the **ADSI Router** – a COM object which is able to enumerate the ADSI Providers on the system. And we can see the providers listed as children of the router. ADSI uses providers in the same way as OLE DB does: an ADSI Provider is what allows us to connect to certain types of directories just as an OLE DB Provider is what allows us to connect to certain types of data source. So the providers roughly correspond to the directories available on a system – IIS, LDAP, WinNT, etc. Don't worry about what these directories are for now – we'll go over that soon. For now we'll concentrate on Active Directory.

We saw earlier that there is an industry standard protocol for communicating with directories – the LDAP protocol. Active Directory is an LDAP-compliant directory, which means the LDAP node in the tree view is the one that connects us to Active Directory.

So we'll expand that node and see what we get:

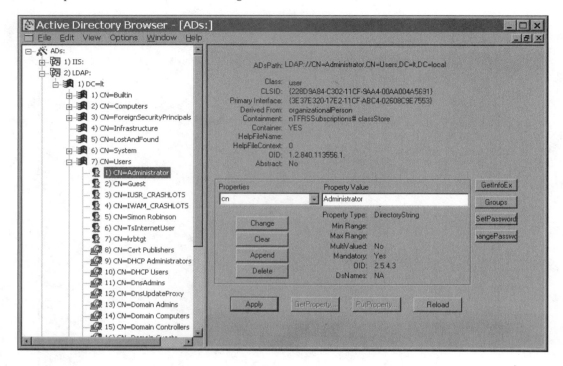

Under **LDAP:** is a node that corresponds to my local domain, **DC=lt**. From there, we've navigated down through a node that contains the user accounts (**CN=Users**) to select the domain's Administrator account, **CN=Administrator**. At this point, we have quite a bit of new terminology and several concepts that we need to introduce.

Firstly, we note that each node in the tree view below **LDAP:** corresponds to a directory object – that is to say, an identifiable object in a directory. The directory objects that can contain other nodes are known as **containers**, while the other nodes are **leafs**.

The prefixes in front of the names of the objects (e.g. **CN**) come from LDAP. All objects in LDAP-compliant directories are named with a prefix that in principle indicates something about the type of object it is. Common prefixes that we'll come across in Active Directory include **DC** (**Domain Component**), **OU** (**Organizational Unit**), and **CN** (**Common Name** – a generic prefix for any directory object that doesn't have its own specific prefix).

Now we'll move on to the information displayed in the right-hand pane for the **CN=Administrator** object. The first item listed is something called the ADsPath. The best way to understand this is to think about the Windows file system. I'm currently editing a file called ChADSI.doc, but the full path name to this file is F:\Simons Chapters\Pro ASP Data Access\ChADSI.doc. To uniquely identify the file, the full path name, specifying the drive, the folders, and finally the file, is what we need here. For the directory objects, the name corresponds to ordinary file names, and the ADsPath corresponds to the full path name. To identify a directory object with ADSI, we need the ADsPath.

Let's look at the `ADsPath` of the administrator's user account in more detail. This is:

```
LDAP://CN=Administrator,CN=Users,DC=lt,DC=local
```

The first part of this is the name of the ADSI provider, followed by `://`. All names of ADSI objects start in this way. The precise syntax of what follows depends on the provider, but Active Directory, being LDAP-compliant, follows the standard LDAP format. This works up the directory tree from the object itself (in contrast to file system names, which work down the hierarchy), and separates names of containers with a comma. In LDAP-parlance, this name (i.e. everything after the `LDAP://`) is called a **distinguished name** (**DN**), or sometimes a **fully qualified distinguished name**.

Note that for our example there's an extra DC=local on the end of the DN. This is because the full name of my domain is `LT.local` (the `local` indicates that it's on a private network and not connected to the internet; `LT` is just what I decided to call the domain).

> *With Windows 2000, we are able to give domain names the same name as the corresponding internet domain for our organization if we want to, but Active Directory LDAP-izes the names, so, for example, LT.local becomes dc=lt, dc=local (note that this is case-insensitive).*

Other than ADsPaths, there's still a lot more information we can gather from that screenshot. If we read on down the right-hand pane, we see a long set of other information about the object that represents the Administrator user account. Most of this information is beyond the scope of this chapter, but we will comment on the field called Class. The class of an object is the name of the type of object. To understand the class, we can note that Active Directory stores information about many types of objects, including, for example, user accounts, group accounts, and computers, as well as others. The class of the object says which of these objects the Administrator account is. And – not surprisingly, we find the class of the user account is User.

Below the list of information in the screenshot are a list box marked Properties and a text box marked Property Value. Each object in a directory has a lot of information stored about itself – for example, user accounts will have information such as the user name, details about when they last logged in, and whether the account is enabled. Each piece of information is called a **Property** or an **Attribute** (the two terms are interchangeable). The Properties box allows us to select a property, and the Property Value box lets us view or modify its value.

Before leaving `adsvw.exe`, we'll take a brief look at some of the various containers that can be seen under the DC=lt container in the screenshot.

- ❏ DC=lt represents the domain itself. The nodes under it are all containers that group together objects of similar types.

- ❏ CN=Users, as we've already seen, stores user accounts, as well as some group accounts. (In the screenshot, the objects represented by faces are user accounts; the ones represented by the icons showing faces in front of a computer are domain groups.)

- ❏ CN=BuiltIn is there specifically to hold certain other domain groups that are set up by the operating system and essential to the running of Windows 2000.

- ❏ CN=Domain Controllers (not visible in the screenshot) holds computer accounts for those computers which are domain controllers.

- ❏ CN=Computers holds computer accounts for all the other computers in the domain – the member workstations. The remaining containers hold various bits of system information, which we won't need to go into in this chapter.

Directory Services

Our little tour of Active Directory has actually told us a lot about the structure of directories. We've seen how they are composed of directory objects, with each object being composed of a number of different properties. We've also seen how each directory object belongs to a certain class, which indicates what type of object it is.

However, one of the most important characteristics of directories is something that we've actually passed over without any comment, because it fell so naturally out of those screenshots:

> **Directories have a hierarchical, rather than a relational, structure.**

The hierarchical structure explains why adsvw.exe allowed us to navigate around Active Directory using a tree control. It would be difficult to do that with a relational database. The hierarchical structure is also one of the main reasons why we have a different API, ADSI, to access directories. When we come to examine how to write code using ADSI, we'll see that ADSI is well suited to hierarchical data – something that's not true of ADO. It's true that ADO can simulate a hierarchical structure using its data-shaping provider, but that provider is really there just to convert relational data so that it appears hierarchical, and does add some overhead in the process. When it comes to it, ADO was just never designed for natively hierarchical data.

Before we look at some of the common directories around, we'll go over what the main characteristics of directories are.

The following list gives some of the characteristics of directories and shows how they are distinguished from databases. It's important to bear in mind, however, that data sources come in many different varieties, so it's not really possible to lay down sharp divisions about what is a directory and what isn't. This list gives *typical* characteristics, but they won't be shared by all directories, and you'll notice that many of them also apply to relational databases:

Characteristics of Directories	Comment
Tree Structure	Directories usually have a hierarchical data structure.
Primarily for Lookup	Directories are optimized for frequent reading. The data they store doesn't change often, but it needs to be accessed frequently.
No Transaction Monitoring	Directories often don't have the same sophisticated transaction support that can be found in databases such as Oracle and SQL Server. It's simply not as important for the sort of data they contain.
Contain Real Objects	Partly due to the hierarchical structure, entries in directories often correspond in an obvious way to external objects such as users and computers. This is not always the case for entries in a table in a database.

Characteristics of Directories	Comment
Open	Directories will normally be accessible through some standard protocol (LDAP being the obvious one), which means we don't have to learn to use a different API to access each directory (although databases do have a standard protocol –SQL – the LDAP protocol is applied far more vigorously).
Scaleable/Replicated	Good directories will be able to handle many thousands of users querying them for data. In other words, they are highly scalable. A common way of achieving this is to replicate them over several servers. In other words, all the servers have independent copies of the directory.
Complex Search Queries	Most directories can understand and respond to complex search queries, such as 'return the names of all user accounts that are members of the administrators group but have not logged on for the last week'. We'll cover searching later in the chapter, but we'll note here that LDAP includes a language for formulating such queries.

These characteristics are certainly all present in Active Directory. To run through them, we've seen how Active Directory has a tree structure. It is also there primarily for look-up; every time we log in or perform any action that requires access to any network resources, it will need to be checked whether we do actually have the appropriate permissions and privileges. And this will involve the relevant objects in Active Directory being accessed. But changes to the information stored in Active Directory are much less frequent.

The lack of transaction monitoring isn't as serious as it sounds. It doesn't mean that no checks are made when changes are made to the directory – clearly, routine checks to ensure that we are not destroying the integrity of the directory will be made before any modification to the information is allowed. What it means is that directories tend not to have the sophisticated facilities to group operations together and roll them back that we'd find in relational databases.

Active Directory is open – it's based on the LDAP protocols, and it's replicated because every domain controller stores a copy of it. This actually brings up a point relating to the transaction monitoring: if the directory is replicated, isn't there a danger of the replicas getting out of sync? Well, yes, but Active Directory is designed to accommodate this. It is implemented with sophisticated algorithms that regularly compare recent changes to the different copies of Active Directory to ensure that the most up-to-date data is propagated throughout all the replicas, but this will mean that there will be short periods of time – perhaps a few minutes – when a given update isn't yet stored on all replicas. Directories are designed to hold the type of information where this delay doesn't matter.

Finally, complex search queries are supported as part of the standard LDAP protocol – we'll look at these later in the chapter.

Other Directory Services

In this section, we'll take a tour through some of the other common directories which can be accessed through ADSI.

Netscape Directory Server and the OpenLDAP Directory Server

I've grouped these together because although they are different directory services, they both serve a similar purpose. These directories are general-purpose directories. They are designed to store any data we want in them, in much the same way that, for example, SQL Server or Oracle are designed as general purpose database services that allow us to store any information. Both of these directory services are fully LDAP-compliant, which means that ASP pages will access them using the same ADSI LDAP provider that we've been using to explore Active Directory.

Netscape Directory Server has for some time been widely regarded as the most scalable and sophisticated directory service on the market, though at the time of writing it's not yet clear how or whether the arrival of Active Directory has changed that. Netscape Directory Server is available for Windows NT, as well as for many other platforms including Unix, Redhat Linux and Solaris.

> *The **OpenLDAP Server** is free for download from*
> `http://www.openldap.org/software/download.`
> *Netscape Directory Server is available for purchase from Netscape at*
> `http://www.iplanet.com/downloads/download/index.html.`

The IIS Metabase

This is a directory that stores all the configuration information for Internet Information Server (for IIS 4 onwards). For example, it contains details of virtual directories, permissions for users for each directory, the default home directory and default files, etc. We can use the Internet Services Manager to view and set these settings, but we can also access them programmatically using ADSI, through the ADSI IIS provider. In fact, if you've ever used the web version of the Internet Services Manager, you might be surprised to discover that this page itself uses ADSI internally.

The IIS Metabase has the same hierarchical structure as we've seen in other directories, but it is more specialized and has more restricted functionality – for example, it doesn't support searching.

Novell Directory Services

The various versions of **Novell Netware Directory Services** basically perform the same task as Active Directory. However, they have been around for some years now. They are accessible using ADSI using the ADSI NDS and NWCompat providers. We'll examine this in depth in Chapter 19.

The Exchange Directory and the Site Server Membership Directories

These are LDAP-compliant directories, and are therefore accessed from ADSI using the ADSI Provider for LDAP. The **Exchange Directory** stores information about distribution lists, users and contacts and other configuration information for Exchange Server, while the **Site Server Membership Directory** stores information about users who connect to your web site from browsers, along with what permissions they have.

We won't look in any detail at these directories here. However, at the time of writing, the latest non-beta versions of these products are Exchange Server 5.5 and Site Server 3.0, which use separate directories to store this information. Microsoft has indicated that in future versions these directories will be integrated into Active Directory to form a single unified directory.

> *One interesting point that illustrates how it is possible to transform data is that the Site Server Membership Directory is actually stored internally as a relational database – in either SQL Server or Access depending on the options selected when Site Server is installed – and is transformed automatically into a hierarchical structure for access via ADSI.*

WinNT

This leaves only the WinNT ADSI Provider. This provides access to certain information about a domain, and, unusually for ADSI Providers, doesn't connect to a directory service. We'll look at this in more detail later in this chapter.

Introducing ADSI

We've now seen something of the nature of directories and taken a look at what directories we might want to talk to from ASP pages. And, since the aim of this chapter is to investigate how to write ASP pages that can access the information in directories, we need to learn about the API we'll need to do so – ADSI.

ADSI works by using COM components to provide wrappers around directory objects. We'll illustrate this with an example. Let's go back to that administrator account – the one that had the ADsPath. Suppose we want to examine the administrator account in our Active Directory installation, which we happen to know has the distinguished name:

```
CN=Administrator,CN=Users,DC=lt,DC=local
```

And so has the ADsPath:

```
LDAP://CN=Administrator,CN=Users,DC=lt,DC=local
```

And let's say we want to display its name. We can do that with this bit of VBScript in an ASP page:

```
Dim objAdmin
Set objAdmin = GetObject("LDAP://CN=Administrator,CN=Users,DC=lt,DC=local")
Response.Write objAdmin.Name
' do any other processing on the object
Set objAdmin = Nothing
```

The key line in this bit of code is the call to the VBScript GetObject function. GetObject works in a similar way to Server.CreateObject. That is to say, it instantiates a COM object and returns a reference to it. The difference between GetObject and Server.CreateObject is that we supply the name of the type of the object we want to CreateObject, whereas GetObject takes a name that is unique for that very object, not just that *type* of object. In formal COM terms, GetObject takes something that's called a **Moniker**, but we're not going to go into that in this book, since Monikers require fairly advanced knowledge of COM, and GetObject hides all this stuff from us.

What this code does is instantiate a COM object which wraps around the corresponding object in the directory – a process that's known as **binding** to the directory object. This is an incredibly neat system. The COM object is an in-process object, so access to it is very efficient. We don't need to worry about the fact that the object in the directory may actually be located on a server on the other side of the world. We don't need to worry about what protocols or APIs are needed to talk to the directory service – the COM object takes care of all that for us. We can just call up methods and properties on this object, and it's as if we're talking to the actual object in the directory.

The only noticeable difference is that because the COM object stores a local (client-side) copy of all the information in the directory object, we will occasionally need to call a couple of methods on it to resynchronize its data with the data in the underlying directory service. The copy of the data held by the local COM object is known as the **property cache**. In most of this chapter I'll informally refer to the COM object as the ADSI object. That's not the correct technical term, but it's in common use. And it's simpler than saying: 'the COM object that wraps the underlying directory object' everywhere!

> *GetObject has been introduced at this point because it's the easiest way of binding to a directory object and is great for illustrating how ADSI works. Normally, we'd also want to pass some authentication credentials to the directory – which we can't do with GetObject. We'll see how to get round this problem later in the chapter.*

That code snippet has given us a glimpse of how simple ADSI is to use. Before we go on take a look at more code samples, we'll take a quick break to list the main ADSI Providers that are available, then we'll examine ADSI's object model in more detail.

The ADSI Providers

Just like the OLE DB Providers, it's not possible to give an exhaustive list of ADSI providers, because anyone can write a new provider if they want to. However, depending on our installation options, we'd usually find that ADSI comes with the following Microsoft-written providers installed for us. To some extent, this list recaps the earlier list of the directory services available. But here we are taking a different emphasis, looking at what providers are available rather than what directory services are available, and it's not always a one-to-one mapping.

- ❑ **LDAP**: This is used to access any directory that is LDAP-compliant.

- ❑ **WinNT**: This allows access to details of computers and users in a domain, as well as some information about individual machines, such as local user accounts.

- ❑ **IIS**: This connects to the IIS Metabase for IIS4 and IIS5. We can use this provider to configure our IIS settings.

- ❑ **NDS** and **NWCompat**: These two providers connect to Novell Directory Services. NDS is discussed in more detail in the next chapter.

Of these, the LDAP and WinNT providers are the ones we'd probably encounter most often. Because of the importance of these two providers, we'll take a further look at them here.

The LDAP Provider

The **LDAP** Provider gives access to any directory service that is LDAP-compliant. Since we may have several LDAP-directories on our system, this means that it might be able to access more than one directory.

We can distinguish between the directories because each directory service must be running on one or more server, and must be configured to be running on a particular port. We can think of ports simply as identification numbers. A given server will be listening for messages coming in, and direct them to the appropriate software to respond to them, based on the port number that each message identifies. For example, by default HTTP requests come in on port 80, and Telnet requests on port 23. LDAP requests by default use port 389, and Active Directory also uses this port.

We can specify an LDAP `ADsPath`, in the following way:

```
LDAP://[server-name][:port][/]<LDAP-distinguished-name>
```

Where the square brackets indicate optional information, and the angle brackets indicate information that we must provide. This means that the earlier `ADsPath` we gave for the administrator account isn't the only way of doing it. We had previously written:

```
LDAP://CN=Administrator,CN=Users,DC=lt,DC=local
```

Since my domain controller is called `CrashLots`, (I've only got one domain controller – I'm a single author, not a huge multinational organization), I could equally use the `ADsPath`:

```
LDAP://CrashLots/CN=Administrator,CN=Users,DC=lt,DC=local
```

Or:

```
LDAP://CrashLots:389/CN=Administrator,CN=Users,DC=lt,DC=local
```

Thus, we indicate first that we want to use the LDAP provider. Then we can optionally indicate the name of the server that we want to respond to our request, and the port number. If we omit these, the LDAP Provider will just query the nearest available domain controller, using port 389.

> *Although the documentation claims that ADSI will automatically locate the nearest domain controller, in practice, if ASP scripts are run on a member workstation, it usually doesn't manage to do this and returns an error instead. For this reason, it is good practice to supply the server name explicitly in LDAP ADsPaths, and we will do so in the examples in this chapter.*

It's quite possible to have different LDAP directory services hosted on the same machine, provided they respond to different port numbers. For example, we might have Active Directory listening on port 389, while Netscape Directory Server is listening on a different port (say 1025), and the Exchange Server 5.5 directory is on port 1026. Port numbers above 1024 are reserved for us to use as we want – they are not used for standard protocols in the way ports like 80 and 389 are.

The WinNT Provider

As mentioned above, WinNT gives access to a lot of domain information, though it's not restricted to just that. We can also use it to control print queues and file shares, and to start and stop NT services. There is nevertheless quite a bit of overlap between the information exposed through WinNT, the information exposed through Active Directory, and that available through the LDAP Provider. This may leave us wondering which to use.

The key point here is that the LDAP Provider can connect to Active Directory, which means it can get to *all* the information in Active Directory. That makes it very flexible, but also means we can only use it if our domain is controlled by W2K domain controllers. And – as is common in software development – flexibility comes at the price of increased complexity.

By contrast, the WinNT Provider doesn't necessarily use Active Directory. Internally, it uses Windows API calls to find out about a domain. That means it will also work on NT4-controlled domains where there is no Active Directory installation. But, even on Windows 2000, we may find the WinNT Provider easier to use for simple tasks. This is because it has been designed to expose only a small well-defined set of information. It has a simple schema and doesn't support schema extensions. `ADsPaths` are simpler in WinNT.

For example, compare the ADsPath of my local Administrator account with the WinNT Provider:

```
WinNT://LT/Administrator
```

With the LDAP Provider:

```
LDAP://Crashlots/CN=Administrator,CN=Users,DC=lt,DC=local
```

The ADsPath using WinNT is simpler, partly because of the simpler hierarchical structure exposed by the WinNT Provider, and partly because of its simpler format for forming ADsPaths – unlike LDAP, WinNT doesn't use the prefixes like CN, etc. It also separates components with slashes instead of commas.

> *We won't be using the WinNT provider in this chapter, but the WinNT* ADsPaths *and the data exposed by WinNT can be explored using* adsvw.exe.

One interesting point about the WinNT Provider is that it doesn't actually connect to an integrated directory. It uses Windows API calls and registry information from the various computers on a network, and gathers this information together to present it *as if* it is a unified directory. That's why, earlier on, we didn't list any directory corresponding to WinNT.

The ADSI Interface Model

This is the point in the chapter where, if we'd been talking about ADO, ADOX, RDO, or any of many other technologies, we'd probably give this section the heading 'The Whatever Object Model'. But we haven't – we've entitled this section 'The ADSI *Interface* Model'. The reason for this is that ADSI doesn't really have a small set of objects in the way that a technology such as ADO has. The design of ADSI is, to a far greater extent, based on interfaces. So much so that we'll very rarely even be aware of the type of object we are using.

To see why it works like this, think about how we query a data source with ADO. We might do it by instantiating an ADO command object, and using it to send an SQL statement to the data source. Something like this:

```
Set oCommand = Server.CreateObject("ADODB.Command")
oCommand.ActiveConnection = sConnString
oCommand.CommandType = adCmdText
oCommand.CommandText = sSQL
Set oRS = oCommand.Execute
```

In this code, sConnString is assumed to contain the appropriate connection string, and sSQL the SQL statement we want executed.

This works because the ADO Command object – as with all the other ADO objects – is a generic object that is capable of sending a command to any data source as long as an OLE DB provider for that source exists.

But remember that an ADSI object works by providing a wrapper around the corresponding directory object. For example, if we execute the code from our previous example:

```
Set objAdmin = GetObject("LDAP://CN=Administrator,CN=Users,DC=lt,DC=local")
```

We'll get an object that is specifically connected to the Administrator object. This object cannot be used to perform operations on any other object in the directory – it's specific to this directory object. But think of all the different directory objects around. Active Directory can store users, computers, groups, organizational units, domains, as well as objects that contain group policy information and other objects that contain details of the directory schema, to name a few, and there are many more directories.

Add to this the possibility of independent software vendors (ISVs) writing their own directories that are accessible through ADSI, and LDAP's ability to accept custom schema extensions, and the numbers of different possible types of directory object, each with its own different set of properties, becomes endless. So with ADSI it's not practical to base the object model on objects – because there are so many objects we might want to use. It's not like ADO where 7 or 8 different COM objects give us all we need. Instead, ADSI is based on interfaces.

Recall, from Chapter 6, that an interface is essentially a contract that says what methods, properties, events, and collections an object supports. In ADSI we are not interested in what type of COM object an ADSI object is, but we know that ADSI does require all ADSI objects to implement certain interfaces, which means we can still say that ADSI objects will expose certain properties, methods and collections. (ADSI doesn't support events – and we can't use events in ASP anyway).

> *An interface can be thought of as a set of properties, collections and methods that an object can implement. There is a lot more behind how interfaces work than that, which we'd need to be aware of if we were coding in C++, but the ASP script engines take care of all those details for us.*

As an example, all ADSI objects have a property, Name, which gives the name of the object. So given any ADSI object, we can always do this:

```
' sADsPath contains an ADsPath
Set objObject = GetObject(sADsPath)
Response.Write objObject.Name
```

Just as we did for the Administrator account in Active Directory. For example, this will work exactly the same for the object that corresponds to my domain controller, Crashlots, with the WinNT provider:

```
Set objDC = GetObject("WinNT://LT/CRASHLOTS")
Response.Write objDC.Name
```

And again, in exactly the same way for the object that represents my IIS WWW Service running on CrashLots:

```
Set objWWW = GetObject("IIS://CRASHLOTS/W3SVC")
Response.Write objWWW.Name
```

I could go on, but we should get the idea by now.

The property, Name, exists because it's part of an interface called IADs, which all ADSI objects implement.

There are a lot of ADSI interfaces; nearly 60 in total, but most of them are rarely used. In the next section, we're going to look at a couple of the most common ones, then we'll see how to use them.

The IADs Interface

The **IADs Interface** is arguably the most important interface because every ADSI object must implement it. This means that whenever we instantiate an ADSI object, we know that we will be able to talk to its IADs interfaces. This means that in principle all the methods and properties of this interface are available, although in practice we will find that there are a few ADSI objects for which some of the properties are not relevant, so we should still allow for the theoretical possibility of an error being raised when we attempt to reference some properties on some objects.

The **IADs properties** are all read-only and are as follows:

Property Name	Purpose
Name	The name of the object (usually the same as the least significant component of the ADsPath).
ADsPath	The full ADsPath of the object (in other words, the string we probably supplied to GetObject when we instantiated this object.
Class	The name of the class of this object.
Schema	The ADsPath of a class schema object which describes the properties of this class.
Parent	The ADsPath of the parent of this object – the container which contains this object.
Guid	Not always implemented. A string containing a unique GUID that can identify this object.

And the **IADs methods** are:

Method	Purpose
Get	Returns the value of a property from the cache.
GetEx	Similar to Get but returns the value in a slightly different format (we'll look at this a little later).
Put	Sets the value of a property in the cache.
PutEx	Similar to Put but has extra options to allow setting of multi-valued properties (for example, we can choose to add another property to the list, or remove a particular value, or remove all the values).
GetInfo	Populates the cache from the directory.
SetInfo	Updates the underlying directory by writing the information in the cache to it.
GetInfoEx	Similar to GetInfo but refreshes only a particular named property.

There are no IADs collections.

This list of methods is where we first see the distinction between the local COM object, containing the property cache, and the underlying directory object. All the properties and the Get, GetEx, Put and PutEx methods work with the local cache only. Then three extra methods are provided, GetInfo, SetInfo and GetInfoEx, which synchronize the cache with the directory object. Of these, SetInfo is the only one we'd normally use. GetInfo is automatically called implicitly on our behalf when the ADSI object first detects that we are attempting to access its cache – which is why the earlier code snippets that displayed the names of objects worked.

As an example of using these methods, user accounts have descriptions associated with them. Each of these contains a description of the purpose of the account. If we want to see what's in the description of the administrator account, we could do something like this:

```
' objADs points to the administrator account
Response.Write objADs.Get("Description")
```

In the table above we saw that GetEx() is similar to Get, but returns the result in a slightly different format. The difference is to do with the fact that some properties contain more than one value and so need to be returned in an array. Get will only return an array if there actually is more than one value, whereas GetEx will always return an array. The Description property only has one value, so Get returns a simple string, whereas GetEx returns an array. So, if we wanted to, we could rewrite the above code in the following way:

```
' objADs points to the administrator account
For Each sValue in objADs.GetEx("Description")
    Response.Write sValue & "<BR>"
Next
```

GetEx is useful if we don't know how many values are going to be returned, because we don't need to worry about what format the results will be returned in, whereas Get is slightly more efficient if we know in advance that only one value will be returned.

If we want to change the description to something else, we could do it like this:

```
' objADs points to the administrator account
objADs.Put("Description", "This is a powerful account!")
objADs.Put("homePhone", "345333")
objADs.SetInfo
```

Notice the call to SetInfo after the Put operation. If we missed that out then the new description would never get to the underlying directory object and so would be lost as soon as the ASP page finished running. In general, Put is a fast operation because it only acts on the local cache while SetInfo is slow because it will need to talk to the directory service, which is running in a different process, possibly on a different machine. Because of this, we will normally make all our changes in the local cache then call SetInfo once to send all our changes to the directory service in one go, as shown in the sample.

The IADsContainer Interface

IADsContainer is the interface that we need to browse down a directory. For example, to see what children an object has and to bind to them. Where IADs is implemented by all ADSI objects, the IADsContainer methods and properties are only implemented by those objects where the underlying directory object can contain children. For example, the Users container in Active Directory that contains all users clearly contains children, and therefore must implement IADsContainer.

In ASP, the easiest way to check whether an object can have any children is just to set On Error Resume Next, then call an IADsContainer method and see if it succeeds or not. It's not very elegant, but it works!

The neat thing about IADsContainer is that it makes the COM object we are talking to act as a collection. The things in the collection are the references to the ADSI objects that represent the children of the container. Let's illustrate this with an example. We'll take the users container in Active Directory. Recall that this is the object that is the parent to all the users and some of the groups, and which has the ADsPath:

```
LDAP://Crashlots/CN=Users,dc=lt,dc=local
```

The following code snippet binds to the object, displays its ADsPath and class (using the IADs properties) and then displays the names and classes of all its children:

```
Dim objCont, objUser
Set objCont = GetObject("LDAP://Crashlots/CN=Users,dc=lt,dc=local")
Response.Write "ADsPath: " & objCont.ADsPath & "<BR>"
Response.Write "Class: " & objCont.Class & "<BR>"

' now list the users and groups
For Each objChild In objCont
    Response.Write "ADsPath of user: " & objChild.Name"
    Response.Write "Class of user: " & objChild.Class"
Next
```

This architecture is powerful. Notice that each object in the collection is itself a full-blown ADSI COM object, just like the container we started off with, and implements all the normal ADSI interface methods and properties. In fact, if any of the children we've just enumerated over are themselves containers, we can use more nested For Each loops on them to enumerate their children, and so on. By this means, we can explore the entire directory programmatically.

It is worthwhile pointing out that if we want to go the other way – up the directory tree – we'd need to use the Parent property of the IADs interface. This property doesn't return an object – it just returns the ADsPath as a string, so we'll need to bind separately to the object:

```
' to get the parent of an object referenced by objADSI
Dim sParent, objParent
sParent = objADSI.Parent
Set objParent = GetObject(sParent)
```

Or more simply:

```
Dim objParent
Set objParent = GetObject(objADSI.Parent)
```

Besides acting as a collection, IADsContainer exposes the following properties and methods:

The `IADsContainer` properties are:

Property	Description
Filter	Used to restrict children enumerated to those of a particular type. If not set, then all children are enumerated.
Hints	Used to restrict the properties returned from enumerated children. This is provider-dependent, and if this property is not set then all properties on any enumerated children are returned.
Count	The number of children in the collection which satisfy the filter (some providers don't implement this property).

The `IADsContainer` methods are:

Method	Description
GetObject	Binds to a named ADSI object that is a child of the container. Allows us to bind to an object by specifying its name instead of its `AdsPath`.
MoveHere	Moves an ADSI object from anywhere within the same directory structure to be a child of this container.
CopyHere	Copies an ADSI object to be a child of this container.
Delete	Deletes an ADSI object which is a child of this container.
Create	Creates a new ADSI object which is a child of this container.

As we can see, besides allowing us to bind to children, `IADsContainer` includes the methods we need to move, copy, create and delete objects in the directory. We won't go into how to do that in this chapter, but full details of how to use these methods can be found in the MSDN documentation.

Of the properties, the `Filter` is the most interesting. To see how it's used, consider our earlier example of enumerating all the users and groups in a container. By itself, the `For Each` loop will pick up all the children. If, for instance, we were only interested in user, not groups, then that would be quite inefficient as we'd have to enumerate all the children, then pick out the ones we wanted (using the `Class` property). By using the `Filter` property on the container, we can restrict the enumeration so it only returns the Users:

```
' now list the users only
objCont.Filter = Array("User")
For Each objChild In objCont
    Response.Write "ADsPath of user: " & objChild.Name"
    Response.Write "Class of user: " & objChild.Class"
Next
```

Note that, when setting this property, we need to use an array. That's to allow us to specify more than one class of object to be returned.

Enumerating Children of an Object

So far, all the code we've presented is in the form of little code snippets. We've now got far enough to attempt a full ASP page. What we're going to do is attempt to reproduce a part of the tree that we saw displayed in `adsvw.exe`. We'll list out the containers under the domain object. That is, all the ones under `DC=lt,DC=local`. So far, that doesn't sound too useful, but we'll move on to more realistic operations soon.

Our first stab of the code isn't going to work quite how we might anticipate, because of the problem of authenticating to the directory service. We haven't tackled this yet, but we'll investigate this in the next section.

The complete code for the page is as follows. It shouldn't need any further explanation, as we've already gone over all the concepts used in it. We bind to the object representing my domain in Active Directory, display most of its `IADs` properties, and then list its children. For each child we give the name, class, and the description (if one exists):

```
<%@ Language = VBScript %>
<% Option Explicit %>

<!DOCTYPE HTML PUBLIC "-//W3C//DTD HTML 4.0 Transitional//EN">
<HTML>
<HEAD>
<TITLE>Enumerate Children</TITLE>
</HEAD>

<BODY>

This page binds to an ADSI object, displays its IADs properties
and lists its children.
<P>

<%
On Error Resume Next

Dim sADsPath
sADsPath = "LDAP://crashlots/dc=lt,dc=local"

' bind to the object
Dim objCont
Set objCont = GetObject(sADsPath)

If Err.number <> 0 then
   Response.Write "Problem authenticating to the object" & "<BR>"
   Response.Write Err.description & "<BR>"
   Response.Write Err.number & "<BR>"
Else
   Response.Write "<STRONG>Container object:</STRONG><BR>"
   Response.Write "ADsPath: " & objCont.ADsPath & "<BR>"
   Response.Write "Name: " & objCont.Name & "<BR>"
   Response.Write "Class: " & objCont.Class & "<BR>"
   Response.Write "Schema: " & objCont.Schema & "<BR>"
   Response.Write "Parent: " & objCont.Parent & "<BR>"
```

```
        Response.Write "<P>Children are:"
        Response.Write "<TABLE BORDER=2>"
        Response.Write "<THEAD><TH>Name</TH><TH>Class</TH>" & _
                        "<TH>Description</TH></THEAD>"
        Response.Write "<TBODY>"
        Dim oChild
        For Each oChild In objCont
            Response.Write "<TR><TD>" & oChild.Name & "</TD>"
            Response.Write "<TD>" & oChild.Class & "</TD>"
            Response.Write "<TD>" & oChild.Get("Description") & "</TD></TR>"
        Next
        Response.Write "</TBODY></TABLE>"
    End If
%>


</BODY>
</HTML>
```

Note that error checking in this script is fairly basic. We pick up on any failure to bind to the parent object and display an error message. Otherwise, we just charge through displaying its properties and the children's properties, relying on our `On Error Resume Next` to get us out of any trouble if any properties aren't defined for any particular objects (which does happen).

So far so good. The problem comes when we attempt to view the page. Here's what it produces on my system:

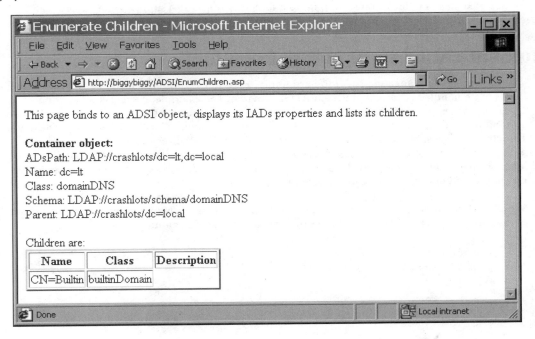

The page seems to have worked (although the `Description` property is clearly missing for the `BuiltIn` object), but it's only come up with one child, the `BuiltIn` node, which contains certain system-supplied groups. If we look back at our earlier `adsvw.exe` screenshots, we'll see that we're expecting quite a few children; the `Users` container, for a start, then the containers for the computers, the domain controllers, and several others. So what's gone wrong?

Well, the answer has to do with security. As I mentioned earlier, we've not attempted to supply any authentication credentials to the directory service. This page is running under IIS, which means it's running under the `IUSR_<machine name>` account, which has virtually no privileges. So we'd expect that Active Directory, being security-conscious, isn't going to hand over much information. In fact we'd probably be very worried if the Internet Guest account was able to query Active Directory for any of the confidential information stored there!

What's happened is that Active Directory has supplied the only information this account has access to read – which is basically the fact that a `BuiltIn` container exists. So our enumeration of children produced only the one result. We didn't encounter this problem when running the `adsvw.exe` screenshots, because we were there using the Windows user interface, logged in as a domain administrator!

It should be pointed out that the previous screenshot shows what happened on one particular system with specific security settings. If you have your security set up differently, then you may find different results, depending exactly what the Internet Guest account is allowed to access, or if IIS is set up to require authentication. For example, with lower security settings you may find all containers are correctly returned. Alternatively, with high security settings, you may get a timeout (authentication failures sometimes take a long time to return which can time out the page).

So our next step is to look at how to bind to a directory object *and* supply some authentication credentials to say who we are.

Authenticating to Directory Objects

The process of authenticating isn't too hard to master, but it's complicated by the fact that authentication needs to be handled separately by each ADSI Provider. For example, we're asking to connect to Active Directory, which is serviced by the LDAP Provider, and that means that the LDAP Provider needs to sort out the authentication. But the LDAP Provider couldn't help us with authenticating to, say, Novell Directory Services, because it only knows how to talk to LDAP directories. This means that authentication has to be a two-stage process. First we get talking to the provider we are interested in. Then we have to pass that provider some authentication credentials (a username and password) that it can use to authenticate to the directory service on our behalf.

We get talking to the provider by binding to what's known as the **Namespace Object**. That's the object whose `ADsPath` is just the name of the provider, followed by a colon:

```
Dim objNamespace
Set objNamespace = GetObject("LDAP:")
```

Or, if we want to authenticate using the WinNT Provider, for instance, we would use the following:

```
Dim objNamespace
Set objNamespace = GetObject("WinNT:")
```

Now, to actually pass in our user name and password, we need to call up a special method, `OpenDSObject`. This method is *only* implemented on the namespace objects. `OpenDSObject` needs four parameters: the `ADsPath` of the object we want, a user name and password, and a directory-dependent flag to indicate the authentication method we want to use. For authenticating using Windows security this flag has the value 1.

> `OpenDSObject` is the only method exposed by another ADSI interface, `IADsOpenDSObject`, which must be implemented by all namespace objects.

If we put all this together, then what we need to do to our previous ASP page is to remove the call to `GetObject` that did the binding to the original `DC=lt, DC=local` container, and replace it with this. Here we've used the administrator account for simplicity, though in a real project, for security reasons, we'd probably prefer to set up another account specifically for use in ASP pages that need to access Active Directory.

```
Dim sADsPath
sADsPath = "LDAP://crashlots/dc=lt,dc=local"
```

```
' bind to the object supplying a username and password
Dim sUserName, sPassword
sUserName = "CN=Administrator, CN=Users,dc=lt,dc=local"
sPassword = "Nice Password"

Dim oNamespace
Set oNamespace = GetObject("LDAP:")
Dim objCont
Set objCont = oNamespace.OpenDSObject(sADsPath, sUserName, sPassword, 1)
```

```
If Err.number <> 0 then
    Response.Write "Problem authenticating to the object" & "<BR>"
    Response.Write Err.description & "<BR>"
    Response.Write Err.number & "<BR>"
Else
    Response.Write "<STRONG>Container object:</STRONG><BR>"
    Response.Write "ADsPath: " & objCont.ADsPath & "<BR>"
    Response.Write "Name: " & objCont.Name & "<BR>"
End If
```

Now if we run the page we find it works correctly:

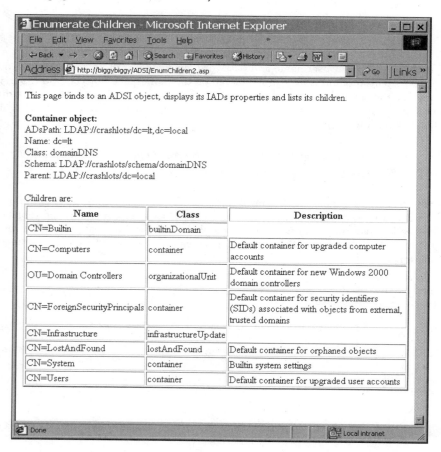

You might be wondering about the username we supplied, and why we didn't just give the username Administrator. The reason is that the way LDAP directories work is they expect us to authenticate *as an object in the directory*. In other words, the username we give should be the actual distinguished name of the administrator's user account in Active Directory.

To simplify things, Microsoft has allowed a couple of alternatives for Active Directory. We could have supplied the downlevel login name LT\Administrator (the downlevel name has the format *<domain-name>\<account-name>*). We could, alternatively, supply an e-mail address, if one has been set up in the user's directory object. But Administrator by itself won't work, (although if we were using the WinNT Provider, Administrator by itself would be the correct way of authenticating).

Listing Domain Users

Although our example works fine, it's probably still not the sort of ASP page we'd find very useful in a production environment. One thing, however, that we might realistically want to do is list the users registered in a domain. We can do this very simply by just changing the `ADsPath` of the object we bind to be the container of the users:

```
On Error Resume Next

Dim sADsPath
sADsPath = "LDAP://crashlots/cn=users,dc=lt,dc=local"

' bind to the object supplying a username and password
Dim sUserName, sPassword
sUserName = "CN=Administrator,CN=Users,dc=lt,dc=local"
sPassword = "Nice Password"
```

Remember, though, that we only want to list the users, not any other objects. So we'll set the filter before we enumerate. We'll also make one other change. Instead of displaying the `Name` of the ADSI object (which gives us those annoying `CN=` prefixes), we'll display a property called the `sAMAccountName` – this is just the name that we'd type into the Windows login dialog to login to that account.

```
Response.Write "<P>Children are:"
Response.Write "<TABLE BORDER=2>"
Response.Write "<THEAD><TH>sAMAccountName</TH><TH>Class</TH>" & _
               "<TH>Description</TH></THEAD>"
Response.Write "<TBODY>"
Dim oChild
objCont.Filter = Array("User")
For Each oChild In objCont
    Response.Write "<TR><TD>" & oChild.Get("sAMAccountName") & "</TD>"
    Response.Write "<TD>" & oChild.Class & "</TD>"
    Response.Write "<TD>" & oChild.Get("Description") & "</TD></TR>"
Next
Response.Write "</TBODY></TABLE>"
```

With these few changes in place, we now have an ASP page that tells us about all the user accounts in the domain:

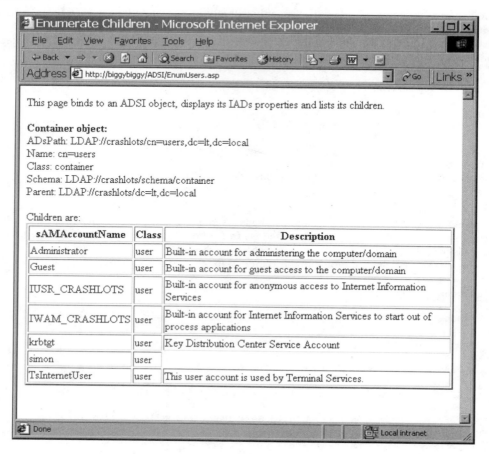

Clearly, there are not many user accounts in this particular domain – but then this is just a home domain.

We have seen that we can access quite a bit of useful information without having to write that much code. The sorts of application we might want to utilize this information with would be, perhaps, a web page that allows administrators to remotely administer user accounts.

Searching

So far in this chapter we've seen how to use the ADSI interfaces to browse through a directory. But often we're not really interested in doing that. What we want is to look for specific information. We might, say, want to know which of the administrator user accounts haven't seen a log in for at least a week, or which of our print queues is currently not working. These kinds of queries can involve combining several properties into a single request.

Another aspect of such queries is that we frequently wouldn't care about the location of the objects, we just want to know what their properties are. In other words, we might not know anything about the directory structure. If we're looking for, say, user accounts, we might not know or want to know where in the directory they are. It's possible that some accounts may be stored at one location in the directory hierarchy and others are located somewhere completely different in the hierarchy. A search allows us to pick out all these users anyway.

This is a very different situation from what we've seen so far, in which we bind to a particular object using the fact that we know exactly where it is in the directory (because we know its ADsPath). And it requires a somewhat different programming solution. In fact, we are actually going to go back to using ADO. Although ADSI does supply an interface, IDirectorySearch, which is designed to let us perform searches, this interface is really designed for use by C++ clients and cannot be used directly from VB or scripting languages. Instead, for these languages, Microsoft has supplied an OLE DB Provider for ADSI; in other words, an OLE DB Provider that talks to the IDirectorySearch interface on our behalf, allowing us to request search queries. At present, this provider exists solely for that purpose. We cannot use it, for example, to write to a directory.

This means that when we search directories using ADSI, our request passes through a chain like this:

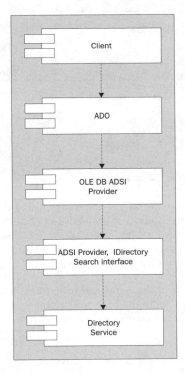

We're going to see how to use the OLE DB Provider for ADSI, but first we're going to get a flavor of what searching involves by using the adsvw.exe user interface tool to request some searches.

To do this we bring up `adsvw.exe`, and request a new **Query**:

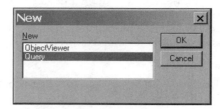

This brings up another dialog box asking us to specify our query in detail. In this screenshot, I've filled in this dialog with the values needed to request that all users be returned:

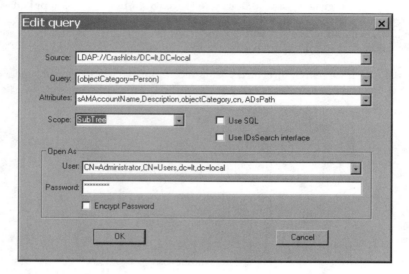

In this dialog, the **Query** specifies what we're looking for, using the special language that LDAP defines for this purpose. We'll look at this in just a short while. **Attributes** specifies the names of the attributes that we're interested in. We've asked for the usual sAMAccountName, Description and ADsPath. We've also asked for the objects' common names (cn) and a multivalued property called objectCategory, which is another way of indicating the nature of the object.

Searching only gives us the values of the requested properties, it doesn't give us references to any ADSI objects. So if we want to be able to actually bind to the objects returned, we'll need to make sure that we specify the ADsPath as one of the properties we want returned, then use the ADsPath to bind separately to the objects.

The Source and the Scope between them tell the directory service whereabouts in the directory to search for the objects. The way they work is that we need to specify the ADsPath of an object, the source (more commonly called the **search base**), and the search will be conducted only among that object and objects below it in the directory hierarchy.

How far down the hierarchy is determined by the search scope, which can have one of three values:

Base	Only the base object is examined. This option is useful if we just want to check if a given object exists and satisfies certain criteria.
OneLevel	The children of the base object (but not the base object itself) will be examined. This is similar to enumerating the children of a container, except that we can apply a much more sophisticated filter to the results.
SubTree	The most common option. The base object will be searched as will all its descendents; its children, and their children, and so on. This is the option we'd use if we don't know where in the directory tree the objects we are looking for are located.

In this example, we've specified the base to be the domain object at the top of the Active Directory hierarchy and the scope to be SubTree, which in this case means that the whole of Active Directory will be searched. Clearly, the more we can narrow down the search, the more efficient it will be.

Finally, in the above dialog box we've specified a user name and password. We don't strictly need to do this since we're already logged in, running adsvw.exe as a domain administrator anyway, so if we left these blank, the resultant default credentials would still get us almost unlimited access to the directory.

When we OK this dialog box, we'll get another dialog asking us to specify some more advanced options that mostly affect the efficiency of the search, but we can just OK the second dialog without filling anything in. We then get this result:

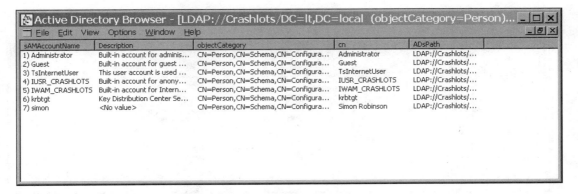

At first sight it looks like all we've done is enumerate the users inside the user container. But we've actually done more than that. Remember that these search results are based on searching the entire directory. Although users get put in the container CN=Users,DC=lt, DC=local by default, there's nothing to stop systems administrators from placing user accounts elsewhere in Active Directory.

In fact, for a large organization, the whole idea is that we can organize accounts better by creating hierarchies of containers to place them in (for example, this can make it easier to apply security policies by applying permissions, etc. to entire containers). If we'd been browsing containers in such a system, we'd have a lot more work to do to find all the users. But doing a search will locate all of them, wherever they are, in one go. Of course, if we want to modify the properties of any users, we'd still have to bind to them and use the IADs interface in the normal way.

The other place where we see the power of searching is when we come to apply more complex search filters. Let's see how LDAP search filters work. The one we used was:

```
(objectCategory=Person)
```

This specifies a property and says what value the property has to have. This filter worked here because all Active Directory objects happen to have a multi-valued property called `objectCategory`, which includes the value, `Person`, for objects that represent user accounts, as we can see from the previous search results.

We can use wildcards, and we can combine conditions using the operators & (and), | (or) and ! (not). The only somewhat unusual feature is that these operators have to precede the conditions rather than coming between them, in a notation that mathematicians sometimes call *Reverse Polish Notation* (after some early calculators that used a similar way of entering data before the days of mass-electronics). This syntax is similar to that used in LISP.

So, for example, to find all user accounts whose `sAMAccountNames` begin with s we might write:

```
(&(objectCategory=Person)(sAMAccountName=s*))
```

Or, for a massive condition, suppose for some reason we wanted to find all user accounts that equalled or came later than `guest` alphabetically, and all the computer accounts. The condition we'd need is:

```
(|(&(objectCategory=Person)(sAMAccountName>=guest))(objectCategory=Computer))
```

It looks complex, but if we carefully expand out the brackets we should be able to see how this expression leads to the required condition.

Here's the result of trying out that particular filter in `adsvw.exe`:

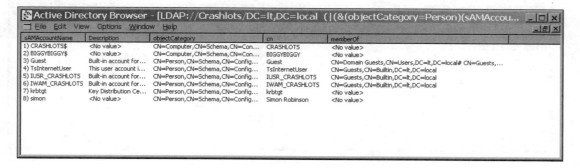

It seems that not only do I not have that many users on my home computer network, I don't have too many computers either!

One point to watch out with search filters is that while >= (greater than or equal) and <= (less than or equal) are accepted, < and > are not recognized. If we wanted to modify the above search to only return results greater than `guest` alphabetically, we'd have to combine the <= and ! operators to do it:

```
(|(&(objectCategory=Person)(!(sAMAccountName<=guest)))
    (objectCategory=Computer))
```

In the process of experimenting with adsvw.exe, we've actually picked up all the concepts we need to be able to code up searches from ASP pages. That's the final thing we'll look at in this chapter.

Searching with ADO

Searching with the OLE DB ADSI Provider works in much the same as issuing queries with any other ADO Provider. We make the query by executing a command from any of the Command, Connection or Recordset objects. And the results are returned in a recordset. As we might expect, the rows of the returned recordset correspond to the objects returned and the columns to the properties. All we need to look at here is the syntax of the commands.

The name of the OLE DB ADSI Provider is ADsDSOObject. The syntax is somewhat more complex as there are two different syntaxes in common use. One is designed to look a bit like SQL, and the other (which Microsoft calls the LDAP syntax) involves listing the parameters of the search separated by semi-colons. (This Microsoft name is somewhat misleading, since it has little to do with any syntax defined by the LDAP protocol, beyond the fact that both the LDAP and SQL syntaxes contain the LDAP search filter.)

It's entirely a matter of preference which we use. We'll opt for the LDAP syntax here, since it does lead to slightly shorter command strings. With this syntax, we form the command string as follows:

```
<base>;filter;properties;scope
```

In other words, we just list the four strings that we typed into the dialog in adsvw.exe, separating them by semicolons, and enclosing the ADsPath of the base object in angled brackets. So, for example, our initial attempt to search for all users becomes:

```
<LDAP://Crashlots/dc=lt,dc=local>;(objectCategory=person);
sAMAccountName,Description,objectCategory,cn,ADsPath;subtree
```

To demonstrate this, we're going to do an ASP page that searches for all users. To keep the table down to a reasonable size, we won't ask for all the properties we asked for before, we'll just go for the sAMAccountName, the common name, and the ADsPath. Here's the code for the page:

```
<%@ Language = VBScript %>
<% Option Explicit %>

<!DOCTYPE HTML PUBLIC "-//W3C//DTD HTML 4.0 Transitional//EN">
<HTML>
<HEAD>
<TITLE> Search for users</TITLE>
</HEAD>

<BODY>

This page uses ADSI to search Active Directory for all users <P>

<%
On Error Resume Next

' set up and display command text
Dim sSearchBase
sSearchBase = "LDAP://Crashlots/dc=lt,dc=local"
```

```
Dim sFilter
sFilter = "(objectCategory=person)"
Dim sAttribs
sAttribs = "sAMAccountName,cn,ADsPath"
Dim sScope
sScope = "subtree"

Dim sCommandText
sCommandText = "<" & sSearchBase & ">;" & _
              sFilter & ";" & sAttribs & ";" & sScope
Response.Write "<STRONG>Command Text is: </STRONG><BR>"
Response.Write Server.HTMLEncode(sCommandText) & "<P>"

' bind to Active Directory and execute search
Dim objConnection
Set objConnection = Server.CreateObject("ADODB.Connection")
objConnection.Open "Provider=ADsDSOObject", _
                   "CN=Administrator, CN=Users,dc=lt,dc=local", _
                   "Nice Password"
Dim objRS
Set objRS = objConnection.Execute(sCommandText)

' display search results
Response.Write "<TABLE BORDER=2>"
Response.Write "<THEAD><TH>sAMAccountName</TH><TH>cn</TH>" & _
              "<TH>ADsPath</TH></THEAD>"
Response.Write "<TBODY>"

While Not objRS.EOF
   Response.Write "<TR>"
   Response.Write "<TD>" & objRS("sAMAccountName") & "</TD>"
   Response.Write "<TD>" & objRS("cn") & "</TD>"
   Response.Write "<TD>" & objRS("ADsPath") & "</TD>"
   Response.Write "</TR>"
   objRS.MoveNext
Wend
Response.Write "</TBODY</TABLE>"

Set objRS = Nothing
Set objConnection = Nothing

%>


</BODY>
</HTML>
```

The guts of this code are where we create the ADO connection object and use it to execute the command:

```
Dim objConnection
Set objConnection = Server.CreateObject("ADODB.Connection")
objConnection.Open "Provider=ADsDSOObject", _
                   "CN=Administrator,CN=Users,dc=lt,dc=local", _
                   "Nice Password"
Dim objRS
Set objRS = objConnection.Execute(sCommandText)
```

Notice that all we need for the connection string is the name of the provider. We pass in the user name and password as separate parameters to the Open method of the connection object.

The command string we've constructed ends up looking like this:

```
<LDAP://Crashlots/dc=lt,dc=local>;(objectCategory=person);
sAMAccountName,cn,ADsPath;subtree
```

And when we run the page we get these results:

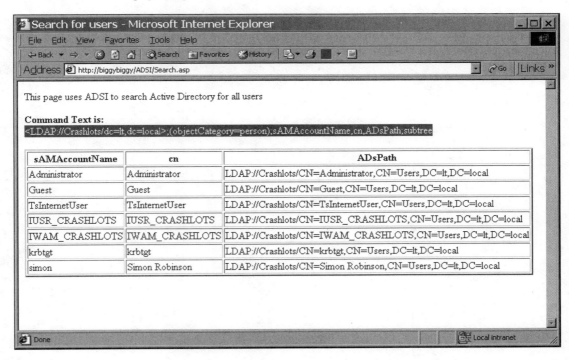

We can confirm that the search has executed already by comparing this with the adsvw.exe screenshot that we saw earlier.

Summary

ADSI is a large subject; there are a huge number of ADSI interfaces which we can use to access far more functionality than we've had space to discuss here. For example, we can use ADSI to start and stop NT services, to manage print queue, file shares, IIS configuration, and the data in the Exchange directory. We can also use it to read and modify any information stored in LDAP-compliant directories on a system.

What we have seen in this chapter is how easy it is to use ADSI to bind to directory objects and perform simple operations on those objects, as well as complex searches, and how to do this from ASP pages.

19

NDS and ASP

In this chapter, we're going to investigate the use of Novell Directory Services (NDS). In particular, we'll look at:

❑   A brief history of NDS

❑   The NDS structure

❑   Extending the schema

❑   Using tools (such as ADSI and ActiveX Controls)

Directory services (DSs) are primarily used as network administration tools (for such things as handling user's rights) but DSs don't have to be used only in this way. DSs also have the ability to handle and receive large amounts of data and return values in a very efficient manner. This chapter also discusses this little-used aspect of DS's and how we can use this feature in our web application development.

What is NDS?

Directory services became popular, and came to be seen as essential, around the same time as the Internet began to be widely available. Directory services were called on to handle multiple server addresses or IPs and the ever-increasing amount of e-mail addresses. In 1986, a group was formed called ISO/CCITT. This created the X.500 standards on which LDAP (Lightweight Directory Access Protocol) is based.

Novell was one of the first companies to create a formal directory based upon this X.500 standard. This began with the release of NetWare 4.0 in 1993. NDS – or Novell Directory Services – was used to replace the old Bindery system that existed on previous versions of NetWare. It should be noted that NDS is *not* NetWare, as is commonly assumed. NetWare is the Network OS, and NDS is an application that runs on NetWare. NDS is important to NetWare, but NDS runs on many different Network OSs.

NDS is a scalable, replicable database of objects in the network. This includes printers, other servers, workstations, and individuals. It allows simple administration of these various network objects including rights, usage logs, and personal information. This information is stored in a hierarchical format similar to a tree layout, hence the term "NDS tree".

This layout has many advantages, similar to hierarchical Java classes. Objects and users can gain specific rights depending on which branch they are in. So for example, the marketing branch of the NDS tree uses the marketing printer. We only have to enter that information once in the NDS tree, and everyone that is added to the marketing branch automatically has access to that printer. Now assume someone in marketing gets transferred to IT, the appropriate user object gets transferred to the IT branch and inherits all the rights of being in IT.

NDS trees can be replicated over many servers in many different locations. The replication can be automatically set, forced to certain time intervals, or fired when a specific event happens. The main advantage of replication is that it can improve data availability. If a server goes down in New York, the information can still be available in San Francisco, for instance.

Data validity is maintained as both directory services loosely contain the same information. They only *loosely* contain the same information, because so much depends on the replication method used. If we have two servers, A and B, and our replication event is fired when either DS is updated, then if server A goes down, server B would have more up-to-date information.

If we have a DS that is constantly being updated, we can update A whenever B is updated. However, this could increase network traffic quite considerably. An alternative would be to use a timed interval. With a timed interval of replication, we would only run the risk of losing the data entered into the DS during a specific period. The same issues arise when dealing with replication issues with large databases.

NDS is **LDAP** (**Lightweight Directory Access Protocol**) compliant. Using LDAP we can easily access NDS via the web or across various networking connections. It also enables us to modify, search, and delete entries in the NDS tree.

So NDS is more than just a network administration tool. It also acts as a fast, efficient data store. And the newest version of NDS, **eDirectory**, runs on virtually all network operating systems: Linux, Unix, Sun Solaris, Windows NT and 2000, Tru64, and, of course, NetWare.

NDS is a mature package. Over the years Novell has changed, enhanced, and expanded NDS to become very scalable and easy to administer. Novell has developed an NDS tree with 2 million objects which has a seek time of 250 milliseconds.

> *More NDS performance benchmarks may be found at*
> `www.novell.com/competitive/nds/bench.html`
>
> *Detailed information and a 90 day trial of eDirectory can be found at*
> `www.developer.novell.com`

NDS Layouts and Rules

NDS is based on the X.500 standards. These standards also apply to NetWare. Because NDS is a mature directory service, the layouts have been expanded somewhat to further enhance the DS.

Since there is a hierarchical structure – like a tree – we have a root object, container objects, and leaf objects:

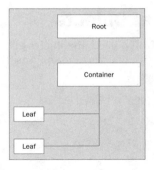

It is important to note that there can only be one root object to the tree. We can have many container objects off that root object, but only one root object.

Container Objects

Container objects are by definition objects that contain other objects, including other container objects and leaf objects. NDS has many different types of container objects. Each container has its own pre-defined properties. Some of the container objects available are:

- ❏ Country
- ❏ Organization
- ❏ Organizational Unit
- ❏ Locality

These are defined so as to aid in the development of our tree. For example, assume we are building a tree for a large multinational corporation. Our container layout could look like this:

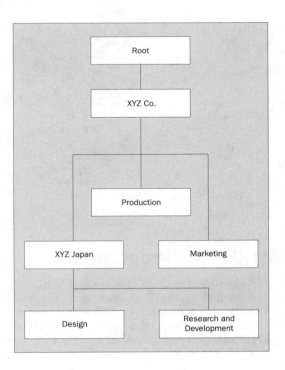

Leaf Objects

Leaf objects are objects that do not contain other objects. These objects are to be used in conjunction with the container objects. Each one has its own predefined set of attributes. Some of the predefined leaf objects are:

- ❑ User
- ❑ Organizational Role
- ❑ Group
- ❑ Printer
- ❑ Printer Queue
- ❑ Server

For an example of using the leaf objects we will just expand on the aforementioned example. Joe, Sally, and Printer are leaf objects contained in the Marketing container:

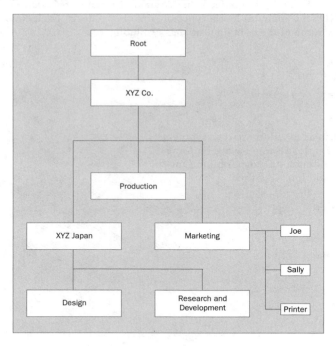

Attributes/Properties

The container and leaf objects come with some predefined attributes or properties. These might include such things as Name, Network address, and SecurityEqualTo. Each object contains a large number of properties, not all of which need to be used. A definitive list of the NDS objects and their corresponding properties is beyond the scope of this book. We can view the available properties of the various objects using ConsoleOne or ScheMax, both which are available for free download at http://www.novell.com/download/#NDS

It is important to know that some attributes can contain more than one value. It is important to realize this before trying to retrieve values from the DS.

Custom Objects

Although we can implement NDS right out of the box by using the predefined objects in the schema, certain situations may require that we customize NDS to meet our own needs. We can define our own objects to suit our needs by using **ConsoleOne** or **ScheMax**. ConsoleOne is a Java-based application that allows administration of NDS and has a built-in Schema Manager which allows us to create our own custom objects as well as to modify the schema to suit our needs. ScheMax is a similar tool which allows us to extend, delete, and move objects around the NDS tree easily.

> *A word of caution on extending the schema. We will want to develop our extended schema in a stand-alone environment separate from any production trees. The reason is that the schema changes can inadvertently replicate throughout the network if we don't want them to and some cannot be undone.*

Naming Objects

An NDS object can be referenced either by its **Fully Distinguished Name** (FDN, or simply DN), or by its **Relative Distinguished Name** (RDN). The FDN of an object must always be unique in its tree. The names are important to NDS as a whole because it allows NDS to easily locate information. The naming system is designed so that the FDN points all the way back to the root of the tree, thus ensuring uniqueness within our directory.

FDNs work in this way so that we can distinguish uniqueness inside our directory. Objects inside the directory existing in different branches can have the same name, so we can have two John Smiths; one in Marketing, and another in Programming. FDNs will enable us to distinguish between the two.

To put all this into perspective, let's consider the adjacent tree layout:

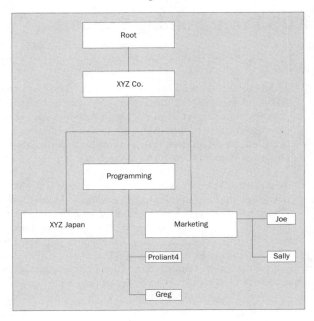

The FDN of Joe would be CN=Joe.OU=Marketing.O=XYZCorp. The FDN of Proliant4 would be CN=Proliant4.OU=Programming.O=XYZCorp. These names are created by walking up the tree from the CN.

For example, we start with Joe, and walk up the tree to the container object; Marketing. Marketing is an Organizational Unit container and therefore it is described in the FDN as OU=Marketing. Again we step up the tree and come to XYZ Corp. This container is an Organization type and is therefore denoted by O=XYZCorp. This type of naming is often referred to as **typeful** naming.

There is another naming convention type called **typeless** naming. This convention allows us to name the objects without including the type of object. For example, in the above mentioned example we included the type of objects (CN=Joe.OU=Marketing.O=XYZCorp). Using a typeless naming convention allows the user to use Joe.Marketing.XYZCorp to trace the route back to the root.

Developing for NDS

Now that we have a basic overview of NDS we can start developing NDS enabled applications.

NDS is basically a type of database. We can programmatically add, edit, and remove objects much like records in a normal relational database. We can also query the database using various methods such as ActiveX controls, JavaBeans, ODBC, and JDBC drivers to retrieve information for a web page or a client/server application.

As we saw earlier, NDS can be implemented on *any* Network OS. The advantage of this is that information can be shared throughout a network. A single tree can run on a hybrid network with little to no extra configuration. This allows us to expand beyond use of a single platform, and increases the scalability of our application.

NDS Programming Support

ADSI

Microsoft and Novell have released an **ADSI** (**Active Directory Service Interfaces**) provider for NDS. ADSI providers work much the same way as the ADO object, and are based on Microsoft's COM (Component Object Model). These providers allow us to program to multiple directory services. In order to be able to communicate to these different directory services, the appropriate provider must be installed. In much the same way as the appropriate ODBC, JDBC or OLE DB object must be installed when we want to connect to a database.

Microsoft's ADSI Provider for NDS relies on the Microsoft NetWare Client being installed. For client machines that are not using Microsoft NetWare Client (which is installed by default when NDS for Windows 2000 or NT is installed), Novell provides its own ADSI provider, which can be downloaded free from http://developer.novell.com/downloadablefiles/download/binaries/novelldeveloperkit/adsi.exe. You will need to install either this provider or the Microsoft NetWare client in order to use ADSI with NDS. To install the provider, simply unpack the downloaded .exe and run the setup.bat file. This is unpacked to the /NDK/ADSI/install folder under the directory to which the .exe was unpacked.

> We looked at ADSI in more detail in Chapter 18. A very detailed look at using the
> Microsoft ADSI providers can be found in Professional ADSI Programming, ISBN 1-
> 861002-26-2, also from Wrox Press.

Novell's ADSI provider closely follows the Microsoft specifications for ADSI providers.

Accessing NDS Objects from ASP

Because we looked at ADSI in the previous chapter, and because there is little difference between using
the NDS provider and other ADSI providers, we'll just show a very quick example here. This page
simply allows the user to input the ADsPath, and displays a list of the optional and mandatory
properties for the object:

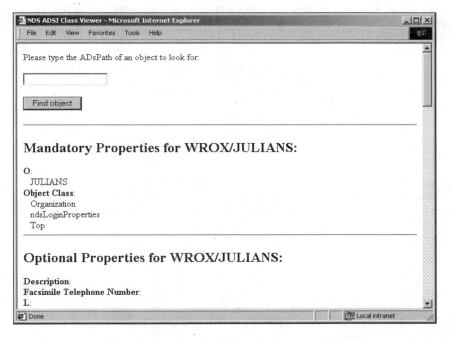

The page contains a form with the ACTION set to itself, where the user can input the ADsPath to look
for, so when we load the page, the first things to do are display this form and check whether an
ADsPath has already been submitted:

```
<TITLE>NDS ADSI Class Viewer</TITLE>
<FORM ACTION="adsi.asp" METHOD="POST" NAME="myForm">
    Please type the ADsPath of an object to look for:<BR><BR>
    <INPUT TYPE="TEXT" NAME="ADsPath"><BR><BR>
    <INPUT TYPE="SUBMIT" VALUE="Find object">
</FORM>
<%
On Error Resume Next
ADsPath = Request.Form("ADsPath")
If ADsPath <> "" Then
```

Note the `On Error Resume Next` line here – attempting to get a reference to a non-existing object will generate an error, so we need to include this basic error handling.

If an ADsPath has been submitted, we try to retrieve the object with the VBScript `GetObject` function. We're only interested in the NDS namespace here, so we prefix the string `"NDS://"` to our ADsPath. We then check whether this object exists; if it doesn't, we display an error message:

```
    Set objNDS = GetObject("NDS://" & ADsPath)
    If objNDS Is Nothing Then
        Response.Write "The object <B>" & ADsPath & "</B> does not exist " & _
                        "in the NDS namespace."
```

If the object does exist, we first iterate through the `MandatoryProperties` collection of its `Schema` object. For each of these properties, we retrieve an array of values by calling the `GetEx` method of our object, and iterate through this array to display each value:

```
    Else
        Response.Write "<HR><H2>Mandatory Properties for " & ADsPath & ":</H2>"
        Set objSchema = GetObject(objNDS.Schema)
        For Each prop In objSchema.MandatoryProperties
            Response.Write "<B>" & prop & "</B>:<BR>"
            For Each Value In objNDS.GetEx(prop)
                Response.Write "   " & Value & "<BR>"
            Next
        Next
```

Next we loop through the `OptionalProperties` collection. Apart from the collection name, this code is identical to the previous section. There's one point to bear in mind, though. All of the mandatory properties will have at least one value, but this isn't the case for optional properties. Our call to `objNDS.GetEx(prop)` will actually generate an error if the property has no values. This is another reason why we need our `On Error Resume Next` line above:

```
        Response.Write "<HR><H2>Optional Properties for " & ADsPath & ":</H2>"
        Set objSchema = GetObject(objNDS.Schema)
        For Each prop In objSchema.OptionalProperties
            Response.Write "<B>" & prop & "</B>:<BR>"
            For Each Value In objNDS.GetEx(prop)
                If Value <> "" Then
                    Response.Write "   " & Value & "<BR>"
                End If
            Next
        Next
    End If
End If
%>
```

LDAP

LDAP (**Lightweight Directory Access Protocol**) is expected to be the standard for accessing directory information through a browser. It is also expected that in the near future browsers will have standard LDAP features built-in.

LDAP allows us to create applications and deploy them over LDAP compliant directories such as NDS and Microsoft's Active Directory. This minimizes our cross-platform development time and still allows us to create extremely powerful web applications without extensive load on servers.

LDAP can be used through many of the standard server languages/components on the market such as Java (through JNDI – Java Naming and Directory Interface), and ActiveX.

LDAP programs can be written using C++ or Java to create server applications that are not necessarily required to run through a browser. Such applications could be designed to undertake certain sorts of administration, or anything else that requires accessing directory information.

Developing with LDAP

NDS is LDAP compliant and has been for a while. Novell has several libraries to use when developing with LDAP for NDS. These include C and Java libraries.

Novell also has an Internet Directory ActiveX control that enables users to be able to utilize LDAP in their web pages and VB applications. These are also available from the DeveloperNet website at `http://developer.novell.com/ndk/`. Each component includes proper documentation for its use.

ActiveX

Novell has released a series of ActiveX controls, among other things, enable easy access to NDS through IIS web and one of the many OLE-enabled languages such as VB or VC++. These controls can work as efficiently as ADSI, while considerably reducing development time. Having a good understanding of these controls allows us – the developer – to build stand-alone, client and server side applications.

The controls specific to NDS are as follows:

Control	Application
Browser Control	The browser control has a GUI component that allows us to use it in conjunction with other controls to retrieve information from NDS and other LDAP directories. This provides a solid front-end to the Directory, Inter Directory, and Volume Administration controls.
Catalog Administration Control	This control is used with the NDS catalog objects, and allows us to refresh, set dredging properties, update, and limit the Catalog database.
Directory Administration Control	This control allows us to work with the replicas and partitions of the NDS tree. The features include allowing someone to access, create, merge, and modify the partitions and replications.
Directory Control	This is the primary control used to interact with NDS. This control allows us to work with the information stored in the tree including allowances to extend the schema, modify entries, and add, delete and search entries.
Directory Query Control	As its name suggests, this control allows us to query entries in the NDS tree. This allows us to set time limits, filters, and the number of returns from a query.

Table continued on following page

Control	Application
Internet Directory Control	This control allows us to create LDAP applications to access LDAP-compliant directories.
Internet Directory Query Control	This control is identical to the Directory Query Control but is used for creation of LDAP applications.
User Group Control	This control allows us to work with the User and Group objects in the NDS tree. This includes add, modify, delete, and search.
Session Control	The Session control allows us to log in and out of the NDS tree.

Downloading and Installing the ActiveX Controls

The ActiveX controls can be downloaded and installed in one bundle. After this has been done, we can register or unregister the controls from the Novell Controls for ActiveX item on the Start | Programs menu. We need to ensure that the controls are also installed on the same machine as our web server.

We are going to use the NWDir control in our example, so we would copy the NWDir.ocx file to the System folder. We can then register it in the familiar way with:

```
Regsvr32 nwdir.ocx
```

This will register the ActiveX control with the system for use.

JavaBeans

Novell has also released **JavaBeans**, which can be used with JSP (JavaServer Pages) and ASP. These are similar to the corresponding ActiveX controls, so we will not go into any great detail on them.

These NDS-related JavaBeans are available from the Novell website:

❑ Directory

❑ Session

❑ Volume Administration

Universal Component System (UCS)

The **Universal Component System** (**UCS**) is a component system that enables us to use different objects such as JavaBeans, Perl Objects, and ActiveX controls in server scripts running on a NetWare server.

UCS is native to the NetWare platform, and consequently has some of its own components called UCX. These include the NDO object and others.

Programming NDS for the Web

Since this is a book about accessing data from Active Server Pages, we might wonder what NDS can do for our web programming?

Well, NDS is fast and extremely scalable. It outperforms Microsoft's Active Directory by a long way (http://www.novell.com/competitive/nds/bench.html). As we have seen, it is extremely scalable as it enables us to scale out over different platforms.

NDS can be used to store user information and provide high levels of security to our web site. However, even if we have Admin access, we cannot view and edit the tree except via ConsoleOne or some other application. The DS files cannot be removed from the server, and viewing them requires the use of a particular console such as Rconsole.

These files are hidden even from the system itself. Therefore, if people break into our web site and they think that they can get at important information, they won't even be able to see the file from which such information could be retrieved.

There are utilities that provide administrators with access to the DS in various capacities, and allow administrative tasks such as backups to be undertaken. However, such backup utilities need to be run at the console itself.

Using NDS for Security

This is a simple application, but we will get a solid understanding of logging into a web site using NDS and how it can be of some use to us.

Let's begin with a main page on which users have to enter a username and password in order to enter our site (which we will call index.htm).

To process the user request, we need to grab their login and password information. In our example, we will use the HTML form fields text and password to receive the input, and will post that information to another web page called login.asp. The login page has modes; a processor mode, success mode, and fail mode.

Here is the working part of the HTML code for index.htm:

```
<FORM METHOD=POST ACTION="login.asp?mode=login">
    <P>Login:<INPUT ID=txtLogin NAME=txtLogin></P>
    <P>Password:<INPUT ID=txtPassword NAME=txtPassword TYPE=password></P>
    <P><INPUT TYPE="submit" VALUE="Submit" ID=submit1 NAME=submit1></P>
</FORM>
```

The login web page (login.asp) has two processes. One to create the NWDir object (the Directory ActiveX control), retrieve the header information (login and password entered), and check it against the tree. The second process takes the information pulled from the tree and, depending on the content of this information, will either make the user login again, give them access, or politely ask them to leave.

Let's look to at the first section of code:

```
<HTML>
<HEAD>
</HEAD>
<BODY>
<%
On Error Resume Next
vMode = trim(Request.QueryString("mode"))
If vMode = "login" Then
    vLogin = trim(Request.Form("txtLogin"))
    vPassword = trim(Request.Form("txtPassword"))
```

This section gets the information from the query string mode and, if in login mode, grabs the header information. The header information was passed when the user clicked the submit button. The information is passed into the appropriate variables for later processing.

In the next section of code, we create an instance of the NWDir control:

```
dim entry
dim NWDir1
set NWDir1 = CreateObject("NWDirLib.NWDirCtrl.1")
```

Now we need to give the NWDir control the full name context. The control will look in the Developers Tree for the OU Programmers. For our tree, Developers will be the tree name and Programmers the first container in that tree. We will expand this name until the proper context is reached:

```
NWDir1.FullName = "NDS:\\DEVELOPERS\Programmers"
```

Next we must use the FullNameFromTreeAndContext method to construct the full name of the user object. The parameters for this command are TreeName and Context. In this case, we are assuming that the users are stored in the Developers tree, so this can be static.

However, the context could change with each user. Since we know part of the Fully Distinguished Name, we can enter that in the string (Programmers). This saves the visitor from having to enter or even know it.

Next, we have to grab the variable vLogin, which contains the login name the user entered, and add it to the string:

```
NWName = NWDir1.FullNameFromTreeAndContext("Developers", "." & vLogin & _
                                    ".Programmers")
```

We then tell the NWDir control to find the entry:

```
Set entry = NWDir1.FindEntry(NWName)
```

Next, we will use the ValidatePassword method to check against the password object in the NDS tree, followed by some clean up code:

```
retCode = entry.ValidatePassword(vPassword)
Set NWDir1=Nothing
```

Since the login is now processed, and the results are all stored in variables, we can have a look at what we have retrieved and process.

The first thing we are going to look at is the entry object. We used the entry variable to store the results of the FindEntry method. The FindEntry method returns nothing if the query is not successful. This is the first test to see if the login name is correct.

We are using Session variables to store the information such as TryCount which keeps track of how many times user, attempt to log in. If they have tried three times, they are ejected. Further security can be implemented by storing the IP of the offender and preventing subsequent returns of that user for a given length of time.

The variables `vReject` and `vLogin` are used as flags for use later in the scripting:

```
If entry is nothing then
    'session login name failed
    Session("TryCount") = Session("TryCount") + 1
    If session("TryCount") > 3 Then
        vReject = True
        vLogin = False
    Else
        vLogin= True
    End If
```

Next we have a variable: `retCode`. This was used with the `ValidatePassword` method. It returns a Boolean response, `True` if password is valid, `False` if password is incorrect:

```
Else
    If retCode=True Then
        'login name found and password works
        Session("Auth") = "y"
    Else
        'login password failed
        Session("TryCount") = Session("TryCount") + 1
        If session("TryCount") > 3 then
            vReject = True
            vLogin = False
        Else
            vLogin=True
        End If
    End If
End if
End If
```

Next, we use the flag `vLogin` we created to tell the ASP page to redisplay the login page, as the previous entry was incorrect:

```
If vLogin=True Then
%>

<HTML CODE HERE>
...

<%
```

Next, if they have maximized their tries, then the value of `vReject` is changed to `True`. This displays the reject page:

```
ElseIf vReject=True Then
%>

<HTML CODE HERE>
...

<%
End if
```

Next, we need to be able to tell the users that they passed with honor if the login was successful. For that, we use another session variable named `Auth`. The reason we use a `Session` variable is so that we can then use the `Auth` variable on each of the secure pages to see if the user has logged in. (I do realize that Session variables *should not* be used. However, this is a chapter about NDS, and using session variables enables us to keep the code that little bit easier to read.)

```
If Session("Auth") = "y" Then
%>

<HTML CODE HERE> .
...

<%
End if
%>
```

Now we can use a little bit of scripting in each of the secure pages to see if the user has logged in, and if they haven't, they will be redirected to the login web page:

```
<%
If Session("Auth") <> "y" Then
    Response.redirect "index.htm"
End if
%>
```

And voila: we now have an NDS-authenticated web site. The final code listing for `login.asp` would be as follows:

```
<%@ Language=VBScript %>
<HTML>
<HEAD>
</HEAD>
<BODY>
<%
On Error Resume Next
' TreeName is the name of the tree
' OU1 is the OrganizationUnit used to build the context of the user
' We can increase the number of OU's used to build our context appropriately
TreeName = "Developer"
OU1 = "Programmers"
vMode = trim(Request.QueryString("mode"))
If vMode = "login" then
    vLogin = trim(Request.Form("txtLogin"))
    vPassword = trim(Request.Form("txtPassword"))
    dim entry
    dim NWDir1
    Set NWDir1 = CreateObject("NWDirLib.NWDirCtrl.1")
    NWDir1.FullName = "NDS:\\" + TreeName + "\" + OU1
    NWName = NWDir1.FullNameFromTreeAndContext(TreeName, "." & vLogin & _
                                               "." & OU1)
    Set entry = NWDir1.FindEntry(NWName)
    retCode = entry.ValidatePassword(vPassword)
    Set NWDir1=Nothing
    If entry Is Nothing Then
        'session login name failed
```

```
            Session("TryCount") = Session("TryCount") + 1
            If session("TryCount") > 3 Then
                vReject = True
                vLogin = False
            Else
                vLogin= True
            End If
        Else
            If retCode=True Then
                'login name found and password works
                Session("Auth") = "y"
            Else
                'login password failed
                Session("TryCount") = Session("TryCount") + 1
                If Session("TryCount") > 3 Then
                    vReject = True
                    vLogin = False
                Else
                    vLogin = True
                End If
            End If
        End if
End If
If vLogin=True Then
%>
<P><IMG ALT="progtoprog.jpg (18030 bytes)" HEIGHT=50 SRC="progtoprog.jpg"
        WIDTH=762 ></p>

<TABLE BORDER="0" WIDTH="100%">
    <TR>
        <TD WIDTH="18%"></TD>
        <TD WIDTH="82%">
            <SMALL>Welcome to the support site of Wrox Press.  Here we can get
                    the latest information on our books and the best technical writers
                    in the world.  </SMALL>
            <P><SMALL>If we are an author log in.  </P>
            <P>If we are not an author just click here to get the latest updates.
            </P>
            <FORM METHOD=POST ACTION="login.asp?mode=login" ID=form1 NAME=form1>
                <P>Login:     
                <INPUT ID=txtLogin NAME=txtLogin></P>
                <P>Password:<INPUT ID=txtPassword NAME=txtPassword TYPE=password>
                </SMALL>
                <INPUT TYPE="submit" VALUE="Submit" ID=submit1 NAME=submit1></P>
            </FORM>
        </TD>
    </TR>
</TABLE>
<%
ElseIf vReject=True Then
%>
<P><IMG ALT="progtoprog.jpg (18030 bytes)" HEIGHT=50 SRC="progtoprog.jpg"
        WIDTH=762></P>
<TABLE BORDER="0" WIDTH="100%">
    <TR>
        <TD WIDTH="18%"></TD>
        <TD WIDTH="82%">
            <P>We have exceeded our limit in failed attempts.</P>
            <P>If we are trying to break into this site, we hope Voldemort comes down
                on we like a month of Sundays :)</P>
            <P> </P></td>
```

```
      </TR>
   </TABLE>
   <%
   End if
   If Session("Auth") = "y" Then
   %>
   <P><IMG ALT="progtoprog.jpg (18030 bytes)" HEIGHT=50 SRC="progtoprog.jpg"
        WIDTH=762></P>
   <TABLE BORDER="0" WIDTH="100%">
      <TR>
         <TD WIDTH="18%"></TD>
         <TD WIDTH="82%">
         <P>We may now proceed into the site. Thanks for coming, and we hope we
            enjoy our stay.<P>
      </TR>
   </TABLE>
   <%
   End if
   %>
   </BODY>
   </HTML>
```

Let's see how we can use the NDS tree in a real-world scenario using the same code.

Storing Customer Information in an NDS Directory

Assume we want to build an e-commerce site. We don't really need our customers to be constantly entering their credit information into our web pages, we can store them using NDS.

Since NDS is by its very nature meant to handle network resources, we will need to extend the schema somewhat to facilitate this type of operation.

Initially, we need to look at the objects that already exist on the tree to determine whether there are any that would be appropriate for our purposes.

Let's look at the properties of the user object. Even if there are properties that we don't really need, it is always more straightforward to use existing objects before creating our own. Since the User object doesn't have a dedicated attribute to store user numbers and credit card information, we will have to create one. We will also need to create an order object to store order information. Although such information as order details would be accessed infrequently, and would therefore, in a real world situation, be better stored in an ordinary database, we will store this information in NDS for illustrative purposes.

How do we want the information to be stored in NDS? By users grouped with all their orders, or some other way? How we do this will have effects on how the tree will ultimately perform and how we might extend the schema.

Regardless of how we choose to store the information, we can retrieve it to generate reports, using, for instance, the JDBC or ODBC drivers, or even one of the ActiveX controls mentioned earlier.

Let's have the order objects stored inside the visitor objects. In order to do this, the visitor object would be a container object like an OU object, and the order object would be a leaf object to the visitor object. The layout would look like this:

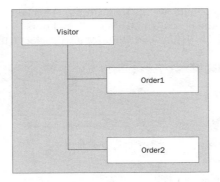

This layout is going to be used so that all the visitor information, including what they ordered, will be stored together. This can be used so that when a user logs in, their order history can be accessed and manipulated with ease. Also, the leaf object (order1) would inherit information from the container object (Visitor), such as Name and Address. When we query specific orders, we will be able to easily retrieve information about who purchased it.

So, how do we extend the schema? Well, we could use one of the consoles, such as ConsoleOne or Schemax. We could also write an application using the aforementioned ActiveX.

We'll create a new schema which we'll call customer, using ConsoleOne. However, before creating this, we will have to create a couple of new attributes. This is because we will want to associate a Credit Card attribute with our customers, and also use a customer ID for uniquely identifying customers, but there are not ready made credit card or CustomerID attributes.

Creating Attributes

A new attribute can be created using Schema Manager (found in the Tools menu of ConsoleOne). Under the Attributes tab we can find a list of existing attribute types:

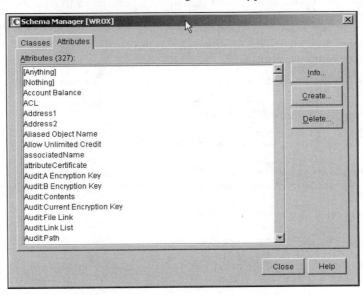

As we want to create a new attribute, we click on **Create**. This takes us to a screen in which we are asked to provide a name for the new attribute. We will call ours `Credit Card`. On the following screen we select the format (syntax) for the new attribute. We will select **Numeric String**:

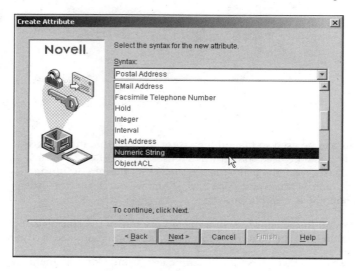

We next have to specify the flags for our attribute. The options here are:

- ❏ **Single Valued**: this allows only one value to be entered in this field.

- ❏ **String**: as we would expect, this indicates a string value type. If the attribute is to be used in naming, it must be a string type.

- ❏ **Synchronize Immediately**: selecting this will mean that any changes made to the value of this attribute will be automatically and immediately propagated to replicas.

- ❏ **Public Read**: this enables all objects in a tree to read this attribute, irrespective of their rights.

- ❏ **Write Managed**: this means that the value of this attribute may only be changed on a read/write or master replica.

- ❏ **Per Replica**: selecting this will mean that the value of this attribute may differ over replicas.

- ❏ **Sized**: this may only be used with formats which are sizeable. We will be asked to specify upper and lower limits if we select this.

For our Credit Card attribute, we only need to select **Single Valued**.

On the following screen, we are presented with a summary of our attribute. We select **Finish**, and NDS will create our new attribute. We can create the `CustomerID` attribute in exactly the same way.

Let's now look at how we create our new class.

Creating a New Class

A new class can be created using the Schema Manager. This will initially present us with a list of already existing classes:

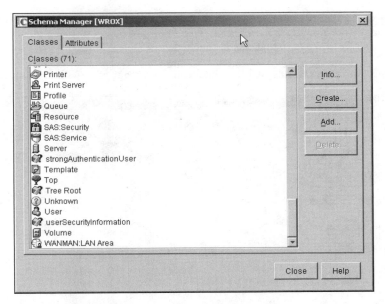

Selecting **Add** will start up the Create Class Wizard. After an initial opening screen, this prompts us to enter the name and ASN.1 ID of our new class. This latter is optional, and should only be used if you have an ASN.1 string registered by an authorized institution.

The next screen requires us to set the flags for the class:

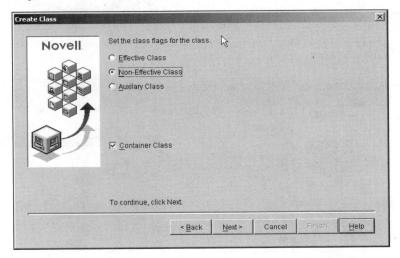

The flags are of three kinds:

❏ Effective Class: we use this if we want to use our class to create objects.

❏ Non-Effective Class: this cannot be used to create objects, but its attributes can be inherited by other classes.

❏ Auxiliary Class: this can have attributes which may only be associated with individual objects.

651

As we will be wanting to create objects from our class, we select **Effective Class**. We are also asked here if we wish to make our new class a container class. We want our `customer` objects to contain our `order` objects, so we make sure that this is checked.

On proceeding, we are asked to select the class from which our class will inherit attributes:

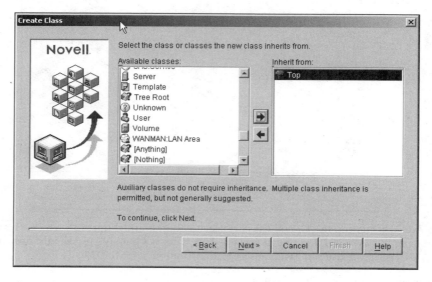

We do not wish to inherit attributes for our `customer` class, so we select **Top**. However, even though we select **Top** here, we will still be presented with the **Object Class** attribute for our new class.

We next face the task of selecting the required *mandatory* attributes for our class. We select the attributes as specified in the schema (which is given below):

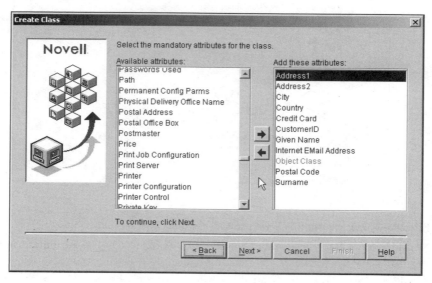

After selecting the mandatory attributes for our class, we are given a screen that allows us to specify optional attributes. We won't be using any optional attributes for our class.

We're next asked to specify the naming attributes for our class, this is the attribute that will be used to identify instances of our class. So we select CustomerID:

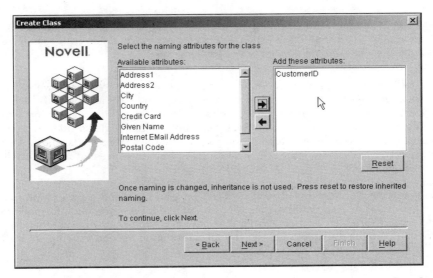

We then have to select which type of container class we wish it to go in. We here select Organizational Unit (OU). After this, just as with the Attribute Wizard, we are given a summary of the class we are about to create. After we select Finish, NDS will create our new class for us.

After creating our Customer class, we can create another class for our leaf objects, which we will call Order Info. The Price attribute isn't predefined, so, as above, we will have to create it for ourselves.

The attributes for our two new classes are as follows:

Class	Attributes
Container Class Customer	CustomerID
	Given Name
	Surname
	Address1
	Address2
	City
	Postal Code
	Country
	Internet Email Address
	Credit Card
Leaf Object Order Info	Product ID
	Price

All the objects that we create from these classes will be stored in an `Organization` container called `WroxWeb`.

Being able to use already existing attributes is a big benefit as this reduces the time spent redesigning the NDS and building lots of new attributes.

> *We could have used the existing attribute `Postal Address` instead of using `Address1`, `Address2`, `City`, `Postal Code` and `Country`, but segregating the different address components could be useful for market research purposes.*

What we want to make mandatory and optional is entirely up to us. We can, if we wish, make a particular field seem mandatory to the user using scripting while it is an optional attribute to the NDS tree. There are advantages and disadvantages to this methodology. First, mandatory attributes are automatically inherited by the sub-object. So, for example, if all the visitor information is mandatory to the NDS tree, that information is automatically passed into the `Order Info` object. A strong disadvantage is that we have to have error checking in place to ensure that mandatory fields are filled out, or we will get errors.

We can then use the aforementioned sample of checking for login and password information using the object name (`Customer name`) and the password in the field. The resulting information would then be stored into session variables for users. Order information could be added using the `NWDir` control using the `Add` method, adding the object and the various information needed to complete the transaction.

Adding Users Via the Web

With these controls, we can easily build web applications to add users to our NDS tree.

In this next exercise we will build a web application that allows us to add users to our NDS tree over the Internet. We can use similar code to add customers or the like to our NDS tree.

First, we need a web page that allows users to input the important information.

We used the following HTML code to grab the information:

```
<FORM ACTION="add.asp?mode=add" METHOD=POST ID=form1 NAME=form1>
    <TABLE BORDER=1 CELLPADDING=1 CELLSPACING=1 WIDTH="75%">
        <TR>
            <TD>Customer ID</TD>
            <TD><INPUT ID=txtObjectName NAME=txtObjectName></TD>
        </TR>
        <TR>
            <TD>Surname</TD>
            <TD><INPUT id=txtSurname name=txtSurname></TD>
        </TR>
        <TR>
            <TD>Given Name</TD>
            <TD><INPUT ID=txtGivenName NAME=txtGivenName></TD>
        </TR>
        <TR>
            <TD>Full Name</TD>
            <TD><INPUT ID=txtFullName NAME=txtFullName></TD>
        </TR>
        <TR>
```

```
              <TD>Other Name</TD>
              <TD><INPUT ID=txtOtherName NAME=txtOtherName></TD>
        </TR>
        <TR>
              <TD>Title</TD>
              <TD><INPUT ID=txtTitle NAME=txtTitle></TD>
        </TR>
        <TR>
              <TD>Location</TD>
              <TD><INPUT ID=txtLocation NAME=txtLocation></TD>
        </TR>
        <TR>
              <TD>Department</TD>
              <TD><INPUT ID=txtDepartment NAME=txtDepartment></TD>
        </TR>
        <TR>
              <TD>Telephone</TD>
              <TD><INPUT ID=txtTelephone NAME=txtTelephone></TD>
        </TR>
        <TR>
              <TD>Email Address</TD>
              <TD><INPUT ID=txtEmail NAME=txtEmail></TD>
        </TR>
        <TR>
              <TD><INPUT ID=submit1 NAME=submit1 TYPE=submit VALUE=Submit></TD>
              <TD><INPUT ID=reset1 NAME=reset1 TYPE=reset VALUE=Reset></TD>
        </TR>
    </TABLE>
</FORM>
```

Two modes are used, one to enter the data and the other to process the data. When the information is submitted, a query string is added to the URL telling the web page to process the information. If no query string is present, then we display the above HTML. The following code was used to affect this:

```
<%
vMode = trim(Request.QueryString("mode"))
If vMode <> "add" Then
%>
```

Next we must take the input the user entered and change it to variables. This is much easier to debug as the lines of code are significantly shorter:

```
<%
Else
    'grab the information entered and store to variables
    vObjectName = Trim(Request.Form("txtObjectName"))
    vSurname = Trim(Request.Form("txtSurname"))
    vGivenName = Trim(Request.Form("txtGivenName"))
    vAddress1 = Trim(Request.Form("txtAddress1"))
    vAddress2 = Trim(Request.Form("txtAddress2"))
    vCity = Trim(Request.Form("txtCity"))
    vPostCode = Trim(Request.Form("txtPostCode"))
    vCountry = Trim(Request.Form("txtCountry"))
    vEmail = Trim(Request.Form("txtEmail"))
    vCard = Trim(Request.Form("txtCard"))
```

We used the Trim command to erase all trailing spaces from the entry and thus make them more accurate.

Next on the agenda is to create an instance of the `NWDir` control. This is done as before using the following code. We must also at this point tell the control where to start to add. This is done through the `FullName` property:

```
Dim NWDir1
Set NWDir1 = CreateObject("NWDirLib.NWDirCtrl.1")
NWDir1.FullName = "NDS:\\DEVELOPERS\programmers\wroxweb"
```

The following is the code to take the variables and enter them into the tree:

```
Dim MyEntry
Set MyEntry = NWDir1.Entries.Add("Customer",vObjectName)
Call MyEntry.SetFieldValue("Surname",vSurname)
Call MyEntry.SetFieldValue("Given Name",vGivenName)
Call MyEntry.SetFieldValue("Address1", vAddress1)
Call MyEntry.SetFieldValue("Address2", vAddress2)
Call MyEntry.SetFieldValue("City", vCity)
Call MyEntry.SetFieldValue("Postal Code", vPostCode)
Call MyEntry.SetFieldValue("Country",vCountry)
Call MyEntry.SetFieldValue("Internet Email Address", vEmail)
Call MyEntry.SetFieldValue("Credit Card",vCard)
Call MyEntry.Update
Response.Write "User successfully added"
End If
```

First we add the object using the `Entries.Add` method with the type of object (in this case `Customer`) and the object name (`vObjectName`). Once this has been done, the object is cached, and we then need to set the values of the fields using the `MyEntry.SetFieldValue` method. We put the name of the object, followed by the variable that contains the information to be stored. When this is all done, we then call the `Update` method to actually create the object in the NDS tree.

Voila, we just added a user. This is an easy way to enter new users into the NDS tree. This way, we can allow the HR department to enter the information of a new user when they are hired, thus reducing the amount of time we spend adding new users to the system.

Next, we are going to see how to update user information in the NDS tree.

Updating User Information Through the Web

Updating information in NDS from ASP is achieved using precisely the same techniques that we just encountered in creating a new object. That is, the following line of code would alter the contents of the `Credit Card` field of an object:

```
Call MyEntry.SetFieldValue("Credit Card", vNewCreditCardNumber)
```

Adapting the above code to implement this functionality should be fairly straightforward.

Summary

We have only scratched the surface of using NDS in conjunction with ASP. However, as directory services are becoming more prevalent, accessing and manipulating the information that they contain over the Internet is becoming more common.

In this chapter, we have seen how to control access to a web site through using NDS. We have also seen how to create and manipulate the information stored in NDS.

20

Indexing Service

Introduction

Back in July 1997, Dr Jakob Nielsen wrote that "... the search is one of the most important user interface elements in any large web site. As a rule of thumb, sites with more than around 200 pages should offer [a] search [facility]." (You can find his article at www.useit.com/alertbox/9707b.html.) Dr Nielsen goes on to explain that his studies show that half of all site users prefer to use a search function to navigate a site. Therefore, it is not surprising that when sites fail to offer a search facility, whether a full or limited search, it actually discourages users from delving into the site's resources. There are several possible explanations why search engines are not implemented more. Search engine technology is something of an arcane art and few people understand how best to implement such an engine. Also, developing front-ends for search engines can be a messy and involved task.

> *Dr Nielsen is a noted expert in the fields of User Interface design and usability. He has written several books on these topics. "Design Web Usability" is highly recommended reading.*

This chapter discusses how you can integrate a search feature into your web sites using the Indexing Service for Windows 2000. We will start with an overview of how the Indexing Service works and how you can configure it for use. Next, we will cover the Index Query technology and demonstrate how it can be used to generate search results. The last parts of the chapter demonstrate how you can integrate the Indexing Service into your web sites and web Applications.

When Microsoft released Internet Information Server version 3.0 (IIS3) in 1996, a new optional service shipped along with it – **Index Server**. This tool took much of the labor out of building web site searches by providing both a search engine and a content indexing engine. The search engine received search requests and returned HTML-formatted result sets. The content indexing engine scanned the local host's file system and built a database-like structure for holding information about the documents and references to them. However, this implementation still had problems. In addition to mastering HTML, developers who wanted to use it had to master the Index Query file (.idq) and HTML template files (.htx). Although functional, having to learn the technology provided another obstacle for busy developers to overcome.

In 1998, Microsoft introduced Internet Information Server version 4.0 (IIS4). This dramatically improved life for web developers by providing a much better ASP run-time environment. It also introduced version two of the Index Server (IS2), which took a major step forward, from a developers prospective, because it provided COM objects for defining and executing searches. It also provided a way to make use of ADO programming skills. In effect, Microsoft made developing a web site search application as easy as implementing a database search.

As nice as the new version of Index Server was, it still had some shortcomings. First, additional installation work was required – either as part of the IIS4 installation or afterwards. By design, IS2 was meant to be used only by server-side applications, and it was not installable on other Windows platforms, such as NT4 workstation, Windows 9x, and Windows 3x. A major issue for some sites was the large amount of extra time that IS2 service imposed on the server when it started up. Also, it was unable to retain a reliable list of what had, or had not been, indexed. Frequently the service would rescan the entire file system during start-up. Since the service started by default at boot, this behavior frequently increased the time it took a server to return to service after booting (or a dreaded blue screen of death).

At the beginning of the year 2000, Microsoft introduced Windows 2000 and a new version of the Index Server: The **Indexing Service for Windows 2000**. This was far more than a name change. Designed from the outset to be a native, integral part of the operating system, the Indexing Service is installable on any Windows 2000 platform host with a minimum of effort. It also takes advantage of the journaling capability of the Windows 2000 file system to determine if a file needs to be processed or not. This allows the Indexing Service to search all parts of the file system, not just web-related ones. The service is so integrated, in fact, that the ever-so-annoying "Find Fast" can be replaced with it in the "Start | Search | Find Files or Folders" option.

In this chapter, we will show how the Indexing Service can be used as a data store and give examples of how to construct web searches using it. It will be important to understand the atomic units of the Service, such as catalogs, properties, scopes and queries. There are two approaches to constructing web searches: either through COM objects, or by using the OLE-DB Provider for the Indexing Service. We will dissect a search engine designed using both of these methods. Of course, this chapter cannot and will not cover all there is to say about the Indexing Service, so we will conclude with some additional reading resources.

Indexing Service from a Database Perspective

Since you are reading a book about data access using ASP, it is probably safe to make two assumptions. First, you understand the general vocabulary of databases, and second, that you understand the relationships between elements of data within a database. Such knowledge is vital to the developer who wants to make use of the Indexing Service for his or her application. Fundamentally, the Indexing Service can be thought of as little more than just another data provider. You can query it for result sets. You can specify restrictions on the returned data to fine-turn your search. You can even exclude 'records' containing information you do not want included. To really understand this data, you must understand where it comes from, how it makes its way into the database, how to query it, and how to render it in a meaningful way for the viewer. To help you make sense of these concepts, we will relate them to terms that may already be familiar.

Catalogs

Catalogs are the fundamental data source for the Indexing Service. Through the filtering process, the Indexing Service populates the catalogs with keywords and references to source files. The filtering process is discussed in a following section.

> *Catalogs are stored in multiple files, in directories. These directories can be placed anywhere within the file system of the host server*

> *You should not, however, place the catalogs in the same directories as you have FrontPage (or Visual InterDev) web sites. When an attempt is made to open or publish these web sites, a conflict arises because the Indexing Service has a lock on the files in the catalogs.*

Think of **catalogs** as being like both databases and tables Catalogs – both contain the index data and expose that data. Catalogs are like databases in the sense of being the containers of data. They are also like tables in that they directly expose the data. In SQL Server 7.0, for example, databases contain tables, stored procedures and views. You query the tables or views, or execute stored procedures, to obtain results from the database. If you query a table, you are getting directly exposed data. If you query a view or execute a stored procedure, you are getting indirectly exposed data. In the Indexing Service, you query the catalogs directly. While creating views of Indexing Service is possible, you cannot currently create stored procedures within the Indexing Service.

When organizing a database, you probably follow the rules of **normalization**. That is, you successively distribute the data between tables, based on the concepts that the data represents, until achieving a satisfactory level of distribution. Thankfully, you will not have to normalize the Indexing Service database by hand, as the service does this automatically. However, you should normalize data in the catalogs by having as many catalogs as required pointing at specific content. For example, if you have an intranet web site for your accounting department and a other web site for your Marketing Department, you should create separate catalogs for each department rather than combining them in one. We will cover this topic in a following section.

Data must come from some place. In the SQL Server world, data gathered from sources as diverse as spreadsheets, legacy databases, and line-of-business applications gets loaded into the database. The data is typically scrubbed for consistency beforehand before being processed by a program or utility that populates the tables. By contrast, in the Indexing Service, data comes from the file system of the host server. The filtering and indexing processes populate information gleaned from the system into the catalog. Since the locations of all the documents are known at the time it is processed, this address is stored in the catalog.

There are two ways to create a catalog:

❑ Microsoft Management Console (MMC) snap-in for the Indexing Service

❑ Indexing Service Administration Automation Objects (ISAAO)

Using the MMC snap-in for the Indexing Service to create a catalog is roughly the same as using the SQL Server Enterprise Manager MMC snap-in for creating databases on SQL Servers. The ISAAOs are roughly the same as using the SQL-DMO or ADOX objects.

We will also discuss a Windows Script Host script file that uses the ISAAOs for creating a catalog later on in this chapter.

Catalogs are essentially references to file system directories and folders and can be tied to the root directory of a hosted web site. All directories – even the virtual directories – are included in these catalogs by default. The system and users may create additional catalogs of the file system. When installing the Indexing Service, it creates two default catalogs, one file system catalog called "System", and the default web site catalog called "Web".

Result Sets

If you are comfortable with querying SQL Server databases through ADO, you already know about recordsets. **Result sets** are to the Indexing Service what recordsets are to SQL queries. Another cool feature of the Indexing Service is that any result sets returned using the methods we discuss in this chapter are also ADO recordsets. This probably eliminates much of the learning curve you would otherwise have to deal with when coding the rendering of the result set. It also means that you are able to persist the result set to an XML stream or file for subsequent transformation.

Keywords

In SQL Server, we tend to think of a database as holding data in tables. Specific instances of data are stored in **columns**. A table holding purchase orders will probably have a column containing data for a given client, whereas a table holding patient data will probably have a column containing a reference to a particular physician. But how would a search engine for a hospital be able to show all of the purchase orders involved in stocking medications frequently prescribed by a physician? And how would that same engine be able to associate modem setting strings with operating system information in a database used by an Internet Service provider?

Conventional techniques for organizing data cannot do this. For such associations to be made, key concepts like "purchase orders", "prescriptions", "modem strings", and "operating system" must be derived from the data and associated with the source. These phrases, or **keywords**, can be entered into the catalog along with a reference to the source file. The search engine can then construct the relationships between files that contain the keywords.

So then, what makes a word or group of words a keyword? Is everything a keyword? The answer to the second of these is much easier to answer – no. Words and phrases that are not keywords are called "noise words", and as such are not included in the catalog. Determining what a keyword is relies on a complex algorithm based on the code page in use on the system and the native language of the document. The exact nature of this process is beyond the scope of this book.

Certain elements within a document are specifically associated with entries in the catalog. These specific entries are known as properties. For example, an HTML file may contain one or more <H1> tags. The text between these tags is entered into the catalog and is associated with that tag. The Indexing Service can also generate an **abstract** of the document, a feature that is also known as a **characterization**. The abstract will be presented to the user as a brief description of the document's subject matter.

File Properties

All documents included in the catalog have their file properties included, such as the location of the file, the date created, the last time saved and the last time accessed. If the filtering process knows that other information in the file should be treated as a property, this information is added to the catalog. For example, when indexing a Word document, the title, subject, and author are also included in the catalog.

Scopes

In most bookstores, books are typically shelved by topic: computer titles are clustered with other computer books; cookery books are arrayed with other cookery books and magazines are racked with other magazines. This establishes a scope for the books. So when you need to find information about the latest developer technology, you know where to go to get it. The Indexing Service scopes serve the same purpose – scopes are used to include (and exclude) directories (and thus files), from the result set. By default, all of the directories in a scope are included in the result set, including sub-directories. These types of queries are known as deep traversals. If you want to just include a single directory, you will need to perform a shallow traversal.

Dr Nielsen's article advises us to avoid defining scopes as constraints on searches. If a site contains several sub-sites that you might be tempted to search against, you should explicitly state the scope of the search and you should offer a link to a sites global search engine. That is, if you have a master site and three sub sites, the sub sites should not have an option that allows searches on the other sub sites. However, it is recommended that the master site is allowed to search all sites or any of the sub sites.

The Filtering and Indexing Process

As we noted before, the populating of the catalogs occurs through the filtering and indexing processes. The filtering process finds and opens candidate files within the catalog's scope. The service passes each file to a registered filter (sometimes called an iFilter), which act like DLLs – loaded and unloaded as required by the Indexing Service. The service determines which filter to use by examining the file's extension. The filter then opens and parses the file, and creates lists of keywords. It also determines what file properties should be included in the catalog. The indexing process enters the keyword lists into the catalog along with the file properties.

This design makes it possible to write a filter for virtually any file format. A classic example of a third-party filter is the Adobe Acrobat PDF iFilter. This filter knows how to open, decompress, parse, and return keyword lists for PDF files.

Queries

Of course, being able to get information out of the catalogs is what Indexing Service is all about. To get the most appropriate result set from the service, both the user and the developer must work together to write the most efficient query. As the developer, you must recognize which options to offer the user for defining the search type to the Indexing Service. Users must know use the search options and accurately choose terms to search on. Confusingly, "restriction" may be used as a synonym for query. This occurs because the query restricts what documents are included in the result set. There are essentially three types of queries commonly used with the Indexing Service: **content**, **relational** and **pattern-matching** queries. Relational and pattern-matching queries are subsets of the more general "property value" query type.

The most commonly used type of query is the content query. With this type of query, the keywords expressed in the query must be present in the document in order to be included in the result set. There are two modes for content queries: **phrase** and **free text**. In phrase mode, the exact phrase must be in the document. In free text, the words in the search phrase must be in the document, but they do not have to be in exact order, nor do they have to occur consecutively. For example, consider the search phrase "pirates beat cubs". In free text mode, any document with "pirates", "beat" and "cubs" will be included in the result set. In phrase mode, only documents with "pirates beat cubs" will be included in the result set. For more information on constructing content queries, see "Content Queries" in the MSDN library (navigate through the following pages: Platform SDK/Base Services/Indexing Service/About Indexing Service/Query Languages for Indexing Service/Index Server Query Language/).

Relational queries tend to be used heavily when querying document properties. A query like "Size > 10000000 and CreateDate >= -7d" returns the documents that are both larger than 10 megabytes in size and have been created in the past seven days. For more information on constructing relational queries, see "Relational Queries" in the MSDN library (from the same page as the previous MSDN reference).

Pattern-matching queries are ideal for advanced search needs. Powered by UNIX-style regular expressions, pattern-matching searches are well suited for very finely tuned property and content searches. Optionally, making use of wildcard searches (think MS-DOS) can achieve the same thing. For more information on constructing pattern-matching queries, see "Pattern-Matching" in the MSDN library.

There is one other type of query: vector space. This query method allows for precise control of the calculated ranking, as well as the documents gathered into the result set. In other words, vector space queries allow us to do weightings. For example, we can use a free text search to find all of the documents containing "Cats" and "Dogs". The rankings of the document will depend on the number of occurrences of "Cats" and "Dogs" equally. With vector searches, you can define how important a term is. Thus, with a vector search, you could make "Cats" three times as important as "Dogs" when the ranking is calculated. Vector space queries are quite potent but exact a heavy price in terms of proper construction.

Query Languages

The Indexing Service supports two different languages: the Indexing Service Query Language (ISQL) and SQL. Complicating matters further, ISQL has two dialects, "Dialect 1 for Index Server 2.0" and "Dialect 2". The important issue to note here is that scripting using the COM objects provided by the Indexing Service or custom-written ISAPI extensions, should use one of the ISQL dialects. Any application can perform queries provided that it has access to ADO and can use the SQL language and the OLE DB Provider for Indexing Service. For the best performance, you should use the ISQL and the COM objects instead of the SQL language wherever possible.

The difference between ISQL's Dialect 1 and Dialect 2 essentially boils down to this: Dialect 1, by default, works in content mode, whereas Dialect 2 works in free text mode. Consider the search phrase "cats and dogs". In dialect 1, only documents with "cats and dogs" – literally in that sequence – meet the restriction and are included in the result set. In Free-Text mode, any document with both "cats" and "dogs" – regardless of sequence or proximity – will be included in the result set. If you upgrade a server to Windows 2000 and start getting different search results, this may be the reason why. The delimiters for vector-space queries are different. The Boolean operators are now available in the localized language and not just English or short form. Technically, Dialect 1 is an incomplete part of Dialect 2's "short form". Dialect 2 is the default.

The SQL utilized by the OLE DB Provider is not exactly what we would use in relational databases. It is based on the standard SQL but with some extensions included to both the properties and the query stem itself. The extensions to properties provide access to metadata about the documents in the catalog. The extensions to queries provide the ability to define views, define scopes and different types of operations in the WHERE clause.

Query Methods

There are several different approaches to querying the Indexing Service:

❑ The first method involves the use of COM objects. Some of these – known as the **helper objects** – can be used in any COM-enabled environment, including the Windows Scripting Host, Visual Basic, and scripting languages. As stated before, you should use ISQL when calling the helper objects.

❑ Another method is to use ADO objects and the OLE DB Provider for the Indexing Service. The major benefit of this approach is that the developer is already familiar with the core technologies – ADO and SQL. All the Indexing Server internals are taken care of by OLE DB.

❑ C++ programmers can take advantage of the Indexing Service API through the OLE DB Provider. This makes it possible to write high-performance ISAPI filters and extensions that access the service. However, if you do this, you will need to use ISQL.

The first two methods – the query helper and ADO/OLE DB – are both valid means to an end to ASP developers. Which one should you use? From the performance standpoint, the query objects are usually the best choice. However, if you were not familiar with these objects, using the OLE DB method would be a less steep hill to climb when cranking out a prototype or pilot site. As you become familiar with the COM objects, you will probably find them just as easy to work with.

Virtual Web Sites and Catalogs

System administrators and developers alike face a question when developing a new web site. Should the site be a sub-web of the default web or created as a new virtual web site? Both have advantages. Sub-webs tend to be easier to define and easier to allocate file system space to. Virtual web sites provide easier to administer spaces to work with and process isolation providing system stability. Also, it is easy to create and associate a catalog with a virtual web site using the Microsoft Management Console or with scripts.

Security Issues

The Indexing Service does not implement any security itself with respect to the query results it returns. The service normally runs in the system account context, thus it "knows all and sees all" when filtering and indexing. This means that all of the documents in the catalog could be included in the result set provided they meet the restrictions (query criteria). The Indexing Service determines the user context of the process making the request. The service then compares user context against the Access Control Lists (ACL) for each document in the result set. If the user context allows access to the document, the document will be included in the result set. For example, if you are searching an "allow anonymous" web site, the IUSR_ account for that host must have access (either a specific user or group ACL entry) to a given file if it is to be included in the result set.

Only users with explicit or inherited administration rights may manage the Indexing Service. This includes pausing, starting, and stopping the service; adding or removing catalogs, and adding or removing scopes.

The Indexing Service Administration objects

The Indexing Service provides five COM objects used for managing the service, managing catalogs and conducting queries. All of these objects are dual-interfaced, so they are available to both C/C++ and Visual Basic developers. They are also available to any ActiveX scripting language. Two different DLLs house these objects. The first, ciodm.dll, contains objects for service administration: AdminIndexServer, CatAdm and ScopeAdm. The other library is ixsso.dll which hosts the objects used for conducting queries: Query and Admin.

AdminIndexService Object Methods

The AdminIndexServer object manages the indexing service. It can detect if the indexing service is running and can programmatically start and stop the service.

Method Name	Description
AddCatalog	Creates a new catalog.
Continue	Continues Indexing Service.
FindFirstCatalog	Initializes catalog enumeration. TRUE if a catalog exists and can be retrieved.
FindNextCatalog	Enumerates the next catalog. TRUE if the next catalog exists and can be retrieved.
GetCatalog	Retrieves the current catalog during an enumeration.
GetCatalogByName	Retrieves a catalog object by name.
GetLongProperty	Retrieves a content index registry value of type REG_DWORD, as described in Registry Entries. Accessed as type Long in Visual Basic.
GetSZProperty	Retrieves a content index registry value of type REG_SZ, as described in Registry Entries. Accessed as type String in Visual Basic.

Method Name	Description
IsPaused	Checks to see whether Indexing Service is paused.
IsRunning	Determines whether Indexing Service is running.
Pause	Pauses Indexing Service.
RemoveCatalog	Removes an existing catalog.
SetLongProperty	Sets a content index registry value of type Long (REG_DWORD) as described in Registry Entries.
SetSZProperty	Retrieves a content index registry value of type String (REG_SZ) as described in Registry Entries.
Start	Starts Indexing Service.
Stop	Stops Indexing Service.

CatAdm Object Properties

The CatAdm object is the name of the catalog administration object. This object defines the set of files to index by specifying the list of directories which are to be used by the indexing service.

Name	Data Type	Access	Description
Catalog Location	String	Read-only	Case-insensitive path.
CatalogName	String	Read-only	Case-insensitive catalog name.
Delayed FilterCount	Long	Read-only	Count of documents delayed for indexing. This reflects the number of documents that could not be indexed during a previous pass for various reasons, such as sharing violations.
Documents ToFilter	Long	Read-only	Number of documents to index.
Filtered DocumentCount	Long	Read-only	Number of documents indexed since the Indexing Service was last started.
IndexSize	Long	Read-only	Total size of the index in megabytes. Includes master and shadow indexes, and the property store. The master index is the final destination of all Indexing Service "index" data. It is persistent, disk-resident, highly compressed, and optimized for querying. All indexed content eventually is merged into the master index. Shadow indexes are an intermediate part of the Indexing Service index that are persistent, disk-resident, and highly compressed. They result from word lists and eventually merge with the master index.

Table continued on following page

Name	Data Type	Access	Description
IsUpToDate	Boolean	Read-only	Flag indicating whether index is up to date.
PctMerge Complete	Long	Read-only	Percentage of merge process completed.
Pending ScanCount	Long	Read-only	Number of directories that are to be scanned.
Persistent IndexCount	Long	Read-only	Number of persistent indexes that currently exist.
QueryCount	Long	Read-only	Number of active queries since Indexing Service started.
StateInfo	Long	Read-only	A combination of CI_STATE_* constants reflecting the state of the service.
Total DocumentCount	Long	Read-only	The document count in the set of documents that are to be indexed.
Unique KeyCount	Long	Read-only	Number of unique keys. Includes existing persistent indexes and non-persistent wordlists.
WordListCount	Long	Read-only	Number of existing word lists.

CatAdm Object Methods

Method Name	Description
AddScope	Creates a new scope.
ContinueCatalog	Starts the catalog and returns its previous state.
FindFirstScope	Finds the first scope in an enumeration.
FindNextScope	Finds the next scope in an enumeration.
ForceMasterMerge	Begins a master index merge for the catalog.
GetScope	Retrieves current scope object.
GetScopeByAlias	Retrieves scope object by alias name.
GetScopeByPath	Retrieves scope object by path name.
IsCatalogPaused	Checks whether the catalog is in read-only mode.
IsCatalogRunning	Checks whether the catalog is in read/write mode.
IsCatalogStopped	Checks whether the catalog is stopped.
PauseCatalog	Pauses the catalog and returns its previous state.
RemoveScope	Removes an existing scope object from a collection.
StartCatalog	Starts the catalog and returns its previous state.
StopCatalog	Stops the catalog and returns its previous state.

ScopeAdm Object Properties

The `ScopeAdm` is the Scope Administration object. It manages the scope definition for a catalog in the Indexing Service.

Name	Data Type	Access	Description
`Alias`	`String`	Read-write	Friendly name for the scope object.
`ExcludeScope`	`Boolean`	Read-write	TRUE disables indexing for this scope.
`Logon`	`String`	Read-only	Logon name.
`Path`	`String`	Read-write	Case-insensitive path.
`VirtualScope`	`Boolean`	Read-only	TRUE if this scope refers to a virtual root.

ScopeAdm Object Methods

Method Names	Description
`Rescan`	Full or incremental rescan trigger.
`SetLogonInfo`	Sets name, password pair.

Creating a Catalog with the Administration Objects

The MMC can be used for querying, but scripting is more effective. For the rest of this chapter, we will be working on an example virtual web site called "Sample". We will first look at a script to create the virtual web site, and then a script to create the catalog. This provides us the opportunity to examine part of the Indexing Service COM object library. In the following sections, we will look at how to develop a search engine solution with ASP scripts.

Scripting the Virtual Site

The basic steps for creating a virtual web site is:

- ❏ Back-up the IIS metabase
- ❏ Find the last web in the service
- ❏ Create a new web in the service
- ❏ Establish the key properties for the service
- ❏ Start the newly created web

IIS manifests itself in something called the **metabase**, which is a hierarchically structured storage format like the Active Directory. It combines data storage with compiled methods and event generators. The IIS metabase persists itself to and from a file when the service starts and when the host shut downs. Programmatic access to IIS is very similar to that of LDAP or Active Directory.

669

You would most often want to run the script as a system script (.vbs file), rather than as an ASP script. This would allow an administrator to run the script and manipulate the results. Bear in mind that the person using these scripts *must* have administrative rights on the host where the script is executing. In some cases, developers may have such rights and in other cases, they may not. Thus, it makes sense to make the script as easy to use as possible. One way to accomplish this is to write the script so that only a few changes are required to use it over and over again, making sure that the constraints needing changes are clearly labelled.

Note: the source code for this script is available from the Wrox web site at (www.wrox.com). This particular script is CreateSite.vbs. We will now look at the script in detail.

We will define seven key variables at the start of the script.

strHostToUse defines what server this virtual web site server will be created on. This can be an IP address, or a TCP/IP host name or NetBEUI machine name. Of course, "localhost" refers to the system on which the script is executing. You would need to change this to be the host name you want to use (if it is not localhost):

```
' set this next time to the name of the host you want
' to create the virtual web site on
strHostToUse = "localhost"
```

We will use the strDescription to hold the name of the web site as it appears in the MMC snap-in list. You will want to change this to something that has meaning for your site or application:

```
' Set the description to use for this web
strDescription = "Sample Documentation"
```

Every virtual web space must have a root directory (folder). This path may either a reference to the local file system or a Universal Naming Convention (UNC) path to a different server. For our "Sample" web site, we will set the root directory to the start of the HTML-formatted documentation. Unless you are "overlaying" a virtual web site over existing content, this will probably be a folder under the \Inetpub directory:

```
' Set the Home directory for this site
strRootPath = "c:\Sample\HTML"
```

Since all web sites need an IP address, we will provide a variable to define it, as well as the port to listen on. IIS5 supports two types of virtual web site: dedicated IP and shared IP. When each site on the host is associated with a unique IP address, the site is dedicated. When several sites are using a common IP address, it is a shared IP site. Shared IP addresses are practical because they allow the maximum number of sites to be supported by a minimum number of IP addresses. In order to know what site is being requested, IIS looks at the actual host name requested, a process also known as **host-header resolution**. The script implements the shared IP solution with a host header:

```
' Set the IP address, port and host header name for the site
strIPAddress = "172.16.1.131"
strPort = "80"
strHostHeaderName = "sample.w2ktegels.org"
```

The last variable our script defines is a list of candidate documents. If no document is specified in an HTTP GET request, and one of these documents exists in the root directory, the response will be the first of these documents found. Being able to define this priority list as you see fit is convenient if you are porting web sites from Apache servers.

```
' Set the default document string
strDefaultDocList = "index.html, default.asp, default.htm"
```

Before creating a virtual web site, you should first back up the current metabase. Doing so will save valuable time should something go wrong later on. We'll come to this procedure very shortly. However, we have to define some constants first – just in case the numeric values associated with the constants change.

```
' Constants used in backing up
const MD_BACKUP_SAVE_FIRST = 2
const MD_BACKUP_FORCE_BACKUP = 4
const MD_BACKUP_NEXT_VERSION = &HFFFFFFFF
```

The **IIS Administration Objects** enable us to create a metabase backup in one step. Essentially, a backup is no more than a dump of the metabase to a file. The purpose of the backup is to provide a quick, point-in-time restoration of the metabase should you need it – it is not a backup of the whole web service or a way to transfer web sites between servers. It is an undo at best.

The backup method requires three parameters: a name for the backup, a version, and one or more flags. The MD_BACKUP_NEXT_VERSION constant simply tells IIS to create a new backup set. The MD_BACKUP_SAVE_FIRST flag tells the service to save any pending data before making the backup. The MD_BACKUP_FORCE_BACKUP tells the service to backup even if the "save first" fails.

```
' Backup Metabase first
' The backup will be called BeforeAdd. Change the name as you like
Set objComputer = GetObject("IIS://" & strHostToUse)
iFlags = (MD_BACKUP_SAVE_FIRST or MD_BACKUP_FORCE_BACKUP)

' The actual backup step
objComputer.Backup "BeforeAdd", MD_BACKUP_NEXT_VERSION, iFlags
Set objComputer = Nothing
```

Now we can move on to finding the next available spot to create our web site. In order to do this, we must loop through each of the indexes of the web sites already existing to find the index of the last one.

```
' Connect to the WebService on the desired host.
Set objIIS = GetObject("IIS://" & strHostToUse & "/W3SVC")
' Loop through each of existing webs to find the last one used
' This is essentially finding an index for the next web.
For Each objInst In objIIS
    If isNumeric(objInst.Name) Then
        If objNextInst < objInst.Name Then
            objNextInst = objInst.Name
        End If
    End If
Next
```

Having found the index of the last web site, we know what the index of the next one will be:

```
' The next web follows the last web...
objNextInst = objNextInst + 1
```

When we get around to creating a catalog for the site, we will need to know the index for the site we are about to create. If you create the virtual web site and catalog in one shot (such as the CreateSiteAndCatalog.vbs script does – we will discuss the CreateCatalog.vbs script later), you will not need this:

```
MsgBox "This will be virtual web site will be #: " & objNextInst, vbOkOnly
```

We can now create a container for the new site. Remember that since IIS uses structured data , you first need to create a container for all those properties, methods and event sources:

```
' Create a new container for our virtual site
Set objNewIIS = objIIS.Create ("IIsWebServer",objNextInst)
```

The next thing you should do is provide a description for that web site. Failing to do this can cause errors in the MMC snap-in for IIS. The SetInfo method immediately commits the current state of the container to the metabase:

```
' Set the description for this web
objNewIIS.ServerComment = strDescription
objNewIIS.SetInfo
```

Unless acting as a redirector to other sites, a web site will have content and that content must be kept in some file system location. That web site will probably have other properties you want to fine tune. Our next step does this fine tuning by defining the root directory and our desired setting for the Web. Since we will want to run scripts from this web site, we must create an application root as well:

```
' Set the root path for this site
Set objIISNewRoot = objNewIIS.Create("IIsWebVirtualDir"",Root")
objIISNewRoot.path = strRootPath
objIISNewRoot.SetInfo
objIISNewRoot.AppCreate True
Set objIISNewRoot = Nothing
```

Since this is a shared IP virtual web site, we have to bind the site to a specific address, port and host header name:

```
' Build and bind to the desired address
strBoundTo = strIPAddress & ":" & strPort & ":" & strHostHeaderName
objNewIIS.ServerBindings = strBoundTo
```

And we can now set some properties of virtual web site as well:

```
' Set the web as read enabled and indexed. Also set the desired
' order of default documents.
objNewIIS.AccessRead = True
objNewIIS.ContentIndexed = True
objNewIIS.DefaultDoc = strDefaultDocList
objNewIIS.AccessRead = True
objNewIIS.AccessScript = True
objNewIIS.SetInfo
```

With the web set up and committed, we can now start it running and clean up any now unused objects:

```
' Start up the new Web and clean up
objNewIIS.Start
Set objIIS = Nothing
Set objNewIIS = Nothing
```

An important fact to keep in mind is that virtual web sites will inherit settings from the master web service settings, regardless of how created. Unless you specifically override those settings when creating the web site, they remain in effect until you otherwise change them. However, this does not apply to the Application space settings. If you want to run scripts on a web site, you must explicitly set it that way via the `CreateApp` method.

> *There is another "gotcha" to watch out for: The documentation for IIS 5.0 states that if the FrontPageWeb is set to true, the FrontPage manager installs the files required for FrontPage Server Extensions. Setting it to false removes the extensions. However, neither of these seem to work. Your best bet is to call* `fpsrvadm.exe` *See The MS Knowledge Base Article Q247864 (http://support.microsoft.com/support/kb/articles/Q247/8/64.ASP?LN=EN-US&SD=gn&FR=0) for details on the FrontPage server administrator program.*

Scripting the Catalog

With the virtual site created, we can now turn our attention to creating a catalog specifically for it. The basic algorithm for that is:

- ❑ Set up the variables as we did before.
- ❑ Create an Indexing Service `AdminIndexServer` object and a Scripting `Shell` object.
- ❑ Add registry values that associate the catalog with the virtual web site.
- ❑ Restart the Indexing Service and clean up the objects left.

We will now look at the `CreateCatalog.vbs` script, which can be downloaded from the Wrox web site.

The `ISAdm` object allows us to control to the service and create the catalog. The scripting object provides access to the system registry:

```
'Create the objects we need to create the catalog
Set objAdminIS = Wscript.CreateObject("Microsoft.ISAdm")
Set objWshShell = Wscript.CreateObject("Wscript.Shell")
```

Before we can add a catalog, we have to stop the Indexing Service:

```
' Stop the Indexing service while we create the catalog
objAdminIS.Stop
```

> You need to be careful when creating the catalog. If your application is being hosted on a server that needs to be up "24x7." Stopping the Indexing Service to create a new catalog stops all other catalogs as well. This means that if a user is trying to conduct a search while you are generating a new catalog, they may receive an error. It is prudent to check the value of the IsRunning property of an AdminIndexServer object before conducting a query.

Adding the catalog is simply a matter of calling the `AddCatalog` method. It takes two parameters, the name you want to give the catalog and a path to where the catalog database files will be stored.

```
Set objCatAdm = objAdminIS.AddCatalog(strCatalog, strCatalogPath)
```

Next, we will add five registry keys that bind the catalog to the virtual web site. The key `FilterFilesWithUnknownExtensions` defines if the Indexing Service will use a default filter if no specific filter is registered for document type. By setting this to zero, unknown files will not find their way into the index. The `GenerateCharacterization` key instructs the service to build an abstract of the document. The `IsIndexingW3Svc` defines that this catalog is tied to a given web site. The `MaxCharacterization` key limits the abstract to no larger than the given size, in bytes. Finally, the `W3SvcInstance` key associates a catalog with a given web site.

> You may be asking, "What is the benefit of manually writing registry keys instead of using the Indexing Service Administration Objects?" The answer: there are no objects with methods with this power – at least in the Windows 2000 version of the Indexing Service. Of course, you must be very careful when manually editing the registry. Back up the registry before editing it.

```
' Create the needed registry entries
objWshShell.RegWrite strRegBasePath & _
                      "FilterFilesWithUnknownExtensions",0, "REG_DWORD"
objWshShell.RegWrite strRegBasePath & _
                      "GenerateCharacterization",1",REG_DWORD"
objWshShell.RegWrite strRegBasePath & _
                      "IsIndexingW3Svc",1",REG_DWORD"
objWshShell.RegWrite strRegBasePath & _
                      "MaxCharacterization",lngMaxCharSize",REG_DWORD"
objWshShell.RegWrite strRegBasePath & _
                      "W3SvcInstance",objNextInst",REG_DWORD"
```

Finally, we can restart the Indexing Service and clean up our leftover objects:

```
' Restart the Indexing Service and clean up
objAdminIS.Start
Set objCatAdm = Nothing
set objAdminIS = Nothing
set objWshShell= Nothing
```

Note: the source code for this script is available from the Wrox web site at
(**www.wrox.com**). This particular script is `CreateCatalog.vbs`. **The alternative
script**, `CreateSiteAndCatalog.vbs`, **integrates both of the scripts described thus
far into one easy to use package.**

An important fact to bear in mind is that web catalogs will inherit settings from the "Web" catalog.
Unless you specifically override those settings when creating the web site, those values will remain in
effect until you change them.

The Query Automation Objects

The query automation objects provide an interface to the catalogs. The objects are available to all
ActiveX-enabled scripting languages, as well as Visual Basic and Visual C++. COM objects can also be
included within multi-tier applications.

Technically, you can get by with only the `Query` object so long as you want to search an entire catalog.
The `Utility` object is predominately used to add to or narrow down scopes from a search. We will see
these objects in depth in the following section.

Query Properties

The `Query` object allows you to create queries, and also creates an ADO recordset to display the results.

Property Names	Type	Access	Description
Allow Enumeration	Boolean	Read-write	`True` indicates that enumeration is allowed.
Catalog	String	Read-write	The index catalog name.
CiFlags	String	Read-write	Indexing Service flags. This is a deprecated property. Use `Utility.AddScopeToQuery` instead.
CiScope	String	Read-write	The catalog path. This is a deprecated property. Use `Utility.AddScopeToQuery` instead.
CodePage	Long	Read-write	The character set code page.
Columns	String	Read-write	List of columns available for ADO recordset retrieval for query results.
Dialect	String	Read-write	Query language version.
GroupBy	String	Read-write	Choice for grouping.
LocaleID	Long	Read-write	Language locale ID (LCID) to use when executing query.
MaxRecords	Long	Read-write / Read-only	Maximum number of records to retrieve. Read/write when the recordset is closed and read-only when it is open.

Table continued on following page

675

Property Names	Type	Access	Description
OptimizeFor	String	Read-write	Controls whether queries are optimized for better performance or for a greater number of hits.
OutOfDate	Boolean	Read-only	True if content index is out of date.
Query	String	Read-write	Query string, also known as restriction.
Query Incomplete	Boolean	Read-only	True if query could not be resolved using the Content index and if the AllowEnumeration property was False.
QueryTimedOut	Boolean	Read-only	True if query exceeded time limit for execution.
SortBy	String	Read-write	Choice for sorting.

Query Methods

Method Names	Description
Create Recordset	Execute the query, creating an OLE DB results table or an ADO recordset.
DefineColumn	Defines a column to be used in the query.
QueryToURL	Creates the query string portion of a URL from the internal state of the query properties.
Reset	Clears the state of the query object.
SetQuery FromURL	Sets query and other properties from the query string.

Utility Methods

The utility object implements a dual interface (supports IDispatch). It is an ActiveX control which gives script writers routines for use with the Query object.

Method Names	Description
AddScope ToQuery	Add a new scope restriction to a query.
GetArray Element	Access a safe-array vector element.
HTMLEncode	Encode a string using HTML encoding using a given code page.
ISOToLocaleID	Convert a language code to a Win32 locale identifier (LCID).
LocaleIDToISO	Convert a Win32 LCID into a language code.
Truncate ToWhitespace	Truncate a string at a white-space character.
URLEncode	Encode a string using URL encoding using a given code page.

Constructing a Web Search

The procedure for adding a search to web site is reasonably simple:

- ❑ Create a catalog for a web site.
- ❑ Create a form that gathers the search parameters.
- ❑ Create a script that executes the search and renders the result set.

The process for creating catalogs was discussed in the previous section. Here, we will quickly look at creating a front-end form for gathering the search parameters. We will examine two methods for scripting the search: through the `Query` object and using the Indexing Service OLE-DB provider.

User Interface

In order to do a minimum search, you will need a phrase to base the search on. This phrase restricts what documents are included or excluded from the result set. You may also want to include a limit on the number of results returned. If this is the case, it makes sense to have an element where this limitation can be set. You may also want to provide a way to determine what type of search to conduct, by document title, phrase or by content (free text). In this example, our search for will allow you to set the search method, the maximum number of files to include and to specify the search depth. Here is how the search form renders initially in Netscape Navigator 4.7:

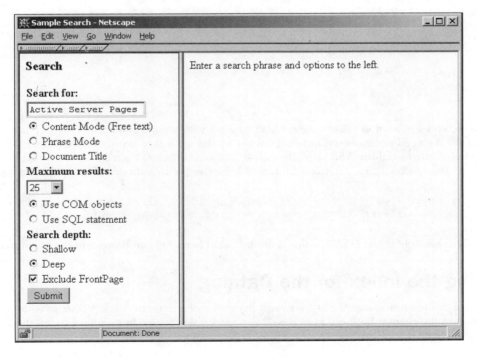

We will now discuss the most interesting bits of the code, which is downloadable from the Wrox web site.

Index.html is just a frameset which contains `search_ready.htm` and `search_panel.htm`. `Search_ready.htm` is the first page, which requests that the user enters their search information:

`Search_panel.htm` is a bit more interesting. The basic web page headers include a `BASE` tag which directs the form's output to the right-hand frame:

```
<HTML>
<HEAD>
<TITLE>Search Panel</TITLE>
<BASE TARGET="main">
```

Next, we will need a bit of client-side script. On the search form, we want to control which type of search method we want to use. We can do this by setting the form's `ACTION` method:

```
<SCRIPT ID=clientEventHandlersJS LANGUAGE=javascript>

function searchForm_onSubmit(theForm) {
   theForm.action = "";
   if(theForm.SearchTypeCOM.checked) {
      theForm.action = "http://sample.w2ktegels.org/search_com.asp";
   }
   if (theForm.SearchTypeSQL.checked) {
      theForm.action = "http://sample.w2ktegels.org/search_sql.asp";
   }
   theForm.submit();
}

</SCRIPT>
</HEAD>
<BODY>
```

Of course, you will want to change these URLs to work with your servers. The next step is to render the form itself. We need to set several attributes in the `FORM` tag for it to do what we want, such as the `ACTION` attribute to call the ASP page, the `LANGUAGE` and `ONSUBMIT` attributes to instruct the browser to execute the `searchForm_onSubmit` function before requesting the search script processor:

```
<FORM METHOD="post" ACTION="search_com.asp" ID="searchForm" NAME="searchForm"
LANGUAGE=javascript ONSUBMIT="searchForm_onSubmit(searchForm)">
```

The rest of this page is just HTML – this is not included here, but can be seen in the downloaded code.

Creating the Index for the Catalog

Before we can use our search facility, we must have an index to search. The VBScript code discussed earlier on in the chapter built our virtual web site and catalog for us, but we have to tell the Indexing Service to create the index.

Open up Computer Management console window from the Administration Tools option of the Start menu, select the Services and Applications tree and then Indexing Service. You will see the new catalog Sample in the list:

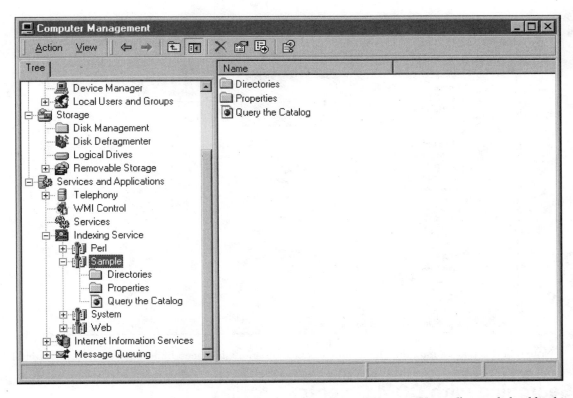

Right-click on the Directory folder under Sample and select New > Directory. You will get a dialog like this:

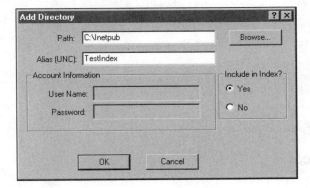

Browse to the root directory of your web site, and if you wish, insert an alias for that directory and press OK. Now right-click on the directory name and select All Tasks > Rescan (Full) which will build your index.

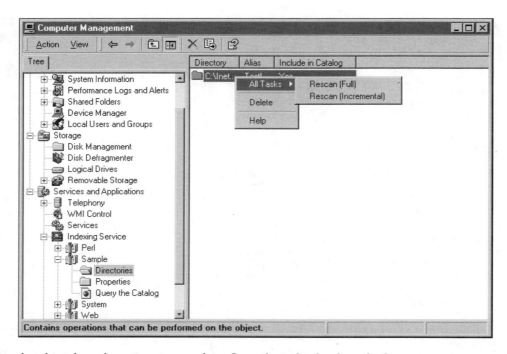

Note that this takes a long time to complete. Once the index has been built, you can start to search it.

Searching with COM Objects

With the search form already out of the way, building a web site search with the COM objects consists of five basic steps:

- ❏ Create an instance of the required objects.
- ❏ Populate the properties of those objects.
- ❏ Execute the query.
- ❏ Render the result set.
- ❏ Clean up any objects you have created.

Creating the Objects

We are writing an ASP script, so we do need provide a minimum set of HTML heading tags:

```
<%@ Language=VBScript %>
<HTML>
<HEAD></HEAD>
<BODY>
<H3>COM Search Results</H3>
<OL>
```

We can then start the actual script. As noted before, the result sets returned by the Indexing Service are also ADO recordsets, so we need to create one of those. We will also need a Query object. Our sample includes an Indexing Service Util Helper Object used to add a scope to the query:

```
<%
set objRS = Server.CreateObject("ADODB.Recordset")
set objQuery = Server.CreateObject("IXSSO.Query")
set objUtility = Server.CreateObject("IXSSO.Util")
```

Populating Properties

The default catalog for Web originating searches is "Web". In this case, we want to search our "Sample" catalog instead, so we need to see the Catalog property of the Query object to that name. Of course, you may set these properties in any order:

```
objQuery.Catalog = "Sample"
```

On the search form, we allow the user to select if they want to search all of the directories represented in the catalog or just the root directory. To implement this choice in our script, we can use the Util object to add the scope:

```
if ucase(Request.Form("SearchDepth")) = "S" then
   objUtility.AddScopeToQuery objQuery, "c:\Sample\html", "shallow"
else
   objUtility.AddScopeToQuery objQuery, "c:\Sample\html", "deep"
end if
```

In reality, we do not need the else part of this statement. By default, all scopes begin at the root and include all sub-directories. However, you never know if this behavior might change, and it is reasonable to code an explicit setting here.

Next, we need to define what metadata we want returned about each document in the result set. This is done by the Columns property. Remember that the Indexing Service is going to return an ADO recordset, so the values used are essentially the column names (and thus the keys) to each element in the recordset:

```
objQuery.Columns = "FileName, Size, Rank, Characterization, VPath, DocTitle,
Write"
```

Our form allows the user to select a maximum number of results desired, which is set on the Query object:

```
objQuery.MaxRecords = Request.Form("MaxRecords")
```

You can also define which constraining factor is more important when building the result set: the least processing time or the quality of hits. The OptimizeFor property controls this decision. If set to performance, the maximum number of matching files are found first, then documents for which the user context lacks security rights are removed. The alternative setting is hitcount, where the documents that the user context cannot access are not added to the result set while it is being compiled:

```
objQuery.OptimizeFor = "performance"
```

Next, we will set the query (or restriction) for the search. Recall that we provided three search options – phrase, content, and document title. By default, the COM objects use ISQL dialect 2, so we have to our query using this standard. The default search method is the content (free-text), so we can set the query equal to that phrase for matching and default search modes. For the phrase-based query, we just need to wrap the restriction in {phrase} and {/phrase} tags. For the document title option, we use a {prop} and {/prop} tag set, where the "prop" is short for property. You need to specify a property to work with, and these will typically be one of the columns you listed for the Columns property:

```
select case UCase(Request.Form("SearchMode"))
   case "P"
      objQuery.Query = "{phrase}" & Request.Form("Restriction") & "{/phrase}"
   case "C"
      objQuery.Query = Request.Form("Restriction")
   case "D"
      objQuery.Query = "{prop name=DocTitle}" & _
                                    Request.Form("Restriction") & "{/prop}"
   case else
      objQuery.Query = Request.Form("Restriction")
end select
```

We also offered users the choice of removing the FrontPage specific files and directories from the result set. This can be done by adding a Boolean constraint to the query that determines if the string "_vti_" is in the virtual path for the file and excludes it if so. This example shows the short hand "!" for "not", "#" for "property", and the pattern-matching operator ("*"):

```
if UCase(Request.Form("ExcludeFrontPage")) = "Y" then
   objQuery.Query = objQuery.Query & "&! #vpath */_vti_*"
end if
```

There is just one more property to set: the SortBy property, which instructs the Indexing Service how to order the result set. This should be the name of the columns in the Columns property and may be followed by the string "[d]" to sort in descending order:

```
objQuery.SortBy = "Rank[d]"
```

Executing the Search

Executing the search takes just one method call: CreateRecordset. You should define what type of recordset you want. Do that by providing a string parameter for the method. This string may be either sequential or non-sequential. If you use the first option, the resulting recordset will be just that: you can only read from the beginning of the result set and progress through the list one item at a time. If you want a result set that you scroll through, use the second option:

```
Set objRS = objQuery.CreateRecordset("sequential")
```

The Indexing Service is able to determine whether or not the files in the catalog have been filtered and indexed. If not, the OutOfDate property will be True. You should check this property and alert the user if the index is out of date. It would also be appropriate to recommend to the user that they retry the search in a few minutes to see if the catalog query has been completed:

```
If objQuery.OutOfDate Then
   Response.Write "<P><STRONG>Warning: </STRONG>" & _
      "Results may not be accurate as the catalog is out of date.</P>" & vbCrLf
End If
```

It is somewhat rare to have the `QueryIncomplete` property set to `True`. This happens if the restriction is too complex to be used by the Indexing Service or too many elements of the restriction were found. However, it is good to check for this situation:

```
If objQuery.QueryIncomplete Then
    Response.Write "<P><STRONG>Warning: </STRONG>" & _
        "Results may not be accurate as the query was incomplete.</P>" & vbCrLf
End If
```

Like all queries, the Indexing Service may not be able to fully complete a search within a given period of time. If that occurs, the `QueryTimedOut` property will be `True`. By default, queries are allocated 10 seconds of CPU time before timing out. That is not the same as ten seconds of real-time – queries may run for a few minutes before reaching this threshold.

> **Where is the `TimeOut` property set?** There is no such property for the Indexing Service (at least, not so far). To change the amount of CPU time searches run before timing out, you have to set the `MaxQueryExecutionTime` registry key.

```
If objQuery.QueryTimedOut Then
    Response.Write "<P><STRONG>Warning: </STRONG>" & _
            "Results may not be accurate as the query timed out.</P>" & vbCrLf
End If
```

Rendering the Result Set

This, at least, will probably seem very familiar. To render the result set, loop through the created recordset and write the columns out. We count how many records are presented so we can alert the user if no matching files were found:

```
IntRecCount = 0
While Not objRS.EOF
    If isNull(objRS("DocTitle")) Then
    Response.Write "<LI>" & j & "<A HREF=" & objRS("VPath") & ">" & " " & _
                    objRS("VPath") & "</A><BR>" & vbCrLf
    Else
    Response.Write "<LI>" & j & "<A HREF=" & objRS("VPath") & ">" & " " & _
                    objRS("DocTitle") & "</A><BR>" & vbCrLf
    End If
    Response.Write objRS("Characterization") & "<BR>" & vbCrLf
    Response.Write "<strong>Rank:</strong> " & objRS("Rank") & " " & vbCrLf
    Response.Write "<strong>Size:</strong> " & objRS("Size") & " " & vbCrLf
    Response.Write "<strong>Updated:</strong> " & objRS("Write") & "</LI>" & _
                    vbCrLf
    intRecCount = intRecCount + 1
    objRS.MoveNext
Wend
If intRecCount < 1 Then
    Response.Write "<P>No matching Records found"
End If
```

Cleaning Up

Since this script renders all of the result sets at once, we have finished with the recordset object and may close it. In ASP scripts, it is never a good idea to leave objects that you are no longer using lying around, so clean them up by setting them to nothing. We also need to close the HMTL page up so it renders correctly:

```
objRS.Close
Set objRS = Nothing
Set objUtil = Nothing
Set objQuery = Nothing
%>
</OL>
</BODY>
</HTML>
```

The resulting search appears as follows:

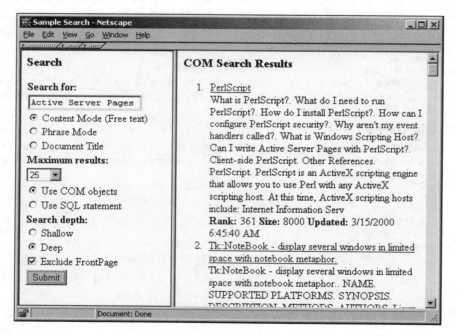

Searching with the OLE DB Provider

If you are familiar with calling OLE DB providers from your ASP Scripts, you might prefer to use SQL statements for querying the catalog. You take a performance hit do to so, but you also gain all of ADO's error-handling features.

Building a Connection String

The first question you have probably been asking is, "What is my connection string supposed to look like?"

```
Provider=MSIDXS.1;Integrated Security="";Data Source=Sample
```

The provider should always be MSIDXS, and you may specify a version as desired. The Indexing Service only supports Integrated Security, so this attribute can be omitted. The Data Source attribute contains the name or names of the desired catalog(s), separated by commas.

Starting the Script

Start the script off with the required HTML elements and an ASP Script start tag:

```
<%@ Language=VBScript %>
<HTML>
<HEAD>
</HEAD>
<BODY>
<H3>SQL Search Results</H3>
<OL>
```

Constructing the Query

The challenge of searching via the OLE DB Provider is getting your query right. Queries to the Indexing Service must have a SELECT clause and a FROM clause. The WHERE clause is technically optional, but since this is where you specify what the result set returns, then you do need one.

The SELECT clause is the easiest one to construct as you simply name the properties (or columns, if you will) that you want included in the result set:

```
<%
strQuery = _
    "SELECT FileName, Size, Rank, Characterization, VPath, DocTitle, Write"
```

The FROM clause is a bit more difficult. When constructing queries against the Indexing Service, scopes essentially fill the roll that tables would if you were querying a SQL Server store. To construct a scope, you need to specify the catalog name, a double dot, the SCOPE function, and a scope description. Note that the double double quotes wrapping the path are required:

```
If ucase(Request.Form("SearchDepth")) = "S" Then
    strQuery = strQuery & " FROM Sample..SCOPE(' SHALLOW TRAVERSAL OF ""/"" ')"
Else
    strQuery = strQuery & " FROM Sample..SCOPE(' DEEP TRAVERSAL OF ""/"" ')"
End If
```

The WHERE clause forms differently as well. The WHERE should be followed by a predicate. Predicates can be any of the following: ARRAY, CONTAINS, FREETEXT, LIKE, MATCHES, NULL or a comparison operation. ARRAY is used to scan multiple properties for a common value. FREETEXT and CONTAINS specify essentially content and phrase searches, respectively. LIKE works as it does in normal SQL (that is, it performs limited pattern matching: "%Wrox%" returns documents with Wrox anywhere in the columns selected against). MATCHES works on the same principal as LIKE, but allows a greater degree of control over the "likeness". You can use the IS NOT NULL construct to weed out empty properties. For CONTAINS and FREETEXT, follow the predicate with the restriction in single quotes.

685

```
Select Case UCase(Request.Form("SearchMode"))
    Case "D"
        strQuery = strQuery & " WHERE FREETEXT (DOCTITLE,'" & _
                                    Request.Form("Restriction") & " ')"
    Case "P"
        strQuery = strQuery & " WHERE CONTAINS (CONTENTS,'""" & _
                                    Request.Form("Restriction") & """ ')"
    Case "C"
        strQuery = strQuery & " WHERE FREETEXT (CONTENTS,'" & _
                                    Request.Form("Restriction") & " ')"
    Case Else
        strQuery = strQuery & " WHERE FREETEXT (CONTENTS,'" & _
                                    Request.Form("Restriction") & " ')"
End Select
```

Since we gave the user the option of excluding FrontPage specific documents from the result set, we need add a predicate phrase to strain them out in our query:

```
If UCase(Request.Form("ExcludeFrontPage")) = "Y" then
    strQuery = strQuery & "AND NOT MATCHES (VPath, '*_vti*')"
End If
```

Adding an ORDER BY phrase is conventional:

```
strQuery = strQuery & " ORDER BY Rank DESC"
```

Creating the ADO Objects

You have probably seen this a few too many times by now:

```
Set objConn = Server.CreateObject("ADODB.Connection")
Set objRS = Server.CreateObject("ADODB.Recordset")
```

Executing the Query

Now we can open the connection, set the maximum number of records and execute the query:

```
objConn.Open "Provider=MSIDXS.1;Data Source=Sample"
objRS.MaxRecords = Request.Form("MaxRecords")
objRS.Open strQuery, objConn
```

Rendering the Result Set

To render the result set, loop through the created recordset and write the columns out. We do count how many records are actually presented, so we can alert the user if no matching files were found:

```
intRecCount = 0
While Not objRS.EOF
    If isNull(objRS("DocTitle")) Then
        Response.Write "<LI>" & j & "<A HREF=" & objRS("VPath") & ">" & " " & _
                                    objRS("VPath") & "</A><BR>" & vbCrLf
    Else
Response.Write "<LI>" & j & "<A HREF=" & objRS("VPath") & ">" & " " & _
                                    objRS("DocTitle") & "</A><BR>" & vbCrLf
    End If
    Response.Write objRS("Characterization") & "<BR>" & vbCrLf
    Response.Write "<strong>Rank:</strong> " & objRS("Rank") & " " & vbCrLf
    Response.Write "<strong>Size:</strong> " & objRS("Size") & " " & vbCrLf
```

```
        Response.Write "<strong>Updated:</strong> " & objRS("Write") & "</LI>" & _
                            vbCrLf
    intRecCount = intRecCount + 1
    objRS.MoveNext
Wend
If intRecCount < 1 Then
    Response.Write "<P>No matching Records found"
End If
```

Cleaning up

Since this script renders all of the result sets at once, we are done with the connection and recordset objects and may close them. In ASP scripts, it is never a good idea to leave objects that you are no longer using lying around, so clean them up by setting them to nothing. We also need to close the HMTL page up so it renders correctly:

```
objRS.Close
Set objRS = Nothing
Set objConn = Nothing
%>
</OL>
</BODY>
</HTML>
```

Summary

In this chapter, we have explored two different ways of implementing searches for your web sites. The first method used the Indexing Service for Windows 2000 helper objects while the second method used OLE DB Provider for the service. We also looked at how you use script to create virtual web sites and Indexing Service catalogs. If you want to learn more about the Indexing Service, the following resources are recommended.

- ❑ Chapter 40 of *ASP 3.0 Programmer's Reference* (www.wrox.com/Consumer/Store/Details.asp?ISBN=1861003234) provides a very complete reference to using the Indexing Service with ASP.

- ❑ ASP Today has a number of good articles about the Indexing Service including *Creating Combined SQL Server and Index Service Queries*, (www.asptoday.com/articles/20000223.htm) *Querying Index Server using ADO*, (www.asptoday.com/articles/19990804.htm) and *Dealing with Ignored Words in Index Server* (www.asptoday.com/articles/19990409.htm)

- ❑ Krishna Nareddy has three very good articles in the collection: *Anatomy of a Search Solution*, (http://msdn.microsoft.com/library/techart/msdn_ss-intro.htm) *Introduction to Microsoft Index Server*, (http://msdn.microsoft.com/library/techart/msdn_is-intro.htm) and *Indexing with Microsoft Index Server* (http://msdn.microsoft.com/library/techart/msdn_is-index.htm).

- ❑ David Lee's *Using HTML Meta Properties with Microsoft Index Server* (http://msdn.microsoft.com/library/techart/msdn_ismeta.htm) is a great explanation of not only how to index meta properties, but provides an in depth explanation of defining and using custom columns.

- ❑ If you plan to make extensive use of the Index Query method, Mark Swank and Drew Kittle's *Designing and Implementing Microsoft Index Server* is priceless.

21

Semi-Structured Data and Internet Publishing

In this book we've been looking at accessing various different sources of data, including relational databases and directories. In this chapter we're going to look at how to use ADO to access another type of data: the contents of your web site. By this I don't mean just browsing a web site; I mean actually getting to the files on your web site so that you can manage it. This includes updating files, moving them around, and so on, *over the Internet* – in other words, without having to be logged on locally to the server on which the site is hosted. The OLE DB Provider that will allow us to do this is the OLE DB Provider for **Internet Publishing**.

This chapter is also going to bring two concepts together, which at first sight you wouldn't think were related: on the one hand, **semi-structured data**, and on the other hand Internet Publishing and the **WebDAV protocol**.

Semi-Structured Data is about data that is – well – just what the name implies, semi-structured. The structure of the data isn't quite regular enough to be stored in ADO recordsets, though it still retains some structure. Files in a file system are a good example of this. You might expect to be able to use a recordset for all the files in a given folder, but that won't work very well because different types of file can have different properties. A recordset expects all its rows to have exactly the same fields, so a new ADO object is needed to store this type of data – the Record object.

Internet Publishing is about managing your web sites, which means things like uploading new pages, modifying files (ASP and HTML files, images etc.) when you need to update your site, or deleting files – basically all the same things you might do on your local file system. This kind of maintenance has traditionally been done using the FTP protocol, but in this chapter we won't be using FTP – we'll be using an OLE DB Provider that is based on the newer, more powerful, WebDAV and FrontPage server extension protocols.

WebDAV stands for **Web Distributed Authoring and Versioning**, and is a standard protocol which allows remote maintenance of web sites. It is an extension to the HTTP protocol, designed to cover operations like moving, copying and deleting files. But it goes further than that, providing the ability, for example, to track versions of files and lock files while editing them. Microsoft have been working hard to make its software WebDAV-aware, and later in this chapter we'll explore some of the ways you can use the Windows user interface to directly use WebDAV to publish documents on web sites.

The reason that we're bringing these topics together is that the OLE DB Provider for Internet Publishing relies heavily on the principles of semi-structured data, so we need to understand those concepts in order to use this provider.

The reason we would use this provider is that it allows us to write scripts that can help us maintain our web sites. For example, you might use the Internet Publishing Provider in the following scenarios:

1. Your company has a policy that all pages on the site that have not been explicitly modified recently should be reviewed at least every two months to ensure they are still up to date. Accordingly, you need to ensure that any pages that have not been modified within the last two months are examined. Since there are many pages in the site spread across numerous folders, using FTP or a Windows Explorer user interface to locate the files in question would be laborious. Instead, you can write an ASP script which hunts through the site to identify the relevant files and automatically e-mails their details back to the person responsible for the reviewing.

2. If your site is hosted remotely by an ISP, you will not have direct access to the server and you need to regularly synchronise the site with your local copy of it, you can write a script that intelligently uploads only those files that have been modified more recently on the local copy than on the actual site.

3. If a number of individuals are responsible for maintaining different areas of your site, you could write some web pages that allow these individuals access to update only their own areas of the site, while restricting their ability to modify or view source code to pages outside their own areas.

4. If you run a large public site for which individuals outside your organisation are allowed to create or modify pages on your site or create their own pages in your domain, then you could write HTML pages that allow these individuals access to do this, while imposing whatever restrictions you wish (for example, that all their pages must begin with certain appropriate heading information – your script could add this information prior to placing the files on the site).

It should be pointed out that there are other ways of accomplishing some of these tasks – the beauty of using ASP and the Internet Publishing Provider is that it allows web site maintenance tasks like these to be carried out by scripting clients – so you can do your site maintenance from any machine connected to the Internet.

The ultimate goal of this chapter is to show you how to write ASP pages that use the Internet Publishing Provider to give access to web sites in order to manage the files there. Unfortunately there's a lot of new concepts involved – which means this is going to be one of those chapters where we'll have to spend quite a while going over the theory before we'll be in a position to start writing any code.

We're going to start by looking at the principles of semi-structured data by using an example of the folders in the Windows file system. In the process we'll introduce the ADO `Record` object, which is available from ADO version 2.5 onwards, and we'll examine how this object is related to the ADO recordset. Then we'll look at what Internet Publishing involves, and in the process, we'll look at the WebDAV protocols. Finally we'll introduce the OLE DB Provider for Internet Publishing, examine its capabilities, and go on to demonstrate our ASP pages that will use it. We'll also have a quick look at how you can do Internet Publishing with Windows Explorer and Internet Explorer. This latter topic isn't strictly related to ASP, but having a quick-and-easy user interface available to demonstrate the principles involved and check whether your code is working is always useful.

Semi-Structured Data

The usual way of representing data retrieved from data sources in ADO is using recordsets. Recordsets are extremely good at representing tables of data as might be stored in a relational database – and you'd generally imagine that each row of the recordset would correspond to a specific object, and each column to a specific field. If you were going to represent – say – the files in a folder on a web server in this way, you might expect to end up with something like this.

NAME	MIME TYPE	DATE LAST CHANGED
index.htm	text/html	3 June 00
MMCMap.htm	text/html	3 May 00
Images		8 Feb 00
Logo.gif	image/gif	8 Feb 00
...	...	...

By the way, if you're wondering, MIME stands for Multi-purpose Internet Mail Extension and is the Internet's equivalent of the Windows file name extensions .txt, .gif etc. Don't be confused by the reference to 'mail' in the name – MIME types were originally used for e-mail but their usage has since evolved to cover any Internet file. On web servers, files always have a MIME type associated with them that indicates how that file should be displayed in the browser. Although browsers don't necessarily rely on this information – for example Internet Explorer version 4 onwards uses a fairly complex algorithm that involves checking the MIME type, the actual contents of the document or image and, as a last resort, the file extension.

So far so good. We are on our way to being able to store information about the files in a recordset. We do have our first potential problem though – `Images`, being a folder, doesn't actually have a MIME type, so we've had to leave that field empty for that row. This is the real indication of how recordsets are going to be inadequate for this data, but we'll persevere with a recordset for the time being to see where that leads us, and then come back to this problem.

The fact that `Images` is a folder also reminds us that files in any kind of file system have a hierarchical structure, with folders being contained in other folders. That's not a problem for recordsets – all we need to do is store a reference to a recordset inside another (parent) recordset in order to represent folders within other folders. So our parent recordset will start to look like this:

NAME	MIME TYPE	DATE LAST CHANGED	SUB-FOLDSER
index.htm	text/html	3 June 00	
MMCMap.htm	text/html	3 May 00	
Images		8 Feb 00	ref to recordset
Logo.gif	image/gif	8 Feb 00	
...	...	...	...

Here ,the recordset referred to under `Images` will be a recordset of all the files and folders in the `Images` folder. In principle this seems no different to the nested or hierarchical recordsets that we cover in Chapter 29.

So, by using a hierarchy of recordsets it looks like we've solved the problem of representing a file system. But we still haven't dealt with the question of different files having different sets of properties. And the `Images` row in the above recordset has now given us a problem even more serious than the earlier fields with blank entries: We've had to create a new field just for this one folder. Given that most file systems will have many more files than folders, this means an awful lot of wasted space in the recordset. Not only that, but it may be hard to tell what additional properties may be needed later on for other files that get added – we're going to end up in a situation where the presence of columns in the folders recordset is dependent on which files happen to be in that folder.

What we really need is a way of storing all the standard properties that will apply to most or all items in a folder in a recordset, and putting any special properties that are specific to a given item somewhere else. It's for this reason that Microsoft provided the ADO **Record Object**.

The `Record` object is similar to a recordset except that it has only one row. So it has roughly the same methods and properties as a recordset, except that the methods that let you move between rows are missing. For the file system, a record represents a single file or folder while the recordset represents the collection of items in a folder. How this works is illustrated in the diagram below. We first connect to a `Record` object that represents the folder containing the entire web site. Records that represent folders each contain an associated recordset which you can use to enumerate over the children of that folder. You access this recordset with a method of the `Record` object, `GetChildren`, which we'll illustrate soon.

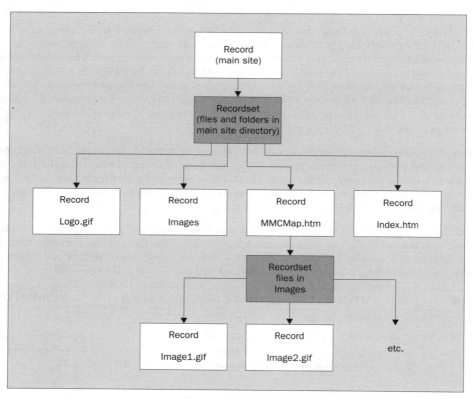

Note that although this example shows the `Record` object that represents the entire web site as the object you first connect to, you can select any file or folder on the site as the entry point. However, if you do this, you won't be able to navigate up from the file or folder you first connect to – you'll only be able to access files and folders below it.

So what we see is that as we move down the folder hierarchy, records and recordsets alternate: Each recordset contains information about a folder and contains one row for each file or folder in that folder. Where a record refers to a folder, then it contains in turn a reference to another recordset which can be used to access the children of that folder – this recordset can be accessed using the `GetChildren` method of the `Record` object. To open a record that represents a row of a recordset, you call the `Open` method of the `Record` object, passing a reference to the recordset as the only parameter.

Internet Publishing

Internet Publishing is all about maintaining the files on your web site. There are a couple of ways you would do this.

❑ **FTP** – The **File Transfer Protocol** is quite commonly used. In the bad old days of command prompts we'd sit there on our FTP commands, saying put `this_file` and put `that_file`. Nowadays, there are many third-party utilities like cuteFTP around, which allows you to swap files around with graphical user interfaces – but the underlying protocol is still FTP. FTP is useful for moving files to and from web sites, but its prime purpose is really for transferring files between machines – which means that's all it can do. As we'll see later, there are many more things you'd want to do with your files than just transferring them to and from the web site.

❑ **WEC** – This is the **Web Extender Client** protocol. It's not an industry standard protocol, but is something that is defined by Microsoft and implemented by the FrontPage Server Extensions. Essentially, if the web server supports the FrontPage Server Extensions and they happen to have been installed there, then you will be able to use this protocol to talk to it. IIS version 4.0 and newer supports WEC, as well as Personal Web Server (PWS). The fact that FrontPage Server Extensions are vendor-specific is regarded as a disadvantage, but having said that, they are available for other web servers such as Apache, and hence are widely supported across the Internet.

❑ **WebDAV** – Web Distributed Authoring and Versioning is intended as the real industry-standard solution.

More About WebDAV

In this chapter, we really don't need to understand much about WebDAV. After all, we're going to be using ADO to talk to our web servers, and one of the main points of ADO is that it hides the details of the underlying protocols and APIs used to talk to the data source. So it is possible to use the OLE DB Provider for Internet Publishing without bothering about how it talks to the site. Nevertheless, WebDAV is an important standard. Parts of it are still being finalized, but it does promise a very rich set of functionality, so it won't do us any harm to know a bit about it and what it can do. You can find the full specifications for WebDAV in RFC 2518.

The ultimate aim of WebDAV is to allow users to work together with documents that are stored on the server, no matter what platform the users are working on, what authoring tools they are using, or what platform the web server is running on.

WebDAV is an extension to the HTTP protocol – in other words it works much like HTTP but adds a number of other commands. With HTTP, essentially all you can do is request files with the GET command or send information from a form using the POST command. WebDAV adds methods to move, copy, and delete files. It's also possible to retrieve the raw version of a file – in other words, if it's an ASP file, to retrieve the actual ASP code, without it having been processed by IIS into an HTML page. Obviously, WebDAV also includes security features – you will need to authenticate before you can start playing about with the site.

What will make WebDAV particularly powerful is the promise that it will eventually be able to handle versioning issues and access synchronization.

Versioning is something that you will have encountered if you use Visual SourceSafe (VSS) or some other source control software in your development projects. In VSS, after modifying a document or code, you can **check it in**, which means that its current state will be stored as a well-defined version. You also need to explicitly **check out** a document before you can make any changes to it. VSS will remember changes you subsequently make to the document so that if you realize a couple of months later you need to view that version of the document, you can recover it. You can also branch out versions. For example, if you have version A of a document, you might create version B by making some changes to version A. Then independently, you might create version C, also by making some changes to version A. Different branches can also later be merged back into a single version, though this process is more complex as some user input may be needed to decide how to merge conflicting changes.

Access synchronization, or locking, is important to prevent different users from simultaneously making conflicting changes to a document, resulting in one user unwittingly destroying the changes that have been made by another user. This can be a particular problem with web servers since different users may be working from different locations and hence unable to speak directly to each other in order to coordinate their work on the site. WebDAV will allow users to temporarily lock files, preventing other users from writing to them.

Details of versioning and locking have yet to be finalized, so in this chapter we'll stick to the simpler operations of moving files around, viewing their properties and viewing their contents.

One point I should mention is that in this chapter we've been talking loosely about accessing files and folders on a web site. WebDAV doesn't really think in terms of files and folders, but in terms of **resources** – which roughly means any object that forms part of the web site. This is in recognition that there are many different items that may be available on a site, for example, if the site is running IIS then there will also be virtual directories. However, in this chapter we'll continue to refer to the objects we access as files and folders since this is how they actually appear to us as the end users, for example a virtual directory in reality just looks like a folder.

The OLE DB Provider for Internet Publishing

You've probably gathered most of what this provider does by now, but we'll quickly go over what's going on.

This provider is called MSDAIPP.DSO and is a fairly standard OLE DB Provider, except that it uses a web server as its data source. It has two ways that it can talk to the web server – it can use the FrontPage Server Extensions or it can use WebDAV. This makes it slightly unusual in that most OLE DB Providers only use one protocol. With MSDAIPP, when you set up your connection string you can optionally specify which protocol you want it to use. If you don't specify one then the provider will try them both out to see which one works. My own tests suggested that it tries the FrontPage Extensions first and only goes for WebDAV if FrontPage doesn't get it anywhere, though that doesn't seem to be documented so I wouldn't rely on it.

The Internet Publishing Provider allows you to do the following when you connect to a site:

- ❏ List the files and folders and navigate through the folders
- ❏ View properties of files and folders
- ❏ Open files to view and edit their contents
- ❏ Move, copy and delete files

One other thing that's unusual about the Internet Publishing Provider is that you never really use the `Command` object or pass command strings to it to execute. Instead, you perform all the operations like retrieving data, navigating through the web site directory hierarchy and moving and copying files by calling methods on the `Record` and `Recordset` objects. Passing in command strings wouldn't really make much sense since the Internet Publishing Provider can use different protocols to connect to the web server, and the commands issued would depend on which protocol it is using.

One potentially confusing point you need to be aware of is that when you are using the Internet Publishing Provider with ASP, you are actually dealing with two web servers as well as the end client machine that you are running the web browser on: The server that is running ASP, and the server that you are using Internet Publishing to manage. This is shown in this diagram:

These applications may or may not be running on the same machine: it's perfectly possible to run a browser to connect to the local host, and/or have the Internet Publishing Provider connect to the same machine again. This is actually quite a plausible scenario if you are posting some ASP pages on your site that use the Internet Publishing Provider in order to manage the same site, and if you are able to log in locally as a site administrator! Nevertheless, we do need to logically distinguish the machines. For the rest of this chapter I'll distinguish the two web servers when I need to by referring to them as the *ASP Web Server* and the *Published Web Server* – these are my terms, not terms that are in general use.

Connecting to MSADIPP

Connecting to the Internet Publishing Provider is in principle very simple – a matter of supplying the correct connection string and a file path name.

> You should note that although it is in principle very simple, there are at present some security issues which can prevent the Internet Publishing Provider from working under ASP on some machines. The problem appears to be to do with the fact that under Windows NT/Windows 2000, the Internet Guest Account, by default, does not have the permissions it needs to access certain files and folders. At the time of writing, we understand Microsoft are investigating the problem, and information about this and the solutions will also be posted on the Wrox Press web site as soon as it is available. In the meantime, we've tested all the code in this chapter on a machine for which Windows 2000 is installed on a FAT32 partition, rather than an NTFS partition, which effectively disables file and folder permissions checking. However, because of the security implications, we strongly recommend that you *do not use FAT32 partitions on your web servers*.

The standard connection string looks like this:

```
Provider=MSDAIPP.DSO;Data Source=http://SiteName;User
ID=AccountName;Password=Password
```

We here substitute the appropriate URL (including the `http://` prefix) into the `Data Source` field, and username and password for the published web server. The URL is the same as the URL you would use if you were using Internet Explorer to browse that site.

Microsoft have, however, provided an alternative version that doesn't explicitly name the provider:

```
URL=http://SiteName;User ID=AccountName;Password=Password
```

If the connection object sees `URL=` as the first item in the connection string then it knows that it needs to look for the Internet Publishing Provider (in much the same way that if you don't supply a provider name at all, OLE DB will by default bind to the OLE DB Provider for ODBC).

If you wish you can also specify the version of the provider name (currently version 1), by using `MSDAIPP.DSO.1` instead of `MSDAIPP.DSO`, though this isn't normally recommended as this ties you down to a specific version, preventing your code from being able to automatically take advantage of new versions, and may cause your code to fail altogether if your preferred version isn't installed on the machine. A connection string that specifies the provider version might, for example, look like this:

```
Provider=MSDAIPP.DSO.1;Data Source=http://SiteName;User
ID=AccountName;Password=Password
```

This is, in fact, the string I will use the later samples – since it happens to be what works on my own computer.

For other OLE DB Providers the connection string is not sufficient to return a recordset – generally you also need a command string, such as an SQL statement. The Internet Publishing Provider doesn't use command strings, but we do still need some extra information besides the connection string to return a result – in this case a `Record` rather than a `Recordset`. The extra information needed is the name of the file you want to initially bind to, so the `Record`'s `Open` method takes the file name as the first parameter and the connection string as the second parameter.

This all means that in ASP, the following code snippets are all legitimate ways of retrieving a record object:

```
Dim oRec
Set oRec = Server.CreateObject("ADODB.Record")
oRec.Open "", "Provider=MSDAIPP.DSO.1;" & _
    "Data Source=http://MyGroovySite.com;" & _
    "User ID=administrator;Password=lego2453"
```

Since the initial file name is blank, this will give you a record that represents the web site itself, allowing you access to the entire site.

Passing a file name as well as a URL may seem redundant because the URL can contain a file name, but the reason for doing it this way is that the URL provided with the connection string indicates the highest level in the directory hierarchy that it is possible to access – in other words you cannot navigate above the file or folder indicated in the connection string, using that connection. This gives you an extra degree of control over security, preventing people who use your script from being able to access areas of the site you don't want them to.

Alternatively, if you are only interested in a subdirectory called `Images`, you could do this:

```
Dim oRec
Set oRec = Server.CreateObject("ADODB.Record")
oRec.Open "Images", "Provider=MSDAIPP.DSO.1;" & _
    "Data Source=http://MyGroovySite.com;" & _
    "User ID=administrator;Password=lego2453"
```

or this:

```
Dim oRec
Set oRec = Server.CreateObject("ADODB.Record")
oRec.Open "", "Provider=MSDAIPP.DSO.1;" & _
    "Data Source=http://MyGroovySite.com/Images;" & _
    "User ID=administrator;Password=lego2453"
```

If you want to use a connection object explicitly you could do it this way:

```
Dim sConnString
sConnString = "Provider=MSDAIPP.DSO;" & _
    "Data Source=http://MyGroovySite.com/Images;" & _
    "User ID=administrator;Password=lego2453"

Dim oConn
Set oConn = Server.CreateObject("ADODB.Connection")
oConn.Open(sConnString)
Dim oRec
Set oRec = Server.CreateObject("ADODB.Record")
oRec.Open "", oConn
```

Or using the alternative `URL=` syntax:

```
Dim oConn
Set oConn = Server.CreateObject("ADODB.Connection")
oConn.Open("URL=http://MyGroovySite.com/Images;" & _
    "User ID=administrator;Password=lego2453")
Dim oRec
Set oRec = Server.CreateObject("ADODB.Record")
oRec.Open "", oConn
```

ADO is traditionally flexible, so you can probably dream up many more possible combinations based on these examples. Whichever one you prefer will depend largely on your own tastes and what you are trying to achieve. Using an explicit connection object is generally recommended for performance reasons, if you want to re-use the same object to open many different records.

You should note that none of these examples use a `Command` object; as mentioned before the command object doesn't really come into the picture with MSDAIPP.

The `Open` method of the `Record` object takes several other optional parameters. The full list is:

```
Open Source, ActiveConnection, Mode, CreateOptions, Options, UserName, Password
```

We've covered the `Source` and `ActiveConnection` parameters. The other parameters are:

`Mode` indicates the permissions you want for reading or writing to the object as well as sharing it with other users. Values are taken from the ADO `ConnectModeEnum` enumeration, which are as follows:

adModeRead	1	This indicates read-only permissions.
adModeReadWrite	3	This indicates read/write permissions.
adModeRecursive	0x400000	This applies permissions recursively.
adModeShareDenyNone	16	This prevents others from opening the connection with any permissions.
adModeShareDenyRead	4	This prevents others from opening the connection with read permissions.
adModeShareDenyWrite	8	This prevents others from opening the connection with write permissions.
adModeShareExclusive	12	This prevents others from opening the connection.
adModeUnknown	0	This is the default value. It indicates that the permissions have not yet been set or cannot be determined.
adModeWrite	2	This indicates write-only permissions.

`CreateOptions` indicates what action to take if the file or folder does not already exist. Its values are taken from the ADO `RecordCreateOptionsEnum` enumeration and can be any of the following:

AdFailIfNotExists	-1	The default value. The attempt to open the record will fail if the requested file or folder does not exist.
AdCreateCollection	0x2000	If the record does not exist then a new folder (collection) will be created. If the record already exists then the `Open` method will fail unless you also specify either `adOpenIfExists` or `adCreateOverwrite`.
adCreateNonCollection	0	If the record does not exist then a new file will be created.
AdCreateOverwrite	0x4000000	Modifies the creation flags `adCreateCollection`, `adCreateNonCollection`, and `adCreateStructDoc` so that if the file or folder already exists then it will be overwritten.
AdCreateStructDoc	0x80000000	If the record does not exist then a new record of type `adStructDoc` will be created.

AdOpenIfExists	0x2000000	Modifies the creation flags `adCreateCollection`, `adCreateNonCollection`, and `adCreateStructDoc` so that if the file or folder already exists then it will be opened instead of a new one being created.

Note that some of these flags can be combined using the bitwise OR operator – for which you can use either + or OR in ASP pages: `adCreateOverwrite + adCreateCollection`, or alternatively `adCreateOverwrite OR adCreateCollection`

`Options` specifies various options for how the record is to be treated. These values can be combined with the + or Or operators. Possible values include:

adOpenRecord Unspecified	-1	The default value. None of the other special options in this table apply. All fields are returned immediately with this option.
AdDelayFetch Fields	0x8000	Fields associated with this record are retrieved only when needed, not when the record is open. Will make opening the record faster at the expense of more round trips to the server when fields are later requested.
AdDelayFetch Stream	0x4000	By default the contents of the file are fetched when it is opened and placed in a stream object. This option delays that process until the stream object is actually requested by the client.
AdOpenAsync	0x1000	Record is opened asynchronously. Not relevant to ASP clients.
AdOpenSource	0x800000	If this record points to an executable script, such as an ASP page, then the source for the script will be returned in the stream rather than the compiled HTML output.

The final two parameters are simply authentication credentials which you can pass in if you need to – though you can alternatively absorb them into the connection string, as we have done in our examples.

We've now learnt about the Internet Publishing Provider and learnt how to bind to it. We're just about ready to dive in and start writing some ASP pages. But before we do that I'm going to quickly show you how you can get a lot of Internet publishing facilities without any coding at all – by using Windows Explorer and Internet Explorer.

Internet Publishing from Windows Explorer

One of the less well-known facilities of Windows Explorer is that you can manage your web sites from it. Yes that's right, I did say Windows Explorer. I didn't say Internet Explorer.

Now this book is about ASP, not about the Windows User Interface. What we really want to do is learn how to code up Internet Publishing stuff in ASP pages. But when I've been debugging my code I've never objected to having a ready-made user interface that I can use to duplicate some of what my code is doing, and hence help check that the code is working properly. So, in that spirit we'll take a quick swipe at Windows Explorer – then we'll see how Internet Explorer can do something similar.

As far as Explorer is concerned, the term for a web site that you are accessing via WebDAV or the FrontPage Extensions is a **Web Folder**. In Windows 98 and NT 4.0 machines, you can find the Web Folders node under My Computer. Web Folders are not a feature of Windows 95:

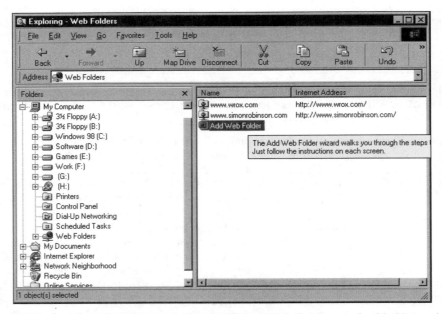

In Windows 2000, the principle is the same, but you'll find Web Folders under My Network Places. If you select Web Folders in the tree view and double click on Add Web Folder you'll be taken through a short wizard that asks you for the URL to the site (which needs to be the same URL that you'd use if you were browsing the site, for example http://www.wrox.com, or just www.wrox.com) and the user name and password to log on. As you can see from the above screenshot I've got two folders set up, to my own web site and the Wrox web site.

If you double click on a web folder, you get to see all the files there – or at least, all the ones that the authentication credentials you supplied will give you access to:

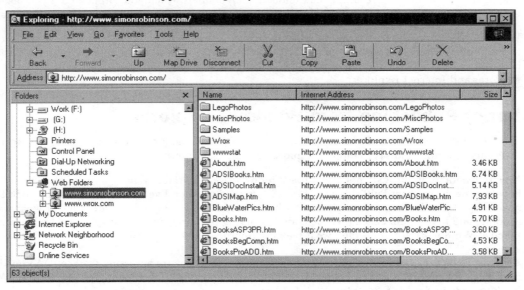

You can download and upload files, or even copy files between different web sites in just the same way you'd move local files around – provided of course you have sufficient security permissions on the web servers to do so. (Though if you try to copy files between different sites you'll find Windows does it by first downloading the file to your local machine then uploading again – there's no way to avoid that.)

Internet Publishing with Internet Explorer

In Internet Explorer 5.0 and above, you can achieve something similar by connecting to a URL and specifying that you wish to connect to it as a web folder. You can't do this by just typing in the URL in the usual edit box. You have to explicitly go to the File menu and select the Open option. This gives you a dialog box to type the URL, with a check box to indicate you want to open the site as a web folder rather than just issuing a straight HTTP request to look at the site. This feature is not available in Internet Explorer 4x:

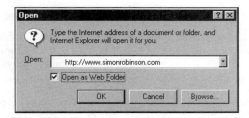

This gives you a view much the same as the Windows Explorer view, and with similar functionality:

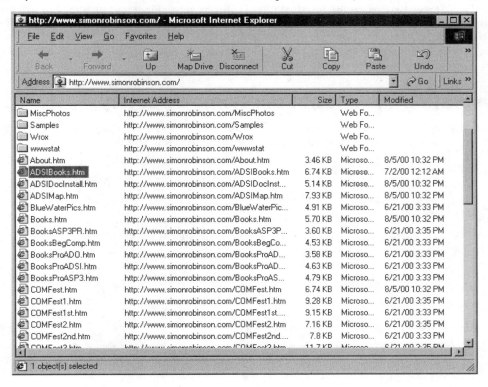

Internet Publishing with ASP

We're at last ready to present some code samples that use the Internet Publishing Provider. We're going to present some simple samples that show the basic operations you can carry out. That means that some of these examples are going to look a bit pointless at first sight, since they are doing things like moving files, which as isolated operations you could do more easily using say Windows Explorer. The point is of course that in practice you will incorporate these operations in larger, more complex, scripts that do perform non-trivial tasks. Before we do that we'll quickly go over what software you'll need to have installed to be able to use the samples.

Software Requirements for Internet Publishing from ADO

As mentioned before there are three machines involved. The client is easy to deal with – you just need a web browser on it.

The ASP Web Server (the server you host your ASP pages on) will need IIS 4.0 or later and at least MDAC 2.5 installed. If you are running Windows 2000 then you will have MDAC 2.5 as part of the operating system, otherwise you will need to install it. You can be running any version of Windows from Windows 95 OSR2 onwards or Windows NT Service Pack 4 onwards. (Though if you are running NT 4.0, you will need to run the server version otherwise you won't be able to install IIS.)

The Published Web Server (the one you try to connect to with MSDAIPP) must be running a web server that supports either the WebDAV protocol or the WEC protocol. If it is running IIS 5.0 then you'll be fine since IIS 5.0 supports WebDAV. If you are running IIS 4.0 then you'll need to ensure the FrontPage Server Extensions are installed (these come as an optional part of IIS). You will also find there are a number of other web servers that support the FrontPage Server extensions including Apache Web Server and Netscape (Enterprise Server and FastTrack Server). You can alternatively use any of these servers provided that the FrontPage Server Extensions are installed. This means that the Published Web Server doesn't even need to be running Windows.

Enumerating the Files in the Home Directory

Our first sample will list all the files in the home directory of a site – that is the main directory of a site. For now we won't try and browse into folders – we'll come to that later.

The ASP script looks like this:

```
<%@ Language = VBScript %>
<% Option Explicit %>

<!DOCTYPE HTML PUBLIC "-//W3C//DTD HTML 4.0 Transitional//EN">
<HTML>
<HEAD>
<TITLE> Enumerate Files</TITLE>
</HEAD>

<BODY>

<H2>List of top level files on a site</H2>

<!-- METADATA TYPE="typelib" UUID="{00000205-0000-0010-8000-00AA006D2EA4}" -->
<!-- you might want to modify the GUID depending on what version of ADO you have.
Above one is for ADO 2.5 -->
```

```
<%
' create and open record
Dim oRec
Set oRec = Server.CreateObject("ADODB.Record")

Dim g_sConnString
g_sConnString = "Provider=MSDAIPP.DSO;Data Source=http://BiggyBiggy;User
ID=administrator;password=spicegirl"
oRec.Open "", g_sConnString

Response.Write "<H3>Connected to URL: " & _
                                 oRec("RESOURCE_ABSOLUTEPARSENAME") & "</H3>"

' check whether this is a folder
If (oRec("RESOURCE_ISCOLLECTION") = True) Then
  ' get recordset to list contained files and folders
  Dim oRS
  Set oRS = oRec.GetChildren

  Response.Write "Files etc. contained in this folder are:<P>"
  Do While Not oRS.EOF
    Response.Write oRS("DisplayName") & "<BR>"
    oRS.MoveNext
  Loop
  oRS.Close
  Set oRS = Nothing
Else
  Response.Write "This object is not a folder."
End If

oRec.Close
Set oRec = Nothing
%>

</BODY>
</HTML>
```

If we go over the script in detail, we see the normal HTML headers, followed by the inclusion of an ADO type library:

```
<!-- METADATA TYPE="typelib" UUID="{00000205-0000-0010-8000-00AA006D2EA4}" -->
```

I should stress that this line is strictly speaking not needed in this particular page – in fact it would be more efficient not to put it in here since it causes the scripting engine to go and read the ADO type library. I've included it so we have access to any ADO named constants that we might need. As it happens we're not going to use any in this page, but to keep things simple and consistent I've just put this line in all the scripts, on the basis that it's there if we do need it.

Next we create the record object in the way we did earlier, and write out the URL we've connected to:

```
Response.Write "<H3>Connected to URL: " & _
                                 oRec("RESOURCE_ABSOLUTEPARSENAME") & "</H3>"
```

Here we're using the record object's property, RESOURCE_ABSOLUTEPARSENAME, which returns the full URL of the object the recordset represents. We'll list the main properties available soon.

Next we enumerate the files in the set:

```
' check whether this is a folder
If (oRec("RESOURCE_ISCOLLECTION") = True) Then
   ' get recordset to list contained files and folders
   Dim oRS
   Set oRS = oRec.GetChildren

   Response.Write "Files etc. contained in this folder are:"
   Do While Not oRS.EOF
     Response.Write oRS("DisplayName") & "<BR>"
     oRS.MoveNext
   Loop
   oRS.Close
   Set oRS = Nothing
Else
   Response.Write "This object is not a folder."
End If
```

The code shows that we use the GetChildren method of the record object to retrieve a reference to a recordset, the individual rows of which correspond to the files and folders in the current record, assuming the current record represents an object which is a folder. If the current Record represents a file then it will not contain other files, and the GetChildren method will raise an error – we get round this by first using the property, RESOURCE_ISCOLLECTION, to check whether the item we are looking at can contain other items. The RESOURCE_ISCOLLECTION property indicates, returns True if the record represents a folder or directory, which can therefore contain other objects, and False otherwise.

This is the kind of output that you will get:

Enumerating the Properties on a File or Folder

The properties of a file or folder are obtained using the Fields collection of the corresponding Record object. Alternatively you can use the Fields collection of the recordset that contains that file or folder – though in this latter case you will only retrieve the standard properties common to all files.

The next sample displays the properties of the main Record object for the web site as a whole. Since the HTML headers etc. are the same for this and all following code samples, we won't show those but will concentrate on the ASP code:

```
<%
' create and open record
Dim oRec
Set oRec = Server.CreateObject("ADODB.Record")

Dim g_sConnString
g_sConnString = "Provider=MSDAIPP.DSO;Data Source=http://crashlots;User
ID=administrator;password=spicegirl"
oRec.Open "", g_sConnString

Response.Write "<H3>Connected to URL: " & _
                              oRec("RESOURCE_ABSOLUTEPARSENAME") & "</H3>"

Response.Write "<TABLE><THEAD><TH>Name</TH><TH>Value</TH></THEAD>"
Response.Write "<TBODY>"

Dim oField
For Each oField In oRec.Fields
    Response.Write "<TR><TD>" & oField.Name & "</TD><TD>" & oField.Value & _
                "</TD></TR>"
Next

Response.Write "</TBODY></TABLE>"

oRec.Close
Set oRec = Nothing
%>
```

This code produces this output:

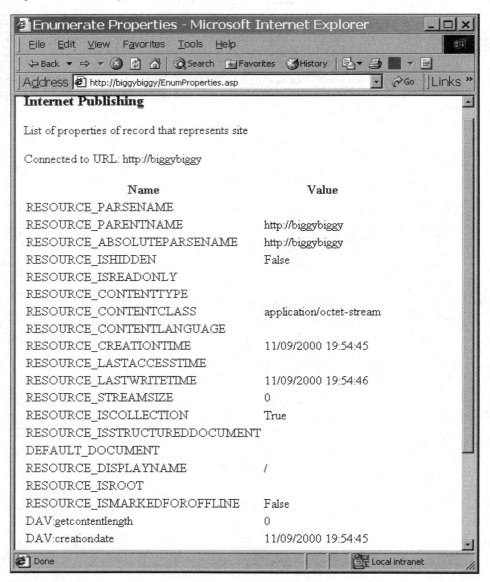

As we can see from the output there are quite a number of properties, although many of them are empty. This is because some of the properties are required by the WebDAV standards, but no value happens to have been set for them by default in IIS.

Because different files can have different properties, it's not really possible to give an exhaustive list of all the possible properties. However, for reference, we'll list the standard properties – the ones that you will find returned by recordsets with the Internet Publishing Provider – you'll normally find records will return all these properties and additional ones:

RESOURCE_PARSENAME	adVarWChar	The relative URL of the resource – in other words the name of the file or folder.
RESOURCE_PARENTNAME	adVarWChar	The full URL of the parent of this object.
RESOURCE_ABSOLUTEPARSENAME	adVarWChar	The full URL of this object.
RESOURCE_ISHIDDEN	adBoolean	Whether the resource is hidden.
RESOURCE_ISREADONLY	adBoolean	Indicates if the resource may not be modified.
RESOURCE_CONTENTTYPE	adVarWChar	MIME type of the document (for example text/html).
RESOURCE_CONTENTCLASS	adVarWChar	Likely use of the document.
RESOURCE_CONTENTLANGUAGE	adVarWChar	Language in which contents are stored.
RESOURCE_CREATIONTIME	adFileTime	The time the resource was created.
RESOURCE_LASTACCESSTIME	adFileTime	The time the resource was last accessed.
RESOURCE_LASTWRITETIME	adFileTime	The time the resource was last modified.
RESOURCE_STREAMSIZE	asUnsigned BigInt	The size of the contents of the resource.
RESOURCE_ISCOLLECTION	adBoolean	Whether the resource can contain other resources (is a folder) .
RESOURCE_ISSTRUCTUREDDOCUMENT	adBoolean	Whether the resource is a structured document (simple files and collections are not).
DEFAULT_DOCUMENT	adVarWChar	Whether this is the default file returned by this web site.
CHAPTERED_CHILDREN	adChapter	This column is required by WebDAV, but is not used by MSDAIPP.
RESOURCE_DISPLAYNAME	adVarWChar	User-friendly display name.
RESOURCE_ISROOT	adBoolean	Whether resource is the root of a collection or structured document.

Moving or Renaming a File or Folder

As far as Internet Publishing is concerned, moving and renaming files are the same thing. They are both done using the MoveRecord method of the record object. The following code snippet demonstrates this by renaming the file index.htm as index2.htm, and then moving the file COMFest.htm to the Events folder (we assume these files all already exist).

```
<%
' create and open record
Dim oRec
Set oRec = Server.CreateObject("ADODB.Record")
Dim oConn
```

```
Set oConn = Server.CreateObject("ADODB.Connection")

Dim g_sConnString
g_sConnString = "Provider=MSDAIPP.DSO;Data Source=http://crashlots"
oConn.Open g_sConnString,MyUserName,MyPassword

oRec.Open "index.htm", oConn
Response.Write "<H3>Connected to URL: " & _
                              oRec("RESOURCE_ABSOLUTEPARSENAME") & "</H3>"
oRec.MoveRecord , index2.htm

oRec.MoveRecord "COMFest.htm","Events/COMFest.htm"

oConn.Close
Set oConn = Nothing
oRec.Close
Set oRec = Nothing
%>
```

Note in this code we use one `Record` object for both moves. The object is initially bound to the `index.htm` file, which we move to `index2.htm` with this line:

```
oRec.MoveRecord , index2.htm
```

The first parameter to `MoveRecord` is the URL (absolute or relative) to the source record, the second is where we want to move it to. However, if we omit the first parameter then the move is applied to the object that this record is attached to. Thus the above line moves the `index.htm` file, because that's the file we specified when we opened the `Record` object.

For the second move, we want the move to apply to a different file so we specify the first parameter:

```
oRec.MoveRecord "COMFest.htm", "Events/COMFest.htm"
```

Note that `MoveRecord` also takes four other optional parameters. The full syntax is:

```
MoveRecord Source, Destination, UserID, Password, Options, Async
```

The `UserID` and `Password` are to authenticate you to the destination URL if necessary – they may be required in the event that you are moving the object to a different location on the web site, access to which requires different user credentials from those used to access the part of the site the file is being moved from.

`Options` is one value taken from the `MoveRecordOptionsEnum`. Possible values are:

adMoveUnspecified	-1	The default value. Operation will fail if the destination already exists, and HTML links will be updated.
adMoveOverWrite	1	If the destination already exists it will be overwritten.
adMoveDontUpdateLinks	2	Doesn't update HTML links.
adMoveAllowEmulation	4	If an attempt to ask the server to perform the move fails, then MSDAIPP will simulate it by downloading the file locally, uploading it with a new name and deleting to old file.

The final `Async` parameter requests the move to be performed asynchronously, and so is not relevant to ASP clients.

708

Copying a File or Folder

This uses the `CopyRecord` method of the record object. The `CopyRecord` object works in exactly the same way as `MoveRecord`, except that it creates a copy of the original file or folder rather than moving it. Thus this code copies the file `index.htm` to the file `index2.htm`, then copies the file `COMFest.htm` to the `Events` folder:

```
Dim g_sConnString
g_sConnString = "Provider=MSDAIPP.DSO;Data Source=http://crashlots"
oConn.Open g_sConnString,MyUserName,MyPassword

oRec.Open "index.htm", oConn
Response.Write "<H3>Connected to URL: " & _
                          oRec("RESOURCE_ABSOLUTEPARSENAME") & "</H3>"

oRec.CopyRecord , index2.htm

oRec.CopyRecord "COMFest.htm", "Events/COMFest.htm"
```

Even the parameter list to `CopyRecord` is identical to that for `MoveRecord`, except that the `Options` are now taken from the `CopyRecordOptionsEnum`, for which possible values are:

adCopyUnspecified	-1	The default. Recursively copies any folders, but fails if the destination already exists.
adCopyOverWrite	1	Overwrites destination if it already exists.
adCopyNonRecursive	2	Does not copy any subfolders of the folder to be copied.
adCopyAllowEmulation	4	If a direct copy attempt fails, attempts to emulate this with download and upload operations.

Creating a New File or Folder

There is no specific method to create a new file or folder. However, it can be done by opening a new `Record` object and specifying, in the `Options` parameter, that a new file or folder should be opened. In other words, open a record, giving it the name of a the new resource you want to create, and indicate either the `adCreateNonCollection` or the `adCreateCollection` flag, depending whether it is a file or folder you wish to create.

Deleting a File or Folder

You delete a file or folder using the `DeleteRecord` method. This code will delete first the file `index.htm` and then the file `COMFest.htm`:

```
oRec.Open "index.htm", oConn
Response.Write "<H3>Connected to URL: " & _
                          oRec("RESOURCE_ABSOLUTEPARSENAME") & "</H3>"

oRec.DeleteRecord
oRec.DeleteRecord "COMFest.htm"
```

As with `MoveRecord` and `CopyRecord`, the first parameter to `DeleteRecord` is the name of the file or folder to be deleted. If the parameter is omitted, as in the first call to `DeleteRecord` in the above code, the file or folder pointed to by this record is the one deleted. (`DeleteRecord` takes one additional optional parameter, an asynchronous flag, which there is no point using from ASP!)

Reading the Contents of a File

The `Record` object itself can't read the contents of a file, but you can do it by opening a `Stream` object associated with the record, and displaying its contents:

```
<BODY>

<H3> Internet Publishing </H3>
<P>List of properties of record that represents site<P>

<!-- METADATA TYPE="typelib" UUID="{00000205-0000-0010-8000-00AA006D2EA4}" -->
<!-- you might want to modify the GUID depending on what version of ADO you have.
Above one is for ADO 2.1 -->

<%
' create and open record
Dim oRec
Set oRec = Server.CreateObject("ADODB.Record")

Dim g_sConnString
g_sConnString = "Provider=MSDAIPP.DSO;Data Source=http://biggybiggy;User
ID=administrator;password=spicegirl"

oRec.Open "index.htm", g_sConnString

Response.Write "<H3>Connected to URL: " & _
                            oRec("RESOURCE_ABSOLUTEPARSENAME") & "</H3>"

Dim oStm
Set oStm = CreateObject("ADODB.Stream")
oStm.Charset = "ascii"
oStm.Open oRec, adModeRead, adOpenStreamFromRecord

Response.Write "<P>Text of this file is: <P>"
Response.Write "<PRE>" & Server.HTMLEncode(oStm.ReadText) & "</PRE>"

oStm.Close

oRec.Close
Set oRec = Nothing
%>

</BODY></HTML>
```

In order to display the contents of a file, we first instantiate a `Stream` object. We set its `Charset` property to `ascii` to indicate this is a plain text file. We then open the stream, using the `adOpenStreamFromRecord` flag, which indicates that the contents of the stream should be taken from the file associated with the given record object. Finally we use the `ReadText` method of the stream object to actually obtain the contents of the stream:

```
Dim oStm
Set oStm = CreateObject("ADODB.Stream")
oStm.Charset = "ascii"
oStm.Open oRec, adModeRead, adOpenStreamFromRecord

Response.Write "<P>Text of this file is: <P>"
Response.Write "<PRE>" & Server.HTMLEncode(oStm.ReadText) & "</PRE>"
```

Note that in displaying the file we HTMLEncode its contents to prevent tags in the file from being interpreted by the browser. We also enclose this text in a <PRE> element in order to preserve formatting from the file.

This sample produces this output:

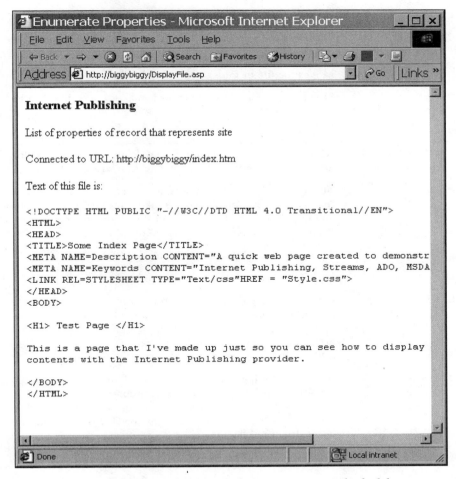

Writing to a file works similarly, except that we use the WriteText method of the Stream object to place the text in the file.

The Record Object

We're going to end this chapter by summarizing the methods and properties that are available on the Record object. They are:

Methods

Cancel	Halts execution of an asynchronous command. Since you cannot use asynchronous calls from ASP you're unlikely to encounter this method in ASP pages!
Close	Closes the record.
CopyRecord	Copies the file or folder pointed to by this record to another location.
DeleteRecord	Deletes the file or folder pointed to by this record.
GetChildren	Returns a recordset that contains the files in the folder pointed to by this record.
MoveRecord	Moves the file or folder pointed to by this record to another location.
Open	Opens the record – in other words makes the connection to the web site.

Properties

ActiveConnection	Reference to the connection object. When the record is closed may alternatively simply hold the connection string.
Mode	The access permissions (that is, is the record open for reading or reading/writing etc). Values are taken from the ConnectModeEnum enumeration – which have been listed and explained earlier in the chapter. The default is adModeUnknown.
ParentURL	Absolute URL of the parent of this object.
Source	URL of the actual object pointed to by this record.
State	Indicates what the object is currently doing – whether it is open, closed, executing a command, etc. Values are taken from the ObjectStateEnum enumeration: adStateClosed, adStateConnecting, adStateExecuting, adStateFetching and adStateOpen.
RecordType	Indicates whether the record is a collection (folder) or not. Values are taken from the RecordTypeEnum enumeration: adCollectionRecord (for a collection resource like a directory), adSimpleRecord (for a simple text or HTML file) and adStructDoc (for a structured document).

Collections

Fields	The properties of the file or folder pointed to by this record.

Summary

We've had a quick tour of Internet publishing and seen how using the Internet Publishing Provider you can very quickly write code that will display and modify the contents of files on a web site, as well as letting you carry out maintenance operations such as copying and moving files. Once the technology has fully evolved to include the versioning and locking components, then we will easily be able to carry out sophisticated distributed maintenance of web sites using WebDAV and ADO.

22

Exchange 2000

Introduction

Microsoft Exchange 2000 Server provides a big step towards seamless integration of a messaging system with web-enabled, data-driven applications. It supplies a somewhat overwhelming collection of integration mechanisms and APIs, which might, at first sight, make it difficult to see the forest for the trees.

In this chapter, we will outline the various methods which can be used to access data within the Exchange 2000 Web Storage System. To begin with, we will briefly recap some of the related technologies, covered elsewhere in this book, and how they relate to Exchange 2000. Then, we will take a deeper look into the different facets of the Web Storage System and a variety of methods to access items from it.

We will look at some folders and items in the Web Storage System from different angles, and will discover how the different access methods bring about a series of remarkable transformations. They will start off as simple files, become web pages, then change into database records, and finally resurface as programmable COM objects.

We will see how to view, create, modify, and delete items in the store and how to perform searches against it. Finally, we will take a look at another core capability of Exchange 2000: sending and receiving various kinds of messages.

At time of writing (Summer 2000), Exchange 2000 was still in beta (RC2). Screenshots and code represent what was publically known at the time. Some details may have changed or been updated in the final version.

What's New with Exchange 2000

Exchange 2000 is a huge topic and cannot be covered in any depth in a single chapter. Therefore, we will concentrate on data access within Exchange 2000, and specifically, the new data integration features.

Microsoft Exchange 2000 Server is a major new release of Exchange and includes significant architectural changes, which enable new and exciting capabilities with every development platform, be it client-side script, an ASP page, or a full-blown, COM-based web application.

Active Directory Integration

Unlike earlier versions of Exchange, Exchange 2000 Server does not include its own directory service. Directory services for Exchange are fully integrated into and provided by the **Windows 2000 Active Directory**. This has a number of very useful consequences. Exchange 2000 benefits from the flexible and scalable design of Active Directory, including its native security support.

Also, this allows us to take advantage of the Active Directory's advanced search capabilities to locate network objects, such as users, computers, and printers. When searching the Active Directory, we can search on specific attributes of an object, not just the object itself. Active Directory is covered in detail in Chapter 18.

Message Transport

SMTP, the Internet Simple Mail Transfer Protocol, is now Exchange's primary messaging protocol. Exchange 2000 makes use of the default Windows 2000 SMTP service and includes additional features. We can further extend it to provide additional capabilities, or customize existing ones, based on a new SMTP event handling system.

When certain events occur, such as when messages are sent or received, custom programs can be invoked. Typical actions of these event handlers include adding a disclaimer to messages, checking for specific files attached to messages, and so on.

Integration with IIS

Exchange 2000 makes intense use of **Internet Information Services** (**IIS**). IIS provides client access to the Exchange Information Store through HTTP, POP3 (Post Office Protocol), IMAP4 (Internet Message Access Protocol), and NNTP (Network News Transfer Protocol).

IIS enables read-write access to the Exchange store through the **WebDAV** (**Distributed Authoring and Versioning**) extensions to HTTP. WebDAV is the underlying communication mechanism of the new version of Outlook Web Access, the built-in web client of Exchange.

Web Storage System

One of the most important innovations in Exchange 2000 is the introduction of the **Web Storage System**. This new storage platform provides a single repository for managing semi-structured information, which is typical of, but not limited to, a messaging system.

Firstly, the Web Storage System replaces the traditional Exchange message store and serves as the repository for e-mail and all other other messaging items. Secondly, it emulates a traditional file system like NTFS and can be used to save and organize ordinary files of any type. It is fully integrated with IIS in that every item in the store is also associated with a URL and accessible from the Web. In this way, the Web Storage System makes use of features and functionality of the file system, the Web, and a messaging system as Exchange into a single location for storing, accessing, and managing information and for building and running applications.

The Web Storage System is really more a platform concept than a specialized messaging store, it's not limited to Exchange 2000, and we can expect it to emerge in other areas in the not too distant future. Time will tell, but conceptually, the Web Storage System could emerge as a great platform for web applications of all kinds, the underpinnings of document - and knowledge - management systems, and could ultimately replace the traditional file system altogether.

Exchange 2000 also includes a new integrated full-text indexing and search engine, which significantly increases client-side search performance. Full-text indexing not only includes the message body text, but reaches into attachments such as Microsoft Office documents.

Rich Application Programming Interfaces

The new architecture enables programmatic access into Exchange with a variety of existing, and new APIs. Some of the more prominent COM interfaces include **CDO** (**Collaboration Data Objects**) and its companion libraries for workflow management (CDOWF) and system management (CDOEXM), as well as **ADO** (**ActiveX Data Objects**).

The user interface piece is programmable through Outlook Web Access, where we can create custom forms for display in a browser, or we can create custom ASP solutions.

Scalability

Last, but not least, Exchange 2000 should also come with a number of improvements to help scalability, such as the ability to run multiple messaging databases and support for active clustering.

Exchange 2000 and the Active Directory

Prior versions of Exchange always came with their own user and e-mail directory, which was not integrated with the NT domain structure and security database. This directory no longer exists in Exchange 2000, which simply uses the directory service of the underlying operating system, the Windows 2000 Active Directory.

The installation process simply upgrades the Active Directory schemas with the necessary additional structures to support Exchange. This is clearly another step towards tighter integration of systems and services, as it unburdens administrators from having to maintain two or more directories. It also offloads application developers from building and maintaining different access mechanisms and code into the directories.

Consequently, the Exchange Directory information is stored and accessed in exactly the same way as we have seen in Chapter 18, where we have used Active Directory Service Interfaces (ADSI) to programmatically access Active Directory.

Exchange 2000 and WebDAV

In the previous chapter, we looked at the principles of WebDAV and how the **Internet Publishing Provider** (known as MSDAIPP) uses this extension of the HTTP protocol to get write access to the Web. Exchange 2000 also exposes the contents of its message store via the WebDAV protocol, but, unfortunately, the Internet Publishing Provider does not work properly with Exchange's store. Microsoft explicitly states that the MSDAIPP is not supported in this situation.

This is not too much of a problem, so long as we are only concerned with the server. Exchange 2000 Server itself comes with the **ExOLEDB** Provider, which is specifically designed for server-side use and which makes the equivalent of MSDAIPP functionality available on the server. We will take a detailed look at this functionality later in this chapter. However, for client-side applications, there is currently no OLE DB Provider, which we can plug into ADO and gain access to the Exchange Store.

On the other hand, we can still use WebDAV without going through an OLE DB Provider. It just means that we will have to dig into a few more details of the WebDAV protocol and use a lower-level communication mechanism. We will lose some of the abstraction of the Internet Publishing Provider, but, as we might have guessed, the low-level WebDAV functionality gives us a few capabilities beyond what we can do with ADO.

Later in this chapter, we will see an example of a WebDAV dialogue between a client and a server, and we will see a feature of the store which we would not be able to activate in any other way.

The Web Storage System Described

The **Web Storage System** is a new database technology that can be used to store, share, and manage many types of data, not just e-mail messages.

It is important to recognize that the Web Storage System is architected with a much broader purpose than just a message store. As we would expect from a messaging system, we can store e-mail messages, but also web content, ASP script pages, multimedia files, and Office documents together in the Web Storage System. In the long term, it is not unlikely that this storage system will play an important role in just about everything that we do.

At first glance, the Web Storage System is organized much like a traditional file system – that is as a hierarchy of folders containing items (files). Folders can contain other folders as well as any number of leaf items. However, the Web Storage System is more than just another file system. In the remainder of this section, we will briefly discuss its key capabilities and features, which extend beyond that of a traditional file system.

The Web Storage System Protocols

There is a confusing plethora of protocols and APIs, which can access the Web Storage System, ranging from the traditional Win32 file I/O and MAPI APIs to the POP3 and IMAP4 Internet messaging protocols, ADO and OLE DB data access components and CDO objects for messaging and collaboration. Let's take a closer look at how some of these access the Web Storage System.

POP3 and IMAP4 Access

POP3 and IMAP4 are *the* standard Internet protocols for client access to e-mail systems. It comes as no surprise that the Web Storage System in Exchange 2000 supports these protocols and can be accessed with traditional e-mail clients like Outlook, Outlook Express or any other POP3/IMAP4 compliant application. Moreoever, Exchange 2000 has become much more open than previous versions of Exchange and natively supports these Internet standards, as illustrated by the screen shot. In this particular case, we have chosen Outlook Express as the client and IMAP4 as the communication protocol against an Exchange 2000 server.

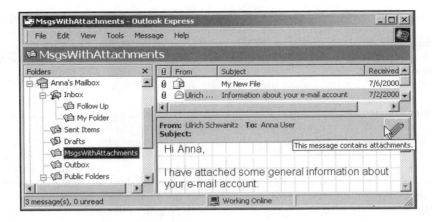

HTTP and WebDAV Access

The previous version of Exchange also included **Outlook Web Access** (**OWA**), a set of ASP pages which provided a web interface for the conventional message store. The OWA user interface still exists, and has been greatly improved, but the underlying technology is completely new and based on the new capabilities of the Web Storage System.

By definition, every item in the Web Storage System is identified and accessible by its URL. For example, http://mars.planets.be/anna/Inbox/RE%3A A note from Anna to Bart.eml might be the URL identifier of an e-mail message in the store. Consequently, when we type this identifier into a browser's address bar, and our security rights allow us access, the Web Storage System will find the message, render it into HTML, and return it to us. The rendering process is handled completely within the Web Storage System, but is customizable.

As an example, we have included a screen-shot of the OWA browser interface into the mailbox of our fictitious user Anna:

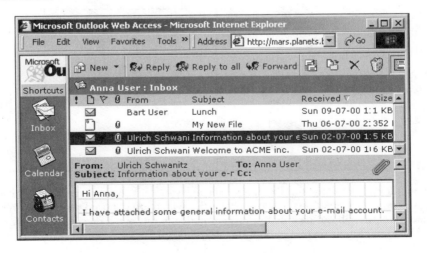

The rendering engine will even detect the capabilities of the user's browser software and act accordingly. It will generate rich DHTML content for Internet Explorer 5.0. For less powerful browsers it will fall back and generate content in HTML 3.2. Exchange 2000 comes with predefined forms (templates with rendering instructions) for Outlook Web Access, but these can be overridden, and we can add our own Web Storage System forms for any folder in the store. Creating and registering form templates is relatively straightforward and is documented in the Exchange 2000 SDK.

It is important to note that the message lookup and rendering functionality is provided by the Web Storage System. Unlike the previous version of Exchange, where similar behavior was accomplished with some intermediate ASP pages and COM objects, the message in the store is not only *accessible* via a web page, every message, as well as any other store item, *is* a web page. The internal representation of the items in the store (the bits and bytes on the hard disk) can be in a completely different format, but as soon as you address them via their URL, the rendering engine in the Web Storage System transparently transforms them into appropriate HTML pages for your browser. This is an important architectural change, and undoubtedly a big step forward towards full Internet integration.

The Web Storage System and Exchange 2000 fully support write access to the store via the WebDAV protocol, which turns the Web, and thus the Web Storage System, into a fully writable medium. We will take a deeper look at that later in this chapter.

File System Access

On the Exchange server itself, the Web Storage System does not only surface as a set of web pages, but will also be visible as a virtual hard drive containing folders and files. The drive, or any of the folders within, can be shared out over the network to provide a more traditional file-level view into the storage system. This can be particularly useful when file-level access to the content of Exchange Public Folders is required.

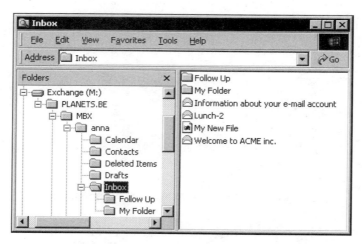

This simple method of accessing the Exchange message store has some charm, but we also need to realize that we can only gain access to those properties which are exposed through theWin32 file system APIs. For example, we will not be able to programmatically retrieve a message's *importance*, because the file system APIs don't know anything about this property.

The ExOLEDB Provider

Exchange 2000 comes with the Exchange OLE DB Provider (ExOLEDB), which is similar to, but more advanced than, the Internet Publishing Provider (MSDAIPP).

The biggest difference between the two is that the ExOLEDB Provider is specifically designed for server-side use, making it a very suitable data access platform for web applications. On the down side, this provider is not currently available as a stand-alone component. It can only be installed with Exchange 2000 and cannot be used from client-side applications.

The ExOLEDB Provider allows server-side components to access the Web Storage System with the familiar ADO toolkit. We can navigate along the folder tree, enumerate any of the properties in records and recordsets, as well as programmatically create or manipulate store items. This gives us a fairly easy and powerful avenue into the store, using familiar programming techniques.

We can search entire folder hierarchies using an extended SQL syntax. The extensions allow us to specify deep and shallow searches as well as loosely matched full-text queries of words or groups of words.

Collaboration Data Objects

While the ExOLEDB Provider and ADO give us a fine-grained access to the Web Storage System, they are not involved with the dynamics of a messaging system, such as sending e-mails, scheduling meetings, or handling workflow. These are covered by **Collaborative Data Objects** (**CDO**).

New versions of the CDO libraries come with both Windows 2000 and Exchange 2000. The Windows 2000 libraries are a proper subset of the Exchange libraries. Applications written against the Windows libraries will continue to function after an installation of Exchange.

CDO consists of the following libraries:

- ❑   **CDO for Windows 2000** (cdosys.dll) allows us to create basic messaging applications that can send e-mail messages using the SMTP and NNTP protocols. The message can be a simple text message or a message formatted according to the **Multipurpose Internet Mail Extensions** (**MIME**) specifications.

    We can also create transport event sinks to intercept incoming messages and examine the message contents and envelope fields. Based upon the content, sink code can alter the message contents or block the delivery of the message. CDOSYS does not work with the Web Storage System.

- ❑   **CDO for Exchange 2000 Server** (cdoex.dll) includes the core collaboration functionality such as folder and item access, messaging, scedule planning, and contact management. It extends the bare-bone functionality of CDOSYS with the capabilities of the Web Storage System.

- ❑   **CDO Workflow for Exchange 2000 Server** (cdowf.dll) provides us with workflow management tools.

- ❑   **CDO Management Objects for Exchange 2000 Server** (cdoexm.dll) is used for programmatic access to system management functionality for the Web Storage System and Exchange 2000.

In this chapter, we will concentrate on the functionality of CDOSYS and CDOEX, but we will not be able to consider the CDO workflow and management objects in any detail, as these don't have much to do with data access.

Unlike the previous versions, CDO for Windows 2000 and its companion libraries are no longer MAPI-based. The underlying transport mechanisms of CDO are always the Internet standard SMTP and/or NNTP protocols. In the past, you may have used the CDONTS library to send SMTP messages, for example, to add e-mail functionality to your web applications. The new capabilities of CDO have rendered this library completely obsolete. The older libraries are still provided for compatibility. However CDONTS-based applications can be easily upgraded.

All CDO components integrate with ADO to provide us with a consistent data-access interface to the Web Storage System and Active Directory. For example, we can use an ADO-based search to locate Exchange messages in the store and seamlessly pass the data objects to CDO for the manipulation of addressing properties. As we set values for CDO properties or access Web Storage System properties, CDO saves data to the correct locations for us, whether it be in the Web Storage System or in Active Directory.

Supporting Capabilities

When using one or more of the APIs, we will make use of some of the supporting capabilities of the Web Storage System. These capabilities are not typically limited to being used with a single API, but will be available to several, if not all of them. In this section, we will briefly discuss how the Web Storage System supports schemas, namespaces, and events.

Schemas and Namespaces

A schema is the meta-description of types of items in the store. The Web Storage System supports schemas, which are organized into a series of namespaces. Exchange 2000 comes with a fairly long and comprehensive list of namespaces with lots and lots of properties. For most reasonably sized messaging applications, the predefined schemas will be fully sufficient, though the schemas are customizable and you can define your own namespaces and properties.

Items in the Web Storage System can carry any number of predefined or custom properties. To avoid possible naming conflicts, every property name has to be associated with a namespace and carries a locally unique name. The namespace is again a unique string that acts as a scope for the name. For example, every store item will have a `DAV:creationdate` property. e-Mail messages in the store will carry values for this and other `DAV:` properties, but will also have a `urn:schemas:mailheader:date` property, which contains the date on which the message was sent.

At first glance, we may be a little puzzled by the many predefined Exchange 2000 namespaces and long property lists, but they are well organized and grouped quite logically. Some of the more prominent namespaces include:

- ❏ `DAV` – Properties related to storage and WebDAV access, such as the URL (`href`), the size of an item (`getcontentlength`), or the number of items in a folder (`childcount`).

- ❏ `urn:schemas:mailheader` – Properties directly extracted from the RFC-822 mail header, such as `from`, `to`, `subject`, and `date`.

- ❏ `urn:schemas:httpmail` – Very similar to the above, but the property values have all encoded characters converted back to Unicode. This namespace will be the primary source of information about messaging properties.

- ❏ `http//schemas.microsoft.com/exchange` – Custom properties, which are only found in Exchange, but not defined by any Internet standards, such as `sensitivity` or `outlookmessageclass`.

- ❏ `urn:schemas-microsoft-com:office:office` – Specific properties of Microsoft Office documents, such as `Author`, `TotalTime`, and `LastPrinted`. This namespace is used for Word, Excel and other document formats, but also for simple HTML files.

You may want to consult the Exchange 2000 SDK (accessible via http://msdn.microsoft.com/exchange) for a complete list of predefined namespaces and their property lists. There are no hard naming rules for custom namespaces, but the SDK gives us some guidelines, which would help to maintain uniqueness. We should get the general picture from the samples above.

Besides holding messaging and storage related properties, the Web Storage System schemas also provide information about a document's content class. Content classes are names identifying the intent or purpose of an item along with a set of properties that this item normally has. A good example of a content class is an expense report, which could be in Excel, Word or PDF format, or it could be a simple e-mail message. Regardless of the format (as described by the content type), there would be set of common properties associated with the expense report, like the approval state. Each item stored by the application can have these properties defined, irrespective of the item's content type.

For custom applications, we can further extend the existing definitions and define our schemas, namespaces, and content classes. One of the benefits of doing this would be that the Web Storage System's query processor would know about our custom properties, such that a SELECT * statement or WebDAV response would include custom properties.

Web Storage System Events

Before we move on to the next section and start looking into some of the details of accessing data in the Web Storage System, I simply could not resist mentioning another exciting capability; **Web Storage System Events**.

The Web Storage System provides a powerful set of store and system events. An event occurs when there is some activity or action within a folder or store, and we can hook custom event handlers (or event sinks) to the following store events:

- ❑   OnSyncSave – before an item is saved into the store.
- ❑   OnSave – after an item is stored.
- ❑   OnSyncDelete – before an item is deleted.
- ❑   OnDelete – after an item is deleted.
- ❑   OnTimer – after a certain period of time.

Event sinks can interact with data in the Web Storage System using the ExOLEDB Provider and ADO.

There are a million possible applications for Web Storage System Events, and they are not limited to Exchange messages. We can easily implement simple notifications (such as "A new item has arrived in the XYZ folder"), automatic classification of items, prevent propagation of viruses propagated by e-mail – by aborting the save operation, prevent deletion of files which are referenced elsewhere, and much more.

Imagine we were system administrators of a web server, concerned about users who store large MP3 files on their site. Instead of running the sites directly off the hard disk, we could now run them from the Web Storage System. On every file save (when using OnSyncSave, it actually happens before the file is saved), we could implement a little event sink which rejects MP3 files which exceed a certain size or quota.

Programming the Web Storage System

As you have seen so far, there is an extremely rich set of access paths into the Web Storage System. We will not be able to discuss all of our options in detail in this chapter. For the most part, we will be using the technologies that fall under the **Universal Data Access** (**UDA**) umbrella. The bulk of the following samples will be using properties and methods from ADO 2.5 and will demonstrate its integration with CDO.

However, we will occasionally take a little detour and sneak a quick look at other, sometimes very helpful technologies, like Outlook Web Access, WebDAV, and a tiny bit of client-side XML.

OLE DB Access – ExOLEDB

The Exchange OLE DB Provider (ExOLEDB) is a server-side component which exposes the Exchange Web Storage System as a semi-structured database. ADO makes this database accessible as `Record` and `Recordset` objects. In the upcoming section, we will take a deeper look at how to use ADO to work with the Web Storage System and how to read and manipulate the items therein. We will get to know some of the many properties of web store items and see how they are logically organized into a series of namespaces.

Establishing a Connection

As with any other OLE DB provider, we need to specify a database connection string to get access to the store. We can explicitly create a connection, or we can immediately jump to a `Record` object and let it create the connection for us.

Suppose there is an Exchange mailbox for user `anna` on server `mars.planets.be`, then Anna's mailbox will be located at `http://mars.planets.be/exchange/anna`. We can use this string in an ASP application to establish a connection to her mailbox. Our application could also connect to any subfolder `therein`:

```
Set oConn = Server.CreateObject("ADODB.Connection")
oConn.Provider = "ExOLEDB.DataSource"
oConn.Open "http://mars.planets.be/exchange/anna"
```

However, there is a potential catch with this approach. Connection strings starting with `http://...` are by default registered with the **Internet Publishing Provider**. If we do not explicitly specify the ExOLEDB Provider before opening the connection, we will end up using the wrong provider. Therefore, the Exchange provider has registered the prefix `file://./backofficestorage/...` as its default. So, to avoid the potential conflict, we can use the following syntax:

```
Set oConn = Server.CreateObject("ADODB.Connection")
oConn.Open "file://./backofficestorage/planets.be/exchange/anna"
```

The prefix `file://./backofficestorage/` is essentially a synonym for the virtual `M:` drive that Exchange establishes at installation. In production applications, we certainly don't want to hard-code server or domain names. We can also see that both connection strings contain references to either the exchange server or its domain. To avoid hard-coding strings, these objects from the Windows 2000 ADSI interfaces may come in handy:

```
Set oInfoNT = Server.CreateObject("WinNTSystemInfo")
Set oInfo   = Server.CreateObject("ADSystemInfo")

vNtName = oInfoNT.ComputerName
vDomainName = oInfo.DomainDNSName
```

The first property call will return the server name, while the second will return the server's domain name. The fully qualified domain name can be formed by concatenating the two.

Working with Record Objects

Once we have a valid connection object, it can be used to open any number of store items. In the ADO object model, every item, be it a folder or anything else, can be opened as a record. The source URL to the record can be given as a complete, absolute reference, but you may find it more convenient to specify a relative URL. The code snippet below will open a read-only record object pointing to the Follow Up folder in Anna's Inbox:

```
Set oRec = Server.CreateObject("ADODB.Record")
oRec.Open "Inbox/Follow Up", oConn, adModeRead
```

> Note that, you might get problems with permissions when using the Record object from ASP. For more information, look up the discussion on this topic in Chapter 21.

Records have properties (or, in ADO terminology, fields) and eventually children. Lets have a look at the properties first.

Items in the Exchange store have many properties, and not all of them are always populated. To make things worse, different items have different lists of properties, and we can add any number of custom properties to the lists. For now, it may be a good idea to just look at what's available by default. ADO records carry a Fields collection. We can enumerate this to see what's available:

```
For Each oField in oRec.Fields
  vFieldName = oField.Name
  vFieldValue = GetVariantOf(oField.Value)

  ' output
Next
```

This snippet should look very familiar. The only unknown piece is probably the GetVariantOf() function, which is essentially an error handler. Some of the Exchange properties come in a format which VBScript cannot handle, such as byte arrays. This function will just check the format of each property and either returns its value, or nothing, if it cannot handle it. As an added convenience, it will also return the underlying data type, so long as it can interpret it:

```
Function GetVariantOf(vVar)
  Dim vTmp(1)
  On Error Resume Next

  vTmp(1) = TypeName(vVar)
  If Err <> 0 Then
```

```
      vTmp(1) = Err.Description
   ElseIf Instr(1,vTmp(1),"()") = 0 Then
      vTmp(0) = vVar
   End If

   GetVariantOf = vTmp
End Function
```

Now that we have all the properties to hand, it's not difficult to embed all this into an ASP page. There is just one more thing to consider before we look at a more complete code fragment. Throughout the remainder of this chapter, I have stripped off almost all decorative HTML, in an attempt to make the code fragments more readable, and I have also replaced code which requires excessive string concatenation, such as:

```
Response.Write "<a href='" & vTheHref & "'>" & vTheText & "</a>"
```

With extremely simple helper functions, for example:

```
Response.Write Atag(vTheHref, vTheText)
```

Where the helper function is defined by:

```
Function Atag(vHref, vInnerHTML)
   Atag = "<a href='" & vHref & "'>" & vInnerHTML & "</a>" & vbCrLf
End Function
```

The purpose of these helper functions should be self-explanatory, which is why they won't be presented here.

We have already discussed most of the code that we see below. However, we have included the ability to accept the URL to the store as an input variable, giving us some added flexibility for testing. Another change to note is how the HTML output is generated:

```
<%
' declarations and such

vDavHref = Request("href")

Set oConn = Server.CreateObject("ADODB.Connection")
oConn.Provider = "ExOLEDB.DataSource"
oConn.Open vDavHref
%>

<!-- some HTML goes here -->

<%
Set oRec = Server.CreateObject("ADODB.Record")
oRec.Open ".", oConn, adModeRead

For Each oField in oRec.Fields
  vFieldName = oField.Name
```

```
    vFieldValue = GetVariantOf(oField.Value)

  With Response
    .Write "<dl></dl><dl>"
    .Write DTtag( Btag(vFieldName) )
    .Write DDtag( vFieldValue(0) )
    .Write DDtag( Itag(vFieldValue(1)) )
    .Write "</dl>"
  End With

Next
%>
```

When our fictitious user Anna browses to the `ShowProperties.asp` page and enters the URL of one of her e-mail messages, she will see an output like this:

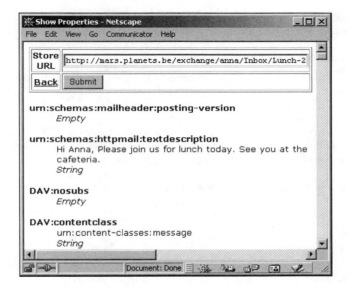

Namespaces

As you can see from the size of the vertical scrollbar in the above screenshot, the page comes back with a long list of properties, and to discuss each and all of them in detail would be a tedious process. Instead, we will make a general overview of the more important properties.

The DAV: Namespace

The `DAV:` namespace holds all standard WebDAV properties, which are very similar to the properties of an ordinary file system object. DAV does not know anything about the Microsoft-specific implementation of the Web Storage System, nor about e-mail messages or Exchange. The most useful properties in the `DAV:` namespace are:

- ❑ `href` – the absolute URL.

- ❑ `displayname` – the mail subject, file or folder name.

- ❑ `creationdate` – the creation date.

- ❑ `getcontentlength` – the size of the item.

727

We always have to pre-pend the DAV: namespace qualifier to these and other property names.

Quite a number of Boolean and numeric properties are related to the folder hierarchy. For example, the type of an item can be determined by inspecting these properties:

❑ isfolder – whether it is a folder.

❑ hassubs – whether is has sub-folders.

The count of contained items in a folder is returned in:

❑ childcount – count of contained items.

❑ objectcount – count of leaf objects (files) excluding subfolders.

And, last but not least, the contentclass property will tell us about the document classification, a value which determines the other namespaces and properties applicable to this item.

The urn:schemas:httpmail: Namespace

The httpmail namespace holds properties related to Internet standard messages. Here, we can inspect the contents of the RFC-822 message header and body. Many of the properties are directly derived from the underlying urn:schemas:mailheader namespace.

Properties in the mailheader namespace are directly derived from the RFC-822 message headers and may therefore be 7-bit encoded. When a property value is transferred from mailheader namespace to the httpmail namespace, this 7-bit encoding is taken out again.

It's not difficult to guess that all of the following can be found in this namespace:

❑ from (also fromname and fromemail)

❑ to

❑ subject

❑ datereceived

It is also important to realize that some properties, like the subject property, will automatically be carried forward into the DAV namespace and also show up there. In this case, the subject property will also set the DAV:displayname.

The httpmail namespace is not only limited to the mail header, we can also derive the message content via properties such as:

❑ textdescription – the bare ASCII text.

❑ htmldescription – the HTML message body.

❑ hasattachment – whether the item has attachments.

Finally, in a multi-lingual environment, where we cannot be sure that the name of a user's Inbox is really "inbox", we may find properties like inbox, calendar, or sentitems useful. These properties will contain the absolute URL of the localized folder.

The http: //schemas.microsoft.com/exchange/ Namespace

The exchange namespace is fairly specialized and is Microsoft's implementation of the Exchange Web Storage System. Nevertheless, the permanenturl property is of general interest. This property contains a machine-generated URL pointer for every item in the store, which never changes even if the item is moved or renamed. This machine-generated permanent URL looks like a large hex number and is not identical to the ordinary URL or the position of the item in the folder hierarchy.

Think about this for a moment. The Web Storage System is not limited to Exchange. We can run an entire site from it. If we changed all the URLs in this site to their permanenturl equivalents, programmatically or otherwise, our links could never break again.

Other Namespaces

Depending on the nature of the store item, and its DAV: contentclass property, there are quite a number of other namespaces for appointments, contact, tasks, office documents and more. A complete discussion of these namespaces would extend far beyond the scope of this chapter. Please consult the Exchange SDK for further information.

Navigating the Folder Tree

After this lengthy, but necessary discussion of namespaces and properties, let's get back to another example. The next thing that we should look at is how to move from one item to another. So far, we have established a connection to a folder or item and asked for a record object, which returned us an overwhelming number of properties, but not the items contained in the folder. Let's build a new page (ListChildren.asp), which performs this task.

One of the key capabilities of the ADO Record object is the GetChildren method, which will return a recordset with information about all the contained items. In theory, this recordset would only contain a few properties common to all the items, but very little detailed information. In reality, though, the recordset has exactly the same property list as the underlying record.

The following code fragment uses a Record's property from the DAV namespace to check whether an item is a folder, and if it is, grabs the corresponding Recordset object. It then loops over the recordset and formats it into a list. Remember how I have encapsulated most of the HTML code generation into a series of very simple tag() functions. For every row in the recordset, it will display:

The DAV:displayname followed by:

- ❑ A link to the ShowProperties.asp page, which passes the item's URL in the href parameter. This will direct the target page to enumerate the item's properties.

- ❑ For folders only, a link to the current page (vMe) with the href parameter pointing to the subfolder. Thus, it will recurse back and allow us to walk down a folder tree.

- ❑ A hyperlink to the item itself – we will look at this in a moment.

```
Set oConn = Server.CreateObject("ADODB.Connection")
oConn.Provider = "ExOLEDB.DataSource"
oConn.Open vDavHref
'
Set oRec = Server.CreateObject("ADODB.Record")
oRec.Open ".", oConn, adModeRead
If oRec("DAV:isfolder") Then
```

```
Set oRs = oRec.GetChildren

Do While Not oRs.EOF
  vDavDisplayName = oRs("DAV:displayname")
  vDavHref = oRs("DAV:href")
  vDavIsFolder = oRs("DAV:isfolder")

  With Response
    .Write "<dl></dl><dl>"
    .Write DTtag(Btag(vDavDisplayName))
    .Write DDtag( _
      Atag("ShowProperties.asp?href=" & vDavHref, "Properties"))

    If vDavIsFolder Then
      .Write DDtag( _
        Atag(vMe & "?href=" & Server.URLEncode(vDavHref), "Children"))
    End If

    .Write DDtag(Atag(vDavHref, "View"))
    .Write "</dl>"
  End With

  oRs.MoveNext
Loop

Set oRs = Nothing
End If
```

You may be asking yourself why we use the DAV:isfolder property and not DAV:iscollection. According to the WebDAV specification, iscollection is a superset of isfolder. A collection (in the WebDAV sense) is either a folder or a compound document. The specification is a little vague about what a compound document is, and the Microsoft implementation of WebDAV currently does not have any provisions for them. As this may change in the future, isfolder appears to be the better choice.

Calling up the page in a browser yields the following:

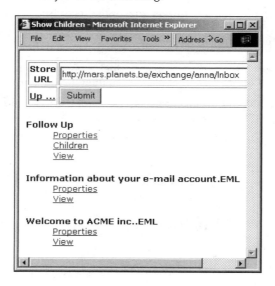

Anna's Inbox contains one folder and two messages. Clicking on a Properties link will return the verbose list of all properties of the respective item or folder. Clicking on a Children link will loop back into the same page, but now show the contents of the child folder. In effect, we have implemented a rudimentary mechanism to navigate the entire folder tree.

Being able to navigate the tree is one thing, but we will also want to look at message contents. During the discussion of namespaces and properties, we saw that the `Record` object gives us access to the message content. We could indeed write an ASP page, which accesses these properties and somehow formats them into an HTML page, but there is another, often easier way to accomplish the same result.

Finally, there is a View hyperlink for every item. Recall that these links are nothing but the URLs of the respective items. Clicking on one of them will bring up a window like the one below, easily identified as the Outlook Web Access interface.

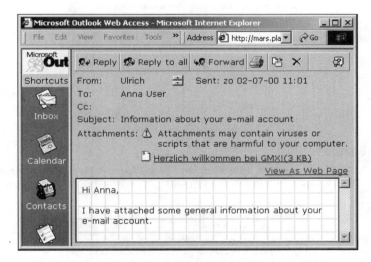

We will return to this behaviour and the Outlook Web Access interface a little later. For now, let's continue with the ADO discussion.

Add, Change, and Remove Store Items

The next step is to manipulate some items in the Web Storage System. The ExOLEDB Provider and ADO make this easy and the code will look familiar. Before we begin, we need to add a few more links to the `ListChildren.asp` page. The updated script will generate links to add, change and remove items, these links will just take us to the respective input forms, where the actual work is done. The code behind this page is not discussed here, but can be downloaded from www.wrox.com.

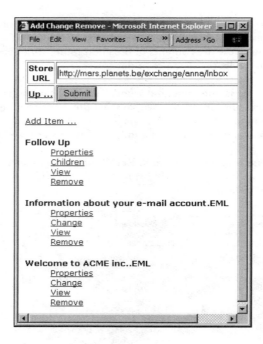

Adding Items to the Store

The Add Item… link will take us to a little form, where we specify the essential parameters necessary for creating the form. When this form is submitted, it will call up the script, which performs the addition.

The code fragment below assumes that we have already captured the incoming parameters, which relate to the form fields as follows:

❑ Name – vDavDisplayName

❑ CreateFolder/CreateFile – vCreateOptions

❑ Allow Overwrite – vAllowOverwrite

It is also assumed that the ADO connection to the parent folder has already been established. Adding a new item to this folder is as easy as opening the Record object with the desired name. The option parameters were carried over from the input form and can be either adCreateCollection (0x2000) or adCreateNonCollection (0), and eventually adCreateOverwrite (0x4000000):

```
Set oRec = Server.CreateObject("ADODB.Record")

oRec.Open vDavDisplayName, oConn, adModeReadWrite, _
                            vCreateOptions + vAllowOverwrite
```

The most fundamental property of these items is their content class, which determines their default list of properties. Appropriate values are urn:content-classes:folder and urn:content-classes:document. The latter associates the entire set of Microsoft Office properties with the item:

```
If vCreateOptions = adCreateCollection Then
   oRec("DAV:contentclass") = "urn:content-classes:folder"
Else
   oRec("DAV:contentclass") = "urn:content-classes:document"
   ' ...
End If
```

We could leave the newly created document empty, but it is worthwhile showing how to add some content to it. For the sake of this sample, we will turn this into an HTML document, which means that we have to set the document's content type to text/html.

The next few lines are a very typical example of how to handle document contents with ADO records and **streams**. Details of handling data streams have already been discussed in Chapter 21. When working with ADO records, a document's content stream is available as the value of its adDefaultStream (-1) field. Here, we just write a small piece of HTML into the document and save all our changes back to the Web Storage System:

```
If vCreateOptions = adCreateCollection Then
   oRec("DAV:contentclass") = "urn:content-classes:folder"
Else
   oRec("DAV:contentclass") = "urn:content-classes:document"
   oRec("DAV:contenttype") = "text/html"

   Set oStm = oRec(adDefaultStream).Value
   oStm.WriteText "<html><head><title>" & vDavDisplayName & _
                  "</title></head><body></body></html>"
End If

oRec.Fields.Update
```

Changing Documents

The code for changing an existing document is very similar to what we have just seen, except that the object is tied to an existing record:

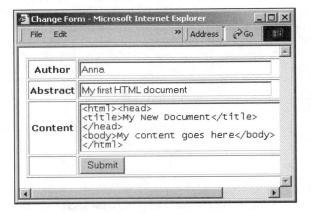

Let's take a look at the code behind the input form.

As usual, the values of the input fields are populated from the existing record. The interesting aspect is really the wealth of attributes that the Web Storage System keeps for every item, even if it's a simple HTML document. The code to retrieve the document's content via the stream object is as follows:

```
oRec.Open ".", oConn, adModeReadWrite

vDavAbstract = Server.HTMLEncode( oRec("DAV:abstract") )
vOffAuthor = Server.HTMLEncode( _
  oRec("urn:schemas-microsoft-com:office:office#Author") )

If oRec("DAV:contenttype") = "text/html" Then
  Set oStm = oRec(adDefaultStream).Value
  vStmContent = Server.HTMLEncode( oStm.ReadText )

  Set oStm = Nothing
Else
  vStmContent = "-not applicable-"
End If
```

Removing a Store Item

Deleting items from the store is also very easy. In fact, it's almost too easy. It takes a single method call to remove a store item, and this call applies equally to folders *including all its subfolders and documents*. We should be extra careful when experimenting with the DeleteRecord method, and make sure our code contains the appropriate protection. In the sample below, we check the value of the DAV:childcount property, and will not do anything unless it's 0, that is, it is an empty folder:

```
oRec.Open ".", oConn, adModeReadWrite

If oRec.Fields("DAV:childcount") = 0 Then
  vDavDisplayName = oRec("DAV:displayname")
  oRec.DeleteRecord
```

```
      Response.Write "Item <i>" & vDavDisplayName & "</i> removed"
   Else
      Response.Write "Folder<i>" & vDavDisplayName & _
        "</i> is not empty. Item not removed."
   End If
```

Manipulating Message Items

As this chapter is supposed to be about Exchange 2000, we might have expected to have seen something about manipulating e-mail messages. While we *can* create and modify messages with ADO alone, it's usually more laborious and error-prone than doing it with a *combination* of ADO and the Collaboration Data Objects (CDO). We will come back to this point later in this chapter.

Reusing Outlook Web Access

In the course of this chapter, we have already seen a few instances of the new Outlook Web Access application. Although it is primarily intended as a stand-alone web interface into Exchange, it provides some simple but effective methods of integrating web applications with Exchange. Earlier, we said that every item in the Web Storage System is not only accessible via a web interface, but that every item is a web page. Remember, when we clicked a View link in one of the sample scripts above, the Web Storage System suddenly started Outlook Web Access and displayed the message.

In fact, it only does this with e-mail, appointments, other message items or folders. Files which are not message-related will just load normally in the browser window or the respective application. So why does the Web Storage System make this distinction and how?

If you have seen the previous version of OWA, you may recall that it comprised a series of ASP pages, somewhat similar to the samples that we have been looking at. The new version is different. There are no longer any of these ASP pages as the Web Storage System controls the entire rendering process itself, and the user interface of OWA is defined as a series of Web Forms. These forms are associated with messaging items and folders, such that whenever we address a store item with the messaging attribute, the Web Storage System will automatically apply the OWA forms to this item.

Unfortunately, we cannot go into a lot of detail about this process, but we can use some features of the OWA user interface. For example, we might want an application that looks up and classifies items in a public folder, and displays a clickable list of hyperlinks. Clicking the hyperlink would, of course, open the item, but it should not be displayed in the context (or frameset) of Outlook Web Access.

It would save us a lot of time if we could tie just that one piece of OWA right into our site, and there is a way to achieve this. We can simply append a query string to the message URL and give Outlook Web Access some directions. The command syntax follows a simple pattern:

- ❑ Cmd= – to initiate an action
- ❑ View= – to call up a specific view
- ❑ Sort= – to sort by a column

Commands Applicable to Message Items

The following commands can be used against existing message items. They will open the respective HTML pages or input forms from Outlook Web Access:

❏ Cmd=Open – to open the message without the surrounding OWA frame

❏ Cmd=Reply – to reply to an existing message

❏ Cmd=Forward – to forward an existing message

Commands Applicable to Folders

The following commands can be used against folders:

❏ Cmd=Contents – to open the folder without the surrounding OWA frame

❏ .../Drafts/?Cmd=New – to create a new message

❏ Cmd=Contents&View=Unread Messages – to force a specific view

A number of other parameters are also mentioned in the Exchange SDK, but I could not get them to work against the RC2 pre-release.

This is certainly not a very sophisticated set of capabilities, but nevertheless, it opens up a number of possibilities. It can save us from writing our own content renderer for message items or notes in public folders. We may also find the Cmd=New switch useful. I can definitely think of some instances where this could replace the ubiquitous mailto:... hyperlinks.

Searching the Store

One of the most beautiful aspects of using ADO against the Exchange 2000 Web Storage System is the ability to perform extremely powerful searches with the familiar SQL SELECT syntax, including extensions to support hierarchical data structures and full-text searches. These are the same extensions as defined by the Microsoft Indexing Service Query Processor. The Indexing service is discussed in Chapter 21.

We can search the Web Storage System with ADO, which delivers the results in the form of recordsets. We can also search the store directly from a client computer using WebDAV, which delivers the results as an XML-formatted message. There is more about XML in Chapters 24-27 of this book.

In this section, both methods will be demonstrated. We will implement a simple, yet flexible ASP/ADO-based query application. We will be able to formulate our own SQL strings and send them to the server for execution. Later on, we will use WebDAV to persist the results of a SQL string into a Search Folder and access it from a client.

Before We Begin

Before we begin, we should check whether full-text indexing is enabled and active on the Exchange Server. If it isn't, our full-text queries will not do what we want them to do.

Call up the Exchange System Manager console application and drill down into the Mailboxes Store of the server. The full-text indexing icon will report the status of the index. If the index is not available or needs to be rebuilt, right-click the Mailbox Store's icon and select the option to enable full-text indexing:

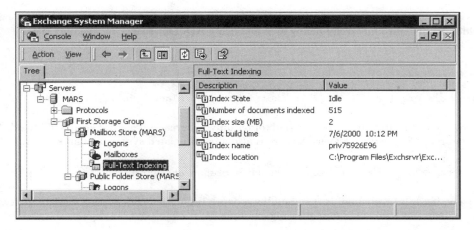

When the index is built and up-to-date, it needs to be made available to client applications. There is checkbox on the Mailbox Store's **Full-Text Indexing** property tab, which is unchecked by default and easy to overlook:

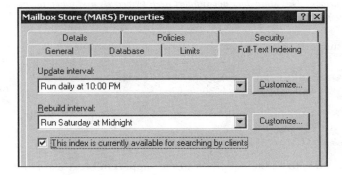

Syntax of the SELECT Statement

You can use a SQL SELECT statement to query for items in a particular folder or a branch of folders within a store. The general syntax of the SELECT statement is as follows:

```
SELECT select-list | *
FROM SCOPE(resource-list)
[WHERE search-condition]
[order-by-clause]
```

The `select-list` is used to restrict the recordset to specific properties. We have to specify the fully qualified property name, including the namespace qualifier, and enclose each property name in quotation marks, for example:

```
SELECT "DAV:href", "DAV:parentname" FROM SCOPE(...)
```

We may be tempted to avoid specifying `select-lists` and use just the SELECT * syntax. While this is possible and will return the long list of properties defined by the item's content class, it will significantly reduce performance. It is just as laborious to assemble the complete, and very long list of properties as it would be picking a few of them.

In the `resource-list`, we specify the URL of the starting folder and whether we want to search just that folder or the entire hierarchy below it. When using ADO for searching, we may specify a folder relative to our connection's URL. For example:

```
'shallow traversal of "Inbox/"'
'deep traversal of "http://mars.planets.be/public/"'
'deep traversal of "file://./backofficestorage/planets.be/MBX/anna/"'
```

A shallow traversal will search the specified folder only, whereas a deep traversal will include the entire folder hierarchy. For shallow traversal, there is also an abbreviated syntax available:

```
SELECT * FROM "http://mars.planets.be/exchange/anna/Inbox"
```

Conversely, if a `SCOPE` element is specified but a depth is not, the Web Storage System query processor assumes a deep traversal, as in the following example:

```
SELECT * FROM SCOPE("http://mars.planets.be/public")
```

For reasons of backward compatibility, one public store in the Web Storage System is designated for MAPI clients, such as Outlook. This store does not support deep traversals and when we attempt to execute one, the Web Storage System query processor will return an error message stating this.

The `WHERE` clause supports basic comparison operators, for example:

```
... WHERE "DAV:creationdate" > '2000-07-04' AND
          "DAV:creationdate" < '2000-07-10'
```

and:

```
... WHERE "DAV:isfolder" = True
```

This has been extended with additional predicates to support full-text searching of the selected fields, such as:

```
... WHERE CONTAINS (*, '"season greetings"')
```

```
... WHERE FREETEXT ("urn:schema:httpmail:subject", '"christmas xmas santa"')
```

```
... WHERE CONTAINS ('FORMSOF(INFLECTIONAL, "garden", "plant")')
```

The query processor is a little picky in respect to the use of single and double quotes. All property names within the `SELECT` statement must be enclosed within double quotes. The search specification, though, must be in single quotes. Strings within the search specification require an additional pair of double quotes. For example, the following clause will not work:

```
... WHERE CONTAINS ('Anna User')
```

and needs to be changed to:

```
... WHERE CONTAINS ('"Anna User"')
```

Other predicates support ordering, grouping, and ranking of items. Check out the Exchange SDK or other references for details.

Searching with ADO

We can take a copy of the `ListChildren.asp` page and, with only a few modifications, build a search capability into it. First, we have to add an input field where we would just type a proper SELECT statement. The text input area is pre-filled with a statement, which retains the previous behavior of the page.

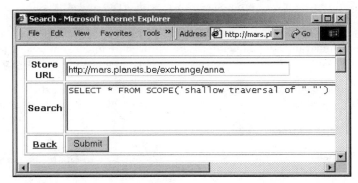

Recall the previous example in which we generated the list of items in a folder. The incoming URL was used to get a connection object and open a record on the URL. We asked that Record object for its children, which gave us a recordset. We looped over the recordset to generate the list of items and hyperlinks to other pages:

```
oConn.Open vDavHref
'
Set oRec = Server.CreateObject("ADODB.Record")
oRec.Open ".", oConn, adModeRead
Set oRs = oRec.GetChildren

Do While Not oRs.EOF
  ' ... formatting some output ...
  oRs.MoveNext
Loop
```

To implement our search-enabled page, we only need to implement a different way of getting at the Recordset object. The Recordset object is no longer required and can be eliminated altogether, and we can simply pass the incoming SELECT string (vSQL) to the connection's Execute method. This will return a recordset with exactly the same property list as before, just the rows in the recordset will vary with the SELECT statement. It cannot be much easier than this:

```
oConn.Open vDavHref

Set oRs = oConn.Execute vSQL

Do While Not oRs.EOF
  ' ... formatting some output ...
  oRs.MoveNext
Loop
```

We can now try this new search page against private mailboxes as well as public folders. As long as we manage to construct the proper SELECT statements, which can sometimes be a little tricky, it will always report the expected list of messages.

Things will undoubtedly be more complex in a real-life application. However, the fundamental methods of working with the Exchange Web Storage System are almost identical to working with a relational database.

Creating a Search Folder

There is another, client-side access path into the Web Storage System. It is based on the WebDAV protocol and gives us read-write access to the store via the HTTP protocol. A full discussion of WebDAV's capabilities in an Exchange environment is beyond the scope of this book, but we will demonstrate one feature which we cannot accomplish with ADO and ASP alone.

We can save a SELECT statement into the Web Storage System, where it will show up as a Search Folder. Conceptually, this is similar to a saved query or stored procedure in conventional database systems. Once the Search Folder has been created, it can be used from other applications as if it were a real one.

In the previous chapter, we looked at the principles of WebDAV and how the Internet Publishing Provider (MSDAIPP) uses this protocol to get write access to the Web. Exchange 2000 and the Web Storage System also expose their content via the WebDAV protocol, but unfortunately, MSDAIPP does not work against the Web Storage System.

Without an OLE DB Provider on the client, there is only one way to talk to the store: by using XML, the native language of WebDAV. Fortunately, two very helpful COM components are installed together with Internet Explorer 5.0:

- ❑ XMLHTTP is a COM component, which can issue any HTTP request and receive the server's response. With WebDAV being just a variation of HTTP, this is the ideal component to manage communication with the Exchange server.

- ❑ XMLDOM allows us to build and analyze XML documents and streams. Recall, from the previous chapter, that WebDAV messages contain an XML-formatted message body, making the XMLDOM component the tool of choice for building WebDAV message bodies and analyzing the results.

With the help of these two components, we can construct and analyze every conceivable WebDAV message. To keep this sample a little easier to understand, and to keep it focused on the creation of a Search Folder, we won't use the XMLDOM component but will just hard-code the XML message body. However, we will still need the XMLHTTP component to communicate with the server.

The following sample WebDAV request will create a Search Folder. The SELECT command walks through all folders (doing a deep traversal) and find all messages with attachments, by checking the urn:schemas:httpmail:hasattachment property.

There are two essential pieces in this WebDAV message; the HTTP request header containing a MKCOL (make collection) command which tells the server to create a new folder, and the request body containing the SELECT statement in the middle of a bunch of XML tags which specifies the desired search command. The exact hierarchy and meaning of the XML tags is not important in the current context:

```
MKCOL /exchange/anna/MsgsWithAttachments/ HTTP/1.1
Host: mars.planets.be
Content-Length: ???
Content-type: text/xml

<?xml version='1.0'?>
<a:propertyupdate xmlns:a='DAV:' >
  <a:set><a:prop><a:searchrequest><a:sql>
    SELECT "DAV:displayname" FROM SCOPE(
    'deep traversal of "/exchange/anna/"') WHERE
    "urn:schemas:httpmail:hasattachment" = True
  </a:sql></a:searchrequest></a:prop></a:set>
</a:propertyupdate>
```

Such a request is not difficult to build and execute, and the following code fragment demonstrates that. We will run it as a stand-alone VBScript file, but we could also paste it into a VB program or embed it in an Internet Explorer script.

We are currently not interested in the odds-and-ends of the XML tags, so we just hard-code them into two string variables. The script will pop up an input dialog asking where to create the search folder. The response will be stored in the vUrl variable. In the second dialog, we ask for the SELECT statement, wrap the XML around it, and store the result in vXML. Not very sophisticated code, but it will do the job.

```
vXmlPre = "<?xml version='1.0'?>" & _
          "<a:propertyupdate xmlns:a='DAV:'>" & _
          "<a:set><a:prop><a:searchrequest><a:sql>"

vXmlPost = "</a:sql></a:searchrequest></a:prop></a:set>" & _
           "</a:propertyupdate>"

vUrl = InputBox("Enter Target URL")
vXml = vXmlPre & InputBox("Enter SELECT statement") & vXmlPost
```

Next, we instantiate an XMLHTTP object that will help us to send the XML request string to the server. This object serves two purposes. First of all, it helps build the message header containing the all-important command verb and the target URL. It will take care about splitting the host name and the folder specification to adhere to the HTTP and WebDAV specifications, and it will calculate the length of the message and send it together with the other HTTP headers.

Before sending the message, we must not forget to explicitly declare the content type of the message, otherwise, the server will not process it. The remainder of the code fragment is truly self-explanatory – we don't even worry about parsing the response apart and simply display it in a message dialog:

```
Set oXmlHttp = CreateObject("Microsoft.XMLHTTP")

oXmlHttp.open "MKCOL", vUrl, False
oXmlHttp.setRequestHeader "Content-type", "text/xml"
oXmlHttp.send vXml

MsgBox oXmlHttp.responseText
```

The successful creation of a search folder will return an XML-formatted message like the one below.

```
<?xml version="1.0"?>
<a:multistatus xmlns:a="DAV:"><a:response>
  <a:href>http://mars.planets.be/exchange/anna/MsgsWithAttachments</a:href>
  <a:status>HTTP/1.1 201 Created</a:status>
    <a:propstat>
      <a:status>HTTP/1.1 200 OK</a:status>
      <a:prop>
        <a:searchrequest/>
      </a:prop>
    </a:propstat>
</a:response></a:multistatus>
```

Now that the Search Folder is there, we can access it from other applications and with other protocols. For example, Anna can use Outlook Express (using the IMAP4 protocol) to view all of her messages with attachments:

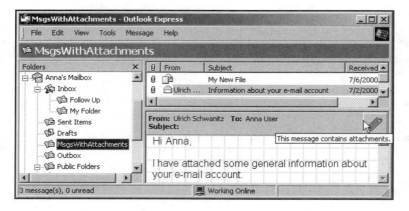

The ability to persist search commands into the store is a great way to persist dynamic views of the store database as virtual folders. Search Folders can even be nested, that is, we can reference an existing Search Folder in another statement. When we inspect the Search Folder's property list, we will see that the original SELECT statement is made available in the DAV:searchrequest property.

Messaging and Collaboration

So far, our discussion was centered on viewing and manipulating folders and items in the Web Storage System, which acts as the underlying message store of Exchange 2000. However, we have not yet touched on the dynamics of a messaging system, the ability to send e-mails around.

ADO and the other components of the UDA architecture give us a great new way of looking at hierarchical data from a database viewpoint, but they are not concerned with the transport and movement of messages from one place to another. Also, the data access components will happily store and retrieve any content stream for us, but they don't have any idea about its internal structure. This is where Collaboration Data Objects (CDO) come into play.

CDO has been around for some time and has essentially been an OLE Automation interface into MAPI. Not very many database and web developers have spent much time looking at CDO, as it was so poorly integrated with most data access toolkits.

This has changed with the newly architected CDO 2.0 libraries for Exchange 2000. They seamlessly integrate with the Exchange OLE DB Provider and ADO in a way that they complement each other's capabilities. In the remainder of this chapter, we will look into a few fundamentals of sending messages with CDO and will see how CDO fills some of the gaps in the ADO data access model.

Sending Messages

With CDO, it's very easy to mail-enable web applications. We first need a little input page from where we can enter some basic information, such that it can be submitted to an ASP page:

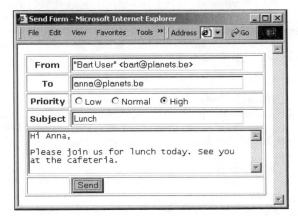

The receiving page captures the incoming parameters into some variables and starts to process the message. To do this, the script just instantiates a CDO message object and assigns the relevant parameters; From, To, Subject and the message body. The priority flag is a little special; we will look into that in a moment. When the required properties are set, the script simply invokes the message object's Send method:

```
vMailFrom = Request("mailFrom")
vMailTo = Request("mailTo")
vMailPriority = Request("mailPriority")
vMailSubject = Request("mailSubject")
vMailBody = Request("mailBody")

Set oMsg = Server.CreateObject("CDO.Message")
With oMsg
  .From = vMailFrom
  .To = vMailTo
  .Subject = vMailSubject
  .TextBody = vMailBody
End With

oMsg.Send
```

The CDO message object carries a few more properties, but not an extensive list of fields as it was exposed through ADO records. However, there is nothing which would come even close to a Priority property, though we can easily get access to the underlying ADO Fields collection through the CDO Fields collection, which makes setting the priority very easy:

```
' ...

Set oMsgFields = oMsg.Fields 'CDO object returns an ADO collection
With oMsgFields
  .Item("urn:schemas:mailheader:x-priority") = vMailPriority
  .Update
End With

oMsg.Send
```

What we see here is a common coding pattern which we can use almost anywhere in Exchange 2000. Whether we want to send a message, create an appointment, set properties of an addressee or something else, these standard operations are directly supported by the respective CDO object. If we want to do something *special*, we grab the corresponding ADO object, manipulate a property or anything else which is specific to the ADO record or recordset and continue working with the CDO object.

The same approach also works the other way around. While we are working with some ADO record or recordset, we might need a property or method which is only provided by the CDO interfaces. It is normally very easy to hop from ADO into the corresponding CDO object. To better understand what this means, let's have a look at an example.

In the earlier section about Search Folders, we created a virtual folder containing all messages with attachments. This was easy enough by specifying a WHERE clause which checked the urn:schema:httpmail:hasattachment field. However, there is no ADO-accessible field telling us about the number of attachments in a message. This information is only available in CDO.

To build an example of how to report the attachment count on every message in a specific folder, we can build on our previous ListChildren.asp page. None of the ADO code needs to change:

```
' ... get connection, get record
Set oRs = oRec.GetChildren
```

Before we loop through the recordset, we instantiate an empty CDO Message object. This object will be used later to obtain the message, which is associated with the current row. Inside the loop, we check to see whether we are dealing with a message (via the DAV:contentclass property).

```
Set oMsg = Server.CreateObject("CDO.Message")
Do While Not oRs.EOF
  vDavDisplayName = oRs("DAV:displayname")
  vDavHref = oRs("DAV:href")

  With Response
    .Write "<dl></dl><dl>"
    .Write DTtag( Btag(vDavDisplayName))

    vDavContentClass = oRs("DAV:contentclass")
    If vDavContentClass = "urn:content-classes:message" Then
```

The most important line in the following fragment is the next statement. We associate the previously created CDO message object with the current row in the recordset. When this is done, it's a routine task to get at the attachment count and to generate the output:

```
      oMsg.DataSource.Open vDavHref, oConn, adModeRead

      vAttCount = oMsg.Attachments.Count
      If vAttCount > 0 Then
        .Write DDtag( "Attachment Count : " & vAttCount )
      End If
    End If

    ' ... more output ...
  End With

  oRs.MoveNext
Loop
```

When we call up the page, the script will generate the output shown below. Everything is seamlessly integrated, and there are no traces that we have used two, formerly independent, access mechanisms to achieve this result:

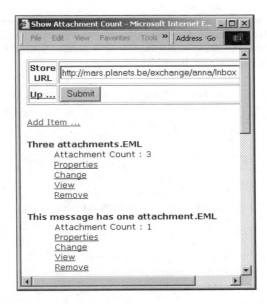

What we have just seen is a very important integration feature of ADO and CDO. Each of the two sets of interfaces has its particular strengths and weaknesses. ADO is better at handling structured data, CDO is better at handling the dynamics of messages and complex document structures. However, it is extremely easy to hop between the two interfaces and to combine the best of both worlds. Typically, it involves just a single line of code to switch between the two.

❑ To jump from a CDO object to ADO:

```
Set adoFields = cdoObject.Fields
```

❑ To jump from an ADO object to CDO:

```
CdoObject.DataSource.Open Source, adoConnection
```

Manipulating Message Properties

There is a certain overlap in functionality of ADO and CDO. For example, we can get at a message's subject line in two different ways. We can either use an ADO record or recordset and work with the field value; oRec("urn:schemas:httpmail:subject"). Or we can work with a CDO Message object and manipulate the oCdoMsg.Subject property. We may ask ourselves which of these two access methods is better.

In general, there is nothing wrong with reading all available message properties from ADO Fields collection. We would find this more convenient when working with lists of messages or when applying a SELECT statement or sort criteria.

However, when it comes to updating messaging-related fields (`From`, `To`, `Subject`, and so on), it's much better to take one extra step – obtain a CDO object and perform the update there, in a similar way to how it was demonstrated above.

There is a reason for this. Messages are stored and sent in the RFC-822 format. This is an ancient specification, originating from a time when nobody was concerned about structured data handling or even object orientation. An RFC-822 compliant message contains both the messaging information and the body of the message in a single file, like this:

```
Received: from mail pickup service by mars.planets.be with Microsoft SMTPSVC;
    Sun, 9 Jul 2000 11:02:26 +0200
Thread-Topic: Lunch
thread-index: Ab/phGc1ukHK63buSRC1NtWtH99DhQ==
X-Priority: 1
From: "Bart User" <bart@planets.be>
To: <anna@planets.be>
Subject: Lunch
Date: Sun, 9 Jul 2000 11:02:26 +0200
Message-ID: <000d01bfe984$67378570$6800a8c0@planets.be>
MIME-Version: 1.0
Content-Type: text/plain
Content-Transfer-Encoding: 7bit
X-Mailer: Microsoft CDO for Exchange 2000
Content-Class: urn:content-classes:message
Importance: normal
Priority: normal
X-MimeOLE: Produced By Microsoft MimeOLE V5.00.2919.6700
X-OriginalArrivalTime: 09 Jul 2000 09:02:26.0831 (UTC)
FILETIME=[675609F0:01BFE984]

Hi Anna,

Please join us for lunch today. See you at the cafeteria.
```

When a message arrives at the store, the header fields are separated from the body and stored, in a structured fashion, in the Web Storage System database. The original message file is also kept in the store, but ADO never touches this file again. When we retrieve a field value, it is not read from, nor written back to, the original message file. Updating any of these fields with ADO can easily create inconsistencies between the RFC-822 message text and one of the other properties of the store item.

On the other hand, CDO is aware of this dualism, so when we update a message's subject line, or any of the other messaging-related properties, it will change both the entry in the Web Storage System data source and in the underlying message file.

What's Next

There is much more in Exchange 2000 and CDO than we can reasonably cover in a single chapter. This is a topic with a huge potential and I would expect it to play a more significant role for ASP-related application development than it has in the past. Watch out for upcoming publications on Exchange 2000 to learn more.

Summary

In this chapter, we have taken a brief look at some of the new capabilities of Exchange 2000, mostly from a data access perspective. We have taken a deeper look at the new Web Storage System and the principal APIs and protocols that it supports.

One of the most prominent access mechanisms into the Web Storage System is via the Exchange OLE DB provider, which enables us to read and write to the store via the familiar ADO toolkit. We have looked into the store search capabilities, which include the ability to perform full-text searches with extensions to the well-known SQL SELECT syntax.

We have briefly looked at WebDAV and how this protocol can be used from client computers to access the store. We have used WebDAV to persist a SELECT statement as a virtual folder.

Last, but certainly not least, we have used Collaboration Data Objects (CDO) to send messages and also to obtain information about message items, which are otherwise not available from ADO. We have talked about the tight integration between ADO and CDO and how easy it is to jump between objects from the two libraries.

23

Legacy Data

Data forms the basic building block of many businesses. It is the key that allows companies to unlock the information they need to make critical business decisions. Companies track data about their customers, sales, market share, and many other aspects of their business. They use this for self-analysis and for tracking industry trends, for targeting marketing and sales efforts, to run their financial system, and to provide services to their customers.

For most of today's enterprise organizations, this data is mission critical. Having the right data in the right place at the right time is essential to keep these companies running. Banks, insurance agencies, hospitals, and many other businesses would be unable to operate without access to the data that they maintain. Customers expect these businesses to store their data in a reliable and secure manner. Any amount of downtime can cost a company large amounts of money and customer loyalty. Because of this, businesses must store this information only on systems with the highest levels of reliability and performance.

Although PC server-based systems are now available that can provide the capacity, performance, and reliability to store this mission critical information, much of this data has traditionally been stored on legacy host systems. Legacy hosts include mainframes, midrange systems, minicomputers, and a variety of other systems. Some of these host systems have been around for upwards of thirty years, and because of this, the businesses that use these host systems have invested a lot of time, money, and effort in building and maintaining these systems, and have thirty year's worth of data stored on them. Although many of these companies are moving this mission-critical data to PC server-based systems, it is safe to say that these legacy host systems, and the need to access the data on these legacy host systems, are going to be around for quite some time.

In fact, with the rise of the Internet, the need to access data on these legacy host systems has never been greater. Businesses want to web-enable their data to allow their employees to quickly access the information they need to do their jobs. Customers want to use a simple browser to gain easier access to their accounts and personal information. Companies want to give customers direct access via a web-based application to cut back on the expensive costs of employing customer service representatives. These are some of the driving factors behind many of today's web-based applications.

In this chapter, we are going to explore some of the ways of integrating legacy data on host based systems with PC Server based ASP applications. Specifically, we will be discussing ways to access data on IBM Mainframe and AS/400 systems. We'll start the chapter with an overview of how these host systems function, and the different types of data that they store. We'll be talking about accessing relational data stored in DB2 databases on IBM mainframe and AS/400 systems, as well as non-relational data files such as AS/400 physical files and files stored in VSAM databases on mainframe systems.

The tools we're going to use in this chapter to access this data are the OLE DB Provider for DB2, and the OLE DB Provider for AS/400 and VSAM, which are part of Microsoft SNA Server and Microsoft Host Integration Server 2000. These are both OLE DB Providers that allow consumer applications (such as ASP applications using ADO) to use standard OLE DB interfaces to gain access to host data. We will briefly cover the setup and configuration of SNA Server and Host Integration Server 2000, as well as go through step-by-step instructions for configuring each of the data providers mentioned above. We will then finish off the chapter by putting our new knowledge to work in setting up an ASP application that retrieves data from a demo host system.

IBM Hosts and SNA Networks

Over the years, IBM has been one of the biggest suppliers of host systems. It has produced many different systems to address the needs of enterprise customers, and each of these systems has evolved through many iterations. With all these different systems, the need arose in the mid-1970s to allow these systems to communicate and share data with each other. To address this need, IBM developed its **Systems Network Architecture**, or **SNA**.

SNA is IBM's proprietary network architecture that defines the methods and protocols that can be used to enable these legacy systems to communicate with each other. At first, SNA was defined as a purely hierarchical model, in which the host system centrally managed and controlled the functions of the network. But as time moved on, the flexibility and economic benefits of distributed data processing began to create demand for midrange systems.

Distributed data processing differs from a hierarchical model in that multiple systems, usually with lower individual processing power, work together to process data, rather than one high performance system doing all the processing. In the early 1980s, SNA was expanded to include **APPN** (**Advanced Program-to-Program Networking**), which allows these SNA networks to support distributed data processing. First, we will look at some of the key pieces of an SNA network, and we will then discuss how these pieces fit into two different SNA networking models: the hierarchical model, and the peer-oriented model.

There are two key elements of an SNA network that we need to understand in order to accomplish our goal of accessing legacy data from our ASP applications. These two elements are **physical units** and **logical units**.

Physical Units

Physical units (PUs) are devices on an SNA network that perform very specific tasks, and play a key role in managing the resources on the network. Although the name implies that a physical unit is a specific piece of hardware, the software controlling the hardware must also be considered an integral part of the physical unit. IBM has defined several different types of physical units, each with specific responsibilities on the SNA network. The physical units that are important for us to understand are:

- **PU 5** is the top of the hierarchical model. It represents an IBM mainframe system and the software programs that control the SNA networking functions of the mainframe. Generally, these software programs are **VTAM** (**Virtual Telecommunications Access Method**) and **SSCP** (**System Service Control Point**). As we will see in the upcoming description of the hierarchical SNA networking model, the PU 5 is responsible for managing all of the resources on the SNA network.

- **PU 4** is a device that is used to offload some of the communications processing from the PU 5 device on an SNA network. This is typically called a front-end processor (**FEP**). It works closely with the PU 5 device to handle network communications, and performs many of the addressing and routing functions to free the PU 5 device from having to deal with that work.

- **PU 2.0** defines a cluster controller. A cluster controller is a device to which terminals, printers, and other end-user devices can be connected. It controls the physical communication paths to these devices, as well as providing a way to group these end-user devices together.

- **PU 2.1** nodes are an extension to the PU 2.0 specification, and are the core component of peer-oriented SNA networks. They not only provide a connection point for end-user devices, but also manage their own processing and network communications as well. When we examine the peer-oriented SNA networking model, we will see that PU 2.1 devices communicate with each other directly, and are not down level devices to a PU 5. In fact, when a mainframe acts as part of a peer-oriented network, it functions as a PU 2.1 device. Mainframes, midrange systems, and any other system that implements the required functionality can act as a PU 2.1 device.

Logical Units

Logical units (LUs) represent resources on an SNA network. More specifically, a logical unit defines the logical resource that an end-user device or application uses to communicate with a host system. IBM defines several different types of logical units. The specification for each type of logical unit defines both the type of resources that can be accessed and the formats used for data flows to and from the resource. This will make more sense if we take a look at some of the different LU types that IBM has defined:

- **LU 0** is the most loosely defined of all the LU specifications. Application developers are free to define their own data flows. Many people use this to provide access to non-standard devices, such as bar code readers, cash registers, and other such devices. These are also sometimes referred to as LUA or LU/A (Logical Unit Applications).

- **LU 1** is defined for IBM 3287-type printers.

- **LU 2** is defined for IBM 3270-type terminals (3278, 3279, and others).

- **LU 3** is defined for IBM 3284-type printers.

- **LU 6.2** has been defined to provide **APPC** (**Advanced Program-to-Program Communication**). It defines the data flow that is used between programs that communicate over an APPN (peer-oriented) network. A form of LU 6.2 (dependent LU 6.2) can also be used in hierarchical SNA networks to provide access for APPC applications. It provides a great deal of functionality and flexibility for applications that need to communicate with each other over SNA networks.

Now that we've defined some of the elements of an SNA network, let's take a look at the way these elements are structured in an SNA network. As SNA is defined today, we basically have two different models. The first is the hierarchical model supporting the centralized processing capabilities of IBM mainframe systems. The second model is the peer-oriented model, which allows IBM mainframes and midrange systems, such as IBM AS/400s, to work together to process data and run applications. The two models are illustrated in the following diagrams.

Hierarchical SNA Network Model

In the hierarchical model, the IBM mainframe system provides a central point for processing data, running applications, and managing network communications. All resources on the network are defined on the mainframe (PU 5) and the other PU devices on the network exist to enable end-user devices to gain access to these resources. For the most part, all applications and data processing run on the mainframe system itself. The end-user devices gain access to the applications and data they need via the logical units that have been defined on the host system.

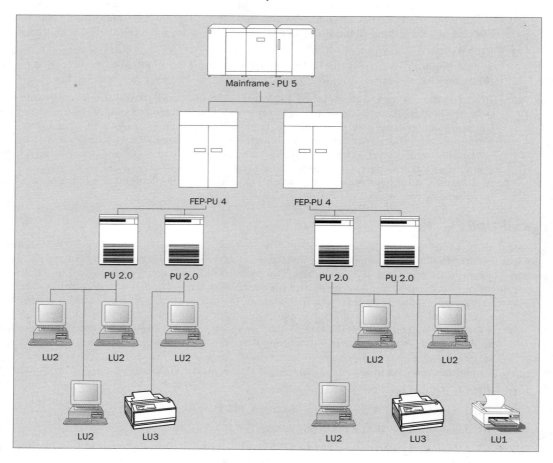

Many of the devices in a hierarchical SNA network are referred to as "dumb" devices because they only understand how to format and display the data, they do not actually perform any of the processing for the applications that are running. A good example of this is a standard IBM 3270 terminal. A 3270 terminal only displays the screen data that the host system sends down to it, and returns the keystrokes that are pressed by the user back to the host. All processing is then done at the host, and the next screen of information is sent down to the terminal.

For these types of applications and devices, the hierarchical model works well enough. The resources of the high-powered mainframe are utilized well and most environments can support thousands of end-user devices.

Peer-Oriented SNA Network Model

In the peer-oriented SNA networking model, PU 2.1 devices each manage their own resources and communications. PU 2.1 devices work co-operatively to establish network connections, and to allow APPC applications to communicate with each other over the network. There is no central point of resource management as in the hierarchical model:

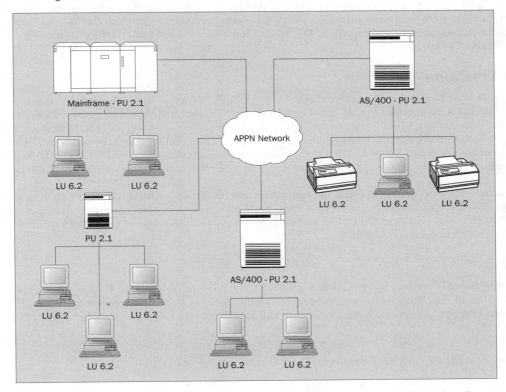

Generally, only LU 6.2 resources are used in a peer-oriented SNA network. Applications that communicate with each other over these resources are referred to as transaction programs. The communication between the two transaction programs is usually referred to as a conversation. In contrast to the hierarchical model, each transaction program does its own processing of the data.

The peer-oriented SNA networking model provides good performance, scalability, and flexibility and provides a much more economical solution for companies with a need for host system integration.

Types of Legacy Data

Now that we understand a bit more about the need to access legacy systems, and how these legacy systems operate, we can examine the different types of legacy data that we might need to access.

When talking about data stored on any kind of system, there are really two different categories that data can be classified under. In fact, if we go back and look at the table of contents for this book, we will see that the chapters defining different types of data have been organized into these same two categories; relational data, and non-relational data.

Relational Data

For the purposes of this chapter, we will define relational data as data that is stored in a tabular format and that contains meta data describing the format of the data. For the most part, this means data is stored in tables, which are organized into rows and columns (also referred to as records and fields). The data itself is usually normalized into different tables, with keys defined between the tables to define the relationship between the two. In most cases, this data is maintained through the use of a relational database management system (RDBMS). We looked at several different RDBMS systems back in Chapters 14 through to 17.

Non-Relational Data

Non-relational data is just what we might expect it to be: data that is not in relational database format. In fact, most non-relational data has no set format at all. Non-relational data could be a document, an e-mail, a directory listing, or any other piece of data we care to conceive of. The format is generally known only to the application that created the data, and cannot be easily accessed by other applications (a notable exception being XML). Of course, as we saw earlier in this book, OLE DB has been designed to allow applications easier, standardized access to non-relational data as well as relational data.

So which type of data is available on legacy host systems? Host systems actually contain both kinds of data. There are RDBMS systems that run on hosts, as well as a number of systems that provide methods for storing non-relational data. Let's examine the most common forms of each that we'd find in use on IBM mainframes and AS/400s.

DB2

For relational database systems, IBM's DB2 is by far the most widely used RDBMS on host systems. Versions of DB2 have been designed for many different host operating systems, as well as PC server-based operating systems. In this chapter we will specifically be looking at DB2 for MVS, OS/390, and OS/400.

The DB2 RDBMS itself is covered in more detail in Chapter 16.

VSAM and IMS/DB

Non-relational data on host systems comes in many forms. Many host-based applications store their data in non-relational files. Most choose to do so in a record based format, but without specifically organizing and defining fields to partition the records contained in the file. Because these files are not in a table format, and do not contain metadata describing the data in the file, they are considered non-relational data files. Many AS/400 physical files are stored this way, and VSAM and IMS/DB are popular systems for storing non-relational data on mainframe systems.

Distributed Data Management

Because this host data is so critical to the businesses that use the data, many applications need to gain access to this information. To access these different types of host data, IBM has created a specification called **Distributed Data Management** (**DDM**). DDM defines an architecture for applications to access these different types of host data. It defines rules and protocols that govern how data can be exchanged between different systems, resulting in standardized ways of accessing both non-relational and relational data on host systems.

This is implemented using a standard client/server approach, in which a DDM server program resides on the host system, and a DDM client application communicates with the DDM server to perform the desired data exchange. The OLE DB providers that we will look at later in this chapter are examples of this kind of client application.

DDM defines several protocols for accessing different types of data. For our purposes, we will examine two of these protocols:

- ❏ **DRDA** (**Distributed Relational Database Architecture**)
- ❏ **RLIO** (**Record Level Input/Output**).

DRDA is the DDM protocol used for accessing relational data. DB2 has a built-in interface for DRDA, thus allowing DDM client applications to gain access to the relational data stored in DB2 databases.

RLIO is the DDM protocol used to provide record level access to non-relational data files. With record level access, a DDM client application can navigate through the records of non-relational data files without having to use the application that created those data files.

We are now starting to understand the types of data that are available on IBM mainframe and AS/400 systems, and the methods that IBM has exposed for gaining access to that data. We will now look at the tools that we will be using to gain access to this host data, and then we'll be ready to put these to work to start using legacy data as part of our ASP applications.

Microsoft SNA Server and Host Integration Server 2000

There are several solutions available today that help PC-based applications integrate with legacy data. In this chapter, we will be focusing on one such solution; **Microsoft SNA Server**, and the next generation, called **Microsoft Host Integration Server 2000**. Before we dig into the data integration features of SNA Server and Host Integration Server 2000, we'll go through a quick overview of the products and the features that they provide. We will also see where they fit into the SNA networking models that we looked at earlier.

SNA Server

SNA Server is part of Microsoft's BackOffice product line, and runs on Windows server-based platforms (Windows NT and Windows 2000). It provides many features that allow integration between PC systems and legacy host systems. The main features are:

- ❏ **SNA gateway functionality**. At its core, Microsoft SNA Server acts as a standard gateway between PC networks and SNA networks. It can function as a PU 2.0 device for integrating with hierarchical SNA networks, and as a PU 2.1 device for integrating with peer-oriented SNA networks. It uses a client/server architecture on the PC network, allowing SNA Client systems to communicate with an SNA Server over a variety of network transports.

  SNA Server handles the translation between the PC network protocols and standard SNA network protocols. It provides for standard 3270 and 5250 terminal emulation, printing, and file sharing. It also features a TN3270 server and a TN5250 server to provide Telnet services to clients using Telnet emulation software.

  SNA Server also provides support for LU 6.2 to allow access for APPC-type applications. It is fully integrated with the Windows server platforms, allowing secure, encrypted (up to 128-bit) client/server communication.

❑ **Application integration**. The **COM Transaction Integrator** (**COMTI**) feature of SNA Server allows programmers to define PC based COM objects that act as proxies for transaction programs that run in CICS and IMS systems on an IBM mainframe. By using Microsoft Transaction Server on Windows NT 4.0, or COM+ services on Windows 2000, application developers can then use these COM objects with languages such as Visual Basic, and ASP, allowing easy integration of host-based transactions with PC-based applications.

There is also a feature called the MSMQ-MQ Series Bridge. This feature allows interoperability between Microsoft Message Queue server and MQ Series messaging servers residing on IBM host systems.

❑ **Security integration**. The Host Security Integration feature of SNA Server provides two main services. The first is single sign-on support. Because PC systems and IBM host systems use different user account databases, users have to log on to both systems, and often have different user IDs and passwords for each. By using the single sign-on feature of SNA Server, host user credentials can be associated with Window NT domain credentials, which gives the users the ability to log in only to the Windows NT domain, and still gain access to their host resources.

The second service Host Security Integration can provide is synchronization of user account and password information from Windows NT to the host system.

❑ **Data integration**. SNA Server provides three data integration components to allow access to legacy data contained on IBM host systems. We will go into more detail on the first two (the OLE DB Provider for DB2 and the OLE DB Provider for AS/400 and VSAM) later in this chapter.

The third component is the ODBC Driver for DB2, which allows ODBC applications to gain access to relational host data.

❑ **Load-balancing and fail-over support**. SNA Server provides several load-balancing options as well as fail-over support for most of the features in the product. Up to 15 SNA Servers can be grouped together to balance the client load and provide backup resources should one of the servers go down. Another way to provide fail-over support is through backup connections. Backup connections can be configured as On-Demand. For example, if the primary connection to the host is over a LAN connection, a backup connection over dial-up lines could be configured to activate in situations when the LAN connection was lost.

Host Integration Server 2000

Host Integration Server 2000 is the next generation of the SNA Server product line and maintains almost all of the same functionality in addition to adding several new features. Most notably, support for the OS/2 client has been dropped, as well as support for banyan vines. Here's a list of some of the more impressive new features:

❑ The OLE DB Provider for DB2 now supports distributed transactions. This means that applications will now be able to ensure data integrity through two-phase commit protocols. This allows us to rollback all changes to the database if part of the overall transaction fails.

❑ Load balancing now provides support for Sync Point enabled LUs. Sync Point enabled LUs are necessary to allow applications like the OLE DB Provider for DB2 and COMTI to use two-phase commit protocols. Previously, these types of resources could not be load balanced across servers.

❑ Integration with Windows 2000 Active Directory Services.

- ❏ Programmatic configuration and monitoring of Host Integration Server via **WMI** (**Windows Management Instrumentation**). WMI is a new feature from Microsoft that allows its Windows platforms and other applications to enable programmatic access to configuration and status information via a standard COM interface.

- ❏ Host Security Integration now uses the Microsoft Data Engine (MSDE), allowing for better performance and better recovery mechanisms.

- ❏ AS/400 Data Queues are now supported via a COM Automation control.

Configuring SNA Server and Host Integration Server

In the following section, we'll briefly go over the steps needed to configure SNA Server and Host Integration Server 2000. However, the OLE DB providers that we'll be configuring in the next few sections also support direct connections to IBM host systems via TCP/IP. So, if you're planning on connecting directly to your host system via TCP/IP, you can probably skip this and dive right into the sections on configuring the OLE DB providers.

If you need to connect to your host system via standard SNA networking transports, then you'll need to get the basics on configuring your connection to the host from this section. Similarly, if you plan on setting up the examples using the demo hosts at the end of this chapter, you'll need to read this section.

Note that the screen shots in this section, and throughout the rest of the chapter, are taken from Host Integration Server 2000. If you're using SNA Server, the screens may look slightly different, but the required connection parameters are the same.

When configuring SNA Server and Host Integration Server 2000 for use with the data integration features, there are five main things that need to be configured:

- ❏ **Link Services**: a link service defines the physical connection to the host system. The types of link services supported include 802.2 DLC, SDLC, X.25, DFT, Twinax, and Channel. For more information on these link service types, refer to the Host Integration Server 2000 Online Books.

- ❏ **Connections**: a connection represents the server's appearance as a PU to a host system. Depending on the connection type, the server can act as either a PU 2.0 or PU 2.1 device. The server can support multiple connections, and thus can provide access to resources from multiple SNA networks at the same time.

- ❏ **Local LU**: a Local LU is the definition of an LU 6.2 type LU representing the local server.

- ❏ **Remote LU**: a Remote LU is the definition of an LU 6.2 type LU representing the resource available on the remote host. In most cases, this represents the application that we will be talking to on the host system.

- ❏ **APPC Mode**: an APPC Mode description defines characteristics of the sessions between APPC applications. When a conversation between APPC applications is started, a Local LU, Remote LU, and APPC Mode are required. The LUs represent the resources on either end of the conversation, and the APPC Mode defines the characteristics of the conversation between the LUs.

To configure these, we'll need to start up the SNA Manager program. Here's a view of the SNA Manager from Host Integration Server 2000:

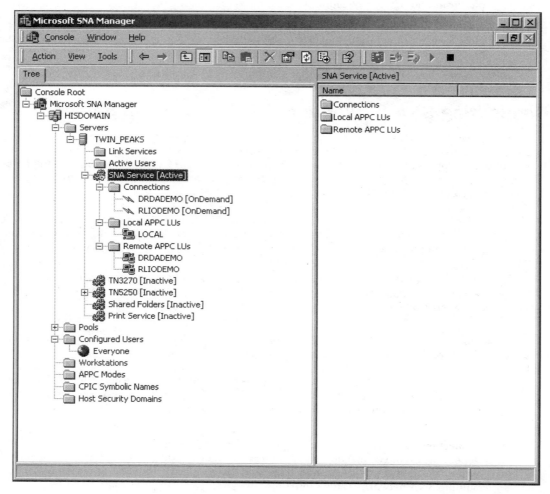

The easiest way to configure the server to communicate with a host system is to use the following steps:

❑ We add the appropriate Link Service for our physical connection to the host system. The 802.2 DLC link service and some SDLC link services ship with SNA Server and Host Integration Server 2000. Otherwise, you will need to obtain the link service from the manufacturer of your card, whatever kind of card that may be.

❑ We start either the **AS/400 Connection Wizard** or **Mainframe Connection Wizard** from the tools menu in the SNA Manager program. If you're connecting to an AS/400, you'll need to follow the instructions on each of the wizard screens. If you're connecting to a mainframe system, you should see the following screen:

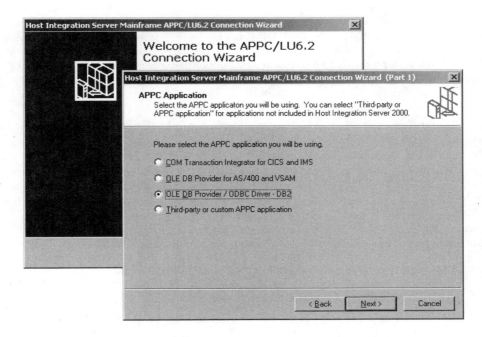

We choose the appropriate OLE DB provider, depending on whether we need access to relational or non-relational data on the host system. We fill in the rest of the screens on the wizard as appropriate. We can also print worksheets from the wizard that will help to track down the configuration information needed for the host connection. These can be very helpful, especially when trying to talk to a host administrator about what settings are necessary for the connection.

❑   Once finished, we save the configuration file and we're ready to go. At that point, we can right-click on the SNA service and choose Start. The SNA service should go Active, and then, if the connection was set to start on server startup, the connection should show Active. Otherwise, we may need to right-click on the connection and start it manually before the connection will go Active.

Should We Run the Data Provider On the Server Or a Client?

SNA Server and Host Integration Server 2000 use a client/server architecture on the PC side to provide access to host resources. Because of this, situations may arise where it may be unclear whether the client software or server software should be used. The data providers that we will be configuring are installed with both the client software and the server software for SNA Server and Host Integration Server 2000. So, which one should we use, and where should it be installed?

For the most part, we're going to want to install the data provider we will be using on the same machine as our web server. If we will be using the SNA Server (or Host Integration Server 2000) for the data providers only, then it might make sense to install the server on the web server. If we want to use the server for other traffic to the host system in addition to the data providers, we will probably want to install just the client software on the web server.

759

Of course, there are a couple of other factors that we will also need to keep in mind. The new distributed transaction support in the OLE DB Provider for DB2 is available only when running directly on a Host Integration Server 2000 server computer. Sometimes we may not have or want a physical connection from our web server to our host system. In this case, we would need to use the client software on the web server, and place the SNA Server (or Host Integration Server 2000) in a location where we have a physical connection to the host.

For more information on which architecture might work best for your environment, refer to the online help included with these products.

Configuring the OLE DB Provider for DB2

The OLE DB Provider for DB2 was first shipped with SNA Server 4.0 Service Pack 2. It is also available in Host Integration Server 2000. It can be installed with the server installation, as well as with the client installations. Please note that the new distributed transaction support in the provider is only available on the Host Integration Server 2000 server installation, not with the client installations.

The OLE DB provider supports several different implementations of DB2:

❑ IBM DB2 for MVS V4R1 or later to support an SNA LU 6.2 connection

❑ IBM DB2 for OS/390 V5R1 or later to support an SNA LU 6.2 or TCP/IP connection

❑ IBM DB2 for OS/400 V3R2 or later to support an SNA LU 6.2 connection

❑ IBM DB2 for OS/400 V4R2 or later to support an SNA LU 6.2 or TCP/IP connection

❑ IBM DB2 UDB for Windows NT V5R2 or later to support a TCP/IP connection

❑ IBM DB2 UDB for AIX V5R2 or later to support a TCP/IP connection

In this chapter we will only discuss configuration issues for systems running MVS, OS/390, and OS/400. We'll start by walking through setting up a new `.udl` with the following configuration (see Chapter 7 for more information about setting up a `.udl` file).

Again, we illustrate this using Host Integration Server 2000. The screens may look slightly different with SNA Server, but the configuration parameters are almost identical. This section only describes the steps necessary to configure the provider. Later in this chapter, we will walk through step-by-step instructions for using the provider to access a demo host:

❑ From the Start menu, go to Programs, then Host Integration Server, then Data Integration, and then OLE DB Data Sources.

❑ This will start up the Data Link configuration utility. Switch to the Provider tab and make sure Microsoft OLE DB Provider for DB2 is selected, then hit the Next button.

❑ We will now be on the Connection tab. Fill in a data source name. This name will be used as the name of the `.udl` file that is created:

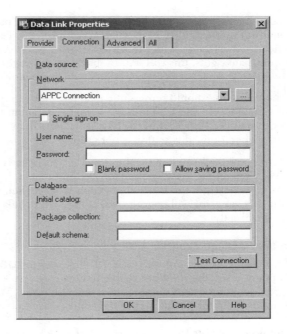

- In the Network section, we need to choose the type of connection we want to make to the host (either APPC or TCP/IP) and then hit the button to the immediate right of that selection box. This will pull up details of the connection parameters for the connection type that we are using:

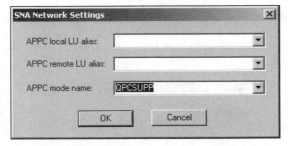

- If you are using an APPC connection, you need to fill in the Local LU, Remote LU, and Mode Name, as defined on your server. If you are using a TCP/IP connection, fill in the host name or IP address and make sure the port number is correct.

- Back on the Connection tab, we enter the login information for the host system that we will be accessing. As we do not want to be prompted for a password every time we use this .udl, we check the Allow saving password box.

- The Initial Catalog setting should be set to the name of the DB2 database on the host system. If this is DB2 on OS/400, we can retrieve this information by using the WRKRDBDIRE command. If this is DB2 on MVS or OS/390, we can retrieve this information from the system table SYSIBM.LOCATIONS.

❑ The **Package Collection** setting should be set to the name of the package on DB2. The OLE DB provider requires the use of a package when accessing DB2. The provider can create the package dynamically when the provider is started. However, if the user of the provider does not have the appropriate rights, this will fail. In that case, packages will need to be set up ahead of time by using the package creation utility, which we look at later in this chapter.

❑ The **Default Schema** setting should represent a qualifier name to be used when the provider queries the host system tables and tries to retrieve metadata about the tables on the system. This parameter can be QSYS2; SYSIBM; SYSTEM; CURLIB; or USERID, depending on the platform. For other operations, this setting is not used.

❑ At this point, the required information for the provider has been configured, and it's time to test things out. We click on the **Test Connection** button to have the provider attempt to connect to DB2 on the host system. If the connection is successful, we're ready to start using the provider. If it fails, an error will be returned, along with details about which parameter(s) were configured incorrectly.

Creating Packages Using the Package Creation Utility

As mentioned in the step-by-step instructions, the OLE DB Provider for DB2 needs to use a package when accessing DB2. In many cases, the provider is able to create this package dynamically when it starts up; however, this could fail if the user does not have enough rights. We can refer to the Host Integration Server 2000 online help for details on the rights necessary to build these packages.

In the case where the end-user is unable to create packages, the packages will need to be pre-built by a user with appropriate rights. This is accomplished by using the package creation utility:

❑ To start the package creation utility, we need to go to the **Start** menu, selecting **Microsoft Host Integration Server 2000**, then **Data Integration**, and then **Packages for DB2**.

❑ Once the utility has started, we need to tell it which host system to connect to. The easiest way to do this is to point it to an existing `.udl` file. From the file menu, we choose **Load Data Source**, and then **OLE DB UDL File**. When prompted, we can select the `.udl` file for our host system:

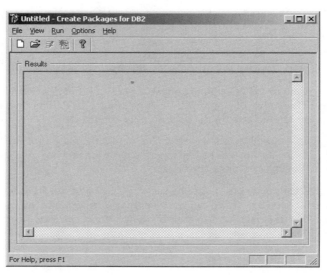

❑ The next step is to start building the packages. To start this process, we need to go to the Run menu and choose Create Packages. This will run through a number of steps. We should be able to read through the information in the results window to determine if everything completed successfully or not. Once successful, users will then be able to use the OLE DB Provider for DB2.

Configuring the OLE DB Provider for AS/400 and VSAM

The OLE DB Provider for AS/400 and VSAM was first shipped with SNA Server 4.0 Service Pack 2. It is also available in Host Integration Server 2000. It can be installed with the server installation, as well as with the client installations.

The OLE DB Provider can access several different types of files as listed below:

❑ AS/400 keyed and non-keyed physical files

❑ AS/400 logical files

❑ Sequential Access Method (SAM) data sets

❑ Virtual Storage Access Method (VSAM) data sets

❑ Basic Partitioned Access Method data sets (PDSE and PDS members)

The OLE DB provider requires the following software on the host system to access these data types:

❑ IBM Distributed File Manager (DFM), a component of IBM Data Facility Storage Management Subsystem for MVS (DFSMS/MVS), V1R2 or later to support an SNA LU 6.2 connection

❑ IBM OS/400 V3R2 or later to support an SNA LU 6.2 connection

❑ IBM OS/400 V4R4 or later to support a TCP/IP connection

Because the files being accessed are non-relational data files, we need some way to describe the records contained in these files. DDM on OS/400 systems can provide this information to the OLE DB provider automatically. However, DDM on mainframe hosts does not, so we need to have some way to describe the format of the records to the OLE DB provider.

The OLE DB Provider for AS/400 and VSAM accomplishes this through the use of **data description files** (.hcd files). The first step in setting up the OLE DB provider is to set up a data description file defining the record format for the file we will be accessing. The easiest way to do this is with the data description utility that comes with SNA Server and Host Integration Server 2000.

Using the Data Description Utility to Create a Data Description File

We can follow the following steps to set up a data description file using the data description utility:

❑ From the Start menu, we choose Programs, then Host Integration Server, then Data Integration, and then Data Descriptions. This will start the data description utility.

❑ Expanding the Data Descriptions folder will show us a sample file. If we expand this sample file, we will see that three tables have been defined. Clicking on one of the tables will display, on the right side of the screen, the columns that have been defined for that table:

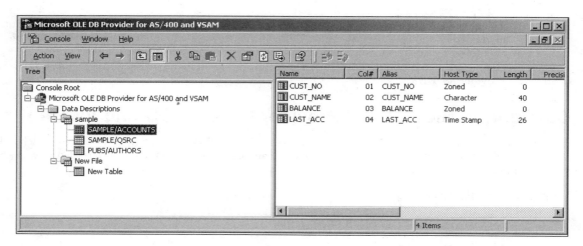

- To start a new data description file, we right-click on the data descriptions folder and choose New and then File. A new file will be created, which we can rename if desired.

- To define a table (or host file) in that data description file, we right-click on the file name and choose New and then Table. Again, we can rename the table if desired:

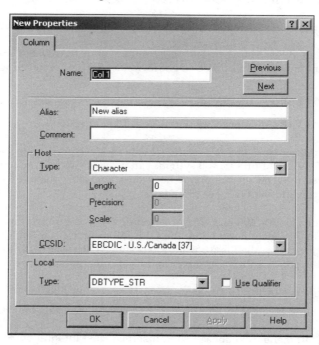

- If we click on the table, we will see that no columns have yet been described for that table. To define a new column, we right-click on the table and choose New and then Column. We fill in the column information and then choose OK. We repeat this step until all the columns have been defined.

The following table will help us to match up our host data types with the OLE DB data types:

Host Data Type	OLE DB Data Type
Binary	DBTYPE_BYTES
Character	DBTYPE_STR
Date	DBTYPE_DBDATE
Double	DBTYPE_R8
Float	DBTYPE_R8
Long Integer	DBTYPE_14
Long Variable Binary	DBTYPE_BYTES
Long Variable Character	DBTYPE_STR
Packed	DBTYPE_DECIMAL
Real	DBTYPE_R4
Short	DBTYPE_12
Single	DBTYPE_R4
Time	DBTYPE_DBTIME
Time Stamp	DBTYPE_DBTIMESTAMP
Variable Binary	DBTYPE_BYTES
Variable Character	DBTYPE_STR
Zoned	DBTYPE_NUMERIC

❏ Once we've described all our columns, we can simply exit out of the data description utility. The file will be saved automatically to the Host Integration Server 2000 system directory as an .hcd file.

Creating the Data Link

With our newly created .hcd file to hand, we are now ready to walk through creating the .udl file. We will do this here with Host Integration Server 2000. The screens may look slightly different with SNA Server, but the configuration parameters will be almost identical.

This section only describes the steps necessary to configure the provider. We will walk through step-by-step instructions for using the provider to access a demo host later in this chapter:

❏ From the Start menu, we need to select Programs, then Host Integration Server, then Data Integration, and then OLE DB Data Sources.

❏ This will start up the Data Link configuration utility. We switch to the Provider tab and make sure Microsoft OLE DB Provider for AS/400 and VSAM is selected, and then hit the Next button:

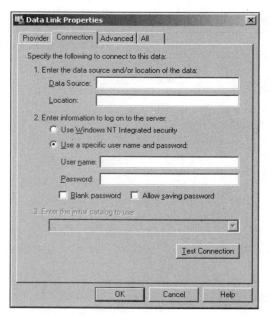

❑   We will now be on the Connection tab. We fill in a data source name and location name. This location name will be used for the name of the `.udl` file that is created.

❑   We next enter our login information for the host system that we will be accessing. If we do not want to be prompted for a password every time we use this `.udl`, we check the Allow saving password box.

❑   We then switch to the All tab. This gives us access to the rest of the configuration parameters for the provider:

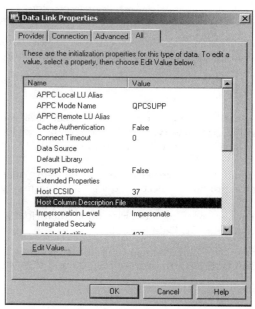

❏ If we are using an LU 6.2 connection to the host system, we fill in the correct APPC Local LU Alias, APPC Mode Name, and APPC Remote LU Alias.

If we are using TCP/IP, we need to change the Network Transport Library setting to TCP/IP and then fill in the Network Address and Network Port number.

❏ In the Host Column Description File setting, we enter the path and file name of the .hcd file that we created using the Data Description utility.

❏ At this point, we switch back to the Connection tab, and hit the Test Connection button. If the test connection is successful, we hit OK, and we've now created a functioning .udl file that we can use with our applications. If an error is returned, we use the error information to try to troubleshoot the problem.

Using the OLE DB Provider for DB2 to Connect to a Demo Host from an ASP Application

We're now ready to put our new knowledge to work. In this example, we're going to set up an ASP application that uses the OLE DB Provider for DB2 to retrieve information from a host system.

Because you may not have a host system to use for testing purposes, and because it would be impossible to provide step-by-step instructions for the live hosts that you may have access to, we will be using a Demo Link Service in Host Integration Server 2000 to simulate accessing a live host. Also, we'll be using LU 6.2 as our transport for this example. This will give us a good look at the configuration steps necessary for LU 6.2 type connections.

We'll start by setting up the necessary elements in the SNA Manager. After starting up the SNA Manager program, we walk through the following steps:

❏ From the Microsoft SNA Manager, we right-click on Link Services and add a new DEMO SDLC Link Service, choosing DB2OLEDB as the script file.

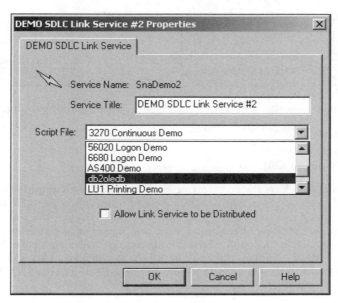

❑ From the Microsoft SNA Manager, we right-click on the server name and select the AS/400 Wizard... from the All Tasks menu option. We walk through the wizard screens using the following configuration options:

    ❑ SNA Service: (select server name)

    ❑ Connection Name: DRDADEMO

    ❑ Link Service: (select the Link Service created in Step 1)

    ❑ Network Name: APPN

    ❑ Control Point Name: DRDADEMO

    ❑ SDLC settings: (leave as default)

❑ Once done with the wizard, we right-click on the Local APPC LUs folder, and choose New and then Local LU...

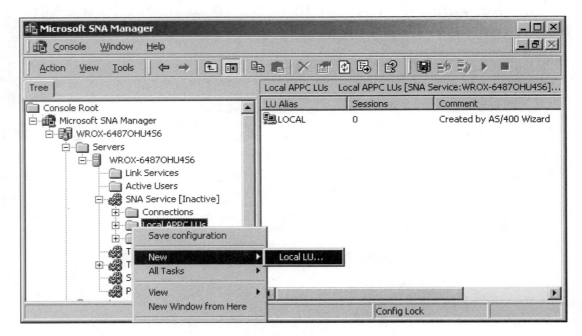

❑ We then configure the new Local LU using the following configuration options:

    ❑ LU Alias: LOCAL

    ❑ Network Name: APPN

    ❑ LU Name: LOCAL

❑ We next right-click on the server name and choose Save Configuration, then start the SNA Service. The newly-created DRDADEMO connection should go to On Demand status.

The SNA Manager part of the configuration is now complete. For use with the demo scripts, Host Integration Server 2000 ships a couple of pre-configured .udl files, so we won't need to create our own from scratch. However, let's pull up the .udl for a second and take a look at a couple of the important parameters to see how they match up with what we just configured in the SNA Manager.

The .udl file is called `drdademo.udl` and should be located in the `C:\Program Files\Common Files\System\OLE DB\Data Links` directory. We double-click on it to pull it up in the Data Link configuration utility. We will see the following screen:

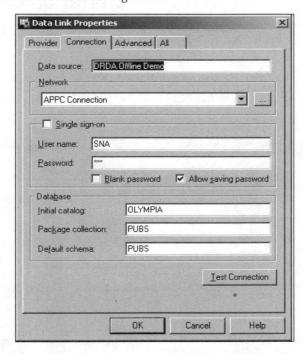

The values here for Initial Catalog, Package Collection, and Default Schema have been coded to match up to the values contained in the demo script file. If we click on the Ellipses button to the right of the Network setting box, we will see the following parameters:

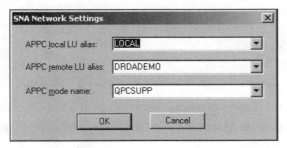

We should recognize these names. They match up to the values that we configured in the SNA Manager program. If we hit the Test Connection button back on the Data Link Properties dialog, the connection should succeed. If it doesn't, we need to double check the values that were entered into the SNA Manager earlier in this example.

We're now ready to use our .udl to retrieve data. We'll start off by using a sample application that ships with Host Integration Server 2000. After we see that working, we'll be ready for the final step in our example: accessing legacy DB2 data from an ASP page! Let's walk through the following steps to use the DRDA_VB sample application to test our .udl:

❑ From the Run line of the Start menu, we type drda_vb and click OK.

❑ We click the Connect button to use the ADO Connection.Open method. This will establish an APPC session between the OLE DB Provider for DB2 computer and the demo AS/400.

❑ When asked to use an existing data link file, we select Yes. When prompted to enter the path to the data link file, we use the following:

C:\Program Files\Common Files\System\OLE DB\Data Links\drdademo.udl

❑ We next click the Open RS button to use the ADO Recordset.Open method.

❑ In the open dialog, we enter SELECT * FROM PUBS.AUTHORS, then click OK to continue. We should see a record containing information about an author.

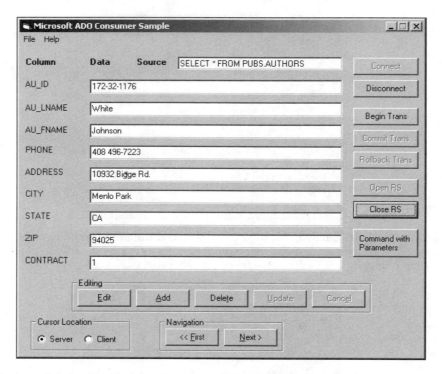

❑ We then click the Next button to sequentially access all of the records in the table.

❑ Clicking the Close RS button will close the host file using the ADO Recordset.Close method.

❑ Clicking the Disconnect button will end the APPC session using the ADO Connection.Close method.

❑ We can then close down the DRDA_VB application.

Accessing Data from ASP

We should have seen several records of data contained in the sample table. Now that we've configured everything and tested out our .udl, we're ready to write an ASP page to present this data.

Here's an example of the kind of ASP code we could use to access this data:

```
<%@ LANGUAGE="VBSCRIPT" %>

<!DOCTYPE HTML PUBLIC "-//W3C//DTD HTML 4.0 Transitional//EN">
<HTML>
<HEAD>
<TITLE>OLE DB Provider for DB2 sample</TITLE>
</HEAD>

<BODY>

<H3>Here are the first ten Authors:</H3>
<BR>

<%

' set our connection string
Dim sConnString
sConnString = "Provider=DB2OLEDB; NetLib=SNA;NetAddr=;" & _
              "NetPort=;RemoteLU=DRDADEMO;LocalLU=LOCAL;" & _
              "ModeName=QPCSUPP;User ID=SNA;Password=SNA;" & _
              "InitCat=OLYMPIA;DefSch=PUBS;PkgCol=PUBS;" & _
              "TPName=0X07F9F9F9;CCSID=37;" & _
              "PCCodePage=1252;BinAsChar=NO;"
'set our command string
Dim sCommand
sCommand = "SELECT * FROM PUBS.AUTHORS"

'execute the command and retrieve the recordset
Dim RS
Set RS = CreateObject("ADODB.Recordset")
RS.Open sCommand, sConnString, 0, 1, 1

%>

<TABLE BORDER=1>
<TR>
<% For i = 0 To RS.Fields.Count - 1 %>
   <TD><B><% = RS(i).Name %></B></TD>
<% Next %>
</TR>
<%
' Put up to 10 rows in a 2d variant array
v=RS.GetRows(10)
%>
<P>
<% For row = 0 To UBound(v,2)  ' iterate through the array %>
   <TR>
   <% For col = 0 To UBound(v,1) %>
      <TD><% = v(col,row) %> </TD>
   <% Next %>
   </TR>
<% Next %>
</TABLE>
<%
RS.close
Set RS = Nothing
%>
<BR>
</BODY>
</HTML>
```

This is just regular old ASP code for accessing data. Because of the standardized interface provided by OLE DB, we can easily integrate host data into our ASP applications.

Of course, the important pieces of code are the connection string, which contains the provider specific information, and the command string, which contains the command to pass up the host system.

There are really two ways to obtain this connection string:

❑   We can configure a `.udl` file by using the data link configuration utility that we walked through earlier in this chapter. Once created, we simply open the `.udl` file in a text editor and cut and paste the connection string into your ASP code.

   However, we would need to watch out for one thing when using this method. Some values in the `.udl` file may contain quotes around the value data. We would need to remove these quotes in order to use the connection string with ASP. ASP expects quotes only at the beginning and end of the connection string, unless, of course, the & _ syntax is used to concatenate multiple strings.

❑   The second way to obtain the connection string is to build it from scratch. The following table defines the valid arguments for the OLE DB Provider for DB2. These are the settings as defined for Host Integration Server 2000, which we are using in this example. Although many of the arguments are the same, the provider that ships with SNA Server 4.0 has slightly different parameters. Refer to the online help in SNA Server 4.0 for more details:

Argument	Description
BinAsChar	When set to true, the provider treats binary data type fields as character data type fields. Defaults to false.
CCSID	The Code Character Set Identifier (CCSID) defines which code page is being used on the host system. Defaults to U.S./Canada (37).
Data Source	Optional data source name.
DefSch	Name of the default schema, which points to the location of the system catalog. See the description in the Configuring OLE DB Provider for DB2 section for more details. There is no default value.
File Name	Can contain pointer to a pre-configured `.udl` file. Cannot be used if the Provider argument is being used.
InitCat	This argument represents the Initial Catalog setting. Again, see the section on Configuring the OLE DB provider for DB2 for details. There is no default value.
LocalLU	Name of the Local LU as configured in the SNA Manager program. If using SNA as the network library, this is required.
ModeName	Name of the APPC mode as configured in the SNA Manager program. If using SNA as the network library, this is required.
NetAddr	TCP/IP address of the host system. If using TCPIP as the network library, this is required.
NetPort	TCP/IP port number being used by the host system. If using TCPIP as the network library, this is required. Default value is 446.
NetLib	Defines which method of network communications will be used. Setting this to SNA will cause the provider to access the host over LU 6.2. Setting this to TCPIP will cause the provider to access the host over TCP/IP. Defaults to SNA.

Argument	Description
Password	Valid host password.
PCCodePage	Code page to be used on the PC. Defaults to Latin 1 (1252).
PkgCol	Location of the packages to be used by the provider. See the description in the Configuring OLE DB Provider for DB2 section for more details. There is no default value.
Provider	Name of provider to use for the connection. For the OLE DB Provider for DB2 this should be set to "DB2OLEDB".
RemoteLU	Name of the Remote LU as configured in the SNA Manager program. If using SNA as the network library, this is required.
TPName	Transaction program name when used with SQL/DS.
UOW	Determines whether distributed transactions (two-phase commit) will be used or not. The two possible values are DUW (distributed transactions used) or RUW (distributed transactions not used). The default value is RUW.
User ID	Valid host user ID.

As for command syntax, DB2 on the host expects fairly standard SQL syntax, so this command shouldn't look particularly unusual. Here's a look at the final output from this application:

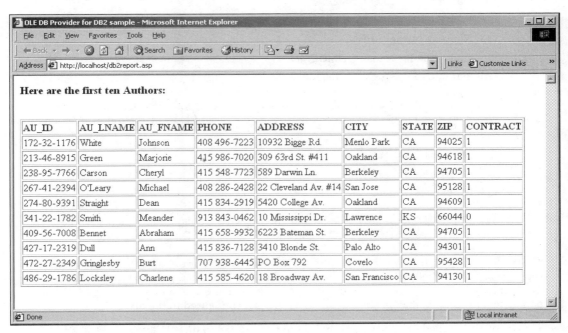

Using the OLE DB Provider for AS/400 and VSAM to Connect to a Demo Host from an ASP application

In this example, we're going to set up an ASP application that uses the OLE DB Provider for AS/400 and VSAM to retrieve information from a host system.

> *Because you may not have a host system to use for testing purposes, and because it would be impossible to provide step-by-step instructions for the live hosts that you may have access to, we will be using a Demo Link Service in Host Integration Server 2000 to simulate accessing a live host. Also, we'll be using LU 6.2 as our transport for this example. This will give us a good look at the configuration steps necessary for LU 6.2 type connections.*

We'll start by setting up the necessary elements in the SNA Manager. We start up the SNA Manager program and walk through the following steps:

❑ From the Microsoft SNA Manager, we right-click on Link Services and add a new Demo SDLC Link Service, choosing SNAOLEDB as the script file.

❑ From the Microsoft SNA Manager, we right-click on the server name and select the AS/400 Wizard... from the All Tasks menu option. We use the following configuration options:

   ❑ SNA Service: (select the server name)

   ❑ Connection Name: DDMDEMO

   ❑ Link Service: (select the link service created in Step 1)

   ❑ Network Name: APPN

   ❑ Control Point Name: DDMDEMO

   ❑ SDLC settings: (leave as default)

❑ Once done with the wizard, we can right-click on the Local APPC LUs folder, and choose New and then Local LU... We configure the new Local LU using the following configuration options:

   ❑ LU Alias: LOCAL

   ❑ Network Name: APPN

   ❑ LU Name: LOCAL

❑ We right-click on the server name and choose Save Configuration, then start the SNA service. The newly-created DDMDEMO connection should go to On Demand status.

The SNA Manager part of the configuration is now complete. For use with the demo scripts, Host Integration Server 2000 ships a couple of pre-configured `.udl` files, so we won't need to create our own from scratch. However, let's pull up the `.udl` for a second and take a look at a couple of the important parameters to see how they match up with what we just configured in the SNA Manager.

The `.udl` file is called ddmdemo.udl and should be located in the `C:\Program Files\Common Files\System\OLE DB\Data Links` directory. Double-click on it to pull it up in the Data Link configuration utility. We should be presented with the following:

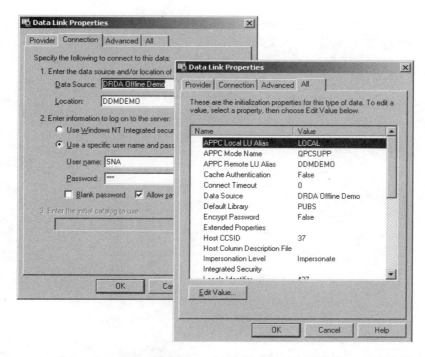

We should recognize the names of the APPC Local LU Alias and APPC Remote LU Alias. They match up to the values that we configured in the SNA Manager program. If we hit the Test Connection button, the connection should succeed.

We're now ready to use our .udl to retrieve data. We'll start off by using a sample application that ships with Host Integration Server 2000. After we see that working, we'll be ready for the final step in our example: accessing legacy non-relational data from an ASP page! Let's walk through the following steps to use the RLIO_VB sample application to test our .udl:

❑ From the Run line of the Start menu, we type rlio_vb and click OK.

❑ Next we click the Connect button. This will establish an APPC session between the OLE DB Provider for AS/400 and VSAM computer and the demo AS/400.

❑ When asked to use an existing data link file, we choose Yes. When prompted to enter the path to the data link file, we enter the following line, then click OK:

```
C:\Program Files\Common Files\System\OLE DB\Data Links\ddmdemo.udl
```

❑ We click the Open RS button to use the ADO Recordset.Open method.

❑ In the open dialog, we enter PUBS/AUTHORS, and then click OK to continue.

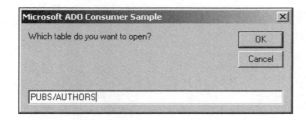

❏   We should see a record that contains information about one of the authors.

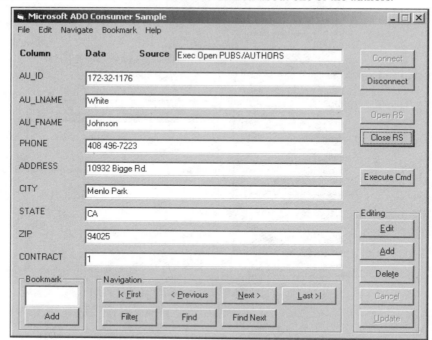

❏   We click the **Next** button to sequentially access all of the records in the table.

❏   We then click the **Close RS** button to close the host file using the ADO `Recordset.Close` method.

❏   Click the **Disconnect** button to end the APPC session using the ADO `Connection.Close` method.

❏   Now we can close down the `RLIO_VB` application.

We should have seen several records of data contained in the sample table. Now that we've configured everything and tested out our `.udl` file, we're ready to write an ASP page to present this data. Here's an example of the kind of ASP code we could use to access this data:

```
<%@ LANGUAGE="VBSCRIPT" %>

<!DOCTYPE HTML PUBLIC "-//W3C//DTD HTML 4.0 Transitional//EN">
<HTML>
<HEAD>
<TITLE>OLE DB Provider for AS/400 and VSAM sample</TITLE>
</HEAD>

<BODY>

<H3>Here are the Authors:</H3>
<BR>

<%
'set our connection string
Dim sConnString
sConnString = "Provider=SNAOLEDB;Password=SNA;" & _
              "User ID=SNA;Data Source=DRDA Offline Demo;" & _
              "RemoteLU=DDMDEMO; LocalLU=LOCAL;" & _
```

```
            "Default Library=PUBS; ModeName=QPCSUPP;" & _
            "BinAsChar=False;Repair Host Keys=False;" & _
            "StrictVal=False; NetLib=SNA;" & _
            "CCSID=37; PCCodePage=1252;"
'set our command string
Dim sCommand
sCommand = "EXEC OPEN PUBS/AUTHORS"

'execute the command and retrieve the recordset
Dim RS
Set RS = CreateObject("ADODB.Recordset")
RS.Open sCommand, sConnString, 2, 4, 1

%>

<TABLE BORDER=1>
<TR>
<% For i = 0 to RS.Fields.Count - 1 %>
    <TD><B><% = RS(i).Name %></B></TD>
<% Next %>
</TR>
<%
' Put up to 10 rows in a 2d variant array
v=RS.GetRows(10)
%>
<P>
<% For row = 0 To UBound(v,2)  ' iterate through the array %>
    <TR>
    <% For col = 0 To UBound(v,1) %>
        <TD><% = v(col,row) %> </TD>
    <% Next %>
    </TR>
<% Next %>
</TABLE>
<%
RS.close
Set RS = nothing
%>
<BR>
</BODY>
</HTML>
```

Again, we can figure out the necessary connection string using the datalink configuration utility, or by building it from scratch.

The following table defines the valid arguments for the OLE DB Provider for AS/400 and VSAM:

Argument	Description
BinAsChar	When set to true, the provider treats binary data type fields as character data type fields. Defaults to 0 (false).
CCSID	The Code Character Set Identifier (CCSID) defines which code page is being used on the host system. Defaults to US/Canada (37).
Data Source	Optional data source name.
Default Library	The name of the default AS/400 library to be accessed. This is an optional setting that is not used when connecting to a mainframe host system.
File Name	Can contain pointer to a pre-configured .udl file. Cannot be used if the Provider argument is being used.

Table continued on following page

Argument	Description
HCDFileName	A pointer to the column description file (.hcd). This should be a fully qualified filename, or a UNC string specifying the location of the .hcd file. This is a required parameter for connection to mainframe systems, optional when connecting to an AS/400 system.
LocalLU	Name of the Local LU as configured in the SNA Manager program. If using SNA as the network library, this is required.
ModeName	Name of the APPC mode as configured in the SNA Manager program. If using SNA as the network library, this is required.
NetAddr	TCP/IP address of the host system. If using TCPIP as the network library, this is required.
NetPort	TCP/IP port number being used by the host system. If using TCPIP as the network library, this is required. Default value is 446.
NetLib	Defines which method of network communications will be used. Setting this to SNA will cause the provider to access the host over LU 6.2. Setting this to TCPIP will cause the provider to access the host over TCP/IP. Please note that the provider only allows TCP/IP connection to AS/400 systems, not mainframe systems. Defaults to SNA.
Password	Valid host password.
PCCodePage	Code page to be used on the PC. Defaults to Latin 1 (1252).
Provider	Name of provider to use for the connection. For the OLE DB Provider for DB2 this should be set to "DB2OLEDB".
RDB	This should be the AS/400 remote database name. We can get this name by using the WRKRDBDIRE AS/400 command. This is optional when connecting to mainframe systems. If this name is the same as the Remote LU, we do not need to specify this value.
Repair Host Keys	Indicates whether the provider should repair any host key values set in the registry. Defaults to false. See the Host Integration Server 2000 online help for more details.
RemoteLU	Name of the Remote LU as configured in the SNA Manager program. If using SNA as the network library, this is required.
StrictVal	Indicates whether strict validation should be used. The default is false.
User ID	Valid host user ID.

The command string contains a syntax that you may not be familiar with. It is basically a DDM command which tells the DDM server on the host side which data we want to access. More information about the details of this syntax may be found in the Developers Guide that comes with Host Integration Server 2000.

Here's a look at the final output from this application:

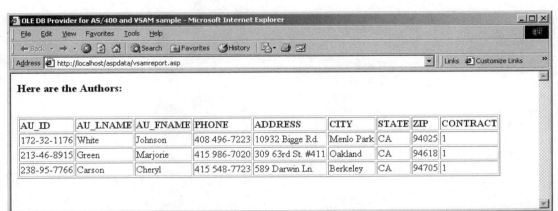

Summary

In this chapter, we have taken a general look at legacy host systems. We looked briefly at the architecture of these systems, and the SNA networks that connect these systems. We also looked at the different types of data available on these host systems. Finally, we used Microsoft SNA Server and Microsoft Host Integration Server 2000 to integrate that legacy data with some sample ASP applications.

What we learned from these exercises is that the OLE DB Providers that enable access to this legacy data are as easy to use in our ASP applications as any other OLE DB Provider. The hardest part about integrating legacy data with web-based applications is understanding the data and systems we are working with, and then configuring the providers to access that data.

Section 6

XML and ASP

24

An XML Primer

The **eXtensible Markup Language** (XML) expands on the information sharing model that HTML had when it was introduced several years ago. At that time, web pages consisted of pretty much just text, with minimal extra objects such as links and pictures. Since then, HTML has evolved quite a bit, and now encompasses advanced graphic elements, scripts and components. Yet these extra elements are still bolted onto the basic text-based HTML content.

XML came to life in the second half of the last decade. It arose from the **Standard Generalized Markup Language** (SGML) and combines the best of both SGML and HTML. Simpler than SGML but not simplistic like HTML, is the slogan that summarizes the essence of XML.

XML has widely been touted as the new and smarter ASCII. Given its nature, and thanks to the wide-range acceptance it has gained from industry, XML transcends programming languages and software platforms. We can find XML just about everywhere, and anything that is expressed through XML becomes magically accessible from just about everywhere. This is the direction in which Microsoft is heading with the .NET framework.

There can be little doubt that XML will be, in a very short time, an intrinsic part of our programming arsenal, in the same way a that the C++ or Visual Basic languages are today. But it is already significant, and has a bearing on almost any area of software development today. Whether we are developing web sites, distributed DNA (or in the future .NET) applications, or Visual Basic programs, XML can help us out. In this chapter, we'll be focusing on the following:

- ❑ The difference between XML, HTML and SGML
- ❑ The structure of an XML document
- ❑ Custom XML languages
- ❑ Parsing XML documents

XML has been a W3C recommended standard since February 1998. You can find more details about W3C and XML on W3C's web site at www.w3.org/XML.

XML, HTML and SGML

XML is intended to replace SGML (too difficult and unwieldy) and HTML (too simplistic). What do these three languages have in common? For one thing, they all are **markup languages**. Secondly, they are all, to some extent, used to describe data in a generalized form. They were developed at different times, and gained different degrees of acceptance from the industry.

If we look only a little farther, it seems that there may be a future for XML only and for HTML as a special-case XML language. More precisely, this special-case XML language is called **XHTML**. Before going on to look in a little more detail at the characteristics of these three languages, we should know what a markup language actually is.

A markup language is a language (not necessarily a text-based language) that allows us to identify a piece of information through a label. This labeled information can be placed anywhere in the document, and its role is determined by the label rather than by the position. For example, in a bitmap, file size and color depth are stored at a very well known offset from the beginning of the file. If we want to create a valid BMP file, we must store that information at that point. Of course, the BMP file format is not a markup language for describing images. The TIFF format instead follows a markup logic, allowing the embedding of RGB and CMYK color data, and extra data such as alpha channels and clipping paths.

The Standard Generalized Markup Language

SGML has been an ISO standard (ISO 8879) since 1986, but was around for a good 20 years before that. SGML is a meta-language for the description of other markup languages. SGML was originally designed by IBM. They wanted a general-purpose tool to model and describe any content in such a way that it could be published in different storage media.

It evolved to become a rich document markup language enabling authors to neatly separate content from presentation. In order to use it, however, it is necessary to come up with our own SGML language. An SGML language is a set of tags, attributes and dependency rules that form a grammar for the application. Before describing anything with SGML, we must create a type definition. Each of our documents will then be written in that made-to-measure markup language.

While elegant and powerful, SGML turned out to be too quirky and time-consuming for general purpose use. For this reason, the industry never had much love for it, and was eager to welcome both HTML and XML – two pre-defined markup languages that inherited many of the principles behind SGML.

The HyperText Markup Language

HTML was created by Tim Berners-Lee, and was originally just a way, much used within the scientific community, of packing together documents to make them accessible from any platform. HTML is much simpler than SGML for two reasons:

❑ Firstly, HTML is a specialized SGML with an already written schema that is used by the web browser.

❑ The second reason is that HTML, unlike SGML, is designed to work in a very specific scenario: the Internet. This made it possible to use the simpler explicit definition of the document's structure.

Another factor that contributes to the success of HTML is its relationship with HTTP. The **HyperText Transfer Protocol** is one of the protocols used on the Internet and sits on top of TCP/IP. HTTP connects heterogeneous networks all over the world, and HTML represents the text that HTTP deals with.

The point where HTML became successful is where it started its decline. Being widely accepted encouraged web browser vendors to customize and enrich its syntax. They came up with a number of different HTML languages and the W3C was forced to alter the nature of HTML with special new tags and behaviors. As a result, HTML is a great, if not excellent, markup language to define the page layout. It is not as good to describe the data it contains and represents. In other words, HTML is about presentation, while we need a better solution for data description. XML is all this and much more.

The Extensible Markup Language

XML has been designed to be more rigorous and flexible than HTML and simpler than SGML. It is a markup language that:

- ❑ Requires a rigorous respect for its syntax rules
- ❑ Supports but does not dictate the type definition for the document
- ❑ Supports an open set of tags and attributes
- ❑ Is cross-platform and language-agnostic
- ❑ Its only purpose in life is to describe data

XML is often associated with the Internet, but this is just one of the possible fields where we can take advantage of it. XML fits in perfectly with the emerging picture of how the Internet will work in future: that of the Internet as a source of *service providers*. In such a scenario, rather then sell software and data, companies would rent their software and data through the Internet. XML seems to be the right format to use in order to overcome platform barriers.

In a world where the Internet has become a source not only of information but also of service providers, companies could rent their data for us to use in a made-to-measure user interface and application. For example, we could sign up with a weather bureau and get real-time information about the weather in a certain area of the globe. We would access that information through XML, process it locally on our web server, and serve it up to our users along with any other ingredients we want.

XML is so central to this model that a question arises. What came first? Was it the business model that found in XML the perfect tool, or was it the opposite? I suspect the latter. The new business model was a natural evolution when people realized the full potential of XML.

One way or the other, XML is a hot topic. Whatever your specialization, chances are that you'll run into it sometime soon, so it is a good idea to have the basics to hand. As we will see, XML is very simple, yet effective.

XML Documents

An XML document is a text file containing tags, attributes, raw text, and a few other parts such as entities, comments, processing instructions, and non-parsable sections. To become usable, an XML document is processed by a special module called a **parser**. An XML parser reads in the file and produces an in-memory representation of it that allows software manipulation of the content. More on this later.

Let's start by considering a simple example:

```
<articles>
   <article title="When Windows'll be sixty-four" author="John Bogus">
      If you already love Windows now, you'll love it even more when she's 64.
   </article>
   <article title="All you need is COM" author="Joe Users">
      COM is love and humans need love. Thus, all you need is COM...
   </article>
   <article title="With a little help from XML" author="Sally Hello">
      More than friends and lovers. XML only can help in life!
   </article>
</articles>
```

The elements enclosed in angle brackets are **tags**. They're also often referred to as **nodes**. In this code snippet, there are only two nodes: `<articles>` and `<article>`. Each node can contain **attributes**. An attribute is a name-value pair which is defined within the start tag. The tag `<articles>` has no attributes, while `<article>` has two of them: `title` and `author`. The text between the opening and the closing tag is the raw unparsable text that qualifies the node. Nodes can have both parsable and unparsable content. Raw text is unparsable content, while subnodes form the parsable content. Here all `<article>` nodes form the content of `<articles>`.

When writing XML documents there are two things to keep in mind. All XML documents have to be **well-formed** – namely they must comply with a general-purpose syntax. In addition, they can have a precise vocabulary of tags called the type definition of the document. If this extra document is defined and linked, an XML document must comply with this one too (this is called validation).

Well-formed

An XML document is said to be well-formed if all of the following conditions apply:

- ❑ There's exactly one root element
- ❑ Tags are case-sensitive
- ❑ All empty tags are properly opened and closed
- ❑ There are no overlapping tags
- ❑ Each non-empty tag has a start and end tag that match properly
- ❑ Each attribute is enclosed by either single or double quotes
- ❑ Special characters, whenever needed, must be replaced by their equivalent escape sequence

These seven XML development issues do not always, or not entirely, apply to HTML documents. For this reason, in contrast to HTML, XML has a reputation for formal severity. Let's look at all these issues in a bit more detail and measure their respective degree of importance.

Single Root

Any XML document must have a single entry-point like the root `<html>` tag in HTML. All the tags must be placed under the umbrella of a single start/end tag that brackets all the XML content. XML creates a hierarchical representation of its data; an XML file is rendered like a tree where each node contains either raw text, references to subnodes, both, or neither.

Case-sensitivity

The names of tags are case-sensitive in XML but not in HTML. For example, the following returns an error in XML but works just fine in HTML:

```
<HTML>
Some text
</html>
```

Empty Tags

An empty tag is a tag that contains no text and no subnodes. An empty tag, though, can have attributes. With XML there's no distinction between empty and nonempty tags. In other words, all of them must be well-balanced. The world's simplest HTML tag:

```
<hr>
```

must be rewritten like this in XML:

```
<hr></hr>
```

However, the allowed syntax proposes a shortcut for empty tags. Instead of <hr></hr> we can resort to a single trailing slash:

```
<hr/>
```

Balanced Tags

In XML, all tags must have a closing tag. Notice that this is not always the rule with HTML. In HTML, in fact, there are tags that require this (e.g., <form>) and others that do not (e.g. <img>). The following code works fine with HTML:

```
<img src="image.gif">
```

But in XML, it would need to be replaced with the following:

```
<img src="image.gif"></img>
```

The image tag is an empty tag, so could also be rewritten in the format for empty tags which was described above:

```
<img src="image.gif"/>
```

Nested Tags

Unlike HTML, XML doesn't accept nested tags whose closing markers overlap. If we have nested tags, we should close them in the reverse order that they were opened. For example, the following is supported by HTML browsers, but not by XML parsers:

```
<img src="image.gif"><span>Look at me!</img></span>
```

The <span> tag, which is placed within the <img>, must close first!

```
<img src="image.gif"><span>Look at me!</span></img>
```

Quotes Required

The content of all attributes must always be enclosed in either single or double quotes. Once again, this is not strictly necessary in HTML.

Special Characters

Special characters are those ones that have been assigned a special meaning. For example, < and &. In addition, we also have vowels with accents, quotes, and $. In particular, < denotes a start tag while & prefixes an XML entity. If we need to use these characters with their original meaning (i.e. < is the less-than symbol) we need to replace them with an equivalent escape sequence. HTML and XML specifications define all the special characters and their respective escape sequence. For example, instead of <, we can use <. More details can be found on the W3C web site at `http://www.w3.org/TR/1998/REC-xml-19980210#dt-chardata`.

XML Nodes

The main component of an XML document is the node, also referred to as **tags** or **elements**. Such nodes represent specific chunks of user-defined information. They have a name and content, sometimes empty content. They can also be qualified by one or more attributes.

XML nodes start with an opening tag given by the name enclosed in angle brackets, and end with a closing tag where the name is prefixed by a slash. The name is case-sensitive. For example:

```
<mytag>
...
</mytag>
```

Start and end tags denote where the element begins and ends. It may contain raw text as well as a subtree of nodes, or both. Provided that we respect the well-formedness rules, we can use any name to identify a node and can insert as a child any other node. This is put under stricter control when the XML document is assigned a **vocabulary** through a type definition (more on this a little later). In this case, both the attributes and the subnodes must comply with the structure defined in the vocabulary.

For an XML node to provide useful information about its role and content, the name is rarely enough. For this reason, it is common to specify a node with **attributes**.

XML Attributes

Attributes are name-value pairs associated with nodes. They give information about the role of the node. In a certain way, attributes are the node meta data. As we saw earlier, the content of an attribute must be enclosed in quotes. Attributes don't affect the XML tree structure, as we can insert them in any order within the parent tag. Attributes can be marked as optional, or take a default value.

Through attributes, we specify the quality and the role of the node. Usually, we choose their names based on the information the parent node represents. However, there's an exception to this. An attribute called ID is assigned a special meaning and serves the purpose of uniquely identifying the node within the whole document. Through the ID attribute, XML parsers can implement indexing and fast-retrieval functionality.

Nodes and attributes are the fundamental units that form an XML document. However, there are other elements that can form parts of XML documents. We'll now take a look at these.

Other Parts of an XML Document

Nodes and attributes allow us to describe data in a significant percentage of cases. However, sometimes we need more advanced tools such as processing instructions, entities and character data (CDATA) sections. Let's see when and how we can take advantage of them.

Processing Instructions

A **processing instruction** (PI) is an XML structural construct. It is given by instructions that are passed through to the processing applications. A PI is composed of two parts: name and content. The syntax for a PI is:

```
<? pi-name content ?>
```

The name is what identifies both the processing instruction and the application that will make use of it, while the content is given by a list of name-value pairs that represent the real informational content for the parser.

A PI is wrapped by `<?` and `?>`. Here are a few frequently used examples of processing instructions:

```
<?xml:stylesheet type="text/xsl" href="employeeTable.xsl" ?>
<?xml version="1.0" encoding="windows-1252"?>
```

The former associates an XSL stylesheet to the XML document. (We'll look at XSL stylesheets in the next chapter.) The second determines the version of the XML standard the document adheres to and the character set chosen for it. These two PIs are for the Microsoft parser.

We can adorn any XML document with as many processing instructions as we need, including different instructions for different applications. The content of the PI section affects the way in which a parser or an XML-aware application works on that document. For example, the following tells the Microsoft parser that the document must be compatible with the 1.0 version of the XML standard and supports a certain character set:

```
<?xml version="1.0" encoding="windows-1252"?>
```

This information is useful during the validation phase. Alternatively, the following doesn't affect the way in which the Microsoft parser works, but tells Internet Explorer (an XML-aware application that processes XML data) that when rendering that XML document, it should apply the specified stylesheet:

```
<?xml:stylesheet type="text/xsl" href="employeeTable.xsl" ?>
```

The following is a perfectly valid processing instruction:

```
<?Articlebazaar device="wap" model="nokia" ?>
```

This passes the name-value pairs to an application, for which Articlebazaar is a meaningful word, that the document can be affected by changes in the name-value pairs. For example, it could tell a certain application to transform the XML document into another XML format suited for the Nokia WAP device.

Reading the content of all the processing instructions can be easy or not depending on the parser's capabilities. For example, the Microsoft's parser exposes the processing instructions through specific objects, making it a snap for any application to test what it needs to test.

789

The DOCTYPE Instruction

Technically speaking, DOCTYPE is not a processing instruction, yet it could be seen as part of the XML prolog. The DOCTYPE directive is a sort of all-parser specific PI. It tells them about the DTD for that XML document.

Entities

An **XML entity** is to XML what a macro is to programming languages. An entity is characterized and identified by a name that begins with a & character, and terminates with a semi-colon. For example:

```
 
```

Each time the parser encounters a text element that it recognizes to be an entity, it expands the entity with the proper text. In HTML, for example, the above entity is automatically expanded to a white space.

Entities are also the structural mechanism behind the management of special characters. The < expression expands to <. Any XML parser supports a number of system entities for special characters, but the same mechanism is available to us programmers to define our own macros.

Entities provide a powerful means to modularize the structure of an XML document. Entities can be divided into two different categories:

❏   Internal entities

❏   External entities

Internal entities are the type we just looked at. The latter, in contrast, are names that evaluate to external XML files. What's interesting is that the XML parser is capable of automatically loading and processing these external references. In practice, an external entity turns out to be a sort of #include directive for XML documents.

We define an **internal entity** through the following processing instruction:

```
<!ENTITY entity_name "value-of-the-entity">
```

For example,

```
<!ENTITY publisher "Wrox Press">
```

We would use it in an XML file like this:

```
<book publisher="&publisher;">
```

The parser recognizes the & character and reads in until it finds a ;. This text is taken as the name of the entity. The next step is searching for a match between the entity name and the expanded text. But where are the entity declarations stored? The point is that we *cannot* store them within the same XML file. For example, we cannot use the following code:

```
<!ENTITY publisher "Wrox Press">
<book publisher="&publisher;">
   <title>Professional ASP Database</title>
</book>
```

This would generate an error message:

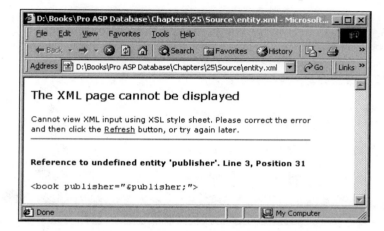

Apparently, the parser isn't able to locate the definition of the entity. Nevertheless, such a definition does exist in the file itself! While we can insert as many <!ENTITY> directives as we want in an XML document, they will be ignored. The right place to insert the instruction is in the DTD.

An **external entity** looks like this:

```
<!ENTITY entity_name SYSTEM "external-XML-file">
```

For example:

```
<!ENTITY outline SYSTEM "proaspdata.xml">
```

Of course, the specified XML file must be a well-formed XML file. Let's put together internal and external entities and write a simple DTD file:

```
<!-- Entity.dtd -->

<!ENTITY publisher "Wrox Press">
<!ENTITY outline SYSTEM "proaspdata.xml">
```

Now we can arrange a XML document like this:

```
<!-- Entity.xml -->

<!DOCTYPE book SYSTEM "entity.dtd">

<book publisher="&publisher;">
    <title>Professional ASP Database</title>
    <outline>&outline;</outline>
</book>
```

The document links to a DTD file through the <!DOCTYPE> processing instruction and then utilizes the definitions it contains. The macro &publisher; is now recognized and handled properly. Notice that the second entity &outline; expands to the whole content of the proaspdata.xml file:

```
<!-- ProAspData.xml -->

<chapters>
   <chapter num="5" title="Introduction to Data Access Technologies">
   abstract of chapter 5
   </chapter>

   <chapter num="6" title="OLE DB">
   abstract of chapter 6
   </chapter>
</chapters>
```

Here's how Internet Explorer 5.0 visualizes this `entity.xml` document:

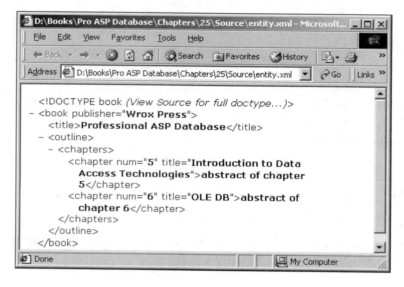

The final source code that the parser processes looks like this:

```
<book publisher="Wrox Press">
   <title>Professional ASP Database</title>
   <outline>
   <chapters>
      <chapter num="5" title="Introduction to Data Access Technologies">
      abstract of chapter 5
      </chapter>
      <chapter num="6" title="OLE DB">
      abstract of chapter 6
   </chapter>
   </chapters>
   </outline>
</book>
```

We'll look in more detail later on at the `<!DOCTYPE>` directive and the role of DTD.

CDATA Sections

CDATA stands for 'character data'. It is simply a string of text embedded in an XML document and it never gets parsed. Since no parsing operations are performed on data enclosed within CDATA markers, we can insert text that would ordinarily cause problems for the parser.

For example, suppose we need to insert a piece of script code into an XML document. Chances are that we need to use & and < with their language-specific meaning. When writing plain text, using the escape sequence for special characters is not a big issue. On the other hand, it turns out to be fairly tedious when writing script code. The following looks neither elegant nor effective:

```
<code>
If A &lt; B Then
    MsgBox "Hello " &amp; "world"
End If
</code>
```

Moreover, when we embed script code in XML documents, we normally need to extract it later for execution. Not using a CDATA section, we also have the extra burden of manually converting any escape sequence into the original character. Javascript provides the escape/unescape functions, but VBScript does not.

In these cases, the perfect workaround looks like this:

```
<code>
<![CDATA[
If A < B Then
    MsgBox "Hello " & "world"
End If
]]>
</code>
```

If you're writing a DTD for a series of XML documents, then by marking as CDATA the content of a certain node, you can avoid having to wrap its content with <![CDATA[...]]> markers in the body of the XML file.

Comments

Like HTML files, XML documents can contain comments. The syntax is identical:

```
<!-- This is my comment -->
```

Comments can appear anywhere, but cannot be interspersed with attributes. The following is incorrect:

```
<book <!-- comment --> publisher="&publisher;">
```

XML Languages

XML is a generic language that accepts any tag or attribute name provided that the final document is well-formed. This brings us straight to a couple of considerations. First off, we need to make sure we have our own set of unambiguous tags. Secondly, we need to ensure that all tags are given a specific meaning, semantic and, actually, a behavior.

XML Namespaces

XML namespaces are an excellent solution to the problem of having ambiguous tags. They provide an environment in which our tags can be uniquely identified. Tags with different names belonging to different namespaces are, by definition, different tags! A namespace adds a second level of identification and distinction to tag names. Names are too generic to resolve any ambiguities that might arise. How many people do you know that share the same first name? There could be quite a few. But the uniqueness of an individual could be ensured if we were to introduce their name in the context of a particular family (or, in the case of XML tags, a particular namespace). Namespaces are to XML tags what the family name is to first names.

We define a namespace whenever we need to characterize our tag names and assign them a special meaning. A tag called <code> can have a variety of interpretations, all equally valid. It could be an invoice number, an item code, a piece of script code, or an alphanumeric string. Namespaces serve the purpose of disambiguating names by defining the virtual space where they live; in which they have a particular syntax and semantic.

Defining Namespaces

A namespace has a **prefix** and a **name**. We use the prefix to qualify the tag. The name is a **Universal Resource Identifier** (URI). URIs are essentially formatted strings that uniquely identify a resource. There are two types of URIs:

❑ **Universal Resource Locator** (URL)

❑ **Universal Resource Name** (URN)

URLs contain the protocol and the location of the resource. They identify the resource by specifying how to reach it. Conversely, URNs are location-independent and simply identify a resource through its name. URNs are similar to CLSID for COM components. There's no algorithm to automatically obtain the resource from the URN, but the association is established through assignments – much like with COM's CLSID.

In most cases, the URI of a XML namespace is a URL. But it doesn't mean that something gets downloaded when the XML document is accessed! It's only a way to give a unique name to the XML namespace resource because each URL is guaranteed to be unique worldwide.

We define a namespace with the xmlns keyword. The generic syntax looks like this:

```
<prefix:tagname xmlns:prefix=uri>
```

To specify a tag that belongs to a certain namespace (say, articlebazaar) we would use the following notation:

```
<articlebazaar:article>
```

The name of the namespace prefixes the name of the tag, the two being separated by a colon. Let's rewrite the article description we met earlier in terms of a namespace:

```
<ab:articles xmlns:ab="http://www.expoware.com/books/3927/articlebazaar">
   <ab:article title="When Windows'll be sixty-four" author="John Bogus">
      If you already love Windows now, you'll love it even more when she's 64.
   </ab:article>
   <ab:article title="All you need is COM" author="Joe Users">
      COM is love and humans need love. Thus, all you need is COM...
   </ab:article>
   <ab:article title="With a little help from XML" author="Sally Hello">
      More than friends and lovers. XML only can help in life!
   </ab:article>
</ab:articles>
```

The first line of the code defines the namespace:

```
<ab:articles xmlns:ab="http://www.expoware.com/books/3927/articlebazaar">
```

In the example, the URI of the `Articlebazaar` documents is:

```
http://www.expoware.com/books/3927/articlebazaar
```

while `ab` is the prefix for qualifying all the tags.

Getting an XML Vocabulary

As we have seen, an XML language is simply a finite and well-defined set of tags that we want to use. A well-formed HTML (namely XHTML), is an XML-based language as it is well-formed and defines a finite set of tags. The set of tags, their attributes, and the dependency rules between tags form the XML vocabulary. Such a vocabulary is a somewhat abstract concept, and so we will look at how it can be implemented in practice.

How to Write a Vocabulary

Writing a vocabulary of tags means listing the tag names we want your language to support, their attributes, and the way in which they relate to each other. There are two possible approaches open to us:

- ❑ **Document Type Definition** (DTD) files
- ❑ **XML Data schema** (XDS)

A DTD is a text file with the usual extension of `.dtd`. It follows a custom and tagged syntax which looks like XML, but is actually a distant relation to it. XDS files let us express the same information, but using a full XML syntax. In other words, an XDS is an XML file.

XDS provides some additional features, such as the possibility of inheriting from an existing schema, stricter control over tag cardinality (this will be discussed later), and stronger typing. These are soon to become W3C recommendations, but at the moment they're supported only on the Windows platform. Incidentally, XDS is a key element of the BizTalk infrastructure.

DTD is the descendant of SGML, and as such represents the cross-platform standard. They're much more powerful than is commonly believed, even though they cannot reach the same level of flexibility as XDS for the simple reason that XDS has been specifically designed to improve and enhance DTD. But, for most day-to-day tasks, DTD and XDS may be considered functionally equivalent.

> **An in-depth exploration of DTD and XDS may be found in *Professional XML* (ISBN 1861003110), also from Wrox Press.**

In the next section, we'll take a look at how to write and use both a DTD and an XDS to cope with the content of the Articlebazaar Web application that we built from Chapter 10 to Chapter 13.

The DTD for the Language

The DTD syntax is made of three main elements:

```
<!ELEMENT>
<!ATTLIST>
<!ENTITY>
```

We have already looked into `<!ENTITY>`, but let's take a look at the other two.

The <!ELEMENT> Keyword

The `<!ELEMENT>` keyword describes a node in terms of the subnodes and the attributes. For example, the following means that `<ARTICLEBAZAAR>` can have only one child node, called `<ARTICLES>`:

```
<!ELEMENT ARTICLEBAZAAR (ARTICLES)>
```

More nodes need to be separated by commas:

```
<!ELEMENT PARENT     (ONE,TWO,THREE)>
```

In this case, the nodes must appear in the same order for the validation to be successful. We can give a certain cardinality to each node. The **cardinality** of the node specifies how many occurrences of a certain tag are permitted. In particular, by suffixing the node's name with either ?, *, or +, we specify that it can have 0 or 1, 0 or more, or 1 or more occurrences respectively. The default cardinality of a node is 1. For example, the following denotes that `<ARTICLES>` can have 0 or more nodes called `<ARTICLE>`:

```
<!ELEMENT ARTICLES    (ARTICLE*)>
```

If the node can contain text, we use the `#PCDATA` keyword. A node can also be empty. In this case the syntax to use is:

```
<!ELEMENT MYNODE EMPTY>
```

The <!ATTLIST> Keyword

The <!ATTLIST> keyword describes the list of attributes for each node. The syntax puts together the name of the node and all of its declared attributes with name and other meta data. In particular, through using CDATA we specify that the attribute contain unparsable text.

Alternatively, we can force it to take only a string chosen from a given set. For example:

```
<!ATTLIST payment (card | check | cash) #REQUIRED>
```

In this case, valid values for the attribute payment can only be card, check or cash.

Another parameter we can specify for an attribute regards the initial value. #REQUIRED means that the attribute is mandatory, and that the value will be read from the file. #IMPLIED means that the attribute will have a value only if specified. An attribute marked as #IMPLIED is optional and, if we miss it, won't have a value. Another possibility is to assign a default value:

```
<!ATTLIST payment CDATA "cash">
```

In this case, if the attribute is not specified in the XML document, it assumes the default value.

Sample Application: Describing Articles

In Chapter 11, we defined an ASP page that was capable of returning XML streams when passed some parameters. For example:

```
http://expoware/xmlquery.asp?magazine=2&&year=00
```

This would run a SQL query and produce an XML document to be passed to external clients. Since XML data is not always exchanged between modules that know each other's structure and behavior, being able to describe the structure of the XML document that's returned is an important issue. This is precisely what DTD and XDS are for.

The structure we want to obtain is like the following:

```
<ARTICLES found="2">
   <ARTICLE title="…" author="…" magazine="…"
      issue="…" URL="…" keyword="…" >
   abstract
   </ARTICLE>

   <ARTICLE …>
   :
   </ARTICLE>
</ARTICLES>
```

In addition, we define the root tag of the language as ARTICLEBAZAAR, with a couple of attributes to remind the query parameters. All this information has now to be coded in a DTD file. Each tag can have its own set of attributes with specific properties.

Let's see what the final DTD looks like:

```
<!-- Document Type Definition for the "Articlebazaar" Language -->

<!ELEMENT ARTICLEBAZAAR (ARTICLES)>
<!ATTLIST ARTICLEBAZAARmagazine         CDATA #IMPLIED
                        year            CDATA #IMPLIED>

<!ELEMENT ARTICLES      (ARTICLE*)>
<!ATTLIST ARTICLES      found       CDATA #REQUIRED>

<!ELEMENT ARTICLE (#PCDATA)>
<!ATTLIST ARTICLEtitle  CDATA #REQUIRED
                author  CDATA #REQUIRED
                magazine CDATA #REQUIRED
                issue   CDATA #REQUIRED
                URL     CDATA #IMPLIED
                keyword CDATA #IMPLIED
>
```

In the next section, we're going to look in more detail the content of the DTD file.

The ARTICLEBAZAAR Tag

This is the root tag of the language and can contain just the <ARTICLES> child tag plus a couple of optional attributes called magazine and year:

```
<!ELEMENT ARTICLEBAZAAR(ARTICLES)>
<!ATTLIST ARTICLEBAZAARmagazine         CDATA #IMPLIED
                        year            CDATA #IMPLIED>
```

The ARTICLES Tag

ARTICLES is the container for all the single <ARTICLE> subtrees. The contained articles can be 0 or more depending on the result of the query. That's why we see a * symbol trailing the name of the child node:

```
<!ELEMENT ARTICLES      (ARTICLE*)>
<!ATTLIST ARTICLES      found CDATA #REQUIRED>
```

The only attribute is called found. This counts the child nodes.

The ARTICLE Tag

ARTICLE describes an article from the Articlebazaar database. It has as many attributes as the record fields. Four of them have been declared as mandatory. The body of the node is given by the abstract of the article:

```
<!ELEMENT ARTICLE (#PCDATA)>
<!ATTLIST ARTICLE       title   CDATA #REQUIRED
                        author  CDATA #REQUIRED
                        magazine CDATA #REQUIRED
                        issue   CDATA #REQUIRED
                        URL     CDATA #IMPLIED
                        keyword CDATA #IMPLIED
>
```

And now that we have defined an XML language, let's see how it can be used to write actual XML documents.

The DTD in Action

To link a certain XML document to a DTD we use the `<!DOCTYPE>` instruction:

```
<!DOCTYPE ARTICLEBAZAAR SYSTEM "AB.dtd">
```

Notice that the DOCTYPE name must coincide with the root node of the XML document. Of course, everything is case-sensitive here. Let's see how the xmlquery.asp page we've left in chapter 11 changes in order to comply with the DTD:

```
<%
    ' <--- Collect the arguments --->
    argMagazine = Request.QueryString("Magazine")
    argYear     = Request.QueryString("Year")

    ' Set the MIME type
    Response.ContentType = "text/xml"
    ' Write the doctype
    Response.Write "<?xml version='1.0' ?>"
    Response.Write "<!DOCTYPE ARTICLEBAZAAR SYSTEM 'AB.dtd'>"

    Response.Write "<ARTICLEBAZAAR "
    Response.Write "magazine=" & Quote(argMagazine) & " "
    Response.Write "year=" & Quote(argYear) & ">"

    ' Call the necessary components to get the data and convert it to XML
    set o = Server.CreateObject("Articlebazaar.Query")

    if argMagazine = "all" then
        set oRS = o.GetMagazines()
        outBuf = AllMagazines(oRS)
    else
        set oRS = o.GetArticles(argMagazine, argYear)
        outBuf = SelectedArticles(oRS)
    end if
    ' Return the XML data
    Response.Write outBuf
    Response.Write "</ARTICLEBAZAAR>"
    Response.End
%>

<%
Function SelectedArticles(oRS)
    outBuf = ""
    nArts = 0
    while Not oRS.EOF
        outBuf = outBuf & "<ARTICLE "

        outBuf = outBuf & "title=" & Quote(oRS("title")) & " "
        outBuf = outBuf & "author=" & Quote(oRS("author")) & " "
        outBuf = outBuf & "magazine=" & Quote(oRS("name")) & " "
        outBuf = outBuf & "issue=" & Quote(oRS("issue")) & " "
```

```
            outBuf = outBuf & "URL=" & Quote(oRS("URL")) & " "
            outBuf = outBuf & "keyword=" & Quote(oRS("keyword")) & " "

            outBuf = outBuf & ">"
            outBuf = outBuf & oRS("abstract")
            outBuf = outBuf & "</ARTICLE>"
            nArts = nArts + 1
            oRS.MoveNext
        wend
        outbuf = "<ARTICLES found=" & Quote(nArts) & ">" & outBuf
        SelectedArticles = outBuf & "</ARTICLES>"
End Function
```

Pay attention to the case of the attributes that must coincide perfectly with the content of the DTD. The following is a valid XML page:

```xml
<?xml version='1.0' ?>
<!DOCTYPE ARTICLEBAZAAR SYSTEM 'AB.dtd'>
<ARTICLEBAZAAR magazine="2" year="99">
<ARTICLES found="3">

<ARTICLE title="BHO: The browser the way you want it"
    author="Dino Esposito" magazine="MSDN News" issue="9901"
    URL="" keyword="IE,Windows" >
The article explains the basics of the browser helper objects - a new feature of
IE4 and higher. BHO are COM objects written to get in touch witht Explorer and
Internet Explorer.
</ARTICLE>

<ARTICLE title="A Web look for your folders"
    author="Dino Esposito" magazine="MSDN News" issue="9905"
    URL="" keyword="shell,Windows" >
If you have IE5 installed then you're perfectly able to start working with XML.
Learn how you can employ XML to describe the content of a folder customized via
HTT
</ARTICLE>

<ARTICLE title="Talk to your data with MSEQ"
    author="Dino Esposito" magazine="MSDN News" issue="9909"
    URL="" keyword="OLEDB,SQL" >
MSEQ is a module that sits on the top of SQL Server 7 and allows you to issue
queries against a database using your natural language instead of SQL.
</ARTICLE>

</ARTICLES>
</ARTICLEBAZAAR>
```

Checking the DTD

When an XML parser meets a DTD, it has to parse the document in order to verify that it complies with the required syntax. This occurs in addition to the usual checking for the XML well-formedness. The following script code utilizes the XmlHttpRequest object to query Articlebazaar for all the articles that appeared in a certain magazine in 1999. The result is written to a local response.xml file:

```
set xmlhttp = CreateObject("Microsoft.XmlHttp")
xmlhttp.open "POST", _
   "http://expoware/aspdata/xmlquery.asp?magazine=2&year=99", _
   0
xmlhttp.send ""


' write XML to file
set fso = CreateObject("Scripting.FileSystemObject")
Set f = fso.CreateTextFile("response.xml")
f.Write xmlhttp.responseText
f.Close
```

Here is how Internet Explorer 5.0 displays the XML document:

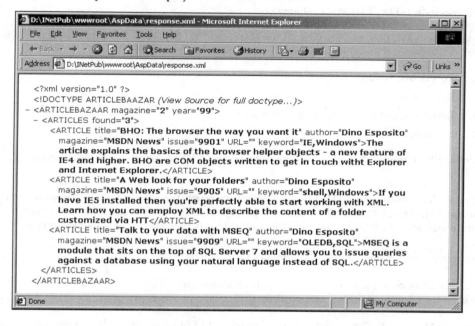

Note that not all the XML parsers are validating. A parser is validating when it checks for DTD compliance. The fact that IE 5.0+ correctly displays the XML document doesn't mean it fully adheres to the DTD syntax. This IE 5.0 behavior is by design. However, the Microsoft parser can be set to work and validate via software. We can use the following script to check the correctness of an XML file that utilizes a DTD:

```
set xmldom = CreateObject("Microsoft.XMLDOM")

xmldom.async = False                    ' load the document synchronously
xmldom.validateOnParse = True           ' validate against a DTD, if any

xmldom.load("response.xml")             ' load the XML document

' Any error occurred?
Set myErr = xmldom.parseError
MsgBox myErr.errorCode & " - " & MyErr.reason
```

If `errorCode` is 0, all is fine with our DTD and the XML document that uses it.

Using a DTD can slow down performance since it takes a while to complete. This happens each time a page is hit or needs to load the document. If we don't have to share documents with someone else, and you can assume that all the client applications know the XML format, then we should consider removing the DTD burden.

The Schema for the Language

While DTDs are an important piece in the XML jigsaw, they aren't particularly powerful. A DTD looks like a grammar file, and doesn't let us provide the language with the particular features we might want. A typical example is provided by typed attributes. To resolve this problem, Microsoft proposed a new way to specify a DTD: XML data schemas.

XDS are pure XML files and provide all the features of DTDs plus a few other things. The main differences between data schemata and DTDs are that XDS provide:

❑   Pure XML syntax

❑   Better support of the attribute's types

❑   Better control for element's position and features

❑   Possibility of inheritance

Inheritance here means that we could take an existing XDS and derive our own, changing or adding what you need.

Writing an XDS basing on a DTD is not particularly hard. We should be familiar with a couple of new elements: `AttributeType` and `ElementType`. They define the elements and the attributes in much the same way as `<!ELEMENT>` and `<!ATTLIST>`. This is how we define an element type:

```
<ElementType name="ARTICLES" content="eltOnly">
```

The `eltOnly` keyword means that it contains elements only. The body of each `<ElementType>` contains a list of child elements and attributes.

Likewise, `<AttributeType>` defines the characteristics of an attribute. When we declare an attribute later on, we must refer to the proper type. This is, however, easier said than done. What follows is the XDS for the Articlebazaar DTD seen previously:

```
<?xml version="1.0"?>
<Schema name="Articlebazaar"
        xmlns="urn:schemas-microsoft-com:xml-data"
        xmlns:dt="urn:schemas-microsoft-com:datatypes">

<!-- Attribute Types -->
<AttributeType name="magazine"   dt:type="string" />
<AttributeType name="year"       dt:type="string" />
<AttributeType name="found"      dt:type="number" />
<AttributeType name="title"      dt:type="string" />
<AttributeType name="author"     dt:type="string" />
<AttributeType name="issue"      dt:type="string" />
```

```
<AttributeType name="URL"          dt:type="string" />
<AttributeType name="keyword"      dt:type="string" />

<!-- Element Types -->
<ElementType name="ARTICLEBAZAAR" content="eltOnly"
   model="closed" order="seq">
   <element type="ARTICLES" minOccurs="1" maxOccurs="1" />

   <attribute type="magazine" required="no" />
   <attribute type="year" required="no" />
</ElementType>

<ElementType name="ARTICLES" content="eltOnly" model="closed">
   <element type="ARTICLE" minOccurs="0" maxOccurs="*" />

   <attribute type="found"        required="yes" />
</ElementType>

<ElementType name="ARTICLE" content="mixed">
   <attribute type="title"        required="yes" />
   <attribute type="magazine"     required="yes" />
   <attribute type="author"       required="yes" />
   <attribute type="issue"        required="yes" />
   <attribute type="URL"          required="no"  />
   <attribute type="keyword"      required="no"  />
</ElementType>
</Schema>
```

With XDS we can also specify whether the `model` is closed or open to other tags beside the ones listed. The attribute value `seq` applied to the `ElementType` tag means that the child elements must be found in the sequence in which they're declared.

When declaring attributes, we can use enumeration like this:

```
<AttributeType name="published" dt:type="enumeration" dt:values="yes no"/>
```

and we can assign a default value too:

```
<attribute type="description" required="no" default="Description" />
```

Notice that we can specify the type of the attribute and this will be checked at run-time. For example, the `found` attribute is clearly a number, since it represents the number of selected articles:

```
<AttributeType name="found" dt:type="number" />
```

We try to create an XML file that complies with the schema and assign it a string and see what happens:

This is what the VBScript program shown above to check XML files returns

```
<ARTICLEBAZAAR xmlns="x-schema:ABschema.xml"
    magazine="2" year="99">
:
</ARTICLEBAZAAR>
```

To force an XML to adopt a schema to qualify the vocabulary, we need to add an xmlns attribute to the root element of the document. The xmlns attribute will point to the XML file to be used for validation.

XML Parsers

The principal tool that works with XML documents is the parser. The parser is a module that reads in the XML code, processes it, and creates an in-memory representation of it. There are two families of parsers:

❑ Those that produce an object model (XMLDOM)

❑ Those that fire events whenever they meet a tag (SAX)

The former family includes the Microsoft MSXML parser, available with IE 5x. SAX parsers don't create anything in particular, but give the users a chance to do whatever they want when the document is scanned. For example, the user can build its own specialized object model. SAX parsers are faster than XMLDOM parsers, since they scan the document only once without executing any particular operation on the various nodes. And of course, SAX parsers have a smaller memory footprint.

XMLDOM parsers return us an in-memory representation of the file content, and make available a hierarchy of objects from which we might retrieve any of the information we want. Let's take a look at the major features of the MSXML parser.

Initializing the Parser

Each time we want to process XML data, we need to load a parser. MSXML is an automation COM object that can be used from virtually any environment that is COM-aware. From an ASP page, we initialize the object in the following way:

```
Set xmldom = Server.CreateObject("Microsoft.XMLDOM")
xmldom.async = False
xmldom.load "file.xml"
```

The async property tells the parser to load the document synchronously so that the line following the call to load or loadXML executes when the object model has been successfully built.

There are two ways to associate an XML document with an instance of the parser; using the load, or the loadXML methods. The former requires a file name while the latter takes a string. When the loading process has successfully completed, we're ready to work with the document and access the tree or add and delete nodes.

The Node Object

We access the root node of the XML tree through the `documentElement` property:

```
Set root = xmldom.documentElement
```

At this point we can run queries for child nodes and attributes, editing the text of the node as well as adding or removing nodes. The programming interface of the node object is particularly rich.

An in-depth look at XMLDOM can be found in Wrox's *Professional XML* (ISBN 1-861003-0), and also in the MSDN documentation.

Traversing an XML Document

Let's see how the XMLDOM works in practice by writing the code that traverses an XML document and outputs nodes and attributes. The following VBScript file opens a XML file and creates an informational HTML page where it stores nodes and attributes:

```
' XmlDom.vbs
' Creates a HTML page with all the nodes and attributes
' of the specified XML document
' -----------------------------------------------------------

Dim xml, nodeAttrColl, n, nodeColl
Dim fso, f

Set xml = CreateObject("Microsoft.XMLDOM")
Set fso = CreateObject("Scripting.FileSystemObject")

fileXML = "file.xml"
fileHTM = "file_info.htm"

' Loads the XML file
xml.load(fileXML)

' Creates the output HTML file
Set f = fso.CreateTextFile(fileHTM)
f.Write("<h1>The document contains the following nodes:</h1>" & vbCrLf)
f.Write "<br>" & "<b>" & xml.documentElement.nodeName & "</b>" & vbCrLf

' Adds the info about the root node and its attributes
Set nodeAttrColl = xml.documentElement.attributes
For Each a In nodeAttrColl
    f.Write "<br>  " & "<i>" & a.nodeName & "</i> = " & _
                a.nodeValue & vbCrLf
Next

' Loops on the child nodes (first level only)
Set nodeColl = xml.documentElement.childNodes
For Each n In nodeColl
    f.Write "<br>" & "<b>" & n.nodeName & "</b>" & vbCrLf
```

```
      Set nodeAttrColl = n.attributes
      For Each a In nodeAttrColl
         f.Write "<br>  " & "<i>" & a.nodeName & "</i> = " & _
                        a.nodeValue & vbCrLf
      Next
   Next


   ' Closes the file
   f.Close
```

It gets a reference to the document element and then prints out the name:

```
xml.documentElement.nodeName
```

The next step is reading the information available for all of its attributes:

```
Set nodeAttrColl = xml.documentElement.attributes
For Each a In nodeAttrColl
   f.Write "<br>  " & "<i>" & a.nodeName & "</i> = " & _
              a.nodeValue & vbCrLf
Next
```

Notice that the `attributes` collection is a collection of node objects. Each element found evaluates to a COM object with a node interface. It's not a string. The output is shown in the figure below:

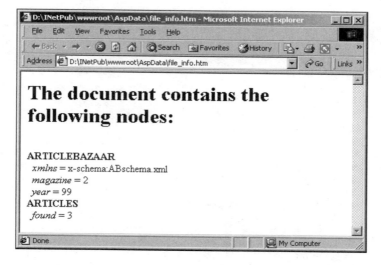

If we want to select a particular node in the subtree of the node where we're positioned, we use the `selectNodes` method and pass the tag name as an argument. This returns a collection of all the nodes that match the criteria.

Alternatively, `selectSingleNode` returns only the first node found. If we want to do a full-text search, we can use the `nodeFromID` method exposed by the root object. It retrieves any node in any part of the document that exposes an `ID` attribute whose content matches our argument.

> The **XMLDOM object model** is looked at in some detail in Alex Homer's *XML IE5 Programmer's Reference* (ISBN 1861001576), also from Wrox Press.

XML Data Islands

The final aspect of XML to consider in this chapter is the **data island**. A data island is a piece of XML code embedded in an HTML page, forming an integral part of the page and downloading with it.

> *XML Data Islands are a feature introduced by IE4.0 and enhanced with IE5.0. However, we can easily simulate data islands on other browsers such as Netscape Communicator.*

IE 50 supports direct browsing features that make it apply a standard stylesheet to each piece of XML code it receives. In addition, it supports COM and Dynamic HTML, so it's relatively easy to arrange a component (the MSXML is just fine) that processes the XML data, and updates the current page accordingly.

If we cannot use COM on the client, and don't have browser-specific support for XML, there's very little that we can do with data islands, unless we have a JavaScript XML parser.

However, if for any reason we need to embed XML code in pages viewed with Netscape browsers, we could insert it in hidden text boxes. Otherwise, data islands are a prerogative of Internet Explorer alone.

The <xml> Tag

Internet Explorer 5.0 supports a new <xml> tag which implements data islands. The content of this tag, a well-formed XML document, is invisible to the users. We can use <xml> with either inline XML code, or when pointing to a remote XML file. In the former case, <xml> contains the entire document, including its root tag, in the following way:

```
<xml id="MyXML">
<book publisher="Wrox Press">
   <title>Professional ASP Database</title>
   <outline>
   <chapters>
      <chapter num="5" title="Introduction to Data Access Technologies">
      abstract of chapter 5
      </chapter>
      <chapter num="6" title="OLE DB">
      abstract of chapter 6
      </chapter>
   </chapters>
   </outline>
</book>
</xml>
```

The XML code is at the page's disposal, and can be used by script code. To retrieve this code, we need to use the ordinary DHTML object model. This means that we always need to assign the tag an ID.

The following HTML page demonstrates how to retrieve the text stored into a data island:

```html
<html>

<script language=VBScript>
function ShowXml
   set o = document.all("MyXML")
   alert o.innerHTML
end function
</script>


<xml id="MyXML">
<book publisher="Wrox Press">
   <title>Professional ASP Database</title>
   <outline>
   <chapters>
      <chapter num="5" title="Data Access Technologies">
      abstract of chapter 5
      </chapter>
      <chapter num="6" title="OLE DB">
      abstract of chapter 6
      </chapter>
   </chapters>
   </outline>
</book>
</xml>
<body>

<input type=button value="Click to see XML data island"
   onclick="ShowXml()">
</body>
</html>
```

When we click on the button, the script code uses the ID as the pointer into the DOM, and uses inner HTML to display the text. At this point, however, nothing prevents us from loading the XML text into the XML parser and using it as we wish.

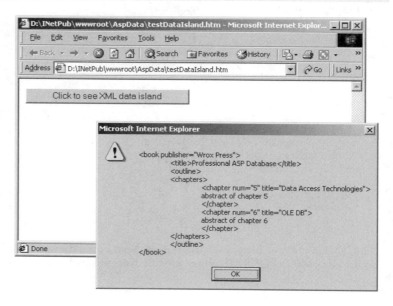

Getting the XMLDOM

We don't in fact need the XML source code to create the XMLDOM. IE 5.0 does this for us. All we have to do is simply call the XMLDocument property on the <xml> node object. This is the root object of the XML document. The following code shows up the XML source code, but this time through the XMLDOM.

```
set o = document.all("MyXML")
alert o.XMLDocument.xml
```

Referencing External Files

The <xml> tag also supports the src attribute through which we can make it point to an external URL. For example:

```
<xml ID="MyXML"
    src="http://expoware/aspdata/xmlquery.asp?magazine=2&year=99">
</xml>
```

This code inserts into a page the XML description of all the articles that match the query. The final HTML code is somewhat more compact and elegant but there's a subtle point to note. The page DHTML object model is built before the XML completely downloads. For this reason, the code that we saw above:

```
set o = document.all("MyXML")
alert o.innerHTML
```

returns an empty string. This happens because the DHTML runtime considers only the physical content of <xml>, which is the empty string at the time of page download. If we attempt to show the outerHTML property, we see the following:

For the DHTML object model, the node <xml> is exactly as it appears in source file. Using external XML files, therefore, the only way to get the source code is through XMLDOM:

```
set o = document.all("MyXML")
alert o.XMLDocument.xml
```

This isn't a big issue, if you consider that in most cases we need the XML source just to create the XMLDOM.

Summary

In this chapter, we have looked at the most important aspects of using XML. We first saw how XML relates to HTML and SGML, and what its differences are. XML was designed to solve problems with the SGML and HTML languages. It has responded to precise industry needs and has redefined the industry's business model to make it more platform-independent.

XML is inherently cross-platform, and so provides us with a high degree of flexibility. XML is not limited to the Web, but things are moving towards a more web-based architecture. So XML and the Web (i.e., HTTP) are the winning couple for developing today.

XML is about data description, and if we look at it as-is, it looks more like a meta-language than a really usable language. For this reason, we need to customize it through a vocabulary of tags and attributes.

In this chapter, you've looked at:

- Whys and wherefores of XML
- Document type definition files and data schema
- Practical examples of how to use the Microsoft XML parser
- How data islands work in Internet Explorer

In the next chapter, we will look at XML stylesheets. These enable us to transform XML into other formats such as HTML and other XML languages.

25

Rendering and Styling XML

As we saw in the last chapter, XML is a generic language that can accept any tag and any attribute provided that the final document is well-formed, that is, it is structured in accordance with a specific set of rules. This poses serious problems when it comes to rendering XML code into something that the user – not the programmers – can understand, use, and interact with.

MSXML version 2.0, that shipped with Internet Explorer 5.0 in early 1999, started support of the **Extensible Stylesheet Language** (XSL). It was an early implementation of what today has become XSLT – **Extensible Stylesheet Language Transformations** – with the blessing of W3C. To get support for XSLT, we need MSXML 2.6, or higher, available for download from the MSDN web site, in the XML developer area: `http://msdn.microsoft.com/xml`.

This book is neither about XML, XSL or XSLT. However, it is about accessing data from ASP applications, and there are many interesting things we can do with XSL(T), in conjunction with XML, in an ASP application. XSL and XSLT have the same objective; to transform XML documents into other formats; HTML, RTF, plain text and XML itself.

> *XSLT support in MSXML 2.6 provides roughly the same functionality as before with XSL. However, now we can rely on a more stable version of the transformation language and a new API and object model.*

For the purpose of this book, we'll concentrate on XSL rather than XSLT. Unless otherwise specified, anything you read from now on applies to a generic XSL(T) platform. This chapter will cover:

❏ XML-to-HTML transformations

❏ Applying XSL on the client- and the server-side

❏ Document/view applications with XML and XSL(T)

> For compatibility purposes, the newest Microsoft XML Parser has been implemented in a new file (`msxml2.dll`) and utilizes brand new `ProgIDs` and `CLSIDs`. So it will not disrupt any current XML-enabled applications, but to take advantage of the new functionality, we need to edit the code to accommodate this new functionality.

Give XML a Stylesheet

As a data description language, XML is ideal for storing data, but not for providing a way of presenting it. This is where XSL(T) is important. This provides a set of transformation rules used to convert XML, tag by tag, from an input format to an output format. In other words, XSL(T) enables us to assign a significance to each custom tag used to describe some data. While we can transform text from XML to any other text-based format, the two most interesting and commonly used transformations are:

❏ XML to HTML

❏ XML to XML

The first turns out to be very helpful if we want to maintain the content of a document in one place, and generate as many different views of it as necessary. The second type of transformation finds its place in the server-to-server, business-to-business scenario, where XML data schemas form an essential part of the plumbing for interoperable systems. Translating documents from format to format to comply with different schemas is exactly what people need. This is where XML and XSL(T) are essential.

Once we have a fixed set of XML tags, we have a language capable of describing a particular type of document. The same document can be rendered in different ways to accommodate different users, different devices, and different operating contexts. By writing more XSL files, that is, more sets of transformation rules, we can provide different views of the same content:

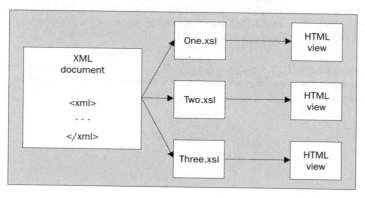

As shown in the picture, the same XML document can be used as the source for many different HTML views (and non-HTML views as well) by referencing a different XSL file.

This feature has an important practical impact. If a client informs us that he or she no longer likes the user interface of his or her web site, we can change it by simply writing a new XSL file and referencing it from all the existing pages. No other change is required – unless, of course, a more structural change is required. Using XSL to drive the user interface of a web solution also means that we can allow the end users to decide how a certain table has to be drawn. It is as easy as pointing the browser to an ASP page with a new XSL directive.

Let's start this XSL(T) tour with a first practical example that takes the rather generic XML output generated by a query to the ArticleBazaar site, and renders it as HTML via XSL. Next, we'll see a more complex example of using XML/XSL in a document/view web application.

In the picture below we can see the typical output of an ArticleBazaar query. The portion of text that appears below the horizontal rule is generated after the query is returned. We encountered this back in Chapter 10. Recall the source code that generated this output; it uses just a `<TABLE>` with some CSS styles to introduce some color and a neat format.

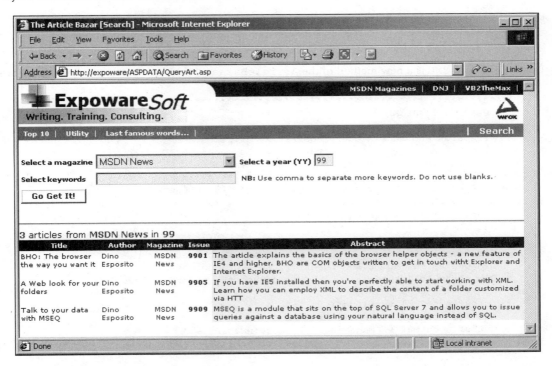

Rewriting the piece of ASP code that generates the report in a more general way is not a bad idea. Achieving a neat separation between data and presentation is one important factor in successful software development. We will now look at a way of doing this using XML.

Our goal now is to rewrite the portion of the code that generates the report and make it XML-based. In particular, we could go further and use two different XSL(T) transformers, one for Internet Explorer and another for Netscape.

The structure of the final part of the `queryart.asp` page could be changed like this. This will detect whether the user is using Netscape Navigator or Internet Explorer, and will access details about the required articles using the appropriate format:

```
<hr>
<%
  if bFirstTime then
    Response.end
  end if

  set o = Server.CreateObject("ArticleBazaar.Query")
  xml = o.GetArticlesAsXML strMagID, strYear

  ' transform XML into HTML
  browser = Request.ServerVariables("HTTP_USER_AGENT")
  bMSIE = (Instr(browser, "MSIE") >0)

  if Not bMSIE then
    ' load the Netscape's XSL
  else
    ' load the IE's XSL
  end if
%>
```

`GetArticlesAsXML` is a new method of the `ArticleBazaar Query` component, defined as follows:

```
' ***************************************************
'     GetArticlesAsXML
' ---------------------------------------------------
'     Prepares and runs a query against My Articles.
'     Returns all the articles that match the magazine ID
'     and the year of publication. In XML format.
' ***************************************************
Public Function GetArticlesAsXML(ByVal nMagID As Integer, _
    ByVal strMagz As String, _
    ByVal strYear As String) As String

    Dim outbuf As String          ' the output XML buffer
    Dim temp As String            ' temporary buffer
    Dim oRS As New ADODB.Recordset ' the ADO Recordset
    Dim nArts As Integer          ' counts the records found

    outbuf = "<?xml version='1.0' ?>"
    outbuf = outbuf & "<ARTICLEBAZAAR "
    outbuf = outbuf & "magazine=" & Quote(nMagID) & " "
    outbuf = outbuf & "year=" & Quote(strYear) & ">"

    ' Call the necessary components to get the data and convert it to XML
    Set oRS = GetArticles(nMagID, strYear)

    nArts = 0
    temp = ""
    While Not oRS.EOF
        temp = temp & "<ARTICLE "
```

```
            temp = temp & "title=" & Quote(oRS("title")) & " "
            temp = temp & "author=" & Quote(oRS("author")) & " "
            temp = temp & "magazine=" & Quote(oRS("name")) & " "
            temp = temp & "issue=" & Quote(oRS("issue")) & " "
            temp = temp & "URL=" & Quote(oRS("URL")) & " "
            temp = temp & "keyword=" & Quote(oRS("keyword")) & " "
            temp = temp & "articleID=" & Quote(oRS("articleID")) & " "

            temp = temp & ">"
            temp = temp & oRS("abstract")
            temp = temp & "</ARTICLE>"

            nArts = nArts + 1
            oRS.MoveNext
        Wend

        temp = "<ARTICLES found=" & Quote(nArts) & " " & _
                "magazine=" & Quote(strMagz) & ">" & temp
        temp = temp & "</ARTICLES>"

        ' Concatenates all and prepare the final output
        outbuf = outbuf & temp & "</ARTICLEBAZAAR>"
        GetArticlesAsXML = outbuf
End Function



'   **********************************************************
'       Quote
'   ----------------------------------------------------------
'       Helper function to wrap a string into quotes
'   **********************************************************
Private Function Quote(ByVal buf As Variant)
    Quote = Chr(34) & Trim(buf) & Chr(34)
End Function
```

We now need some way to present the information we have been passed. So the next step is writing an XSL(T) file.

Writing an XSL(T) File

The principle behind XSL(T) is that we apply templates to tags. An XSL(T) file is a regular XML file with tags coming from two namespaces. One is XSL, and the other is the standard HTML namespace. In an XSL file, we choose a namespace and, once we have done so, all the tags that are part of this namespace aren't parsed and expanded, but copied as they are. This is the principle that lets us 'compile' an HTML page at runtime, expanding all the XSL tags.

An XSL(T) file is like a well-formed HTML file (following the XML syntax rules) with some interspersed XSL tags pointing to the content of the XML file to process. An XSL(T) file begins with a prolog such as this:

```
<?xml version="1.0"?>
<xsl:stylesheet xmlns:xsl="http://www.w3.org/TR/WD-xsl"
                xmlns:html="http://www.w3.org/TR/REC-html40"
                result-ns=""
                language="JScript">
```

Any XSL file contains at least one template that applies to the root of the XML document. It is characterized by the `<xsl:template>` tag and the `match` attribute being set to /, which refers to the root element:

```
<?xml version="1.0"?>
<xsl:stylesheet xmlns:xsl="http://www.w3.org/TR/WD-xsl"
                xmlns:html="http://www.w3.org/TR/REC-html40"
                result-ns=""
                language="JScript">
<xsl:template match="/">
  <!-- XSL main template  -->
</xsl:template>
</xsl:stylesheet>
```

The first portion of the HTML code shows the results of the query. All this information is stored in the XML file we want to process. The XML file is the one we defined in the previous chapter:

```
<!-- Write the top line with results -->

<font face="verdana" size="2">
<span style='color:red;font-weight:bold'>
<xsl:value-of select="ARTICLEBAZAAR/ARTICLES/@found"/>
</span>
articles from
<span style='color:red;font-weight:bold'>
<xsl:value-of select="ARTICLEBAZAAR/ARTICLES/@magazine"/>
</span> in <span style='color:red;font-weight:bold'>
<xsl:value-of select="ARTICLEBAZAAR/@year"/>
</span></font>
```

There are three things to notice:

- ❏ It's absolutely necessary to use quotes for attributes
- ❏ The syntax to locate a node or an attribute
- ❏ The use of the `<xsl:value-of>` tag

The XSL file remains an XML file. As we saw in the last chapter, this means that it must be well-formed. Even though the final document will be an HTML document, which tolerates a fair degree of flexibility, when writing an XSL file we must produce a well-formed document. Actually, the final HTML will be a neat and clean HTML, namely XHTML.

To locate a node or an attribute within the XML document, we have a query language at our disposal with a path-based syntax that allows us to retrieve the `<ARTICLES>` node with the following:

```
ARTICLEBAZAAR/ARTICLES
```

And the `found` attribute of `<ARTICLES>` with:

```
ARTICLEBAZAAR/ARTICLES/@found
```

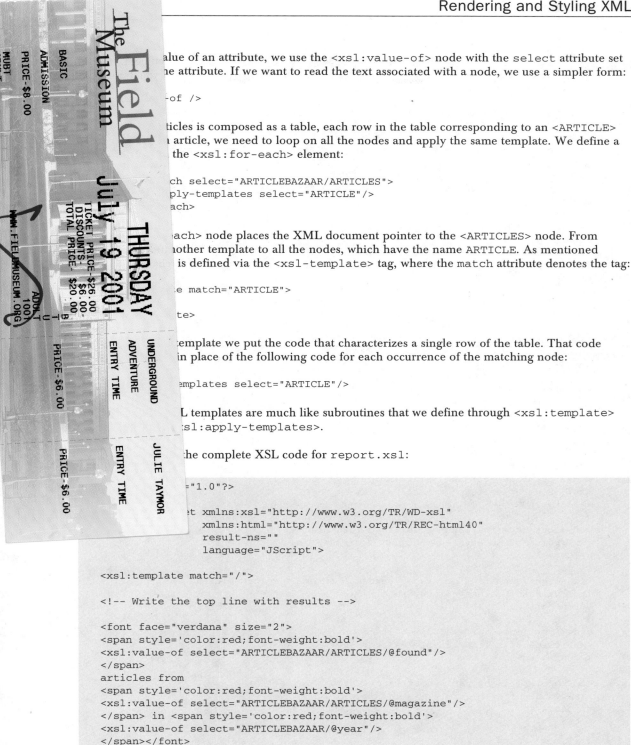

value of an attribute, we use the `<xsl:value-of>` node with the `select` attribute set
the attribute. If we want to read the text associated with a node, we use a simpler form:

```
-of />
```

ticles is composed as a table, each row in the table corresponding to an `<ARTICLE>`
article, we need to loop on all the nodes and apply the same template. We define a
the `<xsl:for-each>` element:

```
ch select="ARTICLEBAZAAR/ARTICLES">
ply-templates select="ARTICLE"/>
ach>
```

each> node places the XML document pointer to the `<ARTICLES>` node. From
nother template to all the nodes, which have the name `ARTICLE`. As mentioned
is defined via the `<xsl-template>` tag, where the `match` attribute denotes the tag:

```
e match="ARTICLE">

te>
```

template we put the code that characterizes a single row of the table. That code
in place of the following code for each occurrence of the matching node:

```
emplates select="ARTICLE"/>
```

L templates are much like subroutines that we define through `<xsl:template>`
sl:apply-templates>.

he complete XSL code for `report.xsl`:

```
="1.0"?>

t xmlns:xsl="http://www.w3.org/TR/WD-xsl"
    xmlns:html="http://www.w3.org/TR/REC-html40"
    result-ns=""
    language="JScript">

<xsl:template match="/">

<!-- Write the top line with results -->

<font face="verdana" size="2">
<span style='color:red;font-weight:bold'>
<xsl:value-of select="ARTICLEBAZAAR/ARTICLES/@found"/>
</span>
articles from
<span style='color:red;font-weight:bold'>
<xsl:value-of select="ARTICLEBAZAAR/ARTICLES/@magazine"/>
</span> in <span style='color:red;font-weight:bold'>
<xsl:value-of select="ARTICLEBAZAAR/@year"/>
</span></font>
```

```
<!-- Prepares the table with the list of the articles -->
<table cellspacing="0" cellpadding="2" border="0" width="100%">
<tr align="center" bgcolor="0">

<td><font face="verdana" size="1" color="#ffffff" style="font-weight:bold">
Title
</font></td>
<td><font face="verdana" size="1" color="#ffffff" style="font-weight:bold">
Author
</font></td>
<td><font face="verdana" size="1" color="#ffffff" style="font-weight:bold">
Magazine
</font></td>
<td><font face="verdana" size="1" color="#ffffff" style="font-weight:bold">
Issue
</font></td>
<td><font face="verdana" size="1" color="#ffffff" style="font-weight:bold">
Abstract
</font></td>
</tr>

<!-- Iterates on all the articles -->
<xsl:for-each select="ARTICLEBAZAAR/ARTICLES">
    <xsl:apply-templates select="ARTICLE"/>
</xsl:for-each>

</table>
</xsl:template>

<!-- The ARTICLE template -->
<xsl:template match="ARTICLE">

<tr valign="top">
<td><font face="verdana" size="1">
<xsl:value-of select="@title" />
</font></td>

<td><font face="verdana" size="1" color="blue">
<xsl:value-of select="@author" />
</font></td>

<td align="center"><font face="verdana" size="1" color="blue">
<xsl:value-of select="@magazine" />
</font></td>

<td><font face="verdana" size="1" color="blue" style="font-weight:bold">
<xsl:value-of select="@issue" />
</font></td>

<td bgcolor="lightcyan"><font face="verdana" size="1">
<xsl:value-of />
</font></td>
</tr>

</xsl:template>
</xsl:stylesheet>
```

This code will render our XML in precisely the way we want for the ArticleBazaar site.

Using a Stylesheet

There are two ways in which we can test a stylesheet file. We can either explicitly associate it with an XML file, or we can apply the transformation rules via script. The former is useful only if we can rely on an XML-enabled browser that fully supports XSL(T). At the moment, only Internet Explorer 5.0 and higher has this capability. Applying transformation via script is a much more interesting possibility, since it enables XML server-side processing.

XSL on the Client

To force Internet Explorer to display an XML file using a certain stylesheet, we just need to put the following line at the top of the XML file we're viewing, referencing the stylesheet we wish to use:

```
<?xml-stylesheet type="text/xsl" href="report.xsl"?>
```

This is a processing instruction, recognized only by Internet Explorer 5.0 and above, that tells it about the XSL file to download and process – such information is ignored by other parsers. Other parsers supporting XSL might choose a different way to associate the same information.

If we don't specify our own XSL(T) transformation from XML to HTML, then IE 5.0 utilizes the default stylesheet. This functionality is also called **XML direct browsing**.

XSL Through Script

We took a look at Microsoft's XML DOM in the last chapter. By using this, we can seamlessly transform XML code into HTML via XSL. This can be done from within a client-side HTML page, VBScript or JScript file, or a server-side ASP page, or even from within C++ or Visual Basic code. The following JScript code takes the name of the XML document and the XSL stylesheet from the command line, and creates a HTML file in the current folder:

```
// XmlToHtml.js
// Converts from XML to HTML via XSL
// ------------------------------------------------------

var xml, xsl;
var fileXML, fileXSL, fileHTM;
var fso, f;

// Read the argument from the WSH command line
fileXML = WScript.Arguments(0);
fileXSL = WScript.Arguments(1);
fileHTM = WScript.Arguments(2);

// Get an instance of the XMLDOM object for handling the XML document
xml = new ActiveXObject("Microsoft.XMLDOM");
xml.async = 0;

// Get an instance of the XMLDOM object for handling the XSL source
xsl = new ActiveXObject("Microsoft.XMLDOM");
xsl.async = 0;
```

```
// Initialize both XMLDOMs
xml.load(fileXML);
xsl.load(fileXSL);

// Create an empty text file
fso = new ActiveXObject("Scripting.FileSystemObject");
f = fso.CreateTextFile(fileHTM);

// Write the result of the transformation down to the file
f.Write(xml.transformNode(xsl.documentElement));
f.Close();
```

We require similar code to redesign the core part of the ArticleBazaar query results page. The following code (called ABReport.xml) does just this:

```
<?xml version='1.0' ?>

<ARTICLEBAZAAR magazine="2" year="99">

<ARTICLES found="3" magazine="MSDN News">
<ARTICLE title="BHO: The browser the way you want it"
  author="Dino Esposito" magazine="MSDN News" issue="9901" URL=""
  keyword="IE,Windows" >
The article explains the basics of the browser helper objects - a new feature of
IE4 and higher. BHOs are COM objects written to get in touch with Explorer and
Internet Explorer.
</ARTICLE>

<ARTICLE title="A Web look for your folders"
  author="Dino Esposito" magazine="MSDN News" issue="9905" URL=""
  keyword="shell,Windows" >
If you have IE5 installed then you're perfectly able to start working with XML.
Learn how you can employ XML to describe the content of a folder customized via
HTT
</ARTICLE>

<ARTICLE title="Talk to your data with MSEQ"
  author="Dino Esposito" magazine="MSDN News" issue="9909" URL=""
  keyword="OLEDB,SQL" >
MSEQ is a module that sits on the top of SQL Server 7 and allows you to issue
queries against a database using your natural language instead of SQL.
</ARTICLE>
</ARTICLES>

</ARTICLEBAZAAR>
```

Running this using the following command produces the IE 5.0 output:

```
cscript xmltohtml.js abreport.xml report.xsl test.htm
```

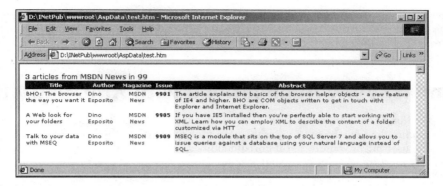

What remains is to adapt the above script and incorporate it in the `queryart.asp` page:

```
<%
  if bFirstTime then
    Response.end
  end if

  set o = Server.CreateObject("ArticleBazaar.Query")
  xmlText = o.GetArticlesAsXML(strMagID, strMagz, strYear)

  ' transform XML into HTML
  set xml = Server.CreateObject("Microsoft.XMLDOM")
  xml.async = False
  set xsl = Server.CreateObject("Microsoft.XMLDOM")
  xsl.async = False

  xml.loadXML xmlText
  xsl.load Server.MapPath("report.xsl")

  Response.Write xml.transformNode(xsl.documentElement)
%>
```

Our ArticleBazaar query page should look like this:

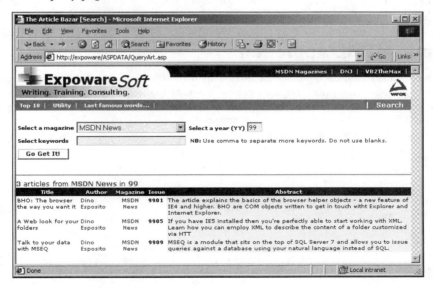

At this point, should we need to change the way in which the list of articles is rendered, a new stylesheet would pay the bill. More interestingly, we can make this a feature of the application and allow users to select their preferred view.

Document/View Applications with XML and XSL

If you're providing a large number of records, or long table reports, it might be nice to give the users a chance to modify the table layout so that they can look at the data in whatever format they prefer. For example, one user might want to scroll horizontal lines of fields, while another might prefer a tree structure, or a more general master-detail schema.

Think of the Windows shell and, in particular, consider the five possible views of a folder available in Windows 2000: large icons, small icons, list, detailed list, and thumbnails. We can switch between them at any moment, and see the changes instantaneously. Despite the different views, the data displayed is always the same.

An ASP Approach

A web XML document viewing application is simply a web page that provides different views of the same data through XSL stylesheets. The content of the page is described by an XML document, and the XSL files are used to produce the views.

The easiest way to code something like this is through ASP. To do this, we put a form on the page and use a combo-box to select the desired view. Each time the selection changes, or each time the user clicks a button to change the view, the form submits the information to the remote ASP page, which then arranges a new page with the selected layout. To accomplish this, it applies a different XSL file to the same XML data.

All this works fine, but there's a significant drawback to this method. Each time we ask to refresh the view, we have to download not only the new view, but also the same data. The same XML content travels unremittingly back and forth between the client and the web server. Ideally, the XML should download once, and only the required XSL should be downloaded.

A Dynamic HTML Approach

A better solution is based on Dynamic HTML. This provides much better performance, but we pay the price of limited browser support. So, how can we manage to download an XML document only once? Data islands provide a good way of solving the issue. We embed the XML data within a data-island, and each time the user changes the view, we simply pass the URL of the XSL file to the XML DOM object, and have that download it for us.

Let's consider the following HTML page:

```
<html>

<script language=javascript>
function chg()
{
```

```
   f = document.forms["Main"];
   s = f["cboMagz"];
   fileXSL = s.options[s.selectedIndex].value;
}
</script>
```

```
<xml id=MyDoc
  src="http://localhost/xmlquery1.asp?magazine=1&year=00">
</xml>
```

```
<body>

<form name=Main>
<font face=verdana size=1><b>Select a view
<select style="background-color:beige;width:200px" onchange="chg()"
  name="cboMagz">
  <option value="http://localhost/report.xsl">One Row Report</option>
  <option value="http://localhost/2rowreport.xsl">Two Row Report</option>
</select>
</font>
</form>

<hr>

<div id="content"></div>

</body>
</html>
```

The `<xml>` tag brings in the XML source code produced by a slightly modified version of the `xmlquery.asp`:

```
<%
   ' <--- Collect the arguments --->
   argMagazine = Request.QueryString("Magazine")
   argYear     = Request.QueryString("Year")

   ' Set the MIME type
   Response.ContentType = "text/xml"

   ' Call the necessary components to get the data and convert it to XML
   set o = Server.CreateObject("ArticleBazaar.Query")
   Response.Write o.GetArticlesAsXML(argMagazine, "", argYear)

   Response.End
%>
```

The `<select>` tag defines two possible views, one where the data is displayed on one row and another where the abstract text is moved to a new row. Both use different server-side XSL files selected from a combo-box as follows:

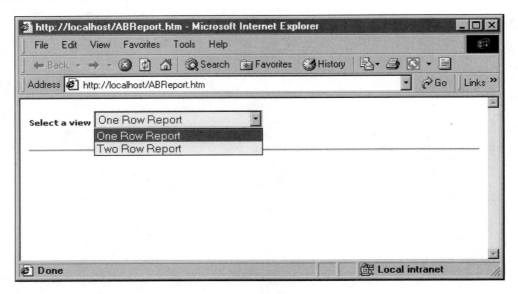

Changing the view causes a little piece of client-side script code to run:

```
<script language=javascript>
function chg()
{
  f = document.forms["Main"];
  s = f["cboMagz"];
  fileXSL = s.options[s.selectedIndex].value;
  xml = document.all("MyDoc").XMLDocument;
  xsl = new ActiveXObject("Microsoft.XMLDOM");
  xsl.async = 0;
  xsl.load(fileXSL);

  o = document.all("content");
  o.innerHTML = xml.transformNode(xsl.documentElement);
}
</script>
```

This calls the XMLDOM `load` method on the specified XSL file. If not already cached, such a file downloads and gets loaded into memory. Next, it is used to transform XML into another piece of HTML code, and the result is assigned to the `innerHTML` property of the `<div>` tag.

The XSL stylesheet used to transform this view is `report.xsl` which we saw earlier:

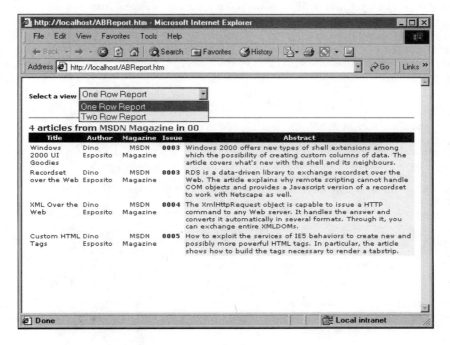

Changing the view results in a new page layout:

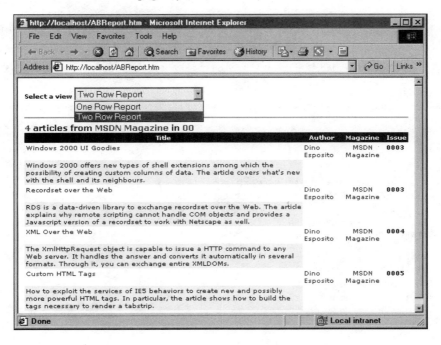

In this case, the abstract is moved to a new row, which makes the display easier to read if you have a small browser window. The stylesheet used to format this page is little different from that for the single row report:

```
<?xml version="1.0"?>

<xsl:stylesheet xmlns:xsl="http://www.w3.org/TR/WD-xsl"
                xmlns:html="http://www.w3.org/TR/REC-html40"
                result-ns=""
                language="JavaScript">

<xsl:template match="/">

<!-- Write the top line with results -->
<font face="verdana" size="2">
<span style='color:red;font-weight:bold'>
<xsl:value-of select="ARTICLEBAZAAR/ARTICLES/@found"/>
</span>
articles from
<span style='color:red;font-weight:bold'>
<xsl:value-of select="ARTICLEBAZAAR/ARTICLES/ARTICLE/@magazine"/>
</span> in <span style='color:red;font-weight:bold'>
<xsl:value-of select="ARTICLEBAZAAR/@year"/>
</span></font>

<!-- Prepares the table with the list of the articles -->
<table cellspacing="0" cellpadding="2" border="0" width="100%">
<tr align="center" bgcolor="0">

<td><font face="verdana" size="1" color="#ffffff" style="font-weight:bold">
Title
</font></td>
<td><font face="verdana" size="1" color="#ffffff" style="font-weight:bold">
Author
</font></td>
<td><font face="verdana" size="1" color="#ffffff" style="font-weight:bold">
Magazine
</font></td>
<td><font face="verdana" size="1" color="#ffffff" style="font-weight:bold">
Issue
</font></td>
</tr>

<!-- Iterates on all the articles -->
<xsl:for-each select="ARTICLEBAZAAR/ARTICLES">
    <xsl:apply-templates select="ARTICLE"/>
</xsl:for-each>
</table>
</xsl:template>

<xsl:template match="ARTICLE">
<tr valign="top">

<td><font face="verdana" size="1" color="blue">
    <xsl:value-of select="@title" />
</font></td>
```

```
<td><font face="verdana" size="1" color="blue">
    <xsl:value-of select="@author" />
</font></td>

<td align="center"><font face="verdana" size="1" color="blue">
    <xsl:value-of select="@magazine" />
</font></td>

<td><font face="verdana" size="1" color="blue" style="font-weight:bold">
    <xsl:value-of select="@issue" />
</font></td>
</tr>

<tr>
<td bgcolor="lightcyan"><font face="verdana" size="1">
    <xsl:element name="div">
        <xsl:value-of />
    </xsl:element>
</font></td>
</tr>
</xsl:template>
</xsl:stylesheet>
```

In this second stylesheet, we have included a new tag: `<xsl:element>`, which is used to dynamically create an XML element (in this a `div` tag to hold the abstract text). There is a similar element `<xsl:attribute>` for creating new attributes.

The document/view architecture implemented over the Web with XML and XSL(T) gives us an idea of what we can do with XML on the client. We'll now take a look at server-side processing of XML

Server-Side XML and XSL(T)

Writing code with XML rather than HTML is much easier and more natural. Moreover, the direct browsing feature of IE 5.0 and higher makes using XML very easy indeed. If we open an XML file in IE, we will see it rendered through the standard stylesheet or through one of our own. It seems that most of the things we want are already there, waiting for us to exploit. This conviction becomes even stronger when we realize that there is really nothing to prevent us from writing ASP pages using XML, instead of HTML, as the underlying language. We can do this seamlessly by just renaming an XML file as an ASP file, and placing it on a directory on our web server.

Consider the following ASP script. It looks like ordinary ASP and HTML code, but it is actually a mix of ASP and XML. All the tags that appear in the text are XML tags rather than HTML tags:

```
<%
  Function Quote(s)
    Quote = Chr(34) & Trim(s) & Chr(34)
  End Function
%>

<articleBazaar>
```

```
<articles>
<%
  Response.ContentType = "text/xml"
  set o = Server.CreateObject("ArticleBazaar.Query")
  set oRS = o.GetArticles(2, "99")

  while Not oRS.EOF
    Response.Write "<article "
    Response.Write "title=" & Quote(oRS("title")) & " "
    Response.Write "author=" & Quote(oRS("author"))
    Response.Write "></article>" & vbCrLf
    oRS.MoveNext
  wend
%>
</articles>
</articleBazaar>
```

It displays the following:

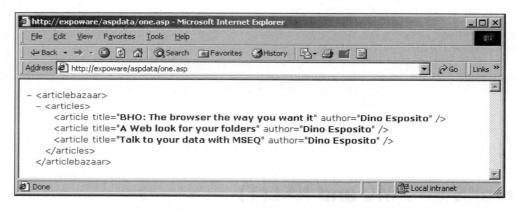

The problem with this kind of page is that we need an XML-enabled browser. Worse still, we need a browser that knows how to treat and render XML streams. For example, Internet Explorer 4.0 can be considered an XML-enabled browser in the sense that it provides a parser, but it doesn't convert XML into HTML. What we need is a browser that provides XML browsing capabilities. To date, this is only Internet Explorer 5.0 and higher.

Write XML and Send HTML

To use XML in our server-side code, we need to make sure that either the browser supports direct browsing through XSL(T), or that we have the means to translate our XML into HTML on the server. In a previous section, we saw how to do just that, namely, how to apply XSL(T) transformation on the server. So what's new this time?

In the previous example, we had a COM object returning an XML string and an XSL transformer to convert it into the proper HTML layout. It was plain script code running in an ASP code block. Wouldn't it be nice if we could write XML and have something taking place on the server to automatically and smoothly convert it into HTML?

There are a few rather quirky possibilities here, but all of them require us to modify the structure of the ASP page. For example, we could accumulate the response code into a variable and then flush it to the browser, invoking the XSL(T) processor. Even though this might sound neat and effective, it forces us into an unnatural programming style. Each time we need to send back some output, we must not use `Response.Write`, but resort to something like this instead:

```
buf = buf & myOutput
```

All this would be unnecessary if the ASP object model provided a `GetResponseBuffer` method to read the text currently buffered. (Remember that with IIS 5.0 and Windows 2000, the ASP buffering is on by default.)

Expanding ASP Code

Another possible approach to the problem requires us to keep ASP and XML in different files. We could call a dispatcher ASP page, which would be the same for all of the XML pages we want to use. We would pass this dispatcher the URL of the XML page and make it process the XML. It works great so long as our XML file has a static content and doesn't contain `<%...%>` code blocks. On the other hand, an XML-coded ASP is only ASP because of these code blocks!

The XML DOM's `load` method can also accept a URL, not just local path names. Interestingly, if this URL points to an ASP page, the method expands it properly. In other words, so long as `foo.asp` outputs well-formed XML, the following code creates an instance of the XML DOM where all the code blocks in the ASP page have been properly expanded:

```
xmldom.load "http://expoware/aspdata/foo.asp"
```

This would be really great news, if it were not for a particular problem, which is explained in the Knowledge Base article Q237906. This article explains that the code seen above will work only if invoked from a client-side context. If we try to run it from within an ASP page, or a COM object running under IIS/ COM+, we'll experience unpredictable results that can vary from an incredibly high response time to problems accessing secure sites through HTTPS, not to mention random runtime errors.

According to Microsoft, this behavior (or bug, as some would say) was designed this way, since `load` method sends HTTP requests through system libraries such as `WinInet` and `UrlMon`. Using the `WinInet` and `UrlMon` from a protected server service like IIS and ASP will end up breaking some of the functionality, which causes the misbehavior. This, we are promised, will be fixed in the final version of MSXML.

To summarize, there's no easy way to write XML-coded ASP pages that work for any client. The main problem lies in the difficulty of fully expanding the XML code. At present, the only workaround is not to use `Response.Write` at all, but dump everything to a string and then convert it through XSL(T).

Can ISAPI Filters Help Us Out?

An ISAPI filter is a piece of code that we register with IIS through the Internet Services applet:

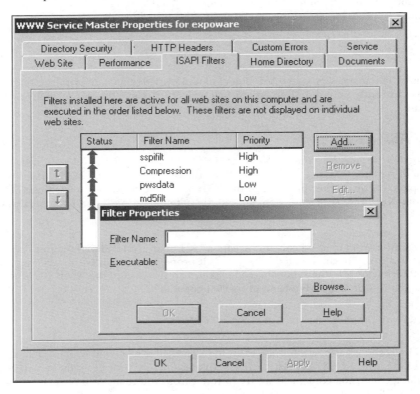

Filters are DLLs that can be written with MFC, taking advantage of a ready-made wizard. Each time IIS is about to accomplish a task, which is customizable through filters, it looks up in the internal table of filters and notifies all of them with event-specific code.

Upon loading, each filter lets IIS know about the events it is interested in. In more fashionable terminology, filters subscribe only to certain events raised by IIS, and get a notification only for those events. One such event is when the web server is sending raw data back to the client. If we write an ISAPI filter that hooks onto this event, we're half way to solving the problem.

Such a filter could detect the browser and do nothing if it is Internet Explorer 5.0 or higher. Otherwise, it could locally buffer the XML code, and, when the final packet arrives, convert it to HTML using XSL(T) and send back the HTML code. All this would be completely transparent to the browser as well as to the server-side code.

ISAPI Filters Details

The code, below, has been obtained by simply running the MFC ISAPI Extension wizard as shown in the figure below:

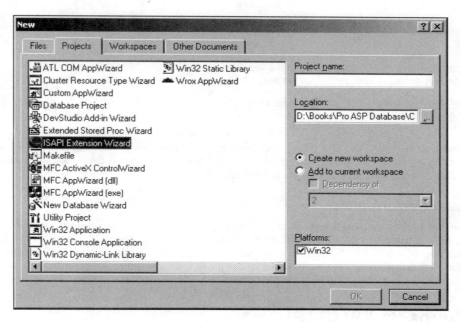

The Outgoing Raw Data and Headers option is selected from the second step:

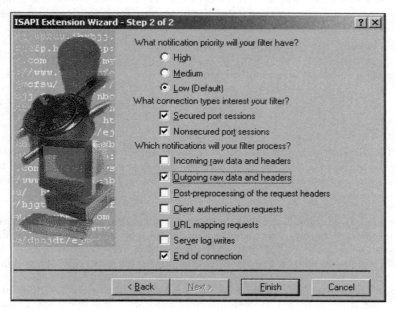

This is what IIS calls when sending data back to the client. The method returns a status code and kills the event:

```
DWORD CMyTestFilter::OnSendRawData(CHttpFilterContext* pCtxt,
  PHTTP_FILTER_RAW_DATA pRawData)
{
  // TODO: React to this notification accordingly and
  // return the appropriate status code
  LPTSTR p = new TCHAR[pRawData->cbInBuffer];
  lstrcpyn(p, (LPTSTR) pRawData->pvInData, pRawData->cbInBuffer);

  return SF_STATUS_REQ_NEXT_NOTIFICATION;
}
```

The p variable points to the text being sent. We can add a piece of code to log this to a file and see what's going on during a connection. (If we're using IIS and the client is on the same machine, we could also use a MessageBox, but this isn't recommended!)

Filters and Performance

However we look at it, using ISAPI filters slows down the performance of the web server. We can set a priority for the filter, but this simply affects the time elapsed from when IIS originates the event until the point the filter is notified. Filters are invoked very frequently, and this ends up constituting an overhead. For this reason, if we really need to use a filter, we should make sure we write lean and highly optimized code.

The Microsoft XSLISAPI

Microsoft recently made available an XSL ISAPI filter that attempts to solve the problem of making XML available to any browser. Version 2.0 of the filter is available for download at:

```
http://msdn.microsoft.com/downloads/webtechnology/xml/xslisapi.asp
```

It is written in plain C++ and is available in source code.

Summary

The beauty of XML is that it lets us concentrate on how our data is structured and enables us to define tags that describe our data better. An XML-derived language accepts the tags we list in our definition file. As a result, we have a specialized language to describe our own data. So much for the logical layout, what about the display?

An XML document is just data, but needs some kind of rendering to become useful to the end user. XML would lose part of its importance and charm if there were no reliable tool to transform it into something else – in particular HTML. But XML doesn't have to be transformed into HTML. In the business world, data needs to be transferred between applications that offer no user interface. So XML conforming to one company's schema can be transformed to another XML document conforming to a different schema altogether, thus enabling the same data to be usable by two different systems. Thus, XML-to-XML and XML-to-HTML are two principal transformations that XML supports.

These transformations can now be achieved with the relatively fresh W3C standard, XSLT – XSL Transformations. The older version of XSL was supported by MSXML 2.0. XSLT, however, now expresses the full potential of stylesheets. Microsoft has implemented XSLT in its latest version of the MSXML parser.

In this chapter, we didn't focus on XSLT as a stand-alone technology, but endeavored to present the main functionality of XSL(T) – a generic mechanism to apply XML transformations. In fact, despite the different names and implementation, both XSL and XSLT share the same goal: compiling input XML into another format. The chapter covered:

❑   How to use stylesheets

❑   The most important XSL tags

❑   Document/view applications with XML and XSL

❑   How to write XML-based server pages

In the next chapter, we will move on to look at the use of XML with ADO.

26

ADO and XML

One important use of XML is as the data-transfer format in **business-to-business** (B2B) applications and **Enterprise Application Integration** (EAI). In most, if not all situations, these applications will need to exchange collections of records shaped in many different ways: tabular, hierarchical or semi-structured. Since B2B applications will often reside on different machines that employ different technologies on different platforms, there has to be a data format that is universally accepted, easy to process, simple, but not simplistic, and extensible. XML fits the bill.

Certainly XML has been designed to act as a universal glue for heterogeneous systems, maintaining the same intuitiveness of the ASCII text but adding the power of markup tags. However, XML is only a data-transfer format, probably the best we have ever had. It cannot create and doesn't destroy anything. It simply provides a means to describe data in a way that can be easily understood and processed anywhere. So, who or what produce this XML? Who's providing the data that XML so remarkably describes, which goes beyond any language, any programming tool and any operating system? These magical entities are data providers.

ADO is Microsoft's preferred technology to talk to data providers from within ASP pages and any other development environment where there is no direct use pointers or calls to `QueryInterface`. In Chapter 5, we explained that ADO comprised a set of objects that sat on top of the OLE DB COM interfaces. Indeed, ADO would be nothing without OLE DB and OLE DB data providers. Everything that we're going to say from now on regarding ADO can also be applied to OLE DB. It is true that ADO simplifies and enriches the OLE DB programming interfaces, but if we need that little bit more power and efficiency then we could, using C++, write our own data access components.

Since ADO is the recommended way of accessing data in the Microsoft world, the ADO `Recordset` object becomes the focus of interest as it is the container for data extracted from the source. It is the contents of a recordset that can be marked up as XML in cross-technology and cross-platform communications. In this chapter, we'll look at all possible relationships and interactions between the ADO recordset and XML, with data transfer and functionality exchange at the forefront of our minds. The main points we'll discuss are:

❑ Recordset persistence

❑ XML-format for recordsets

❑ Working with disk-based recordsets

❑ Recordsets and Stream objects

❑ News from the ADO+ world

We'll try to be as RDBMS-independent as possible, and the code will use the ADO 2.5 object model, whose XML support is very powerful. As far as the functionality of data transfer is concerned, the understanding of the concept of persistence is fundamental. Also, a good implementation of persistence becomes a critical factor for whole system. So let's start with explaining the basics of ADO recordset persistence.

Persisting ADO Recordsets

Ever since version 2.0, ADO has offered automatic recordset persistence. The `Recordset` object has a method called `Save` that has the ability to serialize the in-memory representation of the recordset to disk. In version 2.0, there was no choice for the output format – recordsets could be saved only as a faithful image of their in-memory structure. This image was called an **Advanced Data TableGram** (ADTG), which was a binary representation of the data; a rather compact and unintelligible file format.

With ADO 2.1, Microsoft brought us a second, more intriguing persistence format based on XML. And now, with ADO 2.5 in our hands and with ADO+ on the horizon, ADTG and XML remain the two alternatives for recordset persistence. Let's analyze them in a bit more detail.

The ADTG Format

ADTG is a binary, Unicode-based, but uncompressed format that is proprietary to Microsoft. Basically, it is a sort of disk copy that stores the in-memory representation of the instance of the `Recordset` object to a file. In general, because it is a binary format and not ASCII text with added markup, the ADTG format is more compact than XML. We cab save a recordset in ADTG format like this:

```
Dim oRS as New ADODB.Recordset
oRS.Save "file.adtg", adPersistADTG
```

The `.adtg` extension is only a matter of choice. Feel free to choose the file extension you like.

XML Data Schemas

Microsoft utilizes a particular XML schema to store a recordset. At a first sight, the structure of the XML document might be overwhelming and seem unnecessarily complex. However, as we'll see in a moment, it contains all the information it needs to contain in order to implement a list of additional features. In other words, when we export an ADO recordset to disk storage – no matter whether it is ADTG or XML –it remains an ADO recordset object.

By calling the `Save` method, we simply move the in-memory ADO recordset object to a different storage medium. The object maintains the same functionality and we can work on recordsets recovered from disk in the same way as we would work with those kept in memory. Thus an XML recordset contains much more information than what would appear to be necessary. The figure below shows how Internet Explorer 5.0 displays an XML recordset. So that the entire file fits in the window, the `<s:Schema>` tag has not been expanded:

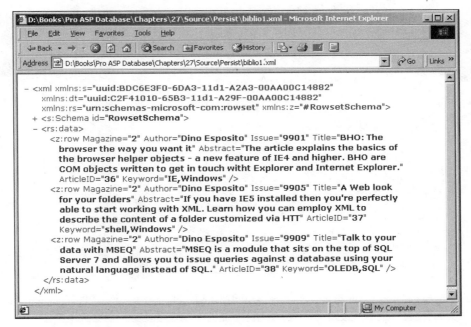

Let's now see its source code in a bit more detail. Supposing we have run the following Visual Basic code:

```
Dim oRS As New ADODB.Recordset
oRS.Open "select * from articles where magazine=2 and issue like '99%'", _
        "uid=sa;Provider=SQLOLEDB;Initial Catalog=My Articles;"
oRS.Save XMLFILE, adPersistXML
```

The resulting XML is divided into two parts: the schema and data. The schema contains the information about the fields that make up the recordset, such as the type of the data and the length and the name of the field. The XML looks like this – reformatted and indented for easier reading:

```
<xml xmlns:s='uuid:BDC6E3F0-6DA3-11d1-A2A3-00AA00C14882'
    xmlns:dt='uuid:C2F41010-65B3-11d1-A29F-00AA00C14882'
    xmlns:rs='urn:schemas-microsoft-com:rowset'
```

```
        xmlns:z='#RowsetSchema'>

  <s:Schema id='RowsetSchema'>

  <s:ElementType name='row' content='eltOnly' rs:CommandTimeout='30'>
      <s:AttributeType name='Author' rs:number='1' rs:nullable='true'
            rs:writeunknown='true'>
         <s:datatype dt:type='string' dt:maxLength='50'/>
      </s:AttributeType>
      <s:AttributeType name='Issue' rs:number='2' rs:nullable='true'
            rs:writeunknown='true'>
         <s:datatype dt:type='string' dt:maxLength='50'/>
      </s:AttributeType>

      <s:AttributeType name='Title' rs:number='3' rs:nullable='true'
            rs:writeunknown='true'>
         <s:datatype dt:type='string' dt:maxLength='50'/>
      </s:AttributeType>
      <s:AttributeType name='Keyword' rs:number='4' rs:nullable='true'
            rs:writeunknown='true'>
         <s:datatype dt:type='string' rs:dbtype='str' dt:maxLength='50'
            rs:fixedlength='true'/>
      </s:AttributeType>

  <s:extends type='rs:rowbase'/>
  </s:ElementType>
  </s:Schema>

  <rs:data>
      <z:row title='BHO: The browser the way we want it'
         Author='Dino Esposito' Issue='9901' Keyword='IE,Windows'/>
      <z:row title='A Web look for our folders'
         Author='Dino Esposito' Issue='9905' Keyword='shell,Windows'/>
      <z:row title='Talk to our data with MSEQ'
         Author='Dino Esposito' Issue='9909' Keyword='OLEDB,SQL'/>
  </rs:data>
  </xml>
```

Note that there are four namespaces characterized by the labels: s, dt, rs, z. This is what each refers to:

Namespace	Content
s	Defines the schema of the recordset. It looks like a XML Data schema and includes information about the element and attribute types.
dt	Defines the type of the XML attributes.
rs	Defines the rowset.
z	Defines the single row of the rowset.

Using this information, ADO is able to rebuild an in-memory image of the recordset object when loading the XML from disk. That's an important aspect to consider: we can save a recordset to, and load from, a disk file.

Nodes or Attributes?

As we may have noticed, the XML schema for recordsets defines its content as attributes rather than as individual elements:

```
<z:row title='BHO: The browser the way we want it'
    author='Dino Esposito' issue='9901' keyword='IE,Windows'/>
```

Each field in a record is rendered through a single <z:row> node which contains as many attributes as required. Is this a good schema? What about using child nodes? Is it better to use nodes or attributes when it comes to defining a custom XML schema?

Attributes are more limited than elements, in that they cannot contain sub-elements and they cannot be made to appear in any particular order. We can specify whether an attribute is required or optional, but an attribute may only appear once per element. However, attributes have some capabilities that elements do not. They may limit their legal values to a small set of strings, and may indicate a default value to be used if the attribute is omitted. More importantly, different element types may have attributes with the same name – the attributes are considered independent and unrelated.

In terms of processing speed, attributes are preferable. In order to handle them, the parser doesn't have to work that hard, unlike a node. This is presumably the reason why Microsoft used attributes to render the recordset's data. On the other hand, a node can be more easily expanded to include subnodes and attributes.

Writing and Loading Recordsets

Open and Save are the methods of the ADO Recordset object. As mentioned earlier, the syntax of the method Save is rather intuitive:

```
rs.Save [Destination], [PersistFormat]
```

The Destination parameter can be either a local file name or any COM object that exposes the IStream interface, for example, the ASP Response object. Another interesting possibility of persisting the recordset is offered by the MSMQ Message object. This can receive and store an entire recordset.

The PersistFormat argument is an enumerated type that lists only two values. The enumerated type is called PersistFormatEnum.

Name	Value	Description
adPersistADTG	0	Saves the recordset using the ADTG binary format
adPersistXML	1	Saves the recordset using the XML Data schema

By default, a recordset is persisted in the ADTG format.

Saving a Recordset to Disk

Before we call the `Save` method, we should make sure the file we're about to write doesn't exist. If it does exist, and we want to overwrite it, we must delete it first.

```
If Dir(strFile) <> "" Then
    Kill strFile
End If
```

`Save` does not close the ADO recordset or the destination file or object – this is intentional and allows us to continue working with the recordset, saving our most recent changes. The destination file or object remains open until the recordset itself is closed. The destination element is in a read-only state for other applications during this time. If `Save` is called while an asynchronous operation is in progress (fetch, update, execute), then the method will wait for the operation to complete before proceeding.

Since the destination object is open, when we subsequently call the method `Save` to update the persisted recordset we must avoid specifying the file or object name. Otherwise we run into the File already exists runtime error. The first time we save the recordset, it is recommended, but not mandatory, that we specify a file name. If we don't, and leave the destination argument blank, then a new file will be created with a name set to the value of the `Source` property of the recordset. This is definitely not what we might expect or want.

Each time we call `Save` with a new target object, the recordset is saved at a new memory location. However, this will not automatically close the file that was previously used – both the new file and the original will remain open.

Recordsets are saved starting from the first row. When the method finishes, the current row pointer is moved to the first row of the recordset.

Filtered recordsets

A filtered recordset is a `Recordset` object where the `Filter` property has been set to a non-zero expression. A filtered recordset exposes only those rows that match the criteria specified in the filter. For this reason, only those rows are saved.

Security Issues

If we plan to use the `Save` from within HTML pages viewed through a browser, then extra security settings will probably apply. In particular, the `Save` method only works from within sites for which we chose low or custom security settings.

> *Saving a* `Recordset` *with* `Fields` *of type* `adVariant`, `adIDispatch`, *or* `adIUnknown` *is not supported by ADO and can cause unpredictable results.*

Reloading a Persisted Recordset

The syntax of the `Open` method we use to reload a previously persisted recordset is more complex than the `Save` method:

```
rs.Open [Source], [ActiveConnection], [CursorType], [LockType], [Options]
```

Except for `Source`, all these arguments are optional. `Open` populates a `Recordset` object by reading the data stream from a source that can be a file or any COM object that exposes the `IStream` interface, for example, the ASP `Request` object.

The `ActiveConnection` argument is useful only if we want to obtain a recordset through a connection to a particular data provider. When we want to recreate the recordset from disk, then the `ActiveConnection` argument is automatically set to `MSPersist`.

`MSPersist` is the name of the OLE DB provider for persistence. It is responsible for persisting an entire OLE DB rowset, including data, metadata and current state. It is also in charge of rebuilding the recordset. Note that this occurs without establishing a new connection with the data provider that originally created the recordset. In fact, ADO recordsets are creatable objects, and any component that has the relevant information to hand can create and make available a fully-fledged recordset object.

`CursorType` and `LockType` represent the cursor and lock types required to open a recordset. By default, they are set to the forward-only cursor and the read-only lock type.

Finally, the `Options` argument indicates how the provider should evaluate the `Source` argument. When we want to restore a recordset from a file, we use the `adCmdFile` constant. If `Source` is a path name to a file, then it can refer to a full or relative path as well as a URL. If no `Connection` object is associated with the recordset, then the `Options` argument defaults to `adCmdFile`, because this will typically be the case for persistently stored objects.

Remember that when we call the `Close` method on a recordset object we're simply closing it and allowing the system to release any internal structure associated with the recordset. When a recordset is open, a few properties, such as `CursorType` and `LockType`, become read-only, and are restored to their read/write status as soon as we close it.

If we pass a `Stream` object as the `Source` argument, we should avoid specifying other arguments; otherwise we get a runtime error.

Working with XML-based Recordsets

To demonstrate that an XML-formatted ADO recordset restored from disk is a normal recordset, let's see what happens when we modify it. Let's create a Visual Basic application with a `WebBrowser` control to display the XML code and a few buttons:

```
' ******************************************************************
'    Constants and Globals
' ******************************************************************
Private g_oRS As New ADODB.Recordset
Const CONNSTR = "provider=sqloledb;initial catalog=my articles;uid=sa"


' ******************************************************************
'    Create a persistent copy of the recordset
' ******************************************************************
Private Sub btnPersist_Click()
    g_oRS.CursorLocation = adUseClient
    g_oRS.Open "select * from articles", CONNSTR
```

```
        ' Navigate to the XML file just created
        RefreshRecordsetView
    End Sub


    ' *****************************************************************
    '    Helper Functions
    ' *****************************************************************
    Private Sub RefreshRecordsetView()
        Label1.Caption = g_oRS.RecordCount & " record(s)"

        If Dir("persist.xml") <> "" Then Kill "persist.xml"
        g_oRS.Save "persist.xml", adPersistXML
        g_oRS.Close

        WB.Navigate App.Path & "\persist.xml"
    End Sub
```

The application will give output like this:

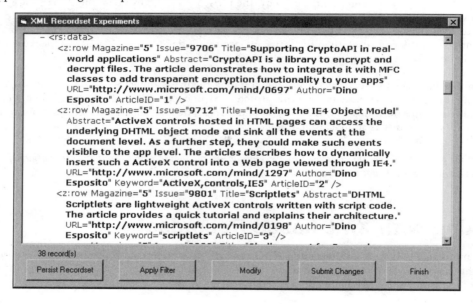

The Persist Recordset button gets a recordset from the My Articles database in SQL Server 7.0, persists it to XML and then closes the recordset. Closing the recordset automatically closes the file too.

Next, for user interface reasons, the WebBrowser control navigates to the freshly created XML document.

Applying Filters

The Apply Filter button loads the persisted recordset and adds a filter to it. Actually, it does nothing that is particularly related to XML and ADO. This piece of code just demonstrates that we can work on a restored recordset in much the same way that we work on a recordset that has come straight from the database. The filter includes only those records whose magazine ID is equal to 2. (This is hard-coded into the source, but in a real-world program we would not want to do this.)

```
    Private Sub btnFilter_Click()
        g_oRS.Open "persist.xml", , , , adCmdFile
        g_oRS.Filter = "magazine = 2"
        RefreshRecordsetView
    End Sub
```

Now the application looks like this:

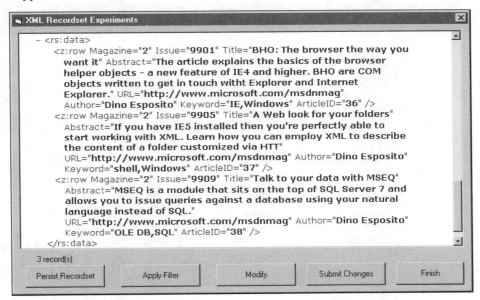

By calling the helper function `RefreshRecordsetView` we save the recordset back to the disk. Now its size is considerably smaller (4 kilobytes from 17 kilobytes) since the recordset consists of four records out of the original forty.

Updating the Recordset

The Modify button loads the recordset from disk, locates the first record that matches certain criteria and updates one of its fields. Notice that in order to update a recordset we must specify a particular lock type. By default, the `LockType` property is set to `adLockReadOnly`, which has a value of 1, which will not allow us to make changes. The value to choose is `adLockBatchOptimistic`, which has a value of 4, which means that the record will be locked before the batch update process starts.

The value of `CursorType` – another critical property – is automatically set to `adOpenStatic` whenever we load a recordset from a file. In fact, loading a recordset from a file clearly requires a static cursor. The value of `CursorType` is silently adjusted during the execution of the `Open` method.

```
    Private Sub btnModify_Click()
        g_oRS.Open "persist.xml", , , adLockBatchOptimistic, adCmdFile

        g_oRS.Find "articleID=36"
        g_oRS("author") = "Francesco Esposito"
        g_oRS.Update
```

```
    RefreshRecordsetView
End Sub
```

`Find` is the method which locates the first record that matches some specified search conditions. Once the article with an ID of 36 is selected, the value of the `author` field is changed and the view is refreshed:

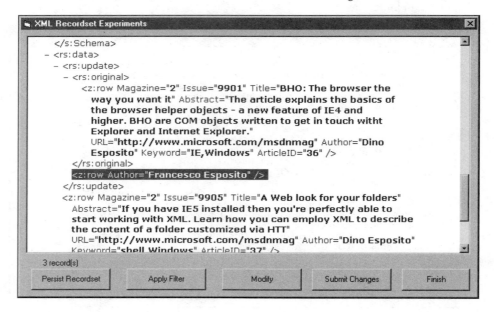

As we can see from the figure, something happened in the XML source code. The updated record changed from:

```
<z:row
    Magazine='2'
    Author='Dino Esposito'
    Issue='9901'
    Title='BHO: The browser the way we want it'
    ArticleID='36'
    Keyword='IE,Windows'
    Abstract='The article explains the basics of the browser helper
objects - a new feature of IE4 and higher. BHO are COM objects
written to get in touch with Explorer and Internet Explorer.'
    />
```

To this:

```
<rs:update>
<rs:original>
    <z:row
        Magazine='2'
        Author='Dino Esposito'
        Issue='9901'
        Title='BHO: The browser the way we want it'
```

```
        ArticleID='36'
        Keyword='IE,Windows'
     Abstract='The article explains the basics of the browser helper
     objects - a new feature of IE4 and higher. BHO are COM objects
     written to get in touch witht Explorer and Internet Explorer.'
     />
</rs:original>
    <z:row Author='Francesco Esposito'/>
</rs:update>
```

The XML code now shows that a change has occurred. The original row is retained and a new row element added with the field that has been modified. Persisting the recordset, persists all this extra information too.

Deleting Records

The overall ADO behavior changes only for a minor particular if we decide to delete one or more records instead of updating. Suppose we had a delete button, which called the recordset's Delete method like this:

```
Private Sub btnDelete_Click()
    g_oRS.Open "persist.xml", , , adLockBatchOptimistic, adCmdFile

    g_oRS.Find "articleID=36"
    g_oRS.Delete

    RefreshRecordsetView
End Sub
```

The difference between this and the update we saw earlier is that the affected record is wrapped by a <rs:delete> tag:

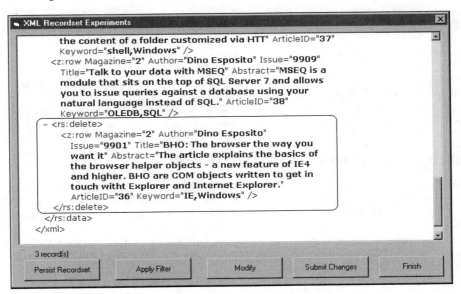

Inserting Records

The same support also exists for insertions. This example Visual Basic code would produce the XML that follows:

```
Private Sub btnInsert_Click()
    g_oRS.Open "persist.xml", , , adLockBatchOptimistic, adCmdFile
    g_oRS.AddNew FieldList:=Array("Magazine", "Title", "Author"), _
                 Values:=Array(9, "Kill the killer-app", "Joe Users")
    RefreshRecordsetView
End Sub
```

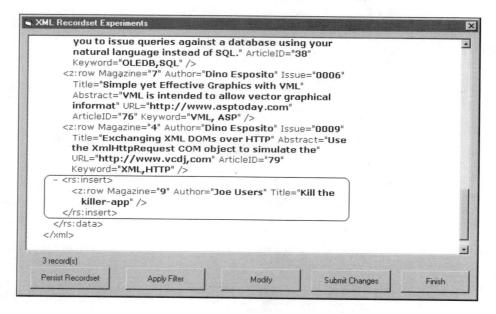

The new record is wrapped by <rs:insert> tags.

Whatever data access operation we carry out on an persisted recordset, the text is immediately updated and it can be kept up-to-date on a local disk. All the changes remain isolated from the original code and are clearly marked by special rs tags. Since a persisted recordset is obviously a disconnected recordset, the last problem we have to tackle is how to submit the changes to the database.

Submitting Changes

When it comes to reconnecting a disconnected recordset, we have to get the connection string, which would be the very same string used when the recordset was extracted – with the value stored as a constant. Either we can assign the connection string to the ActiveConnection property of the recordset, or we can create an ADO Connection object (with the same settings and properties) and assign it to the same ActiveConnection property. This would be done after we'd already opened the persisted recordset. With this done, all we do is call UpdateBatch. Don't forget to choose the proper lock type, such as adLockBatchOptimistic.

```
Private Sub btnSubmit_Click()
    g_oRS.Open "persist.xml", , , adLockBatchOptimistic, adCmdFile
    g_oRS.ActiveConnection = CONNSTR
    g_oRS.UpdateBatch
End Sub
```

Notice that the syntax to open a persisted recordset can be rewritten like this:

```
g_oRS.Open "persist.xml", "Provider=MSPersist", , adLockBatchOptimistic
```

If we explicitly invoke the OLE DB Persistence Provider, then we don't need to specify adCmdFile as the final argument. If we miss both out, we will get a runtime error complaining about stored procedures.

At this point, if we run the code, we get this:

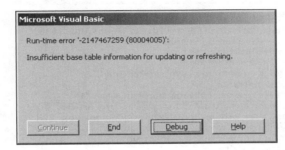

ADO gently informs us that it does not have enough information about the data source to apply the changes. In other words, ADO doesn't even know what the database is called and what the column names are. Such information was not persisted in the recordset. Let's see why this is.

Persisting Data Source Meta-data Information

Whether or not the data source meta data is persisted will depend upon the settings of two of the Recordset object's properties, CursorType and LockType, at the time when the recordset was opened in the first instance – that is, on the database. The recordset must be created with a client-side cursor and a read/write lock type. These two settings, however, are *not* the default ones.

Client-side Cursors

A client-side cursor (with a value of adOpenStatic) implies a disconnected recordset, and thereby one that might need to be reconnected in due course and any pending changes submitted to the database. For this reason, the recordset embeds and then persists the data source meta-data information.

We obtain the same effect by setting the CursorLocation property to adUseClient. If the cursor location is on the client, in fact, the only cursor type we can have is adOpenStatic. In this case, ADO would silently adjust incorrect settings.

Read/write Locks

By default, the LockType property is set to adLockReadOnly (a value of 0), which means that the given recordset cannot be modified, and as such, there would be no chance of reconnecting to the database and submitting any changes. That's why the data source meta-data information is not added to the in-memory image of the recordset. To enable updating, we can use any value apart from adLockReadOnly, for example, adLockBatchOptimistic.

Persisting the Metadata

The code that allows the recordset to reconnect to the database and submit any changes is therefore:

```
Private Sub btnPersist_Click()
    g_oRS.CursorType = adOpenStatic
    g_oRS.LockType = adLockPessimistic
    g_oRS.Open "select * from articles", CONNSTR
    RefreshRecordsetView
End Sub
```

Notice that this must be done in the procedure that gets the data directly from the data provider.

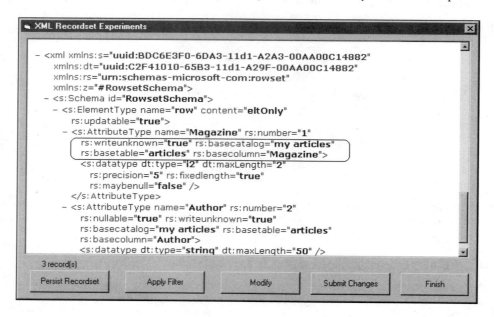

The figure above shows the additional XML formatted meta-data that describes the recordset. All the `<s:AttributeType>` nodes now include three more attributes:

- ❑   `<rs:basecatalog>`
- ❑   `<rs:basetable>`
- ❑   `<rs:basecolumn>`

The content of the above fields is straightforward as they refer to the database, the table and the column respectively. Now the code that submits the changes to the database works correctly and the result can be seen in the figure after.

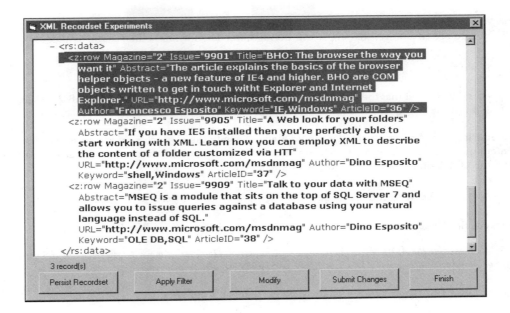

Streaming a Recordset

So now we know how to persist a recordset in XML. As pointed out earlier in this chapter, this feature is nothing new and dates back to ADO 2.1. However, what is new in ADO 2.5 is the ability it offers to stream a recordset into any COM object that exposes the `IStream` interface, such as the ASP `Response` and `Stream` objects.

A stream is simply a block of memory whose contents can be accessed and manipulated through the methods and the properties that the `Stream` object makes available. They enable us to transfer contents between objects without writing to disk or using a file. We can use streams programmatically in a variety of ways, for example:

- ❑ To connect to a URL and receive data from a resource – which is what an ASP page or a CGI application sends out

- ❑ To access the content of `Record` objects

- ❑ To create a custom in-memory representation of data

Here's a simple example of what we can do with a `Stream` object:

```
Const adModeRead = 1

Set oSTM = CreateObject("ADODB.Stream")
oSTM.Charset = "windows-1252"
oSTM.Open "URL=http://expoware/aspdata/xmlrec.asp", adModeRead
MsgBox oSTM.ReadText
```

The VBScript code utilizes the OLE DB Provider for Internet Publishing to connect to the specified URL. There are two things that are worth noting here. The former is the custom syntax for the query:

```
URL=http://...
```

The second is the fact that the provider is one of the first to fully support the OLE DB 2.5 specification. In fact, it returns an object that implements the `IStream` interface, as explained in Chapter 6.

When using the `Stream` object, we should always specify the character set we need. By default, the content of a `Stream` object is written in Unicode. If we want a different set of characters we have to reset the `Charset` property, as in the example above:

```
oSTM.Charset = "windows-1252"
```

This tells the object that we want the text to be returned as standard Windows text.

> We looked at the ADO object model back in Chapter 7. However, a more detailed look at this may be found in Professional ADO 2.5, ISBN 1861002750, also from Wrox Press.

Let's see how recordsets and the `Stream` object can work together.

From Streams to Recordsets

As we can see, streams and recordsets are to some extent interchangeable objects. In other words, we can convert from a stream to a recordset and vice versa. Here's how to proceed in an ASP page:

```
<%
    Const adModeRead = 1
    Const adLockBatchOptimistic = 4
    Const adUseClient = 3

    set oSTM = Server.CreateObject("ADODB.Stream")
    oSTM.Charset = "windows-1252"
    oSTM.Open "URL=http://expoware/aspdata/xmlrec.asp", adModeRead
    Set oRS = Server.CreateObject("ADODB.Recordset")
    oRS.CursorLocation = adUseClient
    oRS.LockType = adLockBatchOptimistic
    oRS.Open oSTM
%>
```

Provided that the stream contains what is needed to build a recordset, we can pass the `Stream` object directly to the `Recordset`'s `Open` method.

From Recordsets to Streams

When would converting a recordset into a `Stream` object be useful? The `Recordset`'s `Save` method simply creates a file. To get the content of the recordset into a non-COM format, we are required to read the recordset back from disk. This can be done, but is not particularly efficient.

For example, if we need a function that, given an ADO recordset, returns an XML string, we could use code like this:

```
<%
    Function GetRecordsetAsXML(oRS)
        oRS.Save "temp.xml", 1          ' adPersistXML
        oRS.Close

        Set fso = Server.CreateObject("Scripting.FileSystemObject")
        Set f = fso.OpenTextFile("temp.xml")
        GetRecordsetAsXML = f.ReadAll()
        f.Close
    End Function
%>
```

The same functionality could be obtained much more efficiently using streams. The idea is that we first persist the recordset into a `Stream` object. Since this object is a memory object, and provides a programming interface, it's really easy to create the corresponding XML string without the burden of accessing the disk.

The following code shows how to persist a recordset object to a `Stream` object:

```
<%
    Set oRS = Server.CreateObject("ADODB.Recordset")
    oRS.Open "select * from authors", & _
            "provider=sqloledb;uid=sa;initial catalog=pubs"

    ...

    oRS.Save oSTM, adPersistXML
%>
```

At this point, re-writing the `GetRecordsetAsXML` function is easy:

```
<%
    Function GetRecordsetAsXML(oRS)
        ' Create the new stream
        set oSTM = Server.CreateObject("ADODB.Stream")

        ' Write the XML version of the recordset to the stream
        oRS.Save oSTM, 1                ' adPersistXML
        oRS.Close

        ' Return the string
        GetRecordsetAsXML = oSTM.ReadText()
    End Function
%>
```

Notice that in this case we don't need to specify the character set, since it is determined by ADO when writing to the stream. Indeed we must not set the `CharSet` property.

To demonstrate the `GetRecordsetAsXML` facility, let's adapt this code to work on this client through a `.vbs` file and Windows Script Host:

```
set oQRY = CreateObject("ArticleBazar.Query")
MsgBox GetRecordsetAsXML(oQRY.GetArticles(2, ""))

Function GetRecordsetAsXML(oRS)
    set oSTM = CreateObject("ADODB.Stream")

    oRS.Save oSTM, 1                    ' adPersistXML
    oRS.Close

    GetRecordsetAsXML = oSTM.ReadText()
End Function
```

Finally, if we need to persist the stream to a file, the `Stream` object has functionality to do this. `LoadFromFile` and `SaveToFile` do just what their names suggest.

Data Transfer with Recordsets

As we have seen from the content of this chapter, transforming an ADO recordset into XML is really quite easy. However, this does raise some new architectural considerations. Is XML really enough to ensure interoperability? Should we use XML or recordsets when communicating from tier to tier? And, most importantly, is the proposed XML schema the best approach to stream recordsets?

There are advantages and disadvantages of using ADO recordsets. On the plus side, they provide a rich and attractive programming interface, and can be used from many programming and scripting languages. On the other hand, they are strictly COM-based in nature and as such are not that portable when it comes to real-world heterogeneous web environments involving non-Windows platforms.

Interoperability and scalability are two important requirements for the modern distributed web system. The means to meet such requirements will be considerably improved through the forthcoming member of the ADO family: **ADO+**.

The Reason Behind ADO+

ADO recordsets provide a great way of manipulating data in a Windows and COM-based scenario. Unfortunately, they progressively lose their appeal and strength as soon as our system evolves in the direction of total Internet interoperability. The crucial area is the middle-tier where we have one or more layers of business objects exchanging data in response to the user's input. These components may need to pass data to each other, but in doing so, they need a common data format that is both easy-to-use, powerful and mutually understandable.

The questions to answer are:

❑   Are ADO recordsets always a good format to exchange data between tiers?

❑   Are XML recordsets always a good schema to exchange data between heterogeneous tiers?

The transfer of disconnected ADO recordsets between components involves COM marshaling and therefore only COM business objects will be able to use these recordsets. In a homogeneous Windows-based architecture where only COM/DCOM is involved in the business tier, this presents no problem at all. However, this dependence on COM turns out to be a great inconvenience when the system we're considering uses other platforms. If one of our business objects is running on a UNIX workstation, direct communication is simply impossible, and we need to resort to the services of special modules such as Host Integration Server or a similar third-party product.

As a further note, consider that the advent of web services can only make this type of scenario more common. The same happens if we want our browser to manipulate recordsets through Remote Scripting or Remote Data Service. We always need a COM-aware client.

From this, it seems that ordinary ADO recordsets aren't suitable for a truly distributed environment, just in case applications on non-Microsoft platforms need to access them. But, we may argue, we can always persist recordsets to XML strings either through the disk file procedure or more directly through a `Stream` object. XML is text and as such can be easily transmitted and understood by any business object on any platform. This is correct, but with ADO+ we have a brand new data model to comply with. This has been developed from scratch with interoperability in mind.

Recordset Marshaling

Transferring a recordset from one component to another may require marshaling. That means that the COM runtime needs to recreate the same object context in another process or on another machine for the object to work. While COM acts to make this completely transparent to users and programmers, it is a time-consuming operation and ends up constituting a significant overhead for the overall system.

The impact is different if the components are in the same process or on the same machine. In the former case, there's no marshaling whatsoever and simply a pointer is passed. Of course, cross-process marshaling is much faster than cross-machine marshaling.

The figure below shows a view of the interfaces that the `ADODB.Recordset` object implements. As we can see, one of them is called `IMarshal`, which means that the recordset supports **custom marshaling** – that is, a non-standard, manually written and optimized way of transferring records. The ADO programming interface to this is the `MarshalOptions` property:

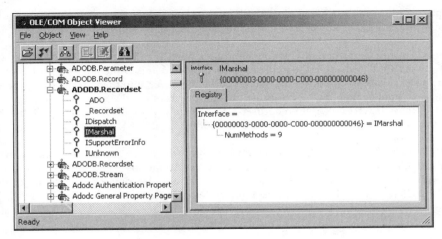

Thus ADO does its best to minimize the impact of marshaling, yet it remains a hurdle to overcome and a performance limitation whenever different processes or machines are involved in running communicating components.

XML Marshaling

The term "XML marshaling" is not exactly a common expression. What we mean by this is that we can stream recordsets into XML to make it easier to transfer them across processes and machines. Even if we defined a specific XML schema, it remains a rather generic description of the data with no code or behavior associated with it. The component that receives the XML stream must figure out a way to parse it. While XML parsers are available for all platforms, they quite frequently do not provide the same capabilities in terms of supported features.

In a nutshell, transforming an ADO recordset into a document that complies with the standard ADO XML schema serves the purpose of enabling interaction between remote and heterogeneous components at the inevitable price of rebuilding a usable representation of the data stream at the final destination.

Sending XML has a number of advantages:

❑ XML doesn't need either COM marshaling or expensive type conversions to accommodate COM specific data types.

❑ XML can be understood and processed on any platform.

❑ XML over HTTP can penetrate corporate firewalls (although this could also be a disadvantage).

There's just one drawback. ADO employs a particular XML schema that is well suited for the purpose of ADO, but is unnecessarily complex when it comes to data exchange between other object types. ADO inserts meta-data information about both the data source and the records. While this is critical when rebuilding a recordset for use by other ADO applications, it is verbose and unwieldy when our only goal is sending usable data to other business objects. In order to address this problem, the whole concept of a recordset has been redefined for ADO+.

ADO+ Datasets

ADO+, part of Microsoft's **.NET** platform, will be the standard data access technology for the next version of Visual Studio products, and it will be supported by Visual Basic .Net and ASP+.

ADO+ provides a new object model whose central element is called the **dataset**. A dataset evolved directly from ADO recordsets and comprises a disconnected and in-memory view of the database. There's no strict relationship between a dataset and a data source in that we can have datasets created dynamically without a single byte of information coming from a DBMS. In other words, datasets take advantage of these features of ADO recordsets: the ability to work disconnected and the ability to be programmatically created and populated with any sort of data.

A dataset can contain any number of **datatables**, each of which can correspond to a database table or view. A datatable object is simply a collection of rows and columns. Each row retains its original state together with the current state. Another element that can enrich a dataset is the table relation, which is basically a foreign-key relationship between datatables.

An example ADO+ dataset may be illustrated in the following way:

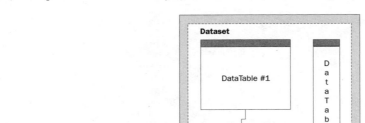

The dataset is a collection of child objects each of which contains data. The whole dataset structure can be persisted to XML reflecting only the internal structure, without any reference to the physical data providers from where the information may have originated. ADO+ datasets describe data, whereas ADO recordsets describe a collection of records taken from a table.

Architecturally Speaking

Most developers, when optimizing the performance of their distributed, multi-tiered and heterogeneous systems, will only extract and send the significant part of XML recordset data. That is, this code is sent:

```
<customer>Joe Users</customer>
```

Rather than this:

```
<xml xmlns:s='uuid:BDC6E3F0-6DA3-11d1-A2A3-00AA00C14882'
    xmlns:dt='uuid:C2F41010-65B3-11d1-A29F-00AA00C14882'
    xmlns:rs='urn:schemas-microsoft-com:rowset'
    xmlns:z='#RowsetSchema'>
<s:Schema id='RowsetSchema'>
<s:ElementType name='customer' content='eltOnly' rs:CommandTimeout='30'>
<s:extends type='rs:rowbase'/>
</s:ElementType>
</s:Schema>
<rs:data>
    <z:row customer='Joe Users'/>
<rs:data>
```

It does not matter that we do not have enough information to automatically rebuild the recordset. Indeed, we might not even need it, since ADO itself might not be available where the data is being sent. What ADO+ generalizes and standardizes is exactly what skillful developers are already doing.

In terms of architecture, here's how ADO+ fits in distributed systems:

Notice that .Net and B2B applications, web services, and existing XML-aware systems are all able to take advantage of ADO+ data access components. What matters is that they are able to prepare and deliver XML packets over HTTP. More importantly, they don't need to employ the ADO data schema, but make use of what can be called the **natural language XML** interface.

The Interop Challenge

As we can see, this architecture is inherently interoperable since once the XML arrives on the middle tier it can be processed by an ADO+ enabled component as well as by an ordinary XML parser written, say, in Java or Perl. What our business-tier component receives is plain XML. Lucky us if we could leverage the power of ADO+ components to build an easy-to-program object model on the top of it. Otherwise, we just handcraft our processing code through the poor man's object model: the keyboard!

Summary

ADO and XML are highly integrated technologies –ADO manufactures data and XML takes care of delivery. It sounds like the perfect business model.

ADO is a great tool for data access, but works best only within a homogeneous system that is based on the Windows platform. However, the distributed systems of the future will require total Internet interoperability. In this scenario, the ADO model has some serious shortcomings. XML can be of considerable help in streaming recordsets into more manageable, cross-platform formats that web services and B2B applications can exchange. With ADO+, which is supposed to ship as part of Microsoft's .Net platform, and is supported by all Visual Studio .Net products, we have a new data model built from scratch with interoperability and scalability in mind.

In this chapter, we've run through:

- ❑ Recordset persistence using XML and ADTG
- ❑ Working with disconnected XML-based recordsets
- ❑ How the ADO 2.5 `Stream` object is used
- ❑ Changes expected in ADO+

XML and Relational Databases

ADO is an excellent way to get relational data to and from XML, but relational database vendors are not content to leave such popular (dare we say well hyped?) access to middleware. All the major relational vendors are developing or have released native support for XML in their database engines. The pattern is familiar: we pose an SQL statement to the engine and receive an XML document representing the rowset. All have some way to adjust the form and nomenclature of the returned document. In this chapter, we will look at the in-built features for XML in SQL Server 2000, Oracle, and DB2.

XML and SQL Server 2000

SQL Server 2000 embraces XML in several ways. These are web access, querying using the **XPath** (XML Path Language) syntax, and SQL Update Grams. Taken together, these features give a web-like view of SQL Server's data while allowing programmers to deal with that data using the format and syntax of XML.

> *If you are using SQL Server 7.0 or 6.5, an XML SQL Technology Preview is available from*
> `http://msdn.microsoft.com/workshop/xml/articles/xmlsql`. *This will enable*
> *you to similarly access data in XML format.*

This access is enabled by HTTP: we can issue a query in a URL, issue a query based on an XML document, update a database, and execute stored procedures in the database. We can get recordsets in one of several formats. If our data is targeted toward human users of web browsers, we can even use XSL to style the XML results as richly formatted HTML.

Web Access

ADO, like ODBC before it, is a programmatic interface to relational data. SQL Server 2000, however, will provide a view of relational data that is more like a web site. We will use an administrative tool to create virtual web directories for databases. These virtual directories will control access to particular databases through XML documents. These documents will either be passed to SQL Server as part of a URL, or will be parameterized XML documents residing on the server. By configuring access and providing some XML documents, database administrators will be able to provide standard views of their data to web clients.

XPath Syntax for Queries

SQL is a language based on relational algebra. It provides access to data using the syntax and semantics of the relational model. It is very powerful, but it is not the only way to view data. It is best for ad hoc queries. Paths through data rather than relations between data better describe some kinds of queries. This is particularly true of data meant to be read more often than it is written, or data that expresses a hierarchy. Retrieving user profiles for members of a structured organization is one such type of query. This is why directory services use LDAP syntax rather than SQL for their queries.

XML is another hierarchical view of data. The XPath query syntax is designed to retrieve XML elements or attributes based on a path through an XML document or the context in which an element or attribute appears. SQL Server 2000 will support such XPath queries on its data. Consider the following SQL query and its equivalent XPath query:

```
SELECT * FROM publishers WHERE pub_name="Wrox Press Ltd"
```

The XPath equivalent of this would look like this:

```
publisher[@pub_name="Wrox Press Ltd"]
```

The XPath statement retrieves all publisher elements whose pub_name attribute has the value "Wrox Press Ltd". Either syntax will work for a simple query like this. The point is not to produce a more efficient or compact query expression, but to choose a query language that most naturally fits the task at hand.

XPath queries will be implemented by an ISAPI extension that applies XPath statements to the XML documents provided by an administrator as part of configuring a virtual web directory. As a consequence, both web access and XPath queries, while part of the SQL Server 2000 product, operate outside the core SQL Server engine.

Update Grams

Although originally intended for release with SQL Server 2000, this feature has been delayed and may be released as a separate download. Unlike the two previous forms of access, update grams will be implemented in an OLE DB provider named **OpenXML**. An update gram is an XML document written according to a schema provided by SQL Server. It is used to modify the database.

Update grams work by providing elements that express a before and after view of a particular row. The before view is the state of the row prior to the modification. SQL Server uses this to locate the row. The after view is the state of the row after the modification is applied. Update grams map to SQL commands as follows:

❑ An after element without a before element is equivalent to a SQL INSERT statement.

❑ A before element without a corresponding after element maps to a DELETE statement.

❑ A transaction in which both elements appear is a SQL UPDATE.

SQL Server XML Architecture

SQL Server Meta Data Services is implemented as an ISAPI extension (sqlxmlx.dll). Queries issued in a URL via HTTP are parsed by this extension and submitted to SQL Server. The recordset is then converted into XML, according to the conventions of the tool, and returned as XML. Configuration is simplified through the provision of a snap-in for the **Microsoft Management Console** (**MMC**). The snap-in allows us to configure access to a database as if it were a virtual directory on our IIS server. The underlying settings are made for us so that the ISAPI extension may correctly configure its connection.

To configure XML support, we can simply select Configure SQL XML Support in IIS under the Microsoft SQL Server menu.

Configuring Access

Consider the most common case: a user sitting in front of a web browser wanting to access his relational data. Since HTTP sends URLs in clear text, we would either need to implement XML SQL as secure HTTP (necessitating a server certificate) or hide connection details on the server. Since the goal is to allow ad hoc access from any location in an easy-to-use form, the latter approach is the right one. So we must perform some configuration steps before our users can get access to the data.

We create a virtual directory by right-clicking on the appropriate web server in the MMC snap-in, and then selecting the New Virtual Directory menu item. Once the new virtual directory appears in the right hand pane, we select it and click on the Properties menu item.

Configuring a Virtual Directory for SQL Access

We will see a different property page dialog to the one we are accustomed to receiving through the Internet Services manager. The dialog includes the following tabs:

❑ General – for naming the virtual directory and locating the corresponding physical folder

❑ Security – for selecting the log in method.

❑ Data Source – for selecting the SQL Server and database.

❑ Settings – for specifying how users may access the data.

❑ Advanced – for locating the ISAPI extension and specifying the IIS version in use.

In the General tab, we establish a virtual root for the virtual directory from which we will be accessing our SQL Server data. It is useful to think of the data as a web site. This is only a metaphor, however; we cannot mix physical content (ASP and HTML pages) and SQL Server access in the same virtual directory.

If we are fielding this tool as part of a larger web application, we should ensure that our SQL Server accesses a virtual directory off the main application directory. Next, we go to the security tab and select the log in method we want to use. All the authentication methods available in SQL Server are available. We may choose to log in under a fixed account, or force a prompt when the user tries to access the data.

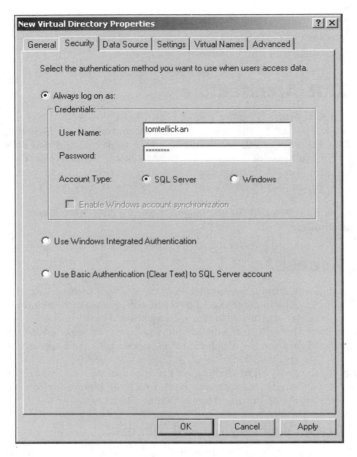

In the Data Source tab, we select the physical SQL Server and database we wish to access. And finally, we go to the Settings tab and specify how the user may access the data. We are offered three different types of access:

❑ URL queries – the SQL statement appears as a parameter of the URL.

❑ Template queries – the URL refers to a canned query specified in an XML document.

❑ XPath – users can execute XPath queries against SQL views defined in schemas.

Since template queries are under the control of the administrator, this is the most secure access method. It is therefore the only method enabled by default.

> **If you are working with a version of IIS prior to 5.0, or if you have moved the ISAPI extension, go on to the Advanced tab and make the appropriate configuration changes.**

SQL Queries in URLs

When we want to access our data in XML form through HTTP, we need to specify a query in the URL. This is done in one of two ways: as a SQL string or as a template file embedded in the URL. The first form looks like this:

```
http://myserver/pubs_db?sql=SELECT * FROM authors FOR XML AUTO
```

This query will return all the columns of the `authors` table in the default `pubs` database, provided we have configured access through a virtual directory named `pubs_db` on the IIS server named `myserver`.

> Note that the XML returned from SQL Server by default is *not* well-formed, in that there is more than one top level element. Because of this, Internet Explorer will generate an error message when it tries to display it. A way of getting around this is shown in the next form.

Note that we are taking advantage of IE's nonstandard feature by which it preprocesses URLs for HTTP. That is, we've left the spaces for clarity; IE will convert them to %20 literals so that the URL conforms to HTTP requirements. The second form, embedded template files, looks like this:

```
http://myserver/pubs_db?template=<ROOT>
            <sql:query xmlns:sql="urn:schemas-microsoft-com:xml-sql">
                        Select * from authors for XML
AUTO</sql:query></ROOT>
```

Note the insertion of the `<ROOT>` element. This ensures that there is a unique top level element. Note also that the line breaks in the above example have been added for clarity. In the **Address** box of our browser, we would have the XML document in a single line. Entering either of these URLs and making the HTTP request returns an XML document with the requested relational data. The general syntax for a URL based query is:

```
http://servername/virtual_directory?{sql=string | template=xml_file}
        [&param=value[&param=value]...]
```

where `servername` and `virtual_directory` are the names of the IIS server and the virtual directory root we configured, `string`, is a SQL statement, and `xml_file` is the content of a template file in string form. The multiple `param` entries are named parameters in the SQL query. This is just the format of any HTTP script, e.g., CGI or ISAPI, with the named `sql` and `template` parameters, and zero or more parameters specific to our query.

At this point we may be wondering why there are two forms. The template form seems to be unnecessarily complicated, not to mention redundant. The main use of template files is to offer canned queries on the server. We will go into that form later. In such a case, the nature of the SQL is hidden from the user and is managed by the system administrator in a file residing on the server. Having this form available directly through the URL, as in the above example, is useful primarily for development.

There are two additional parameters that may be used with the URL that are not shown in the above syntax. These are `contenttype` and `outputencoding`. These let us control the MIME type and character set encoding, respectively, of the returned XML. The default value `contenttype` is text/xml, the usual MIME encoding for XML markup. It is this MIME type indicator that lets IE5 know to invoke its default stylesheet for rendering XML.

If we are using another browser, we will want to change this value to text/plain. Many browsers will show the textual content of the XML when it does not recognize the XML tags. It will be ugly, but visible. In other cases, such as when we know the server is using XSL for formatting XML as HTML, we may need to specify other values. For HTML, we use text/html. If we know we are returning binary data, e.g., a JPEG stored in the database, we use the MIME type for the binary format that will be returned. Here's what the above query would look like if we requested text/plain as the MIME type:

```
http://myserver/pubs_db?sql=SELECT * FROM authors FOR XML
AUTO&contenttype=text/plain
```

We will seldom need to get involved with specifying the character set. By default, UTF-8 (Unicode) is returned. This is adequate for most purposes. If we will be further manipulating the XML that is returned, as in script access, we need to specify UTF-16 so that Windows can work with it.

Format Modes

One thing we didn't explain in the preceding section is the meaning of the FOR XML AUTO clause in the samples. This has to do with how the returned recordset is formatted. The phrase FOR XML tells the ISAPI extension to return XML markup. More importantly, it sets up the **mode** in which the XML markup is returned. The structure of the FOR clause is:

```
FOR | [XML mode [, schema] [, ELEMENTS]]
```

Where `mode` denotes how the XML is structured, `schema` is an option for requesting the DTD or schema to which the returned markup conforms, and `ELEMENTS` controls how columns are marked up.

The mode parameter must take one of the following values:

- ❑ RAW
- ❑ AUTO
- ❑ EXPLICIT

Let's take a look at these different options.

RAW Mode

In RAW mode, each row of the recordset is represented as a row element. The columns of the recordset are attributes on the row element. This results in a generic, flat representation of the recordset. Thus, the sample query we showed earlier:

```
http://myserver/pubs_db?sql=SELECT * FROM authors FOR XML RAW
```

results in the following XML:

```
<?xml version="1.0" encoding="UTF-8" ?>
<root>
    <row au__id="172-32-1176" au__lname="White" au__fname="Johnson"
         phone="408 496-7223" address="10932 Bigge Rd." city="Menlo Park"
         state="CA" zip="94025" contract="1" />. . .
```

AUTO Mode

Sometimes we want more structure in the XML document that is returned. This is particularly true if the consumer of the data is a COM component rather than a web browser. In this case, we would use AUTO mode:

```
http://myserver/pubs_db?sql=SELECT * FROM authors FOR XML AUTO
```

in this results:

```
<?xml version="1.0" encoding="UTF-8" ?>
<root>
    <authors au__id="172-32-1176" au__lname="White" au__fname="Johnson"
            phone="408 496-7223" address="10932 Bigge Rd." city="Menlo Park"
            state="CA" zip="94025" contract="1" />. . .
```

How do the rows get named in AUTO mode? Each table in the query from which at least one column is retrieved becomes an element. Nesting is based on the relationship between the tables. For example, we wanted to get year to date sales information by author from the pubs database, so we might use the following SQL statement:

```
http://myserver/pubs_db?sql=SELECT au_fname, au_lname, title, ytd_sales FROM
titles
        INNER JOIN (authors INNER JOIN titleauthor on
authors.au_id=titleauthor.au_id)
        ON titles.title_id=titleauthor.title_id FOR XML AUTO
```

We're selecting columns from the author and titles tables. Authors and titles have a one-to-many relationship, so titles elements are children of authors elements. The attributes of each element are the columns drawn from the underlying table:

```
<?xml version="1.0" encoding="UTF-8" ?>
<root>
    . . .
    <authors au__fname="Marjorie" au__lname="Green">
        <titles title="The Busy Executive's Database Guide" ytd__sales="4095" />
        <titles title="You Can Combat Computer Stress!" ytd__sales="18722" />
    </authors>
    . . .
</root>
```

EXPLICIT Mode

The EXPLICIT mode is a more complex construction, but one which affords the query author the maximum control over the structure of the returned XML document. This mode allows the query designer complete control over the structure and nomenclature of the recordset XML document at the cost of taking total responsibility for the validity of that structure.

A recordset in this mode is augmented with two columns of meta data which the tool uses to define the structure of the XML document. The first column, Tag, consists of an integer denoting the level of the element. The other column, Parent, also consists of an integer. The value of the Parent column must be the level that is the immediate parent of the current element. Any row whose Parent value is NULL denotes elements that are the immediate children of the root element.

Consider a query that would return all titles of the pubs database by the publisher. We want the data returned as Publisher elements with Book children:

```
<?xml version="1.0" encoding="UTF-8" ?>
<root>
   <Publisher pubName="Algodata Infosystems">
      <Book title="The Busy Executive's Database Guide" />
      <Book title="Cooking with Computers: Surreptitious Balance Sheets" />
      <Book title="Straight Talk About Computers" />
      <Book title="But Is It User Friendly?" />
      <Book title="Secrets of Silicon Valley" />
      <Book title="Net Etiquette" />
   </Publisher>
   . . .
```

Apart from renaming the elements, this isn't very different from the structure we'd get if we used the AUTO mode. Let's consider the structure in terms of the XML tree:

A table in this format is called a **universal table**. The metadata columns – Tag and Parent – provide the linkage between levels, while the data that corresponds to the elements at the particular levels are organized into separate rows in a parent-child relationship.

How Do We Obtain a Universal Table?

We need to communicate some information in the query in a form that the XML SQL tool will recognize. First, we need to create the metadata columns. Next, we need to provide names for the columns in a form that allows the SQL Server to create the appropriate element names. Finally, we need to provide a SQL query that will give us the structure of a universal table.

The vehicle for providing the first two pieces of information is the column name. Column names are composed in the following form:

```
Element_name!Level_num!Item_name!Directive
```

The components of this form are provided according to the following table:

Component	Meaning
Element_name	Name of the resulting element.
Level_num	Integer denoting the level of nesting, i.e., 1 for immediate children of the root, 2 for their children, etc. This is the value that must appear in the Tag column of the universal table.
Item_name	Name of the attribute or element containing the data column. If Directive does not appear, the column will appear as an attribute of the element named by Element_name, otherwise, Item_name becomes a child element of Element_name whose textual content is the data.
Directive	An optional directive controlling how data columns are displayed.

For example, if we want the pub_name column to appear as the pubName attribute of a Publisher element, as in the example we used earlier, and the Publisher element is an immediate child of the root element, then the name for the pub_name column must be:

```
Publisher!1!pubName
```

This is the simplest form; the Directive component does not appear. Before considering the contents of the Directive component, let's look at the SQL needed to generate the universal table for our sample XML document. All such queries consist of a UNION of two queries. The first sets up the meta data columns:

```
SELECT 1 as Tag, NULL as Parent,
    publishers.pub_name as [Publisher!1!pubName], NULL as [Book!2!title]
    FROM publishers
```

This gives us a resultset consisting of the columns Tag, Parent, Publisher!1!pubName, and Book!2!Title. Note that the query returns rows with 1 in the Tag column, NULL in the Parent column, and pub_name in the Publisher!1!pubName column. The remaining column, which we shall need for book titles, is empty, as we would expect rows that will be used to populate the Publisher level of the XML document tree.

Next, we need to retrieve the book title information. We also need the publisher names to perform the UNION properly:

```
SELECT 2, 1,
    publishers.pub_name, titles.title
    FROM publishers, titles
    WHERE titles.pub_id = publishers.pub_id
```

Note that 2 becomes the value of the Tag column, 1 is the value of its Parent, and the data we want goes into the remaining columns. Now we put it all together with the UNION keyword and add an ORDER BY clause to organize the universal table. The complete SQL statement is:

```
SELECT 1 as Tag, NULL as Parent,
    publishers.pub_name as [Publisher!1!pubName], NULL as [Book!2!title]
    FROM publishers
UNION ALL
SELECT 2, 1,
    publishers.pub_name, titles.title
    FROM publishers, titles
    WHERE titles.pub_id = publishers.pub_id
    ORDER BY [Publisher!1!pubName] FOR XML EXPLICIT
```

As noted, all that this query did differently from what the equivalent query in AUTO mode did was to rename the elements. If we want to do more, we have to explore the values permitted for the Directive component.

Directive Value	Meaning
ID	Causes the named attribute to be of type ID; no effect unless DTD or XMLDATA is specified in schema option.
IDREF	Causes the named attribute to be of type IDREF; no effect unless DTD or XMLDATA is specified in schema option.
IDREFS	Causes the named attribute to be of type IDREFS; no effect unless DTD or XMLDATA is specified in schema option.
hide	Attribute will not be displayed; useful for ordering by an attribute that does not appear in the final result.
element	Causes the data item to be generated as a child element rather than an attribute of the parent; content is rendered as an entity to preserve characters reserved by XML.
xml	Like element, except textual content is not rendered as an entity.
cdata	Renders the data item as a CDATA section; item must be a text database type. This directive may not be combined with any other directive, and Item_name should not appear, e.g., Book!2!!cdata.
xmltext	Causes column content to be wrapped in a single tag that will be integrated within a document; useful in fetching overflow XML data stored in a column by OPENXML.

With the Directive component available to us, we can begin to modify the structure the XML SQL tool returns to us. For example, we can use the element directive value to force an item to be returned as an element rather than an attribute. Here's our preceding query with titles.title rendered as an element and the title_id added:

```
SELECT 1 as Tag, NULL as Parent,
    publishers.pub_name as [Publisher!1!pubName],
    NULL as [Book!2!Title!element],
    NULL as [Book!2!title_id]
    FROM publishers
UNION ALL SELECT 2, 1,
    publishers.pub_name,
    titles.title,
    titles.title_id
    FROM publishers, titles
WHERE titles.pub_id = publishers.pub_id
ORDER BY [Publisher!1!pubName] FOR XML EXPLICIT
```

Note that while title becomes the Title child element of Book, its Tag value is still 1. It is being treated as a single construct, much as an attribute is treated. Even though the generated element resides at a lower level, we are specifying it at the same level of detail as the attributes and any other item associated with the Book element. Here are some partial results:

```
<?xml version="1.0" encoding="UTF-8" ?>
<root>
    <Publisher pubName="Algodata Infosystems">
        <Book title_id="BU1032">
            <Title>The Busy Executive's Database Guide</Title>
        </Book>
        . . .
```

XML has its own facility for handling relationships within a document. It provides three attribute types – ID, IDREF and IDREFS – to associate two or more elements. The value of an ID type attribute is an identifying key unique to the document's scope. If the same value is used for an IDREF attribute, the element possessing that attribute points back at the first element. The value of an IDREFS attribute is a series of one or more ID values delimited by whitespace.

IDREFS models the singular end of a one-to-many relationship by pointing back at all the elements whose ID attribute value is found in the IDREFS value. We can also impose ID and IDREF constraints on attributes when posing a SQL query. If this is set, we can use methods in an XML parser to trace various relationships in the completed document. Here's a version of the query that uses publishers.pub_id as an ID and titles.pub_id as an IDREF:

```
SELECT 1 as Tag, NULL as Parent,
    publishers.pub_id as [Publisher!1!pubID!id],
    NULL as [Book!2!title],
    NULL as [Book!2!titleID],
    NULL as [Book!2!pubID!idref]FROM publishers
UNION ALL SELECT 2, 1,
    publishers.pub_id,
    titles.title,
    titles.title_id,
    titles.pub_id
FROM publishers, titles
WHERE titles.pub_id = publishers.pub_id
ORDER BY [Publisher!1!pubID!ID] FOR XML EXPLICIT
```

Here's a partial result:

```
<?xml version="1.0" encoding="UTF-8" ?>
<root>
<Publisher pubID="0736">
    <Book title="You Can Combat Computer Stress!" titleID="BU2075" pubID="0736" />
    . . .
```

There's a slight problem here – there is no mention of ID and IDREF. In fact, the partial result gives no indication that we used the ID and IDREF directive values. The problem is that these constraints are imposed in the DTD or schema that governs the document. In the next section we will see how to obtain this meta data in a returned XML document.

Whether this is a problem or not, depends on which parser we use to manipulate the returned document and how we use it. The XML 1.0 Recommendation requires a parser to implement this feature, but does not specify how. In Microsoft's parser, MSXML, we typically handle this by calling the getNodes or getSingleNode methods with a pattern that looks for the IDREF/IDREFs value. This does not depend on meta data, so we could leave off the directive and obtain the same result. Strictly speaking, though, we should communicate our intentions with these directives so that parsers have as much information as possible.

Special XML Structural Settings

There are a few miscellaneous settings that may be useful to us. We might want the DTD or schema that describes the XML document. If we include the keyword DTD in the FOR clause, an internal DTD will be generated for the XML document. The sample query becomes:

```
http://myserver/pubs?sql=SELECT * FROM authors FOR XML AUTO, DTD
```

which results in the following document:

```
<?xml version="1.0" encoding="UTF-8" ?>
<!DOCTYPE root [
   <!ELEMENT root (authors)*>
   <!ELEMENT authors EMPTY>
   <!ATTLIST authors au__id CDATA #IMPLIED
                     au__lname CDATA #IMPLIED
                     au__fname CDATA #IMPLIED
                     phone CDATA #IMPLIED
                     address CDATA #IMPLIED
                     city CDATA #IMPLIED
                     state CDATA #IMPLIED
                     zip CDATA #IMPLIED
                     contract CDATA #IMPLIED>]>
<root>
   . . .
```

We can also get an XML schema to describe the document. The schema is written to the nonstandard
XML – Data Reduced (XML-DR) format previewed by Microsoft in the XML parser that shipped with
IE5. Since that format is a subset of the XML Data proposal, the keyword is XMLDATA and the query
URL becomes:

```
http://myserver/pubs?sql=SELECT * FROM authors FOR XML AUTO, XMLDATA
```

resulting in an embedded schema:

```
<?xml version="1.0" encoding="UTF-8" ?>
<root>
   <Schema xmlns="urn:schemas-microsoft-com:xml-data"
           xmlns:dt="urn:schemas-microsoft-com:datatypes">
   <ElementType name="authors" content="textOnly" model="closed">
      <AttributeType name="au__id" dt:type="string" />
      <AttributeType name="au__lname" dt:type="string" />
      <AttributeType name="au__fname" dt:type="string" />
      <AttributeType name="phone" dt:type="string" />
      <AttributeType name="address" dt:type="string" />
      <AttributeType name="city" dt:type="string" />
      <AttributeType name="state" dt:type="string" />
      <AttributeType name="zip" dt:type="string" />
      <AttributeType name="contract" dt:type="boolean" />
      <attribute type="au__id" required="no" />
      <attribute type="au__lname" required="no" />
      <attribute type="au__fname" required="no" />
      <attribute type="phone" required="no" />
      <attribute type="address" required="no" />
      <attribute type="city" required="no" />
      <attribute type="state" required="no" />
      <attribute type="zip" required="no" />
      <attribute type="contract" required="no" />
   </ElementType>
   </Schema>
      <authors . . .
```

A validating parser should accept the DTD form and perform validation without complaint. The IE5 parser, MSXML, won't automatically accept the schema form for validation, so some manipulation will be necessary. For more on validating documents using the XML-DR format, see Professional XML, ISBN 1-861003-11-0, also from Wrox Press.

So far we've seen the recordset columns returned as attributes on an element corresponding to a database table. We can also instruct the XML SQL ISAPI extension to return the columns as child elements. To do this, we specify the ELEMENTS keyword after the format mode (and the schema option if it appears):

```
http://myserver/pubs/sql=select * FROM authors FOR XML AUTO, ELEMENTS
```

This results in the following document:

```
<?xml version="1.0" encoding="UTF-8" ?>
<root>
    <authors>
        <au_id>172-32-1176</au_id>
        <au_lname>White</au_lname>
        <au_fname>Johnson</au_fname>
        <phone>408 496-7223</phone>
        <address>10932 Bigge Rd.</address>
        <city>Menlo Park</city>
        <state>CA</state>
        <zip>94025</zip>
        <contract>1</contract>
    </authors>. . .
```

Note how the column names are child elements rather than attributes of the authors element.

Parameters

We can also pass parameters to a query just as we would in any normal SQL statement. Suppose we wanted to find all the titles in the pubs database published by Algodata InfoSystems. This publisher has the pub_id value 1389. The query, using a parameter for the pub_id, would be:

```
http://myserver/pubs?sql=SELECT titles.title, publishers.pub_name FROM titles
        INNER JOIN publishers ON titles.pub_id = publishers.pub_id
        WHERE titles.pub_id=? FOR XML AUTO&pub_id=1389
```

By itself, this is inefficient – we could have specified the pub_id directly. This will become useful, however, when we get into template files, or if we want to use a parameter driven query with an HTML form.

Executing Stored Procedures

Suppose our publishers want to be able to check their year to date sales from a remote location – say, a poolside in the tropics:. A stored procedure executed from a web browser would be ideal. Assume our system administrator has created a stored procedure, YTDsales, that retrieves authors, titles, and year to date figures for all authors in the pubs database. Here's the DDL for the stored procedure:

```
CREATE PROCEDURE YTDsales AS
    SELECT authors.au_fname, authors.au_lname, titles.title, titles.ytd_sales
    FROM titles INNER JOIN (authors INNER JOIN titleauthor
    ON authors.au_id=titleauthor.au_id) ON titles.title_id=titleauthor.title_id
```

The URL to execute it would be:

```
http://myserver/pubs?sql=execute YTDsales FOR XML AUTO
```

Note how the keyword `execute` replaces `SELECT`. The query above covers all publishers. Suppose, however, we wanted to restrict the query to a particular publisher. We call our system administrator and ask him to add a parameter to the query as follows:

```
CREATE PROCEDURE YTDbyPub @pubID char(4) AS
    SELECT authors.au_fname, authors.au_lname, titles.title, titles.ytd_sales
    FROM titles INNER JOIN (authors INNER JOIN titleauthor
    ON authors.au_id=titleauthor.au_id) ON titles.title_id=titleauthor.title_id
WHERE
    titles.pub_id = @pubID
```

Remembering that the `pub_id` for Algodata InfoSystems is 1389, the URL becomes:

```
http://w2ktest/pubs?sql=execute YTDbyPUB @pubID="1389" FOR XML AUTO
```

Here we've explicitly named the parameter for which we are furnishing a value. We could also have relied on its position in the stored procedure. Since there is only one parameter in this procedure, we could have written the URL in the following form with no ambiguity:

```
http://w2ktest/pubs?sql=execute YTDbyPUB "1389" FOR XML AUTO
```

If there is more than one parameter in the stored procedure, the parameter values replace the parameters in the order in which they appear, the first parameter value in the URL replacing the first parameter in the stored procedure, and so forth. Note that these are parameters and values in the sense of SQL, not HTTP. The parameter name is prefaced with the @ character, not an ampersand (&), and it is separated from the name of the stored procedure by a space (or %20 or + once prepared for HTTP).

Limitations on the FOR XML Clause

The `FOR XML` clause is a flexible extension to SQL, but it has limits. It can only be used, practically speaking, on the outermost `SELECT` statement. It is not valid with `INSERT`, `UPDATE`, or `DELETE` statements, and it will not work with a `SELECT` statement that includes a `COMPUTE BY` clause. The `FOR XML` clause is basically an extension that post processes SQL output into XML. Mixing it into clauses within a `SELECT` statement will not work because XML SQL does not parse out such clauses. SQL Server would receive these clauses and reject the statement.

Template Files

URL queries are useful for ad hoc access, but we can't expect our users to type in such URLs. We might make such URLs the target of hyperlinks, but a better way is to keep our queries to ourselves. Our users want access, not SQL text. A technique we can use for this is to make use of the **template file**. Such files contain one or more canned queries that may be executed by naming the file that contains them. Template files offer several advantages:

❑ Queries are controlled on the server, permitting database schema changes to be accommodated with a single change.

❑ Updates can be made from template files, allowing DELETE, UPDATE, and INSERT statements.

❑ Template files can be combined with HTML forms and parameters to encapsulate database access logic.

Basic Template Files

A template file is an XML document written according to a specific vocabulary. Such files consist of a root element containing one or more query elements drawn from the namespace denoted by urn:schemas-microsoft-com:xml-sql. Here is the general form:

```
<root xmlns:sql="urn:schemas-microsoft-com:xml-sql">
    <sql:query name1="value1" name2="value2" ...>SQL statement here</sql:query>
    . . .
</root>
```

The named attributes are optionally included to pass parameters into the SQL statement contained in the query element. Template files are an exception to the rule about not including content in the physical folder that implements our virtual directory. We place the following file in the pubs directory and name it allauthors.xml:

```
<?xml version="1.0"?>
<root xmlns:sql="urn:schemas-microsoft-com:xml-sql">
    <sql:query>select * from authors FOR XML AUTO</sql:query>
</root>
```

Now we request the URL http://myserver/pubs/allauthors.xml. We will see the same recordset returned that we would have expected had we issued the query in the URL itself.

Another benefit of template files is that any ODBC errors that result from a template file query will be returned in the body of the XML document. If we are having trouble getting a URL query to work, we can write it as a template file and call it to see the error message.

Executing Stored Procedures from a Template File

Let's execute our YTDSales stored procedure from a template file:

```
<?xml version="1.0"?>
<root xmlns:sql="urn:schemas-microsoft-com:xml-sql">
    <sql:query>exec YTDSales FOR XML AUTO</sql:query>
</root>
```

Name this file YTD.xml and place it in the pubs virtual directory. When requested, we get the same result as when we executed it from a URL query.

Parameters in Template Files

Let's invoke the YTDbyPub stored procedure for a template file. Here is the XML document saved as YTDbyPub.xml:

```
<?xml version="1.0"?>
<root xmlns:sql="urn:schemas-microsoft-com:xml-sql">
    <sql:query pubID="1389">exec YTDbyPub ? FOR XML AUTO</sql:query>
</root>
```

If we call it without an explicit parameter, the default value of 1389 is used and we see the results for that publisher. If instead we pass in a parameter by name

```
http://myserver/pubs/ytdbypub.xml?pubID=0736
```

we get the results for New Moon Books. What if we want to pass multiple parameters to a stored procedure or query requiring parameters? Try the following template file, `TwoQueries.xml`:

```
<?xml version="1.0"?>
<root xmlns:sql="urn:schemas-microsoft-com:xml-sql">
    <sql:query pubID="1389">exec YTDbyPub ? FOR XML AUTO</sql:query>
    <sql:query zip="94705">select * from authors where zip= ? FOR XML
AUTO</sql:query>
</root>
```

This template has two queries, one to execute the parameter driven YTD stored procedure and one that is a SQL SELECT statement that includes a zip code parameter for authors. If we execute it with no parameters – `http://myserver/pubs/TwoQueries.xml` – we get an XML document that combines the two resultsets, one after the other within the root element. We can explicitly pass in one or both parameters with a URL like this:

```
http://myserver/pubs/TwoQueries.xml?pubID=0736&zip=97330
```

HTML Forms and Templates

Template files don't need to live on disk on the server. We can embed them in an HTML form to provide dynamic access to a canned query. The text of the template file is placed in a hidden element named template. Another hidden element has the name contenttype and the value text/xml (or text/html if we choose to style the template's results with XSL). Any parameters in the SQL statement are filled by providing an input element whose name is the name of the parameter. When the ISAPI extension receives a POST, it matches the posted values with the template to get a template file execution.

Here is the source for the html file `form_template.html`. It retrieves year to date and advance figures for an author when given his ID. Note that the target of the form is the pubs virtual directory. The ISAPI directory determines what to execute based on the posted fields.

```
. . .
<BODY>
Enter an author ID and retrieve advance payments and YTD sales for the author.
<FORM action="http://w2ktest/pubs" method="POST" id=form1 name=form1>
    <FONT face=Verdana>
    <B>Author ID:</B>
    <INPUT style="LEFT: 9px; TOP: 15px" name="au_id" id="au_id">
    <INPUT type="hidden" name="contenttype" value="text/xml">
    <INPUT type="hidden" name="template" value = '
        <root>
        <sql:query xmlns:sql="urn:schemas-microsoft-com:xml-sql" au_id="1">
            SELECT authors.au_fname,
                   authors.au_lname,
                   titles.advance,
                   titles.ytd_sales
            FROM (authors INNER JOIN titleauthor
                  ON authors.au_id = titleauthor.au_id)
```

```
            INNER JOIN titles ON titleauthor.title_id = titles.title_id
            WHERE authors.au_id=? FOR XML AUTO</sql:query>
       </root>'></P>
   <P><INPUT type="submit" value="Submit"></P></FONT>
 </FORM>
 </BODY>
 . . .
```

Caching Template Results

A common use for templates is to provide standard database reports. It is highly likely in this type of usage that we will have many users wishing to view the exact same results. For this reason, SQL XML Meta Data Sevices can cache the results of template file execution. If we have performed XSL formatting on the server, the results will be retained as HTML. If our template returned XML, that is what remains in memory.

Caching is implemented through a processing instruction inserted in the template file immediately following the XML declaration. The syntax for this instruction is:

```
<?servercache [cache-timeframe="hh:mm:ss" |
               cache-time-point="hh:mm:ss" |
               cache-forever]?>
```

The meaning of the attributes is as follows:

Attribute	Meaning
cache-timeframe	Output is cached for the specified duration, for example, cache for ten minutes: cache-timeframe="00:10:00"
cache-timepoint	Output is cached until the specified time, for example, cache until 8:00 AM: cache-timepoint="08:00:00"
cache-forever	Output is cached until IIS, or the IIS application, is restarted.

There are a few behavioral points of which we should be aware. The duration or timepoint must be expressed in hh:mm:ss format, for example, we cannot leave off the hours or seconds if we specify a caching duration of some number of minutes. Cached output is only refreshed when a new request comes in outside the caching boundary. If the cache expires, but no request for the results is received, the ISAPI extension does not make any requests of the SQL Server. This makes sense, when we think about it. An ISAPI extension cannot initiate any activity of its own without some cumbersome time out mechanism, and we don't want the load on the database unless we actually need results. Caching, obviously consumes memory on the HTTP server. There is not yet any administrative or automatic means of releasing this memory other than restarting IIS or the web application.

Database Updates

We can do more than just query for results. We can also perform UPDATE, DELETE, and INSERT statements from a template file. This is not done, as we might expect, by simply writing a SQL statement of this form and using it as the text of a URL query or template file. Instead, it is accomplished with XML documents termed **update grams**. An update gram is similar in spirit to a template file in that it usually resides on the server, it is an XML document, and elements within the document control the generation of SQL commands that result in XML output.

Update Gram Structure

Rather than trying to compose a single SQL command that identifies a row we wish to update and changes it, an **update gram** uses a `before` element to identify the rows to be changed, and an `after` element to perform the change itself. Here is the form of an update gram XML document:

```
<root xmlns:sql="urn:schemas-microsoft-com:xml-sql">
    <sql:sync>
        <sql:before>
            . . .
        </sql:before>
        <sql:after>
            . . .
        </sql:after>
    </sql:sync>
</root>
```

We have a `sync` element with a `before` element and an `after` element, as mentioned. The entire `sync` element is processed as a single transaction. The `before` and `after` elements are optional, depending on what we want to do. Both have element only child content that is not part of the XML SQL namespace but whose form is as follows:

```
<Table [sql:id="value" | sql:at-identity="value"] col="value" . . . col="value"/>
```

`Table` is the name of the SQL Server table to modify. If we want to update the `authors` table, we need to have one or more `authors` elements inside our `before` and `after` elements. The `col` attribute is the name of a database table column, and `value` is the data we want to locate or modify.

The `id` and `at-identity` attributes are provided for use with identity columns. Such columns have values provided by the system. The `id` attribute lets us mark a position. For example, if we want to update a row and the primary key changes, we would include `id` attributes in the `before` and `after` elements. The value of the attribute is an arbitrary placeholder. The `at-identity` attribute is used to retrieve the latest value of an identity column. For example, if an identity column were a foreign key into another table, we would use `at-identity` to retrieve the value of that column in the table to which the foreign key points, then specify the value as part of the update to the table where it is used.

Inserting Rows

Our favorite publisher, Wrox Press, does not appear in the `publishers` table of the `pubs` database. Let's use an update gram to rectify this grievous error. An `INSERT` is specified with a `sync` element that has no `before` element. Here's the source of the update gram.

```
<root xmlns:sql="urn:schemas-microsoft-com:xml-sql">
    <sql:sync>
        <sql:after>
            <publishers pub_id="9900" pub_name="Wrox Press" city="Birmingham"
            country="UK" />
        </sql:after>
    </sql:sync>
    <sql:query>select * from publishers for xml auto</sql:query>
</root>
```

Within the `after` element, we have a single `publishers` element, telling the ISAPI extension we want to insert a row into the `publishers` table. The attributes of this element are column names in the table.

> *Note especially the value of the `pub_name` attribute. The only attribute type that can accept embedded spaces is IDREFS. Apparently, the ISAPI extension uses this to allow us to update textual columns. In addition, we need to use a double underscore in the `pub_id` and `pub_name` attributes.*

A `query` element also appears. This is not required, but it is not prohibited, either. It is a useful way for us to check the results of the insertion.

> *You may have noticed that 9900 isn't the Wrox Press identifier which is found in the ISBN of books from Wrox. This value is required to get around a column check constraint in the pubs database.*

Updating Rows

An update gram that modifies an existing row uses both the `before` and `after` elements. Unfortunately, there are some limitations on the `before` element. Columns of database type `text`, `ntext`, `image`, `binary`, and `varbinary` are not supported in the before element. This precludes us from updating the Wrox entry directly; we would have to delete it and re-insert it with the new information.

Suppose, however, we decided that the position of Chief Executive Officer was being filled with insufficiently experienced people. This is controlled by the `jobs` table; specifically, the `min_lvl` field of the `jobs` table. Upon creation, the minimum level is 200. Let's increase that to 210:

```
<root xmlns:sql="urn:schemas-microsoft-com:xml-sql">
   <sql:sync>
      <sql:before>
         <jobs job__id="2" />
      </sql:before>
      <sql:after>
         <jobs job__id="2" min__lvl="210" />
      </sql:after>
   </sql:sync>
   <sql:query>select * from jobs for xml auto</sql:query>
</root>
```

The `job_id` column is typed as a numeric, so we can use it in the `before` element. In the `after` element, we use the same `job_id` (that is 2) and specify the new `min_lvl` value. As before, we issue a select statement to check the results of our transaction.

Deleting Rows

Deleting a row or rows consists of locating elements in the `before` element but not including them in the `after` element. A simple deletion would thus consist of a `sync` element with a `before` element and no `after` element. Here's what we need to do to delete Wrox Press from the database:

```
<root xmlns:sql="urn:schemas-microsoft-com:xml-sql">
   <sql:sync>
      <sql:before>
         <publishers pub__id="9900"/>
      </sql:before>
      <sql:after>
      </sql:after>
   </sql:sync>
      <sql:query>select * from publishers for xml auto</sql:query>
</root>
```

879

Although it would appear that we can mix operations – say, adding a modification in with the deletion – errors may result. It is best to keep our database operations distinct.

Multiple Operations

Fortunately, XML SQL lets us combine multiple operations into one XML document. Removing Wrox Press from the `publishers` table doesn't seem like a very good idea to us.

Suppose we want to restore Wrox to the `publishers` table, reset the CEO's minimum level to 200, but also want to increase the maximum level for the lowly editors up to 250. We could do this in the following way.

The XML file `multiple_ops.xml` combines operations in two ways. First, we'll have two `sync` elements. The first transaction will restore Wrox to the `publishers` table. Next, we'll have another `sync` element that updates multiple rows: one to reset the CEO (job_id="2") and one to modify the editors (job_id="12"). Here's what it looks like:

```
<root xmlns:sql="urn:schemas-microsoft-com:xml-sql">
   <sql:sync>
      <sql:after>
         <publishers pub_id="9900" pub_name="Wrox Press"
                     city="Birmingham" country="UK" />
      </sql:after>
   </sql:sync>
   <sql:sync>
      <sql:before>
         <jobs job_id="2" />
         <jobs job_id="12"/>
      </sql:before>
      <sql:after>
         <jobs job_id="2" min_lvl="200" />
         <jobs job_id="12" max_lvl="250" />
      </sql:after>
   </sql:sync>
   <sql:query>select * from publishers for xml auto</sql:query>
   <sql:query>select * from jobs for xml auto</sql:query>
</root>
```

We can combine the capability to work on multiple rows, with the `at-identity` attribute to add rows with foreign keys whose value is assigned by the system. In the `jobs` table, the `job_id` column is an identity column. If we want to add an employee, we need the `job_id` as a foreign key. This poses a problem if a newly hired employee is assigned to a newly created position. The `at-identity` attribute solves the problem by retrieving the value assigned for later use. Let's test this by hiring the CEO's nephew:

```
<root xmlns:sql="urn:schemas-microsoft-com:xml-sql">
   <sql:sync>
      <sql:after>
         <jobs sql:at-identity="x" job_desc="CEO nephew"
               min_lvl="10" max_lvl="100"/>
         <employee emp_id="ABC12345M" fname="Tony" lname="Davis"
                   job_id="x" job_lvl="50" pub_id="9900" hire_date="2000-02-
03"/>
      </sql:after>
   </sql:sync>
   <sql:query>select * from jobs for xml auto</sql:query>
   <sql:query>select * from employee for xml auto</sql:query>
</root>
```

We added a new position just for this young man. The placeholder value x for the at-identity attribute in the jobs element is then used in the employee element as the value for the job_id attribute.

Formatting the Results

If you've been following through these exercises with SQL Server and IE5, you'll have seen a flurry of XML in your browser, formatted according to IE's default stylesheet for XML. That's okay for debugging, and if the consumer of the relational data is a program rather than a person, we don't care about formatting. In fact, in that case, we don't want anything getting in the way of the XML.

One of the chief uses of templates, though, is to provide users with access to common queries. That calls for styling. Because we can't count on the capabilities of the different browsers, we are better off using server-side XSL to turn our XML into HTML. In fact, if we do that, our data is accessible from more browsers than it is in raw XML format. SQL Server Meta Data Services makes things easy for us. It encapsulates the XSL features of Microsoft's parser to make recourse to XSL simple for query designers.

Examine the following template file, titles_styled.xml. It retrieves all the columns of the titles table:

```
<?xml version="1.0"?>
<?xsl-serverstylesheet xslfile="./xsl/titles.xsl" ?>
<root xmlns:sql="urn:schemas-microsoft-com:xml-sql">
    <sql:query>select * from titles FOR XML AUTO</sql:query>
</root>
```

Notice the second line. It is a preprocessor instruction, consumed by the ISAPI extension, to locate and use a separate XSL stylesheet. If we are not familiar with XSL, it is a declarative form in which we specify, often recursively, rules for the transformation of XML into some other XML form. Each rule consists of a pattern against which the rule must match – some combination of context and element name – and a specification for output. The xslfile attribute of the processing instruction has as its value a relative path to the XSL stylesheet. This path must be below the virtual root in which the template file is found for security reasons – we'd hardly want to access a template file in one application and have it point to a stylesheet in another application!

Here is the stylesheet we used:

```
<?xml version="1.0"?>

<xsl:stylesheet xmlns:xsl="http://www.w3.org/TR/WD-xsl">

    <xsl:template match="/">
        <xsl:for-each select="root">
        <HTML><HEAD/><BODY>
            <xsl:apply-templates />
        </BODY></HTML>
        </xsl:for-each>
    </xsl:template>

    <xsl:template match="titles">
        <DIV style="background:red; color:white;font-family:Verdana; font-
size:12pt">
            <xsl:value-of select="@title"/>
        </DIV>
```

```
        <DIV style="font-family:Verdana">
            Price: $<xsl:value-of select="@price"/>  YTD Sales:
                    <xsl:value-of select="@ytd_sales"/>
                    <xsl:value-of select="@price"/></DIV>
        <DIV style="font-family:Verdana; color:blue">
            <xsl:value-of select="@notes"/>
        </DIV>
        <P/>
    </xsl:template>

</xsl:stylesheet>
```

A complete explanation of the syntax and functioning of the rules we see here is beyond the scope of this chapter. Basically, though, when the XSL processor matches against the root of the XML document, it generates the shell of an HTML document, then proceeds to lower levels of the XML. When it matches against any `titles` element, it generates HTML `DIV` elements with style attributes that provide nice formatting of the desired attribute values found in the XML. Note that the HTML generated is therefore a subset of the XML data retrieved from the database; we've stripped out information we don't want to present.

> *Complete information on XSL in general and its implementation in the IE5 parser may be found in Professional XML (Wrox, 2000, ISBN 1-861003-11-0) and XML in IE5 Programmer's Reference (Wrox, 1999, ISBN 1-861001-57-6).*

Here is the result of the transformation:

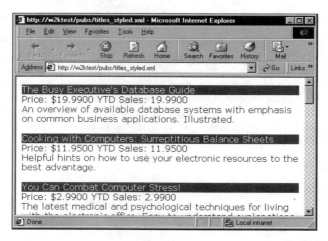

The combination of template files and XSL stylesheets is a productive way for us to handle user requests for common database reports. We manage the SQL in one file and the styling rules in another. Either can be modified separately, and no programming is required.

XML and Oracle

XML support in Oracle is provided through the **XML SQL Utility**, a set of special components which allow us to retrieve an XML document from the database by executing a SQL query, and to update a database by parsing an XML document.

The XML SQL Utility

The XML SQL Utitlity (often abbreviated to XSU) can be downloaded from Oracle's TechNet site at:

```
http://technet.oracle.com/software/tech/xml/oracle_xsu/software_index.htm
```

The Windows version of the utility can be downloaded as a single Zip file, named `XSU12_ver1_2_1.zip` (for XSU 12), or `XSU12_ver1_1_1.zip` (for version XSU 111). To install the XSU, extract all the files from this Zip archive. This will create a directory named by default `C:\OracleXSU12` (for XSU 12), which contains the installation files, documentation files and samples.

XSU Components

The XSU consists of three separate components:

- ❑ A client-side front end. This is a command line utility which acts as a front end to the XSU.

- ❑ A Java API, for access to the XSU from Java programs.

- ❑ A PL/SQL API, which allows us to use the XSU from within PL/SQL (for example, in stored procedures).

We won't look at the first two of these components in depth, because they may not be particularly useful for ASP developers. Since the front end is command line based, it cannot be used from an ASP application, although it is useful for testing. The Java API will be useful if you call Oracle stored procedures from your ASP application, but otherwise it is more likely to be used by JSP developers than ASP programmers.

Setting up the XSU

To use the XSU, we need to have certain components already installed. The actual components we need installed on the machine, vary according to whether we are using that machine as a client or as the database server. If the same machine is serving both as a client and server (for example, if the web server and database server are on the same machine, or if we are developing on a single test machine), then of course, all the components must be installed.

	XSU 12	XSU 111
Client-side	Java JDK 1.2.x or later.	JDK 1.1.x or later.
	Oracle's JDBC 2.0-compliant drivers.	Oracle's JDBC 1.x-compliant drivers.
	Oracle XML parser v. 2+	Oracle XML parser v. 2+
Server-side	Oracle 8.1.6 or later.	Oracle 8.1.5
	Oracle XML parser v. 2+	Oracle XML parser v. 2+

The Oracle XML parser is installed with the XSU itself; and the JDK (Java Developer's Kit), and Oracle JDBC (Java DataBase Connectivity) drivers are installed with Oracle.

The installation itself is simply a matter of running a couple of scripts which are supplied with the XSU. To enable the command line front end and Java API on the client, run the `env.bat` batch file in the XSU's install directory (e.g. `C:\OracleXSU12`). If you didn't install the XSU or Oracle to the default directory, then you may have to edit the file to ensure all the directories are correct.

To install the Java and PL/SQL APIs on the database server, we just need to run the `oraclexmlsqlload.bat` file (installed by default to the `lib` directory of the XSU directory, for example `C:\OracleXSU12\lib\oraclexmlsqlload.bat`). The only alteration we need to make to this file is the username – password pair, which is set at the start of the file:

```
set USER_PASSWORD="scott/tiger"
```

This batch file performs four tasks:

❏ It installs the Oracle XML parser. If this is already installed, we can comment out the line:

```
call loadjava -r -v -u %USER_PASSWORD% xmlparserv2.jar
```

❏ It loads the classes for the XSU's Java API into the database.

❏ It installs the PL/SQL API on top of the Java API.

❏ It tests that the PL/SQL API has correctly installed.

The xmlgen Package

Now that we've got the XSU installed, it's time to see what we can do with it. As we said above, we'll restrict ourselves to the PL/SQL API, since that is the component that is most likely to be useful to an ASP developer.

The PL/SQL API is essentially a wrapper which sits on top of the Java API, and consists of a single Oracle package called `xmlgen`. This package contains too many functions to go through each one, so we will look instead at how we can accomplish the most important tasks using the XSU, and see how we can use these features from an ASP application.

Retrieving an XML Document From the Database

The most common Oracle/XML task will probably be to retrieve a recordset in XML format as a result of a database query. True, we can do this easily enough with ADO – as we saw in the previous chapter – but the structure of ADO XML recordsets is hardly intuitive. Fortunately, Oracle allows us to retrieve far more intuitively structured XML documents from a database using the `getXML` function of the `xmlgen` package. The syntax for this function is:

```
XMLDoc := xmlgen.getXML(sql_statement, [meta_type])
```

Where:

Name	Data Type	Description
XMLDoc	CLOB	The generated XML document.
sql_statement	varchar	The query which will be used to generate the XML document.
meta_type	number	Optional. Specifies whether a DTD is to be generated with the XML document.

The following stored procedure illustrates the use of this function. In this procedure, we will simply pass a hard-coded SQL query into getXML and return the generated XML document as a varchar output parameter:

```
CREATE OR REPLACE PROCEDURE spGetEmpXml
(strXML OUT varchar)
AS
clobXML CLOB;
intLength integer;
BEGIN
    intLength := 4000;
    clobXML := xmlgen.getXML('SELECT * FROM EMP');
    DBMS_LOB.READ(clobXML, intLength, 1, strXML);
END;
```

The getXML function returns a CLOB (Character Large Object), rather than a varchar, so we need to convert this to a string before returning it from our procedure. To do this, PL/SQL provides the DBMS_LOB.READ method. This takes four parameters: the CLOB we wish to read from, the number of characters we want to read, the offset (the position in the CLOB where we want to start reading), and a varchar variable which will be used to hold the result. Note that the second of these parameters is in/out, so it cannot be passed in as a literal – we have to use a variable.

The getXML function returns an XML document in the following format:

```
<?xml version="1.0" ?>
<ROWSET>
    <ROW num="n">
        <column>value</column>
        <!-- an element for each column -->
    </ROW>
</ROWSET>
```

Each row in the resultset is represented by a <ROW> element in the XML document, and these are enclosed by a root <ROWSET> element. The individual <ROW> elements are identified by a num attribute. Each column is represented by an element with the same name as the column, and contains the column's value in a child text node.

Calling the Stored Procedure From ASP

Now that we've got our XML document as a stored procedure output parameter, it's a very simple job to access this via ADO from an ASP page or an ASP component. After connecting to the database, we simply create an ADO Command object, set its CommandType to adCmdStoredProc, and create a Parameter object. This should be an output parameter of type adVarChar, with a length of 4000 characters, since that's the number of characters we read from the CLOB in our stored procedure. Next, we call the Command object's Execute method to call the procedure, set Response.ContentType to "text/xml", and display the XML document. This is returned as an output parameter from our procedure, so our Parm1 Parameter object is populated when we call cmd.Execute:

```
<!-- METADATA TYPE="TypeLib"
            FILE="C:\Program Files\Common Files\System\ADO\msado15.dll" -->
<%
Set cn = Server.CreateObject("ADODB.Connection")
```

```
cn.Open "Provider=MSDAORA;Data Source=orcldb.julian_new.wrox.com;" & _
         "User ID=scott;Password=tiger"

Set cmd = Server.CreateObject("ADODB.Command")
Set cmd.ActiveConnection = cn
cmd.CommandText = "spGetEmpXML"
cmd.CommandType = adCmdStoredProc

Set Parm1 = cmd.CreateParameter("strXML", adVarChar, adParamOutput, 4000)
cmd.Parameters.Append Parm1

cmd.Execute

Response.ContentType = "text/xml"
Response.Write Parm1.Value
%>
```

When viewed in IE5+, the output from this ASP page will be:

Retrieving the DTD

Before moving on, let's just make a couple of small changes to our stored procedure so that our generated XML document contains an in-line DTD. As we saw earlier, the getXML function can take an optional parameter meta_type. If we set this to the value one, the XSU will include a DTD with the document. This DTD is automatically generated according to the structure of the data returned by the SQL query.

```
CREATE OR REPLACE PROCEDURE spGetEmpXml
(strXML OUT varchar)
AS
DTD CONSTANT NUMBER := 1;
clobXML CLOB;
intLength integer;
BEGIN
   intLength := 4000;
   clobXML := xmlgen.getXML('SELECT * FROM EMP', DTD);
   DBMS_LOB.READ(clobXML, intLength, 1, strXML);
END;
```

Alternatively, the `xmlgen` package also has a `getDTD` function, which will generate and return a DTD on its own from a supplied SQL query. This has the syntax:

```
DTD := xmlgen.getDTD(sql_statement, [with_version])
```

Where:

Name	Data Type	Description
DTD	CLOB	The generated DTD.
sql_statement	varchar	The query which will be used to generate the DTD.
with_version	number	Optional. Specifies whether the DTD is to include the XML declaration with the version information, `<?xml version = '1.0'?>`.

The following stored procedure calls this function to retrieve a DTD. The code is very similar to that for retrieving an XML document:

```
CREATE OR REPLACE PROCEDURE spGetEmpDtd
(strDTD OUT varchar)
AS
intLength integer;
clobXML CLOB;
BEGIN
    intLength := 4000;
    clobXML := xmlgen.getDTD('SELECT * FROM EMP', TRUE);
    DBMS_LOB.READ(clobXML, intLength, 1, strDTD);
END;
```

The DTD returned by this stored procedure is:

```
<?xml version = '1.0'?>
<!DOCTYPE ROWSET [
<!ELEMENT ROWSET (ROW)*>
<!ELEMENT ROW (EMPNO, ENAME?, JOB?, MGR?, HIREDATE?, SAL?, COMM?, DEPTNO?)>
<!ATTLIST ROW num CDATA #REQUIRED>
<!ELEMENT EMPNO (#PCDATA)>
<!ELEMENT ENAME (#PCDATA)>
<!ELEMENT JOB (#PCDATA)>
<!ELEMENT MGR (#PCDATA)>
<!ELEMENT HIREDATE (#PCDATA)>
<!ELEMENT SAL (#PCDATA)>
<!ELEMENT COMM (#PCDATA)>
<!ELEMENT DEPTNO (#PCDATA)>
]>
```

Inserting Rows Into the Database

Now that we've seen how to retrieve XML data from an Oracle database, you're perhaps wondering how we can use an XML file to update the database, and insert and delete rows. Again, the `xmlgen` package contains functions which allow us to do this.

To insert rows into a database table, we use the `insertXML` function. This takes an XML document and decomposes it into a row in a specified table. If the document contains elements which do not match a column name in the table, or if data integrity constraints are infringed, an error will be raised.

The syntax for `insertXML` is:

```
numRows := xmlgen.insertXML(strTableName, strXML)
```

Where:

Name	Data Type	Description
numRows	number	The number of rows successfully inserted into the database.
strTableName	varchar	The name of the table into which the rows should be inserted.
strXML	varchar	The XML document which contains the data to be inserted into the table.

So, let's have a look at a stored procedure which calls this function. We pass into the procedure two input parameters, `strTable` (the name of the table to update) and `strXML` (our XML document), which we pass directly into the function. We also have one output parameter – the number of rows inserted. This is passed directly from the return value of the function into an output parameter:

```
CREATE OR REPLACE PROCEDURE spInsertXML
(strTable IN varchar,
 strXML IN varchar,
 intRows OUT integer)
AS
BEGIN
    intRows := xmlgen.insertXML(strTable,strXML);
END;
```

An XML file for updating the `EMP` table using this procedure might look like this:

```
<ROWSET>
   <ROW num='1'>
      <EMPNO>7503</EMPNO>
      <ENAME>ROBINSON</ENAME>
      <JOB>CLERK</JOB>
      <MGR>7902</MGR>
      <HIREDATE>10/21/1980 0:0:0</HIREDATE>
      <SAL>1700</SAL>
      <DEPTNO>20</DEPTNO>
   </ROW>
</ROWSET>
```

As we stated above, there must be no elements within a `<ROW>` which do not correspond to a column in the table. Also, if we try to insert a row which infringes any constraints (for example, if we attempt to insert a row with no value for a column which is not nullable, or if we try to insert a duplicate primary key or `UNIQUE` column), an error will be raised.

The following page shows how we might call this stored procedure from an ASP page. It is similar to the previous example, but we create three parameters (two input and one output) to match the parameters of our stored procedure. We read in the XML document from a file on the server using a `TextStream` object and the `FileSystemObject`:

```
<!-- METADATA TYPE="TypeLib"
          FILE="C:\Program Files\Common Files\System\ADO\msado15.dll" -->
<%
Set cn = Server.CreateObject("ADODB.Connection")

cn.Open "Provider=MSDAORA;Data Source=orcldb.julian_new.wrox.com;" & _
        "User ID=scott;Password=tiger"

Set cmd = Server.CreateObject("ADODB.Command")
Set cmd.ActiveConnection = cn
cmd.CommandText="spInsertXML"
cmd.CommandType=adCmdStoredProc

Set objFSO = Server.CreateObject("Scripting.FileSystemObject")
Set objTStream = objFSO.OpenTextFile
                    ("C:\inetpub\wwwroot\xml\oracle\insert.xml")
strXML = objTStream.ReadAll
objTStream.Close

Set Parm1 = cmd.CreateParameter("strTable", adVarChar, adParamInput, 4000, _
                                "scott.emp")
Set Parm2 = cmd.CreateParameter("strXML", adVarChar, adParamInput, 4000, _
                                strXML)
Set Parm3 = cmd.CreateParameter("intRows", adInteger, adParamOutput)

cmd.Parameters.Append Parm1
cmd.Parameters.Append Parm2
cmd.Parameters.Append Parm3

cmd.Execute

Response.Write Parm3.Value & " rows inserted."
%>
```

Deleting Rows From the Database

If we can insert rows using an XML document, then we must be able to delete them as well; right? And, sure enough, `xmlgen` provides a `deleteXML` function which does just that. The syntax is very similar to that for `insertXML`:

```
numRows := xmlgen.insertXML(strTableName, strXML)
```

Where:

Name	Data Type	Description
numRows	number	The number of rows successfully deleted from the database.
strTableName	varchar	The name of the table from which the rows should be deleted.
strXML	varchar	The XML document which indicates which rows are to be deleted from the table.

The XML document we pass into this function acts very much like the WHERE clause in a SQL DELETE statement. We don't need to include elements for all the rows, and any rows that match the criteria we do specify will be deleted. For example, if we call this function on the EMP table with the XML document;

```
<ROWSET>
    <ROW num='1'>
        <ENAME>SMITH</ENAME>
    </ROW>
</ROWSET>
```

This will be equivalent to the SQL command:

```
DELETE FROM EMP WHERE ENAME='SMITH'
```

The following stored procedure can be used to call the deleteXML function; it is virtually identical to the spInsertXML procedure we saw earlier:

```
CREATE OR REPLACE PROCEDURE spDeleteXML
(strTable IN varchar,
 strXML IN varchar,
 intRows OUT integer)
AS
BEGIN
    intRows := xmlgen.deleteXML(strTable,strXML);
END;
```

We won't show the code for calling this procedure from an ASP page, since it's identical to the code for calling spInsertXML: all we need to do is change the name of the stored procedure that we are calling:

```
cmd.CommandText="spDeleteXML"
```

And possibly also the name of the XML file to load.

Updating the Database

So, we can use XML documents to retrieve, insert, and delete rows in the database. But can we modify existing rows with the XSU? Again, the xmlgen package provides a function (called updateXML) to meet our needs. The syntax for this function will come as no surprise either:

```
numRows := xmlgen.updateXML(strTableName, strXML)
```

Where:

Name	Data Type	Description
numRows	number	The number of rows successfully updated in the database.
strTableName	varchar	The name of the table where the rows should be updated.
strXML	varchar	The XML document which specifies which updates are to occur.

But how does the XSU know which rows to update? This is where things get a bit more complicated than the last couple of examples. Before we call this function, we must tell the XSU which columns we want to use as key columns for identifying individual records. We can add a column to the list of key columns using the `setKeyColumn` procedure;

```
xmlgen.setKeyColumn(strColumnName)
```

Where:

Name	Data Type	Description
strColumnName	varchar	The name of the column to add to the list of key columns.

If we call the `updateXML` function without specifying the key column(s), or with a value for the key column which is not found in the database, no update will occur, although no error will be generated.

We can clear the list using the `clearKeyColumnList` method:

```
xmlgen.clearKeyColumnList
```

A similar list of columns is maintained to indicate which columns should be updated. Any columns not in this list will not be updated by the `updateXML` function, even if they are included in the XML document. We can add columns to the list using the `setUpdateColumn` procedure;

```
xmlgen.setUpdateColumn(strColumnName)
```

Where:

Name	Data Type	Description
strColumnName	varchar	The name of the column to add to the list of columns that can be updated.

If a value isn't specified in the XML document for one of the update columns, it will be set to NULL. This will generate an error if the column is not nullable.

We can clear this list of updateable columns using the clearUpdateColumnList method:

```
xmlgen.clearUpdateColumnList
```

So let's see an example stored procedure which updates the database based on an XML document. It is similar to the insert and delete procedures, but before calling the `updateXML` function, we first clear the key column list. We will identify rows based on the primary key of the EMP table, the EMPNO column, since this is guaranteed to be unique, so we add this to the key column list. Then we clear the update column list and add the ENAME column. This will ensure that users can only change this column when updating the table, and can't change, for example, the salary details.

```
CREATE OR REPLACE PROCEDURE spUpdateXML
(strTable IN varchar,
 strXML IN varchar,
 intRows OUT integer)
AS
BEGIN
    xmlgen.clearKeyColumnList;
    xmlgen.setKeyColumn('EMPNO');
    xmlgen.clearUpdateColumnList;
    xmlgen.setUpdateColumn('ENAME');
    intRows := xmlgen.updateXML(strTable,strXML);
END;
```

Oracle XML Example

We'll finish off this section on Oracle and XML by providing a simple example which makes use of the Oracle XML SQL Utility, and IE5 data binding to allow client-side editing of our Oracle data over the Internet or over an intranet. We will look at data binding in depth with relation to RDS in Chapter 32. It is a feature of IE5+, (although an earlier version also existed in IE4), which allows us to bind HTML elements to a data source. This data source can be an RDS `DataControl`, as we will see in Chapter 32, but it can also be an **XML data island**. These are islands of XML data embedded into an HTML page, enclosed in `<XML></XML>` tags. Data binding allows us to bind an HTML table to the XML document contained in one of these data islands, and to bind the cells in the table to individual elements in the document.

The Stored Procedures

This application will use very slightly modified versions of the select and update stored procedures we looked at above. In the case of the update procedure, the only difference is that we only retrieve three columns from the `EMP` table – `EMPNO`, `ENAME` and `JOB`:

```
CREATE OR REPLACE PROCEDURE spGetEmpXml2
(strXML OUT varchar)
AS
clobXML CLOB;
intLength integer;
BEGIN
    intLength := 4000;
    clobXML := xmlgen.getXML('SELECT EMPNO, ENAME, JOB FROM EMP');
    DBMS_LOB.READ(clobXML, intLength, 1, strXML);
END;
```

For the update procedure, the only change is that we will allow both the `ENAME` and `JOB` columns to be updated:

```
CREATE OR REPLACE PROCEDURE spUpdateXml2
(strTable IN varchar,
 strXML IN varchar,
 intRows OUT integer)
AS
BEGIN
    xmlgen.clearKeyColumnList;
    xmlgen.setKeyColumn('EMPNO');
    xmlgen.clearUpdateColumnList;
    xmlgen.setUpdateColumn('ENAME');
    xmlgen.setUpdateColumn('JOB');
    intRows := xmlgen.updateXML(strTable,strXML);
END;
```

The ASP Page

The rest of the code is contained entirely within an ASP page. The page submits to itself. When the user opts to update the database, the entire XML document will be posted to the page in a hidden element, hdnXML. We therefore start by checking the Request.Form collection to see if an XML document has been submitted. If so, we call our update stored procedure, display a link to return to the edit page, and end the execution of the page:

```
<!-- METADATA TYPE="TypeLib"
            FILE="C:\Program Files\Common Files\System\ADO\msado15.dll" -->
<HTML>
<HEAD>
   <TITLE>Oracle XML Example</TITLE>
</HEAD>
<%
If Request.Form("hdnXML") <> "" Then
   strXML = Request.Form("hdnXML")

   Set cn = Server.CreateObject("ADODB.Connection")

   cn.Open "Provider=MSDAORA;Data Source=orcldb.julian_new.wrox.com;" & _
           "User ID=scott;Password=tiger"

   Set cmd = Server.CreateObject("ADODB.Command")
   Set cmd.ActiveConnection = cn
   cmd.CommandText="spUpdateXML2"
   cmd.CommandType=adCmdStoredProc

   Set Parm1 = cmd.CreateParameter("strTable", adVarChar, adParamInput, _
                                4000, "scott.emp")
   Set Parm2 = cmd.CreateParameter("strXML", adVarChar, adParamInput, _
                                4000, strXML)
   Set Parm3 = cmd.CreateParameter("intRows", adInteger, adParamOutput)

   cmd.Parameters.Append Parm1
   cmd.Parameters.Append Parm2
   cmd.Parameters.Append Parm3

   cmd.Execute
   varRows = Parm3.Value
   Set Parm1 = Nothing
   Set Parm2 = Nothing
   Set Parm3 = Nothing
   Set cmd = Nothing
   cn.Close
   Set cn = Nothing
   Response.Write varRows & " rows were updated.<BR><BR>"
   Response.Write "<A HREF='update.asp'>Return to edit page</A>"
   Response.End
End If
```

If no XML document has been submitted, we call our stored procedure to retrieve the XML document from the database:

```
Set cn = Server.CreateObject("ADODB.Connection")

cn.Open "Provider=MSDAORA;Data Source=orcldb.julian_new.wrox.com;" & _
        "User ID=scott;Password=tiger"
```

```
Set cmd = Server.CreateObject("ADODB.Command")
Set cmd.ActiveConnection = cn
cmd.CommandText="spGetEmpXML2"
cmd.CommandType=adCmdStoredProc

Set Parm1 = cmd.CreateParameter("strXML", adVarChar, adParamOutput, 4000)
cmd.Parameters.Append Parm1

cmd.Execute

varXML = Parm1.Value
Set Parm1 = Nothing
Set cmd = Nothing
cn.Close
Set cn = Nothing
%>
```

Once we have this, we can store it in an XML data island embedded in the HTML page, so we can access it on the client:

```
<XML ID="dsoEmp"><%= varXML %></XML>
```

Now we display our data-bound table. The table itself will be bound to the XML document as a whole, while each cell contains a textbox which is bound to one of the columns we retrieved from the database. We use textboxes (rather than, say, <SPAN> elements) because this will allow the user to change the entries. Any changes made here will be reflected in the XML document stored on the client:

```
<TABLE ID="tblData" DATASRC="#dsoEmp">
   <THEAD>
      <TH>Employee Number</TH>
      <TH>Name</TH>
      <TH>Job Description</TH>
   </THEAD>
   <TBODY>
      <TR>
         <TD><INPUT TYPE="TEXT" ID=txtHireDate DATAFLD="EMPNO"></TD>
         <TD><INPUT TYPE="TEXT" ID=txtName DATAFLD="ENAME"></TD>
         <TD><INPUT TYPE="TEXT" ID=txtSal DATAFLD="JOB"></TD>
      </TR>
   </TBODY>
</TABLE>
<HR>
```

Finally comes the form we use to submit the updated XML document, and a short piece of client-side JScript which will store the XML document in the hidden element before submitting the form;

```
<FORM ACTION="update.asp" NAME="frmUpdate" ID="frmUpdate" METHOD="POST">
<INPUT TYPE="HIDDEN" ID="hdnXML" NAME="hdnXML"></INPUT>
<BUTTON NAME="btnSubmit" ONCLICK="fnSubmit()">Update database</BUTTON>
</FORM>
<SCRIPT>
function fnSubmit() {
   hdnXML = document.all['hdnXML'];
   hdnXML.value = dsoEmp.xml;
   frmUpdate.submit();
}
</SCRIPT>
</HTML>
```

And this is how our page looks:

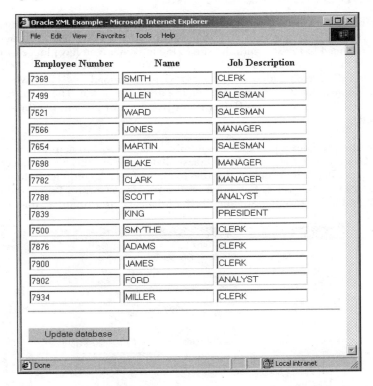

We've kept things as simple as possible, so there are no fancy graphics here, and we've kept functionality to a minimum, too. We haven't incorporated the ability to insert or delete records, although this would be easy to do with the `deleteXML` and `insertXML` functions we saw earlier in the chapter. Finally, remember that this code will only work in IE5+, so at present XML data binding is of limited use in an Internet scenario. However, the data binding techniques shown here are very useful if you can rely on the IE5 browser; and the Oracle XML SQL Utility is a great way of extracting XML data, for example for business-to-business applications. We haven't covered all of the XSU's functionality here, but we have shown how you can accomplish the most important data manipulation tasks, and how you can use the XSU from within an ASP application.

XML and DB2

Like Oracle, IBM provides a set of components for use with DB2 which enables us to store XML data in columns in an XML enabled database table. The **DB2 XML Extender** also provides a number of stored procedures which allow us to retrieve a resultset from the database in the form of an XML document.

Installing the DB2 XML Extender

The XML Extender can be downloaded from IBM's DB2 Personal Developer Edition web site at `http://www6.software.ibm.com/dl/db2pde/db2pde-p`. After choosing an operating system and language, you will need to register with the site to log in. When you have logged in, the XML Extender appears as one of the download files for DB2. On the Windows platform, the XML Extender is downloadable as a Zip file named `xmlv7_nt.zip`. This download file is 27.4 MB in size. To install the XML extender, unpack this Zip archive and run the `setup.exe` file. The XML Extender requires DB2 version 6.1 or greater; it also requires JDK 1.1.x or JRE 1.1.x or greater, but these are installed with the DB2 server itself.

The XML Extender provides a Java based Administration Wizard to help with a number of tasks such as enabling XML support for a particular database. Before we use this, we will need to add a number of entries to the `CLASSPATH` environment variable to allow the Java compiler to find the classes used. To set the `CLASSPATH` variable, select **System** from the Windows Control Panel, and then select **Environment Variables...** from the **Advanced** tab of the **System Properties** dialog box:

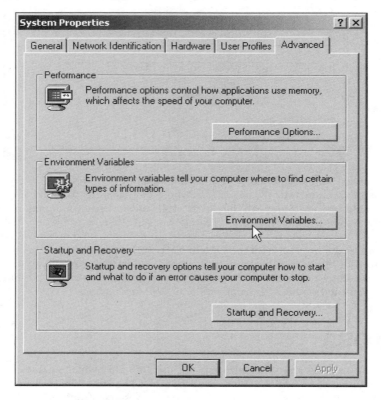

This will cause the **Environment Variables** dialog to be displayed. The `CLASSPATH` variable will appear in the **System variables** list box:

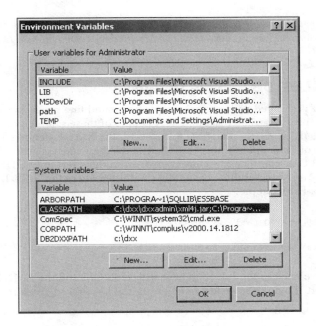

To change the value of this variable, click on the bottom Edit... button:

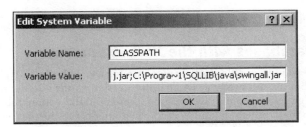

The CLASSPATH variable consists of a semicolon-delimited list of folders and files which can be accessed from any directory. The entries we need to add to use the XML Extender are:

Path	Description
`C:\dxx\dxxadmin\xml4j.jar`	Contains the class libraries for IBM's XML parser.
`C:\Progra~1\SQLLIB\java\swingall.jar`	Java GUI classes (the `javax.swing` package and related classes).
`C:\dxx\dxxadmin\dxxadmin.jar`	The classes used by the XML Extender Administration Wizard itself.
`C:\Progra~1\SQLLIB\java\jdk\lib\classes.jar`	Standard Java language classes.

Note that these paths assume that DB2 and the DB2 XML Extender were both installed to the default directories. If you installed them to other directories, you will need to change these paths accordingly.

Installing the SALES_DB Sample Database

The XML Extender is shipped with several sample command line programs, which are by default installed to the `c:\dxx\samples\cmd` folder. A couple of these sample programs can be used to create a small sample (called `SALES_DB`) database for use with the XML Extender. We will use this sample database in most of our examples in this section. The database itself is created using the `getstart_db.cmd` DB2 command line program. To run this, start up the DB2 Command Window, change to the `samples/cmd` subdirectory under the folder where the XML Extender was installed, and type `getstart_db`. For example:

```
C:\PROGRA~1\SQLLIB\BIN>cd\dxx\samples\cmd

C:\dxx\samples\cmd>getstart_db
```

After this has run, we need to bind the database with DB2 CLI and the XML Extender, and enable XML support. To do this, we just need to run the `getstart_prep.cmd` program, in the same directory:

```
C:\dxx\samples\cmd>getstart_prep
```

Now we're ready to use the XML Extender with this database.

Enabling Other Databases with the XML Extender

However, what if we want to enable another database for use with the XML Extender? This requires slightly more work, but it's still pretty easy. First, we need to connect to the database to bind the database to the XML Extender and to CLI. Again, there are DB2 command-line utilities we can use to achieve this. Start up the DB2 Command Window and connect to the database. For example (using the `SAMPLE` database):

```
C:\Progra~1\SQLLIB\BIN>db2 "connect to SAMPLE"
```

Now change to the `bnd` directory under the XML Extender's installation folder and bind the database to the XML Extender:

```
C:\Progra~1\SQLLIB\BIN>cd\dxx\bnd

C:\dxx\bnd>db2 "bind @dxxbind.lst"
```

Next, change to the `bnd` subdirectory under the main DB2 directory (for example, `Program Files\SQLLIB`) and bind the database to CLI:

```
C:\dxx\bnd>>cd\Progra~1\SQLLIB\bnd

C:\Progra~1\SQLLIB\bnd>db2 "bind @db2cli.lst"
```

We can now close the connection to the database;

```
C:\Progra~1\SQLLIB\bnd>db2 "terminate"
```

and we're finally ready to enable XML support in the database. This takes just one command-line instruction. This can also be done from the XML Administration Wizard, but we've got the Command Window open already, so we might as well use it:

```
C:\Progra~1\SQLLIB\bnd>dxxadm enable_db SAMPLE
```

The XML Extender Administration Wizard

The DB2 XML Extender comes with a handy GUI-based utility called the Administration Wizard which can help with most of the tasks we'll need to perform when working with XML data in DB2. DB2's XML support is in some ways more powerful than that of SQL Server or Oracle, in that we can define very precisely how our database tables will map to elements and attributes in XML documents. However, this power comes at the price of ease of use, and the Administration Wizard is designed to alleviate this problem.

The wizard can be started be selecting Programs | DB2 XML Extender | XML Extender Administration Wizard from the Start menu. The first screen allows us to connect to any available DB2 database:

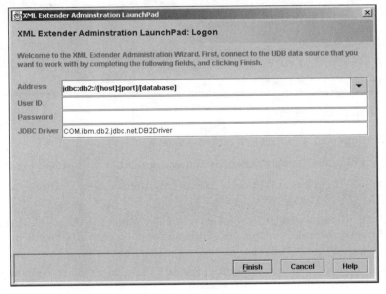

The Address field should contain a JDBC address in the form:

```
jdbc:db2://server_name:port_number/database_alias
```

For example, to connect to the SAMPLE database running on machine JULIANS1 on port 50000, the address would be:

```
jdbc:db2://JULIANS1:50000/SAMPLE
```

If we're connecting to a local instance of DB2, no port number should be specified (that is, we would just use `jdbc:db2://JULIANS1/SAMPLE`).

After entering the appropriate User ID and Password information, click on Finish and the Administration Wizard's main menu will be displayed:

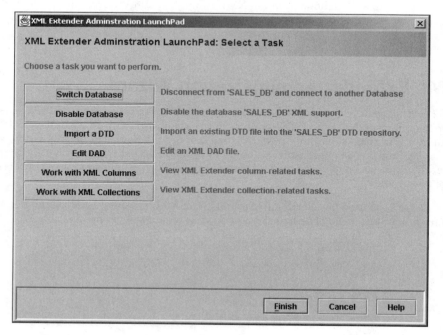

The wizard presents us with options to:

- ❏ Switch Database. Connect to a different database.

- ❏ Enable Database/Disable Database. Enable or disable XML support in the current database.

- ❏ Import a DTD. Import a DTD into the current database. DB2 can use imported DTDs to validate XML columns in the database.

- ❏ Edit DAD. Create or edit a Document Access Definition file. These files are XML documents which specify how the columns in a DB2 table map to an XML document. We will look at these files shortly.

- ❏ Work with XML Columns. Enable an existing column in a table to contain XML documents, or create a new column for XML support.

- ❏ Work with XML Collections. XML collections are used to indicate how XML documents are to be decomposed into relational data, or how the XML is to be composed from DB2 data. XML collections can be specified in the DAD file, but we can also create them from existing DADs and work with them directly.

We will look at some of these administrative tasks now, before seeing how we can use the XML Extender in conjunction with ASP pages.

Importing DTDs

Clicking on the Import a DTD button allows us to register a pre written DTD in the DTD repository for the current database. Enabling XML support in a database causes a table named DTD_REF to be created. This table includes one row for each registered DTD, containing the contents of the DTD, an ID we'll use to identify the DTD in our DAD files, as well as other optional information such as the author and creator of the document.

The wizard allows us simply to specify the path and file name of an existing DTD, together with an ID string, and, optionally, the author of the DTD:

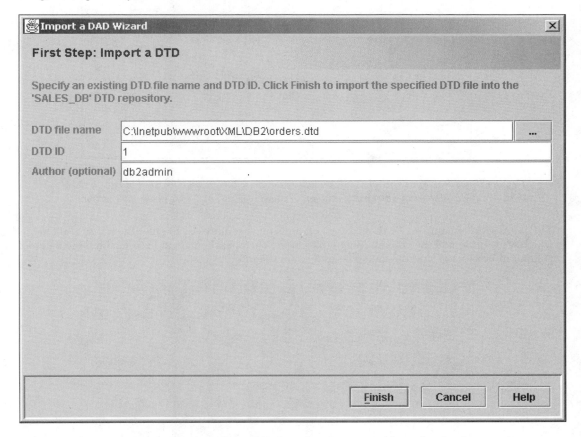

Clicking on Finish will register the DTD and update the DTD_REF table in the database.

Enabling XML Columns

One of the tasks we can accomplish through this wizard is to add XML columns to an existing table in an XML-enabled database. To do this, select Work with XML Columns from the Administration Wizard's main menu. As well as the option to create a new XML column, the wizard gives us options to enable XML support in an existing column, and to disable an existing XML column:

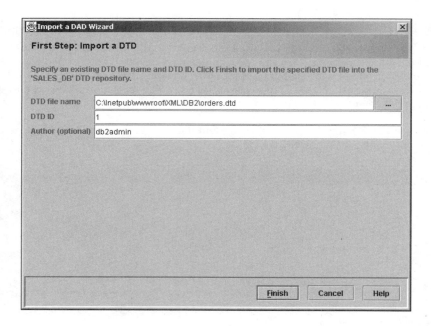

Here we'll just look at adding an XML column to database tables, since we need to have a DAD file to enable XML support in an existing column. We will look at DAD files in the next section.

The last step in creating an XML-enabled column simply requires us to enter the name of the table to which we want to add the column (only tables in the current schema will be available), the name of the column to be created, and the data type of the new column:

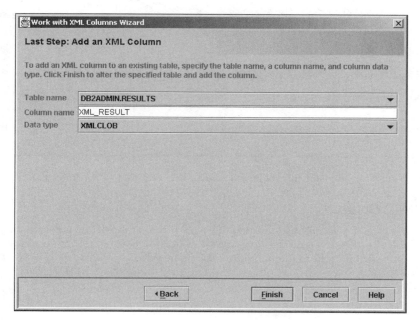

The XML Extender supports three XML data types:

- ❑ XMLCLOB. Stores an entire XML document as a Character Large Object (CLOB).

- ❑ XMLFILE. Stores the XML document itself in a file on the server, and stores the path and file name of this file in the XML column.

- ❑ XMLVARCHAR. Stores the entire XML document as a varchar.

Finally, click on Finish to create the column.

Document Access Definitions

Document Access Definitions, or DADs, are XML documents which specify how the XML elements will be mapped to the columns in the database. These files are absolutely essential for working with XML data in DB2. The structure for a DAD is specified in the file dad.dtd; this is supplied with the XML Extender, so we won't reprint it here.

There are three different types of DAD, and these can all be created either through the wizard or manually (writing the XML which comprises them by hand). The type of DAD we need depends on the tasks we want to use it for:

- ❑ XML Column. Used for enabling XML support in an existing column.

- ❑ SQL Node Mapping. Used for creating an XML collection for composing XML documents from the database. The columns to be included in the collection are specified using a SQL SELECT statement.

- ❑ RDB Node Mapping. Used for creating an XML collection for both composing and decomposing XML documents. The tables and columns to be included in the collection are specified with <table> and <column> XML elements.

The latter two types can also be used instead of an XML collection when composing or decomposing XML documents using the stored procedures which are supplied with the XML Extender.

We'll look first at creating a SQL Node Mapping DAD with the Administration Wizard, before seeing how we can create an RDB Node Mapping DAD ourselves. For both of these examples, we'll use the SALES_DB database.

Creating a DAD With the Wizard

To create a DAD with the Administration Wizard, select Edit DAD from the main menu. This will load the Work with DAD Files Wizard. The first step of this wizard invites us to enter the file name of a DAD to edit. If we want to create a new DAD, rather than edit an existing one, we just leave this blank:

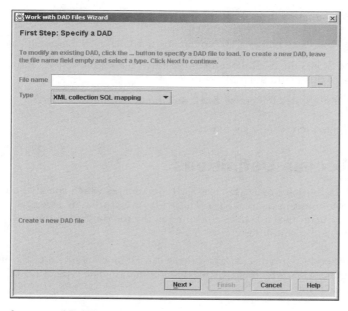

We must also select the type of DAD we want to create; this can be any of the three types we mentioned earlier. We will use the wizard to create a SQL Node Mapping DAD, so select XML collection SQL mapping here, and click Next.

Selecting a DTD

The next screen allows us to state whether we want our XML documents to be validated by DB2, and if so, to choose one of the DTDs from the repository. We need to have an existing DTD which has been stored in the database to do this, so select Do not validate and press Next:

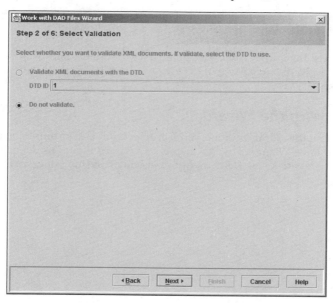

The DTD specified here will be used by the external application to which the XML document is returned, not by the XML Extender itself.

> **If no DTDs have been imported into this database, we will not be able to select the option to validate our XML documents.**

Defining the Prolog

The next step allows us to enter the prolog and document type declaration. The text we enter here will be used to build the XML declaration and document type declaration in XML documents generated by our DAD. We should enter these nodes exactly as they will appear in our documents, but without the opening and closing angled brackets:

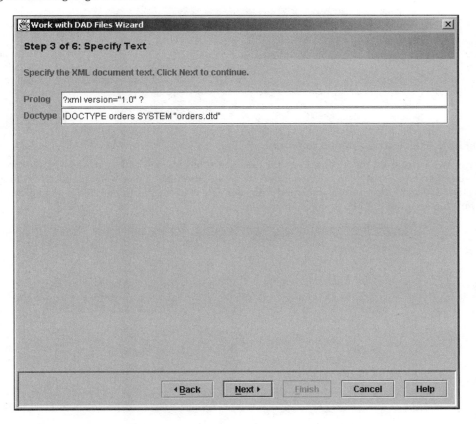

Specifying the SQL Statement

The next step is to specify the SQL SELECT statement which we will use to determine which columns are to be included in the XML document generated using this DAD. For this example, we'll perform an INNER JOIN on the ORDER_TAB and PART_TAB tables:

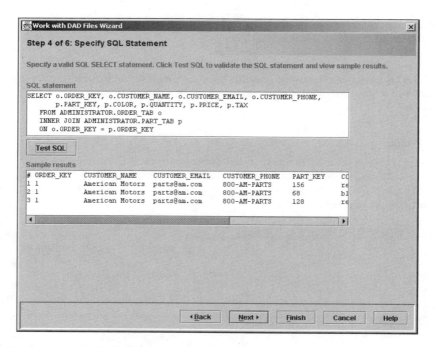

Mapping XML Nodes to Database Columns

When we've composed the SQL statement, the wizard lets us check its syntax, displaying sample results from the query so that we can be sure it does what we intended. Then we can click Next to go onto the next step, and map the columns returned from our select statement to the elements and attributes which we want the generated XML documents to contain:

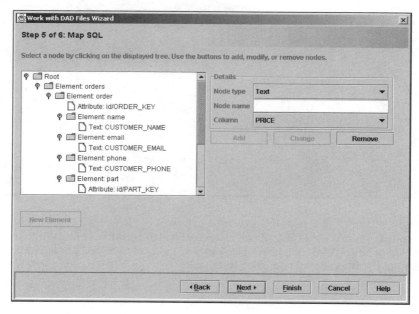

The wizard provides a graphical interface for mapping columns in the database to XML nodes. We will generate XML documents with the structure:

```
<?xml version="1.0"?>
<!DOCTYPE orders SYSTEM "orders.dtd">
<orders>
    <order id="...">
        <name>...</name>
        <email>...</email>
        <phone>...</phone>
        <part id="...">
            <color>...</color>
            <quantity>...</quantity>
            <price>...</price>
            <tax>...</tax>
        </part>
    </order>
</orders>
```

Where the `<order>` element represents a row in the ORDER_TAB table, and the `<part>` element a row in PART_TAB. The `id` attributes of these two elements correspond to the ORDER_KEY and PART_KEY columns respectively, and the other columns are represented by elements. The DTD for the document is:

```
<?xml version="1.0" ?>

<!ELEMENT orders (order*)>
<!ELEMENT order (name, email, phone, part)>
<!ATTLIST order id CDATA #REQUIRED>
<!ELEMENT name (#PCDATA)>
<!ELEMENT email (#PCDATA)>
<!ELEMENT phone (#PCDATA)>
<!ELEMENT part (color, quantity, price, tax)>
<!ATTLIST part id CDATA #REQUIRED>
<!ELEMENT color (#PCDATA)>
<!ELEMENT quantity (#PCDATA)>
<!ELEMENT price (#PCDATA)>
<!ELEMENT tax (#PCDATA)>
```

For each element that our document will contain, we need to create an Element node with the same name in the Map SQL dialog box. To create a new node, select the parent element for the node and click on New Element. We can set the type to Element, Attribute or Text. For Attribute and Text nodes, we can use the Column dropdown box to specify that they should contain data from one of the columns returned by our SELECT query. Click on Add to add the node to the tree.

> Text and attribute nodes must be added to the tree before they can be mapped to columns in the database. When adding these nodes, click on Add first, then select the column to map to, and click on the Change button.

When you've added all the nodes in this way, click on <u>N</u>ext for the final step.

907

Saving the DAD

The wizard now has all the information it needs to generate the DAD, so we just have to give a path and file name to specify where the DAD file should be saved:

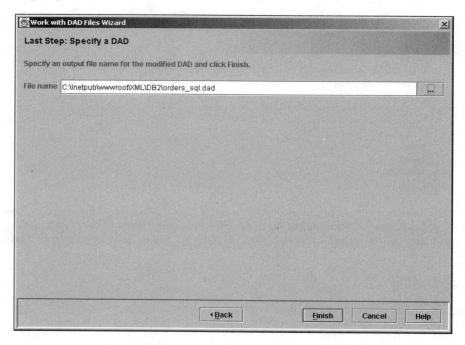

When we click on Finish, the DAD will be generated and saved to the specified file. The DAD we generated has this format:

```
<?xml version="1.0"?>
<!DOCTYPE DAD SYSTEM "../dtd/dad.dtd">
<DAD>
  <validation>NO</validation>
  <Xcollection>
    <SQL_stmt>SELECT o.ORDER_KEY, o.CUSTOMER_NAME, o.CUSTOMER_EMAIL,
                     o.CUSTOMER_PHONE, p.PART_KEY, p.COLOR, p.QUANTITY,
                     p.PRICE, p.TAX
              FROM ORDER_TAB o
              INNER JOIN PART_TAB p
              ON o.ORDER_KEY = p.ORDER_KEY</SQL_stmt>
    <prolog>?xml version="1.0" ?</prolog>
    <doctype>!DOCTYPE orders SYSTEM "orders.dtd"</doctype>
    <root_node>
      <element_node name="orders">
        <element_node name="order">
          <attribute_node name="id">
            <column name="ORDER_KEY"/>
          </attribute_node>
          <element_node name="name">
            <text_node>
              <column name="CUSTOMER_NAME"/>
```

```
                    </text_node>
                  </element_node>
                  <!-- Same for email and phone elements -->
                  <element_node name="part">
                    <attribute_node name="id">
                      <column name="PART_KEY"/>
                    </attribute_node>
                    <element_node name="color">
                      <text_node>
                        <column name="COLOR"/>
                      </text_node>
                    </element_node>
                    <!-- Same for quantity, price and tax elements -->
                  </element_node>
                </element_node>
              </element_node>
            </root_node>
          </Xcollection>
        </DAD>
```

The Structure of DAD Files

Let's look quickly at the structure of this file, before we go on to build an RDB Node Mapping DAD by hand.

The root element for the document is the `<DAD>` element. The first element underneath this is `<validation>`. This contains a text element with a value of either YES or NO, and indicates whether XML documents generated using this DAD should be validated against a DTD. If set to YES, the DTD must be registered with the DTD repository for the database, and the next element should be a `<dtdid>` element containing the ID which we assigned to the DTD when we registered it in the database.

The next element is the `<Xcollection>` element, which contains our XML collection – that is, this is where we actually map the nodes in the XML document to the columns in our database tables. The first element within this is `<SQL_stmt>`, which contains our SQL SELECT statement.

After the SQL statement, we specify a `<prolog>` and a `<doctype>`. The text in these elements is what we entered in Step 3 of the wizard.

We then come to the `<root_node>` element, which represents the automatically created Root node at the top of the node tree (Step 4). Within this element, there are `<element_node>`, `<attribute_node>`, and `<text_node>` elements to specify the structure of our XML document. These correspond to the Element, Attribute and Text nodes we added in the wizard. The name of attribute and element nodes is specified using the name attribute. To indicate that a text or attribute node is to take its value from a particular column in the database, we use `<column>` elements within the appropriate `<attribute_node>` or `<text_node>`.

Creating an RDB Node Mapping DAD

RDB DADs are very similar to SQL DADs, but they don't contain a SQL statement to define which columns are to be included in the XML document. Instead, we use `<table>` elements to indicate which tables to include, and which tables to take data from. We also use `<condition>` elements to specify the conditions for table joins, etc., taking the place of the ON clause of a SQL INNER JOIN.

Although the Administration Wizard allows us to create RDB Node Mapping DAD files, it doesn't allow us to enter the table information at the start of the document. This means, in effect, that we can't use it to create working RDB DAD files. Unfortunately, that means that if we want to use the XML Extender to insert records into a database, we're going to have to write an RDB DAD file by hand. Therefore, we will look now at creating a DAD manually. To make the example easier to follow, we'll create an RDB DAD which corresponds exactly to the SQL DAD we saw above.

The start of the file is identical, except for the omission of the `<SQL_stmt>` element. The outermost element is the same `<DAD>` element, followed by the validation information and an `<Xcollection>` element. Again, this element contains a `<prolog>`, a `<doctype>`, and a `<root_node>` element:

```
<?xml version="1.0"?>
<!DOCTYPE DAD SYSTEM "c:\dxx\dtd\dad.dtd">
<DAD>
<validation>NO</validation>
<Xcollection>
    <prolog>?xml version="1.0"?</prolog>
    <doctype>
       !DOCTYPE Order SYSTEM "c:\inetpub\wwwroot\xml\db2\orders.dtd"
    </doctype>
    <root_node>
```

Next comes our outermost `<element_node>` element. As with a SQL DAD, this will be used to form the root element of our generated XML files. However, before we specify any other elements beneath this, we must indicate the tables we want to include. We do this with an `<RDB_node>` element; this contains one `<table>` element for each table to be included. We indicate the name of the table using the `name` attribute. We can also specify the primary key of the table using a `key` attribute. This is optional if we only want to use the DAD for composition, but mandatory if we also want to use it for decomposition.

If the `<RDB_node>` element contains more than one table, we must also specify a `<condition>` element to indicate the relationship between the tables. These elements correspond to the `WHERE` clause of a SQL `SELECT` statement, or the `ON` part of an `INNER JOIN` clause:

```
<element_node name="orders">
    <RDB_node>
       <table name="order_tab" key="order_key"/>
       <table name="part_tab" key="part_key"/>
       <condition>
          order_tab.order_key=part_tab.order_key
       </condition>
    </RDB_node>
```

We can now proceed to map our XML nodes to database tables. We use the same elements as in the SQL DAD, except that `<attribute_node>` and `<text_node>` elements contain an `<RDB_node>` element. This in turn contains a `<table>` element to specify the table from which the data will be taken, and a `<column>` element for the column. We can also include a `<condition>` element if we don't want to return all rows. Note that the `<column>` element must have a `type` attribute to specify the data type of the column if this DAD is to be used for decomposing XML into relational data.

So, the definition for the `id` attribute of our `<order>` element looks like this:

```
<element_node name="order">
    <attribute_node name="id">
        <RDB_node>
            <table name="order_tab"/>
            <column name="order_key" type="integer"/>
        </RDB_node>
    </attribute_node>
```

Similarly for the `<name>` element:

```
<element_node name="name">
    <text_node>
        <RDB_node>
            <table name="order_tab"/>
            <column name="customer_name" type="varchar(16)"/>
        </RDB_node>
    </text_node>
</element_node>
```

And so on for the remaining columns in ORDER_TAB.

Again, the `<part>` element is represented by an `<element_node>` nested within the node for the `<order>` element, with its own nested `<attribute_node>` and `<element_node>` elements:

```
<element_node name="part">
    <attribute_node name="id">
        <RDB_node>
            <table name="part_tab"/>
            <column name="part_key" type="integer"/>
        </RDB_node>
    </attribute_node>
    <element_node name="color">
        <text_node>
            <RDB_node>
                <table name="part_tab"/>
                <column name="color" type="character(6)"/>
            </RDB_node>
        </text_node>
    </element_node>
    <!-- Repeated for the quantity, price, and tax elements -->
    </element_node>
    </element_node>
    </root_node>
    </Xcollection>
</DAD>
```

Retrieving XML Data From DB2

So now we've got our DAD files, what can we do with them? Let's start by retrieving an XML document from our DB2 data. To achieve this, we will use a stored procedure that ships with the XML Extender, called `dxxGenXML`. This, and the other stored procedures which ship with the XML Extender, reside in the DB2XML schema. This will compose an XML document from our database tables, and store it in an XML-enabled column in a named table.

The syntax for this stored procedure is:

```
CALL db2xml.dxxGenXML (objDAD, strTabName, intOverride, strOverrideType,
                       intMaxRows, intNumRows, lngRetCode, strRetMsg)
```

Where:

Name	Data Type	Description
objDAD	CLOB	The DAD which specifies how the nodes in the XML document will map to the columns in our database table.
strTabName	char	The name of the table in which the XML document will be stored.
intOverrideType	integer	Indicates whether the condition in the DAD file is to be overridden. Possible values are NO_OVERRIDE (0), SQL_OVERRIDE (1, for overriding SQL Node Mapping DADs), or XML_OVERRIDE (2, for overriding RDB Node Mapping DADs).
strOverride	varchar(1024)	If the override type is SQL_OVERRIDE, the SQL statement which will be used to override the SQL statement in the DAD. If the override type is XML_OVERRIDE, an XPath-based expression. If there is no override, an empty string.
intMaxRows	integer	The maximum number of rows which we want to retrieve into the XML document.
intNumRows	integer (output)	The actual number of rows retrieved.
lngRetCode	long (output)	The return code from the stored procedure.
strRetMsg	varchar(1024) (output)	The return message from the stored procedure.

Because this syntax is quite complex, we'll wrap this call to dxxGenXML up in a SQL stored procedure, so we don't have to specify all the parameters every time we want to call the procedure. We'll also execute a SELECT statement against the table where the generated XML document is stored, so that we can retrieve it directly from our SQL stored procedure.

We will hard-code most of these parameters into our stored procedure for the sake of simplicity, just passing in the DAD document, and returning the number of rows, the return code and the return message as output parameters. We will specify that the XML document is to be stored in the RESULT_TAB table, that there is to be no override, and that a maximum of 255 rows are to be retrieved into the XML document:

```
CREATE PROCEDURE DB2ADMIN.uspXML (IN objDAD varchar(4000),
                                  OUT numRows int,
                                  OUT retCode int,
                                  OUT retMsg varchar(4000))
    RESULT SETS 1
    LANGUAGE SQL
```

```
P1: BEGIN
    -- Declare variables
    DECLARE numRows_TMP int DEFAULT 0;
    DECLARE retCode_TMP int DEFAULT 0;
    DECLARE retMsg_TMP varchar(4000) DEFAULT ' ';

    DECLARE intOverride int DEFAULT 0;
    DECLARE strOverrideType varchar(4000) DEFAULT '';
    DECLARE strTabName varchar(4000) DEFAULT 'RESULT_TAB';
    DECLARE maxRows int DEFAULT 255;

    -- Declare cursor for selecting the XML column from our results table
    DECLARE cursor1 CURSOR WITH RETURN FOR
        SELECT * FROM RESULT_TAB;

    -- call the supplied stored procedure
    CALL db2xml.dxxGenXML (objDAD, strTabName, intOverride, strOverrideType,
                           maxRows, numRows_TMP, retCode_TMP, retMsg_TMP);

    -- Set output parameters
    SET numRows = numRows_TMP;
    SET retCode = retCode_TMP;
    SET retMsg = retMsg_TMP;

    -- Open the cursor to send the XML to the client
    OPEN cursor1;
END P1
```

We can now call this SQL stored procedure from an ASP page. This consists mostly of standard ADO code. We create and open a connection, open a `TextStream` object with the `FileSystemObject` to load the DAD file into a string, create the input and output `Parameter` objects, and call the stored procedure. If no error occurs (that is, if the return code is zero), we simply stream the XML document to the client (this assumes the client is IE5); otherwise, we display the error message returned from the `dxxGenXML` procedure:

```
<!-- METADATA TYPE="TypeLib"
            FILE="C:\Program Files\Common Files\System\ADO\msado15.dll" -->
<%
Set cn = Server.CreateObject("ADODB.Connection")

cn.Open "Provider=IBMDADB2.1;Data Source=SALES_DB;User ID=db2admin;Password="

Set cmd = Server.CreateObject("ADODB.Command")
Set cmd.ActiveConnection = cn
cmd.CommandText="uspXML"
cmd.CommandType=adCmdStoredProc

Set objFSO = Server.CreateObject("Scripting.FileSystemObject")
' Load the DAD file. We could use either DAD we created earlier.
Set objTStream = objFSO.OpenTextFile("orders_sql.dad")
strDAD = objTStream.ReadAll
objTStream.Close
Set Parm0 = cmd.CreateParameter("objDAD", adVarChar, adParamInput, _
                                4000, strDAD)
Set Parm1 = cmd.CreateParameter("numRows", adInteger, adParamOutput)
Set Parm2 = cmd.CreateParameter("retCode", adInteger, adParamOutput)
Set Parm3 = cmd.CreateParameter("retMsg", adVarChar, adParamOutput, 4000)
```

```
cmd.Parameters.Append Parm0
cmd.Parameters.Append Parm1
cmd.Parameters.Append Parm2
cmd.Parameters.Append Parm3

Set rs=cmd.Execute

If Parm2.Value = 0 Then
    Response.ContentType = "text/xml"
    Response.Write rs(0).Value
Else
    Response.Write "Error Message is:<BR>"
    Response.Write Parm3.Value
End If
%>
```

The output of this, viewed in IE5, is:

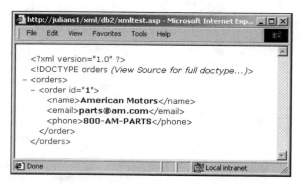

Inserting Rows into the Database

The second major task we can achieve with the XML Extender is to insert rows into a DB2 database by decomposing an XML file into relational data. Again, the XML Extender provides a built-in stored procedure which we can use to do this. The dxxShredXML stored procedure has the syntax:

```
CALL db2xml.shredXML (objDAD, objXML, lngRetCode, strRetMsg)
```

where:

Name	Data Type	Description
objDAD	CLOB	The DAD which specifies how the nodes in the XML document will map to the columns in our database table.
strXML	CLOB	The XML document which will be decomposed (or 'shredded') into relational data.
intRetCode	long (output)	The return code from the stored procedure.
strRetMsg	varchar(1024) (output)	The return message from the stored procedure.

There's less obvious need to wrap a call to this procedure in a SQL stored procedure, but the XML Extender stored procedures weren't really designed for use with ADO, and can be a little temperamental, so it's probably advisable to do this anyway. So, in this case, we will create a SQL procedure which simply passes a DAD and XML file to the dxxShredXML procedure, and returns the output code and message back to the caller:

```
CREATE PROCEDURE DB2ADMIN.uspShredXML
    (IN strDAD varchar(10000),
     IN strXML varchar(10000),
     OUT intRetCode integer,
     OUT strRetMsg varchar(4000))

     LANGUAGE SQL

P1: BEGIN
    DECLARE intRetCode_temp integer;
    DECLARE strRetMsg_temp varchar(4000);

    CALL db2xml.dxxShredXML(strDAD, strXML, intRetCode_temp, strRetMsg_temp);

    SET intRetCode = intRetCode_temp;
    SET strRetMsg = strRetMsg_temp;
END P1
```

The XML file we'll use for updating the database must follow the structure we defined in our RDB Node Mapping DAD:

```
<?xml version="1.0" ?>
<!DOCTYPE orders SYSTEM "orders.dtd">
<orders>
    <order id="2">
        <name>Wrox Cars</name>
        <email>parts@wrxcrs.com</email>
        <phone>555-5555</phone>
        <part id="25">
            <color>red</color>
            <quantity>5</quantity>
            <price>2000</price>
            <tax>0.055</tax>
        </part>
    </order>
</orders>
```

We can then call our SQL Procedure from an ASP page. This page is very similar to the previous ASP page, except that we also have to load the XML file, again using a TextStream object. Also, for updating the database, we *must* use the RDB DAD – we can't use a SQL DAD for decomposing XML. This makes sense, because it must contain a SQL SELECT statement – it can't contain an INSERT, UPDATE or DELETE.

```
<!-- METADATA TYPE="TypeLib"
            FILE="C:\Program Files\Common Files\System\ADO\msado15.dll" -->
<%
Set cn = Server.CreateObject("ADODB.Connection")
```

```
cn.Open "Provider=IBMDADB2.1;Data Source=SALES_DB;User ID=db2admin;Password="

Set cmd = Server.CreateObject("ADODB.Command")
Set cmd.ActiveConnection = cn
cmd.CommandText="uspShredXML"
cmd.CommandType=adCmdStoredProc

' Load the DAD file. We can only update the database using an RDB DAD.
Set objFSO = Server.CreateObject("Scripting.FileSystemObject")
Set objTStream = objFSO.OpenTextFile
                    ("C:\inetpub\wwwroot\xml\db2\orders_rdb.dad")
strDAD = objTStream.ReadAll
objTStream.Close

' Load the XML file which contains the data to be inserted
Set objTStream = objFSO.OpenTextFile("C:\inetpub\wwwroot\xml\db2\orders.xml")
strXML = objTStream.ReadAll
objTStream.Close

Set Parm0 = cmd.CreateParameter("strDAD", advarchar, adParamInput, 10000, _
                                strDAD)
Set Parm1 = cmd.CreateParameter("strXML", advarchar, adParamInput, 10000, _
                                strXML)
Set Parm2 = cmd.CreateParameter("intRetCode", adInteger, adParamOutput)
Set Parm3 = cmd.CreateParameter("strRetMsg", adVarChar, adParamOutput, 4000)

cmd.Parameters.Append Parm0
cmd.Parameters.Append Parm1
cmd.Parameters.Append Parm2
cmd.Parameters.Append Parm3

cmd.Execute

If Parm2.Value = 0 Then
   Response.Write "Database updated successfully!"
Else
   Response.Write "Error Message is:<BR>"
   Response.Write Parm3.Value
End If

Set cmd = Nothing

cn.Close
Set cn = Nothing
%>
```

We haven't by any means exhausted the complete functionality of the DB2 XML Extender in this section; but we have had a good look at how we can use it to retrieve XML documents from the database, and to insert rows into database tables by decomposing an XML document, and how we can make full use of this functionality from within our ASP applications. As we mentioned above, the necessity of writing DAD files makes XML support in DB2 more difficult to use than in SQL Server or Oracle, but it does give us a fine level of control over how our XML document will be structured. In effect, writing a DAD may avoid the need to transform the XML with an XSLT stylesheet. Since DADs are likely to be less painful to write than XSLT stylesheets, DADs may in fact be a benefit in disguise.

Summary

We have seen how SQL Server Meta Data Services give us the ability to perform basic data access tasks using XML. From a browser, we can make ad hoc relational queries. With templates, site administrators can provide standard database reports in XML format. Finally, with update grams, we can modify the state of a database by constructing an XML document and passing it to SQL Server.

XML support in Oracle is provided by the XML SQL Utility, or XSU. This consists of three components; a client-side front end, a Java API, and a PL/SQL API. The PL/SQL API can be accessed from stored procedures and these in turn can be called from an ASP application. We looked at how we can use this API to retrieve an XML document from the data in an Oracle database, to insert rows into a database table, and to update an existing table.

Finally, we looked at XML support in DB2. This is provided by the DB2 XML Extender. The XML Extender makes use of special XML files, called Document Access Definitions, which specify how elements and attributes in an XML document relate to columns in a DB2 database table. So, after looking at the installation and configuration of the XML Extender, we discussed how to create DAD files, and how to use them to retrieve data in XML format from the database and to 'shred' an XML document to insert rows into the database.

Relational databases host the bulk of business data today. Web interfaces are quickly becoming a popular client interface, offering an alternative to traditional client-server applications. Within the web development world, there is increasing demand for XML as the format of choice for data exchange. These trends place a premium on our ability as programmers to deliver relational business data productively in a web-compatible form. Each of the three biggest selling database systems offers its own way of meeting these challenges and allowing us to combine the power of a traditional RDBMS with the flexibility of XML data.

Section 7

Advanced Topics

28

E-commerce and E-business

Embarking on any form of e-business project will typically mean using at least one, and perhaps all, of the data access techniques we've already seen.

E-business usually denotes any form of commercial activity undertaken with the assistance of the Internet (although it could include commercial activity undertaken over a private network or an intranet). It's primarily a way of making communication more efficient. These efficiencies typically give rise to other business benefits, such as being able to find more customers, cutting costs, and making it easier and cheaper to manage the customers we already have. Our job is to work out how to implement a technical solution when given a particular business need.

What's the difference between e-business and e-commerce? Well, to simplify somewhat, e-commerce is strictly "selling goods and services online". E-business, on the other hand, covers many more aspects of a business's activity, such as the automation of stock control, marketing, and so on.

Improving the Customer Experience

Here's a typical problem. The person in charge of customer service in our company brings it to our attention that each of our support staff is answering 20 calls a day from people wondering where their orders are. This is not only a drain on resources, but is not convenient for our customers. A way to provide a solution to this is to allow customers to visit a web page and determine where their orders are, whenever they like. We would then face certain technical problems. Solving these would quite probably involve the integration of many different systems and the cooperation of many different people.

Storing Customer Data

An existing company would probably already have a considerable customer database in one form or another, or perhaps multiple data stores. Depending on the company's industry sector and size, such data stores could be anywhere from an Outlook contacts database, to a dedicated contact management tool such as ACT! or Goldmine, through to a massive multimillion row database held in an Oracle database somewhere.

A new company, on the other hand, would have a good opportunity to build an infrastructure from scratch that would take the company through its first years of growth successfully.

Whichever type of company we are dealing with, if we want to create a compelling e-commerce site, perhaps making use of **Personalization and Membership** (**P&M**), we need to build each part of the system around this central customer database (we look at P&M later in the chapter). This means that our e-commerce site must have access to the same information about each of our customers as our customer support people do through their **Customer Relationship Management** (**CRM**) software. We will look at CRM later in the chapter.

In most real-world situations, it's often necessary to write bridging software to keep everything in sync, because although there is often a master copy of the customer data, we find many different systems copying that information for its own needs.

> *An alternative to writing our own bridging software would be to use Data Transformation Services (DTS), if appropriate.*

Imagine a customer changes his billing address when placing an order on the e-commerce site. Without a centralized store of customer information, it would be necessary to replicate that change over to other systems. For example, if we send out catalogs in the mail every few months, we'd need to note the new address in whatever system is used to provide the names for the catalog mailings.

New companies usually start in a really strong position because they can ensure that all the relevant information about their customers is kept in a central data store. In the long run, this leads to less complicated systems and lower maintenance costs.

Here's an example of how customer data might be distributed around an organization. All elements of the company need to have access to the same set of data, even though there's no common location where it can all be found:

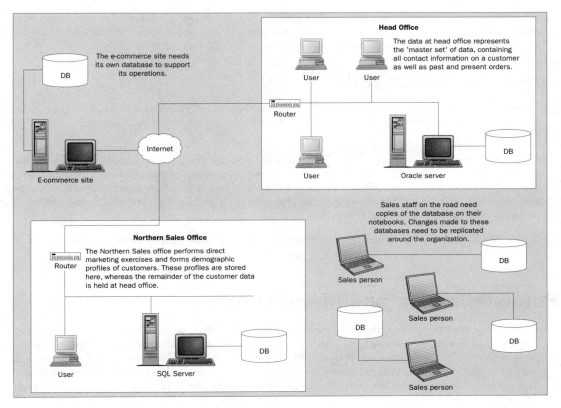

A problem with developing e-business solutions is that they must be based on the information that powers the business. And, as we can see from this diagram, this information is frequently spread over a number of different types of data stores in a number of different locations. So, if we identify a business problem that can be solved through some form of e-business strategy, we need to develop a way of integrating this information.

Sales Chain Integration

Integration is the bugbear of most e-business solutions. Chances are, if our company has already been trading and our e-business systems are part of a reengineering strategy, we already have considerable sets of data to support that system. Even if we are a brand-new company, we'll want to integrate our new custom-made systems, such as an e-commerce site, with off-the-shelf packages, such as an accounting system.

If we already have an existing order processing system, such as one that might be used by a direct telesales team, our e-commerce site can be considered as an alternative front-end to that sales system. In small solutions where cost is a key factor, many companies choose not to integrate their e-commerce site with the order processing system that supports their telesales team. (In this instance, the e-commerce site is often known as "the electronic channel".) Rather, when an order is placed on the site, the details of the order are e-mailed to a sales executive who then rekeys the order into the system. As we can imagine, this approach is extremely error-prone. But, it imposes virtually no development costs on the organization (although, in the long run, the costs of such a system could well outstrip those of a properly automated e-commerce system).

When the e-commerce site can place orders directly into the existing sales system, some type of **sales chain integration** has been performed. In this instance, the role of the sales executive is eliminated and the job of entering the order information into the system is performed by the customer.

Supply Chain Integration

If our company buys products for resale from another company, either as a wholesaler buying direct from a manufacturer or as a retailer buying from a wholesaler, we can take advantage of "supply chain integration".

In this scenario, our sales support systems (which include our electronic channel implemented through our e-commerce site) are integrated with the sales support systems of our suppliers. For example, when our stock level of a certain product is running a little low, our system can directly communicate with and place an order on our supplier's system. This is another example of how e-business solutions can make an organization run more efficiently.

Alternatively, we may download prices directly from our supplier on an hourly, daily or weekly basis, allowing us to check and update our prices on an ongoing basis.

Personalization and Membership

E-commerce sites wishing to make the customer interaction process more involving have popularized **Personalization and Membership**, or P&M. In P&M, if we visit an online bookstore, that bookstore will present us with books that we are likely to have an interest in. So, if the site knows that we have an interest in child rearing, perhaps because we've just bought some baby accessories from another department of the store, it's likely to offer us children's books alongside our usual diet of technical books and contemporary fiction.

P&M can cross boundaries of privacy. For example, if we haven't specifically told the site we've just had a baby, how did it find out? P&M can be a very useful tool for enhancing the customer experience, providing it's done with sensitivity. If the site worked out we've just had a baby by matching our credit card number with sales records at a nationwide chain of baby stores, many people would regard that as an invasion of privacy and take their custom elsewhere. However, if browsing one day we stumble across a suitable book and click the "I like books like these – show me more" button, most customers would not mind being offered particular types of books by the site.

Because e-commerce is arguably the most visible kind of e-business functionality, P&M is usually used in this context. However, companies adopting a broader scope with their e-business strategy will find that P&M techniques have their uses throughout all parts of the strategy to create a richer, and more efficient experience for the customer.

Directories versus Databases

Since the wide scale adoption of directory services, such as Microsoft's Active Directory and NDS, there has been a debate about whether P&M information should be best stored in a directory or in a relational database, such as SQL Server or Oracle.

There's no hard and fast rule about which is better, so we can choose either. One point to consider, however, is that if we do choose to go down the directory route, we may experience difficulties down the line with integration. People have been storing customer information in relational databases since they were invented several decades ago, whereas storing customer information in directories is, by comparison, a very new technique. Integrating these two very different types of data may be very difficult.

Worked Example of P&M and Customer Database Integration

Let's now look at how we can create a personalization and membership system for a simple e-commerce site. In this example, we're going to assume that we have a central store of customer information in our office while our e-commerce site is hosted by a dedicated Windows NT/Windows 2000 hosting company at a separate location. We'll assume that software is in place to synchronize these two databases. Specifically, this will ensure that:

❑ Any new customers added to, or existing ones changed on, the central database by customer service and sales staff is replicated to the off-site e-commerce database.

❑ Any new customers added to, or existing ones changed on the e-commerce site directly, through that customer placing an order, is replicated to the central database.

❑ The customer database includes their P&M profile – a topic we'll cover later.

Here's an overview of the system:

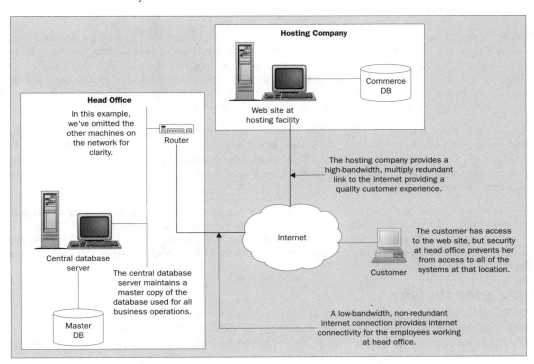

Customer Profile

As we've mentioned before, P&M is based on a customer profile. A profile is simply a set of data that describes the customer such that we can derive, among other things, how the site should be presented to the customer. It includes typical customer data, including:

- ❑ Name
- ❑ Address (or addresses)
- ❑ Company name (or names)
- ❑ Phone numbers (switchboard, direct lines, mobiles, fax, etc.)
- ❑ E-mail address (or addresses)
- ❑ Age, and other demographics, such as marital status and gender
- ❑ Hobbies, and other personal information

As well as these standard items, it can also include things like:

- ❑ Last time the site was visited
- ❑ Number of times the site has been visited
- ❑ Average spend per transaction
- ❑ Preferred types of products
- ❑ Preferred genres of product
- ❑ Upcoming birthdays and other personal special events

In our example, we're going to concentrate on a fictional e-business that operates a fictional e-commerce site selling books, CDs and DVDs. What we're interested in doing is engineering the site to concentrate on selling the products that our customer is most likely to buy, but also offering other products, so that the customer remains aware of our full range of products. So, if our customer mostly buys DVDs, we want to appear to be a site that sells 80% DVDs, and 20% everything else. Likewise, if our customer buys mostly CDs, we want to appear to be 80% CDs, and so on.

As we work through the example, it's this feature of adjusting the product range to suit the customer that we're going to concentrate on. We'll also implement code that handles information about the last time the site was visited and the number of times the site has been visited, but we're assuming that once we understand this foundation work, adding more diversity and richness to our profile will be straightforward.

Whatever we choose to do, all customer profile data can and should be stored in a database or directory of some kind, accessible to all the other systems within our organization. So, if a customer uses an e-commerce site for a year and is only ever interested in CDs, if we wanted to send that customer a catalog through traditional mail, we could include a special offer on CDs, rather than wasting resources including a special offer on books.

Building the Profile

Building the profile itself is reasonably complex because we don't really want to present our customers with such questions as "what do we buy more of?" the first time they visit the site. Apart from anything else, a customer might gradually change his or her buying habits over time, starting off concentrating on books, and then slowly move into DVDs.

The trick is to derive the profile from the customers' activity. If, for example, a customer visits our sites 100 times, but only ever clicks on DVDs, we know that that customer really only wants to know about DVDs, so that's where we should concentrate our selling efforts. However, we should still make sure we tell the customer that we sell CDs and books in case he or she starts to look around for an alternative vendor for these goods.

To do this, all we have to do is keep track of how many items in total the customer looks at, and how those are distributed among the available sets. Here's an example:

	Hits	Percentage of total hits
Books	50	37%
CDs	75	55%
DVDs	10	8%
Total	135	100%

We define a product hit as an activity involving a specific product. This could be the customer drilling down into the product to find out more about it, or adding it to his or her basket. Here, we're aggregating product hits by linking them to a type of product. For the remainder of this example, we're going to refer to a type of product as a department. So, whenever a customer clicks on a particular CD, we increment the hits on the CDs department.

But what do we do with this information? Well, let's imagine that in each of the three product groups we have ten products we're interested in selling on the front page. This concept of "special sale" items is commonly found in e-commerce sites. Of those possible 30 items, we want to display a dozen, but we want that list to be weighted by the customer profile. Looking at the percentages we have so far for our customer, we know that he's most interested in CDs, followed by books, and then DVDs. Taking the weightings from our example, we also know that roughly six of the dozen should be CDs, followed by roughly four books, then two DVDs. We might also take into account the types of CDs or DVDs the customer is interested in. The listing on the front of our site might read:

- ❑ CD – The Middle of Nowhere, Orbital
- ❑ CD – Risotto, Fluke
- ❑ CD – Basement Jaxx, Remedy
- ❑ CD – Blue Wonder Power Milk, Hooverphonic
- ❑ CD – Little Earthquakes, Tori Amos
- ❑ CD – Wide Angle, Hybrid
- ❑ Book – Permutation City, Greg Egan
- ❑ Book – Slab Rat, Ted Heller
- ❑ Book – Beyond Lies the Web, Phillip K Dick
- ❑ Book – Contact, Carl Sagan
- ❑ DVD – Boiler Room
- ❑ DVD – Rushmore

Remember, though, that our entire product catalog is available to the customer – all we're doing at this point is skewing the home page to suit his or her profile. If the customer wants to buy some DVDs and doesn't like the two we're offering, he or she can search for more using the search tools, or click on a "DVD Department" link. We might also want to define a click on the "DVD Department" link itself as a click on the DVDs.

Now let's see what happens if on the next few visits to the site, the customer clicks on the "DVD Department" link, and drills down into a few movies and perhaps even purchases a couple. During those few visits, the customer adds 50 hits to his or her DVD profile.

We now know that the customer is as interested in DVDs as he or she is in books, and that there's now a more even spread across all three departments. The listings that are presented to this customer would change accordingly.

The weightings are adjusted against the customer profile, so we can now see how as he or she uses the site, to present a site that's most suited to the customer. We can now look at how to start building this solution.

Building the Product Catalog

An e-commerce product catalog is simply a set of database tables that describes the set of products and services that our company wants to sell on the Internet. To keep this example simple, we're not going to build a complex structure for holding our product catalog, which will contain just ten products from each of the three departments. Our example here will not be as scalable or maintainable as a real-world solution would require.

> *If you're interested in learning how to build an e-commerce site suitable for real-world deployment, try Beginning E-Commerce, ISBN 1-861003-98-6, also from Wrox Press.*

We first create a new SQL Server database called MyStore, and create this Products table:

We then create this Departments table:

We're going to have a reasonable amount of sample data in this database. The first table to deal with is the Departments table, so we add this data:

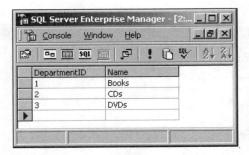

Now we enter the product data. Remember, we're using an Identity flag on the ProductID column, so our product IDs may not match the ones here. It's not a problem if they don't.

ProductID	Name	Author	Description	DepartmentID	Price
1	Permutation City	Greg Egan	<NULL>	1	10
2	Slab Rat	Ted Heller	<NULL>	1	10
3	Beyond Lies the Web	Phillip K Dick	<NULL>	1	10
4	Contact	Carl Sagan	<NULL>	1	10
5	Prometheus Rising	Robert Anton Wilson	<NULL>	1	10
6	3001 : The Final Odyssey	Arthur C Clarke	<NULL>	1	10
7	Bright Messengers	Gentry Lee	<NULL>	1	10
8	Convergent Series	Charles Sheffield	<NULL>	1	10
9	Navohar	Hilari Bell	<NULL>	1	10
10	Hunted	James Alan Gardner	<NULL>	1	10
11	The Middle of Nowhere	Orbital	<NULL>	2	16
12	Risotto	Fluke	<NULL>	2	16
13	Remedy	Basement Jaxx	<NULL>	2	16
14	Blue Wonder Power Milk	Hooverphonic	<NULL>	2	16
15	Little Earthquakes	Tori Amos	<NULL>	2	16
16	Violator	Depeche Mode	<NULL>	2	16
17	Beaucoup Fish	Underworld	<NULL>	2	16
18	Wide Angle	Hybrid	<NULL>	2	16
19	Behind the Sun	Chicane	<NULL>	2	16
20	2Future4U	Armand Van Helden	<NULL>	2	16
21	Boiler Room	Ben Younger	<NULL>	3	20
23	Rushmore	Wes Anderson	<NULL>	3	20
24	Fight Club	David Fincher	<NULL>	3	20
25	The World is not Enough	Michael Apted	<NULL>	3	20
26	Being John Malkovich	Spike Jonze	<NULL>	3	20
27	Dogma	Kevin Smith	<NULL>	3	20
28	Bringing out the Dead	Martin Scorsese	<NULL>	3	20
29	The Insider	Michael Mann	<NULL>	3	20
30	Three Kings	David O Russel	<NULL>	3	20

For simplicity, we have here left the description fields empty. But of course, on a real site, we would want this information to be given.

The final activity to undertake for our database construction is to build a view called vProducts. This view will enable us to instantly cross-reference the department ID to determine the department name. We create the view as shown here:

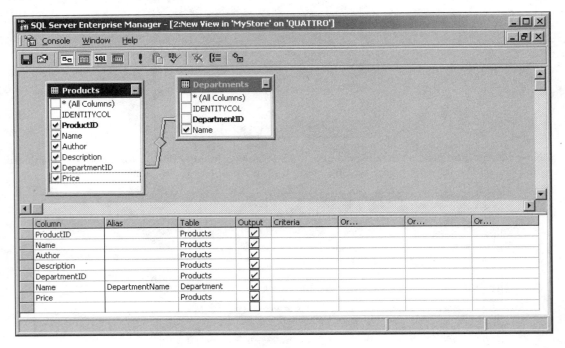

To make sure everyone's on the same page, here's the SQL command that makes up the view:

```
SELECT Products.ProductID, Products.Name, Products.Author,
    Products.Description, Products.DepartmentID,
    Departments.Name AS DepartmentName, Products.Price
FROM Products INNER JOIN
    Departments ON
    Products.DepartmentID = Departments.DepartmentID
```

Building the Customer Database

Now that we've built the catalog tables, we can turn our attention to the Customers table. This table is a fairly simple representation of data that we may hold for a customer. Remember, we may well already have a database of customers somewhere in our organization that is ideal for this purpose.

Here's the table that we're going to use in this example:

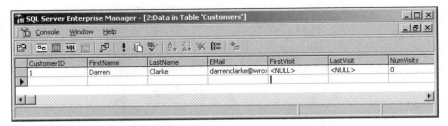

We can see that only four of those columns are traditional customer data, that is ID, first name, last name and e-mail. The rest are the customer profile, and define their action on the site. In this example, we will be keeping track of the first visit, last visit and number of visits the customer makes. We won't be implementing "checkout" code for the site, so a number of purchases and spending columns will not be used. However, it's straightforward to see how they could be used. Finally, the last three columns describe the weighting of the departments.

Notice that we've set the default value for these three columns at 100 hits. We want to start their weighting at a relatively high point so that the first few times the customer visits the site the product ordering doesn't jump around too much. As the weightings get higher, the adjustments will get smoother as each hit has less impact when taken across the entire distribution.

We're only going to use one customer in this demonstration. We enter Darren Clarke into our `Customers` table:

Building the Business and Presentation Tiers

Now that we have the data tier squared away, we can concentrate on the business and presentation tiers. We want to try and keep this example fairly limited, so here's the functionality we wish to provide:

❑   Display a dozen products on the front page, the content of which is weighted according to a customer profile.

❑   Each product will be "clickable", each click adjusting the weightings against the department of the product.

We're not going to concern ourselves with allowing customers to log onto the site either. When the session is first created, we're going to choose a customer at random and he or she will be the user throughout that session. Of course, in a real life situation, we would want to supply a logon page.

Building the Business Tier

We'll be implementing this example as a pure 3-tier distributed application, so we need to start putting together the object model for the application.

To keep this example simple, we're going to keep the object model very simple – in fact, we're only going to have a single object: `Visit`. This object will represent a single visit to the site, which translates to exactly one page view. One instance of this object will be created per page view, and each instance will be destroyed when the page no longer needs the object.

We create a new Visual Basic **ActiveX DLL** project. Using the Project Explorer, we change the name of the project to `MyStore`, and the name of the new class module to `Visit`.

Before we start adding methods to this object, we need to create references to the two libraries we'll be using – Microsoft **ActiveX Data Objects** and the Microsoft **Scripting Runtime library**.

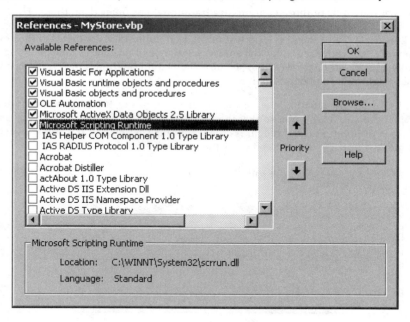

In our example, we've created a reference to Microsoft ADO 2.5. This is installed by default in Windows 2000, but is also available in Visual Studio Service Pack 4.0, or may be downloaded from `www.microsoft.com/data`.

There is quite a lot of code we need added to the `Visit` object. This may be downloaded from the Wrox website at `www.wrox.com`. Most of the methods and properties are very straightforward.

Without further ado, let's take a look at the code:

```
Option Explicit

' we need somewhere to hold the database details...
Private m_strDBString As String
Private m_objConnection As Connection

' we also need somewhere to hold the customer id...
Dim m_lngCustomerID As Long
```

These will form the member variables for the object properties. We keep track of the OLE DB connection string, the ADO object used to hold the open connection, and the currently logged in user:

```
' DBString - store the database string in the object...
Public Property Let DBString (ByVal strNewVal As String)
    m_strDBString = strNewVal
End Property
```

The DBString property simply stores the OLE DB string in the member variable:

```
' DB - get the ADO Connection object (create it if we don't have it)
Private Property Get DB() As Connection

    ' do we already have a database?
    If m_objConnection Is Nothing Then

        ' create a new connection...
        Set m_objConnection = New Connection

        ' open the connection using the database string we set before...
        m_objConnection.Open m_strDBString

    End If

    ' return our database...
    Set DB = m_objConnection

End Property
```

This is an example of **just in time activation**, which is a great technique to use when building scalable distributed applications. When building such applications, it's important that we try to limit the "resource footprint". This footprint is a measure of the amount of resources an application is using at a specific moment in time. Even though the Visit object may have been around for a number of seconds, if none of the methods or properties has needed a database connection, one will not have been opened.

Instead, the very first call to the DB property creates an ADO connection object and uses the m_strDBString member variable to create it:

```
' Shutdown - stop the object, including closing the database
Public Function Shutdown()

    ' if we have a connection, close it...
    If Not m_objConnection Is Nothing Then
        m_objConnection.Close
        Set m_objConnection = Nothing
    End If

End Function
```

933

The `Shutdown` method closes the database connection. We should always remember to do this:

```
' Visit's destructor...
Private Sub Class_Terminate ()

    ' call shutdown to make sure we've cleaned up, even if not explicitly called
    Shutdown

End Sub
```

Although `Shutdown` should be called properly, we've created a terminator on the class so if the ASP developer forgets to close the connection, we still clean up our database connection. If, on the other hand, the ASP developer has closed the connection, this code is skipped:

```
' CustomerID - set the ID of the customer...
Public Property Let CustomerID(ByVal lngNewVal As Long)
    m_lngCustomerID = lngNewVal
End Property

' CustomerID - return the current ID...
Public Property Get CustomerID() As Long
    CustomerID = m_lngCustomerID
End Property
```

The `CustomerID` property gets and sets the ID of the logged in customer using the `m_lngCustomerID` member variable:

```
' IsLoggedOn - determines if a customer is logged on...
Public Function IsLoggedOn() As Boolean
    If CustomerID = 0 Then
        IsLoggedOn = False
    Else
        IsLoggedOn = True
    End If
End Function
```

The `IsLoggedOn` helper method examines the `CustomerID` property and returns a Boolean value indicating the logged on state of the user:

```
' SetCustomerVisit - call on the start of the session to introduce a customer...
Public Function SetCustomerVisit()

    ' now make some changes to the database to set his or her first visit,
    ' last visit and total visits...

    DB.Execute "update customers set firstvisit=getdate() where " & _
               "customerid=" & CustomerID & " and firstvisit is null"
    DB.Execute "update customers set lastvisit=getdate(), " & _
               "numvisits=numvisits+1 where customerid=" & CustomerID

End Function
```

The ASP developer calls the `SetCustomerVisit` method when the customer logs into the site. It records the first time he or she visits the site, and records his or her last visit and total number of visits:

```
' Customer - return the customer...
Public Property Get Customer() As Recordset

    ' do we have a customer?
    If CustomerID <> 0 Then

        ' select the customer out...
        Set Customer = DB.Execute("select top 1 * from customers where " & _
                                        "customerid=" & CustomerID)

        ' don't return anything if the id is invalid...
        If Customer.EOF Then
            Customer.Close
            Set Customer = Nothing
        End If

    End If

End Property
```

The `Customer` property returns a properly configured recordset containing a row from the `Customers` table that represents the logged in customer.

That's the end of the standard set of properties and methods on the `Visit` object. Now we can start using the model.

Building a Basic Page

For this exercise, we're going to require two ASP pages: `default.asp` and `site.asp`. `default.asp` will provide our front page listing of the products on offer, whereas `site.asp` will provide support functionality to the application.

site.asp

To start with, we create a new page called `site.asp` and add the following code. For simplicity, we have here used session variables, however, as we have explained in many places in this book, we should, ideally, avoid using them:

```
<%
    Dim m_objVisit

    ' Visit...
    Function Visit

        ' do we have a visit?
        If IsEmpty(m_objVisit) Then

            ' create it...
            Set m_objVisit = Server.CreateObject("MyStore.Visit")
            ' set its database string...
            m_objVisit.DBString = _
            "driver=sql server;database=mystore;uid=sa;pwd=;server=beetle"

            ' do we have a customer in the session?
            If IsEmpty(Session("CustomerID")) Then
```

```
                      ' set the session... use any row we like from
                      ' our customers table for this demo...
                      Session ("CustomerID") = 1
                      m_objVisit.CustomerID = Session("CustomerID")

                      ' set the last visit details...
                      m_objVisit.SetCustomerVisit

              Else
                      m_objVisit.CustomerID = Session("CustomerID")
              End If

          End If

          ' return it...
          Set Visit = m_objVisit

      End Function

      ' Shutdown - make sure Visit has been cleaned up...
      Function Shutdown

          ' close visit...
          If Not IsEmpty(m_objVisit) Then
              m_objVisit.Shutdown
              Set m_objVisit = Nothing
          End If

      End Function
  %>
```

Our goal with `site.asp` is to provide very easy access to the object model through a function called `Visit`. In later ASP pages, the `Visit` function will provide a fully configured instance of our `MyStore.Visit` object. To configure the object, all we have to do is supply an OLE DB connection string. The neat thing about using this method is that the object is not instantiated or configured until the very first time `Visit` is called. This is another example of just in time activation.

> *We'll need to alter our connection string to point to our database server and use a correctly configured user ID and password. In our example, our "sa" user has no password and our server is called "beetle". By default, SQL Server uses the NetBIOS client access library to communicate with its servers, so our database server name will typically be the Windows Networking name of the server itself.*

We're also forcing a customer to be logged in all the time – in this case the customer with an ID of "1"; Darren Clarke. We'll need to find an appropriate ID from our `Customers` table and use that to get our example to work. We're using the `Session` object here to use ASP's default session manager to keep track of the currently logged in user. Although we're forcing a user to be logged in, in a real-world application we'd provide a method for the user to log into his or her account.

In this example, we provide this functionality to ensure that `SetCustomerVisit` is only called once per session. If we recall, this function records their first visit to the site (in the case of customer data being imported from an existing customer database), their last visit to the site, and the total number of visits they have made.

The other function in `site.asp` is `Shutdown`. This function checks to see if `Visit` has ever been called and, if it has, calls `Visit.Shutdown`. This method in turn closes the database connection if one has been opened.

Default.asp

Now we can turn our attention to a basic `default.asp` page. To start with, we just want to display the first name of the logged in customer. Here's the code:

```
<% Option Explicit %>
<HTML>
<HEAD>
<TITLE>MyStore</TITLE>
</HEAD>
<BODY>
<!-- #include file="site.asp" -->

    <%
        ' do we need to welcome the visitor?
        If Visit.IsLoggedOn = True Then

            ' get the customer...
            Dim rsCustomer
            Set rsCustomer = Visit.Customer
            Response.Write "<b>Hello "
            Response.Write rsCustomer("FirstName")
            Response.Write "!</b><br><br>"
            rsCustomer.Close
            Set rsCustomer = Nothing

        End If
    %>

</BODY>
</HTML>

<%
    Shutdown
%>
```

The `Visit.IsLoggedOn` call first calls the `Visit` function which instantiates and configures a `Visit` object that we'll use throughout the page. The call to the `Shutdown` function at the end of the page properly cleans up this `Visit` object. We then ask this object if the customer is logged in. If so, we receive a recordset containing the customer's information and we render his or her first name. Here's how it looks:

Of course, now we have to get that page displaying the product list! Let's look at that now.

Customer Profiles and Product Selection

With the core business objects in place, we can turn our attention to the fun part of the project – writing the code that selects out the dozen products we're interested in.

There are a number of rules this code needs to adhere to:

❑ We want a single recordset containing the dozen products, in order.

❑ We always want to include at least one item from each of the three departments.

❑ If equal weightings are found, the default order must be "Books" then "CDs" then "DVDs".

We add this `GetFrontPageItems` method to the `Visit` object:

```
' GetFrontPageItems - get the items that should appear on the front page...
Public Function GetFrontPageItems (Optional ByVal lngNumProducts As Long = 12, _
             Optional ByVal boolAsKeyset As Boolean) As Dictionary

    ' firstly, select all of the departments from the database.
    ' the order in this Recordset will determine the default
    ' order on the site...
    Dim rsDepts As New Recordset
    Dim lngNumDepts As Long
    rsDepts.Open "select * from departments order by departmentid", DB, _
            adOpenKeyset, adLockOptimistic
    lngNumDepts = rsDepts.RecordCount
```

Our first job is to select the departments. Although this is a limited example, we're trying to build some code that can grow, so if we add another row to the `Departments` table, this function and its siblings will continue to work as normal.

We open the recordset as a keyset so that we can quickly find the number of departments that we're dealing with. By adding an `ORDER` directive to the statement, we always bring out the departments in the same order. This activity also provides the default order of the listing should the scores be equal.

One slight problem with this is that we have to make an association between the name of the department and the name of the column as it appears in the `Customers` table. The assumption is that if we take the last letter off the department name (so "Books" becomes "Book"), adding the word "Hits" to the end forms the name. In the departments we have so far, this works fine: "Books" becomes "BookHits", "CDs" becomes "CDHits" and "DVDs" becomes "DVDHits". We'll see this in action in a moment:

```
    ' first of all, set up the default weightings...
    Dim lngHits(lngNumDepts) As Long
    Dim lngDeptIDs(lngNumDepts) As Long
    Dim lngTotalHits As Long
```

Once we have the departments, we create two dynamic arrays. `lngHits` will first be populated with the raw score drawn from the customers table. `lngDeptIDs` will store the ID of each department:

```
    ' get the customer back...
Dim rsCustomer As Recordset
Set rsCustomer = Customer

    ' loop the departments, loading the hits from the profile on each one...
    ' or, if we don't have a customer, setting a default value...
Dim intC As Integer
Do While Not rsDepts.EOF

    ' do we have a customer? if so, use the name of the department as the
    ' basis of the column in the profile...
    If Not Customer Is Nothing Then
        lngHits(intC) = _
        Customer(Left(rsDepts("Name"), Len(rsDepts("Name")) - 1) & "Hits")
    Else
        lngHits(intC) = 100
    End If

    ' adjust the total...
    lngTotalHits = lngTotalHits + lngHits(intC)

    ' store the department id...
    lngDeptIDs(intC) = rsDepts("DepartmentID")

    ' next
    rsDepts.MoveNext
    intC = intC + 1

Loop
rsDepts.Close
Set rsDepts = Nothing
```

Before walking the departments, we use the `Customer` property to select a recordset containing the customer information. As we walk the departments, if we have a customer logged onto the site we take their score from their profile and add it to the `lngHits` array. Notice how we use `Left` and `Len` to construct the column name in the `Customers` table based on the `Name` column in the `Departments` table.

If we have no customer, we default the score to "100". Finally, we keep track of the total number of points and store the department ID in `lngDeptIDs`:

```
    ' now, adjust the scores for each of the departments such that each fits into
    ' the number of products we want (a default of 12)...
    For intC = 0 To lngNumDepts - 1

        ' set it...
        lngHits(intC) = _
            CInt(CDbl(lngNumProducts) * (CDbl(lngHits(intC)) /
CDbl(lngTotalHits)))

        ' check it...
```

```
        If lngHits(intC) = 0 Then lngHits(intC) = 1
        If lngHits(intC) > lngNumProducts - (lngNumDepts - 1) Then
            lngHits(intC) = lngNumProducts - (lngNumDepts - 1)
        End If

    Next
```

Once we've loaded the scores, or we've set default scores, we adjust each score as a percentage of the total number of items we want returned. By default, this number is "12" and is passed through the optional parameter `lngNumProducts`. So, if we have 1000 hits in total, and 500 are for books, 250 for CDs, and 250 for DVDs, we end up with 50%, 25%, and 25%, or 6, 3, and 3 actual rows. As we want to make sure that we list every type of product, if we get zero products we change it to 1, and if we end up with too many products, we drop down the total such that we always have room for the other product types:

```
    ' sort the order, based on the scores...
    Dim boolDidMove As Boolean
    Dim lngIDBuffer As Long, lngHitBuffer As Long
    Do
        ' loop the first departments, checking to see if the value
        ' beneath it is more...
        boolDidMove = False
        For intC = 0 To lngNumDepts - 2

            ' check the next item...
            If lngHits(intC) < lngHits(intC + 1) Then

                ' swap them...
                lngIDBuffer = lngDeptIDs(intC)
                lngDeptIDs(intC) = lngDeptIDs(intC + 1)
                lngDeptIDs(intC + 1) = lngIDBuffer
                lngHitBuffer = lngHits(intC)
                lngHits(intC) = lngHits(intC + 1)
                lngHits(intC + 1) = lngHitBuffer

                ' flag the fact we did something...
                boolDidMove = True

                ' quit the loop so we can start again...
                Exit For

            End If

        Next

        ' Loop until the customer does something
    Loop While boolDidMove = False
```

Once we have the adjusted scores, we run a quick bubble sort so that the biggest score is on the top (a bubble sort simply sorts a series of integers by size). This sort preserves the default order as defined when we selected the departments, so the default order of "Books" then "CDs" then "DVDs" is preserved:

```
' check the scores to make sure they don't exceed lngNumProducts...
Dim lngMaxDept As Long, lngMaxScore As Long, lngCheckTotal As Long
lngMaxDept = -1
lngMaxScore = 0
For intC = 0 To lngNumDepts - 1

    ' found highest...
    If lngHits(intC) > lngMaxScore Then
        lngMaxScore = lngHits(intC)
        lngMaxDept = intC
    End If

    ' add to the total...
    lngCheckTotal = lngCheckTotal + lngHits(intC)

Next

' did the total exceed lngNumProducts?
' take the excess of off the maximum score...
If lngCheckTotal > lngNumProducts Then
    lngHits(lngMaxDept) = lngHits(lngMaxDept) - _
                                (lngCheckTotal - lngNumProducts)

End If
```

Once we have the sorted scores, we want to make sure that the total adjusted scores we have (That is the number of rows we want from each department) don't exceed the number of products we require. This can happen because we're converting between integers and real numbers and back again, which introduces rounding errors.

Paradoxically, these errors are useful for sorting, but returning more results than we've asked for is sloppy. To do this, we find the department with the maximum score and subtract the excess from this department:

```
' run all of the queries and return them as an array...
Dim strSQL As String
Dim rsResults As Recordset
Dim objResults As New Dictionary


For intC = 0 To lngNumDepts - 1

    ' form the sql...
    strSQL = "select top " & lngHits(intC) & _
                    " * from vproducts where departmentid=" & _
                            lngDeptIDs(intC) & " order by productid"

    ' run the query. if we want a keyset cursor, handle that...
    If boolAsKeyset = False Then
        Set rsResults = DB.Execute(strSQL)
    Else
        Set rsResults = New Recordset
        rsResults.Open strSQL, DB, adOpenKeyset, adLockOptimistic
    End If
```

```
        ' add it to the dictionary...
        objResults.Add intC, rsResults

    Next

    ' return the dictionary...
    Set GetFrontPageItems = objResults

End Function
```

Finally, we create a `Dictionary` object into which the results will be added and returned from the function. As we walk through each of the scores in order, an individual recordset is created and added to the dictionary. The ASP developer can then walk through the items in this dictionary to return and render each recordset.

To present the results we have to adjust our listing for `default.asp`. We add this code in the appropriate place:

```
<% Option Explicit %>
<HTML>
<HEAD>
<TITLE>MyStore</TITLE>
</HEAD>
<BODY>
<!-- #include file="site.asp" -->

    <%

        ' do we need to welcome the visitor?
        If Visit.IsLoggedOn = True Then

            ' get the customer...
            Dim rsCustomer
            Set rsCustomer = Visit.Customer
            Response.Write "<b>Hello "
            Response.Write rsCustomer("FirstName")
            Response.Write "!</b><br><br>"
            rsCustomer.Close
            Set rsCustomer = Nothing

        End If

        ' retrieve the default front page products from the database
        ' and render each one...
        Dim objProducts
        Set objProducts = Visit.GetFrontPageItems

        ' loop the Recordsets that we have...
        Dim rsItems
        For Each rsItems in objProducts.Items

            Response.Write "<b>" & rsItems("DepartmentName") & "</b><br>"
```

```
        ' loop the products...
        Dim lngLastDeptID
        lngLastDeptID = -1
        Do While Not rsItems.EOF

            ' render the item...
            Response.Write "<li><a href="""
            Response.Write """>" & rsItems("Name") & "</a>"
            Response.Write "<br>"

            ' next
            rsItems.MoveNext

        Loop
        rsItems.Close
        Set rsItems = Nothing

    Next
%>

</BODY>
</HTML>

<%
    Shutdown
%>
```

As we can see, getting a list of the products is virtually no problem for the ASP programmer: one call to GetFrontPageItems and, by default, a dozen products are displayed to loop through and render. Here's what the page looks like by default when Darren is logged into the site:

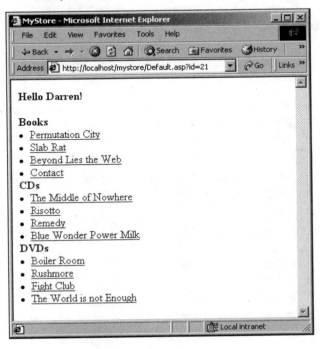

Adjusting the Profile

In order to make the personalization and membership actually do something, we need to provide a way to adjust the weighting depending on the customer activity. We're going to do this in two ways – one method deals with hits to a product, the other deals with hits directly to a department.

Firstly, we add this `AddDepartmentHit` method to the `visit` class:

```
' AddDepartmentHit - add a hit for a department...
Public Function AddDepartmentHit(ByVal DepartmentID As Long)

    ' are we logged in?
    If IsLoggedOn Then

        ' get the department that we're dealing with...
        Dim rsDept As Recordset
        Set rsDept = DB.Execute("select top 1 * from departments " & _
                                "where departmentid=" & DepartmentID)
        If Not rsDept.EOF Then

            ' get the column name...
            Dim ColumnName As String
            ColumnName = Left(rsDept("Name"), Len(rsDept("Name")) - 1) & "Hits"

            ' update the database....
            DB.Execute "update customers set " & ColumnName & "=" & _
                        ColumnName & "+1 where customerid=" & CustomerID

        End If
        rsDept.Close
        Set rsDept = Nothing

    End If

End Function
```

Notice how we're using the `Left` and `Len` functions to construct the appropriate column name once we've selected the department. Once we have this, we call `DB.Execute` to run a simple SQL statement that updates the profile. Also notice how we're checking to make sure the customer is logged in before we do any of this work.

A good extension here would be to store default customer profiles at an alternative location in the database – that way we can monitor the activities of customers who aren't logged in and learn more about our business.

It's time now to add the other method of the pair – `AddProductHit`:

```
' AddProductHit - adds a hit for a product...
Public Function AddProductHit(ByVal ProductID As Long)

    ' get the product so we can find the department...
    Dim rsProduct As Recordset
```

```
            Set rsProduct = DB.Execute("select top 1 * from products" & _
                                "where productid=" ProductID)
    If Not rsProduct.EOF Then

        ' add a hit to the department...
        AddDepartmentHit rsProduct("DepartmentID")

    End If
    rsProduct.Close
    Set rsProduct = Nothing

End Function
```

The last time we changed `default.asp`, we created the items as links, but didn't provide anywhere for those links to go. We'll do this now by making each link call back into the page, providing the ID of the product in the query string. When the page is executed, we'll check for the existence of this variable in both the query string and form variables and, if it's there, call `AddProductHit` with the appropriate ID. Here's the modified `default.asp`:

```
<% Option Explicit
    ' did we click a product? if so, we need to adjust the rating...
    If Request("id") <> "" Then
        Visit.AddProductHit Request("id")
    End If

%>
<HTML>
<HEAD>
<TITLE>MyStore</TITLE>
</HEAD>
<BODY>
<!-- #include file="site.asp" -->

    <%

        ' do we need to welcome the visitor?
        If Visit.IsLoggedOn = True Then

            ' get the customer...
            Dim rsCustomer
            Set rsCustomer = Visit.Customer
            Response.Write "<b>Hello "
            Response.Write rsCustomer("FirstName")
            Response.Write "!</b><br><br>"
            rsCustomer.Close
            Set rsCustomer = Nothing

        End If

        ' retrieve the default front page products from the database
        ' and render each one...
        Dim objProducts
        Set objProducts = Visit.GetFrontPageItems
```

```
    ' loop the Recordsets that we have...
    Dim rsItems
    For Each rsItems in objProducts.Items

        Response.Write "<b>" & rsItems("DepartmentName") & "</b><br>"

        ' loop the products...
        Dim lngLastDeptID
        lngLastDeptID = -1
        Do While Not rsItems.EOF

            ' render the item...
            Response.Write "<li><a href="""
            Response.Write Request.ServerVariables("script_name")
            Response.Write "?id=" & rsItems("ProductID")
            Response.Write """>" & rsItems("Name") & "</a>"
            Response.Write "<br>"

            ' next
            rsItems.MoveNext

        Loop
        rsItems.Close
        Set rsItems = Nothing

    Next

%>

</BODY>
</HTML>

<%
    Shutdown
%>
```

To try this example, we refresh the page to get the links working and then click on one of the DVDs once. If we examine the Customers table, we'll see something like this:

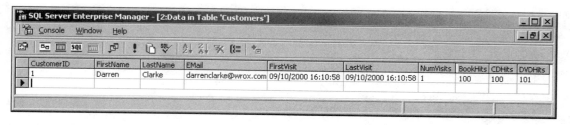

What this shows is that Darren's DVD weighting has been affected. This indicates that Darren is more interested in DVDs that anything else. However, no change will appear on the first page because taken across the entire distribution, that change is not significant enough to affect our algorithm. However, if we change DVDHits to 121, we'll see this:

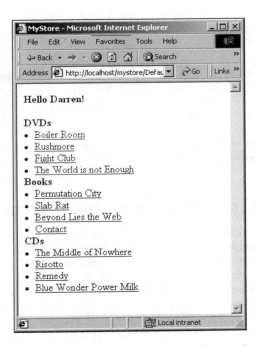

So by watching what Darren clicks on, we can make it easier for him to find the products he wants, which makes for a more useful customer experience for him. To round off this discussion, let's examine what happens if Darren brings his DVD hits to 1000, but never clicks on a book or CD:

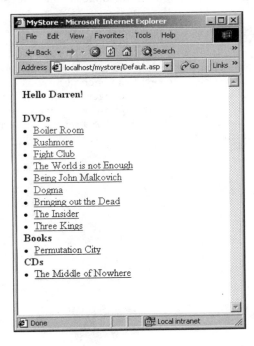

Security

All e-business systems need to be secure, in terms of ensuring that the data that powers our system is available only to the select few bits of hardware and software that it comprises. For example, an e-commerce site that allows hackers to intercept our customers' credit card numbers is doomed to failure. Likewise, any business partner we deal with will typically insist that data passing between our systems is subject to rigorous security procedures.

Security can be considered as two separate sections. Firstly, data traveling to or from our system must be impervious to interception. Secondly, data held on our system must not be readable, or changeable, to outsiders.

Protecting Data as it Travels to Our Server

The best way to protect data as it moves from system to system is to use encryption. By using encryption, we can rest assured that should the messages be intercepted (which, when transmitted over the public Internet they may well be) they cannot be understood by the interceptor.

Today, the most popular kind of cryptography is **Public Key Cryptography**, or **PKC**. In PKC, two massively long prime numbers are multiplied together to get an even bigger prime number. This bigger number is then applied to the message we're trying to encrypt through a relatively simple mathematical process. The end result is an encrypted message.

For example, if we started with the credit card number *4111 1111 1111 1111*, we'll end up with something unreadable, such as *jk_d#h(*&#$0SLHY&*(*9[p3844GV*%(*. Once we have the encrypted message, to read it all we have to do is perform the opposite mathematical number, again using the bigger prime number.

The smart thing about PKC is that it provides a **public key** and a **private key**. Both of these are created together as a single "key pair". By having two keys, I can give my public key to anyone I want. Anyone having the public key can use their private key and my public key to create a message that only I can decrypt. And, with someone else's public key, I can encrypt messages that only they can decrypt (with my public key and their private key). There's no danger that anyone will be able to decrypt my message with just my public key; only a person with the appropriate private key can have access to it. In fact, many people using PKC will put their public keys onto a server where anyone wanting to send them a private message can download the key:

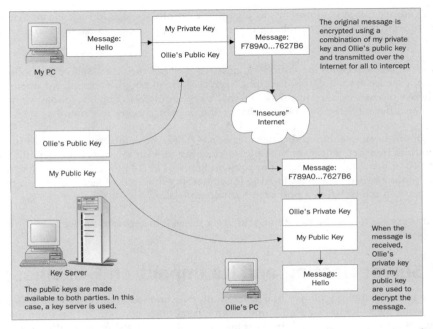

When accepting sensitive information over the Web from the general public – for example, when taking a credit card number as part of an e-commerce purchase – our only option is to use **Secure Socket Layer**, or **SSL**. SSL uses PKC to encrypt communications, but all of the negotiation to determine which keys should be used is handled by the browser and server without user intervention. This makes it very easy for the customer to securely pass information to us, and today the public perception of SSL is sufficiently good that whenever the padlock icon appears in the status bar of the browser, the customer knows his or her information is secure.

The only caveat about SSL is that we have to obtain a "server certificate". This certificate proves to the visitor that the server is operated by the legal entity they're entering into a contract with. For example, if we're buying something from Amazon.com, their server certificate proves that the server is operated by "Amazon.com Inc, Seattle, WA". Certificates are issued by a Certificate Authority (CA), and they go to considerable lengths to ensure that any application is legitimate.

Protecting Data on Our Server

When the data has found its way onto our server, we need to protect it to ensure that parties cannot download or change that data. One type of data that's been attracting attention from a security perspective in recent years is that of credit card numbers. Several e-commerce sites attempt to make it easier for customers to make repeat purchases by storing customer's credit card numbers in their database, and this can cause problems.

However, can we imagine what would happen if a high profile e-commerce site happened to have a copy of their customer database, complete with credit card numbers, stolen? Chances are, that such a venture would go bankrupt as customer trust in the operation collapsed. This is why some companies choose not to store credit card numbers and ask the customer to enter it each time he wants to make a purchase. They are, of course, still open to the risk of someone stealing their customer list and selling it to a competitor.

In order to ensure our system remains as secure as possible, we should seek the advice of a professional security consultant, although there are a couple of easy things we can do straightaway to help boost security.

Firstly, we can use extremely random, long passwords. Passwords like "secret" or "john" are simply not suitable for a secure system. Passwords like "secret15" are getting better, but, for maximum security, we should choose passwords like "ppiL744AZ83hG". We should also make sure that we don't use the same password for different things, and try to change the password every few months.

Secondly, if our hosting solution dictates that our SQL Server database is accessible through TCP/IP over the public Internet, wherever possible we're going to want to change the default port. SQL Server uses port 1433 by default, so change it to something else, like 14128. Of course, a hacker is in a position to scan all of the ports on a server, looking for something that looks like SQL Server, but there are tools available that can tell us when a port scan has taken place.

Thirdly, if we're hosting in-house, we should use a firewall to separate the web site from the rest of our public network.

Shared Server Hosting and its Impact on E-business

One of the issues that many people find when deploying an e-commerce solution is that their hosting company won't allow them to install homegrown Visual Basic components on their shared servers. As this is often the most inexpensive hosting route, many people developing smaller e-business systems find this a bit of a problem.

Hosting companies don't like to allow people to install software they don't understand, and, typically, homegrown VB components fall into this category. Their fear is that someone will run some code that compromises the integrity of the system, or unfairly takes processor cycles away from the other customers on the server. With ASP pages, they can easily examine the pages to make sure that no one's doing anything questionable.

So, typically, this means that if we wish to run our e-business system on a shared host, and engineer the solution using the techniques set out earlier, we can't use shared hosting (although there are a few hosting companies that would allow us to do this). Our only solution is to rent a dedicated server (that is become the only customer on the machine, so we cannot affect their other customers) or "co-locate" a server (that is give them a machine to put into their data center). As we can imagine, both these options are more expensive than shared hosting.

Before throwing our hands up in despair, it's worth noting that our security requirements will prevent us from using shared hosting anyway! It simply is not a sound proposition to run our e-business system from a shared host. There are three reasons for this:

❑ The first reason is that, just as we could hog all of the resources and prevent other sites from operating properly, so could other people on our server. One badly written ASP page on our neighbor's site, and suddenly our site will stop responding. If this happens regularly, and we have to solve the problem, tracking down the problem would be particularly difficult. This difficulty would be compounded, as there would be no way of isolating our site from the others sharing the server.

❑ The second reason is that we would not have a fine level of control over the server, as we would have over our development server and dedicated production server. All dedicated web hosts provide remote control software, either through Terminal Services, Symantec's pcAnywhere or the excellent, freeware VNC (`http://www.uk.research.att.com/vnc/`). This means we can stop and start services, install or uninstall any software we want, and configure anything just how we like it, without having to struggle with a potentially difficult systems administrator.

❑ The third reason is probably the most important. There is a very real security risk in using shared servers because we are *no longer physically isolated from our neighbors*. This increases the chance that someone could contravene our security. Here's an example: our shared server is configured relatively sloppily (remember, without administrative control, we can't easily check for or remedy security issues) and a neighbor runs some ASP pages using the `FileSystemObject` object that examines each page on our site looking for a database connection string. Once the string has been found, he or she connects to the database and downloads our customer database.

In a dedicated hosting environment, we have the control to determine exactly how the security on the server is configured, and we have an extra boundary of physical isolation. We have the ability to make it harder for the hacker to find his way into our system and act maliciously.

It's mainly for this reason that if we're running *any* form of software requiring approval or cooperation from a bank, they will reject any infrastructure based on shared hosting. If we want to take credit cards, we cannot use a shared host.

Although dedicated NT hosting was once quite rare, a lot of hosting companies are now offering it. A number of these companies are also hosting on Windows 2000 Server. A good source of companies is CNet's Web Host List at `http://www.webhostlist.com/`.

Summary

In this chapter we looked a little at e-business and e-commerce and discussed the various kinds of integration that are involved in e-business systems. We then looked at Personalization and Membership ("P&M"), and put together a system for providing personalization for a site that sells books, CDs and DVDs. Finally, to round off the chapter, we looked at securing our e-business solution, both in terms of protecting data as it travels between systems and protecting data once it's there.

29
Data Shaping

In this part of the book we are looking at different types of data which, for various reasons, are not really suited to being stored in a relational database. For instance, in Chapter 18 we looked at directories and the reasons why it is sometimes preferable to store certain forms of data hierarchically.

This chapter also has a hierarchical theme, but the emphasis is slightly different. The data we will examine here is merely *accessed* hierarchically. In the database, it is still stored relationally. We will *transform* the structure of the data as we extract it from the database.

Why would we want to do this? Well, primarily to maximize the performance of the server, and also to minimize the amount of data sent to the client. When the relational data we are interested in is spread over several tables, we will normally need to do some sort of join in order to view it. That not only gives a lot of work for the database to do, but often leads to a fair amount of duplication of data in the results. If the data is being transmitted over a network or over the Internet, then that duplication of data can be one of the most significant factors impairing performance. Transforming the data to a hierarchical form avoids this overhead.

The tool we're going to use in this chapter is the **OLE DB Data Shaping Provider**, which comes with ADO/MDAC version 2.1 onwards. This provider can *shape* our data, converting it to various different hierarchical structures, or shapes.

We saw back in Chapter 6 that there are broadly three categories of OLE DB: providers, consumers, and service providers. The data shaping provider will normally obtain data from another OLE DB provider (termed the **data provider**), then supply the transformed data to the consumer. As far as the consumer is concerned, the data shaping provider is just a normal OLE DB provider, while as far as the data provider is concerned, it's a client.

The data shaping provider can take as its data source any other OLE DB provider – which means that we can use it to view data from any of the relational databases accessible through OLE DB – but we get the benefit of being able to use a highly efficient hierarchical arrangement of recordsets. We can even change this arrangement according to the way we want to view the data without having to go back to the actual data source. There are also facilities to calculate various aggregates and averaged results over the data.

In this chapter we're going to kick off by examining the problem of doing a simple INNER JOIN on a couple of tables. A pretty simple task in SQL, but we're going to look at it in detail in order to see precisely why the performance problems with using straight SQL occur, and how they can be solved by transforming the data and retrieving it hierarchically. After this we'll move on to an example, looking at how we can use the data shaping provider to provide an alternative to using a JOIN. After that, we'll look at some slightly more advanced topics, such as aggregating data. In the process we'll become familiar with the Shape data-shaping language. We use this to send commands to the data shaping provider.

Throughout this chapter, we're going to use the pubs sample database that comes supplied with SQL Server. This contains data concerning books, their authors and publishers, and where the books are sold. The database is moderately complex, but for most of the chapter we'll only need to work with a few of the tables in it, so familiarity with the database is not really necessary.

Why We Need Data Shaping

In this section we're going to examine why a SQL join is inefficient and how data shaping can solve this problem.

As an example, consider the portion of the pubs database that stores details of the publishers and the employees. That bit looks like this:

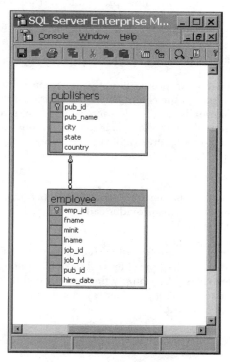

What we see is a pair of tables with a one-many relationship between them represented by a primary key in the `publishers` table related to the foreign key, `pub_id`, in the `employee` table. The relationship is this way round because there are many employees working for a given publisher.

Let's say we want to retrieve details of employees working for all publishers– we want the first and last name, publisher's name, and city of each employee. That's not hard to do in SQL – the statement that will do that is this:

```
SELECT      dbo.employee.fname, dbo.employee.lname, dbo.publishers.pub_name,
dbo.publishers.city
FROM        dbo.employee
INNER JOIN dbo.publishers ON dbo.publishers.pub_id = dbo.employee.pub_id
```

If we create a new View in SQL Server using the above SQL statement we can see the results:

This looks OK, and is relatively easy to do. The trouble is, the process of generating this result actually involves more work than we really require in order to see the employee details. If we look at the `pub_name` column of the results, we can see that the string 'Binnet & Hardley' is repeated many times. And the same goes for the names of every other publisher, and for the city names in the fourth column.

These strings aren't repeated in the actual database, because the publishers' details are stored in a separate table from the employees' details. This allows details of each publisher to be stored only once. In other words, the database was sufficiently normalised to avoid the repetition of data. But in the process of doing the `INNER JOIN`, we de-normalised the data and so generated results with each publishers' details repeated as many times as the number of employees for that publisher. For the actual example here, in which we're using the Enterprise Manager to view the data, this isn't really an issue, but if we were viewing the data on an ASP page, using ADO to communicate with the database, this data duplication would give us a fair bit of extra work on two counts.

Firstly, the database server has to do a lot of work in copying the data to generate the query results. Secondly, there's quite a good chance that the ASP page may be running on a different machine from the database server. This means a lot of duplicated data is going to be transmitted over the network – or possibly even over the Internet. Over a network, the extent to which performance will be impaired may be insignificant. However, over the Internet it could make a very large difference.

This problem will be more acute if we use RDS to actually send the recordsets to the client (browser) machine, and have them processed there. Another potential problem is the extra memory that needs to be allocated on the client or the web server to store the duplicate data – though this is less serious and only likely to be an issue if we are retrieving enormous sets of results that are being transmitted with large page sizes.

So we have a situation where the data we need is being stored efficiently in the database but needs to be duplicated substantially in order to generate a query. But since the data can be stored OK, isn't there a way of having it transmitted efficiently as well? Well the answer is yes in principle. The problem is to do with the relational structure of the data. If we'd been storing the same data in a hierarchical manner, the problem would probably never have arisen. To see this, examine how the first few rows of the same data would look if we'd stored it hierarchically (perhaps in a directory) instead of a relational database:

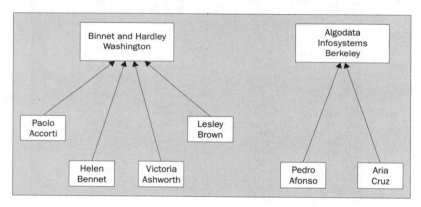

Now there's no duplication. To retrieve the data, we'd probably go through an algorithm that looks something like this:

- ❑ Get the first publisher.
- ❑ Enumerate all the first publisher's children.
- ❑ Display details of these children, along with the pub_name and city fields of their parent.
- ❑ Free up memory for this publisher.
- ❑ Get the next publisher and repeat the process until we've covered all publishers.

This algorithm means that details for each publisher are retrieved just once and this data is shared by each of the children – so there's a lot less data that needs to be transmitted over the network, and much of the work the database had to do in copying data to perform the join is eliminated. This looks like a much better solution.

So, if having a hierarchical directory is so efficient, why didn't we just store *all* the data in one in the first place? Why use a relational database at all? The problem there is that we've only examined two tables in the pubs database. When you've got just two tables, it's easy. The primary key/foreign key relationship maps naturally to a parent/child hierarchical relationship. If we start to include more of the database in our analysis, mapping it to a hierarchical structure isn't so easy. The pubs database actually looks like this:

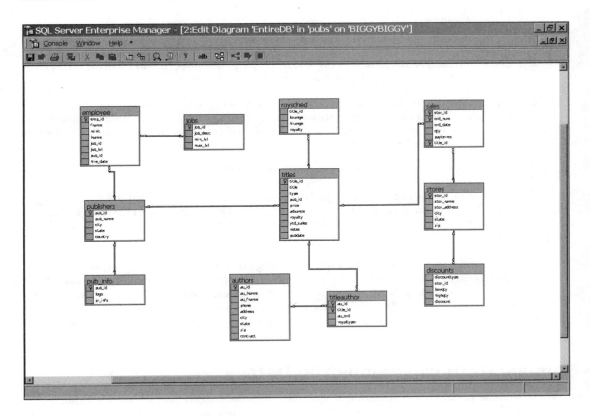

There's another primary key/foreign key relationship between the `publishers` table and the `titles` table – so we'd presumably put each title as another child of the corresponding publisher. So far so good. But then what about the `jobs` table? There's one job corresponding to many employees – reflected in the fact that the `job_id` field in the `employee` table is related to the primary key of the jobs table. So the job needs to be another parent of the employee (as well as the publisher). But hang on – in a hierarchical database each object is only supposed to have one parent. How are we going to manage that?

Well I hope I don't need to go on. By now you should have got the point that if we try to store any reasonably sized database in a hierarchical structure, the result is going to be one huge mess. Hierarchical directories are great for performance when you're doing queries, but they're basically hopeless when it comes to representing complex relationships between many different types of data.

So we're stuck with a relational database. But we want better performance for our query. What we really need is to be able to still have our relational database, but to be able to access it as if the tables we need for our particular query were hierarchical. That's where the data shaping provider comes in.

For our example, we need information from the `publishers` and `employee` table – and we need to be able to treat the publishers as a parent. That's exactly what the data shaping provider will do for us. What the provider can do is this:

1. Query the pubs database for details of employees.

2. Separately, query the database for details of the publishers. In other words, no `JOIN` is being performed – two independent recordsets are returned.

3. On the client machine (client here means the ADO client, not necessarily the web browser client), rearrange the recordsets so that the employees end up as children of the publishers (this involves a new concept – a recordset where one or more fields is another recordset – a child recordset).

4. Present the ADO client with the rearranged recordsets.

Powerful, huh! And this is just the beginning – we'll see later in the chapter that the data shaping provider can do a lot more than this. For example, it can work out aggregates of results, and it can rearrange the recordsets it's retrieved so we can look at them in a different way – the process of reshaping.

Of course, the usual penalty for having a new technology that makes things easy for us is that there's some extra learning to do upfront to know how to use the technology. In the case of the data shaping provider, that penalty is largely concerned with needing to learn the **Shape** language – the language which we use to tell the provider what recordsets to retrieve and how to arrange them. But the Shape language isn't too difficult, and we'll see later how a tool called the **Data Environment Designer** can write our Shape commands for us.

Sample: Retrieving Employee Details

We're going to present our first sample program that uses the data shaping provider – a simple ASP page which presents the same employee data we used from our previous example. Except that instead of using an SQL join, it uses data shaping to retrieve the same data more efficiently.

The page when displayed looks like this:

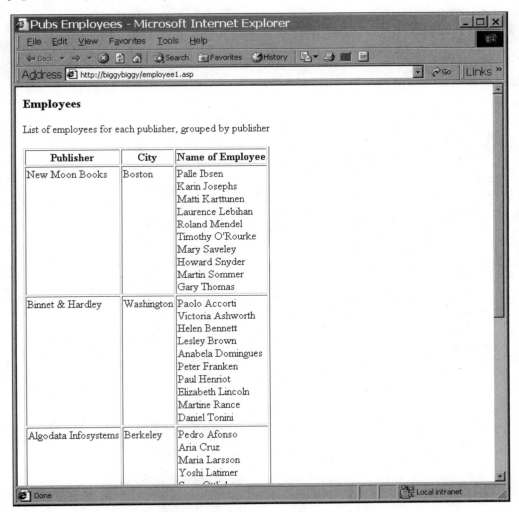

We'll present the entire source code for the ASP page in one go – then we'll go over the interesting bits of it. The ASP code is as follows:

```
<%@ Language = VBScript %>
<% Option Explicit %>

<!DOCTYPE HTML PUBLIC "-//W3C//DTD HTML 4.0 Transitional//EN">
<HTML>
<HEAD>
<TITLE> Pubs Employees</TITLE>
</HEAD>

<BODY>
```

```
<H3> Employees </H3>
<p>
List of employees for each publisher, grouped by publisher <P>

<!-- METADATA TYPE="typelib" UUID="{00000200-0000-0010-8000-00AA006D2EA4}" -->


<%

' set up connection string and Shape command
Dim g_sConnString
g_sConnString = "Provider=MSDataShape;Data Provider=SQLOLEDB;" & _
    "Data Source=BiggyBiggy;Initial Catalog=pubs;" & _
    "User ID=sa;Password=tardis885"

Dim sCommand
sCommand = "SHAPE {SELECT pub_name,city,pub_id FROM publishers} " & _
    "APPEND ({SELECT fname,lname,pub_id FROM employee} AS rsEmployee " & _
    "RELATE pub_id TO pub_id)"

' retrieve recordset from datashaping provider
Dim oRS
Set oRS = CreateObject("ADODB.Recordset")
oRS.Open sCommand, g_sConnString, adOpenStatic, _
    adLockReadOnly, adCmdText

' write out data from recordset into a table
Dim oRSEmp
Response.Write "<TABLE BORDER=1>" & _
    "<THEAD><TH>Publisher</TH><TH>City</TH><TH>            Name of
Employee</TH></THEAD>" & _
    "<TBODY>"
Do While (Not oRS.EOF)
    Response.Write "<TR><TD VALIGN=Top>" & oRS("pub_name") & "</TD>" & _
        "<TD VALIGN=Top>" & oRS("city") & "</TD><TD>"
    Set oRSEmp = oRS("rsEmployee").Value
    Do While (Not oRSEmp.EOF)
        Response.Write oRSEmp("fname") & " " & oRSEmp("lname") & "<BR>"
        oRSEmp.MoveNext
    Loop
    Response.Write "</TD></TR>"
    oRS.MoveNext
Loop
Response.Write "</TBODY></TABLE>"

oRSEmp.Close
Set oRSEmp = Nothing
oRS.Close
Set oRS = Nothing

%>

</BODY>
</HTML>
```

If we go through this code, we see that we first display the standard HTML header information. Then we include the ADO type library – this is just so that we can refer to the ADO constants like adCmdText by their names:

```
<!-- METADATA TYPE="typelib" UUID="{00000200-0000-0010-8000-00AA006D2EA4}" -->
```

The code then sets up the connection and command strings. Here we'll just remark that the connection string specifies the data shaping provider MsDataShape as the provider, and the command string is a command in the Shape language, though embedded in it are the two SQL commands to retrieve the two recordsets that the data shaping provider will arrange into a hierarchy.

Retrieving the recordset is also pretty standard ADO stuff:

```
' retrieve recordset from datashaping provider
Dim oRS
Set oRS = CreateObject("ADODB.Recordset")
oRS.Open sCommand, g_sConnString, adOpenStatic, _
    adLockReadOnly, adCmdText
```

The interesting part is where we iterate through the recordsets to retrieve the data:

```
Do While (Not oRS.EOF)
    Response.Write "<TR><TD VALIGN=Top>" & oRS("pub_name") & "</TD>" & _
        "<TD VALIGN=Top>" & oRS("city") & "</TD><TD>"
    Set oRSEmp = oRS("rsEmployee").Value
    Do While (Not oRSEmp.EOF)
        Response.Write oRSEmp("fname") & " " & oRSEmp("lname") & "<BR>"
        oRSEmp.MoveNext
    Loop
    Response.Write "</TD></TR>"
    oRS.MoveNext
Loop
```

Let's go over this in more detail. We've asked for the pub_name and city fields of the records from the publishers table (If that's not obvious now, you'll see when we examine the Shape command string that that's what we've done). These fields go into the first recordset in the normal way. This 'parent' recordset, however, also contains another field, named rsEmployee. The value of this field is not a simple string, but another embedded, 'child' recordset. This recordset stores the details of the employees – we've requested the employees' first and last names, which we concatenate to form their full names. So looping through the records in this child recordset gives us all the employees – but note that by 'all the employees' I actually mean all the employees for the publisher that we are currently looking at. In other words, as we move through the parent recordset, the data in the child recordset gets filtered so that we only see the information we need. It's as if the data shaping provider hasn't just created two recordsets for us: It's created one parent publishers recordset – publishers – and one employee recordset for each publisher.

> *Personally I find it easier to think of it as if we have lots of child recordsets, one for each publisher. However, the MSDN documentation indicates that the internal implementation is that there may be just one child recordset, and different filters get applied to it as we move through the parent. However, since that's just an implementation detail and the end results are the same as far as writing the clients goes, we won't worry about it.*

This code shows how easy it is to read the results of Shaped recordsets – and remember that this is with all the performance benefits provided by the data shaping service. Now we'll have a look at the connection and command strings and see how these gave us the recordsets in the parent-child hierarchy that we needed.

Data Shaping Connection Strings

Our connection string for the above example looked like this:

```
Provider=MSDataShape; Data Provider=SQLOLEDB; Data Source=BiggyBiggy;Initial
Catalog=pubs;User ID=sa;Password=tardis885
```

This looks fairly complex, until we realise that if we'd wanted to connect directly to the OLE DB provider for SQL server, our connection string would be this:

```
Provider=SQLOLEDB; Data Source=BiggyBiggy;Initial Catalog=pubs;User
ID=sa;Password=tardis885
```

In other words, if you want a simple rule for how to construct your data shaping connection strings, all you need to do is take the string you would have used to get to the actual database, and prefix it with:

```
Provider=MSDataShape;Data
```

The first part of this prefix tells us that the OLE DB provider we need is the data shaping provider. We are going to ask the data shaping provider to connect to the 'real' OLE DB provider on our behalf, so we just give it the connection string that it needs to use. And the remainder of the connection string is basically that. The one modification is that we can't call this source provider the 'Provider' – because that would mean we have two different Provider fields in the connection string! Instead, we refer to it as the 'Data Provider' – meaning that that's the ultimate provider that we want MsDataShape to talk to. The arrangement may be clearer from the diagram:

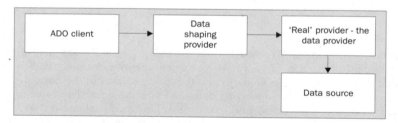

This chapter refers to three machines: There's the browser client machine, then there's the web server which is running ASP. I refer to this one as the client as it's a client to the data source. Then there's the machine running the DB, which is referred to as the server.

The Command String

This is where we get our first introduction to the Shape language. We'll take a practical approach here – learning what we can about the language by dissecting the command we passed in our Employees ASP page. That command string was:

```
SHAPE {SELECT pub_name,city,pub_id FROM publishers}
APPEND ({SELECT fname,lname,pub_id FROM employee} AS rsEmployee
RELATE pub_id TO pub_id )
```

The first part of this command is the keyword SHAPE, which tells the provider that we are about to tell it how to arrange some recordsets. Then, enclosed in a pair of curly braces, is a SQL statement – this is the statement that will retrieve the parent recordset. And as you can see it's a plain SQL command to retrieve the fields we're interested in from the publishers table. Apart from the fields we want, pub_name and city, we also ask for the pub_id. We need this even though we're not intending to display it because it's the primary key field that the employees table will link to.

Now we come to the APPEND keyword. This tells the datashaping provider that we want to create a child recordset. And the syntax is basically the same as for the Shape keyword – we stick the SQL statement that will retrieve the recordset inside a pair of curly braces. Again we ask for the pub_id field, as well as the fields we actually want to display.

After the APPEND clause comes the AS keyword followed by a name. The significance of the name we've chosen here – in this case rsEmployee – is that this will be the name of the field in the modified parent recordset that the data shaping provider presents to us, which will allow us access to the child recordset. In other words, it's the same name that we later use in this bit of ASP script:

```
Set oRSEmp = oRS("rsEmployee").Value
Do While (Not oRSEmp.EOF)
    Response.Write oRSEmp("fname") & " " & oRSEmp("lname") & "<BR>"
    oRSEmp.MoveNext
Loop
```

Notice that I have specified the Value property of the field explicitly. This is necessary, as it will default to returning a recordset otherwise.

Finally we get to the RELATE clause. The reason for this clause is that we've so far told the data shaping provider what our parent and child recordsets are – but we haven't told it how it can figure out which employee corresponds to which publisher. In other words, how, given a row in the employees recordset, it can tell which row in the parent recordset to associate that employee with. If you were doing an SQL join, you'd use the primary and foreign keys for this – and if you look back at our earlier SQL statement you'll see that we explicitly specify in it how to use these keys to match the rows when performing the inner join:

```
SELECT      dbo.employee.fname, dbo.employee.lname, dbo.publishers.pub_name,
dbo.publishers.city
FROM        dbo.employee
INNER JOIN dbo.publishers ON dbo.publishers.pub_id = dbo.employee.pub_id
```

Our RELATE clause in the Shape language does the same thing as the ON clause in the SQL statement: it tells the data shaping provider what test to use when matching employee to publisher. The employee goes with the publisher that has the same value of the pub_id column in each of the two recordsets. That's why we needed to ask the database to return this column even though we weren't going to want to display it.

Now we've seen how this works from the point of view of coding up the client ASP page, it's worth reminding ourselves what exactly the data shaping provider will do when we ask it to return a recordset:

❑   It will bind to the provider we've specified as the Data Provider, acting in this context as an OLE DB client.

❑   It passes to the data provider each of the SQL statements that are embedded in the Shape command, thus retrieving two recordsets, one for the publishers and one for the employees.

❑   It now creates a parent recordset, which will contain the data from the publishers recordset, along with an extra field named `rsEmployee`, which will contain references to the child recordsets. (The documentation doesn't say whether it works by creating a new recordset or by modifying the recordset it got back from the data provider – but it doesn't make any difference to us either way).

❑   It sets up the child recordset, putting a filter on it which changes as we move through the parent recordset. What it looks like to us is as if for each row in the parent recordset, the data shaping provider creates a child recordset, and populates this data with the fields for all those employees corresponding to that publisher. The filtered child recordset is known as a **chapter**.

As you can see, there is some processing involved here. All the processing that the database would have had to do had we requested an inner join hasn't quite been reduced to nothing. But we have successfully lost all of the data duplication that an inner join would have entailed.

Note, by the way, that the `pub_id` field which we used solely for matching the employees to publishers is still present in the parent and child recordsets – so if we'd wanted to we could have displayed that as well in the browser.

This example really completes the core functionality of the data shaping provider. If you want to you can stop reading now, and you'd have all the knowledge you need to efficiently perform joins. However, there is more that you can do with data shaping. We'll now go on to look at some of the more advanced topics.

Grandchild Recordsets

In our earlier example we had one parent recordset and one child recordset. But in hierarchical databases and directories, objects can in principle be nested to arbitrary depth. And the same is true with data shaping. You can put multiple child recordsets inside other child recordsets.

The employee data isn't a good part of the pubs database to illustrate this concept, since there are no other tables in the database that are suitable to be children of the employees, so instead we'll look at the `publishers` – `book titles` – `sales` part of the database:

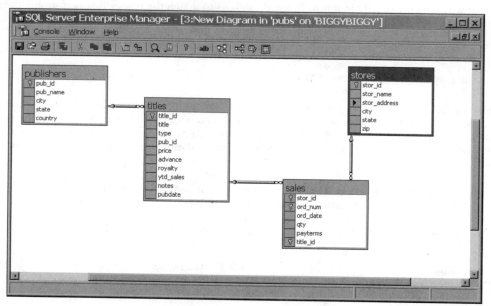

Each publisher publishes a number of titles, and there are many sales corresponding to each title, so it would make sense to have the titles as a child recordset of the publishers, and again to have the sales as a child of the titles. We'll leave the stores table for the time being – we'll need to introduce this table soon in order to display the name of the store instead of the ID. Note, by the way, that as far as the pubs database is concerned, a sale isn't a sale of an individual book to an end reader – it's an order for a quantity of books placed by a store. The number of books is stored in the qty field in the sales table.

So we have our hierarchy, and we know what our three recordsets are going to be. We'll assume that the information we want is the pub_name and city from the publishers table, as before. We also want the title from the titles table and qty from the sales table. We're not actually going to use the stores table here as we're only going to display the quantities, not the names of the stores. But I've left it in the diagram both to remind you that we would need that table there, and because I want to comment on it later in the chapter.

We also need the pub_id to link the publishers and titles tables, and the title_id to link the title to the sale. The Shape command that we need to accomplish all of that is this:

```
SHAPE {SELECT pub_name,city,pub_id FROM publishers}
APPEND ((
    SHAPE {SELECT title_id,title,pub_id FROM titles}
    AS rsTitles
        APPEND (
            {SELECT title_id,qty,stor_id FROM sales}
        AS rsSales
            RELATE title_id TO title_id))
RELATE pub_id TO pub_id)
```

This probably looks a bit much to take in – it's the sort of command you need to work through carefully to figure out what's going on, but rest assured it is logical.

We start off with the SHAPE keyword as normal – with the SQL statement that grabs the appropriate data from the parent level publishers table. We then APPEND the child to it. But instead of appending a simple SQL statement, we have another full-blown SHAPE command inside it. This SHAPE command grabs the data from the titles table into a recordset which it refers to as rsTables, and appends the data from the sales to it in another child recordset, called rsSales.

The indentation of the lines is my doing to make the command easier to read – the shape provider just ignores white space so you can format the command however you want.

Once you've generated a recordset with this Shape command, you can access it in much the same way as before, but this time with nested child recordsets:

```
' write out data from recordset into a table
Dim oRSEmp, oRSSales
Response.Write "<TABLE BORDER=1>" & _
    "<THEAD><TH>Publisher</TH><TH>City</TH><TH>   Name of Employee</TH></THEAD>" &
_
    "<TBODY>"
Do While (Not oRS.EOF)
    Response.Write "<TR><TD VALIGN=Top>" & oRS("pub_name") & "</TD>" & _
        "<TD VALIGN=Top>" & oRS("city") & "</TD><TD>"
```

```
         Set oRSEmp = oRS("rsTitles").Value
         Do While (Not oRSEmp.EOF)
            Response.Write oRSEmp("title")  & ": "
            Set oRSSales = oRSEmp("rsSales").Value
            Do While (Not oRSSales.EOF)
               Response.Write oRSSales("qty") & ", "
               oRSSales.MoveNext
            Loop
            Response.Write "<P>"
            oRSEmp.MoveNext
         Loop
      Response.Write "</TD></TR>"
      oRS.MoveNext
   Loop
   Response.Write "</TBODY></TABLE>"
```

This code is largely lifted from the previous employees sample, but with the modifications needed to display the new recordsets added. This page produces the following:

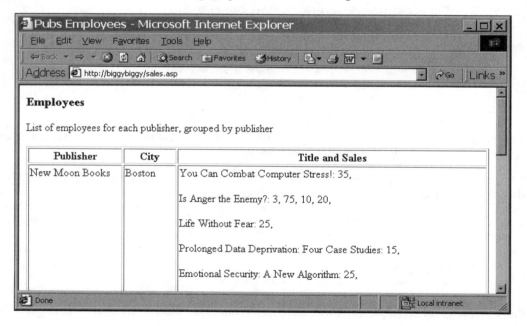

Aggregating a Quantity

The above page gives the titles of all the books for each publisher, then for each book it lists out the quantities of each sale, separated by commas (I didn't use more table rows here as trying to nest three levels of rows in one HTML table would be very hard to read!). However, more often we're going to be interested in the total sales of each book. In other words the sum of all the individual quantities. It is possible to do that using SQL and the SUM function, however we don't need to because the data shaping provider has its own SUM function to aggregate quantities like this.

Here's how we would use it:

```
SHAPE {SELECT pub_name,city,pub_id FROM publishers}
    AS rsPublishers
    APPEND ((
        SHAPE {SELECT title_id,title,pub_id FROM titles}
        AS rsTitles
        APPEND ({SELECT title_id,qty,stor_id FROM sales}
            AS rsSales
            RELATE title_id TO title_id)
            AS rsSales,
            SUM(rsSales.qty) AS TotalSales)
            AS rsTitles
            RELATE pub_id TO pub_id) AS rsTitles
```

The keyword needed is SUM. This SHAPE command is essentially the same as for the previous example. We form a hierarchy from the publishers table to the titles to the sales. The difference is that we also request the totals of the sales to be summed up, or aggregated. The SUM command takes all the records in the recordset in question, which are the children of the same record in the parent recordset. The entries in the named field in these child records are summed, and the result is stored in the *parent* record, in an extra field with the name specified in the AS clause – in our case TotalSales. As an example, for the title Is Anger The Enemy, there are five individual sales (child records) with quantities 3,75,10, and 20. These add up to 108, so the record in the rsTitles recordset for this title will store the value 108 in the TotalSales field.

To check this, we can modify our sales ASP page to include the above Shape command, and also modify the commands to write the output in the table as follows:

```
Do While (Not oRS.EOF)
    Response.Write "<TR><TD VALIGN=Top>" & oRS("pub_name") & "</TD>" & _
        "<TD VALIGN=Top>" & oRS("city") & "</TD><TD>"
    Set oRSTitle = oRS("rsTitles").Value
    Dim sSales
    Do While (Not oRSTitle.EOF)
        sSales = ""
        Response.Write oRSTitle("title")  & ":  Total Sales: " &
oRSTitle("TotalSales")
        Set oRSSales = oRSTitle("rsSales").Value
        Do While (Not oRSSales.EOF)
            If (sSales <> "") Then sSales = sSales & ", "
            sSales = sSales & oRSSales("qty")
            oRSSales.MoveNext
        Loop
        Response.Write "  (" & sSales & ")<BR>"
        oRSTitle.MoveNext
    Loop
    Response.Write "</TD></TR>"
    oRS.MoveNext
Loop
```

This produces the following output:

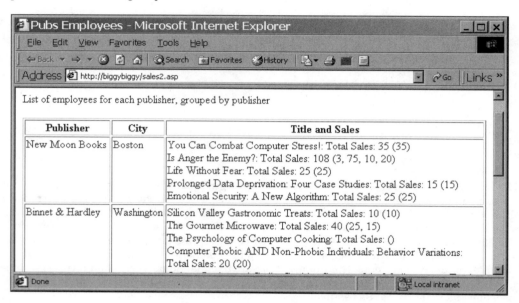

The SUM command isn't the only aggregate we have available. The full list is:

Command	Description
SUM	Sum of the values in the field
AVG	Mean of the values in the field
STDEV	Standard deviation of the values in the field. The standard deviation provides a measure of how similar the values are. It has the value 0 if all the values in the field are the same, and gets larger the more different the values become
MIN	The minimum of all the values in the field
MAX	The maximum of all the values in the field
ANY	Assumes the values are all the same and just returns any one of them
COUNT	How many records there are

Parameterized Recordsets

I'll start off by saying what parameterised recordsets are not. The name is rather suggestive of ADO parameters, which when used with other OLE DB providers allow you an alternative means of passing data into command strings, and retrieving data from the database. Parameterized recordsets in the context of the data shaping provider have nothing to do with this. Rather, they amount to an alternative way of requesting data, which has some performance implications.

Let's go back to our employees example. Recall that the SHAPE command used was:

```
SHAPE {SELECT pub_name,city,pub_id FROM publishers}
APPEND ({SELECT fname,lname,pub_id FROM employee} AS rsEmployee
RELATE pub_id TO pub_id
```

When the shape provider executes this, it will first grab the names of the publishers from the database. Then it will grab the names of all the employees from the database into a separate recordset. As you might expect for a subsidiary table, there is going to be data for an awful lot of employees. This all means that when the Shape command is first executed, there will be an awful lot of work going on – the client will have to wait while the recordsets are populated. But after that, subsequent queries will be very fast because all the data is now held locally by the data shaping provider.

There may be situations in which you would prefer not to have to wait at the start for all the data to be fetched. Perhaps, for example, you're intending to present a list of the publishing companies to the end user, who will then select which one he or she wants to view for all the employees. In that situation it's a bit silly to fetch the data for all the employees of all publishers in advance, since most of that data will just be discarded. And since the main reason for using the data shaping provider in the first place was to improve performance you'll have defeated the whole object! There may be other cases where you do want all the data, but you'd rather fetch it gradually, in order not to keep the end user waiting too long initially.

That's where parameterised recordsets come in. What happens is that we modify the Shape command, as follows.

```
SHAPE {SELECT pub_name,city,pub_id FROM publishers}
APPEND ({SELECT fname,lname,pub_id FROM employee WHERE pub_ID = ?} AS rsEmployee
RELATE pub_id TO PARAMETER 0 )
```

We don't need to make any other changes to our code sample, other than replace the shape command.

The new command will now retrieve the same data, but in a slightly different manner. When the command executes, the details of the publishers (the first SQL query) will be fetched. But no employee data will be retrieved.

Rather, the employee data will be retrieved by publisher where it is specifically requested. So when you first attempt to access employee data for the first publisher, the data shaping provider will send a SQL request to the data provider to obtain just the employee data for that publisher. It will do this again when you first attempt to access employee data for the next publisher, and so on.

Notice that you as the client don't need to create any ADO parameters – but it's not hard to guess from the format of the Shape command that the data shaping provider is probably using parameters internally to make its requests to the data provider.

Other Topics

We've looked at the basic things you can do with the data shape provider. We'll just mention a couple of other areas that you may want to look up. Details of these areas are beyond the scope of this chapter, but can be found in MSDN.

ReShaping

You'll have noticed by now that the Shape commands can become quite complex. It's not actually necessary to construct complex recordset hierarchies in their entirety with one command. Instead, we can reuse the results of previous Shape commands. This has two benefits: Firstly, it means you can break one complex command down into a series of simpler commands. Secondly, it means that once you have obtained recordsets from the data shaping provider, you can reuse them to construct different hierarchies, without needing to return to the data store for the information. This latter benefit is the reason why the process of reusing the results of previous commands is known as reshaping.

Creating New Parents

We saw how when using the aggregation commands we can use the data in child recordsets to add new fields to their parent recordsets. It is also possible to use a similar technique to create a new parent recordset (as opposed to a new field in an existing parent). This is achieved using the command, COMPUTE. COMPUTE can be used with any of the aggregates we've mentioned here.

VBA Functions

It is also possible to create new columns in an existing recordset using any of the functions available in VBA. For example, if you have a column in a recordset that represents the date-time and you need to know the actual day of the week, then you can create a new column calculated using VBA's Day function.

Note that this is different from the aggregation functions, since here the operations are performed individually on each row (the day of the week is calculated in our example from another column in the same row) – there is no aggregation performed and no writing of data to parent recordsets.

For details of this feature you should refer to the CALC Shape command in MSDN.

The Data Environment Designer

We're going to finish off this chapter by mentioning this tool because it provides a useful way of getting your SHAPE commands written for you – something that can be a Godsend given how complex we've seen some of the SHAPE commands can become. What makes the Data Environment Designer (DED) even more important is that the data shaping provider is, at present, not very good at generating explanatory error messages. In my experience, all you ever get if there's a problem with the command you've tried writing is a plain 'syntax error' – which in a command spanning 10 or more lines isn't always very helpful.

The DED comes as part of the Visual Basic Integrated Developer Environment (VB IDE) – the tool you'd normally use to write VB programs (you need either the professional or enterprise edition, not the learning edition). But don't worry if you've never used VB – you don't actually need to write any VB code – you just need to start the VB IDE to get to the DED.

You can normally find the DED under the Project menu in VB. It's the Add Data Environment option. You might, however, find at first that this option isn't there. If so, you need to select Project | Components. This gives you a tabbed dialog – select the Designers tab and ensure that the Data Environment check box is checked:

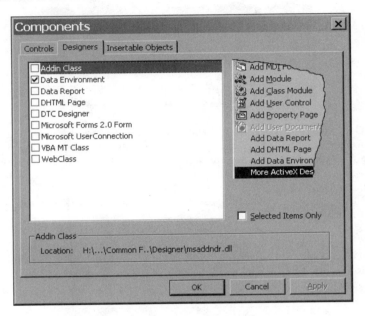

You'll now be ready to start up the DED. We'll go through the steps needed to generate a Shape command since it's not actually very obvious from the user interface.

When you create a DED you get presented with a tree structure which is intended to describe your data source:

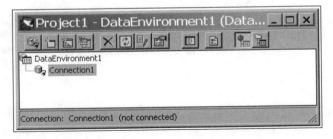

You need to start by setting up the connection – do this by right-clicking on the Connection1 item and selecting Properties from the context menu. This brings up the standard data link wizard used by OLE DB. You should go through the wizard, specifying the details of the connection. Note, however, that it is the connection to the actual data source you need to set up, not a connection to MsDataShape.

Now right-click on the Connection1 item again and select Add Command from the context menu. This extends the tree structure a bit:

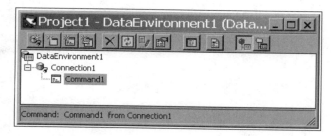

Right-click on Command1 and again select Properties. The Properties sheet you get will let you specify the details of the command. As an example, I'll demonstrate how to set up the command we used in our initial example of displaying employees and publishers. Recall that the Shape command I used was:

```
SHAPE {SELECT pub_name,city,pub_id FROM publishers}
APPEND ({SELECT fname,lname,pub_id FROM employee} AS rsEmployee
RELATE pub_id TO pub_id
```

To get the DED to generate this command, we need to bear in mind that Command1 is actually the first command we need to send to the data provider – in other words the SQL statement. (Recall that we set up the connection to point to the data provider, not to MSDataShape.) So we set the first tab in the Command1 property sheet to the relevant SQL statement:

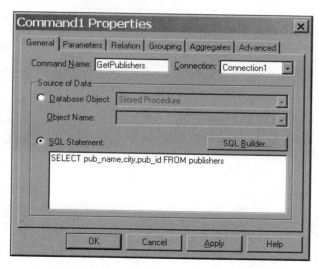

Note that in the process I've taken the trouble to change the name of the command from the rather unhelpful 'Command1' to GetPublishers.

We click OK to this dialog – we don't need to worry about any of the other tabs for a while. Don't worry either about a couple of other dialogs that appear asking you to confirm the password for the database and warning you that executing this statement may alter the database contents. (It won't – it's a SELECT statement!)

Now is when we get to see why we didn't need to specify a connection to `MsDataShape` – the DED has an awareness of data shaping built into it. We can right-click again on our newly renamed command and select **Add Child Command**. This gives us a new command, which will be our second SQL statement, so we set its properties just as we did for the first command (note that the first parameter is Lname, and not I name):

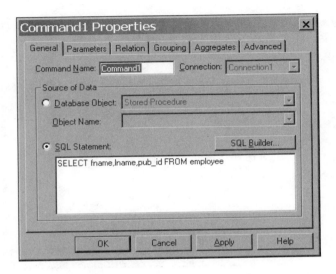

Now however, before we click **OK**, we must define the relationship between the two statements. So go to the **Relation** tab and select the appropriate fields from the list boxes and click the **Add** button to add the relation:

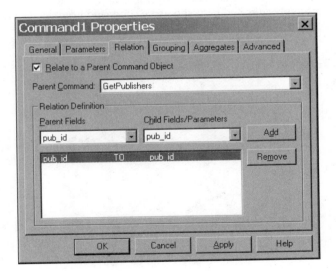

Note that the DED designer is intelligent enough to have executed the commands and determined which fields get returned from each – so it is able to populate the list boxes sensibly. Note also that if there's any problem with how you've set up your command or the connection string, this will probably be given away by the Parent Fields and Child Fields list boxes not displaying the appropriate set of fields.

If you want to set up any aggregates, you can do that too using the Aggregates *tab.*

Once you've set up the relation, you can click OK and see the hierarchy of commands:

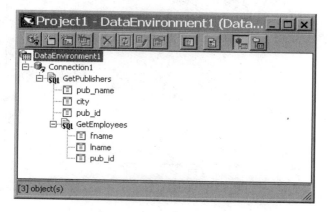

The tree view also displays the fields returned from the queries. You've now given the DED all the information it needs to generate the Shape command. To see the result, right-click on the topmost command (GetPublishers) again, but this time select Hierarchy Info from the context menu. You'll get this dialog in response, and you can simply copy and paste the shape command from the dialog into your code:

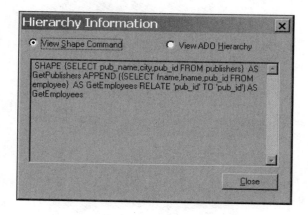

Simple, huh!

Summary

In this chapter we started off by showing why SQL JOINs can be inefficient, and why it would be useful to be able to represent the data hierarchically instead. Then we went on to show how Microsoft's data shaping provider, MSDataShape, can be used to do just that.

The data shaping provider can't really do anything that you couldn't achieve with SQL commands (or manually yourself by manipulating recordsets if you're willing to do the work), but it does allow you to retrieve the results from complex queries very efficiently without making your code any more complicated. If you are expecting to be handling SQL JOINs that will be returning thousands of results, and performance is an issue, then it's certainly worth checking out the data shaping provider to see if it can help you speed up your applications.

30

Multi-Dimensional Data

This chapter focuses on a way of achieving a broad overview of the contents of a large relational database. For example, when given a table of sales, we want to see which products or geographical areas are getting us our best results, or what the trend has been over the last 6 months. We need a way of utilizing our data which will give us this information. The technology we need to do this is something called **OLAP (On Line Analytical Processing)**. We will explore this in some detail, before going on to take a look at how it may be used in ASP pages.

If you've never encountered OLAP before, you may be wondering why we need this chapter. After all, doesn't SQL let us get any information we need from our database? Well, yes it does. But it's not always the most efficient tool to do so. And as we've already seen, relational databases aren't always the best structures to hold data in. For example, in Chapter 18 we looked at directories and examples of data which is best stored hierarchically. In Chapter 29, in which we covered data shaping, we showed how even when a database is relational, sometimes it's more efficient to convert it to a hierarchical form when retrieving data, using the OLE DB data shaping provider.

It turns out that another area where SQL and relational data structures aren't really the best tool for getting at the information we want is when we need an overall picture of our data rather than the ability to access individual records – even when the individual records are stored relationally. For such situations, the ideal data structure isn't hierarchical, but is a structure known as a **data cube** (sometimes referred to as a **multi-dimensional database**).

Relational structures are best suited to making frequent updates to data, where the updates consist of adding, modifying, or deleting single records (and any cascaded records) in a database. And most commercial relational database systems are optimised for this sort of operation; in particular, for write operations that are protected by transactions. But in this chapter we're concerned with combining records in such a way that we can find out, for instance, which geographical region is giving us our best sales, or whether our recent advertising drive aimed specifically at the teenage market has actually worked.

If we're working for a large company, and our database contains an entry for each individual sale, we could be combining literally millions of records from several tables in the queries to gain this kind of information. That not only means that our query is going to take a long time, but if we're doing a lot of this kind of analysis, it won't be long before we bog down our database so it becomes less responsive to the people trying to do the kind of updates and simple queries that the database was supposedly there for! OLAP is designed to provide a solution for exactly this sort of situation.

The approach we're going to take in this chapter is to base it around a real world example; a sports centre that wants to get a broad picture of its sales. We'll begin by outlining the example so we can see in more detail the problem that we're faced with, and why just sending SQL queries to the database isn't a realistic way of getting the data we need. From there we'll move on to investigate Microsoft's own OLAP solution, which was introduced under the banner SQL Server OLAP Services with SQL Server 7.0, and renamed **Analysis Services** in SQL Server 2000.

We'll also look at the process of setting up an OLAP database using the **Analysis Manager**, the UI tool that comes with Analysis Services. At that point we'll have the necessary background to start coding.

From ASP, we use ADO to talk to OLAP databases – specifically a variant of ADO called **ADO Multi-Dimensional (ADO MD)**, which has a slightly different object model more suited to OLAP. This is done via an OLE DB provider known (oddly enough) as the OLE DB provider for OLAP. We'll look at how to use this provider and in the process develop an ASP page that provides analyses of the sports centre's sales. In doing this, we'll take a look at **MDX** (**Multi-Dimensional Extensions**), which is Microsoft's language used for making queries against cube databases. When using ADO MD to make queries, we'll pass in MDX command strings, in much the same way that we use ADO to make queries against relational databases by passing in command strings written in SQL.

There's not going to be a great deal of coding in this chapter – that's simply because although ADO MD is simple to use, we've got quite a lot of new concepts to learn before we'll be ready to use it. But there'll be enough code to get started writing ASP pages that use ADO MD to access multi-dimensional databases.

The RocksWorks Sports Centre

The RocksWorks sports centre provides a wide range of facilities to its members, including aerobics and other keep-fit classes, a well-equipped weights room, and various indoor and outdoor sports facilities. It also has a modern computer system, with a large database that records every sale or booking. In other words, every time anyone uses any of the facilities, an entry is made in the database.

We're not going to need to examine the RocksWorks database in detail, but suffice to say that the portion of it that deals with customer bookings probably looks something like this:

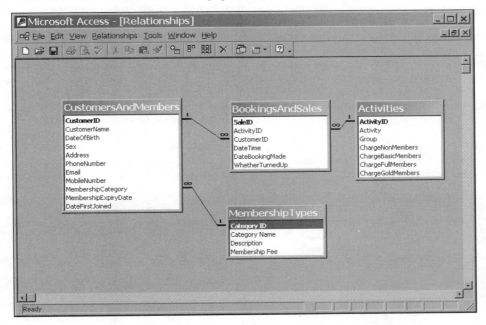

If you've any experience with relational databases it should be pretty clear how this stores details of bookings and sales as well as membership details.

The database will be used to add bookings, record visits to the gym, and do things such as mail out membership renewal reminders. But we're not interested in that in this chapter. What concerns us here is that in order to plan future expansion and better target advertising and promotions, the management need to know which of their facilities are being used most. They also need to know what kinds of people (for example male or female, and what age ranges) are using the centre most, and about any seasonal variations. In other words, they need to see this sort of thing:

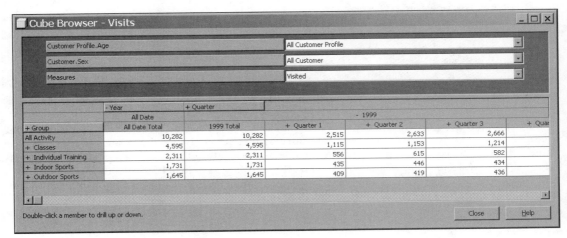

This table gives the numbers of customers visiting the various facilities at RocksWorks, both for the entire year, and then in different columns for each quarter of 1999. The All Date column, which appears to duplicate the values for 1999, would indicate the values for all years, but for this example I've only stored data for 1999 in the database. So, for example, the figure of 10282 in the top left cell of the table shows the total number of visitors to the sports centre throughout the whole period for which figures were collected. In the cells below this we can see how those 10282 visits were distributed amongst the different activities – 4595 for sports classes etc. On the other hand reading along the first row we can see an alternative breakdown of the 10282 visits – by which period of which year they occurred in.

The table we've just shown above is what's generally known as a **pivot table**, and it shows the total figures from the database, aggregated up and then broken down in various ways. In this case we've shown the numbers of times the facilities were used broken down by time of year and by the general category of facilities. This would give management an idea of when certain facilities are most popular. We might decide we're not interested in the date, but we are interested in the profile of people using the facilities, by both age and sex, in which case we might want to look at the same data this way:

Cube Browser - Visits

Date — All Date

Group	Sex	MeasuresLevel	+ Age Range Visited		
		All Customer Profile	+ 15-24	+ 25-34	+ 35
All Activity	All Customer	10,282	3,903	2,407	
	F	5,231	1,833	1,246	
	M	5,051	2,070	1,161	
+ Classes	All Customer	4,595	1,726	1,353	
	F	3,489	1,309	1,052	
	M	1,106	417	301	
+ Individual Training	All Customer	2,311	870	214	
	F	520	216		
	M	1,791	654	214	
+ Indoor Sports	All Customer	1,731	810	306	
	F	719	308	97	
	M	1,012	502	209	
+ Outdoor Sports	All Customer	1,645	497	534	
	F	503		97	
	M	1,142	497	437	

Double-click a member to drill up or down.

Close   Help

We've now got three different ways we want to break down the total of 10282 visits: Nature of facility used, customer age, and customer sex. Unfortunately there are only two dimensions to the table – rows and columns! We've solved this by putting two breakdowns along the rows – sex and activity type. So, for example, if we look at the first column, first three rows we see that 10282 visits were made in total, of which 5231 were by women and 5051 by men. The next three cells for the first column show the equivalent figures for just those visits to sports classes.

The tool we're looking at is the user interface tool Microsoft provides for browsing data in OLAP tables – we'll see how to access this tool later in the chapter. The cube browser is a very flexible tool – it allows us to select and remove items to break down data by clicking them and dragging them between the actual table and the list of items at the top of the screen. We can also expand out categories into more detail by double-clicking on the + signs. For example, if we want to examine the particular fitness classes being attended, we'd double-click on +Classes to get this:

Cube Browser - Visits

Date | All Date

Group	Activity	Sex	MeasuresLevel All Customer Profile	+ Age Range Visited + 15-24	+
All Activity	All Activity Total	All Customer	10,282	3,903	
		F	5,231	1,833	
		M	5,051	2,070	
- Classes	Classes Total	All Customer	4,595	1,726	
		F	3,489	1,309	
		M	1,106	417	
	Aerobics	All Customer	1,119	298	
		F	1,019	298	
		M	100		
	Cardiofunk	All Customer	2,181	1,140	
		F	1,564	821	
		M	617	319	
	Step	All Customer	1,295	288	
		F	906	190	
		M	389	98	
+ Individual Training	Individual Training Total	All Customer	2,311	870	

Double-click a member to drill up or down.

Close   Help

The process of expanding out fields to see the data in finer detail is known as **drilling down**, while the reverse process is **drilling up**.

> *In case you're wondering how I managed to get a database for a fictitious gym with records for over ten thousand visits in it – I coded up a VB application that simulated visits by different customers according to various statistical rules. Even so, the database size is small – a decent-sized real gym with the facilities RocksWorks has would be more likely to have over a hundred thousand visitors a year. But there's enough data there to illustrate how OLAP may be used.*

It's a useful tool – but what it's doing is not quite the sort of thing you're used to doing with SQL. If we wanted to use SQL in conjunction with the database we saw earlier, there are several problems:

Performance

Each figure in the pivot table is an aggregate over a lot of records. In the above example, over hundreds or thousands of records. In real life it could be millions. Databases like SQL Server and Oracle might be highly scaleable and efficient, but even they are going to have problems if they are getting hit by perhaps several tens or hundreds of queries for these aggregated results at the same time – one query for each cell in the pivot table. We really need a database in which these aggregates are pre-calculated and stored in advance.

Database Design

If we compare the table structure of the RockWorks database with the information presented in the pivot table, they are very different. The information in the pivot table is spread over several tables in the database. And the core statistic, the number of visits, isn't directly stored in the database at all – we have to get that by counting records. So any SQL query is going to have to do joins of tables – quite a few tables in a larger, more realistic, example. This hits performance again, as well as making for complex SQL statements.

SQL Design

Finally, SQL just isn't suited to the kind of queries we'd need to run to generate a pivot table. It's designed to allow individual updates and reads. The SQL queries we'd need to write to get the summary information we need out of disparate tables are going to be complicated – and we'd need a detailed understanding of the structure of the database to be able to write them at all.

There are really two separate but related problems here:

❏ For performance reasons, we probably don't want to be using the same database for these analysis queries as the database we would be using for day-to-day transactions.

❏ Our database doesn't really have the right structure for this type of query anyway – the information we need is spread out over many tables and the database stores lots of individual records whereas we are more interested in summaries.

At the core of our database is the `BookingsAndSales` table that stores each individual transaction in a two-dimensional table consisting of rows and columns. It also has various linked tables. But if we tried to imagine the database that we really need to be looking at to get our overall queries, that database would have to look something more like this:

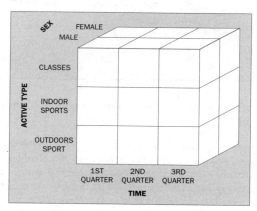

The first thing that stands out is that this database does not contain any two-dimensional tables; it's a three-dimensional block. Three-dimensional, because we've picked on three things to analyse; date, customer sex, and activity type. In fact, for our RocksWorks example, there are four things to analyse; the three I've just given, plus the customer age. So our database is really a four-dimensional hypercube (if you've not heard the term before, a hypercube is just the name for the shape that a cube would look like if you could draw one that had more than three dimensions). For each new way that we want to break down our data, we get another dimension. At this point you can probably start to see why this chapter is called 'Multi-Dimensional Data', and why the ADO API that interacts (via OLE DB) with OLAP is called ADOMD (ADO Multi-Dimensional).

This is the kind of problem tha OLAP and ADOMD is designed to solve. We're going to move on now to look at Microsoft's solution.'

Introducing Analysis Services

Analysis Services – Microsoft's implementation of OLAP – comes on the same CDs as SQL Server, although it is not actually a part of SQL Server and is installed separately. When you install Analysis Services, you will get the back-end software that performs the analyses of databases, as well as the pivot table user interface tool and the OLE DB providers to allow you to talk to Analysis Services from ADO clients.

> *Note that we'll be using the terminology that applies to SQL Server 2000 here. All the material in this chapter applies equally to SQL Server 7.0, but you'll find some of the names used in the screenshots differ in line with Analysis Services' former name having been SQL Server OLAP Services.*

Essentially, what Analysis Services does is analyse a relational database and present us with what looks like a database in the form of the cube that we saw above, so that we can easily get the statistics we want from it. The database we think we're accessing might or might not actually exist as a cube, depending on the options selected when OLAP generated it. OLAP can generate a database with a cubic (as opposed to a relational) structure, or it can be set so that it will continue to query a relational database. When we generate a database, we'll be presented with the following options for how we want to store it:

- ❑ **MOLAP** (Multi-Dimensional OLAP). All the data is copied to a new database, and stored in a cubic structure (though there are efficient algorithms to keep the storage requirements down, for example by not allocating memory to empty cells). This option is most suitable if we intend to query the data cube for large scale statistics often, since it gives the highest performance, though at a cost of higher disk space requirements. It's also more suitable if we don't need to update the data cube from the original database very often (in other words, if we don't need our statistics to be bang up-to-date) since updating the cube is a very computationally intensive process.

- ❑ **ROLAP** (Relational OLAP). Instead of creating a new cube database, OLAP will use the existing data warehouse for queries. This is slower but uses less disk space, and is most suitable for large databases that we will not be querying for statistics very often (since a query takes more time to process in ROLAP, as we have to refer back to the original database) but which need to be up-to-date (there's no need to build a new data cube to get up-to-date statistics). Note that if your database is really large, this might be the only option because of the amount of disk space that MOLAP data cubes will occupy.

- ❑ **HOLAP** (Hybrid OLAP). An intermediate solution in which some data is queried from the data warehouse while other data is copied to the OLAP database. There are various sophisticated algorithms to optimise which data is stored where, based on our usage of the database.

Note that an important part of the process – at least for MOLAP and HOLAP databases, is that the aggregates we will need to access are pre-calculated and stored, so that queries for statistical data no longer need to sum over thousands or millions of individual database records. This means that they can run a lot faster.

Separately, the ADOMD object model gives us access to an OLAP cube database, so we can query the data in it from ASP pages (or VB, C++, C# or any other COM-aware language).

Although OLAP comes with SQL server, that doesn't mean it needs to use a SQL Server database. It will happily read in any database accessed through SQL Server 6.5 onwards, Access 97 onwards, or Oracle 7.3 and Oracle 8. From SQL Server 2000 onwards it'll even read in data stored in LDAP-compliant directory services for conversion to a data cube. This means, for example, that if you have details of all your company employees stored in a directory such as Active Directory or Netscape Directory Server, you'll be able to do things like use OLAP to get breakdowns of salaries or numbers of employees in different departments.

For the RocksWorks example in this chapter, we will use an Access database, simply because Access provides the easiest user interface to create the new database.

When OLAP is installed, a sample database, the FoodMart2000 database, is automatically set up. This comes all set up to analyse using OLAP. We've stayed away from FoodMart2000 in this chapter because it's a very realistic sample – which means the database is huge and complex – and I don't want to get bogged down explaining how the database structure works. But FoodMart2000 is well worth a look at when you've installed OLAP.

We're next going to look at how to use Analysis Services to generate an OLAP database, but first, it's about time we introduced some of the technical terms used to describe these databases.

Measures and Dimensions

The item of data that we want to analyse is called the **measure**. So, in our case, the measure is the number of visits. In other examples, measures might include sales, total cost, net revenue, etc. Each variable we might want to use to break down our data is called a **dimension**. For a large organization, possible dimensions might include the ones we've used here, as well as product, department or geographical area. The basic table of data is termed a **cube**.

*As has been said earlier, despite the name **cube**, we're not confined to three dimensions. Microsoft's OLAP service, which we're using in this chapter, will actually let you go up to a combined total (for no. of measures plus no. of dimensions) of 64 dimension*

We also need to mention **hierarchies**. Hierarchies are very similar to dimensions, but in some cases there may be more than one way to break up a dimension. For example, in the RocksWorks sample in this chapter, we can break customers down by age and sex. There are two ways of looking at this – one is to regard customer age and customer sex as different dimensions. An alternative way, which makes little difference programmatically but is conceptually more correct, is to regard age and sex as two hierarchies of the customer dimension.

Levels

We also need to understand the concept of a **level**. We can think of a level as a subdivision of a dimension. Look again at our breakdown of the activity in the earlier pivot table screenshots. The dimension is `activity type`, but we've separated it into two levels. The first one gives the broad category of activity – whether members have been going to a fitness class, playing a competitive sport, or working out by themselves. The second level gives a more precise indication of the nature of the activity. For example, if the activity is classified as a fitness class, the second level indicates whether it is aerobics, step-aerobics or cardiofunk. We might even go to a further level and separate out beginners, intermediate and advanced aerobics. Having these different levels gives us a choice of how finely we break down the data.

The difference between level and dimension is a subtle one. The dimension indicates the way the measures are broken down, while the level indicates how finely they're broken down. As other examples, you might have the dimension of time period. The levels could be annually, quarterly, monthly, weekly, and daily – giving you five levels. Or if you were running a multinational company and wanted to look at the profitability of your regional offices, you might have a dimension corresponding to geographical area. Then the successive levels might be continent, country, region, and town.

Axis

This is similar to a dimension, but indicates the row or column on a report of the data. Generally, we would put one dimension along an axis, but we might want to combine some dimensions for a particularly detailed report – just as in one of the earlier pivot table screenshots we placed customer, sex, AND activity type on the rows of the table. It is possible to have more than two axes, though that tends to lead to data that is quite hard to read (you have to represent them by displaying more than one 2-dimensional table).

Generating the OLAP Database.

There are really two steps to generating the database. Firstly, we have to create a new relational database called the **data warehouse**. Then we bring Analysis Services in to analyse the data in the data warehouse and possibly generate a new database that has a cubic structure.

Step 1. The Data Warehouse

The main reason for generating the data warehouse is that the main database of an organization is very unlikely to be in a form that Analysis Services can read easily. Analysis Services is reasonably sophisticated, and there is some flexibility in how we can design the database that it's going to read, but it does need to be able to easily identify the measures and dimensions, and they need to be related in a relatively simple way, which isn't necessarily always the case for the main database.

> In the next chapter we'll look at the principles of data warehouses in a lot more detail and discuss various different designs for them. Here we're focusing on developing a simple database that can be read by Analysis Services, so we're going to focus on the simplest possible design, known as a Star Schema. This is efficient and clearly illustrates the concepts involved in designing a database that can be interpreted by Analysis Services. Because of this, you'll find that the next chapter presents data warehouses that are more complex and flexible than the one presented here.

The easiest way to see the structure we want for the data warehouse is by going over the data warehouse for RocksWorks. This was created in Access, in the following way:

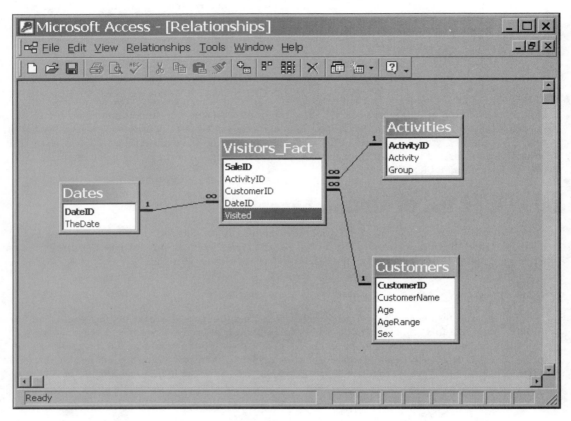

In the data warehouse, we've eliminated all the data that is not required by OLAP.

The central table of the warehouse is the Visitors_Fact table. This approximately contains the data from the sales table of the original database (approximately because I've picked out some columns, left out a couple of others, and added the visited column); it's got a record for each time someone uses the facilities. The key point about this table is that it contains the measure we're interested in. This is the table from which the cube will be formed. The table which performs this role is generally called the **fact table**, which is why I've named it Visitors_Fact. The actual measure comes from the field highlighted in the diagram, called Visited.

We can see how this works if we look at a section of the data in the table:

If we were interested in counting the income generated, the measure would come from a field that stored the income for each visit. However, in this case we're only interested in the number of visits, so we actually need to just add 1 on for each visit. To simulate this we've introduced the column, Visited, which just contains the number 1 for each entry. The other entries are all numbers and apart from the SaleID primary key, they are foreign keys linked to primary keys in other tables.

Linked to the Visitors_Fact table are the other tables that give the data for the dimensions, and there's one table for each dimension (You don't have to do it that way, but we're trying to keep things simple here). And the form of the linking is fairly precise; the primary key in each dimensions table is linked to a foreign key in the fact table. It has to be this way for the dimension to make sense, because in order to compute the aggregates OLAP needs to be able to associate each row in the fact table with one member of each dimension.

*This isn't the only possible arrangement for the data warehouse, but it's the most efficient way of doing it, and is known as the **star schema**. We're not going to go into details of the other possible arrangements in this chapter, but details can be found in the OLAP documentation. Generally speaking, the other arrangements allow some further separation of the tables increasing flexibility at the cost of reduced performance.*

The idea of having the dimensions in separate tables leads to some interesting consequences. Look, for instance, at the date in the Visitors_Fact table. In the original database this was stored directly as a column in the SalesAndBookings table, but now in the data warehouse it is a foreign key to an entry in the Dates table. The Dates table just stores a list of dates through the year in the canonical form, MM/DD/YYYY:

OLAP is able to understand dates, so we only need to store a single date and Analysis Services will be able to figure out how to break the measure down into quarters, months, etc. However, for the other dimensions, this isn't the case, and we need to make sure that the tables include all the information needed for the different levels. To see how to do this, let's have a look at the data in the Activities table a bit more closely:

This is quite a small table, which gives the details of the different facilities available at RocksWorks. And the table has actually been designed to make it easy for OLAP; it has the levels already there. Notice that each activity has a field for the activity type, then a separate field for the Group (meaning the general category of the activity). In order to generate the reports we've seen, we need to inform OLAP that there will be a dimension, Activity Type, and that the data for it can be read from the Activities table. We also need to inform OLAP that the first level is taken from the Group column, and the second is from the Activity column.

That's actually all we will need to do because OLAP is fairly intelligent. It will read the Group column, looking for all the different possible values the rows in it have. So it will deduce that the possible values for this level are Classes, Indoor Sports, Outdoor Sports, and Individual Training. Then it will take each of these values and read the Activity column, to see what values for Activity exist that correspond to each activity. Hence it will, for instance, deduce from the table that the possible children of Classes are Aerobics, Step, and Cardiofunk, while the children of Indoor Sports are Squash, Table Tennis, and Badminton.

> *This design means there is some duplication in the data in the table. For example,* Classes *appears several times. In general, data warehouse databases won't be normalized to the same extent as the main company database.*

We've now taken a look at the structure of the database from which OLAP will read its data; the so-called data warehouse. The last thing we need to look at is how to generate the data warehouse. Unfortunately, OLAP can't help us here. If we want a data warehouse that doesn't have the same structure as the original database, then we'll have to create one, most likely using either ADO or (probably more efficiently) some stored procedures in the main database. This will take some work, but since the data warehouse is still a relational database, the difficulties shouldn't be too great. We'll also need to periodically update the data warehouse with whatever new records have been added to the main database. Note here that it is our responsibility to arrange for these updates – including deciding how often we want them to take place, and arranging for the code we've written that performs the updates to be executed at the scheduled times – this isn't something that analysis services will do for us.

How often we want the updates to take place is a decision that must be made based on the balance between performance and how up-to-date we need the data warehouse to be. The more often you do it, obviously the more up-to-date the warehouse will be. On the other hand we're talking about processing and copying a substantial part of the database, which isn't a trivial task and for a very large database may take many hours. You probably don't want to tie up the database in this way very often. And then you'll need to separately update the data cube from the updated data warehouse as well.

You'll see from this discussion that the data warehouse is generally at least slightly out-of-date. That's in the nature of the data warehouses – they are there to store information stretching back into history for analysis. They don't need to be totally up to date because the usual business transactions are not being performed on them, those are happening to the original database.

We can now have a look at the next stage – how to generate the OLAP database from the data warehouse.

Step 2. The Cube Database

Analysis Services has a pretty good user interface based on an MMC SnapIn. For SQL Server 2000 it can be found in the Start Menu under Programs | Microsoft SQL Server | Analysis Services | Analysis Manager (if you have SQL Server 7.0 you'll find the menu names change to Programs | Microsoft SQL Server 7.0 | OLAP Services | OLAP Manager). This is what it looks like with SQL Server 2000:

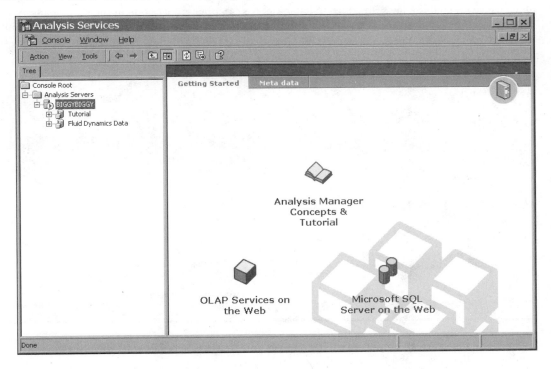

The scope pane (that's the left hand tree view in an MMC snapin) is similar to the one for the SQL Server Enterprise Manager, insofar as the hierarchy goes through the available servers to the databases available on each one. This screenshot shows that we currently have two OLAP databases installed, Tutorial and Fluid Dynamics Data. If there's no data for the selected node in the scope pane, the results pane defaults to a taskpad presenting us with a few other options, as shown in the right hand pane, including an extensive tutorial on how to use the analysis manager.

We're going to quickly run through the process of setting up the OLAP database for RocksWorks. Since the user interface is fairly intuitive, we won't show every step – just enough to see how the process works.

We start off by right–clicking on the server name in the scope pane and selecting **New Database**. This gives us a dialog asking for the database name and description:

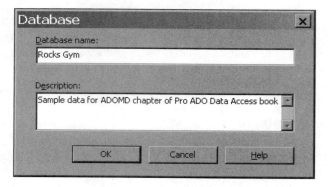

Once we've created the new **Rocks Gym** database, we can open up its node in the scope pane. We can then see that the similarity with the **SQL Server Enterprise Manager** is only skin deep. At this point, we are presented with a display of the items for the database, represented in the cube structure of OLAP databases, rather than the relational structure of SQL Server databases:

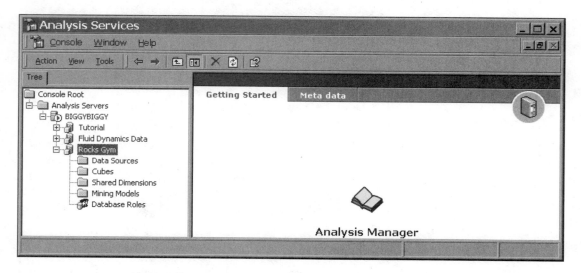

So far, these items are all empty, as we haven't yet told Analysis Services what data is to go into our new database. Initially, we need to specify the data source.

If we right-click on Data Sources and select New Data Source, we get the usual property page supplied by OLE DB, asking us to select a data source. Since our data source is an Access database, we select the Jet 4.0 OLE DB Provider. (Note, it's the data source for the data warehouse we are interested in – don't select the provider for OLAP!).

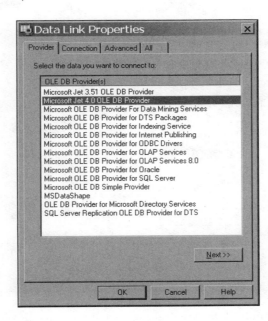

Then enter the path to the RocksGym.mdb file in the Connection tab:

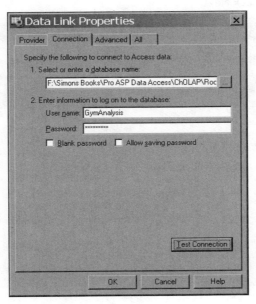

Now we can actually generate the cube. So we select **Cubes** in the scope pane, and then select **New Cube** from the context menu. We also get offered a choice of using an editor or a wizard to supply the information needed to generate the cube. For starting off, the wizard is easiest.

After an initial welcome dialog, we get presented with the following screen:

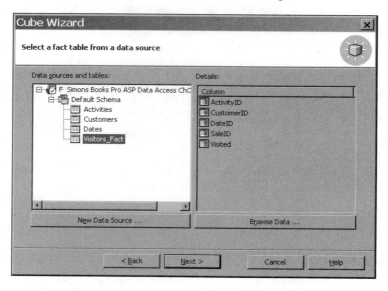

Analysis Manager has examined the Access database and presented us with a list of tables. From these, we may select which table is to supply the data for the cube. For our example, we will select the Visitors_Fact table and click **Next**:

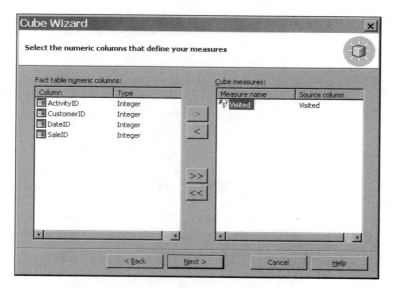

At this point we need to select which of the columns of the Visitors_Fact table will give us our measure. This is one of those dialogs that gives us a pair of list boxes, along with buttons to shift items between the list boxes. Our measure is the Visited column, which as we saw earlier, just contains the number 1 to allow us to count visits. So we need to ensure that the Cube measures list box contains the Visited item.

Clicking Next takes us to the next step in the wizard, which asks us to select the dimensions.

At this point, we need to select which of the tables will give us our dimensions:

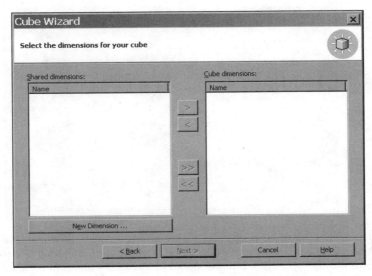

It is possible to pick any of the dimensions listed in the shared dimensions list. As we have not yet created any shared dimensions we'll click on New Dimension. Clicking on that button gives us the next dialog, asking us to specify the table structure of the dimension. Note that a **shared dimension** is just a dimension that you define which is available to be used in any other cubes you might want to create. You would normally define a dimension to be shared, as you don't lose anything by doing so:

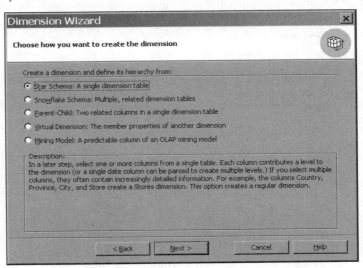

We're keeping things simple here by sticking to the **Star Schema** – that's the schema in which each dimension is a table linked to the main fact table, just how we created our data warehouse. The other schemas allow for various more complex arrangements of the tables in the data warehouse.

Next we need to specify which table is going to supply the information for the dimension:

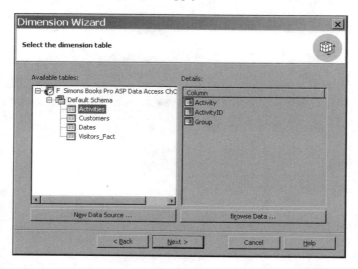

We're going to have to work through this several times to specify all the dimensions. We'll start off by going for the **Activities** dimension. Notice that the wizard has even provided us with a **Browse Data** button, in case we want to see what's actually stored in any of the tables in the database.

The next dialog is where things start getting interesting. We're presented with another 2-list box, in which we select which columns of our chosen table will form the levels. Notice that in this case there are also buttons to shift columns up or down, since we need to have the columns in the correct order to form the sequence of levels. For **Activities**, the first level (strictly speaking, the 2nd level, since the first level will by default be the aggregation of everything in **Activities**) is **Group**, and the final level is **Activity**:

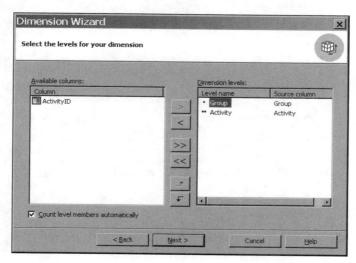

The Count level members automatically checkbox tells the dimension wizard to look up the values in the table for each level. For example, it can tell that the possibilities for Individual Training are Exercise Studio and Weights Room. You'd normally leave that checked as it makes your life easier!

We then get several dialogs that confirm the names of our levels, and ask us to select some more advanced options such as whether we want to be able to modify the structure of our dimension later on. There's no need for us to look at these dialogs at the moment, as the default values are fine, and they're not really relevant to understanding how to set up a dimension. The final dialog asks us to confirm the name of the dimension:

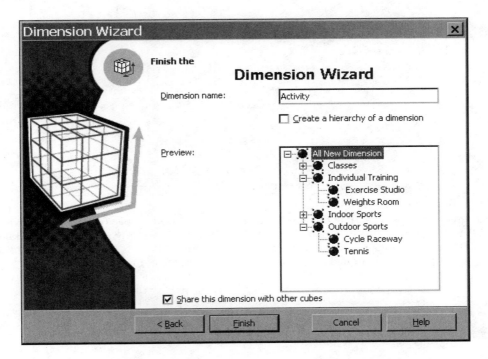

Notice the tree control that lets us verify the structure of the dimension. There's also a check box which lets us specify whether we want to create a hierarchy. We'd need to check that button if our dimension was going to have more than one hierarchy, which we don't want to do here. But we will want to do this for Customers, since they can be organised by sex and age.

When we click on Finish we get returned to the cube wizard and are invited to create further dimensions. To create the Rocks Gym database, we will need to work through the wizard again to create the Customer and Date dimensions. We won't go through these processes in detail, since they are basically the same as for Activities. We'll just mention a couple of differences.

When we try to create the Dates dimension, the wizard will notice that there's a date column, and as a result, presents us with an additional dialog asking if this is a standard Time dimension:

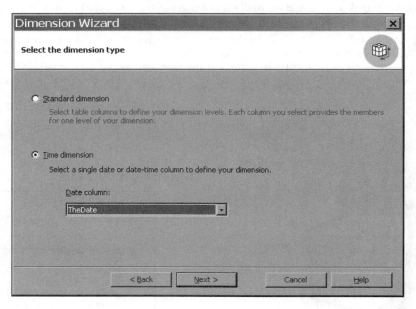

If we agree to this being a Time dimension, then there is no need to specify the levels individually; OLAP can break down the time data automatically. This is why we only needed one TheDate column in our Dates table in the original Access database. All we need to do is tell the Analysis Manager how far we want the time data to be broken down; in our case by Year, Quarter and Month:

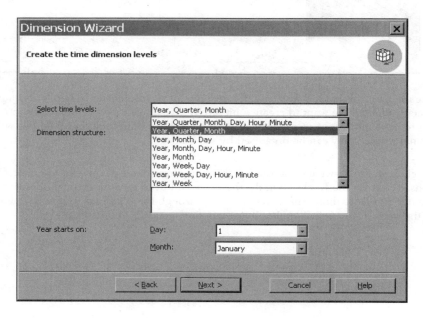

We also need to be careful for the customer profile, since as mentioned earlier `Age` and `Sex` are really two hierarchies of the same dimension rather than two separate dimensions. (Actually you could create them as two independent dimensions and everything would still work fine, but from the point of view of code maintenance, it's probably best to represent them in the correct way).

To create Age and Sex as hierarchies, the process is exactly the same as for the Activity Type, except that in the final dialog of the Dimension Wizard we ensure that the Create Hierarchy checkbox is ticked as shown in the next screenshot. This creates another edit box for the name of the hierarchy in the dialog, so you need to enter the name of the dimension and the hierarchy. Here we enter Customer for the name of the dimension and respectively Age and Sex for the name of each hierarchy. (We go through the whole process once for each hierarchy.):

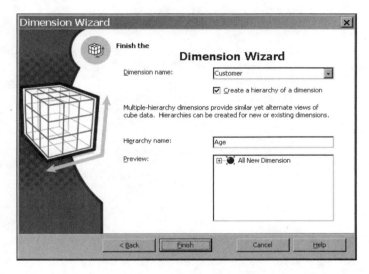

Once we've finished adding dimensions we click Finish in the Dimension Wizard and are returned to the Cube Wizard. We can then click Next in the cube wizard, at which point the final Finish dialog appears, and we get asked to confirm the name of the cube:

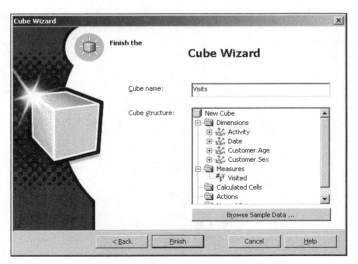

After clicking on Finish, we are led straight into the Cube Editor dialog, in case there is any further editing that needs to be done:

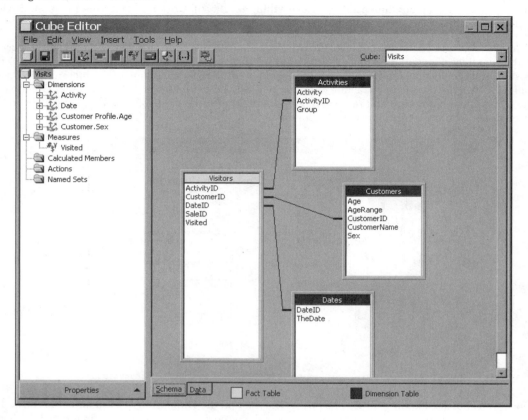

There's nothing to do here so we Save the cube and exit.

We're not finished yet. Saving the cube only saves the details of how we want the cube to be set up, it doesn't store the complete database. There are two more things to be done. One is to select the storage options for the cube, including whether we want to use MOLAP, ROLAP, or HOLAP, and the other is to process it. Here I'm going to go for MOLAP since the database is fairly small.

Setting the storage options is the next stage. When you exit the cube editor from the previous screenshot you will immediately be presented with a dialog asking you if you want to do this:

Clicking Yes results in a Welcome to the Storage Design Wizard dialog followed by the actual steps of the storage design wizard. The first stage is to choose the storage format:

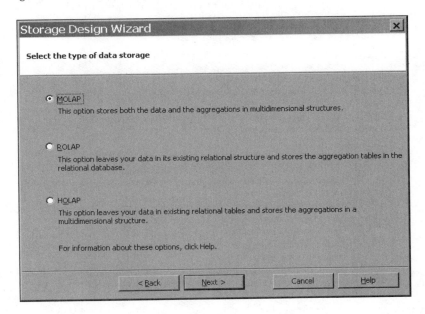

No matter which option you pick the next step invites you to choose the extent to which you want aggregates of data to be calculated – this uses disk space but increases performance, and the wizard allows you to specify how much disk space to use, or what performance gain to aim at, or how long to spend actually calculating the aggregates (Until I click Stop):

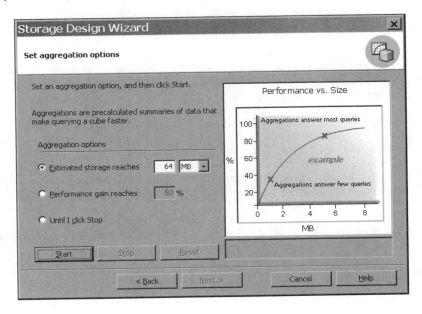

The final stage after the aggregates have been calculated is to actually process the cube. This is an important task, and one which we'll have to repeat whenever the data in the source database has changed, that is when we want the updated data to be made available to OLAP. When processing is complete, the Analysis Manager presents us with a detailed report on whether the processing succeeded or not, and where any problems occurred:

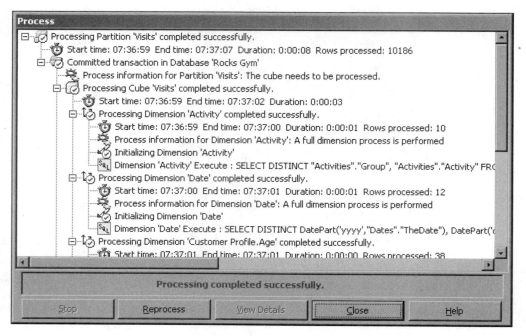

We can reprocess the dimensions and the cube through context menu options in the scope pane of the Analysis Manager.

Once the cube is set up, we don't actually need to do any programming in order to look at the breakdown of our data. We've already seen the tool that can be used to browse the data; it's just the pivot table tool that we saw when we first introduced the RocksWorks gym. We can bring up this tool by selecting the appropriate data cube in the scope pane, right clicking, and selecting **Browse Data**.

One other point before we start coding; we will need to make sure that we have permission to read the OLAP database from whatever account that our code will be run under. If we try to use ADO MD to access the database from an account that doesn't have suitable permissions without supplying an appropriate username and password in the connection string, our code will obviously generate an error. Confusingly, I found it doesn't give us an **Access Denied** error – it simply returns '**Object does not support this method or property**' as soon as we try to read something we're not allowed to.

We can edit the permissions to access the data cube under the **Roles** node of the scope pane in Analysis Manager. The process involves creating roles (just as with SQL Server), indicating which groups the roles apply to, and which cubes each role has permission to read.

Coding Analysis Services Using ASP

We've pretty much got all the background we need to start writing code using ADO MD; which is, after all, the core component of this chapter!

Writing code to hook up to OLAP databases using the ADO MD library is very simple. We're going to quickly go over the object model here, then present some sample code to show the sorts of things we can do using ADO MD.

The ADO MD object model can be broken into two sections. These allow access to both the original database structure, and a given view of the database. The part that lets us access the database structure looks like this:

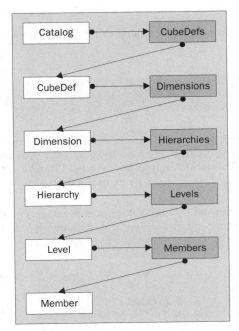

In this diagram, the shaded boxes represent collections, and the white boxes represent objects. As we can see, the structure is entirely hierarchical, with each object containing a collection of the next object in the hierarchy.

If we run down the hierarchy, the objects are:

❑ The Catalog, which identifies the Server and Database. This serves a purpose that is in some ways analogous to the ADO connection object, in that it is the object that actually connects us to OLAP services.

❑ The CubeDef, which represents an individual cube. In our RocksWorks example there will be one CubeDef object, representing the Visits measure.

❑ The Dimension, which represents each dimension applied to the cube. In RocksWorks we will have three dimensions – customers, dates and activities.

- ❑ The `Hierarchy`, which represents a way of breaking down the dimension. In RocksWorks, `Activities` and `Dates` each has only one hierarchy, while `Customers` has two – age and sex.

- ❑ The `Level`, which gives the levels of a hierarchy. For example, the `Dates` hierarchy and `dimension` has levels representing year, quarter and month. Note that where in the database each level is a child of the level above, this is not the case in the ADO object model: each level object exists directly within the Levels collection of the hierarchy. For example, in the database, under the date hierarchy, the level Quarter is a child of the level Year, while the level Month is a child of the level Quarter. The ADO object model simply puts the levels together so all three levels Month, Year and Quarter are all contained in the same Levels collection. Where the level exists in the hierarchy is indicated by its properties.

- ❑ The `Member`, which represents an individual item within a level, for example `Aerobics`, `Step`, or `Cardiofunk`.

The `Catalog` object is the main entry point, and can be instantiated in the following way:

```
Dim objCat
Set objCat = CreateObject("ADOMD.Catalog")
objCat.ActiveConnection = "Provider=MSOLAP; Data Source=BiggyBiggy;User
ID=GymAnalysis;Password=Cybermat"
```

Setting the `ActiveConnection` property of the `Catalog` object automatically opens the connection. The connection string is fairly intuitive. We have to specify the provider and the data source. The provider for connecting to Microsoft Analysis Services is MSOLAP, and the Data Source is the name of the server you're running OLAP on (not the name of the database).

The collections work in the normal way for VBScript collections. For example, to display the name of the `Catalog` created in the code snippet above, and the names of all the `CubeDefs` in it, we'd use the following code:

```
Response.Write "Catalog Name: " & objCat.Name & "<BR>"
    Dim objCubDef
For Each objCubDef In objCat.CubeDefs
    Response.Write "Cube Name: " & objCubDef.Name & "<BR>"
Next
```

Alternatively, to access a particular cube, we could use this:

```
Dim objCubDef
Set objCubDef = objCat.CubeDefs("Visits")
Response.Write "Cube Name: " & objCubDef.Name & "<BR>"
```

We won't go into detail with the methods and properties available on the various objects, but in general most of the objects have a property called Name, which gives the name of the object and also have a property, UniqueName, which provides a full path name through the hierarchy. The UniqueName is what is needed to identify the underlying database object when passing MDX commands to the database.

This part of the ADO object model allows us access to the database structure; we can see how the cube can be broken down. However, it doesn't let us get at the actual data in the cube. For that, we need the other half of the ADO MD object model; the hierarchy of objects based on queries:

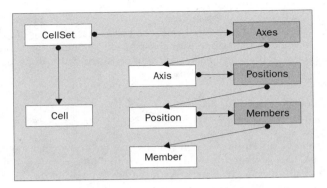

The objects in this structure are:

- CellSet: provides a connection to the cube and is used to request a query.

- Cell: represents an individual cell in the pivot table. This is the object from which we retrieve the values in the table.

- Axis: represents axes in the table; rows and columns, for instance.

- Position: gives the data for what each position along an axis represents.

- Member: if we have asked for data from more than one dimension to be placed on one axis, then each position will represent combined data from more than one source. Each member gives one of the sources.

We'll have a quick look now at how we might use some of these objects.

The object at the top of this hierarchy is the CellSet. This performs a similar role to the Catalog, but the CellSet provides both the connection to the cube and the particular query leading to the retrieval of a set of data intended to form a pivot table. The Cell is the unit that contains each item of data. As an example, if we wanted to look at the data in the cube broken down by activity and customer gender, we could instantiate a CellSet with the following code:

```
Dim objCellSet
Set objCellSet = Server.CreateObject("ADOMD.CellSet")

' set the connection string and MDX command up
Dim sConnection
sConnection = "Provider=MSOLAP; Data Source=BiggyBiggy"
dim sMDX
sMDX = "SELECT [Activity].Children ON COLUMNS, " & _
    "[Customer.Sex].Children ON ROWS FROM Visits"
objCellSet.Open sMDX, sConnection
```

The Open method of the CellSet object connects to the database and retrieves all the values of the cells.

This bit of code also gives us our first introduction to MDX, the language used to pass commands to cube databases using Analysis Server. We'll look at how the syntax of the command we've provided works in the next section – for now, we can just accept that it will give us the breakdown we want – showing the results by activity and customer gender.

Once we've got the `CellSet`, the individual cells can be accessed through the `Items` property of the `CellSet` – they are stored as a multidimensional array. For each cell, the value is strictly given by the property, `Value`, but both of these properties are actually the default properties of the `CellSet` and `Cell`. This means we can access the values like this:

```
Response.Write "Value at 1st column, 1st row is" & objCellSet(0,0) & "<BR>"
Response.Write "Value at 3rd column, 2nd row is" & objCellSet(2,1) & "<BR>"
```

Of course, accessing the values in this way only helps us if we know what the third column and second row actually represent. This is where the other objects in the hierarchy come in; they tell us what data corresponds to each position on a given axis. We'll see how to extract this information from the ADO MD objects in the code sample at the end of this chapter.

MDX

MDX is a rich language, with a lot of sophisticated features. We don't have space here to go into it in detail, but we should get a good idea of how it works by looking in more detail at the command used in the previous section.

MDX syntax is quite similar to SQL, though it serves a somewhat different purpose. Let's look again at the command we used earlier:

```
SELECT [Activity].Children ON COLUMNS, [Customer.Sex].Children ON ROWS FROM Visits
```

This command tells the database what dimensions we're interested in. Specifically, it does the following:

- ❏ The final `FROM` clause says that the cube we want to extract the data from is the `Visits` cube.

- ❏ The `ON COLUMNS` and `ON ROWS` statements indicate the axes that we want to put the data on. Recall that an axis is just an axis of the pivot table. As far as the `SELECT` command is concerned, we are actually going to retrieve the results in the form of a multidimensional array, and the axis really just indicates which dimension of the array to put the results in. `COLUMNS` will give the first dimension, and `ROWS` the second. If we need more dimensions, we can specify `PAGES`, `SECTIONS`, and `CHAPTERS`. After that, we just use `AXIS(n)` where n is the number of the axis (`PAGES`, `SECTIONS`, and `CHAPTERS` would be `AXIS(3)`, `AXIS(4)`, and `AXIS(5)`). If we need that many dimensions, then our query must be incredibly complex!

- ❏ Finally, we need to specify what dimensions/hierarchies and levels are going on each axis. We want the columns to display the `Activity` and the rows to display the `Customer` sex. The square brackets are optional in the above example, but would be needed if the name of the dimension contained any special characters or spaces. We've also suffixed each hierarchy name by `.Children`. This indicates to MDX that we just want to break the data down as far as the first level. So for `Activity` we'll get the categories `Classes`, `Outdoor Sports`, etc. but we won't get the further breakdown into `Aerobics`, `Step`, `Tennis`, etc.

If we wanted to break down the data into it's smallest possible unit, we'd specify `.Members` instead of `.Children`, which does a complete drill down, giving all the members at all levels (that is, not just the lowest level):

```
SELECT [Activity].Members ON COLUMNS, [Customer.Sex].Members ON ROWS FROM Visits
```

For the case of the `Customer.Sex` hierarchy, there is only one level, so `.Members` and `.Children` will give identical results. For `Activity`, `Children` will give us Classes, Indoor Sports, Outdoor Sports and Individual Training. `Members` will give us those members as well as Aerobics, Cardiofunk, Squash, etc.

Samples

To round off the chapter, we're going to quickly present two very simple ASP pages that make use of OLAP services and the Rocks Gym OLAP database. The first sample displays the names of the hierarchies in the database, while the second actually uses the `CellSet` to display a table of number of customers at RocksWorks, simultaneously broken down by sex, age and type of facility attended.

Displaying the Hierarchies

This short sample displays the dimensions and hierarchies in the Rocks Gym database. For each dimension it shows the name of the dimension, while for the hierarchy, the name and the unique name are displayed. Recall that the unique name is the name that needs to be used to identify the hierarchy in MDX statements.

The ASP page looks like this when displayed in a browser:

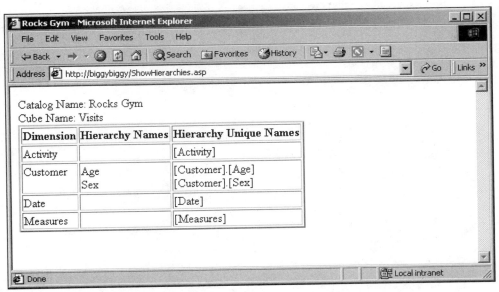

Notice how this shows that the hierarchy only has a (simple) name when necessary.

The code used to generate this page looks like this:

```
<%@ Language = VBScript %>
<% Option Explicit %>

<!DOCTYPE HTML PUBLIC "-//W3C//DTD HTML 4.0 Transitional//EN">
<HTML>
<HEAD>
<TITLE>RockWorks Gym</TITLE>
</HEAD>

<BODY>

<p>

<%

    ' set up the catalog object and obtain the CubeDef
    Dim sConnection
    sConnection = "Provider=MSOLAP; Data Source=BiggyBiggy"
        Dim objCat
        Set objCat = CreateObject("ADOMD.Catalog")
        objCat.ActiveConnection = sConnection
    Response.Write "Catalog Name: " & objCat.Name & "<BR>"
        Dim objCubDef
    Set objCubDef = objCat.CubeDefs("Visits")
    Response.Write "Cube Name: " & objCubDef.Name & "<BR>"

    ' display the dimensions and hierarchies
    Response.Write "<TABLE BORDER=2>"
    Response.Write "<THEAD><TH><STRONG>Dimension</STRONG></TH>" & _
        "<TH><STRONG>Hierarchy Names</STRONG></TH>" & _
        "<TH><STRONG>Hierarchy Unique Names</STRONG></TH></THEAD>"
    Response.Write "<TBODY>"
    dim objDimension
    For Each objDimension In objCubDef.Dimensions
        Response.Write "<TR><TD VALIGN=Top>" & objDimension.Name & "</TD><TD>"
        Dim objHierarchy
        For Each objHierarchy In objDimension.Hierarchies
            Response.Write objHierarchy.Name & "<BR>"
        Next
        Response.Write "</TD><TD>"
        For Each objHierarchy In objDimension.Hierarchies
            Response.Write objHierarchy.UniqueName & "<BR>"
        Next
        Response.Write "</TD></TR>"
    Next
    Response.Write "</TBODY></TABLE>"

    Set objHierarchy = Nothing
    Set objDimension = Nothing
    Set objCubDef = Nothing
    Set objCat = Nothing

%>

</BODY>
</HTML>
```

This page starts by displaying the usual HTML headers, then sets up a catalog object to connect to the database. Then we display headers for the table and go on to list the dimension and hierarchy names in this part of the code:

```
dim objDimension
  For Each objDimension In objCubDef.Dimensions
    Response.Write "<TR><TD VALIGN=Top>" & objDimension.Name & "</TD><TD>"
    Dim objHierarchy
    For Each objHierarchy In objDimension.Hierarchies
      Response.Write objHierarchy.Name & "<BR>"
    Next
    Response.Write "</TD><TD>"
    For Each objHierarchy In objDimension.Hierarchies
      Response.Write objHierarchy.UniqueName & "<BR>"
    Next
    Response.Write "</TD></TR>"
  Next
```

This code shows how we use some of the hierarchy of objects and collections in the ADO MD object hierarchy, with the `hierarchies` collection being contained in the `dimension` object, the `dimensions` collection in turn being contained in the `CubeDef` object.

Finally we clean up our objects:

```
Set objHierarchy = Nothing
Set objDimension = Nothing
Set objCubDef = Nothing
Set objCat = Nothing
```

Displaying a Table of Results

The next sample is designed to display a table rather like the pivot tables we've seen earlier (although without the ability to manipulate the table – it's strictly a read only fixed format table). The table will display the number of visitors broken down by class type, age range, and sex. The page when running looks like this:

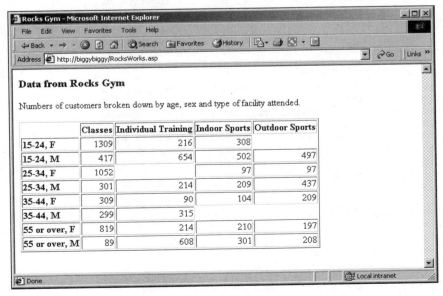

Data from Rocks Gym

Numbers of customers broken down by age, sex and type of facility attended.

	Classes	Individual Training	Indoor Sports	Outdoor Sports
15-24, F	1309	216	308	
15-24, M	417	654	502	497
25-34, F	1052		97	97
25-34, M	301	214	209	437
35-44, F	309	90	104	209
35-44, M	299	315		
55 or over, F	819	214	210	197
55 or over, M	89	608	301	208

It's a static table of numbers of attendees. Along the columns it is broken down by the nature of the activity, while along the rows the data is broken down by both the age and gender of the visitors.

As a user interface, this is a pretty basic page. For example, there's no facility for the user to modify the data displayed, and we haven't even bothered with any code to tidy up the appearance of the cells that display zero results. In a real application, we'd almost certainly be concerned with both of these, but that's just plain ASP coding. Here we want to focus on the code that's relevant to ADO MD, so we've stuck with the simple user interface.

The MDX statement needed to pick out these results is this:

```
SELECT [Activity].Children ON COLUMNS, CROSSJOIN([Customer.Age].Children,
[Customer.Sex].Children) ON ROWS FROM Visits
```

The statement uses a CROSSJOIN to combine the two different dimensions onto the ROWS axis.

Let's go over the code that generates this page. We'll first present the entire ASP page in its entirety, then go over the pertinent bits:

```
<%@ Language = VBScript %>
<% Option Explicit %>

<!DOCTYPE HTML PUBLIC "-//W3C//DTD HTML 4.0 Transitional//EN">
<HTML>
<HEAD>
<TITLE> Rocks Gym</TITLE>
</HEAD>

<BODY>

<H3> Data from Rocks Gym </H3>
<p>
Numbers of customers broken down by age, sex and type of facility attended.<P>

<%

    Dim objCellSet
    Set objCellSet = Server.CreateObject("ADOMD.CellSet")

    ' set the connection string and MDX command up
    Dim sConnection
    sConnection = "Provider=MSOLAP; Data Source=BiggyBiggy"
    dim sMDX
    sMDX = "SELECT [Activity].Children ON COLUMNS, " & _
        "CROSSJOIN([Customer.Age].Children, [Customer.Sex].Children) ON ROWS FROM
Visits"
    objCellSet.Open sMDX, sConnection


    ' write out the column headers
    Dim objAxis
    Dim objPosition
    dim nColumns
```

```
    Response.Write "<TABLE BORDER=1>"
    Response.Write "<THEAD><TH></TH>"
    Set objAxis = objCellSet.Axes(0)
    nColumns = objAxis.Positions.Count
    For Each objPosition in objAxis.Positions
        Response.Write "<TH>" & objPosition.Members(0) & "</TH>"
    Next

    ' write out the rest of the table
    Response.Write "</THEAD><TBODY>"
    Dim iRow, iColumn
    Dim sRowHeader, sValue
    Dim objMember
    Set objAxis = objCellSet.Axes(1)
    For Each objPosition in objAxis.Positions
        iRow = objPosition.Ordinal

        ' figure out the caption for the row
        sRowHeader = ""
        For Each objMember In objPosition.Members
            if (sRowHeader <> "") Then sRowHeader = sRowHeader & ", "
            sRowHeader = sRowHeader & objMember.Caption
        Next
        Response.Write "<TR><TD><STRONG>" & sRowHeader & "</STRONG></TD>"
        For iColumn = 0 To nColumns-1
            sValue = objCellSet(iColumn,iRow)
            Response.Write "<TD ALIGN=Right>" & sValue & "</TD>"
        Next
        Response.Write "</TR>" & vbCrLf
    Next
    Response.Write "</TBODY></TABLE>"

%>

</BODY>
</HTML>
```

In this code we start off by instantiating a `CellSet` object and using it to prepare the query. Then we write out the headers for the columns. The way we figure out the headers is as follows:

```
Set objAxis = objCellSet.Axes(0)
nColumns = objAxis.Positions.Count
For Each objPosition in objAxis.Positions
    Response.Write "<TH>" & objPosition.Members(0) & "</TH>"
Next
```

The `Axes` collection of the `CellSet` gives all the axes. However, there's no point in our using a `For Each` loop to loop over them, since we know that the columns are the first axis, and so given by the first element of the collection. Instead, we just use `objCellSet.Axes(0)` to retrieve this axis object.

Now the `Positions` collection of the axis contains an object for each position along the axis, so it follows that the count of these elements gives the number of columns of data (excluding the row-header column). Which is why we declared:

```
nColumns = objAxis.Positions.Count
```

We then need the names of each column. This is retrieved by the `Caption` property of the `Members` object in each position. However, since our MDX query only specified one dimension for the columns, we know there will only be one `Members` object in each collection; which we've referenced as `Members(0)`. In doing so we've taken advantage of the fact that the `Caption` is the default property.

Getting the headers for the rows involves a similar process:

```
For Each objPosition in objAxis.Positions
    iRow = objPosition.Ordinal

    ' figure out the caption for the row
    sRowHeader = ""
    For Each objMember In objPosition.Members
        if (sRowHeader <> "") Then sRowHeader = sRowHeader & ", "
        sRowHeader = sRowHeader & objMember.Caption
    Next
    Response.Write "<TR><TD><STRONG>" & sRowHeader & "</STRONG></TD>"
```

In this case, however, we have requested two dimensions to go on the ROWS axis, so we do need to loop through all the objects in the `Members` collection to get the caption names. We've also been explicit in this case about our use of the `Caption` property. Notice we've also used the `Ordinal` property of the `Position` object to find out which row we're on. The `Ordinal` is just what its name implies; a number that is zero for the first row, 1 for the second, and so on.

At this point we've written out the row header, and we've stored the index of the row in the `iRow` variable, so we can just write out the values of our measure straight from the array that stores them:

```
    For iColumn = 0 To nColumns-1
        sValue = objCellSet(iColumn,iRow)
        Response.Write "<TD ALIGN=Right>" & sValue & "</TD>"
    Next
    Response.Write "</TR>" & vbCrLf
Next
```

Summary

This has been a pretty quick tour of OLAP and ADO MD. As you probably suspect, there is a lot more we can do with the various ADO MD objects. And with a bit of ASP coding, we can use them to build quite sophisticated pivot tables, or to write pages that focus in on the data that management wants to be able to do their planning. In the course of this chapter, we've also seen how Microsoft's Analysis Services is able to build a database with a multi-dimensional structure, conceptually very different from the kind of structure we're accustomed to using in relational databases. By using Analysis Services in conjunction with SQL Server, or whatever other relational database you might normally use, we can construct a solution that not only gives us all the normal transactional facilities of a scaleable database, but enables us to efficiently analyse the overall statistics of the transactions, and hence provide high quality data with which to assess the position and future strategies of an organization.

31

Data Mining

We live during the information age, which means that we have a lot of data at our disposal. Companies are playing their part in adding to this mass of data by gathering information at every opportunity. When we buy something from a retail store, we're often asked for addresses, zip code or phone numbers. When we subscribe to a web site, we are often asked to give personal information so that the presentation of the site can be tailored to our needs. When we purchase items, what we buy is recorded.

So, we see that there is a mass of information out there, which, when used properly, can be extremely valuable, and in today's fast moving markets, can be the key to having a competitive advantage. This competitive advantage is often the motivation for a company acquiring this their data in the first place. However, now that companies have acquired all of this data, they are frequently unsure as how to gain any benefit from it – it's not the data that is so valuable but the knowledge contained within the data!

The knowledge is buried inside the data, but it is often extremely difficult to extract. This is where **data mining** comes in. Data mining can help us gain value from the data we have collected by giving us the methods to retrieve knowledge from that data. When applied correctly, this knowledge can often result in benefits for the business.

Data mining is the semi-automatic process of extracting hidden trends and patterns within data. These patterns can help us make key business decision that can radically change our business direction. The data mining process naturally requires large amounts of data, so we'll look initially at data warehousing, and then move on to data mining.

The Foundation: Data Warehousing

Since data mining is intended to dig into data in order to extract valuable information, it's imperative that we have quality data to mine. The quality of that data will affect the success, or otherwise, of the entire data mining process. This massive amount of data is often stored in data warehouses. As such, data warehousing is the foundation for the entire data mining process.

Like much technological jargon, **data warehousing** is one of those terms that many people use but few really understand. Companies frequently feel that a data warehouse is necessary – consultants are hired, projects started, software evaluated, expensive hardware purchased, and massive amounts of resources are spent, all in the name of data warehousing. Yet if you ask many of those involved what 'data warehousing' means and what benefits it will eventually bring, we would likely receive many different answers, if indeed we get any answers at all.

W. H. Inmon, often referred to as the father of data warehousing, is typically credited with coining the phrase 'data warehousing' in the mid-1980's. Since then there's been a lot of excitement about it, but very little understanding. To some, a data warehouse is simply a large database. To others, it's a repository of data from more than one data source. And to others, it's a central database fed by other operational databases, intended primarily for the purpose of query access to provide management information. While all of these ideas may be true of a data warehouse, they fall way short of fulfilling what a data warehouse was defined to be.

The vision for a data warehouse should be to provide a model to collate valuable data from operational systems into a central decision support database. A data warehouse becomes the foundation for decision support and data analysis by gathering information together for the purpose of making more educated business decisions. To help understand a data warehouse, lets look at the traits of a data warehouse. A data warehouse is "subject-oriented, integrated, time-variant, and nonvolatile", (see W.H. Inmon, Building the Data Warehouse, 1992).

❑ **Subject-Oriented**: Information in a data warehouse is subject-oriented as opposed to functionally or process oriented. Typically, applications are modeled to meet the day-to-day function and process needs of operations. For instance, operational data would be designed around specific transactions, orders, shipping and tracking information, current pricing, etc. In contrast to these operational systems, the organization of a data warehouse should be based on business related subject areas such as customers, products, and vendors.

❑ **Integrated**: The information in the data warehouse is taken from non-integrated operational systems and must be transformed so that it follows naming conventions, units of measure, and semantics that are consistent throughout. Data from the different operational systems must follow the standards that we have set for our data warehouse. **Cleansing** is the process of both transforming the data that will be placed in the data warehouse and stripping off any unwanted information that come from the operational systems that provide the data.

❑ **Time-variant**: Information in the data warehouse is accurate at some point in time. The information retrieved from our operational sources was valid at a certain point of time and before it was placed into the data warehouse. This time-variant is important in our decision analysis, as it helps us to evaluate how the results fit into real-time. For instance, an operational system may not keep a record of sales after 90 days. However, our data warehouse may have sales information for periods of 10 years or more.

❑ **Nonvolatile:** A data warehouse is designed to be a read-only database. It is not an operational database with daily insert, delete, and update activity. Data is loaded at the very beginning and it is updated periodically with cleansed operational data as part of the data warehouse model. However, data should only be updated as part of the data warehousing model and not through direct user interaction. The data in the warehouse is not subject to constant changes as in the case of operational systems. From the user perspective, the data warehouse will be read-only! However, the architecture of the data warehouse may (and probably will) change over time to meet changing business needs, but the data itself would not change.

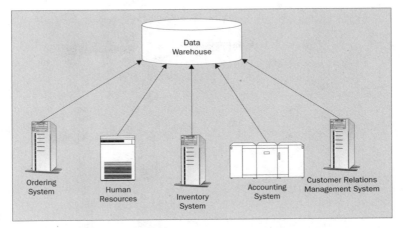

The above figure helps us see the big picture. The data from various operational systems is cleansed and then fed into our centralized data warehouse. Typically, we have unconnected operational systems scattered throughout our enterprise, each with the goal of getting a specific job done. They are designed to meet various business needs, often built on various technologies using various standards. The data is contained in many different places and is stored in many different forms. By implementing data warehousing, we are able to pull all of that data into a single database system for decision support.

Implementing a data warehouse is no small undertaking. However, the benefits are enormous when implemented correctly. One problem generally associated with data warehousing is that each department will often have its own data warehousing project underway to meet its specific needs. However, a properly implemented data warehouse can meet the needs of most, if not all, of the business units in a company.

Project management is as critical to the success of data warehousing projects as technical expertise. It's not uncommon for companies to have several data warehousing projects occurring simultaneously, which complicates the purpose of setting up a central all-encompassing data warehousing. Helping business units understand that a single company's data warehousing initiative can meet all of their business needs is critical. A good rule of thumb is that 80% of a company's data warehousing data is valuable to all business units. It's also important to know that the process of extracting, cleansing, and loading the data will be the most expensive aspect of the entire project; it's not uncommon for this cost to be 80% to 90% of the total project cost. To have multiple projects doing the same thing is a poor use of company resources. The most successful company-wide data warehousing projects often require a great deal of internal company marketing to get everyone on board.

Data Warehousing Designed for Data Mining

A data warehouse should be designed as a long-term solution for the management of information. The data in our data warehouse should have an enterprise scope and not be specific to departmental level requirements. However, after convincing those departments that an enterprise-wide solution is best for the company as a whole, how do we meet their individual departmental needs? One solution is to implement **data marts**, which are departmental or workgroup specific databases that are much smaller in size and scope than a data warehouse and are designed to meet the individual needs of the various departments. The data mart is fed data from the data warehouse and this is where the user interacts with our enterprise data warehousing system. The vast majority of user queries are directed at data marts and not the data warehouse itself. As departmental needs change, these data marts can be changed much easier than the enterprise data warehouse.

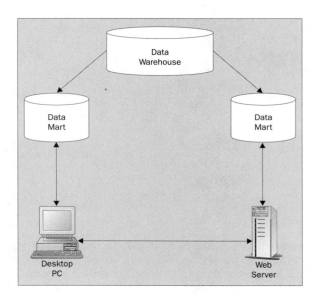

Overview of Data Mining

Now we have this well designed data warehouse regularly being populated with information about our business. Data is regularly extracted from our operational systems, cleansed, and imported into our data warehouse. The data warehouse contains a wealth of information that can help us to make critical business decisions. How can data mining help? Can't we just run queries against our data warehouse (or even better, against data marts) to get answers to our questions?

We certainly can do this. But what if you are a technology manager trying to find ways to increase business in your consulting division? Questions like "what is the average age of our customers" or "from what region do most of our sales originate" would provide important information. It is very hard to query a data source for this sort of information. However, data mining may produce the answers that you need. Suppose, data mining returns a pattern like this: "70% of your customers were previously clients from your training division". You might not have thought of this as a possible solution to your business problem. Based on this pattern, you might choose to spend your marketing dollars on your corporate training program as a form of lead generation for your consulting division. In this instance, data mining didn't just return the information but also came up with the hypothesis by detecting patterns and trends in our data using complex algorithms. For this process to be successful, it must shield us from the number crunching and supply us with the information we can use. It also takes the initiative and automatically finds these hidden patterns and trends all by itself. Some have mistakenly considered data mining as simply the process of retrieving data from data warehouses. However, it is much more than this; it attempts to find hidden information within that data. At its core, it is a statistical process, but the goal is always to rise above getting raw data by discovering the knowledge within the data. This is partly the reason why the term 'Knowledge Discovery in Databases' (KDD) has begun to be used to refer to the data mining process.

> A hypothesis is the set of patterns and trends that the data mining tool produces as output. It is a suggested business solution based on the criteria supplied to the tool by the user.

Discovery and Forecasting

In data mining, there are two primary categories of operations: discovery and forecasting:

❑ **Discovery (Descriptive)**: This model enables enterprises to identify hidden patterns or trends in the data without having any prior knowledge about what the pattern may be. The system takes the initiative and pulls out the knowledge buried in our data.

❑ **Forecasting (Predictive)**: As it's name implies, predictive modeling patterns discovered by the data mining process can be used to forecast values based on existing patterns.

Let's look at how both models could benefit an organization. In the discovery model, the data mining process may identify relationships and patterns in our data we hadn't previously thought of. Having automatically explored the data, the data mining process would help the users visualize and understand those patterns. For instance, we may be trying to find the primary causes of accidents during peak traffic times. If our data warehouse has been populated with the records of all accidents for a particular region for the last 5 years, we could query the database for various scenarios using standard query syntax (e.g. falling asleep, driving under the influence of alcohol, etc), but we would be hard pushed to come up with every possible accident cause.

With a data mining tool, we could analyze the data and may pull up information that showed that many accidents are in fact caused by applying makeup, changing a tape, daydreaming, feeding a baby in a car seat, talking on a mobile phone, reading a map and a host of other scenarios that we may have never imagined, just so long as one example exists in the data. The important thing to remember is that this discovery process isn't simply based on a list of possible scenarios, but is found through finding those trends within the existing data. Having found those hidden trends, we must then evaluate our results and verify their validity.

In the predictive model, the system attempts to predict a result for a particular scenario, based on existing patterns within the database. For instance, we may want to predict how much inventory we need in our retail stores, or we may want to forecast what product a return visitor to our web site would buy. With these predictions, we can stock our store accordingly and can make sure that our high probability products are listed in a "personal recommendations" section of our web site, or perhaps emailed out to our customers. As the data warehouse is updated with more data from our operational systems, our predictive information will also be updated, based on any new patterns and trends that are found. As the volume of quality data in our data warehouse increases, so does the probability that our forecasting will be accurate.

Today, data mining is used by companies to evaluate credit approval, improve target marketing, analyze lead generation techniques used by the sales force, and customer profiling, to name a few.

Data Mining Techniques

As data mining has evolved as a technology, more and more techniques have come into the marketplace. In addition, increases in hardware and network performance have made some of the more complex methods much more feasible as solutions for the mass market. Many data-mining vendors are coming up with new methods and variations of existing methods to produce tools that offer maximum efficiency. Most tools on the market today offer several different techniques for the various user goals. In this section, I will go over some of the most common data-mining techniques.

Visualization

Visualization is the process of choosing key attributes and then having those attributes mapped to coordinates that are rendered graphically. For instance, you might choose age, average income, and education as your key attributes. The data-mining tool would then generate a three-dimensional space based on the data. The benefits of visualization lie in the fact that humans like data to be presented visually. For most, being overwhelmed with pure numeric data can be mind-numbing, but a color-coded graph or bar-chart will quickly make its point and will last longer in someone's memory that a page full of numbers. Trends that seem incomprehensible in a spreadsheet can become crystal clear through a chart or a graph.

Clustering

With clustering, the data mining algorithms look through large amounts of data seeking clusters, or groupings, of data that would indicate a pattern or trend. One great feature of clustering is that it requires no user input to execute. The user doesn't need to have an agenda or hypothesis prior to beginning the data mining process. The system takes the initiative and seeks clusters of information within the data. Having found those clusters, it is up to the end user to analyze them and assess their value.

An example where clustering would be used, would be a marketing campaign in which we are trying to determine which periodicals would be most effective for our target audience. Our data mining tools could be set to give us any number of clusters found from within our customers' data. Rather than trying to target all of our customers, we can focus on these clusters and devise a marketing strategy for each of them. As we analyze each cluster, we can determine average income, average education, marital status, gender, etc. to help us target each cluster. The data that was once unmanageable has been segmented into groupings that we can work with.

Decision Trees

Decision trees are a great choice when seeking to predict customer behavior. They produce results that are easy for the user to understand and follow. A simple example would be the production of a decision tree to help a marketing campaign. Based on existing data, a decision tree may show that of those responding to an auto leasing campaign, 72% were homeowners whereas 12% lived in rented housing/apartments. Having identified that homeowners are a market we'd like to target, we can break homeowners down further. For instance, the tree could then branch off and show how many of the 72% of homeowners were first time homeowners. With this information, a marketing department may choose to focus their efforts on flyers packaged with mortgage companies' monthly billing statements.

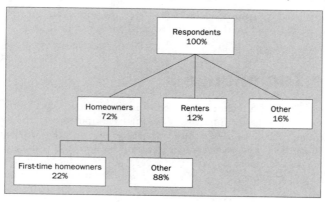

Neural Networks

Neural Networks are composed of large numbers of interconnected nodes. As such, they bear a structural similarity to the neural structure of the brain (and much is often made of this). They are generally useful in analysing data which is affected by a large number of different factors, and in which the relationships between these factors are difficult to unearth. In analysing a set of sales data, for instance, we might want to find out what kinds of factors influence buying patterns.

Normally, the nodes of a network are arranged into three distinct layers; an input layer, a hidden layer, and an output layer:

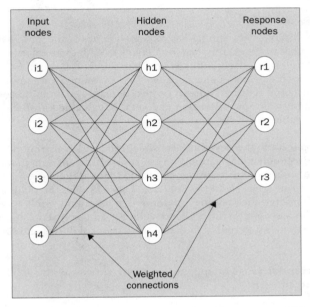

Each node in the network can have a certain activation value. Data is entered into the network by assigning appropriate activation values to the nodes in the input layer. These activation values are propagated through the network via the connections. These are *weighted*, so that the activation values of nodes in the subsequent layer are a function of the activation values of all the nodes in the preceding layer and the connection weights.

The output of the network (the activation values of the output nodes) is compared with the desired output (normally taken from the data we are working with). The difference between these two represents the current *error*. This is used to determine, via an appropriate algorithm, how the connection weights should be adjusted. Adjustments are typically quite small, and the amount of data passed through the network is normally very large, so the network only slowly comes to generate the desired output.

However, the network ends up being configured in such a way that the hidden relationships between the variables in the data are 'learned', and it becomes capable of yielding accurate predictions from large sets of complex data.

Neural networks are often referred to as paradigm examples of *distributed* processing. However, we should make it clear that they aren't distributed in the ordinary sense of running over numerous computers, but are simulated, normally on just one machine.

Data Mining and ASP Applications

The primary goal of data mining is to return knowledge that will help us make better business decisions. This decision support system can be invaluable for the key decision makers in a company. For data mining to reach its full potential, that knowledge must be made accessible to everyone in the company, particularly executive management. They should be able to generate the information and have that knowledge returned to them in an understandable format such as graphs, charts, and tables. This last step of the data mining process has often proved to be a drawback of many data warehousing/data mining projects. Technical resources are able to extract and understand the information, but this information doesn't necessarily reach those that need it, at least not in a form they find easy to work with.

Throughout its early history, data mining has remained in academic circles at universities and research laboratories, and this has only recently begun to change. With the explosion of computer technologies (and particularly the Internet), data mining is now moving in to position to become a viable solution for the mass market. Many a data-warehousing project has consumed vast amounts of resources, both in man-hours and dollars, and returned little or no real benefit. Data mining combined with ASP changes all that, and applications can now be written that get that valuable knowledge that is buried inside the data and make it available to the key business decision makers.

Through an ASP application, the developer can shield the end user from having to learn the various data mining tools. Most tools today support a vast array of current data mining techniques. However, learning to use these tools requires training, and those being trained are highly technical, but they would not necessarily be the one who would use the data. Those in sales, marketing, and upper-level management rarely undergo this training and those that do attend won't necessarily to become proficient in using the tools. However, a web developer can use ASP to simplify this process and make various levels of functionality available to match the various skill sets and business needs of the end user.

Using ASP opens up a wide range of options. Let's look at twoways in which ASP applications can be used with data mining projects:

- ❑ **Report Generation**: Through an ASP interface, a developer can give the user a web-based interface from which to generate data mining reports. By controlling the application, the developer can control how complicated the process of accessing reports is by limiting the number of options available to the user. One of other great things about an ASP application is that the developer can provide online help to the user that is easily updateable by the developer. Often, the vendor documentation supplied with today's data mining tools is intended for advanced users. However, with ASP, we can customize our help system to target the level of our user base. We can also update this information based on feedback from our users. This process, while time consuming, will ensure that all of the previous efforts and expenses are not in vain. Through ASP, Excel web controls can be used on the client to enable *ad hoc* pivoting and displaying of data graphically. By pushing this to functionality to a user-friendly interface, management can quickly generate reports, analyze and verify the data and either except the results or modify the process to produce more valid results.

- ❑ **Presentation**: Having generated the reports, it's important that the results are made available to others for review. Presentation allows us to distribute the results from the ASP-generated reports to those who only need to see the results, not generate new reports. At this point, we have implemented a data warehouse with quality data from our operational systems, we've implemented data mining, we've given the user an interface to mine that knowledge, and now a format is needed to present the findings to the key decision makers. This is where ASP really comes into its own. Having generated the information, we can now simply point others to an ASP page which generates the view of our stored results. We can use this medium during the presentation from any location where we have access to the web server. For a national or global sales force, we could make this information available on the Internet, or an intranet or extranet for others to view.

As said before, ASP can be used to generate the presentation of the results of the data mining process. The web application can be used to display forecasting results from our data mining process, for instance, required inventory estimates could be exposed through web parts and made available on a digital dashboard, where office managers could glance at the recommended ordering level for a particular product. Another example would be to make sales forecasts available on an intranet. Here end-users would be able to look up regularly updated sales projections for the month, quarter, or year. As data is loaded from our operational systems into our data warehouse, the data mining process is updated and the new results displayed through ASP pages. ASP gives us the flexibility to incorporate our results into web applications that are easily accessible to our end users.

In the figure below, we can see how data flows from the data-mining server to our web application. Note that we can also add third party data to the process by feeding our data mart with data from both our corporate data warehouse and third-party databases. Our corporate data warehouse has data cleansed and updated from our internal operational systems but third party data may include data packages with demographic information, industry statistics, or other information purchased from the third-party vendor. This data can add validity to our data mining process by providing data we are unable to get internally.

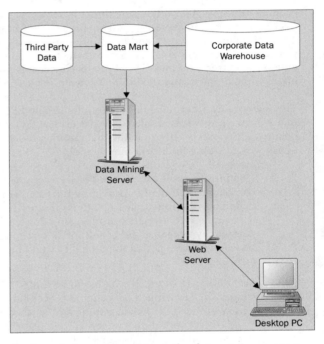

ASP is not the only technology that can make the knowledge gathered from the data mining process available to everyone in your organization – other client server applications could also be used to do this. However, ASP can make this information available to others much easier. I want to emphasis the importance of presentation of our data findings. This step is critical as we seek to give others the ability not only to read the information but also to validate it. Computers can't decide whether a piece of data is useful or not; this requires a uniquely human skill. As we scan the data, we are the ones who decide if it is relevant or determine whether extra data is needed. In the latter case, we can move to include that information in our data warehouse and begin the process again. Otherwise, data mining has done its job and produced a wealth of useful information. It will then be up to the business to respond accordingly.

Data Mining Tools

Data mining tools have come a long way in the last few years. While some are still very complex, and tailored to statisticians and mathematicians, more and more products are being released that, while sophisticated enough to perform advanced analysis, are quite usable by a much wider user base.

Before we begin to evaluate particular data mining tools, its critical to first stop and evaluate our business needs. There are a lot of tools on the market today, but they are not of the same type, or targeting at the same user base. Most offer features that make them a better choice for a particular business need or skill set. It is essential to get a solid understanding of our company's needs before beginning the process of selecting a tool.

Today's tools cover the spectrum of functionality and technical skill required to utilize them efficiently. Some desktop tools, such as Holos, by Seagate Software (www.seagatesoftware.com), use Microsoft Excel as its user interface. Most users are familiar with Excel, or at least some form of a spreadsheet, so training on using the product isn't difficult. However, these programs won't offer the power and control over more advanced server-based systems such as Oracle's Darwin or IBM's Intelligent Data Miner. These systems offer power and flexibility but are expensive to purchase and complex to use. Another solution is Microsoft's Analysis Server, which is included with SQL 2000. While only offering clustering and decision tree data mining techniques, the cost is much lower for MS SQL implementation, yet it offers enough power and flexibility to meet the needs of most companies.

There are many other tools in between the simple Excel-based tools and the powerful enterprise tools that we have just talked about. Again, its critical that we first identify the functionality we need before beginning the process of evaluating data mining tools. Here are some general guidelines and questions to ask when looking for a data-mining tool:

❑ **Complexity and Cost**: If a tool is very complex, training will become a major issue. Is our company committed to providing the training required? If so, are the employees committed to dedicating the time to learn and use the product? If the tool is too complex, and the commitment to using the product isn't there, its unlikely that users will push through the complexity to realize the benefit of data mining. It may be wise to trade some flexibility for less complexity. Added functionality won't be of much benefit if people find the product too difficult to use.

❑ **Scalability**: How much data has to be mined? How much data do we expect to have five years from now? How much data should be kept and how much will need to be discarded after a period of time? With data mining and data warehousing, we should always think long term. A trend over a period of one day will not be as valuable as a trend over five years. Ask the software vendors just how much data their applications can support. Be careful and analyze their answer. They may state that their tool will work with terabytes of data, but what will be the performance with that volume of data? If you find reports are taking weeks to generate, your entire project will most likely be a failure. What hardware does your tool support to handle this growth? Products range from desktop systems to products that support parallel processing. Be careful to avoid overkill that may leave your project short of funding. However, you should purchase a product that can scale and grow with your business for years to come.

❑ **Support**: Who will be supporting the design, implementation, and maintenance of this tool? Will consultants be hired? Or will this be done using existing staff? Tough questions but questions that a critical to the success of this project. It really comes down to two primary options: use outside consulting (outsourcing) or using internal resources (in-house). This is an over simplification and your answer might be both; a good solution is to contract outside consulting during the implementation phase with the ultimate aim of internally supporting the process long term. This requires a knowledge transfer at the end of the project cycle to train your internal employees to take over these processes. This quickly gets you the experience you need in data warehousing/data mining but doesn't leave you dependent on another company indefinitely. Of course the best mix of consulting versus in-house must be made based on skill set of internal employees, core competencies, and business direction. Keep in mind that data warehousing and data mining are very complicated processes.

❑ **Integration**: What technology does this data-mining tool use? How well will it integrate in with the existing IT environment? For instance, your company may be primarily a Microsoft based network. You may have a Microsoft network, MS file/print servers, MS Exchange server, etc. with everything running on Windows 2000. This is obviously your IT department's area of expertise. If you purchase a solution that requires UNIX hardware, it may be difficult to support this internally. Your IT department will probably find it difficult to monitor, difficult to maintain, hardware failures will be an ordeal, and essentially your servers will most likely be orphaned. Problems will be detected when end users call to complain that nothing is working and then someone will reluctantly find the server buried somewhere in a computer room and begin troubleshooting. Naturally, this is to be avoided. Performance and cost issues are of course important in choosing a data-mining tool, but think with a company focus as well. If this system doesn't integrate with your existing technology, performance will most likely suffer and support cost can rocket. Bear in mind that this isn't just about server integration. Make sure that your tool is based on a technology that can be supported by your internal developers *and* external partners. After using a data mining tool to predict inventory needs, business units may require that an operational system automatically place orders. Many vendors offer several supported platforms and technologies so make sure you keep integration in mind when evaluating your tool. As more and more vendors support XML, integration will get easier from disparate systems.

❑ **Broad selection of data mining techniques**: As I mentioned earlier, there are several data mining techniques available today. Some work better for certain types of data analysis, but often the best results come from trying multiple methodologies. This is why many of today's top tools include multiple algorithms and hybrid algorithms to try to get the best of various techniques. Your needs will change but it is important to have a data mining tool that is flexible enough to meet those changing needs. There are efforts underway to standardize data mining techniques but don't assume that a particular vendor adheres to those standards. Make sure you pick a product that offers several options concerning the data mining techniques available.

One last consideration is whether we need a data-mining tool at all. A product designed for a particular business function that has data mining functionality built in might better suit our needs.

Microsoft's Site Server Commerce Edition 3.0 is an example of this type of product. Site Server has a feature called "intelligent cross-selling" which starts by identifying items in the current shoppers order history, for instance. It then compares that to orders of previous customers with those same products in order to suggest to the customer any other items that may be of interest to him or her. While this is not as flexible in that we may not be able to find other trends (such as demographics, age), if we are only looking to generate an intelligent product recommendation for our customers, this may be all we need.

Another kind of product that might suit our needs is what is known as a **Customer Relationship Management** (CRM) program. Some CRM programs also offer specific data mining processes for trend analysis to generate reports on lead patterns and customer profiling. For example, Pivotal (**www.pivotal.com**), a popular CRM package, has what is known as a Pivotal Intelligence Engine that allows us to data mine our CRM data.

Below is a list of vendors and tools on the market today:

Vendor	Tool(s)	URL
Angoss Software	KnowledgeStudio, Knowledge Seeker	www.angoss.com
Attar Software	XpertRule Mine	www.attar.com
IBM	Intelligent Data Miner	http://www-4.ibm.com/software/data/iminer/
Knowledge Discovery, Inc.	KD Data Mining Suite	www.datamining.com/dmsuite.htm
Magnify Inc.	PATTERN	www.magnify.com
MegaPuter Intelligence Inc.	PolyAnalyst	www.megaputer.com
Microsoft	Analysis Services in SQL 2000	www.microsoft.com/sql
NCR	TeraMiner	www.ncr.com
Oracle	Oracle Darwin	www.oracle.com/datawarehouse/products/datamining/index.html
SAS Institute	Enterprise Manager	www.sas.com
Silicon Graphics Inc.	MineSet	www.sgi.com
SPSS	Clementine, Answer Tree and Neural Connection)	www.spss.com

The above list of tools is by no means exhaustive. Picking a data-mining tool can be an enormous task. One company that can help is Two Crows (www.twocrows.com), who offer an annual report evaluating over two-dozen data mining tools. Their *Data Mining '99: Technology Review* gives details on each product including features descriptions as well as application screen shots. Their technology review also includes a non-technical overview of data mining.

Another good source of information about data mining can be found on the KDNuggets website (www.kdnuggets.com). This site is a great place to find out what tools are available as well as keep up with the latest information in the data mining field.

Microsoft® SQL Server™ 2000 Analysis Services

One of the many great enhancements in SQL Server 2000 is the addition of Analysis Services. Analysis Services is the new name for what use to be called OLAP Services in SQL Server 7. In addition to the change of name, it has been extended to include many new features. One of the new features included with Analysis Services is data mining, which can be used to discover information in both OLAP cubes and relational databases. Analysis Services support two of the data mining techniques we mentioned earlier, Microsoft Clustering and Microsoft Decision Trees. The data mining features included in Analysis Services are incorporated into Microsoft's implementation of OLE DB for Data Mining specification. For more information on OLE DB, visit
http://www.microsoft.com/data/oledb/default.htm.

Now, anyone running SQL 2000 has access to data mining tools without purchasing third party software. Microsoft provides numerous wizards and user-friendly interfaces to help us discover the knowledge buried in our data but they also provide us with ways to access our Analysis Server programmatically. In this chapter I won't be able to cover Analysis Services in depth, but what I will do is demonstrate how to use ASP to retrieve information from Analysis Services. I think that once you see the code, you'll be surprised how easy it can be.

Installing Analysis Services

To install Analysis Services, you'll need to have a copy of SQL Server 2000 Enterprise Edition, Enterprise Evaluation Edition, or Developer Edition. (I'll be using the Developer Edition since I like to work on my laptop which is running Windows 2000 Professional Edition and not a server version.)

1. On the first screen on the installation, select SQL Server 2000 Components

2. Select Install Analysis Services.

You may install both SQL 2000 Database Server and Analysis Services or just Analysis Services. It isn't required that Analysis Services run on the same computer as SQL 2000 Database Server.

3. At the Welcome screen, select Next.

4. If you accept the terms of the licensing agreement, select Yes.

5. At the Select Components window, select Next to accept the defaults.

6. At the Data Folder Location window, select Next to accept the default location or Browse to make a change.

7. At the Select Program Folder window, select Next to accept the default folder or type a new folder or select an existing folder.

8. At the Setup Complete window, select Finish.

That's it. It can't get much simpler than that. Analysis Services should now be installed on your computer. In the next section we'll start to use Analysis Manager to work with our new installation of Analysis Services.

Analysis Manager

Analysis Manager is a console application that allows you to manage Analysis servers and their meta data repositories. Analysis Manager provides many functions but we will limit our attention to using it to browse and create data mining models. To start Analysis Manager (assuming a default installation) select Start | Programs | Microsoft SQL Server | Analysis Services | Analysis Manager.

1. Double click on the Analysis Servers folder to show the available Analysis Servers. Your server as well as any other servers on your network running Analysis Services will be displayed. My computer is MSBD-LT10132 so this is my 'localhost' computer. Since there are currently no other Analysis Servers on my network, it's the only server listed.

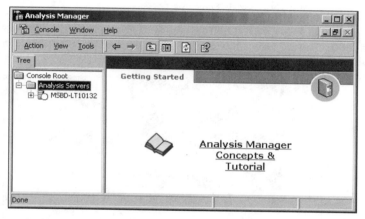

Double click on your server to display the available databases. The default install is FoodMart 2000. Double click on FoodMart 2000 and then Mining Models.

To browse any of the Mining Models, simply right click on one and select Browse.

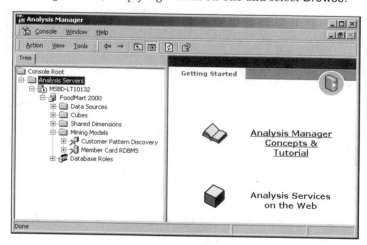

Browsing starts the Data Mining Model Browser and allows you to view the results of the data mining model. By right clicking on Mining Models and select New Mining Models, you can walk through the "Mining Model Wizard" to create new custom Mining Models. Let's quickly create a Microsoft Clustering mining model.

Right click on Mining Models and select New Mining Model... At the Welcome to the Mining Model Wizard, select Next. At the "Select Source Type" window, select OLAP data and click Next.

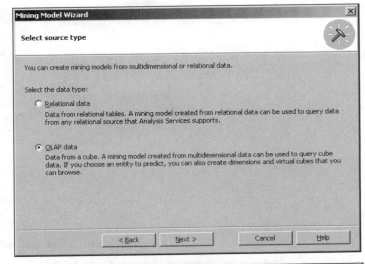

At the Select source cube window, select Sales for the cube and click Next.

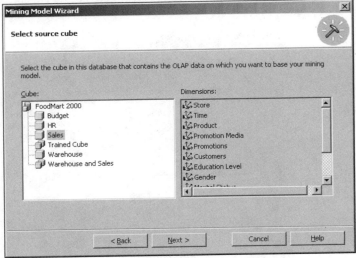

At the Select data mining technique window, select Microsoft Clustering and click Next.

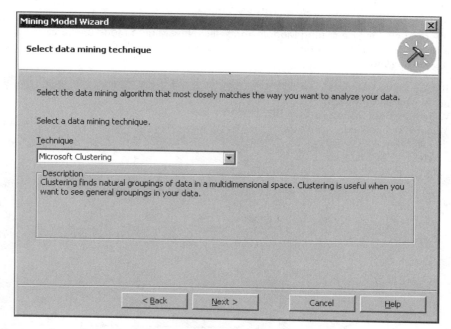

At the "Select case" window, select Customers for the Dimension and Name for the Level and click Next.

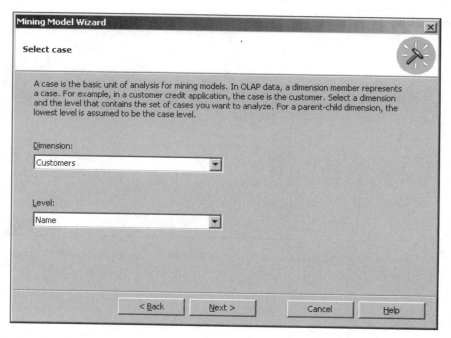

At the Select training data screen, scroll down to Customers and de-select Country, State Province, and City and click Next.

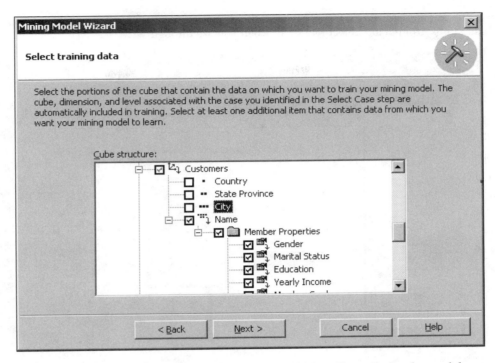

At the Finish the Mining Model Wizard window, enter Clustering_Example for the model name. With Save and process now selected, click Finish.

When Analysis Server finishes processing our new mining model, click Close.

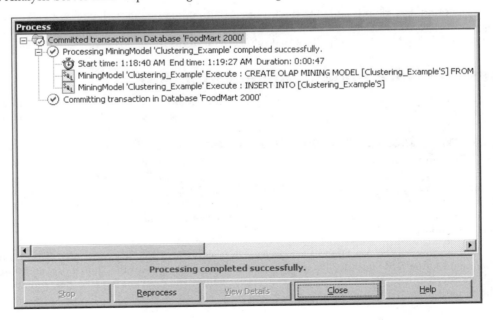

This will bring up the OLAP Mining Model Editor for our mining model with 10 clusters mined from our data. Look around and Select File | Exit when you are through.

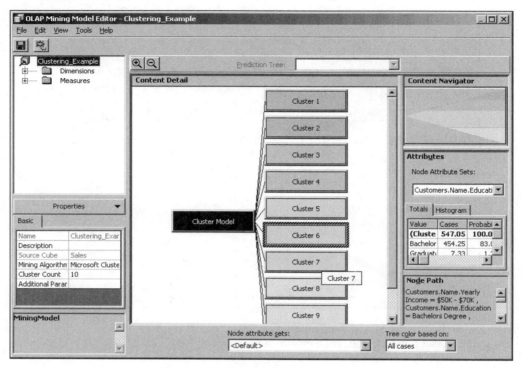

Now Clustering_Example is added to the list of current mining models. Digging in to all of the options is beyond the scope of this chapter, but hopefully you did get a feel for what it takes to create a basic mining model. Now lets look at pulling that information from ASP.

Accessing Data Mining Models from ASP

Here's were we get down to the bits and the bytes and really hit some code on working with Analysis Server. First we'll look at how to retrieve data from our mining models and display it in our ASP pages.

Working with Decision Support Objects and Data Mining

COM access to the many features of Analysis Server is made available through Decision Support Objects (DSO). Through DSO, Analysis Services are made available through any development environment that supports COM such as VC++, VB, and VBScript. Decision Support Objects will be available if you are working on the same computer that Analysis Services was installed on. If you are working from a computer that doesn't have Analysis Services installed, you may need to register msmddo80.dll.

Let's look at how we can use DSO to access Analysis Server functionality from ASP. The following code will connect to the DSO and display a list of available DataSources on the "localhost" computer. If Analysis Services is not installed on the same server where you are running IIS, then replace local host with the path to the Analysis Server.

You may receive an error if the user account under which the ASP page is running does not have OLAP admin privileges. These can be given to the IUSR account, but it would be more secure to set up a new account with OLAP privileges to run the page with.

```
<%@ language="VBScript" %>
<% option explicit %>

<%
dim dsoServer, dsoDS, dsoDMM

set dsoServer = CreateObject ("DSO.Server")
dsoServer.Connect ("LocalHost")

for each dsoDS in dsoServer.MDStores
    Response.Write dsoDS.name & "<br>"
Next
%>
```

For a default installation, this will return only FoodMart 2000 but if there were other datasources available, this would retrieve them as well. We could then put this in a drop down list for our users to select their datasource. Since we know we are using Localhost for the server, and FoodMart 2000 for the datasource, I'm going to assign those to variables to keep the code simple. Now let's loop through to get a list of data mining models available from our FoodMart 2000 data source.

```
<%@ language="VBScript" %>
<% option explicit %>

<%
dim strServer, strDB
dim dsoServer, dsoDB, dsoDMM

strServer = "LOCALHOST"
strDB = "FoodMart 2000"

set dsoServer = CreateObject ("DSO.Server")
dsoServer.Connect (strServer)
set dsoDB = dsoServer.MDStores(strDB)

For each dsoDMM in dsoDB.MiningModels
    Response.write dsoDMM.name & "<br>"
Next
%>
```

This will print out the available data mining models, which will be the same as the ones available through Analysis Manager. We can retrieve the mining model data as XML and then parse that to display the information to the user. Now that we have the name of the mining models (dsoDMM.name), we can retrieve the data from that model as an XML document. We know Clustering_Example is in the list since we just created that model in our previous walk through so let's set that mining model to a variable and retrieve that XML data.

By using the dsoDB.MiningModels collection, we are able to bind to our mining model object (dsoDMM) to our selecting mining model. Now we can easily pull the results out in XML format by simply using the XML Document Object Model to load dsoDMM.xml. The code below just gives us an easy way to view the XML results from different Mining Models. This is important, as XML structures will be different for Microsoft_Clustering models and Microsoft_Decision_Trees models. Now that the output is XML, getting to the data is an issue of displaying XML and not one of accessing Analysis Server. In the code below, we'll create a drop-down list of available mining models. Then by selecting a mining model and submitting the form, we'll be able to view the XML document returned for that mining model.

```
<%@ language="VBScript" %>
<% option explicit %>

<%
' WROX_viewXML.asp

dim strServer, strDB, strDMM, strXML
dim dsoServer, dsoDB, dsoDMM, xmldoc, formDMM

strServer = "LOCALHOST"
strDB = "FoodMart 2000"
formDMM = Request.Form("mining_model")

set dsoServer = CreateObject ("DSO.Server")
dsoServer.Connect (strServer)
set dsoDB = dsoServer.MDStores(strDB)
Response.Write "<title>Displaying Data Mining Models as XML</title>"
Response.Write "<html>"
Response.Write "<body>"
Response.Write "<center>"
Response.Write "<form method=post>"
Response.Write "<select name=mining_model>"

For each dsoDMM in dsoDB.MiningModels
  Response.Write "<option value=""" & dsoDMM.name & """>" & dsoDMM.name & _
               "</option>"
Next

Response.Write "</select>"
Response.Write "  <input type=submit value=Continue>"
Response.Write "</center>"
Response.Write "</form>"

If FormDMM <> "" then
  Display_XMLresults(formDMM)
End if

Response.Write "</body>"
Response.Write "</hmtl>"

Function display_XMLresults (strDMM)
  set dsoDMM = dsoDB.MiningModels(strDMM)

  set xmldoc = CreateObject ("Microsoft.XMLDOM")
  xmldoc.async = false
  xmldoc.loadXML(dsoDMM.xml)

  strXML = strDMM & ".xml"
  xmldoc.save (Server.MapPath (strXML))

  Response.Redirect strXML
End Function
%>
```

While not very complicated, this little ASP file can be extremely useful in helping us view the XML structure for various mining models. Now that we are pulling XML data from our data mining models, let's put it all together in a good working example that allows the user to select a Microsoft_Clustering mining model and display the results in ASP.

Displaying Selected Clustering Data Mining Models

In this example, we'll give the user an option to select from available mining models and then display the results in our ASP page. We'll assume the server is the Localhost and the datasource is FoodMart 2000 though you could of course add code to make these all user selectable options. In this example, the code is only set to parse through XML structures for Microsoft_Clustering. Remember earlier I mentioned that the XML structure is different for each of the different Microsoft algorithms.

```
<%@ language="VBScript" %>
<% option explicit %>
<%
'    WROX_viewClusteringModel.asp

dim strServer, strDB, strDMM
dim dsoServer, dsoDB, dsoDMM
dim xmldoc, total, formDMM
dim pmml_node, pmml_nodeattributes
dim OLAPschema_node, OLAPschema_nodeattributes
dim segmentmodel_nodelist, datadistribution_nodelist
dim simpleattribute_node, simpleattribute_nodeattributes
dim state_nodelist, state_nodeattributes
dim i, x, y, z

strServer = "LOCALHOST"
strDB = "FoodMart 2000"
formDMM = Request.Form("mining_model")

set dsoServer = CreateObject ("DSO.Server")
dsoServer.Connect (strServer)
set dsoDB = dsoServer.MDStores(strDB)

Response.Write "<title>Data Mining Models</title>"
Response.Write "<html>"
Response.Write "<body>"
Response.Write "<center>"
Response.Write "<form method=post>"
Response.Write "<select name=mining_model>"

For each dsoDMM in dsoDB.MiningModels
    If dsoDMM.MiningAlgorithm = "Microsoft_Clustering" then
        Response.write "<option value=""" & dsoDMM.name & """>" & _
                dsoDMM.name & "</option>"
    End if
Next

Response.Write "</select>"
Response.Write "  <input type=submit value=Continue>"
Response.Write "</center>"
Response.Write "</form>"

if formDMM <> "" then
    display_cluster_results(formDMM)
end if

Response.Write "</body>"
Response.Write "</html>"
function display_cluster_results (strDMM)
    set dsoDMM = dsoDB.MiningModels(strDMM)
    set xmldoc = CreateObject ("Microsoft.XMLDOM")
    xmldoc.async = false
```

```
xmldoc.loadXML(dsoDMM.xml)

set pmml_node = xmldoc.documentElement.selectSingleNode("/pmml")
set pmml_nodeattributes = pmml_node.attributes
set OLAPschema_node = pmml_node.selectSingleNode("OLAP-schema")
set OLAPschema_nodeattributes = OLAPschema_node.attributes

Response.Write "Database: " & _
    OLAPschema_nodeattributes.getNamedItem("database").value & "<br>"
Response.Write "Data cube: " & _
    OLAPschema_nodeattributes.getNamedItem("cube").value & "<br>"
Response.Write "Name: " & _
    pmml_nodeattributes.getNamedItem("name").value & "<br><br><br>"

set pmml_node = nothing
set pmml_nodeattributes = nothing
set OLAPschema_node = nothing
set OLAPschema_nodeattributes = nothing
set segmentmodel_nodelist = _
                xmldoc.documentElement.selectnodes("/pmml/segment-model/node")

'loop through each <node> node
for i=0 to (segmentmodel_nodelist.length -1)
    Response.write "<b><font color=blue>Cluster " & i + 1 & "</font></b>"

    set datadistribution_nodelist = _
                segmentmodel_nodelist.item(i).selectNodes("data-distribution")


    'loop through each <data-distribution> node"
    for x=0 to (datadistribution_nodelist.length -1)
        Response.write "<table>"
        total = 0

        set simpleattribute_node = _
        datadistribution_nodelist.item(x).selectSingleNode("simple-attribute")
        set simpleattribute_nodeattributes = simpleattribute_node.attributes
        set state_nodelist = _
                        datadistribution_nodelist.item(x).selectNodes("state")

        Response.write "<tr>"
        Response.write "<td colspan=2><b>" & _
        simpleattribute_nodeattributes.getNamedItem("name").value & "</b></td>"
        Response.write "</tr>"
        Response.write "<tr>"
        Response.Write "<td><u>Name</u></td>"
        Response.Write "<td><u>Support</u></td>"
        Response.Write "<td><u>Probability</u></td>"
        Response.Write "</tr>"

        ' loop through each <state> node to calculate the total number for
        ' support
        for y=0 to (state_nodelist.length -1)
            for each state_nodeattributes in state_nodelist.item(y).attributes
                if state_nodeattributes.nodeName = "support" then
                    total = total + state_nodeattributes.nodeValue
                end if
            next
        next
```

```
            'loop through each <state> node, display values and calculated
            ' probabilities
            for z=1 to (state_nodelist.length -1)
                set state_nodeattributes = state_nodelist.item(z).attributes
                Response.Write "<tr>"
                Response.Write "<td>" & _
                state_nodeattributes.getNamedItem("value").value & "</td>"
                Response.Write "<td>" & _
                formatNumber(state_nodeattributes.getNamedItem("support").value) & _
                    "</td>"
                Response.Write "<td>" & _
   FormatNumber((state_nodeattributes.getNameDItem("support").value/total)*100) & _
                    "%</td>"
                Response.Write "</tr>"
            next

            Response.Write "</table><br><br>"
        next
        set datadistribution_nodelist = nothing
    next

    set segmentmodel_nodelist = nothing
    set xmldoc = nothing

end function

%>
```

The following screenshot displays the results of running the page:

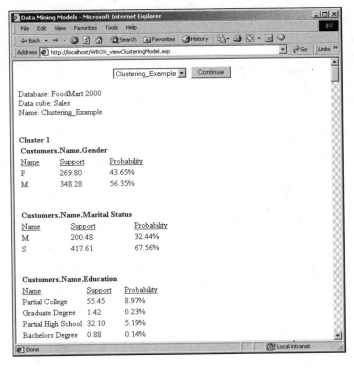

Let's walk through the ASP code. First we connect to the `FoodMart 2000` datasource and get a collection of the available mining models. We also run `Request.Form("mining_model")` and assign the result to a variable so we can check later if the user has already selected a mining model to process.

```
strServer = "LOCALHOST"
strDB = "FoodMart 2000"
formDMM = Request.Form("mining_model")

set dsoServer = CreateObject ("DSO.Server")
dsoServer.Connect (strServer)
set dsoDB = dsoServer.MDStores(strDB)
```

Now that we have a collection of mining models, we display that in a select element drop down list. Since our code is only set to parse the XML structure returned for Microsoft Clustering, we check the `.MiningAlgorithm` value and only display options that use `Microsoft_Cluster` algorithm.

Then we check our `formDMM` variable to see if our user has already selected a mining model to display. If they have, then we submit our XML object to our `display_cluster_results ()` function to parse and display in our ASP page. If we want to display Microsoft_Decision_Tree models, then we could check for that value here and instead go to a function to handle an XML structure based on Microsoft_Decision_Tree models. If no selection has been previously posted, we only display the select drop-down list and wait for them to pick and click Continue to submit our form.

```
Response.write "<form method=post>"
Response.Write "<select name=mining_model>"
For each dsoDMM in dsoDB.MiningModels
    If dsoDMM.MiningAlgorithm = "Microsoft_Cluster" then
        Response.write "<option value=""" & dsoDMM.name & """>" & dsoDMM.name & _
            "</option>
    End if
Next
Response.Write "</select>"
Response.Write "  <input type=submit value=Continue>"
Response.Write "</form>"

If formDMM = <> Then
    Display_cluster_results(formDMM)
End If
```

The `display_cluster_results()` function parses the XML. Displaying the information is just like handling any XML document. I'm using Microsoft's XML Document Object Model and looping through the nodes to get to the need information. The only calculations we do is to loop through each `<state>` node and add up the `support` value to give us the total support for each node.

```
'loop through each element to calculate the total number for support"
for y=0 to (state_nodelist.length -1)
    for each state_nodeattributes in state_nodelist.item(y).attributes
        if state_nodeattributes.nodeName = "support" then
            total = total + state_nodeattributes.nodeValue
        end if
    next
next
```

Now we can determine what percentage support is for each `<state>` case and format our results with `formatNumber()`.

```
'loop through each element, display values and calculated probabilities
for z=1 to (state_nodelist.length -1)
    set state_nodeattributes = state_nodelist.item(z).attributes
    Response.write "<tr>"
    Response.write "<td>" & state_nodeattributes.getNamedItem ("value").value & _
        "</td>"
    Response.write "<td>" & _
        formatNumber(state_nodeattributes.getNamedItem("support").value) & "</td>"
    Response.write "<td>" & _
    formatNumber((state_nodeattributes.getNamedItem("support").value/total)*100)&_
        & "%</td>"
    Response.write "</tr>"
Next
```

So there we have it. We've allowed our user to select from the available "clustering" mining models and then we've displayed that output on our ASP page. Hopefully, you've seen a lot of places to dress this up and make it more presentable to the user. The possibilities are certainly there. The key is that we have demystified the process of getting data mining information to our end-users through ASP.

Creating a New Data Mining Model

In this section, we'll take a quick look at the code required to create a new data mining model. In this example, we'll create a mining model using Microsoft_Clustering for the algorithm and we'll limit the number of clusters to 3.

```
<%@ Language="VBScript" %>
<% option explicit %>

<%
Dim dsoServer, dsoDB, dsoDMM, dsoColumn, dsoRole
Dim strServer, strDB, strAlgorithm, strCluster_Count
Dim form_newDMM

strServer = "LOCALHOST"
strDB = "FoodMart 2000"
strAlgorithm = "Microsoft_Clustering"
strCluster_Count = "3"
form_newDMM = Request.Form("new_mining_model")

Response.Write "<title>Creating a new clustering data mining model</title>"
Response.Write "<html>"
Response.Write "<body>"
Response.Write "<center>"
Response.Write "<form method=post>"
Response.Write "Name <input type=text name=new_mining_model><br>"
Response.Write "<input type=submit value=Continue>"
Response.Write "</center>"
Response.Write "</form>"

If form_newDMM <> "" then
    CreateClusterOLAPMiningModel (form_newDMM)
    Response.write "<b>Process complete.</b>"
End if
```

```
Response.Write "</body>"
Response.Write "</html>"

Sub CreateClusterOLAPMiningModel(strMiningModel)
   set dsoServer = CreateObject ("DSO.Server")
   dsoServer.Connect (strServer)
   set dsoDB = dsoServer.MDStores(strDB)

   dsoServer.Connect "LocalHost"
   Set dsoDB = dsoServer.MDStores("FoodMart 2000")

   ' Check for the existence of the model on this computer.
   If Not dsoDB.MiningModels(strMiningModel) Is Nothing Then
      dsoDB.MiningModels.Remove strMiningModel
   End If

   ' Create a new OLAP mining model, set to sbclsRelational to create a
   ' relational mining model
   Set dsoDMM = dsoDB.MiningModels.AddNew(strMiningModel, sbclsOlap)

   ' Create a new mining model role called All Users
   Set dsoRole = dsoDMM.Roles.AddNew("All Users")

   ' Set the needed properties for the new mining model.
   With dsoDMM
      .DataSources.AddNew "FoodMart", sbclsRegular
      .Description = "ASP generated clustering model"
      .MiningAlgorithm = strAlgorithm
      .SourceCube = "Sales"
      .CaseDimension = "Customers"
      .TrainingQuery = ""
      .Parameters = "Cluster_Count=" & strCluster_Count
      .Update
   End With

   ' Set the column properties pertinent to the new model.
   ' When columns are automatically added to the model in this fashion,
   ' they are disabled. You must choose which columns are to be enabled
   ' before you can process the model, at least one column must be enabled,
   ' or an error will result.

   ' Enable the Name column. As this column is the
   ' lowest enabled level on the Customers case dimension, it becomes the case
   ' level for the data mining model.

   Set dsoColumn = dsoDMM.Columns("Name")
   dsoColumn.IsDisabled = False

   Set dsoColumn = dsoDMM.Columns("Gender")
   dsoColumn.IsInput = True
   dsoColumn.IsDisabled = False

   Set dsoColumn = dsoDMM.Columns("Marital Status")
   dsoColumn.IsInput = True
   dsoColumn.IsDisabled = False

   Set dsoColumn = dsoDMM.Columns("Education")
   dsoColumn.IsInput = True
   dsoColumn.IsDisabled = False

   Set dsoColumn = dsoDMM.Columns("Yearly Income")
   dsoColumn.IsPredictable = True
   dsoColumn.IsDisabled = False
```

```
    ' Save this data mining model.
    With dsoDMM
        ' Set the LastUpdated property of the new mining
        ' model to the present date and time.
        .LastUpdated = Now
        .Update
    End With

    ' Process the data mining model.
    With dsoDMM
        .LockObject olapLockProcess, "Processing the data mining model in ASP code"
        .Process processFull
        .UnlockObject
    End With

    Set dsoRole = Nothing
    Set dsoColumn = Nothing
    Set dsoDMM = Nothing
    dsoServer.CloseServer
    Set dsoServer = Nothing
End Sub
%>
```

The code above was pretty straightforward so I won't step through it section by section. I do want to point out a couple of settings that could be changed to create differences in our mining model. The most obvious is setting the algorithm to be used. This is set by setting the `MiningAlgorithm` property to either `"Microsoft_Clustering"` or `"Microsoft_Decision_Trees"`. Another key setting that I've changed is the number of clusters to be generated. If left unspecified, the default number of clusters created is 10. Ten is a little too high for many scenarios. For instance, if your marketing department wants to target several market segments for a marketing campaign, ten may be too many. However, by selecting 3 clusters we may find some real patterns that the marketing campaign can target. Good luck in finding how to select the number of clusters in the Microsoft documentation. It's not a separate parameter that you can set. To set this value, you'll need to pass it as a value in the `.parameters` property.

```
dsoDMM.Parameters = "Cluster_Count=3"
```

I found this parameter by analyzing the XML document generated from a Microsoft_Clustering model. In that XML I saw the `cluster-count` setting in the `data-dictionary` node of the returned XML document.

```
<data-dictionary column-ordering="ORDINAL" column-count="5" cluster-count="3">
```

To verify that the code works, enter the name new_clustering_asp into the web page and click Continue. When the page is complete and displays "Process complete", run the WROX_viewClusteringModel.asp covered earlier or go to Analysis Manager to see if it is now an available mining model.

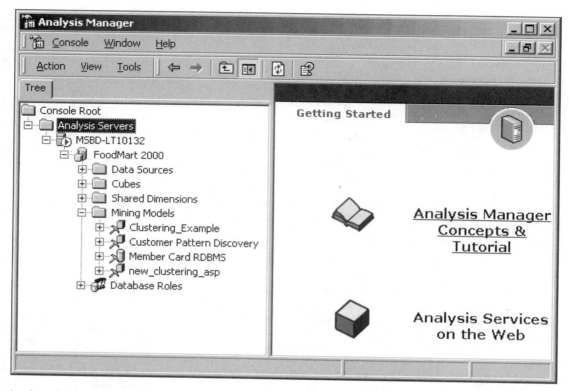

Analysis Manager shows that indeed we have created a new mining model. Microsoft has done an excellent job of bringing data mining functionality to the developer. In these examples, I've deliberately kept it very basic so you could focus on the code needed to connect to the Analysis Server through the Decision Support Object. Normally, I wouldn't use so many `Response.Write` statements but I wanted it to be obvious what I was doing in the code. The key is that much of the work is ASP and handling XML. You can use client side scripting to make the page come alive, use XSL to transform your XML document, and all of the other normal tricks of that trade to improve performance and functionality when working with ASP. Through DSO, we can view existing mining models, extract the data as an XML document, process an existing mining model, or create new mining models. The bulk of the work will not be focusing on DSO but instead focusing on straight ASP and XML as we find ways to get the valuable information in a format our users can use. SQL 2000's Analysis Services and ASP makes getting knowledge from our data and out to our end-user easier than ever before.

The Future of Data Mining

I think we'll see much more from data mining in the years to come. It will be used in ways we haven't even considered yet. Until now, most vendors have been working on proprietary data mining tools. As the market share increases, many have started working to industry standards. Microsoft, for instance, in a joint effort with several vendors, has released OLE DB for DM Specification version 1.0. This is part of Microsoft Universal Data Access strategy for providing access to information across the enterprise. For more information, go to www.microsoft.com/data.

Also, the Data Mining Group has released the Predictive Model Markup Language (PMML). PMML is an XML based language, which provides a quick and easy way for companies to define predictive models and share models between compliant vendor applications. For the specs on PMML, check out www.dmg.org.

Another joint effort by NCR, SPSS, Daimler Chrysler, and OHRA is the Cross Industry Standard Process for Data Mining (CRISP-DM) project. Rather than focus on technology, this project focuses on providing a process structure for carrying out data mining. The CRISP-DM project strives to bring benefit to small-scale data mining projects as well as large scale projects. Information on CRISP-DM may be found at www.crisp-dm.org.

And then there's of course the enormous growing acceptance of XML. As these standards become commonplace, data mining will no longer be reserved for highly costly projects but will begin to be available at much more economical levels.

Web technologies and the Internet will also play a very important part in the future of data mining. The Internet is all about speed, and as such customers will no longer be satisfied with submitting a credit card application and waiting several weeks for a reply. Now Internet-based companies, using data mining, can evaluate your application online and give you a status within 30-60 seconds.

Another reason why the growth of the Internet will lead to an increase in the need for data mining is the amount of data that e-commerce transactions generate. In physical retail stores, you do not normally keep information on a particular customer who has made a cash transaction, though credit card details would be retained should a customer use this payment method. However, on the Web, everything can be tracked. Typically, a user will be required to register on a web site and from that moment on, all subsequent transactions can be linked with that user's data. For every online purchase a customer makes, you can use that information to build a profile for that customer. With this data stored and available, data mining can give you a better understanding of your customer base than was ever possible before.

Data mining will be an even hotter technology in the years ahead. It may still be a few years before it reaches its critical mass, but as more and more operation systems support XML, the extraction process will become a much simpler process and we'll see a increase in the number of data warehouse implementations as well as an improvement in the quality of data in those data warehouses. XML won't prevent us from needing to cleanse the data but it will greatly reduce the time needed to extract it.

Summary

Data mining has just really started to come into its own in the last several years and the future looks even more promising. More and more companies are using data mining to gain an advantage over their competitors and gain a better understanding of their business needs. It can help companies understand where they are today and how to get where they want to be tomorrow. Like most technologies that give companies an advantage, it may well be required by e-businesses if they are to continue to be competitive. As tools continue to improve, in both functionality and ease of use, data mining will to grow in popularity. Finally, we may start to gain some real information from all the data out there!

32

Remote Data Services

So far, we've seen how we can access data in a data source on the server via ADO and utilize that data in our ASP application. This is fine, but there is one potential problem: if the user wants to change his query request, or wants a different view of the data, we need to make a round-trip to the server, requery the database and resend a new web page with the new data. Wouldn't it be great if we could actually send an entire recordset to the client, and simply apply a new filter there, or change the sort order of this recordset if the user decides to change their view of the data? To satisfy this need, Microsoft introduced **Remote Data Services**, or RDS, with ADO 2.0. RDS can do all this, and more. In fact, with RDS you can remote *any* COM object to the client – including custom objects that you've written yourself. We can also use data binding to bind HTML elements to our recordset, so that text boxes and the contents of table cells, etc., will be automatically refreshed when we navigate through the recordset. In this chapter we'll look at the objects which comprise RDS, and see how to use them to cache an ADO recordset on the client and how to bind HTML elements to this recordset. We'll also look at how we can use RDS to instantiate our own business objects remotely on the client.

What Is RDS?

RDS is a technology that allows us to instantiate on the client a COM component which resides on a remote server. RDS provides a default COM component called the `DataFactory`, which we can use to return an ADO `Recordset` object to the client; however, we can actually instantiate any COM component. The client application could be any application that supports COM, such as a web page containing DHTML script hosted in Internet Explorer 4.01+, a Visual Basic application, or a Visual C++ application. We saw in Chapter 9 that we can use **Distributed COM**, or DCOM, to communicate between COM objects across machine boundaries. So how does RDS manage this cross-machine communication? DCOM is fine over a network connection, but no use over the Internet (chiefly because it requires configuration of the client computer).

The answer is that RDS allows us to use any of four different protocols, according to our needs:

❑ DCOM, for use over a network connection.

❑ HTTP, for use over an intranet/internet connection.

❑ HTTPS, for use over a secure intranet/Internet connection over SSL.

❑ In-process, for a local connection when the client and server are the same machine. (This adds nothing to the normal functionality of COM, but can be used for testing RDS-enabled applications on a single machine.)

> **Remember that RDS has a fairly serious limitation when used over the Internet. RDS requires support for COM, so it won't work with non-Microsoft browsers. It also requires that ADO and the client-side RDS components are installed, so may not work with versions of Internet Explorer prior to 4.01.**

Why Use RDS?

The main use of RDS is, as its name suggests, to enable the remote manipulation of data on the client (in the form of an ADO recordset). This allows us to integrate our data fully into our client-side DHTML script. The most obvious advantage of this is that it saves on network traffic and server resources. We can show records one at a time, or one page at a time, without the need for a costly round-trip to the server when the user moves on to a new record. Because the data is all downloaded in one go, our client-side application can manipulate it at will without reconnecting to the server until changes need to be marshaled to the database or the client-side recordset needs to be refreshed. This can significantly reduce the amount of work our server has to do, and so make our application far more scalable, as well as improve performance, since we need fewer round-trips.

Moreover, because we are caching our data on the client, we can run much more of our application on the client-side, too. RDS allows us to move almost any code that interacts with the data from the server to the client (there may be code we don't want to be visible on the client, or code such as data validation that we want to run on the server for security reasons). This further reduces the burden on the server and on the network. For example, suppose we want to implement a filter for the recordset. The user will select the field for the filter from one <SELECT> element, and this will cause another listbox to be populated with the possible values. Without RDS, that would mean one round-trip to the server to find out the possible values for the second listbox, and another to actually implement the filter (by requerying the database) and return a new set of data:

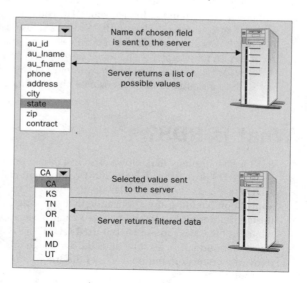

With RDS, we can populate our <SELECT> element dynamically using client-side code, rather than having to rely on ASP. Because there's no trip to the server involved, we can react to the <SELECT> element's OnChange event, and automatically populate the second listbox whenever the user selects a new field. Without RDS, we probably wouldn't want to go all the way to the server unless we were sure that's what the user really wanted, so we'd wait for a button to be pressed. Subtle touches such as this can help to make for a much richer and more interactive experience for the user.

When Not to Use RDS

However, that doesn't mean that all your data-centric ASP applications should make use of RDS. There are three chief reasons for not using RDS. The first has already been mentioned – RDS isn't supported by early versions of IE, or by non-Microsoft browsers. While these are used by a decreasing proportion of visitors, the percentage of visitors using Netscape browsers, in particular, is still significant, and it would be a brave webmaster who decided that his company could safely forfeit this share of the market! This means that, in the real world, RDS is unlikely to be used by Internet applications, unless browser-specific pages are maintained. However, RDS is still a good choice for intranet applications, where the webmaster may be able to dictate that a particular browser must be used, or for certain business-to-business or other applications where restrictions can be enforced on our users.

The second reason is that downloading a complete recordset involves a certain trade-off: we may gain increased performance during the running of the application in return for a longer start-up time while our recordset is downloaded. The data itself can be downloaded asynchronously, but there is also a cost involved in serializing the data into a string, and rebuilding the Recordset object on the client. In most situations, this trade-off is probably well worthwhile, but if the user is unlikely to require different views of the data (for example, if all the relevant data can be displayed in a single page and the user is unlikely to want to sort through it or filter it), then it is possible that the original costs of serializing and unserializing the data won't be repaid as the application runs.

Finally, it is worth remembering that one of the prime advantages of RDS is that it uses disconnected recordsets. This means that any changes made to the data won't be saved to the database until a specific call to update the database is made. This greatly improves performance, but does increase the risk of data conflicts causing by multiple users attempting to update the same row simultaneously. For this reason, it is inadvisable to use RDS if it is essential that your data is kept up-to-date at all times.

> There is a fourth consideration: security. In its simplest configurations, there are serious security holes in RDS. However, there are ways round this, and we will look at security issues with RDS later in the chapter.

The RDS 2.6 Object Model

Because RDS is concerned chiefly with marshaling data between machines, it requires both server- and client-side components. Two of the three RDS components, the DataSpace and DataControl reside on the client and are used to instantiate server-side objects, while the DataFactory resides on the server and can be instantiated remotely on the client. The entire RDS object model therefore looks like the figure overleaf:

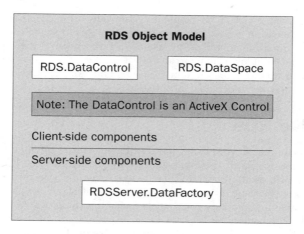

COM objects cannot communicate *directly* with each other if they reside in different processes (and, of course, processes cannot cross machine boundaries). We can get round this problem by creating a **proxy** of the server object in the process of the calling client object. This proxy object exposes exactly the same interface as the real server object, so the caller is not aware that it isn't talking directly to the real object.

Similarly, a **stub** object is created in the server object's process. The proxy sends its message to this stub, which in turn passes the message to the real server object. Again, the server isn't aware that it isn't communicating directly with the client object. The following diagram illustrates this entire procedure:

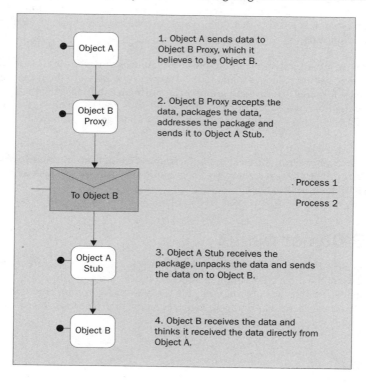

RDS therefore provides a client-side object (the RDS.DataSpace object), which allows us to create proxy objects in the client process for our server-side COM objects. It also provides a server-side component (the RDSServer.DataFactory object), which acts as a simple middle-tier business object specifically designed for creating disconnected recordsets for transfer to a remote client. The following diagram shows the interaction between these objects:

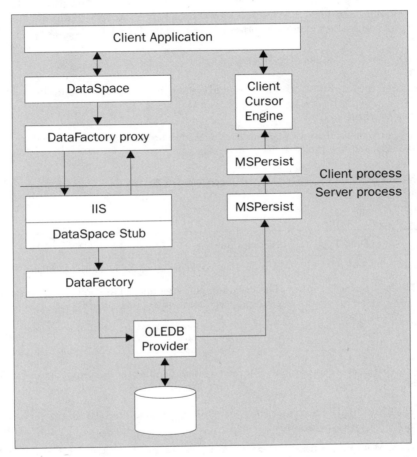

The DataFactory object queries the data source and returns an ADO Recordset object. This is persisted in ADTG (Advanced Data TableGram) format by the MSPersist provider and marshaled over to the client. We can, of course, replace our own business object for the DataFactory. Because the DataFactory always returns a disconnected recordset, the OLE DB Client Cursor Engine will be used to provide cursor services such as filtering and sorting on the client. This is the OLE DB service provider that gives us the ability to manipulate the recordset on the client side with no active connection to the database.

RDS also provides a third object, the DataControl (RDS.DataControl), which allows us to bind HTML elements in a web page to a recordset returned by the DataFactory or another business object. The RDS control uses the functionality of the DataSpace and (by default, although this can be overridden) of the DataFactory objects. However, the DataControl shields the programmer from explicitly coding against the other RDS objects.

The DataSpace Object

The `DataSpace` object is the client-side component that RDS provides for instantiating COM components on a remote server. As this is the only functionality it needs, it has only one method – `CreateObject` – and a single property, `InternetTimeout`. This read-write property merely sets or retrieves a long value that specifies the timeout period (in milliseconds) when RDS is attempting to instantiate an object over an HTTP connection. We can instantiate the `DataSpace` object by calling VBScript's `CreateObject` method (or JScript's `ActiveX` constructor) in our client-side script, using the Prog ID `"RDS.DataSpace"`:

```
Set objDS = CreateObject("RDS.DataSpace")
```

As we will see later, the same method can be used to instantiate our own custom business objects.

The CreateObject Method

The `CreateObject` method, as we might expect, is used to instantiate the object on the remote machine, and returns a reference to the proxy. It takes the syntax:

```
Set Object = objDS.CreateObject(strProgID, strServer)
```

Where:

Name	Data Type	Description
`Object`	Object	A reference to the proxy of the instantiated object
`strProgID`	String	The Programmatic Identifier of the object to be instantiated (for example `"myComponent.myClass"`)
`strServer`	String	The URL or server name of the machine on which the object to be instantiated resides

The `strServer` parameter can take one of three forms, depending on the protocol used to communicate with the server:

- ❑ For HTTP and HTTPS connections, `strServer` will be the URL of the server's domain, for example `"http://mydomain"`.

- ❑ For DCOM connections, `strServer` is simply the machine name, for example `"myserver"`.

- ❑ For local connections, `strServer` is the empty string `""`.

For example, to instantiate the `DataFactory` object over an HTTPS connection, we would use:

```
Set objDS = CreateObject("RDS.DataSpace")
Set objDF = objDS.CreateObject("RDSServer.DataFactory",
                               "https://mySecureDomain")
```

The DataFactory Object

The `DataFactory` object is used, as we have seen, as a default server-side business object for use with the `DataSpace` object. It has a few methods which provide the basic functionality we might need from a middle-tier object in an RDS application, such as querying a data source and returning a disconnected recordset, creating a new recordset, and submitting changes to the data source.

While we can instantiate the `DataFactory` locally, there isn't a lot of point – we can just use plain ADO. To instantiate it on a remote server, we use the `CreateObject` method of the `DataSpace` object, specifying a Prog ID of `"RDSServer.DataFactory"`:

```
Set objDS = CreateObject("RDS.DataSpace")
Set objDF = objDS.CreateObject("RDSServer.DataFactory","http://JULIAN")
```

Using the DataFactory to Query and Update the Data Source

The most important method of the `DataFactory` object is the `Query` method. This allows us to execute a query against a database from the remote `DataFactory` object, and it returns us a disconnected recordset to the client. The syntax is:

```
Set objRS = objDF.Query(strConnection, strSQL, [lngMarshalOptions])
```

Where:

Name	Data Type	Description
objRS	Recordset object	The returned disconnected recordset.
strConnection	String	The connection string to connect to the data source. This will be visible from the client and could include the username and password for the database, so this has very severe security implications. We will look at a way round this later in the chapter.
strSQL	String	The SQL query to be executed against the data source.
lngMarshalOptions	Long	Optional. One of the `MarshalOptionsEnum` values: `adMarshalAll` (0, the default) or `adMarshalModifiedOnly` (1).

If we make any changes to our recordset, we'll need a way to marshal these changes back to the database. This is provided by the `DataFactory`'s `SubmitChanges` method:

```
objDF.SubmitChanges strConnection, objRS
```

Name	Data Type	Description
strConnection	String	The connection string to connect to the data source
objRS	Recordset object	The updated recordset with changes that we want to save to the data source

The following example uses the `DataFactory` to retrieve a recordset from the data source, changes a record, and then calls the `SubmitChanges` method to update the source database:

```
' Create the DataSpace object
Set objDS = CreateObject("RDS.DataSpace")
' Instantiate the DataFactory remotely
Set objDF = objDS.CreateObject("RDSServer.DataFactory", "http://JULIAN")

' Execute the query and get a recordset
' Remember that this password is visible from the client
strConn = "Provider=SQLOLEDB;Data Source=JULIAN;Initial Catalog=pubs;" & _
          "User ID=sa;Password="
strSQL = "SELECT au_lname FROM authors WHERE au_lname='White'"
Set objRS = objDF.Query(strConn, strSQL)

' Check that at least one record was returned, and change the name
If Not objRS.eof Then
    objRS("au_lname") = "Black"
    objDF.SubmitChanges strConn, objRS
End If
```

Creating Programmatic and Persisted Recordsets

There are two more methods of the DataFactory, which we'll take a quick look at before moving on to the DataControl object. As well as the methods above, which connect to a data source, the DataFactory provides a couple of methods for working with recordsets without a connection. The simpler of these two methods is the ConvertToString method, which converts an ADO Recordset object into a string in MIME 64 format:

```
strData = objDF.ConvertToString(objRS)
```

Name	Data Type	Description
strData	String	The MIME 64 string representation of the recordset
objRS	Recordset object	The recordset to convert into a string

The ConvertToString method is used by the DataFactory when passing data from the server to the client over HTTP, since the recordset is passed in MIME format and rebuilt by RDS as an ADO Recordset object on the client.

Note that this method can be inefficient if the size of a row exceed 1024 bytes, or if there are more than 400 rows.

The last method we'll look at is the CreateRecordSet method, which we can use to create a recordset programmatically with no connection to a data source. It has the syntax:

```
Set objRS = objDF.CreateRecordSet(arrColumnInfo)
```

Name	Data Type	Description
arrColumnInfo	Variant array	An array containing information about the columns in the recordset we wish to create
objRS	Recordset object	The fabricated recordset returned by the method

The *arrColumnInfo* variant array is an array of arrays – each column is defined by an array of four fields, containing the name of the column, the data type for the column (one of the ADO DataTypeEnum values), the column size, and a Boolean indicating whether or not the column can contain null values. This is easier to see in practice, so let's look at a quick example:

```
Dim arrColInfo(1)     ' The array which will contain all the info
                      ' for all the columns
Dim arrCol1Info(3)    ' The array for the first column's info
Dim arrCol2Info(3)    ' The array for the second column's info

' Create the array for the first column
arrCol1Info(0) = "FirstName"  ' Column name
arrCol1Info(1) = 200          ' Data type = adVarChar
arrCol1Info(2) = 25           ' Column size
arrCol1Info(3) = True         ' Can contain nulls

' Create the array for the second column
arrCol2Info(0) = "LastName"   ' Column name
arrCol2Info(1) = 200          ' Data type = adVarChar
arrCol2Info(2) = 15           ' Column size
arrCol2Info(3) = False        ' Can't contain nulls

' Store these two arrays in arrColInfo
arrColInfo(0) = arrCol1Info
arrColInfo(1) = arrCol2Info

Set objDS = CreateObject("RDS.DataSpace")
Set objDF = objDS.CreateObject("RDSServer.DataFactory", "http://JULIAN")

' Create the recordset with this info
Set objRS = objDF.CreateRecordset(arrColInfo)
```

The DataControl Object

The final RDS object is the DataControl object, which we can use to bind HTML elements to a recordset, and to avoid writing the code for the DataSpace and DataFactory objects. We'll spend most of the rest of this chapter looking at how to use this object, so in this section we're only going to have a quick run through its basic functionality.

To create a DataControl on our page, we must use an <OBJECT> tag, since we cannot bind HTML elements to an object created dynamically using client-side code. The CLASSID for the object is "BD96C556-65A3-11D0-983A-00C04FC29E33", so we instantiate it using the code:

```
<OBJECT CLASSID="clsid:BD96C556-65A3-11D0-983A-00C04FC29E33" ID="myDC"
        NAME="myDC" WIDTH=0 HEIGHT=0>
</OBJECT>
```

Accessing the Data Source with a DataControl

Once we've got our `DataControl`, we'll need to connect to a database and retrieve a recordset. To do this, we'll need to supply information about the server we want to connect to, the data source we want to access, and the query we will execute against this data source. This information is passed into the `DataControl` using three of its properties, or using `<PARAM>` elements within the `<OBJECT>` element.

To specify the server to connect to, we use the `Server` property. This is a string value in the same format as the *strServer* parameter of the `DataSpace.CreateObject` method, depending on whether the connection to the server will be via HTTP, HTTPS, DCOM or in-process. For example (using HTTP):

```
myDC.Server = "http://myserver"
```

To specify the server within the `<OBJECT>` element, we use a `<PARAM>` element with a `NAME` attribute set to `"Server"` and a `VALUE` attribute equal to our server name or HTTP address:

```
<PARAM NAME="Server" VALUE="http://myserver">
```

To connect to the database from the `DataFactory`, we'll need an ADO connection string. Again, this can be passed in through code, by setting the `Connect` property:

```
myDC.Connect = "Provider=SQLOLEDB;Data Source=JULIAN;" & _
               "Initial Catalog=pubs;User ID=sa;Password="
```

> Remember that this will be visible from the client, so in real code you shouldn't use an administrator account here, but a guest account with very limited permissions. You should also ensure that the user ID and password for the administrator account have been changed from their default values.

Or using a `<PARAM>` tag with the `<OBJECT>` element:

```
<PARAM NAME="Connect" VALUE="Provider=SQLOLEDB;Data Source=JULIAN;
                             Initial Catalog=pubs;User ID=sa;Password=">
```

Finally, we need to specify the SQL query we want to execute against the data source. To do this, we can set the `SQL` property:

```
myDC.SQL = "SELECT * FROM authors"
```

Or using a `<PARAM>` tag:

```
<PARAM NAME="SQL" VALUE="SELECT * FROM authors">
```

If we specify all these parameters within the HTML `<OBJECT>` element, the query will be executed automatically when the page loads. However, if we specify them by setting the `DataControl`'s properties using client-side code, we will need to refresh the `DataControl` explicitly to retrieve a recordset:

```
myDC.Refresh
```

This method takes no parameters; it causes the `DataControl` to re-execute the query and refreshes the data.

So, to instantiate a `DataControl`, instantiate a `DataFactory` on the remote server, and execute a query against a data source, we can either use HTML code such as this:

```
<OBJECT CLASSID="clsid:BD96C556-65A3-11D0-983A-00C04FC29E33" ID="myDC"
        NAME="myDC" WIDTH=0 HEIGHT=0>
   <PARAM NAME="Server" VALUE="http://JULIAN">
   <PARAM NAME="Connect" VALUE="Provider=SQLOLEDB;Data Source=JULIAN;
                                Initial Catalog=pubs;User ID=sa;Password=">
   <PARAM NAME="SQL" VALUE="SELECT * FROM authors">
</OBJECT>
```

Or we can set the `Connect`, `Server` and `SQL` properties of the `DataControl` directly using code, and then call the `Refresh` method to execute the query:

```
<OBJECT CLASSID="clsid:BD96C556-65A3-11D0-983A-00C04FC29E33" ID="myDC"
        NAME="myDC" WIDTH=0 HEIGHT=0>
</OBJECT>
<SCRIPT LANGUAGE="VBScript">
   myDC.Connect = "Provider=SQLOLEDB;Data Source=JULIAN;" & _
                  "Initial Catalog=pubs;User ID=sa;Password="
   myDC.Server = "http://JULIAN"
   myDC.SQL = "SELECT * FROM authors"
   myDC.Refresh
</SCRIPT>
```

This second approach is useful when we don't want to execute the query as soon as the page loads (for example, if the query depends on user input, or if we are using a custom business object rather than the default `DataFactory`). It is also probably easier to read.

Downloading the Data

The `DataControl` has a couple more properties we can use to control executing queries and downloading the data. Firstly, we can specify whether the recordset will be refreshed synchronously or asynchronously using the `ExecuteOptions` property. This is a short integer which can be one of the two `ExecuteOptionsEnum` values:

Name	Value	Description
adcExecSync	1	The query will be executed synchronously (the program's execution will pause until all the data is sent).
adcExecAsync	2	The query will be executed asynchronously (the default).

Generally, in web-based applications, it is better to use asynchronous execution, due to the potentially longer loading time of the data. This is particularly true if a very large recordset is being sent to the client. Synchronous execution is better suited to client/server scenarios on a LAN where we can rely on very high bandwidth.

Secondly, we can use the FetchOptions property to specify how the DataControl will fetch data from the remote server. This can be one of the three FetchOptionsEnum values:

Name	Value	Description
adcFetchUpFront	1	The DataControl will wait until all the data has been fetched before returning control to the application.
adcFetchBackground	2	The DataControl will wait for the first batch of records before returning control to the application.
adcFetchAsync	3	The DataControl will return control to the application immediately (the default).

As well as setting these options dynamically in client-side code, we can also set them in our <OBJECT> element using <PARAM> tags:

```
<PARAM NAME="ExecuteOptions" VALUE="2">
<PARAM NAME="FetchOptions" VALUE="1">
```

If we are fetching our data asynchronously, we may need to know the current state of play – whether data is accessible, whether all the data has downloaded, etc. – before we carry out any operations on it. For this purpose, the DataControl provides the read-only ReadyState property, which returns a long value indicating the availability of the data in the DataControl. This may be one of the ReadyStateEnum values:

Name	Value	Description
adcReadyStateLoaded	2	No data is yet available for reading.
adcReadyStateInteractive	3	Some of the data is available.
adcReadyStateComplete	4	All the data has loaded and is available.

Sorting the Data

Once we've created our DataControl and executed the query, we can access the data through the DataControl's read-only Recordset property. This returns a full ADO Recordset object, which we can manipulate just like any other ADO recordset (for example, we can navigate through it using myDC.Recordset.MoveNext, etc.).

However, the DataControl also provides properties of its own which we can use to sort and filter the recordset. To sort a recordset, we need to set two properties: to specify the column to use as the basis for the sort, we set the SortColumn property; and to set the order (ascending or descending) for the sort, we specify the SortDirection. This property takes a Boolean value: True for ascending (the default), or False for descending.

When these properties have been set, we call the Reset method to cause the sort to take effect. The syntax for this method is:

```
myDC.Reset([blnRefilter])
```

The optional *blnRefilter* parameter specifies whether any previous filters should still be applied (True, the default), or whether these should be lost when the new sort or filter is applied, and the new sort or filter be applied to all rows in the recordset (False). So, to sort a recordset on the au_lname column in descending order while retaining previous filters, we would use:

```
myDC.SortColum = "au_lname"
myDC.SortDirection = False
myDC.Reset(True)
```

If we want to sort the recordset on more than one column, we therefore have to run this procedure more than once, calling Reset with the blnRefilter parameter set to True (or omitted) the second time. For example, to sort a recordset on the au_lname and au_fname fields:

```
myDC.SortColum = "au_fname"
myDC.SortDirection = True
myDC.Reset(False)
myDC.SortColum = "au_lname"
myDC.SortDirection = True
myDC.Reset(True)
```

Note that we perform the sorts in reverse order: we sort on the primary sort field (here au_lname) last, because we want that to be the last sort which is applied.

Filtering the Data

Filtering allows us to hide any records that do not match a given criterion. These records are not deleted from the recordset, but are invisible until a new filter is applied or the recordset is refreshed. Filtering with the DataControl works in a similar way to sorting, but here there are three properties to set. Firstly, we must specify the column to use as the basis for the filter by setting the FilterColumn property. Then we specify the FilterCriterion: whether we want to filter for rows where the value of the column is less than, greater than, equal to, etc., a specific value. The possible values for the FilterCriterion property are "<", ">", "<=", ">=", "=" and "<>". We set the value against which we want to compare the rows, using the FilterValue property. Again, to apply the filter we call the Reset method.

For example, to filter all records (regardless of any currently applied filter) for birth dates later than the first of January 1960, we would use:

```
myDC.FilterColumn = "BirthDate"
myDC.FilterCriterion = ">"
myDC.FilterValue = "1/1/1960"
myDC.Reset(False)
```

As with sorting, if we need to apply multiple filters, we have to set these separately, and call Refresh with blnFilter set to True after each time that we set a new filter.

Updating the Data Source

When we've made changes to the data in the client-side recordset, we'll need a way to marshal these to the server so we can update the data source. If we're using the control with the default DataFactory business object, this is as simple as calling a single method. The SubmitChanges method takes no parameters, and has no return value. Calling this method has the effect of calling the DataFactory's submit changes method with the DataControl's current recordset and connection string as parameters. We will see in a later section how to update the data source using a custom business object.

If we want to cancel changes made in the client recordset, we can call the `CancelUpdate` method. This will restore the original values for any changed fields that have not been saved to the data source; these values are kept on the client by the Client Cursor Engine (CCL). When `CancelUpdate` is called, the CCE will discard any changes and refresh the bound controls with the original values, with no need for a round-trip to the server.

DataControl Events

The `DataControl` also exposes two events, which we can access in our client-side script. The `OnReadyStateChange` event is called whenever the `DataControl`'s `ReadyState` property changes. We can use this event to check whether data is available for reading:

```
Sub myDC_OnReadyStateChange
    If myDC.ReadyState = adcReadyStateComplete Then
        ' All data has loaded
    End If
End Sub
```

The second event of the `DataControl` object is the `OnError` event. This is raised whenever an error occurs during an operation. The syntax for the `OnError` event handler is:

```
Sub myDC_OnError(intStatus, strDescription, strSource, blnCancelDisplay)
    ' Event handler code here
End Sub
```

Where:

Name	Data Type	Description
intStatus	Integer	The status code for the error which occurred
strDescription	String	A description of the error which occurred
strSource	String	The SQL command which caused the error
blnCancelDisplay	Boolean	Indicates whether the error can be trapped by VB (the default is `True`)

Data Binding with the DataControl

One of the major new features introduced in IE4 (and refined in IE5) is that of **HTML data binding**. This involves binding HTML elements such as tables or text boxes to a **Data Source Object** (DSO). A DSO is a client-side ActiveX component used for remote data access. The DSO makes a recordset available to DHTML elements within a web page. This works in a very similar way to binding (say) a text box on a VB form to an ADO or DAO data control: the element is populated with the value of the field to which it is bound, and this value is automatically updated as we navigate through the recordset. Also, changes made to the bound element are automatically reflected in the client-side recordset.

The Data Source Object used with RDS is (as you might have guessed) the `DataControl`. As we saw above, we instantiate this in our page using an `<OBJECT>` tag, optionally supplying information that can be used to instantiate the `DataFactory` on the server and query a data source:

```
<OBJECT CLASSID="clsid:BD96C556-65A3-11D0-983A-00C04FC29E33" ID="myDC"
        NAME="myDC" WIDTH=0 HEIGHT=0>
   <PARAM NAME="Connect" VALUE="Provider=SQLOLEDB;Data Source=JULIAN;
                               Initial Catalog=pubs;User ID=sa;Password=">
   <PARAM NAME="Server" VALUE="http://JULIAN">
   <PARAM NAME="SQL" VALUE="SELECT * FROM authors">
</OBJECT>
```

> We're not limited to one `DataControl` per page: we can have as many as we like, if we
> need to use multiple recordsets in our page (for example, if we need to access data from
> more than one data source).

Binding to the DSO

Once we've created an instance of the `DataControl` DSO in our page, we can bind HTML elements to it.
To do this, we need to specify a `DATASRC` attribute for the element which points to our `DataControl`
object. We indicate that this is a DSO by prefixing the name with the # symbol (for example,
`DATASRC="#myDC"`). We can bind to specific fields in the recordset using the `DATAFLD` attribute. For
example, to bind an input box to the `au_lname` field from our `DataControl`, we would use:

```
<INPUT TYPE="TEXT" DATASRC="#myDC" DATAFLD="au_lname">
```

We can also set these properties dynamically using code:

```
<INPUT TYPE="TEXT" ID="myText">

<SCRIPT LANGUAGE="VBScript">
    myText.DataSrc="#myDC"
    myText.DataFld="au_lname"
</SCRIPT>
```

There is one final data-binding property we can set: `DATAFORMATAS`. If the field value contains HTML tags,
we can specify for some elements that these are to be rendered or to be ignored. To cause HTML tags to be
rendered, we set the `DATAFORMATAS` attribute to `"HTML"`, and to have them ignored, we set it to `"TEXT"`.

Bindable HTML Elements

Not all HTML elements can be bound to a DSO (after all, it wouldn't make much sense to bind a `<B>`
element to a data source). Of those that can, not all can be used to update the recordset (again, this makes
sense if you consider that we can type text into a text box, but not into a `<SPAN>`), and not all elements
support HTML rendering. Also, the way in which binding occurs differs between element types: the data
from the `DataControl` populates a specific property or attribute of the element. For example, binding a
span causes the element's `InnerText` and `InnerHTML` properties to be set, whereas for a data-bound `<A>`
element, it is the `HREF` attribute that takes its value from the data source.

The following table shows which elements support data binding, the properties that are data-bound, whether
or not the element supports updating the data source, and whether HTML tags can be rendered:

Element	Data-bound Property	Updateable	HTML Rendering
A	href	No	No
APPLET	param	Yes	No
BUTTON	innerText, innerHTML	No	Yes
DIV	innerText, innerHTML	No	Yes
FRAME	src	No	No
IFRAME	src	No	No
IMG	src	No	No
INPUT TYPE=CHECKBOX	checked	Yes	No
INPUT TYPE=HIDDEN	value	Yes	No
INPUT TYPE=LABEL	value	Yes	No
INPUT TYPE=PASSWORD	value	Yes	No
INPUT TYPE=RADIO	checked	Yes	No
INPUT TYPE=TEXT	value	Yes	No
LABEL	innerText, innerHTML	No	Yes
MARQUEE	innerText, innerHTML	No	Yes
OBJECT	param	Yes	No
SELECT	value*	Yes	No
SPAN	innerText, innerHTML	No	Yes
TABLE	None	No	No
TEXTAREA	value	Yes	No

The value of a <SELECT> element can only be set if the element already contains an <OPTION> element with this value. If no <OPTION> exists with the same value as the field to which it is bound, no value will be displayed in the <SELECT> element.

Tabular Binding

As the table shows, data-bound tables are a little different to other elements, in that no individual property is bound to the DSO. The reason for this is that the <TABLE> element supports **tabular binding**; that is, it allows us to bind the table to the entire recordset. Whereas other elements can only be bound individually to a DSO, tabular binding allows us to bind the <TABLE> element as a whole to the DSO, and child elements within the table to specific fields in the recordset. To do this, we set the DATASRC attribute of the <TABLE>, but set the DATAFLD attributes for child elements within the table's <TD> elements. We only need to specify the bindings for one row – tabular binding ensures that the table will contain one row for each record in the recordset.

We can't bind the table cells themselves to the DSO, since <TD> elements don't support data binding.

For example, to bind a `<TABLE>` element to our DSO, and `<SPAN>` elements in its cells to the `au_id`, `au_fname`, and `au_lname` fields:

```
<TABLE ID="tblData" DATASRC="#myDC" BORDER="1">
    <TR>
        <TD><SPAN ID="spnID" DATAFLD="au_id"></SPAN></TD>
        <TD><SPAN ID="spnFName" DATAFLD="au_fname"></SPAN></TD>
        <TD><SPAN ID="spnLName" DATAFLD="au_lname"></SPAN></TD>
    </TR>
</TABLE>
```

This gives us the following table:

Table Paging

A data-bound table will often contain too many rows to display nicely in one page. Even if you don't mind your page scrolling down for an eternity, it will be difficult for the user to find information in a huge table. Fortunately, IE tabular data binding provides an easy way to limit the number of records displayed at any one time in the table. We can simply specify a "page size" for the table using the `DATAPAGESIZE` attribute. Navigation from one page to another is provided by the methods `NextPage`, `PreviousPage`, `FirstPage`, and `LastPage`, which are exposed by a data-bound table. The following code limits the table to showing five records per page, and provides buttons for navigating to the previous or next page of data. The `OnClick` event handlers for these buttons call the table's `NextPage` and `PreviousPage` methods:

```
<SCRIPT LANGUAGE="VBScript">
Sub btnNext_OnClick
```

```
      tblData.NextPage
  End Sub

  Sub btnPrev_OnClick
      tblData.PreviousPage
  End Sub
  </SCRIPT>
  <TABLE ID="tblData" DATASRC="#myDC" BORDER="1" DATAPAGESIZE="5">
      <TR>
          <TD><SPAN ID="spnID" DATAFLD="au_id"></SPAN></TD>
          <TD><SPAN ID="spnFName" DATAFLD="au_fname"></SPAN></TD>
          <TD><SPAN ID="spnLName" DATAFLD="au_lname"></SPAN></TD>
      </TR>
  </TABLE>
  <BUTTON ID="btnPrev">Previous page</BUTTON>
  <BUTTON ID="btnNext">Next page</BUTTON>
```

DHTML Data-Binding Events

As well as the two events of the DataControl object, there are a number of DHTML events which are available to us when we bind HTML elements to a Data Source Object. These events are raised partly on the DSO itself, and partly on the bound element. Some of these events allow us to cancel the action which triggered them, by returning False from the event handler function:

Event	Raised On	Cancelable	Description
OnBeforeUpdate	Bound element	Yes	Raised before changes to data in a bound element are passed to the DSO
OnAfterUpdate	Bound element	No	Raised after changes to data in a bound element are passed to the DSO
OnErrorUpdate	Bound element	Yes	Raised if an error prevents the data being passed to the DSO
OnBeforeUnload	Window object	No	Raised before the current page is unloaded
OnDataAvailable	DSO	No	Raised periodically while data is being downloaded to the DSO
OnDataSetComplete	DSO	No	Raised when all the data has been downloaded from the data source
OnDataSetChanged	DSO	No	Raised when the data set changes, such as when a filter is applied or the data is sorted
OnReadyStateChange	DSO	No	Raised when the ReadyState property of the DSO changes

Event	Raised On	Cancelable	Description
OnRowEnter	DSO	No	Raised for a row when it becomes the current row in the recordset
OnRowExit	DSO	Yes	Raised for a record when another record becomes the current one
OnRowsDelete	DSO	No	Raised just before rows are deleted from the recordset (IE 5 only)
OnRowsInserted	DSO	No	Raised just before rows are inserted into the recordset (IE 5 only)
OnCellChange	DSO	No	Raised when the data in a bound element changes and focus moves from that element (IE 5 only)

These events are implemented in the same way as the `DataControl`'s own events. We will see an example using the `OnAfterUpdate` event in our example towards the end of this chapter.

RDS and Custom Objects

If we want to use our own custom business object, rather than the default `DataFactory` with RDS, there are a couple of extra things we must do. After we've installed and registered our DLL as usual on our RDS server machine, we need to make further modifications to the registry to indicate that this component may be instantiated remotely. The steps we need to take to do this vary depending on whether we want our object to be instantiated via HTTP (or HTTPS) or DCOM.

Registry Modifications for HTTP Connections

We only need to add one key to the Registry if we want to instantiate our object over an HTTP or HTTPS connection. Namely, we must add a registry key with the name of our object's Prog ID under `HKEY_LOCAL_MACHINE\SYSTEM\CurrentControlSet\Services\W3SVC\Parameters\ADCLaunch\`. We can do this using `Regedit` or another registry editing tool. Open up Registry Editor by selecting Start | Run... and type `regedit`. Navigate to the `ADCLaunch` key with the path shown above, right-click on the key, select <u>N</u>ew | <u>K</u>ey, and then rename the newly created key (New Key #*n*) as the Prog ID of our object:

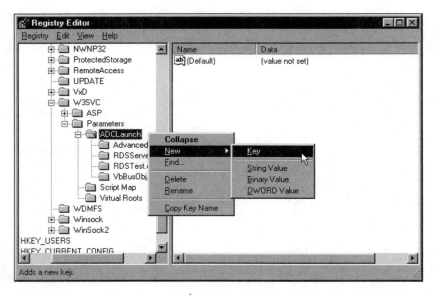

Alternatively, we can run a Registry script to update the Registry. Type the following lines into Notepad or other text editor, save the file with the extension .reg, and double-click on the file in Windows Explorer to run it:

```
REGEDIT4

[HKEY_LOCAL_MACHINE\SYSTEM\CurrentControlSet\Services\W3SVC\Parameters\
ADCLaunch\MyObject.MyClass]
```

Where *MyObject.MyClass* is the Prog ID of our object.

Registering an Object with DCOM

Unfortunately, if we're going to use DCOM, then we've got quite a bit more to do. DCOM gives us more control over who instantiates our objects than HTTP, so we've got more configuration to do. Firstly, we must add a new key named LocalServer under our DLL's registry entry with the path to dllhost.exe as its value. To do this, find the Class ID of your object by opening up Registry Editor and looking under the HKEY_LOCAL_MACHINE\Software\CLASSES*MyObject.MyClass*\Clsid key (where *MyObject.MyClass* is again the Prog ID of your object):

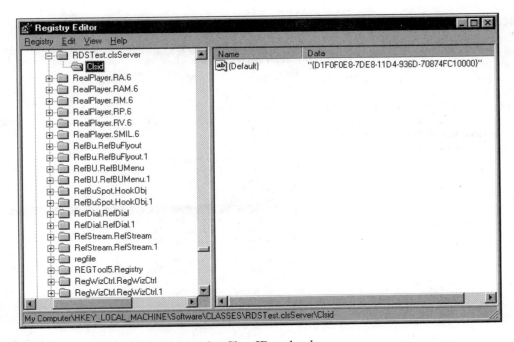

Now find the key with the same name as this Class ID under the
HKEY_LOCAL_MACHINE\Software\CLASSES\CLSID\ key. For example:

```
HKEY_LOCAL_MACHINE\Software\CLASSES\CLSID\{D1F0F0E8-7DE8-11D4-936D-70874FC10000}
```

Under this key, add a new key named LocalServer by right-clicking on the Class ID, selecting New | Key
and renaming the newly created key to LocalServer. Finally, change the value for this key to the path to
dllhost.exe (this file resides in the system32 directory, e.g. c:\WinNT\System32\dllhost.exe),
by right-clicking on the existing (Default) value and entering the path name. The registry key for your object
should now look like this:

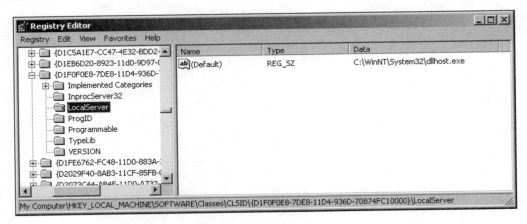

Granting DCOM Launch Permissions

Sadly, we're not done yet. Now we have to assign permissions to given users to instantiate our object via DCOM. We can do this using the `dcomcnfg` utility. Load this by selecting **Start | Run...** and entering `dcomcnfg`. On the **Applications** tab, select your business object from the drop-down list and choose **Properties...**

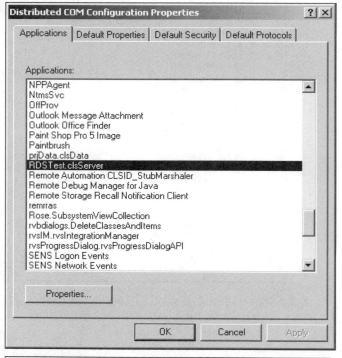

Selecting the Security tab on the Properties dialog box allows us to configure permissions for instantiating the object remotely. To change the permissions for invoking the object, we need to **Use custom launch permissions**, so click on the radio button for that option, and click on the **Edit...** button in this middle section:

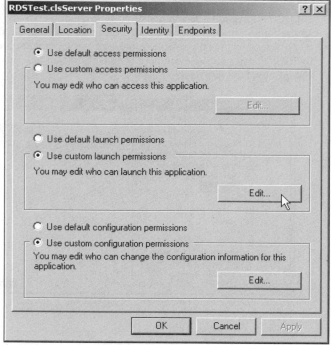

This launches the **Registry Value Permissions** dialog box, which allows us to add and remove launch privileges for our object. We should grant permissions only to those specific users and groups who will need to access our object:

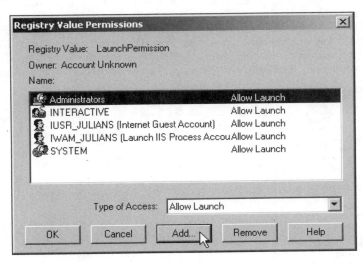

Selecting **Add...** launches the **Add Users and Groups** dialog, from which we can select individual users and groups of users from the Active Directory or NT User Manager to whom we want to grant permission to instantiate our object:

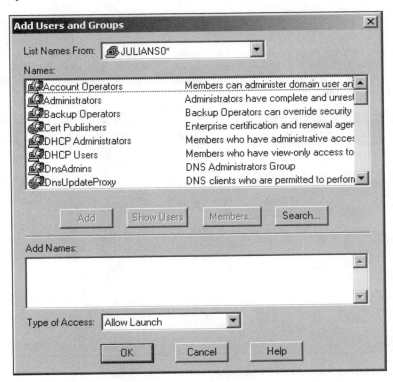

Configuring the Client

We've finished with server configuration now, but, unfortunately, there's still more to be done. In order to instantiate an object remotely using DCOM, we need to configure the client as well as the server. Specifically, we must create a key in the client machine's Registry so that our script can recognize the Prog ID. This is the main reason why DCOM isn't a viable solution over the Internet. Firstly, add a new key directly under the HKEY_CLASSES_ROOT key with the same name as the Prog ID of your business object. Then, under this new key, create another key named clsid, and change the default value of this to the Class ID of the component that we used when configuring the Registry on the server. The Registry should now look something like this:

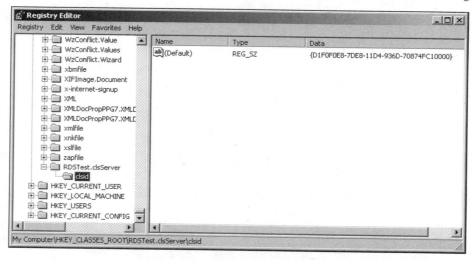

Now create a new key under HKEY_CLASSES_ROOT\CLSID\ and give this the name of your object's Class ID. Create another new key under this, named Implemented Categories, and under *this* key create two more new keys, named {7DD95801-9882-11CF-9FA9-00AA006C42C4} and {7DD95802-9882-11CF-9FA9-00AA006C42C4} – these mark the class safe for scripting and initialising. The client machine's Registry should now look like this:

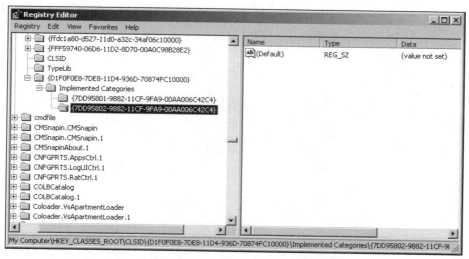

And finally we're ready to instantiate our business object via DCOM!

Invoking Custom Business Objects

Once we've performed this configuration, invoking our business objects remotely is a simple matter. We can call the `DataSpace`'s `CreateObject` method as usual, specifying the Prog ID of our object, rather than `RDSServer.DataFactory`:

```
Set objDS = CreateObject("RDS.DataSpace")
Set objRDSTest = objDS.CreateObject("RDSTest.clsServer", "http://myserver")
```

We can now call the methods and properties of this object from our client-side code exactly as if it existed on the client.

Data Binding with Custom Objects

We can also bind HTML elements to a recordset retrieved from our business object by setting the `SourceRecordset` property of a `DataControl` object. This property specifies the ADO `Recordset` object that the `DataControl` will use for binding HTML elements, so if we set this to equal a `Recordset` object that is returned from a method call to our remote business object, we can use data binding with our own object rather than the standard `DataFactory` object. Because we're instantiating our object programmatically, this of course means that we have to use the script code approach to executing the query (rather than <PARAM> elements):

```
<OBJECT CLASSID="clsid:BD96C556-65A3-11D0-983A-00C04FC29E33"
        ID="myDC" NAME="myDC" WIDTH=0 HEIGHT=0>
</OBJECT>
<SCRIPT LANGUAGE="VBScript">
' Instantiate the DataSpace object and our custom business object
Set objDS = CreateObject("RDS.DataSpace")
Set objRDSTest = objDS.CreateObject("RDSTest.clsServer", "http://myserver")

' Retrieve a recordset from our object
Set objRS = objRDSTest.GetRecordset

' We don't need the custom object or DataSpace any more
Set objRDSTest = Nothing
Set objDS = Nothing

' Set the DataControl's SourceRecordset
Set myDC.SourceRecordset = objRS
</SCRIPT>
```

Updating a Data Source with a Custom Business Object

One point to note about using custom business objects with a `DataControl` is that we can't call the control's `SubmitChanges` method, since that calls the `DataFactory`'s `SubmitChanges`. This means that we're going to have to write our own method to achieve this. The easiest way to do this is to write a public method for our component which takes an ADO `Recordset` object as a parameter. Note that this parameter must be passed in by value, since objects are by default passed by reference to avoid the footprint of two resource-intensive objects. However, since we are passing the object across machine boundaries, we need the object itself to be passed into the method, not simply a variable reference.

Within our method, we need to re-establish our connection to the database. We can then call the `Recordset`'s `UpdateBatch` method to save any changes in the data to the data source. We will see a simple example of this technique in our worked RDS example later in the chapter.

Security Issues and RDS

We've seen that we need to make a number of changes to our server's Registry if we want to allow our business object to be instantiated, but we don't have to make any modifications to allow the standard RDSServer.DataFactory to be instantiated remotely. This begs the question: if our script can instantiate this object from client-side code, why can't everyone else's? And the answer, unfortunately, is that it can. And that means that, if we haven't changed our administrator user name and password for our database (a frighteningly common phenomenon), or they can be guessed, then anyone can instantiate a DataFactory object remotely and do what they like with our data.

Fortunately, we can remove this functionality and prevent the DataFactory from being invoked remotely, while still allowing our custom objects to be instantiated through RDS. This is simply the reverse of the operation we used to allow our business object to be instantiated over HTTP: whereas then we added a key to the ADCLaunch key, now we must remove one. Again, the key has the name of the object's Prog ID, in this case RDSServer.DataFactory. To delete this key, we simply run Registry Editor, find the HKEY_LOCAL_MACHINE\SYSTEM\CurrentControlSet\Services\W3SVC\ Parameters\ADCLaunch\RDSServer.DataFactory key, right-click on it and select Delete:

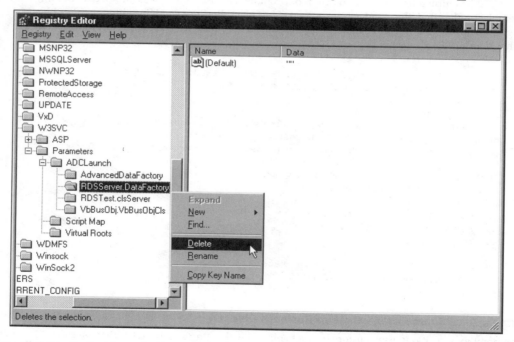

This will delete the key from the Registry, and prevent the DataFactory from being initiated over HTTP or HTTPS connections.

> *There isn't a problem with the DataFactory being invoked illegitimately over DCOM, since we have to grant permissions to specific users and groups to invoke objects over DCOM.*

RDS Customization Handlers

However, even if we don't use a custom object, and decide to use the default RDS objects, all is not quite lost. We can customize RDS by specifying a COM object on the server to use as a **customization handler**. These handlers are associated with .ini files, which contain details of the connection strings used to connect to the data source, the SQL queries that can be executed, and the users who can open specific connections. The handler uses this information to authorize users and validate queries before this information is passed to the DataFactory. We can also provide the location of a log file, where errors occurring on the connection can be logged. RDS customization provides two main security advantages over uncustomized RDS:

❑ The connection details are stored in the .ini file on the server, so are not visible in client-side script.

❑ We can assign to specific users the ability to open any given connection, or to execute a stated SQL query, denying all access to unknown users, and preventing the execution of unknown queries.

There is one disadvantage, though: the handler is interpreted, not pre-compiled, so there is a performance cost.

By default, RDS is set to allow access to the data source where no handler is specified. Obviously, this isn't much use if we're using this feature for security. Fortunately, RDS comes supplied with a registry script that will update the Registry to prevent access to the DataFactory without a handler. This script is called handsafe.reg, and resides in the Program Files\Common Files\System\msadc directory. Should you wish to allow access to the DataFactory again without a handler, the Registry can be reset by running the script handunsf.reg, which is also shipped with RDS, and resides in the same directory.

The Customization File

The connection and query details used by a handler are stored in a special .ini file stored on the server and read when the component is created. This text file is (like all .ini files) stored in the Windows directory (for example C:\WinNT). RDS comes shipped with a sample handler named msdfmap.dll (in the Program Files\Common Files\System\msadc directory) and an associated customization file named msdfmap.ini. It is possible to write our own handlers in VB or in C++, but this topic is beyond the scope of this book, and in any case, we can achieve the functionality we need for much better security with the MSDFMAP handler.

The customization files consists of a number of sections supplying information about the connection strings and SQL queries we want to allow access to, the users we want to allow to access our data, and the log files where we want to record any errors. We can give these sections names (with the exception of the log section), so we can reference them when we call our handler from RDS. Note that we can have more than one section of each type in our file, so we can assign different rights to different groups of users.

The Connect Section

The most important sections of the customization file are the connect sections. These sections are used to specify the connection strings we want to use to access the data. The format for this section is:

```
[connect connect_name]
Connect=connection_string
Access=NoAccess | ReadOnly | ReadWrite
```

The connect_name is the name by which we will refer to this connection configuration from RDS. We can also specify default here; this indicates that this connection string should be used if no connection is specified, or if an unrecognized connection is specified.

The `Connect` line under this section simply specifies the connection string we want to associate with this connection configuration. This can include a reference to a DSN which is set up on the server.

The connect section can also contain an `Access` line, which specifies the level of access we will grant on this connection. This can be `NoAccess` (used in the `[connect default]` section to prevent access if no connection information is given), `ReadOnly` to allow only select access on this connection, or `ReadWrite`, to allow both reading and updating on this connection.

The SQL Section

The `SQL` section of the customization file allows us to specify the query that will be executed against the data source. Again, we can assign this query a name, so it can be called from RDS. The syntax is:

```
[SQL query_name]
SQL=query
```

Where `query` is the SQL query that will be passed to the data source. This query can contain parameters; these are identified by a question mark (?) in the query. For example, if we want to select an author based on first and last name, we might have a SQL section as follows:

```
[SQL AuthorByName]
SQL="SELECT * FROM authors WHERE au_fname=? AND au_lname=?"
```

Again, we can specify a default query to execute if no valid name is specified. To ensure that this raises an error, we can use an invalid SQL query (such as a single space) (note that an empty string will cause the entire section to be ignored):

```
[SQL default]
SQL=" "
```

The Userlist Section

The `userlist` section is where we assign permissions to specific users on a given connection. The name of the `userlist` should be the same as the name of the `connect` section for which these users will be given rights. The syntax for the `userlist` section is:

```
[userlist connect_name]
user_name=NoAccess | ReadOnly | ReadWrite
```

Where `user_name` is the name of the user to whom we want to grant or deny access over this particular connection. Again, we can specify for each user whether they are to be denied all access, granted read-only access, or granted read-write access.

The Logs Section

The final type of section in the customization file is the `logs` section, where we can specify a log file where any errors raised during the `DataFactory`'s operation are recorded. It has the syntax:

```
[logs]
err=filename
```

Where filename is the full path and filename to the log file where errors occurring in relation to this handler will be logged.

Sample Customization File

We've now seen enough to construct a customization file, but it will probably help to see a complete simple example. This file contains details for connecting to the SQL Server pubs and Northwind databases, for extracting records from the authors and customers tables based on the author/customer ID. We will also specify a log file and a list of users to whom we will grant privileges. Note that we can include comments in the customization file by preceding the line with a semi-colon (;):

```
; Prevent access if no valid connection
[connect default]
Access=NoAccess

; Disallow invalid queries
[SQL default]
SQL="SELECT * FROM authors WHERE au_id=?"

[connect cnPubs]
Connect="Provider=SQL Server;Data Source=JULIAN;Initial Catalog=pubs;User
ID=userid;Password=password;"

[connect cnNWind]
Connect="Provider=SQL Server;Data Source=JULIAN;Initial Catalog=Northwind;User
ID=userid;Password=password;"

[SQL AuthorById]
SQL="SELECT * FROM authors WHERE au_id=?"

[SQL CustomerById]
SQL="SELECT * FROM customers WHERE CustomerId=?"

; Users for the pubs connection
[userlist cnPubs]
Administrator=ReadWrite
Sales=NoAccess

; Users for the Northwind connection
[userlist cnNWind]
Administrator=ReadWrite
Sales=ReadOnly

[logs]
err="C:\logs\handler.log"
```

Using a Customization Handler

Once we've specified a customization file, we can set up our DataControl to use this handler. The first way to do this is to set its Handler property. This should contain a reference to the handler we want to use (using the extension .handler, rather than .dll; for example msdfmap.handler), and if we're not using the default customization file for this handler, the .ini file we are using should be specified after a comma. We can then set the Server, Connect, and SQL properties as normal, except that the Connect and SQL properties should contain references to connect and SQL sections in our customization files respectively. Any parameters to be passed in to our SQL query should be contained in a comma-delimited list in parentheses after the name of the SQL query:

```
<OBJECT CLASSID="clsid:BD96C556-65A3-11D0-983A-00C04FC29E33" ID="myDC"
```

```
            NAME="myDC" WIDTH=0 HEIGHT=0>
  </OBJECT>
  <SCRIPT LANGUAGE="VBScript">
    myDC.Handler = "MSDFMAP.Handler,MyCustFile.ini"
    myDC.Server = "http://JULIAN"
    myDC.Connect = "cnPubs"
    myDC.SQL = "AuthorById('172-32-1176')"
    myDC.Refresh
  </SCRIPT>
```

On calling the Refresh method, the DataControl will be populated as normal, so long as the current user has the requisite permissions (as specified in our customization file) to make the requested connection.

Customization files provide a convenient 'middle way' for managing security with RDS. They allow us to control who has access to our database, and what queries can be executed, without the need to write our own business object. However, they still depend on the somewhat limited functionality of the DataFactory, so for full flexibility you should consider using a custom object.

RDS Example

Now let's put what we've seen so far in this chapter together by building a sample mini-application that uses client-side RDS code to manipulate a recordset without needing round-trips to the server. To avoid sending connection details to the client, we will use a very simple middle-tier object to connect to the database. This will have two public methods, for retrieving the recordset from the database, and for updating the database respectively.

Our recordset will be bound to an HTML table. To keep the code as simple as possible, we will only get data from one table (the authors table in the SQL Server pubs database). Our data-bound table will support paging through the recordset, and we will also build in support for filtering the recordset on any field, sorting in either ascending or reverse order on any field by clicking on the table header, and for updating, inserting, and deleting records. Our web page will look like this:

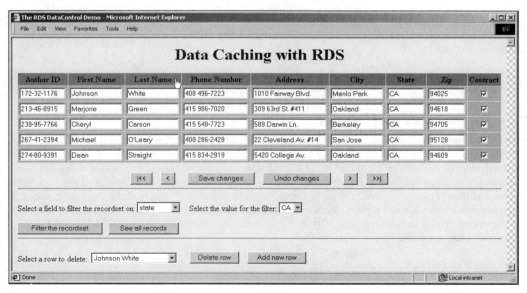

Building the Middle-Tier Object

Our first task, then, is to build the middle-tier object that will perform the actual database access. Since this is a chapter on RDS, not COM, we're going to keep it as simple as possible. Create a new ActiveX DLL project in Visual Basic; I've called this `RDSTest` and renamed the default class `clsServer`, but feel free to give these more useful or exciting names.

Retrieving the Recordset

As we've already indicated, this class will have two public methods. The first of these, `GetRecordset`, will simply return a disconnected ADO `Recordset` object containing all of the fields in the `authors` table. Because we're going to be disconnecting the recordset, we need to set its `CursorLocation` to `adUseClient` before we open it. This tells ADO that we're going to be using OLE DB's Client Cursor Engine (see Chapter 7 for more information about creating disconnected recordsets). Notice that we set the `CursorType` to `adUseStatic`, since only static cursors are supported by the Client Cursor Engine, and that's what we'd get even if we specified another cursor type. We also set the `LockType` to `adLockBatchOptimistic`. This specifies that records will only be locked while updating is in progress (optimistic locking), and that multiple updates will occur in one go (batch updating).

We can disconnect our recordset immediately by setting its `ActiveConnection` to `Nothing`, and we can then close the connection and release our `Connection` object. Finally, we return the disconnected `Recordset` object. Notice that we don't close the recordset, since that would also close the recordset we want to return – the `Set` command sets a new reference to the object we already have; it doesn't create a new object. So the full code for this method is:

```
Public Function GetRecordset() As ADODB.Recordset

Dim objConn As ADODB.Connection
Dim objRS As ADODB.Recordset

' Open the connection
' ***** CONFIGURE THIS CONNECTION STRING *****
Set objConn = New ADODB.Connection
objConn.Open "Provider=SQLOLEDB;Data Source=JULIAN;" & _
             "Initial Catalog=pubs;User ID=sa;Password="

' Open the recordset
Set objRS = New ADODB.Recordset
objRS.CursorLocation = adUseClient
objRS.Open "SELECT * FROM authors", objConn, adOpenStatic, _
           adLockBatchOptimistic

' Disconnect the recordset and tidy up
Set objRS.ActiveConnection = Nothing
objConn.Close
Set objConn = Nothing

' Return the recordset
Set GetRecordset = objRS

End Function
```

Updating the Database

The second method is no more complicated. This takes an ADO `Recordset` object passed in as a parameter, opens a new connection to the database, reconnects the recordset and updates the database. We return a Boolean value to indicate whether the update was successful, or whether errors occurred.

Notice that when we pass in the recordset, we specify the `ByVal` keyword. This is because object parameters are by default passed by reference – that is, only the reference to the object is passed in, not the object itself. This is fine in many circumstances, but in our case the recordset will actually be on another machine, so we need to specify that the parameter is passed in by value (so that the actual value of the variable is passed in – that is the object itself – not just a reference to that variable).

Once we have this recordset, we simply create a new ADO `Connection` object with exactly the same properties as the connection in the previous method, and set the `Recordset`'s `ActiveConnection` property to this object. We can reconnect the recordset in this way because the recordset was originally created on the same connection. If we had programmatically created the recordset (that is without a database connection), it would be impossible to connect it to a database.

After reconnecting the recordset, we can simply call its `UpdateBatch` method to perform a batch update of all the changes made to the recordset on the client. We can then close and release our object references and return `True` if all went well:

```
Public Function UpdateDB(ByVal objRS As ADODB.Recordset) As Boolean

Dim objConn As ADODB.Connection

On Error GoTo UpdateError

' Open the connection
' ***** CONFIGURE CONNECTION STRING *****
Set objConn = New ADODB.Connection
objConn.Open "Provider=SQLOLEDB;Data Source=JULIAN;" & _
             "Initial Catalog=pubs;User ID=sa;Password="

' Reconnect the recordset and update the database
Set objRS.ActiveConnection = objConn
objRS.UpdateBatch

' Close and release objects
objRS.Close
Set objRS = Nothing
objConn.Close
Set objConn = Nothing

' Everything went well - return True
UpdateDB = True

Exit Function

UpdateError:
' Return False if an error occurred
UpdateDB = False

End Function
```

Registering the Component with RDS

Once we've compiled this component, we need to register it under RDS, so that it can be instantiated remotely. We're only going to use the HTTP protocol, so we just need to add the registry key under the `ADCLaunch` key. We can do this using `Regedit`, or simply by running a `.reg` file containing the following lines:

```
REGEDIT4

[HKEY_LOCAL_MACHINE\SYSTEM\CurrentControlSet\Services\W3SVC\Parameters\
ADCLaunch\RDSTest.clsServer]
```

To create and run this file, simply type these lines into a text editor such as Notepad, save this file with the extension `.reg`, and double-click on this file in Windows Explorer.

Remember to change the Prog ID if you gave different names to the VB project or class.

Coding the Web Page

Now we've created our business object, we can look at the code for our ASP page itself. Because RDS can only be used with Internet Explorer, we're going to write our client-side code in VBScript rather than JScript. The first thing we must do is create our `DataControl`, instantiate our remote business object, retrieve a recordset by calling our `GetRecordset` method, and set the `DataControl`'s `SourceRecordset` property to this object. We'll also set the `DataControl`'s `SortDirection` property to False, for reasons that will become apparent later...

```
<HTML>
<HEAD>
<TITLE>The RDS DataControl Demo</TITLE>
<OBJECT CLASSID="clsid:BD96C556-65A3-11D0-983A-00C04FC29E33"
        ID="myDC" NAME="myDC" WIDTH=0 HEIGHT=0>
</OBJECT>
<SCRIPT LANGUAGE="VBScript">
Set objDS = CreateObject("RDS.DataSpace")
Set objRDSTest = objDS.CreateObject("RDSTest.clsServer", "http://julian")
Set objRS = objRDSTest.GetRecordset
Set objRDSTest = Nothing
Set objDS = Nothing
Set myDC.SourceRecordset = objRS
myDC.SortDirection = False
```

Implementing Table Paging

We're going to bind an HTML `<TABLE>` element called `tblData` to this `DataControl`, and we're going to implement table paging. The user will navigate through the pages using buttons, so next let's write the code for the event handlers for these buttons. Remember that all we need to do is call the `FirstPage`, `PreviousPage`, etc., methods on our table:

```
Sub btnFirstPage_OnClick
    tblData.firstPage        ' Move to the first page of data in the table
End Sub
```

```
Sub btnPrevPage_OnClick
   tblData.previousPage    ' Move to the previous page
End Sub

Sub btnNextPage_OnClick
   tblData.nextPage        ' Move to the next page
End Sub

Sub btnLastPage_OnClick
   tblData.lastPage        ' Move to the last page
End Sub
```

Updating the Data Source

The data fields will be displayed in editable input boxes, so next let's implement the code for updating the data source and saving any changes in the client recordset. Again, we'll provide a button (named btnUpdate) for the user to save changes. Within the OnClick event handler for this button, we need to instantiate our RDSTest.clsServer object again, and call our UpdateDB method. We pass into this method the DataControl's recordset, which we extract from its Recordset property. However, before we do this, note that we set myDC.Recordset.MarshalOptions to adMarshalModifiedOnly. This means that only updated rows in the recordset will be sent back to the server, rather than the entire recordset, and so is much more efficient. Finally, depending on the value of the Boolean returned from the UpdateDB method, we display a message box informing the user whether or not the update was successful:

```
Sub btnUpdate_OnClick
   myDC.Recordset.MarshalOptions = 1  ' adMarshalModifiedOnly
   Set objDS = CreateObject("RDS.DataSpace")
   Set objRDSTest = objDS.CreateObject("RDSTest.clsServer", "http://julian")
   blnResult = objRDSTest.UpdateDB(myDC.Recordset)
   Set objRDSTest = Nothing
   Set objDS = Nothing
   If blnResult = True Then
      MsgBox "Update succeeded!"
   Else
      MsgBox "Unable to update database"
   End If
End Sub
```

Canceling Changes

So what if the user wants to undo any unsaved changes? We'll first check that they really mean it (we know what users are like) by calling the Window.Confirm DHTML method. This method takes a string parameter containing the message we would like to ask the user and displays a modal dialog box with this message and OK and Cancel buttons. The method returns a Boolean value – True if the user selected OK, False for Cancel – so we check this value, and call the DataControl's CancelUpdate if the user really did mean to discard changes:

```
Sub btnUndo_OnClick
   strMsg = "Are you sure you want to reject changes?"
   If Window.Confirm(strMsg) = True Then
      myDC.CancelUpdate
   End If
End Sub
```

Inserting New Records

Now let's see about letting the user insert a new record. To do this, in theory we just need to call `MyDC.Recordset`'s AddNew method, which adds a new, empty row to the recordset. However, in practice there are a couple of other loose ends to tie up. Firstly, we set the value of the Boolean `Contract` field in the new row to `False`, since this field is represented by a checkbox in our table, and we cannot set the value of a checkbox to `Null`. We also need to ensure that the new record will be displayed in the table – that is, we need to move to the correct page in the table where the new record resides. Since the fields in our new record are blank, it will be the first row if the recordset is sorted by any field in ascending order, or the last row if it is sorted in reverse order. Therefore, we check the value of the `DataControl.SortDirection` property and move to the first or last page accordingly. Our only problem is if the recordset hasn't been sorted yet – `SortDirection` will be `True`, but the new record will be added at the end of the recordset. That's why we set `SortDirection` to `False` when the page opened:

```
Sub btnInsert_OnClick
    MyDC.Recordset.AddNew
    MyDC.Recordset("Contract") = False
    If MyDC.SortDirection = True Then
        tblData.FirstPage
    Else
        tblData.LastPage
    End If
End Sub
```

Deleting Records

The last piece of functionality we need for editing the data is the ability to delete records. To do this, we'll allow the user to select a name from a list of all the names in the recordset (populated by ASP script when the page loads), and then press a **Delete row** button. The corresponding row will be deleted from the recordset. The `au_id` field will be stored as the value of the selected option in the `selIDs` <SELECT> box. This field is the primary key of the `authors` table, so it is unique. For this reason, we'll filter the recordset using this value. This causes the selected record to be displayed on its own, so the user can be certain that the right field will be deleted. We'll call the `Window.Confirm` method again, to check that the user really does want to delete this row. If the user clicks on **OK**, we delete the record by calling the `DataControl.Recordset`'s `Delete` method. We don't need to pass any parameters into this, because we're only deleting the current record (which is the only one in the group). Finally, we refresh the select list from which the user will select rows to be deleted (so the user can't attempt to delete the same row again), by calling a subroutine named `subRefreshIDs`, which we'll look at next:

```
Sub btnDelete_OnClick
    strID = selIDs.Value
    MyDC.FilterColumn = "au_id"
    MyDC.FilterCriterion = "="
    MyDC.FilterValue = strID
    MyDC.Reset(False)
    strMsg = "Are you sure you want to delete row " & strID & "?"
    If Window.Confirm(strMsg) = True Then
        myDC.Recordset.Delete
    End If
    myDC.FilterColumn = ""
    myDC.Reset(False)
    subRefreshIDs
End Sub
```

The `subRefreshIDs` subroutine is used to refresh the options in the `selIDs` `<SELECT>` element whenever a change occurs to the data in the recordset. First, we reset the list by setting its `length` (the number of elements it contains) to zero. We then loop through the `DataControl`'s `Recordset` from the start. For each record in the recordset, we create a new HTML `<OPTION>` element. We set the `Text` of this option (which the user will see in the listbox) to a concatenation of the `au_fname` and `au_lname` fields, and its `Value` (which our delete routine above uses) to the `au_id` field. We then add this `<OPTION>` element to the `<SELECT>` element, before moving on to the next record:

```
Sub subRefreshIDs
    selIDs.options.length = 0
    MyDC.Recordset.MoveFirst
    While Not myDC.Recordset.EOF
        Set optID = Document.CreateElement("OPTION")
        strName = CStr(myDC.Recordset("au_fname") & _
                       " " & myDC.Recordset("au_lname"))
        optID.Text = strName
        optID.Value = myDC.Recordset("au_id")
        selIDs.options.add optID
        MyDC.Recordset.MoveNext
    Wend
End Sub
```

In order to refresh the list every time a change occurs in the recordset, we'll use the `OnAfterUpdate` data-binding event. This event applies to HTML elements bound to a DSO (here, our `tblData` table), and is raised whenever the value in the element (in this case, in a table cell) is changed when focus moves to a different element, or to a different cell in the table. Within the event handler routine, we'll just call our `subRefreshIDs` routine:

```
Sub tblData_OnAfterUpdate
    subRefreshIDs
End Sub
```

Sorting Records

Our next task will be to sort the fields. We'll implement this in a way modeled on Windows Explorer, Outlook and other Windows applications. When the user clicks on a header in the table, the recordset will be sorted in ascending order on that field; however, if the recordset is already sorted on this field, we will sort it in the opposite direction to the one in which it is currently sorted. That is, if it's sorted in ascending order, we will sort it in reverse order, and vice versa. To do this, we will add an `ONCLICK` attribute to each `<TH>` element in our table, and this will call a sub named `subSort`, passing in the name of the field to sort on as a parameter. To perform the sort, we will check whether the passed-in field name is the same as the current `SortColumn` of the `DataControl`. If it is, we need to reverse the sort direction, so we store `Not(myDC.SortDirection)` in the variable `blnOrder`; otherwise, we simply set `blnOrder` to `True` to sort the field in ascending order. We then set the `DataControl`'s `SortColumn` property to the selected field name, and the `SortDirection` to our `blnOrder` variable. Finally, we call the `Reset` method to perform the sort:

```
Sub subSort(strFieldName)
    If myDC.SortColumn = strFieldName Then
        ' Recordset already sorted by this field,
        ' so reverse the value
        blnOrder = Not(myDC.SortDirection)
```

```
      Else
          ' Recordset not sorted by this field,
          ' so we'll sort in ascending order
          blnOrder = True
      End If
      myDC.SortColumn = strFieldName
      myDC.SortDirection = blnOrder
      myDC.Reset    ' perform the sort
  End Sub
```

Filtering the Recordset

That leaves just one piece of functionality we're going to implement: the ability to filter the recordset. We will allow the user to select any field name from a <SELECT> box (called selFields), which we will populate using ASP script before the page loads. Whenever the user chooses a new field in this list, the <SELECT> element's OnChange event will fire. We can add code to this event handler to populate another <SELECT> element (selValues) with every value in that field. This is very similar to the procedure for populating the selIDs listbox we saw above – we loop through the recordset, creating an <OPTION> element for each record, setting its Text and Value properties to the value of the field for the current record. However, since the values aren't guaranteed to be unique, we need to ensure that we don't add the same option twice. We do this by setting the ID property for each option, as well as the Text and Value. We can then check whether an element with this ID already exists in the select box's options collection, and only add the option if it doesn't:

```
  Sub selFields_OnChange
      strField = selFields.Value
      selValues.options.length = 0
      MyDC.Recordset.MoveFirst
      While Not myDC.Recordset.EOF
          Set optValue = Document.CreateElement("OPTION")
          strValue = CStr(myDC.Recordset(strField))
          If selValues.options.item(strValue) Is Nothing Then
              optValue.Text = strValue
              optValue.Value = strValue
              optValue.ID = strValue
              selValues.options.add optValue
          End If
          MyDC.Recordset.MoveNext
      Wend
  End Sub
```

Now, when the user clicks on the button to filter the recordset, we can just set the DataControl's FilterColumn property to the value in our selFields select box, and the FilterValue to the value of selValues. We're only going to allow filtering where the value of a field is the same as one of the values in the recordset, so we set FilterCriterion to "=" in all cases. Finally, we call Reset to perform the filter:

```
  Sub btnFilter_OnClick
      myDC.FilterColumn = selFields.Value
      myDC.FilterCriterion = "="
      myDC.FilterValue = selValues.Value
      myDC.Reset
  End Sub
```

When the user wants to see the entire recordset again, we just set a new filter, specifying that we don't want to filter by any column, so we set `FilterColumn` to an empty string. Then we call the `Reset` method, passing in a parameter of `False`, to indicate that we want any currently applied filter to be discarded:

```
Sub btnUnfilter_OnClick
    myDC.FilterColumn = ""
    myDC.Reset(False)
End Sub
```

Creating the Table

That's all of our client-side script, but we've still got a bit to do. Firstly we need to create our data-bound HTML table, `tblData`. We set the `DATASRC` property to `"#myDC"` to bind to our `DataControl` DSO, and we specify a `DATAPAGESIZE` of `"5"` to implement table paging.

```
</SCRIPT>
</HEAD>
<BODY BGCOLOR="#EEEEFF">
<CENTER>
<H1>Data Caching with RDS</H1>
<TABLE DATASRC="#myDC" CELLPADDING=3 CELLSPACING=1 BORDER=0
       DATAPAGESIZE=5 ID="tblData" WIDTH="100%">
```

Next comes the table head. We'll set the `STYLE` attribute of the `<THEAD>` to `"cursor:hand"`, because clicking on the header will cause the recordset to be sorted. In each `<TH>` element, we'll add an `ONCLICK` attribute that will call our `subSort` routine. We pass in the name of the field as a parameter, so the sub knows which cell has been clicked on:

```
<THEAD BGCOLOR="#888888" STYLE="cursor:hand">
    <TH ONCLICK=subSort("au_id")>Author ID</TH>
    <TH ONCLICK=subSort("au_fname")>First Name</TH>
    <TH ONCLICK=subSort("au_lname")>Last Name</TH>
    <TH ONCLICK=subSort("phone")>Phone Number</TH>
    <TH ONCLICK=subSort("address")>Address</TH>
    <TH ONCLICK=subSort("city")>City</TH>
    <TH ONCLICK=subSort("state")>State</TH>
    <TH ONCLICK=subSort("zip")>Zip</TH>
    <TH ONCLICK=subSort("contract")>Contract</TH>
</THEAD>
```

Now we have the table body. Remember that we only need to have one row in the table, and that we have to specify the `DATAFLD` attribute in a child element of each cell in this row to implement tabular binding. We want our data to be updateable, so we will use text `<INPUT TYPE="TEXT">` elements for most of the fields. The only exception is the `contract` field. This is a Boolean field, so we will use a checkbox rather than a textbox in this case:

```
<TBODY>
    <TR BGCOLOR="#BBBBBB">
        <TD><INPUT TYPE="TEXT" DATAFLD="au_id" ID="txtID" SIZE=11></TD>
        <TD><INPUT TYPE="TEXT" DATAFLD="au_fname" ID="txtFirst" SIZE=13></TD>
        <TD><INPUT TYPE="TEXT" DATAFLD="au_lname" ID="txtLast" SIZE=13></TD>
        <TD><INPUT TYPE="TEXT" DATAFLD="phone" ID="txtPhone" SIZE=17></TD>
```

```
    <TD><INPUT TYPE="TEXT" DATAFLD="address" ID="txtAddr" SIZE=20></TD>
    <TD><INPUT TYPE="TEXT" DATAFLD="city" ID="txtCity" SIZE=13></TD>
    <TD><INPUT TYPE="TEXT" DATAFLD="state" ID="txtState" SIZE=8></TD>
    <TD><INPUT TYPE="TEXT" DATAFLD="zip" ID="txtZip" SIZE=8></TD>
    <TD ALIGN="CENTER"><INPUT TYPE="CHECKBOX" DATAFLD="contract"
                              ID="chkContract"></TD>
  </TR>
</TBODY>
</TABLE>
```

The Rest of the Page

Next we have the buttons for navigating through the table pages, and for saving and rejecting changes to the data on the client:

```
<BR>
<BUTTON NAME="btnFirstPage">  |&lt;&lt;  </BUTTON>
   
<BUTTON NAME="btnPrevPage">  &lt;  </BUTTON>
     
<BUTTON NAME="btnUpdate">Save changes</BUTTON>
   
<BUTTON NAME="btnUndo">Undo changes</BUTTON>
     
<BUTTON NAME="btnNextPage">  &gt;  </BUTTON>
   
<BUTTON NAME="btnLastPage">  &gt;&gt;|  </BUTTON>
</CENTER><HR>
```

Of the three `<SELECT>` elements on the page, we're going to populate two using server-side ASP script, and leave the other (`selValues`) empty – this will only be populated when the user selects a field for filtering on. To populate the `selFields` element, which contains a list of all the field names in the recordset, we will instantiate our business object again – but this time on the server in ASP code. We call the object's `GetRecordset` method (using `Server.CreateObject`), iterate through the fields in the returned recordset, and create an `<OPTION>` element for each one. We could in fact do this on the client as well, but since the field definitions can't be updated by our application, we're only going to have to populate this select box once before the page loads, so we can just as easily use ASP:

```
<P>Select a field to filter the recordset on:
<SELECT ID=selFields>
<%
Set objRDSTest = Server.CreateObject("RDSTest.clsServer")
Set objRSServer = objRDSTest.GetRecordset
Set objRDSTest = Nothing
For Each objField In objRSServer.Fields
   Response.Write "<OPTION VALUE='" & objField.Name & "'>" & _
                  objField.Name & "</OPTION>"
Next
%>
</SELECT>
   Select the value for the filter:
<SELECT ID=selValues></SELECT>
</P>
<BUTTON NAME="btnFilter">Filter the recordset</BUTTON>   
<BUTTON NAME="btnUnfilter">See all records</BUTTON><HR>
```

Our next bit of ASP code is used to populate the list of names that will be used when the user wants to delete a row. We iterate through the recordset, creating an <OPTION> element for each row. As we indicated above, we set the VALUE attribute of each option to the au_id field for internal use by our 'Delete' subroutine, but we set the TEXT attribute to a concatenation of the author's first and last names, so that a more user-friendly list will be displayed in the select box:

```
<P>Select a row to delete:  <SELECT ID=selIDs>
<%
objRSServer.MoveFirst
While Not objRSServer.EOF
    Response.Write "<OPTION VALUE='" & objRSServer("au_id") & _
                   "'>" & objRSServer("au_fname") & " " & _
                   objRSServer("au_lname") & "</OPTION>"
    objRSServer.MoveNext
Wend
%>
</SELECT>
     
<BUTTON NAME="btnDelete">Delete row</BUTTON>
   
<BUTTON NAME="btnInsert">Add new row</BUTTON>
</P>
</BODY>
</HTML>
```

And that completes the code for the application! In order to avoid complicating the application and adding too much code that isn't directly related to RDS, we've left out quite a bit that would have been very desirable; error handling has been kept to the barest minimum, for example. We've also kept the functionality fairly simple for the same reason. However, the example does give an idea of what can be achieved with RDS, and does provide a few features that would be very difficult (if not impossible) without RDS, such as automatic refreshing of select boxes whenever a value in the data is changed.

Summary

We haven't seen a huge amount of ASP in this section, for the simple reason that we've been looking at a technology that can take some of the burden off our server and off the network. RDS allows us to transfer an ADO Recordset object from a business object on our web server to the client, and work with the data locally using client-side script (or a client application). As well as the obvious savings in network traffic and server resources, this technology has the added advantage of allowing us to integrate our data fully into our application, without needing a round-trip to the server every time the user's view of the data needs to be refreshed.

We also looked at some of the limitations of RDS – its inability to work with non-Microsoft browsers, the footprint required to send and build Recordset objects across machines, and above all, the potential security risks if RDS is carelessly implemented. However, so long as these security and performance considerations are taken into account, RDS can be a very important piece of our Internet or intranet application, which allows us to create genuinely rich client-side applications.

Advanced Query Interfaces

The declared goal of Microsoft's **Universal Data Access** (UDA) strategy is to make it easier for developers to integrate different data sources, and different data *types*, within applications. OLE DB, the practical counterpart of the UDA philosophy, provides the means of accessing any data store through a common set of COM interfaces.

There's an area in data access, though, where even the high-level approach of UDA and OLE DB together cannot provide a unified solution; data query. While it is not that hard to come up with a common API for special providers to expose proprietary data in a standardized way, creating a similar general-purpose and universally valid mechanism for querying data has not proved that easy.

In this chapter, we'll look at the various options we have today to use a generalized query language. What has been put under the umbrella of 'Advanced Query Interfaces' consist of basically two technologies:

❑ The SQL Server 7.0 (and higher) OLE DB Heterogeneous Queries

❑ The SQL Server 2000 English Query

Throughout the chapter, we'll describe the architecture and operation of heterogeneous queries before moving on to the more intriguing capabilities of English Query.

Beyond SQL

SQL – an ISO standard since 1992 – has become the *de facto* standard language for database query. Such a specification, also known as SQL-92, is articulated into three levels of adherence: entry, intermediate, and full.

All top-industry RDBMSs available today support SQL, but years of real-world experience prove that not even SQL can be considered a standard if we move beyond the entry level of the SQL-92 specification. As a result, we no longer have a standard language for data query. Nevertheless, SQL represents the closest the software community has come to the definition of a truly universal query language.

Although SQL has been exclusively defined for and used with relational databases, there are now some Windows 2000 Management Instrumentation providers (WMI) that come with an inbuilt query language that mimics SQL.

From the SQL-92 specification, we get a query language that is standardized enough to work with ODBC drivers and relational data. From the UDA specification, we need a query language, that will be as universally accepted as SQL is today, but that will be more powerful and more widely supported than SQL-92. With UDA also covering non-relational and hierarchical data types, this makes things even more complicated. There is just one certainty: SQL-92 was not developed with anything other than relational tables in mind.

The Query Language of OLE DB Providers

If we write custom OLE DB providers, we may define our own query language, or we are free to invent and set up the syntax that we want our module to understand. There are no guidelines on how to do this, and a set of directives seems rather inconceivable.

Each OLE DB provider – from an RDBMS to ADSI or Indexing Services, and from ODBC to custom providers – can be made to understand a different language. The lack of a universal query language means that a developer writing an OLE DB provider has complete control over how to make data available to queries.

Heterogeneous Queries

A **heterogeneous query** (also known as a distributed query) is one that involves more than one data provider; for example, a query that gets a recordset made up of some records coming from a SQL Server database and others from an AS/400 machine. Since a universal language, and consequently a universal query processor, doesn't exist today – and probably won't exist in the foreseeable future – any heterogeneous query must pass through a module that can understand the overall syntax, identify and run all the sub-queries, and put the various pieces together. Or to put it another way, running a distributed query requires the involvement of a specialized application behaving like a 'distributed query coordinator' (as opposed to the Distributed Transaction Coordinator that we find in the MTS/COM+ architecture).

Architecting Distributed Queries

Versions of SQL Server prior to 7.0 allowed access to external data sources through remote stored procedures running on other SQL Server machines. However, the distributed query mechanism introduced with SQL Server 7.0 is more flexible because now objects in remote data sources (that is, tables and views) can be directly referenced using local T-SQL statements such as SELECT, INSERT, UPDATE, and DELETE.

Distributed queries rely on OLE DB as the underlying technology and access non-relational data as long as an OLE DB provider exists for it. SQL Server 7.0/2000 distributed queries go beyond the traditional relational DBMS systems with SQL query processors. If a piece of software exists that is capable of exposing data in a tabular format (rowset) through the OLE DB interfaces, then we can treat the data as a SQL Server table and combine and process it via a slightly extended version of T-SQL.

Through the use of special syntax, the SQL Server 7.0/2000 query mechanism recognizes a distributed query and is able to break the command text into pieces and run the resulting sub-queries. As mentioned earlier, we can join together data coming from a SQL Server and an AS/400 table, but we could also ask SQL Server to retrieve and join data from heterogeneous sources such as Access or a custom OLE DB provider.

Let's see how the SQL Server 7.0 mechanism for distributed queries actually works and how to take advantage of it in real-world applications.

Linked Servers

Central to distributed queries are logical elements called **linked servers**. In the figure that follows, we can see where all the existing linked servers are listed in the SQL Server Enterprise Manager:

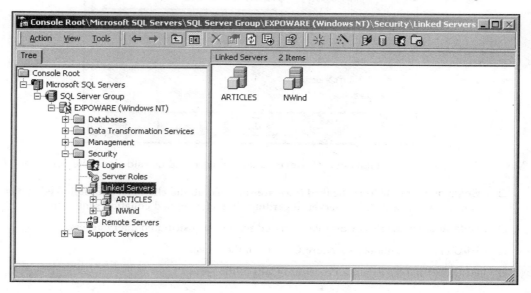

A linked server is the place in the SQL Server environment where all the information needed to execute OLE DB queries on remote machines or spanning over non-SQL Server databases is gathered. Linked servers provide remote server access as well as the ability to run queries and execute commands on heterogeneous data sources across the enterprise information system. In addition, they provide a uniform interface for working with different data sources.

When configuring a linked server, we just specify an OLE DB provider and the data source. We can do this in two possible ways: either manually through the SQL Server Enterprise Manager or programmatically via a stored procedure on the system.

Manually Creating a Linked Server

To create a linked server interactively, right-click the Linked Servers node in the SQL Server Enterprise Manager and then select the New Linked Server... menu command:

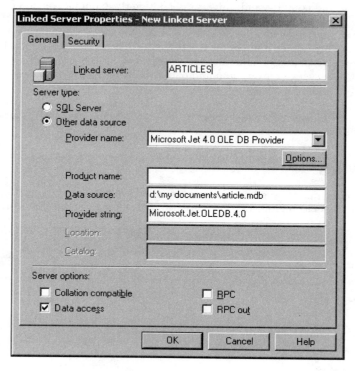

Most of this is fairly self-explanatory. However, a few things could be said about the Server options:

❑ Collation compatible is checked if we are sure that all the characters in the linked server are compatible with the local server, regarding character set and collation sequence.

❑ Data Access enables or disables a linked server for distributed query access.

❑ RPC enables Remote Procedure Calls from the server.

❑ RPC out enables Remote Procedure Calls to the server.

Another way of creating linked server configurations is through the Query Analyzer or any other environment that allows us to run stored procedures. For example, an ADO application.

Programmatically Creating a Linked Server

The following code creates a linked server to a Microsoft Access database:

```
EXEC sp_addlinkedserver 'NWind', '',
    'Microsoft.Jet.OLEDB.4.0',
    'd:\nwind.mdb'
```

The stored procedure can accept up to seven arguments, as illustrated here:

```
sp_addlinkedserver [@server =] 'server'
    [, [@srvproduct =] 'product_name']
    [, [@provider =] 'provider_name']
    [, [@datasrc =] 'data_source']
    [, [@location =] 'location']
    [, [@provstr =] 'provider_string']
    [, [@catalog =] 'catalog']
```

The first is the name of the new server, and all the others serve to identify the data source and the OLE DB provider that wraps it. When a user attempts to execute a distributed query that accesses a linked table, the local server must be able to log onto the linked server on behalf of the user.

Login Issues

While creating a new linked server, sp_addlinkedserver also establishes a default mapping between all logins on the local server and the logins on the remote servers. Such a mapping assumes that SQL Server utilizes the local login's user credentials. If this doesn't suit our needs, we can use another system stored procedure, sp_addlinkedsrvlogin, to specify the new settings.

If we choose the interactive approach, we can use the **Security** tab instead:

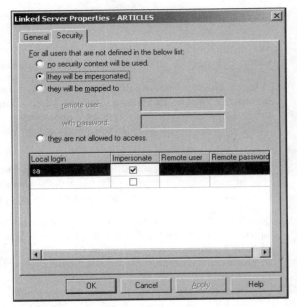

The three important options here are:

❑ **No security context will be used**: specifies that users with logins not listed will not be able to connect to the linked server.

❑ **They will be impersonated**: specifies that, for users not listed, their existing login and password will be used. If their login and password do not exist on the linked server, access will be denied.

❑ **They will be mapped to**: specifies that users who are not listed will be mapped to the given user login and password.

SQL Server can use the Windows NT/2000 username and password to connect to a linked server and run a query on behalf of the current user. This requires a user to be connected to SQL Server using Windows NT authentication. In addition, the provider must support the same authentication mode. The linked server is responsible for the permissions on the various objects contained in the remote database.

Removing Linked Servers

To remove the mapping between a local SQL Server login and a linked server's login, we can use the `sp_droplinkedsrvlogin` stored procedure. To remove a linked server altogether, we use `sp_dropserver` instead.

We can also remove linked servers from the SQL Server Enterprise Manager by simply selecting the appropriate server and pressing the *Delete* key.

The OPENROWSET Keyword

Once we have a fully functional linked server, we can use it wherever we would use a native SQL Server table:

```
SELECT * FROM NWind.Northwind.dbo.Employees
```

We should always use complete names when working with linked server objects. The fully qualified name includes the linked server name, the catalog, the schema, and the object name.

When it comes to issuing distributed queries, a linked server provides a predetermined mapping between a local and a remote database object. However, there might be circumstances where we might want to dynamically specify a query string and get a rowset from a non-SQL Server data source. The SQL Server 7.0/2000 T-SQL language provides a made-to-measure keyword called OPENROWSET to do this.

Functionally speaking, OPENROWSET and linked servers provide the same capability. However, we should use linked servers for data sources that we use regularly, and use an *ad hoc* connector like OPENROWSET where an occasional or one-off access to a remote OLE DB data source is required.

OPENROWSET is defined to include all the connection information that is necessary to access a data source for which an OLE DB provider exists. It establishes a connection and can be used as the target of a FROM clause or an INSERT or DELETE statement. All the information contained in an OPENROWSET statement can be used wherever a table name or view is needed.

> Note that OPENROWSET returns a single recordset, even though the query is designed to return multiple sets of records. It only takes the first one and ignores all the others.

Using OPENROWSET

The syntax for OPENROWSET looks like this:

```
OPENROWSET(
  'provider_name'
  {'datasource';'user_id';'password' | 'provider_string'},
  {[catalog.][schema.]object | 'query'}
)
```

The catalog and schema names are not always necessary and can be omitted, if the provider does not support them. The query string is any string the specified provider can understand and process, which includes SQL. Once again, a unified query language or a unified model for issuing distributed and heterogeneous queries would be of great benefit here.

Let's see a few practical examples of how to use the OPENROWSET keyword with T-SQL. Open the SQL Query Analyzer and enter the following:

```
SELECT *
FROM OPENROWSET('Microsoft.Jet.OLEDB.4.0',
  'd:\my documents\articles.mdb';'admin';'', Magazines)
```

The first argument is the ProgID of the OLE DB provider. The second argument identifies the data source and includes login parameters, with all the tokens separated by a semicolon. This is pretty much like using a connection string with ADO.

For Access tables, such information corresponds to the name of the MDB file, username, and password. The third argument contains the object to access – the table or the query to run. In the previous example, we used the table name (Magazines):

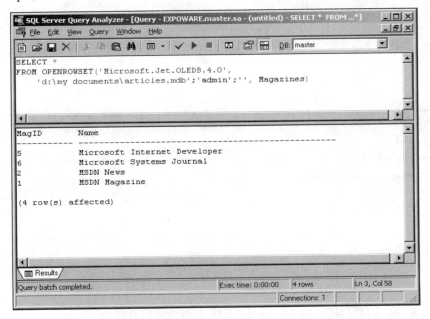

The power of distributed queries is particularly evident when heterogeneous data sources are involved. In the following SQL script the final recordset is a combination of a SQL Server table and an Access table:

```
USE [My Articles]
SELECT m.[Name], m.Periodicity, a.Title
FROM Magazines AS m
INNER JOIN
  OPENROWSET('Microsoft.Jet.OLEDB.4.0',
  'd:\My documents\articles.mdb';'admin';'', Articles)
  AS a ON m.MagID = a.Magazine
  WHERE a.Magazine = 1
```

Here we are using the same SQL Server database called My Articles that we used for several other examples. The Access database contains the same information – indeed, it was used to populate the SQL Server database in the first place. The code snippet above executes an inner join on the value of the magazine ID field. Here are the results of this query in the SQL Server Query Analyzer:

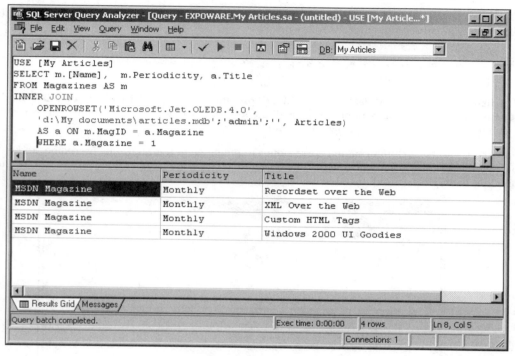

Of course, the above command is only a query string that SQL Server 7.0 runs. However, we can issue similar commands from other programming environments, including Visual Basic, Visual C++ and ASP – wherever ADO and OLE DB can be used.

In a real-world application we would normally not use SQL Server and Access together. During development, and in case of critical legacy data, we will need to gather data together from many diverse sources.

Towards a Universal Query Language

The heterogeneous query mechanism supplied by SQL Server 7.0/2000 attempts to provide a common means (through SQL or T-SQL) of querying data. It provides a kind of general-purpose tool to gather data from a variety of data providers. However, it falls way short of a **universal query language**.

Is a Kind of UQL in Order?

The computing world of tomorrow will probably be completely ruled by XML. Consequently, anything that can help searching and retrieving data within XML documents will become the best candidate to provide the foundation for "UQL" – the hypothetical "Universal Query Language".

To answer the question raised in the heading above, we cannot detract from the overall objectives of XML. In my opinion, if UQL does become a reality one day, it will be an XML-related technology. Of particular interest at the moment is **XPath**, a W3C (see http://www.w3.org/TR/xpath) recommendation that Microsoft already supports in the latest version of the MSXML parser.

In short, XPath defines the official syntax that standardizes the abstract data model of XML version 1.0. Such a data model, also called **Infoset**, comprises a set of objects and properties that characterize a well-formed XML document. And it is this data model that XML parsers should make available to clients. For more information about the Infoset specification, see http://www.w3.org/TR/xml-infoset.

Based on a common data model, it will be easier to devise a query language, which is exactly where XPath fits in.

XSL Patterns and XPath

If you're familiar with the Microsoft XML parser and object model (XMLDOM), then you're probably already familiar with what selectNodes or selectSingleNode achieve. Let's take a look at how they work.

Given the following XML document:

```
<?xml version="1.0"?>
<xml>
  <books>
  <book specialty="textbook">For children</book>
  <book specialty="cookbook">For mummies</book>
  <book specialty="adventure">For daddies</book>
  </books>
</xml>
```

We can query for a particular node like this:

```
...
Set xmlDoc = CreateObject("Microsoft.XMLDOM")
xmlDoc.async = False
xmlDoc.load("books.xml")

set n = xmlDoc.documentElement.selectNodes( _
  "books/book[@specialty = 'adventure']")

MsgBox n.item(0).xml
...
```

And this is the resulting output:

The original syntax was called **XSL Patterns**, and was based on an early dialect of what today is XPath 1.0. As databases expose their content through XML, the importance of XPath will increase. In fact, it is easy to imagine it becoming the basis of some kind of UQL.

What About the Natural Language?

Although SQL is relatively straightforward to use, we might still find ourselves having to constantly refer to the documentation for explanations of the syntax and how to use certain commands. We might even have breathed a sigh of relief when the first version of **Microsoft English Query** (MSEQ) came out, about two years ago.

Personally, I neglected MSEQ until a client of mine asked me whether there was a more natural way of issuing database queries. The question was whether a query like this:

```
show me all the customers
```

could be used rather than the standard SQL command:

```
select * from customers
```

To get the same information, why should we learn SQL? Can't the database learn Italian instead, or, at the very least, English?

In responding to such a need, Microsoft English Query was developed – a tool that sits on the top of SQL Server 7.0/2000 and lets the user issue queries against it using everyday language instead of the limited grammar offered by SQL. Stated this way, it might seem like magic. But be warned, it is only software!

English Query

In the search for a universal query language, we might look at various technologies, or platforms, or meta-languages, yet the best solution might also be the most obvious one and the easiest to run – using natural language.

My client was definitely right when she brought up the idea of a database that communicates using everyday language. Once we have MSEQ installed and properly configured, that's exactly what the user experiences; the database now understands a human-intelligible language! How does this work?

As we may have guessed, MSEQ carries out a simple translation from everyday English into SQL. In this way, both the database and the users can continue doing their respective jobs using their own language. Architecturally speaking, all the complexity of such a communication is encapsulated in MSEQ.

Originally, MSEQ was only an English-to-SQL translator for SQL Server 7.0, which did little more than whet the user's appetite. The version of MSEQ that ships with SQL Server 2000 supports only English as the user query language, but it extends the database-side query language to include **MDX** (**Multi-Dimensional Extensions**), a SQL-like language defined for querying OLAP cubes that we encountered in Chapter 30.

At this time, MSEQ only understands English, but Microsoft is currently redeveloping the internal architecture to make it accept different languages as a configuration parameter. MSDN subscribers can download MSEQ from http://www.microsoft.com/sql/eq.

MSEQ and Databases

Originally, MSEQ was only capable of working with SQL Server. MSEQ 2000 still only works directly with SQL Server as the database. However, we can now access any data source, which is externally linked to SQL Server 2000 through the mechanism of heterogeneous queries. Today MSEQ does not support any OLE DB providers natively, which means we cannot connect to any provider without the help of SQL Server 2000.

The reason for this is very simple – MSEQ only knows how to translate from English to T-SQL or MDX. On the other hand, not all OLE DB providers support SQL as the query language. We have providers, such as those for Active Directory or Indexing Service, that define their own custom language for commands. This is why MSEQ can't directly support them. However, passing MSEQ queries through SQL Server heterogeneous query processor fixes this since SQL Server acts as an additional level of translation from SQL to the provider's supported language. To summarize, MSEQ lets us always query against a SQL Server database, but by exploiting the heterogeneous query mechanism we can access virtually any OLE DB provider that we have available:

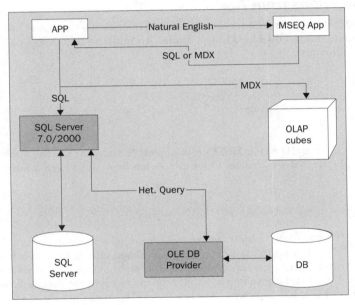

MSEQ is not a module that returns recordsets or cellsets. It is a simple translator that takes a string in plain old English and, according to its configuration, returns a corresponding SQL or MDX command. The application can then use that string at its leisure to issue the real query against the data source.

How Applications Use MSEQ

MSEQ 2000 integrates well with Visual InterDev, which provides wizards to create an **EQ application**.

An EQ application is a block of data that the MSEQ runtime utilizes to attempt the translation from English to SQL or MDX. Even though MSEQ cannot retrieve any data itself, it does need to know about the organization of database tables in order to create a meaningful query string.

Writing EQ Applications

An EQ application is always bound to a specific data source, and the questions we define are used to manipulate the content of the data source. In order to create EQ applications, two steps are required:

❑   Define the questions that MSEQ must translate

❑   Define a set of logical entities and relationships to map verbs and nouns to tables and fields

We can do all this in a graphical manner using Visual InterDev making use of drag-and-drop, context menus, and other UI facilities. Within the IDE, there is also a runtime environment to let us submit questions and test the corresponding SQL/MDX code.

When we finish defining our queries, we compile everything into an `.eqd` file. This is our entire EQ application. An EQD file, also called an **English Query Domain**, groups all the information about entities and relationships in an XML-based language called **Semantic Modeling Format** (SMF).

Using EQ Applications from ASP

When we install MSEQ on our web server, actually we're enabling our server-side applications to take advantage of a brand new COM-based object model. To initialize the MSEQ object model we use code such as the following:

```
<%
  Set eq = CreateObject("Mseq.Session")
  eq.InitDomain ("myfile.eqd")
%>
```

`Mseq.Session` is the ProgID of the MSEQ root object. `InitDomain` is the method that starts processing the EQD file that we created. Once all this has been done successfully, we can submit our query string:

```
Set eqResponse = eq.ParseRequest(myEngQuestion)
```

What we get back is a `Response` object (`Mseq.Response`) that has nothing to do with the ASP `Response` object. The EQ's `Response` object contains typed information. It can also contain executable, SQL or MDX strings, a direct answer, or an error message. In certain cases, MSEQ can answer the question itself and doesn't need to pass the query on to the database. Such frequently used questions are "what time is it?" and "what day is it today?"

In general, the question may require more commands. Here's how to get the command text to pass to ADO or ADOMD:

```
for each cmd in eqResponse.Commands
  strCmd = strCmd & cmd.SQL & vbCrLf
next
```

The `Response`'s `Commands` collection contains all the executable commands returned for that question. MSEQ also rephrases the question in more rigorous terms. For example, this:

```
List customers that issued an order
```

becomes this:

```
Which customers issued an order?
```

This intermediate string doesn't affect the success of the translation but can help to train users. By issuing the question in the right form we can get a faster response. The rephrased sentence is available through `Response.Restatement` property.

For developers, writing MSEQ-aware applications means determining which questions the application is supposed to answer before mapping the questions to the fields in the tables.

It's worth noticing that, while SQL can be used to carry out highly complex database operations, MSEQ supports only queries. We can use SQL to insert or delete records, but we cannot ask MSEQ to do this.

Putting MSEQ to Work

The first thing to do when putting MSEQ to work is to teach it a few sentences and explain what it has to do in response to them. Of course, both sentences and the corresponding behaviors will depend upon the structure of our database and the logical entities that populate the problem's domain. Writing an MSEQ application means defining relationships between tables and grammar elements such as verbs, nouns and adjectives.

MSEQ Entities and Relationships

An EQ application consists of a collection of entities and a set of pre-defined relationships between them. Visual Interdev allows us to create entities and define relationships in a relatively easy way. As soon as we install MSEQ 2000, on setting up a new project in Visual Interdev, we get a window like this:

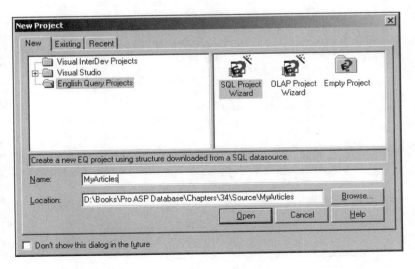

We choose the SQL Project Wizard, define a database connection using a standard data link window, and then select the tables we want as part of the final EQ domain:

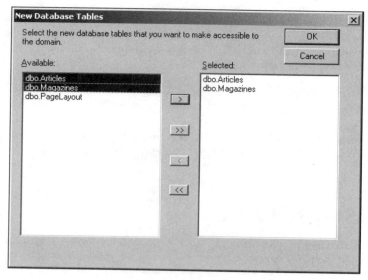

In this case, we're working with the My Articles SQL database. The questions that we want to ask relate only to the magazines and articles tables. The third concerns the layout of the web UI, which we won't be using.

Click OK and MSEQ will create and display all the entities and the relationships between them, all based on the data source information. As we can see, an entity maps to a database table, whereas a relationship represents a link between two or more entities:

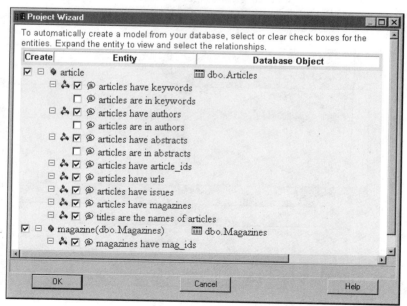

MSEQ extracts all this information from the data source itself by looking at the tables, indexes, and the relationships between the tables. The window can be used to remove all the entities and the relationships we do not want, by unchecking the box by each unneeded element.

What we include and what we remove will depend upon the questions we want our EQ application to answer. Entities and relationships can be more easily reviewed within the Visual Interdev IDE through the workspace window:

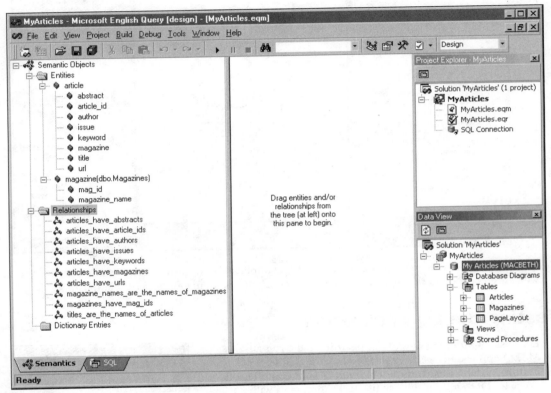

The workspace window provides a graphical representation of the semantics of the database query language we're about to define. Notice that all this information is actually stored in a .eqm file whose content is formatted in XML. The IDE provides us with context menu and drag-and-drop support to help us use the product. For example, by dragging and dropping two relationships (articles_have_magazines and articles_have_authors) into the right panel, we get this graphical representation on the right hand side:

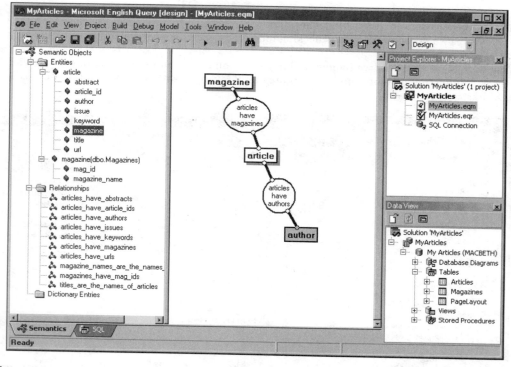

At this point, we can compile and build the EQD application for testing. At the moment, the questions we can successfully ask the application are based on the existing entities and relationships.

Testing the EQ Application

Let's ask about the names of all the articles. To run an MSEQ application we have just to click the standard **Start** button on the Visual Interdev toolbar. MSEQ compiles the `.eqm` text into a `.eqd` binary file and prompts us with a user interface like this:

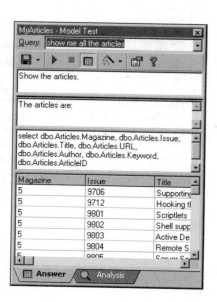

The original question is:

```
Show me all the articles
```

This question has been automatically restated as:

```
Show the articles
```

The corresponding SQL code is:

```
select dbo.Articles.Magazine, dbo.Articles.Issue, dbo.Articles.Title,
dbo.Articles.URL, dbo.Articles.Author, dbo.Articles.Keyword,
dbo.Articles.ArticleID
```

A polite 'sorry, I didn't understand that' is what we get if we submit a question that MSEQ cannot understand.

Defining the Entity Representation

MSEQ selects the fields based on the description of the entities involved. For instance, the `article` entity is initially associated with all database fields. We have to narrow down the number of associated fields.

To change the fields that an entity is associated with, we can right click on the entity name and select Edit. In the dialog box that follows, we can set the fields we need as illustrated here:

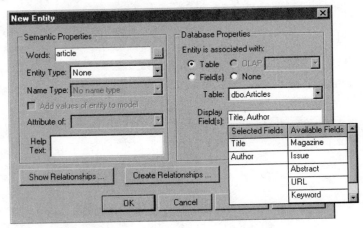

Now issuing the same command in the MSEQ test window produces a different SQL statement:

```
select dbo.Articles.Title, dbo.Articles.Author from dbo.Articles
```

At this point, we have a fully working, albeit basic, EQ application. The next step is teaching it to answer special questions. For the purposes of our Article Bazaar application, we're interested in the following couple of questions:

❑ All articles written for <MagazineName>

❑ All articles written for <MagazineName> in <year>

Given the current set of entities and relationships, such questions would generate error messages.

Managing Specific Questions

Our work at this stage is the same as that of a trainer. We must teach the EQ application how to understand and answer our users' questions. In most cases, we have to map database objects onto the specific expressions we want to use. MSEQ duly defines several phrasing types to help us sort this out.

Articles Written For ...

The new relationship we want to define is between articles and magazines and is fixed in terms of 'articles that are written for magazines'. To define a new relationship, just right-click on the Relationship node and select Add Relationship... The wizard asks us to specify the entities involved in the definition. One is `article`, while the other is the `magazine_name` of the magazine. Notice that `magazine` denotes the ID of the magazine since, by default, the names of the entities match the names of the fields. If we choose `magazine`, then we couldn't ask for 'articles written for ASPToday', but should resort to a syntax like 'articles written for 9' (9 is the ID of ASPToday):

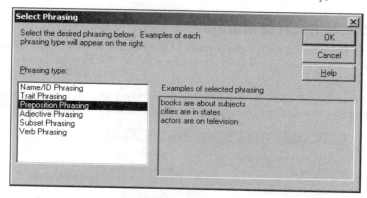

The next step is defining the phrasing. What we need here is "preposition phrasing"; phrasing which has a structure which will match well with the type of question we want to ask:

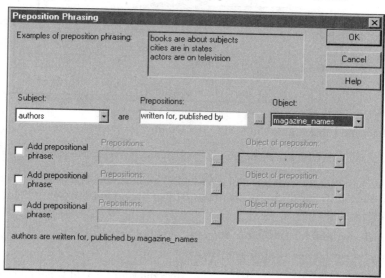

The subject is `articles`, and the object is `magazine_names`. In the middle, we enter two (or more) comma-separated prepositions:

- ❏   `written for`
- ❏   `published by`

Once we've saved the relationship, sentences like these can be understood by MSEQ:

- ❏   Show me all the articles written for MSDN News
- ❏   Show me all the articles published by MSDN News

Not completely convinced? Look at the figure below:

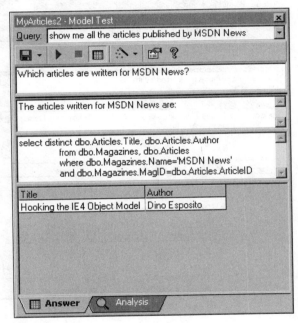

Articles Written for ... in ...

Let's make things a bit more complicated and try to combine the magazine and the year of publication. There would be no need for this extra relationship if the publication information had been expressed as a number. In this case, the following English query would work OK:

```
show me all the articles written in 1999 published by MSDN News
```

However, in our example, the year is only a part of the `Issue` field, and we've used the following syntax in all earlier queries:

```
Like Issue '99%'
```

To associate articles with a particular magazine, we need to fix the principle that magazines publish articles. This relationship will be expressed through a verb phrasing. As before, we right-click on the Relationship node and select Add Relationship... The wizard asks us to specify the entities involved in the definition, which are the same as before: article and magazine_name. We next choose Verb Phrasing and then the subject verb object type. The subject is article, the object is magazine_name, and the verb is "publish".

To force MSEQ to use the Like operator, we could use the expression 'begins with'. For example:

```
Show me all the articles whose issue begins with 00
```

will yield this:

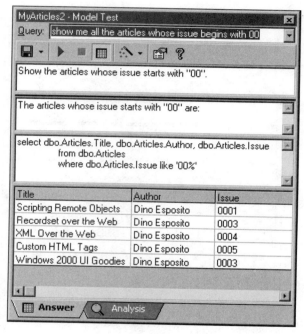

Now a question such as:

```
Show me all the articles whose issue begins with 99 published by MSDN News
```

produces the expected result, but the wording is stilted and unnatural. We can simplify it by introducing synonyms. These are expressions that MSEQ replaces with other ones. For example, we would normally use the phrase:

```
written in
```

instead of:

```
whose issue begins with
```

At the moment, MSEQ only understands the latter phrase, so we define a synonym, by right-clicking on the Dictionary Entries node and selecting Add Dictionary Entry:

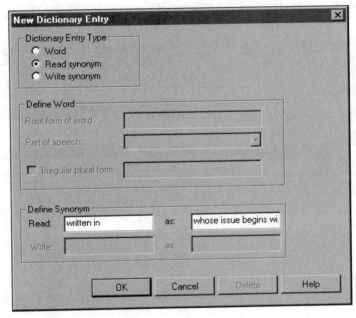

The figure that follows shows how this sentence is subsequently processed:

```
Show me all the articles written in 00
```

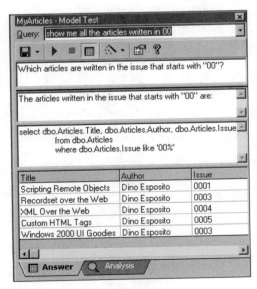

Note that this is now a legitimate EQ command.

Enhancing the Article Bazaar Web Site

Wouldn't it be good if we could add EQ support to the Article Bazaar web site? Just add a new link to the default page and build a brand new page like this:

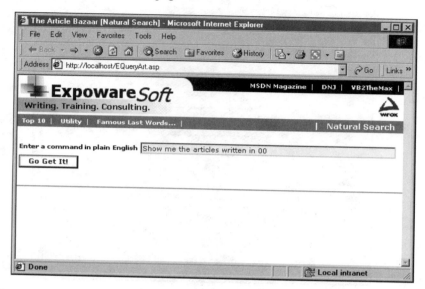

To process the input string, we use a Visual Basic COM object (`ArticleBazaar.NaturalQuery`) that returns an ADO recordset:

```
Option Explicit

' ***********************************************************
'  GetArticles
' -----------------------------------------------------------
'  Prepares and run a EQ query against My Articles.
' ***********************************************************
Public Function GetArticles(ByVal strCmd As String) As ADODB.Recordset
    Dim strSQL As String              ' the SQL statement
    Dim strConn As String             ' the connection string
    Dim oRS As New ADODB.Recordset    ' the ADO Recordset
    Dim oEQ As New Mseq.Session       ' the EQ Session object
    Dim oRSP As Mseq.Response         ' the EQ Response object
    Dim cmd As Mseq.QueryCmd          ' the EQ command object

    ' *** get in touch with the EQ application
    oEQ.InitDomain App.Path & "\myarticles.eqd"
    Set oRSP = oEQ.ParseRequest(strCmd)

    strSQL = ""
    If oRSP.Type = nlResponseCommand Then

        For Each cmd In oRSP.Commands
            strSQL = strSQL & cmd.SQL
        Next
```

```
        Else
            Exit Function
        End If

        ' *** prepares the connection string...
        strConn = DATASOURCE

        ' *** runs the query...
        With oRS
            .CursorLocation = adUseClient
            .Open strSQL, strConn
            Set GetArticles = oRS
        End With

        ' *** disconnect the recordset
        Set oRS.ActiveConnection = Nothing
    End Function
```

It requires early binding to the EQ type library:

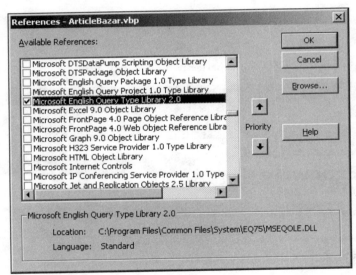

What the component does is prepare a SQL string ready to pass to ADO. To call the component from ASP we have a new ASP page called `equeryart.asp`, which is only slightly different from the other query page:

```
<hr>
<%
  if bFirstTime then
    Response.end
  end if
%>

<table cellspacing=0 cellpadding=2 border=0 width=100%>

<tr align=center bgcolor=0>
<td><font face=verdana size=1 color=#ffffff style=font-
weight:bold>Title</font></td>
```

```
<td><font face=verdana size=1 color=#ffffff style=font-
weight:bold>Author</font></td>
</tr>

<%
  set o = Server.CreateObject("ArticleBazar.NaturalQuery")
  set oRS = o.GetArticles(CStr(strPhrase))

  while Not oRS.EOF
    Response.Write "<tr valign=top>"
    sFont = "<font face=verdana size=1>"
    Response.Write "<td>" & sFont
    Response.Write oRS("title")
    Response.Write "</td>"
    sFont = "<font face=verdana size=1 color=blue>"
    Response.Write "<td>" & sFont
    Response.Write oRS("author")
    Response.Write "</td>"
    Response.Write "</tr>"

    oRS.MoveNext
  wend
%>
</table>
```

The figure demonstrates that EQ works perfectly through the Web:

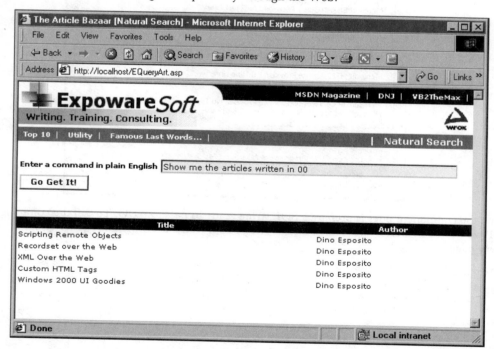

Deploying an EQ application is as easy as shipping an EQD file.

Querying OLAP Cubes

Using MSEQ 2000, working against either a SQL database or an OLAP data cube turns out to be indistinguishable as far as the user in concerned. There are a number of factors that contribute to this. Microsoft SQL Server OLAP Services plays a key role, since it allows us to create multidimensional structures to summarize and organize a massive amount of working data. Once we have an OLAP data source at our disposal, the next problem is determining an effective way to get rapid responses to complex queries. Basically, we need a couple of things: an easy to use programming tool to connect to the OLAP Services and a language to interrogate it. This is where ADOMD and its custom query language MDX come to the rescue. We looked at using OLAP in depth back in Chapter 30.

Querying Cubes with EQ

To create an EQ application to work against an OLAP data source, we first need to create an OLAP project from the Visual Interdev Project Wizard. It immediately asks us to specify the OLAP Server, the database, and the particular cube to use.

We can carry out our tests locally on the server machine by connecting to the FoodMart OLAP data source, which contains two OLAP cubes called Sales and Warehouse. Once we select a cube, EQ fills the Cubes tab on the Model Editor, as shown below:

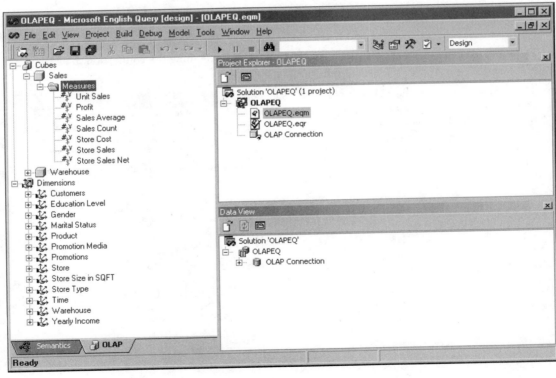

During setup, EQ creates a default set of entities and relationships that we can work with in exactly the same way as for SQL data. This is because there is no distinction between SQL and MDX within EQ. To see how powerful EQ is when working with OLAP cubes, let's suppose we want to know which stores in which cities have unit sales of greater than 20,000. A human-readable way of posing such a question might be:

```
show the store cities with unit sales greater than 20000
```

Assuming that the FoodMart database is called, the above question evaluates to the following hard-to-read command string:

```
SELECT
{Measures.[Unit Sales]} ON COLUMNS,
FILTER([Store].[Store City].members,
Measures.[Unit Sales]>20000) ON ROWS
FROM [SALES]
```

At this point, we can can pass this command to the ADOMD object model to get a CellSet object, which can be displayed by ASP.

```
set connFM = Server.CreateObject("ADODB.Connection")
connFM.Open "data source=expoware; provider=MSOLAP;"
connFM.DefaultDatabase = "FoodMart"
set csFM = Server.CreateObject("ADOMD.Cellset")
csFM.Open strMDX, connFM
```

Note that we need to specify the data source token when defining the connection to an OLAP server.

This figure shows how the EQ runtime compiles and builds an application based on the FoodMart database.

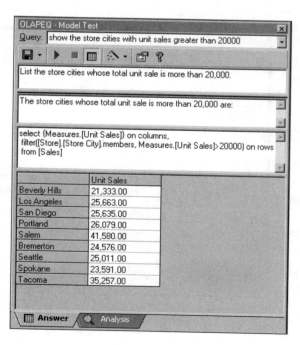

While EQ enables an ordinary user to work with SQL or MDX query strings using a similar syntax, for an application developer, using SQL or MDX is not exactly the same thing. EQ is well designed since it exposes a common set of user tools to translate from English to database-readable syntax. However, getting the same kind of uniformity within applications is another story. With the same effort on the user's part, EQ can give SQL or MDX, but then the final call to the database is up to us.

Summary

Querying for data is an important programming issue. For a long time, the problems associated with querying seemed to have been solved once and for all with SQL. However, with the anticipation of a Universal Data Access (UDA) and the rise of XML, it has become clear that there would soon have to be a more universal query language than SQL to enable non-SQL data sources to be accessed.

In the meantime, though, what's better than a natural language to talk to a database and query for data?

In this chapter, we covered:

❑   Special functionality available in SQL Server 7.0/2000 to access heterogeneous data

❑   How and why XPath runs for the position of universal query language of the near future

❑   How to use natural language to query for data with MSEQ

Section 8

Performance and Security

34

Scalability and Performance

To say that every developer wants his or her applications to perform quickly is stating the obvious. Although we never intentionally build applications that are slow, it is often the case that when the application hits production, its responsiveness is not what was hoped for. With many applications, there is not one specific cause for poor performance. Usually there are a number of reasons that compound upon each other.

This chapter addresses a number of issues that have an effect on performance. Not all of these issues will come into play in every application, but if taken as guidelines, what is discussed can make a significant difference in the overall operation of an application.

Before we can evaluate how applicable each of the issues mentioned in this chapter are to an application, it is necessary to determine priorities. Every application should satisfy the business needs, and performance is usually just one of these. In many cases there are tradeoffs when choosing between priorities: a cluster of web servers provides faster access but is more costly, greater volumes of data can affect access speed, adding an index to a database table may provide faster selects but slow down inserts and updates, and so on. In order to set priorities, we need to determine how an application will be judged by the customer it is being built for. There are many different measures that may be used, some directly related to some business need, while others are related to how the technology is working.

With these in mind, we will take a look at the typical measures of performance. We will also discuss aspects of scalability. Although scalability is not the same as performance, the two usually have a direct influence on each other. Reliability is another performance-related issue that we'll discuss. If an application crashes every hour, performance will definitely be affected! And so will the business. For a web-based business, frequent crashes or frequent unavailability of the site are highly detrimental to building customer relationships.

Judging An Application

Performance is a word that can mean different things to different people. When we say that we want a computer application to perform well, some may interpret this as a measure of how the application provides its basic services. Others may think that this means that the application should execute as fast as possible, while yet others may think that performing well means that the application does not crash. Although there is no single correct answer to what performance actual is, we software engineers tend to think of performance as how quickly the application completes its functions. When talking about the likelihood that an application, or some portion of it, will fail or crash, we typically refer to its **reliability**.

Scalability... Performance

When we consider Web Applications, what do scalability and performance mean? As we have just discussed, performance can have different meanings to different people, but an underlying concept of most of these meanings is a measure of *speed*. Scalability differs from performance, although the two terms are often used together to help describe the overall quality of an application.

> *According to the online dictionary* Dictionary.com, *Scalability is defined as: "How well a solution to some problem will work when the size of the problem increases." For example, a central server of some kind with ten clients may perform adequately but with a thousand clients it may fail to meet response time requirements.*

As we can see, the definition of scalability includes a reference to "performance". Even when we consider performance as concerning the speed of the application, there are different ways we can measure performance. Are we talking about how many lines of code are executed each second? Perhaps we are talking about how many transactions are processed within some time frame. We may even be talking about how fast the application is perceived to be by the user. The point is, an application will be judged to be a success or failure by someone. What we need to do is find out what criteria they will use when the application is evaluated.

Any good quality assurance professional knows that it is necessary to quantify and qualify how the application will be evaluated. As a general rule of thumb, this topic should be discussed at the very start of the project-planning phase. When a client has us build an application, it is because there is a business need. It is often true that the customer expects the application to perform its functions at the highest possible speed, although they may not state that explicitly. Given the choice between having an application that is error free but slow or one that is fast but prone to errors, most customers will of course say that they want *both* a fast application and one that is robust and full featured. Unfortunately, having both isn't always a choice, so when pressed they will usually go with "slower but more accurate". Why? Because they have a business need to resolve, and accuracy is usually more important to businesses than sheer speed. Fulfilling the business need is the priority.

There are other priorities that must be considered, and with each item in a list of priorities there will probably be some tradeoff. Faster machines cost more money. More features take more time and resources, money, and people. A shorter deadline means fewer or less robust features. With almost every approach we can take to increase performance, there will be a trade off. In many cases, we can throw more money at a problem to buy better solutions, but funding is almost always limited.

Where to Look for Performance Gains

In order to get the best possible performance, you need to consider every layer or portion of your application and the environment your app will run under. This means you should consider the impact of the hardware, operating system, and server software as well as the application itself.

Better hardware can help solve many performance issues, but often we developers have little control over what hardware will be used. Similarly, we often don't have much influence over what operating system and server software will be used. If your client has a big investment in Windows 2000 boxes running Oracle, then it may be hard to justify developing an app that doesn't use these products.

Assuming that we, the developers, have some influence on what is used for hardware, operating system, and such, we need to consider the architecture of the application to make the most appropriate selections. Is the application going to be 2-tier or N-tier? Will we be running clusters of servers or standalone boxes? By asking questions such as these we can help estimate the demand upon each tier and therefore determine how much or how fast our hardware needs to be. Knowing these demands will aid us tremendously with making our selections.

If we are trying to increase performance in an existing application, then we should ask ourselves where we should concentrate our efforts to get the best gains. In many cases, you won't be able to change the hardware radically. Sure, you may be able to suggest adding more memory to a server or possibly adding an extra server or two, but these gains may only be marginal. Similarly, there is little you can do with the operating system and RDBMS beyond configuration changes, although correcting a poor configuration may be significant. With existing applications, it is generally best to start looking for performance enhancement in the application and the database that it uses. It is these areas that developers have the greatest control over, and therefore, the best chance of making improvements:

Where to look for performance improvements in existing applications

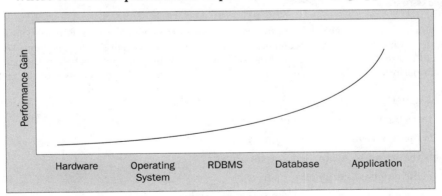

But where in the application should we focus our optimization efforts? The best places to start to examine are the most frequently used activities in your site or application. You can determine user behavior with IIS service logs or by using utilities such as the Usage Import and Report Writer component of Microsoft Site Server. Making even incremental performance in the most-commonly used parts of the app or site will be more likely to give you better overall performance.

Web Application Performance

Since every application is essentially unique, it is unreasonable to suppose that we can decide on a unique way of optimally meeting requirements, however, we can discuss what may be done and, together with the client, can evaluate each option and produce a list of priorities. But again, any list of prioritized items will be a direct reflection of how the application will be judged. So what are typical measures used for evaluating an application? There may be qualitative assessments, such as the perceived ease of use of the user interface or the perceived speed of the application. Often, the measures used are more quantitative, such as:

- Seconds required to load pages
- Time required to service a request, such as a credit card validation or sending a confirming e-mail
- The number of simultaneous requests/users that may be serviced
- Transactions processed per minute by the database
- The availability of services 24 hours a day, seven days a week
- Zero errors or some statistically insignificant number of errors

The ideal is to achieve or exceed each of these measurements. To do so, we *may* need to write efficient code, *may* need fast and robust hardware, and *may* need to consider installing a high-speed segmented network. The word "may" is important here. There are many scenarios where even the best approach to performance wouldn't help or isn't needed. If a site displays only small, static HTML web pages, there may be no need for multiple web servers. We may have the fastest database server on the market, but the data won't reach the user quickly if our site is bottlenecked because of a slow connection from our web site to our ISP. Similarly, if our web page content is heavy with graphics and streaming media, the load time may be so slow that many users will move on to a new web site, so our ultra-fast shopping cart feature will rarely be seen. When addressing performance issues, care must be taken to address the bottlenecks first.

So how do we determine where the bottlenecks are? Sometimes they are easy to spot; sometimes they are more elusive. Often, finding performance bottlenecks is like debugging code. Just because there is an error on line 114 doesn't mean the problem is at that line. Often the problem lies before the error is seen. When we look at performance, we need to evaluate the components used at every level of the application:

- Are the network cards fast enough?
- Does the server have enough memory?
- Is the operating system configured correctly?
- Is the server software configured correctly?
- Is the database designed properly?
- Are we implementing security inappropriately?
- Is the application distributed using tiers of components?
- Is there a single point of failure in the application?
- Is the code written efficiently?

Asking the right questions is half the work. Finding out the answers to these questions and then taking the appropriate actions is the other half.

It should also be noted that many of these questions concern areas that are more typically outside the domain of programmers. Applications that have been developed with an eye towards the environment that will be used will often be more successful. Increasingly, a developer of applications needs to think not just as a programmer, but also as a network engineer, a database administrator, and a network architect. Unfortunately, with the accelerating pace of technologies, it is very difficult for a single developer to have the time or energy to stay current with such a broad range of topics. It is almost always a good move to consult with others who are specialists in these areas to gain a wider perspective for your design, and to enlist them in developing the infrastructure your application will run in.

Web Application Scalability

If we define performance as how quickly a web page loads or allows a user to complete a transaction, then scalability can be measured in terms of how well performance is maintained as more and more web users use our application. One obvious solution to the performance problems of a web application is to throw more hardware at the problem – install bigger machines with greater memory and faster processors. However, we will soon reach a point when throwing more hardware will not produce a corresponding improvement in performance, because of the types of bottlenecks we mentioned earlier.

In such a scenario, we would need to consider adding more web servers to meet the increased user demands. When we add multiple web servers, each containing a copy of our web site, it will be possible to meet the increased user demands on our application. This solution, however, adds to the implementation, administration and maintenance chores we need to perform on our web servers.

Scalability can therefore be measured in terms of how easily a web application can scale across multiple web servers, and be implemented, administered and maintained. We shall take a look at the different techniques available to implement multiple web server web applications later in this chapter.

Solving Scaling issues is usually approached using three techniques:

- ❑ Scaling hardware vertically – by adding more memory, faster processors, and upgrading hardware while still maintaining the physical footprint and number of servers in use. The advantage to this approach is simpler site management, but there is a limit to how much we can upgrade in this way. This approach can also be costly since high-end machines demand premium prices.

- ❑ Scaling hardware horizontally – by adding additional web servers, additional database servers and additional machines to handle business tier components. Web farms are a good example of horizontal scaling. Each machine in the farm is effectively a clone of the others and therefore, performs the same functions. The advantage of this method is usually lower up-front cost, but it results in greater site management issues. Also, this solution has the advantage that it will work more or less without limit to the number of servers, while vertical scaling has a definite ceiling defined by the biggest server on the market at any given time.

- ❑ Improving architecture – by identifying similar operations and isolating these operations on dedicated servers. For example, a single high-end machine that hosts both the web server software and database probably would not perform as well as two lower-end machines where one machine acted as a dedicated web server and the other a dedicated database server.

Hardware Performance

Although the typical developer wouldn't have direct control over what hardware the application will run on, they often are asked to provide recommendations for what hardware should be used. In fact, many consulting firms are doing more than just writing applications – they are involved in architecting the infrastructure that the application will run under. To help meet these requirements, a quick look at hardware resources is in order.

When considering hardware performance issues, we have to think of all of the physical components the application uses to transport and process data. This includes not just hardware, but how the hardware is configured. This means looking into how each component interacts with the network, the operating systems used, and our application itself. Some of the most common measures for these interactions are **throughput** and **response time**. Although these terms are related, they are not identical. Throughput is a measure of how much information can be processed at one time, while response time is concerned with the amount of time required to process that information. If an application is inefficient, the response time can be improved with greater throughput. Conversely, response times may be maintained at reasonable levels when throughput is poor by designing an efficient application.

The speed and efficiency of the hardware used will have a direct impact upon throughput and response time. There isn't usually any specific piece of hardware that can be identified as slowing down a system. Although a single hardware component may cause a bottleneck, typically, a number of components should be evaluated. These should include:

❑ amount of memory

❑ clock speed of the CPU

❑ number of processors

❑ available disk space

❑ access speed of the disk drives and disk drive controllers

❑ number of disk drives and disk drive controllers

❑ speed of devices used for backup and restore operations

Memory

The single easiest – and usually cheapest – way to increase performance on a given machine is to increase its memory. Like most hardware, the price of memory has been steadily decreasing year after year, and with today's prices we can easily maximize the amount of RAM on the typical machine for a few hundred dollars. If increasing the amount of memory to the maximum isn't an option, then we should consider adding enough additional memory to insure that our server isn't being constrained by the amount of memory we currently have.

Memory Utilization – Task Manager

One easy way to get a rough estimate of how much memory a server requires to handle its demands is to take a look at Windows **Task Manager**. The Performance Tab will show a Memory Usage History graph that shows how much memory has been in demand over the last few minutes.

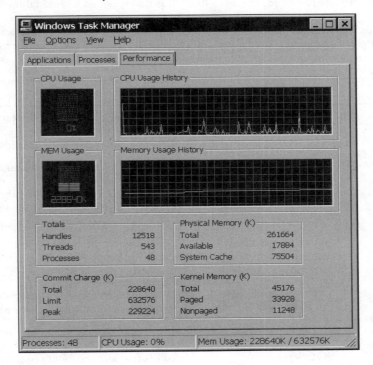

Using the View menu, set the update speed to Low and watch the graph for a few minutes. If the memory usage is consistently higher than the amount of physical RAM, your system is performing well below its capabilities. When the memory demand exceeds the amount of physical memory in the machine, Windows will copy the data from the least recently used segments of RAM onto disk. As fast as today's disk drives are, they are magnitudes slower than RAM, so when memory is copied to disk, performance suffers.

> *Usually, the most important machine to maximize the memory in is the database server. This machine should usually get the best hardware, because it cannot be scaled horizontally as easily as say, a web server, and so it should be scaled vertically as much as possible.*

Memory Utilization – Performance Monitor

To get a much more accurate estimate of memory demand over a longer period of time, use the **Performance Monitor**. This utility, which is run by selecting Programs/Administrative Tools/Performance from the Start menu, provides a series of counters that may be used to monitor the server's activity. The counters available to Performance Monitor depend upon what software is installed. As part of the installation process of any given product, new counters may be installed and are grouped by object. For descriptions of any of the counters installed, double click on the System Overview log in the Counter Logs folder, click Add... in the System Overview Properties dialog box, then select the object and counter names and click the Explain button.

Two useful counters to begin the examination of memory usage are the Pages/sec and % Committed Bytes In Use counters for the Memory object. By monitoring Pages/sec we get a measure of how much activity there is within the system's virtual memory. Similarly, the % Committed Bytes In Use represents the amount of virtual memory in use. The greater both of these numbers are, relative to the amount of memory already fitted, the more likely it is that we need additional memory.

There are other Performance Monitor counters that are more informative when analyzing the memory demands on a particular server. Below is a table describing some of the counters for each type of server that are useful in determining memory demands:

Server	Object: Counter	Notes
IIS	IIS Services Global: Cache Hits %	Measures the effectiveness of the cache. If this value is very low, then a larger cache size may be needed. A value of 80-90% should be considered excellent.
	Process: Working Set: Inetinfo	The physical memory visible to an IIS process. Compare this value with the value of the Memory: Available Bytes counter. If this value continually decreases, you probably have a memory leak in one of your components.
	Active Server Pages: Memory Allocated	The total amount of memory, in bytes, currently allocated by Active Server Pages.
	Cache: Pin Read Hits %	Measures the effectiveness of the *file system cache* used for frequently and repeatedly used file system data.
SQL Server	SQL Server: Buffer Manager: Buffer Cache Hit Ratio	Measures the percentage of requests that were serviced from cache. A ratio of 85-95% should be considered excellent.
	SQL Server: Buffer Manager: Free Buffers	If this value is consistently low, it may indicate that more memory is required.
	SQL Server: Memory Manager: Total Server Memory	If this value is consistently high compared to the amount of physical memory in the computer, it may indicate that more memory is required.
	SQL Server: General Statistics Object: User Connections	This identifies the number of user connections. Monitoring this helps to verify whether connection pooling is working properly – if it is not, then fixing this problem will greatly improve db performance.

Disk Drives and Drive Controllers

It is common to think that disk drives impact performance only insofar as disk access speed may be slow or fast. While it is true that such factors as seek time, latency, and internal data transfer rate of a drive will affect performance, it should be noted that the number of drives and each hard drive's configuration play an even greater role.

When possible, use at least three different drives, each with a separate controller. By having separate controllers, each drive can be accessed concurrently and therefore a huge increase in performance may be realized. But why a minimum of three drives? Well, we would need one drive for the operating system, and at least one drive for our applications and data. In general, we should always separate the operating system from the applications and data. If we wish to add fault tolerance to protect data if one drive goes bad, we will need at least two drives just for our data.

For the sake of our discussion, let's assume that we have already obtained our drives, or, if we haven't, that we would buy the fastest drives within our budget. How would we configure these drives for optimal performance? To answer this question we need to consider the tradeoffs between fault tolerance and performance. There are several approaches for configuring hard drives. These range from **disk spanning**, which combines multiple partitions into a single logical disk, to **disk striping**. These approaches are referred to as **RAID** (Redundant Array of Inexpensive Disks). Fault-tolerant disk systems are categorized in six RAID levels, 0 through 5. Each level offers various mixes of performance, reliability, and cost. Each level uses a different algorithm to implement fault tolerance. Let's look at these in more detail:

RAID Level 0

RAID level 0 is commonly referred to as **disk striping** and uses a disk file system called a **striped set**. Data is divided into 64K blocks and is spread equally, in a fixed order, among all the disks in the array. RAID level 0 improves read and write performance by spreading operations across multiple disks, so that operations can be performed independently and concurrently. Although RAID level 0 offers performance benefits when used with multiple disk controllers, it does *not* offer fault tolerance. If any of the drives in the array goes down, all of the drives may be unusable.

RAID Level 1

RAID level 1 is commonly referred to as **disk mirroring** and uses a disk file system called a **mirror set**. Disk mirroring provides a redundant, identical copy of a selected disk. All data written to the primary disk is written to the mirror disk. This approach offers fault tolerance since the data is duplicated across two drives. The advantage of this approach is that if one drive goes bad, another drive will automatically take over. This mirroring approach generally improves read performance but may degrade write performance unless each drive has its own controller since data is written twice.

RAID Level 2

This is often referred to as **Disk Striping with Error Correction**. Error correcting information is recorded with the striped data that is interleaved among the disks in the array. This approach offers poor disk utilization and is not widely used.

RAID Level 3

This approach is similar to RAID level 2, but uses parity information rather than the Error Correcting information. As with RAID level 2, this approach offers poor disk utilization and is not widely used.

RAID Level 4

Rather than interleaving correction information with the data, this approach writes complete blocks of data on each disk in the array and incorporates parity check information as well. Although RAID level 4 is more robust and has better disk utilization than RAID levels 2 and 3, it suffers from slow performance.

RAID Level 5

RAID level 5 is commonly referred to as **striping with parity** and is the most popular of the RAID levels. It stripes the data in large blocks across all the disks in the array and it writes parity information for those blocks across all the disks. The data redundancy is provided by the parity information. The data and parity information are arranged on the disk array so that the two are always on different disks. Striping with parity has better performance than mirroring (RAID level 1).

Hardware vs. Software RAID Support

Some manufacturers provide RAID support at the hardware level. Windows NT/2000 also supports several fault-tolerant strategies, including RAID 0, 1, and 5. There are advantages and disadvantages with using either approach. The decision on what level of RAID to use and whether it will be implemented as part of the hardware or from the operating system needs to be determined before the server software is installed:

	Advantages	Disadvantages
Hardware-based RAID level 5	Has excellent performance. Does not compete for processor cycles.	Cost
Hardware-based RAID level 1	Has best redundancy. Does not compete for processor cycles.	Cost
Windows based RAID level 1	Has good redundancy. Low cost.	Uses system processing resources.
Windows based RAID level 5	Has excellent read performance. Low cost.	Uses system processing resources.

If you are going to use a cluster of web servers, each server is effectively a backup for any other server in the cluster, so there is little need for anything other than RAID 0. On the other hand, database servers are not often in a cluster, so fault tolerance is more important for them. Database servers often use RAID 5.

I/O Processing

As a general rule, Input/Output (I/O) slows down an application. Reading and writing to physical devices is very slow compared to using memory, so the less disk access your application has the better it will most likely perform.

There are two kinds of I/O, **Sequential** and **Random**. Sequential I/O can be described as when the disk drive is reading information in a contiguous stream, one section of the hard disk after another. This type of access doesn't require the disk drive arms to move around much, which results in faster access. The speed of access with disk drives is often measured as "seek time". In general, we want to use hard drives with a low average seek time (although there are other metrics that may be used to measure the performance of disk drives). Sequential I/O gives us higher throughput since there are fewer and longer accesses to the disk. Sequential I/O offers better performance. Random I/O can be described as when the disk drive head must move from section to section of the drive to acquire data that is not stored contiguously. Random I/O requires much more movement of the disk drive's heads, which results in longer seek times.

When possible, our goal is to reduce the amount of I/O but when it is necessary, maximize the amount of Sequential I/O and minimize Random I/O. There are a number of ways to do this. Here are a few suggestions:

- ❑ Use efficient queries. Don't perform joins against tables unless those tables are needed. Also, when issuing a query, return only the fields and records you are interested in rather than selecting all fields from an entire table or tables.

- ❑ Reduce the number of hits to the database by caching frequently used values in variables rather than repeatedly querying the database.

- ❑ It is important to use indexes in our databases. Using indexes, especially clustered indexes in Microsoft SQL Server, can help substantially to reduce Random I/O.

- ❑ Regularly using tools such as Windows' Disk Defragmenter to help make sure that the files stored on your drives are not spread across the disk will also help to reduce Random I/O.

- ❑ Turn off logging on the web server.

- ❑ Set Response.Expires appropriately so that proxy servers can intelligently cache information that doesn't change often.

- ❑ Schedule I/O intensive operations, such as backing up the server or database, to run during periods of low demand. For any given time zone, the lowest average usage on Internet is around four in the morning.

Network Performance

Just as the speed and efficiency of the hardware used will have a direct impact upon performance, the same may be said about the network that an application runs on. The network must be considered in at least two parts – the Internet and our intranet. We have little control over how fast the external network will behave. The best that we can do is make sure that the bandwidth we subscribe to from our ISP is adequate to meet the needs of our traffic. But within the LAN we do have a great deal of influence on performance. Within our LAN, we want to make sure that incoming requests can be accepted without delay and that these requests are processed quickly.

Network Cards and Subnetworks

The first component of a LAN to look at is the **Network Interface Card** (**NIC**). Each machine in the network must have at least one card to connect it with the network. Since 1986, the majority of NICs that have been installed have been 10 Mbps 10BaseT Ethernet cards. Although 10 Mbps may be adequate for day-to-day intranet office activity, they are far too slow for servicing the Internet. Even if only one machine in a network is connected to the Internet and it has a fast 100 Mbps card, the slower cards found in the other machines can still have an impact on that machine. This is because these machines must still communicate with each other, and if one machine is slow, the faster machine has to wait for it.

One way to prevent slow network cards from degrading the performance of faster cards is by segmenting our intranet. By using a hub or switch we can group like-speed machines together to create sub-networks. Even if all of our machines have 100 Mbps cards, there are some significant benefits to segmenting the network.

We should consider creating a separate sub-network dedicated to our Internet applications. This idea isn't as elaborate as it might first seem. If we plan on investing significant amounts of money into development of an application, spending a little more to insure that the application has the network to support it is certainly justified. By having our Internet servers in a separate sub-network, we reduce the amount of "broadcast noise" or "chatter" that the servers have to listen to that would normally come from the office intranet. This translates to better performance for applications, better security, and a more robust environment for our Intranet.

Notes:

❑ For increased performance, we should consider using a switch rather than a hub. Although switches cost significantly more than hubs, they provide much better throughput

❑ 100 Mbps network cards are not the only option for high-speed communications. 1000 Mbps Ethernet cards are now available. For the latest on the Gigabit Ethernet standard take a look at http://www.gigabit-ethernet.org

Software Performance

When discussing software-related performance issues, we need to consider efficiencies in code and in the environment that the code executes in. Poorly written code or poorly designed algorithms can have a major impact on how long it takes operations to complete. In addition, our application should efficiently utilize available resources, such as disk space, memory, and the processor.

Operating System and Server Software

At the level of the operating system and server software, we can make numerous changes to the settings and configurations that can affect performance. These may include optimizing the amount of virtual memory used by the OS, removing unused network protocols, limiting resources accessible by any single user, and disabling unused services. Here are a few suggestions on how to tune your servers at this level.

Use Performance Monitor

Use Performance Monitor to measure the health and performance of your server to identify issues. One of the first things to do when trying to make performance enhancing configuration changes is to understand what is currently going on and to find out where your bottlenecks are.

This tool is included with both Windows 2000 Advanced Server and Windows 2000 Professional. Performance Monitor allows you to add **counters** that monitor various activities and resources. By adding counters, you can track almost every aspect of your server with visual graphs. Performance Monitor also includes facilities for reporting and alerting based on ongoing activity. Performance Monitor also lets you connect to other machines on your network to evaluate their performance.

Web Server Master Properties

Master properties allows us to define default settings for all of the web sites on our server. Master properties are ideal for establishing common parameters between web sites, such as connection limits and bandwidth consumption.

You can access these properties from Computer Manager. Select Internet Information Services in the tree tab, right-click, and select Properties. You will be presented with a tabbed dialog:

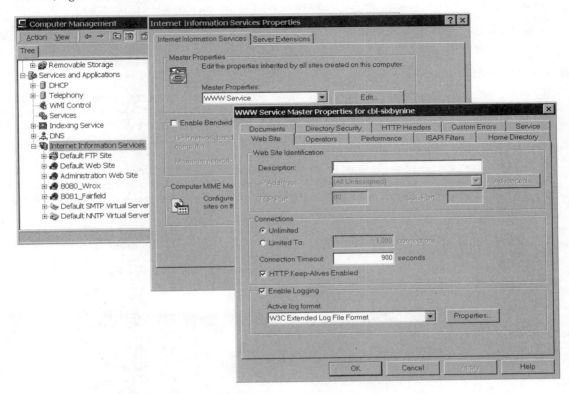

There are a number of properties that we can control that directly influence server performance, such as Connection limitations and Bandwidth throttling. Each of these properties may affect each other, so you will need to experiment to find which combinations of settings work best for your sites. Each of these properties can be modified for individual web sites you can fine-tune how each site works.

Connection Llimitations

Although we want to attract as many users to our sites as possible, it is only realistic to accept that there is a limit to how many people we can service at one time. On the Web Site tab is a group of connection limitation options. The first setting allows us to place a cap on how many simultaneous connections may be served by any given site. By limiting the number of connections, we are less likely to have our server performance fall to a crawl while trying to service a large number of visitors. You need to make a business decision before using this option. Is it more desirable to service *any* number of users although that service may be *extremely* slow or is it more important to service a limited, but still very large, number of users with a minimum level of response?

In addition to limiting the number of simultaneous connections, you can also define the web service connection time-out. This time-out is used to determine when a visitor's session is closed if a network error occurs, rather than leave the session open indefinitely. A timeout value should *always* be used.

Establishing connections to a server is costly in terms of time and resources. The HTTP Keep-Alives setting allows a client to maintain an open connection with our server, rather than re-opening the client connection with each new request. Although enabling this setting may have performance advantages, it does come with a price – it will require more connections to be used. You should experiment to see if using this setting, in combination with connection limits, gives you a performance boost. If you enable this setting, you may need to increase the number of simultaneous connections that are allowed.

Bandwidth Throttling

If you want to limit the overall network bandwidth usage by the web service, you can define an upper limit. This is convenient if you want to ensure that your entire network pipe is not used up by your web server. All values for bandwidth throttling are based on kilobytes per second (KB/s).

Performance Tuning Based Upon Volume of Hits

On the Performance tab of the Master Properties dialog, you will find a slider control that will adjust the number of resources allocated for servicing connections. This setting is based upon how many hits per day your site will get. If this setting is too high, you will be reserving resources for hits that never come, and therefore are never used.

The default value for this setting is "Fewer than 100,000". It may be too optimistic for your web site to have tens of thousands of hits per day, especially when it is first published. You should start with the lower setting of "Fewer than 10,000" and when your volume exceeds 10,000, consider adjusting this setting upwards:

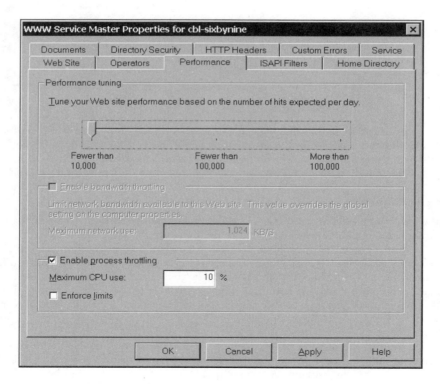

Operating System Performance

As far as what can be done to configure an efficient, high performance operating system is concerned, much is beyond the developer's control but there are some options available to us. Here are a number of performance tweaks that you should consider. You will need to work with your network administrators to make sure that any of these suggestions will not cause conflicts with other servers' software that resides on the same machine. Of course, you should experiment with these settings to determine which ones give you the best overall performance.

❑ Place the operating system's virtual memory swap file on the fastest disk drive you have. If you have more than one disk drive controller in your server, consider splitting this virtual memory across different drives that use different controllers. This way, you can access multiple drives simultaneously.

❑ Remove any network protocols that are not needed. For example, most Internet communications use TCP/IP, so there may not be a need to have the AppleTalk Protocol installed.

❑ Another performance tweak for servers is to reduce the priority of the foreground application and increase the priority of services. This can be done via the Advanced tab of the System Properties dialog. Change the setting in the Application response group to use Background services:

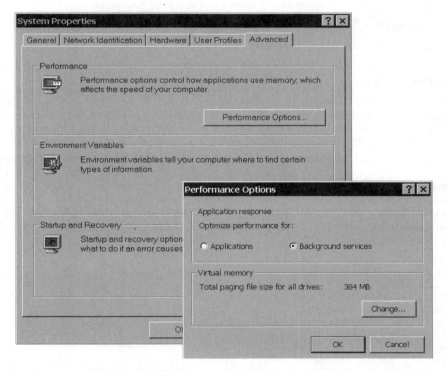

❑ Leave the server logged off. When no one is logged onto the server, the operating system doesn't load a lot of system components needed for an interactive account and thus can give the application added resources.

❑ Don't use a screen saver on your servers. When screen savers kick in they become the server's "foreground application", which usually means they will command the greatest attention of the system's resources. It is much more efficient not to use a screen saver and simply to turn off the server's monitor when not in use.

Application Performance

When developing ASP web applications, we should always have performance in mind. Even if we are developing a small site for a small audience, there is no harm in developing with slightly better performance as a design objective. For that reason, tips and techniques for improving performance, and advice on what to do when developing ASP applications are given in various chapters of this book. This section elaborates on some of them.

When we are developing large-volume web applications, better performance is not only a design objective; often it is a mandate from the business owners of the project. We can use guidelines to improve our ASP code performance. There are several key elements we can use that would especially benefit a large volume web application:

❑ Reduce hits and fetches against the data store by caching data that does not change often – data that is usually used to populate list boxes and combo boxes on a page

❑ Reduce unnecessary ASP parsing and ASP execution of pages that are relatively static – pages that do not change very often

❑ When accessing the data store, do so in a fast and efficient manner

❑ Optimize the content that is sent to the client

❑ Optimize the ASP Scripting code

Reducing Database Hits

If data is fetched from the database to populate an HTML select control on a form, we can reduce this database hit the next time the same or a different user requires the same data by caching the relevant information. Remember that the data from the database will be fetched in the form of a recordset in order to create the SELECT statement. We *do not* want to cache the recordset variable, either in the Session object or in the Application object; we need to cache the information from the recordset.

Consider the following pseudocode for a typical approach where we would populate an HTML SELECT control with data from a database. First, we establish a connection to the database. Second, we query the database to populate a recordset with data. Next, we "walk" the recordset and build an OPTION item tag for each row in the recordset. Finally, we close the recordset and disconnect from the database:

```
Open Connection to the Database
Get a recordset filled with data you need to display

Output the <SELECT> tag for the SELECT control
Do while not Recordset.EOF
   Ouput the <OPTION> item tag for each row of the recordset
   Recordset.MoveNext
Loop
Output the </SELECT> tag to end the SELECT control definition
Close Recordset
Close Connection
```

Each time a user accesses the page containing the SELECT control, the above cycle is repeated, forcing a database hit again and again for data that does not change often.

Alternatively, consider the following pseudocode that changes this cycle:

```
Open Connection to the Database
Get a Recordset filled with data you need to display
'
Do while not Recordset.EOF
    Build a list of <OPTION> item tags,
        one for each row of the recordset
    Recordset.MoveNext
Loop
Close Recordset
Close Connection
'
Output the <SELECT> tag for the SELECT control
Output the list of <OPTION> tags built previously
Output the </SELECT> tag to end the SELECT control definition
```

As we can see, the outputting of the <OPTION> tag list is separated from the actual process of acquiring it from the database. We did not really gain anything with this change.

However, we can refine this method to store the data in the Application object and reuse it over and over again. Consider this refined pseudocode:

```
Check the Application Object containing <OPTION> tags for data
If no data exists Then
    Open Connection to the Database
    Get a Recordset filled with data you need to display
    '
    Do while not Recordset.EOF
        Build a list of <OPTION> item tags,
            one for each row of the recordset
        Recordset.MoveNext
    Loop
    Close Recordset
    Close Connection
    '
    Store the list in the Application Object for the next cycle
End if


'
Output the <SELECT> tag for the SELECT control
Output the list of <OPTION> tags built previously
Output the </SELECT> tag to end the SELECT control definition
```

With this refined code, we see that the items for a HTML SELECT control are obtained from a cached Application Object variable. The first time any user hits the web site and requests the page containing the SELECT control we make a database hit. We immediately store the items in an Application variable. For every subsequent hit on the page, we access the data directly from the Application Variable. If there are 1000 requests to the page, there will be only 1 database hit.

Using the Database Server's Capability to Optimally Fetch Data

Instead of writing SQL statements in ASP code, and then executing them against the database server, we can use database server side capability. We should use SQL stored procedures instead of SQL statements in the ASP page. Executing a stored procedure on the database server will be faster than executing native SQL statements. If we are building dynamic SQL statements based on parameters obtained from the user, we should create stored procedures that accept arguments and generate dynamic SQL statements that include the name of the stored procedure and its arguments, or use the Command object to pass parameters to the stored procedures.

Within stored procedures, we can build temporary tables that will hold data in the format that we want our ASP page to display. We can use these temporary tables to gather data from different sources within the database and return the temporary table data to the ASP page. The ASP page then just needs to dump the data back to the browser without having to manipulate it further. Since all the processing is handled by the database server, and assuming the amount of data being passed back to the ASP page is smaller, we will obtain a performance improvement.

Access the Data Efficiently

Stored procedures should be used, whenever possible, to access the database for a number of reasons. Stored procedures are SQL code modules that are precompiled and saved on the server. Because stored procedures can contain multiple SQL statements as well as programming logic, you can perform a series of related operations together by executing a single stored procedure. This means that the database avoids having to parse and process each SQL command separately, therefore using stored procedures is more efficient. Using stored procedures may also reduce network traffic since only the call to the stored procedure and parameter values needs to be transmitted rather than successive SQL statements.

You should also optimize the queries used by your application as well as in the stored procedures. A poorly constructed query may take many times longer than a more efficient one. Use tools such as Microsoft SQL Server's Query Analyzer to examine the steps required to process the query. By seeing the overall distribution of effort taken by the query engine, you can better target where to optimize your SQL code:

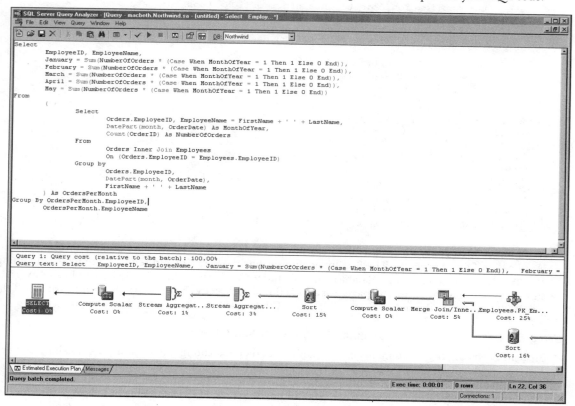

❑   Chapter 14 discusses how to use SQL Server's Query Analyzer.

Minimize Connection Time

With a high volume site that uses a database, you want to avoid maintaining a connection to the database as much as possible. As far as possible, we should open a database connection and execute a database action as late as possible in our code, process or cache the results, and then disconnect immediately. By disconnecting as soon as possible, you are making those connections's resources used by the RDBMS available to other users.

For example, we should not open a database connection and then take time to process variables, create a SQL statement, validate the data and finally execute the SQL Statement. For the brief time when all the activity is taking place, we are holding on to a database connection that could otherwise be used by another process. Instead, we should ensure that all the processing is carried out, data is validated, and the SQL statement is generated, before the connection is opened. After the SQL statement is executed, the connection should be shut down as early as possible.

Releasing Objects As Soon As Possible

As soon as we are done with an object – whether it's a COM component or an ADO object, we should release it by setting its value to nothing. By setting the value to nothing, you destroy the object's reference and the object's resources then can be reclaimed and made available for others.

Streamlining HTML

We should examine our HTML code to see if it is possible to make improvements that will enable browsers to render the page faster. For example, we should always use the WIDTH and HEIGHT attributes with any IMAGE (IMG) tags. This allows the browser to draw a placeholder of the appropriate size on the page and continue to render the text content while the image is downloading. When the image has finished downloading, it is placed into the spot where its placeholder resides. The result – the page appears on screen faster. If we do not supply the WIDTH and the HEIGHT attributes, the text content is rendered on the page, but when the image has downloaded completely, the text content needs to be redrawn to accommodate the new image.

Most browsers will not render the contents of a table until the ending table tag, </TABLE>, has been encountered. If we are displaying a long list of data from a database in the form of table rows and columns, we should break up the list into multiple tables. Each table will sit on top of the one below, and together, they will appear to be one large table. However, as soon as the ending table tag is received by the browser, it will render it on screen.

Again, the result is a page that appears on the browser faster. While the user is still going through the beginning rows of the first table, the browser can download and render the other table data. One good technique we practice in our company is that when we display data from a database in the form of a long table of rows and columns, we keep track of the number of rows being displayed. When the row count reaches 20 or so, we break the table and generate a fresh set of column headers for the next table, and continue processing the data. The result is a long list that the user can scroll, and still be able to see the column headers, without having to scroll back all the way to the top to figure out what the third column, for instance, contains.

We should pay close attention to the size of our HTML output page, as well as the size of the graphics we have included in our page. We can use graphic tools to reduce the size of graphics and optimize them for web delivery.

If we are mixing ASP code with HTML code within a page, we should try to reduce the amount of "context switching." This refers to the interspersing of script blocks and HTML text. When the web server has to alternate between ASP code and HTML it will take a small performance hit as it switches between the scripting engines. This performance hit is negligible in most circumstances, except for within large loops.

For example, instead of writing code as follows:

```
<%
    Do While Not objRS.EOF
%>
<TR>
<TD><%= objRS("field1") %></TD>
<TD><%= objRS("field2") %></TD>
<TD><%= objRS("field3") %></TD>
<TD><%= objRS("field4") %></TD>
<TD><%= objRS("field5") %></TD>
</TR>
<%
        objRS.MoveNext
    Loop
%>
```

We should use the following code snippet that produces the same result, but performs all of the work as part of ASP code. Rather than alternating between HTML and scripting code, this approach uses only VBScript to store the combination of the HTML tags and the data from the recordset as a string and then outputs that variable's content:

```
<%
    Dim strBuff
    Do While Not objRS.EOF
        StrBuff = "<TR>" & _
        "<TD>" & objRS("field1") & "</TD>" & _
        "<TD>" & objRS("field2") & "</TD>" & _
        "<TD>" & objRS("field3") & "</TD>" & _
        "<TD>" & objRS("field4") & "</TD>" & _
        "<TD>" & objRS("field5") & "</TD>" & _
        "</TR>"

        Response.write strBuff

        objRS.MoveNext
    Loop
%>
```

Choose Your Files Wisely

Because everything you send to a user from your site is a file, you should be conscious of file size and delivery speed of those files. File size and delivery speeds are closely linked, but not necessarily mutually inclusive. Much will depend upon what is required to process the files. When you are planning your site, it is important to consider what file type will have the most profound effects on your site's performance, for both speed and size.

Browsers can handle simple files like JPEG, bitmaps, and GIF, but streaming media may be an issue. Audio files also have a variety of file types, ranging from WAV and AU files to RealAudio RAM files. Streaming video also comes in a variety of formats. If you plan on supporting multiple formats, you may need to have more than one product running to service these streaming formats. Each streaming engine will cause overhead for the server – more server resources are used, connections are open longer, more memory and bandwidth is used, and of course storage space is consumed.

You should also consider the file formats used for your graphics. When should you use a GIF and when should you use a JPEG image? What about bitmaps? The answer concerns which one produces the smallest file and whether or not you need special effects. Our goal is to use that format which gives us what we want in the smallest possible file. If we choose the wrong format, we may end up with images that are 300K in size rather than 16K.

Unless you need some special effect, such as a transparent background or animation, the rule of thumb is that JPEG images are best used for "continuous tone" photographic images, the GIF format is best for images that have large areas of solid color, and bitmaps (BMP) should be altogether avoided. There is little that a bitmap can offer you that a JPEG or GIF can't, and bitmap files are not compressed so they tend to be huge in comparison to the other formats. The way to find out which format to use is simple: you save an image in each format and then compare file sizes and how they look. Because of color pallet differences in the formats, you may need to use a larger format to keep the appropriate colors. If you do need an image with a transparent background or simple animation, you will need to go with a GIF or use some more advanced technology such as Flash.

Reducing Unnecessary ASP Parsing and Execution

If a page displays data that does not change often, we can pre-generate the page and either save it as an ASP page or save it as an HTML page on our web site. So we can build web applications that mix ASP pages with static HTML pages to improve performance.

If we change the page extension to an HTML page from an ASP page, we will also need to update the links from other pages that refer to the changed page. We can either achieve this manually or use tools that automatically crawl through our web site creating static versions of our dynamic pages and automatically update the links in all pages that refer to a particular static page. One such tool is XBuilder from http://www.xbuilder.net. XBuilder converts selected pages to static HTML, readjusting links and renaming pages to make pages download faster. XBuilder also compresses the static HTML to add additional speed improvement. We can choose to compile an entire site or only selected pages, creating a hybrid site that can then be deployed. You can also use languages such as Perl, Visual Basic, or Visual C++ to build static pages from dynamic content and then host those pages on a server.

Apart from the above two techniques, which have a major impact on web applications, there are a host of different techniques that can be used to improve performance. None of these by themselves will make a dramatic change but their cumulative effect will enable our applications to perform better.

Reducing Object Name Lookups

If we are using the Session object, Application object, Response object or Request object in ASP pages, then it is possible to reduce the overhead caused by the VBScript engine performing name lookups of the object variable.

Instead of using the Session("var") syntax each time, we can cache this value in a variable at the beginning of our page, and then later on, use the variable:

```
Dim objSession, strVar
Set objSession = Session

    later on in your code

strVariable = objSession("var")
```

We can use a similar approach for the `Application`, `Request`, and `Response` objects. Similarly, if there is a value within the collections of these built-in objects that is used frequently, we can place it in a local variable early on, and then use the local variable value in our code:

```
Dim strVar
StrVar = Session("var")

     later on in your code

Response.write strVar ' Instead of Response.write Session("var")
```

When Possible, Avoid Using CreateObject

Here's a tip for those of us not yet using IIS 5.x. As a general guideline, within our ASP pages running under IIS 4, we should use the `Server.CreateObject` function, rather than the `CreateObject` function. However, if we are not deploying our application using MTS, or if the object we are trying to create is not an MTS object, `CreateObject` is slightly faster than `Server.CreateObject`. This is because it reduces activation time, since no MTS context wrapper is created for the object when the `CreateObject` method is used directly. Another alternative is to use the `<OBJECT>` tags when possible.

Disable the Session Object

Disable the `Session` object on a page-by-page basis with the `<%@ EnableSessionState = False %>` statement. This declarative allows ASP to process scripts concurrently, rather than sequentially.

Optimize Your VBScript Code

There are a number of simple techniques to help your VBScript perform faster:

❑ Avoid redimensioning arrays. This action is very costly and slow, especially if the `Preserve` option is used. Rather that redimensioning arrays, declare them with a size that is likely to handle the highest volumes of data. The loss in performance from using the extra memory required for over-estimating the size of arrays is greatly outweighed by not having to resize the arrays.

❑ Use ordinal references rather than name of items in a collection. Referencing a variable by ordinal value is significantly faster than referencing it by name. For example, a call to a Field object such as `rsClientPhones(1)` will be faster than using `rsClientPhones("LastName")`.

❑ Retrieving values from collections is relatively slow. Store retrieved values in local variables if you need to access them more than once.

❑ When referencing more than one member of an object, make sure that you use the `With...End With` block. This will provide faster access to the object. For example:

```
'-- Create the connection object.
Set cnDB = Server.CreateObject("ADODB.Connection")
'-- Configure the connection object.
With cnDB
    .ConnectionTimeout = 60
    .Open "File Name=D:\Webs\808_Pubs\data\pubs.UDL"
End With
```

❑ Always explicitly declare your variables. Declared variables are faster to process than undeclared variables as undeclared variables are referenced by name. Declared variables, on the other hand, are assigned an ordinal, either at compile time or run time, and this ordinal value is always used for referencing the variable.

❏   Rather than using an include file for constants, such as those for ADO, use the `METADATA` tag to reference the type library of the object model:

```
<!-- METADATA TYPE="typelib"
     FILE="C:\Program Files\Common Files\System\ado\msado15.dll" -->
```

If you are using IIS 5.0, you may also try:

```
<!-- METADATA NAME="Microsoft ActiveX Data Objects 2.5 Library"
     TYPE="TypeLib" UUID="{00000205-0000-0010-8000-00AA006D2EA4}" -->
```

For you to use this second method, you will need to know the exact name and type library identifier. To find out this information, you can search the system's Registry for the name of the type library under `HKEY_LOCAL_MACHINE\SOFTWARE\Classes\TypeLib`. For example, a search for "Microsoft ActiveX Data Objects" will eventual find, if installed, the ADO 2.5 type library. The folder immediately above the folder for version 2.5 will be named with the value required for the UUID attribute:

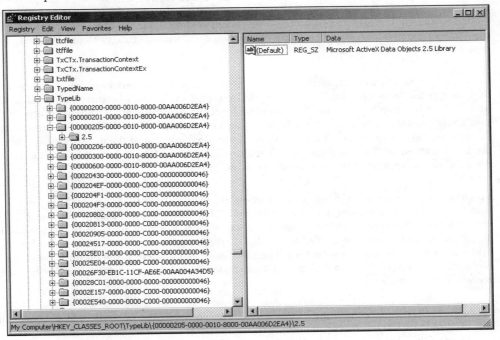

Scalability and Reliability through Clustering

Hopefully, any Internet site that we develop will be visited by lots of people. As the number of visitors rises, more demand will be placed upon the network, the servers, and the application. Eventually the load on the system will become great enough for performance to be affected. One way of responding to greater demand is to replace the existing servers with bigger, faster machines. Another way is to simply use more machines. It is recommended, when possible, to keep the database server and IIS web server on different machines. If and when these services are located on different boxes and performance is still an issue, we should look into using multiple machines for each service. This is called **clustering**.

Even if an application isn't expected to draw enough demand to justify using multiple servers, there is another reason for using them. What happens if one machine needs to go down for maintenance or simply fails? For many commercial sites, a guaranteed 24 hours a day, seven days a week uptime must be maintained. By using clustering, the different machines act as backup devices for each other.

If you have used Windows Domains, you are probably already familiar with some of the concepts used in clustering. In every Windows domain there is at least one **Domain Controller (DC)** that is used for authentication purposes. During normal operations, the various domain controls replicate the security information between themselves on a regular basis. If one of the DCs goes offline, another DC will be able to take over that failing DC's responsibilities. Since each DC will have been regularly updated with security information, any of the DCs can take over authentication seamlessly. In many clustering scenarios, a similar failsafe mechanism takes place.

Clustering with Microsoft SQL Server

Microsoft SQL Server provides clustering features in its Enterprise edition. There are two configurations for clustering with SQL Server: **Active-Passive** and **Active-Active**. The former configuration uses one machine to perform the work and the second machine takes over if the first one fails. The Active-Active configuration, on the other hand, has *both* servers providing database services at all times, thus distributing the demands between them. In both configurations, changes to one database must be replicated in the other.

In order for this database clustering to work, the two database servers must be in constant contact. Each SQL Server machine has installed in it an additional network card which is used to establish a **heartbeat** between the two machines. If the first machine loses the heartbeat of the second, it attempts to reestablish contact using the first machine's other network card. This failsafe mechanism ensures that the two machines can stay in contact with each other even if one of the network cards dies. Because of the traffic caused by this heartbeat, and from the replication of data, it is generally a good idea to place the database servers within their own subnetwork.

To enhance performance and reliability even more, the database files used by SQL Server to store content are placed on a third device – an *external RAID device*. With this approach, each SQL Server machine only holds the stored procedures, views, triggers, etc. that are used to manipulate the data. The data itself is located on a highly redundant RAID device connected to the servers with a high bandwidth cable, such as a fiber optic connection. The advantage gained here is the elimination of the constant replication between the two machines. Without having to perform replication, there is less load on the servers and less network traffic.

As useful as SQL Server clustering is, unless we have the Enterprise editions of SQL Server and Windows NT, or Windows 2000, this type of clustering isn't an option. So, if we don't have access to the Enterprise edition of SQL, what can we do to utilize two SQL Server machines to increase performance?

Well, we can partition the functionality of the database across the two servers. Exactly how we would do this would depend upon the application, but here are a few examples of how this could be achieved:

❑ If an application requires that the user logs onto the system by supplying a username and password that is stored in a database table, this operation may be a good candidate for offloading onto another SQL Server.

❑ We might locate some of the tables in the database on each server. When queries are run using tables from both servers, we can simply use the `server.database.owner.tablename` syntax to reference each remote table. This works very well so long as a certain amount of aged or historical data needs to be kept in the database but is not frequently referenced. We can set up a regularly scheduled task that transfers this historical data from the main SQL Server to the secondary one, then construct views that, when invoked, perform a union join between the tables from both servers.

❑ If we need to perform replication to remote machines over some slow link, such as some non-dedicated line, we can utilize the second SQL Server as a **distributor**. Replication can occur between the primary (**publishing**) SQL Server to the distributor over a high-speed LAN. The distributor then contacts the other SQL Server machines that are to receive the data (the **subscriber machines**) over the slow link. This replication model frees up the publishing server to be more responsive to the minute-by-minute activities of the application.

It should be noted that these partitioning schemes may be used with more than two servers – not just SQL Servers – and some partitioning approaches may even be used in conjunction with SQL Server clusters.

Clustering with Web Farms

Like SQL Server clusters, we can group together more than one web server into a cluster called a **web farm**. Using web farms increases the number of simultaneous users that an application can service as well as providing increased availability, since each server can act as a fail-over for the others.

To understand how web farms work, let's review how a request from a browser is processed within a *single* web server. First, the request arrives at the web server from the Internet. The request is parsed, analyzed, and then processed. Typically, this request requires some communication with the database. The database acquires the data and sends it back to the web server where server-side ASP code integrates it with HTML to produce a page. This page is then sent back to the requesting browser.

What happens when the number of requests increases? The server's response time increases and delays occur. What happens when there are too many requests for the server to handle? At best, there is a delay in processing the request, but more likely the connection times out. If the number of connections that the web server can accept is exceeded, then the request never even makes it to the server. Also, if the web server goes down, because of failure or, perhaps, because of necessary maintenance, the whole site goes down.

Now consider having four web servers. Requests may be serviced by any of the servers. If the requests are distributed equally among the servers they can process more requests concurrently. Since the demand on each server is kept relatively low, they can each perform quickly. If any server goes offline, then there are others that will continue to service requests.

So, the more web servers we have, the faster our web site will be? No, not always. Web servers have the ability to cache used pages and objects. Ideally, the majority of objects being served will be found in the cache, so the server will not have to waste time performing slow disk reads. If we have too many web servers, then the demands on any single server may not be enough to efficiently use this cache. But if we have too many servers, it's an easy problem to deal with compared to not having enough. We can always opt not to use the extra web server, or servers, except when one of the other servers goes down.

This begs the question of how we know which servers to send requests to? The answer is **load balancing**. Load balancing may be implemented through hardware, such as products from Cisco Systems and Cabletron, or through software, such as from Microsoft. Regardless of the implementation, the overall concept of what load balancing does is essentially the same. That is, it distributes the traffic among the various web servers. By using load balancing, all of the servers in the web farm appear as one big virtual server, and client requests are distributed across a cluster of servers.

Load Balancing Schemes

There are several approaches to determining which server will receive an incoming request. Some use sophisticated hardware to monitor traffic, while others are software based and are relatively inexpensive (or free). We'll take a brief look at some of the more widely used approaches and see how they balance load and provide fault tolerance.

Round Robin Load Balancing

When users make a request from their browser, the URL they entered is sent to their ISP. At the ISP, the address of this URL's domain is referenced and the request is routed to our domain's Domain Name Server (DNS). It is in the DNS Server where the exact IP address of the requested machine on our network is determined. **Round Robin Load Balancing** works by assigning the IP addresses of each of our web servers to the same name:

```
www.acmeaquarium.com    196.196.196.1    Web Server A
www.acmeaquarium.com    196.196.196.2    Web Server B
www.acmeaquarium.com    196.196.196.3    Web Server C
```

When the DNS Server resolves the first address for this name, it uses the first IP address for web server A. The next request will be resolved to web server B, and so on. Using a Round Robin approach, the number of requests across each server should be equal.

The problem with this scheme is that although the number of requests may be balanced among the servers, no consideration is made as to how active the server is or how much horsepower the server has. In the event of a server failure, Round Robin doesn't realize that the server is offline and continues to route requests to the failed server.

However, even with these failings, there are some advantages to using Round Robin loading balancing. It is very easy to maintain and has no impact upon the hardware configuration of our servers. And best of all, it doesn't cost anything.

Dispatcher Load Balancing

Dispatcher Load Balancing (**DLB**) software is a bit more sophisticated than the Round Robin scheme. Rather than relying solely upon the DNS Server, a different server on the network accepts all requests to the web servers from the DNS Server and then routes the requests to the appropriate server. Like Round Robin, Dispatcher Load Balancing still routes requests to the various servers in a formulaic way, but it allows us to specify the percentage of the requests that are sent to each server. This way, we can have servers of different configurations and send more requests to those servers that can handle more. Although this scheme is better than simple Round Robin and is relatively inexpensive, it still doesn't take into consideration how much activity each server has.

To illustrate this problem, suppose that we have three servers, A, B, and C. Server A is a dual Pentium 800 MHz box with a half a gigabyte of memory while servers B and C are single processor Pentium 400 MHz machines with 128 Mb of memory each. Load balancing is configured so that 60% of the requests are sent to server A and 20% are sent to each of the others. 9 requests come into the DLB, so 5 are sent to server A and 2 are sent to each of the others. As luck would have it, 8 of the 9 requests were for small static pages that were serviced quickly, but the 9th request, sent to server A, is for a labor intensive ASP page. It is very possible that when a new request comes in, it will be sent to Server A, even though both of the other servers are idle.

Another problem with using dispatchers is that the throughput of the entire site is limited by the speed and processing power of the dispatcher server. For high traffic sites, the dispatcher server must be fast and powerful, or its limitations may be crippling.

Hardware-based Load Balancing

A much more sophisticated approach to load balancing can be found in many hardware-based products. The most notable is the award winning Local Director from Cisco Systems. Local Director is a **Hardware Load Balancer** (**HLB**) that sits between the Internet connection and our web servers. Unlike Round Robin Load Balancing, all of the servers in the web farm appear to have the same IP address to the outside world:

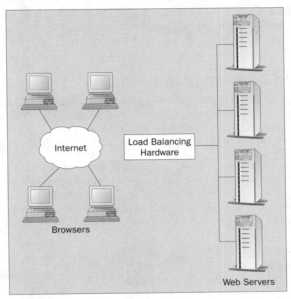

Rather than blindly sending requests in some predetermined order, the HLB monitors network activity and directs incoming requests to the currently highest performing server in the network. This is accomplished by polling the servers. When the least active server is determined, the HLB transparently routes the request to that server.

Hardware load balancing is generally expensive, ranging in the thousands of dollars, but for high-volume sites it is money well spent. Not only do HLBs offer intelligent and efficient routing, but they also provide fault tolerance since, through polling, the HLB can detect when a server goes down and will not send requests to a machine that is offline.

Network Load Balancing and Windows NT Load Balancing Service

Microsoft offers load balancing software for use with Windows domains called **Network Load Balancing** (**NLB**). This product was first introduced for Windows NT Server 4.0 under the name **Windows NT Load Balancing Service** (**WLBS**).

These products install as a standard Windows networking driver and run transparently on an existing LAN. As with other load balancing schemes, client machines access the servers in the cluster by using one IP address. Network traffic is balanced between the clustered computers, and if a server fails or goes offline, the load balancing service automatically reconfigures the cluster to direct the client connections to the surviving computers. Later on, when the offline computer comes back up, it transparently rejoins the cluster and regains its share of the workload.

NLB/WLBS offers a number of additional advantages over other load balancing strategies. With hardware load balancing, if the HLB unit fails, the site goes down unless a redundant device is installed.

Having a second costly HLB unit which doesn't do anything except wait for a failure may not be the best way to spend money. Since NLB/WLBS runs as a service on each machine, there is no single point of failure. Another advantage is that these services have a significantly higher throughput and can even support the newer 1000baseT Gigabit Ethernet standard.

WLBS may be downloaded from Microsoft free of charge at `http://www.microsoft.com/ NTServer/all/downloads.asp#WindowsNTServerFeatures.`

Load Balancing and Segmented Networks

Unless we are using Round Robin Load Balancing, there will be some additional network traffic generated. Although the traffic generated is about one broadcast per second, this additional noise on the line (called "chatter") may merit segmenting the cluster from other portions of the network. This additional network traffic becomes more and more significant as the number of servers in the cluster increases.

Take a look at the following illustration. When a user request comes to the site from the Internet, the request is processed by a high-speed switch. This switch directs requests to the appropriate subnetwork. The first subnetwork includes a hardware load balancer that distributes requests to the web farm. The second subnetwork contains a firewall that leads to the database cluster. The databases are configured for Active-Passive use and are connected to an external RAID device using high-speed fiber cables:

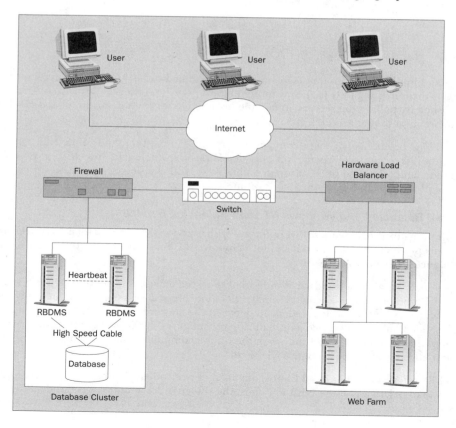

This design offers a number of advantages. First, the two subnetworks are isolated from each other to reduce network chatter. The servers that comprise the web farm are load balanced for performance and redundancy. Note that the web farm is not behind a firewall, so as not to avoid any issues with authentication, as we will in Chapter 35. 100% uptime is achieved by having the database cluster set up in an Active-Passive configuration and the external storage device that houses the database is configured with RAID 5.

ASP Considerations with Web Farms

If we plan to implement web farms, there are some ASP programming issues that need to be in place, while there are other techniques that we can use to improve scalability. Many of these issues and techniques concern stateless programming. State becomes a big issue when using a web farm since the server serving any given page may be different from the server that served the prior page.

Typically in an internet application, state is maintained through the use of session variables. Session variables have two characteristics that are a distinct disadvantage when we are building web farms; they consume memory and are limited to a single server.

Session variables use up precious computer memory and hold on to this memory for the duration of the session (usually 20 minutes). As the number of users increases, the amount of memory being used on the machine increases dramatically, degrading performance.

Session variables reside in the memory of the web server where they were created. In a web farm scenario, an ASP page can be accessed from one physical web server and a subsequent page can be accessed from a different web server. If the first ASP page created the session variable and the second ASP page requires the value in that session variable, we will encounter trouble. The session variable has been created on the first web server. When the second page is requested, there is no session variable in place on the second web server and the ASP page code will fail.

We can get around this limitation by making sure that once a user acquires a page from a specific web server, all other requests from the same user are always routed to the same web server. This feature, often called "establishing a sticky connection", is available in many hardware and software load balancing products. If we use sticky connections, we can still continue to use Session variables. However, this workaround defeats the very purpose of a web farm – which is that all requests may be serviced by any machine in the farm.

As alternatives, we can send whatever state information is needed along with each request to the server. This state information can be saved on the client machine using cookies and/or stored in hidden fields on an HTML form. For example, we may need to send some identifier for the user each time they access a secured page. When the user first successfully logs into the system, we can record this fact, along with their userID in a cookie. This cookie then may be used to populate a hidden field in the HTML forms used in later pages. When the form is submitted, the user's userID will be sent and used as the identifier for accessing their information in the database.

Summary

Performance is important to any application, but more so for Internet applications. There is seldom any one specific reason why a given application may perform poorly. Usually there are a number of reasons that compound the effect of diminished performance. These may be design issues, poor technique, hardware-related, or poor configurations. As we have discussed, performance is difficult to define clearly since it means different things to different people, but a good working definition of performance includes some measurement of how fast the application completes its operations.

Performance is not the same thing as scalability. Scalability is related to performance, but deals with how well an application functions when the number of users increases significantly. Reliability is another related concept that is concerned with how consistently an application will be able to perform.

In this chapter, we addressed a number of issues that have an effect on performance. These issues were broken down into several areas: hardware, network, operating system, server software, and the application. Although we discussed a number of topics at each level, for the developer, we found that making improvements to the application gives us the best return for our efforts.

Regardless of where the inefficiencies occur, our first job is to find out where the bottlenecks are in our application. By using such tools as Performance Monitor, we can examine the health and load of our servers to discover where our efforts are best placed.

Improvements in the efficiency of the application's coding can have a tremendous impact on overall performance. Similarly, the architecture of the application influences performance greatly. By using an N-tier approach, we can add clustering so take advantage of web farms and database clusters to increase performance and add scalability and reliability.

35
Security

When discussing security, we could consider a wide range of topics, from firewalls, proxy servers and the physical security of the machines being used, through to the secure processing of e-commerce transactions and the prevention of hackers. However, what we will discuss in this chapter are those security topics that are most important to ASP developers and we will try not to concentrate on those aspects of security that are normally the domain of network administrators and other IT professionals.

But what are the security topics that are most important to ASP developers? This will vary from developer to developer depending upon the nature of the application being developed, but the most common topics include:

- ❑ Allowing restricted access to the application and its data by users.
- ❑ Providing appropriately secured e-commerce transactions.
- ❑ Building appropriate safeguards into each tier of your application to prevent hacking and unauthorized use.
- ❑ The development of "safe" components that identify your organization, so that, if needed, users can install these components on their clients.
- ❑ Allow for "confidential personalization" in your applications.

In order to address these concerns we have a number of tools and technologies at our disposal including those built into Windows 2000, Internet Information Services (IIS), database management systems, and custom solutions developed through coding:

- ❑ IIS is integrated with Windows NT/2000 file security which requires that every file and application must be accessed by a Windows user account – either the IIS anonymous user or a user that has been authenticated to the server. We can specify which users are allowed access to our web sites or individual folders or files.
- ❑ The authentication of users can be performed using several methods to support the widest possible range of browsers, including encrypted password information and digital certificates.
- ❑ Data can be kept confidential and secure over the network through the use of encryption.
- ❑ Users may be tracked through the use of cookies.

Windows 2000 and Security

If you haven't yet started to use Windows 2000, or are new to Windows 2000, there are a number of security features that make it worth considering. Windows 2000 includes a new, highly advanced security technology known as **Kerberos**, that can replace the existing security technology, the NT LAN Manager (NTLM). Windows 2000 still supports Windows NTLM for backward compatibility with earlier versions of Windows and Windows NT. However, the default network authentication protocol is now Kerberos.

> *Kerberos originated at MIT and is defined in Internet RFC 1510, making use of security tokens as defined in Internet RFC 1964. Microsoft has extended the protocol to support smart card-based log on using public key certificates that are based on a draft specification already submitted to the Internet Engineering Task Force (IETF).*

Kerberos operates in a way similar to using certificates. It uses a mutual authentication strategy between machines utilizing the concept of **shared secret-based encryption**. This allows a client to encrypt data transmitted over the network, knowing that only the destination machine is able to decrypt it. When users log onto an NT system, the Kerberos engine obtains a security key, which is analogous to a certificate, from a security database called the **Key Distribution Center** (KDC). This key is known as a **long-term key** and is partially derived from the user's password when the user's account was first created. When a user first attempts to access a resource, the KDC is referenced and a new key is generated, called a **short-term key**. The short-term key is then distributed to the two machines, and each machine encrypts its copy of the short-term key using their own long-term key. The two parties use this key when authenticating each other.

One advantage Kerberos has over NTLM is much better performance. With NTLM, a Security Accounts Manager (SAM) database held all user accounts and access rights. With large networks, the SAM database was queried frequently whenever a user accessed a resource. With Kerberos, the KDC is accessed when the resource is used for the first time where the short-term key is generated. For any additional interactions with the resource, authentication is done using the key. Another reason why Kerberos performs better is that Windows 2000 uses the Active Directory to store users' access controls.

Windows 2000 also offers a number of additional security-related features. It includes a certificate server, a security configuration editor for creating, monitoring, and deploying security settings throughout the department or even corporate-wide, and smart-card support. Trusted relationships between domains have also been enhanced and simplified. Under Windows NT 4, only explicitly defined trusted relationships are supported and these are unidirectional. In Windows 2000, implicit, bi-directional trusted relationships are supported. To illustrate this, consider three domains: A, B, and C. In NT 4, in order to have each domain trust each other, you needed to establish six different relationships:

- ❑ A trusts B
- ❑ B trusts A
- ❑ A trusts C
- ❑ C trusts A
- ❑ B trusts C
- ❑ C trusts B

With Windows 2000, you only need to set up one trusted relationship between A and B and then another between B and C. Since relationships in Windows 2000 can be bi-directional, A trusting B can imply that B trusts A. Also, since A trusts B and B trusts C, then A implicitly trusts C.

Authentication

As a web server, IIS provides files for a browser. Files, as well as all other resources under Windows NT/2000, are considered objects that have access privileges associated with them. When a request is made to use an object, the system performs a security check comparing the user with the permissions assigned to that object. If the user has permission to access the object, then the object is served to the user. If they don't have the appropriate permission, then access is denied.

For example, your site may contain confidential profile data on your users such as credit card information. You want to allow the user to update this information, but only after checking that user's credentials, typically a username and password. This simple example demonstrates two concepts: **authentication** and **authorization**. Authentication is the name given to the process of verifying that the user is who he or she claims to be, whereas authorization is the action of granting (or otherwise) the user access to the site's resources, in this case the credit card information.

When using Microsoft Internet Information Services (formerly known in Windows NT as Microsoft Internet Information Server, though still abbreviated to IIS), you have several authentication choices including built-in authentication models and writing your own custom IIS extensions called ISAPI filters. You can also implement using third-party verification through certificates, or build your own solutions using cookies or some customized database queries from ASPs.

IIS Authentication

For security checks to work with built-in authentication models, two things are needed. The first concerns the access privileges assigned to an object. The second concerns identifying the requesting user. The User Manager for Domains utility defines users and groups of users. The authentication features available in IIS provide ways for you to identify these users. IIS also provides a mechanism for specifying what type of access is permitted on folders that make up your web site.

Authorization is accomplished by the system's **access control** security that determine which system resources the user will have access to – whether they be files, components or other services, and what can be done with those resources. Authorization may be controlled by the NT File System (NTFS) in Windows NT and Windows 2000, and may work in conjunction with Windows 2000's Active Directory.

IIS provides four methods to provide authentication for access to your resources: **Anonymous**, **Basic**, **Digest**, and **Integrated Windows Authentication**, the last of which evolved from the **Windows NT Challenge/Response**, found in Windows NT. You can restrict IIS to use any one of these authentication methods or use them in combination. If you select some combination of methods, IIS will first try the anonymous method, then the basic method, then digest, and finally the Integrated Windows Authentication method.

In deciding which type of authentication to use, it's important to keep the following points in mind:

❑ You want the widest possible audience, along with browser and platform independence.

❑ You want to provide the highest practical level of security to your sensitive data.

❑ You want to maintain the highest possible performance.

Anonymous Authentication

All web browsers support anonymous access. Anonymous authentication works by not authenticating at all and simply assigning that user to a default user profile, called an **anonymous user** logon account. From this anonymous account, the user may access resources based upon the permissions granted for the account. Anonymous access is typical for web applications that provide the same access to every user or when authentication is handled within the application itself, such as requiring the user to provide identification through a sign-in feature that utilizes a query against a credentials database. For example, many sites require that you "sign up" for free access to their site by having you supply your e-mail address and a password. These two pieces of information are then stored in a database table. When you return to the site, you are required to sign in by providing the same e-mail address and password combination. When this information is given, a call to the database is made to find the e-mail address and if found, the supplied password is compared with the stored password. If this challenge is successful, the application directs the user to the secured content.

By default, when the anonymous user tries to gain access, IIS will use the authorizations assigned to a special user account that is installed by IIS specifically for anonymous access. This account has the description of "Internet Server Anonymous Access", has a name in the form of IUSR_machinename, such as IUSR_TERRA, and a randomly generated password. Therefore, when IIS receives an anonymous request to log onto a server or access a resource, it assumes that the user is the IUSR_machinename account. This account must have permission to log onto the server, or use the requested resource. IIS stores resource access permission information in the resource's **Access Control List** (ACL).

Since you may be supporting more than one web site on the IIS server, the access permissions for anonymous access for one web site will probably differ from site to site, so don't use the IIS-installed default anonymous user account. Rather, create a new user account for each site and assign this new account for use when the user accesses the site anonymously. You should also disable or greatly restrict access permissions on the default account created by IIS to prevent hacking. In fact, regardless of whether you'll support multiple sites, this is good practice to avoid using the default anonymous user account. This makes it more difficult for the would-be hacker to guess the name of the anonymous user account, thus adding to your security.

> For added security, if you are not using Anonymous Authentication, you should consider removing the permissions for IUSR_machinename from any secured directory.

Setting up Anonymous Authentication

Setting up Anonymous Authentication is fairly simple, although it differs slightly depending upon whether you are using Windows NT or Windows 2000 and whether or not you are doing this on a domain controller. To illustrate the process, let's step through what is required to set up Anonymous Authentication on a Windows 2000 domain controller.

1. Create a new user account for use when anonymous access to the site is requested. This is done using Active Directory Users and Computers found under Administrative Tools.

If your Windows 2000 machine is not a domain controller, use Local Users and Groups, *also found under* Computer Management. *If you are using Windows NT, try* User Manager *or* User Manager for Domains, *both found in the* Administrative Tools (Common) *folder.*

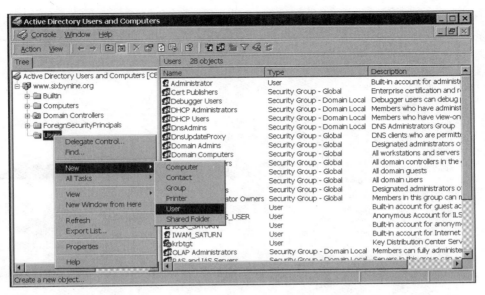

After selecting User from the New menu, fill out the dialog boxes presented by the New User Wizard. You will be required to enter a username and a password for that user.

Using the Internet Information Services folder from the Computer Management applet, select the web site that you wish to protect, or a folder within the web site to protect. Next, right-click and choose Properties from the context menu.

For Windows NT, use Internet Service Manager, which is usually found under the Windows NT 4.0 Option Pack folder.

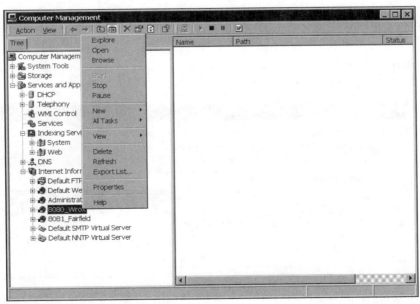

Select the Directory Security tab and then select the Edit button from the Anonymous Access and Authentication Control group to display the Authentication Methods dialog box:

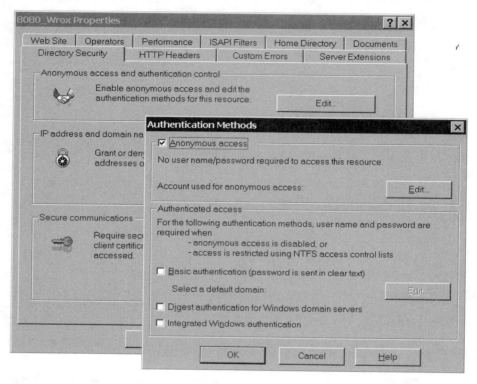

Check the Allow Anonymous Access option.

Select the Edit button from Allow Anonymous Access to specify the user account to be used when anonymous access is requested:

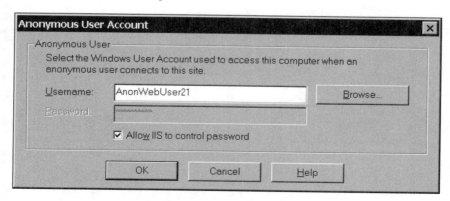

Select the anonymous user account you just created and then select the Allow IIS to control password checkbox. This option lets IIS use the password of the selected user without requiring us to manually enter the password in this dialog. This is convenient for us to use since any changes that are made to the user's password will be detected automatically by IIS. If we choose not to use this option, then anytime this user's password changes in Active Directory Users and Computers, we will be required to manually update the password on this dialog. If we don't, then IIS will not authenticate this user for anonymous access.

Basic Authentication

When your web site must be accessible from browsers other than Microsoft Internet Explorer, Basic Authentication may be a good option. Basic Authentication is also the way to go if you want to use encryption and other advanced security features.

When basic authentication is used, IIS will honor authenticated access for HTTP requests that contain username and password information. Most browsers don't automatically include username and password information with HTTP requests, but if the user attempts to access a secured page or resource, the browser, if it is able to, will display a dialog requesting these credentials. Only after the user has entered this information will the browser actually send an HTTP request that contains username and password information in its header.

Like Anonymous Authentication, the Basic Authentication method uses a Windows user account and it is the client that is responsible for obtaining the requesting username and password information. Unless you implement additional security features, this information is then transmitted to IIS using **clear text**, meaning non-encrypted text characters. The credentials are then encoded (although not encrypted) and sent to the server. If the username and password specified matches the credentials of a user account on the IIS computer or in a trusted domain, the requesting user is authorized based upon the permissions assigned to that user account.

Having authentication credentials transmitted in such an unsecured manner as clear text is not recommended for commercial applications. However, it *may* be acceptable for use within an intranet, although it is not recommended. There are many easily available "packet sniffing" software utilities that can be downloaded from the Internet to easily find out passwords just by analyzing the network traffic a computer is on. These utilities work very well in both the intranet and Internet environments and if Basic Authentication is used, your passwords are at risk.

When using Basic Authentication, you do have some options to make the transmission of data more secure, such as using *Secured Socket Layer* (SSL) and *Certificates,* which we will discuss later, but these options may impact performance.

Don't use IIS Basic Authentication if you are concerned about the security of your user accounts. This method has another potential disadvantage, namely, for every request made IIS needs to make multiple calls to the system, which is expensive in terms of CPU cycles and therefore may cause a performance hit.

Setting Up Basic Authentication

Setting up IIS Basic Authentication is not much different than setting up Anonymous Authentication. You will need to create a user account for each user whom you want to give access to. Create a user group for each level of access that you wish to give to the application and then add the users to each group accordingly. The users must have the *Log On Locally* right on the IIS server. A user who has the Log On Locally right can start an interactive session on the Windows NT/2000 server. Next, you will need to use Internet Information Services to turn on Basic Authentication. To do so, select the Directory Security tab and then select the Edit button from the Anonymous Access and Authentication Control group to display the Authentication Methods dialog box:

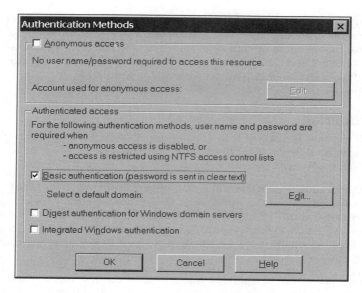

Turn off all of the options in this dialog, except for Basic Authentication. You will be warned that your usernames and passwords will be transmitted without being encrypted, and asked to confirm your selection.

If you have more than one domain in your organization, you may use the Edit button on this dialog to select a default domain for each user using Basic authentication. Choose Yes and then select the OK button

Digest Authentication

Digest Authentication provides the same functionality as Basic Authentication, but provides added security by encrypting the credentials rather than using clear text. It also works with firewalls and proxy servers.

The credentials are secured by using an encryption process that is called **hashing**, which produces a 160-bit binary code called a **message digest**. The hashing process uses information from both the client and the server, such that the final encrypted data can only be used between the two machines.

There are a few important limitations with Digest Authentication. Most notably, only Internet Explorer supports it. Because Digest Authentication is based upon the new HTTP 1.1 industry standard, you can expect that new versions of other browsers will, in time, support this authentication model. Another limitation is that, currently, Digest Authentication is supported only for domains with a Windows 2000 domain controller.

Setting Up Digest Authentication

The process for setting up IIS Digest Authentication is exactly like the process for Basic Authentication. The only difference is that, when presented with the Authentication Methods dialog, you select Digest authentication rather than Basic authentication.

Integrated Windows Authentication

When using Integrated Windows Authentication, the client machine uses its currently established Windows 2000 user logon information to identify itself securely to the server, so the user doesn't need to provide credentials. Because of this fact, you cannot use Integrated Windows Authentication if Anonymous Authentication is enabled. This makes a lot of sense since the Windows file system permissions would have been set when the user logged onto the network, which is well before the user tries establishing a connection with restricted content.

Although authorization will have occurred before the user attempts to connect to the secured content, the client's browser still will need to provide the user's password, which will prevent anyone from impersonating the client. The password sent will be encrypted using hashing, so this communication will be secure.

Integrated Windows Authentication is the preferred choice for intranet applications on a Windows 2000 network, but it is usually impractical for Internet applications. The main reasons for not being able to use this authentication model for Internet applications include the requirement that both the client and the server are located in the same or trusted domains, and lack of support from browsers other than Internet Explorer.

Notes on Integrated Windows Authentication

❑   Integrated Windows Authentication was previously known as NTLM or Windows NT Challenge/Response Authentication.

❑   Integrated Windows Authentication can use both the Kerberos authentication protocol and its own challenge/response authentication protocol. If Directory Services is installed on the server, and the browser is compatible with the Kerberos authentication protocol, both Kerberos and the challenge/response protocol are used; otherwise only the latter is used.

❑   Integrated Windows Authentication does not work across proxy servers or other firewall applications.

Setting Up Integrated Windows Authentication

To set up Integrated Windows Authentication, follow the same procedure as Basic authentication except that in the Authentication Methods dialog box, select Integrated Windows Authentication. You will still need to create a Windows user account for each user you want to provide access for, and you should remove the permissions for IUSR_*machinename* from the secured directory.

Cookie-Based Authentication

To service the broadest number of users, Internet applications must be platform-independent at the client level, meaning, your application should work equally well for a client using a Mac, PC or UNIX box. Because the client operating system is unknown in advance, Internet applications are not supposed to write anything to the user's machine. Also, the nature of the HTTP protocol is **stateless**, meaning that each time a browser requests the URL of a web page, the web server treats the request as a new interaction without any knowledge of prior requests. There are situations where keeping some tidbit of information on the client may be extremely useful. To address this issue, a standard was developed by the Netscape Corporation where small amounts of data, called **cookies**, may be stored on the client.

The ability to save information about a web user on the browser machine allows us to use cookies to identify returning customers. Although cookies may be used for authenticating users, many companies also use cookies to compile information about web users, which in turn is used by advertising clients to deliver targeted advertisements. This is just one way some popular search engines can display a seemingly random banner ad when you first contact the site. After you've entered a word search, for example "books for sale", the banner ad suddenly starts displaying an advertisement for Barnes & Noble. What appears to be magic is instead an example of high-tech marketing analysis in this Internet age. Opinions vary widely about the safety and intrusiveness of cookies, but very few can argue with their convenience.

For as clever as cookies may be, cookie-based authentication with ASP pages does have some limitations, such as:

❑ The amount of data that can be stored in a single cookie is limited.

❑ Cookie-based systems can be susceptible to "spoofing", a technique of impersonating the IP or domain addresses in the code that reads cookies in an attempt to recover information stored in the cookies.

❑ Reading and writing cookies may be slow.

❑ Although most modern browsers support cookies, a few browsers do not and all modern browsers provide the user with options to disable cookies and users can delete them from the client machines.

A cookie stores a small amount of information, often no more than a short session identifier that the HTTP server sends to the browser when the browser connects for the first time. The browser can then send a copy of the cookie's data to the server each time it reconnects. By having the cookie send some identifier of the user, the server is able to maintain the illusion of a session that spans multiple pages.

You can use the cookie-based session variables of ASP to capture a username and password from a sign on form, validate the username and password, then set a session variable to indicate the user has correctly logged in. When the user returns to the site, the cookie can be "read" to supply the user's ID and password.

Notes on Cookies

❑ For sensitive portions of your applications, you should probably encrypt the entire channel between browser and server using a version of SSL. The cookie will be encrypted along with the rest of the data stream in such a way that network eavesdroppers cannot intercept the cookie without first cracking the encryption. To avoid the cookie being inadvertently disclosed across a non-secure channel, you should set the secure attribute so that the browser only transmits the cookie when SSL is in effect. SSL is described later in this chapter.

Another technique for making cookies more secure is to encode the data that is saved in the cookie. For example, you can write a simple routine that transforms every character "A" to a "B", a "B" to a "C", and so on. Of course, when you read the values stored in the cookie, you will need to reverse this encoding.

❑ To support older browsers that can't use cookies, Microsoft has made a utility available that simulates cookies so that you can maintain session state. This utility, *Cookie Munger*, is available as part of the IIS Resource Kit and is described at http://msdn.microsoft.com/workshop/server/toolbox/cookie.asp.

Using Cookies

There are two HTTP headers used with cookies: `Set-Cookie` and `Cookie`. When a client application makes an HTTP request, it sends the `Cookie` header as part of the request. In turn, the Server manipulates the value of the cookie and then sends the `Set-Cookie` header back to the client. Both the `Set-Cookie` and the `Cookie` request headers used the values shown in the table below:

Parameter	Description
`name=value;`	Returns a string of all the cookies that apply to the page. The server must parse the string to find the values of individual cookies.
`expires=date;`	Deletes the cookie when the browser is closed if no expiration is set on a cookie. The cookie is saved across browser sessions if an expiration date is set (using Greenwich Mean Time). Setting an expiration date in the future causes the cookie to be saved across browser sessions.
`domain=domainname;`	Pages on a domain made up of more than one server can share cookie information.
`path=path;`	Allows the current document to share cookie information with other pages within the same domain. If no `path` is specified, it is assumed to be the path of the resource associated with the `Set-Cookie` header.
`secure;`	Allows the stored cookie information to be accessed or sent only from a secure environment.

If you want to see what the content of a cookie looks like, check your hard drive. With Microsoft Internet Explorer, cookies are saved in the `WinNT\Profiles` folder, such as `C:\WINNT\Profiles\Cathy\Cookies\`. For Netscape users, take a look at the `cookies.txt` file found under each user's personal settings folder, such as `Program Files\Netscape\Users\Cathy\cookies.txt`. You can read the cookie data in any text editor.

The `Set-Cookie` response header uses the following syntax:

```
Set-Cookie: name=value;expires=date;domain=domainname;path=path;secure
```

When setting cookies, there are a few things to consider:

❑   The only required item in the header is its name and value. The other items are optional.

❑   The format for the expiration date is "DD-MMM-YYYY HH:MM:SS GMT" where the DD represents the day of the month using leading zeros, MMM is the three-letter abbreviation for the month, and the time is expressed using a 24 hour clock.

❑   The `domainname` item is used for persistent cookies and is used to indicate the domain for which the cookie is valid. If the specified domain name ending, such as ".microsoft.com", matches the request, requests to `home.microsoft.com` and `support.microsoft.com` would be honored, if it is possible.

- Setting the `path` item is used to specify a subset of the URLs for which the cookie is valid. If a path is specified, the cookie is considered valid for any requests that match that path. For example, if the specified path is `/store`, requests with the paths `/storefront` and `/store/checkout.htm` would match. If no path is specified, the path is assumed to be the path of the resource associated with the `Set-Cookie` header.

- When the cookie uses the `secure` item, it will only be sent to a server providing a secured version of the HTTP protocol, called HTTPS.

Here is a demonstration that uses JavaScript routines to show how cookies may be used to save and read information about the users. This code will save the user's name and keep track of how many visits the user has had to the site and then display this information on the page. When you reload the page, the counter for the number of visits will increment:

```
<SCRIPT LANGUAGE="JavaScript">
<!--BEGIN Script

var ExpireDate = new Date();
var Duration = 90;
ExpireDate.setTime(ExpireDate.getTime()  + (Duration*86400000));

function InitializeCookie(){
   UName = prompt("Please enter a UserName: ");
   WriteToCookie ('UserName', UName, ExpireDate);
   WriteToCookie ('NumberOfVisits', 0, ExpireDate);
   document.location="SetCookies.html";
}

function NameOfUser(){
   var CookieValue = ReadFromCookie('UserName')
   if (CookieValue == null) {
      CookieValue = prompt("Please enter your UserName:");
      WriteToCookie ('UserName', CookieValue, ExpireDate);
      }
   return CookieValue;
}

function GetNumberOfVisits(){
   var NumberOfVisits = ReadFromCookie('NumberOfVisits')
   if (NumberOfVisits == null) {
      NumberOfVisits = 0;
   }
   else
      NumberOfVisits++;
   WriteToCookie ('NumberOfVisits', NumberOfVisits, ExpireDate);
   return NumberOfVisits;
}

function ValueOfCookie (ItemPosition) {
   var LengthOfData = document.cookie.indexOf (";", ItemPosition);
   if (LengthOfData == -1)
      LengthOfData = document.cookie.length;
   return unescape(document.cookie.substring(ItemPosition, LengthOfData));
}

function ReadFromCookie(ItemName) {
   var RetVal = null;
   var ItemRef = ItemName + "=";
   var PosOfLastChar = document.cookie.length - ItemRef.length;
   var i = 0;
```

```
      while (i < PosOfLastChar) {
         var j = i + ItemRef.length;
         if (document.cookie.substring(i, j) == ItemRef) {
            RetVal = ValueOfCookie (j);
            break;
         }
         i = document.cookie.indexOf(" ", i) + 1;
         if (i == 0) break;
      }
      return RetVal;
   }

   function WriteToCookie (ArgName, ArgValue) {
      var ArgumentValues = WriteToCookie.arguments;
      var NumberOfArguments = WriteToCookie.arguments.length;
      var ExpireDate = (NumberOfArguments > 2) ? ArgumentValues[2] : null;
      var Path = (NumberOfArguments > 3) ? ArgumentValues[3] : null;
      var Domain = (NumberOfArguments > 4) ? ArgumentValues[4] : null;
      var Secure = (NumberOfArguments > 5) ? ArgumentValues[5] : false;
      document.cookie = ArgName + "=" + escape (ArgValue) +
         ((ExpireDate == null) ? "" : ("; expires=" +
         ExpireDate.toGMTString())) +
         ((Path == null) ? "" : ("; path=" + Path)) +
         ((Domain == null) ? "" : ("; domain=" + Domain)) +
         ((Secure == true) ? "; secure" : ""));
   }

   // End -->
   </SCRIPT>


   <CENTER>
   <SCRIPT LANGUAGE="JavaScript">
   document.write("UserName: " + NameOfUser() + ". ");
   document.write("Visits: " + GetNumberOfVisits());
   </SCRIPT>
   <P>
   Reload this page to view the counter increment.<BR>Click <A
   HREF="JavaScript:InitializeCookie()">here</A> to reinitialize the cookie.
   </CENTER>
```

Certificate-Based Authentication

Certificates are an advanced form of authentication that uses a trusted third-party, called a **Certificate Authority** or CA, which can be used to identify you to a web server and to other users. With a certificate, you can establish secured, encrypted communications, send and receive encrypted e-mail messages, verify the identity of the person who sent you an e-mail message, or prove your identity to a web server.

Used mostly by companies, certificates are the electronic equivalent of a business license. Similar to having the office of the Secretary of State issue Articles of Incorporation for a company, a CA can also issue digital certificates to companies or individuals. Before issuing a certificate, the CA reviews your credentials – such as your organization's Dun & Bradstreet number or Articles of Incorporation – and completes a thorough background checking process which ensures that your organization is what it claims to be, and is not claiming a false identity. Then the CA issues you a certificate, which can be used to prove your identity. Having a certificate bolsters the confidence of customers whom you are asking to submit confidential data, such as credit card information. In turn, you know that your company is receiving accurate information that the customer cannot later refute.

Private individuals can also obtain certificates, although at the moment they are not widely used on the Web. Still, certificates are growing in popularity, since they are easily available and cost little or nothing from many CAs. The major use of personal certificates is within corporate intranets, where they are used to control access to confidential information on the corporate web server. However, personal certificates are being used more and more and are now legally binding electronic signatures in the United States for Internet-based financial and legal transactions. Once certificates are installed, they offer a much more convenient way to identify users than having them supply a user name and password.

How Does Security with Certificates Work?

Certificates use **public key cryptography** to sign and authenticate signatures. When you apply for a digital certificate, a **private key** is automatically generated for you and saved to the hard disk of your computer. During this generation process, you are prompted for a password, which will be used to encrypt the private key before saving it to disk. With the certificate and private key, you can offer secured communications using **Secured Sockets Layer** (SSL) by enabling SSL client authentication on your web directory.

SSL is a low-level encryption scheme used to encrypt transactions in higher-level protocols such as HTTP, NNTP and FTP. The SSL protocol includes provisions for server authentication, encryption of data in transit, and optional client authentication. SSL is supported on many commercially available browsers, including Netscape Navigator, Secure Mosaic, and Microsoft Internet Explorer. Many web servers also support SSL as well, including those from Microsoft, IBM, Netscape, Apache, Quarterdeck, and OpenMarket.

The procedure followed when using SSL to ensure secure communications parallels that of the hashing that is performed under Digest Authentication. Unlike Digest Authentication, which encrypts username and password information, SSL uses the private key of the server (and, if requested, from the client). The result is called a **session key**, rather than a message digest. Once the session key has been established, it is used to encrypt and decrypt all communications between the two machines.

The encryption used may be 40-bit or 128-bit SSL sessions, but don't expect to use the stronger 128-bit version. Until recently, United States export laws have prohibited the distribution of 128-bit encryption technologies, so for the roughly 50% of Internet users that are outside the United States, 40-bit encryption will suffice. The 128-bit encryption is much stronger and it has been claimed that a 128-bit encryption has never been broken.

When a secured connection is in use, visitors to your site are presented with the following cues, depending upon which browser and version is being used:

❑ The URL in the browser window displays https at the beginning, instead of http.

❑ In Netscape Communicator, the padlock icon in the lower left corner of the Navigator window will be closed instead of open.

❑ In Netscape Navigator versions 3.X and earlier, a solid key with three teeth means 128-bit encryption, a solid key with two teeth means 40-bit encryption.

❑ In Internet Explorer, a padlock icon will be displayed in the status bar found at the bottom of the IE window.

If a user attempts to submit information to a server that is not secure, most browsers will provide some sort of warning to them. Microsoft Internet Explorer and Netscape Navigator will, by default, show a warning. If your browser doesn't show a warning, check your browser's options since you can suppress the display of these warning messages:

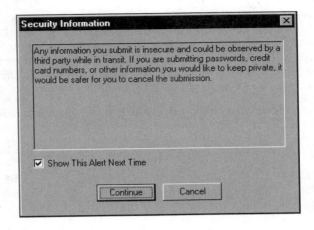

Obtaining a Certificate

After installing an SSL-enabled server you will need to obtain a *server certificate* from a certifying authority. Certificates are available from several companies, such as:

❑ VeriSign Corporation (http://www.verisign.com)

❑ Thawte Consulting (http://www.thawte.com) – now part of VeriSign

❑ Entrust (http://www.entrust.com)

❑ GTE (http://www.baltimore.com/cybertrust)

❑ Entegrity Solutions (http://www.entegrity.com)

❑ SoftForum (http://www.softforum.co.kr/english)

The process of obtaining a server certificate is slightly different from CA to CA, but each follows the same general approach. Connect to the CA's web site and find the server certificate application section and fill out the appropriate form. You will have to provide such information as your domain name, company name, e-mail address, phone number, etc. You will also be asked to provide documentation to verify yourself or your company. These documents may be your company's articles of incorporation, or some other notarized document.

Next you will need to create a public/private key pair on your computer following the procedures set by the issuing CA. The CA-supplied software will also generate a file containing a key request, which you send through regular, non-electronic mail to the CA. They will process the request and eventually send you a signed certificate. You then complete the process by installing the signed certificate on your server.

Using the Certificate

Under Internet Information Services, select the directory you want to protect, right-click to display the context menu and select Properties. From the Directory Security property sheet, choose the Server Certificate... button from the Secure communications section and install the certificate you obtained. Once the certificate has been installed, click the Edit button and select the Require client certificates option.

Since HTTPS is slower and more resource-intensive than HTTP, you may not want to secure every page in your web site. In most e-commerce sites, the catalog portion of the site will typically be displayed using HTTP while ordering and payment pages will be secured using HTTPS. This is possible because HTTP and HTTPS are different protocols and they typically reside on different ports (by default, 80 and 443, respectively), so your server may use both protocols simultaneously. You also have the option of using two different servers, one for secured content and another for unsecured content.

The syntax for creating a secure hyperlink in a web page is not much different from an unsecured one. Simply replace the `http://` portion of the protocol with `https://`.

```
<A REF="https://www.acmeaquariums.com/orders.htm">Secured Order Form</A>
```

You may also force the use of SSL by using an ASP page to redirect a user from an HTTP page to a page utilizing HTTPS. To do so, first create a file named `SSL.inc` in the root of your web server that contains the following:

```
<%
If Request.ServerVariables("SERVER_PORT")=80 Then
    Dim strURL
    strURL = "https://" & Request.ServerVariables("SERVER_NAME") _
                        & Request.ServerVariables("URL")
    Response.Redirect strURL
End If
%>
```

For each page that you wish to use SSL with, include the `SSL.inc` file created above:

```
<%@Language="VBSCRIPT"%>
<!--#include virtual="/SSL.inc"-->
```

Now when a page is requested that uses this include file, the ASP code determines which port is being accessed, and if HTTP is being used, the browser will be redirected to the same page using HTTPS.

Custom Authentication with ASP

You may decide to implement authentication using ASP code. This may be done by prompting the user for a username and password and then checking to see if these credentials match the records in a database. This approach is extremely easy to implement, and when used with HTTPS is extremely secure. You will also need to implement Basic Authentication if you want the added protection of HTTPS. Since this approach uses a query, you will need to establish a user login account for the database. It is recommended that this login be granted minimal rights and access only to a single view or table that provides the login information.

This approach uses an HTML page and an ASP page. The first page uses an HTML form to submit the user's credentials and the second processes those credentials:

```
<HTML><HEAD>
<TITLE>customlogin.asp</TITLE>
</HEAD><body bgcolor="#FFFFFF">
<FORM ACTION="Authenticate.asp" method="POST">
Username: <INPUT NAME="username" size="40"><BR>
Password: <INPUT NAME="password" size="40"><BR>
<INPUT TYPE="submit"><INPUT TYPE="reset">
</FORM></BODY></HTML>
```

```
<HTML><HEAD>
<TITLE>authenticate.asp</TITLE>
</HEAD><body bgcolor="#FFFFFF">
<%
   dim strDB, strUsername, strPassword, cnAuthenticate
   dim strSQL, rsCount, intResult, strMsg

   '-- Get credentials from user.
   strUsername =request.form("username")
   strPassword =request.form("password")

   '-- Create the connection and start a session.
   Set cnAuthenticate = Server.CreateObject("ADODB.Connection")
   cnAuthenticate.ConnectionTimeout = 60
   cnAuthenticate.ConnectionString = _
       "PROVIDER=SQLOLEDB;DATA SOURCE=MyServer;" _
       & "USER ID=authenticator;PASSWORD=" & gstrPassword 'password in global.asa
   cnAuthenticate.Open

   '-- Query database to validate credentials.
   strSQL ="SELECT COUNT(*) FROM Users WHERE Username=" _
       & "'" & strUsername & "' AND Password='" & strPassword & "'"
   Set rsCount = cnAuthenticate.execute(strSQL)
   IntResult = rsCount(0)
   rsCount.close
   Set rsCount = Nothing
   cnAuthenticate.close
   Set cnAuthenticate = Nothing

   '-- React to success or failure.
   If rsCount(0) = 0 Then
       StrMsg = "Invalid Username or password<BR>" & _
               "<A HREF='Authenticate.asp'>Try again</A>"
   Else
       session("username")= strUsername
       '-- Redirect to secured area of site.
       '-- Write cookie to mark that the client has been authenticated
   End If
%>
</BODY></HTML>
```

Web Server Authorization

So far, we have discussed several approaches to authentication. The authentication models provided through IIS allowed us to determine who the user was so that we could authorize them for access to various objects on the machine. This authorization is performed on a user-by-user basis, or a user group-by-user group basis. We can also set permissions for individual web sites. Web Permissions allow us to provide a different level of authorization by controlling access to virtual directories of your web site, regardless of who the user is.

Web Permissions control such things as whether or not a user can view the folder or file contents, change the contents of files, and run scripts and executables. Since every authentication model requires that the user be associated with a user account, which has its own set of restrictions, Web Permissions will further define what the user can or cannot do. If the Web Permissions and user authorization differ for a particular directory or file, the more restrictive settings are used.

The permissions that may be set for a web site folder are:

Read	Users can view directory or file content and properties, as well as download files. (The default is "on".)
Write	Users can change folder or file content and properties. Write can only be done with a browser that supports the PUT feature of the HTTP 1.1 protocol standard. (The default is "off".)
Script source access	Users can access source files. If Read is selected, then source can be read, if Write is selected, then source can be written to. Script Source Access includes the source code for scripts, such as the scripts in an ASP application.
Directory browsing	Users can view the files and subfolders of a folder as a hypertext list. Virtual directories will not appear in directory listings; users must know a virtual directory's alias.
Log visits	A log entry is created for each visit to the web site.
Index this resource	Allows Indexing Service to index this resource so that its contents may be included as part of searches of your site.
Execute Permissions	Selects the appropriate level of script execution, which includes the following options:

	None	Execution of executables and scripts, such as ASP applications, not allowed. Only static files, such as HTML or image files, can be accessed.
	Scripts only	Allows execution of only scripts, such as ASP applications, on the server.
	Scripts and Executables	All file types can be accessed or executed, such as ASP applications, and executables on the server.

Setting up Web Permissions

To set web server permissions for web content, use the Internet Information Services snap-in found in the Services and Applications folder in Computer Management. Expand this folder to display all of your web sites. Right-click on a web site, file, or virtual directory to display its context menu and then select Properties:

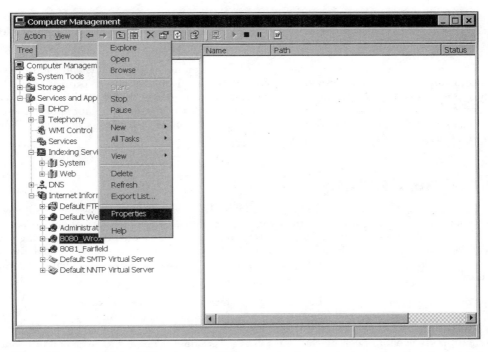

On the Home Directory, Virtual Directory, or File property sheet, select or clear the appropriate checkboxes to configure the ability to read or change the contents, directory browsing, logging, and indexing and select the level of script execution:

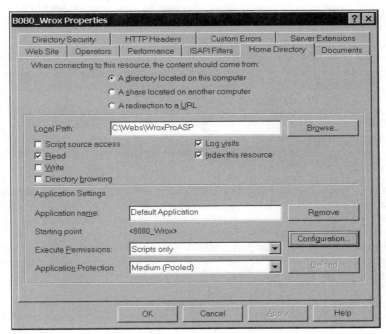

This dialog provides a checkbox for Script Source Access. This option allows users to examine the contents of your ASP scripts. This may pose a serious security risk and is not recommended for most applications.

Also found on this dialog is the Application Protection drop-down list that lets you choose whether application are run in the same process as web services, in an isolated pooled process with other applications, or in an isolated process separate from other processes. Although this is not strictly a security feature, it is possible that an application sharing process space with your application could be used to gain unauthorized access. Running your application in its own process space is the most secure, but it does cause a performance hit since additional resources will be required.

Preventing Hacking

With an Internet application, you are not limited to only a few users. You hope that the site will be well received and visited frequently. Unfortunately, with an increase in the number of visitors comes an increase in the likelihood of malicious and unscrupulous individuals (that is, hackers) using your application. To make matters even more challenging, many of your clients may not have the resources to properly secure their site, so you may need to provide such services as part of delivering your application.

Today's developer not only has to be a good programmer, but also take on roles and responsibilities to ensure that your application will function properly in spite of what users may try to do with it. Sure, your application has to be designed well and meet your business requirements, but it also needs to operate properly even if under attack. Your job as a developer is not just to write and test code, or just develop specifications, but also to create a working product that will function correctly and will survive in the hostile world of the Internet. To do this, you need to be part business analyst, part database administrator, and part systems engineer, and the way to do this is not to give a malicious user the opportunity to wreak havoc with your system. In a nutshell, an essential part of any Internet application is **security**.

This section discusses a number of topics that can help with protecting your application and the site from unauthorized and malicious users. What is covered here is by no means a complete coverage of security. Whole books have been dedicated to the topic. Keep in mind that *no site will ever be 100% secure*, but by taking a few simple actions you can go a long way in eliminating much of the risk.

There are many resources available for finding out more about security. Most of the major software vendors and Certificate Authorities have very good white papers and articles dealing with the subject. You can also find out a great deal by visiting hacker sites on the Net. Although many of these sites are legitimate ones, others are managed by dangerous hackers. You should be careful about what information you might give to them and be wary of anything you might obtain from them.

To be fair, many of these security-related web sites are run by honest people who are doing some very interesting and creative work. Some of the coolest applications can be found on them, and they serve a beneficial purpose since they let you know where your security holes are and suggest ways of patching them up. Often these sites exist to embarrass software companies into better protecting our privacy, and sometimes this tactic works. For example, Lotus credits a hacker site, L0pht Heavy Industries, with flagging a potential security issue in some of its software. The individuals that run these sites have even testified before the US Congress and offered advice on computer security.

> For an interesting article on hackers testifying before the US Congress, take a look at:
> www.abcnews.go.com/onair/WorldNewsTonight/wnt_991220_CL_L0pht_feature.html.

Here are a few resources that you can check out to find out more about security and what hackers are up to:

Hacker News Network	http://www.hackernews.com
L0pht Heavy Industries	http://www.l0pht.com
Microsoft	http://msdn.microsoft.com/workshop/security http://www.microsoft.com/security
Netscape	http://home.netscape.com/security http://home.netscape.com/security/securesites/ecommerce.html
Symantec	http://www.symantec.com
Verisign	http://www.verisign.com
Astalavista.Box.sk	http://hack.box.sk

Use the Latest Versions of Software

One very simple way to keep up with security holes is to keep up with the latest software available. As products are used in the marketplace, software vendors learn of potential security failings and offer updates and enhancements in response. Microsoft release new versions and service packs for their products on a regular basis. Many of these releases include some sort of security enhancement bundled in with a multitude of other features. They do this, in part, because it is in the public's best interest to have their products be as secure as possible. You should regularly check the Microsoft site (as well as other vendor sites) for information on the availability of updates.

It should also be pointed out that "keeping up with the latest software" doesn't necessarily mean go out and install every patch or utility as soon as it becomes available. Although the latest software may have new and improved security features, by virtue of being brand new, it is unproven and untested. It may contain security bugs that haven't been discovered yet – and they will be discovered if they are there. You may wish to wait awhile before installing that latest patch or service pack and see if any information about its security and reliability is mentioned on one of the web sites listed above.

Using SYSKEY to Protect Password Data

If you haven't yet moved to Windows 2000, you are using an operating system that has long been explored by hackers. Although NT has been around long enough that major security holes have been addressed, over the years many hacker utilities have been developed (and are available as free downloads) that can extract sensitive system and user account information from the registry of Windows NT 4 systems. Such software can crack passwords in literally a matter of seconds. In response to this problem, Microsoft released the `sec-fix` hot fix to be applied after Service Pack 2 for Windows NT 4.0. This hot fix introduced the capability to protect the account password data contained in the registry with the aid of *strong* (128-bit) encryption. This capability is retained in later service packs of Windows NT 4.0.

The program used to apply this encryption on the passwords in the registry is called `SYSKEY.EXE`. It allows you to generate a 128-bit key that makes hacking the passwords extremely difficult. Once the encryption had been applied, the key is required by the system every time it is started. The `SYSKEY` utility allows you to store the key on the machine, or on a floppy, or prompt the user to manually enter a secondary key upon system startup that can be used to derive the system key.

For details on using SYSKEY refer to the following article on Microsoft's site:
http://support.microsoft.com/support/kb/articles/Q143/4/75.asp.

Here are a few words of warning about using SYSKEY that you should know before you attempt using the utility. First, SYSKEY only protects the password data contained in an NT system's local registry, so you should use SYSKEY on every domain controller in the network. Second, you can't undo the encryption once SYSKEY has been applied. Once you use it, *the only way to stop using it is to wipe the machine clean and reinstall the operating system from scratch!*

To install SYSKEY, you need to be logged in as an administrative user. You start SYSKEY from the Run menu in the Start menu with:

```
C:\WINNT\system32\Syskey.exe
```

The first time you run SYSKEY, you will see that encryption is currently disabled:

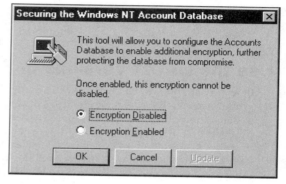

To enable encryption, simply select Encryption Enabled and then select OK to continue. A warning message will be displayed to remind you that the encryption cannot be disabled after it has been enabled.

Next, you will need to choose where the key will be stored – either on a floppy or, on the machine itself, or require the user restarting the machine to enter in a password:

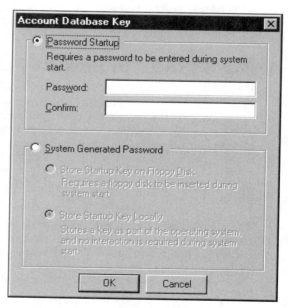

For this demonstration, we will use the Password Startup method. Enter a password of your choosing. The utility will then use this password to derive the encryption key. The password should be a *strong* one, meaning some nonsense word that is at least eight characters and contains a combination of upper and lower case letters along with at least one number. A convenient way to come up with a meaningful password that is hard to hack is to use the first characters of some phrase or sentence, such as "I was born on May 23 in 1964 in Bridgeport, Connecticut" to produce a password of "IwboM23i1964iBC".

Once you have entered your password and re-entered it in the confirmation box, select OK to proceed. The utility will go to work at generating the key and encrypting your registry's passwords, and then display a confirmation message:

Now restart the system to make sure that everything worked properly. As the system restarts, a prompt appears asking you for the startup password. Once the password is entered correctly, startup proceeds as usual:

Now that you have encrypted the registry you should create a new Emergency Repair Disk using the RDISK utility with the /S option.

Security Through Folder Permissions

It is important that the permissions applied to a folder through NTFS agree with the permissions set up under IIS. Permissions granted using IIS are not the same as permissions granted using NTFS. NTFS offers a read-write permission that is quite different from IIS's read-write Web Permissions. The NTFS read-write permission is used to determine if a user has access to the resources on the hard disk, whereas Web Permissions let the web resources control the HTTP verb commands that are sent in headers requesting actions.

Consider the scenario where your web site is located in D:\Webs\8082_Acme. Say the NTFS permissions for this folder are set to read and write, while the Web Permissions are set to read-only. When a browser points to this folder, it will not be able to write to the web site due to the Web Permissions, though a network client could, because of the NTFS permissions. However, if the settings were reversed, that is, the NTFS settings for the folder become read-only and the Web Permissions become read-write, neither the network client nor the browser will be able to write to the folder.

Also, when organizing the files for your web site, use multiple folders rather than a single folder. Place only your ASP files in one folder, and place your "sensitive files" in another. Use different folders for "non-sensitive files" such as graphics or help files and set permissions for each folder. By segregating like files into different folders you can apply permissions more easily than securing files individually. The following is an example of how you can organize your folders:

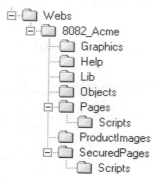

Each sub-folder is explained as follows:

8082_Acme	The web site root
Graphics	Images and icons used in pages
Help	Help and support text
Lib	Common utility routines
Objects	Data sources and COM objects
Pages	Unsecured pages
Pages/Scripts	Scripts used for unsecured pages
ProductImages	Graphics used to display products
SecuredPages	Restricted-use pages
SecuredPages/Scripts	Scripts used for restricted-use pages

Security Through Process Isolation

As we discussed in the earlier chapter on COM objects, applications can share their memory with the components they use or can have those components execute in a separate memory space. One of the advantages of sharing the same process space is speed, but this benefit comes with a risk. This risk is that if one component dies, it may corrupt the shared memory and crash the entire process. Typically server applications are loaded into the same memory space as that of the requesting client application. If a component fails, either through some bug or an attack by a hacker, your entire server may be in jeopardy.

By segregating the IIS/ASP code and COM components into different memory spaces, if there's an exception in the component, IIS will not be affected by it. In other words, by running in a separate process space, an error will be confined to that process space, leaving all other processes on the machine running normally.

Security Through IP Address and Domain Restrictions

There are some situations where you want to prevent or allow access to your site based upon the location of the user. For instance, you may only wish to allow site access to individuals coming from your company's domain. Perhaps you wish to deny site access to your competitors. To do this, you can take advantage of the fact that when the web client makes a request to the web server, the IP address is sent along with the header information. By using this information, you can accept or reject the request.

Typically, this filtering is done through Internet Service Manager, by using Grant Access to block access to everyone except to the IP address you want. You can achieve the same results by using a bit of ASP code. The following code snippet denies access to all users except those coming from a specific IP address:

```
<%
If Request.ServerVariables("REMOTE_ADDR") <> "164.171.1.3" Then
    Response.Buffer = True
    Response.Status = ("401 Unauthorized")
    Response.End
End If
%>
```

Access to Databases

Some developers may cut corners when coding the access to databases by hard-coding login IDs and passwords into their applications. This is an obvious security risk, but is still carried out much too often. Another common practice is to hard code SQL statements into applications. Although not as severe a security risk as exposing the login IDs and passwords, it does reveal the names of your databases, tables, and other objects. Knowing the name of a table may not seem like much of a security breach, but that extra piece of information may still be used against you. One common approach with hackers is that they try a variety of different activities in the hope that they will get a tidbit of information here and there. And then, like putting together the pieces of a puzzle, they amass enough information to penetrate your system.

A much safer approach is to implement all database access using stored procedures and views. Not only will this add an additional layer of protection, it will usually improve performance. In addition, all SELECT/INSERT/UPDATE and DELETE permissions on the database objects should be removed so that the hacker would not be able to use utility tools like Microsoft Query to get to the data in the database.

You should even consider eliminating all logins to the database except for the single login used to access the stored procedures, and of course, the system administrator. If you do need to have access to the database from outside your application, consider constructing multiple versions of your views. By having two (or more) views for your tables, you can separate how your application accesses your data from how other users would access it. The views can be completely identical, except for the access permissions. The first view could be accessible by your application's stored procedures and the second accessible by groups defined in your NT domain using NT security.

Microsoft SQL Server also provides application roles, which are very useful in preventing users from accessing your database without using your application.

Most RDBMSs allow you to specify a default database. Unless you specify otherwise, the default is usually the system database. This is not good practice! Try creating a new, empty database and assign that as the default. This way, if an unauthorized person does gain access to your database server, they should be directed to this benign database.

Another risk factor worth considering is from internal attacks – people within your own organization. Unauthorized access by employees and contractors is probably the primary concern for many corporations. In many development environments, the application is developed on one server, tested on a different server, and finally installed on a third server for production. Often developers will create a single DSN or UDL file and simply edit the name of the server in the file when the application moves from server to server, using the same login ID and password on each. A more secure approach is to create three different data source files, each using a different login and password for the servers they access. Not only will this add another measure of security, it helps to eliminate the application from accidentally pointing to the wrong server and keeps the development team from accessing potentially sensitive production data.

Summary

We have seen in this chapter a number of options available to secure our web sites. Through authentication, we can determine who is attempting to access our site and its resources. Once we know who the user is, we can authorize them so that they are able to operate on the site. IIS provides several different authentication models that range from no authentication (Anonymous Authentication) through secured authentication via the operating system (Integrated Windows Authorization). We also provided the option of using outside resources, such as Certificate Authorities, to verify credentials and to provide additional security.

We also discussed how we may set up permissions on the web site itself, so that we can control what an authenticated user may or may not do while using our web site's resources. Used together, user authorization and web site permissions give us a great deal of security. This security may be further enhanced, by taking some fairly simple steps to better secure our databases, IP addressing, and the system registry.

Of course, you should work closely with your network engineers to determine how security should be implemented best with your organization's applications, but by following what was discussed in this chapter, you will be able to build into your applications the security needed to carry out e-commerce transactions.

Section 9

Case Studies

Case Study 1: Web-Based Reports

With any business, there are needs for summarizing and reporting upon that business' activities. With the preference of many organizations to display information online, there is a demand for producing reports using web pages. This case study demonstrates how ASP pages may be used to produce such reports using an N-tier architecture.

This case study demonstrates many of the basic concepts and techniques described in the previous chapters: it uses multi-tiered components with ASP pages to access a database. We'll see how the ASP pages can utilize COM+ applications that are managed by Windows 2000 Component Manager to invoke stored procedures, which in turn acquire data from tables using views. The resulting data is merged with HTML and JavaScript by using VBScript to produce an attractive green bar report in the browser.

The most important aspect of this application is that it demonstrates a framework, not just an application. Rarely will we need to build a single report, so having a solid framework to build upon is essential to expand the application for additional reports.

The application described in this chapter is based upon development work performed for a number of different applications, drawing from each of the applications to produce a reporting framework that will allow for easy generation of reports *en masse*. Some of the complexities found in the applications that this case study draws from have been simplified so that we can illustrate the concepts more clearly. By having a clear understanding of how this application is constructed, you will be better able to enhance and expand it to meet your particular needs.

The code and scripts required to create this case study can be downloaded from the Wrox Programmer to Programmer web-site at www.wrox.com.

Business Objectives

The fictitious company developing this application has an e-commerce web site. Currently, the site monitors the movement of customers on the site as they move from page to page, and keeps track of the contents of each customer's shopping cart. This information is stored in a Microsoft SQL Server 2000 database. The company wishes to develop a facility to summarize the activities of the customers on the site. The application to provide this service must meet the following objectives:

❑   The application must have the ability to summarize the activity on the site as well as historical information in a standardized report format.

❑   A number of options must be available to summarize the information on a daily, weekly, and year-to-date basis.

❑   The data presented shall be downloadable to allow for further analysis.

❑   The application should be accessible by any authorized manager regardless of the computer they are using.

❑   Adequate security must be used to insure that unauthorized users do not have access.

❑   The interface for the application should be easy to understand and to use.

❑   Initially, the application must be able to support as many as a dozen simultaneous users, and be capable of eventually supporting several dozen simultaneous users.

❑   The number of connections to the database should be limited so that the cost of additional server licenses will be kept to a minimum.

❑   The application should allow for the addition of new reports without affecting existing reports.

❑   When calculating statistics concerning the customers' shopping carts, those customers that did not place any items in their carts should be excluded.

With these objectives in mind, a browser-based solution is ideal. By using a series of ASP pages on a web site, access to the application and its data can be limited to the appropriate parties. To provide the scalability required without having to buy many additional client licenses for the database, OLE DB and Component Services will be used to pool the connections to the database. To provide access to the most current web site statistics, views will be used to directly reference the tables in the database.

By acquiring the data using ASP pages, the information can be assembled for display within a browser as well as for download into a client-side application, such as Microsoft Excel. There are several advantages to providing a download feature. First, using a spreadsheet for analysis has become commonplace in today's office, so most end users appreciate being able to actually work with the numbers and not just view them. Secondly, by having the reporting and download features together, it makes managing security a bit easier than having two different applications. Not only will end users like the ability to obtain the data from a report, but this feature also provides us with another mechanism for testing the application.

The requirements for an easy-to-use interface and to allow for additional reports in the future will be addressed by developing a standardized framework of ASP files. By creating each report using a framework, there will be consistency in the user interface making them easier to use. Another advantage of taking a framework approach is that the development of future reports will be relatively easy since we will be able to leverage the existing code in the framework.

Using the Application

One of the goals for the application's design was to make it easy to use and understand. One way to accomplish this was to use a wizard-type interface. Wizards have become more and more popular in recent years, and many people are used to working with them, so having such an interface is appropriate in many cases.

After the user navigates to the start page and enters their username and password, they are presented with a list of available reports:

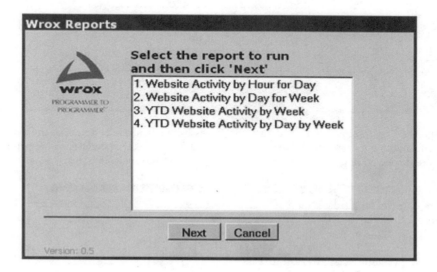

This illustration shows only four reports, but many more can easily be added. We will demonstrate using these reports by selecting the first report in the list. Since each report has a similar interface, by walking through the pages of one report, we will get a look and feel for the other reports as well.

To select a report to execute, the user may double-click the report to run or highlight it and then select the Next button. Choosing Cancel redirects the user to a page of our choosing, in our case the Wrox web site. After selecting the report, a page is displayed with the parameters required to run the selected report.

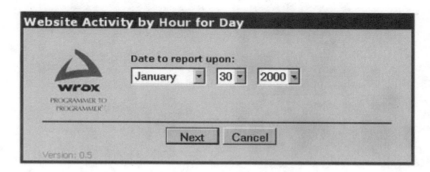

In this case, the report selected requires only a date to be selected by the user, so drop-down lists provide month, day, and year selections. As with the first page, a pair of Next and Cancel buttons is displayed at the bottom. When the user selects the Next button, a new form is displayed allowing the user to choose how they want the report to be displayed: as an HTML page in their browser, an Excel spreadsheet in their browser, or as a downloadable **Comma Separated Values** (**CSV**) file:

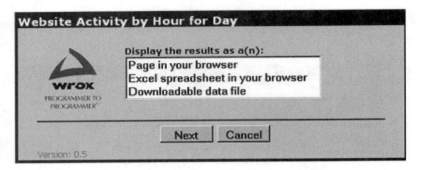

Selecting the Next button invokes a third page that accesses the database and merges the data and the appropriate formatting to produce the results. The Cancel button returns the user to the prior page. When the results are displayed in the browser, the end result of this report looks like this:

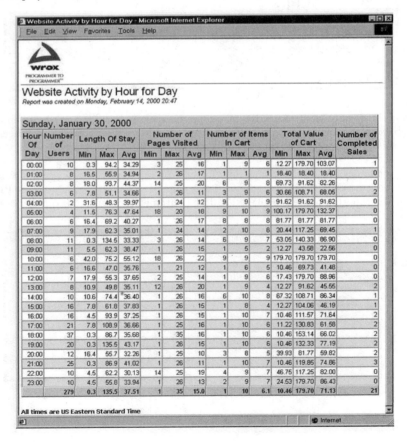

Website Activity by Hour for Day
Report was created on Monday, February 14, 2000 20:47

Sunday, January 30, 2000

Hour Of Day	Number of Users	Length Of Stay			Number of Pages Visited			Number of Items In Cart			Total Value of Cart			Number of Completed Sales
		Min	Max	Avg	Min	Max	Avg	Min	Max	Avg	Min	Max	Avg	
00:00	10	0.3	94.2	34.29	3	25	16	1	9	6	12.27	179.70	103.07	1
01:00	8	16.5	55.9	34.94	2	26	17	1	1	1	18.40	18.40	18.40	0
02:00	8	18.0	93.7	44.37	14	25	20	6	9	8	69.73	91.62	82.26	0
03:00	6	7.8	51.1	34.66	1	26	11	3	9	6	30.66	108.71	68.05	2
04:00	2	31.6	48.3	39.97	1	24	12	9	9	9	91.62	91.62	91.62	0
05:00	4	11.5	76.3	47.64	18	20	18	9	10	9	100.17	179.70	132.37	0
06:00	6	16.4	69.2	40.27	1	26	17	8	8	8	81.77	81.77	81.77	0
07:00	9	17.9	62.3	35.01	1	24	14	2	10	6	20.44	117.25	69.45	1
08:00	11	0.3	134.5	33.33	3	26	14	6	9	7	53.05	140.33	86.90	0
09:00	11	5.5	62.3	38.47	1	26	15	1	5	2	12.27	43.58	22.56	0
10:00	6	42.0	75.2	55.12	18	26	22	9	9	9	179.70	179.70	179.70	0
11:00	6	16.6	47.0	35.76	1	21	12	1	6	5	10.46	69.73	41.48	0
12:00	7	17.9	55.3	37.65	2	25	14	1	9	6	17.43	179.70	88.96	0
13:00	8	10.9	49.8	35.11	12	26	20	1	9	4	12.27	91.62	45.55	2
14:00	10	10.6	74.4	36.40	1	26	16	6	10	8	67.32	108.71	86.34	1
15:00	16	7.8	61.8	37.83	1	26	15	1	8	4	12.27	104.06	46.19	1
16:00	16	4.5	93.9	37.25	1	26	15	1	10	7	10.46	111.57	71.64	2
17:00	21	7.8	108.9	36.66	1	25	16	1	10	6	11.22	130.83	61.58	2
18:00	37	0.3	86.7	35.68	1	35	16	1	10	6	10.46	153.14	66.02	2
19:00	20	0.3	135.5	43.17	1	26	15	1	10	6	10.46	132.33	77.19	2
20:00	12	16.4	55.7	32.26	1	25	10	3	8	5	39.93	81.77	59.82	2
21:00	25	0.3	86.9	41.02	1	26	11	1	10	7	10.46	119.85	74.86	3
22:00	10	4.5	62.2	30.13	14	25	19	4	9	7	46.75	117.25	82.00	0
23:00	10	4.5	55.8	33.94	1	26	13	2	9	7	24.53	179.70	86.43	0
	279	0.3	135.5	37.51	1	35	15.0	1	10	6.1	10.46	179.70	71.13	21

All times are US Eastern Standard Time

As we can see, the top portion of the report, called the masthead, has the company logo on the left. Clicking the company logo will return the user to the report selection page.

When the option to display the results as an Excel worksheet within the browser is selected, an instance of Excel is started and runs within the browser window and displays the report:

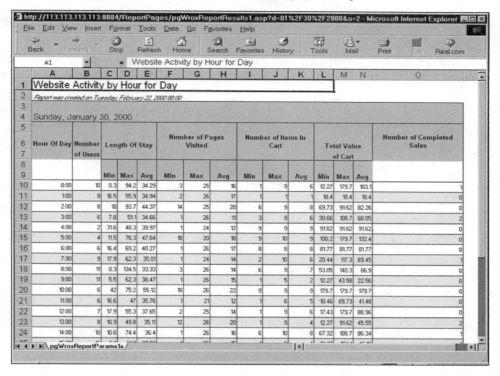

If the user chooses to download the data, they will be presented with the standard dialog allowing them to either open the file or save it to disk:

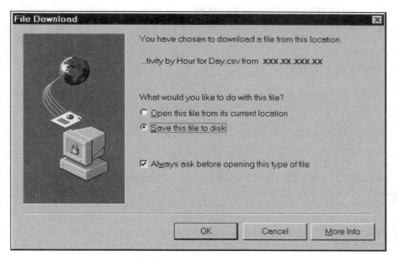

The downloaded file is formatted as a comma separated values file. When the file is opened, either directly or after being saved to disk, the raw data will be available for analysis. Since the data is stored as a CSV file, it may be opened in Excel, Word, and many other desktop applications. When opened, the file displays only the raw data values and no formatting, so some minor effort will be needed to clean up the display of the data. This is what the information looks like when opened in Microsoft Excel:

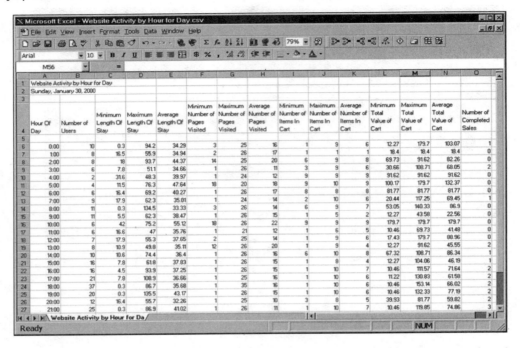

Hour Of Day	Number of Users	Minimum Length Of Stay	Maximum Length Of Stay	Average Length Of Stay	Minimum Number of Pages Visited	Maximum Number of Pages Visited	Average Number of Pages Visited	Minimum Number of Items In Cart	Maximum Number of Items In Cart	Average Number of Items In Cart	Minimum Total Value of Cart	Maximum Total Value of Cart	Average Total Value of Cart	Number of Completed Sales
0:00	10	0.3	94.2	34.29	3	25	16	1	9	6	12.27	179.7	103.07	1
1:00	8	16.5	55.9	34.94	2	26	17	1	1	1	18.4	18.4	18.4	0
2:00	8	18	93.7	44.37	14	25	20	6	9	8	69.73	91.62	82.26	0
3:00	6	7.8	51.1	34.66	1	26	11	3	9	6	30.66	108.71	68.05	2
4:00	2	31.6	48.3	39.97	1	24	12	9	9	9	91.62	91.62	91.62	0
5:00	4	11.5	76.3	47.64	18	20	18	9	10	9	100.17	179.7	132.37	0
6:00	6	16.4	69.2	40.27	1	26	17	8	8	8	81.77	81.77	81.77	0
7:00	9	17.9	62.3	35.01	1	24	14	2	10	6	20.44	117.25	69.45	1
8:00	11	0.3	134.5	33.33	3	26	14	6	9	7	53.05	140.33	86.9	0
9:00	11	5.5	62.3	38.47	1	26	15	1	5	2	12.27	43.58	22.56	0
10:00	6	42	75.2	55.12	18	26	22	9	9	9	179.7	179.7	179.7	0
11:00	6	16.6	47	35.76	1	21	12	1	6	5	10.46	69.73	41.48	0
12:00	7	17.9	55.3	37.65	2	25	14	1	9	6	17.43	179.7	88.96	0
13:00	8	10.9	49.8	35.11	12	26	20	1	9	4	12.27	91.62	45.55	2
14:00	10	10.6	74.4	36.4	1	26	16	6	10	8	67.32	108.71	86.34	1
15:00	16	7.8	61.8	37.83	1	26	15	1	8	4	12.27	104.06	46.19	1
16:00	16	4.5	93.9	37.25	1	26	15	1	10	7	10.46	111.57	71.64	2
17:00	21	7.8	108.9	36.66	1	25	16	1	10	6	11.22	130.83	61.58	2
18:00	37	0.3	86.7	35.68	1	35	16	1	10	6	10.46	153.14	66.02	2
19:00	20	0.3	135.5	43.17	1	26	15	1	10	6	10.46	132.33	77.19	2
20:00	12	16.4	55.7	32.26	1	25	10	3	8	5	39.93	81.77	59.82	2
21:00	25	0.3	86.9	41.02	1	26	11	1	10	7	10.46	119.85	74.86	3

Some minor formatting has been applied here: the row containing the column headings was selected and Wrap Text cell formatting was applied.

How the Application Works

Before we delve too deeply into the details of the application, let's discuss at a high level what happens at each step in the process. Once we see how the various parts fit together, we can drill down and take a closer look at how the code was assembled.

The core of the design is a series of ASP pages, and the code in these pages is organized by function. The code that is specific to a given report is saved in separate files: code that may be used by multiple reports in a different page, and general use code stored in other files, again according to use. Many of these files contain functions that return standardized HTML code and are used to merge the data obtained from the data store to dynamically format the pages.

These HTML functions, along with a series of global constants, provide a convenient method for assembling a consistent look and feel for the application. They also help relieve us from getting bogged down writing repetitive HTML tags and allow us to concentrate on the logic required to construct the application. For example, since we are using a wizard interface for many of the pages, making a function call at the start of each page to produce the HTML code for the wizard is much more convenient than reconstructing the code for each page.

The initial page for this application is pgWroxReports.asp, This page would typically be available as a link from the existing web site. We store this page and the other files for the reporting application in a different folder from the rest of the site. By keeping these pages in their own folder, we can more easily apply the necessary security features governing access. By applying such security, we meet one of our business objectives to make the application available only to authorized managers.

As we have seen, the pgWroxReports.asp file provides the user with a list of available reports. Depending upon which report is selected, a second page is displayed to prompt the user for the parameters needed for that report. Once the parameters have been obtained, a third page is invoked that does the majority of the work. This third page calls a function that creates an instance of our data access components and uses this instance to access a stored procedure in the database.

The stored procedure used is specific to the report being executed, but each operates generally the same way. The stored procedure executes a query that selects data from database views, getting only those records that match the parameters selected by the user. The first view used returns detail information and the second view returns summary values. The records returned are then processed by the ASP to provide the necessary formatting for output as either an HTML page or a downloadable comma separated values file.

Below is a breakdown of the various files used in the application, as well as the folders where they are stored.

Data folder

This folder contains files relating to the content displayed in the site. Although this application obtains all of its content from a database, other applications would store text or help files here.

File	Description
WroxReports.UDL	The **Universal Data Link** (UDL) containing the connection information needed to access the database. We look at using UDLs later in the chapter.

Objects folder

The Objects folder holds the various dynamic link libraries and applets used by the site.

File	Description
App.dll	A component with an application-specific interface.
MTSDAL.dll	A data access component used by App.dll to access the database.

Library folder

This folder provides a single location for commonly used files found in most applications, as well as template and default files.

File	Description
CommonRoutines.asp	Commonly used routines for such actions as instancing objects, using cookies and detecting browser settings.

Table continued on following page

File	Description
`DefaultFooter.asp`	The HTML code for a default footer for each page.
`DefaultMeta.asp`	Standardized META tags.
`ReportingRoutines.asp`	Functions used by all reports.
`WizardRoutines.asp`	Routines for constructing the HTML to display a wizard interface.

Images folder

All graphics used in the construction of the site are placed here, but not product or inventory graphics.

File
`rule.gif`
`spacer.gif`
`wrox_logo100.gif`

ReportPages folder

This folder contains files specific to this reporting application.

File	Description
`default.asp`	Default pages, used for redirection to main report page
`IncGlobals.asp`	Defines global constants, variable, and default assignments
`IncMastHead.asp`	Defines standard HTML code for a banner at the top of each page
`IncPageBottom.asp`	Defines standard HTML code for the bottom of each page: uses an include file for a standard footer as well as `</BODY>` and `</HTML>` codes
`IncPageComments.asp`	Writes standardized comments, notifications, etc. for a page
`IncPageHeader.asp`	Defines standard HTML for `<HEAD>` with a title
`IncPageTop.asp`	Common location for assembling the top of a page with include files and possible navigation bar.
`pgWroxReportParams1.asp`	Prompts the user for parameters for running the first report and validates those parameters
`pgWroxReportParams2.asp`	Prompts the user for parameters for running the second report and validates those parameters
`pgWroxReportParams3.asp`	Prompts the user for parameters for running the third report and validates those parameters
`pgWroxReportParams4.asp`	Prompts the user for parameters for running the fourth report and validates those parameters

File	Description
pgWroxReportResults1.asp	Acquires the data for the first report and merges that data with the appropriate formatting codes (usually HTML) for display as a report
pgWroxReportResults2.asp	Acquires the data for the first report and merges that data with the appropriate formatting codes (usually HTML) for display as a report
pgWroxReportResults3.asp	Acquires the data for the first report and merges that data with the appropriate formatting codes (usually HTML) for display as a report
pgWroxReportResults4.asp	Acquires the data for the first report and merges that data with the appropriate formatting codes (usually HTML) for display as a report
pgWroxReports.asp	Provides the list of reports that may be executed by the user

The Start Page

As we have seen, the initial page of the application, named pgWroxReports.asp, allows the user to select a report to execute. This page is the simplest of the three. It does little more than display a form with a series of OPTION tags to produce the list of available reports. It contains a number of include files to provide a standard layout for the pages, a set of variables and constants, as well as access to a module of routines used to generate the wizard interface. These wizard routines are used to generate the HTML for the top and bottom portions of the wizard dialogs.

The reports listed on this page are hard coded, which is perfectly adequate for our purposes. Although reports may be added in the future, the list of available reports will not change frequently enough to justify dynamically generating this list.

When the user selects a report, a small bit of JavaScript code redirects the user to the appropriate page to choose the parameters for the report. When the first report is selected, pgWroxReportParams1.asp is accessed. If the second report is selected, then pgWroxReportParams2.asp is used, as is pgWroxReportParams3.asp for the third, and so on. By using this standard naming convention, the JavaScript code can use the numeric value of the OPTION tag selected to construct the filename of the next page to be invoked.

```
<SCRIPT LANGUAGE="JavaScript" TYPE="text/javascript">
<!--
function ProcessUserSelection() {
    if (document.frmWizard.cboSelections.selectedIndex >= 0) {
        location.href = 'pgWroxReportParams' +
        (document.frmWizard.cboSelections.selectedIndex +1) + '.asp';
    }
}
//-->
</SCRIPT>
```

As seen from the code snippet above, the JavaScript references an HTML form named `frmWizard`. The form is defined to invoke the `ProcessUserSelection()` JavaScript routine when any of the option controls are clicked or when the Next button is selected.

Since we will want to have the same set of Next and Cancel buttons at the bottom of the form on each page, the function `ConstructButtonsOfWizard` is called that produces the HTML required for these buttons. This function takes two arguments. The first argument identifies the action to be taken if the Next button is selected, and the second identifies the action to be taken when selecting the Cancel button.

```
<FORM NAME="frmWizard" ACTION="#" METHOD="POST" ONSUBMIT="return false;"
ALIGN="center">
<%
   ' -- Generate the Wizard interface upto our contents
   ' -- code in included file library/WizardRoutines.asp
   ConstructTopOfWizard "Wrox Reports", "../images/wrox_logo100.gif", _
      "Wrox Reports", "pgWroxReports.asp"
%>
   <FONT FACE="VERDANA, ARIAL, HELVETICA" SIZE="2" COLOR="#000000"><P>
   <STRONG>Select the report to run<BR> and then click 'Next'</STRONG>
   <BR>
   <SELECT NAME="cboSelections" SIZE="10" ONDBLCLICK="ProcessUserSelection();">
      <OPTION VALUE="1">1. Website Activity by Hour for Day</OPTION>
      <OPTION VALUE="2">2. Website Activity by Day for Week</OPTION>
      <OPTION VALUE="3">3. YTD Website Activiy by Week</OPTION>
      <OPTION VALUE="3">4. YTD Website Activiy by Day by Week</OPTION>
   </SELECT></FONT>
<%
   ' -- Generate the Wizard interface after our contents
   ' -- code in included file library/ WizardRoutines.asp
   ConstructBottomOfWizard 1
   ' -- Note, in the next line, the $ sign is required.
   ConstructButtonsOfWizard _
      "$ProcessUserSelection();", "'http://p2p.wrox.com/'"
   ConstructBottomOfWizard 2
```

There is an advantage to using JavaScript here. By using client-side code to assemble the name of the next ASP file to be invoked, we avoid having to make another round trip to the server.

The Parameters Page

Most reports will require that the user provide a number of parameters for generating the output. With some designs, one ASP page will be used to display an HTML form to collect the parameters and when that form is submitted, another ASP page is used for validation. If more than one set of parameters is needed, the validation page would invoke a third ASP page, which in turn uses yet another page for validation. This approach is cumbersome and prone to maintenance problems since the code used to gather the parameters is separated from the code that validates those parameters.

The approach taken with our application is to collect and validate all of the parameters required for any given report in a single page. When the parameters form is submitted, it calls itself to validate the parameters. Depending upon the number of parameters that need to be provided for the report, this page may be called many times.

The first time the page is displayed, the initial parameter request form is displayed. After the user fills out the form and selects the Next button, the page calls itself, passing the values of the parameters entered as part of the query string. A variable named `mintVisitCount` is also passed to indicate that the other arguments passed in the query string should be validated. This indicator is also used to display a second parameter form should the arguments pass their validation tests.

Here is the routine that is called to determine which data validation routine should be used, as well as the validation routines themselves for the first report:

```
InitializePage

If mintVisitCount = "1" Then
    '-- If this is the initial call to page, no error msg is needed
    mstrErrMsg=""

ElseIf mintVisitCount = "2" Then
    '-- Validation for the first page of parameters.
    '-- If parameters are not valid, then mstrErrMsg describes the issue
    If Not ValidateParameterSet1 Then
        mintVisitCount = "1"
    End if

ElseIf mintVisitCount = "3" Then
    '-- Second page of parameters, if needed.
    '-- If parameters are not valid, then mstrErrMsg describes the issue
    If Not ValidateParameterSet2 Then
        mintVisitCount = "2"
    Else
        DisplayResultsPage
    End if

Else
    mintVisitCount = "0"
    mstrErrMsg=""
End If
```

Here are the routines to initialize all the variables, validate parameters, and redirect the user to the results page:

```
Sub InitializePage

    '-- Acquire values from Query String.
    mintVisitCount = Request("vc")
    If mintVisitCount = "" Then mintVisitCount = "1"
    mdtStartDate = Request("d")
    mintOutputFormat = Request("o")
    If mintOutputFormat = "" then mintOutputFormat = "-1"

    '-- Assign defaults.
    gPageCurrent = gPageHome
    gPageSubsequent = ""

End Sub
```

```
Function ValidateParameterSet1

    Dim dtStartDate
    Dim strDay, strMonth, strYear
    Dim blnReturnValue

    blnReturnValue = False
```

```
      strYear = Trim(Request("cboYear"))
      strMonth = Trim(Request("cboMonth"))
      strDay = Trim(Request("cboDay"))

      If strYear = "" Or strMonth = "" Or strDay = "" then
         mstrErrMsg = "Please choose a date before continuing."
         mintVisitCount = ""    '-- Redisplay the initial parameters form
      Else
         If CInt(strMonth) < 10 Then
            strMonth = "0"  & strMonth
         End If
         If CInt(strDay) < 10 Then
            strDay = "0"  & strDay
         End If
         dtStartDate =  strMonth & "/" & strDay & "/" & strYear

         If Not IsDate(dtStartDate) then
            mstrErrMsg = "An invalid date was selected. " _
              & "Please try again."
            mintVisitCount = ""    '-- Redisplay the initial parameters form
         Else
            mdtStartDate = dtStartDate
            blnReturnValue = True
         End If
      End If
   ValidateParameterSet1 = blnReturnValue
End Function


Function ValidateParameterSet2

   Dim intOutputFormat
   Dim blnReturnValue

   blnReturnValue = False
   intOutputFormat = Trim(Request("cboSelections"))

   If intOutputFormat = "" then
      mstrErrMsg = "Please choose an output format before continuing."
      mintVisitCount = "1"    '-- Redisplay the initial parameters form
   Else
      If Not IsNumeric(intOutputFormat) then
         mstrErrMsg = "An invalid selection was made. Please try again."
         mintVisitCount = "1"    '-- Redisplay the initial parameters form
      Else
         mintOutputFormat = intOutputFormat
         blnReturnValue = True
      End If
   End If
   ValidateParameterSet2 = blnReturnValue
End Function


Function DisplayResultsPage
   ' -- Invoke the page that generates the results of the report.
   Response.Redirect "pgWroxReportResults1.asp?" _
```

```
        & "d=" & Server.UrlEncode(mdtStartDate) _
        & "&o=" & Server.UrlEncode(mintOutputFormat)
    Response.End
End Function
%>
```

Each time the form is displayed, the contents of the `mstrErrMsg` variable are shown in the middle of the form. When the page is first loaded, this variable is set to a zero length string, so no message is presented to the user. If invalid data is passed, the `mstrErrMsg` variable is assigned some feedback message, so when the form is redisplayed, this message is shown.

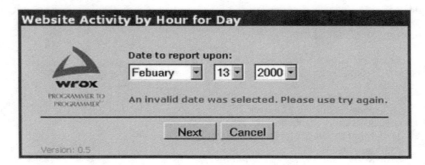

When the second parameters form is used, the Next button on the first form will again call `pgWroxReportParams1.asp`. We keep track of which form is to be displayed by incrementing the value for the variable `mintVisitCount`.

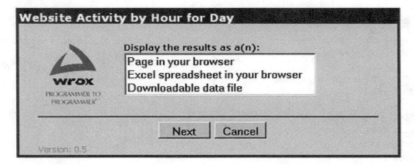

When the last set of parameters is validated, a new page that generates the report results is called. We display the results in a different page. We do this because as Netscape has a peculiarity which prevents the printing of a page that calls itself.

The Results Page

The majority of the work is performed by the last page, `pgWroxReportResults1.asp`. The code for this page starts by validating the query string parameters passed. Although these parameters should have been validated in the `pgWroxReportParams1.asp` file, it is always good practice to double-check the arguments passed.

If the parameters contain valid values, a subroutine named `ConstructReport` is called. This routine is the heart of the code. It is here that we call the stored procedure to acquire the data and "walk" the resultset to construct the appropriate formatting code to display these results.

Let's take a look at the code for this routine, and then go through what it does step-by-step:

```
'-- ConstructReport -----------------------------------------------------------
'
' PURPOSE:
'    This routine makes the call to the database to acquire the data. If data is
'    returned, then the recordset is processed and the appropriate formatting
'    code (usually HTML) is generated to display this data in a table format.

Function ConstructReport()

    ' -- Data Retrieval argument for this report.
    mstrSQL = "EXEC spReportActivityForDay " & " '" & dtDay & "'"
    If PopulateRecordset(mobjRS, mobjCOM, mstrSQL) Then

        ' -- Process the results of the stored procedure.
        WriteTopOfReport mstrReportTitle
        If (mobjRS.BOF and mobjRS.EOF) Then
            ' -- No Data was found
            DisplayMessage gSeverityWarning, _
              "No Data available in report for " _
              & "the parameters that you have requested. Please try again"
            Exit Function
        Else
            ' -- We have results to display.
            WriteGroupHeader   ' Show the column headings.
            Do While Not mobjRS.EOF
                WriteRowOfTable   ' Display the data from the current record.
                mobjRS.MoveNext   ' Advance to the next record
            Loop
            WriteBottomOfReport
        End if

        ' -- Clean up.
        On Error Resume Next
        mobjRS.close

    Else
        Response.Write "An unexpected condition prevented accessing the data."
    End if
    set mobjRS = Nothing
    set mobjCOM = Nothing

End Function
```

At the top of this routine we construct an SQL statement to invoke the stored procedure appropriate for this report, passing the selected parameters to it. In this first report, only the day to be processed is passed to the stored procedure. The actual call to the database is performed by the `PopulateRecordset` function, which returns a boolean value to indicate success or failure. We'll take a close look at this routine later on, but for now, we just need to realize that the function populates the recordset object `mobjRS`.

1190

If the `PopulateRecordset` is successful, we call the routine to generate the HTML for the masthead of the report. Next, we check if we had any records returned in the recordset. If both the BOF and EOF properties of the recordset object are True, then we have no data to report upon, so we add warning text to the page to notify the user of this.

If we do have records to display, we then proceed to generate the opening table tags in HTML with the first row of the table containing our column headings.

Next, we walk through the recordset using a loop. For each record in the recordset, we call a function that adds the HTML for a new row in the table and encloses the recordset's field values in the cells of that row. Once the recordset has been processed, we then call the `DisplayReportBottom` routine which adds the end table tag and writes any additional report footer information as needed.

Finally, we destroy the objects that we used and gracefully exit the routine.

Accessing the Middle-tier Components

The `PopulateRecordset` function called from `ConstructReport` is located in a file called `ReportingRoutines.asp`. Since this routine will be called by all of the reports, it is kept, along with other report related functions, in a separate file. The purpose of this routine is to create the COM objects specific to our application and then use those objects to have the database populate a recordset with the data needed for our reports.

```
'--------------------------------------------------------------------
' --   PopulateRecordset -----------------------------------------------
'
' PURPOSE:
'   Queries the database and sets up the passed recordset object with the
'   results.
'
' RETURNS:
'   True upon success, false otherwise
'
Function PopulateRecordset(ByRef objRS, ByVal objCOM, ByVal strSQL)

    PopulateRecordset = False
    ' -- Invoke COM component using a standard routine
    ' -- so that errors are handled centrally
    ' -- Routine in ../library/CommonCode.asp
    If SetupObjects(objRS, objCOM, gDALClassName) Then
        ' -- Data Retrieval argument for this report.
        set objRS = objCOM.ExecQuery(gConnectionInfo, strSQL, _
            gADOConnectionTimeout, gADOCommandTimeout)
        PopulateRecordset = True
    End If

End Function
```

The function accepts three arguments used to acquire data. The first argument, `objRS`, is passed by reference so that the calling routine, `ConstructReport`, will have access to the data returned by the database. The other two arguments specify the command object used to connect to the database and the SQL string that identifies the stored procedure call.

The recordset and command objects are in turn passed to the SetupObjects function that creates an instance of a COM object provided by the Windows 2000 Component Manager. The COM object is specified by its class name, which we identify by the constant gDALClassName. This constant is defined in the IncGlobals.asp file.

```
'-------------------------------------------------------------------
' -- SetupObjects ----------------------------------------------------
'
' PURPOSE:
'    Creates the Data Access Objects with error checking
'
' RETURNS:
'    True upon success, false otherwise
'

Function SetupObjects(ByRef objRS, ByRef objCOM, ByVal strObjectName)

    SetupObjects = False

    Set objRS = Server.CreateObject("ADODB.Recordset")
    If Err <> 0 Then
        Set objRS = Nothing
        Response.Write "Error in creating recordset: " _
          & Err.Description & "<BR>"
        Response.End
    End if
    Set objCOM = Server.CreateObject(strObjectName)
    If Err <> 0 Then
        set objCOM = Nothing
        Response.Write "Error in creating COM object: " _
          & strObjectName & ": " _
          & Err.Description & "<BR>"
        Response.End
    End If

    SetupObjects = True

End Function
```

But why have a different routine to create the instance of the COM object? Why not do all this work in the PopulateRecordset function? The reason goes back to one of the original goals for this application – to establish a framework so that we can create new pages easily by using as much of our existing code as possible. The PopulateRecordset function, although fairly generic, does provide us with a layer to add code specific to reporting. It also holds the connection string information found in the UDL. The SetupObjects function is more generic and may be used with any ASP page that requires a middle-tier component that accesses a database.

In our application, we will use two Visual Basic components:

❑   Capplication

❑   CdataAccess

The CApplication class is used to execute SQL queries. It uses the following signature when calling its ExecQuery method:

```
Function ExecQuery _
  (ByVal scCONNECT As Variant, ByVal strSQL As Variant, _
   Optional ByVal lngConnectionTimeout, Optional ByVal lngCommandTimeout) _
   As ADODB.Recordset
```

The two optional arguments allowed in this method are used to specify timeout values for the connection and command objects. This is provided as an alternative to setting these properties using the objects' interfaces. By passing these properties as part of the call to the method, we avoid having to make additional round trips to the server.

The `cdataAccess` class returns a disconnected recordset object when passed a valid connection string and a SQL statement.

Since these components are to be managed by Component Manager, we need to make sure that **MTSTransactionMode** and **Instancing** properties are set correctly. We specify **Multiuse** instancing to minimize the number of component instances that will be needed to service our database requests, and thus allow for greater scaling of our application. This also helps meet the business objective to minimize the number of client licenses required for the application since Component Manager, along with OLE DB, will utilize connection pooling.

When the Data Access Components connect to the database, they use the connection information found in the `WroxReports.UDL`. This configuration file uses OLE DB to access the server to maximize connection speed and take advantage of connection pooling. The settings used in this file are shown opposite:

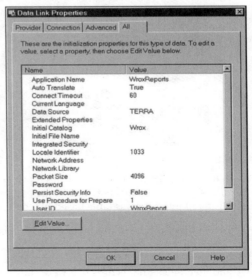

1193

We identify the name of the UDL file and the class name for our component in the `IncGlobals.asp` file as constants:

```
'-- Data Access-related constants
const gConnectionInfo="FILE NAME=K:\WEBS\Wrox\data\WroxDAL.UDL"
const gDALClassName = "App.CApplication"    ' COM Class Name
```

The Database

The database itself can be set up by running the scripts available at the Wrox web site. The objects in the database include a table that holds the data accessed, some views used to access this data, and a number of stored procedures used to select against these views. In a live web site, there will be many more objects. In order to more clearly impart the techniques used in this case study, we have eliminated from the database those objects that do not directly relate to our application.

The data accessed for the reports in this application comes from a single table. This table, `StatisticsByHourByUser`, contains data describing the activities of different visitors to the site on an hourly basis.

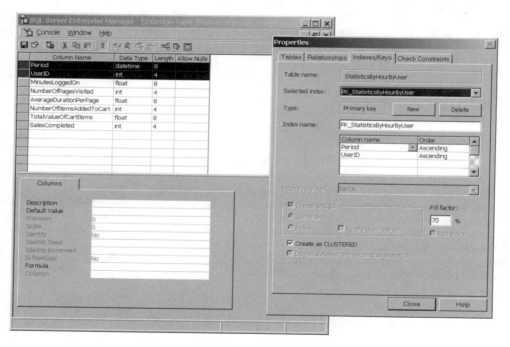

We assume that this table will be used primarily for reporting purposes, and that when it is used we will be most frequently selecting data by specifying a range of dates. To improve performance, we applied a clustered index on this table based first on the `Period` field and then the `UserID`.

In a live environment, this table would be populated in one of two ways. The first is by directly updating the table as users interact with the web site. The second way is to have the users' activities recorded in a different table and then use some regularly scheduled task that would calculate these statistics from the source table and then delete the records that were summarized.

This approach keeps the original source tables relatively small, and allows us to perform in advance many of the calculations that would normally be required when summarizing historical data. The task used to perform these calculations may be scheduled to run as frequently as desired, say every 10 minutes, to provide descriptions of the web site's current usage. Regardless of the approach used, the reports will have access to data that is sufficiently current to meet the business objective.

When this table is accessed from the application, we must use one of several views. The permissions applied to the table do not permit direct access except from the database administrator. This is done to help prevent unauthorized access to the data, as well as to facilitate modifications that may be required in the future. By accessing the data with views, if we ever need to make changes to the table structure, the likelihood of breaking our existing code will be reduced. This lends itself to supporting another business objective: to allow for the addition of new reports without effecting existing reports.

The business objectives also stated that when calculating statistics concerning the customers' shopping carts, we are to exclude those customers that did not place any items in their carts. In order to facilitate this, we will need to calculate the cart-related fields by only those records that show that items were placed in the cart, while other fields are calculated using all records. By using a view, we can easily combine multiple select statements to produce a single resultset The code below lists the definitions of two of these views to illustrate how this is accomplished.

The following code generates a report of activity over an hour.

```
CREATE VIEW dbo.vwStatisticsByHour
AS

SELECT
    A.Period,
    UserCount,
    MinutesOnsiteMax,
    MinutesOnsiteMin,
    MinutesOnsiteAvg,
    NumberOfPagesVisitedMax,
    NumberOfPagesVisitedMin,
    NumberOfPagesVisitedAvg,
    NumberOfItemsAddedToCartMax,
    NumberOfItemsAddedToCartMin,
    NumberOfItemsAddedToCartAvg,
    TotalValueOfCartItemsMax,
    TotalValueOfCartItemsMin,
    TotalValueOfCartItemsAvg,
    SalesCompletedCount

FROM
(
    SELECT
        Period,
        UserCount = Count(UserID),
        MinutesOnsiteMax = MAX(MinutesOnSite),
        MinutesOnsiteMin = MIN(MinutesOnSite),
        MinutesOnsiteAvg = AVG(MinutesOnSite),
        NumberOfPagesVisitedMax = MAX(NumberOfPagesVisited),
        NumberOfPagesVisitedMin = MIN(NumberOfPagesVisited),
        NumberOfPagesVisitedAvg = AVG(NumberOfPagesVisited),
        NumberOfItemsAddedToCartMax = MAX(NumberOfItemsAddedToCart),
        TotalValueOfCartItemsMax = MAX(TotalValueOfCartItems),
```

```
            SalesCompletedCount =SUM(SalesCompleted)
        FROM
            StatisticsByHourByUser
        GROUP BY
            Period
    ) As A
    LEFT JOIN
    (
        SELECT
            Period,
                NumberOfItemsAddedToCartMin = MIN(NumberOfItemsAddedToCart),
                NumberOfItemsAddedToCartAvg =
            AVG(CONVERT(float,NumberOfItemsAddedToCart)),
             TotalValueOfCartItemsAvg = AVG(CONVERT(float,TotalValueOfCartItems)),
             TotalValueOfCartItemsMin = MIN(TotalValueOfCartItems)
        FROM
            StatisticsByHourByUser
        WHERE
            NumberOfItemsAddedToCart > 0
        GROUP BY
            Period
    ) As B
    ON (A.Period = B.Period)
```

And the following generates a report of activity over a day:

```
CREATE VIEW dbo.vwStatisticsByDay
AS

SELECT
    A.DayOfYear,
    UserCount,
    MinutesOnsiteMax,
    MinutesOnsiteMin,
    MinutesOnsiteAvg,
    NumberOfPagesVisitedMax,
    NumberOfPagesVisitedMin,
    NumberOfPagesVisitedAvg,
    NumberOfItemsAddedToCartMax,
    NumberOfItemsAddedToCartMin,
    NumberOfItemsAddedToCartAvg,
    TotalValueOfCartItemsMax,
    TotalValueOfCartItemsMin,
    TotalValueOfCartItemsAvg,
    SalesCompletedCount

FROM
(
    SELECT
        Convert(datetime, CONVERT(varchar(14), Period, 110)) AS DayOfYear,
        UserCount = Count(UserID),
        MinutesOnsiteMax = MAX(MinutesOnSite),
        MinutesOnsiteMin = MIN(MinutesOnSite),
            MinutesOnsiteAvg = AVG(MinutesOnSite),
            NumberOfPagesVisitedMax = MAX(NumberOfPagesVisited),
```

```
            NumberOfPagesVisitedMin = MIN(NumberOfPagesVisited),
            NumberOfPagesVisitedAvg = AVG(NumberOfPagesVisited),
            NumberOfItemsAddedToCartMax = MAX(NumberOfItemsAddedToCart),
             TotalValueOfCartItemsMax = MAX(TotalValueOfCartItems),
            SalesCompletedCount =SUM(SalesCompleted)
    FROM
        StatisticsByHourByUser
    GROUP BY
        Convert(datetime, CONVERT(varchar(14), Period, 110))
) As A
LEFT JOIN
(
    SELECT
        Convert(datetime, CONVERT(varchar(14), Period, 110)) AS DayOfYear,
            NumberOfItemsAddedToCartMin = MIN(NumberOfItemsAddedToCart),
            NumberOfItemsAddedToCartAvg =
        AVG(CONVERT(float,NumberOfItemsAddedToCart)),
            TotalValueOfCartItemsAvg = AVG(CONVERT(float,TotalValueOfCartItems)),
            TotalValueOfCartItemsMin = MIN(TotalValueOfCartItems)
    FROM
        StatisticsByHourByUser
    WHERE
        NumberOfItemsAddedToCart > 0
    GROUP BY
        Convert(datetime, CONVERT(varchar(14), Period, 110))
) As B
ON (A.DayOfYear = B.DayOfYear)
```

Although views can be created to execute sophisticated SQL statements, they do not allow parameters to be used within their definitions. Since our application must select records for any given report based upon certain date ranges, we need a stored procedure to select only particular records. In addition, we want to calculate the summary values for the time frame and return these along with the rest of the recordset. The stored procedure listed below is used by the first report.

```
CREATE PROCEDURE [spReportActivityForDay]
(
    @dtDateToProcess datetime
)
AS
BEGIN

    Select 0 as RecordType, *
    From vwStatisticsByHour
    Where
        DatePart(dy,Period) = DatePart(dy,@dtDateToProcess)
        and
        DatePart(yy,Period) = DatePart(yy,@dtDateToProcess)
    Union
    Select 1 as RecordType, *
    From vwStatisticsByDay
    Where
        DatePart(dy,DayOfYear) = DatePart(dy,@dtDateToProcess)
        and
        DatePart(yy,DayOfYear) = DatePart(yy,@dtDateToProcess)
```

```
        Order By
            RecordType, Period

    END
```

This simple stored procedure queries against both the hourly and daily views. It adds a new field, `RecordType`, at the start of the resultset that is used to indicate if the record contains summary data or detail data. This field is later used by the ASP page to properly format the display of each record.

Processing the Results

After the `PopulateRecordset` function is called from `ConstructReport`, the variable `mobjRS` will be populated with any records returned by the database. Our next task is to merge the values found in these records with the required formatting. First we construct the top portion of the report by calling the `WriteTopOfReport` routine, passing it the title of the report. This routine, like the other formatting routines we will see, checks the value of the variable `mintOutputFormat` in order to choose the correct formatting code. This variable gets its value from the query string passed to the page.

```
'-----------------------------------------------------------------------------------
'-- WriteTopOfReport ---------------------------------------------------------------
'
' PURPOSE:
'   Writes the top portion of the report, either as an HTML doc or CSV file;
'   includes the title for the report.
'
Function WriteTopOfReport(ByVal strTitle)
    Dim value
    If mintOutputFormat = gOutputToHTML Then
        '-- Generate the HTML for top of the page.
        value = ConstructTopOfHTMLPage (strTitle)
    ElseIf mintOutputFormat = gOutputToExcel Then
        '-- Generate the top of the page w/o HTML heading codes
        Response.ContentType = "application/vnd.ms-excel"
        Response.AddHeader "Content-Disposition", _
            "filename=" & mstrDefaultXLSFilespec & ";"
    Else
        '-- Specify result as a Comma Separated Values file.
        Response.ContentType="application/csv"
        Response.AddHeader "Content-Disposition", _
            "filename=" & mstrDefaultCSVFilespec & ";"
    End if
    value = value & ConstructReportTitle()     ' Display the titles report
    Response.Write value
End Function
```

If the output is to be either a CSV file or an Excel spreadsheet to be displayed in the browser, we skip inserting the `<HTML>`, `<TITLE>` and `<BODY>` tags. Instead, we assign the `ContentType` of the `Response` object and add a **Content-Disposition** header. Content-Disposition headers are used to allow the content to be tagged in a way that indicates how it should be presented or saved as a file. In our application, when we assign a filename as part of the Content Disposition header, the extension of the filename is associated with an application by the client. By default, `XLS` and `CSV` extensions are associated with Microsoft Excel.

Once the top of the report has been constructed, we call a function that constructs the code for the column headings and we then loop through the recordset, calling the `WriteRowOfTable` function for each record. Once all records have been processed, we use the `WriteBottomOfReport` function to add any required closing codes, such as </BODY> and </HTML>, as needed.

```
WriteGroupHeader     ' Show the column headings.
Do While Not mobjRS.EOF
    WriteRowOfTable     ' Display the data from the current record.
    mobjRS.MoveNext    ' Advance to the next record
Loop
WriteBottomOfReport
```

The `WriteRowOfTable` function operates on the current record of `mobjRS`. First, it checks to see if the record contains detail or summary information by examining the `RecordType` field. If the record contains detail data, the `ConstructDetailCell` function is called for each field in the record. When the record contains summary data, the `ConstructSummaryCell` function is called instead. As each field is processed, the content of the page is constructed and saved in the `value` variable. At the end of the `WriteRowOfTable` function, the value variable is written to the output file using `Response.Write`.

```
'------------------------------------------------------------------
' -- WriteRowOfTable -----------------------------------------------
'
' PURPOSE:
'   Writes the formatted content for the current record of the opened recordset.
'
Function WriteRowOfTable()

    Dim value, tmpvalue
    Dim sngRecType

    sngRecType = CSng(mobjRS(mintRecordType))
    If (sngRecType = mintDataDetail) Then
        '-- The current record contains detail data, not summary data.

        intGroupRowCount = intGroupRowCount + 1    ' -- increment row counter

        value = value & ConstructDetailCell(mintPeriod)
        value = value & ConstructDetailCell(mintUserCount)
        value = value & ConstructDetailCell(mintMinutesOnsiteMin)
        value = value & ConstructDetailCell(mintMinutesOnsiteMax)
        value = value & ConstructDetailCell(mintMinutesOnsiteAvg)
        value = value & ConstructDetailCell(mintNumberOfPagesVisitedMin)
        value = value & ConstructDetailCell(mintNumberOfPagesVisitedMax )
        value = value & ConstructDetailCell(mintNumberOfPagesVisitedAvg )
        value = value & ConstructDetailCell(mintNumberOfItemsAddedToCartMin )
        value = value & ConstructDetailCell(mintNumberOfItemsAddedToCartMax )
        value = value & ConstructDetailCell(mintNumberOfItemsAddedToCartAvg )
        value = value & ConstructDetailCell(mintTotalValueOfCartItemsMin )
        value = value & ConstructDetailCell(mintTotalValueOfCartItemsMax )
        value = value & ConstructDetailCell(mintTotalValueOfCartItemsAvg )
        value = value & ConstructDetailCell(mintSalesCompletedAvg  )

        If mintOutputFormat <> gOutputToCSV Then
            value = ConstructReportTR(rptPlain) & value _
```

```
                & ConstructReportTR(rptEndTag)
        else
            value = value & vbNewLine
        End if

    Else
        '-- The current record contains summary data, not detailed data,
        '   so we need to format the row as a group footer.

        intGroupRowCount = 0 ' reset counter of records within the group.

        tmpValue = ConstructSummaryCell(mintPeriod) _
            & ConstructSummaryCell(mintUserCount) _
            & ConstructSummaryCell(mintMinutesOnsiteMin) _
            & ConstructSummaryCell(mintMinutesOnsiteMax) _
            & ConstructSummaryCell(mintMinutesOnsiteAvg) _
            & ConstructSummaryCell(mintNumberOfPagesVisitedMin) _
            & ConstructSummaryCell(mintNumberOfPagesVisitedMax) _
            & ConstructSummaryCell(mintNumberOfPagesVisitedAvg) _
            & ConstructSummaryCell(mintNumberOfItemsAddedToCartMin) _
            & ConstructSummaryCell(mintNumberOfItemsAddedToCartMax) _
            & ConstructSummaryCell(mintNumberOfItemsAddedToCartAvg) _
            & ConstructSummaryCell(mintTotalValueOfCartItemsMin) _
            & ConstructSummaryCell(mintTotalValueOfCartItemsMax) _
            & ConstructSummaryCell(mintTotalValueOfCartItemsAvg) _
            & ConstructSummaryCell(mintSalesCompletedAvg)

        if mintOutputFormat <> gOutputToCSV Then
            value = ConstructReportTR(rptGroupFooter)
            value = value &  ConstructReportTD(rptEndTag, 1, 1, 0, 42)
            value = value & tmpValue
            value = value & ConstructReportTR(rptEndTag)
            value = value & "</TABLE></P>"
        Else
            value = " ," & vbNewLine & tmpValue & vbNewLine & vbNewLine
        End if

    End If
    Response.Write value
    WriteRowOfTable = value

End Function
```

The `WriteRowOfTable` function and the functions it calls rely upon a number of helper functions that actually assemble the formatting code. For example, the `ConstructDetailCell` function is passed the ordinal position of a field and, based upon this position, we know how to display the field value:

```
Function ConstructDetailCell(ByVal i)
    Dim value

    If IsNull(mobjRS(i)) Then
        mobjRS(i) = 0
    End If

    If i = mintPeriod Then
```

```
        value = FormatDatetime(mobjRS(i),4)

    ElseIf i = mintMinutesOnsiteMax Then
        value = FormatNumber(mobjRS(i),1)
    :
    :
```

Other functions, such as `ConstructReportTR`, return HTML:

```
'------------------------------------------------------------------------------
' -- ConstructReportTR ------------------------------------------------------
'
' PURPOSE:
'   Returns the appropriately formatted <TR> or </TR> tag according to the type
'   of table row code that is passed.

Function ConstructReportTR(ByVal intType)
    Dim value
    If intType = rptPlain Then
        value = "<TR>"
    ElseIf intType = rptEndTag Then
        value = "</TR>"
    ElseIf intType = rptGroupHeader Then
        value = "<TR BGCOLOR=""" & gstrHeaderRowBGColor & """>"
    ElseIf intType = rptGroupFooter Then
        value = "<TR BGCOLOR=""" & gstrFooterRowBGColor & """>"
    End If
    ConstructReportTR = value
End Function
```

By using these helper functions, our code is much easier to construct and maintain, and we produce much more consistent content.

Security

A number of security-related features are implemented with our application. The business objectives required that the reporting portion of the web site allows only authorized users access. In addition, these authorized users should be able to access the reports, regardless of the computer they are using. Implicit with all application development is the need for a certain measure of security applied to the data itself. To meet these needs, our application employed security on both the web site and in the database. Let's take a look at what was done.

Security on the Web Site

The first level of security is very simple, namely by not making the URL to the reports a visible link from the main web site. Since only the managers in the company will be provided with the URL, we are not advertising the site and therefore not encouraging unauthorized access.

The second level of security comes from the organization of the ASP files in the folders of the site. By placing the report files in their own folder, `ReportPages`, we can easily add folder-level permissions. Under the Directory Security tab of the Properties dialog for the site, we applied Windows Integrated Authentication so that the user will be required to enter a username and password. By taking this approach, the user will be able to access the pages from any computer as long as he or she provides the proper credentials.

Security in the Database

All access to the database from the application to the database uses the connection information provided in a UDL located on the web server. This file is stored in an NTFS protected folder called objects. The NTFS permissions applied to this folder allow only administrators to access it. Furthermore, we set the identity of the COM components to use the same administrative account:

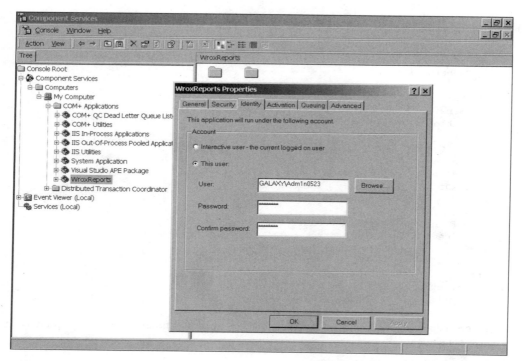

When the MTS components access the database, they do so only as the WroxReport user. This user is given very limited access to the server, and only to certain stored procedures in the Wrox database:

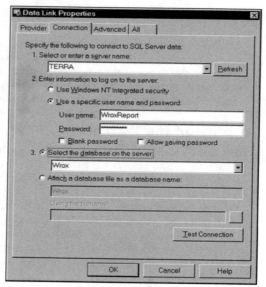

Even if the UDL was used by some other application, such as Microsoft Query or Microsoft Excel, by limiting access for the WroxReport user to only the reporting stored procedures, direct access to the data is prevented. As an additional layer of protection, these stored procedures reference only views. Only the database owner has permission to access the tables directly.

Summary

In this chapter we have seen how ASPs may be used to provide the common business task of reporting. From a developer's point of view, one of the most interesting aspects of this application is that it is constructed using a series of modules that establish a framework for future development and for easy maintenance. We illustrated how to apply many of the concepts covered in many of the previous chapters: ASP pages, HTML, client-side and server-side scripting, Visual Basic COM components, Component Manager, stored procedures, views, table indexes, and security.

From the business perspective, we were able to meet all of the business requirements laid out at the start of the chapter. These requirements are very typical of many business applications. To meet these requirements we:

❑ Created a browser-based solution that allows access to the application from virtually any computer with an internet connection.

❑ Provided adequate security so that only authorized users gained access by using NTFS folder permissions, Windows Integrated Authentication, SQL Server database log ins, and Component Manager identities.

❑ Kept the number of database connections low by utilizing OLE DB and the Component Manager, which allows for connection pooling.

❑ Allowed the data for the report to be presented in several ways, including downloads into Excel.

❑ Allowed for the development of new reports without effecting existing reports by keeping our code modular.

❑ Provided an easy-to-use wizard interface.

❑ Allowed for scaling to a great many users by using SQL Server, components, and by using a stateless design.

❑ Made the appropriate calculations in a database call by using views rather than the more costly approach of using multiple SQL statements.

Case Study 2: Dynamic Elements

As more and more web applications are being developed for the Internet, intranet, and extranet, the level of complexity of these applications has increased. We have come to rely on Dynamic HTML more and more to create web applications that provide a sophisticated interface for our users. In fact, as our users become more internet-aware, they have come to expect and even *demand* more sophisticated web applications. In addition this increase in sophistication in our web applications is the fact that our databases have also become more complex.

This case study addresses a particular need to create a web form that provides **dynamic HTML element creation**. The relationship of these dynamic elements also brings about a need to create some tables in SQL Server that provide **one-to-many** and **many-to-many relationships** – these will be discussed later in the chapter.

In this case study we will examine:

- ❏ The Problem
- ❏ The Solution
- ❏ Creating Table Relationships
- ❏ Creating Dynamic HTML Elements On The Client
- ❏ Server Side Processing Of Dynamic HTML Elements

All examples in this case study are written for Internet Explorer 4.0 or greater, and use a database stored in SQL Server.

The Problem

We are going to build a project manager web page – this page will allow you to name your project and list various tasks that you may want to complete. You want to be able to add any number of tasks that need completing, and for each of these tasks that you add, you want to add any number of sub-tasks from a selection.

The implementation scenario is that we need to create a web page that allows a user to input data on a form. While most of the fields on the form are static, we need to allow the user to enter data on the form in a one-to-many relationship. That is, the user could enter any number of fields for this record. There is no way to determine ahead of time how many fields the user may need to enter.

The next problem is that the user needs to be able to select data for each field that they entered. Again there could be multiple selections for each field that they entered and this becomes a many-to-many relationship. There is no way to determine ahead of time how many selections for each field there could be.

The screenshot below shows the form that we will be creating later on, with sample data entered. The number of dynamic fields added is unlimited and the number of dynamic select fields required for each dynamic field could also be unlimited.

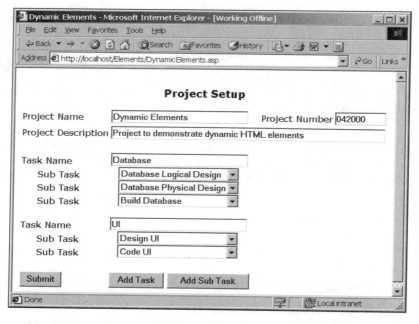

There are two problems that come to mind when we look at this scenario. First, how do we allow the users to dynamically input text on the form and to select one or more items for each field they enter? The next question that comes to mind is how do we define these relationships in SQL Server?

We will address these questions in detail in the sections that follow.

The Solution

The solution to this problem is not as difficult as one might expect. We need to allow the user to create as many text fields as they need, and for each field we need to allow them to display as many combo boxes as necessary, and to select an item from each combo box.

All of this can be accomplished using **Dynamic HTML**. All we need to do is to provide some buttons that will create the Dynamic HTML elements on the form. This is also possible using ASP and standard HTML, but this would require a round trip to the server to get the data and rebuild the page.

Looking at the form represented in the figure on the previous page, we can determine that we need to dynamically create HTML INPUT Type=Text elements. For each of these elements that we create on the form, the user can choose to create none or many combo boxes, which are represented by HTML SELECT elements. The OPTION data in the SELECT elements is populated from data in the database.

A prototype of what this form should look like is shown in the figure below:

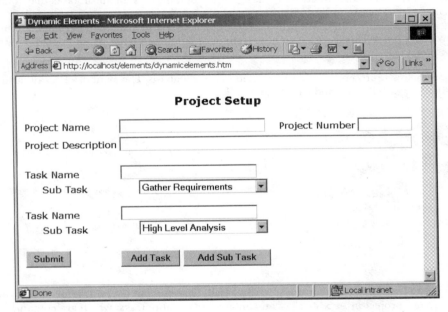

As we can see in the figure, we have two buttons (**Add Task** and **Add Subtask**) that allow the user to add Dynamic HTML elements on the form, an INPUT Type=Text element for entering a task name, and a SELECT element for selecting a subtask. We will examine creating these Dynamic HTML elements in detail later in this case study.

The database part of this solution is just a matter of creating the appropriate relationship tables, which tie together all of the dynamic elements that the user has created.

We will start our examination of the detailed solution by creating the database, which contains the relationship tables.

All the code in this chapter is available to download from the Wrox web site at
`http://www.wrox.com`.

Creating Table Relationships

Before we set out to create our web form we need to address the database issue at hand. From the previous figure, we can visually get an idea of what is needed in our database.

We are going to set up a table called `Project_T` that contains basic information about our project that will relate to the *static* fields on the form (these are static as they are always present on the page - the information in them can be changed), and another table called `Task_T` that contains all the fields that the *user creates*. This second table will provide the *one-to-many relationship*: one project relates to many tasks.

Next we will create a table called `Sub_Task_T` that contains a list of all subtasks that could be related to a particular task. Then in order to tie the subtasks to a task, we will create a table called `Task_Relationship_T` that will provide the *many-to-many relationship* in our database: many subtasks relate to many tasks. This is called an intersection, or a junction table. We'll explain how this all works in just a moment.

The figure below represents the tables needed in our database. The symbol <PK> indicates a primary key while the symbol <FK> indicates a foreign key.

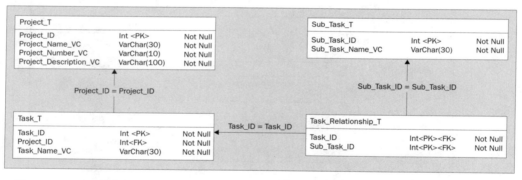

The table `Project_T` is the main table in this small database that contains information about different projects. Every project in `Project_T` can contain one or more tasks, which are contained in the `Task_T` table. This provides our one-to-many relationship. Notice that the `Task_T` table has a foreign key reference to the `Project_T` table.

The `Sub_Task_T` table contains common project-related subtasks. These subtasks can be related to one or more tasks for a project. The `Task_Relationship_T` table provides the relationship between `Task_T` and `Sub_Task_T`. This is where the many-to-many relationships between tasks and subtasks are stored. This table simply contains a foreign key reference to the `Task_T` and `Sub_Task_T` tables. The columns `Task_ID` and `Sub_Task_ID` are combined to make up the primary key to this table.

Given the simple design and the small number of tables in our database, we will create a SQL script to create the database and build the tables. This will allow those readers who are not familiar with creating databases and tables through script to learn how to perform this task. We will create and execute this script in the Query Analyzer.

Creating A Database Script

```
-- ***************************************************************************
-- Use The Master Database
-- ***************************************************************************
USE Master
Go
```

This code can be found on the Wrox web site, named `create_db.sql`. The first part of our SQL script will switch to the `Master` database, all SQL statements that are executed after this statement will be executed in the `Master` database. The `Go` command is not a SQL statement, but is recognized by the Query Analyzer and instructs it to send the preceding batch of SQL statements to the SQL server for processing.

```
-- ***************************************************************************
-- Create Projects Database
-- ***************************************************************************
CREATE DATABASE Projects
    ON PRIMARY
    (NAME = Projects,
    FILENAME = 'c:\mssql7\data\projects.mdf',
    SIZE = 2MB)
Go
```

Now we have switched to the `Master` database, we create our new `Projects` database. The `CREATE DATABASE` statement has many parameters, of which we are only going to use a small subset. We need to specify the database name, `Projects`. Then the `ON PRIMARY` parameter tells SQL Server that the disk files used to store the data portions of our database should be created on the `Primary` file group.

Next we specify the `NAME` parameter, which specifies the logical name for our database file. This name is sometimes used in SQL statements to reference our database files for this database, for example when backing up files and file groups. We are using a name of `Projects` as our logical file name for our database.

The next parameter that we have specified here is the `FILENAME` parameter. This parameter specifies the physical name of our database file. The file name that you specify here must be fully qualified and point to a directory on the same machine in which SQL Server is installed - you can't use mapped network drives here.

The last parameter we have specified is the `SIZE` parameter. This is the initial size of our database file and has been specified here as 2 megabytes. After all parameters have been specified, we code the `Go` command again so the database will be created before any other SQL statements are processed.

```
-- ***************************************************************************
-- Use The Projects Database
-- ***************************************************************************
USE Projects
Go
-- ***************************************************************************
-- Create Table Project_T
-- ***************************************************************************
CREATE TABLE Project_T
    (
    Project_ID                INT IDENTITY(1) NOT NULL,
    Project_Name_VC           VARCHAR(30)    NOT NULL,
    Project_Number_VC         VARCHAR(10)    NOT NULL,
    Project_Description_VC    VARCHAR(100)   NOT NULL
    )
GO
```

We switch to our newly created Projects database, so the rest of our SQL statements get executed on it. We now want to create the tables in the database. The first table that we want to create is the main table, Project_T. We are using the CREATE TABLE SQL statement, which like the CREATE DATABASE SQL statement has many parameters. Again, we are only using a small subset of these parameters.

We use the CREATE TABLE statement to create the Project_T table. Next, we specify column names, their data types, and whether or not the column will accept null values. The first column however, also has some additional arguments which define this column as an IDENTITY column. This argument specifies the initial seed value (the starting number), and increment value, both of which have been specified as 1. This column will be our primary key on the table and will be specified as such in just a little while.

You could use the Project_Number_VC column as the primary key for the table. However, I like to use integer data types as the primary key, especially when the primary key will be used as a foreign key in another table. Using an integer value for a primary and foreign key is more efficient than using a character value.

```
-- ********************************************************************
-- Create Table Task_T
-- ********************************************************************
CREATE TABLE Task_T
   (
   Task_ID       INT  IDENTITY(1,1)   NOT NULL,
   Project_ID    INT                  NOT NULL,
   Task_Name_VC VARCHAR(30)           NOT NULL
   )
GO


-- ********************************************************************
-- Create Table Sub_Task_T
-- ********************************************************************
CREATE TABLE Sub_Task_T
   (
   Sub_Task_ID INT IDENTITY(1,1) NOT NULL,
   Sub_Task_Name_VC VARCHAR(30)  NOT NULL
   )
GO
```

This process is repeated for the Task_T and Sub_Task_T tables.

```
-- ********************************************************************
-- Create Table Task_Relationship_T
-- ********************************************************************
CREATE TABLE Task_Relationship_T
   (
   Task_ID      INT NOT NULL,
   Sub_Task_ID INT NOT NULL
   )
GO
```

Notice that we have not specified an IDENTITY column on this last table we are creating. This table is a *relationship* table where the primary key will be made up of the only two columns. Both of these columns are also foreign key columns to their respective tables, Task_T and Sub_Task_T – that's why we don't have an identity column.

```
-- ***********************************************************************
-- Add Constraints (Primary Key) To Project_T
-- ***********************************************************************
ALTER TABLE Project_T
    ADD
    CONSTRAINT PK_Project_T PRIMARY KEY CLUSTERED (Project_ID)
GO
```

After all of the tables have been created, we add our constraints to the tables through the use of the ALTER TABLE statement. Here we are adding a PRIMARY KEY constraint as a CLUSTERED index to the Project_T table. Project_ID has been specified as the column that we want to be the PRIMARY KEY.

```
-- ***********************************************************************
-- Add Constraints (Primary and Foreign Keys) To Task_T
-- ***********************************************************************
.ALTER TABLE Task_T
    ADD
    CONSTRAINT PK_Task_T PRIMARY KEY CLUSTERED (Task_ID),
    CONSTRAINT FK_Task_T_Project_T FOREIGN KEY (Project_ID)
        REFERENCES Project_T (Project_ID)
GO
```

The next table, Task_T, has two constraints being added. One is for the PRIMARY KEY and the second is for the FOREIGN KEY.

First we specify the PRIMARY KEY constraint on the column Task_ID. Then we specify that the column Project_ID is a FOREIGN KEY to the column with the same name in the Project_T table.

```
-- ***********************************************************************
-- Add Constraints (Primary Key) To Sub_Task_T
-- ***********************************************************************
ALTER TABLE Sub_Task_T
    ADD
    CONSTRAINT PK_Sub_Task_T PRIMARY KEY CLUSTERED (Sub_Task_ID)
GO
```

We need only add a PRIMARY KEY constraint on the Sub_Task_ID column in the Sub_Task_T table. This table will be referenced by other tables and has no foreign keys to related tables.

```
-- ***********************************************************************
-- Add Constraints (Primary and Foreign Keys) To Task_Relationship_T
-- ***********************************************************************
ALTER TABLE Task_Relationship_T ADD
    CONSTRAINT PK_Task_Relationship_T PRIMARY KEY CLUSTERED
        (Task_ID,Sub_Task_ID),
    CONSTRAINT FK_Task_Relationship_T_Sub_Task_T FOREIGN KEY (Sub_Task_ID)
        REFERENCES Sub_Task_T (Sub_Task_ID),
    CONSTRAINT FK_Task_Relationship_T_Task_T FOREIGN KEY (Task_ID)
        REFERENCES Task_T (Task_ID)
GO
```

The last table that we want to create primary and foreign key constraints on is the
`Task_Relationship_T` table. This table's primary key is actually made up of two columns, `Task_ID`
and `Sub_Task_ID`. While both of these columns combined make up the `PRIMARY KEY` for this table,
separately they are `FOREIGN KEY`s to the `Task_T` and `Sub_Task_T` tables respectively.

After your script has been entered, execute it. Once your database has been created and the tables
added, you will need to populate the database with some data.

Populating The Sub_Task_T Table

The only table that needs to contain data at this point is the `Sub_Task_T` table. The rows in this table
will be used to populate a list on the web form. These subtasks will be selected by the user and related
to one or more tasks that the user defines.

> **Before running this script, ensure you select the Projects database in the Database
> combo box on the toolbar in the Query Analyzer. You also need to make sure that the
> user, specified in the connection string later on, has permissions to run the stored
> procedures and edit the tables.**

```
INSERT INTO Sub_Task_T (Sub_Task_Name_VC) VALUES('Gather Requirements')
INSERT INTO Sub_Task_T (Sub_Task_Name_VC) VALUES('High Level Analysis')
INSERT INTO Sub_Task_T (Sub_Task_Name_VC) VALUES('Detailed Analysis')
```

The code fragment above, taken from the file `populate_subtask.sql`, shows the first couple of the
`INSERT` statements which populate the `Sub_Task_T` table. The `Sub_Task_T` part of the statement
specifies the table name we want to insert data into. The next part of the `INSERT` statement specifies a
list of column names each separated by a comma. However, in our case we only have one column that
we are inserting data into. The `IDENTITY` column does not get included in the column list, as SQL
Server will automatically insert the next available number into that column, we get an error if we try to
insert it. The last part of the `INSERT` statement specifies the values that we want to insert. The values are
specified in the same order as the columns. However, since we are only specifying one column, we only
specify one value to be inserted. This is a string value and must be enclosed in single quotes.

Run the SQL script in the Query Analyzer to insert the values into the `Sub_Task_T` table.

Stored Procedures

When we work with Active Server Pages, we always want to ensure that we get as much performance
out of them as possible. This helps to reduce the load on our web server so that time can be spent
serving other client requests. To that end, we want to use stored procedures in our Active Server Pages
instead of in-line SQL statements. Stored procedures are more efficient than in-line SQL statements
because they are prepared and optimised in the database.

Another reason stored procedures are more efficient is the fact that you do no have to transmit as much
data across the network. When you execute a stored procedure, you are only sending the stored
procedure name along with any parameters it requires. When you use in-line SQL statements, you must
send all of the SQL statements and any parameters they require.

All of our stored procedures will be created using the Query Analyzer.

Subtask Select Stored Procedure

We now look at the stored procedure, `sp_upselect.sql`, that will select all subtasks from the `Sub_Task_T` table. This is a simple SELECT stored procedure that will be used to populate the combo box on the form. The following code will retrieve the stored procedures in the order in which they were entered.

```
CREATE PROCEDURE up_select_sub_tasks AS

SELECT Sub_Task_ID, Sub_Task_Name_VC
    FROM Sub_Task_T
    ORDER BY Sub_Task_ID
```

We start this stored procedure by specifying the CREATE PROCEDURE statement followed by the stored procedure name. Since this is a simple SELECT stored procedure, it does not have any input or output parameters.

Next, we specify our SELECT statement and list the column names that should be returned by this stored procedure. We are selecting data from the Sub_Task_T table and want the results sorted by the Sub_Task_ID so we have specified the ORDER BY clause and this column name.

Project Insert Stored Procedure

Once again, looking at the web form illustration, we can determine that we need a stored procedure - `sp_parmins.sql` - to insert our project name, number and description. Since we do not know how many dynamic fields the user will create, this stored procedure will just handle the project name, number and description.

```
CREATE PROCEDURE up_parmins_project (@Project_ID INT OUTPUT,
    @Project_Name        VARCHAR(30),
    @Project_Number      VARCHAR(10),
    @Project_Description VARCHAR(100)) AS

-- ****************************************************************************
-- Insert the new project into Project_T
-- ****************************************************************************
INSERT INTO Project_T
    (Project_Name_VC, Project_Number_VC, Project_Description_VC)
    VALUES(@Project_Name, @Project_Number, @Project_Description)

-- ****************************************************************************
-- Get the Project_ID just inserted and return it as an output parameter
-- ****************************************************************************
SELECT @Project_ID = @@IDENTITY
```

We start this stored procedure, as we did the last one, by specifying the CREATE PROCEDURE statement followed by the stored procedure name. Where this stored procedure differs is that it needs to accept parameters, so we have specified the parameters that it will need following the stored procedure name.

Notice that the first parameter specified, @Project, is an OUTPUT parameter. This parameter will be used to return the IDENTITY value that was inserted as the primary key. The next three parameters are INPUT parameters and are all VARCHAR data types.

Then we code the INSERT statement and specify Project_T as the table name that we want to insert data into. The next line of this INSERT statement lists the columns in the table that we want to insert data into. The last line of this INSERT statement contains the parameters that contain the data to be inserted.

The last part of our stored procedure places the IDENTITY value that was just inserted into our OUTPUT parameter using a SELECT statement.

Task Insert Stored Procedure

Since we have no way of knowing how many tasks or subtasks a user will create, we need to create a stored procedure - sp_parminstask.sql - which inserts a single task. We will then execute this stored procedure as many times as necessary.

If you recall our table design shown earlier, the Task_T table contains a foreign key reference to the project in the Project_T table. This key will need to be an input parameter to the stored procedure we create here.

```
CREATE PROCEDURE up_parmins_task (@Task_ID INT OUTPUT, @Project_ID INT,
   @Task_Name VARCHAR(30)) AS

-- ******************************************************************
-- Insert the task into Task_T
-- ******************************************************************
INSERT INTO Task_T
   (Project_ID, Task_Name_VC)
   VALUES(@Project_ID, @Task_Name)

-- ******************************************************************
-- Get the Task_ID just inserted and return it as an output parameter
-- ******************************************************************
SELECT @Task_ID = @@IDENTITY
```

This stored procedure looks very similar to the last INSERT stored procedure we created. Again, the first parameter this stored procedure has is an OUTPUT parameter. This is because we need the IDENTITY value that will be inserted to form the relationship for the subtasks as it will be used in our next stored procedure.

We also need to relate this task to the project, so we are using the Project ID that was returned from our last stored procedure as an INPUT parameter to this stored procedure. The last parameter of this stored procedure is the actual task name that the user has entered.

The rest of our stored procedure looks like the last INSERT stored procedure that we created. We have included comments to make the stored procedure easy to read and maintain. The last part of this stored procedure returns the IDENTITY value that was inserted as the primary key.

Task Relationship Insert Stored Procedure

Just as we do not know how many tasks a user will create, we also do not know how many subtasks a user will create for any given task. Given that, this stored procedure will insert a single relationship between a task and a subtask. We will execute this stored procedure, sp_relationship.sql, for every subtask that the user creates.

Since this stored procedure inserts a many-to-many relationship between tasks and subtasks, we need to pass the `Task_ID` and `Sub_Task_ID` of the relationship that we want to create. These IDs will be used as foreign keys their respective tables.

```
CREATE PROCEDURE up_parmins_task_relationship (@Task_ID INT, @Sub_Task_ID INT) AS


--    ***************************************************************************
--  Insert the task into Task_T
--    ***********************************************************************
INSERT INTO Task_Relationship_T
    (Task_ID, Sub_Task_ID)
    VALUES(@Task_ID, @Sub_Task_ID)
```

This `INSERT` stored procedure varies slightly from the last two stored procedures that we created, in that it does not return an `OUTPUT` parameter. We simply want to insert the `Task_ID` and `Sub_Task_ID` into the relationship table `Task_Relationship_T`.

If you recall the database diagram, this table consists of a primary key that is made up of the two values that we are inserting here. These two values also serve as foreign keys to their respective tables.

Select Project Stored Procedure

Once we have inserted a project and all of its related tasks and subtasks, we will want to select the project from the database and see the project details. That is where this stored procedure, `sp_parmsel.sql`, comes into play. However, given the nature of our project with the one-to-many and many-to-many relationships, this stored procedure introduces a little more complexity.

We want to create a `SELECT` stored procedure that will select the project details from the `Project_T` table; all of the tasks assigned to this project from the `Task_T` table; and every subtask for each task from the `Task_Relationship_T` table. The `Task_Relationship_T` table only contains foreign keys pointing to the `Task_T` and `Sub_Task_T` tables. Therefore we will also need to include the `Sub_Task_T` table to get the names of the subtasks.

```
CREATE PROCEDURE up_parmsel_project_details (@Project_ID INT) AS
SELECT Project_T.Project_ID, Project_Name_VC, Project_Number_VC,
    Project_Description_VC, Task_T.Task_ID, Task_Name_VC,
    Task_Relationship_T.Sub_Task_ID, Sub_Task_Name_VC

    FROM Project_T
```

The only input parameter this stored procedure accepts is the Project ID, the primary key of the project we want to display. Our `SELECT` statement starts with all of the columns that we want to select. Notice that since some of the column names have the same name in more than one table, we have prefixed those column names with the table name. This ensures that we don't get an "ambiguous column name" error in SQL Server.

```
--
--  Join the Task_T table to get all tasks
--
JOIN Task_T ON Project_T.Project_ID = Task_T.Project_ID
```

The main table that we want to select data from is the `Project_T` table and this is the table specified in the `FROM` clause. It is assumed that at least one task and one subtask exists for every project. Therefore, we are using a simple `JOIN` clause. If it were possible that a task or subtask did not exist for a project then we would want to use a `LEFT OUTER JOIN` to ensure that all records were returned in our query and null values were returned for columns that do not exist.

```
--
-- Join the Task_Relationship_T table to get all of the foreign keys for
-- each subtask
--
JOIN Task_Relationship_T ON Task_T.Task_ID = Task_Relationship_T.Task_ID
```

The first table that we want to join is the `Task_T` table. This table is joined to the `Project_T` table using the `Project_ID` column. This will give us all tasks for this project. The next table that we want to join is the `Task_Relationship_T` table. We are joining this table to the `Task_T` table using the `Task_ID` column. This will give us the foreign keys for all subtasks related to a specific task.

```
--
-- Join the Sub_Task_T table to get the names of the subtasks contained
-- in the Task_Relationship_T table
--
JOIN Sub_Task_T ON Task_Relationship_T.Sub_Task_ID = Sub_Task_T.Sub_Task_ID
```

In order to get the subtask names for a given task we need to join the `Sub_Task_T` table on the `Task_Relationship_T` table using the `Sub_Task_ID` column.

```
WHERE Project_T.Project_ID = @Project_ID

ORDER BY Task_Relationship_T.Task_ID
```

The `WHERE` clause limits the selection of data to a specific project that we specify in the `@Project_ID` input parameter. The `ORDER BY` clause ensures our tasks are selected in the order that they were inserted.

Creating Dynamic HTML Elements On The Client

Now that our database has been built and the stored procedures created, it's time to focus our attention on the Active Server Page that will contain the form for user input. Remember that this form will contain data from the database, so for this reason we need to make it an Active Server Page. If the form did not contain any data from the database or did not need any server-side processing before being displayed, we could create this form as a static HTML web page.

Remember the screenshot from earlier, showing the page that we are going to build? Here it is again to refresh your memory:

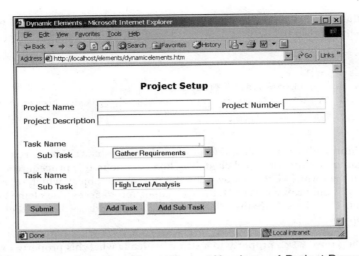

The first three fields on the form, Project Name, Project Number and Project Description, are the only static fields on the form. The Task Name field and Subtask combo box are dynamically generated. To that end we want to talk about dynamically adding fields.

The SPAN element is a powerful part of Dynamic HTML because it is a container for text. This text can be in the form of regular text or HTML that can be set or retrieved at runtime. Using regular text allows us to use a SPAN element to display messages dynamically or to display information for an OPTION in a SELECT element.

Using a SPAN element allows us to modify the HTML within the element, such as changing the formatting of text (e.g. changing the font attributes) or inserting script into the page. The most important feature however, is that a SPAN element allows us to dynamically create HTML elements on a page. That is where we are going to be focusing our attention.

> We can also set the display style of a SPAN element at runtime so we can dynamically show
> and hide text and HTML contained in the SPAN element. However, that discussion is beyond the
> scope of this case study, but is something that you should be aware of.

To create Dynamic HTML elements on a form, we must create a SPAN element in the form that will be used to house the elements created. We will use the innerHTML property to change the contents of the SPAN element and therefore create the Dynamic HTML elements. The code fragment below shows how we would code a SPAN element in our form.

```
<FORM ACTION="Some.asp" METHOD=POST ID=Form1 NAME=Form1>
    <SPAN ID=spnElements></SPAN>
    <INPUT Type=Button Name=btnCreate Value="Create Element">
</FORM>
```

Here we have defined a SPAN element in our form and have assigned a name to the ID property of the SPAN element so we can address the reference it in code.

In order to set the `innerHTML` property of the SPAN element in code, we would write some client-side script similar to that shown below:

```
<SCRIPT Language=VBScript>
Sub btnCreate_OnClick()
    Document.All.spnElements.innerHTML = _
        "<INPUT Type=Text Name=txtElement Value=""Dynamic Element"">"
End Sub
</SCRIPT>
```

So what does all this code mean? Well, the subprocedure `btnCreate_OnClick` is the code that gets fired when the button on the form is clicked. The line of code in this procedure starts by addressing the SPAN element on the form. We do this by using the `Document` object, which represents the entire HTML document in the browser. We use the `All` collection to access the elements within the `Document` object. Then we specify the SPAN element's ID to address the SPAN element and the `innerHTML` property.

We are setting the `innerHTML` property to a string, which is what this property expects. Notice that our string represents an INPUT Type=Text element. This will create a Dynamic HTML element within our SPAN element on the form. The end results when we click the button would look like this:

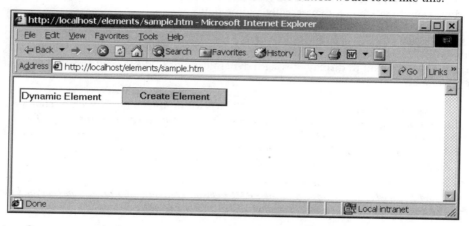

Now that we have a general idea of how to create Dynamic HTML elements on the client side, let's put this knowledge to use in order to solve the problem at hand.

Creating The Dynamic HTML page

Given the explanation and example above, we want to create an Active Server Page like the one shown at the start of the chapter. This Active Server Page will need to execute the `up_select_sub_tasks` stored procedure. This data will be used to load the OPTION elements of the SELECT element on the form.

There will be a button to allow the user to add a task, and a button to add a subtask. The first button will create an INPUT Type=Text element on the form, and the second button will create a SELECT element on the form. The user will be able to add as many tasks and subtasks per task as they wish.

Each task and each group of subtasks will be given a unique name. This will keep track of which task the subtasks are related to.

There are four **include files** that we include in all of our Active Server Pages. These include files contain common code that is shared among all pages in our small web application. All of these include files are plain text files with an .inc extension, and contain server-side VBScript. You can create these include files using NotePad, Visual Interdev, or your favourite text editor. We chose to place these include files in a sub directory called Includes in the web site for easier maintenance and to provide separation of code. You can place your include files in a subdirectory or in the same directory as your Web pages.

```
<%
Option Explicit
Response.Expires = 0
%>
```

The first of these files is the Header.inc include file, shown above. This code simply sets the Option Explicit statement. This requires us to declare all variables and helps reduce errors due to keying the wrong variable names.

The next line of code sets the Expires property of the Response object to 0. This expires the page in the browsers cache immediately. This will cause the browser to make a trip back to the server when the user revisits the page. This ensures that the user gets the most current information from the database and any server-side processing that needs to be done to build the page will be executed.

The next include file in our Active Server Page is the adovbs.inc file. This file is installed with the ActiveX Data Objects (ADO) and can be found in the directory where ADO was installed. This file contains all of the ADO constants that we will use when accessing ADO. This file is not listed here due to its size, and because it can be found on your machine by searching for adovbs.inc.

```
<%
'Create and open the database connection object
Dim objConn
Set objConn = Server.CreateObject("ADODB.Connection")
objConn.Open "Provider=SQLOLEDB;Data Source=SQLServer;Initial
Catalog=Projects;User ID=sa;Password="
%>
```

The next include file that is contained in our Active Server Page is the Connect.inc include file. This include file contains the common code that declares the Connection object and opens a connection to the database. The ConnectString parameter of the Open method uses the SQL OLE DB provider. The rest of the connection string specifies the SQL Server instance name, the data base name, and the username and password. You should change these to reflect the settings on your machine.

It should be noted at this point that all error handling has been omitted due to space. You should include the appropriate error handling to ensure your connection was successful.

```
<%
' Close the connection object
objConn.close
Set objConn = Nothing
%>
```

The last include file that we need to create is the DisConnect.inc include file. This include file will be included at the bottom of our web pages and will provide code to disconnect from the database. The code for this include file is listed above.

Here we are closing the database `Connection` object and setting it to nothing to release the object from memory.

The Web Page

The start of the `DynamicElements.asp` web page contains the first three include files that we discussed. We are using the `#INCLUDE` directive to include these files. Notice that the include files are in a sub directory on this web site called `Includes`.

```
<!-- #INCLUDE FILE="Includes/Header.inc" -->
<!-- #INCLUDE FILE="Includes/Adovbs.inc" -->
<!-- #INCLUDE FILE="Includes/Connect.inc" -->
```

We are going to use some specific styles in our web page and thus we have defined an in-line **Cascading Style Sheet**. This is also a good way to test your CSS styles before coding them in an external Cascading Style Sheet.

```
<STYLE TYPE='Text/CSS'>
/* Style for table header */
TH
{
    font-family: verdana, arial;
    font-size: 12pt;
}
/* Style for text */
.Normal
{
    font-family: verdana, arial;
    font-size: 10pt;
}
/* Style for controls */
.Controls
{
    font-family: ms sans serif;
    font-size: 10pt;
}
</STYLE>
```

We start the definition of our in-line style sheet by specifying the `STYLE` element. The `TYPE` attribute retrieves the language the style sheet was written in.

```
<BODY>
<FORM Action="ProcessDynamicElements.asp" Method=Post Name=frmTasks>
```

We start the `BODY` of our web page with a form by specifying the `FORM` element. The `Action` attribute specifies the URL the form will send its content to for processing. The `Method` attribute specifies how the form will send its content to the server for processing. We've specified the `Post` method, which sends the data through an HTTP post transaction. The last attribute that we have specified is the `Name` attribute, which assigns a name to the form so that we will be able to access it in our client-side script.

```
<TABLE Border=0 Class=Normal>
    <TR Height=60>
        <TH ColSpan=5 Align=center>Project Setup</TH>
    </TR>
```

Within the form, we use a table to keep our **Project Name** form elements properly aligned. Notice that on the TABLE element we have specified a Border attribute of zero, which causes no border to be drawn around the table. We have also specified the Class attribute, which sets the style class for this element using a style defined in our in-line style sheet. This style will be applied to all text with in this table.

The first row in our table has the Height attribute specified and set to 60 pixels. This provides the appropriate spacing between the first and second rows, which causes the header column to be separated from the form elements. The header column, <TH>, is specified and has its ColSpan attribute set which specifies the number of columns to span. The Align attribute specifies how our text will be aligned within this column and we have set it to Center.

```
<TR>
    <TD>Project Name</TD>
    <TD><INPUT Type=Text Name=txtProjectName Size=30 _
        MaxLength=30 Class=Controls></TD>
    <TD Width=15> </TD>
    <TD>Project Number</TD>
    <TD><INPUT Type=Text Name=txtProjectNumber Size=10 _
        MaxLength=10 Class=Controls></TD>
</TR>
```

The next row in our table contains five columns. The first column contains the text that will identity the INPUT element for the user. The next column contains the INPUT Type=Text element. Within this, we have specified the Name attribute, which assigns a name to this element. This will allow us to access by name in client-side script. The Size attribute specifies the number of visible characters in this element and is used to control its size on the web page. The MaxLength attribute limits the number of characters that a user can enter. Both of these attributes have been set to 30. The Class attribute sets the style class for this element using a style defined in our in-line style sheet. This style will override the default style.

The next column is used as a spacer and has its Width attribute set to 15 pixels. We are using an HTML blank space defined by   to force a blank space in this column. This provides a physical separation between the Project Name and Project Number making the form more visually attractive.

```
<TR>
    <TD>Project Description</TD>
    <TD ColSpan=4><INPUT Type=Text Name=txtProjectDescription _
        Size=62 MaxLength=100 Class=Controls></TD>
</TR>
```

The next two columns define the Project Number, and the INPUT Type=Text element is defined the same as the first one with the Size and MaxLength attributes containing a smaller number.

The next row in our table contains the text that will identify the INPUT Type=Text element for the user. The second column in this row has the ColSpan attribute set to 4, because we want the INPUT Type=Text element to span four columns. The INPUT element itself has the Size attribute set to 62 which lines up its end with the end of the last INPUT on the previous row. This will need to be adjusted to the default screen resolution that the web application will be running on ,as the alignment varies with different screen resolutions. The MaxLength attribute has been set to 100 to allow up to 100 characters to be entered.

```
<TR>
    <TD ColSpan=5><SPAN ID=spnTasks></SPAN></TD>
</TR>
```

The next row in our table contains the SPAN element that will contain all of our Dynamic HTML elements. Notice that the ColSpan attribute of the TD (column) element has been set to 5. This allows our Dynamic HTML elements to span across five columns should they need to. Notice that we have specified the ID attribute of the SPAN element. We will use this ID to access the SPAN element in our client-side script.

```
<TR>
    <TD> </TD>
</TR>
```

This row in our table simply provides whitespace between the SPAN elements and the buttons.

```
<TR>
    <TD>
        <INPUT Type=Button Name=btnSubmit Value="Submit" _
            Class=Controls>
    </TD>
    <TD ColSpan=2>
        <INPUT Type=Button Name=btnAddTask Value="Add Task" _
            Class=Controls>
        <INPUT Type=Button Name=btnAddSubTask Value="Add Subtask" _
            Class=Controls>
    </TD>
</TR>
```

The last row in our table contains the INPUT Type=Button elements. The first INPUT Type=Button element is the button that will be used to submit the form. This element has the Name attribute specified so we can access this button in our client-side script. The Value attribute is the caption on the button, which is what the user sees. The Class attribute sets the style class for this element using a style defined in our in-line style sheet.

The second INPUT Type=Button element in this row is the button that the user will use to dynamically create a new task. Again we have specified the Name, Value and Class attributes.

The last INPUT Type=Button element in this row is the button that the user will use to dynamically create a new subtask and also has the same attributes as the last two INPUT Type=Button elements.

```
    </TABLE>
</FORM>
```

After the last row in our table, we specify the closing tags for the TABLE and FORM elements.

Now that our form is complete, we start our client-side script by specifying the SCRIPT element. We have specified the Language attribute, which specifies what language the script is in. Since our script is being coded using VBScript, we have specified VBScript for this attribute.

```
<SCRIPT Language=VBScript>
'Declare Local Variables
Dim intTask
Dim strOptions
```

The first lines of code in our script contain variable declarations. These are variables that will be used by multiple procedures in our script. The `intTask` variable will be used as a counter containing the number of tasks that a user creates. The `strOptions` variable will be used as a string that contains the `OPTION` elements for the `SELECT` element. This string will be populated in the `Window_OnLoad` procedure.

```
Sub Window_OnLoad()
    'Collections are zero based on the client side so set
    'the number to -1 so the first task counter is zero
    intTask = -1
```

The `OnLoad` event for the `Window` object fires immediately after the browser loads the Window. There are multiple tasks that we want to perform in the `Window_OnLoad` procedure.

The first thing that we want to do is set the `intTask` variable to −1. We will increment this variable by one before using it. Thus the first task created will be zero, because all collections on the client are zero based.

```
    'Build the OPTIONs for the SELECT element in a string
<%
    'Declare variables and objects
    Dim strSQL
    Dim objRS

    'Create and open recordset
    strSQL = "dbo.up_select_sub_tasks"
    Set objRS = Server.CreateObject("ADODB.Recordset")
    objRS.Open strSQL, objConn, adOpenForwardOnly, _
        adLockReadOnly, adCmdStoredProc
```

The next task that we want to perform in this procedure is to open a recordset containing all subtasks in the `Sub_Task_T` table. Notice that this code is being executed as server-side code, as is evident by the server-side scripting tags `<%` and `%>`. We first declare the variables that we will need. Then we set the `strSQL` variable to the stored procedure name that we will be executing. Next, we set the `objRS` variable to a valid ADO `Recordset` object.

The last thing we do in this section of code is to open the recordset using the `Open` method of the `Recordset` object. The `Source` parameter of the `Open` method is set to our string variable, which contains the stored procedure to be executed. The `ActiveConnection` parameter contains the `Connection` object variable that we defined and opened in the `Connect.inc` include file.

Since we only want to read this recordset in one direction, we have specified the `adOpenForwardOnly` constant for the `CursorType` parameter. This ADO constant is defined in the `adovbs.inc` include file. The `LockType` parameter has been set using the `adLockReadOnly` constant since we only want to read this recordset. The `Options` parameter specifies how the provider should evaluate our `Source` parameter. Since we are executing a stored procedure, we have specified the `adCmdStoredProc` constant.

Once again, notice that error handling has been omitted. You will need to include the appropriate error handling to ensure the `Open` method is successfully executed.

```
    'Load resources
    Do While Not objRS.EOF
%>
```

After our recordset has been opened, we want to loop through the recordset building our strOptions variable. (Note - we're not actually building the variable here - just creating the DHTML code which will do the building on the client, when the page is loaded into the browser). We accomplish this task using a Do While loop, looping through the recordset until an EOF condition occurs on the recordset.

```
        strOptions = strOptions & _
           "<OPTION Value=" & <%=objRS("Sub_Task_ID")%> & ">" & _
           "<%=objRS("Sub_Task_Name_VC")%>"
    <%
        objRS.MoveNext
    Loop
```

Switching back to client-side code, we set the Sub_Task_ID field of the recordset as the Value attribute of the OPTION element. Notice that we have enclosed the Recordset object in server-side scripting tags. The text that will be displayed for this OPTION element is being set from the Sub_Task_Name_VC field of the recordset. Again this has been enclosed in server-side scripting tags.

Each time through the loop we append a new line to the client-side code that adds a new OPTION element to the strOptions variable when it is executed. We then specify the MoveNext method of the Recordset object to move to the next record.

```
    'Close the recordset
    objRS.Close
    Set objRS = Nothing
%>
End Sub
```

After we have processed all records in the Recordset object, we close it and set it to nothing to release it from memory.

```
Sub btnSubmit_OnClick()
    'Submit the form
    frmTasks.Submit
End Sub
```

The code for the OnClick event for the btnSubmit is listed next. This procedure simply calls the Submit method of the form.

Dynamically Adding Elements

The next two procedures are the heart of our example. These two procedures contain the code that will be executed when a user clicks on the btnAddTask and btnAddSubTask buttons. This code will create our Dynamic HTML elements.

```
Sub btnAddTask_OnClick()
    'Increment the task counter
    intTask = intTask + 1

    'In the SPAN element (spnTasks) we want to create a DIV element.
    'Within the new DIV element we will create a SPAN element and
    'an INPUT 'Type=Text' element.
    Document.All.spnTasks.innerHTML = Document.All.spnTasks.innerHTML & _
        "<DIV ID=divTask><SPAN ID=spnTask><BR>Task Name  " & _
        "           " & _
        "<INPUT Type=Text Name=txtTask" & intTask & _
        " Size=30 MaxLength=30 Class=Controls></SPAN></DIV>"
End Sub
```

When a user clicks on the `btnAddTask` button, we increment the `intTask` counter by one. This counter is then used as part of the `Name` attribute assigned to the new `INPUT Type=Text` element being created - this allows the processing page to recognize individual tasks.

We then address the `SPAN` element's `innerHTML` property using the `Document` object and the `All` collection. Using the `innerHTML` property we are able to specify HTML elements to be created. Notice that we have specified that the `innerHTML` property is equal to itself plus the new element to be created. This appends the new HTML element to any existing HTML elements that we may have already created.

When creating a new HTML element, we want to create a `DIV` element first. The `DIV` element keeps our dynamic HTML elements aligned vertically. If we did not specify a `DIV` element, all elements created would be aligned horizontally. Within the `DIV` element, we create a new `SPAN` element and within that `SPAN` element we create the new `INPUT Type=Text` element. Notice that the `INPUT` element created has its `Name` attribute set to `txtTask` plus the number contained in the `intTask` variable. Thus the first `INPUT Type=Text` element created would have a name of `txtTask0`, the second `txtTask1`, and so on. We have also specified the `Size`, `MaxLength` and `Class` attributes for this `INPUT Type=Text` element.

Using the same `ID` attribute for the `DIV` and `SPAN` elements each time effectively creates a collection of these elements with the first item in the collection being item number 0.

We create a new `SPAN` element so that we can keep all tasks and subtasks grouped together. Within the new `SPAN` element that we created we have included some other HTML elements. These include the `BR` element, which inserts a line break. This keeps each group of Tasks and Subtasks separated from each other providing a visually pleasing interface. We have also specified several HTML blank spaces using ` `. This provides the separation of the `INPUT Type=Text` element from the text that we have specified and keeps it aligned with the `INPUT Type=Text` elements above it.

Notice also that we have specified that the `SPAN` element, `spnTasks`, is equal to itself plus the new Dynamic HTML elements that are being created. This appends all new Dynamic HTML elements to the existing Dynamic HTML elements that we have already created.

```
Sub btnAddSubTask_OnClick()
    'Ignore errors if a user tries to create a subtask without
    'first creating a task
    On Error Resume Next

    'Within the SPAN element (spnTask) that we created when we added a task,
    'we want to create one or more SELECT elements.
    If intTask = 0 Then
        'Only one span tag named 'spnTask' exists so reference it as such
        Document.All.spnTask.innerHTML = Document.All.spnTask.innerHTML & _
            "<DIV ID=divSubTask>     " & _
            "Subtask     " & _
            "       " & _
            "<SELECT Name=cboSubTasks" & intTask & " Class=Controls>" & _
            strOptions & "</SELECT></DIV>"
    Else
        'The span tag 'spnTask' is a collection now so reference it
        'in the collection.
        Document.All.spnTask(intTask).innerHTML = _
            Document.All.spnTask(intTask).innerHTML & _
```

```
              "<DIV ID=divSubTask>     " & _
              "Subtask     " & _
              "       " & _
              "<SELECT Name=cboSubTasks" & intTask & " Class=Controls>" & _
              strOptions & "</SELECT></DIV>"
      End If
  End Sub
```

When the user clicks on the `btnAddSubTask` button we execute the code above to dynamically add an HTML `SELECT` element to the current task.

Since we are creating the `SELECT` element within the `SPAN` element created when a user added a task, we must check to see if this is the first `SPAN` element created. We do this by checking to see if the `intTask` variable is equal to zero. If it is, we address the `SPAN` element, `spnTask`, as a normal element. If `intTask` is greater than zero then we address the `SPAN` element, `spnTask`, as a collection and specify the index position within the collection.

Using the same format as the last procedure, we dynamically create the `SELECT` element in the `SPAN` element `spnTask`. Notice that once again, we are appending this new HTML element to any existing HTML elements that might exist in the `spnTask` `SPAN` element. And also once again we are using a `DIV` element so our new dynamic HTML elements are created vertically instead of horizontally.

In creating the `SELECT` element, we use the variable `strOptions` as the `OPTION` elements within the `SELECT` element. The `SELECT` element has its `Name` attribute set to `cboSubTasks` plus the value contained in the variable `intTask`. Remember that the variable `intTask` is only incremented when a new task is created. So if the user creates more than one subtask per task, then the second subtask creates a collection of subtasks with the same name. This keeps the group of subtasks related to a specific task.

We are also creating an HTML blank space using ` ` and have assigned the style `Controls` to the `SELECT` element.

```
  </SCRIPT>
  <!-- #INCLUDE FILE="Includes/DisConnect.inc" -->
  </BODY>
  </HTML>
```

This is all of the code contained in our client-side script, so we end the `SCRIPT` element and specify the `#INCLUDE` directive to include the `DisConnect.inc` include file. If you remember from our discussion on the include files, this file closes our database connection and sets the `Connection` object to equal to nothing. We end the page by specifying the closing `BODY` and `HTML` elements.

At this point you should be able to open the web page in a browser (IE 4 or later) and create as many Tasks and Subtasks as you want. A Task does not have to have a Subtask but a Subtask cannot be created without a Task.

You should be able to create a page that looks similar to the one shown in the figure below.

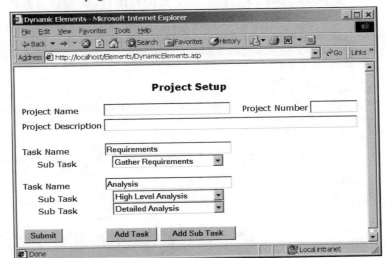

Server-Side Processing Of Dynamic Elements

At this point you may be thinking "Cool, I have a web page that creates all of these dynamic elements". And then the excitement wears off and you realize that your work has just begun. Because what good is it to have all of these dynamic elements in a form if you can't process them?

When we create Dynamic HTML elements on a form in a web page, those elements become part of the form's `Elements collection`. We are then able to access those dynamically created HTML elements in this collection.

You can access an item (HTML element) in the `Request.Form` collection by either the item's name or index position. The syntax to access an element by its name, and then its position, is shown below:

```
strText = Request.Form("txtInput")
strText = Request.Form.Item(1)
```

If the `INPUT Type = Text` element named `txtInput` is a collection itself, you can access its elements with the following syntax:

```
strText = Request.Form("txtInput")(intSubIndex)
strText = Request.Form.Item(1)(intSubIndex)
```

The `Count` property allows us to determine the number of items in a collection, shown in the first line of code; or a subcollection, shown in the second line:

```
number = Request.Form.Count
number = Request.Form("txtInput").Count
```

Now that we know how to process items in the `Request.Form` collection, let's look at how we are going to process the Dynamic HTML elements we created on the client side.

ASP Page To Process Dynamic Elements On The Server

Now that we have a web page to create dynamic HTML elements, we need to create an ASP page to process these elements. When we created our stored procedures, we created a stored procedure to insert one task and one subtask at a time. Thus we will process one task and one subtask from the `Request.Form` collection at a time.

The web page that we will be creating will be a server-side web page. That is, the only thing this Web page will contain is server-side code. Once we have processed all data from the `Request.Form`, we will display a message on the web page using the `Response` object. We will not create any forms or tables in this web page.

Let's look at the code for this page - which can be found in `ProcessDynamicElements.asp`:

```
<!-- #INCLUDE FILE="Includes/Header.inc" -->
<!-- #INCLUDE FILE="Includes/Adovbs.inc" -->
<!-- #INCLUDE FILE="Includes/Connect.inc" -->
```

The first thing we want to code in the web page is the `#INCLUDE` directive. Once again, we are using the same three include files that were used at the beginning of the last active server page that we created. These include files provide the common code used in all of our web pages.

```
<HTML>
<HEAD>
<META HTTP-EQUIV="REFRESH" CONTENT="5;URL=DynamicElements.asp">
```

After the include files, we code the `HTML` and `HEAD` elements. After the server-side processing, this web page will load in the user's browser and display a message that processing has been completed. Then, after five seconds, the `META` element will cause a refresh of the browser and will load the `DynamicElements.asp` web page.

Using this method is just another way that we can redirect a user to another web page.

```
<%
'Declare variables and objects
Dim lngProjectID, lngTaskID
Dim intIndex, intSubIndex
Dim objCmd
```

We start our server-side code by declaring the variables that we will need for processing. We have declared a couple of variables that will be used to hold the return values from our stored procedures, and a couple of variables to be used as indexes when accessing the `Request.Form` collection and subtask collections. Then we declare a variable that will be set to the ADO `Command` object.

```
'*******************************************************************
'* Process the static fields from the request form first
'*******************************************************************

'Set a reference to the ADO command object
Set objCmd = Server.CreateObject("ADODB.Command")

'Set the command objects properties
Set objCmd.ActiveConnection = objConn
objCmd.CommandText = "dbo.up_parmins_project"
objCmd.CommandType = adCmdStoredProc
```

We want to process the static fields from the `Request.Form` first. These are the `txtProjectName`, `txtProjectNumber` and `txtProjectDescription` fields. These fields will always be there.

So, we set a reference to the ADO `Command` object, and then set the `Command` object's properties. We set the `ActiveConnection` property to the `Connection` object that is created in the `Connect.inc` include file, and set the `CommandText` property to the name of the stored procedure we want to execute. Then we set the `CommandType` property to the `adCmdStoredProc` constant, which specifies what type of command we are processing, in this case a stored procedure.

```
'Append the parameters to the parameters collection
objCmd.Parameters.Append objCmd.CreateParameter("ProjectID", _
    adInteger,adParamOutput)
```

Next, we append the parameters to the `Parameters` collection using the `Command` object's `CreateParameter` method. The `CreateParameter` method accepts several parameters. The first parameter, `Name`, specifies the name of the `Parameter` object that we are creating. This name is a string value and does not map to the parameter name in the stored procedure. You can use any name that you like that describes the `Parameter` object in the `Parameters` collection.

The second parameter of the `CreateParameter` method is the `Type` parameter and specifies the data type for the `Parameter` object in the `Parameters` collection. The third parameter is `Direction` and specifies the `Parameter` object's direction. The `Size` parameter is a value that specifies the maximum length of the `Parameter` object. This parameter is normally used for `VarChar` and `Char` data types. The last parameter in the `CreateParameter` method is the `Value` parameter and specifies the value of the `Parameter` object being created.

The stored procedure that we are executing, `up_parmins_project`, expects four parameters. The first of these parameters will be used to return the Project ID that was inserted and thus this parameter is specified as an `OUTPUT` parameter. Notice that since this is an output parameter and a SQL Server `Integer` data type, we have not specified the `Size` and `Value` parameters of the `CreateParameter` method.

```
objCmd.Parameters.Append objCmd.CreateParameter("ProjectName", _
    adVarChar,adParamInput,30,Request.Form("txtProjectName"))
```

The next parameter that our stored procedure expects is the Project Name and this is the next `Parameter` object that we append to the `Parameters` collection. Since this parameter is a SQL Server `VarChar` data type, we have specified the `Size` parameter of the `CreateParameter` method. We are using the `txtProjectName` field from the `Request.Form` as the `Value` parameter of the `CreateParameter` method.

```
objCmd.Parameters.Append objCmd.CreateParameter("ProjectNumber", _
    adVarChar,adParamInput,10,Request.Form("txtProjectNumber"))
objCmd.Parameters.Append objCmd.CreateParameter("ProjectDescription", _
    adVarChar,adParamInput,100,Request.Form("txtProjectDescription"))
```

The next two parameters that we append to the `Parameters` collection are the `ProjectNumber` and `ProjectDescription`.

```
'Execute the command object to insert the project
objCmd.Execute
```

After all parameters have been appended to the `Parameters` collection, we execute the `Command` object. Once again, please note that error handling has been omitted and should be included in your code.

```
'Save the Project ID that was returned
lngProjectID = objCmd("ProjectID")

'Dereference the command object
Set objCmd = Nothing
```

After the `Command` object has been executed, the data has been inserted into the database and the `Command` object now contains the Project ID that was inserted. Remember that this parameter was defined as an `OUTPUT` parameter and we can now retrieve the value that was inserted by accessing the parameter by name. This code uses the default collection of the `Command` object, which is the `Parameters` collection. That is why we do not have to specify the `Parameters` collection directly.

Once we have retrieved the output parameter and assigned it to our local variable, we set the `Command` object to nothing to release it and destroy the `Parameters` collection.

```
'**********************************************************************
'* Process the dynamic fields from the request form
'**********************************************************************

'Loop through the collection of elements on the Request.Form
For intIndex = 1 To Request.Form.Count
```

Now that we have our project details inserted into the database, we need to loop through the `Request.Form` collection and insert all tasks and subtasks. We are going to set up a loop and process from item 1 to the last item contained in the `Request.Form.Count`.

```
'If this is a task then insert it
If InStr(Request.Form.Key(intIndex),"txtTask") Then
```

The first thing we do in this loop is to see if the name of the item in the `Request.Form` collection begins with `txtTask`. This is accomplished using the `Key` property. This property contains the name of the item in the `Request.Form` collection that we are working with. Since we named all of our task elements `txtTask` followed by a number, we can check to see if the name partially matches.

Using the VBScript `InStr` function, we see if any part of the `Key` property matches the character string `txtTask`. The `InStr` function will return the starting position if a match was found, and zero if no match was found.

Thus if a match is found the results would be `True`, indicating that this item is a task that the user created, and processing would continue immediately after the `If` statement.

```
'Set a reference to the ADO command object
Set objCmd = Server.CreateObject("ADODB.Command")

'Set the command objects properties
Set objCmd.ActiveConnection = objConn
objCmd.CommandText = "dbo.up_parmins_task"
objCmd.CommandType = adCmdStoredProc
```

Once again, we set a reference to the `Command` object and set the `CommandText` property to `up_parmins_task`, which is the stored procedure we want to execute to insert a task.

```
'Append the parameters to the parameters collection
objCmd.Parameters.Append objCmd.CreateParameter("TaskID", _
    adInteger,adParamOutput)
objCmd.Parameters.Append objCmd.CreateParameter("ProjectID", _
    adInteger,adParamInput,,lngProjectID)
objCmd.Parameters.Append objCmd.CreateParameter("TaskName", _
    adVarChar,adParamInput,30,Request.Form.Item(intIndex))
```

Again, the first parameter that we append to the `Parameters` collection is an `OUTPUT` parameter. The second parameter that we append uses the local variable that contains the Project ID that was inserted by our last stored procedure.

The last parameter that we append is the value from the dynamically created `INPUT Type=Text` element that contains the task name. We retrieve the value from this element from the `Request.Form` collection using the `Item` property and the index of the item within the `Request.Form` collection.

```
'Execute the command object to insert the task
objCmd.Execute

'Save the Task ID that was returned
lngTaskID = objCmd("TaskID")

'Dereference the command object
Set objCmd = Nothing

End If
```

We then execute the `Command` object and retrieve the Task ID that was inserted from the `TaskID` `OUTPUT` parameter and assign it to our local variable. We then set the `Command` object to nothing to release it from memory and destroy the `Parameters` collection.

```
'If this is a subtask, then enumerate the subtask collection
'for the task and insert the relationships
If InStr(Request.Form.Key(intIndex),"cboSubTasks") Then
```

If the item in the `Request.Form` collection is not a task, then we check to see if it is a subtask. This is accomplished similarly to the way we checked for a task. This time however, we are checking the name of the item in the `Request.Form` collection to see if it begins with `cboSubTasks`. Remember we named all dynamically created `SELECT` elements `cboSubTasks` followed by the number of the task that was created.

```
'Loop through the collection and insert all relationships
For intSubIndex = 1 To Request.Form(Request.Form.Key(intIndex)).Count
```

If this item is a subtask then we get a count of subtasks in the subtask collection using the `Request.Form(Request.Form.Key(intIndex)).Count` property. If there is only one item and this is not a collection then the `Count` property will be 1. If it is indeed a collection then the `Count` property will contain the number of items in this collection. Either way we perform this loop until all subtasks for a given task have been added.

```
            'Set a reference to the ADO command object
            Set objCmd = Server.CreateObject("ADODB.Command")

            'Set the command objects properties
            Set objCmd.ActiveConnection = objConn
            objCmd.CommandText = "dbo.up_parmins_task_relationship"
            objCmd.CommandType = adCmdStoredProc

            'Append the parameters to the parameters collection
            objCmd.Parameters.Append objCmd.CreateParameter("TaskID", _
                adInteger,adParamInput,,lngTaskID)
            objCmd.Parameters.Append objCmd.CreateParameter("SubTaskID", _
                adInteger,adParamInput,, _
                Request.Form.Item(intIndex)(intSubIndex))
```

If this is a subtask then we will process this loop at least once. Here we set a reference to the `Command` object and set its properties. The stored procedure we want to execute this time is the `up_parmins_task_relationship` stored procedure. This stored procedure accepts two `INPUT` parameters and has no `OUTPUT` parameters.

The first parameter that we create and append to the `Parameters` collection is the Task ID of the last task that was inserted.

The next parameter is the ID of the subtask that was selected by the user. We retrieve this value using the item number of the item in the `Request.Form` collection and the item number of the item in the subtask collection.

```
            'Execute the command object to insert the task
            objCmd.Execute

            'Dereference the command object
            Set objCmd = Nothing

        Next

    End If
```

We then execute the `Command` object to insert the subtask, and then set the `Command` object to nothing to release it from memory and to destroy the `Parameters` collection. Again, we need to point out that you need to include your own error handling to ensure the `Command` object executes successfully.

```
    Next
```

We continue processing the `For` loop until all items in the `Request.Form` collection have been processed.

```
    'Display a message that the project has been inserted
    Response.Write "<B><FONT COLOR=Navy>The Project has been added to the " & _
        "database.<BR>You will be automatically redirected in 5 seconds.</FONT></B>"
%>
```

After all items in the `Request.Form` collection have been processed, we display a message on the page informing the user that the project has been inserted. Notice the use of HTML in the string that is written using the `Write` method of the `Response` object. This just helps format a more appealing message for the user.

```
    <!-- #INCLUDE FILE="Includes/DisConnect.inc" -->
    </BODY>
    </HTML>
```

The last part of our Active Server Page has the `#INCLUDE` directive that specifies the `DisConnect.inc` include file to close the `Connection` object.

Testing The Web Pages

When you fill out the `DynamicElements.asp` web page and add some tasks and subtasks and then click the Submit button, this Active Server Page will be executed.

Let's run through both forms again and enter a small project. The figure below shows the project that I have chosen to enter. You can follow along entering the same data that I have, or enter your own data.

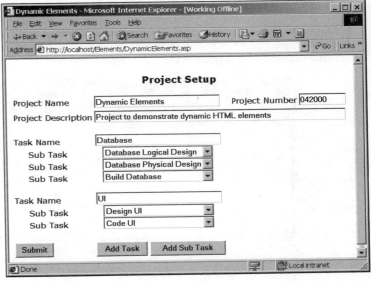

After you have entered all of the information that you want, click on the Submit button. The form will be submitted and the data posted through an HTTP post transaction. The `ProcessDynamicElements.asp` page will execute and process the data. Remember that it will loop through the entire `Request.Form` collection and add each task and subtask separately.

When the `ProcessDynamicElements.asp` has finished its database processing, it will display a message like the one shown below. Remember that the results will only be shown for five seconds and then the `DynamicElements.asp` page will be displayed again.

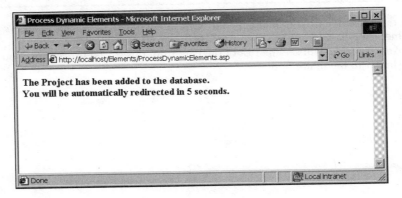

Viewing The Results

If you recall, we created a stored procedure to view the results of our processing. The up_parmsel_project_details stored procedure expects just one parameter, the Project_ID. Since this is the first record you have inserted into the database, the Project_ID should be 1. (This is the third project that we have inserted and so the Project_ID for our project is 3.) You can check the Project_ID in several ways. First, you can open the Project_T table in the Enterprise Manager and view the data. Another way to check this is to run a SELECT query in the Query Analyzer to select all rows from the Project_T table.

Once you know the Project_ID of the project you want to view, execute the up_parmsel_project_details stored procedure, passing it the Project_ID of your project. The results should look similar to the ones shown below.

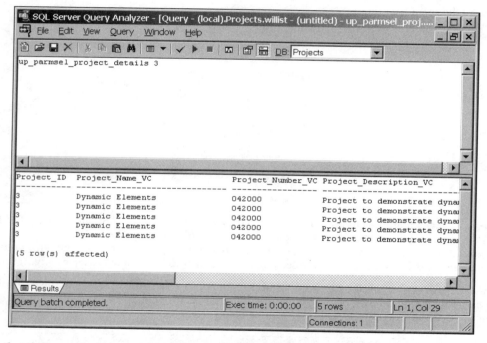

Notice that there are five rows of data, one for each subtask. The figure above shows the Project ID, Project Name, Project Number and Project Description. If you scroll to the right in the Results pane in the Query Analyzer, you will see the rest of the data from this stored procedure. You should see something similar to the figure opposite.

This figure shows the bulk of our data. Here we see each task and subtask that was inserted and also the IDs of the tasks and subtasks.

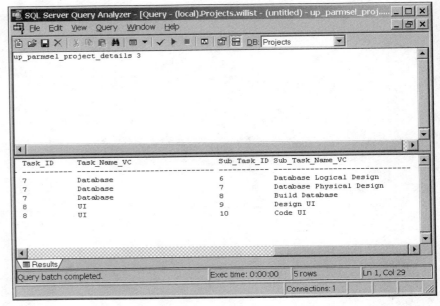

As you can see, this stored procedure could be used to build an edit screen to allow a user to edit their project data. With a little imagination, you could even allow the user to dynamically add more subtasks to a task on the edit screen.

Summary

This case study has taken a look at how to dynamically create HTML elements on a form in a Web page. We have examined the code that is needed to do this and have demonstrated dynamically creating INPUT Type=Text and SELECT elements. This can be expanded upon and other HTML elements can be dynamically created. we're sure you can think of a couple of situations where this might be useful.

Along with dynamically creating HTML elements, we have demonstrated how to process those elements using server-side script and looping through the Request.Form collection examining each element's name. We have also shown how to process an element that has a collection of its own, as we did with the subtasks.

The database side of our case study has shown how to create relationship tables that contain one-to-many and many-to-many relationships. These tables were used in both our INSERT and SELECT stored procedures.

In summary, we have seen:

- How to create relationship tables.
- How to code INSERT and SELECT queries and stored procedures against those tables.
- How to create dynamic HTML elements.
- How to process dynamic HTML elements.
- How to process dynamic HTML element collections.

The ASP 3.0 Object Model

The ASP object model is made up of six objects. The following diagram shows conceptually how these objects relate to the client and the server, and the requests made by the client and the responses sent back to them from the server:

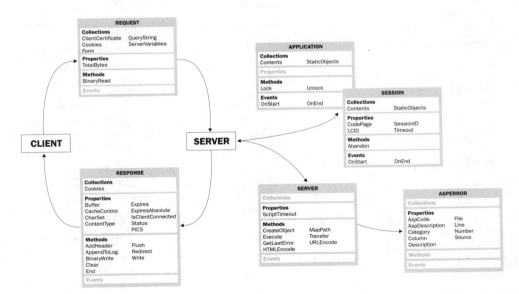

The Application Object

The Application object is created when the ASP DLL is loaded in response to the first request for an ASP page. It provides a repository for storing variables and object references that are available to all the pages that all visitors open.

Collection	Description
Contents	A collection of all of the variables and their values that are stored in the Application object, and are not defined using an <OBJECT> element. This includes Variant arrays and Variant-type object instance references.
StaticObjects	A collection of all of the variables that are stored in the Application object by using an <OBJECT> element.

Method	Description
Contents.Remove ("variable_name")	Removes a named variable from the Application.Contents collection.
Contents.RemoveAll()	Removes all variables from the Application.Contents collection.
Lock()	Locks the Application object so that only the current ASP page has access to the contents. Used to ensure that concurrency issues do not corrupt the contents by allowing two users to simultaneously read and update the values.
Unlock()	Releases this ASP page's lock on the Application object.

* You *cannot* remove variables from the Application.StaticObjects collection at run-time.

Event	Description
onStart	Occurs with the first instance of a user requesting one of the Web pages in the application, before the page that the user requests is executed. Used to initialize variables, create objects, or run other code.
onEnd	Occurs when the ASP application ends. That is, when the web server shuts down. This is after the last user session has ended, and after any code in the onEnd event for that session has executed. All variables existing in the application are destroyed when it ends.

The ASPError Object

The ASPError object is a new object in ASP 3.0, and is available through the `GetLastError` method of the Server object. It provides a range of detailed information about the last error that occurred in ASP.

Property	Description
ASPCode	*Integer.* The error number generated by IIS.
ASPDescription	*Integer.* A detailed description of the error if it is ASP-related.
Category	*String.* Indicates the source of the error. E.g. ASP itself, the scripting language, or an object.
Column	*Integer.* The character position within the file that generated the error.
Description	*String.* A short description of the error.
File	*String.* The name of the file that was being processed when the error occurred.
Line	*Integer.* The number of the line within the file that generated the error.
Number	*Integer.* A standard COM error code.
Source	*String.* The actual code, where available, of the line that caused the error.

The Request Object

The Request object makes available to the script all the information that the client provides when requesting a page, or submitting a form. This includes the HTTP server variables that identify the browser and the user, cookies that are stored on the browser for this domain, and any values appended to the URL as a query string or in HTML controls in a <FORM> section of the page. It also provides access to any certificate that may be being used through **Secure Sockets Layer** (SSL) or other encrypted communication protocol, and properties that help to manage the connection.

Collection	Description
ClientCertificate	A collection of the values of all the fields or entries in the client certificate that the user presented to our server when accessing a page or resource. Each member is read-only.
Cookies	A collection of the values of all the cookies sent from the user's system along with their request. Only cookies valid for the domain containing the resource are sent to the server.

Table continued on following page

Collection	Description
Form	A collection of the values of all the HTML control elements in the `<FORM>` section that was submitted as the request, where the value of the `METHOD` attribute is `"POST"`. Each member is read-only.
QueryString	A collection of all the name/value pairs appended to the URL in the user's request, or the values of all the HTML control elements in the `<FORM>` section that was submitted as the request where the value of the `METHOD` attribute is `"GET"` or the attribute is omitted. Each member is read-only.
ServerVariables	A collection of all the HTTP header values sent from the client with their request, plus the values of several environment variables for the Web server. Each member is read-only.

Property	Description
TotalBytes	*Integer*. Read-only value holding the total number of bytes in the body of the request sent by the client.

Method	Description
BinaryRead(*count*)	Retrieves *count* bytes of data from the client's request when the data is sent to the server as part of a `POST` request. It returns as a `Variant` array (or `SafeArray`). This method *cannot* be used successfully if the ASP code has already referenced the `Request.Form` collection. Likewise, the `Request.Form` collection *cannot* be successfully accessed if you have used the `BinaryRead` method.

The Response Object

The Response object is used to access the response that is being created to send back to the client. It makes available the HTTP variables that identify the server and its capabilities, information about the content being sent to the browser, and any new cookies that will be stored on the browser for this domain. It also provides a series of methods that are used to create the returned page.

Collection	Description
Cookies	A collection containing the values of all the cookies that will be sent back to the client in the current response. Each member is write only.

Property	Description
Buffer = True|False	*Boolean.* Read/write. Specifies if the output created by an ASP page will be held in the IIS buffer until all of the server scripts in the current page have been processed, or until the Flush or End method is called. It must be set before any output is sent to IIS, including HTTP header information, so it should be the first line of the .asp file after the <%@LANGUAGE=..%> statement. Buffering is on (True) by default in ASP 3.0, whereas it was off (False) by default in earlier versions.
CacheControl "*setting*"	*String.* Read/write. Set this property to "Public" to allow proxy servers to cache the page, or "Private" to prevent proxy caching taking place.
Charset = "*value*"	*String.* Read/write. Appends the name of the character set (for example, ISO-LATIN-7) to the HTTP Content-Type header created by the server for each response.
ContentType "*MIME-type*"	*String.* Read/write. Specifies the HTTP content type for the response, as a standard MIME-type (such as "text/xml" or "image/gif"). If omitted, the MIME-type "text/html" is used. The content type tells the browser what type of content to expect.
Expires minutes	*Number.* Read/write. Specifies the length of time in minutes that a page is valid for. If the user returns to the same page before it expires, the cached version is displayed. After that period, it expires and should not be held in a private (user) or public (proxy) cache.
ExpiresAbsolute #*date[time]*#	*Date/Time.* Read/write. Specifies the absolute date and time when a page will expire and no longer be valid. If the user returns to the same page before it expires, the cached version is displayed. After that time, it expires and should not be held in a private (user) or public (proxy) cache.
IsClientConnected	*Boolean.* Read-only. Returns an indication of whether the client is still connected to and loading the page from the server. Can be used to end processing (with the Response.End method) if a client moves to another page before the current one has finished executing.

Table continued on following page

Property	Description
PICS ("PICS-label-string")	*String.* Write only. Create a PICS header and adds it to the HTTP headers in the response. PICS headers define the content of the page in terms of violence, sex, bad language, etc.
Status = "code message"	*String.* Read/write. Specifies the status value and message that will be sent to the client in the HTTP headers of the response to indicate an error or successful processing of the page. For example "200 OK" and "404 Not Found".

Method	Description
AddHeader ("*name*" , "*content*")	Creates a custom HTTP header using the *name* and *content* values and adds it to the response. Will *not* replace an existing header of the same name. Once a header has been added, it cannot be removed. Must be used before any page content (i.e. text and HTML) is sent to the client.
AppendToLog ("*string*")	Adds a string to the end of the Web server log entry for this request when W3C Extended Log File Format is in use. Requires at least the URI Stem value to be selected in the Extended Properties page for the site containing the page.
BinaryWrite (*SafeArray)*	Writes the content of a Variant-type *SafeArray* to the current HTTP output stream without any character conversion. Useful for writing non-string information such as binary data required by a custom application or the bytes to make up an image file.
Clear()	Erases any existing buffered page content from the IIS response buffer when Response.Buffer is True. Does *not* erase HTTP response headers. Can be used to abort a partly completed page.
End()	Stops ASP from processing the page script and returns the currently created content, then aborts any further processing of this page.
Flush()	Sends all currently buffered page content in the IIS buffer to the client when Response.Buffer is True. Can be used to send parts of a long page to the client individually.
Redirect ("*url*")	Instructs the browser to load the page in the string *url* parameter by sending a "302 Object Moved" HTTP header in the response.
Write ("*string*")	Writes the specified *string* to the current HTTP response stream and IIS buffer so that it becomes part of the returned page.

The Server Object

The Server object provides a series of methods and properties that are useful in scripting with ASP. The most obvious is the `Server.CreateObject` method, which properly instantiates other COM objects within the context of the current page or session. There are also methods to translate strings into the correct format for use in URLs and in HTML, by converting non-legal characters to the correct legal equivalent.

Property	Description
ScriptTimeout	*Integer*. Has the default value 90. Sets or returns the number of seconds that script in the page can execute for before the server aborts page execution and reports an error. This automatically halts and removes from memory pages that contain errors that may lock execution into a loop or those that stall while waiting for a resource to become available. This prevents the server becoming overloaded with badly behaved pages. You may need to increase this value if your pages take a long time to run.

Method	Description
CreateObject ("*identifier*")	Creates an instance of the object (a component, application or scripting object) that is identified by "*identifier*", and returns a reference to it that can be used in our code. Can be used in the `global.asa` page of a virtual application to create objects with session-level or application-level scope. The object can be identified by its ClassID (i.e. "{CLSID:FDC8-...-37A9}") value or by a ProgID string such as "ADODB.Connection".
Execute ("*url*")	Stops execution of the current page and transfers control to the page specified in "*url*". The user's current environment (i.e. session state and any current transaction state) is carried over to the new page. After that page has finished execution, control passes back to the original page and execution resumes at the statement after the `Execute` method call.
GetLastError ( )	Returns a reference to an `ASPError` object that holds details of the last error that occurred within the ASP processing, i.e. within `asp.dll`. The information exposed by the `ASPError` object includes the file name, line number, error code, etc.
HTMLEncode ("*string*")	Returns a string that is a copy of the input value "*string*" but with all non-legal HTML characters such as '<', '>', '&' and double quotes converted into the equivalent HTML entity—i.e. <, >, &, ", etc.

Table continued on following page

Method	Description
MapPath (" *url*")	Returns the full physical path and filename of the file or resource specified in " *url*".
Transfer (" *url*")	Stops execution of the current page and transfers control to the page specified in " *url*". The user's current environment (i.e. session state and any current transaction state) is carried over to the new page. Unlike the Execute method, execution *does not* resume in the original page, but ends when the new page has completed executing.
URLEncode (" *string*")	Returns a string that is a copy of the input value "*string*" but with all characters that are not valid in a URL, such as '?', '&' and spaces, converted into the equivalent URL entity—i.e. '%3F', '%26', and '+'.

The Session Object

The Session object is created for each visitor when they first request an ASP page from the site, and remains available until the default timeout period (or the timeout period determined by the script) expires. It provides a repository for storing variables and object references that are available just to the pages that this visitor opens during the lifetime of this session.

Collection	Description
Contents	A collection of all the variables and their values that are stored in this particular Session object, and are *not* defined using an <OBJECT> element. This includes Variant arrays and Variant-type object instance references.
StaticObjects	A collection of all of the variables that are stored in this particular Session object by using an <OBJECT> element.

Property	Description
CodePage	*Integer*. Read/write. Defines the code page that will be used to display the page content in the browser. The code page is the numeric value of the character set, and different languages and locales may use different code pages. For example, ANSI code page 1252 is used for American English and most European languages. Code page 932 is used for Japanese Kanji.

Property	Description
LCID	*Integer.* Read/write. Defines the locale identifier (LCID) of the page that is sent to the browser. The LCID is a standard international abbreviation that uniquely identifies the locale; for instance 2057 defines a locale where the currency symbol used is '£'. This LCID can also be used in statements such as FormatCurrency, where there is an optional LCID argument. The LCID for a page can also be set in the opening <%@..%> ASP processing directive and overrides the setting in the LCID property of the session.
SessionID	*Long.* Read only. Returns the session identifier for this session, which is generated by the server when the session is created. Unique only for the duration of the parent Application object and so may be re-used when a new application is started.
Timeout	*Integer.* Read/write. Defines the timeout period in minutes for this Session object. If the user does not refresh or request a page within the timeout period, the session ends. Can be changed in individual pages as required. The default is 20 minutes, and shorter timeouts may be preferred on a high-usage site.

Method	Description
Contents.Remove ("*variable_name*")	Removes a named variable from the Session.Contents collection.
Contents.RemoveAll()	Removes all variables from the Session.Contents collection.
Abandon()	Ends the current user session and destroys the current Session object once execution of this page is complete. You can still access the current session's variables in this page, even after calling the Abandon method. However the next ASP page that is requested by this user will start a new session, and create a new Session object with only the default values defined in global.asa (if any exist).

* You *cannot* remove variables from the Session.StaticObjects collection at run-time.

Event	Description
onStart	Occurs when an ASP user session starts, before the first page that the user requests is executed. Used to initialize variables, create objects, or run other code.
onEnd	Occurs when an ASP user session ends. This is when the predetermined session timeout period has elapsed since that user's last page request from the application. All variables existing in the session are destroyed when it ends. It is also possible to end ASP user sessions explicitly in code, and this event occurs when that happens.

B

P2P.WROX.COM

Join the Pro ASP 3 mailing lists for author and peer support. Our unique system provides **programmer to programmer™ support** on mailing lists, forums and newsgroups all in addition to our one-to-one email system. Be confident that your query is not just being examined by a support professional, but by the many Wrox authors and other industry experts present on our mailing lists.

We've extended our commitment to support beyond just while you read the book, to once you start developing applications as well. We'll be there on this crucial second step of your learning. You have the choice of how to receive this information, you can either enroll onto one of several mailing lists, or you can just browse the online forums and newsgroups for an answer. Go to p2p.wrox.com. You'll find three different lists, each tailored to a specific support issue:

❑ **Errata**
You find something wrong with the book, or you just think something has been badly or misleadingly explained then leave your message here. You'll still receive our customary quick reply, but you'll also have the advantage that every author will be able to see your problem at once and help deal with it.

❑ **Code Clinic**
You've read the book, and you're sat at home or work developing your own application, it doesn't work in the way you think it should. Post your code here for advice and supports from our authors and from people in the same position as yourself.

❑ **How to?**
Something you think the book should have talked about, something you'd just like to know more about, a completely baffling problem with no solution, then this is your forum. If you're developing an application at work then chances are there's someone out there who's already done the same as you, and has a solution to your problem here.

How To Enroll For Support

Just follow this four-step system:

1. Go to p2p.wrox.com
2. Click on the Professional ASP 3.0 cover graphic
3. Click on the type of mailing list you wish to join
4. Fill in your email address and password (of at least 4 digits) and email it to us

Why this system offers the best support

You can choose to join the mailing lists or you can receive them as a weekly digest. If you don't have the time or facility to receive the mailing list, then you can search our online archives. You'll find the ability to search on specific subject areas or keywords. As these lists are moderated, you can be confident of finding good, accurate information quickly. Mails can be edited or moved by the moderator into the correct place, making this a most efficient resource. Junk and spam mail are deleted, and your own email address is protected by the unique Lyris system from web-bots that can automatically hoover up newsgroup mailing list addresses. Any queries about joining, leaving lists or any query about the list should be sent to: moderatorproasp3@wrox.com.

Index

A Guide to the Index

The index is arranged hierarchically, in alphabetical order, with symbols preceding the letter A. Most second-level entries and many third-level entries also occur as first-level entries. This is to ensure that users will find the information they require however they choose to search for it.

Stream object (*continued*)
OLE DB 2.5, for semi-structured data, 199
persistence into a file, 854
reading website file contents, 710
ReadText method, 710
WriteText method, 711
streaming
converting streams into recordsets with ASP, 852
data streams, ADO records, 733.
introduced, and as applied to recordsets, 851
specifying character sets, 852
stress testing
performance tuning technique, 66
third-party products for, 67
strHostToUse variable
CreateSite.vbs system script, 670
stylesheets *see* CSS; XSL; XSLT.
styling *see* formatting.
SubmitChanges method
DataControl object, 1055, 1067
DataFactory object, 1049
sub-networks *see* segmented networks.
sub-queries, SQL *see* nested queries.
subRefreshIDs subroutine
RDS application example, 1078
SUM function
of data shaping provider, 966
summary tables
conditions where use is acceptable, 52
violate normalization rules, 51
superuser permissions
apply to all MySQL server databases, 567
supply chain integration, 924
Sybase
OLE DB provider for, expected, 196
Synch Point
enabling of LUs under Host Integration Server 2000, 756
synchronization primitives, 282
synonym control
MSEQ application, 1104
SYSKEY.EXE
Windows NT 4.0 security deficiencies and, 1167
system architectures
client-server generally two-tiered, 18
component tiers as additional physical tiers, 275
logical and physical tiers, 272
n-tier, Windows DNA, 265, 271
performance and, 1117
problems with two-tier, 265
three tier
client-server application restructured with Windows DNA, 266
e-commerce example application, 932
web applications built with Windows DNA, 266
Windows DNA, 20
Windows DNA example advantages over two-tier, 23
System Identifiers (SID)
Oracle8 database connections, 481
System Service Control Point (SSCP)
used by SNA PU5 units, 751
Systems Network Architecture *see* SNA

T

table joins *see* joining database tables.
table paging
HTML data binding to an ADO recordset, 1059
HTML data binding, RDS example application, 1080
user navigation with buttons, 1075

table relations
ADO+ feature linking datatables, 856
<table> tag
browser neutrality in Article Bazaar example, 345
recordset display in Article Bazaar example, 353
tables
pivot tables, 980
tables, database
websites display faster with breaks in, 1133
tables_priv table
MySQL user authentication, 570
tabular binding
HTML elements to a recordset, 1058
Tagged Image File Format (TIFF), 784
tags, XML, 786
balanced, empty and nested, 787
case-sensitivity, 787
namespaces, 794
nodes, 788
Task Manager
memory utilization estimation with, 1121
TCP/IP (Transmission Control Protocol/Internet Protocol)
HTTP sits on top of, 785
MySQL servers communicate with, 561
OLE DB access to IBM host systems via, 757
template queries
advantages over SQL queries in URLs, 874
form of basic template files, 875
formatting results using XSL, 881
HTML forms embedding, 876
parameters and stored procedures, 875
SQL hidden from users, 864, 865
XML access to SQL Server, 864
testing *see* performance optimization.
third normal form (3NF), 45
extends 2NF functional dependency test, 45
stage of database normalization process, 39
third-party information
enriching data mining output, 1021
threading
COM and COM+ components, 428
COM threading models, 282
issues managed by COM+, 301, 302, 426
MTS thread management, 299
MTS working, processes and threads, 270
throughput
web applications, performance measure, 1120
TIFF file format, 784
Time dimensions, 996
timeouts, 303
TLA (Three Letter Acronyms), 186
TNS (Transparent Network Substrate)
Oracle Net8 service names, local naming, 480
transaction monitoring
relatively unimportant for directory data, 606
transaction programs
SNA peer-oriented network model, 753
transaction support
see also MTS.
MySQL, requires declaration of BDB tables, 577
MySQL, status of, 559
transactional processing
COM+ components, 302
commands for commiting or rolling back, 105
defined for SQL, 104
locking, minimizing performance effects where RDBMS allows, 106
transactions must exhibit ACID properties, 104